PANDORA'S BOX

PANDORA'S BOX

A History of the First World War

JÖRN LEONHARD

Translated by Patrick Camiller

THE BELKNAP PRESS OF HARVARD UNIVERSITY PRESS

Cambridge, Massachusetts | London, England | 2018

FIRST PRINTING

This book was first published as *Die Büchse der Pandora: Geschichte des Ersten Weltkriegs*
© Verlag C. H. Beck oHG, München 2014

The translation of this work was funded by Geisteswissenschaften International—
Translation Funding for Humanities and Social Sciences from Germany, a joint initiative
of the Fritz Thyssen Foundation, the German Federal Foreign Office, the collecting society
VG WORT, and the Börsenverein des Deutschen Buchhandels (German Publishers and
Booksellers Association).

LIBRARY OF CONGRESS CATALOGING-IN-PUBLICATION DATA
Names: Leonhard, Jörn, author. | Camiller, Patrick, translator.
Title: Pandora's Box : a history of the First World War / Jörn Leonhard ; translated by
    Patrick Camiller.
Other titles: Büchse der Pandora. English
Description: Cambridge, Massachusetts : The Belknap Press of Harvard University Press, 2018. |
    "This book was first published as Die Büchse der Pandora: Geschichte des Ersten
    Weltkriegs © Verlag C. H. Beck oHG, München 2014." | Includes bibliographical
    references and index.
Identifiers: LCCN 2017040904 | ISBN 9780674545113 (alk. paper)
Subjects: LCSH: World War, 1914–1918—History.
Classification: LCC D521 .L36513 2018 | DDC 940.3—dc23
LC record available at https://lccn.loc.gov/2017040904

To the brothers
Ludwig Leonhard (1893–1917)
and
August Leonhard
(1898–1976)

CONTENTS

MAPS

PANDORA'S BOX

1

LEGACIES

The First World War and Europe's Long Nineteenth Century

IT WAS REMEMBERED as a glorious summer. During the coming weekend, the children and some friends of theirs in the neighborhood were planning to perform a play based on the Greek myth of Pandora's box. Recounted in one of Gustav Schwab's well-known collections of tales from classical antiquity, it tells in parable form the story of Zeus's rage against Prometheus after he steals fire from the gods. The father of the gods orders Hephaistos, the god of blacksmithing, to produce a life-size figure of a maiden, who is then endowed by the other gods with many ways of inflicting calamity on human beings. Zeus himself leads this woman, Pandora (literally, "the All-gifted"), to Prometheus's brother Epimetheus. And though warned by his brother never to accept a gift from the gods, Epimetheus, to save humans from harm, invites Pandora into his home: "In her hands she was carrying her gift, a finely crafted golden box with a lid. She carefully lifted the lid from the receptacle—and at that very moment a swarm of evils rushed from it and spread in a flash over the whole earth. A single good lay hidden at the bottom of the box: hope. But before it could escape, Pandora—acting on divine inspiration—quickly snapped the lid shut. And now all forms of misery filled land, sea and air; all manner of fevers laid siege to the earth, and death, which used to creep up slowly on mortals, quickened its step."[1]

The children eagerly awaited the day of the performance. Wearing specially designed costumes, they were in the midst of the final full dress rehearsal in the garden of their vacation home on Saturday, August 1, 1914, when it was interrupted by their nanny: "Just you take them off again; you can't play at theater today. War has broken out." The puzzled children found their parents on the terrace. Mother had her head buried in a newspaper, while Father, "gazing into the distance" and not without a touch of theatricality of his own, remarked, "Before long a fiery sword will probably appear in the sky." That, anyway, is how the children remembered it.

This was the family of Thomas Mann, which had been spending the summer in their chalet at the idyllic Bavarian resort of Bad Tölz. On that August afternoon, the German Reich had declared war on Russia. It struck the children as odd that their father should be thinking just then of Leo Tolstoy, the writer and apostle of radical nonviolence, who had died in 1910. "It's strange," he mused, "but if the old man were still alive—he wouldn't need to do anything, just be there at Yasnaya Polyana—this would not be happening; *it wouldn't dare to be happening.*"[2]

Four years and three months later, in November 1918, Thomas Mann commented in his journal on the collapse of the order in which he had grown up and by which he had been so deeply marked: the order of the nineteenth-century bourgeois world, with its distinctive values and symbols. Through his novel *Buddenbrooks,* he himself had become its chronicler. But now it seemed to have foundered beneath a twin wave of revolution and military defeat. This was no mere change in the political form of the state. The novelist's entry for November 9, 1918, in which he points to the hollowing out of that order by the long years of war, has a laconic feel. He is no longer surprised by the turn of events: "All in all, I am rather calm and no longer feel horror. Revolutions happen only when they encounter no resistance (it was so with this one too), and this very lack proves that they are natural and justified. At heart the old rulers are happy to be rid of their power—which was no longer real power—and it has to be conceded that their authority is not adequate to the situation as it is and as it will be in the near future."[3]

What was the First World War? With the hindsight that we have today, it appears as the formative prelude, elemental crisis, or early turnaround of the still young twentieth century.[4] Soon after its outbreak, people experiencing the war had already begun searching for the right words to describe what was so vast, novel, even monstrous about it: in Britain they spoke of the Great War, in France of the *Grande Guerre,* in Germany of the *Weltkrieg.* Or else, like Ernst Jünger a few years later, they emphasized its universal, indeed revolutionary, character: "The war [was] not the discharge of revolution but its opening fact. No one can escape this fact; every being is directed and shaped by it, however he may regard it ideologically."[5] Today's labels, by contrast—"seminal catastrophe" of the twentieth century, "crisis of modernity," "collapse of civilization," "second Thirty Years' War" (from 1914 to 1945), beginning of a period in which Europe became a "dark continent" of violence—were formulated only with the knowledge of consequences that no one living in August 1914 could have guessed.[6] The unprecedented violence of the world war did not end with the formal peace agreement after 1918, but persisted and intensified in Europe and elsewhere in the name of new radical ideologies. This is what made the war an epochal turning point, which people living after 1918 were just beginning to understand. For Thomas Mann, the "extraordinary pastness" of the narrative in his novel *The Magic Mountain* resulted from the "rift that has cut deeply through our life and consciousness" since "the old days of the world before the Great War, with whose beginning so many things began, whose beginnings, it seems, have not yet ceased."[7] This deep rift became the defining feature—whether in stylized memories of childhood or as a reference point for the post-1918 generation that experienced the results of the war.[8] In December 1937, the Social Democrat politician Wilhelm Dittmann wrote in the party paper *Neuer Vorwärts,* "Prewar Germany is almost a *terra incognita* for today's generation, so much did the war shatter the link between what went before and what came after."[9]

The conflict reached completely new quantitative and qualitative levels of violence, killing ten million soldiers and nearly six million civilians; bringing about an unprecedented mobilization of societies and mass media, economies, and finances; and eliciting a plethora of explanations and justifications. It also marked a profound change in the relative weight of the world's regions and especially in Europe's place in the world.[10]

What was the First World War? Anyone who wishes to understand it must grasp the experiences and expectations of the world it affected. William Gladstone, who, as Britain's Liberal prime minister, left his stamp on the

Victorian age, was born in 1809 and died in 1898. In his childhood he heard the sound of cannons firing from Edinburgh Castle to mark the abdication of Napoleon, and toward the end of his life he listened to his own recorded voice and became familiar with the newly invented telephone as the twentieth-century means of communication.[11] The great tensions and dynamics of change in the nineteenth century, bridging the period before 1800 and the prehistory of the contemporary world, were concentrated in a single man's lifespan; the century was, so to speak, illustrated in his biography. How should this legacy of the long nineteenth century be characterized, and what did the First World War mean for it?

(1) Emancipation was a leitmotif running through the nineteenth century. In Europe as a whole, despite regional differences, demographic growth resulted in the mobilization of ever larger segments of the population, as the industrial mode of production imposed itself and transformed a feudal society of estates resting on legal privileges into a complex class society. Social and economic criteria increasingly came to define the locus of the individual within society. The legacy of the nineteenth century thus included the experience of economic growth and the ideal of not only political but also social equality—evident, for example, in the recurrent struggles for a republican form of state with socially defined rights, which erupted in France in 1848–1849 and among the forces of the democratic Left in Germany. By the end of the century, the specific momentum of economic and social differentiation became evident, contrasting with the political-ideological image of an elemental class conflict between capitalist bourgeoisie and proletarian working class that could only be solved by revolutionary means. Indeed, such simple rhetoric had masked the many nuances characterizing European societies in practice, which were discernible, for example, not only in the appearance of new groups such as skilled workers and white-collar employees but also in the question of whether the concept of revolution was still applicable at all in highly complex industrial societies. Disputes in the workers' parties between supporters of proletarian revolution and evolutionary reform reflected this dynamic.

At the same time, social classifications and demarcations were changing at the turn of the twentieth century. In 1934 the Hungarian writer Sándor Márai recalled how new social and religious dividing lines had developed.

Describing a new-style apartment building in his native Košice (then part of the Slovak region of Hungary), he wrote, "I think it was an ugly, inhospitable house. No one knew how they had ended up there; no ties of friendship, and scarcely even of neighborliness, bound its occupants together. It already had different castes, classes, and confessions living in it. In the old ground-story houses, families had lived side by side as friends or enemies, but in any case as people inextricably linked to one another."[12] During the First World War, traditional social roles and functions were called into question, as shifts in society brought new stratifications and created new definitions of winners and losers. Above all, the war became a test for societies: it demonstrated whether they were capable of integrating different social, ethnic, and political groups under the conditions of a protracted conflict in which the "home front" played an ever more important role in the mobilization of resources.

(2) Emancipation and mobilization also had a political dimension. One of the key consequences of the European revolutions between 1789 and 1848–1849—however much they varied in their details—was the transition from a monarchic-absolutist form of rule to one based on the regulated political participation of parts of the population. Governance could no longer function as a series of arbitrary acts; it was now bound up with suprapersonal legitimacy, with written constitutions, the rule of law, and parliamentary activity. In practice, this entailed a wide spectrum of forms of government ranging from constitutional parliamentary monarchies to constitutional republics. In this context, new ideological movements and political parties took shape in Europe, which, in the form of liberalism, conservatism, and socialism, developed blueprints for the political and social order. Among the legacies of Europe from the long nineteenth century were therefore not only the experience of ideological competition and political conflict but also the triad of crisis, revolution, and reform. European societies changed through revolutionary upheavals, but even more so through the kind of reforms introduced in Prussia after its defeat at the hands of Napoleon in 1806, which were meant to obviate a violent French-style revolution.

When war broke out in 1914, it seemed to many to reflect a clash between two rival conceptions: on the one hand, the "ideas of 1789" associated with France's revolutionary tradition or, more generally, a western European tradition that also included English parliamentarism and the republican liberty espoused by the American Revolution of 1776; on the other hand, the "ideas of 1914" that supported calls for Germany to distance itself from that tradition and to uphold such values of its own as "culture" and "community," *Kultur* and *Gemeinschaft*. The nineteenth-century liberal inheritance was thus in crisis, because its political forms of electoral and parliamentary participation and of basic human rights, as well as its other constitutional achievements, came up against the new reality of the *Kriegsstaat* (the "war state"). Between 1914 and 1918, this state geared to war represented a challenge to the civil authorities, the role of the constitution, the policy-shaping powers of parliament, political parties, and basic political rights not only in Germany but elsewhere in Europe. The disputes over the franchise and the limits of political participation that dominated the scene in many societies around the year 1900 became deeper and sharper in the context of the war.

(3) The nineteenth century was also the century of the state, which confronted its citizens not only in elections and parliaments but also in law courts and government departments, schools, and universities. Based on constitutional legality, but operating through bureaucratic administration, social intervention, and early welfare-state measures, the state encroached on more and more areas of life that had been private spheres or the province of churches or corporate institutions. Its dealings with subjects were different from those of the monarchic tax-raising and military state of the eighteenth century. It not only claimed the right to register and classify but took on new responsibilities, as in the embryonic social insurance systems established after the 1870s. These processes of "statification," as we may call them, were considerably expanded throughout the First World War and its military, political, social, and economic mobilization. Until August 1914 "a sensible, law-abiding Englishman could pass through life and hardly notice the existence of the state, beyond the post office and the policeman."[13] Then a fundamental change occurred: the state became not only a decisive military actor in the war overseas, but a social state at home, the organizer of the war economy, the grand administrator. As the war dragged on, the limits of these trends and their political and social costs became ever clearer.[14]

(4) Revolutions were a feature of both the beginning and the end of the long nineteenth century. But it was not only an age of connected chains of political revolution, with highpoints in 1789, 1830, and 1848–1849. It was

also an era of multiple revolutions in communications, linked to the political upheavals in many ways, but often surpassing them in their long-term impact. A number of developments lent enormous importance to communications and the media: not only higher literacy rates, the dissemination of printed texts and images with the help of new technologies (from lithography through the daily press to illustrated magazines, from photography and telegraphy to the telephone), and greater access to knowledge among wide sections of the population, but also the increased significance of the public sphere, the publication of parliamentary debates, and the rise of a popular press. The First World War continued trends that had been present since the wars of the French Revolution, only now these had acquired a new dimension thanks to technological innovations and their spread among the broad masses. The world war was also a media war. Communication and information became military factors, whether through the new, institutionalized relationship between army and press, the posters appealing for war loans, or developments in photography and cinema that gave visual form to war experiences and images of the self and others. In this way, the world war fueled hopes and expectations that, given the independent dynamic of the conflict, could often not be realized or fully satisfied. All of this went far beyond the usual understanding of propaganda as a massaging of information in the service of the military establishment and the war state. The war itself would reveal how the impact of the media, and the uses to which this was put, often escaped the intentions of soldiers and politicians.

(5) In the long nineteenth century, the nation, the nation-state, and nationalism became central markers orienting the state's self-assertion in the world, as well as in the political order and the shaping of society at home. Based on the French revolutionary ideal of a self-determining sovereign power, the nation and the state, as well as the people and the territory, were supposed to be harmonized with one another. Yet the actual formation of nations was often associated with wars; for example, in the establishment of the new nation-states of Italy and Germany between 1859 and 1871. At the same time, it involved the internal "nationalization" of societies: the loading of institutions, symbols, and traditions with a national significance in virtually all European societies. This could entail the marginalization or exclusion of groups whose loyalty seemed questionable and who were included in the

core nation only with certain reservations: whether religious groups such as Jews or Catholics in the post-1871 German Reich, ethnic groups such as Danes or Poles in Germany, Irish in the United Kingdom, South Tyrol Italians or Czechs in Austria-Hungary, or political movements such as the socialist workers parties before 1914. Religious and ethnic markers frequently overlapped, as in the case of Catholic Irish in the UK or Catholic Poles in the German nation-state. The world war brought with it new aggressive manifestations of nationalism that continued and exacerbated the prewar forms. The wartime mass mobilization increasingly refined the criteria by which the national loyalty of various sections of society was measured, and in many countries social tensions and distribution crises combined with ethnic or religious factors to exclude certain groups from the nation. Such processes became radicalized as the war went on, often being accompanied with violence. Toward the end, they could even threaten the cohesion of societies and the stability of political regimes.

Between 1500 and 1914, the number of state players in Europe shrank from some five hundred political-territorial entities to approximately thirty states at the time of the First World War. In central Europe, a special connection between war and internal or external state-formation manifested itself above all in the period from 1792 to 1815.[15] Another legacy of the nineteenth century was the recasting of the principle of popular sovereignty: what had been argued out in France in 1830 and 1848 mainly in terms of class conflicts became overlaid with the criterion of nationality in Italy, Germany, and the multinational empires. Here, social confrontations expressed themselves not so much in street fighting and revolutionary barricades as in ethnic differentiation and territorial borders. In the course of the nineteenth century, these divides deepened. From western to eastern and southeastern Europe, the panorama shifted from "barricades into borders."[16]

On pre-1914 maps, the world of states was marked by clear borders and colors. But the imperial red of the British Empire, the green of the Russian Empire, or the blue of the German Reich suggested a uniformity that corresponded to the model of the homogeneous nation-state, not to the complexities of the real world. In stark contrast to the demand for cohesion and loyalty stood the reality of the multinational Habsburg, Tsarist, and Ottoman Empires. Around the year 1900, the borders between nation-states and empires became more porous: Germany, France, and Italy pursued an imperial policy involving the creation of overseas colonies to justify their self-assertiveness and power ambitions both internally and externally, whereas in Britain attempts were made to derive the national concept of "Britishness" from the existence of a maritime empire. Even such small western European countries as Portugal, the Netherlands, and Belgium (whose colonial possessions were 80 times larger than the motherland) acted in an imperial spirit; the ratio was 140 to 1 in the British case.[17] The national state was the engine of empire building, a visible display of the strength and self-assertiveness of each nation in the midst of international rivalry. Ernst Troeltsch, in his essay "Das Neunzehnte Jahrhundert" (1913), argued that both democratization at home and the capitalist way of life—which he could imagine only as the "internationality of capital and business"—were part of the essence of the national state.[18]

But nation-states were not the only political entities in flux; the Russian, Habsburg, and Ottoman Empires were also in transition, engaging in a series of competitive thrusts of nationalization that underlined the model of the homogenizing nation-state. But insofar as attempts at Russification, Germanization, or Turkification gave rise to countermovements, the situation within these empires grew more complex—although their dissolution into breakaway nation-states did not yet seem as inevitable as it would to many living after 1918.[19] Nevertheless, the First World War did mark a decisive change: while none of the three multinational continental empires survived the war, and a host of new nation-states took shape out of their legacy in east-central and southeastern Europe, relations among European states and their colonial empires entered a new age, as the examples of Britain and France demonstrate. At the same time, the weight of new players such as Japan and the United States was keenly felt.

(6) The nineteenth century already brought new, multifaceted forms of interdependence to the relationship between Europe and non-Europe, as well as among the various other regions of the world. This was not only a question of European expansion and the formation of dependent colonies, which, in a climate of increased international competition, led to conflict over the distribution of what many at the time still saw as "free" territories in Africa and Asia. These ties were also evident in migratory flows and the interchange of goods and knowledge. Only because Europe was still a decisive

reference for other societies can the nineteenth century be talked about in terms of a "European global history," as characterized by Hans Freyer. At the same time, the impetus to globalization, with its multiplicity of transfers and interdependences among economic, financial, and knowledge markets beyond national borders, in no way put the European nation-states into question. In fact, those processes restabilized them again and again.[20]

The mainly British-shaped, though not fully British-controlled, economic and legal order operated far beyond Europe in the nineteenth century. This influence no longer rested only upon territorial possession, but on the prevalence of economic and legal models.[21] The Royal Navy itself had a special significance, symbolizing not only military superiority in the narrow sense but also the imposition of norms in a politics of maritime order.[22] This constellation changed in the course of the nineteenth century, as the criterion of ethnic belonging associated with occupation of a territory became more and more important. The nation-state became the model—as form of rule over a particular territory, as basis for legal and political decisions, and as space of experience grounding images of the self and others, as well as nationally defined loyalties. From the 1860s, territoriality was decisive in measuring the capability and legitimacy of states and empires. The tradition of informal empire structures weakened in favor of formal colonial rule.[23]

The First World War marked a watershed in the relationship between Europe and non-Europe, as well as among various regions of the world. This change did not manifest itself only in the dissolution of the European pentarchy (Britain, France, Russia, the Habsburg monarchy, and Prussia / Germany) that had shaped international relations since the eighteenth century. In addition, the reallocation or reversion of Germany's colonies after 1918, as well as the breakup of the Ottoman and other multinational empires, created new scope for action and influence, while the European powers, especially Britain, became much more dependent on the military contribution of their colonial empires. But the First World War did more than usher in a new phase of colonization and decolonization for Europe. Equally important were the worldwide mobilization of manpower and raw materials, the various migration flows, and the wartime experiences of colonial societies outside Europe. And as the British dominions of Canada, Australia, and New Zealand showed, these experiences did not begin and end with the provision of troops and war materials.

Above all, the war changed the weight of these societies within the Empire and helped form them as nations.

(7) The conception of international order that applied in Europe until 1914 originated during the period between 1792 and 1814–1815, the era of the French Revolution and the ensuing Napoleonic Wars. Its primary aim had been to stabilize the European interstate order through a system of balances, which was supposed to block hegemonic projects such as those of the French Revolution and the Napoleonic Empire. This conception of security was designed to de-ideologize conflicts and to prevent war between states from becoming an international civil war. Accordingly, "conference diplomacy" was based on the idea that relations among European states should not be the subject of public discussion; instead, secret talks among government representatives should deal with disputes early on, in accordance with the

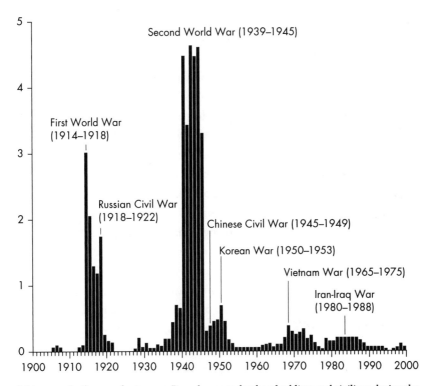

Major wars in the age of extremes. Bars show war deaths of soldiers and civilians during the twentieth century, in millions.

principles of state sovereignty. This war prevention policy was thoroughly successful between 1815 and 1871; even the national unification wars in Italy (1859–1870) and Germany (1864–1871) never involved more than bilateral conflicts, and until the end of the century there were no comprehensive and exclusive alliances involving a number of states.[24] However, while a major conflict was averted in the European core areas that had repeatedly been theaters of war since the seventeenth century, new zones of tension arose in the colonies, particularly in southeastern Europe on the Balkan Peninsula. There the conceptions of order developed in 1815 did not apply, but the fact that power conflicts could be channeled away into those regions served indirectly to stabilize the international order. Even the flashpoints that led to war in Summer 1914 were located in the southeastern zones of tension, where the withdrawal of the Ottoman Empire and the clash of interests between Russia and the Habsburg monarchy had caused a dangerous power vacuum to turn into a highly volatile source of crises.

(8) A key requisite for the conception of international order, and hence also for the relatively long period without major military conflicts in Europe, was the capacity and preparedness of individual states to wage war. Not least because of its deterrent value, this potential was essential for the international balance of power and for the stabilization of internal relations within each country—particularly in the second half of the century, when every large European power save Britain engaged in accelerating arms drives and the development of conscription-based mass armies. At the same time, however, the preparedness in principle to wage war outside Europe was demonstrated, especially in the opportunity space of the colonies. Only in Summer 1914 did the general parameters of the situation change, introducing an unprecedented cascade of violence in the twentieth century.[25]

War readiness in the nineteenth century was also an expression of the economic and technological achievements of industrial societies and of their ability to integrate new social groups, assert themselves politically, and demonstrate their staying power in an age of growing international competition. Not by chance did war fleets acquire enormous symbolic and political value in the wake of colonial expansion;[26] they conveyed the economic strength and technological advances of the country in question, its mobility on the world stage, and its preparedness for military intervention. The existence of these war fleets shaped the strategies of naval combat in an industrializing world and produced a new way of looking at the relationship between war on land and at sea, as well as between continental states and global empires.[27] These developments in turn gave rise to new pressures and dynamics, so that constellations began to emerge in which military elites and their insistence on strategic necessities changed the latitude for policy decisions.

In the end, this orientation to war and the military had a far-reaching social dimension, as it asserted itself in public debate, the educational system, literature, and the press. In all European societies in the second half of the nineteenth century, this war readiness tended to have great importance for the conception of the nation and its massive public dissemination—in material ranging from the culture of flags and uniforms through war memorials and commemorations, to soldiers and veterans associations, and the widespread impact of naval construction in Germany and Britain. On the other hand, it should not be inferred that these trends within society, which point to a close association between martial themes and definitions of the nation, actually led to increased violence in the wars of the nineteenth century. It was not a totalization of war-related violence, but the successful containment of conflicts that constituted the special legacy of the nineteenth century. Its experiences of war, after the period between 1792 and 1815, were restricted to brief conflicts: in 1853–1856 in the Crimean War; in 1859–1861 in the process of Italian unification; and in 1864, 1866, and 1870–1871 in the wars to establish a German nation-state. Although the mass media and retrospective accounts promoted these as national and popular wars, they were in practice limited to conflicts between states in which the primacy of politics was never called into question. The totalization of violence in the name of "the nation in arms" was not yet part of the actual course of conflicts, but it did become an important leitmotif in popular histories and instrumental politics, and especially in images of what future wars would look like.[28]

However, this relative limitation of martial violence remained confined to the core of the European continent. On its southeastern periphery in the Balkans, a distinctive mix of factors—a multinational population, a political vacuum left by the gradual withdrawal of the Ottoman Empire, rivalry between two great powers (Russia and the Habsburg monarchy), and increasingly radical national movements competing with one another in a context of weak state authority—had already resulted in a series of wars before Summer 1914, with a rising tide of violence against various ethnic and religious groups. The limits of containment were all the more apparent in the colonial wars of European powers against indigenous peoples in Sudan (1898) and South Africa (1899 and 1902), and in the German crushing of revolts by the Herero and Nama peoples in and after 1904. In these conflicts, the war aim was not to inflict military defeat on an adversary, but to achieve total subjugation by destroying the economic, social, and political foundations of the enemy's existence.[29] Punitive practices were driven by such purposes as revenge and mass deportations, which after 1914 would also become operative in the war in Europe.[30] Although the unfettering of violence in the colonies did not lead directly, by a kind of causal link, to the totalization of European war after 1914, it was clearly part of the wider historical context. If the long nineteenth century offered partial instances of the violence that the future might present, then they were to be found in the Crimean War of 1853–1856 and, most of all, in the American Civil War. Between 1861 and 1865, 2.1 million troops were mobilized in the Northern states and 880,000 in the Confederate South; the war toll amounted to 750,000 deaths, including more than 620,000 soldiers, or just under 2.5 percent of the North American population—roughly the same as the total number of Americans killed in the revolutionary wars of the eighteenth century, the war of 1812, the Mexican-American war, the Spanish-American war, the two world wars of the twentieth century, and the Korean War combined. These nineteenth-century wars demonstrated the new links between mass mobilization and official justifications of unprecedented casualty figures, between increased violence (also against enemy civilians) and doubts about the loyalty of certain groups in the home population.[31]

(9) Another feature of the nineteenth century was the initially widespread vision of all-around progress: the future would become ever better and open to human design, as a result of wider political participation, economic growth and social equality, improved education and scientific advances, higher mobility and hygiene levels, and the worldwide spread of an idea of civilization conceived in Europe. However, from the last third of the nineteenth century on, more and more doubts beset this faith in progress as the core of what the bourgeois future offered. Cultural criticism, the reception of the writings

of Friedrich Nietzsche, and the manifold reform movements and artistic currents active around the year 1900 revealed that the promise of progress had become increasingly shaky. We cannot infer from these tendencies that there were widespread hopes in liberation through war or even an actual longing for a great war, but neither can we fail to see the extent to which the themes of progress, growth, and expansion had already come under pressure before 1914. Part of the reason for these doubts was a major change in the understanding of reality. In physics, Max Planck's quantum hypothesis and Albert Einstein's theory of relativity had shattered the previous image of the world. The same was happening with the discovery of the unconscious in the psychoanalytic theory of Sigmund Freud. The First World War began under the aegis of these two developments: disillusionment with the promise of progress and turmoil in the perception of reality. Moreover, after 1914 a specific connection between war and science became apparent, as numerous researchers were prepared without further ado to place their knowledge at the service of their country, whether in a flood of justificatory tracts penned by historians, theologians, economists, and sociologists or in the exploitation of new scientific breakthroughs and new technologies for the development of the means of war and substitute materials in everyday life.

(10) All these developments were connected to a final aspect: the changing self-image of individuals and their position in the historical process. A preoccupation with history at a variety of levels—in monuments, museums, and historical associations; in an endless stream of historical novels; and in the rise of history (especially in Germany) as an academic discipline giving a sense of direction to the bourgeoisie—became a central theme of the nineteenth century. Motivating this preoccupation was the quest for individual and collective certainty in an epoch that, especially since the 1860s and 1870s, seemed gripped by the mode of acceleration. This sense of ever-greater speed was different from the distinctions between "before" and "after" that might have been used in relation to events such as wars or revolutions. In contrast to the early nineteenth century, the experience of time had developed a novel quality, side by side with a subjective perception that space itself was shrinking. A number of technological achievements around the turn of the twentieth century contributed to these changes. Steamboats, railroads, and automobiles provided faster and denser transportation, increasingly

replacing the natural propulsion of sailing ships and coaches; and the global cable-and-wire news network entered a new age in 1899, when the first successful wireless transmissions took place between Britain and France, followed in 1901 by a similar transatlantic breakthrough. These accelerations shrank perceived space and hence the distance between events and their reporting as news.[32] But at the time they also produced new crisis symptoms in many people, as historically experienced time and the individual-biographical experience of time grew further and further apart. Indications of this trend in the early twentieth century were the "counting compulsion" and "rush disorder" observable in the heroes of Robert Musil's novels and short stories and especially "shock," "trauma," and "nervousness" as symptoms of a sick age. Thomas Mann's *The Magic Mountain* (1924) was in two senses a *Zeitroman*, since it focused not only on the historical time before the First World War but also, consciously, on the subjective splitting of time into competing conceptions.

Another leitmotif in the quest for self-certainty was discernible in cultural critiques and debates around the turn of the twentieth century. The relationship of the individual to the expanding mass society, particularly the self-assertion of the individual in the crowd, had become for many a deeply ambivalent result of demographic growth, economic development, and social mobility—all legacies of the nineteenth century. Many of the contemporary debates on the popular press and mass consumption, moral improvement, sexuality and the body, and the opposition between anonymous society and identity-building community revolved around the individual's role among the masses.[33]

The world war fundamentally changed people's time-consciousness. Expectations and experiences differed more and more widely between the military front and the home front, and they could no longer be straightforwardly synchronized with each other. Although Oswald Spengler's *Decline of the West* was written before 1914 in anticipation of the coming war, his diagnosis of an age of "gigantic conflicts" and a cycle of civilizations as "organisms" only came into its own after the reality of world war had exceeded any metaphors of decline.[34] The relationship to the future would also change, as would the identification of ideas of progress and theories of order. For after 1917, the promise of new models of political and social order no longer appeared to come from western or central Europe, but rather from Russia and eastern Europe and the other side of the Atlantic: Vladimir Ilyich Lenin and Woodrow Wilson symbolized these imagined futures.

Around the year 1900, Europe was an unsettling tangle of diverse and ambiguous currents. Robert Musil, in his novel *The Man without Qualities*, sketched a panorama of this unrest and contradictoriness: "Suddenly, out of the becalmed mentality of the nineteenth century's last two decades, an invigorating fever arose all over Europe. . . . Talents of a kind that had previously been stifled or had never taken part in public life suddenly came to the fore. They were as different from each other as could be, and could not have been more contradictory in their aims. There were those who loved the overman and those who loved the underman; there were health cults and sun cults and the cults of consumptive maidens; there was enthusiasm for the hero worshipers and for the believers in the Common Man; people were devout and skeptical, naturalistic and mannered, robust and morbid; they dreamed of old tree-lined avenues in palace parks, autumnal gardens, glassy ponds, gems, hashish, disease, and demonism, but also of prairies, immense horizons, forges and rolling mills, naked wrestlers, slave uprisings, early man, and the smashing of society."[35] Also part of this tense configuration was the juxtaposition of rationality and subjectivism. In view of the strong tendencies toward rationalization in economics, politics, and public administration, political and social theorists diagnosed a lack of instinct, intuition, or subjectivity—and hence also of irrational elements—as a source of feelings of loss and isolation. In particular, Max Weber's focus on ecstasy and charisma underlined the perceived limits of regulating social and political activity through rational, bureaucratic, and legal processes alone. Attitudes to violence were another area of tension. Its interpretation as a purely irrational force, to which those like Georges Sorel or the Futurists signed up programmatically, was one thing. But at the same time, Max Weber emphasized that systematic violence was also inherent in legitimate, well-run, peaceful states: every form of social and political order rested on the state's monopoly of violence. Lenin wove precise political analysis, strategic calculation, and rational organization by the revolutionary vanguard together with a high preparedness to use force. Around the year 1900, the nineteenth-century idea that rationality always goes together with progress toward peace, and reason with liberal constitutions and the containment of violence, was being questioned, at least at the level of political and social theory.[36]

It would be wrong to try to elucidate the First World War solely in terms of the nineteenth century. Such an approach would make that century a mere prehistory, guiding one's attention only to processes and contexts that fit one's putative explanation of the war, and not those that speak against it. No history can be merely a prehistory of what came later—that is the misguided perspective of those who expect the structures of the pre-past to explain the past. The "future past" of the nineteenth century had many possible developments, and their multiplicity should not be dismissed too lightly because only one prevailed in the end. Neither should we forego explaining such historical connections—if we did, it would be impossible to understand the zones of tension and constellations of conflict, and ultimately the causes of the war and the escalation of Summer 1914. Underlying these connections is a question that has a deep historical dimension. Why did the tradition of containing crises and channeling violence—a tradition that, after the seventeenth century and against the background of bloody religious and civil wars, had become such an important feature of European history—break down in 1914? Why did the principle of trusting in an internal and external peace order fail so spectacularly?[37]

The dual historical dimension of the First World War, its function as a pivot between the nineteenth and twentieth centuries, has to do with the fact that the destruction and violence, and the inability to construct a lasting peace, persisted well beyond 1918. It may be possible to say quite precisely when the war began, but on closer examination the question of exactly when it ended proves to be incomparably more difficult. In this respect, the First World War resembles other events such as the French Revolution, which for nineteenth-century historians like Alexis de Tocqueville or Jacob Burckhardt had at most a beginning but not a chronologically definable end; the postrevolutionary era involved a continuation of the revolution through other means, so that what became known as the Age of Revolution ground to a halt neither in 1799 nor in 1815. In the case of the First World War, to see the difficulty of defining its end means to grasp the *longue durée* of its consequences. It was the inability to remain at peace with others and oneself that kept the war going in peacetime and characterized the twentieth century until well beyond

1945. In 1955 Hannah Arendt wrote, "No history of the causes leading to the First World War, and no analysis of explicit and ulterior motives, can eluci-date what happened in Europe on August 1, 1914. . . . We cannot 'explain' the First World War from the history of the nineteenth century; but we can do nothing other than understand in the light of that catastrophe the century that came to an end in it. Perhaps the event would have been less dramatic if that one catastrophe had been the end of the matter. But the sorrowful calm that descends on the scene of a great disaster has still not materialized. The first explosion was like the start of a chain reaction, which to date it has not been possible to end."[38]

The First World War, therefore, cannot be explained solely with reference to the nineteenth century, with the latter reduced to a mere prehistory; nor can the war be reduced to its twentieth-century consequences, unfolding as a result of the global upheaval of 1914–1918. Rather, the two centuries are intertwined in the history of the conflict, although ultimately the war went beyond even this complex entanglement. The war had its own particular history of dynamics and logics, of elements beyond what went before and what came after, beyond the apparent causal chains and lines of continuity. It is necessary to take account of this particular history and to engage with it.

2

ANTECEDENTS
Crises and Containment before 1914

HELMUTH VON MOLTKE knew all about war. Born in 1800 into an old noble family in Mecklenburg and educated in a Danish cadet school, he entered the Prussian army at the age of 22 and was soon afterward promoted to the general staff, where he was mentored by Carl von Clausewitz, the foremost theorist of war in the early nineteenth century. His rapidly advancing career reached its peak in 1857, when he was promoted to major general and appointed head of the general staff. In the campaigns of 1864 against Denmark, 1866 against Austria, and 1870–1871 against France, he acted as the top military leader. The trio of victories soon cast him as a strategic genius in the eyes of the public, and he contributed more than a little to the myth of the Großer Generalstab, a Greater General Staff that not only ruled on narrowly military matters but also made decisions with considerable political import.[1]

In contrast to his public image at the time, which fused the legendary grand strategist with the omniscient "man of few words," Moltke was a cautious observer of war. He knew from his own experience how much the reality of an actual war diverged from any theories or plans. He conceived of strategy as a system of makeshift plans or moves, and in his view a campaign could at most be planned only in its initial phase. Once it had broken out, a war should be decided as soon as possible, with the help of all the technical and logistic means available; the introduction of the Prussian needle rifle and, most important, the use of railroads for troop transport had played a decisive role in the Prussian victories of the 1860s.[2] But Moltke always remained aware that wars have a dynamic and logic of their own that cannot be controlled.[3]

After the Franco-Prussian War ended in 1871, Moltke became active as a Conservative Party deputy in the Reichstag and, as its oldest member, served as its interim president in 1881. As he had learned from Clausewitz, he maintained that the traditional *Kabinettskrieg* (cabinet war) between princes, conflicts that involved fairly small armies and were limited in both time and materiel, should be carefully distinguished from the people's war initiated by the French Revolution, with its large national armies and theoretically unrestricted effects. The Austrian war of 1866, for example, had been of the desirable *Kabinett* type, with no excesses of violence, especially against civilians, no humiliation of the enemy, and no ideological gloss on the war aims. Only in this way, Moltke believed, had it been possible to assert the primacy of Prussian politics. The war had not arisen out of "self-defense against a threat to our existence" nor "as a result of public opinion and the nation's voice." Rather, it had been a "struggle deemed necessary in the Cabinet, long envisaged and calmly prepared." The war of 1866 had been waged "not for the incorporation of states, territorial expansion, or material profit," but for the strengthening of Prussia's "power." The Battle of Königgrätz accordingly settled the rivalry for supremacy between Prussia and Austria.[4]

The short war, Moltke wrote in 1880 with the Franco-Prussian War in mind, is the result of a historical learning process. In contrast to the "savagery of the Thirty Years' War," it brings a new "humanity to warfare," avoiding unnecessary excesses of violence, even though the enemy in 1870–1871 suffered more than just symbolic humiliation; for example, the loss of Alsace-Lorraine and the imposition of high reparation payments. Yet unlike in the eighteenth century, it was not only enemy troops who were targeted in these short wars: "The greatest blessing in war is the swift ending of the war, and for this all means that are not actually reprehensible must be freely available." Use should be made of all possible "resources of the enemy government": "its finances, railroads, and food supplies, even its prestige." This was not yet a total people's war or guerrilla warfare, but still war against an enemy state and all its military, political, economic, and ideological instruments of power. In principle, this precise combination seemed to have proven successful in 1870 within a matter of weeks. Only after the defeat of Napoleon III at

A glimpse of total war: Richmond, Virginia, at the end of the American Civil War, 1865

Sedan, when the French side declared a people's war and deployed irregular *franc-tireurs* and guerrilla tactics, did the violence escalate: "The last war against France was waged with this energy, yet with greater restraint than ever before. After two months the campaign was decided, and only when a revolutionary government prolonged it for four more months, bringing ruin on its own country, did the fighting take on a more bitter quality."[5]

The moment in Fall 1870 when the military defeat of the Second Empire became apparent, but the war was not yet over, marked the beginning of a crisis. Philip Sheridan, the former Union general in the American Civil War, was observing the conflict at Prussian headquarters on behalf of the U.S. government, and he saw Prussia after its victory at Sedan in the same position that the Northern states had faced six years earlier in relation to the Confederacy, at the beginning of a spiral of violence and unpredictable guerrilla warfare. The response of the Northern states had been to make a conscious military turn against the civilian population of the South, culminating in General William Sherman's "March to the Sea." Looking at photos taken at the time of Southern cities after their occupation by Northern troops, it is not easy to spot the differences from the images of bombed-out cities at the end of the Second World War. In Fall 1870, Sheridan advised the German generals to employ this "scorched-earth" tactic to force France to sue for peace. Count Waldersee later recalled Sheridan's words: "You know how to strike an enemy, as no other army does, but you haven't got the hang of annihilating him. There should be more smoke from burning villages, or else you won't finish the French off." Such ideas found no echo in Moltke.[6]

In May 1890, just a few weeks after Bismarck left office, Moltke gave his last speech in the Reichstag. At first sight, it was a warning about a new war in Europe, but there was more to it than that. He looked skeptically into the future and saw that, as politics and the conduct of war came increasingly under the spell of new developments, governments would lose their influence in wars. Looming on the horizon stood the horrifying specter of an uncontrolled people's war: "But . . . princes and governments in general are really not the ones who wage war in our times. The age of cabinet wars lies behind us— all we have now is people's war, with all its unpredictable consequences, and any level-headed government will decide on that only with great difficulty. No, . . . the elements that threaten peace are to be found among the people. Internally, they are the greed of less fortunate classes and their occasional attempts to achieve an improvement of their lot through violent measures. . . . Externally, they are the strivings of certain nationalities and races, and the discontent everywhere with things as they are. This may bring about a war at any time, without or even against the will of governments." Given the arms drives underway in all European powers, Moltke feared that a war of incalculable length would exclude a peace agreement of the kind negotiated in 1864, 1866, and 1871: "Should such a war break out, no one can foresee how long it will last or when it will end. The great powers of Europe, armed as never before, will enter the fray against one another; none of them can be defeated so thoroughly in one or two campaigns that it declares itself vanquished, accepts harsh peace conditions, and never picks itself up to renew the struggle even after a year's delay."[7]

In 1911 Alfred von Schlieffen—architect of the German offensive plan that Moltke's grandson, Helmuth von Moltke Jr., would apply against France in 1914—published an influential essay on the new mass army: *Über die*

Millionenheere. He argued that the wars of the future, their length, and their quantitative or qualitative increase in violence were altogether beyond human calculation.[8] They might last "seven" or even "thirty years," and their consequences were so unpredictable that the foundations of the German nation-state, itself a result of war, might suddenly be called into question. Future war therefore contained the potential for revolution. Moltke had already feared the arming of industrial workers in new-style conscription armies. His gloomy, skeptical survey had offered food for thought especially because he considered the implications of the fact that future wars could no longer be restricted. Unlike the traditional "cabinet wars," they might no longer lead only to limited territorial losses; the stakes would be "the survival of the Reich, perhaps the continuation of the social order and civilized existence, and at any event hundreds of thousands of human lives."[9]

Things had not yet gone that far, and despite all the crises over prospective wars, the expected struggle for the survival of European nations did not materialize after the Franco-Prussian War of 1870–1871. Why was this so? Why was war contained despite all the epicenters of crises and zones of tension in Europe? Why, after the end of the wars against Revolutionary and Napoleonic France between 1792 and 1815, was there no other major war until 1914—no war involving not only Britain, France, Russia, Germany, and the Habsburg monarchy, but all the other European powers that had established a long, stable, and successful peace in 1814–1815? But, also, how unavoidable was a great war in 1914, against the background of the nineteenth century and especially its final third? When, therefore, did the prehistory of the First World War begin?

1. BALANCES OF POWER AND DYNAMICS OF CHANGE

To understand why the containment of war in Europe broke down in July and August 1914, we need to look back to the origins of this concept.[10] Efforts to limit wars to interstate conflicts and to contain violence especially against civilians began in reaction to the religious civil wars of the early modern period. After the Reformation there had been an unprecedented ideologization of the grounds for war. It rested on the identification of each individual combatant with grounds for war that were considered "just," "genuine," or "morally superior"; the soldier was not a paid mercenary, but a convinced fighter for a cause, and especially for his faith. This justified an increase in wartime violence, making the boundaries between combatants and non-combatants relatively porous; it brought bloody civil war right to the midst of society, as in the 1560s in France or the 1640s in England. Out of this traumatic experience of civil war, with its unleashing and mobilization of unprecedented violence, came the idea of the sovereign princely state—a state that, as it were, cut itself off from the outside through a new concept of sovereignty, made diplomacy a *domaine réservé,* and thereby supposedly prevented interference in the internal affairs of other states. Internally, the princely monopoly of violence checked the rival systems of force of various social and religious groups; the separation between external and internal politics became clearly distinguishable. The modern law of nations and war, which came out of the great European peace agreements signed in Münster, Osnabrück, and Utrecht between 1648 and 1713, was one consequence of these experiences. Its purpose was to prevent civil wars by creating a European legal order, a *ius publicum Europaeum,* that was supposed to permit only limited interstate wars in accordance with clearly defined rules, to rid war of ideological overload, and to decriminalize the enemy-image by means of the *iustus hostis* formula.[11] In the language of the mechanics of the time, states resembled closed spheres that could be positioned in such a way that the resulting equilibrium prevented any one state from securing hegemony over the others.[12]

The French Revolution and the wars fought after 1792 in the name of the sovereign nation were a fundamental challenge to this regulatory framework. Although the revolutionary wars soon exposed the idea of an international civil war of the oppressed against their oppressors as a naïve myth—nowhere, Robespierre pointed out, do people like "armed emissaries"—contemporaries were aware of the dangers within society of a war unleashed in the name of ideological principles.[13] For a long time the most powerful interpretation of this change between 1792 and 1815 was the one provided by Clausewitz. For the period before the French Revolution, he noted that the "limited, constricted form of war" was due to the restricted finances and personnel available to the absolute monarchies. Clearly this meant it was essential to contain conflicts, to restrict war to armies, and to spare the civilian population: "if the army was pulverized, he [the commander] could not raise another, and behind the army there was nothing. That enjoined the greatest prudence in all operations." The army soon came to constitute a "state within the state." But with the French Revolution and its ensuing wars, a new link developed between violence in the name of the nation and the participation of citizens as defenders of the fatherland: "Suddenly war again became the business of the people—a people of thirty millions, all of whom considered themselves to be citizens. . . . The people became a participant in war; instead of governments and armies as heretofore, the full weight of the nation was thrown into the balance. The resources and efforts now available for use surpassed all conventional limits; nothing now impeded the vigor with which war could be waged, and consequently the opponents of France faced the utmost peril."[14]

After 1815, the generation of politicians around the Austrian chancellor Metternich and the French minister Talleyrand, who had lived through the almost uninterrupted period of wars between 1792 and 1815, tried to draw out the implications of this experience.[15] The point was to avert another revolution at home or another hegemony of a single state within Europe. In sharp contrast to the ideal of the self-governing nation, and without regard for the hopes of early national movements in Germany, Italy, and elsewhere, the politicians who attended the Vienna Congress backed the return of the monarchic state and an international balance of power. To stem outbreaks of violence in the name of national or constitutional principles would require military action abroad, as in the repeated interventions by Austrian forces in Italy or by French troops in Spain. In pursuit of such equilibrium, the Congress of Vienna also redrew territorial boundaries, without regard for traditional claims, established loyalties, or the people's wishes—in this respect, revolution itself became "monarchical."[16]

In 1822, the Prussian general, military author, and diplomat Georg Wilhelm von Valentini emphasized that the contemporary world could remain at peace only if "national hatred" was proscribed and war was left to the princes.[17] However, the practice of war increasingly clashed with its interpretation in the course of the nineteenth century. On the one hand, the national wars of Italy and Germany from the 1850s on were often waged in accordance with the rules of classical interstate warfare; they were, as Moltke rightly pointed out, short wars that did not question the primacy of politics and were not meant to humiliate the enemy. On the other hand, the civil war legacy—in which each individual committed himself to the cause—was unmistakable in the depiction and interpretation of these national wars in books and newspapers, pictures and monuments. The ideal of the contained war remained under threat, and it proved precarious indeed when civil wars developed, as in the United States between 1861 and 1865, with new technologies and infrastructures. Here the boundaries between the military and the home front became blurred, and violence escalated to a degree previously unknown to contemporaries.

The European state system of the long nineteenth century rested on a protracted and relatively flexible juxtaposition of multiple principles: the recognition of state sovereignty and the principle of equal status existed side by side with efforts to prevent a major European war. The main players at first were the traditional pentarchy: Great Britain, an island nation and sea power, which, unlike mainland Europe, experienced wars as geographically remote events, and whose great colonial possessions made long-term alliances seem superfluous, accounting for the ideal of "splendid isolation"; and the Continental powers, France, Prussia, and the multiethnic empires of Russia and the Habsburg monarchy. Lesser players were Italy, a newly established nation-state after 1859–1861, and the Ottoman Empire, which had lost its great power status and, from the early nineteenth century on, found itself on the political retreat in southeastern Europe. According to the Vienna settlement, dangers of single-nation hegemony were to be contained by ad hoc alliances, as France's hegemony had been by various anti-French coalitions before 1815. In the Crimean War of 1853–1856, it was primarily a coalition between France and Britain that prevented Russian hegemony in southeastern Europe. Bismarck's strategy of preserving the conquests made in the limited war in 1870–1871 still maintained the idea of equilibrium, although the order of Congress Europe had been fundamentally altered by the foundation of the German Empire. Spatially and strategically limited wars, as far as possible respecting the primacy of politics and refraining from an increased military input, remained the dominant ideal, even though the period between 1871 and 1914 was increasingly one of *armed* peace.[18]

The pressure on this model after 1815, especially in the second half of the century, and changes in international relations were due to a new constellation in which the boundaries between internal and external politics shifted and became more porous. A nexus connecting the international order with social trends and economic dynamics became discernible at four levels.[19] First, the national question—now carried over into the congruence of nation and state, of ethnic / national boundaries and state borders—acquired a new dynamic, one cause of this being that many aspects such as economic dynamism, greater mobility, new-style communications, and expectations of political, social, or cultural progress could be rolled together in the attractive ideal of the nation-state. Sooner or later these aspirations came into conflict with the practice of territorial redefinition established in 1815, the aim of which was to maintain a balance of power and to block claims to hegemony. For their part, imagined national communities played no role in the post-1815 Congress diplomacy, which is why this system would become an enemy-image for the early national bourgeois movements. This tension between national emancipation and the interests of international security was evident in an age of ever-threatening revolution. But what contemporaries criticized, especially in Metternich as the ostensible symbol of monarchic restoration and arbitrary authoritarian rule, was at the same time a condition for the relative international stability and security in early nineteenth-century Europe.[20]

At any event, whereas in western Europe national—and that usually meant linguistic—boundaries largely coincided with borders between states, the typical situation in eastern and southeastern Europe was a complex mix of ethnic groups. There a simple definition of nation-states was scarcely possible. Indeed, the question of ethnic minorities promised to be one of the basic problems of the late nineteenth and twentieth centuries. The various models of nation-state formation—whether through constitutional or revolutionary acts of political will, a unification of existing territories, or a secession of new states from multiethnic empires—usually rested on violence of widely varying proportions.[21] In any case, it was clear that for many liberals and democrats, expectations of political-constitutional progress went hand in hand with a real preparedness for war in the framework of nation-building. Unification took place mainly against external foes, who were identified with the experience of occupation by a foreign power. This was the underlying ideological justification for the Italian national war against the Habsburg monarchy or for the Prussian-German War against France, which many in 1870 regarded as a follow-up to the anti-Napoleonic wars of 1813. Secession from existing empires—as underlined by the many crises in southeastern Europe, the Polish revolts against the Russian Empire in 1830 and 1863, and the Irish and Boer national movements against British rule—involved a particularly high degree of violence. The example of the United States between 1861 and 1865 powerfully demonstrated how fluid the boundaries between wars of secession and civil wars could become.

The second key factor lay in the dramatic breakthrough to industrial society. The criteria determining a country's power changed: no longer just the possession of territory but, most prominently, the development and mobilization of economic resources in the form of raw materials, investment capital, and labor determined that power. Beginning in the second half of the nineteenth century, limited wars were also tests of a country's economic strength, as it had crystallized in major infrastructure projects. This made railroad construction a key area in which industrial performance, capital investment, and military-strategic considerations were closely bound together. In this sense, Russia's defeat in the Crimean War of 1856 reflected the economic backwardness of the Tsarist Empire, while Prussia's victory over the Austrians in 1866 at Königgrätz was a token of its economic strength and superior logistical infrastructure. But the industrial potential of major

Comparative index of industrial potential (Britain = 100 in year 1900)

	1880	1900	1913
Austria-Hungary	14.0	25.6	40.7
Great Britain	73.3	100.0	127.2
France	25.1	36.8	57.3
Germany	27.4	71.2	137.7
Italy	8.1	13.6	22.5
Russia	24.5	47.5	76.6
Japan	7.6	13.0	25.1
USA	46.9	127.8	298.1

Sources: Bairoch, "International Industrialization from 1780 to 1980," p. 292; Herrmann, *The Arming of Europe,* pp. 233–237; Stevenson, *Armaments and the Coming of War,* pp. 2–8; Mulligan, *The Origins of the First World War,* p. 181.

countries around the world varied considerably before 1914; this entailed a gap in naval capacity and in the production of artillery and ammunition that would be of decisive significance in a future war. British fears of falling behind in this competition were confirmed by the industrial dynamic in Germany and the United States.[22]

A third, closely related, factor was the transition to mass mobilization and the development of new military technologies. For the first time, European societies were demographically and economically in a position to raise and equip mass armies, and to keep them supplied for short periods. Despite the many improvements, however, the level of armament remained quite low in comparison with what developed after 1914. Only after the Second World War, when it no longer seemed to make economic or military sense to maintain mass armies on a long-term basis, would their importance lessen. Between 1850 and 1950, new conscription armies came into being all over Europe. Only Britain relied (until 1916) on the volunteer principle.[23] At the same time, a dynamic arms drive before 1914 eventually led to a full-fledged upward spiral, most noticeable in relations among Germany, France, and Russia. Beyond the strictly military logic, rearmament became a demonstration of industrial capacity; war readiness and warlike postures now increasingly presupposed a stable industrial society. Military spending rose against the background of more frequent crises after 1911, and by 1913 it had reached

Military expenditure after 1900 (in millions of pounds sterling)

	1900	1906	1911	1912	1913
Great Britain	69.6	62.2	67.8	70.5	72.5
France	41.5	46.2	60.8	62.8	72.0
Russia	44.5	109.3	71.0	86.2	101.7
Germany	43.2	57.1	68.1	72.0	93.4
Austria-Hungary	11.4	13.7	17.0	20.6	25.0
Italy	14.1	14.8	22.9	29.9	39.6
Japan	13.7	40.9	23.2	22.8	22.0
United States	39.3	50.9	65.2	65.7	68.9

Sources: Hobson, "The Military-Extraction Gap," pp. 464–465; Mulligan, *The Origins of the First World War*, p. 184.

unprecedented levels in the major countries; the increase was most striking in France, Russia, and Germany, while in Britain the figures remained relatively constant and in Japan, following its victory over Russia in 1905, spending even declined.

The burden of the arms race in Europe was very uneven, however. A comparison of figures for the period between 1911 and 1913 shows that it was especially high for Russia, Italy, and France, which was attributable in part, in Russia and Italy, to their relatively low per capita GDP. Hidden behind the military expenditures were major social and political costs that would only increase with the outbreak of war.

The nominally rising arms expenditures should not, however, lead us to infer a general depletion of national economic resources or a militarization of every sector. Given the high industrial growth rates, the share of military spending in the total budget remained more or less constant: between 30 and 40 percent in Britain from 1853 to 1913, approximately 30 percent in France from 1815 to 1914, and 27 percent in Germany in 1907. Although military spending rose as a proportion of GNP, it was still fairly low in comparison with later periods in the twentieth century: in 1910 it accounted for 3.6 percent in Britain and in 1914 for 4.8 percent in France, 4.6 percent in Germany, 3.5 percent in Italy, 6.3 percent in Russia, 0.8 percent in the United States, and 4.8 percent in Japan. Similarly, the proportion of the population serving in the military was still quite low before 1914: only 1.53 percent in

Comparative real burden of arms spending 1911–1913 (Great Britain = 100)

	1911	1912	1913
Great Britain	100	100	100
France	138	130	149
Russia	132	138	160
Germany	96	96	122
Italy	100	125	158
Japan	190	170	160
United States	35	29	30

Sources: Hobson, "The Military-Extraction Gap," p. 479; Mulligan, *The Origins of the First World War*, p. 184.

France and 0.79 percent in Germany in 1910.[24] Although these figures indicate the scale of militarization in prewar societies, they say nothing about the social presence and cultural function of the military. In this regard, conscription, national-patriotic war memories, and cultural militarization worked in synergy. In 1913, the Deutscher Flottenverein (the German naval interest group) alone had more than 1.1 million members. But this presence of the military in regional capitals and seats of power, at festivals and parades, and in clubs and societies, as well as the tendency for military associations to become political, was not unique to Germany. For all the differences in detail, it was a Europe-wide phenomenon.[25]

The fourth and final factor was the European rivalry for territories outside Europe. This process of imperialist expansion, unlike earlier colony formation, embraced virtually all countries—established colonial powers such as Great Britain as well as new nation-states such as Germany or Italy that sought to strengthen their position in Europe by acquiring imperial aprons. With this expansion came new techniques and strategies of imperial rule, resulting from the asymmetry between colonial players and indigenous peoples. Any state that wished to have a military presence outside Europe also needed battle fleets, and by the 1880s at the latest, these became a symbol of performance capacity. The very rise of the United States and Japan seemed to confirm the significance of international navalism, while between 1904 and 1914 the laws of naval warfare exemplified both the international stake in the containment of conflict and the growing sense of a clash of interests among European powers.[26] However, the asymmetry of colonial force manifested itself even more strongly in the deployment of machine guns, which enabled quantitatively inferior colonial troops to prevail against indigenous armies. An impressive demonstration of this was the battle of Omdurman in 1898, which Winston Churchill characterized as "the most signal triumph ever gained by the arms of science over barbarians. Within the space of five hours the strongest and best-armed savage army yet arrayed against a modern European Power had been destroyed and dispersed, with hardly any difficulty, comparatively small risk, and insignificant loss to the victors."[27]

How did the interstate system change from mid-century onward under the impact of these factors? No matter how wide the range of goals and experiences they involved, the revolutions of 1848–1849 were an important turning point. In France the conflict centered on the struggle for a social republic, whereas in the German and Italian territories and in Hungary it had a two-fold aim of political liberty and national unity, which soon overburdened the respective protagonists. The attempts to create new nation-states "from below," by revolutionary action or parliamentary decision, ended in failure, as did the campaigns of Prussia against Denmark or Piedmont against Austrian forces in northern Italy, both of which were presented as national wars. At any event, revolutions in society were not supposed to result in civil wars that might spill over into the international system. The national question, the formation of new nation-states out of formerly stateless nations, was of such fundamental importance because it marked the interface between political-constitutional and social tensions and international constellations. But in 1848–1849 the system of external interventions operated to maintain the balance of power: this explains Britain's preparedness in autumn 1848 to move against the formation of a German nation-state through war and thus against the will of the Frankfurt National Assembly. In that sense, the Malmö armistice, which sealed the withdrawal of victorious Prussian troops from Denmark, underlined the existence of a functioning international order that offered no place for new nation-states. In 1849, the Russian intervention against anti-Austrian national revolutionaries in Hungary saved the Habsburg monarchy. There internal stability to prevent revolution was inseparably bound up with international pacification. That too was a dimension of *Realpolitik* amid the wave of European revolutions.

At first sight, the European pentarchy seemed to have been reestablished after the revolutions ran their course in 1849–1850, especially since Britain and Russia, the two major powers not directly affected, found their positions strengthened by the outcome. Yet unlike in the period before 1848, governments could no longer brush aside the concerns of the national movements in Germany and Italy, and the political framework was also modified as Prussia and Piedmont became states based on a constitutional order. In the end, the revolutions of 1848–1849, with their clubs, press, and political parties, their mass petitions and parliamentary debates, changed the communicative conditions of politics. Public interest in international relations also rose appreciably, since they were expected to have secondary effects for national politics.

This became apparent a few years later, during the Crimean War. In 1853–1856, the new political constellation was centered on a conflict between Britain and Russia, often viewed in the expressive image of a struggle between a whale and a bear. What lay behind this conflict, however, was a wider clash of interests: in Europe the key issue was control over sea straits and Russian naval access from the Black Sea to the Mediterranean; in Afghanistan and Persia it was the demarcation of colonial spheres of interest. Russia's attempt to profit from the weakness of the Ottoman Empire failed, while the future integrity of the Ottoman Empire became a question of interest for the whole of Europe—an internationalization that contained the potential for both escalation and de-escalation. France strengthened its position through involvement in the Crimean War, its first international conflict since 1815, and drove this point home at the Paris Peace Conference; its assistance in 1859–1861 in the formation of the Italian nation-state against Austria built on this newly acquired power. But with more than 640,000 dead, the war in Crimea was also Europe's costliest in the hundred years from 1815 to 1914.[28] The high toll owed less to pitched battles than to siege warfare, where supply problems and disease were superimposed on each other. Specialized war correspondents and the arrival of photography made the war a novel European media event, in which the distance between event and news began to narrow, and the journalistic mystique of authentic frontline reporting had to offset, as in all subsequent wars, the gap between the ideal of public information and the reality of censorship.[29]

Between 1859 and 1871, it became clear that the ostensible failure of the 1848–1849 revolutions at the level of national politics had not defused the explosiveness of national issues. The wars to establish nation-states in Italy and Germany proved two things: the "nation in arms" became a visible presence in the media of the time, to the point that the wars acquired "holy" status in the public imagination; yet in practice they were relatively brief campaigns that followed the model of a limited war between states. This was apparent especially in the role of certain new concepts. When Giuseppe Garibaldi sought to lead a veritable people's war against nobility and church, the political leaders Camillo Cavour and King Victor Emmanuel of Piedmont-Sardinia responded all the more vehemently with a monarchical strategy of "cabinet war." At the Battle of Aspromonte in Summer 1862, this conflict was fought out *manu militari* between Garibaldi's volunteers and regular Piedmontese troops, highlighting a strategic line of divide within the Risorgimento, the movement to unify Italy. In 1870, at German headquarters in France, Moltke insisted on a contained war and did not respond to the guerrilla tactics of the *franc-tireurs* with a scorched-earth strategy. At heart both of these conflicts were still short wars, in which there were only two opponents, and domino effects in wider alliances were prevented. When active border conflicts seemed to be resolved after 1871, at least in central Europe, the focus of possible military conflict shifted increasingly to southeastern Europe and the colonial sphere outside Europe.

Southeastern Europe as a crisis zone and the Balkans as the powder keg that exploded in Summer 1914 and lit the worldwide conflagration: these reductionist images present a complex history only in terms of its outcomes. For the southeastern European focus of conflict was nothing new, and earlier crises there had not issued in a great war. The backdrop was the so-called Oriental or Eastern question, which essentially grew out of the long-term erosion of the Ottoman Empire and its declining power and influence in Europe. In the period between 1774 and 1923, between the treaties of Küçük-Kaynarca and Lausanne, the successive loss or renunciation of territory in the Balkans repeatedly gave rise to a power vacuum, which in turn fueled rivalry between Russia and the Habsburg monarchy for influence in the region, precipitating outside intervention but also marking the Oriental policy of the German Reich as part of its *Weltpolitik*.[30] From a Russian viewpoint, its geostrategic interest in control over the Black Sea straits became ever more important, and in the end it would lie behind Russia's war on two fronts against Germany and Austria-Hungary, as well as against the Ottoman Empire in the Caucasus.[31] On the other hand, the fear in Vienna was that the balance between the Austrian and Hungarian parts of the Habsburg Empire—the *Ausgleich* reached with difficulty in 1867—might be jeopardized by developments on its southeastern periphery. Before 1914 this constituted the kernel of the South Slav question: that is, how to handle within the Dual Monarchy the strivings for autonomy and independence of Catholic Croats and Slovenes, as well as Orthodox Serbs. Russia's support for Serbia meant that, long before 1914, this conflict too was not simply a regional problem.

From the 1850s on, therefore, the Eastern Question referred to latent but variously internationalized centers of conflict. These have persisted up to the present day: the three major crisis areas making up the Eastern Question—the former Yugoslavia, the Kurdish regions, and the Near East (now Israel-Palestine)—have remained centers of international conflict. In the last third of the nineteenth century, radical national movements in southeastern Europe, with outside support mainly from Russia as the self-proclaimed defender of the Slavs, bet their future on separation from the Ottoman or Habsburg imperial federations. The result was a latent propensity to violence, still below the threshold of open military confrontation. Yet international attention to the region meant that the danger of escalation was initially quite limited. Various initiatives following the Ottoman-Russian wars of the 1870s, exemplified by Bismarck at the Congress of Berlin in 1878, showed how southeastern Europe could serve not only as a "powder keg" but also as a "lightning conductor"—a kind of European bank in which various powers had invested, and with whose help conflicts of interest could be accommodated.[32] Thus, the Ottoman Empire functioned as a tension-deflecting space between Russia and the Habsburg monarchy, with a stabilizing effect also for the core of Europe.[33] Leopold von Ranke wrote of the compromise reached by the major European powers in 1878, but he also emphasized how precarious a solution it was with regard to the new national movements: "What is the force that holds sway in our Europe? It is the agreement among the great powers, which excludes the domination of any single one and consists of them all together. War will begin when this agreement can no longer be achieved. But it is ceaselessly endangered by new events. In fact, the interest of the so-called Eastern Question lies in this danger: for the possibility of a general conflict stems from the fluctuating conditions in the East, which are directly related to all others. At times such a conflict has been averted, but at another time a misunderstanding actually broke out among the great powers, and they went to war with one another. This is a matter of great importance in itself, but it is all the more so because of the autonomous tendencies developing in the East."[34]

The shape of the pentarchy changed with the formation of new nation-states in the period before 1871.[35] Instead of ad hoc alliances like the one in the Crimean War, fixed peacetime alliances began to appear on the scene. But the price for maintaining the status quo was that the international system lost some of its flexibility: it no longer had the elastic buffer that had offered room for maneuver in earlier crises. This by no means necessarily determined the confrontation between blocs in Summer 1914 or the domino effect of alliances and war declarations, but it was an important change nonetheless. The Imperial chancellor, Bismarck, had pronounced that the new German nation-state was "saturated." Having been established as a great power in Continental Europe, it would concentrate on maintaining the status quo, isolating France internationally, avoiding further conflicts, and offering itself as a force for peace and an anchor of stability—as it did at the Berlin Congress of 1878. This ruled out global political ambitions and colonial expansion. However, Bismarck's conception foundered on the clash of interests between Russia and the Habsburg monarchy in southeastern Europe, forcing Berlin in 1879, after the Berlin Congress, into a formal alliance with Austria, which in 1882 was expanded to include Italy. Even this defensive alliance bristling with internal tensions—Italy demanded annexation of the so-called *irredenta* (the "unreclaimed territories"), including the Austrian South Tyrol, to complete the Risorgimento—provoked the signing in 1892–1894 of a Franco-Russian alliance, which enabled France to break out of the diplomatic isolation it had endured since 1871.[36] A classical "balance of power" thus prevailed on the Continent as a result of the two alliances. This was further reinforced by Britain's neutrality, but after the colonial spheres of influence were demarcated (with France in Africa and with Russia in Asia), rivalry with Germany became an ever more important factor in British overseas policy. Germany's rapid economic strides, especially in the Second Industrial Revolution, hinged on chemicals and electrical engineering, as well as its dynamic population growth; also its modern educational institutions and early social insurance schemes to integrate industrial workers made it a model to be reckoned with, against which the efficiency of other countries had to be measured. But only after 1890, with the shift from Bismarck's policy of protecting the status quo of a "saturated" Continental power to the vision of a world power on an equal footing with others, did the classical British policy of neutrality come seriously into question. This ambivalent relationship of rivalry and fascination found a symbolic focus in the German navalism that got underway in 1898, accompanied by the building of an oceangoing battle fleet and large-scale domestic propaganda on the part of the Flottenverein. At the same time,

British experts were busy studying the foundations of the German social insurance system.[37]

2. CONFLICT AREAS AND ACTION LOGICS

Despite the modifications since 1850, especially the development of new nation-states and a two-alliance system, the European concert of powers warded off a major conflict until the summer of 1914. But the situation had been changing. The Triple Alliance linking the German Reich, Austria-Hungary, and Italy, as well as the alliance between France and Russia, expanded in 1907 with Britain to form the Triple Entente, shaped the scope for diplomacy in the years before 1914. By 1913 it was beyond doubt that European statesmen—whether Berchtold in Vienna, Bethmann Hollweg in Berlin, Sasonov in St. Petersburg, or Poincaré in Paris—were prepared to take greater risks than ever before.[38]

Although this constellation by no means made a great war inevitable, the intensity of conflicts increased from the late 1890s on, especially in relation to areas outside Europe. In 1898, a key year in this respect, global tensions affected Europe in various ways.[39] The Sino-Japanese war of 1894–1895 and the Italian-Ethiopian conflict of 1895–1896 had already revealed, in very different regions, the expansionist claims of new players such as Japan and Italy. This applied all the more to the United States, where, after the Pacific coast had been reached, the westward settlement frontier was finally closed. The "frontier" now shifted to a global sphere of political interests, through a mixture of economic penetration, infrastructure development, and military force. The conquest of the Philippines in the Pacific and Cuba in the Caribbean, both in 1898, marked the beginning.

The year 1898 was also critical for European colonial conflicts. After the battle of Omdurman in early September, French and British colonial troops encountered each other at Fashoda on the Upper Nile. The crisis ended—against the background of the Boer uprising in South Africa and France's ongoing clash with Germany—in a demarcation of colonial spheres of interest. In return for French recognition of the British zone of influence in the Nile basin, Britain accepted French rule in Chad and recognized Morocco as a French sphere of interest.

This *mise au point* gave Britain a free hand to suppress the Boer independence movement in South Africa. The curve of violence in this colonial conflict showed how war making could massively escalate outside Europe in a short period of time. Against 80,000 Boers, Britain eventually had to mobilize almost 450,000 men, drawing (against the initial opposition of the chief commander, Lord Kitchener) on contingents from other white colonies and dominions, as well as native black Africans. Faced with successful guerrilla tactics on the part of the Boers, the British responded by taking systematic action against the civilian population: 30,000 villages were burned; 20,000 civilians, including white women and children, died out of a total of 120,000 interned in "concentration camps"; and 14,000 blacks who had worked on Boer farms lost their lives in special camps reserved for them. Britain's early military difficulties against the Boers intensified the crisis of "imperial defense." There was debate back home about the country's capacity to wage war, and some wondered whether the course of the South African conflict did not show that British soldiers had physically degenerated as a result of the Industrial Revolution. John Atkinson Hobson, in his book *Imperialism* (1902), criticized the whole project of imperial expansion and fueled discussion of the costs of empire. Meanwhile, the war in South Africa was feeding back into Europe and demonstrating that the global crisis areas had long been interlinked with one another. The Irish and the Finns, with an eye on South Africa's dominion status, stepped up their demands for autonomy, while Kaiser Wilhelm II sent a friendly telegram to the Boer leader, Paul Krüger, trying to extract political capital from the conflict. In Britain itself, criticisms raised by pacifists and Liberals contributed in no small measure to the Conservative Party defeat in the general elections of 1906.

It was therefore not only European states that sought to carve out spheres of influence as a way of strengthening their international position. This became quite apparent in 1904–1905, with the escalation of conflict between Japan and Russia over Korea, Manchuria, and other spheres of influence in East Asia. Russia had occupied Manchuria after the Boxer Rebellion and pushed through railroad construction in northwestern Manchuria following the 1896 agreement with China, but then Japan's victory over Russia sealed the rise of a new power in Asia. The tsarist regime, in signing the Portsmouth peace treaty negotiated through the mediation of U.S. president Theodore

Roosevelt, was forced to accept Japan's interest in Korea (it would annex it in 1910) and to hand over the Manchurian railroad and coal areas, as well as the southern part of Sakhalin island. To people at the time, the crushing Japanese victory over Russia's Baltic fleet in the Tsushima Strait seemed to underline once more the importance of a modern navy equipped for battle.

In the end, even these were limited clashes: they might strengthen thinking in terms of war or reflection about the future capability of states and empires, but they did not result in a world war. When such a war erupted in 1914, it did so in the Balkans, not outside Europe because of a crisis between colonial powers. Yet, especially in Britain's case, imperial jockeying for position had an impact in Europe. In 1900, Whitehall still had no formal alliances with the Continental states, but after the experience of the South African War the search was on for military and foreign-policy partners. The informal Entente Cordiale with France in 1904 was not an alliance but an understanding, a deal to balance colonial interests in Africa; it confirmed, after the Fashoda crisis and the Boer War, French recognition of British dominance in Egypt and British support for French influence in Morocco. The perception of this as a blow to Germany's *Weltmacht* ambitions was further reinforced in 1905–1906, in the First Moroccan Crisis, when German opposition to French colonial expansion—which reached its peak with Wilhelm II's landing in Tangier and the dismissal of French foreign secretary Delcassé under German pressure—involved an attempt to weaken the Franco-British Entente Cordiale. But although the Algeciras Conference in 1906 upheld the formal sovereignty of the sultan of Morocco, it mainly demonstrated that the German Reich could rely on the support only of Austria-Hungary on the world stage, while the cooperation between France and Britain now extended to military planning.

A further shift in the international order came in August 1907, when Russia and Britain reached a compromise over disputed spheres of influence in Persia, Afghanistan, and Tibet. As a result, British diplomacy was able to secure the frontiers of India, not only safeguarding the crown jewel of the Empire but also stabilizing the military-strategic power base for British dominance in Asia. The Triple Entente, then, was not an alliance fixed by treaty but a set of agreements consisting of the Franco-Russian military convention of 1894, the Entente Cordiale of 1904, and the Russo-British agreement of 1907, supplemented in Spring 1914 by secret negotiations between the naval top brass of the two countries. The point, as the Russians saw it, was precisely to convert the Entente—whose existence the Russian foreign minister thought "as unproven as that of the sea dragon"[40]—into a formal defensive alliance.

These developments were increasingly seen, above all in Germany, as a process of "encirclement"; Chancellor von Bülow warned of this danger for the first time on November 14, 1906, in a speech to the Reichstag setting forth his reaction to the Entente Cordiale. But such scenarios were mixed with great self-confidence on the German side (especially vis-à-vis France) and had nothing to do with a perception of German decline.[41] Even if France and Russia came to actual military arrangements, between 1906 and 1912 it was impossible to speak of a Russo-Franco-British triple alliance directed offensively against Germany. Still, a basic problem was becoming apparent that would be exacerbated in the following years: a dynamic in which each side imputed intentions to the other, postulating effects of certain events and feeling a subjective pressure to react in the interests of prestige, came increasingly to mark the thinking of the political and military elites. The importance of such tendencies was that they limited lateral thinking, the capacity to formulate and assess other options. A sense that there were no alternatives, an inability to question certain ideas for fear that it would entail too high a price and too great a loss of prestige, became widespread in Germany, and not only there, placing army officers and politicians under a pressure to act that was mainly in their own heads.

In Germany, the so-called Schlieffen Plan of 1905 was the expression of wide-ranging commitments that produced specific logics of action, but it failed to take into account factors that would prove of major importance to the future war. This operational plan, devised by the head of the General Staff, Count Alfred von Schlieffen, assumed a war on two fronts against Russia and France, and relied on a quick decisive victory over France to compensate for the ostensible military imbalance between the Central Powers and France and Russia. The strategic disadvantage of Germany's central location, which was the decisive geographical point of reference in pre-1914 thinking, made a short war absolutely essential. In the eyes of the conservative military elite, this short duration would also reduce the danger that a limited war between states would pass over into a people's war with unpredictable political and social consequences. The result was that time pressure became central to German military planning. But, at the same time, one-sided concentration on *the* decisive battle led to neglect of important aspects such as logistics and the security of supplies.[42] The rapid overwhelming of France was supposed to be followed by victory over Russian forces in the East. Originally, the plan accepted the violation of Belgian, Dutch, and Luxembourgian sovereignty, thereby contradicting the attempts in July 1909 of the new chancellor, Theobald von Bethmann Hollweg, to reach a compromise agreement with Britain that would end the perceived encirclement of Germany.[43]

In a memorandum "On the Military-Political Situation," written on December 21, 1912, the head of deployment, Colonel (later Quartermaster-General) Erich Ludendorff, argued as follows: "In view of Germany's central location— and unless the political situation in Europe changes—we shall always be compelled to operate on several fronts. We shall therefore have to defend on one front with weaker forces, so that we are able to take the offensive on others. The latter front can only ever be France. Here we can hope for a quick decision, whereas an offensive war into Russia would have no foreseeable end. But in order to take the offensive against France, it will be necessary to violate Belgian neutrality. Only by passing through Belgian territory can we hope to attack and defeat the French army in the field. By this route, we shall come face to face with the British expeditionary corps . . . as well as Belgian forces. Nevertheless, this operation has better prospects than a frontal attack against the fortified French eastern front. Such an attack would give the war the character of fortress warfare, cost us a lot of time, and deprive our army of the momentum and initiative that will be all the more necessary, the more numerous the enemy is with whom we have to reckon."[44] This position followed a closely defined logic of military action, but it failed to recognize the fundamental change in Germany's political situation. In comparison with 1905, the German Reich after 1907, and *a fortiori* after 1911, found itself in a much more problematic situation because of the closer links among France, Russia, and Britain; their agreements on military cooperation; and the fact that railroad construction had made it possible for Russia to carry its armies to the eastern frontiers of Germany and Austria-Hungary much faster than before. Furthermore, the German

plan of attack relied entirely on land forces, turned a blind eye to the possibility of a British naval blockade, and continued to include violation of the
sovereignty of Belgium and Luxembourg.[45] Still, it was recognized among
the pre-1914 general staff that an onslaught against France in the west would
not settle the war; that, given the military buildup in France and Russia and
the possibility of a people's war with full-scale mobilization of resources, it
would at best signal the favorable opening of a long war, whose end would
become less and less certain with every passing year.[46]

Not only in Germany but in every European country the military drew
up definite war plans from 1900 on, continually refining and updating them
up to 1914. In 1911, the French chief of staff, Joseph Joffre, also allowed
for a violation of Belgian neutrality to enable his troops to invade Germany
around the fortified positions inherited from 1870–1871. The plan of attack
that the French eventually developed, the so-called Plan XVII, also envisaged
the possibility of a frontal attack on Lorraine, so as not to alarm the British
with a violation of Belgian sovereignty, although such an offensive would
have been riskier and more time consuming.[47]

In Russia, too, military scenarios became more and more important after
the war with Japan and developed a powerful dynamic of their own. Secret
service reports of enemy troop movements—which essentially meant those
of Austria-Hungary—acquired huge significance in the focus on mobilization
plans, recruitment in military districts, and army transportation around the
vast country. Military and political circles set great store by such information, especially after experiences in the so-called winter crisis of 1912–1913.
Prior to and during the first Balkan War, parallel mobilization rehearsals or
maneuvers took place on the border between Galicia and the Russian military districts of Kiev and Warsaw in which parts of the Austro-Hungarian
and Russian armies stood directly facing each other.[48] The Russian secret
service drew from this a possible future war scenario, in which the Austro-
Hungarian army moved first against Serbia to the southeast and then against
Russia to the northeast. Troops would already be mobilized in Galicia while
a swift blow was being delivered in Serbia. In July 1914 these hypotheses
would strongly influence the thinking of Russian generals and politicians
and serve as the basis for mobilization orders. Pressure to avoid being caught
unawares, to deny the enemy any time advantage that might prove decisive

at the beginning of a war, was a fateful result of all this military planning in the years before 1914.[49]

But why did war eventually break out in the Balkans? Why was south-eastern Europe particularly susceptible to military conflict? This peculiarity became apparent after the Young Turk Revolution of Summer 1908, when the South Slav question brought Europe to the brink of war. In the fall, as its new rulers sought to stem the erosion of further Ottoman territories, Austria-Hungary reacted by formally annexing Bosnia-Herzegovina, which since 1878 had been ruled by Austria but remained under formal Ottoman sovereignty. But Austrian hoped that a modernization drive in the region would help to curb the rise of nationalism encountered ever greater resistance, notably among educated Bosniacs who rejected the idea of a supranational state and believed that democratic participation was feasible only within the nation-state. Moreover, in the eyes of many, the reality of the Dual Monarchy, with its favoring of Hungarians over other national groups, contradicted Vienna's touted vision of supranational institutions and rendered it implausible.[50]

The annexation of Bosnia-Herzegovina in 1908 led to an international crisis that threatened to escalate. Particularly sharp reactions and protests came from Russia—which felt cheated because its agreement to the annexation had not produced any of the progress in the question of the naval straits promised in return by Vienna—and from Montenegro and Serbia, which saw the Austro-Hungarian move as a brake on their plans for a Greater Serbia; with Russian political backing, Montenegro and Serbia mobilized their troops. There was also a boycott of Austrian goods in the Ottoman Empire. To be sure, the German chancellor, von Bülow, who resolutely backed Vienna in a speech to the Reichstag in December 1908, helped negotiate a compromise between Austria-Hungary and the Ottoman Empire. But as in virtually all earlier diplomatic crises, the head of the Austrian general staff, Franz Conrad von Hötzendorf, was pushing for war. His argument was that hostilities with Serbia should begin at once, while Russia had not yet recovered sufficiently from its defeat in the war of 1905 with Japan. His preparedness to settle the South Slav conflict by force remained a constant all the way from 1906 to 1914.[51] Conrad von Hötzendorf gambled on a violent expansion of Austria-Hungary in the Balkans, going so far as the incorporation of Serbia into a South Slav kingdom and the widening of Habsburg dualism into a new "trialism"; it was an aggressive project, which before 1914 set him at odds with the Austrian heir apparent, Archduke Franz Ferdinand. At the same time, relations between Italy and the other two members of the Triple Alliance were strained because Rome demanded some compensation for the territorial gains of the Dual Monarchy.[52] Under German pressure, Russia and Serbia finally recognized the annexation in 1909; Russia did not yet feel capable of bearing the costs of a major war and advised Serbia to play a waiting game. But this only strengthened and radicalized the mass base of the South Slav movement against Austria-Hungary. The annexation crisis underlined the fact that the Balkans were an area of latent unrest, which could at any time ignite a wider European conflict. But each sharp crisis before 1914 also showed that the outbreak of a major war was not the only conceivable outcome.

This was true also of the Second Moroccan Crisis, in 1911, when France made claims on Fez as the seat of the sultan and Germany dispatched its *Panther* gunship to Agadir, making the year a decisive one for international relations.[53] The Morocco-Congo Treaty eventually signed by the two powers represented another balancing of colonial interests: while Germany recognized a French protectorate and therefore de facto French rule in Morocco, two strips of territory in the French Congo were ceded to the German colony of Cameroon. The outcome of the crisis was thus a land swap, like those carried out in early nineteenth-century Europe to bolster the idea of equilibrium, except that in 1911 the redrawing of boundaries occurred in the imperial outreaches of the European powers, not on the European continent. Rather more important than the actual transfers, however, were the changes in the internal politics and military thinking of European states.

In France there was a political reorientation toward nationalism in the name of the moral unity of the nation and the demonstration of strength against Germany and what Paris saw as its attempts at blackmail. From now on, internal, external, and military politics were very closely bound up with one another.[54] After his appointment as head of the general staff, Joffre was able to translate his dogmatic offensive strategy into Plan XVII, while the Left Republican government under Joseph Caillaux had to give the military a practically free hand because of the increased danger of war with Germany.

The succeeding government under Poincaré then consciously boosted the public prestige of the armed forces and systematically increased the power of the executive in relation to parliament, so as to be able to pursue a decisive foreign policy. Part of this policy of strength vis-à-vis Germany was the Briand government's law of 1913, introducing a three-year period of service in the active army. However, this law sparked political conflicts rooted in tensions between the military and society since the Dreyfus affair, the crisis over the Jewish army captain who was wrongly convicted of espionage for Germany and won rehabilitation only after a long public campaign. The three-year draft contradicted the Left Republican idea of the *nation armée* going back to the French Revolution, according to which all fit and able males were supposed to ensure the common defense of the fatherland. It also stoked old concerns that a powerful standing army might be used at home to repress the Left. Even in the July crisis of 1914, the fear that a left-wing parliamentary majority might change the law later that year fueled the willingness of the French government to support the Russian position unconditionally and to consolidate its alliance with Russia.[55]

The Second Moroccan Crisis also made Britain more ready to redefine its position and, in particular, to develop a Continental security strategy.[56] On July 21, 1911, the British chancellor of the exchequer and future wartime prime minister, David Lloyd George, gave the traditional banquet speech at Mansion House, the residence of the mayor of London, to the City's financial elite. Having consulted beforehand with Prime Minister Asquith and Foreign Secretary Grey, he emphasized with unusual asperity that Britain could not tolerate any unilateral colonial enlargement of the German Empire at the cost of France. If this section of his speech could still be interpreted as a British push for participation in the ongoing talks on the status of Morocco and the Congo, the next took things a step further. Great Britain was indeed prepared to make great sacrifices for the sake of peace: "But if a situation were to be forced upon us in which peace could only be preserved by the surrender of the great and beneficent position Britain has won by centuries of heroism and achievement, by allowing Britain to be treated where her interests were vitally affected as if she were of no account in the Cabinet of nations, then I say emphatically that peace at that price would be a humiliation intolerable for a great country like ours to endure."[57]

The publication of the speech in *The Times* the next morning conveyed a dual message. At first sight it supported France and a more closely knit Entente Cordiale, but at the same time it appealed for international accommodation with British involvement. Earlier that month, when the British foreign secretary had asked that the German demands be made public and that the two countries work together to find an international solution, the German authorities had not responded in any way. Lloyd George's speech was thus not simply another of many steps on the road to war; it also illustrated the ongoing quest for ways to de-escalate conflicts. With regard to the political situation in Britain, it signified a turn in the radical pacifist wing of the Liberal Party (which included Lloyd George himself) to a position that no longer ruled out war as the last option in all circumstances; but most important, amid the crisis of July 1911, it was an attempt to move the German Reich toward a course of international accommodation. In Germany, however, the speech intensified negative perceptions of Britain among the political and military elites, as well as the general public. In addition to the frightening prospect of encirclement on the Continent, there was a widespread sense—as the massive protests of the Pan-Germanic League testify—that Germany's colonial expansions were being restricted.

Finally, a noteworthy domino effect manifested itself in the Second Moroccan Crisis. Inter-imperial distribution conflicts continued to occur because politicians did not wish to be accused of a compromise that damaged their country's prestige and position in the world. A vivid example of this was the Italo-Turkish War that came hard on the heels of the Moroccan crisis. Italian troops attacked territories belonging to the Ottoman Empire in North Africa and the Mediterranean, and in November 1911, Italy actually annexed Tripoli and Cyrenaica, as well as Rhodes and the rest of the Dodecanese island group in the southeast Aegean. Its aim was to take advantage of the precarious situation of the Ottoman Empire to counterbalance France's colonial expansion in Morocco.

In analyzing this chain of events, some have tried to interpret the outbreak of war in August 1914 as an inescapable consequence of the fact that the international order was being shaken by crises at ever-shorter intervals. But a closer look shows that things could have developed differently. The so-called Haldane mission of 1912, the last shot at reconciliation in the British-German naval dispute, made it clear that, even in a situation supercharged by colonial conflicts, it was still possible to seek routes to détente and equilibrium. When the British war minister, Richard Burton Haldane, put colonial concessions on the negotiating table as a quid pro quo for limits on the German navy, his proposal was rejected by Wilhelm II and Grand Admiral von Tirpitz, who, as secretary of state at the Imperial Admiralty since 1897 and the leading champion of German navalism, had been charged with construction of a German battle fleet. This cut across efforts by Chancellor Bethmann Hollweg to reach an agreement with Britain, while in the long term the obsession with the navy weakened the land army.[58] Yet the continuing hope among German politicians that Britain would remain neutral in a crisis on the Continent showed that escalation from regional conflict to major European war was by no means a foregone conclusion. The British nervousness was obvious enough, however, and by now it had a global dimension. Since 1911, a worldwide intelligence network had been keeping London informed about German battleships that might constitute a danger to the British merchant navy.[59] Last but not least, the cult of warships as tokens of national strength and identity became a key feature in the years before 1914, pointing to a close association of politics and diplomacy with national self-images. This applied to the high profile of the navy in the media and the public mind, both in Germany and in Britain.[60]

This constant ambiguity, in which tendencies sharpening regional crises coexisted with attempts to prevent further escalation, was abundantly clear in the Balkan wars that broke out in 1912. These marked for southeastern Europe the beginning of a state of war that would last up to and beyond 1918—indeed, if we also include the Turkish campaigns to revise the Paris peace treaties up to the signing of the Treaty of Lausanne, then the war in this extended region may be said to have begun in 1912 and continued until at least 1923. The significance of the Balkan wars for the prehistory of the world war can hardly be overstated; they maintained the dynamic of violence and counterviolence that had marked the region since the early modern wars of the Habsburg and Ottoman Empires.[61]

The original core was a military conflict between the Balkan League, comprising Serbia, Greece, Romania, and Bulgaria, on one side, and the Ottoman Empire on the other. After a series of severe defeats, the Turkish armies were forced to withdraw almost to Constantinople, and the effective collapse of Ottoman rule in the Balkans cut the ground out from under

the Austro-Hungarian strategy of maintaining the Ottoman Empire against
Russia and the new nation-states supported by it. At first, an international
ambassadors' conference in London managed to contain the conflict, insofar
as the territorial gains of Bulgaria and Serbia were offset by the creation of
an independent Albania that served Austro-Hungarian interests by imped-
ing Serbian access to the sea. But in the Second Balkan War of Summer 1913,
the allies fell out over the sharing of the booty. The military collapse of
Bulgaria at the hands of Serbia, Romania, and Greece, together with the
conquest of Albania that gave Serbia access to the Adriatic, confirmed top
Austro-Hungarian politicians and generals in their view that the situation
in the Balkans could no longer be stabilized in the long term. While the
opposition to Serbia intensified, Bulgaria drew closer to Austria-Hungary
in the wake of its huge territorial losses. Meanwhile, the Ottoman Empire
followed up its catastrophic defeats with a comprehensive overhaul of the
military that would contribute to its relative efficiency as a fighting force in
1914 and thereafter. One element in this was a greater reliance on German
military advisers in the country.[62]

The Balkan wars were a turning point for yet another reason: the military
operations were accompanied by war crimes against the civilian population
on a massive scale. These included the forced resettlement of some 800,000
Muslims and a series of atrocities, mainly against Muslims and Albanians,
as well as between Serbs and Bulgarians in the Second Balkan War. Many
Muslims from parts of the Balkans fled to Constantinople or Anatolia—which
convinced leading figures in Turkey to move away from the concept of Ottomanism and eventually to embrace an aggressive Turkish nationalism. Leon
Trotsky, working as a war reporter for a Kiev newspaper, fully grasped the
novelty of systematic ethnic cleansing, related violence, and scorched-earth
policies operated by soldiers and irregular national units.[63] The events had
an international echo, as an investigation by the Carnegie Foundation demonstrates. Its careful documentation led to an unambiguous conclusion: "The
second war was only the beginning of other wars, or rather of a continuous
war, the worst of all, a war of religion, of reprisals, of race, a war of one
people against another, of man against man and brother against brother. It
has become a competition, as to who can best dispossess and 'denationalize'
his neighbor. . . . A dark prospect, which however, might become brighter

if Europe and the great military Powers so wished. They could, in spite of everything, solve the problem if they were not determined to remain blind."[64]

The Balkan wars therefore represented a dual historical watershed: the boundary between military violence against enemy armies and attacks on civilians became more porous; but at the same time the world became more attentive to ethnic cleansing and atrocities against minorities, even if this could not prevent a further radicalization of such practices during the world war.[65]

While the Ottoman Empire and Bulgaria sought ways to revise the new boundaries, the Constantinople peace conference in 1913 for the first time provided for a full-scale population swap to segregate the multiethnic region. This was quite different from the kind of simple territorial exchanges that had featured in earlier peace treaties, showing the degree to which the ideal of an ethnically homogeneous nation-state had become a guide for action already before 1914. The alternative—provisions for minority rights—never came to fruition. Whereas Turks were openly expelled in Serbia and Greece, they were able to achieve a relatively secure status in Bulgaria and even had some representation in parliament.[66] Intensive media reporting elsewhere in Europe made it clear that the Balkan wars were not just about national liberation but also involved an intensification of the Eastern Question and were therefore a problem for the whole continent. Above all, the conflict seemed to confirm the ultimate purpose of war. The *Kölnische Zeitung* wrote on October 1, 1912: "When, in the development of nations, the obstacles become so great that no advice can help, but it seems reasonable to think that the obstacle can be removed through violence, we shall also experience wars."[67] Even in Scandinavia, governments were making preparations for the eventuality of war.[68]

The main reason why the Balkan wars were so important, however, is that they signaled a substantial change in Russo-French relations—with fundamental consequences for the crisis of Summer 1914.[69] From 1912 on, relations between St. Petersburg and Paris were closely bound up with the Balkans: there was a "Balkanization of the Franco-Russian alliance."[70] No longer improvised and reactive, France's Balkan policy had the aim of giving Russia a clear signal to take proactive decisions.[71] Until Summer 1912, Paris had construed the Franco-Russian military convention mainly in defensive terms; it had, for example, refused to see the Bosnian annexation crisis of 1908–1909 as a threat to the vital national interests of either France or Russia.[72] In 1911, the convention had actually been modified under French pressure, so that immediate mutual assistance would come into play only if there was a general mobilization in Germany. Further consultations between France and Russia would be required in the event of a partial or total mobilization in Austria-Hungary.

When Poincaré took office as French foreign minister and prime minister, however, a new political course came into play, its main thrust being to clarify policy toward Russia and to recommend France as a reliable ally in possible conflicts. This indirect formalization, however, brought with it a loss of flexibility. There was also a change in both the internal and external situation, which increasingly restricted the room for maneuver of the French government. The Second Moroccan Crisis in 1911 had unleashed a wave of nationalism in the French public, and the scenario of a war with Germany, in which France would have to take an offensive posture, came to the fore. This made the focus on military strength all the more important. A final element behind Poincaré's strategic shift was the further instability introduced by the Italian attack on Libya and the likely breakup of the Ottoman Empire.

In March 1912, Poincaré assured Count Izvolzky, the former Russian foreign minister and ambassador in Paris, that France did not distinguish in principle between a local conflict in the Balkans and its higher strategic interests. Thus, Paris was tying itself to developments in this crisis region and losing some of its capacity to influence Russia in the direction of moderation. The French were also aware that a Balkan crisis might lead to war between Russia and Austria-Hungary, thereby activating the German-Austrian alliance and, on the other side, the Franco-Russian entente.[73] Probably the current foreign minister Sazonov informed Poincaré as early as August 1912 about the substance of an agreement between Serbia and Bulgaria, so that Paris was *au fait* with the degree of Russian support for the Serbian position. Perhaps, too, Poincaré already considered that a major conflict with Russian involvement was unavoidable, and he felt under pressure to clarify the French position in such an event.

This linkage of the Franco-Russian alliance to developments in southeastern Europe was consolidated in the run-up to the First Balkan War. In September 1912, Poincaré and much of the French military assumed that a war in the Balkans would lead indirectly to a conflict between Russia and Germany plus Austria-Hungary; the French government would regard this as a *casus foederis* and not hesitate to fulfill its alliance obligations to Russia.[74] Indeed, in mid-November Poincaré assured the Russian government several times that France would support it militarily in such a crisis.

In view of these developments, any involvement by a European power in southeastern Europe was bound to have an unsettling effect, especially in the Ottoman Empire. The governments in Berlin, Paris, and London had earlier used the financing of major infrastructure projects to acquire political influence in Constantinople—for example, when the Deutsche Bank won the contract to build the strategically important railroad from Konya in Turkey to Baghdad and on to Basra. Begun in 1903 and finally completed in 1940, this project served not least as the basis for German military cooperation with the Ottoman Empire, which aroused many a suspicion in Russia and Britain. Thus, when the German general Liman von Sanders was sent out in 1913 to assist with reorganization of the Ottoman army, it elicited British protests and fueled Russian fears that Germany would take control of the Bosporus. Yet these protests changed little in the planned cooperation: in 1914, Sanders became inspector-general of the Ottoman army, and in 1915 he took part in the successful defense of the Dardanelles against Allied attack.[75] The reactions in Paris, London, and St. Petersburg to these developments testify to the climate of great nervousness following the Balkan wars.

The Balkan wars did not, however, only affect France's position toward its Russian ally; they also had an impact on the Franco-British relationship. At first, the British government remained in the role of observer, but then, together with German diplomats, it pushed for a de-escalation of the crisis, not least because London was interested in stabilizing the Ottoman Empire as a force for order in the region. The ensuing resolution of the conflict in 1912–1913 confirmed a recasting of the concert of powers under the changed conditions. Yet London's behavior fueled uncertainties in Paris because it seemed that the cooperation between Germany and Britain might loosen the cohesion of the Entente—and this in turn reinforced the tendency in France to support Russia unconditionally in a new conflict.[76]

The outcome of the Balkan wars also had a political dimension inside Britain that would prove important in July and August 1914. Left Liberals were under the impression that British diplomacy under Foreign Secretary

Edward Grey took seriously their criticism of the rapprochement with the tsarist autocracy and was moving closer toward a pacifist position. In fact, the British government in particular recognized how tsarist policies were calling its own position into question and undermining stability in southeastern Europe. But foreign policy orientations around the year 1913 tended to mask these issues: the decisive factor for Grey was not just the status quo in the Balkans but—in view of the security interests of the British Empire—also the alliance with Russia.[77]

In Austria-Hungary, the government and military leadership reacted with alarm to the Balkan wars, but they were by no means automatically committed to the idea of a future major war—despite Serbia's access to the Adriatic and Russian troop reinforcements in Galicia in Winter 1912. Against the military pressures for war, there was also a search for diplomatic solutions, such as an alliance with Romania to isolate Serbia, although this found no support in Berlin. When Colonel Redl's espionage activity was uncovered in 1913, it strengthened the feeling that Russia posed a threat to Austria-Hungary. But since Western capitals knew of German war plans—an opening attack on France—months before the unmasking of the Russian spy, French pressure on Russia to build up its combat strength was all the greater, so that it could provide some relief by launching an early offensive in the east of the German Reich. In this context, French investments came in useful for the improvement of Russian communications and railroad links.[78]

As early as December 1912, in the aftermath of the First Balkan War, Wilhelm II invited top army and navy officers to a meeting to discuss strategy. The subsequent designation of this as a "war council" derives from Chancellor Bethmann Hollweg, but he was being altogether sarcastic, criticizing the fact that the civilian leadership of the Reich was not invited to the occasion. The record of the meeting reveals that the top brass and Wilhelm II himself engaged in one-track thinking that obeyed a logic of its own. This was nothing new in principle: it followed a number of earlier statements, even if the atmosphere at the meeting was one almost of panic. For the German monarch, things were perfectly clear: "Austria must deal firmly with the Slavs living outside its borders (the Serbs) if it does not want to lose control over the Slavs under the Austrian monarchy. If Russia were to support the Serbs . . . , war would be inevitable for us." If southeastern European countries such as

Bulgaria or the Ottoman Empire sided with Austria-Hungary, "it [would] free us up to throw our full weight behind a war against France," while the navy would "naturally have to prepare for war against England" with "immediate submarine warfare against English troop transports on the Schelde River or near Dunkirk," as well as "mine warfare up to the Thames." Grand Admiral Tirpitz pointed out that naval preparations would require another one and a half years before the navy could fight in a "major war," while Chief of the General Staff Helmuth von Moltke stated, "I consider a war inevitable— the sooner, the better." He added, however, obviously thinking of the Social Democrats (the strongest party in the Reichstag since the 1912 elections), that it would be necessary to justify the war in the eyes of the German public; he therefore considered it essential to "do a better job of gaining popular support for a war against Russia."[79]

This was an argument for greater war readiness in Germany, but it did not predetermine the war. Nor is the so-called war council straightforward proof that an offensive was planned long in advance and simply had to be implemented in the context of the July crisis;[80] such a judgment uncouples the Kaiser's statements from the erratic nature of his personality, postulating a purposive-strategic continuity and a consistent action logic that never actually existed. Evidence of this is Bethmann Hollweg's policy of seeking an understanding with Britain, as well as the chaotic entanglement of competencies in the Wilhelmine leadership, which made the realization of any such objective improbable. What the "war council" shows, with its missing government figures, is not a single-minded intention of going to war all the way up to August 1914, but rather the problematic scope for action in a field of tension that included the monarchic entourage, the military leadership, and the civilian government of the Reich. One-track thinking; erratic, almost panicky reactions; a tendency to "actionism" without a realistic assessment of the medium to long-term consequences—all this was, to be sure, already discernible, and much of it would repeat itself in like fashion in the crisis of late July 1914.

If, despite the burdens they produced, the Balkan wars are not overhastily interpreted as another step on the road to the Great War, the possibility of de-escalation, or even full-blown détente, in 1912–1913 becomes apparent. Beginning in December 1912 at the London ambassadors' conference, British influence over Russia and German influence over Austria-Hungary succeeded in containing the conflict. The plain language of the British war minister, Haldane, warning that Britain would not stand idly by if France was overrun by German armies, led Berlin to treat the forces in Vienna pushing for war with Serbia quite differently from the way in which it behaved toward them in July 1914. On the basis of this German-British cooperation, a provisional agreement was eventually reached in March 1914 on the construction of the Baghdad railroad.[81] These were visible signs of international détente.

3. PANORAMAS OF PROGRESS, SCENARIOS OF WAR

The war scenarios of Helmuth von Moltke were just one example of the countless conceptions of future war that had emerged since the last third of the nineteenth century, ranging from studies by military experts and academics through policy statements to literary works of fiction. In December 1887, Friedrich Engels prominently used the term "world war" as a synonym for a conflict spanning Continental Europe: "No war is any longer possible for Prussia-Germany except a world war and a world war indeed of an extent and violence hitherto undreamt of. Eight to ten millions of soldiers will massacre one another and in doing so devour the whole of Europe until they have stripped it barer than any swarm of locusts has ever done. The devastations of the Thirty Years' War compressed into three or four years, and spread over the whole Continent." Engels predicted not only economic ruin—"hopeless confusion of our artificial machinations in trade, industry, and credit, ending in general bankruptcy"—but also the breakdown of political systems: "collapse of the old states and their traditional state wisdom to such an extent that crowns will roll by the dozen on the pavement and there will be nobody to pick them up." What was "absolutely certain," though, was that "the system of mutual outbidding in armaments, taken to the final extreme," would not only produce "general exhaustion" but establish "the conditions for the ultimate victory of the working class."[82]

Arms spending, racial violence in colonial wars outside Europe, the rise of the United States and Japan as new players in international politics, ever shorter gaps between conflicts—all this undoubtedly fueled a sense that the world was beset with crises. But it is not possible to draw a simple line from these developments to a major European war. For in parallel various forms of transnational cooperation were also taking shape, exemplified not only by the plethora of expert meetings, academic conferences, and harmonization agreements covering everything from legal regulations to postal services but also by the global dimension of large corporations and financial flows that did not stop at national frontiers.[83] Moreover, in the twenty years or so before the world war, international pacifism achieved a high level of visibility and attracted unprecedented public attention.[84] It was precisely in the period before 1914 that the European workers' parties, organized in the Socialist International, experienced major growth. The Peace Congress that they staged in Basel in November 1912, against the background of the Balkan wars, was attended by no fewer than 555 delegates of social-democratic and socialist parties from twenty-three countries. Yet the confident appeals, the demands for disarmament and courts of arbitration, the optimism that it was possible to prevent war were only one side of the story. The other side was the view of German participants, among others, that the peace movement should not misjudge its power at the various national levels. There was no general agreement about the possibility of organizing a strike in the armed forces; representatives of the most successful parties of the Left feared that such a strategy would endanger what they had achieved as a parliamentary force pursuing an evolutionary path.[85]

Not the least of the ambiguities of the period around 1900 was the contradiction between, on the one hand, conflict frequency and crisis perception and, on the other, transnational cooperation and peaceful internationalism as signs of progress. In his widely read, richly illustrated book on the Paris World Fair of 1900, Georg Malkowsky gave special attention to the "gigantic picture" representing today's world and history; "the point was to make the huge advances of the last decade in art, science, and technology understandable in relation to the immediate past." In his eyes, the much talked-of "peaceful competition among nations" did not denote a competitive struggle inevitably leading to war: "It was not only a question of competing, but also of learning. The striving to convert arena into gymnasium was apparent in the numerous conferences that brought together scholars and technicians, commercial and social policy experts, artists and literary figures from all countries, to exchange opinions and experiences on the terrain of the exhibition. Not only were the results of the mighty movement of progress presented for judgment; their intellectual originators agreed to assess them retrospectively in consultation with one another and to take a broad view in regulating them." Especially noteworthy was the great value that Malkowsky attached to efforts to solve the social problems of advanced industrial societies: "An important reflection of the times was the glittering presentation of social policy and workers' welfare institutions—the safety valves that our century has created as inescapable accompaniments of mass production. They added a new ethical element to the national competition documented in Paris, creating a kind of neutral ground on which it was possible to come together without ill will in the same endeavor."[86] The convention prohibiting women's night work, signed in Berne in 1906, showed the potential of internationalized social policy when governments recognized the value of multilateral agreements and proceeded to make concrete advances.[87]

Alongside these optimistically juxtaposed expectations of progress and security, which the world fair symbolized for many at the time, the clash over future war scenarios and how to prevent them had been intensifying since the 1880s, and especially around the turn of the century. As early as 1883, Lieutenant General Colmar Freiherr von der Goltz had published a widely circulated book under the eloquent title *Das Volk in Waffen* (The People in Arms), itself an allusion to the wars against France in and after 1813. Unlike Moltke, however, he saw the arming of the people not as a threat that might lead to revolution, but as a necessary mobilization of all social, indeed mental, resources. Future wars between nations would know no bounds: "Nations collide with one another in solving their cultural tasks. . . . Where such forces set major resources in motion, it appears that wars can end only with the annihilation of one of the two sides or the complete exhaustion of both. In fact, the growing national consciousness and the political realization of the nationality principle have remarkably increased the resistance of states." Such a war would also place novel demands on the political leadership, which could no longer have its hands tied by constitutional or parliamentary constraints: "The most favorable situation for the deployment of wartime energy is to have a dictator at the top in the hour of danger. His powers are similar to those of an unfettered king."[88]

Remarkably, Alfred von Schlieffen, the author of the eponymous plan that seemed to offer a way of limiting war through a decisive early battle, outlined in 1909 a scenario that directly contradicted his plan's presumed effects. From the perspective of military experts, technological changes were crucial, because they called into question all previous assumptions about war: "The science of arms is celebrating its most magnificent triumph. [But] that for which both Germany and France endeavored and that which all the remaining powers desired—an alleviation in battle, a superiority over the enemy—was given to no one." This necessitated a "complete change in tactics." It was no longer possible, as in the eighteenth century, to march up in lines and then, according to the range of the weapons, open fire on the enemy from a close distance. "In the space of a few minutes, rapid fire would wipe both armies off the face of the earth." So, future battlefields would have to be much larger in extent and look totally different to an observer: "However large these battlefields may be, they will offer little to the eye. Nothing will be visible across the wide expanse of wasteland. If the thunder of cannon would not deafen the ears, only weak flashes of fire would betray the presence of artillery." The classical field commander with his aura, standing on a hill and taking everything in, was already a thing of the past; the future belonged to the communications expert: "No Napoleon stands on a rise surrounded by his brilliant retinue. . . . The *Feldherr* finds himself further back in a house with a spacious office, where telegraphs, telephones, and signals apparatus are to hand, and where fleets of cars and motor cycles, equipped for the longest journey, patiently await orders." Above all, barely four years after his plan for the war of the future, Schlieffen no longer thought it possible to decide the issue with a clever offensive strategy. War would present itself as an arduous war of attrition waged by states and societies: "The campaign will drag on. Yet such a war is impossible in a time in which the existence of the nation is founded upon an unbroken flow of trade and industry and the gears that have been brought to a halt must be set in motion again by a speedy decision. A strategy of exhaustion [*Ermattungsstrategie*] is impossible when the maintenance of millions necessitates the expenditure of billions."[89]

These scenarios, involving an interpretation of war as a necessary test for the nation, contrasted starkly with various other positions. In a memorandum of August 24, 1899, the Russian tsar confessed to foreign ambassadors that "preservation of the general peace and perhaps a reduction of the excessive weaponry that burdens all nations today" were "ideals for which all governments should strive." He noted a general tendency to international understanding, which should be strengthened through a great peace conference, a "joyful herald of the coming century." With this initiative, Russia could present itself to world opinion as a progressive and civilized country. Scarcely one European politician believed in the long-term efficacy of disarmament proclamations, and yet in 1899 the first Hague Peace Conference ended with a convention on the conduct of war; this included a ban on certain weapons—for example, the dropping of projectiles and explosives from airships, gas warfare, and the use of dum-dum bullets—and provided for better treatment of wounded enemy soldiers and prisoners. A compulsory international arbitration court failed to materialize, not least because of German resistance to the idea. In 1907, the second Hague Peace Conference adopted a convention on "the laws and customs of war on land," which also covered the right to neutrality, but a number of participants managed to block arms limitation measures, especially in relation to the navy. Still, the two conferences and their public resonance showed that war was by no means universally accepted as a kind of necessary evil.[90]

In 1898, the very year when so many global conflict areas were becoming visible, the Russian businessman Ivan Bloch, who had made a fortune in railroad development, published his 4,000-page book on the future of war; none other than Tsar Nicholas, he boasted, read it before he outlined his plan for an international peace conference. Translations into other European languages soon followed. Unlike most pacifists of the age, Bloch did not seek to disqualify war as immoral. Rather, he based its futility on rational and empirical grounds, meticulously analyzing the implications of the industrial-technological dynamic for future wars. Back in 1884, in *The Man versus the State*, Herbert Spencer had identified war with traditional society and argued that industrial progress was making it irrelevant in the contemporary world.[91] Fourteen years later Bloch could refer to the development of smokeless powder; the magazine rifle, accurate up to 1,500 meters, which had increased the rate of firing from one or two rounds per minute to four or five; and the Maxim machine gun and new heavy artillery. These weapons had so strengthened defensive warfare, he argued, that the classical infantry attack with fixed bayonets had become an impossibility. In the fundamentally altered battlefield, opposing armies had to dig in along mile-long frontlines; since there could be no decisive battle, future wars would drag on endlessly. The most remarkable of Bloch's predictions, however, concerned the social impact of new weapons technology behind the lines. For protracted war would bleed societies dry, to the point where they would eventually collapse: "War has become a terrible prospect as a result of extraordinary advances in weapons technology and the introduction of high-precision firearms with enormously deadly power. The next great war may therefore well be described as a rendezvous with death! . . . No less terrible [will be] the economic and social shocks resulting from conscription of almost the entire male population, from congestion in trade and industry, huge price rises, cessation of credit, budgetary problems, and the difficulty of maintaining the sections of the population that remain. And finally—when the war is called off because of general exhaustion—will the soldiers, some of whom come from socialist districts, be willing to lay down arms?"[92]

Against these pacifist currents, outspoken champions of war held the social Darwinist view that it was essential to the evolution of nations, vitalizing both societies and states. According to the retired cavalry officer and military author Friedrich von Bernhardi—whose *Deutschland und der nächste Krieg*, first published in Spring 1912, went through seven editions before the outbreak of world war, and soon appeared in English, French, Italian, and Japanese translations—pacifists had a dangerous tendency "to discard war in general and to deny its necessary place in historical development." "This aspiration," he wrote, "is directly antagonistic to the great universal laws which rule all life. War is a biological necessity of the first importance, a regulative element in the life of mankind which cannot be dispensed with, since without it an unhealthy development would follow, excluding every advancement of the race and therefore all real civilization."[93]

In the realm of science fiction, H. G. Wells depicted in *War of the Worlds* (1898) a society that, shortly after an extraterrestrial invasion, broke up into small and extremely small groups, with no state order to hold them together. In later books, he also showed how future wars fought with new weapons—submarines, armored vehicles, and flying machines (in a work published in 1908, *The War in the Air*)—would remove any boundary between the military and home fronts. On the other hand, he also believed that "military compulsion" was required to keep in check the excessive egoism of modern societies. Military service seemed to him a necessary learning process, a corrective to the lack of discipline in mass society, because "order and discipline, the tradition of service and devotion, of physical fitness, unstinted exertion, and universal responsibility" were values without which peace would no longer be possible.[94]

In 1910 the British journalist Norman Angell published a book with even greater resonance, *The Great Illusion:* not only did it become one of the early bestsellers of the twentieth century but it also launched a wave of new clubs and associations devoted to "Angellism." Angell, too, argued against war on essentially rational grounds: the historical era when military strength was the basis of prosperity was well and truly over. In the age of the division of labor, economic performance depended above all on dynamic transport links and a worldwide exchange of goods, ideas, and people. Modern societies could no longer afford to go to war, since this flew in the face of their interconnectedness. Economic gain no longer resulted, as in earlier periods, from the occupation of new territory, but rather from trade relations, from the exchange of goods and capital. Thus, Germany's annexation of Alsace-Lorraine and its insistence on French reparation payments after 1871 had been a costly mistake, since it had had the effect of weakening a potential trade partner.[95]

In contrast to the moral strictures associated with such pacifists as Bertha von Suttner, Bloch and Angell attempted a rational, scientific refutation of war. Both men argued that the technological and economic progress of modern society had made war too great a risk, since it would call into question all previous achievements. The social Darwinists, on the other hand, positively feared the setting of limits to war. To them it was the supreme test of a nation's performance, its psychological resolve, strength of nerve, and biological superiority: in short, of its capacity for existence into the future.

4. MASTER NARRATIVES AND OPEN OUTCOMES

How unavoidable, then, was the First World War? Ever since Thucydides, historians have been aware of the difference between structural and immediate causes of war; they have also understood the need to subject official justifications of war to an ideological critique.[96] Distinctions can be made in this area, as in the search for causes of revolutions; the identification of long-term, medium-term, and short-term causes involves separating out determinants, catalysts, and contingencies. Especially with regard to the outbreak of war, moreover, the question of external and internal factors continues to play a key role to this day. To what extent does the root cause of a war lie in the system of international relations, and to what extent does it lie in the internal composition of states and societies? Such questions are legitimate. Yet if various individual factors are simply amassed, without an assessment of their relative weight, they often contribute little to the explanation of an event.

There is certainly no lack of structural approaches in the historiography of the First World War; many have become classical explanatory models, indeed master narratives in their own right. In particular, imperialism, nationalism, and militarism are repeatedly cited in this connection, since they are highly suggestive leitmotifs for the prewar period up to July 1914. On closer examination, however, the limits of these approaches become apparent too.[97]

(1) Many contemporary critics of colonial expansion, from camps as far apart as those of Hobson and Lenin, pointed to pre-1914 high imperialism as the reason for the war. The distinctively German variant, which gave explanatory primacy to internal politics and interpreted social imperialism as a diversion from tensions and integration deficits within the *Kaiserreich*, saw the combination of naval construction and protective tariffs in terms of a compromise between large agrarian and heavy industrial interests, and hence as a factor that tended to stabilize the system.[98] In this view, Wilhelmine global policy was an attempt to shield the traditional elites of the latecomer nation-state from internal threats on both the Left and the Right. But to see the cause of international conflicts in the increasing vulnerability of capitalism is to explain the war in terms of a systemic crisis that did not exist as such in the period before 1914. In most of the future belligerent countries, what was on the agenda was not social revolution, but a balancing of opposed economic interests. It was therefore no accident that, in the run-up to 1914, welfare-state interventionism and social liberalism were being widely discussed in Europe's two most advanced industrial countries, Germany and Britain. The social

measures undertaken by a number of governments triggered bitter disputes in the parties of the Left over whether they should choose a path of conflict and revolution or one of limited cooperation. For all the rhetorical affirmations, neither France nor Britain nor Germany stood on the threshold of a social revolution, and it did not even seem likely that workers' strikes would or could prevent a major war. Most important of all, the references to high imperialism do not explain why the war eventually broke out in southeastern Europe and could not be kept in check by a Socialist International of peace.

(2) There is no doubt that nationalism changed in the second half of the nineteenth century after the establishment of new nation-states and the development of imperial expansion, heightened international rivalry, and critiques of mass society. Racial and social-Darwinist ideas, based on fears that the nation could not face the future successfully, gained ground in every European country. But these tendencies did not lead to war by any direct route; they did not determine diplomacy and international relations, nor was the new Right strong enough politically to impose such positions against the pacifist, internationalist orientations of the workers' parties. Although the media, especially the daily press, grew in importance in all European countries, there was no "democratized foreign policy" to provide a national springboard for war. Diplomacy—we know this from the host of international meetings, as well as talks and memoranda involving military elites and government spokesmen—remained a largely arcane affair, even if it did respond more to press reports in the home country and abroad.[99] Where aggressive nationalism really did sharpen conflicts was in regions with a multiethnic or multireligious population, since a breakaway from larger entities such as the Ottoman or Habsburg Empire was combined with the ideal of an ethnically homogeneous nation-state, and external support for the movements in question meant that the spiral of violence might at any time become internationalized. In those areas, as the Balkan wars of 1912–1913 demonstrate, the threshold to violence against the civilian population was lowered.

(3) It is also difficult to conclude that the militarism of prewar societies led to the outbreak of war in 1914. The social presence of the military, in a plethora of army and navy clubs and veterans associations, did have much in common with the folkloristic cult of the "nation in arms" that dominated the landscape in France, Germany, and elsewhere in Continental Europe.

With the beginning of the war, however, public parades and colorful uniforms suddenly vanished, as earnest rituals and proud demonstrations of military-technological superiority appeared in the place of popular festive holidays celebrated under the aegis of the armed forces.[100] More convincingly, the martial spirit and the pre-1914 arms buildup can be connected to a climate of expectancy of, indeed fixation on, a future war; the omnipresence of martial themes in the media was a reflection of this climate. Yet beyond the cult of war as an instrument of vitalist renewal and selection of the fittest states and nations, and beyond the cult of the all-deciding offensive war and the problem of civilian control over the military, there was also a line of rational argument against the glorification of war. Its focus was not on ethical considerations but on rational consideration of the nature of modern weapons technology, arms races, and related economic development, making war seem pointless because the danger of its consequences far outweighed any possible gain in prestige. Not only the visions of H. G. Wells or Friedrich von Bernhardi but also the books by Ivan Bloch and Norman Angell became bestsellers of the age. Nevertheless, we should not underestimate another new factor: the top military brass, and not only in Germany, had a clear tendency to develop scenarios in which there seemed to be only one option. Arms races, the hardening of bloc alliances, and, above all, the autonomous logic of offensive strategies and the dynamics of mass mobilization (call-up, equipment, and transportation) on the eve of war were all factors contributing to this lack of perceived alternatives. This tendency was particularly strong in Germany, where there was no effective civilian control over the military and a vacuum could arise in which panicky visions of encirclement and overhasty reliance on standard reactions could gain preponderance. In this respect, too, there was no simple path to the decisions of Summer 1914, but the one-track thinking and failure to allow for possible consequences inevitably weighed heavily in international crises.

Those who seize on pre-1914 militarism as the root cause of the First World War fail to appreciate that, despite the social and cultural presence of the armed forces, the threshold for a major war became considerably higher after 1815 and after 1871 than in previous centuries. The negative costs and consequences could not but have increased because of the large conscript armies, the arms buildup, and the improvements in weapons technology.

Prewar militarism therefore drew less on anticipation of a future war than on the need for self-reassurance, on memories of bygone wars, and on pride in the armed forces as a symbol of national success, economic achievement, and a higher level of civilization. It is true that the risk of war might be contained precisely because of the nature of mass armies and high-power weapons technology, but the dangers of war once it had broken out were so much the greater.[101] The two went hand in hand, as twin sides of a single logic, since deterrence and risk limitation could be credible only if the costs of a war were seen as excessively high. Despite the efforts of pacifists and other critics before 1914, war was by no means excluded as a legitimate instrument of politics. Readiness to wage even a major war, if necessary, remained a key criterion for the strength and status equality of states within international relations. Against this background, the outcome of international crises depended on how governments operated on the ever thinner tightrope between deterrence and assertions of strength within an international state system dominated by ideas of prestige.

(4) Another approach to the First World War, which gained particular currency after it was over, focuses on the international state system and the tradition of secret diplomacy. No doubt there was a change in international relations in the nineteenth century: the relatively stable system of short-term alliances to prevent unequal power constellations lost some of its flexibility in the period before 1914, but it was by no means so sclerotic that the outbreak of a great war just depended on the date of the next crisis. Neither the Triple Alliance of Germany, Austria-Hungary, and Italy nor the agreements among France, Russia, and Britain were the foundations for offensive alliances. Conflicts of interest, whether between Austria and Italy over the *irredenta* (the "unreclaimed" territories of Trentino, Istria, and Dalmatia) or, still latent, between Britain and Russia over the borders of the British Empire, contradicted the image of homogeneous blocs with no latitude for disagreement. In the end, Europe had no offensive alliances geared to fundamental changes in the political-territorial status quo, only an ever more detailed set of diplomatic early-warning systems, which reacted to the slightest sign and tended to trigger an autonomous dynamic of misunderstandings through overinterpretations.[102] The German plans, in particular, arose out of a growing panic that Germany would be encircled in Europe and

thwarted in the wider world, being robbed thereby of the reward of their development successes. Paradoxical though it may seem, the resulting theory of offensive war and decisive battles, which marked the Schlieffen Plan and the mentality of the Kaiser and the military leadership, lacked objectives and contours. All it offered was a well-rehearsed model of reactions in the event of war: it concentrated on issues of mass mobilization, combat on two fronts, and tactical time windows, but it did not present a long-term conception, a strategic war aim, or even an aim involving any fundamental change in the international order. To read a systematic objective into the often erratic reactions of politicians and generals would be to impute a rationality that can only come with hindsight. The so-called war council of December 1912, like many of the responses of European political and military leaders in the crisis of Summer 1914, displayed a startling degree of reality loss and individual inability to cope.

(5) An analysis of the causes of the war that dwells only on the growth of international conflicts and secret diplomacy since the turn of the century therefore falls short of the mark. In itself the greater frequency of crises tells us little; only with retrospective knowledge of the outcome does each new crisis become another step on a road without an exit. But if the perspective is reversed, each successful de-escalation confirms the relative elasticity of the international system and its effectiveness in preventing a major war. In that optic, the years between 1871 and 1914 were one of the longest periods of peace in the history of Europe, when the deflection of tensions to the southeastern periphery (in the case of Austria-Hungary and Russia) or to outlying imperial theaters (in the case of Britain, France, and Germany) was not the least factor in the prevention of war between two or more European great powers. But the price for this deflection was that the situation in those regions became even more prone to conflict.[103]

(6) The concatenation of crises did increase the likelihood of war, since it accustomed people to the idea of military conflict and, in many cases, made them obsessed with it. Even so, examples of successful détente, such as the collaboration between Britain and Germany during the Balkan wars, spoke against the notion that events were predetermined. The real problem was the widening gap between alternative policy options and the self-reinforcing negative perception of all crises and changes as threats to which

there had to be some response. This gap marked the German leadership elite, the monarch, and the military top brass, but it was not confined to them; very similar patterns were discernible in Vienna, Paris, St. Petersburg, and London. Only in this social-psychological perspective does the category of expectation acquire its meaning as a catalyst of the war; only then does it become clear how the subjective expectation of war objectively reduced the options available, setting up a time pressure that led to the neglect of consequences and gave a dangerous weight to the logic of alliances, domino effects, and autonomously driven military reactions.

(7) Before 1914 there was certainly no lack of war scenarios, whether in works of fiction, in the writings of popular military authors, in the action plans of military experts and general staff officers, or in the nightmare visions of peace movement activists and opponents of war. All these emphasized the incalculable risks of war once it had broken out, arguing that they would be quite different from all previous experiences of military conflict. While these anticipations of the changed realities of war remained to a large extent theoretical, the American Civil War and the wars of European powers in their colonies before 1914 brought with them new and tangible experiences of violence. There, on the periphery, the contours of classical "cabinet wars" and interstate conflicts crumbled away, as did the principle of the agonal sovereignty of state belligerents; there, for the first time, the asymmetrical violence of war became intelligible as a mass phenomenon. This disinhibition of violence under the experimental conditions of colonial rule remained unaffected by attempts in the late nineteenth century to limit the violence of war—for example, through the banning of certain weapons and practices in the Hague convention on land war. No international instruments of prohibition or arbitration could keep up with the visible technological asymmetry and practical experience of killing in those overseas lands.

(8) Although a great war was by no means an inevitable result of the slide of international relations into a system of closed alliances with irreconcilable aims and fixed reactions, there were clearly crisis factors before 1914 that made a war more likely and fueled the idea that one was in the offing. Imperial outreach and overseas conflicts between European powers were not among the most prominent factors, however, since diplomats continued to hope—as the British did in the case of Germany—that their consequences

could be kept under control. In the end, war broke out in a region of Europe where the dangers had been multiplying and reinforcing one another, not in the Asian or African colonies or other crisis zones where they could be dealt with on a case-by-case basis. Only in southeastern Europe, in the Balkan Peninsula, did ethnic and religious diversity sharpen into a radical standoff between multiethnic empires and an aggressive nationalism that pursued a secessionist agenda involving violence, expulsions, and the formation of ethnically homogeneous nation-states. Only there, with the decline of the Ottoman Empire, had a power vacuum come about in which these goals ran increasingly rampant and ostensibly clashed with the integrative ideologies of the three empires active in the region: Pan-Germanism, Pan-Slavism, and Pan-Turkism. Only there did the position of Serbia and the South Slav question produce more than just a proxy conflict between Austria-Hungary and Russia, for the underlying issue was where and how the Habsburg monarchy could convincingly demonstrate its capacity for survival. All this played into the hands of those who, like Conrad von Hötzendorf as early as 1911, had been calling for a preventive war against Serbia. Since the Bosnian annexation crisis of 1908, in fact, the ground had existed for a conflict to break out at any time, and since the last third of the nineteenth century there had been a relative continuity of wars and, therefore, a growing culture of violence against ethnic-religious groups that lowered the threshold for the use of force. Nowhere else was there such a fine line between trust in the international regulation of regional conflict and the danger that internationalization would itself make matters worse.

It cannot be said, however, that contemporary perceptions were limited to these overlapping crises. Rather, the world appeared many-sided and dynamic at the turn of 1913–1914, with its promise of further progress expressed in new competitions and records.[104] The thought of another Balkan crisis seemed almost to vanish amid the flurry of worldwide events. In *The Man without Qualities,* Robert Musil puts these laconic words into the mouth of his hero Ulrich: "Was there a war actually going on in the Balkans? Some sort of intervention was undoubtedly going on, but whether it was war was hard to tell. So much was astir in the world. There was another record for high-altitude flight; something to be proud of. If he was not mistaken, the record now stood at 3,700 meters and the man's name was Jouhoux. A black boxer had beaten the white champion: the new holder of the title was Johnson. The President of France was going to Russia; there was talk of world peace being at stake. A newly discovered tenor was garnering fees in South America that had never been equaled even in North America. A terrible earthquake had devastated Japan—the poor Japanese. In short, much was happening; there was great excitement everywhere around the turn of 1913–14."[105]

3

DRIFT AND ESCALATION
Summer and Fall 1914

THE ASSASSINATION did not come without warning, and it did not make war unavoidable. "We were driving down the Appel Quay to City Hall. I was sitting next to the driver in the front of their Majesties' car, when a loud bang suddenly rang out. . . . Thereupon my driver drove off at great speed. At that moment a bang like that of cannon fire rang out, filling the air with gun smoke. Shortly afterwards His Imperial Highness called a halt. . . . The reception at City Hall went ahead as planned. Their Highnesses displayed the greatest sang-froid. . . . There were also discussions about possible changes to the program. . . . As I was sure there would be another attempt, I left the seat next to the driver and placed myself on the running board alongside His Imperial Highness, in such a way that his whole body was covered on the left by mine. We drove to the Latin Bridge and turned to enter Franz-Joseph Gasse, and at that moment His Excellency Provincial Governor Potiorek, having probably discussed it with His Imperial Highness, ordered the driver to go back along the Appel Quay as they had come. Naturally the car came to a stop for two or three seconds as it was executing the turnaround. Then a shot rang out from the line of people on the right, and a second one a moment later from very close by."[1]

After the first assassination attempt, it was decided to change the route so the archduke and his wife could visit wounded members of the visiting delegation in the hospital. But the driver of the first car in the column knew nothing of this change in plan and followed the original route. Since his car had no reverse gear, he then had to execute a long turning maneuver by hand—and this left the successor to the throne and his wife in a defenseless position. The assassin hit Franz Ferdinand in the neck and his wife, Sophie von Hohenberg, in the abdomen. The report on the events of June 28 by Count Harrach, the archduke's adjutant, reveals a barely comprehensible naïveté on the part of the authorities, despite advance warnings in the run-up to the visit to Sarajevo; none other than the Serbian prime minister, Nikola Pašić, had informed the governor of Bosnia-Herzegovina that assassination plans might be afoot, fearing that they would put his government in a difficult situation. Yet the visit was allowed to go ahead, with no changes to the schedule and no strengthening of the security precautions. Only 120 policemen were deployed to protect the motorcade's whole route through the city.[2] The blame for this was subsequently laid at the door of the governor of Bosnia and Herzegovina, Oskar Potiorek, who as the Austro-Hungarian commander would also later preside over the first, abortive offensives against Russia and Serbia.[3]

1. INCUBATION OF THE WAR
Spirals of Crisis, Parallel Actions, and Failed Risk Management

The trigger of the crisis of Summer 1914 may have been an amateurishly planned and executed assassination attempt, which succeeded only because of defective security provisions, but the place and date of the event had great symbolic and historical significance.[4] The visit by the crown prince and inspector-general to the provinces of Bosnia and Herzegovina was meant to consolidate the claim of the Austro-Hungarian monarchy to rule this crisis region that it had annexed in 1908. However, the date chosen for the arrival in Sarajevo, June 28, marked in the Gregorian calendar St. Vitus's Day, the anniversary of the Battle of Kosovo in 1389—a defeat at the hands of the Ottomans that had acquired great significance for the cause of the martyred Serbian nation and was being celebrated for the first time in 1914 as a national holiday in Serbia. The archduke's visit therefore had a provocative effect in Serbia, and all the more for the Young Bosnia national movement out of whose ranks came the actors and planners of the assassination.[5] The actual assassin, Gavrilo Princip (b. 1894), was a Bosnian Serb student who had first encountered the Young Bosnia movement in 1911 and had had to leave high school a year later because of his involvement in anti-Austrian demonstrations. In Belgrade, Princip made contact with Unification or Death, also known as *Crna ruka* (Black Hand), a militant underground organization founded in 1911 by Serb officers in the context of the Balkan wars and led by the head of the army secret service, Dragutin Dimitrijević (aka Apis). Referring to the example of radical Italian irredentists, Black Hand used terrorist actions to promote the unification of all South Slavs within a Greater Serbian nation-state. Until 1913 it had been closely linked to ministers in the Serbian government, and the Serbian crown prince had even funded its journal *Pijemont,* another mark of identification with the Italian Risorgimento. In the year of the assassination, the government under Nikola Pašić saw the growing influence of the movement as a threat to the more cautious policies pursued in Belgrade after the Balkan wars and did not wish to give the war party in Vienna any pretext to strike. Nevertheless, the group of three assassins had at least indirect links to the Serbian government in the person of Apis; they were brought together by Vojislav Tankosić, a Serbian officer and leading member of Black Hand, and trained for their task by the Serbian secret service officer Milan Ciganović; Tankosić reported directly to Apis. The assassins received firearms instruction in Belgrade, and their weapons—four revolvers and six small grenades—came from the Serbian state arsenal in Kragujevac. Black Hand members also assisted their clandestine border crossing into Bosnia.[6]

The assassins' behavior shows how little the government in Belgrade was able or willing to rein in the radical nationalists, who had for a long time placed themselves outside the state monopoly of violence. Nothing hindered their trip to Bosnia or their drawing on Serbian army supplies. Princip consciously placed his act in the tradition of tyrannicides, modeling himself on Bogdan Žerajić, who in 1910 unsuccessfully tried to kill the Bosnian governor Marijan Varešanin, before taking his own life, and above all on Miloš Obilić, who, according to the legend of the Battle of Kosovo, infiltrated the camp of the Ottoman sultan and assassinated him.[7] But did Franz Ferdinand—though representing a foreign power in the eyes of the assassin and his sympathizers—really correspond to the image of a latter-day tyrant?

Born in 1863 as a nephew of the emperor then in power, Franz Ferdinand became heir presumptive to the throne only after the suicide of Crown Prince Rudolf and the death of his father in 1896. His marriage to Countess Sophie Chotek caused trouble with his uncle Franz Joseph, who did not accept the bride's family as equals of the Habsburgs and permitted only a morganatic marriage, the offspring of which would have no claim to the throne. Unlike his uncle, Franz Ferdinand was critical of the *Ausgleich* of 1867 enshrining a compromise between the two halves of the Habsburg monarchic empire, and in particular of the extensive concessions to Hungary. His aim was a remodeling of the state that would strengthen the monarchy and armed forces as central institutions, thereby ensuring the long-term stability of the Empire. But above all it was Franz Ferdinand's position on the South Slav question that revealed a basic dilemma for the pre-1914 Habsburg monarchy. His plan to unify Croatia, Bosnia, and Dalmatia into a single South Slav kingdom would have turned Austro-Hungarian dualism into a wider trialism, and this earned him the hatred not only of Serb nationalists. For the trialist project, which would have meant dissolving the union of Croatia with Hungary, also put a strain on his relations with Hungary.[8] Even the Sarajevo assassins feared Franz Ferdinand's reform policy, which favored a greater say for minorities. At his trial, Princip would later emphasize, "As the future ruler, he would have introduced a number of reforms that obstructed [Serbia's] unification."[9]

A third fault line manifested itself in Franz Ferdinand. Although, in the eyes of the assassins, he stood for the Habsburgs' detested foreign rule, he had repeatedly opposed the plans for a preventive war espoused by his chief of staff, Franz Conrad von Hötzendorf.[10] On the other hand, in 1906 Franz Ferdinand had pushed for von Hötzendorf's appointment and in 1912 urged the emperor to take back the man he had dismissed a year earlier. A further problem was discernible behind this contradictory behavior: Franz Ferdinand wanted to prevent a war with Serbia and the related confrontation with Russia, because he looked to monarchical-dynastic solidarity with the Tsar as a means of countering the threat of internal revolutions; yet, like Conrad von Hötzendorf, he relied on a strong military to ensure the existence of the Habsburg monarchy. It is more than doubtful whether the heir presumptive would have been an engine driving reforms to stabilize the Empire; many of his contemporaries described him as a quick-tempered and generally unlikable person. In his obituary, Karl Kraus wrote that he had not been a welcoming soul and had never been interested in "that unexplored territory the Viennese call their heart."[11] At any event, his murder strengthened the hand of those who had been pushing for a military solution to the South Slav question and who wanted at all costs to avoid another humiliation like that of the two Balkan wars.

The assassination was the top news story all over Europe—and the reactions to it immediately displayed notable differences. The London *Times* reported on the terrible "tragedy at Sarajevo," King George V ordered a week's mourning at court, and Kaiser Wilhelm II expressed shock at the death of the Austrian successor to the throne who had been so close to him. But these were not the only voices. In Italy the government reacted with barely concealed satisfaction in the death of a political opponent, whereas in Bucharest the Serbian envoy reported genuine grief on the streets of a city that valued Franz Ferdinand's efforts on behalf of national minorities.[12] Although diplomatic, political, and military leaders throughout Europe officially condemned the murder, it cannot be said that the sense of shock was universal or continuous, least of all in Austria-Hungary itself. A few hours after the news began to circulate, Stefan Zweig recalls, there were no longer "signs of genuine mourning": "The throngs laughed and chattered and as the evening advanced, music was resumed at public resorts. There were many on that day in Austria who secretly sighed with relief that this heir of the aged emperor had been removed in favor of the much more beloved young Archduke Karl."[13] On account of Franz Ferdinand's unequal marriage, Franz Joseph ordered a modest funeral ceremony. For him the deaths in Sarajevo continued a series of drastic personal losses: his younger brother Maximilian had been shot in Mexico in 1867 as a French-backed puppet ruler; his son Rudolf had taken his life in 1889, and his wife Elisabeth had been murdered by an anarchist in 1898. The bodies of Franz Ferdinand and his wife were brought back to Vienna and, after a brief lying in state at the Hofburg Palace, were taken to be interred at Artstetten Castle in Lower Austria. Only Franz Ferdinand, and not his wife, would have been granted a resting place in the Imperial Crypt in the capital.

By the Thursday after the assassination, the *Neue Freie Presse* in Vienna was already commenting on the exaggeration of its political consequences.[14] The mood in the Austrian public had in no way been thoroughly anti-Serbian since the annexation crisis of 1908 and the two Balkan wars. Serbs living in Vienna felt the mood change only with a certain delay.[15] But even then the press inculpation of the Serbian government contrasted with the relative sang-froid of the general population: "Neither banks nor business houses nor private persons changed their plans. Why should we be concerned with those constant skirmishes with Serbia which, as we all knew, arose out of some commercial treaties concerned with the export of Hungarian pigs?"[16]

The attitude of the military top brass was quite different. As far back as 1906 Chief of Staff Conrad von Hötzendorf had advocated an aggressive policy toward Belgrade; he felt vindicated by the outcome of the Balkan wars and was once again calling for a preventive war against that country in 1914. This assertive stance already reduced the leeway for political solutions. But leading advisers, such as Count Hoyos at the Außenamt (the foreign office), noted with concern the growing unrest among Serbs and Croats within the Habsburg monarchy and feared a general destabilization of the imperial order; the erosion of the Ottoman Empire showed the implications of an aggressive, secessionist nationalism. Especially in view of Russian support for Belgrade, military and political leaders in Vienna increasingly regarded the handling of Serbia as a life-and-death issue for the monarchy. Well before the June assassination, in the spring and fall of 1913, the only way to force the withdrawal of Serbian and Montenegrin troops from Albania had been through the issuing of ultimatums. A military solution of the latent conflict was thus by no means a strategy that had to be invented after the Sarajevo assassination.[17] The Foreign Ministry, under Leopold Graf Berchtold, had already explicitly advised the emperor to take a tough line with Serbia and to ensure that it had the support in principle of the German Reich: "There should be a new political offensive to restore the balance in the Balkans that has been disturbed by Serbian expansion and Romania's hegemonic position, as well as to raise again the influence of Austria-Hungary from the low level to which it has fallen. In this way, the dangerous machinations of the Greater Serbian and Greater Romanian irredenta, which have received such a powerful impetus, will be driven back."[18]

From the beginning, therefore, European reactions to the killing of the Austro-Hungarian heir to the throne and his wife were closely bound up with the prestige and the great power status of the Habsburg monarchy; this is what differentiated the assassination in Sarajevo from all previous crises, not least for people at the time who were aware of the potential for conflict. On June 30, for example, Sir Arthur Nicolson at the British Foreign Office wrote to the British ambassador in St. Petersburg: "The tragedy which has recently occurred in Sarajevo will not, I hope, lead to further complications." But immediately after the assassination, Austrian and German politicians focused on the idea that Habsburg would now have to demonstrate its political will to survive. At the beginning of July, the well-informed Berlin journalist Victor Naumann emphasized to Hoyos that Austria-Hungary would be "lost as a monarchy and a great power" if it "did not make use of this moment." And just five days after the assassination, the Austrian plenipotentiary in Athens, Count Tanczos, wrote to Conrad von Hötzendorf: "War would overnight make us a state that 'dares' to wage a war. Whereas the whole of Europe—the Balkans excepted—has a crazy fear of war, the simple courage to have declared war would make us so respected that our vested rights . . . would be secure for decades to come."[19]

Politicians and diplomats in the capitals of Europe expected a military operation to teach Serbia a lesson once and for all and to stabilize the entire monarchy. Beyond that, however, it was altogether unclear whether Vienna would pursue other far-reaching objectives and, if so, which ones. Although political leaders supported a punitive campaign against Serbia, they opposed any territorial consequences, let alone a further annexation. For the Hungarians, in particular, the resulting strengthening of the Slavs within the Dual Monarchy would have threatened the carefully constructed balance among ethnic groups and established a permanent hotbed of tension within the Empire.[20]

During the time between the assassination and July 23, 1914—the day when, around 6:00 P.M., Baron Giesel von Gieslingen delivered an ultimatum in Belgrade on behalf of the government in Vienna—the prevailing calm seemed to bear no relation to the high drama of the following days. With the ultimatum things began to speed up; no fewer than twenty-two declarations of war followed by the end of the war, beginning on July 28 with

Austria-Hungary's on Serbia and ending on November 6 with France's on the Ottoman Empire.[21] This chain reaction turned the regional conflict into a European war and, within the first few days, into a global conflict. Why, unlike in the Second Moroccan Crisis of 1911 or after the Balkan wars of 1912–1913, did a previously successful approach—containment of colonial and regional conflicts, compensatory balancing of interests within Europe—fail to work? The question is all the more pertinent because, in the four weeks between the assassination and the Austrian ultimatum, the immediate shock at the crime abated and there was enough time to achieve an international de-escalation. The reactions of leading politicians and heads of state did not suggest a particularly explosive situation that might lead at any moment to the outbreak of war. While Franz Joseph remained in his summer residence at Bad Ischl and Kaiser Wilhelm began a trip to Norway on July 6, President Poincaré and Prime Minister Viviani of France set out from Dunkirk on July 16 for a long-planned official visit to St. Petersburg from which they were not expected to return until July 29.[22]

The surface normality, however, concealed something very different. The Austrian chief of staff, Conrad von Hötzendorf, supported by the foreign minister Count Berchthold and a group of young diplomats around Hoyos, called for an immediate declaration of war on Serbia. But the Hungarian premier Count Tisza among others warned of the possible consequences: he feared that Austria-Hungary would become the "disturber of the peace" by fueling a "great war under unfavorable circumstances," that Russia was certain to intervene, and that German support for Vienna was questionable.[23] To clarify this last, decisive issue, Hoyos traveled to Berlin at the beginning of July, and on July 5 he received an assurance that Wilhelm II had given him in virtually the same terms in October 1908, on the occasion of the Bosnian annexation crisis: Franz Joseph could rest assured that "His Majesty [Wilhelm], in accordance with his alliance obligations and his longstanding friendship, would stand alongside Austria-Hungary." By this time, the German side too was aware of the danger that the conflict might escalate. In discussions between Chancellor Bethmann Hollweg and Wilhelm II shortly before the Kaiser left for his summer trip to Norway, it was emphasized that all means should be used to prevent "the Austrian-Serbian dispute from growing into an international conflict"; nevertheless, "Germany's vital interests" required "undiminished support for Austria."[24] Hoyos wrote the following about his meeting with the German chancellor: "Bethmann Hollweg told me that it was not Germany's affair to give us advice regarding our policy toward Serbia. It would cover our backs with all its power and fulfill its alliance duties in every way, if we found it necessary to act against Serbia. If I wanted to know his view regarding the opportunity of the moment, he would tell me that if war was inevitable, then the current time was better than a future one."[25]

This ambivalence about a high-risk venture, together with a view that Germany's allies could not be abandoned just when they needed to demonstrate external strength, left the space for interpretation dangerously open. What came to be dubbed the German "blank check" was thus at first a form of encouragement as Berlin ceased to operate a moderating policy as it had done during the Balkan wars, which at the same time created a lack of clarity with regard to the possible consequences. Once he was back in Vienna, Hoyos reported to the two prime ministers of the Dual Monarchy in the presence of the German ambassador, von Tschirschky. The joint Council of Ministers, which had responsibility for foreign policy, finances, and the armed forces, eventually overruled Count Tisza and opted for punitive military action, "a settlement as quickly as possible of the dispute with Serbia, in a martial or hostile sense." But whereas the war minister argued for a secret mobilization and, with the last Balkan war and the Russo-Japanese war of 1904–1905 in mind, wanted to attack without a formal declaration of war, Tisza won acceptance that there should be a preparatory diplomatic stage. Mobilization would follow only "after specific demands had been placed on Serbia and rejected, and after the issuing of an ultimatum" that the Serbian government would presumably fail to implement. A "purely diplomatic victory, even if it ended with Serbia's resounding humiliation," would be worthless. What was needed was "to place such extensive demands on Serbia . . . that their foreseeable rejection would open the way for a radical solution through military intervention."[26] To ensure that Russia and France did not jointly react to the ultimatum during Poincaré's and Viviani's official visit to St. Petersburg, it was decided to delay issuing it until the French president had begun his journey back to France.

In the days after Hoyos returned to Vienna, the war plans against Serbia continued beneath the appearance of calm. On July 19, the Council of

Ministers decided to insist on border revisions and cessions of territory that would make Serbia a small state dependent on Austria-Hungary both economically and politically. In London, rumors spread about Austro-Hungarian demands on Belgrade, and in France, too, the secret service reported as early as July 17 on the details of the planned ultimatum. For the moment Vienna seemed to be playing for time: "First they have calmed the stock exchange. Next they want to avoid disturbing the tourist season, which brings millions into the spas in Bohemia, . . . the Tyrol, and other Alpine regions. Then they will have to bring in the harvest, and while they are waiting they will try to create a favorable international public opinion."[27]

During this period, political survival and regional self-assertion of the Dual Monarchy were decisive considerations for the government in Vienna, but at another level a competing logic of military action followed long-established plans and conceptions. In roughly mid-July, in parallel with the political reactions, the military staffs in Germany, France, and Russia began to prepare for the possibility of war. As early as May 20, the chief of the German general staff, Helmuth von Moltke, had spoken of his fears in a private conversation with Foreign Secretary Gottlieb von Jagow. According to Jagow, "the prospects for the future" had weighed on him heavily: "In two to three years Russia would have finished arming. Our enemies' military power would then be so great that he did not know how he could deal with it. Now we were still more or less a match for it. In his view there was no alternative but to fight a preventive war so as to strike the enemy while we could still emerge fairly well from the struggle. The chief of the general staff therefore put it to me that our policy should be geared to bringing about an early war."[28] Although nothing precise had been agreed before 1914 between the German and Austro-Hungarian general staffs, the German military command therefore gambled that, with time still on its side, it would have some prospect of success in a war that was anyway unavoidable.

This assessment began increasingly to overlie the heart of the crisis: a limited punitive action against Serbia. Leading officials at the Foreign Office judged that the prospect of national uprisings in Poland and Finland, among other factors, would weaken Russia in a wider war and that France's army was not in a good state.[29] The army also wagered that Britain would not intervene in a conflict in Continental Europe, especially as it was paralyzed by domestic strife over home rule in Ireland. Since the 1870s, the Nationalist Party had been struggling for the establishment of an autonomous Irish parliament within the British Empire—hardly a viable solution in view of the revolutionary aspirations of radical groups in Ireland. By mid-July, then, a special logic of military planning was operating in Germany. In the early phase of the crisis it may not have had decisive weight, but it could quickly come to limit the room for maneuver and lock policy makers into rigid scenarios and military options that allowed for no alternative.[30]

This background explains why the conduct of the German political leadership under Bethmann Hollweg was so central in the weeks following the Hoyos mission in early July, amid the vacuum that arose when the Kaiser and much of the military top brass left for their summer vacation. The two possibilities then were de-escalation of the crisis by restraining the war party in Vienna or enlargement of the conflict to an international level. Bethmann Hollweg—seen by the army as a weak civilian figurehead, from whom no policy independence was to be feared—actually used the period between July 7 and the ultimatum of July 23 both to press Vienna to take a hard line against Serbia and to prepare the ground in Berlin for a military mobilization. In this way, he played a key role in ensuring that the crisis spread and that de-escalation strategies did not take hold.

But what lay behind this "calculated risk" vis-à-vis Russia, so markedly different from the German chancellor's policy of crisis containment in cooperation with Britain during the Balkan wars? Was it a limited intervention to eliminate the southeastern European trouble spot once and for all, or did it consciously accept the danger of a major war—and if so, for what purpose?[31] Kurt Riezler, a close adviser to the chancellor during those critical weeks of Summer 1914, kept a diary at the time, which, though published in an incomplete and problematic form, gives some insight into Bethmann Hollweg's thinking.[32] One element was his impression of Austro-Hungarian weakness, at a time when Russia's arms program and westward railroad construction were calling German war plans into question and challenging the position of the Dual Monarchy in the Balkans; these Russian actions threatened to complete the international isolation of Germany. Another element was his fear that disintegration of the Habsburg Empire, together with British-Russian naval cooperation (which he had known of since early summer), might seriously jeopardize the status quo of Germany's position as a great power. Thus, what lay behind Bethmann Hollweg's troubling image of a "leap in the dark"—as reported by Riezler—was not so much a sense of fatalism or heroism, or even his Hamlet-like nature that some after the war saw as Germany's undoing, but rather an uncertainty as to whether he could possibly succeed in his strategy of pushing Russia back in the Balkans, strengthening the Triple Alliance, and probing the weak points of the Entente or even blowing it apart.[33] The increased risk of war that this strategy involved cannot be simply equated with the preventive war option advocated by Moltke and the general staff—although, as the crisis unfolded, it played into their hands. A final calculation on Bethmann Hollweg's part was that, if the confrontation with Russia was postponed to a later date, it would cause even greater problems for Germany and face it with even more imponderables.

On the other hand, the chancellor's stance was plausible only if he gambled on British neutrality in the event of war, without actually returning to the earlier path of cooperation with London. Through the Foreign Ministry he notified the German ambassador in London, Prince Lichnowsky, that everything should be done to avoid giving the impression that "we are egging Austria on to war."[34] Although Bethmann Hollweg was realistic about Austria's war plans, his sporadic criticism still gave Vienna great leeway in the weeks before its ultimatum to Serbia. And even when he could assess the content of the ultimatum, he emphasized this point to the British Foreign Office: "Since Austria's actions are protecting vital interests, interference by its German ally is ruled out." Germany would "reach for the sword" only if it was forced to do so.[35]

With its pressure on Vienna until July 23 to seize the opportunity to deal with the Serbs, Germany undoubtedly bore a special responsibility in the July crisis. But the picture would not be complete if it left out developments in other European capitals, particularly St. Petersburg and Paris. In the space of just ten days, Russian foreign minister Sazonov developed his own version of events to justify support for Serbia. Rather than focus on the Serb assassins and the question of Belgrade's knowledge of the preparations for their action, he presented the Austro-Hungarian heir to the throne as an aggressive warmonger—which was not the case—and concluded that Russia, as the main Slav power, was duty bound to defend its Serbian brothers under all circumstances.[36] Sazonov further stated to the German ambassador in St. Petersburg that his country would not tolerate "threatening language or military measures" against Serbia on Austria's part.[37] Russia could not accept "the annihilation of Serbia. . . . This was a matter for Europe; the Austrian investigation was extremely untrustworthy; all the great powers should take part in the enquiry into the origins of the murder in Sarajevo."[38]

This hard line was only possible, however, because it could count on the willingness of Russia and France to activate their alliance even in the case of a Balkan conflict. This commitment did not suddenly appear in July 1914; it had first been formulated in 1912. Hence, after the assassination in Sarajevo, the Russian envoy in Belgrade supported Serbia's position vis-à-vis Austria-Hungary, even before Vienna had expressed its terms to the Serbian government. In principle Russia did not accept that Vienna had a right to "satisfaction," and it was prepared to escalate the crisis at the least challenge to Serbian sovereignty.

This position, in line with Russia's demonstrative closing of ranks with Serbia in 1913, gave a boost to Greater Serbian nationalism. But it also implicated France (which supported Russia's policy on Serbia) and made it dependent on developments in the Balkans. This fundamental new element in the European situation, going back to the Balkan wars of 1912–1913, weighed heavily again in the July crisis, lending great importance to the visit of July 21–23 to St. Petersburg by the French prime minister and president. The Russian capital was by no means a side stage in the crisis. Indeed, Poincaré used his trip there to assure Russia of full French support for its Serbia policy. In his diary for July 21 the French president noted the Tsar's reaction to events and, in particular, his interest in the action that Austria-Hungary would take following the murder in Sarajevo: "He repeats that, in the present circumstances, the complete understanding between our two governments is more important to him than ever." The attaché at the French embassy in St. Petersburg registered the change in mood shortly before the beginning of the visit: "It was noticeable in conversations that the atmosphere had changed since the day before . . . ; there was open talk about a war, whereas a few days earlier no one had taken that into consideration."[39]

This considerably increased the likelihood that the situation in the Balkans would grow into a European crisis. In a way, the French posture during the state visit to Russia may be compared to the blank check that the German government gave to Austria-Hungary—although German political leaders, in pursuing such a policy early in the crisis, consciously built a hardening of positions in Vienna into their own calculations. Poincaré's behavior in St. Petersburg can hardly be attributed to a conscious strategy of shattering Germany's position in Europe and gaining revenge for the national defeat of 1871.[40] At the time, France was not really pursuing a goal of hegemony, and the idea of *revanche* had tended to lose its salience in the years before 1914. Poincaré's far-reaching statements had more to do with the situation in France—and this overlap of diplomatic maneuvering and internal political constraints added a further element of complexity to the July crisis. Parliamentary elections in May 1914 had given a clear majority to the Left, which led the president to assume that the government would no longer support his pro-Russian course in its previous form. Poincaré therefore wanted to give a clear sign to the Russian government that it could rely on France's foreign and military policy.[41] In another parallel with Germany, many contemporaries were strongly affected by risk calculations and a subjective impression that France's future room for maneuver would be increasingly reduced. The guiding idea—"sooner rather than later"—apparent in how the German and Austro-Hungarian military viewed the rise of Russia, also informed Poincare's attitude to political developments within France. Both he and the French ambassador in St. Petersburg, Maurice Paléologue, backed the Russian war party around Sazonov in its resistance to the Tsar's misgivings. And after Poincaré left for Paris, Paléologue assured the Russian government of "France's complete readiness, if the need arose, to fulfill its alliance obligations"—which was a considerable overstepping of his authority.[42] Moreover, by deliberately sending reports to Paris late and patchily, he arbitrarily helped fuel the crisis. A deeper problem is also visible here: the loose character of the alliances reinforced the tendency of many players to give demonstrative tokens of support, on the grounds that their commitment might otherwise be doubted. Large sections of the French military and political elite believed that, without such assurances, France might find itself alone, especially as no conclusive judgment could be formed about how Britain would act in the event of a war.

On July 23, while the French delegation was on the high seas homeward bound from Russia, Austrian emissaries delivered the Viennese ultimatum in

Belgrade. Holding the Serbian government jointly responsible for the murder of the heir to the throne and his wife, the ten-point document demanded that it disown the South Slav movement, dissolve the secret irredentist organizations, cease all anti-Austrian propaganda, and above all involve Imperial officials in the investigation into the assassination and in "suppression of the subversive movement against the territorial integrity of the monarchy."[43] The government in Vienna thereby sought to demonstrate, with the threat of war, that it was capable of taking resolute action; this hardly came as a surprise after what had happened in Sarajevo. Josef Redlich noted after a conversation with Hoyos, "Our note is very strong; it will . . . create a dreadful storm in Europe. So, we are still in there with a will. We shall not and cannot be a sick man." Rather than that, it would be better to "go under straight away. . . . A great day is dawning: hopefully it will lead to Austria's recovery."[44]

The ultimatum was not as sharp as it might have been, however, given the enormity of the assassination and the apparent toleration shown to terrorist networks inside Serbia. This made it all the more surprising that the government in Vienna provided no actual evidence of the involvement of the Serbian government. Belgrade was already fearful of a detailed investigation, but now panic broke out in the Serbian political leadership. Russia was immediately asked for support; only its "powerful word" could save Serbia—as Serbian prince regent Alexander put it to the Russian *chargé d'affaires*, Strandtmann. In St. Petersburg, Sazonov told the Serbian ambassador Spalajković on July 14 that no state could meet the conditions in the ultimatum without committing "suicide." Matching Germany's blank check to Vienna in early July and the similar commitment during the French state visit to St. Petersburg, Russia now issued a far-reaching declaration of support for Serbia: Russia could not be "indifferent" to the fate of Serbia.[45]

With the Austro-Hungarian ultimatum, the danger of an international conflict became plainly visible. On July 24, Britain's foreign secretary Grey tried to come up with a solution by proposing an extension of the deadline for a Serbian response, the calling of an international conference, and efforts by the great powers not directly involved in the crisis (Britain, Germany, France, and Italy) to mediate between Austria-Hungary and Russia. However, German political leaders rejected this approach, arguing that no international disputes commission could constrain their ally in its justified course of action. Once again the two dimensions of internationalization manifested themselves: on the one hand, the British still hoped to localize the conflict by bringing outside influence to bear on governments; on the other hand, the crisis continued to spread as other players intervened and exacerbated the conflict.

The Serbian reply, drawn up by Prime Minister Nikola Pašić and other members of his cabinet, was presented by Pašić in person to the Austrian legation in Belgrade, only just within the ultimatum time limit of forty-eight hours. At first sight it seemed accommodating enough, but its content was less conciliatory than its form. It promised little of substance, but did so in an obsequious tone that secured the kind of international reactions foreseen in Belgrade. Consequently, it would be too simple to see the reply as a reason for the sharpening of the conflict. The Serbian government agreed to remove anti-Austrian propaganda from school textbooks, to dismiss public officials and army officers who had wounded the integrity of the Habsburg monarchy, and to open an investigation into the people behind the assassination. But on two key points there were no concessions, since it was felt that they would violate the sovereignty of the Serbian state. These were the demands that "organs of the Imperial government in Serbia [should participate in] suppression of the subversive movement against the territorial integrity of the Monarchy" and that "organs delegated" by the government in Vienna should be free to participate in a judicial investigation into terrorists and their associates in Serbia.[46]

The Serbian government rejected such involvement of Austrian officials as a "violation of the constitution and judicial process."[47] But precisely this was the crux of the matter: since some of its own members were implicated in the planning and preparation of the assassination, the Serbian government could not be assumed to have an interest in clearing up the affair. The conciliatory form of its reply disguised this fact. Formally speaking, the government in Belgrade could have quite easily accepted Austro-Hungarian observers without infringing its own penal code, let alone its constitution; the task then would have been to find common ground with the formulations in the ultimatum. The calculated Serbian reply therefore followed a conscious strategy: the main fear underlying the insistence on national sovereignty was that the origins of the assassination in Serbia, and the extent to which

Serbian state figures and institutions were implicated in it, would become known to the world.[48]

The Austrian envoy in Belgrade, Giesl von Gieslingen, reacted as he had previously agreed with Vienna. Without entering into the details of the Serbian reply, he informed the prime minister that Austria-Hungary was breaking off diplomatic relations with Serbia and set off for Budapest by train on the evening of July 25. When the German Kaiser learned of the Serbian position, an easing of tensions seemed possible: "It seems that things are starting to disentangle," wrote Moritz Freiherr von Lyncker of the Kaiser's trip to Norway. Wilhelm II did in fact emphasize that the Serbian reply satisfied Austria's demands. "A brilliant performance for a deadline of just 48 hours," he noted. "That's more than could have been expected! A great moral victory for Vienna; but it removes any grounds for war, and Giesl should have calmly stayed put in Belgrade! Then I would never have ordered mobilization."[49]

But that is exactly what happened. Following the envoy's departure from Belgrade on July 25 and the severing of diplomatic relations with Serbia, the armies in both Austria-Hungary and Serbia began to mobilize their troops. When the British foreign secretary submitted new mediation proposals on July 27, pushing for Germany to restrain Austria-Hungary and proposing that the Serbian reply should at least form the basis for new negotiations, the reactions in Vienna showed that the basic decision for war had already been taken. The great fear in the Austrian capital was that an international conference might bring about another change. Foreign Minister Berchthold urged the emperor to sign the official declaration of war, because he "did not rule out" the possibility "that the Triple Entente would make another attempt to reach a peaceful settlement of the conflict, unless a declaration of war created a clear situation."[50] During his visit to Franz Joseph at Bad Ischl on the morning of July 28, Berchthold mentioned rumors of initial skirmishes near Temes-Kubin on the north bank of the Danube, hoping that these would dispel the emperor's last doubts. Franz Joseph eventually signed the declaration of war at about 11 A.M.: "The Imperial government finds itself having to provide for the protection of its rights and interests, and for this purpose to call upon the force of arms. From this moment on, Austria-Hungary therefore considers itself to be in a state of war with Serbia."[51] The very first of the many declarations of war took place under the impact of rumors about a supposed outbreak of hostilities. But these rumors seemed plausible at the moment of decision and therefore created a reality of their own. It was this mechanism, this way of operating in the realm of the diffuse and speculative, which contained a possible, imaginable reality. Insofar as people adjusted their actions to it, a special kind of reality took shape out of the speculation. On the day after the Austrian reply was communicated to Belgrade, on July 29, 1914, Austro-Hungarian forces on the opposite shore of the Danube began shelling the Serbian capital. This marked the start of the regional war. After the ultimatum of July 23, the Austro-Hungarian declaration of war on July 28 was Vienna's second, decisive step toward escalation.

Attempts to keep the conflict local now became more intensive. This was true first of all on the German side, where, faced with a possible British declaration of war, and supported by his chancellor, Wilhelm II proposed that Austria should refrain from further annexations and simply occupy Belgrade, until a conclusive investigation had been agreed to by both sides. However, since Bethmann Hollweg assumed that such a solution would no longer be acceptable to Russia, and since he feared the Kaiser's erratic reactions, he forwarded the proposals to Vienna late, and only in part, on July 30.[52] One key to Bethmann Hollweg's inconsistent behavior was the situation in the German parliament: he thought that, with war now looming, it was essential to identify Russia as the aggressor and to avoid making Germany appear to be the country pushing for war; only if Russia was seen as the guilty party would it be possible to build a political bridge to the Social Democrats, who regarded the autocratic tsarist regime as Germany's principal adversary. On the afternoon of July 27, Wilhelm II arrived back in Potsdam from his Norwegian trip and held a meeting with the Reich chancellor. The head of the Kaiser's military cabinet, Moritz von Lyncker, summarized as follows the outcome of their discussion: "The aim of our policy is to push Russia into the role of provoker. But we do not seek to restrain Austria from further action."[53] In this light, German willingness to enter seriously into the talks initiated by London appears distinctly modest.

Nevertheless, Britain continued to push for international mediation, and on July 29 it proposed that the Austro-Hungarian army should stop its advance and that Vienna should seek mediation in its conflict with Russia.

Because of political preoccupations at home and the threat of civil war in Ireland, Whitehall had paid scant attention to the Balkans until the delivery of the ultimatum on July 23. At this point, however, the British foreign secretary was looking to play the role of "honest broker," with sufficient leeway to find a solution. But British neutrality was no more than a theoretical option, for by Summer 1914 the ties to the Entente had long been too strong to allow such a position. In 1912, Britain had entrusted its coastal defenses to a naval agreement with France, and this was no longer negotiable. Furthermore, many politicians and military people were increasingly nervous about the future strength of Russia, which might be in a position to threaten the British Empire in India and elsewhere. They liked to think they could get along with a hostile Germany, but a hostile Russia placed the foundations of the Empire in question. Grey therefore tried to exert influence on all sides, as a result of which he gave out signals that were fatefully contradictory. At the cabinet session on July 29 it was noted with resignation: "It seems we can do nothing right." Grey did not play the honest broker because he feared that a clear statement on his part—a declaration of neutrality vis-à-vis Berlin and Vienna, or an expression of support for Paris and St. Petersburg—would encourage one side or the other to take even more aggressive action.[54]

Grey eventually made a final attempt on July 31. But since July 29, Germany's attitude, Austria-Hungary's rejection of talks with Russia, and the incipient military mobilizations had greatly narrowed the chances for an international conference. In Russia the military mobilization was gathering speed, and on July 26 the German chief of staff had already drawn up an ultimatum to Belgium that was due for delivery on August 2—one symptom of the primacy of the military over the civilian leadership during this decisive phase.[55]

At a personal level, there seemed to be the glimmer of a solution. The harder line taken by Russian foreign policy contrasted with the Tsar's efforts to prevent the outbreak of war: Nicholas and Wilhelm were cousins, and at this moment they symbolized monarchy and dynastic solidarity as the basis of a legitimate order over and above the antagonism of nation-states. Nicholas turned to Wilhelm, in a personal letter, and asked him "in the name of our old friendship" to restrain Austria-Hungary: "An ignoble war" had "been declared on a weak country. The indignation in Russia, which I fully share, is immense. I foresee that I will soon yield to the pressure on me and be forced to take extreme measures that lead to war."[56] But such personal interventions had long been overtaken by military logic. Since the Russian military assumed that twenty-six days were needed for mobilization—more than twice as long as in Germany—the government had already decided on the evening of July 25 to order a partial mobilization of combat forces in four army districts.[57] This was another watershed: partial mobilization made no practical sense to the military, particularly because an advance was unimaginable without the railroad links in the Warsaw district, and so the chief of the general staff, Nikolai Yanushkevich, issued an ultimatum for Sazonov to press the Tsar into ordering a general mobilization. The Tsar eventually signed such an order on July 30, and around noon the next day this became known in Berlin.[58]

On the one hand, news of a Russian general mobilization triggered relief in Berlin, since the military could press ahead with its own mobilization from which it had been held back only with difficulty. The Bavarian military representative reported the mood at the War Ministry: "Beaming faces everywhere, handshakes in the corridors; people congratulate each other that the ditch has been crossed." The initiative in Germany had now passed for good to the military commanders. In his "Review of the Political Situation," dated July 29, Moltke stressed that Austria would not only face the Serbian army but would also have to reckon on war with Russia, and then, "if the clash between Austria and Russia is unavoidable," Germany would "mobilize and be ready to take the struggle to two fronts." In the Prussian House of Representatives, Bethmann Hollweg recognized that the "politics of bluff" had failed: "Things are out of control and the ball has started rolling."[59] Even now, however, the chancellor of the Reich remained ambivalent: on receiving news of the Russian mobilization, he sent several dispatches to Vienna in which he urgently called for a resumption of talks with Russia. Germany was ready to do its duty as an ally, he said, but it must refuse "to be drawn into a global conflagration by Vienna"[60]—a very different attitude from the one he had struck before July 23 and the delivery of the Austro-Hungarian ultimatum to Serbia. At the same time, Moltke was in Vienna pushing for Austria-Hungary to mobilize against Russia. Tactical oscillation by the civilian leadership, pressure for action by the military: this combination again points to a more general feature of the crisis, namely, the mix of contradictory signals and competing action logics that ruled out any consistent position and gave rise to various misperceptions. Above all, no more thought was given to the far-reaching consequences of decisions.

Having received reports of Russian troop movements on the East Prussian border, Wilhelm warned his Russian cousin that "responsibility for the security of [his] realm" was forcing him to take "preventive measures." Lyncker, in his diary entry for July 31, describes the point at which the mobilization mechanism stripped the last monarchical efforts at containment of their credibility: "Remaining in the Sternensaal [Hall of Stars] with Generals von Moltke, von Plessen, von Falkenhayn and myself, the Kaiser again set out the situation to us, with the help of nine telegrams. The culmination was that the Tsar still professed his love of peace and, in his last telegram to the Kaiser, pledges his 'sacred word of honor,' but that the Russian mobilization is continuing because, as the Tsar apologetically claims, it is 'actually not possible' to cancel the military measures, and in particular the mobilization. This points to the most obvious factor: the Tsar has no will of his own and is being driven by the Russian war party."[61] On the afternoon of July 31, an "impending danger of war" was announced in Berlin.

Years later, when employees were looking for lead in the composition room shelves at the Ullstein publishing house in Berlin, they found the already set leading article by the journalist Arthur Bernstein for the *Berliner Morgenpost,* dated July 31, 1914. The official "impending danger of war" announcement meant that the article was never published. But it was a lucid analysis by a well-informed journalist of the time, who had no special knowledge of the behind-the-scenes diplomacy, and what he concluded was that all the premises of those pushing for war were false. The result would be a European war with worldwide consequences and a novel combination of war and revolution: "Therefore, at the last minute: the warmongers are making a mistake. First, there is no Triple Alliance. Italy will not join in, or anyway not with us; if anything, it will be on the side of the Entente. Second, Britain will not remain neutral but will stand by France; either straight away or at the point when France seems to be in serious danger. Nor will Britain tolerate that German army units march through Belgium, according to a strategic plan that has been public knowledge since 1907. But if Britain fights against us, the whole English world—and especially America—will stand against us. . . . Third, Japan will not attack Russia, but it probably will attack us, in fond memory of our hostile intervention at the Peace of Shimonoseki. Fourth, the Scandinavian countries (our 'Germanic' brothers) will sell us what they can spare, but otherwise they are not favorably disposed to us. Fifth, Austria-Hungary is scarcely a match for the Serbs and Romanians militarily. Economically, it can just starve its way through for three to five years. And it won't be able to give us anything. Sixth, a revolution in Russia will come at most only if the Russians are defeated. So long as they fight Germany with success, a revolution there is unthinkable."[62] In its main points Bernstein's analysis accurately predicts later developments; it shows that some people at the time knew what might happen. If we read the text against the background of the escalating crisis of Summer 1914, with its political and military decision-making processes and its competing action logics, then it reveals how hermetically sealed the different layers and players had long been from one another, and how a distinctive "imagined" reality had taken shape in which no-exit scenarios precluded lucid analysis of the overall situation or alternative ways of thinking.

Events following the Russian mobilization order reinforce the impression of mechanisms that could no longer be halted politically. German military doctrine did not allow for last-minute diplomatic solutions: a tight schedule foresaw occupation of the Belgian transport hub at Liège in the first few days of war. This enormously strengthened the position of the military in Berlin. Things were very different in London, however. When Russia's general mobilization was announced on July 31, with Germany's expected to follow immediately and France's soon afterward, the British general and director of military operations Henry Wilson resigned himself: "We did nothing. . . . A terrible day . . . no military opinion from the Cabinet, although it is they who decide on the question of war."[63]

Military leaders on the Continent now thought primarily of how to mobilize hundreds of thousands of troops and to transport them in close succession to the planned theaters; the clockwork of war was set in motion. Such issues were of special concern to the German general staff, which reckoned on an imminent war on two fronts and sought to achieve the optimum starting position for implementation of the Schlieffen Plan. Yet even at this late hour, it is striking how little the political and military leadership contemplated the long-term consequences. On July 31, German ultimatums were still being issued for Russia and France to stop their ongoing or expected mobilization, although no one in Paris or St. Petersburg took any notice. Days earlier, official Paris had already stopped betting on the prevention of war; its only aims were to achieve a favorable starting position and to appear to be the country under attack. Indeed, the government initially refrained from calling up the reserves, despite explicit requests from the military. While the political leadership in Berlin staked everything on presenting Germany as the target of Russian aggression, the French government made every effort to appear as the innocent victim of a German attack.[64]

In contrast to the Prussian War Ministry, Bethmann Hollweg insisted on a formal declaration of war. "Moltke came and said it didn't matter, the war was already on. The chancellor replied that under international law we still needed confirmation. . . . Moltke said, okay, fine, the first shots at the border were from the Russian side. Then the chancellor: So that's clear, the Russians started it, and I'll get the nearest general to hand over the declaration of war at the frontier."[65] On August 1 there was a final delay, when news arrived from London about a supposed declaration of neutrality. While the Kaiser, Bethmann Hollweg, and Jagow interpreted this as a success resulting from their policy of threats, refusing to rule out a diplomatic solution and urging Moltke to withdraw his order for German troops to invade Luxembourg, the chief of the general staff suffered a nervous breakdown—this illustrated the huge pressure under which everyone was operating in the final phase of the crisis. Moltke demanded that the war plans be implemented, his main argument being that the mobilization mechanisms had an autonomous dynamic that it would be very difficult to halt.[66] Finally, when the British denied that they had declared neutrality in the German sense of the term, Wilhelm signed the necessary papers. About 5:00 P.M., a policeman announced in front of the Berlin Palace that the Kaiser had ordered a general mobilization. At the same time, the German ambassador in St. Petersburg handed over the German declaration of war on Russia.

Austria-Hungary's declaration of war on Serbia on July 28 marked the beginning of the pan-European war; it had already moved a long way from the original causes. Hostilities were now spreading to new places. On August 2, the Belgian government was faced with an ultimatum: it must allow German troops to march through its territory, or else the German Reich would be "regretfully compelled to treat the kingdom as an enemy." On the same day, a secret German-Ottoman defensive pact was signed against Russia.[67] In the shadow of the European conflict, then, the war was already directly involving non-European territories and populations in the Ottoman Empire, while the violation of Belgian neutrality was drawing Britain into the war and threatening to mobilize the whole of the British Empire. At least among the general staffs of the Central Powers, however, focused in Vienna on Serbia and Russia and in Berlin on the Schlieffen Plan, this wider dimension played little role; the dawning war remained a confrontation between the major powers of Continental Europe. At no point did Bethmann Hollweg succeed in correcting this egregious misjudgment.

The declaration of war on France immediately confronted German politicians with a problem that would keep reappearing in the later course of the war. For, leaving aside the autonomy of military logic and France's obligations to its Russian ally, there were no specific grounds for war with France and therefore no specific war aims on the German side. When the German declaration of war was finally delivered in Paris on August 3, it made reference to alleged border violations by French airmen. The French president Poincaré noted in his diary: "Never had a declaration of war been met with so much satisfaction."[68]

Massive misjudgments on the German side were already impossible to overlook. Just before the German ultimatum expired on August 3, the Belgian government declared that any violation of its country's sovereignty was completely unacceptable. Neutrality was a basic condition for the founding of the Belgian state in 1830 and—as the Franco-German war of 1870–1871 had recently shown—constituted a guarantee of independence in the eyes of its population. An invasion by foreign troops would not only be a breach of international law but would threaten the right of this small country to exist. The German chancellor tried to reassure Grey, the British foreign secretary, by arguing that any violation of Belgian sovereignty through the entry of German troops was purely a result of Russia's mobilization. The German ambassador in London was told to inform Grey: "Hemmed in as we are between East and West, we must now grasp every means to save our skin. This is by no means an intentional violation of international law, but the action of a man fighting for his life."[69]

On August 2, there was still no majority in the British cabinet for entry into the war against Germany; it met twice that day, while German troops were already on the march into Luxembourg. Britain's protective role toward Belgium was a premise of its foreign policy, but was this sufficient reason to break with the principles of non-intervention by entering a major war on the Continent, especially at a moment when colonial flashpoints and conflicts with Germany over influence in the Ottoman Empire appeared to be less explosive than before? Commenting in the House of Commons on the German threat to Belgium, Grey insisted that Britain could not escape its obligations under international law to uphold Belgian neutrality. Otherwise, he warned, it risked forfeiting all moral credibility.[70] The following day, he went on to say that "if we are engaged in war, we shall suffer but little more than we shall suffer even if we stand aside." For some time, however, British calculations had centered not on the violation of Belgian neutrality but on a future threat to India from a stronger Russia—in the cabinet, there had scarcely been any talk of the question of Belgian neutrality.[71]

On August 4, 1914, at about 8:00 A.M., long columns of German infantry and artillery units began their advance into Belgium. From that moment on, although the war had its beginnings in the heart of Europe, it was no longer simply a European war. Bethmann Hollweg himself was well aware of the massive breach of international law. As he pointed out to the Reichstag that very afternoon, "The wrong we thereby commit we will try to make good as soon as our military aims have been attained. He who is menaced as we are and is fighting for his highest possession can only consider how he is to hack his way through. Gentlemen, we are now in a state of necessity (*Notwehr*), and necessity (*Not*) knows no law."[72] A twofold apologetics, combining subjective reference to threats with justification in terms of necessity, is clearly on display here. Despite all the advance warnings, the chancellor reacted with bewilderment when at 7:00 P.M., the British ambassador in Berlin, Edward Goschen, delivered an ultimatum with a five-hour deadline, demanding an immediate end to the German invasion and the cessation of all hostilities. Goschen reported Bethmann Hollweg's reaction as follows: "Just for a word—'neutrality' . . . —just for a scrap of paper Great Britain was going to make war on a kindred nation who desired nothing better than to be friends with her. All his efforts in that direction had been rendered useless by this last terrible step, and the policy to which, as I knew, he had devoted himself since his accession to office had tumbled down like a house of cards."[73]

The British declaration brought to five the number of major European major powers that had gone to war in the space of four days. By the end of the year there would be twenty-two declarations of war, to which were added another five in 1915, six in 1916, and eight in 1917, so that in the end thirty-eight belligerents became involved with a total of forty-one declarations of war.[74] All the tried and tested strategies of de-escalation had failed to produce results, both at the diplomatic or military level and on the part of individuals and movements that embodied tradition and the avant-garde, legitimist, and progressive models of order. Neither monarchs nor the Socialist International had been able to prevent war, although they would be especially affected by it. Neither fear of antimonarchic revolution and civil war nor the danger that the international solidarity of workers' movements would regress into loyalty to nation-states had been able to halt the spiral.

What had become of the movement that before 1914 had been identified as no other with the ideals of pacifism and internationalism? What precisely was the attitude of the Socialist International to the July crisis?[75] In parallel with developments in the chancelleries and military headquarters, all parties of the European Left had to take a position on the possibility of a major European war. In France, in particular, parliamentary elections in April and May 1914 had once more underlined the resistance of the Left to the raising of the length of military service to three years, which President Poincaré had pushed through in July 1913, not least because of the growing danger of war with Germany associated with the Morocco crises and the Balkan wars. Large demonstrations against this law had taken place in July 1913, organized by the Trade Union Federation, the Socialists, and the Radical Socialists under their new leader, Joseph Caillaux. When Poincaré, after the elections, appointed the Socialist René Viviani as prime minister, he did so partly to win Socialist support for the course he had been pursuing. After the gunshots in Sarajevo, the French Socialists held an extraordinary congress on July 15 and 16. Before the ultimatum was issued to Serbia, they threatened a general strike to pressure the government to pursue an international solution to the conflict. But it was already becoming clear that, in the event of war, there would be no repetition of 1870–1871: the French Socialists emphasized that they were prepared to stand by the Third Republic and the nation and not, like the radical Left in 1870, opt for civil war—a choice that had become a dual burden weighing on the Left in the aftermath of military defeat and the Commune. In 1914, France as a republic could wage war with greater strength than before.[76] The general strike was no longer a disguised threat of revolution against the government. Together with the renunciation of offensive war, there was a readiness among the Socialists to side with the nation in the event of an external attack. Jean Jaurès, the leader of the French Socialists, proclaimed on July 18 in the Party daily *L'Humanité:* "There is no contradiction between fighting with all our strength for peace and fighting with every means for the independence and unity of the nation, if, despite our efforts, war should break out."[77]

Through the end of July this dual attitude informed the many resolutions and antiwar demonstrations of all the parties of the European Left. On July 25, the Social Democratic *Vorwärts* in Germany criticized "Austrian imperialism," warned of the dangers of "the fury of war" unleashed, and underlined the pacific, solidaristic, and internationalist stand of the German workers' movement: "The class-conscious proletariat of Germany raises its voice in protest against this criminal pursuit. No German soldier must sacrifice a single drop of blood for the power thrill of the Austrian rulers."[78] Yet when the leaders of the main French and German unions, Léon Jouhaux and Carl Legien, met in Brussels on July 27, Jouhaux found his assumption confirmed that the German unions would not support an international general strike against war. In France itself, where it was thought that in case of war the authorities would arrest union leaders listed in the notorious "Carnet B," the government and the union leadership reached an original compromise on July 31 that gave up any idea of either detentions or a general strike. This anticipated the political attitude of the Socialists to the war credits.[79]

When the SPD parliamentary fraction sent one of its deputies, Hermann Müller, to a final exploratory meeting in Paris in late July, he could not have suspected what the war would bring for the German Social Democrats and for him personally. Born in 1876 the son of a sparkling wine producer, Müller had had to leave school without taking the final *Abitur* examination, and after a truncated business apprenticeship had graduated through the SPD, the free trade unions, and local politics to become an important party functionary. As recently as early 1914, at the congresses of the French Socialist Party and the British Labour Party, he had hailed the ever-closer friendship among the European workers' organizations. Yet during the war, though initially considered part of the left wing of the SPD, he moved steadily rightward, eventually negotiating with the mutinous Kiel sailors in 1918 and signing the Treaty of Versailles in his capacity as Reich foreign minister in the government of Gustav Bauer.[80]

When Müller went to Paris in late July 1914 to meet the French Socialist leader Jean Jaurès, the policy of international solidarity among the European Left had already broken down. Both the French and the German Left had an overwhelming sense of being part of a nation under attack, which had to defend itself and had a claim to the loyalty of all political forces in the respective countries. Just as this position was becoming apparent among French Socialists, on the eve of the planned meeting with Müller, a right-wing nationalist shot Jaurès in a Paris restaurant, accusing him of having betrayed the nation. The next day, Müller's French interlocutors made it clear that the Socialists would vote for war credits if France was attacked by Germany. In reality, the causes of this collapse of the International went much further back; in August 1907, in a sharp debate at its Stuttgart congress, the French Socialist and passionate antimilitarist Gustave Hervé, following the traditions of revolutionary syndicalism, had called for international workers' resistance and an army strike in the event of war—a position to which Jaurès also subscribed at the Copenhagen congress in 1910. However, in 1907 the SPD chairman August Bebel had vigorously rejected this approach, fearing that the implied threat of revolution would jeopardize the political position his party had achieved with much effort inside Germany.[81] Hervé, who since 1912 had been editor of the journal *La Guerre Sociale,* declared in his July 1914 meeting with Müller that the French reaction to the break with internationalism by the German Socialists and their trade unions could only be a return to the 1793 principle of revolutionary patriotism and national defense; bourgeois democracy and socialism should therefore come together in France. Hervé programmatically changed the title of his journal to *La Victoire*.[82] Unlike in 1870, however, the reference to the French Revolution did not arouse tensions within French society, let alone create a climate of civil war. The Socialists, too, realized that this time France was not isolated internationally. Behind their commitment to defense of the republican nation lay a self-image that defined the task of the nation at war in terms of universalist goals and highlighted France's exemplary role in this war for the whole of humanity. In his speech at Jaurès's graveside on August 4, the day after the German declaration of war on France, Jouhaux proclaimed, "If Jaurès were with us now, this is what he would tell us his comrades: Beyond the national cause in this hard struggle that is now beginning, you shall defend the cause of the International as well as the cause of civilization, of which France itself is the cradle."[83]

After Hermann Müller reported in Berlin on the talks he had had in Paris, a straw poll showed that ninety-two SPD Reichstag deputies favored approval of the government request for war credits, while fourteen were against. Among the opponents was one of the two party chairmen, Hugo Haase, who the next day, against his own convictions, presented the SPD position: "The consequences of the imperialist policy have crashed over us like a storm tide. Now we face the iron law of war. In this we shall make a reality what we have always emphasized. We shall not desert our fatherland in the hour of danger."[84] This was the position of the leading party full-timers, but not that of most workers in Germany. It cannot be said that they showed a general enthusiasm for war, and until a few days before its outbreak their principled opposition to the war remained a predominant feature. While the SPD leaders in the Reichstag behaved in such a way as to avoid the stigma of hostility to the Reich, the main feelings among the workers were skepticism and uncertainty—the kernel for the later growth of discontent and eventually for the split in the party. The often-evoked "August experience" of SPD functionaries, involving a commitment to a "social truce" and a focus on anti-Russian and anti-British enemy images, served to give the party a programmatic basis for the sharp change of direction from pacifism and international solidarity to endorsement of the war and demonstrations of national loyalty.[85]

Despite rhetorical affirmations of solidarity with all the oppressed, and despite the fact that, unlike the pacifists, it represented an institution with millions of members, the International did not prove capable of preventing war. Wide-ranging ideological positions, splits, and infighting, together with actual experiences of politics in European societies, stood in the way of the unity and resolution that would have been necessary in Summer 1914. The spectrum stretched from the radical and revolutionary strategies of the Russian Socialists through the increasingly pragmatic course of the British Labour Party, which in 1914 began to distance itself from the radical pacifism of its left wing, to the majority of the German SPD, which did not wish to jeopardize its gains and its parliamentary role by launching a strike action in the army. The Executive Committee of the Second International therefore seemed to have lost touch with reality when it invited member parties to a special meeting on July 29. Far more realistically, the well-known Austrian Social Democrat Victor Adler saw that international conflict and the impotence of pacifist internationalism were threats to the positions that the European Left had achieved with great effort in many electoral contests before 1914: "The Party is defenseless. . . . We endanger thirty years' work without any political result."[86]

How is the escalation to war in Summer 1914 to be explained? At one level, it is possible to identify the motives of various players. First of all, the political and military leadership of Austria-Hungary was looking to punish Serbia and, in a situation of heightened international rivalry, to affirm its existence as a multiethnic empire. The negative example of the Ottoman Empire highlighted the link between territorial erosion and internal destabilization, as did the whole experience of the Balkan wars, while the reactions of the political-military elite showed that it had a war faction, headed by Foreign Minister Berchtold, and men like Chief of Staff Conrad von Hötzendorf who favored a preventive strike against Serbia. But they also revealed how unprepared the Dual Monarchy was for even a regional war, let alone a conflict engulfing the European continent. There was no detailed military understanding with Germany, on whose political support Vienna tried to build, and whose military help would be needed soon after the outbreak of war. Furthermore, the long interval between the assassination in Sarajevo and the final Austrian ultimatum suggested the lack of a consistent strategy or at least strengthened the impression of unclear signals. The various players seemed to be acting in accordance with a situational rationality, paying little or no heed to the wider consequences. This was evident in the de facto ending of the Triple

Alliance as soon as war broke out, when Italy declared its neutrality and once again underlined the clash of interests within the alliance.[87]

Russia's political leadership had held back from intervention in the Bosnian crisis of 1908 and the Balkan wars of 1912–1913, but their outcome had left it feeling weakened or even humiliated internationally. Considerations of prestige were therefore especially marked in Russia, where the experience of defeat in the war with Japan in 1904–1905 and internal political tensions added to the picture. Unlike the Tsar, who, despite contradictory statements, always worried about the possible consequences of a great war, the group around Foreign Minister Sazonov held that Russia should no longer tolerate the Austrian policy of intimidation that had partly led it to restrain Serbia during the Balkan wars.

At first, the interests of the German Reich were not directly affected by the assassination in Sarajevo. The responsibility of its political leaders for the course of events therefore lay in its support for Austria-Hungary in early July, which, formulated without conditions, covered not only defensive but also offensive scenarios. The military top brass, in particular, who had much greater autonomy than in other countries and had to fear neither political control nor parliamentary counterweights, followed an action logic of their own governed by two decisive factors. On the one hand, they feared a general worsening of the international situation; on the other hand—in view of Russia's long-term potential, the Russian and French arms buildup, and the latent crisis in Austria-Hungary resulting from a lengthy prelude to war—military experts around Moltke did not so much count on a short war as seek to establish a good starting position for a more protracted conflict. Especially in Germany, operational planning, long-term preparations for war, and strategic war aims were by no means synchronized with one another. Thus, war aims and justifications over and above alliance obligations had to be developed on the fly as war was being declared: this was a fundamental difference between the situation in 1914 and earlier wars such as those in 1866 and 1870, or indeed the situation on the eve of the Second World War. A number of elements contradict the idea that the whole German leadership had long been fixated on an aggressive preventive war with clearly defined aims. Against this must be set the erratic statements of nearly all the key players, the manifold contradictions, and the naïve notion, maintained to the last, that war could be limited to Continental Europe, without the involvement of Britain.

This diffuse situation, further complicated by the uncoordinated, sometimes conflicting, agendas of the political leadership, the monarch, and the general staff, imply a special responsibility of the German Reich for the outbreak of war. But similar contradictions were also apparent elsewhere, especially in Russia and France. To qualify later claims that Germany alone bore all the war guilt, by building the responsibility of others into the picture, is not to engage in undue apologetics. Rather, the misperceptions and misrepresentations on all sides, the exaggerated reactions to the slightest move, show how the crisis increasingly stretched everyone's capacity to the limit. The more complex the situation became, the less mutual trust, which is vital for de-escalation, existed.

France and Britain had set aside their colonial conflicts in signing the Entente Cordiale, and a similar course had been charted between Russia and Britain. But no more than in the case of the Triple Alliance should their relations with one another be seen as free of conflict or indicative of an offensive military alliance. Neither Paris nor London had vital interests to protect in the Balkans. And although tensions between Germany and France had undoubtedly grown since the Morocco crisis and the Algeciras conference, the crisis of July 1914 ultimately caught the French leadership unawares. During the decisive stage, both the president and the head of government were at sea on their way back from a state visit to Russia, with only a limited capacity for action. Yet both Poincaré and the French ambassador in St. Petersburg, Maurice Paléologue, backed the Russian war party around Sazonov in its resistance to the Tsar's misgivings. This conduct considerably sharpened the crisis and defined France's share of responsibility for its escalation.[88]

Of all the major European powers, Britain certainly had the least interest in an intensification of the crisis. One reason for this was the country's foreign policy parameters—its focus on security of the Empire, and the continued existence of flashpoints even after the agreements with France, Russia, and (vis-à-vis the Ottoman Empire) Germany—but the domestic political situation, including conflicts over home rule for Ireland, also played a role. London's particular attitude to the crisis, evident at key moments in July and August, led it to send highly ambivalent signals to the German Reich. More than once, the Foreign Office under Grey warned the government in Berlin of the danger of escalation as a result of British involvement, but to the last minute it also repeatedly indicated Britain's preparedness for negotiations and international mediation. This lack of clarity fueled hopes in the German leadership, and in Bethmann Hollweg personally, that Britain would remain neutral, thereby allowing the conflict to be limited, if not to southeastern Europe, then to mainland Europe. Indirectly, this misperception based upon unclear signals strengthened the German war faction.

So, did the European protagonists "sleepwalk" through the crisis, cautious but unseeing, trapped in dream imagery, blind to the horrors that their connivance was bringing into the world?[89] They were certainly not sleepwalking in the sense of behaving unconsciously. They were awake and in many respects oversensitized; the physical and mental overload set in when it became clear to the various players that escalation could no longer be halted. Nor were military specialists blind to the character of modern warfare, whether in relation to the unlikelihood of a short conflict or the consequences of a long one. Nevertheless, the full scale of what would happen on the battlefields in 1916 or 1918, the dimension of ten million or more dead, lay outside the horizon of possibilities of most politicians and military leaders. If they knew of the potential of war, it was an abstract knowledge, a scenario, a part of what people at the time saw as the existing range of possibilities. But the players had no sense of the likely dimensions of the war—and there was no historical point of reference, no previous war that might have served as a warning or a measure against which to weigh the consequences. This was another fundamental difference between August 1914 and September 1939.[90]

Nor were they sleepwalkers in the sense suggested in later bemused accounts of the crisis, which, in seeking to promote reconciliation, based themselves on hindsight and the problems of the peace settlement. In the 1920s David Lloyd George came up with the suggestive metaphor that all countries had "slid" more or less blindly into war.[91] But the real problem had been the nervous overreactions, the multiple early warning systems that had overtaxed people on the ground, and the tendency to test the willingness of the other side to take risks. Mental and physical breakdown among leading politicians and generals was thus not an accidental factor in the crisis.

Beyond the moral category of guilt, no analysis of the July crisis can fail to look at the special responsibility of the key players themselves. On June 28, 1914, at the moment when the shots rang out in Sarajevo, none of the European states was planning an offensive war. But preventive war categories were part of the thinking of the top brass—not only in Berlin and Vienna, but also in Paris and St. Petersburg. The Schlieffen Plan was matched by Russian plans to invade East Prussia and the French Plan XVII for an attack on Lorraine.

In Germany, "sooner rather than later" thinking held sway in the General Staff and in the government that came under pressure from it. In London there was widespread fear that Russia's future strength would pose a threat to the Empire in India, while in Berlin, too, analysts thought they should count on a war with Russia. They knew that this prospect would be much more dangerous in 1916 or 1917 than it seemed then, in the summer of 1914, and this made them all the more willing to adopt a high-risk policy.

The responsibilities in the July crisis did not lie only in the escalation to which everyone contributed, in Belgrade, Vienna, and Berlin, as well as St. Petersburg, Paris, and London. At least equally important is the question of what might have opened the door to de-escalation.[92] There the responsibility attributed to Germany and Britain was especially great, because both had shown in 1912–1913 what a successful solution might look like. When the German government gave a blank check early on to Austria-Hungary, it knew it was taking a huge risk. The idea was to make the conflict between Austria-Hungary and Serbia a test case—in the clear realization that the crisis might grow into a world war. The German risk strategy, in which the issue was how far Russia would go and whether it was ultimately prepared to go to war, ran up against the readiness of Russia and France to make the Balkan crisis the occasion for a major conflict. Britain's position remained too unclear for too long, fueling hopes in Berlin and Vienna that it would remain neutral and, in Paris and St. Petersburg, that it would enter the fray. This whole constellation, in contrast to the situation in 1912–1913, greatly limited the scope for de-escalation.

Other factors existed alongside the motives of the key players, and only the interaction among them set up a dynamic in which each saw its room for maneuver increasingly restricted.

(1) In the years before 1914, war had often been present as a principle, a scenario, or a possibility—in the international conflicts that had become sharper since the 1890s, in the press, in science fiction literature, and in bestsellers by military authors. Yet after 1871 Europe had enjoyed the longest period of peace in its history, and despite all the imperial expansion none of

the crises resulting from it had escalated into a major European war. There was no simple causal continuum leading from overseas crisis zones and the brutality of colonial war to August 1914. On the contrary: each conflict that was successfully contained before 1914 seemed to demonstrate that the international system was capable of solving clashes of interest and power in the colonial areas or in peripheral areas of Europe such as the Balkans. Yet there too the costs of de-escalation were plainly visible: governments became less ready to compromise the more they felt crisis containment policies to be damaging their prestige. For Austria-Hungary and Russia, this threshold was reached at the latest with the Balkan wars.

(2) Another factor was the mismatch between war scenarios and war plans, on the one side, and war preparations and war aims on the other. Before 1914 each major power had many detailed plans and scenarios devised by military experts for the outbreak of war: the German Schlieffen plan, the French Plan XVII, the Russian plan for an invasion of East Prussia and Galicia. But there was a lack of precise war aims and preparedness for a long war. This contrast became all the more conspicuous the more detailed the military plans were before 1914, and the more vehemently generals referred to the autonomous logic and dynamic of arms buildups and mobilizations, thereby increasing the time constraints under which decisions had to be taken. The result was a major conceptual deficit plus a vacuum in the decision-making processes themselves.[93] This lack of clarity allowed an interpretive leeway that favored problematic decisions. The assumption that Britain would remain neutral, widely shared in Berlin to the end, was perhaps the most significant case in point. Individual reactions repeatedly proved to be highly situational, erratic, and unprecictable. Only against this background could the army's assertions of the operational need to act acquire independent weight, since they seemed to promise, amid diverse and contradictory information, a rational basis for action. Thus, despite their responsibility for the outcome of July 1914, the idea that German political and military leaders had a long-standing, uninterrupted intention to wage an offensive war attributes to them a perspicacity and rationality that they demonstrably lacked in the decisive weeks, days, and hours. The key stages of the crisis displayed not so much coolness and consistency of purpose as a loading of the relevant players with more problems than they could handle.

(3) The paradox might be called, with a little exaggeration, asymmetrical risk management. Whereas, until Summer 1914, a number of material factors—from mass conscription to machine guns and artillery firepower—limited the threat of war, the same elements made the potential consequences of conflict all the more dangerous. But the interstate system based on concepts of equilibrium needed the possibility of war in order to function credibly, just as for most people national sovereignty was unimaginable without the principle of war as a legitimate means of politics. Before 1914, a supranational conception of international security had little or no prospect of actual application. What all this largely blanked out were the consequences of war. Yet it would be wrong to think that in Summer 1914 military experts in the general staffs really based their planning on the likelihood of a short war. An all-decisive battle right at the start might be tempting, especially because the idea obscured complex questions concerning war's political, economic, and social consequences. But lessons from the decades before 1914, not least from the American Civil War, had long entered into theories of war and military scenarios for the future. Although no one could precisely define the diffuse transition from war between states to war between peoples, conscription-based armies, new weapons technology, and the resources of large industrial societies seemed to preclude single decisive battles and to favor long wars of attrition, in which total mobilization, perseverance, and loyalty in the face of heavy casualties would play the key role. Moltke himself knew how to make these connections; his dogmatic adherence to the main lines of the Schlieffen Plan was supposed to give Germany a good starting position in the west for a war whose outcome, because of the French and Russian arms drives, seemed ever more uncertain.

(4) There was one final aspect to the international alliances and agreements. People at the time, as well as later historians, focused on the intensive building of blocs before 1914, as exemplified by the Triple Alliance and the so-called Triple Entente. These fixed structures, it seemed, left less and less room for alternative options and severely limited the flexibility of the international system; the fear of "encirclement," so widespread among German politicians and generals, strengthened this mindset and the perceived importance of wider attachments. These were not, however, coherent alliances—on the contrary. The pre-1914 British ententes with France and Russia were agreements that,

while permitting forms of military cooperation, did not lead to offensive war planning. In Summer 1914 colonial flashpoints were defused, but particularly in Asia that represented no guarantee for the future. In the Triple Alliance, the clash of interests between the Habsburg monarchy and Italy over the *irredenta* was plainly visible. In conclusion, it was not a hardening of alliance systems before 1914 but the incomplete formation of blocs that fueled escalation, since it introduced aspects of ambiguity and unpredictability.

In the July crisis, there was a tendency to speculate on the breakup of alliances and the removal of key players from the conflict—witness, for example, Austria's hope of Russian restraint in relation to the ultimatum to Serbia, or German assumptions that Britain would remain neutral if it attacked France through Belgium. However, behavior determined by hopes that certain great powers could be kept out of the conflict actually prompted them to intervene. This was the case for Russia and even more for Britain. Misperceptions on both sides caused the capital of predictability to be eroded by unclear signals. Despite the highly situational risk as war gestated in Summer 1914, a successful solution might have opened up new prospects for international relations.[94] A convincingly strong alliance of Russia, France, and Britain might have made Germany and Austria-Hungary more willing to compromise, and extra-European colonies offered areas where compensation could have been considered. This may have been less likely in the actual situation in 1914 than in the crises of 1911 and 1913, but it was not ruled out. Once again it seems essential not to allow the eventual outcome to obscure the relative openness of the historical situation.

(5) So, was the war absurd in view of the contrast between overplanning, explosive violence, and energetic mobilization on one side, and a vacuum of aims and preparations on the other? Was it even ironic, in the sense that it already involved an imbalance between expectations and realities?[95] Absurdity and irony are terms that come to mind particularly in retrospect and from a bird's-eye view. People living at the time, especially the key political and military players, acted under the impression of a flood of information and subjective perceptions covering an ever shorter time period, and the conclusions they drew often led them to impute certain plans to the other side. Those directly involved tended to do what later historians have also repeatedly done: they operated with assumptions about the thinking of the

other side, about their aims and the effects of events, guessing at intentions without being able to know whether their guesses were accurate; hypothetical enemy plans might seem probably, even necessary, because they justified prior assessments and expectations. In July 1914 this diffuse interaction of events and assumptions yielded a special reality of subjectively reduced options for action. During that summer, individual players again and again displayed a distinctive logic and a distinctive rationality with regard to their own actions. But this logic repeatedly failed to take into account the likely effects of their actions and the ways in which others might perceive them.

(6) All parties and all players operated with the idea that war was theoretically possible; whether desired or feared, it was an imagined possibility. But that was not the war that soon turned into a reality, and never before had images of war and realities of war diverged so radically from each other as they did after August 4, 1914. Although the likelihood of a major conflict in southeastern Europe involving the (externally and internally) threatened multiethnic empires of Russia, the Dual Monarchy, and Ottoman Turkey had increased in the period after 1900, neither the outbreak of hostilities in Summer 1914 nor the escalation of a regional conflict into a European and global conflagration was a foregone conclusion. Other scenarios were perfectly possible. To note this fact is not to overlook the specific features of Summer 1914 or the distinctive starting positions of each country; both are integral to analysis of this dense historical situation.

In Summer 1914, unlike in earlier crises, the flexibility and willingness to compromise previously characteristic of international relations did not take effect, although it is true that isolated efforts continued to the end, such as the attempt to limit hostilities to a temporary occupation of Belgrade or to hold a conference of the major powers to find an international solution to the crisis. By that time such options had little prospect, since they were associated, above all in Vienna and St. Petersburg, with a loss of prestige. A further element was the ever-narrower time frame for political reactions: ultimatums typically set short deadlines, and in the end it appeared, as it did in Berlin on August 1 and 4, that a decision had to be taken in a few moments. This was due essentially to military pressures. Particularly in Germany and Austria, strong political counterweights were lacking in government and parliament that might have offset these autonomous military logics and mechanisms.

Subjective assessments, even panic reactions, involving contradictions and uncertainties caused by excessive demands on individuals, therefore became a deadweight that could no longer be corrected. For by late July any search for alternatives appeared as a weakness, as a wasted opportunity at the very beginning of the war—and no one wanted to be blamed for that later on.

(7) Another dimension is perhaps decisive here. The July crisis was a textbook example of a crisis of trust. As such, it made it more difficult to handle security risks and even prevented a minimum of calculation. Following Niklas Luhmann, we may understand trust as a possibility of complexity reduction that improves the calculation of risks. Since no one can ever assess and direct someone else's actions, since perfect control of others is an impossibility, what is required is a rational strategy to trust others up to a certain point, allowing exchanges between players that break through the logic of mutual assumptions and misperceptions. In the absence of such trust in Summer 1914, there was nothing to offset the growing complexity of a situation with ever more players and action levels, or the multiplicity of imputed plans and aims that put excessive demands on individual players. The trust among individuals that could still sprout at certain moments, as it did between monarchs or even among politicians and ambassadors, could no longer compensate for the lack of systemic confidence in institutions; a basic category of political order was lacking.[96] This social capital, which had to be preserved and expanded if not only individual societies but the system of international relations were to function, was conspicuous by its absence in July 1914. And the loss of this store of confidence could not be counterbalanced. It became clear that one of its main implications was the unavailability of reliable information.[97]

But why did the mutual trust that would have permitted a minimum of calculation fail to materialize in the July crisis? Trust calls for a willingness to take risks, which in turn presupposes a capacity to appraise possible future developments. The risks of war appeared to many leading players in 1914 as evidently lower than the risk of a loss of international prestige through a de-escalation of the crisis. If there was a lack of trust, then, it was because most of the players feared that an advance expression of trust would be interpreted as an expression of weakness. A key element here was the much greater focus on prestige as a result of previous conflict situations, which, as the crisis dragged on, became ever more detached from the assassination in

Sarajevo. In a way, this was the price for the earlier successful de-escalation in the Moroccan crises and the Balkan wars. Top politicians and generals thought they could rely on their own strength, if not autonomy, and on the superiority of their own plans, armies, and weapons; the German military, in particular, laid great emphasis on these in the face of what it saw as international "encirclement." Massive military force seemed to offer a radical way of escaping the complexity of the situation. Finally, once certain thresholds had been crossed, subjectively perceived time constraints and the pressures of problem solving reduced the opportunities to create an effective basis for trust among the various players.

(8) In Robert Musil's *The Man without Qualities,* the mathematician Ulrich decides to take a year's "break from life" in 1913. However, his father instead pressures him to apply for a job with an influential state official. The task—the "parallel action"—is to prepare for a twin jubilee in 1918: the seventieth anniversary of Austrian Emperor Franz Joseph's accession to the throne and the thirtieth year of Kaiser Wilhelm II's time in power. But in the novel all those involved fail in this task; they represent special walks of life, without developing a universal idea on which they might unite. Similarly, the key players in Summer 1914—monarchs and heads of government, foreign ministers and generals—failed because of competing and conflicting action logics, because of assumptions and perceptions about one another that created a reality of their own. The ideas of peacekeeping and stability of the international order had become a smokescreen behind which the clash of interests could no longer be resolved, while the subjective perception of possible alternatives was becoming narrower and narrower. Musil tried to sum up the dual dimension of reality in the prewar world with the concepts of "sense of reality" and "sense of possibility": "But if there is a sense of reality, . . . then there must also be something we can call a sense of possibility. Whoever has it does not say, for instance: Here this or that has happened, will happen, must happen; but he invents: here this or that might, could, or ought to happen. If he is told that something is the way it is, he will think: Well, it could probably just as well be otherwise. So, the sense of possibility could be defined outright as the ability to conceive of everything there might be just as well, and to attach no more importance to what is than to what is not."[98] The players in Summer 1914 were lacking in both respects: their sense of possibility was marked by limited

perspectives and pressures for action, by ways of thinking (most evident in the military) that operated with rigid time frames. Their sense of reality, on the other hand, did not involve the weighing of alternative scenarios, but expressed itself as a set of imputations and negative action logics. In this thinking, it was necessary to defend against purposes ascribed to the other side; to act preventively so as not to be placed in a weak position from the outset. In the end, the subjective image of being under attack and having to defend oneself—an image shared by all the players—made it impossible to halt the spiral of escalation.

2. AUGUST LANDSCAPES
Euphoria, Fear, and the Logic of Retrospect

The war had begun. Its effects reached deep into various societies, even before the first military operations and the first press reports of casualties. And there was already a winner. On August 3, 1914, the American citizen Joseph Clay Walker from Tennessee passed his doctoral exam at the University of Heidelberg on the subject of the ancient migration of the Germanic peoples. His examiner, the history professor Karl Hampe, noted in his diary: "Another doctorate this morning—which seemed pretty fantastical. What do the ancient Germans of the migration period matter to one today! Another terrible migration has begun! The candidate was an American, who in fact only passed because he belonged to a friendly nation. If he'd been Russian, he would hardly have gotten through." Though far from the corridors of state diplomacy, the well-informed Hampe summarized how a middle-class academic saw the tense mood in the German population. There was widespread fear that Britain would enter the war: "A quiet day today; the mobilization is going ahead calmly and effectively. . . . But there was uncertainty about Britain's position. . . . One would have liked to see something like Bismarck's diplomatic effort in 1864," when British intervention was successfully averted in the conflict involving Prussia, Austria, and Denmark. The British declaration of war on August 4 reset the course. That same day Italy declared its neutrality, on the grounds that Austria-Hungary was waging an offensive war against Serbia, whereas the provisions of the Triple Alliance were defensive in intent. A controversy between champions of neutrality and supporters of entry into the war on the side of the Allies then developed in Italian politics and society, growing ever sharper until May 1915. In July 1914 the Auswärtiges Amt, the German foreign office, had recognized that Russia had reason to count on the clash of interests between Austria-Hungary and Italy and that Italy's political and military leadership saw the possibility of gaining the *irredenta* of South Tyrol, Istria, and Dalmatia. In the long run, Berlin believed, this logic would force Italy into the war against Austria-Hungary: "A collapse of the [Habsburg] Monarchy would open up for it the prospect of gaining long-coveted parts of the country."[99] Thus, even before the outbreak of war, the Triple Alliance had ceased to exist. Hampe saw a historical parallel between Germany's situation and the isolation of eighteenth-century Prussia under Frederick the Great in his struggle against the major powers of Continental Europe: "We are mainly reliant on our own forces against a world under arms, and the situation reminds one more and more of the Seven Years' War. Hopefully, the army and navy will get all they can out of it." He based his hopes on a worldwide escalation that would favor Germany, especially as a result of internal and external resistance to the British and Tsarist Empires: "In this situation all the bombs would have to burst: Japan, India, Poland. Will something like that happen?"[100]

A year before Sarajevo, the fifth edition of a widely read novel appeared. It described, in popular science-fiction form, how war might break out and how Germany would carry out a general mobilization. The starting point of this novel, *Krieg-mobil*, was the situation in the German capital after the receipt of a Russian-French ultimatum: "It was whispered from mouth to mouth. Alarm spread like wildfire over the megacity and left behind a leaden quiet. Offices closed their doors, factories knocked off, shopkeepers rolled down their shutters, restaurants remained empty. Pale-faced men hurried home. Trains to the suburbs were stormed. There was no sign of jubilation, but none of fear either. Grim determination radiated from every face. At four o'clock Berlin looked as if it had given up the ghost. By five, people were streaming back from the suburbs. The final decision had to be taken that evening. . . . The crowd wandered the streets in closed groups. Not much was spoken. There was no work for the police. A spell hung over everyone. . . . Then the crowd came to life. A stream flowed down Unter den Linden. The electric advertisements, which had been switched off, suddenly glowed forth. Their fiery characters screamed: War, mobilize. And the crowd shouted in unison: War, war!"[101]

The mood in this work of fiction, already in 1913, was not one of euphoric release—rather, it was a mix of tension and quietness, fear and concentration. This overlapping of feelings was also apparent in August, and the range of emotions was considerable in all European societies. Like the vision of a war caused by circumstances beyond anyone's control, the image of an ecstatic enthusiasm for war uniting all strata and groups in society, the so-called August experience, often featured in retrospective constructions or reflected the logic of a special kind of situational self-censorship.[102] The celebrated scene, captured in a photo of a hat-waving young Adolf Hitler, which is supposed to depict spontaneous war fever in August 1914 before the Field Marshals' Hall on Odeon Platz in Munich, actually shows a crowd that knew of the photographer's presence and was responding to his instructions.[103] An account of the August days would be a central theme and a narrative reference point in numerous later memoirs. For, in comparison with the deep disenchantment in later phases of the war, the period around its outbreak might appear in retrospect to have been luminous, positive, and euphoric. On August 1, 1916, Count Harry Graf Kessler wrote of the earlier mood in Berlin: "Two years of war. Two years ago, Unter den Linden was black with people screaming 'War, war!' This evening I encountered on Luisenplatz and at the Oranienburg Gate troops of boys and girls who had come there to protest against the war. Many policemen but everything took place peacefully. The movement is not threatening. But a great war weariness prevails in all circles."[104] The German ambassador to St. Petersburg, Friedrich Karl von Pourtalès, wrote in the memoirs he published in 1919 of the different reactions in the Russian and German capitals after August 1, 1914, underlining the lack of patriotic fervor in Russia: "Nor was there now the slightest observable enthusiasm for war. Conscripted reservists . . . gave the impression of being pushed into it rather than acting out of enthusiasm. . . . Not one patriotic song or appeal was to be heard. What a contrast with what I saw a few days later in Berlin!"[105]

If we look more closely at public reactions in early August 1914 and free ourselves of retrospect, we can see that, apart from the signs of euphoria, many people panicked and headed straight for their bank to draw money from their savings accounts, or began to squirrel away food for fear of rationing.

Where there was enthusiasm for the war, it was mostly out of relief that the unbearable tension of the preceding days was over. In any case, it cannot be straightforwardly extrapolated to the entire population.[106] In the city centers of European capitals, with their symbolic national sites such as the Berliner Schloss or Buckingham Palace, the picture was different from that in workers' districts, small provincial towns, or rural areas. There, any war fever came in response to the declarations of war and the mobilization orders. The enthusiasm itself was not a causal factor leading to war. It is simply not the case that the decisions of politicians and generals had to take into account popular pressure or even a grassroots movement calling for war.

On July 31, 1914, the 17-year-old Carl Zuckmayer set off for his home in the Rhineland after a stay on the North Sea, taking the last train able to travel unobstructed from the Dutch city of Vlissingen (Flushing) in the Scheldt estuary. Later he described the ways in which his fellow travelers greeted the official announcement of an impending danger of war: "In Vlissingen . . . some Germans got on from the connecting ferry from England. They said that in London one could no longer speak German in the street or in restaurants without being insulted or jostled. They gave the impression, probably as we did too, of being distraught, depressed, or disoriented. It was also like that at the frontier station, late at night. But not long after we crossed the frontier, things became incredibly different. The German customs officials, usually so nonchalant, greeted us with an almost joyful cordiality, as if we were relatives they had not seen for a long time." At the main station in Cologne, Zuckmayer observed the farewells to departing soldiers; the officers on board were "calm, silent, and composed," but he noted a mood of "exaggerated brightness and euphoria" that recurred in his native Mainz: "That's how it was when you were waiting for the Shrove Tuesday [carnival] train to arrive. But the mood was different. Although you heard people calling out, even shouting or laugh-ing, there was a single-minded purpose about the whole operation, no idle curiosity, as if there was something urgent, unpostponable, to be done where everyone was running off to." The mobilization orders did not trigger mass frenzy, but rather a mood of cool concentration: "We hardly spoke, did not talk things over, just looked at one another and exchanged laughing nods: there was nothing to discuss."[107]

Reactions to the outbreak of war were as varied as individual lives. Franz Kafka's laconic diary entry for August 2, 1914—"Germany has declared war on Russia. Swimming in the afternoon"—came closer, in its casual juxtaposition of epochal event and everyday routine, to the average perceptions of the time than did later attempts to cast August as a historic watershed, with a universal significance that could arise only out of the consequences of the war.[108] In Kafka's home city, Prague, Czechs had long experienced internal political tensions and conflicts with Vienna; the regional parliament as well as the Imperial Council in the capital had been prorogued months earlier, and the head of the government in Vienna, Karl von Stürgkh, had been ruling by decree. Yet Kafka noted in his diary that, in the crowds who turned out to send off the troops, shouts of *Heil* and *nazdar,* hurrahs in German and Czech, mingled together.[109] One member of the Wandervogel, the German youth organization, confessed, "I curse the war, because it is agitating my calm and beautiful world, troubling my peaceful heart. But I must also bless it as the purifying storm that may usher in a fresher new age."[110]

After the event, however, the tendency to draw contrasts or to generalize grew stronger. The philosopher and pacifist Bertrand Russell, who in Summer 1914 had collected signatures at Cambridge in support of British neutrality, later recalled with disgust his colleagues' change of mind and the "cheering crowds" in London's Trafalgar Square. In his case, disillusionment colored his look back at public attitudes to the war. Only with knowledge of the results of the war could the German writer Willy Haas detect the end of the Habsburg monarchy in the mood in Prague in August 1914. And Adolf Hitler, in the account he gave of himself in *Mein Kampf,* associated his personal liberation from a precarious existence with the struggle for survival of the German nation. Here too, the "August experience" complied with a retrospective logic: "For me these hours came as a deliverance from the distress that had weighed upon me during the days of my youth. I am not ashamed to acknowledge today that I was carried away by the enthusiasm of the moment and that I sank down upon my knees and thanked Heaven out of the fullness of my heart for the favor of having been permitted to live in such a time."[111]

Police reports from Hamburg, written in July and August 1914 on the basis of conversations overheard in bars, paint a quite different, and much more authentic, picture of changing perceptions in workers' districts. As early as July 4, it was being said among a group of Polish workers that all "Austrian subjects liable to military service" had to report within three days to the military authorities of their hometowns. The Polish workers saw a considerable danger in the multiethnic structure of the Dual Monarchy: "If it comes to war between Austria and Serbia, there will certainly be a revolution inside Austria, for the Croats, Dalmatians, and Czechs will surely not wish to fight against the Serbs." Until late July, the Hamburg workers retained a critical attitude to the approaching war—"I don't feel like getting myself shot for other people" was a typical view—and hoped that Russian Social Democracy would call a general strike to stop its government from going to war. On July 29, this mood also seemed to clash with war patriotism on German streets, posing a threat to public order: "If things go that far here, our hurrah patriots will also lose interest. For now they're shooting their mouths off and have great fun creating mayhem in the streets; the police don't seem to care whether this disturbs the traffic or not. We are warned of parades, and they can do what they like simply because they are prowar and sing [the patriotic song] *Die Wacht am Rhein*." Such statements reflected neither revolutionary sentiments nor exuberant patriotism; indeed, their characteristic ambivalence fit well the situation in which German Social Democrats found themselves in 1914. One is struck by these workers' willingness to be told their duty, with the idea that the state would then have an obligation to reciprocate. When one young man remarked that, as an "enlightened worker," his father could not forsake his family and let himself be sent to war for an Austrian crown prince, the head of the family retorted: "Sure I'm married and have children, but if my country is in danger I'll let the state feed my family. Listen, it's all the same to me whether I die at work or for the fatherland, and you will go just like me, I'm telling you."[112]

This broad spectrum of reactions was also found elsewhere. In the case of France, the gathering international crisis in June and July 1914 was in no way the main issue for the public. Even by July 28, people in Paris were talking not about a further possible escalation but about a political murder two months earlier, when Henriette Caillaux, the second wife of the former premier and finance minister Joseph Caillaux, had shot the editor of *Le Figaro*, Gaston Calmette, in his office. Calmette had published damaging letters that proved she had been having an adulterous relationship with Caillaux before they were married; behind this revelation had been a conservative political campaign against the former prime minister for his alleged indulgence toward Germany during the Second Moroccan Crisis of 1911–1912.[113] Reports of the trial dominated the press in July 1914. Only when the military mobilization began did things suddenly change. Many observations at the time highlight the idea of national unity in France, the political-parliamentary commitment to the *union sacrée*. On August 11, the young lieutenant Louis Gillet wrote to the pacifist writer Romain Rolland (who would spend the war in Switzerland) of the wave of enthusiasm among French soldiers that was sweeping aside all differences and bonding the generations together. This was due to the one war aim that already pointed beyond defense of the fatherland: "If, like me, you could see our army, our soldiers, even these men from the western provinces, you would be fired with admiration for this people. It is the fervor of the Marseillaise, a heroic, solemn, somewhat religious fervor. . . . We shall have driven away the nightmare of materialism, of helmeted Germany, and of armed peace."[114]

In Normandy, at Cuverville-en-Caux near Le Havre, André Gide's experience of the outbreak of war was quite different. On July 30, he noted in his diary the "endless queues" and "the policemen to keep order outside the banks, where everyone has gone to get money. In the restaurants, before

Tension, euphoria, and fear: a snapshot from the Avenue de la Bourdonnais in Paris, early August 1914

serving, waiters warn the customers that banknotes will not be accepted."
Eventually an upper limit of fifty francs was set per transaction. On August 1,
the mobilization was announced not by a special poster but by the local fire
bell that had also tolled before 1800 in the event of accidents or disasters.
The first to be sent off to war were artisans such as bakers', cobblers', and
saddlers' apprentices.

In France the war fever was mainly limited to Paris, although there too
the picture was not uniform. On returning to the capital, Gide reported a
sense of trepidation on August 2 and 3, the day when war was declared: "All
are leaving or have already left. . . . The air is full of a loathsome anguish.
Fantastic appearance of Paris, its streets empty of vehicles and full of strange
people, calm but hypertense also; some are waiting with their trunks on the
sidewalk; a few noisy fellows at the entrance to cafés are bawling the *Marseillaise*. Occasionally an auto loaded down with luggage passes at great speed."
Popular reactions included the looting of stores, a symptom of the state of
emergency and the almost demonstrative suspension of public order: "[In]
the rue du Dragon I witness the sacking of a Maggi dairy store. . . . Two big
fellows, with a sort of tacit approval on the part of the police, are just finish-
ing breaking the shop windows with a kind of wooden rake. One of them
has climbed onto the showcase; he is holding up a big, brown earthenware
coffeepot, which he exhibits to the crowd and then throws onto the sidewalk,
where it crashes noisily. There is much applause."[115] Contemporary photographs confirm this combination of fear, tension, and euphoria, which was
soon distorted into mass-media images of a nation united in enthusiasm
for the war. One random snapshot, taken in Paris in the first few days of
August 1914, shows a number of men and women, including two soldiers, who
are standing around the camera. The actual occasion for the photo cannot
be known—only the general context of the outbreak of war—but nothing
that points to a general enthusiasm for the war can be read on the faces at
that moment. Many other photos from Paris show soldiers marching to the
Gare de l'Est, while local people cheer for them, offer them provisions, and
bid them farewell. But in that one small space a range of reactions is visible:
even the soldiers' laughter speaks more of fear, tenseness, and oppressive
concentration than of unbridled joy or liberating enthusiasm. Similarly, a
questionnaire commissioned by the French education minister testifies to a

Imagined gentlemen's war: British recruits of the College Officer Training Corps, Eton, 1914

wide range of feelings about the war among young schoolchildren in the western *département* of Charente. Of the 330 terms recorded, 57 percent have a negative connotation (dismay, tearfulness, sadness, resignation); 20 percent evince a calm, sober reaction; and only 23 percent express patriotic enthusiasm.[116] If any general tendency can be identified in French responses to the outbreak of war, then it is not so much one of enthusiastic support as a determination across social milieus and political parties to defend France, to prevent at all costs a repetition of the defeat of 1870–1871, and to ensure the continued existence of the Third Republic. But beneath this willingness in principle to accept the war, the skepticism even of mobilized soldiers should not be underestimated.[117]

As in France, most of the British population had not been expecting the sharp turn in the crisis at the end of July. While the French press was preoccupied with the trial of Madame Caillaux, the main story in the United Kingdom was the tense situation in Ireland. Here too, the reactions were more varied than Bertrand Russell's impression of cheering crowds in London would suggest. Hopes of a short war mingled with relief when the days of tension ended at last on August 4. But individuals recorded a range of feelings in diaries and letters. Dorothy Holman in Teignmouth, Devon, moved from shock and fear on August 1 through worry (August 3), excitement (August 5), uncertainty or concern (August 9 to 13), and dread (August 14) to relief (August 19) and despondency (August 25). Three features, in particular, were characteristic of reactions in the United Kingdom. First, the war on the Continent, unlike all other wars since the seventeenth century, was not geographically distant, but directly affected the British population in the form of spy scares, subversive acts by supposed "enemy aliens," and the possibility of aerial bombing and German landings. Before 1914 nightmare scenarios of a German invasion had found a considerable echo in the press and popular fiction, so that a set of collective images could now be readily activated.[118] But contrary to a widespread expectation, this was not a head-on conflict between Britain and Germany, but a war between two alliances, in which Britain, acting to defend its Continental security interests and its maritime dominance, supported France and Russia. The main rallying issue for the public was the German invasion of neutral Belgium, since this made Germany the aggressor.[119] It was not long before thousands of Belgian refugees were bringing reports of the early days of the war—and soon long lists of casualties gave an impression of the scale of the fighting. When 150 civilians were killed in December 1914 as a result of Zeppelin air raids on Whitby, Hartlepool, and Scarborough, the war actually arrived on the British mainland. Second, Britain joined the war with a force of volunteers, in contrast to the Continental conscripted armies. Within a few months its small standing army was transformed into a mass army of 2.5 million, for which there was no tradition of a "nation in arms," but which now carried the experience of war into nearly every family and took the four island nationalities—English, Welsh, Scottish, and Irish—closer to the self-image of United Kingdomers. Ultimately, entry into the war was a major turning point, when the domestic truce raised the question of what the wartime loyalty of Irishmen would mean in the future for their relationship with London.[120]

But how did the outbreak of war affect families in a position between nations and states, who because of their origins, their relatives, or their occupation could not be assigned to a single nation? They experienced August 1914 as an artificial split in personal, familial, and even commercial ties, which, though often continuing, made the individuals concerned especially sensitive to the new situation. The sudden virulence of the question of national belonging made it necessary to take sides and demonstrate one's loyalty, so that any wavering between countries or cultures, any playing with national ambiguities, suddenly aroused suspicions. The writer Elias Canetti, the eldest son of a wealthy Sephardi Jewish merchant family in Bulgaria, had been brought up both there and in Britain. In 1912, after the early death of his father, the family moved to Vienna, and then in 1916 to Zurich, where Canetti attended high school. On August 1, at the age of nine, he learned of the outbreak of war in Baden near Vienna, where he was visiting the spa gardens together with his mother and siblings. When the conductor of the spa orchestra announced that Germany had declared war on Russia, the musicians struck up the Austrian Imperial anthem and then the German hymn *Heil dir im Siegerkranz* (Hail to Thee in Victor's Laurels—the official anthem of the German Reich from 1871 to 1918), whose melody was the same as that of the British *God Save the King*. "I sensed that the mood was anti-British," Canetti later recalled. "I don't know whether it was out of old habit, but perhaps it was also defiance, I sang the English words along at the top of my lungs, and my little brothers, in their innocence, did the same in their thin little voices. Since we were in the thick of the crowd, no one could miss it. Suddenly I saw faces warped with rage all about me and arms and hands hitting at me. My brothers, too, even the youngest, George, got some of the punches that were meant for me, the nine-year-old. Before Mother, who was jostled away from us, realized what was going on, everyone was beating away at us in utter confusion. But the thing that made a much deeper impact on me was the hate-twisted faces. Someone must have told Mother, for she called very loud: 'But they're children!' She pushed over to us, grabbed all three boys, and snapped angrily at the people, who didn't do anything to her, because she spoke like a Viennese; and eventually they even let us out of the awful throng."[121]

A prominent Jewish family like the Ephrussi, which had made its fortune from the grain trade in Odessa and ran two banking houses in Paris and Vienna, also experienced the outbreak of war as an artificial division by country and nation. Whereas the French, Austrian, and German cousins, the Russian citizens, and the British aunts had naturally kept in touch with one another and spent many family holidays together, "all that nomadic lack of love of country" was now "consigned to [different] sides."[122] Jews felt particularly obliged, on the outbreak of war, to underline their loyalty to their respective countries. Nevertheless, even opinion leaders among German Jewry recoiled from the official image of general enthusiasm; they knew how abruptly loyalty tests and an atmosphere of mistrust could turn against the Jews.[123] In Vienna, the Austrian Israelite Union declared in August that "in this hour of danger" Jews were the "most loyal of all Habsburg subjects"; "we want to thank the Kaiser with the blood of our children and with our possessions for making us free"; "we want to prove to the state that we are its true citizens, as good as anyone." Such statements already associated loyalty with the hope that the war would finally prove the patriotic reliability of Jews and cut out the ground from under the anti-Semitic agitation that had gained a massive foothold there before 1914. At the same time, Jews expected that their conduct would entitle them to "full undiminished equality, to unreserved recognition of our citizenship rights."[124] In the *Jüdische Rundschau*, journal of the Zionist Federation in Germany, Jews voiced their hope that the victory of the two allied empires would lead to a new historical epoch of toleration and peaceful coexistence among different ethnic and religious groups: "There are increasing signs that an age of harmony is beginning, in which no nationality will pursue other goals than the blossoming of its culture, and the stronger will nowhere seek to oppress or assimilate the weaker; an age in which each nationality will happily incorporate itself into the state as a whole, and the state will allow national minorities the freedom that their loyalty deserves."[125]

On the afternoon of August 2, a large crowd gathered in front of the Winter Palace in St. Petersburg to hear the Tsar's declaration of war. It was a Sunday, and those who experienced the occasion were mostly schoolchildren and housewives, clerks, civil servants, and craft apprentices, often sent by their superiors, teachers, or employers. It was by no stretch of the imagination a revolutionary crowd. When the crowd members finally knelt down and sang the national anthem, Nicholas thought that, beyond all the social tensions and conflicts, the war would make it possible to achieve the unity of monarch and people that had seemed so difficult in recent years. He confided to his children's tutor: "There will now be a national movement in Russia like that which took place in 1812."[126]

At first, the people's reactions seemed to prove him right. In Russia too, an internal political peace (*vnutrennyi mir*) seemed to prevail at the beginning of the war. Strikes tailed off, many socialists joined the army, while many pacifists and critics of the regime went into exile. But this symbolic unity under the aegis of the Tsar and the Orthodox Church, visible in photos of priests blessing troops and posters presenting the war as a crusade, harbored in reality quite contradictory expectations. Passing through a multifarious stage of transition, Russia was wedged politically between traditional autocracy and constitutional rule. Not only the Tsar but also the radical intelligentsia and the Far Right rejected the new constitutional system. At the same time, the economy had been experiencing a period of dynamic growth. People had become more mobile, but the flow from country to city had put great strain on the urban infrastructure, with often disastrous consequences for working and living conditions. Shortly before Summer 1914, the precarious situation expressed itself in strike waves in the fast-growing cities, while the countryside was in turmoil as many peasants resisted the introduction of private land ownership to replace systems of common ownership. Unrest was also spreading among ethnic minorities, whose identity had grown stronger in recent years.[127]

Thus, the war also came as a test of whether this mobile society was sufficiently cohesive to absorb the various tensions within it or whether a revolutionary situation like that of 1904–1905 would break out.[128] In February 1914, the former interior minister Pyotr Nikolaevich Durnovo warned that a protracted war would end in a social revolution, since the liberal intelligentsia did not have the trust of the masses and a purely political revolution would not hold them back for long. "The trouble will start with the government being blamed for all disasters," he wrote prophetically. Socialist slogans would agitate the masses, so that land distribution would acquire central importance. "The defeated army, having lost its most dependable men, and carried away by the primitive peasant desire for land, will find itself too demoralized to serve as a bulwark of law and order." The Duma and even opposition deputies would eventually lose their authority and be swept along by the masses they had previously stirred up. Russia would be "flung into hopeless anarchy."[129]

In August 1914, however, demonstrations of unity were paramount. Most leading writers spoke out in favor of war, and quite a few volunteered for the army; the intelligentsia, as it were, was looking for long-coveted recognition, for acceptance of it as part of the nation. The destruction of German businesses in the early days of war, or the crowds who toppled the two bronze horses on the German embassy, were seen as insignificant.[130]

While the "unity of Tsar and people" was the main theme in the newspaper reporting of early August, the different expectations associated with it were already discernible in the political press. Conservatives regarded the war as an opportunity to unite the population behind an aggressive military nationalism. In contrast to liberal emphases on political involvement in the mobilization, conservatives saw in the mobilization an ethnic-cultural focus on the Russian nation. They paid no attention to the Duma's statement on the outbreak of war, but concentrated on the struggle against the internal enemy of the nation, against German and other foreign individuals and institutions. The Far Right went even further, stepping up cheap propaganda against Russians of German origin, Poles, Jews, and alleged defeatists, particularly those in the socialist camp. They accused the government of not being sufficiently Russian to represent the interests of its own nation.[131]

The liberal press, which represented the Constitutional Democrats (Kadets), also signed up to the war patriotism. What it foregrounded, however, was not the mystic unity of Tsar and people but a bourgeois concept of the nation: because Russia expected modern government in keeping with its economic development, the Duma, as the parliamentary center of the nation, was therefore the decisive institution to underline its wartime unity. In the liberal perspective, all citizens were present in the gathering of deputies on July 26 to decide on war. This idealized vision closely matched the French model of 1792—and overlooked the differences. In France, at the outbreak of war, people could link up with the successful revolution of 1789, but in the National Assembly war debates of 1792 there had already been shrill voices equating internal and external enemies and calling for greater force to be used against both. The hopes of Russian liberals that the war would help a citizenship-based concept of the nation establish itself marked the starting point for later conflicts. Only a year later the liberals and moderates, bitterly disappointed with the refusal of cooperation between the Duma and the government, went into open opposition and formed a Progressive Bloc. The liberal model was soon on the defensive, and not only because of the exclusion and mass deportation

War against the Central Powers as a crusade for Holy Russia: image of St. George on a Russian war poster, 1914

of Russian citizens of foreign descent.[132] There was also a kind of political-constitutional self-questioning, which was reminiscent of other countries, but expressed something over and above parliamentarism. Indeed, the Duma voluntarily dissolved on August 8, because it did not wish to obstruct the Imperial war effort unnecessarily. While the Duma, in a pompous display of patriotism, suspended its activity until the end of the war (which was expected to be close at hand), foreign visitors reported the somber faces of peasants and workers waiting at railroad stations for a train to take them to the front. In their case, there could be no talk of war patriotism.[133]

The outbreak of war brought momentous changes in neutral countries too, especially the United States. For that land of immigration was immediately confronted with the problem of the national political identification of immigrants, as well as the question of where its own loyalties should lie. On August 5, 1914, for example, the New York Times carried detailed reports on the thousands of Germans, Austrians, Hungarians, French, British, and Russians who had asked their consulates for help in getting them to Europe as quickly as possible to fight in their respective armies; the number of applicants, which it estimated at two to three thousand a day, was stretching consular officials to breaking point. The existence of so many reservists and volunteers, most of whom would be leaving their families behind without provision, illuminated in a flash the kind of problems that the war entailed even for countries not directly involved in it. People of German descent, as well as the German consul in New York, often took care of families left without a male provider, and in some cases a well-off businessman might take drastic action—the druggist Sigmund Kunz, for example, sold his business for a thousand dollars, well below its true value—to pay for passage to Germany. A number of affluent German Americans even tried to hire a special steamer, since the regular shipping services from Germany to America had been interrupted. There were reports of patriotic demonstrations, especially those of Germans and Austrians who shouted "Long Live Wilhelm II and Franz Joseph" and sang the anthems of the two empires. Numerous Americans reported to the French consulate as volunteers, reminding the consul of the transatlantic links between the two nations: "It made us think that in offering their services to France these young Americans had remembered the Marquis de Lafayette." Particularly noteworthy were the patriotic reactions of men whose families had emigrated from Europe and been living in the United

States for generations: "These reservists included wealthy Frenchmen, . . . some of them Legion of Honor men; others were waiters, chefs, and teachers. All became French patriots at the Consulate."[134]

When war broke out, the United States was also feeling the effects of the conflict with Mexico—where it had intervened militarily in 1913—and of its own economic problems.[135] The early British blockade limited exports—which suggested to many that U.S. industry should gear itself more to the Entente countries to compensate for the demand-side loss. This economic orientation, soon complemented with loans to Britain and France, qualified the official emphasis on neutrality. Moreover, the scales were already tipping within the global news market. The Royal Navy cut the sea cables between Continental Europe and the United States in the first few days of the war, so that Britain was able to exercise extensive control over the supply of news and war reporting in North America. German reports got through only after considerable delay, using South American routes or other correspondence networks, whereas the British authorities and British journalists could communicate their version of events almost at once.[136] This would soon have a major impact on the debate concerning U.S. "preparedness" for a world war.[137]

In all the combatant countries, the days between the war declarations and the beginning of hostilities marked a special kind of interlude. The atmosphere of high tension and enormous expectation, together with the limited availability of information, favored the circulation of rumors in which the first popular enemy-images of the war became discernible. Rumors played an important role in collective states of excitement in August 1914, as a form of emotional condensation that stirred intense feeling.[138] But they did not have the same effect everywhere. In Germany, the multiple land borders, as well as the long period of uncertainty, fueled the sense of threat. In Britain, where the shift from peace to war was more abrupt, and where fewer families were directly affected than in France or Germany because of the sealed borders and less extensive call-up, rumors played less of a role in communication. Moreover, the British newspaper market picked up on the general sense of insecurity, helping to channel feelings of danger.[139]

Fear of enemy spies, however, was noticeable in every country in early August 1914, adding to far-fetched rumors that took on a reality and operational patterns of their own. These reflected a threat scenario and a collective urge to specify and personalize the enemy. In the initial phase, when war had broken out but had not yet led to hostilities or fleshed out a military enemy-image, such rumors about spies and conspiracies served the function of preparing people to take on the enemy at home. On August 5, Harry Graf Kessler reported that "fear of spies" was taking "dangerous and grotesque forms" in Germany. Some acquaintances of his were shot at in their car as they were traveling from Silesia to Berlin; others were molested by a crowd on Unter den Linden or threatened "with umbrellas and sticks" on the supposition that they were Russian officers. Kessler himself experienced reactions bordering on hysteria: "On the road from Berlin to Beeskow, . . . I was stopped in every village twice, once on the way in and once on the way out. I had to show my papers although I was in uniform. The peasants have set up roadblocks with hay wagons and wire. They stand around the streets with flintlocks, stopping cars. In Kiekebusch three men blocked the road with flintlocks, and when I asked one to show me his badge he produced his hunting license."[140]

The backdrop to this hysteria was a rumor that French gold was being transported from Germany to Russia. In fact, the presidium of the Düsseldorf government had wired to the Interior Ministry on August 3 that eighty French officers wearing Prussian uniforms were en route through Germany in a secret operation to transport gold to Russia. The hunt for their "gold automobiles" eventually threatened to interfere with the German mobilization, and on August 7 the general staff stepped in and forbade it.[141] Typically, the early wartime emergency situation developed as a mixture of patchy information, hysterical tension, compulsive control, and a propensity to violence that could at any moment turn against civilians who came under suspicion. Waves of spy mania would continue in all the combatant countries over the coming months and years. In France, for instance, conspiracy theories gave rise to the idea that the country's press was being manipulated by German money.[142]

3. MACHINES AND MATERIALS
The Escalation of Killing

Max Weber described the First World War as the first technological-industrial mass war, a "war of machines" waged by the "modern military state," in contrast to the "levies of agricultural tribes."[143] The character of this mechanized warfare, which contemporaries liked at first to identify with rational planning, expert knowledge, and efficiency, asserted itself in the early days and weeks of the war, and it confronted military apparatuses and European societies with casualty figures that, though not unfamiliar from the South African and Russo-Japanese wars, were without precedent in Europe itself. From the beginning, as a result of the overlapping of old military traditions and strategic-operational thinking with advanced techniques and infrastructures of mass slaughter, a peculiar asynchronicity accompanied the war. This was a decisive reason why actual experiences diverged so quickly and radically from people's expectations, increasing the pressure to justify the war and its countless victims. Given the losses in the first weeks, however, it is surprising how stubbornly all military commanders stuck to their conventional strategies and how long millions of soldiers were prepared to endure the nightmarish consequences of those basic decisions.

The French example is especially instructive. In contrast to the assumptions of the army leadership, which, in view of widespread criticism before 1914, was skeptical about a call-up and expected that as many as 13 percent of soldiers would not report for duty, the mobilization was as successful and, for the most part, as efficient as it was in other countries. Between August 1 and August 10, a total of 1.5 million soldiers were transported on 4,300 trains to the border with Germany. Thanks to advances in smokeless powder technology, it had been clear at least since the Russo-Japanese war that camouflage uniforms would be absolutely essential on modern battlefields. But unlike British soldiers, who had been supplied since 1902 with new khaki uniforms, and unlike German infantrymen in their field-gray or gray-green uniforms dating from 1907 (for whom the only individual marking was a red regimental number on their spiked helmet), French, Belgian, and Serbian soldiers marched off to twentieth-century war in their late nineteenth-century parade dress. The French, in their mainly blue frock coats, red trousers, and distinctive kepis, were especially easy to spot on the battlefield—as were the Austrian cavalry, whose commanders continued to wear their traditional blue tunics and red trousers. Only after the huge losses of the early months of war did all the armies hasten the introduction of camouflage battledress and steel helmets instead of kepis and leather helmets.[144]

But a strong adherence to tradition was not confined to matters of uniform. Commanders everywhere were convinced that a war could be decided only through offensives and all-out infantry attacks pursued with a collective will; this obsession would have devastating consequences on all European fronts in 1914.[145] German military thinking and officer training gave primacy to an active war of movement, to the aggressive search for a decisive battle in a short space of time. For all their differences, this linked the starting position in Summer 1914 with the battles of Frederick the Great in the eighteenth century, the short wars of 1866 and 1870–1871, and the culture of violence in the colonial wars of Imperial Germany.[146] The French Plan XVII of 1913 based itself on the *offensive à outrance* (all-out offensive), on trust in the *élan* of French soldiers, and the underlying principle—"advance with all forces united to attack the German armies."[147] The plan failed within a few days in the so-called frontier battles in Alsace-Lorraine and became so much wastepaper. But this catastrophe was due above all to the prior agreement with Russia to launch attacks on the fifteenth day of mobilization, which meant that tactical alternatives such as a temporizing defensive action between the French channel coast and the Swiss border were not available.[148] In those

The burden of war: French infantrymen returning from the Argonne front, 1914

battles, which were decided militarily in less than a week, many units lost up to 80 percent of their strength, and the French incurred the highest losses on any single day of the war—27,000 on August 22—and more than 40,000 between August 20 and 23.[149]

These figures confirmed what Ivan Bloch and other military theorists had predicted before 1914: that soldiers launching an attack, in whichever density or combination, could achieve little, and risked losing a great deal, against coordinated forces of machine guns and massed artillery. Other armies would essentially repeat these experiences in the following weeks and months. On August 26 and 27, the German Fifth Army under Crown Prince Rupprecht of Bavaria lost 24,313 dead and missing—more than 14 percent of its total force of 172,922 men. The German balance sheet of the Battle of the Marne also underlined this new scale of warfare: by the end of September, of the 1.3 million German soldiers deployed, 26,000 were dead, 46,000 missing, and more than 130,000 wounded.[150]

The firepower that defenders could bring to bear from a distance was the principal factor responsible for these terrible casualties. Artillery with a massively increased impact became the prime weaponry shaping this long-range war at the front. Next came the machine gun, which upstaged hand-to-hand combat with saber and bayonet, fundamentally altering the reality of the battlefield. Technically speaking, it used the recoil from each shot to eject the spent cartridge case, to tense the spring for the next shot, and to load a new cartridge into the firing chamber. This was the decisive innovation that the American engineer Hiram Maxim achieved in 1885 with his so-called Maxim gun. It was already in service in Sudan in 1898, and later in the South African and Russo-Japanese wars. Beginning in August 1914, the machine gun transferred the experiences of asymmetrical deadly force from the colonial theaters of war to those of Europe.[151] The models first deployed in 1914 had a firepower of 400 to 600 rounds a minute, a superiority over all conventional repeater weapons that made them so important in battle. However, in 1914 they were still available only in relatively small numbers, and their weight of 40–60 kilograms plus the three to four men required to operate them meant that they were too cumbersome for an infantry attack. The preeminence of this weapon becomes clear if we think of the trends in its use during the course of the war. In 1914 a German infantry division had 24 heavy machine guns at its disposal, but by 1918 it had 108 heavy and 216 light machine guns; the comparable increase in France over the same period was from a total of 24 guns to 108 heavy and 576 light guns, and in Britain from 24 heavy guns to 64 heavy and 336 light machine guns. Only on the Russian side did the machine-gun force stagnate (1914: 32, 1917: 36), while an American division in 1918 could draw on more than 225 heavy and 775 light machine guns. The war also brought new weapons such as gas, hand grenades, and flamethrowers into operational use.[152]

The annihilating effects of artillery fire on unprotected infantry constituted one of the most dramatic experiences of the first days of the war. On August 13, 1914, French Artillery Regiment No. 47 shelled German formations in the Upper Alsace region. According to a French report at the time, "one Württemberg infantry regiment emerging in small columns from the forest was bombarded from a distance of 2,000 meters. The shells could be clearly seen to bounce and explode at a low height, mowing down several columns and forcing anyone not killed to flee to a gully that ran parallel to the edge of the forest at a distance of 150 meters. These men then came under further fire. The next day, an inspection of the area counted hundreds of dead, their bodies mostly blown to pieces. Assault troops had been decapitated by the blade strokes of 75 mm shells. The advance of the regiment and the whole division had been definitively halted by artillery fire alone."[153] Special scatter-projectiles had a particularly devastating effect. These so-called shrapnel shells, which at the beginning of the war formed the bulk of field gun ordnance in all armies, had a delayed fuse that allowed them to be detonated right in front of the object, causing severe and (with successive rounds) multiple injuries among enemy troops, especially if they had no cover. Field shrapnel 96, in regular use by the German artillery, contained 300 lead bullets weighing 10 grams each. The French field artillery also deployed this weapon. Here we can see the hopeless inferiority of cavalry units at the beginning of the war. On August 7, with just sixteen shrapnel salvoes, the German 21st Dragoon Regiment northeast of Verdun was almost completely wiped out from a distance of roughly 5,400 meters. Some 600 to 700 dead and wounded were left lying on the battlefield; none had had a single opportunity even to encounter the enemy.[154]

The first battles showed vividly how well-coordinated defenders could defeat even a numerically superior enemy, especially if they had machine guns at their disposal. On August 22, 1914, near Rossignol in southern Belgium, Regiment No. 1 of the Third Colonial Division, under General Raffenel, was routed by a much smaller force of German troops, partly because of mistakes by its own artillery, but above all because the enemy was able to bring machine-gun fire to bear against the French attackers. The regiment quickly lost some 3,000 of its 3,200 men, including 2,000 dead and 1,000 wounded or captured. In his order of the day on August 24, 1914, the French general Joseph Joffre reported that "whenever we tried to throw the infantry into the attack before the artillery had had its effect," the infantry units suffered huge losses "under machine-gun fire" that "could have been avoided."[155] In general, however, commanders clung to the traditional conception of offensive warfare. They ignored the devastating impact that a combination of artillery and machine guns had on the battlefield. Faced with the constraints on infantry movement and the threat of battlefield stasis, they looked to ways of increasing offensive capacities, in the conviction that the key elements were strength of will, discipline, and bravery and that thick columns of men should direct as much firepower as possible against enemy positions and overwhelm them in close combat.[156] Although military regulations before 1914 had drawn some lessons from the South African and Russo-Japanese wars, paying much greater attention to cover for infantry troops, a strong morale remained the guiding principle. We can see this in the French orientation to the *offensive à outrance*: "Moral forces are the most powerful bearers of success. Honor and patriotism instill the noblest devotion in troops. Self-sacrifice and a will to win ensure success." Staff officers were not keen on trenches and field fortifications, fearing that these would dull their men's offensive spirit and make them more cowardly. In the Russian army, the maxims of General Dragomirov continued to guide thinking: "The bullet is mindless; only the bayonet is a man. . . . There is a national tactics to which modern weaponry must bow, not a modern weaponry to which national tactics has to adapt."[157]

The impact of weaponry did not have only a quantitative dimension. To kill and be killed became anonymous. The operation of heavy guns, also involving radio communication, operated at such a distance from the place where their effects were felt that war came to appear singularly abstract, even bureaucratic—or anyway it acquired a rational-objective dimension.[158] Harry Graf Kessler described his impressions of the deployment of new Krupp mortars in Belgium on August 22, 1914: "One leveled the observation tower, another tossed a great block of concrete on top of it. We observed the destruction as it progressed. The men directing the fire, a captain and a first lieutenant, sat next to us under cover as if in an office, giving orders and numbers via telephone to the cannon two kilometers distant, just as a banker telephones in orders for buying or selling to the bourse, a completely methodical office. The resemblance was heightened by the fact that the captain resembled exactly Herr Rathenau. An order can bring one hundred corpses, between the shots you can lunch and chat. You only realize that the cool calculator kills with his orders when you force yourself to think about it."[159]

Artillery, machine guns, and pinpoint repeating rifles functioned as long-range weapons, which made direct contact between enemies the exception. All told, some 70 percent of soldiers who died in the war were killed by artillery fire, and only 1 percent in close combat from traditional saber or bayonet strikes. It was above all the huge increase in artillery shelling during the war that made death an equal, random danger for all soldiers. The possibility that you might be killed by a shell at any moment, outside the time span of an actual military engagement, gave rise to a novel stress situation and therefore to new pathological syndromes. One aspect of the anonymous killing was that intensive bombardment of quite small areas dismembered the bodies of the fallen so badly that it was later impossible to identify them. The importance of this phenomenon can hardly be exaggerated: 100,000 of the 379,000 French dead at the Battle of Verdun in 1916 were listed as missing, in most cases because body parts could not be fit together to form a whole. The figure of 300,000 missing among the France's 1.3 million dead for the whole war gives only a faint inkling of what this must have meant for family members. The reality of the war not only robbed them of the men's bodies but made it impossible for them to bury and mourn their dead.[160]

The casualties in the first weeks and months of the war overstretched the resources of the military bureaucracy. If there were reliable figures at all, they were subject to strict secrecy. But despite this censorship, people at home soon learned of the exterminatory dimensions of the war. The young Frenchman who in August 1914 could not return to his unit because of an illness, and who by the end of the year was the only one of twenty-seven classmates from his high school still alive, is just one example of thousands in the societies of wartime Europe.[161] The 45-year-old Michel Corday, a senior official in Bordeaux, learned from a lunch he had in November 1914 with Ministers Aristide Briand and Marcel Sembat that even cabinet members had no idea how many soldiers France had or exactly how high the toll had been in the first weeks of the war. Faced with the countless dead and missing, the bureaucracy was not capable of keeping troop lists up to date. When Corday attended the reopening of the Chamber of Deputies in December, he met a general's adjutant who in civilian life was the director of the Opéra Comique and who told him that each evening as many as 1,500 theatergoers had to be turned away. Most of those in the boxes were tearful women in mourning clothes, who had come to cry at the opera and to seek consolation in the music.[162]

Death on a mass scale was soon part of the life of society—indeed, it came to be a leitmotif, a trope. In a joke published in the German *Simplicissimus* in late 1914, a lady says to a young lieutenant: "If you are still alive, you have chosen the wrong profession."[163] In addition to civilians in the immediate vicinity of the front, in Belgium, northern and eastern France, East Prussia and Galicia, whose experience of the war was one of occupation and devastation, those who remained at home in other areas, too, indirectly experienced the war in the first few weeks, and the killing and being killed, as an anonymous event. The war made its presence felt in the ever-longer casualty lists and never-ending troop transports. On September 27, 1914, a columnist in the *Prager Tagblatt* wrote, "The eeriest thing about this war is the secretive way in which it is being conducted. Our sons, brothers, spouses, and fathers board the train—and we do not know where it will take them. Our nearest and dearest are not supposed to write where they are, and if we read their names in the casualty lists, it remains a mystery where they lie buried, or in which battle they received their wounds."[164]

4. BECOMING A SOLDIER, BEING A SOLDIER
From Mobilization to the Mass Army

With *Bebuquin,* the novel he published in 1912, Carl Einstein made his debut as one of the leading writers of German expressionism—yet in August 1914 he was one of those carried away by events who would soon leave behind their old lives along with their convictions. In just a few days he changed from a critical author into a soldier. He wrote to his fellow novelist Robert Musil about his first impressions as a volunteer in the barracks; it was a testimony to the chaos, excitement, and virtual lack of rules that went together with a completely changed rhythm of life. Musil noted in his diary: "Einstein says: In the barracks: disorder, loss of inhibition, except when on duty. Dirt several centimeters thick, makeshift beds, drinking. Stealing is rife. Cases are broken open. One can't leave anything lying around for one moment. He says he doesn't know what it is, but it has got into him, too: he doesn't need a brush but steals two, sees a third, rushes headlong at the man: 'You've got my brush!' and takes it by force. The breech-blocks for the rifles of whole divisions are stolen, hidden for no reason, scattered around. . . . Judges and lawyers say to each other, as if it were a matter of no consequence: 'Was it you who pinched my belt?' One has the feeling that if we're not careful everyone will attack everyone else." The expressionist writer knew only one thing in life: "Einstein is wild with enthusiasm; everything else is obliterated. When he is sleeping with his wife, he is interested only in the stuff he uses to clean his buttons. He never goes into his study."[165]

The call-up of conscripts and reservists began in every country with the coming of war. On the eve of war, only France had nearly completed the draft of servicemen, whereas in other European countries many men liable for service remained without military training. Unlike Continental Europe, the geographically separate Britain and the United States relied on small armies and the recruitment of volunteers; only in 1916 or 1917 did they introduce conscription. Britain's historical tradition of operating on the Continent mainly with the armies of allied powers, or else, as in Wellington's case against Napoleonic France, in close cooperation with the Royal Navy, did not constitute a meaningful alternative in 1914. The answer that Kitchener came up with as war minister was the "new armies," which in a short space of time changed not only the structure of the British armed forces but also their relationship to society. With its medical examinations, conscription, and training, the military state became for the first time a formative experience for hundreds of thousands of young Britons.[166] Starting from a manageable regular army of 247,000, one-third of them stationed in India, the British armed forces saw 5.7 million men, or 22 percent of the male population, serve in its ranks by November 1918. The famous recruitment poster of August 1914, in which Kitchener calls on every young man to enlist ("Britons, Kitchener Wants You!"), became the symbol of the new volunteer armies. Within eight weeks 761,000 men signed up—more than 33,000 on September 3 alone. Typical of the new military units were the so-called Pals Battalions, whose special composition deliberately incorporated local social networks.[167]

Many young Britons first encountered the reality of the war state during the medical examinations that took place in the early months. One recruit, S. C. Lang, recorded, "The sergeant said to me: 'Get on the scales.' He weighed me, took my height, and said: 'Now we'll go round to the doctor for a medical exam.' The doctor told me to take all my clothes off, which embarrassed me very much."[168] The numbers who refused military service—as many as 23,000 men—were strikingly large, considerably more so than in all other countries. A wide range of explanations for this were suggested at the time, ranging from cowardice, degeneracy, and disloyalty to the nation, through to the traditions of Victorian pacifism.[169]

The task of equipping hundreds of thousands of soldiers and deploying them to the front was a huge challenge for the various states, and not only

First encounter with the war state: testing the vision of a British volunteer, 1914

because of the logistical problems it involved. Particularly in the multiethnic empires, recruitment processes at the beginning of the war offered a foretaste of conflicts to come. With the harvest to be collected in August, fear accompanying the mobilization orders ran high in the countryside. This was especially noticeable in the Russian Empire, where in Summer 1914 the various ethnic groups reacted differently to the local recruitment drives; among Armenian families in the southern Caucasus, where incomes were largely dependent on male agricultural labor, wives and mothers were appalled and disoriented when it seemed that their husbands, fathers, and brothers would be called up for the army: "There arose such crying and wailing among the women and children that it immediately became horrible. The din of this weeping prevailed throughout the city both night and day." Other responses to the draft, visible in many rural areas and provincial towns, were the looting of shops and alcohol abuse, which many officers saw as an enemy at least as powerful as the German and Austrian armies.[170]

In the Ottoman Empire, conscription effectively meant a further drive to penetrate the region of Anatolia, so that the war became a vehicle of top-down state-building. In many places, the first experience of the central state was at local recruitment centers—and it was not long before problems arose there, such as the resistance to the draft among Kurds and other groups inhabiting eastern and southeastern Anatolia. Here a mixture of traditional methods and new instruments were used, such as the creation of volunteer units in the Kurdish areas and among distinctive Muslim population groups. This was supposed to improve the image of the Ottoman army in areas with a strong sense of local identity. As to the enlistment of men liable for compulsory service, the authorities sought to forge links between the state and various Muslim organizations—a development that would continue long after the war, marking the formation of the Turkish nation between 1919 and 1923.

When it began to seem that the war would last a long time, increasing the pressure to recruit more and more young men, the state resorted to the creation of a network of paramilitary youth organizations in Anatolia. This tended to equate with a militarization of the population, but the limits of such practices became apparent in rising desertion rates, particularly among Anatolian Muslims. This tendency also reflected the inability of the state to supply both the army and the general population. When its structures began to fray, the authorities often had to strike a deal with local gangs in order to tap more recruits.[171]

The conversion of civilians into soldiers was not an experience limited to young men in Europe; it acquired a global dimension early on. Kande Kamara came from Kindia in what was then French Guinea. Since he could not read or write, his experiences of the war were recorded in a series of interviews in 1976. At the beginning of the war, he was working as a driver in the capital, Bamako, when he heard of the French recruitment drive. He went back to his native village and found that nearly all the men there had hidden from the authorities: "Everyone was in the bush, in the valleys, and in the mountains. The only time they would come into town was in the middle of a dark night." Kamara's father forbade his son to report voluntarily, "as he thought it was stupid and ridiculous to go to a war I didn't understand and to fight in another country." Nevertheless, Kamara ended up enlisting of his own free will. Children from less prestigious families in the villages were registering for military service, because it promised them some improvement in their status—and this made Kamara envious of them. But joining the army also had other consequences. "I felt that, as I was one of the elder children of a chief, it was one of my responsibilities to go to war, if [the white people] needed us. They had already noted down that every slave who went to war would become a chief on return. . . . I was given clothes, money, and food. In the afternoon I presented myself to my people wearing my army uniform. There was a real uproar, there was hysteria, everyone in the village was alarmed at seeing my uniform."[172]

France recruited some 29,000 soldiers from Senegal, the so-called *tirailleurs sénégalais*, of whom 6,000–7,000 were killed in action. In the last two years, in particular, the casualties in these units were two or three times higher than in French regiments. After the mass slaughter of 1916 and the crisis of Spring 1917, many commanders were more sparing with French soldiers and turned increasingly to units from the colonies. In Africa, recruitment practices reflected the complex structure of the colonial societies, and in the urban centers military service was considered an opportunity to achieve political rights. Blaise Diagne, one of the most important Senegalese political leaders and the first deputy of African origin elected to the National

Assembly in Paris, urged his fellow countrymen to enlist and campaigned for the colonial authorities in return to improve social conditions in Senegal and to ensure the fair treatment of war veterans. In country areas, however, fear of recruitment was widespread, and the French authorities often reacted with coercion in the face of local resistance.[173]

In other parts of French West Africa, many local chiefs responsible for recruitment and selection processes tried to protect their tribes in order to preserve manpower for agriculture.[174] In Cameroon, in contrast, the German authorities first had to appoint chiefs to recruit manpower and soldiers— which placed the hierarchies of the indigenous population on a completely new footing.[175] Elsewhere the war helped to boost social mobility among former soldiers; in Kenya, for example, men could buy cattle out of their wages and pensions, becoming more attractive in the marriage market.[176]

The resort to *troupes indigènes* pointed to an intricate interweaving of republicanism, colonial ideology, and racism in France. On the one hand, colonial officials and the army appealed to the republican ideal, which spurned racism in the name of equality. On the other hand, however, this was contradicted by everyday practices. French leaders looked to the aggressive fighting qualities of colonial troops, yet many officers feared that they might strike up relationships with French women. There was strong vocal support for racial equality, and black African soldiers were dressed up in French uniforms in preparation for the occupation of German areas after 1918.[177]

In the British Empire, 2.8 million men were recruited; Great Britain thus mobilized a total of 8.6 million by 1918.[178] The largest contingent was made up of Indians (1.4 million soldiers and laborers), including 150,000 (approx. 90,000 soldiers) on the western front and some 700,000 (approx. 330,000 soldiers) in Mesopotamia.[179] In addition, there were indigenous Canadians, 44,000 black South Africans in the Labour Battalions, soldiers from the West Indies, workers from Africa, and askari soldiers from East Africa, as well as Chinese and Egyptian laborers in the so-called Labour Corps.[180] In Africa alone, two million people were involved in the war effort.[181] Once again, we see the huge importance of the colonies for the conduct of the war, but the war also became a key experience for soldiers from the colonies and their families back home.[182] Many would learn, however, that military service did not improve their rights and status as they had hoped; in many ways, racist segregation and the social hierarchy of colonial society persisted in daily life at the front.[183]

5. DYNAMIC VIOLENCE
Global Zones and Local Experiences

When and how did the war begin? If we ignore the shelling of Belgrade by Austro-Hungarian artillery positioned across the Danube, which began with the declaration of war on July 28, it was August 4 that marked the outbreak of large-scale hostilities in western Europe. But before German troops marched into Belgium, a radio message from the German admiralty reached the commander of the German naval squadron in the Mediterranean. This hastily informed Admiral Wilhelm Souchon that an alliance existed between the Ottoman Empire and Germany and that he should head for Constantinople with the battle cruiser *Goeben* and the light cruiser *Breslau*. The *Goeben* had been launched in 1911 as a ship of the "dreadnought" class (so called after the British battleship of that name). It had a displacement of 20,000 tons and, like all ships of this new type, was equipped with single-caliber twin guns, cemented armor, and a fast drive capable of exceeding 20 knots thanks to low-pressure steam turbines that replaced the older high-pressure piston engines. The formal alliance between the German Reich and the Ottoman Empire was finalized only as a result of the events that followed that radio communication. The combat patrol initiated by the *Goeben* on August 4 became the prelude to the war at sea; it had far-reaching consequences, continuing the policy of German military assistance and cooperation to the Ottoman Empire. The operation was noteworthy because it did not involve a major sea battle with the British navy. Before the war the German naval command had been expecting such an engagement to take place in the North Sea, but on that day in August it was just a question of two German ships in the Mediterranean. Souchon, who on August 4 had found himself in the Adriatic, promptly sailed into the western Mediterranean and shelled the Algerian ports of Bône and Philippeville, in order to hinder the transportation of French colonial troops. Not only did he then shake off his British pursuers but he also managed to get through to Messina in Sicily, to take coal on board there, and, after a brief skirmish with the British warship *Gloucester*, to reach the Aegean at the Dardanelles on August 10. This maritime prelude was followed by a tenacious tug-of-war, which ended when the Ottoman navy took over the *Goeben* and, in late October 1914, under German pressure, led to the entry of the Ottoman Empire into the war on the side of the Central Powers. The influence of the German military on the Turkish land army, which Otto Liman von Sanders had achieved before 1914, was consolidated through Souchon's coup and the presence of his naval firepower at one of the strategic nodal points of the war.[184]

The arrival of the two ships, whose German crews were retained under the formal command of the Ottoman Empire, marked a major strategic success at the outset of the war. From that time on, the Dardanelles and the Bosporus were no longer passable for the Allies, and the Russian Empire had to endure a total blockade of the Black Sea. Since the German navy also largely controlled the Baltic and could quickly move ships through the Kiel Canal linking it to the North Sea, Russia found itself cut off early on from two key supply routes. Only through Arkhangelsk (which was iced up for six months of the year) and Vladivostok (13,000 kilometers from the front) was it now possible to ship exports and, most important, to receive imports vital to the war. The opening in 1916 of a new ice-free port at Romanov-on-Murman (later Murmansk), on the Kola Peninsula north of the Arctic Circle and at the terminus of the Murman railroad, ultimately failed to solve Russia's supply problems.[185] Russia's economy did not have sufficient access to the Allies' industrial and military resources; its exports fell by 98 percent, its imports by 95 percent. This explains the Allies' attempt to capture the Dardanelles Straits by means of large-scale amphibious landings in Spring 1915. For the strategy of the Central Powers, however, the successful blockade of the Black Sea and the Dardanelles also influenced a basic military decision in the region, since all future Allied operations on the territory of the Ottoman Empire—most notably in Mesopotamia and the Near East—would have to be carried out separately, with only very limited Russian involvement. In comparison with the ineffectiveness of the German deep-sea fleet and the lack of an overall strategy against Britain, the *Goeben*'s opening act in the Mediterranean with the small forces at its disposal therefore had quite remarkable consequences.[186] For Russia's military and political leadership, moreover, the de facto blockade demonstrated how important control of the Straits would be in the future. The fact that

Russia did not mass all its forces on the eastern front against Germany and Austria-Hungary, but stepped up the pressure on the Ottoman Empire in the Caucasus, was one more result of this experience at the beginning of the war.[187]

While this course was being set in the eastern Mediterranean, the early months of the war were unfolding quite differently in Continental Europe. Here there was a sharp divergence between expectations and actual experiences. The war began and ended with railroads. This had a symbolic significance, but went far beyond that. The railroad crystallized not only the industrial potential that European societies had developed in the nineteenth century but also their demand for mobility, acceleration, and the opening up of new spaces. Railroads were thus always more than just a transport infrastructure: they symbolized an urge for technological progress, movement, and speed, and they were state enterprises that, alongside the military and the bureaucracy, stood for planning, rational calculation, and efficiency. They therefore played a key role in the military scenarios of the prewar period, whether in relation to the Russian western railroad (on which the speed of mobilization in western Russia depended) or in relation to great projects such as the Trans-Siberian or the Baghdad railroad (in which military motives were from the beginning an essential component). The importance of railroads in supplying the military and the civilian population continued to grow throughout the war, as the example of the Murman line in Russia shows. Whether in Lenin's journey in 1917 from Zurich to Russia in a German sealed wagon, or in the signing of the armistice in November 1918 in a saloon carriage of the Compagnie Internationale des Wagon-Lits, the First World War was also—militarily, economically, symbolically, and in terms of resource policy—a rail war, as Wilhelm Groener, the head of the railroad department at the German general staff from 1912 to 1916, emphasized.[188]

In August 1914 trains were the prime means of carrying men, weapons, and equipment in a swift and orderly manner to their deployment areas. In Germany alone, in the early period of mobilization from August 2 to the capture of Liège (a key railroad junction) on August 16–17, they transported more than three million soldiers and 850,000 horses in approximately 11,000 consignments. Between August 2 and 18, some 2,150 westward-bound trains—an average of one every ten minutes—crossed the Hohenzollern Bridge in

Cologne that had opened over the Rhine in 1911. Given the relatively modest size of the German army railroad department, which before 1914 had consisted of sixty-three officers and thirteen civil servants, this number demonstrates how effectively the railroad was embedded in the military governance and command structure. For people at the time, the success of the mobilization counted as a technical and organizational triumph: "There was a mixed feeling of total confidence in success, pride at the possibility of finally putting into practice years of theoretical labor, and the knowledge that everyone, down to the last worker, would do his duty. . . . On August 1 at five in the afternoon, when the storm broke loose with the mobilization announcement, the machine swung automatically into motion, with outstanding calm, expertise, and cheerful optimism."[189]

If the railroad symbolized the legacy of the industrial age, the potential for technological progress and rational organization of movement, the army's war began by curiously harking back to older traditions and war experiences. Both belonged to the legacy of the nineteenth century. The first German soldiers who, in the early morning of August 4, 1914, advanced onto Belgian soil 110 kilometers east of Brussels were Uhlans of the Marwitz and Richthofen Cavalry Corps, carrying, along with rifles and sabers, their traditional heavy lances more than three meters long and weighing nearly two kilograms. These units were supposed to reconnoiter the positions occupied by Belgian and French troops. At a time when aerial surveillance was still in its infancy and the military did not yet deploy large motorized units, only the cavalry was available for both functions. In 1939 airplanes and tanks would dominate the opening scenes of the Second World War—but in August 1914 it was marching infantrymen and advance guards on horseback. In the villages, the German Uhlan lancers handed out flyers to the civilian population, explaining "with regret" that the invasion had been necessary and warning against "hostile acts" such as the demolition of transport routes. They were not expecting determined resistance from the Belgian army.[190] The units that followed the Uhlans consisted of infantry and field artillery, overwhelmingly drawn by horses. Mobile field kitchens ensured the provision of troops even when they were on the march. The average equipment of a German infantryman weighed roughly 32 kilograms: rifle, ammunition, and kitbag, together with a spare pair of boots and two rations of meat, vegetables, and ship's biscuits, as well as a pack of ground coffee, a bottle of brandy, tobacco, chocolate, and bandages.[191]

The deployments that initially looked like a logical follow-up to the successful mobilization soon escalated into violence of unforeseen proportions. This already demonstrated, in the first few days of war, not only the new killing potential of the military but also the dynamic of hypertrophic expectations among inexperienced troops and their officers, of rumors, false perceptions, and enormous time pressure. It rapidly became clear how little, in certain situations, the civilian population fleeing the cities could be shielded from the use of force against the enemy army. This gave the opening act of the war in the west an exemplary significance that went far beyond military history. Events in Belgium became a reference point both for early political justifications of the war and for the first wave of theoretical explanations

The other face of war: Belgian civilians flee bombed Antwerp toward the Netherlands, Summer 1914

of it. Starting in Belgium, the war waged by the army crossed over into a cultural war waged by intellectuals.

For a long time, German plans had been based on the assumption of a war on two fronts, and also—against the background of the massive French and Russian arms buildup—on the lesser and, in time, declining military strength of the Central Powers in relation to their enemies. The plan developed by Schlieffen in his memorandum of December 1905 and the German deployment instructions of 1906–1907 therefore looked to take on and annihilate the enemy in the west in an all-out campaign before the Russians could complete their troop deployment in the east. Instead of a frontal attack on the French fortifications—a massive line built beginning in 1870–1871 from Verdun, Toul, Nancy, and Épinal to Belfort, a *barrière de fer* of dug-in heavy artillery, infantry bunkers, and machine-gun positions—Schlieffen had envisaged a large-scale operation in the northwest. Violating the neutrality of the Netherlands, Belgium, and Luxembourg in order to begin at once the decisive battle on the western front, the right wing of the German armies would encircle the main French forces (thought to be in the vicinity of the fortified belt) and force them back toward Switzerland. Meanwhile, the left wing would remain thin on the ground, and areas on the Upper Rhine and in the eastern section of the front would scarcely be occupied at all. The ratio between the attacking forces on the right wing and the defending forces on the left wing was supposed to be on the order of seven to one. Only after victory in the west would the focus of military operations shift farther east against Russia by means of fast-moving troop transports.

Schlieffen's successor as chief of the general staff, Helmuth von Moltke, was doubtful about the premise that the French would concentrate on the defensive; he thought—rightly, as it turned out—that they would launch an offensive in Lorraine at the beginning of the war. Unlike Schlieffen, he expected a protracted war, a modern people's war, in which all possible resources would be mobilized; a single decisive battle in the west was not on the cards. For these reasons, Moltke's main concern was to improve the German position as much as possible for a war on two fronts through a successful opening operation. Although in theory he stuck to Schlieffen's idea of a concentrated attack in the west, he strengthened German forces on the Upper Rhine and, out of economic considerations, avoided involving the neutral Netherlands.

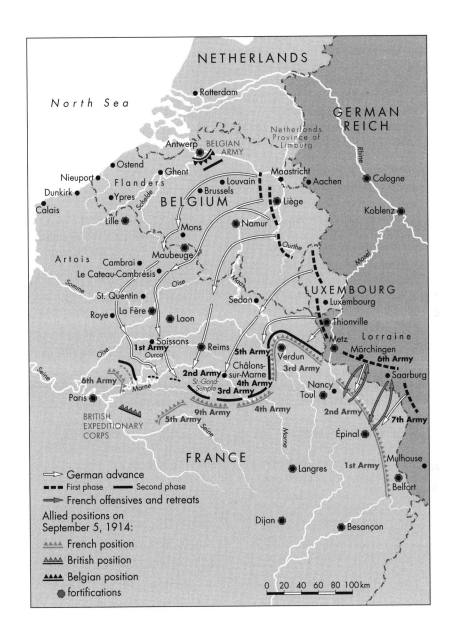

Map 1. Western Front, 1914

This made it essential, however, to conquer Belgium, and especially the Liège transport hub, in short order, since only that would ensure the advance and supply of the extreme right wing of German troops.[192]

Even in its modified form, the Schlieffen Plan left out key political and military factors. The German military leadership, at no point under effective control by the civilian leadership of the Reich, not only kept quiet about the danger of British entry into the war and the mobilization of the military and economic resources of the British Empire against the Central Powers; it also underestimated the speed of Russia's troop deployment on its border with East Prussia and against Austria-Hungary in Galicia. Furthermore, it assumed that there would be highly efficient communication between the German blocs attacking in the west. In persisting with its offensive plan, the German military subjected its inexperienced officers and troops to huge time constraints and pressures to succeed.[193]

Contrary to the expectations of the German top brass, Belgian troops often put up bitter resistance from the beginning. On August 4, even before news had arrived of the German attack, the appearance of King Albert I at the parliament in Brussels unleashed a wave of patriotic fervor. The hero's welcome that the MPs gave him played a symbolic role in the image of a nation fallen victim to a powerful foe. The sharp policy differences between Liberals and Socialists receded before the external threat, and a cross-party government was formed. The country and its 200,000-strong army braced themselves to face the German invasion, the outbreak of war having brought the first major military mobilization in the country's history. After the German capture of Liège and Antwerp, Belgian troops fell back to positions on the River Yser in West Flanders—a marshy plain of great symbolic significance, because it was the last part of the country remaining to be defended. Since the king and the army had decided to save as many soldiers as possible, Belgian troops did not take part in the major Allied offensives. But what now developed in the Yser region was a special microcosm of the front: a total of 40,000 men would die there of epidemics by the year 1918, and the soldiers who served there were the only ones unable to visit their families on home leave for the whole duration of the war. The initial enthusiasm to expel the invaders from the country soon gave way to a strong emphasis on the duty to hold out.[194] In Summer 1917 the war patriotism of the

Belgians on the Yser entered into crisis. Desertions became more frequent, and a *frontbeweging*—a protest movement, directed not least against social discrimination—developed among a nationalistically oriented minority of Flemish soldiers.[195] This reflected the division of the Belgian army into a francophone and a Flemish-speaking component. The movement called for the creation of separate Flemish and Walloon regiments that would emphasize the distinctive cultural unity of Flanders. The Yser front thus became the founding myth of the Flemish nationalist movement.[196] Despite this crisis, in which the limits of the integrative idea of the Belgian nation manifested themselves even in wartime, there was never a mass mutiny on the Yser. The soldiers' will to hold out remained intact.[197]

In August 1914, the capture of the east Belgian transport hub at Liège was of crucial importance for the German plan of attack, particularly for the advance of the First and Second Armies on the far right wing. This city with its population of 150,000 was ringed by twelve fortification systems. A surprise attack on these by the Germans underestimated the strength of the garrisons (some 30,000 men) and the determination of the Belgian troops to resist. Nevertheless, a German brigade under Erich Ludendorff did manage to occupy the city, by then largely empty of civilians, together with its citadel.[198]

The attacks on the forts, which lasted from August 8 to 16, involved the deployment of new weapons. The airship *Cöln* took part in the bombardment of Liège, and heavy 42-centimeter Krupp mortars were used for the first time against the forts. This so-called M-device (*M-Gerät*), mounted on wheels, was so heavy at 42.6 tons that it had to be taken to the front in five loads on special transport vehicles, where it was then reassembled. Its popular and euphemistic soubriquet "Big Bertha"—which probably came from the Morse code's name for the letter B, not from Bertha Krupp—trivialized the devastating effect of this new artillery piece, of which no more than two existed at the beginning of the war. Its shells weighed roughly 800 kilos each and traveled as far as 9,300 meters, pulverizing older fortifications made of quarry stone or tamped concrete. When the mortar first came into action on August 15, scoring a direct hit on the ammunition dump in Fort Loncin, more than 300 Belgian soldiers lost their lives. The role of artillery in the war was already becoming apparent; the original assumption of a war of movement, in which field guns would only support infantry detachments, had led designers to concentrate on weapons with the lowest possible weight; the diameter of most guns was between 7.5 and 8.4 centimeters. With the shift from a war of movement to a war of position, however, the firepower of weapons became a decisive factor in breaking down fortified positions. This brought to the fore heavy weapons—cannons with a diameter of 10 centimeters or more and upright guns starting at 15 centimeters—that were installed behind the actual front with no visual sighting of their targets.[199] The siege of the Belgian forts made apparent for the first time the significance of long-range weapons.

The slight delay in the German advance did not matter much in these first major actions of the war.[200] More important in the long run was the decoration of Erich Ludendorff with the highest military honor, Pour le Mérite, for his role in the siege of Liège. This qualified him shortly afterward for the post of chief of staff of the newly appointed commander in East Prussia, Paul von Hindenburg.[201] In a wider perspective than that of mere military history, however, the Belgian resistance and the actions of German troops were of the greatest significance; they offered the Allies a leitmotif to justify their war against an allegedly uncivilized enemy. The way in which the German army treated Belgian civilians took center stage in Allied propaganda against Germany: "Remember Belgium" and images of a violated woman or a murdered child became iconic elements on countless war posters and postcards. Such cruelty in the conduct of the war would also be a key point after 1918 in the attribution of a special war guilt to Germany.

At any event, the German occupation of Belgium put a huge strain on the civilian population. Approximately 6,400 were killed during the actual invasion; more than 5,500 died in the period up to August 8, including nearly 850 in the Liège area alone, while more than 1,300 buildings were burned out. For the most part, this impact on civilians was due to a variety of causes. The German military often responded in a thoroughly exaggerated manner to the rather scant resistance offered by Belgian civilians, but this also had to do with the fact that most of the German units and their officers had little or no experience of war. Other factors were the feeling that every minute counted in the carefully planned advance and, above all, the fear, already widespread before 1914, that the German army would have to face

French irregulars similar to those who, from October 1870, following the defeat of the French Imperial army at Sedan, had fought on in the tradition of the revolutionary *levée en masse* (mass conscription) of the 1790s. The mere memory of these *franc-tireurs* four decades earlier, regarded as bandits outside the rules of war, was enough to trigger panic reactions among German soldiers in Summer 1914.[202]

Both the range of modern infantry weapons (up to 1,500 meters) and the withdrawal tactics operated by French and Belgian units often made it difficult to locate enemy sharpshooters. The combination of time pressures, wide-reaching expectations, and negative stereotypes gave rise to rumors that took on a dynamic of their own and fed excesses of violence. Attacks on German infantry positions or patrols, as well as "friendly fire" from German artillery, were often attributed to *franc-tireurs,* and ruthless measures were taken against civilians and villages suspected of having given them shelter. The military socialization of German officers heightened such reactions, as did a negative perception of Belgians bound up with anti-Catholic stereotypes from the period of the Bismarckian *Kulturkampf.* The protection extended to noncombatants under the Hague Convention on Land Warfare was not recognized, and even certain provisions covering the German army itself—for example, that anyone accused of a crime was entitled to an independent defense counsel—were widely ignored.[203] The general in command of the Third Reserve Corps, Hans von Beseler, was typical of many senior officers when he wrote to his wife on August 16 that the Belgians "do not behave like a civilized people, but a band of robbers—a pretty result of the priests' domination of Belgium." In Beseler's view, Belgians had brought their fate on themselves by following France and Britain; this justified their harsh treatment: "But the situation has been made thoroughly clear to them. . . . We would not have laid a finger on them, they would have made millions and millions from our transits, and probably their land would not have become a theater of war at all. Instead, they joined the French, incite the British against us and lay waste to their own country! This wretched hybrid state should be either eliminated or at least squeezed in such a way to make them lose their desire to be friends with the French forever."[204] In the Roubaix-Tourcoing zone, the fear of *franc-tireur* attacks was so great that it was forbidden to ring church bells, lest Catholic priests use them as a signal.[205]

Harry Graf Kessler also experienced firsthand some of the excesses. While he found in Andenne the "most peaceful modern rural village, with sleepy philistines in front of the doors, gardens, flowers, springs," nearby Seilles offered the grim image of war unleashed on the civilian population: "This place, which may have had close to three or four thousand inhabitants, has been completely reduced to ashes yesterday and today by our troops. The inhabitants had attacked our pioneers, who were building a bridge across the Meuse, and killed twenty of them. About two hundred inhabitants were tried by court-martial and shot and the place was destroyed. No house has a roof or window left. The bare, burned-out walls stand there, street after street, except where there are household objects, family pictures, broken mirrors, upset tables and chairs, half-burned carpets as witness to the conditions on the day before yesterday." Kessler stressed the effect that these "courts" had on the morale of his own men, since they called into question the legitimacy of what the Germans were doing. Legitimate violence presupposed discipline and composure. But "our soldiers . . . become accustomed to stealing and drinking. In Liège every day whole companies drink themselves unconscious with Bordeaux and schnapps stolen from the burned houses. It will be difficult to root out these habits. In any case, one has the right to carry out terrible executions as in Andenne [only] if our men conduct themselves faultlessly. That is the return payment that the enemy can expect from us. Otherwise this war will degenerate into an expedition of Huns." Although Kessler emphasized the responsibility of the Belgians, he was surprised at the escalation of violence in the early days of the war, which could not be reconciled with traditional ideas of a properly regulated war between states. "Through the fault of the Belgian population," the war had become "much crueler and more barbaric than the war of 1870 or even the Napoleonic wars. You have to go back to the Thirty Years' War to find something similar to the ghastly drama in Seilles / Andenne."[206]

A similar chain of high tension, inexperience, time pressure, wrong information, and negative stereotyping led to violent excesses in Louvain. This Belgian university city was initially occupied on August 19 without a struggle, when the bulk of the German army was already farther west at the French border. A breakthrough by large Belgian units north of Louvain then pushed back German units stationed nearby, which other German troops then mistakenly took to be enemy forces; the widespread fear of Belgian snipers led them to believe that fire was being directed at them from houses belonging to the civilian population. The anti-Catholic enemy image was especially strong, so that the measures taken by the German army soon concentrated on the university as a Catholic institution and educational center of the country's ecclesiastical and secular elite. The library with its 230,000 books was deliberately set on fire, on the false assumption that it was a university building. A total of 248 civilians lost their lives. After the systematic sacking, the remaining population (some 10,000 people) was driven out of the city; 1,500 were deported to Germany, where some 150 women and children were interned in a camp at Munster until January 1915. Although considerably more civilians lost their lives at Dinant on the River Meuse—some 600 were shot out of a population of 6,000—the cultural atrocity at Louvain soon became the most potent symbol of the brutal German conduct of the war.[207]

One reason for this was the systematic, planned character of the destruction: the expulsion of the civilian population was followed by the plundering and burning of their homes. A more important reason, however, was the fact that the events soon became public knowledge and echoed throughout Europe and the wider world. On August 28, Hugh Gibson, the secretary of the American legation in Brussels, recorded what he saw at the Rue de la Station in Louvain: "The houses on both sides were either partially destroyed or smoldering. Soldiers were systematically removing what was to be found in the way of valuables, food, and wine, and then setting fire to the furniture and hangings. It was all most businesslike. The houses are substantial stone buildings, and fire will not spread from one to another. Therefore the procedure was to batter down the door of each house, clean out what was to be saved, then pile furniture and hangings in the middle of the room, set them afire, and move on to the next house."[208] The next day, the London *Times* wrote that a cultural city of European renown, "the Oxford of Belgium," had been destroyed. This proved to be a turning point, especially in neutral countries where German science and culture had enjoyed high prestige. In the Netherlands, the *Rotterdamsche Courant* wrote that the luminaries of German culture must "experience the punishment administered to the population of Louvain as if it were inflicted on themselves. They must be as dismayed as everyone else, whether neutrals or belligerents on both sides, and the wound they have suffered will pain them for evermore."[209]

The war began with multiple areas of violence. In August and September 1914, there were at least four combat zones in Europe: in the west between the Upper Rhine and the North Sea coast, in East Prussia, in Galicia, and in the Balkans. In addition, there were war zones outside Europe and at sea. The complexity of the situation stemmed from the fact that decisive military events came thick and fast in the first few weeks and were often interconnected (as in the case of German military planning) because of resource access requirements or the expansion of alliances. In the west, despite Belgian resistance, the German attack initially went according to plan: Brussels was captured on August 20, and by August 22 the invasion of Belgium had been largely completed. At the same time, French attacks following Plan XVII were mostly repelled in the so-called Battle of the Frontiers in the middle Vosges and Lorraine; German forces successfully crossed the Meuse, taking Longwy and Montmédy, and inflicting a defeat near Mons on the British Expeditionary Force (BEF) that had landed at Ostend.

These early reverses demonstrated the poor preparation and inadequate equipment of the British army for a long war on the Continent. Its commander-in-chief Sir John French, experienced in colonial wars, kept wavering between skepticism, pessimism, and an unrealistic optimism that an attacking spirit would secure a breakthrough. Above all, the BEF suffered from serious structural defects: the regular army, made up of men with a long period of service mostly coming from the urban and rural lower classes, numbered just 250,000 in 1914, with barely 1,000 trained staff officers. A leadership structure for a functioning army did not exist until December 1914. As time pressure intensified with the outbreak of war, the regular army could no longer be used as a cadre force to help train the necessary numbers of additional troops—the British army increased by as many as sixty divisions over a two-year period. In fact, the high losses among experienced soldiers and officers at the beginning of the war increased the proportion of poorly trained young volunteers, who were then killed in the tens of thousands up to the peak at the Battle of the Somme in 1916. Britain thus paid a high price for having pursued a very different military strategy from that of the major Continental powers with their large conscript armies.[210]

Although successful in defense, the German forces in the Vosges and Lorraine lacked the strength to achieve a decisive victory and were unable to break through the fortified French positions in the area of Nancy and Toul. Nevertheless, in late August and early September it looked as if the German offensive plan was generally on course. German forces had been steadily approaching the French capital. "Our right wing is already near Amiens, the cavalry is brushing past. Three and a half weeks after the outbreak of war!" wrote Harry Graf Kessler on August 29. Until September 5 the momentum of the attacks persisted, with considerable territorial gains that appeared to place victory within reach. While German cavalry units penetrated Lille and the First Army under General von Kluck was advancing on Amiens, the Second Army under General von Bülow crossed the Marne and reached Esternay on September 5. The Third Army too, having occupied Reims on September 3, crossed the Marne two days later.[211]

The continual retreat along the front from Oise to Verdun and the German advances in early September caused a political panic in France. The government fled to Bordeaux on September 3, after German long-range artillery began to shell the outer ring of fortifications around Paris. General Gallieni, newly appointed as military governor of Paris, gave the order for trenches to be dug in the metropolitan area and declared that the capital would be defended at all costs. The resolve of the military leadership to avoid a repetition of 1870 was plain to see.[212] Yet the military and political elites found themselves staring defeat in the face. While President Poincaré prepared his country for the possibility of retreat and occupation, the high German expectations of early September crystallized into ambitious visions such as Bethmann Hollweg's "September program." This first comprehensive statement of German war aims, developed after consultations with various authorities and ministries, sought to safeguard the Reich on both east and west through the establishment of German hegemony in central Europe; Belgium would become a vassal state, France's great power status would be destroyed, and a continuous German colonial empire would be established in Central Africa. These aims were not present at the beginning of the war in August; they took shape only under the impact of the seemingly inexorable advances in the west. This projection of objectives to follow the expected victory was so significant because it set a great height from which to fall; it explains the huge sense of disillusionment in Germany following the Battle of the Marne.[213]

Although in early September Helmuth von Moltke may no longer have been so skeptical about Germany's military situation, and indeed entertained far-reaching war aims, he was soon warning of exaggerated hopes in conversations with Karl Helfferich (who, as treasury secretary from February 1915, would organize the financing of the war). In particular, the small numbers of prisoners and captured weapons on the western front led Moltke to conclude that French troops were executing an orderly retreat and that the core of France's military strength was by no means destroyed.[214] It was not long before signs of exhaustion, overextension, and supply defects became apparent among the German forces. In just a few weeks, the units of the extreme right wing of the German army had covered huge distances: the First Army, 500 kilometers in 30 days; the Third Army, 330 kilometers in a fortnight, scarcely pausing in its advance. Many infantry detachments had endured daily marches of 30 to 40 kilometers, each man carrying some 30 kilograms in weapons, ammunition, and baggage in the heat of summer, stopping only to engage in heavy combat. Supply problems meant that many units had to live on raw vegetables they found in the fields.[215] Furthermore, the right wing of the German offensive had been depleted: by losses in battle, by the assignment of troops to guard transport routes in the rear or to besiege Antwerp and the fortress of Maubeuge, and by the reallocation of units to East Prussia after the Russians had invaded it sooner than expected.[216] In the military crisis resulting from the Russian occupation of Gumbinnen and Allenstein on August 20, Moltke diverted two army corps from the western front to East Prussia, although they arrived too late to have a decisive impact in the Battle of Tannenberg. These troop relocations, which later came in for strong criticism, were in line with the long-established doctrine that forces should be moved to the eastern front once a breakthrough in the west was imminent. On August 25–26, that moment seemed to have come.[217]

The weakening of the German right wing in the west changed the relationship of forces with the Allies: twenty German divisions with approximately 750,000 men now found themselves facing thirty French and British divisions with more than a million men. Unlike the German units, the French could use their own railroad lines to bring up soldiers and materiel. Under these circumstances, the dual task of pushing back the French armies and encircling Paris was impossible to achieve. Therefore the First Army under Kluck did not bypass Paris to the south, but headed southeast in the direction of the Marne. The resulting German flank offered British and French troops a golden opportunity to counterattack. In the Battle of the Marne that now developed along 300 kilometers between Meaux and Verdun, the German command gave up its original plan of an encircling battle in favor of a frontal attack, and in the central section of the front, the French Ninth Army under General Foch, indeed came under considerable pressure. But the French attacks to the west on the German First Army had a decisive effect, with fresh reinforcements brought directly from Paris to the front in thousands of taxis. When a 40-kilometer gap opened between the First and the Second German Armies, allowing French and British units to push forward and threaten both army flanks, the situation became critical for the Germans.

The disparity between mobility and territorial gains on the one hand and inadequate communications and coordination on the other made itself felt. With most of the telephone lines down, communications between the two German armies and with headquarters could take place only through improvised radio links. Moltke therefore sent a fellow officer to the general staff, Lieutenant-General Richard Hentsch, who classified the situation of the Second Army as extremely perilous. It was not Hentsch, however, but Bülow who ordered the Second Army to retreat. Thus it was not the judgment of a lieutenant-general together with Moltke's nervous breakdown that decided the battle, but rather the combination of a number of factors. One of these was the complicated, and contradictory, German command structure. Another was Moltke's personal style, which, in contrast to Joffre's strict centralism on the French side, gave quite a large degree of autonomy to the supreme commanders of the two German armies. The striking disparity between modern weapons systems and woefully inadequate communications was a further element. Many German soldiers reacted with disbelief and convulsive weeping when they received the order to retreat. Some officers came close to disobeying it.[218]

The army report on September 10, 1914 in the *Kriegs-Rundschau* read, "Army sections that had advanced in pursuit east of Paris, up to and across the Marne, have been attacked by superior forces from Paris between Meaux and Montmirail. In two days of heavy fighting they have halted the enemy and even made some progress; their wing was withdrawn when strong new enemy columns were reported to be advancing. The enemy did not follow at any point. So far, a booty of fifty artillery pieces and several thousand prisoners has been reported."[219] These dry lines, so far from an admission of defeat, conceal the end of the German offensive in the west and a fundamental turning point in the war. Moltke himself visited the right wing on September 11, when an enemy breakthrough seemed imminent, and gave the order for a general retreat. On September 14, the front eventually stabilized on the Aisne, roughly 40 kilometers north of the Marne.[220] After this decision, the "most difficult" of his life (as he later put it), Moltke returned to headquarters mentally shattered. General Moritz von Lyncker remarked, "Moltke is completely overwhelmed by the events; his nerves are not up to the situation."[221] A few days later, the Kaiser in effect replaced him as chief of the general staff with the Prussian war minister, Erich von Falkenhayn.[222] Fearing, however, that the dismissal might be seen in Germany as an admission of defeat, the authorities took two months to make it known to the public. Until 1917 it was forbidden to publish anything on the Battle of the Marne.[223] Yet news filtered through somehow, and on September 27 Theodor Wolff noted in his diary, "At first we learned of the German retreat from the Marne only from Swiss, Dutch, and Swedish newssheets. General Headquarters told us little about it. . . . We have had to retreat considerably, all along the line. . . . The fact that this is being hushed up, only trickling through here and there, does not make a good impression. The public is full of hope, as before, but no longer raucous with victory. And then there are the endless casualty lists and the sometimes gruesome stories of the wounded who have come home."[224]

Since the enemy was too exhausted to pursue the retreating forces, the front in mid-September 1914 lay along a line from Noyon through Soissons and Reims to Verdun. At this point it was the Germans who had to fear being overrun on their right flank, by a combination of French troops under General Foch and the British Expeditionary Force. A race ensued over the next few weeks that would end only on the Channel coast to the north. Near

Ypres a clash ensued, in which Falkenhayn tried to force a decision by the end of the year after all. But the area along the Yser canal had turned to mud after the Belgians opened the sluice gates; although the battle inflicted heavy casualties, it brought no decision.[225] With the frontlines still holding at year's end, the unresolved war of movement turned into the kind of conflict for which no army and no society, no state and no economy, had been prepared in August 1914—that is, into a war of position focused on organization and attrition, which, despite every effort, would shift back to a war of movement only in its final period. In November the Oberste Heeresleitung (OHL)—the German supreme command answerable directly to the Kaiser and led by the chief of the army general staff—announced the provisional suspension of the offensive; the first trench systems were then constructed to bolster forward positions and to upgrade positions to the rear.

In view of this development, the Battle of the Marne appeared as a turning point in the war, which created a considerable interpretive burden both at the time and in later years. For a long time it was unclear whether the order to retreat was an unauthorized decision or whether it was what Moltke intended. But at that moment at least three characteristics of the German command structures became apparent: Moltke, unlike his French and British counterparts, allowed great operational freedom to his field commanders; this latitude, together with the fixation of the military leadership on attack, movement, and breakthroughs, made coordination extremely difficult; and communication between the armies and the general staff essentially followed a nineteenth-century model. The view of the OHL was supposed to be communicated verbally by adjutants it sent into the field—which left considerable room for interpretation. Thus, the dispatching of Hentsch was not an exception, although Moltke would later distance himself from the orders that Hentsch issued on the spot. In any case, coordination and communication could not keep pace with the hugely increased scale of violence and the speed of the advance.

As it happened, none of the key German military presuppositions passed the test of practice: neither the dogma of the superiority of attack over defense, nor the hopes pinned on an early battle that, if not decisive, would positively affect the course of the war as a whole, nor the assumptions about the speed of mobilization and troop transport. Miscalculations by the German military on the eastern front were especially disastrous, leading as they did to changes in the relative strength of forces on the western front. Most important of all, however, they underlined the tenuousness of detailed war plans, which allowed for little flexibility but permanently overburdened the troops with high expectations and time pressures. Neither the military nor the political leadership was prepared for the reality of the quite different war that set in after the early weeks. The German service regulations of 1906, like those of other countries, had been based on a war of movement and had largely neglected field fortifications; defense was always supposed to be no more than a brief transitional period before the next attack. The French concentration on the *élan* of the offensive corresponded to this way of thinking. It alone was expected to decide the war. Troop mobility thus had primacy over all other operational considerations—and also over weapons technology, as the early shortage of heavy artillery in comparison with lighter pieces clearly shows, especially in the French case.[226]

In a time frame lasting a few weeks, between early August and the middle of September, it became clear on the western front why the basic military assumptions were bound to fail. The decisive right wing of the German attack was overloaded with the task of outflanking Paris and fulfilling the key element of the Schlieffen Plan. Whereas the French benefited from railroad lines in their own country, the Germans soon faced the task of supplying large numbers of troops over great distances, coordinating their various offensive formations, and ensuring effective communication among them.[227] These would be major headaches for all armies in the further course of the war, but they first became fully apparent in the German attack of August and September 1914. Necessary as it was for the Germans to abort their offensive to prevent the collapse of their own position, the crucial aspect lay elsewhere. For although the battle was tactically indecisive, and although the Allies could not take consistent advantage of the German retreat, it marked a strategic watershed after just six weeks of war. For the first time, after the uninterrupted Allied retreat in the west in the early weeks of the war, the battle created the basis for future operations against the German armies.

While France, thanks to the resilience of its troops, managed to avoid a repetition of 1870 and to force Germany to wage a war on two fronts, the initial German successes had ensured that the war would be fought on enemy territory. Belgium, as well as a large, industrially important part of northwestern France, remained in German hands. But the Schlieffen Plan, as modified by Moltke, had failed to bear fruit, making the two-front war a constant strategic dilemma for Germany in the years up to 1917.[228] In a conversation with the Reich chancellor on November 18, 1914, Falkenhayn did not hold back and explained that, in view of the developments on the western front, Germany was no longer militarily capable of dictating the terms of a peace to its enemies; the high losses in officers and men ruled out any large-scale offensive in the west. Thus, after less than four months of war, the head of the OHL was pushing for a separate peace with Russia without territorial annexations, because the Reich would otherwise be threatened with a "war of attrition" that its limited resources would not allow it to win. For Falkenhayn, the aim was nothing less than to call off the two-front war in the east and west, to conclude a separate peace with Germany's enemies on the Continent, and to leave the German navy to continue the war against its main enemy, Great Britain. Bethmann Hollweg did not heed this remarkably critical appraisal or the associated proposals because the German commanders on the eastern front had been communicating to him an altogether different assessment.[229]

On both sides, a distinctive legend grew up around the Battle of the Marne. While the French idealized the heroic salvation and, to take one example, used images of Gallieni's requisitioned Parisian taxis as a metaphor for the national mobilization, the sense of shock in Germany led to the development of a negative myth. The search for someone to blame for the strategic defeat—whether Moltke, Kluck, or Hentsch—concealed the basic failure of German plans to bring the war to a swift conclusion. It even fueled the idea that the Schlieffen Plan had collapsed only because of the inadequacy of certain military leaders, that it might have succeeded if only there had been strong leadership in the west. This mechanism of exculpation, this inability to admit military defeat and the basic failure of strategic planning, foreshadowed the "stab in the back" legend that some German military leaders used after 1918 to explain the eventual loss of the war.[230]

The negativity of the Marne myth contrasted with the German idealization of the Langemarck battlefield. This was similar to the French hero worship of the marines under Admiral Pierre-Alexis Ronarc'h who fought at the Battle of Diksmuide between mid-October and mid-November 1914.[231] To give new impetus to German military operations, Falkenhayn had deployed four new army corps in mid-September made up of students and other young volunteers. Lacking experience and having received only brief training, they suffered heavy losses in the subsequent battles, and also on November 10 near Bixschoote in the face of British machine-gun fire. On November 11, the patriotically tinged order of the day falsified the facts by claiming that the youthful regiments had stormed enemy positions singing *Deutschland, Deutschland über alles.* This had little in common with the grim reality of failed infantry attacks—in any case, charges by men carrying full backpacks left little scope for anthem singing. But the army's media celebration of the young volunteers gathered momentum, presenting them as heroes ready to make the highest sacrifice for the nation. An image emerging from a deliberate instrumentalization on the part of army headquarters thus took on a reality of its own. The claim, for example, that most of the young shock troops had been students would later play a central part in the traditions of the student associations.[232] Thomas Mann, in the closing scene of *The Magic Mountain*, consciously broke with such mythology, replacing confident assertions of victory with a realistic description of the battlefield with its riddled and mangled corpses. Instead of students storming the enemy trenches, it depicts bodies lying prostrate, jumping up, and running aimlessly forward. Nor are there any anthems expressing martial heroism; Hans Castorp "sings to himself" in a kind of "dazed, thoughtless excitement."[233]

The quite different developments on the eastern front, where military successes lent themselves to positive personalization, contributed to the negative myth of the Battle of the Marne.[234] With Paul von Hindenburg, a retired general recalled at the beginning of the war, and Erich Ludendorff, an officer distinguished in the capture of Liège, the military leadership in the east seemed to offer a stark contrast to the army's failures on the Marne, explaining the setbacks there. The political capital that both men could derive from successes on the eastern front had much to do with this contrast. But in fact the symbolically charged victory in the east was less a triumph of command genius than the result of structural factors. All offensive plans failed in

OPPOSITE: Map 2. Eastern Front, 1914–1918

Pskov

Windau ●

Courland ● Riga
Mitau ●

Libau ●

Baltic Sea

Memel ●

Tauroggen ●

Tilsit ●

Königsberg ●

Danzig ●

Kolberg ●

East Prussia

Graudenz ●

Tannenberg

GERMAN
REICH

Thorn ●

Nowo
Georgiewsk ●

Posen ●

Warthe

Lodz ●

Oder

Wrocław ●

Silesia

Katowice ●

Kraków ●

Teschen ●

Austria-
Hungary

Danube

Vienna ●

Daugavpils

RUSSIAN EMPIRE

Lithuania

Lake Narach

Kaunas ●

Gumbinnen ●   Vilnius ●

Olita ●   Minsk ●

Lötzen ●   Suwałki ●

Łyck ●   ● Grodno

Baranovichi ●

Białystok ●

Ostrolenka ●   Pripyet

Bug   Pinsk ●
                                  Pripyet marshes
Warsaw ●   Brest-Litovsk ●

Poland

Ivangorod ●

Lublin ●   Kowel ●
              Lutsk ●   Rovno ●

Zamość ●   Dubno ●

Vistula

Tarnów ●   Lvov ●   Tarnopol ●

Przemyśl ●

Gorlice ●   Galicia   Stryj ●

Dukla Pass   Carpathian Mts.

Tisza   Czernowitz ●

Romania

0   50   100   150 km

→ Austro-Hungarian offensive,
   August 1914

▨ Russia's territorial gains in
   East Prussia, August 1914

■ Russia's territorial gains
   in Austria-Hungary
   (Sept.–Dec. 1914)

=⇢ Central Powers attack on Warsaw,
    East Prussia (Sept.–Nov. 1914)

⇨ Central Powers offensive
   (May–Sept. 1915)

--- Frontline in September 1915

▨ Russia's territorial gains in Brusilov
   offensive, June 1916

East Prussia and in Galicia, as well as in the west, and invading armies proved inferior even if at first they were numerically superior. As early as August it became clear that German calculations about the pace of Russian mobilization had been completely mistaken; there was no question that it would take six weeks to move the necessary troops up to the deployment areas. In fact, the Russian invasion of East Prussia began in the middle of the month, the Army of the Niemen advancing from the east and the Army of the Narev from the south. The numerically inferior German Eighth Army had to break off the opening battle at Gumbinnen, withdraw westward to the Vistula, and hand over large parts of East Prussia to the Russian forces. But the Russian headquarters in Warsaw was then incapable of effectively coordinating the two armies with their 500,000-plus soldiers. Like the Germans in northern France, the Russian armies lacked a reliable supply chain, whereas the German defenders could draw on an intact railroad and telephone network. Most importantly, they succeeded in intercepting the radio communications of Russian commanders, with the result that they were always informed about enemy plans and movements. This combination of superior supply, greater mobility, and better coordination and communication played a key role in the German victory. The two invading Russian armies remained cut off from each other, and while the Niemen Army was kept busy with weak forces, the main German force was able to encircle and defeat the Army of the Narev; the Russian commander Alexander Samsonov subsequently took his own life. Nearly 100,000 Russian soldiers were taken prisoner. After a second major battle in the Masurian Lakes region against the Niemen Army under General Paul von Rennenkampf, the Germans liberated the whole of East Prussia and dashed the Allies' hopes of a victory in the east to offset the weeks of crisis on the western front.

Shadowing the German double front in the west and east was the de facto two-front war of Austria-Hungary, which in Fall and Winter 1914 was already leading to catastrophe both against Russian forces in Galicia and against Serbia in the Balkans.[235] The attack on the southeastern areas of Poland belonging to Russia, which was ordered by the Austrian chief of staff Conrad von Hötzendorf, ended in disaster before the troop deployment was even completed. The cavalry battle of August 21 at Jaroslawice, the largest of its kind during the war for the Imperial army, incurred huge casualties and spelled the end of the cavalry as an independent branch of the armed forces. The Austrian attacks recalled the French concept of an *offensive à outrance,* which led to similarly devastating losses in the frontier battles on the western front. When the Russians captured Lvov on September 2, Conrad von Hötzendorf was compelled for the first time to request German assistance, already reflecting the military, political, and economic imbalance between the two allies that would mark the future course of the war and increasingly call into question the ability of the Dual Monarchy to assert itself in an independent capacity. By September 11, the Austrians had already begun their retreat to the San River, abandoning eastern and central Galicia, and the Russians also managed to surround the San fortress of Przemyśl. By mid-September the Imperial armies had lost 300,000 dead and wounded (plus more than 100,000 prisoners) on this front alone—a figure approaching half of their total active strength. Most important, the loss of large numbers of officers and NCOs had greatly limited the scope for further offensives.[236] In late Fall 1914, in order to relieve the Austrian front in Galicia, Hindenburg and Ludendorff launched an offensive against Russian formations in Silesia, managing to force them back to Warsaw, and on December 6, German troops took Lodz. At the end of the year, however, the fronts became more fixed there too. After General von Mackensen failed in a relief attack, the Austrians were driven back to the Carpathians. Only in 1915 would the fronts in the east become mobile again.

Whereas the high losses in fighting with the Russians in Galicia were the result of strategic mistakes and overconfidence, the Austro-Hungarian attack on Serbia that began on August 11 met stiff resistance from day one. Three armies under the command of General Oskar Potiorek—the same man who in June 1914 had been seated in the automobile carrying Crown Prince Ferdinand in Sarajevo—attacked across the Drina from Bosnia-Herzegovina and soon came to grief. The Serbian troops facing them had the experience of the Balkan wars behind them and were considerably more motivated, while the invading force had to contend with major supply problems.[237] On the Cer plateau it suffered its first major defeat. By the end of the year, the Imperial army had lost 273,000 men (30,000 dead, 173,000 wounded, and 70,000 taken prisoner) out of a total strength of 450,000.[238] Two interrelated aspects soon became evident in the Balkan area of operations.

First, the Austrian top brass treated the civilian population in a brutal manner. According to an official directive, the war was being fought in an "enemy country whose population [was] filled with fanatical hatred toward us"; "any humanity or faintheartedness was inappropriate," because it would endanger the safety of the troops. The fear of partisans (*komitadži*) was even greater than in the *franc-tireur* panic on the western front. The intensity of the violence against Serbian civilians was not primarily due to radicalization associated with wrong information and time pressures, but was essentially the result of official military orders. Systematic pillage, arson, and executions again had a massive echo internationally. At the beginning of the war, some 30,000 Ruthenians and as many Serbs were executed on suspicion of espionage and collaboration with the Russians.[239] In proportion to its size and population, no other country suffered such high losses in such a short period of time; in 1914 alone, Serbia lost 22,000 dead and 91,000 wounded out of a total army strength of 250,000 men, with an additional 69,000 civilian casualties. The death rate in the army for the whole war was in the region of 19 percent. Although Serbian soldiers only really saw action in 1914 and 1915, their proportional losses were nearly as great as those of the whole Imperial army between 1914 and 1918. Moreover, the ethnic expulsions that had been already practiced in the Balkan wars reappeared in the areas in question. Not only did Serbia have to cope with 600,000 refugees fleeing from Austro-Hungarian troops, but approximately 100,000 people died in a typhus epidemic in early 1915.

This background explains a second essential feature of the war: victories against the superior Imperial army, combined with individual sacrifices such as that of the volunteer leader Todorović and the horrific toll of civilian casualties, strengthened the Serbs' perception of themselves as a martyr-nation. The retreat across the Albanian mountains in 1915, with its exceptionally high losses and the brutal crushing of Serbian resistance in Bulgarian-occupied areas were processed in terms of a quasi-religious collective experience. A "national resurrection," centered on the creation of an independent nation state, would follow the Serbian "Golgotha."[240]

Despite heavy setbacks in the early period of the war, it became clear that the multiethnic armies of the Continental empires, especially the Dual Monarchy, were not immediately falling apart because of mass desertions (as many had predicted for the Habsburg Empire) or ethnic contradictions (for example, among German, Romanian, and Slav soldiers). Numerous Croats, Serbs, and Slovenes fought in Potiorek's army, too, comprising as much as 40 percent of some contingents; one such combatant was the 21-year-old Josip Broz, later to become famous, under the name Tito, as the political leader of the trinational Yugoslavia. The Imperial reverses in the Serbian campaign were due not to destabilization resulting from ethnic desertions, but to strategic deficits, supply problems, and massive resistance. Nevertheless, German officers in particular tended to stereotype the Habsburg armies as a force lacking internal cohesion. Harry Graf Kessler, for instance, had the impression of "a traveling cabaret or circus." He noted that many soldiers hardly understood German and compared the Austro-Hungarian front in October 1915 to a "wall pieced together out of ashlars, brick, clay, and all kinds of refuse, with not much greater resistance than the worst of materials."[241]

The long-term military and political significance of events in the east derived from the twin German victory over Russian troops. There a very different war took shape: whereas the frontlines in the west solidified after the Battle of the Marne, movement across large spaces was frequently possible during the first period of the war in the east.[242] Thus, although the Austro-Hungarian setbacks led to a hardening of the front, a major breakthrough against the Russian armies was successfully achieved in Summer 1915. The battles of August 1914 laid the basis for possible territorial expansion, for the creation of a distinctively eastern German military domain that would give a new direction to the Continental war. Furthermore, this war did not unfold in a space with clearly defined national boundaries and populations, but rather in a decidedly multiethnic region with a diversity of religions and denominations. Poles, White Russians, and Ukrainians rubbed shoulders with Russians, Latvians, and Baltic Germans, and Catholicism existed alongside Russian Orthodoxy and Judaism. This distinctive population structure, combined with a possible new form of rule and new visions of a political order, meant that in their experience of the war east central and eastern Europe constituted a space apart.

This development was associated with two individuals who had a pivotal impact both during the war and beyond—one might say on twentieth-century German history as a whole. Paul von Hindenburg and Erich Ludendorff were connected by their military socialization and their absolute dedication to the wartime cause, while bringing to bear quite different experiences from their respective generations. Both men had grown up in Posen (today's Poznan) close to the border with Russian Poland, a peripheral province in the perspective of the post-1871 German nation-state. Born in 1847, a year before the European revolutions, Hindenburg in many respects typified the common experience of a nobleman of his generation in the late nineteenth century— in terms of ancestry, early military socialization, experiences of war up to 1871, and his succession of administrative posts at the War Ministry and staff positions from Stettin and Königsberg to Koblenz and Magdeburg. Having entered a Silesian cadet corps at the age of 11, he was already marked by the short wars of 1864, 1866, and 1870–1871 leading to the formation of a German nation-state. He served as a lieutenant at the Battle of Königgratz (in the Austro-Prussian war of 1866) and represented his guard regiment at Versailles for the proclamation of the German Reich in 1871.

After long years of peacetime service, most recently as general in command of the Fourth Army Corps in Magdeburg, Hindenburg asked to retire in 1911 because he did not think it likely that there would be another war. In 1914, the outbreak of a war in which he could not personally participate was a source of concern for him. He told the Prussian war minister that he felt ashamed to cross the street and asked to be remembered if a post could be found for him somewhere. Unexpectedly, the situation in the east then opened up a new period in his army career, leading to his sudden recall in Summer 1914 as the nominal superior to Ludendorff (who was considered too young for an army supreme command appointment). While Ludendorff operated from the start as the main planner, Hindenburg insisted on his symbolic superiority. His age and sedate air impressed people around him, and to the public this field marshal dressed up as a father figure seemed a real counterweight to the nervous emperor and the ever-tense Ludendorff.[243] Walter Rathenau, the Allgemeine Electricitäts-Gesellschaft company boss and director of the war materials department, described him after a visit in November 1915: "Hindenburg is big, and has rather run to fat, his hands are unusually plump and soft, the lower half of his head resembles his portraits, the upper half is completely different. His forehead is good, the setting of his nose and particularly the nose itself very weak and undefined, his eyes swollen and dull. . . . His voice, soft, deep, elderly, his speech quiet and kindly."[244]

Hindenburg and Ludendorff were, in a way, workers and craftsmen of war, and both men brought with them an unconditional readiness to subordinate themselves to the war and its novel demands. In Ludendorff's case, there was also the special ambition of a social climber lacking the etiquette of nobility. Born in 1865, he was, like Hindenburg, socialized from an early age in a military cadet institution, rising thereafter to become a member of the Greater General Staff in 1894. His mixture of tactical flair, interest in military history, and great ambition carried him into the army's war mobilization department, whose head he became in 1908. There he recognized the central importance of mobility and supply logistics, as well as the necessity of industrial warfare. While Hindenburg brought from the nineteenth century the concepts of controlled war and a jovial aristocratic officer milieu, the tensely concentrated Ludendorff often appeared as an engineer or technocrat with expert knowledge of the new technological and infrastructural possibilities of the modern battlefield, who soon also came to recognize, and ruthlessly exploited, the scope for political action of a new generation of military leaders.[245]

For both men, the early victories in the east carried an enormous symbolic charge. In view of the disappointing news from the western front, Hindenburg managed to present himself—despite his limited personal role in the fighting—as the solid, authoritative figure without whom victory would not have been possible. Above all, he skillfully set the battle in the east within a historical-political continuity, thereby filling with an actual person and narrative the vacuum of meaning and justification that had existed since the beginning of the war. When the Kaiser wanted to congratulate him for the victory at Allenstein or Ortelsburg (the correct geographical site of the battle), Hindenburg pushed for the nearby location of Tannenberg to be chosen instead, because it could be presented as a place of revenge and compensation for the famous defeat there of the Knights of the Teutonic Order, in 1410, at the hands of Polish-Lithuanian forces. The imagined continuity of the medieval monastic state with modern Prussia and the German Reich thus served to cast the battle as a triumph of the Germans over uncivilized powers in the east. At the same time, the vision of a primal German province, a "holy German soil" as a bulwark against the east, fueled fantasies of colonization and a civilizing mission.[246]

Tannenberg and the related glorification of Hindenburg—he was promoted to senior general, awarded the order Pour le Mérite, appointed supreme commander of the eastern front, and, on November 27, 1914, promoted to field marshal—were in keeping with German press coverage of the allegedly uncivilized Russian conduct in the war and "Cossack atrocities" in East Prussia; one function of this coverage was to counter Allied accusations of German barbarity in Belgium. In fact, at the beginning of the war, both Russian and German troops committed excesses against the population in the east; those that took place at Kalisz, on the East Prussian / Russian border, where German troops completely destroyed the city center and killed or expelled many civilians, actually predated the events in Belgium. In Kalisz, too, reports of local hostility had previously lowered the inhibition threshold among the soldiers.[247]

Propaganda about atrocities circulated on both the German and the Russian side, and from the beginning of the war such reports intensified German popular enemy-images of the Russians.[248] Thousands of postcards made the destruction of towns and villages an iconic theme, presenting Hindenburg and Ludendorff as twin geniuses who were saving the fatherland. In particular, Hindenburg's popularity was due to his embodiment of a number of role models: the "savior of Prussia" and the warrior combating "Russian terror" combined with the aura of the experienced general, whose career linked the national unification wars and the founding of the German nation-state with the trio of Wilhelm I, Bismarck, and Moltke. In this continuity with the legacy of the nineteenth century, the image of Hindenburg as "hero of the German nation" grew all the more powerful as the Kaiser's reputation declined in the eyes of the public.[249] At the same time, Hindenburg profited from the fact that people could associate him not only with the Prussian ideal of duty but also with older myths, such as that of Friedrich Barbarossa saving medieval Germany from his castle in the Kyffhäuser range or that of the ancient Germanic chieftain Arminius.[250] The Heidelberg history professor Karl Hampe was representative of German society when he noted on September 15, 1914: "Hindenburg put everything in order when the situation was very threatening."[251]

But it was not only because of military developments that the experience in the east was so distinctive. On the German side, the war produced a new way of looking at Russia that strikingly differed from prewar bourgeois images; it was no longer the cultural nation that people had associated with Tolstoy's novels, the *Ballets Russes,* modern theater, or contemporary painting. What counted was not the dynastic link between Germany and Russia, but a fundamental divide between western and eastern civilization, between Europe and Asia. In fact, attraction and repulsion had always been close to each other in the German perception of Russia. The path from fascination with its "holy literature" (emphasized by Thomas Mann in 1905 in his *Tonio Kröger*) to the kind of literary enemy-image that equated Russia with "Attila's barbarian hordes" (as Alexander Schröder put it in 1914) was shorter than it seemed at first sight.[252] When Harry Graf Kessler was transferred from the western front to Russian Poland, he soon stopped seeing things in the manner of the European man of letters focused on Russia's cultural modernity. On September 22, having crossed the border, he noted, "The road immediately became potholed, wayside trees disappeared, and the village houses, mostly wooden and painted light-blue, seemed poorer and more primitive than back home." This perception expanded into a colonial conqueror's gaze on the Other, on the alien environment, and above all on an ethnic-religious landscape in which anti-Polish and anti-Jewish stereotypes reflected the cultural gulf between west and east: "The Polish and Jewish population vegetates here in a common filth; otherwise they are alien to each other deep down. But the dirt encrusts them in a shared national color, under cover of which the Jew bleeds the Poles white." For General Max von Gallwitz, the border with Russian Poland even marked the beginning of "semi-Asia."[253] The officially commissioned war artist Ludwig Dettmann was reminded of the "map of Russia" in his school atlas: "a vast pale-green, including Poland, against the small patches of color for the rest of Europe. . . . Now the gigantic country lies before me. Not light-green but gray, loamy, dirty-gray, it stretches out as we push forward. The earth appears elongated and broken. To overcome and conquer this immeasurable space is a bold, majestic idea."[254] In comparison with the western front, therefore, German military operations in the east were associated with fundamentally different images of an ethnic-religious divide, and after the successful offensives in Spring and Summer 1915 the

Germans were able to experiment with new models of rule. The east became a space offering the opportunity for a military-bureaucratic order, a new kind of imperial state.

Right from the beginning, the war surpassed the cascade of events on the European continent with the drawing of parallel fronts in the west and east. Societies outside Europe also displayed their importance; the colonies, in particular, were far more than just an extension of the European theater, becoming a space that presented military possibilities of its own. Nor is it the case—far from it—that the global dimension of the war only became evident in retrospect. People at the time, even outside army headquarters, were fully aware of it; it fired their imagination and led to a quite special vision of the war as an intricately interwoven global event. At first, this directed attention to developments in the colonies, to the quest for additional allies, and in the German case to the mobilization of anticolonial forces against the British Empire. Karl Hampe referred as early as September 1914 to "interesting, but as yet unconfirmed, reports of rebellion in India and [to] the Japanese being brought in to fight under difficult conditions for England, which may bring about the future decline of British rule in the Far East. Egypt too appears to be wobbling." Hampe did not share the fear that an "Islamic revolt" might weaken Europe. "Surely we have only to win, and a Turkey raised up with our help is as dear to me as, indeed dearer than, a country like England that uses its culture and its Christianity only to exploit everyone." His exaggerated hopes for a sweeping, systematic "Islamic revolt" eventually led to the vision of a global movement: "It may become something that changes the shape of the world. Keep up the good work!"[255]

The political section of Department IIIb at the general staff considered a whole range of worldwide operations to support national and anti-imperialist movements. The departmental head, Rudolf Nadolny, mentioned among the plans for 1914–1915 "the freedom movements in Finland, Ireland, Georgia, and Morocco, the Senussi movement [in Libya], the movement in Arabia, and the threat of India." The highly symbolic jihad, or holy war, against the British, French, and Russians, which Germany made great efforts to promote, and which Sultan-Caliph Mehmed V declared on November 14, 1914, was also part of this context. Nadolny commented that the Germans had not struck it very lucky with the "declaration of the Holy War," since "the Islamic peoples" were "hardly sticking to it," even though "it had been propagated by Turkey, and therefore by the Sultan." This showed already that the Islamic elites regarded the war as an opportunity to pursue their own interests, which did not simply coincide with the strategies of the Entente or the Central Powers to extend their power and influence.[256] Although most of these operations in support of anti-imperialist revolts failed to have much impact, they reinforced the idea of the war as a global contest with no holds barred. For German, British, or French politicians and generals, the colonies appeared as an extension of the European arena to which the same logic could be applied, but practice soon demonstrated how much this underestimated the autonomous dynamic of the war in the colonial societies. They could not simply be reduced to a pool of recruitment and economic resources for the European war.

When the oceangoing steamer *Moana* put into San Francisco on October 7, 1914, it brought to the United States a number of passengers who had been evacuated from Tahiti a few weeks earlier, including the French actress Miss Geni La France and the New Zealand merchant E. P. Titchener. Both spoke of their experiences in Tahiti to the *New York Times*. La France had spent her holidays there and, on September 22, had been admiring the harbor view from her hotel veranda in Papeete: "I noticed two dark ships steaming up the little river, but was too lazy and 'comfy' to take any interest in them. Suddenly, without any warning, shots began exploding around us. Two of the houses near the hotel fell with a crash and the natives began screaming and running in every direction." Titchener reported how the two battleships had swung around and fired their broadsides at harbor buildings and the docked French gunship *Zélée*. Only parts of the town near buildings flying the American flag were spared the bombardment.[257]

The two German warships were the cruisers *Scharnhorst* and *Gneisenau*, part of the East Asia naval squadron under Vice Admiral Count Spee, which in June 1914 had set off from the Chinese port of Tsingtao (today's Qing-dao). In 1898, Tsingtao had been established as the capital of the German protectorate of Kiao-Chau, a colonial trading station, in accordance with the model used by other European powers; the Germans had used an attack on missionaries as a pretext to send out a detachment of marines and issued an ultimatum forcing China to enter into a 99-year pact. In East Asia gener-ally, the entry of Japan into the war on the Allied side played a key role in

1914; its declaration of war on Germany, on August 23, continued the great power ambitions of its political and military leaders, which the country had first impressively announced to the world in its conflicts with Russia and China. Now the war brought a chance to translate these imperial ambitions into reality.[258] Land grabs in Taiwan, Korea, and the Liaodong peninsula in China, together with the creation of a zone of influence in Manchuria, reflected these pretensions. Japan's entry into the war promised to widen its expansionist policy in China at the cost of the strategically important German territory. Early in September, Japanese troops landed on the north coast of Shandong, and the barely 4,000 soldiers stationed in Kiao-Chau could do little against the invading army of 65,000. Systematic encirclement on land and sea was followed up with constant shelling from October 29 until the German garrison surrendered in early November. Four thousand soldiers became prisoners of war. They were certainly better treated than American and British prisoners in the Second World War, although it was not until 1920 that they were able to return to Germany.[259]

This was more than a mere colonial episode in the Far East. After their experiences in the land war against Russia in 1904–1905, the Japanese troops did not follow European armies by engaging in deadly frontal assaults, but used the opportunities of a methodical siege. The whole operation thus cost them little more than 400 men, while the early redeployment of the German East Asia squadron meant that the Japanese navy did not have to fight a single battle. In comparison with the high losses and minimal rewards on European battlefields, Japan ended 1914 as one of the big winners from the opening period of the war. No other belligerent country made such large territorial and strategic gains in such a short period of time and at such small expense. By the end of the war, Japan would be considerably nearer to its goal of replacing the European powers in China and successfully competing with the United States in the Pacific. Exploiting the confusion after the fall of the monarchy in 1912 and the de facto rule of rival warlords, the Japanese issued a set of "21 demands" in January 1915 that ranged from control over Shandong, Port Arthur, and Dalian to an enlargement of their sphere of interests in Manchuria and Inner Mongolia. Japan, it seemed, was intent on turning China into a Japanese protectorate.[260]

In addition to Kiao-Chau, Japanese forces between August and October 1914 occupied the Caroline, Mariana, and Marshall Islands in the South

Seas without meeting any German resistance. When Tokyo agreed with London in December to take the equator as the dividing line between its own sphere of interests and that of the Australia and New Zealand dominions, Foreign Minister Kato insisted that this was not just a temporary solution: Japan would also claim possession of all formerly German islands north of the equator. Already visible in outline was the constellation of forces that would mark the Pacific theater in the Second World War. Not only would Japan have by 1918 the world's third largest battle fleet after the British and American. Its island bases in Micronesia controlled the bulk of the 6,400 kilometers of ocean separating the U.S. possessions of Hawaii and the Philippines. Japan was in a strong position to assert its great power status in Asia.

Thus Japan and the United States, the two rising great powers since the late nineteenth century and the watershed years of 1898 and 1904, were implicated in the war from early on: the United States economically and financially, but also by virtue of its multiethnic immigrant population from distant theaters of war, and Japan militarily, with early successes against Germany that allowed it to press its claim to hegemony in Asia at very little cost to itself. In 1919 it would obtain one of the four permanent seats in the League of Nations.[261]

Blockaded from its supply base in Tsingtao and eager to avoid a showdown with the Japanese navy, the German East Asia squadron left the Pacific and set sail for South America. Spee decided to wage war on enemy cruisers and merchant vessels, hoping all the while that he would be able to maintain his ships in the neutral countries of South America. At Coronel off the Chilean coast, his squadron annihilated a British cruiser group carrying 1,600 seamen, without suffering significant losses of its own.[262] This first great naval victory over the British bogey triggered euphoric reactions in Germany, and Kaiser Wilhelm had 300 Iron Crosses awarded to Spee's crews. Meanwhile, the British admiralty felt compelled to detach a large group of two modern battle cruisers, four pocket battleships, and two light cruisers from the North Sea and to send them off to destroy Spee's squadron. This they did on December 8, off the Falkland Islands, where Spee, his two sons, and 2,200 German sailors met their end.

The early sea war in East Asia and the Pacific was noteworthy for another reason: Spee's squadron covered 24,000 kilometers, half the earth's circumference, in the six months between June and December 1914. Never before had a naval detachment coped with such a distance under wartime conditions. Traveling this great distance was possible only thanks to an elaborate infrastructure and communications network involving supply ships, radio stations, and coaling bases. Spee also made use of the new wireless telegraphy. Not by chance did his attention turn to the Falkland Islands, where he hoped to destroy the British coaling stations and radio equipment.[263]

What was characteristic of this war, then, was not only the size, weaponry, and armor plating of the battleships central to the pre-1914 naval race between Britain and Germany but also, at least as much, the global supply and communication infrastructures permitting control of access to raw materials and resources. The British reaction to the German sea victory at Coronel showed how tightly intermeshed were the European and global theaters of war. For the transfer of British naval units away from the North Sea was necessary to secure international sea routes, and hence supplies from the Empire, for Britain's war on the European continent. But when it came to disruption of these global links through attacks on enemy merchant and transport shipping, light cruisers with a high propulsive power were much more appropriate than large armored cruisers or heavily armed battleships. And that was precisely what the German naval planners had overlooked in concentrating on a great sea battle with the British in the North Sea. From August on, they spared the high-seas fleet while waiting for the decisive moment to arrive, but this meant that, apart from a handful of ships, the Germans did not have a battle fleet outside Europe capable of cutting enemy sea links. The light cruiser *Emden*, which the Germans left behind in the Pacific in 1914, proved how effectively such ships could be deployed: it managed to tie up large enemy forces, enabling Spee to switch his operations to South America. Within a short time it destroyed sixteen merchant vessels totaling more than 70,000 gross register tons, took out oil storage facilities in Madras, and sank a Russian cruiser and French destroyer in Penang harbor in British Malaya.

When the *Emden* was finally forced out of action in November 1914, a landing party under First Lieutenant Hellmuth von Mücke that had been ashore at the time began an adventurous flight across the Indian Ocean and Arabia to the Middle East, from where it managed to reach Constantinople on the Hedjaz Railway. This "sailors' expedition through the desert" instantly made Mücke one of the best-known naval officers in Germany, but it also demonstrated how the theme of global warfare encouraged the imagining of bold escapades. The ideal of an individual hero, who overcame all geographical distance and all the obstacles of war on land and sea, was all the more attractive the less the European war of position and faceless death lent itself to such narratives. Most of Mücke's five officers, seven NCOs, and thirty-seven men who finally reported on May 23, 1915, to the German naval commander in Constantinople were later spread around the European fronts and killed not long after. Mücke himself became a pacifist, and even after the Second World War he spoke out against rearmament of the German Federal Republic.

The global dimension of the early war period was bound up with four closely related factors: the overseas colonies of the major European powers; the importance of global access to raw materials, resources, and trade and transport links; the worldwide availability of naval units together with a network of supply and communication bases; and the (often overlooked) position of non-European players and their local interests. The example of Tsingtao and the German East Asia squadron illustrates how quickly the European war could spread via the navy to other parts of the world. The attacks on German Pacific bases in Samoa and Rabaul were carried out by troops from Australia and New Zealand—an early sign of the importance of the Empire in the future course of the war. At the same time, a regional player like Japan had enormous opportunities for expansion in the Pacific, without becoming directly involved in the European conflict and paying the heavy price that would have entailed.[264]

Militarily, most of the German colonies could not hold out for long. With the disappearance of these global bases, however, the cruisers and other ships lost their supply and communications infrastructure. By the beginning of 1915, most of the sixteen merchant vessels that had been hastily converted into auxiliary cruisers had been either sunk or detained in neutral ports. It was thus already foreseeable that the German surface fleet would only be able to threaten Allied troop and supply transports in the Mediterranean, the North Sea, and the Baltic. Britain was now assured of the resources of its empire. If a serious threat to Allied merchant shipping and troop ships developed later in the war, this came not from the German battle fleet but from the deployment of submarines, even if their operational range remained limited.[265]

The medium-term loss of Germany's African colonies was in line with these developments. In this colonial theater, however, an autonomous logic soon overtook the intentions of the European players in the war.[266] At the beginning of the war, British and German colonial authorities, civilian governors, and settlers assured one another that it was necessary to cooperate to protect white European supremacy against possible tribal revolts. This changed when the military commanders took the helm, a good example being that of Paul von Lettow-Vorbeck in German East Africa.[267] There colonial policy featured the early incorporation of indigenous soldiers and irregular troops, with the result that the state monopoly of violence tended to fray at the edges.[268]

Whereas the German defenders in Togo surrendered by the end of August, fighting continued in Kamerun (German Cameroon) for a time after superior British, French, and Belgian forces invaded and captured the capital Douala, forcing the Germans to retreat to the north. In German Southwest Africa, in contrast, there was a different set of problems related to conflicts within the British Empire. To relieve the British, the South African prime minister Louis Botha declared that his country would defend itself and use its own forces to intervene against the nearby German colony. Having put down a rebellion by pro-German Boer officers, who had wanted to use the European war to achieve independence, Botha and his war minister, General Jan Smuts, mobilized 67,000 men against German Southwest Africa. In that region, unlike in East Africa, the earlier extermination campaign following the defeat of the Herero uprising in 1904 meant that it was impossible for the small German defense force of 3,000 men to rely on indigenous auxiliaries. In May 1915, the last units under General Victor Franke surrendered.

The German defensive strategy in Togo and Kamerun systematically included the use of indigenous troops. In Togo 300 Germans eventually laid down arms together with 1,200 natives, while in Kamerun, after the fall of Jaunde (today's Yaoundé), not quite 600 Germans and 6,000 Africans crossed into neutral Spanish Guinea. Incorporation was most successful in German East Africa, however, where 90 percent of the units active in

OPPOSITE: Map 3. The War in Africa, 1914–1918

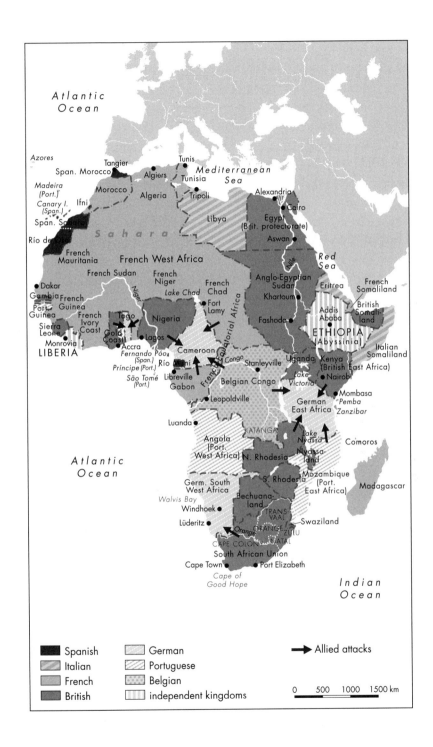

Atlantic
Ocean

Azores

Madeira
(Port.)

Canary I.
(Span.)

Spán. Sahara

Río de

Tangier
Span. Morocco
Morocco
Ifni

Algiers
Algeria

Tunis
Tunisia
Tripoli

*Mediterranean
Sea*

Libya

Alexandria
Cairo
Egypt
(Brit. protectorate)
Aswan

Sahara

*Red
Sea*

Dakar
Gambia
Port.
Guinea
Sierra
Leone
Monrovia
LIBERIA

French
Mauritania
French Sudan

French West Africa

French
Niger
Lake Chad

Togo

Nigeria

French
Chad
Fort
Lamy

Anglo-Egyptian
Sudan
Khartoum

Fashoda

Eritrea

French
Somaliland

Addis
Ababa

British
Somali-
land

ETHIOPIA
(Abyssinia)

Italian
Somaliland

French
Guinea
French
Ivory
Coast
Gold
Coast
Accra

Fernando Póo
(Span.)
Príncipe (Port.)
São Tomé
(Port.)

Lagos

Cameroon

Río Muni

Libreville
Gabon

Leopoldville

Congo
Stanleyville

Belgian Congo

Uganda

*Lake
Victoria*

Kenya
(British East Africa)
Nairobi

German
East Africa

Mombasa
Pemba
Zanzibar

Luanda

Angola
(Port.
West Africa)

KATANGA

N. Rhodesia

*Lake
Nyassa*
Nyassa-
land

Comoros

Germ. South
West Africa

Walvis Bay
Windhoek

Lüderitz

S. Rhodesia

Bechuana-
land

TRANS-
VAAL
Orange ORANGE
CAPE COLONY

Mozambique
(Port.
East Africa)

Swaziland

ZULU
NATAL

Madagascar

South African Union
Cape Town
Port Elizabeth

*Cape of
Good Hope*

*Atlantic
Ocean*

*Indian
Ocean*

Spanish

Italian

French

British

German

Portuguese

Belgian

independent kingdoms

Allied attacks

0   500   1000   1500 km

August 1914 under Lieutenant-General Paul von Lettow-Vorbeck were made up of indigenous troops. In Africa, then, Europeans were fighting Europeans, even competing with one another for the future carve-up of German colonies; Europeans were also relying on indigenous military units, and, above all, indigenous porters, for the conduct of the war. In addition, there was usually a whole baggage train of irregular fighters and women and children. Given the deficient infrastructure and the extreme geographical and climatic conditions, a special kind of war economy developed with as many as a million African porters.[269]

The local *askari,* with their strict selection criteria and draconian training, constituted an elite formation among the German colonial troops. Their active strength—no more than 11,000 during the war—remained manageable, and they were deployed exclusively in Africa, whereas France, for example, recruited more than 200,000 *tirailleurs sénégalais* and shipped them off to the European fronts. Lettow-Vorbeck scored a victory in November 1914 against numerically superior British and Indian troops at Tanga, and another in October 1917 at Mahiwa. His skillful tactics, mainly involving retreats and (after the end of 1916) a de facto guerrilla war, earned him great popularity.[270] Neither Smuts nor his successor, Jacob van Deventer, had managed to defeat him militarily by the end of the war, and it was only in November 1918, having learned of the armistice in Europe, that he surrendered together with his 155 German and 1,156 African soldiers.

In the figure of Lettow-Vorbeck, the contrast between media glorification and the actual practice of colonial warfare was particularly revealing. His military successes rested not least on a precise knowledge of local geography and conditions, as well as a rigorous pragmatism. Thus, he always fielded only as many troops as he could maintain with the available food and medicine, while the South African troops on the other side suffered huge losses from disease and crippling supply problems. As in the case of Spee and Mücke, many Germans identified with Lettow-Vorbeck, considering him the "lion of Africa." The image of an officer struggling against nature and the enemy, relying on his ingenuity to get out of impossible situations, went together with fantasies about a knightly duel in which the enemy was treated with respect. But in practice this chivalry applied at most to the white enemy. Inheriting the racist enemy-images used in the recent past to justify punitive expeditions against Chinese Boxers or insurgent Hereros, Lettow-Vorbeck's way of waging war, like that of the Allies for that matter, showed not the slightest consideration for indigenous noncombatants. Scorched-earth tactics were typical of the war in German East Africa, too, with devastating consequences for the civilian population.[271]

The troop deployment and casualty figures on the African continent appeared to be much lower than on European fronts. This bred a tendency to regard the world war in Africa as no more than a geographical extension involving colonial units made up of European soldiers, in which a romantic ideal of chivalrous combat and individual adventure found outlets that did not exist on the European fronts. Such notions, however, completely failed to grasp the reality of the war in Africa. The numerical calculations usually took into account only the mobilized soldiers, who in fact made up only a small part of the total forces deployed.[272] For a long time, a very different dimension had been shaping up beneath the surface, and now it clashed with the idea of a war waged by Europeans over the fate of European colonies. Much as the British, in the Boer War, had found it difficult to admit that they had an ever-higher proportion of black African troops, so too did General Smuts oppose the deployment of black Africans as regular soldiers, insisting instead that they should be used only as auxiliaries and laborers. Yet in 1917 they made up more than half of the British contingent in East Africa, serving also as soldiers in battle. If we also take into account the large numbers of indigenous porters, who carried essential supplies in areas without a developed infrastructure, then it will be clear how much the war in Africa affected indigenous societies from the beginning. Thus, it is not an exaggeration to compare the effects of the world war on Africa to those of the African enslavement.[273] The British alone recruited more than a million porters in their colonies and in German East Africa, and of those 95,000 did not survive. In Congo, 250,000 porters were mobilized to support fewer than 20,000 Belgian soldiers. According to realistic estimates that included native porters, considerably more than 100,000 men lost their lives in the fighting in German East Africa. The total among the 127,000 British soldiers who served there was 11,200—a death rate of approximately 9 percent. But the number of porters killed there was higher than that of all the Australian or Canadian or Indian soldiers killed in the war. The figure was equivalent to that of all African workers employed at the time in the South African mines.[274] The 45,000 blacks from Kenya alone who died on the British side constituted roughly one-eighth of the male population there. In East Africa, between 1914 and 1918, approximately 650,000 civilians and indigenous porters lost their lives—as a percentage of the population, the highest civilian death rate before the Spanish influenza of 1918. Yet the war in East Africa is still today an almost forgotten chapter.[275]

6. CONTROLS AND SHORTAGES
Militarized States and Improvised War Economies

In September 1914, inspired by reports of German victories, a Stettin landlady by the name of Redepenning wrote a letter to her tenants commenting on the events of the previous week: "The huge turnaround that, through the grace of Almighty God, our troops armed with His power and strength have won for us is making us look toward the great and blessed time ahead. May our people never forget so much grace, nor the Old God who protects the state and people from all evil. From October 1, your accommodation will cost 30 marks more."[276] So it was that the war rapidly entered national societies by many varied paths. It changed political decision-making processes, the functions of parliaments and parties, social composition, and conventional social roles; it called into question the traditional order of public and private finances, economies, production, and commerce. Within a few months of the outbreak of war, these tendencies had coalesced into a home front, which increasingly acquired a weight of its own and marked the ways in which millions of men, women, and children experienced the war. The war was a challenge to all existing societies, since its enormous sacrifices were a test of cohesion, integration, and loyalty; of mobilization and controls; but also of convictions and justifications. However, with the sense of duty and self-sacrifice demanded of millions came new demands for participation and recognition, which put pressure on the legitimacy of the political and social order. With each new year of war, the urgency of the question of how reliably the wartime states could fulfill their functions increased: in the struggle against external enemies, in the just distribution of the burdens of war, in the provision of the population, and in the maintenance of a convincing political-social order in the name of a nation, a monarchy, or a multiethnic empire.

In every country that entered the war in August, a broadly similar development occurred in its parliament and government. Monarchs, prime ministers, and deputies grounded a cross-party image of national unity on the emergency situation resulting from external attack; one of the most symbolically charged moments was the approval of war credits with the support of the parties of the Left. But already differences appeared between various political systems and cultures, especially with regard to the embrace of national unity. In Germany, the events in parliament marked a last fling of monarchic symbolism; the ever-stronger position of the military vis-à-vis the government and Kaiser would henceforth entail the long-term retreat of the monarch. In his two balcony speeches on July 31 and August 1, Wilhelm II set out the leitmotifs of the country's "social truce": "Envious peoples," he asserted "are compelling us to a just defense. The sword is being forced into our hands." This being so, the beleaguered nation was the supreme good that drove all other conflicts into the background: "Should it now come to battle, there will be no more political parties. . . . I no longer know any parties or denominations; now we are all German brothers and only German brothers."[277] For a moment, the nation at war appeared as a community that dissolved all distinctions between Prussians and Bavarians, workers and employers, Jews and Christians, and it was precisely this forging of community that justified the use of force against the enemy. The integrative nationalism of war was based on hatred toward all enemies of Germany.[278] As in a distant mirror, such formulations reflected the bitter domestic conflicts with the Social Democrats and the *Kulturkampf* against Catholicism. But the "civil peace" was also proclaimed as a quasi-feudal act, when the leaders of the bourgeois parties, speaking at the opening of parliament, pledged to follow the Kaiser "through thick and thin, through hardship and death." After meeting to approve the war credits—in a consultative vote, fourteen SPD deputies had initially voted against them, but later in the plenary session they bowed to the pressure of the parliamentary group—the parliament adjourned *sine die.*[279]

In effect, this meant that the German parliament stripped itself of power. The government could now pass laws without its approval; a clause buried in Paragraph 3 of the law extending the validity of checks and bills of exchange empowered the Bundesrat upper house, as the representative of German princes, to take "all necessary measures" in wartime to "compensate for economic damage." In view of the key importance of the economy for the war—in areas ranging from raw materials supply to rent and price controls to the allocation of housing and manpower—this act became the cover for sweeping government powers. Nearly 80 percent of all laws and regulations issued during the war fell under its provisions.[280]

Although the Kaiser formally assumed command of the armed forces, it was Helmuth von Moltke, the head of the general staff, who in fact directed military operations. His OHL, part of general headquarters, soon became the central decision-making body.[281] The Reichstag handed over important legislative powers to it in early August, while Chancellor Bethmann Hollweg, following the SPD's approval of war credits, hoped that he would be able to pursue his integrative "diagonal policy" and balance between left and right. For this purpose the restrictive Law on Associations was modified, and from August 1914 the SPD paper *Vorwärts* could be openly sold at Prussian train stations.[282] Nevertheless, the coming of war brought an extensive shift of executive powers. The Reichstag would become a major factor again only in 1916, when it clashed with the Third OHL under Hindenburg and Ludendorff while the civil peace at home was increasingly strained and the conditions for social integration were changing at an ever-increasing pace.[283]

In the wake of the symbolic scenes in the Reichstag and the Berlin Palace, the declaration of war and a state of siege suspended the existing constitutional order. Executive authority was transferred to the military commanders— which in effect meant the fifty-seven deputy commanders and fortress commanders who remained after mobilization of the twenty-five active army corps in the various home territories. These men were answerable only to the Kaiser, in a direct relationship outside all civilian control, so that they exercised functions of rule that cut deep into the constitutional rights of all Germans. We are not talking here only of military functions such as the organization of army corps materiel, the supervision of reserve troops, or border defense; their tasks also included allocation of prisoners of war, counterespionage, and the general control of public life. Thus, as soon as the war began, they were able to intervene directly in key areas affecting the population. Administrative bodies and local authorities came under the Deputy General Commands, which also decided on matters such as house searches, the opening of mail, press censorship, restrictions on the right of assembly, and the monitoring of aliens. The state of siege also allowed for military detention to be ordered without sentencing by a civil court.[284] This creeping militarization of administration and public life went hand in hand with a mushrooming of military institutions. The Eighth Royal Württemberg Deputy General Command, for example, which had only 7 officers and 14 NCOs in 1914, already counted 135 officer posts in 1917. As the war continued, the OHL tried to counter the strong decentralization tendencies of deputy general commanders by centralizing certain areas of responsibility, founding, for example, the War Press Office (in 1915) and the War Department subordinate to the Prussian War Ministry (in 1916).[285]

Whereas the German Reichstag at least played a visible role in August 1914, the lineup in the Habsburg Monarchy was characteristically different—although the actual consequences (suspension of civil rights, militarization of large enterprises, subordination of civilian administration to military authorities) were similar in the two empires. In Austria-Hungary, the shifting of political power centers and decision-making processes affected a multiethnic population. National groups had quite diverse ways of asserting their interests politically. In the Cisleithanian parts, the Imperial Council in Vienna had already been suspended in March 1914 by the prime minister, Count Stürgkh, and after the outbreak of war the government resorted to the instrument of emergency legislation. The lack of a parliamentary dimension in August 1914, like in Germany and the western democracies, made the role of Emperor Franz Joseph all the more important as an integrative figure and symbol of the monarchy. The parliamentary vacuum, which would end only when Franz Joseph's successor, Karl, recalled the Imperial Council in May 1917, continued for a long time to deepen the gulf between rulers and ruled and helped to give this conflict a national charge. In the Transleithanian parts of the empire there was a functioning parliament, but the non-Magyar nationalities (mostly Slovaks, Romanians, and Serbs) comprising nearly 40 percent of the electorate were largely marginalized in Budapest. This was of great significance for relations between the military leadership and the civilian government; whereas in Hungary the civilian government retained primacy at least in theory, the establishment in Austria of the AOK (Supreme Army Command) and a War Supervision Office introduced a whole new set of institutions dominated by the military, which increasingly sidelined parliament, civilian government, and the monarchy and viewed the Czechs in particular with growing distrust.[286] This climate of suspicion, which bred accusations of disloyalty and treason, soon led to the trial and imprisonment of Czech politicians. Latent tensions therefore intensified, even before the overall situation of the Dual Monarchy was shaken by military defeats and supply crises.[287]

In the Russian Empire as well, a parliamentary and a monarchic dimension coincided. Patriotic demonstrations in support of the Tsar took place in August 1914, particularly in St. Petersburg. And for all the tensions in previous years, the integration of the Empire in his person had by no means been eroded, as the celebrations in 1913 marking three hundred years of the Romanov dynasty had shown. At the decisive session of the Duma on July 16, 1914, only the Social Democrats voted against the war credits, while the non-Russian delegations (from Poland, for example) declared their solidarity with Tsar and Empire and were eager to demonstrate their loyalty in parliament. Here, too, however, the outbreak of war signaled a strengthening of the military executive. Unlike in France and Britain, the parliamentary institution—the Duma first established by the Tsar in 1905 as a constitutional concession—could not operate as an independent factor in the power equation.[288]

The developments in Paris and London presented a striking contrast. The symbolic parliamentary moment underlined the importance of the Chamber of Deputies for France's Third Republic: on August 4, at the key session of the National Assembly, Prime Minister Viviani read out an address from President Poincaré, which by tradition was the only way he could communicate with parliament. For the first time he used the expression that would become central to the national self-image over the following months and years: "In the war that is now beginning, France will have justice on her side, the eternal power of which cannot with impunity be disregarded by nations any more than by individuals. She will be heroically defended by all her sons; nothing will break their *sacred union* before the enemy; today they are joined together as brothers in a common indignation against the aggressor, and in a common patriotic faith."[289]

Even for people at the time, the *union sacrée* was by no means synonymous with the end of political controversies, and on August 10, in the Rhône department, the Socialist Markus Moutet could still win a large majority at a by-election with a high turnout. Yet, despite the stabilization of internal politics in the Third Republic, the bitterness of the Dreyfus affair and more recent conflicts had not been forgotten. Rather, there was a pragmatic truce between the parties in the face of war. And given the secular political culture of the Third Republic, Poincaré's programmatic use of the term *sacré* referred to the duty of everyone to defend the republican nation against German attack, harking back to the language of the 1790s when foreign enemies had threatened the achievements of the Revolution. In August 1914 this was the way to build bridges to the Socialists. On August 2, Socialist leaders meeting in the Salle Wagram decided to participate in the national defense, and in the presence of Jean Longuet, Karl Marx's son-in-law, Gustave Hervé, declared the party's readiness to fight unconditionally "to the last man." The issue here was not revenge for the defeat of 1870–1871 or visions of regaining Alsace-Lorraine, but defense of the republic against external threat. On August 4, on the occasion of Jean Jaurès's funeral, the leader of the CGT union federation, Léon Jouhaux, stated, "Before the great massacre, in the name of the workers who have already left and those who, like myself, will leave soon, I stand at this coffin and cry out all our hatred of the imperialism and savage militarism that are unleashing this horrific crime." Imperialism and militarism, however, were no longer seen as transnational phenomena that should be opposed with the international solidarity of all workers; they were now identified with the German aggressor. This was the turnaround that enabled Jouhaux to place the impending war in the revolutionary tradition of 1793, of the republic in arms. Like the French soldiers of today, those of 1793 had carried out their mission and brought liberty to the world.[290]

In France as in Germany, the war brought a shift of powers from the legislature to the military executive. On August 2, a special decree declared a state of siege in all *départements* of the republic; all civilian authorities, the police force, censorship, and the judiciary were made subject to the military commands of the home army. Except in areas under military administration, the civil institutions of prefects and majors recovered their police powers only in September 1915. After Viviani's first moderate Left government resigned on August 26, he formed a new, expanded government in the spirit of the *union sacrée:* Théophile Delcassé took over the Foreign Ministry, Alexandre Millerand the War Ministry, and two Socialists, Jules Guesde and Marcel Sembat, entered the cabinet—even though Sembat had reemphasized the incompatibility in principle between democracy and war making not long before the war.[291] And in 1915, when a representative of the conservative Right joined the government under Aristide Briand, all major political forces in the country were on board. Later, however, and especially from 1917 under Georges Clemenceau, it became ever clearer that the Right was in the driving seat in the implementation of the *union sacrée.*[292]

In early September, when the government fled to Bordeaux in the face of the German invasion, the cabinet and, in particular, the army headquarters considerably increased their powers. Even a *régime de dictature* did not seem out of the question, and old fears of a conservative military dictatorship were revived. But after autumn set in and held out the prospect of a long war, bringing with it massive supply and munitions problems at the front, parliament—and not primarily the government—came to play an active role again in December. Unlike in Germany, where the Reichstag strengthened its position vis-à-vis the OHL only in 1916, conflicts among the supreme army command, the government, and the Chamber of Deputies developed at a very early stage.

After the recall of parliament on December 22, 1914, to sit in permanence, deputies demanded that the government keep them fully informed of internal military issues and future war strategy. The old lines of suspicion and conflict between parliament (especially the Left) and the generals acquired new force. In response to criticism in parliament of War Minister Millerand—whom some deputies accused of not effectively controlling the commanders at army headquarters—three undersecretaries with far-reaching powers were assigned to work alongside him. In comparison with Germany, the more energetic National Assembly succeeded earlier in asserting a modicum of control over the government and military, thereby linking up with the dominant position of the legislature in the pre-1914 political system of the Third Republic. Although, in view of the military situation, the army high command did not seek to assume political power, it did insist on autonomy in matters of military strategy. The new army commissions of the Chamber and Senate proved to be important for armaments policy and also in military decision-making processes, although commission members did not manage to achieve a position of power comparable to that of the Jacobin *commissaires* in the revolutionary wars of the 1790s. Civilian-military relations generated considerable conflict in the next few years.[293]

When British politicians and the Westminster parliament were confronted with the outbreak of war in August 1914, the country was still reeling from the recent proclamation of home rule in Ireland. The decision to enter the war was controversial up to the last moment even at the cabinet level, with considerable opposition also in parliament, as the government stressed that the expected short war on the Continent would require only a limited expeditionary corps and have no major repercussions for society at home. Still, the decisions had far-reaching societal consequences. On August 7, the Defence of the Realm Act gave the government extensive powers to intervene in the economy and to suspend civil rights and freedoms—a deep inroad in a country whose self-image had long been based on the people's rights and the rule of law.[294] On August 5, a new Aliens Restriction Act compelled aliens to register with the authorities and limited their freedom of movement.[295]

At Westminster, a cross-party truce and a related enlargement of Lord Asquith's minority government took the sting out of conflicts for the duration of the war. The appointment as war minister of General Kitchener, still popular from his role in earlier colonial wars, gave this policy a further symbolic boost.[296] The Liberal government thus opened up to include the Conservatives. But there were limits to this suspension of political hostilities: two Liberal ministers, John Burns and Lord Morley, quit the government over its war policy and supported the position of the group of left-liberal MPs, who, together with the Independent Labour Party, had been refusing to back the government in the lower house.[297] This tendency extended outside parliament, where on September 5, 1914, the Union of Democratic Control (UDC) was founded in protest at Grey's policy in the July crisis. The UDC, which included in its ranks the future prime minister Ramsay Macdonald, the antiwar publicist Norman Angell, the Cambridge philosopher Bertrand Russell, and the economist John Maynard Keynes, soon developed into an extraparliamentary platform embracing all left-liberal and socialist opponents of the war; it already had more than 300,000 members in 1915 and would eventually number 750,000 in 1918. When a broad wartime coalition of Liberals and Conservatives was formed in 1915, the UDC emphasized the division within the Liberal Party and sought closer support from within the Labour Party.[298]

Britain's entry into the war led to bitter conflicts within many families. Charlotte Despard—the sister of Sir John French, who, as head of the British Expeditionary Force (BEF), commanded the largest British army in history—campaigned as a pacifist against the war. The two did remain close until the 1920s, however, when Charlotte sided with the Irish Republican movement, while her brother became Lord Lieutenant of Ireland and fought against nationalist forces there. Despard joined the socialist-pacifist movement of Sylvia Pankhurst, whose own family split apart over Britain's role in the war. At the outbreak of war, Pankhurst's mother Emmeline and sister Christabel (who in 1903 had together founded the Women's Social and Political Union) changed from violent critics of the Asquith government into patriotic supporters of the war, campaigning against Germany on both sides of the Atlantic and championing voting rights for soldiers and sailors to the point that they were prepared to set aside their demands for female suffrage. In contrast, Sylvia and her youngest sister Adela became radical opponents of the war: Sylvia even planned to set up a Women's Peace Expeditionary Force as a pacifist counter to the BEF that would move between the belligerent armies on the Continent; her mother and Christabel subsequently excluded her from the family. The split in the suffragette movement was clear: such a resolute campaigner for women's democratic rights as Millicent Fawcett (the president of the National Union of Women's Suffrage Societies) was convinced that the war against Germany and even the blockade with its effects on the civilian population were unavoidable necessities. She rounded firmly on pacifist members of the Union who saw feminism as an expression of the universal longing for peace.[299]

It was not only for political players and institutions that the outbreak of war marked a watershed; the consequences were immediately felt in the economy. Here the starting points were very different for the Central Powers and the Allies. But size of population (Russia: 171 million, United States: 98 million, Germany: 65 million, Austria-Hungary: 52 million, Great Britain:

42 million, and France: 39 million) said little about economic strength. In terms of per capita GNP, the United States with $377 was ahead of Britain with $244, Germany with $184, and France with $153, while Austria-Hungary ($57) and Russia ($41) trailed far behind. The Central Powers together had only 46 percent of the Entente's population and 61 percent of its GNP. After just a few weeks, the direct economic effects of the war made themselves felt in two developments. First, there was a sharp rise in unemployment due to the economic turbulence: in Germany from 2.7 percent in July to 22.7 percent in September; in Austria-Hungary from 5 percent to 18.3 percent in August; and in France to as much as 40 percent following the mobilization. After this shock wave passed, however, the army and industry had to compete well and hard for ever-scarcer supplies of manpower.[300]

The second bottleneck concerned raw materials. Nowhere did the industrial supply problem associated with global economic warfare manifest itself as early as it did in Germany, where the fighting on two fronts and the blockade of all its commercial sea routes had an especially dire effect. In Britain, in contrast, the image of something close to "business as usual" prevailed at the beginning of the war.[301] The nineteenth-century Army Act permitted the requisitioning of supplies necessary to the war effort, and the government thought that, together with the Defence of the Realm Act, this would provide sufficient basis for intervention in the domestic economy. Once the German naval units operating outside Europe had been eliminated, Britain enjoyed largely unhindered access to the resources of the Empire; nor did it have to endure any effects of fighting on its own territory. But a few weeks into the war, the new war minister Kitchener was already warning against the illusion of a swift victory and pointing to the danger of a supply crisis—a danger that became fully apparent only around the end of 1914 and particularly in Spring 1915.[302] With the appointment of David Lloyd George as minister of munitions, Britain experienced a decisive period of centralization—indeed, a completely new executive approach to the war economy. Yet neither there nor in France did the measures reach the same intensity as in Germany. It is true that France soon suffered from the fact that large parts of its industrial north were a war zone, but important external borders and seaports remained open. Only in 1915, in the context of acute supply problems facing the army, was a special munitions ministry created under the Socialist Albert Thomas.[303]

Germany alone suffered the full force of a new kind of supply problem in the early months of the war. In late October 1914, the government announced the production of so-called war bread, which was supposed to contain as much as 20 percent potato flour in order to save on wheat and rye.[304] In the same month, a war report listed the medical supplies required by one army corps for a single month: it came to the "contents of three long trains consisting of 32 wagons each." The items in question included "50 kilometers of sticking plaster, 50 cubic meters of tube bandages, 16 hundredweight of aluminium acetate, 31 kilograms of digitalis, 800 hundredweight of chlorinated line, 4 hundredweight of hydrogen peroxide, and 200,000 grams of opium."[305] Most important, the effective blockade of seaports was a major threat to the arms industry, which urgently needed imports of raw materials such as chromium, nickel, sulfur, and saltpeter, as well as crude oil and rubber. Given the huge consumption of munitions over a short period of time, it was precisely the interruption of German trade and supply routes that revealed the full scale of global economic interconnectedness.[306]

The saltpeter required for ammunition and artillery shells, which until then Germany had imported mainly from Chile, was a perfect example of the resulting bottleneck. Although it was possible to requisition large quantities early in the war from the ports of Hamburg, Antwerp, and Ostend, the assumptions about military needs proved to be totally inaccurate. The mobilization plan had reckoned on a monthly consumption of 600 tons of explosive and 450 tons of powder, but calculations made in Fall 1914 already pointed to a monthly requirement of 6,500 tons of Chilean saltpeter and another 1,500 tons for the navy by the end of March 1915. In August 1915, the monthly need of the army alone was assessed at 10,000 tons, and in Fall 1916 the Hindenburg program eventually put it as high as 20,000 tons. Nor did these figures include the requirements of either the navy or Germany's Austro-Hungarian ally, let alone agriculture and other branches of the economy important to the war effort.[307]

After the Battle of the Marne, this hypertrophy of resource consumption by the arms industry already led to severe munitions bottlenecks. An existential problem for the German war effort was becoming apparent: "Look around you: everything that surrounds us—machinery and construction, clothing and food, weapons and transport—contains inputs from abroad.

For the economy of nations is indissolubly entangled; wealth flows in from all regions along iron roads and waterways, coming together in the service of life. This is how the expression 'supply of raw materials' acquires its color, and this color emerges all the more seriously in relation to the problem of armament and defense." This analysis stems from Walther Rathenau—the figure who soon took over one of the new agencies of the war economy, but whose whole biography reflected the ambivalent mix of economic performance, cultural hopes, and political skepticism that was part of the early twentieth-century bourgeois legacy. Right at the start of the war, Rathenau clearly saw the geostrategic problem facing the Central Powers: "Yes, of course, we and our allies border on three seas. But what are they? Inland seas. The Baltic, open only via a narrow strait; the North Sea, blocked by the Channel and the Orkney and Shetland islands; and the Mediterranean, locked by the two bases in east and west. Behind these inland seas stretches a needy land with scant supplies of essential raw materials; and to the south, beyond the Mediterranean cauldron, lies a desert fringe through which no paths or transport routes lead to the world's centers of production."[308]

In a memorandum presented a few days after the outbreak of war, Rathenau persuaded the Prussian war minister Falkenhayn to create a new organization to avert the impending crisis of raw materials supply due to the enemy blockade. The War Materials Department (KRA) founded for this purpose began work on August 13, with Rathenau, now holding the rank of general, as its energetic director. His origins and experience made him cut out for the job. Born in 1867 as the son of the German Jewish industrialist Emil Rathenau, he had become familiar at an early age with the late nineteenth-century dynamic of Germany's industrial development; in 1883 his father had founded the Allgemeine Electricitäts-Gesellschaft (AEG). At his father's wish, and despite his own literary and artistic interests, Walther Rathenau studied chemistry, physics, and engineering and launched into an economic career. During the recession that affected the German electrical industry, he pushed for new forms of economic organization to reduce the pressure of competition, getting to know the ins and outs of cartel formation and corporate mergers. In this he was representative of a new generation of economic managers, who saw novel opportunities in the combination of scientific-technological progress, efficient organization, concentration of economic power, and the global linkage of raw materials, manpower, knowledge, and finance. With this primacy of economics in mind, he rejected war in a way that recalled the arguments of Bloch and Angell; the decisive problems were not those of power and imperial expansion, but "questions relating to the economy." "If," he wrote, "Europe's economy fuses into a community—and that will happen sooner than we think—politics too will fuse." World peace was not to be expected as a result, but rather a "softening of conflicts, a saving of energy, and a civilization based on solidarity."[309]

But Rathenau was also marked by a contradiction between external success and outsider status. For the intellectual who, as a Jew, had not been allowed to take the officers' exam after his period of military service in 1890–1891, a critical view of the political structures and culture of Wilhelmine Germany remained paramount. The outbreak of war dashed Rathenau's hopes in a new bourgeoisie active in politics, economics, and culture—but the war also created novel scope for action, and no one in the sphere of the war economy recognized this as swiftly and consistently as he did. Yet even in his conception of the war there were strong elements of ambivalence: on the one hand, he stressed how "internally necessary" the war was, because he expected from it the breakthrough of a new bourgeoisie ("How the old and insupportable dissolves in new hope"); on the other hand, unlike the great majority of educated middle-class Germans and businessmen, he viewed the war as a disaster, and his pessimism about how it would end increased year by year. In this he "painfully separated" himself from the "way of thinking of [his] people . . . in so far as it considers the war to be a redemptive event." So "this war" was not "a beginning but an end; what it will leave behind is ruins."

The fact that, at the beginning of the war, Rathenau did not believe in "our right to give the world a final shape" did not prevent him from later favoring a central European customs union with Austria-Hungary, or even from pursuing in 1915 a plan to force Russia, through extensive conquests, into an anti-British alliance, and promoting a ruthless mobilization of the home front (including the use of Belgian forced laborers). Finally, having quarreled with Ludendorff in 1917 over his plan for unrestricted submarine warfare, he spoke out toward the end of the war for a peace without annexations and a thoroughgoing parliamentarization of Germany. Such contradictions, which may also be found in Max Weber, were typical of bourgeois reactions to the course of the war.[310] When Rathenau resigned as head of the KRA in late March 1915, he had acquired a reputation as the "economic chief of staff behind the frontlines," but his decision to step down also had to do with his disappointment that not he but Karl Helfferich had been appointed the new state secretary at the treasury. In this central function, Helfferich became responsible for financing the war by means of large loans. Rathenau's withdrawal was also a response to the increasing animosity toward civilians and Jews, who were accused of profiting from official directives in their own industrial concerns.[311]

In August 1914, however, the issue was a real crisis in the supply of raw materials to German industry, and the "Raw Materials Office," as it was originally called, soon became a hugely successful economic organization.[312] Rathenau formulated his vision of the war economy when, beyond the tranquil War Ministry garden where he set up shop in mid-August 1914, he saw a chimney pointing to "the vast domain of the German economy that stretched out to our burning frontiers." "This world of thundering trains, smoking flues, glowing furnaces, and whirling spindles, this boundless economic domain, stretched out before my mind's eye, and the task we had been given was to unify this weaving, striving world, to make it serve the war, to impose a single will on it, and to rouse its titanic forces to resistance."[313] A random sample of 900 key firms for the war effort conducted in the first few weeks of the war found that, with the growing needs of the fronts, the country's material reserves would last for scarcely longer than six months. The combination of Rathenau's extensive experience, the KRA's special powers at the War Ministry, and its conversion into a central authority with a staff of three in 1914 that increased to 2,500 by the end of the war, soon led to impressive results. While the KRA introduced monthly balances, confiscated materials, and strictly monitored their allocation, businesses could decide on their own what use to make of them. In the fall and winter of 1914–1915, some corporations were founded in the style of cartels and syndicates to procure and distribute raw materials—for example, War Metals, Inc. or War Wool Supplies, Inc. Looking on the outside like joint stock companies, but also including civil servants or members of boards of trade, this was a new model of economic organization, bringing together elements from the private and state sector to fuse official goals and parameters with autonomous businesses—an idea that Albert Speer would use again as armaments minister in the Second World War.[314]

This semi-state administration did, however, lead to major disputes over fields of competence, since the KRA could not fulfill the demand for a comprehensive central directorate. In 1914, when copper roofs were ruthlessly stripped from Belgian churches and monasteries, conflicts arose with the Catholic Church and the Vatican. Even more important was the question of wood supplies in Russian Poland and oil resources in Romania. Admittedly the model could not be simply transferred elsewhere: the attempt to apply the war economy principle to Austria-Hungary, with the creation of sixteen industrial materials departments, did nothing to ease the shortages of vital materials. It also exacerbated the dualism of government, since economic coordination of the two parts of the Empire, especially in relation to food supplies, remained highly problematic. The military dependence of the Dual Monarchy on Germany was now compounded by economic dependence. The tasks of the new-style authorities rapidly increased: they included the fixing of maximum prices, and in 1917 these were set for iron and steel on the grounds of military necessity, leading to massive price increases that increased the budget deficit. On the other hand, the production of new basic materials was a success. The "Haber-Bosch process" for the industrial production of ammonia from hydrogen and atmospheric nitrogen, which was developed before the war by Fritz Haber and Carl Bosch in close cooperation with BASF, was particularly important, as was the Frank-Caro process of calcium cyanamide synthesis. As the War Ministry promoted the large-scale production of ammonium nitrate and nitric acid from ammonia, a substitute was available soon after the beginning of the war for the saltpeter required in explosives. Not only did this stave off the threatened end-of-year collapse of German munitions; it also maintained the fertilizer output essential to the food supply. In the longer term, this development of ersatz materials was also effective in other areas: the industrial production of aluminium, for example, made Germany independent of copper imports. By the time a central war office reorganized the arms sector in 1916 under the Hindenburg program, the KRA had already been carrying out key structural changes in the war economy since August 1914.[315]

In France and Britain, by contrast, the full economic impact of the protracted war started to make itself felt only in Spring 1915. In Russia, huge problems were already appearing toward the end of 1914, as a result of the German or Ottoman naval blockade of important import-export routes across the Baltic and the Black Sea. As in the case of the British blockade of Germany, the effectiveness of this action put the Russian war economy under major pressure during the following months.[316]

7. LOYALTY AND RECOGNITION IN NATIONS AND EMPIRES

On August 19, 1914, a telling cartoon appeared under the title "A Quick Change of Front" in the British satirical magazine *Punch*. It showed Johann Schmidt, a butcher of German origin, and his display window in an English town, before and after the declaration of war. After August 4, Johann Schmidt became John Smith and removed any reference to Germany in his wares: sauerkraut was replaced with pickles, limburger cheese with Stilton, and frankfurters with Cambridge sausages.[317] The nation at war was omnipresent in Summer and Fall 1914, infusing people's everyday lives with political rhetoric and intellectual position taking. Shortly after the outbreak of hostilities, the Berlin cigarette factory Manoli changed its English brand names that had identified smokers as having an international taste and casual cosmopolitanism. The popular brand "The Kaiser" became "Manoli Kaiser," while "Gibson Girl" turned into "Manoli Bunting." So as not to lose existing customers, the company was careful not to change the pack design and even added a seal that referred to the old name, thereby underlining its patriotic commitment. More generally, the nationalization of language blossomed in distinctive ways: foreign words hailing from enemy countries were removed from restaurant menus, and Oskar Kresse published a lexicon for the "Germanization of superfluous foreign terms."[318] This wave of renaming expressed a programmatic intent to eliminate national ambiguities in public life. In Paris, for example, the change from Avenue d'Allemagne to Avenue Jean Jaurès consciously evoked the national integration of the Socialists in the struggle with Germany.[319]

In St. Petersburg, the city was renamed Petrograd against the advice of the mayor Ivan Tolstoy, who was eager to protect people of German origin from pogroms.[320] Even the International of interrelated noble dynasties disintegrated into rival national branches. From 1917, at the request of the British monarch, the English branch of the Battenbergs was officially renamed the Mountbattens, while the royal house itself forsook any linguistic connection to the House of Sachsen-Coburg-Gotha and renamed itself after its main residence at Windsor.[321]

In all belligerent countries, the invoking of the nation soon became a guide to action. Defense of the nation under attack became the highest principle used by all states to justify the battles ahead, requiring the mobilization of all forces and a readiness to accept sacrifices. In the early months of war, the universal promise of national participation, with its heady mix of "daily plebiscite" and collective memory of earlier lives sacrificed, could once again exert its power over people's minds. Max Weber, referring to this period in 1914, underlined the peculiar integrative effect of war in all modern societies, comparable only to that of religions: "As the consummated threat of violence among modern polities, war creates a pathos and a sentiment of community.

A QUICK CHANGE OF FRONT.

Patriotic labeling as a proof of loyalties: "A Quick Change of Front," *Punch*, 1914

War therefore makes for an unconditionally devoted and sacrificial community among the combatants . . . as a mass phenomenon. . . . In general, religions can show comparable achievements only in heroic communities professing an ethic of brotherliness." The peculiarity of war, for Weber, lay in its unique "concrete significance"; "death on the field of battle differs from death that is only man's common lot"; it "differs from this merely unavoidable dying in that in war, and in this enormity *only* in war, the individual can *believe* that he knows he is dying 'for' something."[322]

In the early weeks of the war, this "for something" referred to the nation and its special promise of participation—a promise that subsequently collided with a very different reality in the trenches and the home fronts, becoming less and less compatible with, let alone justifiable by, the national images of Summer 1914. In the long term, the exaggerated expectations of the nation at war passed over into altogether different formations: frontline communities and bands of war bound up with the soldiers' experience of violence, but also with new internationalisms (as the year 1917 would show), as well as interethnic conflicts in which enemy-images were given an intense ideological charge and directed against more and more people, whether soldiers or civilians. In Summer and Fall 1914, the new framework of nations at war began to take on its defining characteristics: it expressed itself as a great loyalty test, as a verification of the reliability and resilience of each individual's national commitment. Beneath the unity rhetoric, parliamentary sessions, and monarchic symbolism, there was a renewal of many of the prewar social conflicts over participation in the nation, over the question of who did or did not belong to it, who could or could not be trusted. Quite different lineups and reactions began to take shape in the wartime societies, ranging from fear and hysteria through all-consuming suspicion to attempts to make participation in the war an instrument of national integration or a vehicle for the assertion of rights to national autonomy. This explained the ostentatious declarations of loyalty, not only of the workers' parties but also of Catholics and Jews and various national groups. Assurances of loyalty were part of a bargaining strategy associated with expectations of reform. Such questions were by no means confined to academic-intellectual discourse. Within days or weeks, they entered into the daily lives of ordinary people and frequently became associated with violence.

This problem presented itself above all in the ethnically and religiously diverse empires of Russia, the Habsburg monarchy, and the Ottoman Empire. But even in the nation-states there could be no question of ethnic homogeneity. The handling of national minorities thus soon became a measure of trust in the societies at war. Upon its outbreak, the 23-year-old Kresten Andresen served as a soldier in the Prussian army. He belonged to the Danish national minority in Schleswig, which, after the experience of the war in 1864, had been able to identify only superficially at most with the German nation-state founded in 1871. He was an example of the fate of many other national minorities, of Alsatians and Poles, Finns and Slovenes, Balts and South Tyroleans, Czechs and Irish. What war were they fighting, and for whom? At the beginning of the war, Andresen experienced the loyalty test in the form of a police operation involving state-ordered violence: hundreds of Danes were interned, and in some cases beaten, on suspicion of spying or preparing resistance.[323]

For all the skepticism prevalent before 1914, the Tsarist Empire and the Habsburg monarchy were able to mobilize their multiethnic armies successfully. Nor did the military crises of Summer and Fall 1914 cause the empires to fall apart. In the Habsburg monarchy, indeed, the dominant mood was one of solidarity focused on the person of Franz Joseph and his dynasty. But whereas the mobilization of three million soldiers from eleven nationalities was a success, reactions on the home fronts underlined the complexity of the multiethnic experience of the war. The South Slav regions witnessed aggressive behavior toward the Serb population, who were suspected of spying on behalf of the Allies. Serb businesses in Zagreb and Sarajevo were plundered at the beginning of the war, and mass internment followed in Slovenia and Dalmatia. Spy mania swept Galicia, and in Spring 1915, in the run-up to Italy's entry into the war, more than 100,000 Italians were forcibly evacuated from the South Tyrol region. Ethnic violence reached a peak in the campaign waged by Croat general Sarkotić against the civilian population (especially Bosnian Serbs) in South Slav areas. In that region there could be no talk of a distinction between military front and home front, or between combatants and noncombatants, in occupied zones.

In other parts of the monarchy, the balance between official demands and popular expectations was initially stabilized in 1914. In Prague, Germans and Czechs reacted very differently to the outbreak of war, since the Czechs feared that it might strengthen pan-Germanic tendencies and, in any event, did not support Vienna's anti-Russian justifications for war. The power shift in favor of the supreme army command (AOK) strengthened the mutual aversion between the AOK and Czechs thought guilty of disloyalty; nor were such accusations confined to the home front, as the detention and trial of numerous Czech politicians demonstrated. Contradicting the stereotype shared by many officers of German origin, the Czech parties did initially tend to cooperate with the monarchy, but their loyalty was mainly geared to the vision of a postwar federal state. This tension between loyalty, skepticism, and pragmatic temporization also characterized other national groups in the monarchy. The war proved to be a means of improving their own position as the price of their support. In Croatia, for instance, deputies in the officially tolerated Sabor (parliament) tied their loyalty to expectations that Croats would in the future have greater independence and political autonomy within the monarchy.

In September 1914, the 27-year-old British nurse Florence Farmborough reported on her experiences in Moscow. She found that wounded soldiers displayed a group cohesion that made their ethnic affiliation seem secondary: "They nurture a rare comradeship: White Russians get along famously with Ukrainians, Caucasians with people from the Urals, Tatars with Cossacks. Most of them are agreeable, patient men, thankful for the attention they receive; they complain rarely, if at all."[324] In the Russian Empire, too, hundreds of thousands of soldiers from the most diverse regions and ethnicities were successfully mobilized.[325] Proofs of political loyalty came even from centers of resistance to St. Petersburg during the 1905 Revolution—from Transcaucasia and particularly the Baltic provinces, where in Summer 1914 German Balts and other German-speaking settlers supported a war with the German Reich. At the same time, however, the early weeks and months of the war saw the rise of an aggressive Russian nationalism directed against ethnic and religious minorities that were suspected of collaboration with the Central Powers. Violent clashes occurred, especially with ethnic Germans, Poles, and Jews.

The complexity of the home fronts was most evident in the newly conquered territories and in areas bordering the Russian Empire. In East Galicia and Bukovina, Russian wartime nationalism expressed itself most strongly in the idea of incorporating Galicia as "ancestral Russian land"—an expansionism that met hefty resistance in other regions, especially Ukraine. In Lvov a League for the Liberation of Ukraine was founded right at the beginning of the war, with a view to collaboration with the militarily successful Central Powers, but the Russian authorities repressed the Ukrainian national movement by closing schools, banning newspapers, and deporting the head of the Greek Catholic church. In both the Russian and Ottoman Empires, there were hopes that ethnic conflicts would weaken the enemy by spreading tensions beyond their respective borders. In 1915 the founding in Constantinople of a Committee to Defend the Rights of Muslim Turko-Tatar Peoples fueled mistrust toward Turkic-speaking Muslims in Russia, who were seen as an advance guard of Pan-Turkism. While the Ottomans based their calculations on an uprising of Russian Muslims in the Caucasus that would bring closer a holy war against the Allies, the tsarist regime sought to exploit Russia's traditional function as protector of the Christian Armenians—a posture that in turn fanned the hostility of Ottoman military leaders toward the Armenians.

Poland provides a good example of how the war raised national political expectations, but also led to new conflicts. At the beginning of the war, Poland consisted of three parts: the central and largest one was the area of Congress Poland belonging to Russia, while the western and northwestern part, comprising Posen (Poznan) and West Prussia, belonged to the German Reich, and the southern territories of "Galicia and Lodomeria" were part of the Habsburg monarchy. As the war progressed, the partition powers engaged in outright competition over scenarios for a future Polish state, in order to gain the support of Poles against their respective enemies. But in 1914 an independent Poland was the favored option in Petrograd, Berlin, and Vienna. In Germany, however, the idea of an independent state limited to the Russian-Polish part and dependent on Germany encountered massive resistance from advocates of full-blown Germanization. On the Russian side, attempts were made to win the support of Poles by means of the so-called Poland manifesto of August 15, 1914, which promised territorial reunification and full recognition of the Catholic faith and the Polish language. However, the document spoke not of "autonomy" but of self-government in an enlarged Poland including the Prussian and Austrian territories. In Vienna, the aim was to expand Galicia to include the territory of Russian Poland, but the idea of Austrian-Hungarian-Polish trialism ran into massive opposition in Budapest, while any Austro-Polish solution was rejected by Germany. At no point, therefore, did the Central Powers pursue a coherent policy on Poland.

The competition among external players was matched by conflict within Poland itself. On August 16, 1914, the Supreme National Committee met in Lvov under the Krakow city president Juliusz Leo and military leader Władysław Sikorski. Its aim was to seize the opportunity provided by the war to make Galicia a Polish Piedmont in the framework of an Austro-Polish solution: that is, the kernel of an independent nation-state following the precedent of the Italian Risorgimento. Józef Piłsudski, too—who in his struggle against Russia for an independent Poland had taken part in an attempt on the Tsar's life in 1886 and who since 1906, after a number of stints in jail, had run autonomous paramilitary units in Galicia and Silesia with Austrian connivance—backed this policy of alignment with the Central Powers. Anticipating a strategy pursued by many nationalities in the war, he began to organize a number of military formations as the core of a national army and used them to popularize the idea of a sovereign Polish nation-state.[326]

The outbreak of war with Russia was meant to be the signal for Poland to grasp its independence from the historic occupying power. But on August 13, an Austrian ultimatum forced Piłsudski to integrate his units as Polish Legions into the Austro-Hungarian army. Although these special units dissolved after the Russian successes in Galicia and the capture of Lvov, he was later able to draw great political capital from his symbolic action at the beginning of the war.[327] Quite different was the reaction of Roman Dmowski, the leader of the Polish National Democrats, who for years had advocated alignment with Russia and since 1907 had operated as leader of the Polish bloc in the St. Petersburg Duma. On August 8 he made a declaration of loyalty before the assembly, and on November 25 he helped found the Polish National Committee, which advocated reunification in the framework of the Russian Empire under tsarist rule. The bitter conflict between Piłsudski and Dmowski revealed how the war had laid a new basis for debates about the future relationship between multiethnic empires and national political movements but it also sharpened rivalries both externally (between the major protagonists of the war) and internally (between different political groups).[328]

In the Ottoman Empire, the internal political and social constellation that had appeared in outline during the Balkan wars came ever more to the fore after its entry into the war on the side of the Central Powers. Ethnic violence against civilians and mass expulsions had been part of the Balkan wars, accompanying the loss of European territories in the long chain of military defeats that had had such a long-lasting effect on the Young Turk elite. This reinforced an irredentist rhetoric that sought reconquest of the lost territories. For the Young Turk elite, it was even more important to ensure the loyalty of the various ethnic-religious groups in a future war and at the same time to concentrate on the territory of a Turkish nation. The roots of an aggressive wartime nationalism were thus present before 1914. Many a Turkish nationalist called for the European lands in the southeastern Balkans to be abandoned once and for all, and for the regime to concentrate on Anatolia as the "heart and soul" of the fatherland. In parliament, the former military man Cami Bey described such a withdrawal as the only way to regenerate the Ottoman Empire, providing the core "foundations for a civilization of the future."[329] It was another legacy of the defeats, and especially of the Balkan wars, that the supporters of radical Young Turk nationalism operated with the utopian vision of an ethnically homogeneous nation-state.

Young Turk politicians expected a short war that would stabilize the international position of the empire. They did not blindly place themselves in the hands of the German Reich, but they did think they would have to depend on a great power to extract the maximum advantage from postwar bargaining. For as long as possible, they tried to play off the Entente and the Triple Alliance against each other, and it was only the massive military aid offered by Germany that decided them in favor of the Central Powers. Enver Pasha kept trying to put off the deployment of Ottoman forces in battle, while skillfully presenting to the Germans his country's unconditional readiness for war; he continued this procrastination even after the Turkish government had managed, between August and October 1914, to extract everything it had been demanding from Berlin in the way of money, military supplies, ships, and expert advisers without conceding massive influence over Turkish politics or military decisions to the German government or army. At any event, it was not possible to speak of Turkey as a German satellite.[330] In the Second World War, the Turkish president İsmet İnönü leaned more toward the Western Allies, although he stuck in principle to a position of neutrality, and Turkey did not intervene in the conflict. In the First World War, by contrast, the formal ties to an ally proved decisive, since the Young Turk politicians thought these were the only way to ensure the long-term survival of the Empire.[331]

When the Ottoman Empire entered the war and found itself fighting on three fronts—in the Caucasus against Russia, on the Suez Canal and in Mesopotamia against France, and (from Spring 1915) on the Gallipoli peninsula against the British-led Allied landing—the multiethnic structure of its society became a key factor. On November 14, 1914, when the Sultan-Caliph ceded to German pressure and declared jihad, he emphasized not only the common religious basis of the holy war, but even more the hope that the territorial losses of the past could be recovered. "Russia, England, and France never for a moment ceased harboring ill-will against our Caliphate, to which millions of Muslims, suffering under the tyranny of foreign domination, are religiously and wholeheartedly devoted, and it was always these powers that started every misfortune that came upon us. Therefore, in this mighty struggle which now we are undertaking, we once and for all will put an end to the attacks made from one side against the Caliphate, and from the other against the existence of our country."[332] The official flyer emphasized the dual function of the sultanate and caliphate, embodying the connection between patriotism and religion; the holy war would also be a freedom struggle against Allied colonial rule. In this perspective, the text linked "the life of our empire" to the "existence of 300 million suppressed Muslims," whose prayers would accompany the Ottoman soldiers.[333]

In Europe, the idea of an Islamic holy war played a role in capital cities at most; London, for example, at first had its eyes fixed nervously on the situation in India. Much more important was the pervasive tendency in the Ottoman Empire to isolate and stigmatize ethnic-religious groups, which grew stronger in 1915 in the wake of military defeats, but was already discernible in October 1914. The inclusive Ottomanism that fastened the multiethnic empire together was increasingly sidelined by the conception of a homogeneous Turkish nation-state, which the political elite was prepared to impose by radical means and at the expense of ethnic and religious minorities. In Fall 1914 the government began to force through the basic principles of a "national economy." Before 1914, the generally manageable industrial sector, as well as the commerce of the Ottoman Empire had traditionally been in the hands of foreign producers, Ottoman Christians, and Jews—groups that enjoyed, under international treaties, extraterritorial legal status and extensive fiscal privileges. But on October 1, 1914, before the official entry into the war and months before the onset of systematic violence against Armenians, the Ottoman government canceled all the privileges associated with this system. Greeks and Armenians were forced out of their businesses and replaced with Muslim traders and officials. Between 1916 and 1918, a total of eighty new national enterprises incorporated a large part of the Greek and Armenian sector, but the transfer of Armenian property, in particular, began well before that, and from October 1914 numerous Greeks and Armenians fled across the Aegean from the coasts of Asia Minor.[334]

The way in which the war changed complex societies in a short space of time was also apparent in the British Empire. Even before the mobilization of its military and economic resources, which would decisively alter the relationship with the mother country, the first weeks of war reflected the multiplicity of experiences and expectations within the societies of the Empire. Unlike in Continental Europe, the British did not have to face a direct threat from the enemy (except in the special case of East Africa), once they had successfully eliminated Germany's land and sea forces in Asia and Africa. The jihad and other attempts to stir multiethnic populations into revolt against the Empire failed to bear fruit. Indeed, British military and political personnel tried to exploit the multiethnic character of enemy societies, using promises of national independence to gain new allies. This strategy was successful from 1915 onward in the Middle East and Arab regions of the Ottoman Empire, and again from 1917 when the British began to support national committees (of the Czechs, for example) to weaken the Habsburg monarchy. Since the political leadership in London had expected a short war in Europe, and since it did not want to upset the delicate balance of power

"MY BOYS!"

The British Empire as an idealized defensive community: *Punch,* 1914 (orig. 1885).

among dominions, colonies, and territories with a special status such as India and Ireland, it decided at first to involve the Empire as little as possible in the contest with the Central Powers. But the first few weeks of the war forced a rethink in London.

In Egypt, most particularly, the British authorities feared that the Ottoman proclamation of jihad would elicit a mass response. They therefore declared martial law there and established formal control, declaring Egypt a British protectorate in December and rejecting any Ottoman claim to sovereignty over it. Behind these decisions lay the huge strategic importance of the Suez Canal, the key artery of the Empire.

For a short time, Egypt's formal detachment from the Ottoman Empire encouraged hopes that the country was on the road to independence. Many Egyptians therefore accepted the protectorate solution. But the need to sustain large troop contingents, as well as rising inflation and more exacting labor duties, proved to be major burdens for the population. Hopes of a change in

Anglo-Egyptian relations increased with the approach of a ceasefire and were given a powerful boost in 1917 when President Woodrow Wilson embraced the principle of national self-determination.[335]

Contrary to German and Turkish hopes for an anticolonial revolt among Indian Muslims, Summer 1914 saw a wave of declarations of loyalty to London. The Subcontinent was of special importance for the British government and military, since it traditionally counted as the "barracks of the Eastern seas," providing an invaluable recruitment base. In India itself, the Indian National Congress (INC) was fragmented and attracted few delegates.[336] In December 1914, its representatives went out of their way to assure the King-Emperor and the British people of India's "profound devotion to the throne, its unswerving allegiance to the British connection, and its firm resolve to stand by the Empire at all hazards and at all costs." Nor was this mere rhetoric: 1.2 million Indian troops would be deployed in France, Egypt, and Mesopotamia. The young lawyer Mahatma Gandhi, recently returned from South Africa, threw all his weight behind the recruitment drive.[337]

On July 30, after consultation with the War Ministry in London, the viceroy of India, Lord Hardinge, proposed the formation of a special Indian Expeditionary Force. By the fall no less than one-third of the British forces in France came from India, consisting either of Indians or of British troops withdrawn from the Subcontinent. After the Ottoman Empire entered the war, it was feared that the maintenance of such a large contingent in Europe might endanger the Raj, and so the colonial government in Delhi pushed for a separate campaign by British-Indian troops in Mesopotamia.[338]

In other parts of the Empire as well, specific perspectives emerged. Politicians in the former white settler colonies of Canada, Australia, and New Zealand initially used demonstrative avowals of loyalty to affirm their special dominion status and their growing self-confidence within the Empire. Andrew Fisher, the leader of the Australian Labour Party, was prepared to give "our last man and our last shilling" for the common struggle. And Wilfrid Laurier, leader of the Canadian Liberal Party and French Canadian icon, set out his own vision of an imperial civil peace. Canadians would postpone their own demands: "we raise no question, we take no exception, we offer no criticism, so long as there is danger at the front."[339] From 1915 at the latest, however, quite different trends came to the fore: involvement in the war, with its often high cost in lives, became the prelude to nation-building in the dominions, and the introduction of universal conscription led to bitter controversy, especially in Canada.

The most dangerous conflict and threat to British policy came in Ireland. The home rule debate that had dominated British internal politics for a long time came to a head precisely in the weeks and months before August 1914. The Home Rule Bill had cleared its last parliamentary hurdles in May, but it was not seen as a satisfactory solution either by pro-British unionists or by Irish nationalists; the danger of a civil war in Ireland therefore loomed large. When the implementation of home rule was suspended until after the war, the reactions on the two sides were very different. Whereas the nationalists led by John Redmond could claim at best a nominal success, the unionists welcomed the deferment of autonomy status. They presented themselves as loyal and patriotic, but they also demanded assurances that they would not later be punished with home rule against their will in return for their sacrifices. The conflict was therefore merely put on the back burner. But Redmond's declarations of loyalty, like those of Cardinal Logue (who called for military action to defend Catholics in Belgium and France), reflected the hope of many Irish people that, by taking part in the war, they would achieve the goal of far-reaching autonomy on the dominion model. The formation of Irish divisions was also associated with hopes that the common experience of war would foster reconciliation and prevent a slide into civil war. References to the German invasion of Belgium were supposed to remind Irish people of their allegiances and their duty to fight in the war for civilization.[340] Furthermore, the food supplies boom triggered by the war strengthened the prospects for Ireland's largely agrarian economy. At the time, no one could foresee the escalation that would culminate in the armed rising on Easter Monday 1916.[341]

A crisis hit the Empire only in South Africa. When the government headed by Louis Botha declared war on Germany on September 8, the ruling white minority party ignored the majority of the white population (especially the pro-German Boer nationalists), who had been opposed to British policy during the July crisis. Entry into the war was also highly controversial among the black majority; only the small middle classes and tribal chiefs supported the Union government in the hope of achieving greater political rights. When the government, going well beyond what was expected of it, promised London that it would attack the German colony in Southwest Africa, it provoked an open confrontation. The Boer general Christian Frederick Beyers rebelled against the decision, taking with him 12,000 soldiers and deserted officers from the Union army. The dismissal of Colonel Maritz, who had been in contact with German officers, served as the signal for the pro-German group of Old Boers. Government troops, joined by loyal Boers from the civilian militia, quickly put down the mutiny with considerable bloodshed. Although this averted a new showdown over Boer secession from the Empire—which German assurances had fueled in Summer 1914—tensions within the Boer population grew deeper. But the crisis was successfully contained, because two Boers who had fought against the British in 1899 were serving in the government alongside Botha and his war minister Jan Smuts, pledging loyalty to London in order to enhance the status of South Africa within the Empire. In 1916 Botha was able to introduce general conscription as in Britain itself, and Smuts, despite all the military problems, could present the conquest of German Southwest Africa and East Africa as the first great victory of the South African nation, to which Cape British and Boers alike had contributed.[342] Thus, in South Africa in Summer and Fall 1914, the war showed the outlines of a sub-imperialism in which a formerly colonized population now acted as imperial players.[343] Although there would be no rerun of the South African war, the deep split within white society at the end of 1914 could not be overlooked. When elections were held the next year, more than half of Afrikaaners rejected the war. Even the dominion status plus home rule formula advocated by Smuts and Botha—the key achievement of 1905—became less convincing as the war dragged on and the military and economic burdens piled up. The radical nationalism of Barry Hertzog, who insisted on secession and a South African republic outside the Empire, was also an answer to these conflicts.[344]

8. EXPLAINING THE WAR
National Security and Intellectual Empowerment

Since 1912 the German writer Hermann Hesse had been living in Switzerland. In September 1914 he wrote an article that appeared in the November 3 issue of the *Neue Zürcher Zeitung:* its title "O Friends, Not These Tones" (*O Freunde, nicht diese Töne*), referring to Schiller's celebrated *Ode to Joy,* placed it firmly within the tradition of humanist universalism. Hesse pointed out that, since the outbreak of war, the internationalism of art, literature, and science had changed into a sharp mutual antagonism among the intellectual and artistic elites of the belligerent countries: "In recent times, we have noticed distressing signs of an ominous confusion of thought. We hear of a cancellation of German patents in Russia, a boycott of German music in France, and a similar boycott of intellectual works from enemy nations in Germany. In [the] future, very many German newspapers will no longer translate, acknowledge, or criticize works by English, French, Russian, or Japanese authors." The article reflected the writer's ambivalent situation: early on he had reported to the German embassy as a war volunteer, but had been turned down because of his myopia and sent to the prisoners of war welfare center in Berne. He organized book collections for the men there and in 1916–1917 published two newspapers for that particular readership: the *Deutsche Interniertenzeitung* and the *Sonntagsboten für die deutschen Kriegsgefangenen.* In the article quoted earlier, however, he also had criticized German writers and academics— and the German reactions were correspondingly aggressive, many colleagues turning against him and branding him a "traitor." Hesse found himself caught up in a difficult political standoff, which he still described many years later as the decisive turning point in his life.[345] He saw that the intellectuals who in the decades before 1914 had often profited from the internationalization of universities and artistic or literary ventures were now placing loyalty to their nation above any transnational perception. In the post-August clash of interpretations of the war, intellectuals sought to affirm their national identity, to justify the war by conjuring up self-images and enemy-images, and to define the locus of intellectuals in the wartime societies. Precisely because there were at first no political justifications of the war—a serious discussion on war aims began to take shape only in the fall—these intellectual debates filled a certain interpretive vacuum. Academics, publicists, journalists, and artists all seemed to want to make some contribution of their own to the war.

The early reactions of intellectuals were certainly diverse. It made a great difference whether they were expressed in official statements or private chronicles. In Vienna, while Hugo von Hofmannsthal published a euphoric poem "Österreichs Antwort" (Austria's Answer) in the *Neue Freie Presse*, Arthur Schnitzler noted in his diary on August 5, "At the hotel news of Britain's declaration of war on Germany!—World war. World ruin. Immense, atrocious news. . . . We are living through a terrible moment in world history. In [a] few days the picture of the world has completely changed. You think you are dreaming. Everyone has lost their bearings."[346] On August 2, the Heidelberg historian Karl Hampe took part in a meeting at city hall organized by the city and the university. The next day, the *Heidelberger Neueste Nachrichten* reported "that all layers of the population were represented there, from simple workers to scholars, from simple soldiers to senior officers." The speech that made the greatest impression on Hampe, as on most of those present, was the one by the theologian Ernst Troeltsch; it had a resonance that went far beyond the immediate occasion.[347]

Troeltsch had been active in Heidelberg since 1894 as a professor of systematic theology. In addressing the question of how social models of world religions, and particularly of Protestantism, had influenced the shape of European modernity, his works before 1914 had focused on a developmental process that could not be limited to individual nation-states. Now, however, he emphasized the achievements of the new German nation-state, its economic strength, and the transmission of its bourgeois culture into every part of society. But he also warned of the "great disappointments of peace" and the assumption that the general progress would "by itself, through the power of the intellect, necessarily move forward." Rather, there always comes "a point when this intellectual development must be defended and claimed by acting decisively and risking one's life." For Troeltsch, as for many cultured middle-class members of his audience, this necessary alternation between peace and war was a leitmotif of German history, which allowed him to describe the present war as the third Silesian war (after those of 1866 and 1870), and hence to compare the stand of the German nation-state against the "envy and hatred of foreigners" to the struggle of Frederick the Great's Prussia in the Seven Years' War. The enemy-image here focused less on France (with its hopes of revenge for the defeat of 1871) than on a general decline of civilization, with special reference to the Slavs, whose barbarism and lack of freedom made the enemies' unequal alliance lack credibility from the beginning. "Nourished by a thoughtless, badgering style of journalism, working with all the arts of criminal conspiracy, barbaric fury, and Asiatic deceit, the Slav world is breaking loose against us, and a brilliant nation like the French, the nation of European democracy and liberty, seeks in a contradictory alliance with them to overrun us and cook its vengeful soup over this common fire."

Whereas the issue in 1870–1871 had been the completion of nation-building, in 1914 it was the "existence and life" of the nation and the preservation of past achievements, which Troeltsch identified with the "inner freedom of the German citizen" and contrasted with Russia's lack of freedom. The task was not only to shake off the Russian danger but also to shape Germany's freedom in accordance with the demands of political modernity. Troeltsch further recalled that the war, with its burdens and sacrifices that everyone had to bear, would also bring the development of external freedom, of equal political participation, for all Germans. This already pointed to political reforms—of the Prussian *Dreiklassenwahlrecht* (three-class vote franchise), for example, which graded electoral rights according to taxation levels. "We shall bring back with us the survival of our fatherland and the victory of freedom—not only freedom from tsarist absolutism, but also the inner freedom of the German citizen. Where this is still wanting, it will have to be considered that the good of the fatherland was entrusted equally to all men between 17 and 45 years of age, and that only their good will, their joyful enthusiasm for the fatherland, made the great enterprise possible." The unifying wartime sacrifice inspired his vision of a national community over and above traditional class conflicts, where the common man would grasp "the necessity of discipline and unity, not only for the class struggle of farmers and laborers but for the nation in its entirety." This is where Troeltsch's idea of a special German freedom came in—a conception that made him one of the protagonists of German "cultural values" against the foes in the East and West and that culminated in his book of 1916 *Die deutsche Idee von der Freiheit* (The German Idea of Freedom).[348]

Remarkably, then, Troeltsch the liberal expected the war to end in political-constitutional advances and the social reconciliation that had failed to materialize since 1871, which had left all the successes of the young nation-state under a cloud of ambiguity. But Troeltsch the theologian also saw in modern war a contradictory juxtaposition of rationality, planning, and expertise with an irruption of irrationality and unpredictability. This war would no longer be fought with the poetic weapons and chivalrous ethic of the early nineteenth century. With the advent of mechanization, the classical heroism of battle was no longer imaginable: "These difficult technological weapons of modern warfare require endless preparation and calculation, and in the face of an invisible enemy and threats from unknown directions, they involve complex forethought for huge numbers of men and massive backup and protection. They are weapons of calculation, deliberation, and persistence, and only at a few highpoints is there the dramatic heroism for which the soul of youth thirsts." Moreover, the war radically questioned all traditional bourgeois promises of security, the nineteenth-century social and political structures resting on reason, and hence the very basis of bourgeois culture: "Today all rational calculations are collapsing around us. All stock exchange lists and predictions, insurance policies and interest calculations, safeguards against accidents and surprises: the whole elaborate construction of our society has ground to a halt, and over us all lies the immensity, the incalculability, the plenitude of the possible."[349] For all its national self-consciousness and enemy-images, Troeltsch's unusually clear-sighted analysis anticipated many aspects of the military, political, and social experience of the war, not least the basis it laid for later departures from the traditional order.

The influential classical philologist and researcher Ulrich von Wilamowitz-Moellendorff, born in 1848 to a conservative landowning family, who had been on the staff of Berlin university since 1894 and served as president of the Prussian Academy of Sciences since 1902, also took a position on the war in numerous speeches and essays. On August 27, 1914, he spoke in favor of a cross-class German people's army to fight the war, comparing it to the historical Crusades. Oppressed by the tsarist regime, Russian soldiers had no idea "why or for what they were fighting"; whereas the French demonstrated that "they were consciously fighting for their fatherland." But for Wilamowitz-Moellendorff the main ideological enemy was Great Britain: its envy of German economic and scientific achievements and of German freedom, together with its crudely materialistic society, resulted in the waging of a dishonest war. Unlike France, Britain did not send "all its sons off to fight, but specially recruited personnel." For this reason, it was the real origin of "the evil driving spirit that has summoned the war from hell, the spirit of envy and the spirit of hypocrisy. What do they not begrudge us? They want to undermine our freedom and independence, that edifice of order, civilized conduct, and confident liberty. . . . When an English naval officer looks out through fine, beautiful binoculars, casting his eye around at German crusaders, it irks him . . . that the binoculars were made in Jena, and that the cables crossing the ocean were mostly produced in Charlottenburg am Nonnendamm."[350] Wilamowitz is also a good example of how science became the instrument of a new ideological nationalism, which spelled the end of the international research community. In the human and social sciences, Germany had indeed been a model for modern scholarship, evident not least in the study of antiquity that Wilamowitz himself had represented in many foreign academies and universities. Now the international networking was put in reverse, so that in 1915 he was stripped of membership of the Paris Académie des Inscriptions et Belles-Lettres because of his prowar speeches. When his son Tycho was killed in action, he had to recognize that the forms and casualties typical of this war had nothing in common with those of 1870 that he had known as a one-year volunteer.

Wilamowitz-Moellendorff was a signatory of the "Manifesto of the Ninety-Three"—an appeal "To the Civilized World" issued on October 4, 1914—and a co-initiator of the declaration by university professors of the German Reich (October 16, 1914), both of which were featured in the *Krieg der Geister* (War of Minds) collection edited by Hermann Kellermann in the following year. The occasion for this initiative was the destruction of the Louvain library, described earlier. The French writer Romain Rolland, a great admirer of German culture who had emigrated to Switzerland on account of his pacifist principles, heard the news and wrote a letter to the prominent German literary figure Gerhart Hauptmann, contrasting the cultural tradition of Goethe with German martial practices that reminded him more of Attila the Hun.[351] Similar statements followed above the names of British academics, universities, and learned societies. The German reactions—ranging from Hauptmann's response (in which he regretted the destruction, but offset it against a German soldier's shattered breast) to the appeal "To the Civilized World"—triggered a competitive race to provide an explanation of the war. The escalation of military violence led to a wave of intellectual justifications and all-out cultural warfare. This, too, gave Louvain a symbolic media presence that lasted far beyond the opening stages of the war.[352]

The appeal "To the Civilized World," signed by ninety-three prominent writers, artists, and academics, appeared in all the major German dailies on October 4, 1914, and was soon translated into ten languages. Protesting against the international criticism of German militarism and allegations of atrocities committed in Belgium, it countered that German soldiers had been "ambushed" by people "shooting out of houses," that they had not been guilty of "undisciplined cruelty," that Allied troops had operated with dum-dum bullets on the western front, and that in the east "the earth [was] saturated with the blood of women and children unmercifully butchered by wild Russian troops." Most strikingly, however, the signatories identified programmatically with the concept of militarism and criticized a widespread tendency to set it at odds with German culture: "It is not true that the combat against our so-called militarism is not a combat against our civil nation, as our enemies hypocritically pretend it is. Were it not for German militarism German civilization would long since have been extirpated. For its protection it arose in a land which for centuries had been plagued by bands of robbers as no other land had been. The German Army and the German people are one."[353] The idea of this public appeal had been pushed early on by the head of the Imperial Navy news department, Heinrich Löhlein, and the mayor of Berlin, Georg Reicke. The text itself came from the pen of the writer Ludwig Fulda, and in its sixfold repetition of the phrase "It is not true" was reminiscent of Martin Luther's famous theses of 1517. The list of signatories included scientists such as Emil Fischer, Adolf von Harnack, and Gustav von Schmoller, but also such artists as Engelbert Humperdinck and Max Liebermann; while convinced pacifists like Albert Einstein and Hermann Hesse refused to add their names, and others such as the physicist Max Planck and the economist Lujo Brentano distanced themselves from the text soon after its publication.[354] The "Declaration of University Teachers of the German Reich," published on October 16 by four thousand senior academics under Wilamowitz's guidance, similarly emphasized the nexus between German culture and militarism: "It is our belief that, for the whole of European civilization, salvation lies in the victory that German 'militarism'—the discipline, loyalty, and spirit of sacrifice of the united German people—shall secure."[355]

The behavior of many intellectuals who before 1914 had been highly open to the world, and in some cases critical of the German state and the role of the military, underlined the intensity of the pressure on them to prove their loyalty to the nation. It pointed to a widespread feeling, especially among the educated middle classes, that Germany's adversaries looked with envy and resentment on its achievements and its strength. Nevertheless, it came as a surprise that so many German intellectuals seemed oblivious to the international impact of their appeal, to the impression it would give of cultural arrogance as the reverse side of the country's undisputed successes in science and university life. In France, in particular, there were calls for the severing of relations with German academics and university institutions, which were put into practice in the case of Wilamowitz and others. In fact, the isolation of German academia would last in some domains for many years after 1918.

These conceptions that Germans had of themselves found condensed expression in the theme of the "ideas of 1914," with an underlying attempt to interpret the war in terms of a clash between overarching national principles and values. Already in August 1914, the journalist Paul Rohrbach gave notice of a series of articles on "the German war," which would highlight the struggle for a distinctive "German idea" in the world and such values as brotherhood, honesty, and selflessness. Like Wilamowitz, he saw Britain as the main antagonist, synonymous with soulless materialism, uncaring individualism, and moral decadence. Although many German intellectuals did not go along with Werner Sombart's extreme formulations in his book *Händler und Helden* (Merchants and Heroes), published in February 1915, most shared the view that the intellectual-ideological clash between German culture and Western civilization was most clearly traceable in the British foe.

Also in 1914, the Münster-based sociologist and economist Johann Plenge gave a series of lectures *Der Krieg und die Volkswirtschaft* (The War and the National Economy), which appeared in book form the following year. These derived the "ideas of 1914" from a world-historic confrontation with claims that the revolutionary French tradition of 1789 was universally valid. Whereas the "ideas of 1789" had brought forth the bourgeois-capitalist order in a series of stages, now it was up to Germany, with the "ideas of 1914," to establish a completely new political and social model on the basis of the "people's cooperation [*Volksgenossenschaft*] of national socialism." Here lay the epochal change: "Nowhere in the world since 1789 has there been such a revolution as the German revolution of 1914. It is a revolution to develop and combine all the country's forces in the twentieth century against the destructive liberation [that took place] in the nineteenth. . . . For the second time, an emperor roams the world as leader of a people with the immense, world-shaping sense of the power of maximum unity. It may be said that the 'ideas of 1914,' the ideas of German organization, are destined to march across the world as triumphantly as the 'ideas of 1789' once did."[356] This linked up with Troeltsch's idea of a special German conception of freedom, which differed from French or British democracy in the weight it placed on transindividual community, enlightened bureaucracy, and parliamentary control and particularly on efficient organization as the antithesis of traditional class society.[357] In 1915, the Swedish theorist of constitutional law Rudolf Kjellén offered a suggestive formulation of these opposites: the ideas of 1914 were identified with duty, order, justice, community and self-sacrifice, in contrast to atomistic western European individualism.

Whereas Troeltsch began to move away from such ideas in the course of the war, few German writers were as vehement as Thomas Mann in clinging to a distinctive German consciousness and cultural-ideological hostility to the West. Rejected as unfit for military service in 1914 at the age of 39, he was looking for a role for himself as a writer in the service of the nation. His position, which he developed in works from *Gedanken im Kriege* (Thoughts in Wartime; Fall 1914) to *Reflections of a Nonpolitical Man* (1918), was also an attempt to cast himself as a national war writer.[358] The first of these texts, written for Samuel Fischer's journal *Neue Rundschau*, was more than just an author's patriotic *prise de parti*, for it hinted at the conflicts between the Mann brothers, Thomas and Heinrich, which burst into the open with Heinrich's publication of his Zola essay in 1915. In novels such as *Der Untertan* (translated as Man of Straw), Heinrich was fiercely critical of the official Wilhelmine culture and made no secret of his admiration for French republicanism, but at the beginning of the war he found himself without a publisher willing to publish his writings. To his brother Thomas—who, in his enthusiasm for the war, had emphasized on August 7 his "deepest sympathy for this despised, fateful, and mysterious Germany"—he calmly wrote that in his view Germany would go on to lose the war.[359]

In his *Gedanken im Kriege*, Thomas Mann went so far as to identify the clash between culture and civilization as a marker of Germany's special position in the world. He identified culture with "coherence, style, form, composure, and taste," standing for "organization of the mind," whereas civilization referred to "reason, enlightenment, pacification, moral acquisition, analytic dissolution—*intellect*." This counterposition could be expressed even more ideologically in the concepts of Western "politics" and German "morality," allowing Mann to distance himself more generally from the model of western European politics: "For politics is a question of reason, democracy, and civilization; but morality is a question of culture and the soul." The Germans as moralists, as "moral beings," had "seen the visitation coming: indeed, had in a way longed for it."[360] Even the fundamental problem for Mann himself—the rift between artist and citizen, intellect and life, which had still dominated his novella *Death in Venice*—seemed to have been resolved in the war.[361] Tackling British accusations that the Germans' barbaric conduct of the war was overshadowing their earlier cultural achievements, he retorted that everything— hospitals and elementary schools, academic establishments and railroads, as well as modern weapons—was an equal expression of Germany's cultural achievements, that there could be no contradiction between culture and the military side of life. Mann insisted on Germany's special modernity: its social protection meant that it was "in truth a much more modern country than, for example, [France's] unhealthy plutocratic bourgeois republic." Its "social imperium" represented a more convincing model of progress than "any kind of lawyers' parliamentarism, which, when in an exuberant mood, still bandies around straw phrases from 1789." Mann's polemic, directed not only against France but also against his brother's idealization of France, served to underpin the opposition he drew between the German values of 1914 and the French ideas of 1789.[362]

The political thrust of this opposition came down to a fundamentally different, German concept of progress. "One thing is true," Mann wrote, "the Germans are by no means as enamored as their Western neighbors are of the word 'civilization;' they are not used to waving it around in the braggardly French style, nor to using it in the bigoted English manner. They have always preferred 'culture' as a word and a concept. Why so? Because that word has a more human content, whereas in the other one we sense more than a hint of political reverberations." Since Germany was a nation of "metaphysics, pedagogy, and music," a "morally oriented nation," it had also "shown itself to be more hesitant and incurious than others in the political advance toward democracy, the reform of parliamentary government, or even republicanism." However, its distinctive moralism could not be separated from the "soldierly ethos," and whereas other nations "fully assumed the civilian form of doing things . . . German militarism was in truth the form and appearance of German morality."[363]

The cultural mobilization in the early months of war was not in itself unique to Germany; what did differentiate intellectuals there was the programmatic, almost panicky and hysterical rejection of western European models and their insistence on a special road to progress that could not be compared with that of France or Britain. In France, too, many artists, publicists, and academics immediately joined the national self-affirmation, which in the early weeks of the war sometimes took grotesque forms. Thus, Franco-German cultural warfare broke out over the works of Richard Wagner, which had dominated the Parisian music scene around 1900 to the point of obsession, but which now fell under a blanket ban. Bitter debates even persisted after the war. Should Wagner be outlawed as Germany's national composer, it was asked, or could he be admitted as the expression of a musical universalism that escaped all national enemy-images?[364]

In France, unlike in Germany, intellectuals looked to the experience of 1789 and the historic achievements of the nation that had resulted from the revolution. Right from the start, Romain Rolland viewed the army as the bridge between the nation and its history; the "élan de la Marseillaise" was a heroic, religious attitude on the part of all French people, linking the meaning of August 1914 with the revolutionary nation of September 1792, and underlying its preparedness to fight to defend the gains it had made since 1789. War against the external enemy also served to regenerate the nation, to renew it through a relationship with its own history. This self-definition was so revealing because Rolland included the Catholic and conservative camp in the *union sacrée*, thereby binding all ideological currents to the legacy of the revolution.[365] Faced with the mission of combating German militarism, the historical tensions between secular republicanism, conservatism, and Catholicism receded into the background. But the different currents did not disappear, as we can see from the controversy over whether the Königsberg philosopher Immanuel Kant was in some way responsible for the outbreak of the war. Staunch republicans identified with his rationalism and his respect for the moral autonomy of the individual, while anti-republicans condemned in him not only German philosophy but also the traditions of the French Revolution and the Third Republic. This debate, which involved the whole legacy of republicanism, again brought into the open the contradictory positions bound up with the Dreyfus affair.[366]

So, the *union sacrée* did not produce a homogeneous self-image of the French nation, but rather a peculiar amalgam of loci of national memory, by no means without tensions or contradictions, though held together by awareness of a universal historical mission: "We have rung in a new age of world history. . . . France is not yet finished. We are witnessing its resurrection. Always the same: Bouvines, crusades, cathedrals, revolution; always the world's knights, God's paladins," Rolland wrote.[367] The fact that at first there was scarcely any opposition to the *union sacrée,* whether from Catholics, who may well have been disturbed by the secular commitment to a sanctified republic; from syndicalists and socialists; or from political conservatives underlined the unifying effect of the sense that France was under attack from an aggressive militarism. Ideological conflicts were in retreat, without actually being eliminated. It was also clear that the tensions within French society were no longer so great that the outbreak of war could jeopardize the existence of the Third Republic. The association of war and civil war so characteristic of 1870–1871 was not a feature of the situation in August 1914. These unifying aspects were apparent in the reactions of other leading intellectuals such as Henri Bergson, Émile Durkheim, Ernest Lavisse, and Joseph Bédier, while representatives of the Catholic Church, in professing their loyalty, recognized the opportunity to promote reconciliation with the republican state.

In London, the bishop compared British soldiers to none other than Jesus Christ. They were waging a holy war for freedom, honor, and chivalry.[368] Many intellectuals saw the war as a battle between good and evil, arguing for the need to combat Prussian militarism, but also differentiating between the autocratic regime and the German people. The well-known historian Arthur Lionel Smith stressed that only war would create a coherent emotional basis for national unity. This open statement of the foundations of the modern nation, as a community of the living, the dead, and the unborn, was a significant attempt to lend the nation historical legitimacy across time through a vision of shared experience, memory, and future existence.[369] In Britain as in Germany, university professors played a key role in this endeavor. In 1914, influential historians at Oxford University—from which Kaiser Wilhelm II had received an honorary doctorate as recently as 1907—published an essay *Why We Are at War: Great Britain's Case,* which, as we have seen, was a reply to the declarations of German university teachers.[370] Focusing on a philosophical tradition going back to Hegel, in which they saw a dangerous deification of the state, they argued that in the post-1871 history of the German Reich this tradition had finally combined with Prussian-style militarism. Their rejection of this trend thus offered them a basis on which to espouse the British self-image of parliamentary political freedom and, above all, the rule of law.[371] The special laws that suspended parts of this long British tradition were hardly an issue in the first weeks of war, but there too the crisis of the liberal model would make itself felt in 1916–1917.

Russian intellectuals, by contrast, saw the war as an opportunity for spiritual renewal—indeed, as a Day of Judgment for Russia. One Moscow-based philosophy professor stressed that the importance of the war lay in a "renewal of life" that would presuppose "death for the fatherland." In this context, the writer Maxim Gorky was a noteworthy exception, noting with his early skepticism, "One thing is clear: we are entering the first act of a worldwide tragedy."[372]

In many societies not directly involved in the events of August 1914, the war also triggered new ways of thinking about their national destiny. This was true particularly in the United States, where, since the late nineteenth century, debate on the ethnic factors of race, nationality, and language had become more and more pressing in connection with the makeup of the American nation. In view of the high immigration quotas, economic prosperity, and external expansion, the alternatives of multiethnic pluralism and Anglo-driven exclusion were plain to see.[373] The European war made such discussions all the more intense, even before the United States entered the fray. In August 1914, when thousands of immigrants were required by their native countries to return home or to make declarations of support, many sections of the American public were shocked to learn how varied and contradictory were the feelings and reactions within immigrant communities. Another factor in this debate was the influx of war publications appealing to the loyalty of people now living in America.[374] Already before the First World War, Theodore Roosevelt and Woodrow Wilson had emphasized the "melting pot" as the integrative element in national identity and, being historians, recognized its origins in early American history. This ideal now came under increasing pressure, however. In 1891 Roosevelt had lashed out against any idea of visibly incorporating ethnic roots into the national orientation of individual Americans; they were supposed to think of themselves as Americans *tout court,* not as "Irish-Americans, German-Americans, or Native-Americans." With the coming of war and its dangers of polarization, Roosevelt insisted all the more fiercely on this self-perception: "There is no room in this country for hyphenated Americanism. . . . A hyphenated American is not an American at all." Unlike in European societies, reflection on the nation in the United States was not originally tied to an exclusively ethnic consciousness. But things did not remain so with the return to the idea of the melting pot. The very supporters of the "Americanization movement," which set its sights on greater assimilation, stepped up their pressure on German Americans to make a profession of faith in the United States. In the long term, the evocative image of the melting pot, which had arisen in the period of traditional agrarian society, drew more and more criticism and was replaced with an ever more extensive system of controls and restrictions, which reached a climax with the Immigration Act of 1924.[375]

9. FIVE MONTHS ON
Mobilization, Disillusion, and the Irony of War

Contrary to the stream of predictions during the summer mobilization, the war did not end at Christmas. The societies at home therefore adjusted to the conditions of a lengthy conflict. A fundraising appeal for a field chapel automobile, which appeared in the *Kölnische Volkszeitung* on November 6, 1914, was unexpectedly successful, bringing in 113,849.80 reichsmarks by December 22. In addition to stretchers and vestment cabinets in the rear, the car in question had a mobile altar table: "The rear doors seem to open out like altar wings and are decorated . . . with pictures of Archangel Michael, St. Gereon [or] . . . St. Maurice, the two warrior saints of Cologne, and of St. Barbara, the patron saint of artillery. . . . The armored tabernacle is bullet-proof and theft-proof, with Krupp's 5-millimeter thick chrome nickel steel."[376] As people celebrated the first Christmas of the war, the conditions varied enormously at the military fronts; the trenches in the west, east, and south; and in their home countries. Although the festivities were not yet at the mercy of supply problems, the reality of war was already omnipresent, not only in the casualty lists but also in the realm of consumption. While manufacturers of the Sunlicht soap brand coopted the ideal-typical German sailor active all over the world ("Tossed by wind and waves, / Germany's pride keeps watch high above! / The sun's heat browns his skin / Sunlicht soap keeps him clean"), and while the producers of Diana air rifles recalled Lettow-Vorbeck's African troops, the Thalysia Paul Garms GmbH corporation hailed a German victory "in the domain of feminine culture." At last the "rejection of all things foreign" meant that the end was nigh for the "French corset fashions that have made nearly all German women sick"; the "Thalysia-Edelformer" would no longer follow French styles and obstruct women's breathing and movement. Nor was it a "shameless" garment like its French equivalents, for "it changed an overly lavish form into something more delicate and appropriate to Germany." It was a "truly German sanitary marvel."[377] On December 24, 1914, Theodor Wolff reported from Berlin on the "crush in many shops, especially the large department stores." His request for people to give children more modest gifts, "so that the 'war Christmas' leaves a special mark on them," bore little or no fruit, since the distribution of presents was as lavish as in previous years. Their character was not the same, however: there was a prevalence of "soldierly Christmas boxes" and "field gray uniforms" for boys, who now played at "trenches" like "all kids in Berlin. Tin soldiers in toy shops and items of uniform for children nearly sold out."[378]

In the Heidelberg home of the historian Karl Hampe, there was no getting away from the "general mood of sobriety," but hopes were high that the war would end well. On December 25 they performed a "world history in the wood-engraving style," with comic Kasper glove puppets that reviewed the expectations of the previous summer. "The devil is an Englishman, who stirs everyone else up against Kasper, but in the end has to swim as a submarine in the large manure barrel. The Frenchman *Chassepot* and the Russian *Diebich* [Thief], who want to pounce on Kasper together, fail in their attempt, become separated from each other, and are driven into the 'Masurian lakes' of the manure barrel as well. Japs, the infernal crocodile, does finally manage to snatch at Kasper's appendix, but the animal cannot be caught for the moment and is left alive to wreak vengeance for the other enemies."[379]

Conditions were different at the various fronts. While Count Harry Kessler, serving as an officer on the eastern front, celebrated Christmas with "a fir tree from the Imperial forest" and recorded the persistence of "a kind of stifled melancholy," many groups of men saw the holiday out in the trenches.[380] Even "generous gifts" from home and staged visits to the men could not prevent local ceasefires at many points on the western front, especially where British and German troops faced each other across the lines. French units also took part in these on occasion. Often they began with the festivities on Christmas Eve, when the Germans sang carols and put up Christmas trees. After shouts across the trenches that ended in a mutual understanding not to open fire, soldiers from both sides met in no-man's-land, sang songs together, exchanged presents, and even held soccer matches. In some places, the ceasefire lasted for days until the beginning of January. A distinctive soldierly culture became visible, a stubborn mutual understanding that, not allowing itself to become fixated on national enemy-images, reflected the common experience of positional warfare and disillusionment with life in the trenches. On January 3, 1915, the student Karl Aldag wrote home to his family telling them of the previous few days at the front: "New Year's Eve was quite special here. An English officer came over with a white flag and asked for a ceasefire between 11 and 3 to bury the dead. . . . It couldn't go on like that, so we sent someone over to say they might like to get in the trenches, as we would start shooting. The officer replied that he was sorry, but their people were no longer obeying orders. They didn't feel like it anymore. The soldiers say they can't lie in wet trenches any more; France is done for. . . . They're mercenaries really, they just go on strike. Of course we didn't start shooting, because our communication trench is also full of water all the time, and it's good that we could walk under cover without risking our lives. . . . Our lieutenants went over and put their names down in an album belonging to the English officers. One day an English officer came and told us that their people in charge had given an order to start shooting at our trenches, so we might like to take cover."[381]

In December 1914 the region of Armentières, where most of these local ceasefires occurred, did not yet have the reinforced trench systems that became so typical later on. The inadequacy of the existing trenches, which kept filling up with water because of defective drainage, helps explain what happened.[382] The "Christmas truce" was primarily a phenomenon among rank-and-file soldiers and NCOs. When soldiers wrote home about it, isolated reports began to appear in British and German newspapers,[383] catching the military authorities on either side unawares. They responded with closer and more centralized control of frontline sectors, so that the fraternization was not repeated at Christmas in the following years.[384]

The war moved millions of soldiers from their homes to completely new places, where they would never have gone if it had not been for the mobilization. When this was not part of an actual combat deployment, the war became almost like an adventure trip. After the Ottoman Empire joined in, the British supreme command feared an attack on the Suez Canal that would have grave implications for links with all parts of the Empire, and so it was decided to station some 28,000 men from the dominions (mainly Australia and New Zealand) in Egypt. On December 26, 1914, the 21-year-old William Henry Dawkins, an NCO in an Australian engineering unit, wrote home to his mother: "Yesterday was Christmas and our thoughts were in Australia. Some of my section had the most gorgeous dinner—about six courses. They said that they only had to shut their eyes and they could imagine they were home again. Here we have many bands and at daybreak yesterday we had our carols played. Mother—whoever dreamt of having Christmas under the Pyramids—very strange, when one comes to think about it."[385]

Such idylls remained the exception. Every war is ironic, because every war is worse than expected.[386] Paul Fussell's celebrated dictum applies in exemplary manner to the First World War, since a wide gap opened up in the first days, weeks, and months between expectations and actual experiences. This constituted a large part of the reality change in Summer and Fall 1914, and its effects lasted far longer precisely because all the protagonists over the coming months and years would repeatedly attempt to close the gap. As the crisis escalated—from a local conflict over Serbia through the regional showdown in southeastern Europe to the Continental confrontation and eventual global war—a distinctive landscape took shape in which the most diverse theaters overlapped and interacted with one another in complex ways. This panorama included geographically distinct war zones, in the narrow sense of the term, but also radically changed experiential spaces for the soldiers and new social-political maps in the home countries, as well as "mental maps" of national self-images and enemy-images in the context of various media. But where did the war itself stand at the end of the year? What had the preceding five months shown? What expectations had been fulfilled, and where had a wartime reality appeared that no longer corresponded to any prediction and did not lie in a simple continuum with earlier experiences. Where was the distinctiveness of this war becoming visible?

(1) The crisis of July 1914 already demonstrated the dire effects of basic miscalculations, pressure to act, and excessive strain on individuals. But these then intensified during the opening stages of the war—whether in the faulty German assumptions about delayed Russian deployment or in the French underestimation of German attack strength. All such errors guided men's actions and developed a reality of their own. The protagonists in Summer 1914 might have operated with war as a possibility, but soon they were confronted with a reality that exceeded both quantitatively and qualitatively anything they could have anticipated. This gave rise to the paradox of hypertrophied war plans or scenarios plus inadequate preparation, in the munitions short-fall, for example, as well as in supply problems and the failure to shift the economy onto a war footing. The issue was not so much whether it would be a short war from which everyone could be home by Christmas. Neither military commanders like Schlieffen and Moltke (who knew the impact of new weapons systems and the capacity for social mobilization) nor rational pacifists like Angell and Bloch (who had foreseen with some precision the reality of the 1914 battlefield) were convinced in the summer of the likelihood of a short war or one big decisive battle. But the casualty figures right at the beginning of the war pointed to a new quality of killing and dying. They set a new threshold of violence from which it was no longer possible to retreat. Part of the new experience of war, therefore, was the parity and randomness of mass casualties and the constant possibility of death in the trenches. Long-range firepower had enormously increased through the deployment of heavy artillery and machine guns. Although soldiers in the ever-larger network of trenches often faced one another across no more than a few dozen meters,

hand-to-hand combat remained the exception. Effective weapons fire and shelling of battle zones kept the men on the two sides from getting to close quarters; the combination of remote killing with a permanent threat of death thus became a defining characteristic of the war. Anonymous, mechanized killing took the place of a visible enemy. The aiming of artillery fire from a great distance behind the front was redolent of abstract bureaucratic practices, in which the consequences of murderous action remained beyond the field of vision.

The soaring casualty figures set in train a mechanism for justification of the slaughter and ultimately of the war itself. For the higher the toll, the less it seemed possible to abandon the thought of victory or to water it down into a compromise solution. Each new wave of casualties hardened the will to triumph over the enemy, because nothing else would guarantee a fitting acknowledgment or justification of the casualties. But this prolonged the war and exacted an ever-higher death toll.

(2) While the new weaponry and battle conditions reflected the technological and logistical prowess and mobilization energies of the respective societies, military convictions and strategies were in many respects, despite the detailed planning of the prewar years, still marked by the traditions of the previous century. Commanders clung to these until well into the second year of war, and it was only after a period of escalating violence and profound exhaustion in 1916 that a new model began to take shape in the final years of 1917–1918 and to disentangle itself from nineteenth-century thinking.[387] The professionally planned and executed mobilizations, which in a few days carried millions of men in thousands of trains to deployment areas hundreds or thousands of kilometers distant, as well as the significance of worldwide communications and raw materials supply, reflected not only the economic, technological, and infrastructural potential but also the degree of global interdependence. The latter manifested itself most impressively at the very moment when conflicts between states and nations seemed to overshadow any transnational link. It, too, was a legacy of the progress that European societies had made up to the beginning of the war.

But the primacy of the offensive, together with faith in a single decisive battle and an ultimate conviction that the momentum of infantry attack could overpower even superior defenses, suggested conventional notions of honorable male warfare dependent on individual will. In reality, the basic problem of all offensive strategies—the possibility of catastrophic defeats and strategic dead-ends—did not take long to reveal itself. Whether in the so-called frontier battles, the early German attacks up to the Battle of the Marne, the Russian offensives in East Prussia, or the Austro-Hungarian operations in Galicia and Serbia, soaring casualty figures underlined the annihilating power of effective defensive weapons, as well as the supply and communications problem for million-strong armies operating over great distances. The categories of will to victory, infantry momentum, or soldierly *élan* were not enough to master such challenges. In this light, one of the aspects of the Great War that is hardest to understand is that for a long time military commanders blanked out or suppressed the implications of the new integrated weapons systems, particularly modern artillery and machine guns; despite the experience of the first battles, they continued to rely on attack, expecting it to discipline the mass armies even as it broke down in the face of long-range artillery and rapid-fire guns. This basic conviction persisted, even when the goal of a breakthrough could not be achieved through the concentration of men, weapons, and munitions in a small area. The difficult process of shaking off the nineteenth-century theory of war, and of grappling with new weapons or the frictions and contingencies of the battlefield, would accompany this twentieth-century war from the outset. The price for all the countries involved in it would be very high.

(3) Soon after the war broke out, it displayed a quantitatively new scale of bloodshed, but also a preparedness to use violence against civilians in the context of offensive operations, whether in Belgium and France, in eastern Europe, or in the Zeppelin raids on the English coast. The Austro-Hungarian military was particularly violent in its treatment of the Serbian population. Its loss of inhibitions and its ideological criminalization of the enemy were evidence of a long history of conflict and radicalization before 1908. In the case of the German atrocities in Belgium, time constraints and misunderstandings combined with the uncontrollable logic of a military socialization that fanned memories of the French partisans in 1870–1871 and anti-Catholic stereotypes. In war's shadow, a propensity to violence developed in which enemy-images acquired a new ideological and racist intensity, lowering inhibition levels. This was the background

to the occupation regimes in Belgium, northern France, and the Balkans, as well as to wider effects of battlefield violence such as the treatment of the wounded and of prisoners of war. In all these spheres, quantitative scale brought a new quality to the challenges.

(4) At the end of 1914, there were not really any visible winners—only armies that, having suffered extremely high losses, had to recognize that they had achieved few if any of their original aims. The only country to have really profited from the start of global hostilities was Japan, which at minimal cost had decisively strengthened its power in the Pacific. But the dominant impression in Continental Europe was one of failed objectives. After a summer in which all countries had by and large efficiently mobilized, Germany failed to bring off the swift military decision in the west that would at least have given it a favorable starting position for a long war. In the east, on the other hand, the Russian invasion was repulsed and the ground laid for new offensives in 1915. The lack of success on the western front testified to problems of supply and communications, and to the mental and physical overburdening of soldiers and officers, who had to wage a deep offensive under enormous time pressure. At least German troops were fighting on enemy territory, and nothing would change in this respect until Fall 1918. Although back home this repeatedly fueled the idea of a quick victory, the new head of the OHL, Falkenhayn, already had admitted in late November 1914 that Germany's high casualty figures left it with no chance of waging an offensive war in the west. Thus, in the eyes of the country's top military leader, and just a few weeks after the fantasies of its September program of war aims, Germany had forfeited the capacity to dictate the conditions of a future peace to its enemies.

Within a few months, the conflict was raging in three parts of the world— Europe, Asia, and Africa—and the areas outside Europe developed an autonomous dynamic that went beyond the idea of a simple extension of European theaters. This was true especially of the war in Africa, with its high casualty figures among native peoples; but it was also true of Japan's drive for hegemony in East Asia and the incipient U.S. economic and monetary commitment in favor of the Entente, which contradicted its professions of political neutrality.

Outside Europe, Germany soon found itself on the defensive in the communications and information war, and within weeks it lost all scope for military action except in German East Africa. Naval operations in the first few weeks already showed the worldwide dimension of supply and communications, while the loss of maritime bases together with the onset of the British naval blockade denied Germany global access to raw materials, forcing it to place the economy on an especially radical war footing. Germany's capacity for effective action beyond Continental and eastern Europe was now limited to military support for the Ottoman Empire and political destabilization of colonial societies. While the German navy at least helped the Ottoman Empire control the strategically important straits and maintain a blockade of the Black Sea against Russia, the military balance sheet for the Dual Monarchy five months into the war was catastrophic. After the failed operations in Serbia and Galicia, 150,000 men had been killed and the officer and NCO corps decimated.[388]

France's offensive Plan XVII had failed in Lorraine, with extremely high losses. But despite a weeks-long retreat, French troops, reinforced by the BEF, had prevented a German breakthrough on the western front along the lines of the Schlieffen Plan. Although the war in the west was now being fought on large chunks of French territory, and although the loss of coal-mining and industrial areas in northwestern France was a heavy blow, Germany at the end of the year still found itself fighting on two fronts, whereas the French army, for all its losses, remained intact and able to take advantage of short supply and communication lines. Still, there were then "three Frances" occupying different geographical zones and experiential spaces: the France of the fighting front, a strip 5–10 kilometers wide; the France of the home front, which shored up the military front economically and emotionally; and occupied France. The emergence of new internal borders and demographic redistribution were features in Belgium and parts of Italy and Russia as well, whereas no equivalent existed in either Britain or Germany.[389]

In 1914 Britain initially contributed quite small forces to the battles on the western front. While the Irish conflict receded for the time being, the Empire soon experienced the global dimension of the war—not only in the troop recruitment from India and the dominions for the war in Europe but also in the theaters of East Asia; South, West, and East Africa; and the territories of the Ottoman Empire; the latter would soon become foci of military developments on the Suez Canal, in Mesopotamia, and from Spring 1915 in the straits between the Mediterranean and the Black Sea. At first, London was greatly concerned about the proclamation of jihad, and it stationed Indian troops not primarily in western Europe but in Mesopotamia. By the end of the year, despite some impressive actions by German squadrons and individual ships, the British navy had won global supremacy at sea and successfully blockaded German ports. This ensured that Britain would have global access to raw materials and the freedom to transport goods and troops.

Contrary to widespread expectations before 1914, Russia carried out a relatively swift and seamless mobilization. Successes against Austro-Hungarian troops in Galicia were set against the lost encirclement battles and the numerous prisoners taken by German forces under Hindenburg and Ludendorff. Even graver for the long-term supply situation on both the military and home fronts was the German-assisted Ottoman blockade of the Black Sea, which made it difficult for Russia to obtain goods from abroad.

In contrast to the skepticism about the fate of the great empires that had unleashed a wave of doomsday scenarios in the press before 1914, the opening stages of the war by no means brought about an immediate internal collapse in Russia. Nor did they in Austria-Hungary or the Ottoman Empire, which succeeded in mobilizing multiethnic forces and avoiding mass desertions and mutinies. Military reverses, especially in the case of Austria-Hungary, were not a consequence of multiethnic composition, but they did fuel much anti-Czech sentiment in an army high command dominated by Austrian officers. The colonial dimension of the war was visible on the British and French sides in the deployment of black African or Indian troops in western Europe, and Germans in particular responded to this with racist labels and accusations of barbarous, uncivilized warfare.

(5) By late 1914, the question was posed as to why a war so costly in human lives was being fought at all, and later it was asked why it was lasting so long. Although the casualty figures shocked people in every belligerent country, the cohesion of societies and armies was not in question at the end of 1914. At first sight this was a legacy of the nineteenth century: it further underlined the power of nations, states, and empires as points of reference for action and justification. The subjective perception among all players that they were defending themselves from external attack, not waging an offensive war themselves, played a key role in the mobilization of loyalty. At

the same time, however, the war was a point of departure for a new tectonics of loyalty and recognition: workers and trade unions, Catholics, Jews, and ethnic minorities saw their own loyalty as a capital asset, a basis for future recognition and status improvement, for greater integration, autonomy, or national political advances.

Whether flanked by monarchic elements (as in Germany, Austria-Hungary, Russia, and Great Britain) or driven along by images of the *république en danger* (as in France), a war nationalism with at least three dimensions developed right from the beginning. Ideologically, this manifested itself in cultural wars among European intellectuals, writers, and artists, in which the widespread internationalism of the pre-1914 period turned into all the more aggressive nationalisms. The backdrop to these new ideologies was not least a bitter contest over social-political and cultural claims of modernity, over possession of the future, so to speak, as the German reactions showed most clearly. Furthermore, what appeared behind the *Burgfrieden, union sacrée,* or social truce was a much more complex political tectonics than the patriotic rhetoric of unity had suggested in August 1914. The political-ideological suspension of hostilities opened up opportunities for new forms of political recognition and participation. For the workers' parties and trade unions; but also for German and French Catholics; for Jews in Vienna; for Czechs, Croats, or Poles; and for Irish and Indians in the British Empire, the war meant a chance to stake a claim, by virtue of loyalty to the nation, on equal participation and an improved political status. In 1914 this claim was not yet associated with clear-cut programs, but the future was open and the expectations ranged far and wide. It would therefore be wrong to equate the unity rhetoric at the beginning of the war with national homogenization. Rather, what took shape in August 1914 was a new kind of market, in which wartime negotiations and disputes revolved around political positions, social interests, and the capital of national recognition.

The third dimension of the war nationalism was a rigid exclusion of suspect groups and individuals on the grounds of alleged national disloyalty. From the beginning, this went together with various forms of violence: spy mania, campaigns against foreign brands and words, a climate of suspicion, economic dispossession, physical violence against "enemy aliens," and internment in special camps demonstrated how thin the veneer of bourgeois civilization had suddenly become. This development was strengthened by the conversion of wartime states into organs of control and centralization; a genuine alternative would become visible only in 1917, with the mix of war and revolution in Russia. The price for this early habituation in collective endurance, in the ongoing struggle for survival, was the erosion of liberal substance in the wartime states and societies. Freedoms and participatory rights won through long and arduous struggle were revoked or suspended in favor of state centralism and bureaucratic-military controls; new models and categories of social and political order took shape, invoking the objective constraints of war.

In the early months of the war, nation, state, and empire acquired increasing salience in the rhetorical appeals to unity but also in the focus on loyalty in all the belligerent countries. The many promises associated with the nation stepped up the pressure for victory, in order to give meaning to the colossal sacrifices. But the gap between promises and expectations and people's actual experience of the war was already discernible by the end of 1914. It marked a legitimation barrier: when further developments revealed that many expectations were not being fulfilled, it gnawed at the credibility and legitimacy of the discourse of national unity. What soldiers and people at home lived through would undermine some of the power of the traditional conceptions of nation, state, and empire. New reference models of political and social identity appeared alongside them: the soldiers' frontline community, the league of combatants, and from 1917 also the idea of revolution and international organization.

(6) In August 1914 military scenarios and attack plans existed for a major European conflict, but the European powers did not have clearly formulated long-term war aims. As the September program of German chancellor Bethmann Hollweg demonstrated, such objectives mostly developed during the course of military operations over the next few months. This paradoxical contrast between minute, detailed planning and the absence of final strategic goals suggested that neither side had a long-term plan to risk a war. Indeed, there was a political vacuum when it came to justifications and explanations of the war. This may account for the fact that the intellectual debates of the cultural war spread like wildfire: they offered a substitute at the level of interpretations and justifications, filling the strategic policy void at least in the short run. But the ideologically charged counterpositions, with their

resounding either-or categories, also placed any talk of compromise under suspicion of betrayal.

(7) Right from the beginning, the war not only unfolded in well-defined combat zones but also developed a dynamic of its own in different imagined spaces. One important experience, after the first few months, was the contrast between narrow, increasingly fixed positions on the western front and wide zones of great mobility in eastern and southeastern Europe. This situation, which brought the opposition between "boundary" and "frontier" into the experience of war, soon found expression in iconic images: ever-stronger, more sophisticated trenches symbolizing the frozen war in the west, against the repeated possibility of mobile operations in the east, where individuals like Hindenburg or Ludendorff, and later General Brusilov on the Russian side acquired the aura of commanders with real scope for action in a war of machines. They were war heroes, visible soldiers with individual features and experiences, who stood out against the mass anonymity of killing and being killed. Imagined spaces also arose at other levels: in the newly conquered and occupied areas of eastern Europe, with their early colonial connotations, but also in the vision of global theaters of war. Contemporary publicity, media hype concerning military heroes outside Europe, the presence of troops recruited from the colonies, the juxtaposed mobilizations in local areas and remote colonies, and the hopes invested in the worldwide ideological mobilization and instrumentalization of national movements and secessionism—all these ways of thinking about global spaces acquired great suggestive power. At the same time, the early months of war showed how great was the contrast between such global imaginings and the local reality on the ground.

4

STASIS AND MOVEMENT

1915

COULD SPACE be translated into time? Could control over space be converted into a time advantage or, vice versa, was it possible for acceleration and rapid military successes to compensate for an unfavorable spatial position? At the beginning of 1915, space and time were decisive factors in the war, and as the year progressed Britain and Russia in particular would use operational theaters in different ways to obtain a temporal advantage. The blockade of German coasts, combined with global maritime supremacy, would enable Britain to profit from the unexpected lengthening of the war by bringing the global resources of the Empire to bear. The early months had already shown, however, that the war could not be won only with British money and French or Russian soldiers.[1] For Russia too, space could be converted into time. When the Central Powers broke through the front at Gorlice and Tarnów in Summer 1915, the Russian armies withdrew eastward from Poland to the area of the Pripet marshes. Although their military situation worsened considerably as a result, and the Tsar, after a series of defeats, personally assumed the supreme command, the Russian military gained time through this retreat and avoided being forced into a separate peace with Germany. In fact, it redoubled its war effort with Allied help, so that in Summer 1916 it was able to launch a successful counteroffensive under General Brusilov.

Within this same space-time perspective, we may say that in Summer and Fall 1914 Germany ultimately failed to solve its spatial problem and strategic dilemma through a quick military decision on the western front and so was unable to prevent the development of a two-front war in the east and west. But the questions of who would profit from a longer war and how the control of space would permit its continuation became increasingly important in 1915. They applied far beyond Continental Europe, being associated with the problem of global supply links and worldwide communications (British links with the Empire via the Atlantic and the Suez Canal, the cutting of Russia's supply routes by the Central Powers' blockade of the Black Sea and the Baltic).

1. LOOKING FOR MILITARY DECISIONS
Battle Zones and Strategies

At the beginning of 1915, however, these developments were not yet visible; the main focus was on possible ways out of the impasse of positional warfare. This quest for other options would mark the second year of the war. Its consequences were apparent in the involvement of Italy and Bulgaria and in the search for new technological openings. Exploring alternatives on January 5, 1915, Britain's war minister Lord Kitchener warned the commander of the BEF, Sir John French: "Although it is essential to defend the line we now hold, troops over and above what is necessary for that service could better be employed elsewhere."[2]

Initially the BEF on the western front consisted of only six divisions, in comparison with the eighty-two French divisions, and it suffered only a small share of the casualties in the early months of the war. After the strategic success of the Battle of the Marne, and the psychological effects of having stopped the weeks-long advances of German armies and forced them to retreat, the British commanders had to deal with a self-confident French general staff that was pushing to resume a war of movement. Only when the British shouldered a greater burden of the war on the Continent would their de facto subordination to French orders change, and in this initial phase Sir John French's main concern was, through operations of his own, to stake a claim to equal participation in basic strategic decisions.

Despite this widespread feeling among British commanders, the British position had tended to strengthen during these early months. The unpredictable length of the war meant that Britain, more than all other belligerent states, could make the most of its special strategic advantages; the world reach of the Royal Navy ensured access to raw materials and all the economic and military resources of the Empire. Other important factors were the long-distance blockade of German ports and the use of loans to finance the war.[3] Thus, at the beginning of 1915, the political and military leadership in London could seriously ponder alternative strategies to force a decision in the war. While John French pushed for a breakthrough in the west on the Somme, resistance was growing in government circles against any strengthening of British forces in the front against Germany. In view of Whitehall's long pursuit of geostrategic interests in Egypt, the possible threat to the Suez Canal, and the dual blockade of Russia by the German navy in the Baltic and the Turkish navy at the entrance to the Black Sea, the Ottoman Empire soon came into consideration as another possible front. Military action there would secure Russia's supply lines, and the entry of Greece and Bulgaria into the war on the Allied side might uncoil the fixed fronts from the southeast along the Danube.

But while a major anti-Ottoman naval operation was being considered, the possible targets of attack varied considerably. David Lloyd George argued for Salonica (today's Thessaloniki), Kitchener for a strike on Alexandretta in the south of the Ottoman Empire and the eastern corner of the Mediterranean. In the end Winston Churchill, the First Lord of the Admiralty, won approval for his idea of a direct attack by sea on the Dardanelles, which was supposed to start in February 1915.[4] This relied on the scenario of a push through the straits to threaten Constantinople itself. The strategy corresponded to the nineteenth-century tradition of high imperialism, when the dispatch of gunboats was seen as the way to cow inferior colonial adversaries. But it strikingly underestimated the defensive possibilities at the disposal of the Ottomans.

The attack by sea along the Dardanelles coast ensued in February and March 1915. These operations did indeed give a boost to those in Bulgaria, Greece, and Italy who were of a mind to support the Allies and to profit from the expected dismemberment of the Ottoman Empire in the southeastern Mediterranean. The British Admiralty stressed that the use of older ships would not seriously weaken the Royal Navy's overall strength, that no troops would have to be deployed, and that the operations could be called off at any time. Nevertheless, the action ended in military disaster, when three British battleships were sunk in March by mines and coastal batteries, and seven more were so badly damaged that three of them would never again be fit for service. With just one minelayer, built by the Germans in 1912, the Turkish navy had successfully sealed the mouth of the Dardanelles.[5] In this battle too, one could see the asymmetry between attack and defense that was so characteristic of the land war on the western front. Only a small part of the coastal batteries could be eliminated. Churchill, as navy minister, found himself the butt of harsh criticism and eventually had to resign. But the role of military prestige in the dominant thinking prevented an end to the operation. Attempts were made to compensate for the Royal Navy's failure with large-scale troop landings; the plan now was to destroy the shore defenses before undertaking a fresh attack by sea.[6]

A force of 70,000 men, consisting of British and French units and, most prominently, 30,000 troops from the Australian and New Zealand Army Corps (ANZAC), was assembled under Kitchener's command. But the operations that began on April 25 repeated the experience of recent months on the western front: relatively weak defenders, suitably equipped with weapons and dug into fortified positions, were able to throw back a numerically far superior attacking force supported by heavy naval artillery. No will to charge on the part of the infantry could break this asymmetry. Then there were all the contingencies of a large-scale land operation under special geographical conditions. At the southern tip of the peninsula, at Cape Helles, the Turks put up very effective resistance to the actual landings. Some of the ANZAC troops were put down on unsuitable parts of the coast, where they had to cope with small landing strips and jagged cliffs that suited the defenders. In addition, the commander of the Turkish 19th Division, Mustafa Kemal, the later founder of the republic known as Kemal Atatürk, brought up reinforcements that threatened to drive the ANZAC troops back into the sea. In the section where the British troops landed, a combination of barbed-wire fences and machine-gun nests led to dead and wounded figures as high as 70 per cent of the attack units. At the same time, the Turkish units too were almost completely wiped out.

The chain of military defeats before 1914 had left its mark on the thinking of most Turkish officers. A record of Mustafa Kemal's order was found in the uniform of one fallen soldier: "I assume there are none among us who would not rather die than repeat the shameful story of the Balkan war. If we do have such men among us, however, we will immediately arrest them and line them up for execution." But this rhetoric about readiness for the supreme sacrifice sat uneasily with a battlefield on which many officers had to use drawn weapons to force their men to attack. High desertion rates confirm the Turkish troops' growing fear of the forces assembled off Gallipoli. Hopes that universal conscription would create a Western-style "nation in arms" ran up against the reality of murderous positional warfare.[7]

Instead of the planned rapid advance inland, the Allied soldiers could at most establish small bridgeheads. And after this opening attack, the whole enterprise became bogged down in high-loss positional warfare.[8] Attacks by either side did nothing to change this. In May 1915 alone, the Turkish forces lost more than 10,000 men out of 40,000 sent to confront the 10,000-strong ANZAC troops. But on the Allied side too, a British attempt on the night of August 6 to land 20,000 men at Suval Bay to improve the drastic supply situation of the landed troops and to complete the invasion ended in signal failure;[9] once more the steep cliff defenses and the strong Ottoman resistance proved to be insuperable obstacles. Only after this further reverse was London prepared to call off the undertaking and to pull out the remaining troops. This naval evacuation did proceed successfully in December 1915, but the attackers had to leave behind huge quantities of equipment and heavy weaponry.[10]

For the home societies of the ANZAC troops, the battles at Gallipoli were symbolic tests of national worth that would be hard to overestimate. A war narrative took shape that still today serves to preserve national self-images through the medium of public holidays and war memorials.[11] At first the main ideal was the young "citizen-soldier" from Australia or New Zealand, who gave up his farmer's work and took up arms to march into battle and defend the Empire; he was the epitome of a gallant and courageous, heroic, and indestructible soldier.[12] In the collective imagination of the dominion societies, citizen-soldiers were seeking adventure and coming-of-age experiences as boys did back home. To be a soldier expressed the natural qualities of young men: "The average young New Zealander . . . , especially the young New Zealander who lives in the country, is half a soldier before he is enrolled."[13] The home societies of Australia and New Zealand played a large role in these developments. The major newspapers sent special correspondents to Gallipoli whose reports had a huge impact on the public. In their reports, the battle appeared as a great achievement of the countries' troops, while the disastrous military results were hushed up as far as possible. In people's eyes at the time, Gallipoli established a decisive aspect of "Australasia Triumphant," to quote the title of a book by Arthur Adcock that was repeatedly awarded as a school prize during the war years.[14] In this way, Gallipoli became a symbolic site of nation-building in Australia and New Zealand. The journalistic reporting played an important role in army recruitment, stimulating many a young man to sign up and keep the struggle going on the western front. But the quite different face of reality, with its poor equipment and at best amateurish tactics, was not communicated to the antipodean public. For soldiers from the dominions, Gallipoli involved a painful learning process that soon dispelled images of war as one big summer camp or boy scout adventure; it taught them the basics of what training, equipment, and tactics meant in a context of positional warfare.[15] When the Australian and New Zealand units began to be deployed on the western front in 1916, the soldiers knew that no "boys' war" awaited them. The sometimes highly successful stationing of ANZAC forces there up to 1918 also had something to do with their initial experience in the eastern Mediterranean.[16]

In the Dardanelles campaign and at Gallipoli, as in the breakthrough attempts on the western front, there was a glaring mismatch between the high casualty figures and the paucity of visible results. The failed naval operation had shown how effectively a narrow strait could be blocked with mines, and how successfully a protected set of coastal batteries could operate in unison. In the second phase of the battle, a land army in defensive positions was able to fend off a combined assault by naval units and landing forces. The Allies lost more than 140,000 men, and although the Turkish casualties were in excess of 200,000, Gallipoli exposed the dramatic British underestimation of the strength of a Turkish army supported long before 1914 by German officers under Liman von Sanders. Yet, the capacity of the Turkish army for major offensive operations did considerably decline over the course of 1915. In view of the multiple fronts—in the Caucasus against Russia, and in the Near East and (in the medium term) Mesopotamia against British and Empire troops—the Ottoman military had to face massive supply

German aircraft over Egypt, 1915

problems that even German assistance, with aircraft in the Near East, for example, could not offset. After crossing the Sinai Peninsula in ten days, Turkish forces attacked the Suez Canal at the end of January 1915, but this did not have the intended effect of stirring a major anti-British jihad among the Muslim population of Egypt. Still, although the Turkish army withdrew to the Gaza-Beersheba line in southern Palestine, it was strengthened with German units and officers and managed to keep up the pressure on Sinai. It continued to threaten the Suez Canal, the most important link between Britain and East African and Indian parts of the Empire, and in 1916 it would launch another fruitless attack on it.[17]

The successful defense at Gallipoli could not conceal the military disaster suffered by the Turkish army in the Caucasus, which would be decisive for the Ottoman war experience and for the inward radicalization of ethnic-religious violence. Enver Pasha, the deputy supreme commander of Turkish forces, and the German chief of staff Bronsart von Schellendorf had ordered an offensive against the Russian army. But after a Russian attack had been halted, an Ottoman mid-winter counteroffensive across the mountain passes in

January 1915 came to grief at Sarikamish; barely 12,000 of the force of 90,000 Turkish soldiers lived to tell the tale. In spring, when the Russians launched an offensive in Anatolia that was supported by some Armenian nationalists, the violence against Armenians intensified in Ottoman-controlled areas. The defeats before 1914, as well as fears that the invasion in Anatolia would repeat the experience, served as a catalyst for the violence, but the root causes lay deeper.[18]

The close interlinking of the fronts in Continental Europe and the southeastern Mediterranean was evident in Spring 1915. Clashes in the British leadership between "Easterners" and "Westerners" essentially came down to whether the chief military target should be German forces in Belgium and France or whether the Allies should accept the positional warfare on the western front and look for areas of attack elsewhere. While John French, the top British commander, was convinced that the war with Germany could be won only on the western front, Churchill and Lloyd George opted for alternatives that led to the Gallipoli disaster. French, in his reply to Kitchener's inquiry in early January 1915, pointed out that after the heavy casualties of recent months the supply of soldiers and munitions was becoming an urgent problem. His underlying thought was that a strong British presence could stabilize the French positions and ensure that Britain had an equal say in basic strategic decisions.

Since Britain, unlike other European countries, had no conscript army to call upon in August 1914, the war minister, Kitchener, stepped up the publicity effort to attract volunteers. But the quantitative success of his New Armies recruitment campaign could not disguise the fact that previous high casualties had led to a shortage of experienced soldiers, especially NCOs and officers. To some extent, social relationships from civilian life were transferred to the military, as company owners took the leadership of units composed of their former employees.[19] An essential feature of these new units was the inexperience of many of their men, some of whom went to the front before their period of military training was over. True, efforts were made to integrate the newcomers with experienced frontline troops, but losses in the regular army made this increasingly difficult to achieve. Under

OPPOSITE: Map 4. The War in the Near and Middle East, 1914–1918

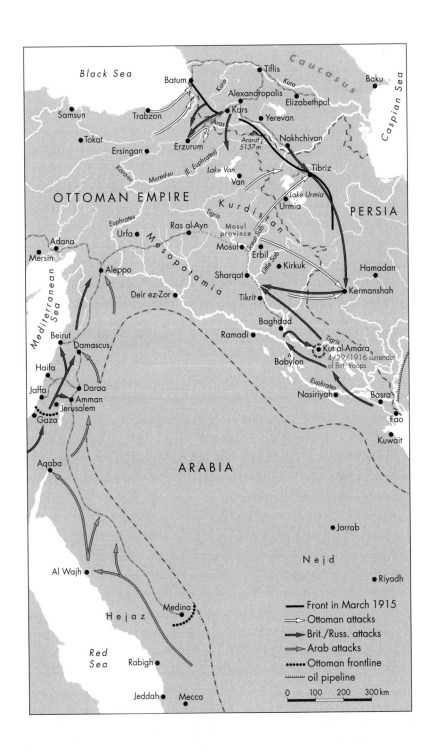

Black Sea

Caucasus

Batum

Tiflis

Baku

Caspian Sea

Samsun

Alexandropolis

Elizabethpol

Trabzon

Kars

Kura

Tokat

Yerevan

Ersingan

Erzurum

Aras

Nakhchivan

Ararat
5137 m

Tibriz

(E. Euphrates)

Karo-su

Mured-su

Lake Van

Van

Lake Urmia

PERSIA

Kurdistan

Tigris

Urmia

OTTOMAN EMPIRE

Euphrates

Urfa

Ras al-Ayn

Mosul
province

Mosul

Great Sab

Erbil

Kirkuk

Hamadan

Adana

Mesopotamia

Sharqat

Little Sab

Kermanshah

Mersin

Aleppo

Deir ez-Zor

Tikrit

Mediterranean
Sea

Baghdad

Beirut

Ramadi

Tigris

Kut al-Amara

Damascus

4/29/1916 surrender
of Brit. troops

Haifa

Babylon

Jaffa

Daraa

Euphrates

Gaza

Amman
Jerusalem

Nasiriyah

Basra

Fao

Kuwait

Aqaba

ARABIA

Jarrab

Nejd

Riyadh

Al Wajh

Hejaz

Medina

Red
Sea

Rabigh

——— Front in March 1915

⇨ Ottoman attacks

➡ Brit./Russ. attacks

➡ Arab attacks

•••• Ottoman frontline

⋯⋯ oil pipeline

Jeddah

Mecca

0   100   200   300 km

the conditions of positional warfare, this lack of experience could have dire effects. The sending of experienced units like the 29th Division to Salonica in February 1915, for example, was seen as putting a particularly onerous burden on the western front. And in the eyes of many British staff officers on the western front, the political decision to attack in the Dardanelles weakened their position in the war with the Germans.[20]

The worsening equipment problems weighed equally heavily in the balance. Special material for positional warfare such as barbed wire, digging implements, and sandbags was in short supply, as was heavy artillery ammunition. Nowhere else was the changed face of war so striking: whereas the British had fired 270,000 artillery rounds in the whole of the Boer War between 1899 and 1902, more than a million rounds were expended between mid-August 1914 and mid-February 1915. Kitchener, who had expected a long war from the outset, commented, "The old-fashioned little British Army was such an infinitely small proportion of the world's demand that looking after its equipment was not much more difficult than buying a straw hat at Harrods. But now I am going to need greater quantities of many things than have ever been made before."[21] The artillery supply problem, already felt by November 1914, came to a head at the beginning of the new year and would have far-reaching political consequences. The munitions crisis on the western front could be effectively invoked against supporters of military operations against the Ottoman Empire—at Gallipoli and elsewhere—since it could be argued that the high casualties in the west were attributable to poor artillery preparation for infantry attacks.

The general situation on the western front, whether in the engagements at Soissons, at La Bassée Canal in January or February, or in the winter battle in the Champagne in February and March 1915, showed a tendency to stagnation. Attacks from trench positions against defensive enemy lines led, if anything, to only inconsequential gains of territory; nowhere did they win greater successes, and they regularly incurred high casualties. One vivid case in point was the British attempt between March 10 and 14 to force a breakthrough at Neuve Chapelle.[22] The commander of the British Fourth Army, Sir Henry Rawlinson, carefully prepared for the infantry assault, deploying 340 artillery pieces (equal to the total number the BEF had sent to France in August 1914). On average, there was one gun every 5.5 meters along the whole of the frontline. Since Rawlinson already had to face the problem of ammunition shortages, he concentrated the shelling over a short time period and thereby secured the effect of surprise. Nevertheless, the massive opening barrage against a small area clearly marked the location at which the infantry troops would go over the top and begin the assault, so that the remaining defenders were able to gear themselves up for it.[23] The British soldiers, emerging from the trenches and establishing a line of fire, carried out a successful initial charge and went on to capture Neuve Chapelle. But since two artillery batteries had arrived late on the scene, a small part of the German trenches remained intact. From there, two companies with barely 200 men of the German 11th Fusilier Battalion raked the British assault units with fire from two serviceable machine guns, inflicting heavy losses in a short period of time and forcing them to call off the initial attack.

The battle of Neuve Chapelle highlighted a number of basic problems. First, there was the difficulty of coordinating infantry operations with artillery fire. If only a few enemy machine guns survived the bombardment, the defenders had the capacity to fight off a numerically superior force. Second, since the defenders occupied an inherently better position, they could use any hesitation in the attack to bring up reserves and prevent a deep breach in their lines. Usually they could operate in areas to the rear less affected by the prior shelling, whereas the attackers in that zone had to advance in a no-man's-land between trench systems that were difficult to overwhelm because of obstacles such as barbed wire and exposure to artillery fire. Third, a considerable imbalance existed between the revolutionary artillery and machine-gun technology, on the one hand, and the relative lack of sophistication of battlefield communications on the other. Field telephone cables could easily be destroyed by enemy action, with the result that links between command posts and combat troops usually had to be assured by messengers. Given the breadth of the front, the generally difficult terrain, and the intensity of fire, effective communication was therefore highly problematic. A further difficulty was to pinpoint the enemy. Although Royal Flying Corps aircraft were deployed over Neuve Chapelle, the quality of aerial observation was not good enough to locate the precise position of German defensive weapons. The fourth and most important factor was the extremely unequal effect of the weapons used by attackers and defenders. In this respect, Neuve

Chapelle was a perfect example of the simultaneous existence of historically unsynchronized aspects, the convergence of a traditional and a modern type of war. The commander of the Royal Scots Fusiliers Second Battalion left it up to his officers to decide whether they wanted to carry swords on that day. Two officers did carry them as tokens of chivalrous hand-to-hand combat reflecting the self-image of the British officer-gentleman, and on the first day of the Battle of the Somme in 1916 a British officer also brandished a sword on the battlefield.[24] Contrast that with the effect of just a couple of German machine guns that repulsed two British battalions! These highly efficient defensive weapons trashed all of the British forward planning. By 9:30 A.M., so many German reserves had been positioned behind the fractured frontline that any further attacks were senseless. By the end of the day, the British had gained at most 900 meters of territory across a width of slightly more than 3.5 kilometers. But the battle continued with further attacks and German counterattacks for another two days. Of the roughly 40,000 soldiers deployed on the British side, 7,000 British and 4,200 Indian were killed, wounded, or listed as missing. The German casualties amounted to approximately 10,600 men.[25] The basic pattern exemplified by this battle would continue on the western front until the end of 1916; only then, on account of the high casualties and paltry results, was there a switch to tactical and technological innovations.[26]

At least at first sight, these contrasting effects of weapons applied even in the case of cavalry units, where the emphasis on honor and tradition was especially pronounced. In fact, the share of mounted units declined sharply— from 9.3 percent in the BEF at the beginning of the war to 3.5 percent in 1915 and finally 1.7 percent in March 1918. However, these figures require closer analysis. On the one hand, given the hardening or indeed locking of the front into positional warfare, it was clear that the age of the classical cavalry attack was over. Yet partial successes were still possible, and not only during the early period of the war, especially in relation to scouting or in favorable conditions of mobile warfare such as those that repeatedly occurred on the eastern front. Until the massive deployment of armored vehicles in the final phase of the war, there was no convincing substitute for the combination of speed and mobility that cavalrymen could offer. In addition, there was the shock effect they could produce on the enemy.[27] This explains their use even at a time when they were hopelessly inferior in firepower.[28] In exceptional cases where the aspects of surprise and mobility came together, individual cavalry units could still operate successfully—for example, German units at the Battle of Lagarde in 1914, or the Canadian Cavalry Brigade at Cambrai in 1917 (which, following a break in the front, advanced 13 kilometers, captured 400 German soldiers, and seized nearly 100 machine guns).[29] Characteristically, the last attack by a major cavalry unit did not take place in Continental Europe, but in an area with no large, strong, or methodically constructed system of trenches. On October 31, 1917, under the command of General Edmund Allenby, the Australian Fourth Light Horse Brigade and the British Fifth Mounted Brigade joined forces in the capture of Beersheba.

After the disappointing spring campaigns in the Artois, the French offensives on the western front in September 1915 secured a breakthrough in the Champagne. The military thinking behind these rested on the assumption that, with sufficient artillery preparation, it would be possible to force a decision. On the eastern front, after successes in the summer, the Central Powers shifted from positional warfare to a war of movement, but the situation in the west continued to stagnate, with high casualty figures. French hopes for a decisive turn of events were therefore great in Fall 1915, as the order of the day issued by the French commander Joffre shows. The aim was to drive the Germans out of France, through a dual offensive in southeastern Champagne and toward Loos and the Vimy Heights in the Artois. The concentration of field guns again increased in comparison with earlier attacks, reaching a new maximum of 2,500 before the battle. The French had learned from previous experiences, particularly the number of devastating head wounds, and improved the equipment available to the infantry. According to the medical statistics, 13 percent of all wounds were to the head, 57 percent of which were fatal. Light steel helmets were therefore developed and distributed for the first time, and short haircuts became obligatory so that head wounds could be treated more effectively.[30] The comprehensive preparations, ranging from large-scale troop deployments and intensive artillery fire, through the stockpiling of ammunition and supply depots, to the building of complex trench systems, further increased the expectations of a breakthrough.

The 22-year-old French infantryman René Arnaud noted with surprise how empty the battlefield seemed; the ever more solid trench systems on both sides made the enemy largely invisible except during an actual attack. He also based hopes of a breakthrough on the increased firepower of the French artillery: "From the protection of the raised ground behind us a battery of 75mm guns has been firing in four pieces one after the other, making the air vibrate as if from the ringing of four bells. The shells whined as they passed over our heads and then, after a short silence, came the four sharp barks as they struck home. Under this torrent of fire we thought that everything in the enemy lines must inevitably be pounded to dust."[31] Yet again the pattern of earlier attacks was repeated: the artillery bombardment, more intense than ever before, still could not completely destroy the echeloned German trench system. A few effectively placed defensive weapons were able to repel the attackers and inflict high casualties on them. Slight and often merely temporary gains had to be offset against the figures of dead, missing, and wounded. In southeastern Champagne, until it was called off at the end of September, the battle raged over a strip of land as little as three kilometers wide. In all the offensives in the Champagne from December 1914 to March 1915 and again in September and October 1915, as well as in the Artois region between May and July 1915, the French lost a total of 204,000 dead, missing, and wounded.[32] Yet until late 1916 and early 1917 commanders on all sides stuck to the cult of the offensive, with the idea that a concentration and disciplining of the soldiers' will could force a military decision on the western front.

Meanwhile, other developments were taking place on the east European fronts. Since Summer and Fall 1915, a fundamental difference in the course of the war and in men's experiences at the front had opened up between western and eastern Europe. In late 1914 the Russian thrust into East Prussia had been beaten back, but Russian forces had at first been successful in operations against the Austro-Hungarian front. Following Hindenburg's appointment as commander in chief (*Oberbefehlshaber*) of all German forces in the east—the German abbreviation "OB Ost" for this military title gave rise to the name "Ober Ost" for the de facto military state and its distinctive occupation regime—and in view of the stalemate in the west, Hindenburg and Conrad von Hötzendorf believed they could force a decision in the war in the east. However, Hindenburg's urging of Falkenhayn to accept his point of view resulted in growing tensions within the German top brass, since the head of the Oberste Heeresleitug (OHL) stuck to the policy of concentrating military forces on the western front. From October 1914 to April 1915, there was no decisive change on the eastern front (which stretched twice the length of the western front, from the Baltic to the Black Sea). While Austro-Hungarian troops in the Carpathians had to defend against Russian attacks from Winter 1914 on, and were several times on the brink of collapse, the Germans managed in February 1915 to repulse in Masuria a new Russian invasion of East Prussia.

Particularly in the extreme conditions of the Carpathian winter war, Austro-Hungarian forces suffered huge casualty rates comparable to those of the British, French, and Germans at the Somme and Verdun in 1916. A combination of military hubris, woefully insufficient preparation for a winter war, improvised field decisions, weak troop concentrations at strategically important points, and inadequate reserves added up to a catastrophe that, in the fight to relieve the fortress at Przemyśl, had some parallels with the Battle of Stalingrad in the Second World War. In order to free this garrison of 120,000 men, the Austro-Hungarian high command eventually sacrificed 800,000 dead, wounded, and missing. When the fortress finally had to surrender in Spring 1915, many Imperial army units had been whittled down to the status of a militia. Under these circumstances, with dependence on German aid stronger than ever, the claim of Conrad von Hötzendorf in particular that the Austro-Hungarian army should continue to make and implement strategic decisions independently became more and more problematic.[33]

Despite German successes in the northern sector of the eastern front, the critical situation in the Carpathians meant that a Russian breakthrough toward Hungary could not be ruled out. For the east European combat zone, Italy's entry into the war on the Allied side in May 1915 therefore spelled a further danger, since Austro-Hungarian troops had to be at least temporarily relocated to the Alpine front. Only then was Falkenhayn willing to support a German offensive to relieve its hard-pressed ally, although unlike Hindenburg he looked only to limited measures, rather than major space gains, to weaken the enemy. At Tarnów and Gorlice southeast of Krakow, the Germans finally succeeded in breaking through the Russian lines in April and May 1915. This led to unplanned or unexpected territorial conquests. Almost the whole of Galicia, including the Przemyśl fortress, and Bukovina were won back. A further offensive, begun in Summer 1915 between the Baltic Sea and the

San River, eventually led to the conquest of much of Russian Poland (includ-ing Warsaw), while a diversionary attack to the north brought Lithuania and its capital Vilnius into German hands. The Russian forces now staged a deep retreat. But the Central Powers offensive slackened only in September 1915, and the front finally stabilized on a line from Riga in the north down through Dünaburg (Daugavpils) to Czernowitz.

In 1915, the main strategic significance of the eastern front lay in its tying up of sizable German forces (two-thirds of the total in September 1915). Despite the crisis that led to the breakthrough by the Central Powers in Sum-mer 1915, Russia did not collapse. Indeed, there was a further mobilization of its economic resources, and even some movement again at the political level. In retreating, the Russian army used space successfully as a military resource against the Central Powers, and the enemy offensives did in fact come to a halt. At the same time, the deployment of more German forces in the east crucially helped France and Britain to gain breathing space in the west, which enabled them to overcome the munitions and supply crisis of Spring 1915. When the Germans ended their offensive in the east at the end of the year and again focused their attention on the western front, they found themselves facing newly strengthened enemies, and it was these who in 1916 sought to decide the war in the great battles of Verdun and the Somme.[34]

2. VIOLENCE IN WAR'S SHADOW
Occupation Regimes and Ethnic Difference

The advances of Summer 1915 brought a completely new power constel-lation to eastern Europe, since large areas came under long-term occupa-tion by the Central Powers. In many other regions too, military occupation would mark the lives of large numbers of people. By 1918 a total of some 17 million civilians were living under regimes imposed by foreign armies: these included 6 million in Belgium, 2.5 million in northern France, and 3 million in the new "Ober Ost" region established in 1915. Austria-Hungary set up its own occupation zones in the "Military Government of Lublin," in Serbia, Montenegro, Albania, Romania, and northeastern Italy.[35] From Sum-mer 1914 on, the occupied parts of northern France experienced a process of administrative, cultural, and economic Germanization.[36]

Belgium found itself in a special situation as both occupied country and combat zone. Moreover, there were fronts not only against the British and French but also against the Belgian troops who defended a small area on the Yser symbolizing the survival of free Belgium. Many other Belgians took the road of exile.

The German occupation of Belgium was established in two different zones.[37] Areas near the front were characterized by a strict military regime, while in the larger territory of the General Government, including the capital Brussels, a combination of civilian and military authorities were in charge. The German invasion of the neutral country, and the role of the king as symbol of resistance, gave rise at first to a broad national consensus, a relatively homogeneous war patriotism. This also included resistance networks, with their own information service and an underground press. Between 25,000 and 30,000 young Belgians were smuggled across the border into the Netherlands, where they could link up with the Belgian army on the Yser front. Each year symbolic protests took place on July 21, the national holiday. In many places, the Catholic Church figured prominently as the basis of religious-national consciousness during the occupation. But no real armed resistance to the occupation developed. Local Belgian authorities worked with the Germans, although the coexistence of a bloated German administrative apparatus with partly competing Belgian institutions made this difficult. A kind of dual structure took shape, as local authorities were subject both to the military commander and to the regional civilian administration.[38] When the Germans suspected a security threat, they imposed draconian punishment for innocuous forms of behavior. This was most evident in 1916, in the context of the great battles on the western front. Since it was feared that spies in the rear might convey information to the enemy by carrier pigeon, flocks of the bird in whole regions were systematically recorded and exterminated. On August 26, 1916, the gardener Petrus Deman and his wife in Ghent were sentenced to two and a half years in prison for violation of the ban on carrier pigeons.[39]

At the same time, the German authorities relied on winning the loyalty and support of Belgium's Flemish population, whom they expected to behave in a friendly manner. They consciously promoted the Flemish language and acceded to other requests from Flemish nationalists. The 15,000 or so

Flemings who actively collaborated with the occupation authorities cast some doubt on the idea of a completely homogeneous patriotism after the experiences of August and September 1914. Another factor was the quartering of many German officers and men in Belgium for the duration of the war. Relations between the German army and the civilian population certainly did not revolve around mass prostitution, such as that observable in Brussels and areas near the front. There were many relationships between officers and men quartered in private homes and Belgian women, and at the end of the war these women were conspicuously excluded from the national community.[40]

As early as Fall 1914 the economic situation of Belgium showed signs of worsening. The population suffered from high unemployment, food supply difficulties, and the emergence of black markets, especially as large farming areas in Flanders and elsewhere were close to the front. But a number of charitable associations also sprang up in response to the shortages. New central distribution agencies were established, and the Comité National de Secours et d'Alimentation, in particular, foreshadowed elements of the later welfare state. Nevertheless, social tensions between employers and workers—which had not at all disappeared in the national consensus—sharpened amid the crisis. Under the occupation it turned out that the burdens of the war were unevenly shared, with workers the main group affected by deportation to Germany.

The 60,000 or so Belgian forced laborers were a striking feature of the German occupation, reflecting the massive labor shortage that hit all the belligerent countries soon after the beginning of the war. But whereas Britain and France could fall back on their colonies or advertise for workers from China, the Central Powers mainly used the territories under their occupation to enlist manpower for their war industries. Until 1916 German manpower practices in Belgium were relatively moderate, and recruitment remained the primary means of hiring workers. When the German war economy mobilized more intensely and casualties in the great battles of the western front worsened the labor shortage, force became a stronger factor in manpower policy. But since the living conditions of the workers in question were precarious, the yield from their forced labor remained limited. Unlike workers deported from the occupied territories in the east, Belgians working in the German economy were the focus of international public attention because of the events of August and September 1914, and the authorities in Germany had to take this into account. By the end of the war, they had reverted to normal recruitment of the necessary manpower.[41]

In 1916 the conflicts in Belgian society came to a head. In addition to the tensions between employers and workers, there were violent riots against merchants accused of price speculation, and the countryside saw the emergence of marauding bands and a space effectively outside the rule of law. The German authorities mainly limited their intervention to the capital and industrial centers such as Liège, where their interests were directly at stake. Yet despite these strains, which reflected the problems facing all the countries at war, Belgian society did not fall apart. Social tensions increased, but they led neither to mass collaboration with the Germans nor to truly revolutionary contradictions. For all the stresses of the occupation, it was clear that the German invasion of Summer 1914 had resulted in a fairly stable basic consensus. Though subject to lapses of patriotism, the collective habitus of endurance and survival remained relatively strong.[42]

The occupation regimes in eastern, central, and southeastern Europe developed differently.[43] The areas on the eastern front occupied by the Central Powers up to Fall 1915 comprised the bulk of the so-called Northwestern Territories of the Russian Empire, including today's Baltic states (Estonia, Latvia, and Lithuania) and parts of Belarus. But the unexpected extent of its successes confronted the German military with a novel situation: the new areas under their rule came with a distinctly multiethnic and multireligious population structure, made up of Estonians, Latvians, Lithuanians, and Baltic Germans; White Russians and Ukrainians; Poles and Russians; and minority groups such as Tatars. Along with Catholics and various Orthodox communities, the encounter with large numbers of eastern Jews was a formative experience for many German soldiers.

From 1915 a distinctive occupation regime developed in the territories of Ober Ost, one in which the military defined the structures of statehood and ruthlessly subordinated them to its own economic requirements. The actions of the German military authorities were therefore two-pronged. In Kovno (Kaunas), for instance, they worked to achieve political and administrative centralization, with the aim of opening up the area and exploiting it economically. They forcibly enlisted manpower and systematically requisitioned agricultural holdings and products. But as well as attempting to exercise total control over the movement of goods and persons, the authorities under Ludendorff's leadership developed an original cultural policy toward the various ethnic and religious groups. This included a language policy that took regional needs into account in schools, theaters, and newspapers in order to gain the loyalty of the different groups to the occupying power. Although the political future of the region was unclear, the scope arose from 1915 on for a wartime imperial-military state, in which fantasies of domination collided with the complexity of multiethnic populations and the problems of a large territory. As the war dragged on, the limits of the penetration of German rule and of the idea of an east European military state became more evident. Many ethnic groups were not prepared to function simply as an extended arm of the German military.[44] In Lithuania, for instance, the strict limits on freedom of movement and the ever-harsher burdens of war meant that attitudes to the German military administration remained negative, and many Lithuanians supported Russian partisans operating behind German lines. Smaller numbers were willing to collaborate with the military authorities, although some groups, such as village elders, received privileges in return.[45]

German policy developed differently between 1914 and 1918 in Ober Ost and the Warsaw General Government. There was therefore not a homogeneous experiential space of wartime rule in the east, any more than there was a simple continuum from colonial conceptions in the First World War to Hitler's *Lebensraum* ideology in the second. In Ober Ost the German military tried to construct an administrative model that would be highly centralized, whereas the German governor in Warsaw, Hans von Beseler, with the help of a civilian administration, charted a more pragmatic course aimed at stronger integration of the Polish population. In both areas, there was considerable leeway for local decision making. Ober Ost might have been conceived as the instrument of an imperial-military state, but in reality this soon ran up against the limits of its effectiveness. The General Government policy of limited cooperation with the Poles produced better results at first. Until Fall

OPPOSITE: Map 5. Balkan Front, 1914–1915

German position

Austro-Hungarian position

Bulgarian position

Serbian/Montenegrin position

Serbian position

Central Powers advance, 1915

Serbian retreat, 1915–1916

Franco-British support

1916 it involved at least no formal compulsion in manpower recruitment, and only then were individuals (mostly Jews from Lodz) at times forcibly enlisted for labor services. Given the proclamation of a Polish state by the Central Powers in November 1916, only volunteers were accepted for work in Germany. Work in the local region, on the other hand, was subject to compulsion.

The situation in Ober Ost was very different: draconian measures and forced labor on roadworks and railroad construction, as well as in agriculture and forestry, violated all the norms laid down under international law. Things grew worse still in Fall 1916, as roundups and kidnappings began to take place in the middle of the street. The military organization of forced labor also took the form of labor columns and civilian work brigades, later renamed "punishment battalions," where the treatment of workers was even harsher. Yet, because of high rates of absence due to illness, as well as frequent escapes by workers, labor productivity remained low. Problems of labor utilization

The enemy everywhere behind the lines: a boy under sentence of death in Ukraine

therefore exposed the limits of the military state—and similarly, Ludendorff failed in his attempt to introduce into Germany Lithuanian-style labor duty on the basis of the auxiliary service law. As the war progressed and the situation on the home front worsened, pressure mounted on the General Government to enlist workers for deployment in Germany itself. But neither qualitatively nor quantitatively was this practice a straightforward anticipation of the forcible deportation of laborers during the Second World War.[46]

The occupation of Serbia followed that country's military collapse.[47] The Austro-Hungarian and German offensive against Serbia began in early October 1915, supplemented by Bulgaria's troop advances after it joined the war. The positioning of Allied (mostly French) forces on the frontline north of Salonica, for which Russia too had been pushing, was unable to improve the situation for the Serbs.[48] Serbia's resistance became increasingly sporadic, partly because its troops fell ill in a major typhus epidemic and had to endure supply problems. After the fall of Belgrade in October and Niš in November 1915, the "great retreat" of some 150,000 Serbian soldiers and innumerable civilians, along with 20,000 prisoners of war, into the mountainous region of Albania and Montenegro got underway. Their trek, with its high death toll, was later elevated to the status of national myth, the Golgotha of a nation once more presented as victim, comparable to the plight of the Serbians who fought the Ottomans at the Battle of Kosovo in 1389.[49] Eventually, a majority of the Serbian troops were evacuated by the French to Corfu.[50]

By the beginning of 1916, with the defeat and occupation of Serbia, the capitulation of Montenegro, and the withdrawal of Italian forces from Albania, Austria-Hungary had in theory achieved its most important war aims in the Balkans. In Serbia it established an occupation regime that savagely bared its teeth time and time again, dividing the country itself between an Austro-Hungarian and a Bulgarian military administration. Control over industry and mining was transferred to the occupation authorities. While industrial output almost ground to a halt, the extraction of minerals for the arms industry was stepped up; 70 percent of the existing livestock vanished by the end of the war.[51] Serbian civilians too were exposed to massive violence, thousands being murdered in Toplica in 1917, for example.[52] As the war kept lengthening, the Austro-Hungarian authorities looked to more cooperative relations with the rural population, in order to improve food supplies to their home society. But the oppression was markedly harsher in the Bulgarian occupation zone.

Violence against civilians played a major role in the areas under Bulgarian occupation, but also later on in the Austro-Hungarian push into Ukraine. Numerous photographs of public executions testify to the way in which military courts dealt with alleged spies. Nevertheless, this practice, attributable in part to strident anti-Serb propaganda in the Austro-Hungarian military, cannot be simply characterized as systematic violence, as a preplanned element in an official campaign against the civilian population.[53] The reasons for the military violence against Serb civilians were manifestly more complex, and in any case the occupation regime was by no means constant after 1915.

It is not enough to argue that the Austro-Hungarian military, in an unbroken line from Metternich's policy in the early nineteenth century, was interested only in establishing a bureaucratic absolutism in Serbia that corresponded to the traditional supranational instrument of rule in the Habsburg monarchy.[54] More important was the fear that many officers had of a general uprising, a Serbian *levée en masse* and guerrilla warfare that they wanted to prevent at all costs. There may have been no objective danger of this in 1915, but the idea that it might develop became a particular factor driving action, much as, in Summer 1914 in Belgium, the imagined specter of Belgian *franctireurs* had repeatedly influenced the conduct of German troops. In Serbia, the Austro-Hungarian authorities first resorted to large-scale arrests and internment, and particularly to hostage taking that reflected the climate of fear in the army. Along with attempts to weaken Serbian nationalism in schools, military justice remained the dominant everyday instrument against anyone suspected of acting outside the conventional norms and rules of war. In this way, the very attempt in 1914 and 1915 to maintain a separation between the army and civil society served to erase the boundary between military and nonmilitary combatants.

When the Austro-Hungarian military government was installed in Serbia in 1916, the reality of the occupation began to change. The security of its own troops remained a central concern, but there was a definite relaxation in the spheres of food supply and justice that would continue in 1917. Austro-Hungarian rule had to appear "just" if conflicts with the population were to be avoided. The principal reason for this shift was that Serbia's role as agricultural producer was becoming ever more important in a context of bottlenecks in Austria-Hungary; only stable cooperation with the rural population could enable the country's resources to be tapped. In the end, the authorities even took pains to protect the peasantry in southern Serbia from guerrilla bands. On the whole, officers of the Imperial army in Serbia tended to pursue rather conservative goals, orienting themselves to the prewar period and adhering to the separation between army and civilian population. This corresponded to their understanding of themselves as guarantors of the peace and stability of the Habsburg monarchy. In everyday experience, however, these boundaries were less clear; the occupation remained dependent on imagined dangers, on overreactions, and on room for maneuvering that began to narrow appreciably in 1916–1917.[55]

The Bulgarian military acted with extreme brutality in Dobruja and large parts of Macedonia. This violence was not only a response to everyday problems under the occupation but also followed the logic of ethnic conflict in the framework of full-scale Bulgarization programs.[56] Furthermore, the state and the military leadership had no resources at their disposal, and army supplies were so abysmal that soldiers lived off occupied land. This led to more and more massive raids, especially against the Turkish and Muslim minorities. Between 1915 and 1918, the mortality rate in Macedonia rose by approximately 60 percent.[57]

The problem of a lack of effective leeway for action also shaped the situation in Romania. When the Central Powers occupied the country in late 1916 following its military defeat, close cooperation soon developed in practice between the military and the local authorities and elites. With their troop strength limited by the fighting on other fronts, the German and Austro-Hungarian military used existing structures whenever this was possible. Here too, attempts were made to draw on earlier experiences of occupation in the west, which had shown that confrontation and repression often did not achieve the desired results, and that there were clear output differences between normally recruited and deported forced labor. Developments on the ground in Romania did not conform at all to the press reports and public image that circulated in the Central Powers. Whereas these repeatedly presented the occupation as a civilizing mission, a much-needed colonization, and, where necessary, forcible opening up of a neglected and underdeveloped country, the authorities and the military were often more restrained, and in general a relatively flexible regime grew up instead of a strict division between occupiers and occupied. Alongside internment and forced manpower recruitment, there was also a system of incentives to gain the trust of the peasantry. And in view of the worsening supply situation in 1916, the authorities threw everything into maintaining agricultural output.[58]

The war of movement in eastern and southeastern Europe, together with regime change, had other dimensions that were most keenly felt by Jews living in the multiethnic environments. Since they fought on both sides, the war between the armies of Austria-Hungary and Russia could also be seen as a tragic fratricidal struggle. One contemporary recalled, "Jews on both sides fought each other, brother against brother. From the start, the Jews were gripped with this horror . . . as in a legend of two soldiers meeting each other in battle. . . . In St. Petersburg I was told about a Jewish patient in a military hospital. During an attack, he had bayoneted an Austrian soldier, and the victim had cried out, 'Hear, oh Israel . . . !' The patient had instantly lost his mind."[59]

It was mostly east European Jews who were affected by the changes in political power accompanying the war of movement in and after 1914. Early Russian successes against Austria-Hungary led to a situation where large parts of Galicia, with their sizable Jewish populations, had to be evacuated. Some 350,000 Jewish refugees left Galicia, and tens of thousands ended up in Vienna, Prague, and Budapest. In October 1915 the total number of war refugees in Cisleithania was 385,645, including 157,630 Jews, more than half (77,000) in Vienna.[60] With the military successes of the Central Powers in Summer 1915, the situation changed again. The picture was especially complex in Galicia. Lvov, for example, experienced a number of shifts between Austro-Hungarian and Russian occupation regimes.[61] In 1915–1916 in Galicia, the German-Austrian offensives brought unemancipated Jews from Russian Poland under Austro-Hungarian rule, while Russian conquests had the consequence that previously emancipated Jews lost their status again.[62] Even within the Central Powers, different ways of treating the Jews prevailed in the former Russian Poland after it was divided between Germany and Austria-Hungary.[63]

From Summer 1915, mainly German troops conquered cities such as Warsaw, Vilnius, and Kaunas in the more northern sections of the front that had a high proportion of Jews. This gave rise, under the occupation, to a further dimension of ethnic-religious diversity in eastern Europe. Many German soldiers and officers found a world completely unfamiliar to them, a multi-ethnic population with a high percentage of Jews who differed greatly from the assimilated Jews in Germany.[64] This encounter with the "eastern Jewish question," all the more intense because of military developments, fed back into society back home. Although Germany's assimilated Jews emphasized their solidarity with *Ostjuden* held legally in subjection in former Russian areas, they were also prone to new worries in this connection. What they feared was that mass immigration of east European Jews would endanger the gains and successes, the laboriously conquered status, of the Jews in Germany. On November 26, 1915, the Breslau (Wrocław) Jew Willy Cohn described the boundary between Jewish solidarity and German Jewish patri-otism in the war: "Unless they are prevented from doing so, the vast human reservoirs in the East will year by year pour forth their masses to the West. We seek to raise up in every way our Jewish co-religionists in the East, who will perhaps, because of the war, enter into closer relations with Germany . . . but we also want and need to draw a dividing line between them and us. . . . To accept them into the community of German Jewry would mean to make Jewry un-German, and the emphasis is and should be on 'German.'"[65]

3. PROGRESSIVE TOOLS OF WAR, VIOLENCE, AND THEIR POLITICAL COSTS
The Mobilization of Technology in Gas and Submarine Warfare

On April 22, 1915, the French general Henri Mordacq received a telephone call near Ypres from Major Villevalleix of the First Regiment of Fusiliers. "The major" he recalled, "was coughing and gasping, broke off several times, and could hardly be understood. His report was: 'I am under heavy attack. Huge yellow smoke clouds are spreading now from the German trenches over the whole of my frontline. The troopers started to abandon the trenches and to fall back. Many fell down suffocated.'" Mordacq rode over at once to the trenches: "But when we were 300 or 400 meters from Boesinghe, we felt a violent prickling in our nose and neck; our ears were whistling; we breathed with difficulty; there was an unbearable smell of chlorine around us. . . . The picture that offered itself to us near the village was more than pitiful—it was tragic. People fleeing everywhere: reservists, Africans, troopers, Zouave infantry, and gunners without weapons—distraught, coats off or wide open, neckbands removed—were running like crazy men into the unknown, screaming for water, spitting blood, sometimes rolling on the ground and vainly trying to get some air. . . . I've never before had to witness such a scene of complete disarray."[66] Four days after the gas attack, the *Berliner Tageblatt* wrote of it in sardonic terms, directly comparing it to the British blockade and its effects on the German population: "The everyday talk is of the 'German fumes' at Ypres. They must be chlorine fumes; more precise analysis is lacking, until the poor victims of the sniff smoke have made it themselves. From what we have heard, there is no danger to life but only a nasty condition lasting four hours or so. . . . The English are touching fellows: they do everything to force us into the hideous death facing the population at home and then complain about a little swelling of the mucous membrane. And not having signed the provisions of international law, they demand that we should respect them. Good vapors!"[67]

A few days later, Fritz Haber—director since 1911 of the newly founded Kaiser Wilhelm Institute for Physical Chemistry and Electrochemistry, which had played a key role in preparing the action—was promoted to the rank of captain and posted to the eastern front to organize further gas attacks in support of a breakthrough against Russian forces. The celebrations in his Berlin home ended in personal tragedy, however. His wife Clara Immerwahr, herself a doctor in chemistry, was appalled by the use of her science in the war, but her husband rebuked her that her conduct was stabbing himself and his country in the back. As a result, she shot herself in the night of May 2, 1915, with Haber's service weapon.[68]

The German use of chlorine gas on a large scale at the Battle of Ypres, on April 22, 1915, changed the character of the war. Pressure to bring about a decision by means of new weapons and technologies became more intense on all sides, and the limits of what was compatible with the Hague Convention were soon reached. In late April 1915, the battlefield use of gas was no longer a novelty, nor was it limited to the German army. In France, there had been experiments with tear gas before 1914; first developed for use by the police, it had proved its military effectiveness only in operations in urban terrain, not in open countryside. The French first employed hand grenades filled with chloroacetone in April 1915. As for the Germans, the lead they had over wartime enemies in industry-related chemical research, which had already been demonstrated in the large-scale production of basic materials such as ammonia, was becoming more apparent. As early as October 1914, at Neuve Chapelle, they had used 3,000 dianisidine / chlorine sulfonate grenades, which irritated the respiratory passages of affected enemy soldiers, but did not have the desired effect of forcing them to abandon their positions. This experience confirms that the development of new weapons did not begin only in the context of the positional warfare of 1915.

Fritz Haber recommended the extensive deployment of chlorine gas from 6,000 pressurized air cylinders, which in favorable wind conditions would drift as clouds over enemy positions. German commanders thought of this as a limited operation, not as a full-blown attempt to break through enemy lines, but it had the effect of provoking the panic-stricken flight described by Mordacq. Since the Germans had no reserves on the spot, however, the action did not lead to a breakthrough, still less to Haber's hoped-for turn in the war.[69]

Measured against the number of soldiers who lost their lives to artillery and machine-gun fire, the 1,200 dead and 3000 wounded in the first gas attack were a small toll. Of all the casualties on the western front up to the end of the war, roughly 3.4 percent (20,000 dead and 500,000 wounded) were the result of gas attacks; this included 186,000 British, 130,000 French, 107,000 Germans, and 76,000 Americans.[70] But the 500,000 victims on the Russian side, as well as the fact that no less than 25 percent of grenade production in Germany was of gas-filled devices, demonstrate the dimensions of this aspect of the war.[71] Yet its significance did not lie only in the number of casualties; all sides invoked the use of gas to accuse the enemy of using inhumane weapons. In particular, it epitomized a qualitatively new mobilization and application of scientific knowledge in war, a mutual radicalization of the tools of war, and a changed perception of war itself. In the contemporary picture of the war, with its iconic images of soldiers in the trenches, the wearing of gas masks already symbolized how every conceivable weapon was being used to attack the bodies of enemy soldiers. Any conventional notion of fair play in positional warfare, involving fixed, transparent rules and a modicum of trust as in the Christmas truce of 1914, went by the board in the face of these new implements of battle. The use of gas also helped make the act of killing more anonymous. In the combat zone, any soldier could be killed at any time by an enemy he hardly ever saw or heard. Furthermore, chemical substances did not suddenly affect the body in the way that gunfire did, and in many cases they led to protracted agonies. The argument used by Haber, for example, that gas was more humane than bullets that tore through the body, was therefore not convincing.[72]

The German army was not alone in using poison gas, but it did resort to it earlier than other armies on the battlefield, and not only as part of the transition from war of movement to positional warfare. The German top brass was prepared to overstep the traditional limits of violence in order to bring about a decision in the war. With the shift to positional warfare, this willingness hardened further and linked to a self-image of technological and scientific superiority in the military sphere. Haber declared to Falkenhayn that Britain was not in a position to develop poison gas and catch up with Germany, because it did not have the scientific base to achieve this.[73]

In contrast to the image of precise planning, the actual use of poison gas initially remained at the level of experimental, often improvised, actions. Then, when tactical advantages resulted, there were usually not enough reserve troops to exploit the panic in the enemy ranks. This failure to think ahead also extended to the dependence on local weather conditions. Since, more often than not, westerly winds prevailed at the front, the Germans soon faced situations in which gas clouds intended for the enemy drifted back to their own positions. Gas warfare intensified on all sides in the course of 1915, demonstrating that German scientists had seriously underestimated the enemy's capacity to hit back with similar weapons. The British, for their part, did more than refine their early improvised measures to protect their troops; by September 1915 they were able to deploy 6,000 pressurized cylinders with 180 tons of chlorine in the vicinity of the front, and on September 25 they used them in an attack at Loos. Local successes there, however, including the capture of more than 3,000 German soldiers, could not disguise their failure to achieve a frontal breakthrough, since the Germans' rear defensive lines proved impregnable.[74]

Later in the war, all sides replaced the pressurized air cylinder with special gas artillery. It did not produce an incoming gas cloud, which made it

New weapons, new victims: British soldiers wearing improvised gas masks, 1915

impossible for the enemy to warn its troops in time of an attack—although the first few months of 1915 already saw improvements in protection. Soon Blue Cross, Yellow Cross, Green Cross, and White Cross gas shells were added to the German arsenal, so called after their color markings. "Multicolored fire," involving a combination of these weapons, began with highly irritating substances such as the Blue Cross, which was supposed to penetrate gas mask filters and induce soldiers to remove their masks. Green Cross substances fired at the same time then did irreversible damage to the lungs. The contending armies developed a veritable race to develop mask-busting chemical substances and filters capable of protecting against them. This led in July 1917 to the targeted use of dichlordiethylsulfide, which was labeled "mustard gas" on account of its distinctive smell. It acted on the skin and after a few hours led to blistering, eye and mucous membrane injuries, and internal burns.[75]

Apart from the question of whether poison gas attacks violated international law, many officers were initially skeptical about its effectiveness and rejected its use in combat. What lay behind this may have been a (by no means uniquely German) conservative attitude to new scientific developments and their application in war. Besides, officers well knew from experience that the enemy would develop similar weapons and that, in this war, traditional ideals of fair and generally accepted rules of combat were no longer enforceable. This had not first shown itself to be the case in relation to gas warfare, and so it served to remind officers of ideals that had been suppressed since the beginning of the war by the reality of new battlefields and combat instruments. In retrospect, the commander of the German Third Army, General von Einem, could write, "But I am furious about the use of gas, which from the beginning struck me as repulsive. We naturally have Falkenhayn to thank for the introduction of this unchivalrous instrument, otherwise used only by rogues and criminals, for the conduct of the war; his adventurous mind thought it could be won in next to no time with this instrument. Now our enemies have it too."[76] Especially on the German side, no consideration was given to the implications of such an evident breach of the rules of war. In this focus on tactical advantage regardless of the political and international consequences, there was an important parallel in 1915 between the use of poison gas and the deployment of submarines against the enemy's commercial shipping and passenger steamers.

The first few months after August 1914 already showed that Germany had no really coherent strategy in the war at sea. A concentration on the battle fleet, which had been a dogma ever since the days of Admiral Tirpitz as state secretary at the Imperial Navy Office, corresponded less and less to the actual situation in the war. Since all thoughts before 1914 had been on a major battle fought by large battleships against the British, the resources were now lacking for the successful deployment of cruisers, and even the ad hoc conversion of merchant ships into auxiliary cruisers could do nothing to change this. After the East Asia squadron under Admiral Spee was annihilated in December 1914 off the Falkland Islands, a few light and auxiliary cruisers still managed to score some eye-catching victories up through the early part of 1915. These demonstrated the importance of such cruiser ships, rather than great battleships, in the context of a global war at sea—but also the extent to which the German navy lacked these instruments to wage economic warfare on the world's oceans.

In November and December, in an attempt to deploy the high-seas fleet, German battle cruisers on several occasions bombarded ports on the English east coast. After the Royal Navy, with its superior radio technology, received news of upcoming attacks, the German squadron under Rear Admiral Hipper suffered a defeat in January 1915 on Dogger Bank in the North Sea.[77] Thereafter the German navy only fought minor engagements in 1915, without taking on British ships in real sea battles. A paradoxical situation therefore developed in 1915: since the German high-seas fleet (which before 1914 had been assigned a key function in any war with Britain) effectively avoided any major battle, finding it more difficult than Britain to make up for any losses, it could not really interfere with the enemy's sea links and was therefore also incapable of breaking the British remote blockade. The original thinking of the German naval leadership had been to establish parity with the British navy by means of small operations in which it had a clear superiority, and only then to risk the great decisive battle. In practice, however, given the British naval blockade, this meant that both sides gave up the idea of a great battle. While Operational Order No. 1 of the German Imperial Navy encouraged North Sea units to keep a low profile, the British Admiralty refrained both from a major battle in the North Sea and from any engagement in the Baltic. There were thus two "fleets in being," which maintained their deterrent power without intervening decisively in the war.[78]

From late 1914 on, after the German U-9 had demonstrated the effectiveness of torpedo attacks by sinking three aging British cruisers at the entrance to the English Channel, the submarine increasingly overshadowed the surface fleet. At first the plan was to use U-boats against enemy battle fleets, not against commercial shipping as in the classical cruiser war, in compliance with international prize rules. This changed only when a U-21 seized the British steamer *Glitra* on its way to Norway on October 20, 1914, allowed the crew to leave in lifeboats, and sank the ship with a weight of 866 gross register tons. By the end of January 1915 seven merchant ships had been sunk in this way.[79] The more the British blockade hit home from early 1915, the more the submarine seemed to offer an answer to the global economic war against Germany. For the naval leadership, a way out of the strategic impasse opened up, now that their two basic assumptions at the beginning of the war (a merely limited blockade of German ports and a decisive sea battle in the North Sea) had proved wide of the mark. As early as November 1914, the chief of staff at the admiralty, Hugo von Pohl, presented the U-boat as a possible weapon in his report to the German chancellor. Rejecting in advance the objection that this would violate international law, he wrote, "The fact that England tries to use all means to crush us economically, not concerning itself whether they comply with the existing principles of international law, makes it appropriate for us, too, to employ sharper means than before in the commercial war. A submarine blockade of the enemy coast promises to be especially successful. . . . The objection that a submarine blockade would not comply with the provisions of international law can be rebutted by simple reference to the British Admiralty's obstruction of the North Sea, which is also not permissible under international law."[80]

The submarine equipped with new-style torpedoes, which in the early years could not yet be reliably located, would develop in the course of the war from a defensive into a decidedly offensive weapon. But the German navy itself began later than other maritime forces to accelerate its construction of submarines. Only with the introduction of underwater diesel engines in 1912 did it become possible to plan extended missions. At the beginning of the war, the German navy deployed more than twenty-eight U-boats, of which only ten had high-performance diesel engines. But many officers initially underestimated the power of the new weapons. U-boats could only

The new war at sea: loading German submarines with torpedoes

load a few torpedoes, so that their main weapon at first was their deck guns. Under international prize rules, they could stop ships, search them, and sink them with explosive charges if a prize turned out to be present. The rules governing commercial warfare at sea specified that castaways had to be picked up and taken on board—which was possible for larger surface ships but not for small submarines. Torpedoes were used only for surprise attacks and dive operations in which the submarines were running on battery power. In addition, German U-boats played an important role as minelayers. Based in Belgian ports, they made the English Channel an important area of operations.

When Tirpitz, reacting in 1915 to the British blockade, claimed that the German navy was capable of torpedoing British ships, it still had no more than fourteen submarines with a wide enough radius to operate in the Atlantic west of the British Isles. The German military's decision on February 4, 1915, to deploy submarines, and its declaration of the British Isles as a combat zone in response to the British blockade, soon led to considerable problems under international law and a danger that the war would be extended to other countries. From February 18, U-boats could seize merchant shipping in accordance with traditional international prize rules and sink them after their crews had been evacuated. But the deployment order also permitted dive operations if the submarine captain had to anticipate possible enemy counteraction (for example, if the merchant ship was armed). Prize rules, as a section of international law, had regulated procedures with enemy ships and goods in wartime, guaranteeing a modicum of safety for the crews of captured ships. With the deployment of submarines as purely destructive weapons against the enemy merchant fleet, however, the war at sea acquired a completely new quality. The sinking of merchant ships and passenger steamers, usually without warning, which was meant to act as a deterrent to neutral vessels as well, made it impossible to rescue crews or allow them to abandon ship in time. The fact that armed merchant ships (or, later, auxiliary cruisers disguised as merchant ships) were a threat to submarines made it difficult to reach a decision in the heat of battle. So, the traditional wartime practice of seizing enemy ships and confiscating their cargo increasingly gave way to indiscriminate destruction of the greatest possible tonnage and the inevitable death of whole crews.

The situation became more difficult in Spring 1915. In February and March, thirty-eight ships were sunk; in April, twenty-nine; and in May, fifty-two.[81] When the U.S. government voiced its concerns about Germany shortly after the U-boat war started, Chief of Staff Falkenhayn asked the admiralty to assess the risk that the United States would enter the war. Tirpitz replied that a U-boat campaign against British shipping could bring Britain to its knees within six weeks. But the actual war at sea soon made absolutely clear the political costs of unrestricted action against merchant ships and passenger steamers. When the German U-20 sank the British liner *Lusitania* on May 7, 1915, the list of 1,198 dead civilians included 128 Americans. Washington reacted sharply, fearing for the safety of its citizens on trips in war zones and seeing the inception of unrestricted submarine warfare as a *casus belli*.[82]

After the sinking of another passenger steamship in August 1915, with three U.S. citizens among the forty-four civilians killed, the German government was forced to call off the attacks on commercial vessels in the Atlantic. Up to that point 379 ships, with 669,000 gross register tons, had been sent to the bottom of the ocean. From that summer, however, U-boats were sent into action only against enemy naval forces or in support of engagements by the Imperial Navy. This policy change led to sharp conflict between the civilian and military leadership. Having almost completely suspended U-boat action in the waters around the British Isles, the Imperial Navy put pressure on the Bethmann Hollweg government to lift the restrictions.[83] Many officers were disappointed that the battle fleet had not been able to fulfill the hopes invested in it and the assumption that submarines alone could decide the war with Britain. Albert Hopman, who from 1909 to 1911 had commanded the *Rheinland,* one of the first German dreadnought-class battleships, and had profited personally from the naval armament program, moved to the Imperial Navy Office in 1911 and was promoted to the rank of rear admiral in 1915. In mid-October 1915 he noted in his diary, "The way to the heart of England, now that our navy has not opened it up and will not soon open it up farther west, will pass through southeastern Europe to Egypt and India. . . . We should no longer look at high politics through the lens of the Navy Act, which is and will remain a dead letter, *pace* S.M. [His Majesty], von Tirpitz, etc. . . . In a few years it will no longer be possible to do anything with big battleships. Cruisers will rule the oceans, submarines, mines, and ship's guns their margins, and even on the high seas submarines will perhaps play a greater role than we suspect today."[84]

Yet, contrary to what the clashes between the navy leadership and the Imperial government suggested, it was clear in the Mediterranean that submarines could be perfectly well deployed in accordance with international prize rules. After Italy joined the war, the Germans sent a number of submarines through the Straits of Gibraltar into the Mediterranean to support the Austro-Hungarian navy, manning them with German crews under Austro-Hungarian command in line with the model of the transfer of the *Goeben* and *Breslau* to the Ottoman Empire. There they managed to sink not only several Italian and French warships but also the British *Majestic* and *Triumph* battleships off the Dardanelles, preventing the bombardment of Turkish coastal batteries from the sea. From Summer 1915, the few U-boats also operated with great success from the Istrian port of Pula against merchant shipping, which they seized under existing prize rules and then sank. Submarines in the Mediterranean sank a total of 102 ships in 1915, 415 in 1916, 627 in 1917, and 325 in 1918—the U-35 boat alone accounting for 224 vessels with a gross registered tonnage of 539,741 tons. The German success rate per submarine was higher in the Mediterranean than in the Second World War. At any event, the unrestricted submarine warfare and violation of prize rules that the navy people around Tirpitz forced through was not the only option from the outset.[85] Much as the German military and civilian leadership in August 1914 had underestimated the possibility that Britain would go to war over the violation of Belgian neutrality, they gave short shrift to the political consequences of the unrestricted U-boat option. By the end of 1915 Falkenhayn was again leaning toward an intensification of submarine warfare, in order to strike at Britain in the context of the military stalemate on the western front, while the navy leadership, given the arming of British merchant ships and the advent of anti-submarine countermeasures, saw no prospect of success unless the restrictions were lifted.[86]

The wavering between restricted and unrestricted submarine warfare revealed a number of problems. First, it reflected the near-compulsive quest of the German navy leadership for a way to decide the war, which did not seem likely to happen on land either in 1914 or in 1915. Second, the top navy people hoped to find an answer to the strategic dilemma resting on the logic of mutual deterrence between Germany and Britain and the fear of irreplaceable losses—a dilemma that had blocked the deployment of heavy battleships. Third, the stationary "fleets in being" underlined the limitations of the navalism of the prewar period. The one-sided trust placed in ever larger battleships and a decisive battle in the North Sea had served to obscure the global dimension of the war at sea and the opportunities for a cruiser fleet operating on a world scale. Much as, on the Continent, the dual doctrine of maintaining the offensive and aiming at a decisive battle had proved mistaken in 1914, making it clear that infantry attacks were hugely vulnerable to heavy artillery and machine-gun fire, so now the advent of the submarine and the growing importance of cruisers in the real war at sea highlighted the vulnerability of battleships, and especially merchant shipping, to enemy action. In fact, there was a remarkable intensification of global economic warfare, in which access to raw materials and a secure supply of men and materials became decisive factors.

Fourth, the unrestricted use of submarines to sink enemy ships without warning called into question the prize rules that were an essential part of international law, creating the danger that civilian deaths would bring other countries into the war. Fifth, this brought out characteristic tensions in Germany between the general staff and the admiralty, which at no point (for example, during the BEF landings on the Continent at the beginning of the war) had managed to coordinate their operations; instead each had dug in their heels and insisted on their respective theories. The Schlieffen Plan and the doctrine of the offensive had ended in failure, as had the navalist concentration on battleship fleets and the vision of one big decisive battle. In 1915, moreover, there were visible conflicts between the civilian leadership of the Reich and the military top brass, in which opposing action logics made themselves felt. The two sides had quite different approaches to the danger that unrestricted submarine warfare would extend the war: whereas the general staff and the admiralty massively underestimated this factor, the civilian leadership under Bethmann Hollweg was able to block escalation until 1916. Things would change, however, when Hindenburg and Ludendorff took over the supreme army command in Summer 1916.

In the shadow of these political developments, the attitude of ordinary ranks and the military hierarchy shifted more in the German navy than elsewhere. This became apparent in naval units that, unlike submarines, often remained docked for weeks or months at a time. Younger officers and NCOs were posted more often as a result of the focus on U-boats, while tensions rose between the remaining older officers and their crews. Long before the real mutinies began in 1917—only to be stamped out with death sentences—the sailor Richard Stumpf on the *Helgoland* battleship noted in April 1915: "There's an agitated, angry mood everywhere. . . . Gone is the early comradeship; it has given way to a grumpy, sullen mood. No wonder everyone longs to get away when volunteers are looked for on U-boats." On Whit Monday 1915, he recorded, "During my period of service, the gulf between officer and men has never been as wide as it is now in wartime." In August, however, something new was added to this irritability and hardly novel tension. Under the special conditions on board ship, with their cramped living space, the inactivity made the officers' glaring privileges in rations, accommodation, and leave appear less and less justified. Criticism of this setup revealed a political potential that included visions of the world beyond the war: "It's amazing how all the men are getting interested in politics. They all agree that the preferential treatment given to officers must stop after the war." By early November 1915 the tension had given way to latent resistance, as on the Russian battleship *Potemkin* in 1905 in the Black Sea: "The atmosphere among the crew is such that everyone would be happy if we got a fat 'cigar' [torpedo] in our belly. Quite seriously, everyone would be delighted for our mousy leadership. . . . There's an evil spirit inside us, and only each man's good training is to thank if the events in the Russian Baltic [sic!] fleet do not have a stronger echo among us."[87]

4. WAIT-AND-SEE NEUTRALITY AND RIVAL PROMISES
New Players and Their Expansionist Fantasies

On May 3, 1915 the Italian writer Gabriele d'Annunzio took the night train from Paris to Genoa. Celebrated in the Parisian art and literature scene, most recently for his collaborative work with Claude Debussy on the play *Le Martyre de Saint Sébastien*, he was traveling to Italy to campaign for the country to join the war on the side of the Allies. In his eyes this would finally end its "cowardly neutrality," which he identified with the figure of Giovanni

Giolitti, the prime minister (with a few interruptions) between 1892 and March 1914.[88] Born in 1863 in Pescara in the Abruzzo, D'Annunzio broke off his study of literature at college and went to work at various newspapers, becoming Italy's leading writer and eccentric representative of the *fin-de-siècle*. A brief stint in parliament ended in 1900, but the highly emotional speeches he made on the floor lingered in people's memory. In these, he argued in the tone of his odes for the expansion of Italy as a great power, until the Mediterranean became again a *mare nostrum*. D'Annunzio combined in his personality and his work a number of conflicts between tradition and modernity. This was also the case with other writers of the time, but his extreme tones mirrored the deep feelings of insecurity in the Italian bourgeoisie, the weak social cohesion, and the failings of the internally heterogeneous nation-state founded in 1861. Convinced that he should make a work of art out of his life, D'Annunzio criticized contemporary Italian culture as a form of plagiarism, a mere transfer from western Europe, especially France. His own work, however, was profoundly eclectic and contradictory: it combined Catholic features with enthusiasm for Friedrich Nietzsche's *Übermensch*, an idealization of the Italian peasantry as the only morally uncorrupted element in Italian society, and the fire of the aristocratic heroes of his novels. At the same time, he developed a futurist aesthetic that found expression in his passion for flying. He began his political career as a vehement anti-socialist, but after a short time he joined the Socialist group in parliament, only to turn radically against it again.

When he arrived in Genoa in May 1915, D'Annunzio gave a series of speeches arguing for Italy to join the war. His idea of a war of liberation resumed an old theme of the Risorgimento and the struggle against the hated Habsburg monarchy, adding to it the aggressive program of a Greater Italian nation-state. In this he was following a strategy rooted in political history and national symbolism: when he unveiled a memorial on May 5, 1915, in Quarto del Mille, from where the "Expedition of the Thousand" to Sicily had begun in 1860, D'Annunzio directly placed himself in the footsteps of Garibaldi, hailing him as an exemplary national liberator and people's hero, a worthy *duce*. As he continued his train journey to Rome, his popularity soared within a few days; he thus became one of the chief advocates of Italy's entry into the war, acting as an extra-parliamentary tribune claiming to represent the real people. The climax of this campaign was his speech before a huge crowd in Rome on May 17, 1915, which he consciously gave on the historically charged Capitol Hill, following several days of street demonstrations in favor of intervention.

D'Annunzio referred to the ideal of ancient Rome to justify an expansionist national drive to found an empire. Above all, however, he invoked the long hostility to Austria-Hungary and the catchy narrative of the *irredenta* (the "unredeemed" territories that, even after the wars of the nineteenth century, still did not belong to the Italian state), arguing the historical necessity of another war to complete the Risorgimento left unfinished in 1861 and 1871. The main ideological target he had in his sights was the liberal system of Giolitti and the *età giolittiana*. D'Annunzio's aggressiveness went far beyond the limits of polemical criticism: it reflected the deep split in the Italian political landscape and the lack of cohesion afflicting the nation-state in 1915. Beneath the surface of patriotic enthusiasm, the war would soon widen this gulf still further. The rounding on Austria-Hungary might have drawn on traditional themes, but the attack on Giolitti's liberalism converted an internal political opponent into a real ideological enemy. D'Annunzio excluded Giolitti's liberal camp from the nation by accusing it of cowardice and betrayal of the national principles symbolized in the army. The "many-sided cowardice of the Giolitti rabble," he declared, was at its "most repulsive" in the "base defamation of our armed forces, of our national defense."[89] If for Italy the world war meant completing the tasks of the Risorgimento, freeing the nation both internally and externally, today's "liberation army" could be placed in the direct tradition of the *garibaldisti* and their "people's war." At the end of his speech, D'Annunzio symbolically kissed the sword that the Risorgimento hero and Garibaldi follower Nino Bixio held out to him.

But D'Annunzio went a step further, appealing in scarcely disguised terms for violence against the ideological enemy within. In this way, he came out openly against the parliamentary-democratic system, which had recently, in 1913, scored another victory with the introduction of universal male suffrage. Every male citizen today, he pronounced, was "a soldier of Italian liberty," but at "the gathering to celebrate our freedom" on May 20 (when a majority of deputies would finally vote in favor of war credits), "we should not tolerate the shameless presence of those who for months have been negotiating with the enemy to sell Italy out. We should not permit that these buffoons clad in tricolored frocks should come with their unclean throats to shout out the holy name. Draw up your blacklist, showing no mercy. You have the right, even the civil right, to do it. Who has saved Italy in these dark days if not you the true people, if not you the genuine people?"[90]

After the declaration of war on Austria-Hungary, D'Annunzio remained an eccentric symbolic figure of Italian nationalism. At the age of 52, he volunteered for service, was initially used by the Italian general staff as a patriotic speechmaker, and then engaged in daredevil propaganda flights, dropping leaflets over Trieste (in August 1915) and even Vienna (on August 9, 1918). He lost one eye in an air accident, later using the episode in his postwar fiction *Notturno,* in which the hero of his prewar novels matured into a *commandante.* Bitterly disappointed with the implications for Italy of the Versailles peace treaty, which he thought of as a "mutilated victory," he ostensibly followed Garibaldi's Sicilian example in September 1919 by occupying the Istrian port of Fiume with a corps of irregulars, to prevent its acquisition of international status and to force its integration into Italy. While D'Annunzio's male band of *arditi* later turned into fascists, the cocaine and morphine-addicted poet himself withdrew to a state-funded villa, Il Vittoriale, on Lake Garda, which he built up into a symbolic site of militarist nationalism. In 1936 Mussolini's fascist regime published his forty-nine-volume collected works at great expense, and in 1937, a year before his death, D'Annunzio became president of the Italian Academy.[91]

In May 1915, Italian national politics were a long way from civic peace—an important difference from the situation in other European countries in August 1914. The Giolitti era from the 1890s up to his withdrawal in Spring 1914 had been a period of dynamic, if uneven, economic growth, especially in northern Italy, but also one in which social conflicts had sharpened. Apart from the successful industrialization and social modernization (introduction of a social insurance scheme in 1912, universal male suffrage based on a census in 1913, and so on), extra-parliamentary mass politics developed, both in and around the Socialist Party and in the Catholic associations. Giolitti appeared the arch survivor in the parliamentary system, but his very pragmatism exposed the liberal heritage of the Risorgimento to ever-greater criticism. Internationally, Italy had most recently distanced itself during the

Bosnian annexation crisis of 1908 from its German and Austro-Hungarian partners in the Triple Alliance and pursued an aggressively expansionist course in the war with the Ottoman Empire in 1911–1912. However, its acquisition of Libya, Cyrenaica, and the Dodecanese did little to dampen internal political tensions. While the Left rejected Giolitti, the nationalist Right felt vindicated by the Libyan war and increasingly drew conservatives and liberals to its side. Different social-political models took shape on both the Left and the Right, rejecting the existing system and its parliamentary foundations. But once the country entered the war, the opposition to the Salandra government's military policy soon decreased.[92]

In Summer 1914, then, the European war found Italy a volatile society and a divided nation. In the *settimana rossa* in June, anti-militarist demonstrations and a general strike supported by revolutionary sections of the trade unions bordered on civil war, and many members of the propertied bourgeoisie supported the formation of armed militias. The effective collapse of the general strike disillusioned the editor of the Socialist *Avanti!,* Benito Mussolini, one of the leading Socialist intellectuals, and when war broke out in August he despaired of a revolution by the Italian proletariat and went in search of a new ideological model beyond socialism. But the main force discredited in the eyes of many in 1914, because of its conspicuously weak foreign policy and parliamentary practice, was political liberalism, the legacy of nation-building and parliamentarism. This disillusionment applied primarily to parts of the bourgeoisie who saw social unrest as a street assault on their gains. For them, it was no longer possible to respond to this threat with Giolitti's strategies of social compensation.

The Italian government, headed since February 1914 by a center-left coalition under Antonio Salandra, initially stuck in July and August to the mutual defense formulas defining the Triple Alliance and declared its strict neutrality, on the grounds that there had been no actual attack on Austria-Hungary. But this position also offered it the opportunity to test the waters, and in negotiations with both the Central Powers and the Allies it could raise the price for either continued neutrality or entry into the war. The wait-and-see neutrality allowed it to bargain with all players, to obtain the maximum political benefit for participation in the war. The government in Vienna initially refused territorial concessions—principally Italian-speaking

Trentino and areas on the Isonzo around Trieste—so as not to encourage similar demands in other parts of the Dual Monarchy that might upset its precarious balance.[93]

Italy's new foreign secretary Sidney Sonnino, who was appointed in November 1914, began to step up the political pressure in March 1915 vis-à-vis the Dual Monarchy and Paris and London. Long a convinced supporter of the Triple Alliance, he was then pursuing a twofold objective—territorial expansion to build a Greater Italian nation-state and internal political stabilization, in the Risorgimento tradition—that he hoped would result from a national war. In view of the military stalemate on the western front, the persistent pressure on Russia, and the problems that arose in Spring 1915 in the fighting with the Ottoman Empire, the Allies had a major interest in widening the front against the Central Powers. They therefore agreed to many of the Italian demands relating not only to the Trentino and Isonzo areas but also to the Brenner frontier and areas in Dalmatia, as well as economic assistance. The other key factor in the decision of Salandra and Sonnino to enter the war, after the long period of maneuvering, was the widespread identification of neutrality with Giolitti's political system and the crisis of liberalism.[94]

The London treaty signed on April 26, 1915, assured Italy of territorial gains in a future peace, far beyond what it had demanded of Vienna. These stretched from the Tyrol to the Brenner, also including the west bank of the Isonzo, Trieste, and the Istrian peninsula without Fiume, as well as northern and central Dalmatia with all its offshore islands. An Italian sphere of influence was confirmed in Albania, Libya, and the Italian-occupied Dodecanese island group in the Aegean; and Rome was promised participation in the carve-up of the Ottoman Empire in the regions of Antalya, Konya, and Smyrna, as well as the German colonies in Africa. These provisions—which were incompatible with Woodrow Wilson's principles of self-determination—contained the germ of deep disillusionment. As far as many Italians were concerned, each unattained objective, each ungained territory, would mean a lost peace following a war won at great cost in human lives. The later poisoning of Italian internal politics would result from these high unattainable expectations.[95]

More critical internally, however, was the pro-war mobilization of public opinion and the deep division in the country on this issue. In the period between August 1914 and May 1915, supporters and opponents of Italy's entry into the war, interventionists and neutralists, campaigned against one another, further sharpening conflicts from the years before 1914. In contrast to D'Annunzio's aggressive rhetoric, for example, there was certainly no general enthusiasm for war; industrial workers and socialist trade unions, small tenant farmers, a section of the Catholic clergy and Pope Benedict XV, as well as many liberal and conservative deputies around Giolitti, rejected Italian involvement. The interventionist camp was even more heterogeneous politically and ideologically; the radical nationalists on the Right drew in many young bourgeois intellectuals who saw the war as an escape from Giolitti's pragmatism and a corrupt parliamentarism, although they vehemently opposed the socialist demands of the workers and the bourgeois-national legacy of the Risorgimento, which was oriented to the British model or the constitutional interpretation of the ideas of 1789. Most significantly, the aggressive irredentism of the nationalists soon developed a dynamic of its own. Their promises of independence regarding Nice, the Savoy, Corsica, and Malta were reminiscent of Russian, German, and Austrian policy toward Poland at the beginning of the war, but in Italy's case these reflected a dizzying degree of hubris.

The pro-war camp also included big industrialists (who hoped that the conflict would ward off the dangers of proletarian revolution and promote economic expansion at the cost of the Dual Monarchy) and the armed forces under their new commander, Luigi Cadorna, who, like the radical nationalists, saw war as an instrument of social Darwinist selection. Meanwhile, a segment of Catholics hoped that a national war would mark the first cautious steps of reconciliation with the secular state—a rapprochement that Cadorna also sought to promote by formally introducing pastoral care in the army. For the first time, the secular state and the Catholic Church agreed to cooperate under the aegis of war patriotism, which was supposed to draw army padres closer to ordinary soldiers. At the same time, many members of the property-owning and cultured bourgeoisie regarded the vision of a Greater Italian empire as a continuation and completion of the Risorgimento.[96]

But the interventionist camp also embraced sections of the Left, such as Gaetano Salvemini's republican democrats, who wanted to fight on the side of the French Republic and saw the main enemy as the autocratic empires of the Central Powers and their repression of national freedoms. On the Far Left, the most prominent was Mussolini, who initially supported a combination of war and proletarian revolution that put him on a collision course with his strictly neutralist Socialist Party; he was formally excluded from it in November 1914. Unlike the media-savvy Mussolini, who cast himself as a people's tribune by publishing his war diary in his new daily paper *Il Popolo d'Italia,* the Italian reform socialist Cesare Battisti paid with his life for his engagement against Austria-Hungary. Scarcely anyone typified more than him the complex situation leading up to Italy's entry into the war and the far-reaching consequences it would have long after 1918. A native of Trento and therefore an Austrian citizen, Battisti entered the Viennese Imperial Council as a Socialist deputy in 1911 and the Tyrol regional parliament in Innsbruck in 1914, where he forcefully championed autonomy status for the Trento region. Unlike the radical nationalists, however, he did not call for the Brenner Pass to become the border between Austria and Italy, but thought more in terms of a linguistic boundary.[97]

Battisti grasped the war as an opportunity to release the Italian-speaking Trentino from the Dual Monarchy and to incorporate it into the Italian nation-state, thereby reconciling Italian Socialists, too, with the national principle. Having previously published articles in favor of Italy's joining the war, he immediately volunteered in May 1915 for service in the Italian army, only to be captured in July 1916 by Austrian troops and, following a sensational court-martial in Trento, found guilty of high treason and executed. Battisti thus became a polarizing symbol: the Austrian military saw him as proof of Italy's betrayal of the Triple Alliance and Austria-Hungary, while for the Italian side—not only the Left but also Mussolini's regime after 1922—he figured as an exemplary national martyr.[98] What this leaves out is that until 1914, despite the growth of irredentist nationalism in Italy, there were few in either the Trentino region or Trieste who wanted to change the political status quo. For most Italians living in the Habsburg monarchy, their *italianità* offered a welcome possibility to delimit themselves from Germans and Slavs within the Empire, without having to tie themselves to Italians in the new nation-state south of the Alps. At first, even many irredentists in the Trentino looked on Italians elsewhere as foreigners; Battisti himself, during his period of service in the Italian army, was reminded of Muslims when he met soldiers from southern Italy, while many Italian-speaking Tyrolians were proud to serve in the Tyrolian Imperial Fusiliers. Only the aggressive conduct of the Viennese government, and above all the army high command, against alleged Italian traitors and spies, including the deportation of civilians from border areas and frontline regions, hardened attitudes and made integration into the Kingdom of Italy a popular option. That did not seem in the cards before 1914, however, nor did it correspond to opinion among the Italian-speaking population.[99]

Until the last minute it was by no means certain that Italy would join the war. In Spring 1915, a survey conducted by prefects showed that a majority of the population opposed intervention, but would be prepared to follow the decisions of the king and government. In parliament, not long before the approval of war credits, hundreds of deputies were still assuring Giolitti that they supported his policy of strict neutrality, and even at the cabinet level there was no talk of a clear course. On May 13, Prime Minister Salandra offered his resignation to the king because he could not obtain a majority for his position. In the end, however, other factors tipped the scales for war. First, the interventionists managed to gain a firm hold over public opinion, as such figures as D'Annunzio and national dailies like *L'Idea nazionale* popularized the idea of war as a national liberation struggle, stirring up the masses against Giolitti's neutralism. Second, while Salandra and Sonnino alarmed the king with the dangers of civil war and an imminent coup d'état if the people was denied the war it supposedly desired, they kept members of parliament in the dark for a long time about the secret talks with the Allies. When the king and premier finally opted to enter the war, and the king again asked Salandra to form a government, the rejectionist front in parliament collapsed. On May 20 and 21, a large majority of 407–74 gave the government special powers in the event of war, and the declaration of war on Austria-Hungary followed on May 23.

Deeply divided politically and ideologically, Italian society entered a war that, though highly contested until the end, immediately became associated with great expectations and political projections. One reason why Giolitti's policy orientation to restraint and neutrality failed in 1915 was the conflict at the level of principle between the Italian nation-state and the multiethnic Habsburg monarchy. Austria-Hungary rejected nationality as the defining principle of political order, challenging as it did the very existence of the multiethnic empire. Italy, in contrast, scarcely had any choice in the matter, since that very principle, the result of the Risorgimento, underpinned its existence as a state. Aggressive nationalism, with its persistent claim to the *irredenta*, might at times appear inopportune, but the government had to keep conjuring it up to justify the expropriation of the princes and the pope and the existence of the state founded in 1861.[100] The demands of 1915 were thus bound up with the legitimacy and moral credibility of the Italian nation-state. In peacetime it was possible to overlook this and to support the Triple Alliance in the spirit of international *Realpolitik*, but at its core this was an alliance between opposing conceptions of state legitimacy and action logics.[101]

The Italian declaration of war added a new conflict zone in the Alps alongside those in the west and east, in southeastern Europe, and on other continents. This new front extended from the Stelvio Pass on the Swiss frontier across the Dolomites and the Carnic and Julian Alps, before bending south to meet up with the Isonzo River on the Adriatic coast. For the German top brass around Falkenhayn, who saw the western front as the main theater of war, it did not have great strategic significance. But for Conrad von Hötzendorf, Italy soon became the number one enemy of the Dual Monarchy. By Summer 1916 these different assessments were having an impact on the conduct of the war, because there was no effective agreement between the two alliance partners either on the eastern European fronts or in the Alpine war. From the Allies' point of view, the new front weakened the position of the Dual Monarchy, since the diversion of Austro-Hungarian troops to the Alps gave the Russian armies a greater chance of breaking through in Galicia. The war would not be decided in the Alps—of that they could be sure—but right from the start the fighting there reached an intensity and brutality that reflected the peculiarities of the terrain, as well as the conduct of the war on both sides. Never before in history had an Alpine war been fought for so long in such inhospitable conditions, at heights more than 2,000 and often more than 3,000 meters above sea level.

Once the front had stabilized within the first few months of war, small units on both sides were able to defend their positions so efficiently that they could not be driven out even at great cost.[102] To maintain supply lines in the

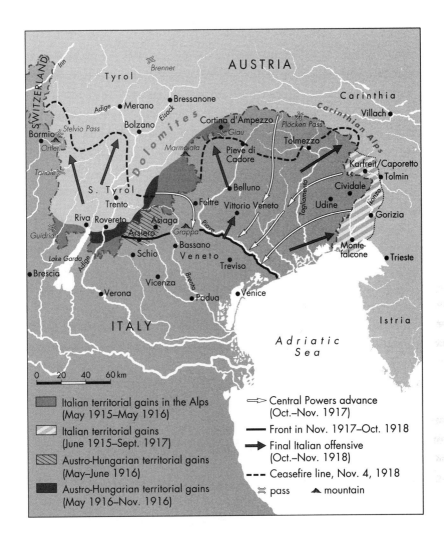

SWITZERLAND

Inn

Tyrol

Brenner

AUSTRIA

Adige • Merano • Bressanone

Carinthia

Stelvio Pass
Bolzano
Eisack
Cortina d'Ampezzo
Plöcken Pass
Villach •

Bormio •
Dolomites
Giau
Tolmezzo

Ortler •
Marmolata
Pieve di Cadore
Carinthian Alps

Tonale
S. Tyrol
• Belluno
Karfreit/Caporetto

Trento
• Feltre
Cividale
Tolmin

Riva
Vittorio Veneto
Udine
Isonzo

Rovereto
Asiago
• Gorizia

Guidriar
Arsiero
Grappa
Piave

Lake Garda
Adige
• Bassano
Monte-falcone

• Schio
Veneto
Brenta
Treviso
• Trieste

Brescia
Vicenza

Verona
• Padua
• Venice

ITALY

Istria

*A d r i a t i c
S e a*

0 20 40 60 km

Italian territorial gains in the Alps (May 1915–May 1916)	⇨ Central Powers advance (Oct.–Nov. 1917)
Italian territorial gains (June 1915–Sept. 1917)	— Front in Nov. 1917–Oct. 1918
Austro-Hungarian territorial gains (May–June 1916)	➤ Final Italian offensive (Oct.–Nov. 1918)
Austro-Hungarian territorial gains (May 1916–Nov. 1916)	--- Ceasefire line, Nov. 4, 1918
	≋ pass ▲ mountain

Map 6. Alpine Front, 1915–1918

often extreme terrain required special logistical efforts—from the carrying of dismantled mortars to barely accessible valleys; through the deployment of artillery pieces in zones of caves, cliffs, and glaciers beneath the Ortler Mountain peak (at a height of 3,900 meters); to the small-scale fortification of exposed positions.[103] From 1916, large mine tunnels were constructed to set off explosions at the heart of enemy positions. But even the densest massing of artillery and the most elaborate infrastructure—in the Marmolada glacier, the Austrians dug a mine system eight kilometers long—could not escape the fact that in this kind of positional warfare nothing was capable of achieving a strategic breakthrough.[104]

The familiar pattern of huge military expenditure for only slight territorial gains repeated itself in a series of eleven battles on the Isonzo; there too, a battle of materiel and a war of attrition were the dominant features.[105] Only in the twelfth battle in October 1917, which had started as a limited offensive by the Central Powers to relieve the beleaguered front, did the depleted Austrian and German forces break through at Caporetto. Until this crisis, attributable mainly to the complete exhaustion of the Italian troops, the same shift from war of movement to war of position, the same combination of attack, counterattack, and mutual attrition, developed as on the western front. But the Alpine conditions, the large troop concentrations and costly supply lines across narrow, difficult terrain, the huge expense of transporting men and materiel—all this meant that the balance between casualty figures, territorial gains, and strategic results was much more skewed than in other theaters, so that even the troops questioned the wisdom of constantly attacking well-defended positions. On the Austro-Hungarian side, the emphasis was on Italy's betrayal; the self-image centered on defense of the fatherland against disloyal ex-partners in the Triple Alliance held good even for soldiers of Slav origin. Until 1918, desertion rates among Austro-Hungarian troops on the Alpine front remained low. On the other side, the lack of tangible successes in return for the high casualties soon led to disillusionment in the ranks of the Italian army and to anger against officers because of poor equipment. The large number of disciplinary proceedings, affecting on average every twelfth Italian soldier until the end of the war, and the draconian justice system, which meted out a total of 4,000 death sentences and more than 15,000 terms of life imprisonment,

War in geographical and climatic extremes: Austrian mountain ranger, 1915

reflected the combination of pressure to perform, high casualty rates, and creeping demoralization.

In contrast to the interventionist rhetoric, it soon turned out that the Italian army was ill prepared for offensive warfare. In particular, inadequate artillery support for infantry attacks placed the defenders in a tactically superior position—even though the Austro-Hungarian army, weakened by its winter campaign against the Russians in the Carpathians, initially had to struggle to cope with the opening of another front. The defense of a front stretching for more than 600 kilometers had to be improvised, with the result that regional forces such as the Tyrol and Vorarlberg militia units were brought into the fray. A special "Alpine Corps," the first separate force of mountain troops ever raised by the German army, further supported Austro-Hungary in the early period and again in the crisis after 1917. Austro-Hungary's defensive war, a child of necessity, proved so successful that until the end of 1917 its forces got by without major German assistance. It was precisely there on the Italian front that Conrad von Hötzendorf sought to assert the AOK's autonomy of German commanders.

In the extreme conditions, both sides relied on experienced elite units such as the Austrian Imperial Fusiliers or the locally recruited Italian *Alpini* (especially important for the heroic image of combat against the enemy and nature). Of the Imperial Fusiliers, some 40 percent came from the Trentino region and a sizable number from the Tyrol, but Italian hopes that many of them would change sides proved unfounded.[106] As the casualty toll rose, it became necessary to deploy troops with no experience of the Alps.

The Italian attack plans in May 1915 envisaged a breakthrough and an advance on Trento across the high plateau near Lavarone. Attempts to achieve this came to grief, however, when they failed to destroy the Austrian defensive barriers softened up by Italian artillery. Even more dramatic was the failure of the open, unprotected infantry attacks on the Isonzo, where the Italian supreme commander, Cadorna, had committed fourteen divisions (half of his entire army) to force a breakthrough whatever the cost and to capture Trieste and the Slovenian capital, Ljubljana, a symbol of the *irredenta*. Once again, as on the western front, the defenders enjoyed a clear tactical advantage, inflicting high losses on the Italians with their artillery and machine-gun fire; there too, the strategy of slowly wearing down the enemy soon came into effect. But as the war dragged on, its huge burdens undermined the strength of military units. By the end of 1915 the Italian Casale Brigade had spent seven months in the trenches, with only nine days of breaks, and had lost 4,276 soldiers and 154 officers.[107] The toll for the whole war, for an army of 2.2 million men, added up to 800,000 men.[108]

Entry into the war soon had a major impact on the politics, society, and economy of Italy, bringing about many of the same developments that had been experienced by other countries since Summer 1914. The parliament in Rome effectively ceded its powers to the government, losing control particularly of state finances. At the same time, there was an enormous expansion of the government and state bureaucracy: new ministries, authorities, and agencies were continually being created, and the Comitato per la mobilitazione industriale, run by an army general, established itself as a dictatorial second government. The war favored a new elite of bureaucrats, officers, and industrialists, which opted more and more for authoritarian solutions and contributed to the loss of credibility of the liberal-constitutional system.[109] The conversion of the economy to a war footing soon produced its winners and losers: while the consumption goods industries suffered, firms of importance to the war effort often profited from the loss of rivals. This combination of soaring demand for military goods and declining competitive pressure explains the enormous boost given to Fiat in Turin, where the number of employees increased from 4,300 to 40,000 and its corporate capital from 17 to 200 million lire.[110]

In southeastern Europe, as well as the Ottoman Empire, the year 1915 was one of war-driven expansion. The Suez Canal illustrated to perfection how essential the security of the British Empire's transport and supply system was to the mother country. The landing of two Indian divisions on the northern shore of the Persian Gulf was supposed to secure the British oil production facilities at Abadan—whose importance had grown considerably with the shift from coal to oil fuel in the Royal Navy. After the failure of the Gallipoli campaign, it became apparent that, despite the relative weakness of the Ottoman army, there would be no walkover in the Ottoman territories that before 1914 had endured one defeat after another; the British top brass had underestimated the will of the Young Turk officer elite to resist the threatened breakup of the Empire. It would take much longer, and require new strategies as well as extensive promises to Arab tribal leaders, before British forces finally managed to capture the key centers of the Near East and Mesopotamia: Baghdad in March 1917, Jerusalem in December 1917, and—the climax of the Arab anti-Ottoman revolt—Damascus in October 1918.[111]

But in 1915 the aftereffects of Gallipoli were also felt elsewhere. By foiling the Allied plan to establish a stable front in the southeastern Mediterranean, the Ottoman Empire could feel secure to its west and also maintain the blockade on Russia's supply lines. Politically, moreover, neither Greece nor Romania could be brought to join the war on the Allied side, whereas Bulgaria went over to the Central Powers. This meant that the situation in southeastern Europe for the Central Powers was much better than it had been in 1914: there was a real chance of defeating Serbia and thereby linking up with the Ottoman Empire by land. Above all, Bulgaria's decision to join the war followed a policy that Italy and other countries had also been pursuing, one of intensive negotiations with both sides in order to extract the maximum territorial gains. For Bulgaria and Italy in 1915, as for Romania in 1916 and Greece in 1917, the aim was to complete the building of their own nation-states through participation in the wider war. The rival promises of the two alliances thus kindled hopes in the "liberation" of unreclaimed national lands, the so-called *irredenta*. In effect, the war incited visions of a Greater Bulgaria, Italy, Romania, and Greece, raising huge expectations in the respective countries and putting politicians there under pressure.

In 1915, in the case of Bulgaria, this strategy eclipsed the traditional pan-Slav orientation to Russia and the pro-Russian attitudes of a majority of the population. The war seemed to offer an opportunity to revive the goal of an ethnically homogeneous Greater Bulgarian state that had failed to be realized in the Balkan wars of 1912–1913. The Allies, having to take Serbia and neutral Greece into account, could not promise Sofia any major territorial expansion, but the Central Powers could accommodate Bulgarian designs on Macedonia and parts of eastern Serbia, and also—in the event that Romania and Greece joined the war on the other side—offer further land grabs in Thrace and southern Dobruja. Furthermore, the Bulgarian government negotiated an indenture with a German-Austrian-Hungarian consortium.[112] It eventually signed the alliance treaty in September 1915, entering the war with a contingent under the command of the German field marshal von Mackensen.[113]

This was a key development for the further course and long-term consequences of the world war. Wait-and-see "bargaining" over territorial demands, with its associated vision of a homogeneous nation-state at the cost of neighboring countries, aroused expectations that could not be fulfilled in the event of defeat and would not necessarily be realized to the full in the event of victory. Either of these outcomes would mean bitter disappointment for these nation-states that had taken shape quite late in the nineteenth century, and so the seeds were sown for an aggressive revisionism that would weigh lastingly on internal politics in many postwar societies of east central and southeastern Europe.

5. CONTINGENCY AND STUBBORNNESS
The Soldier's Experience of the Front and the Limits
of Wartime National Rhetoric

Gabriel Chevallier, a notary's son born in 1895 in Lyon and from 1911 a student at the École nationale supérieure des beaux-arts in Lyon, experienced the war as an ordinary soldier. In his first novel, *La Peur,* published in 1930, he conveyed through the eyes of Jean Dartemont (largely drawn from his own life) the impressions of a French *poilu* on the western front in the year of the great French spring and fall offensives.[114] The *poilu* soon became the symbol of the ordinary French frontline soldier, countless picture postcards making him a fixed part of the collective image of the war back home. He embodied the tradition of the citizen-soldier, underlining the continuity of patriotic defense in the spirit of the French revolutionary wars.[115] The word *poilu* ("hairy" or "bearded") referred to the fact that troops on active service were generally unable to shave, and it was already used in the Napoleonic armies to describe tested soldiers, in contrast to a *bleu* or rookie.[116] It was popularized by Henri Barbusse's novel *Le Feu* (Under Fire) in 1916 as a term for the honorable, courageous, and experienced frontline soldier who had not lost his sense of humor, composure, or staying power. A whole vocabulary tinged with humor and irony developed around the *poilu.* By 1918, the *Dictionnaire humoristique et philologique du langage des soldats de la Grande Guerre de 1914* suggested that there was something alien about the figure: "M. Maurice Barrès also thinks: '*Poilu!* The term has something animal-like. . . . When he is in action, the Poilu stands out because of his admirable spontaneity and unflinching truth. He is just and daring, an embodiment of the warrior. . . .' The term *poilu* is common both at the front and behind the lines. At the front only officers and NCOs use it. When soldiers speak of themselves, they do not use the expression *poilus* but rather *bonhommes,* doubtless out of modesty. The captain would say: 'I need thirty *poilus* this evening.' . . . The Poilu himself would rather use the term *poilu* for civilians or colonial troops—that is, for anyone different from him."[117]

On August 15, 1915, the *poilu* Jean Dartemont first saw a large section of the front from the tower of a church damaged by artillery fire, on Mont-Saint-Éloi in Artois: "From up there you could see right across the plains of

Artois, but it was impossible to make out any real signs of a battle. A few white puffs of smoke, followed by explosions, told us that this was indeed where the war was, but we could not see any trace of the armies on the ground observing and destroying each other slowly in this arid, silent landscape." What the soldier saw from those heights bore no relation to what he knew of the cruelty of battle: "Such a calm expanse, baking in the sunshine, confounded our expectations. We could see the trenches quite clearly but they looked like tiny embankments, or narrow winding streams, and it seemed incredible that this fragile network could offer serious resistance to attacks, that people did not simply step across it to move forward."[118] In the soldier's perception, there were no longer battlefields in the traditional sense, but only individual sectors of the front, segmented spaces, at which long-distance artillery also directed its fire. People thought in terms of a "targeted landscape": land seemed to "come to an end" toward the front, after which followed "nothingness."[119] To the rear lay a different space with phased functions, defined by a network of supply and defense trenches, artillery positions, and finally the communications zone. The shift from a war of movement to positional warfare redrew the cosmos of war. It now consisted of large supply depots for food and munitions, first aid centers for the wounded, holding positions for fresh troops, and rest areas for combatants after they had seen action. Ernst Jünger described this world behind the front in Storm of Steel: "And so we visited the abattoir, the commissariat and gunnery repair workshop in Boyelles, the sawmill and pioneer park in the woods of Bourlon, the dairy, pig farm and rendering plant in Inchy, the aviation park and bakery in Quéant."[120]

If one looks at panoramic photos of the western front taken at the time from elevated positions and compares them with aerial pictures, one gets a strong impression of an invisible war quite unlike the soldiers' actual experience in the zones of death; nor do the innumerable aerial photos give any real hint of the scale and intensity of the artillery barrages.[121] Rather, they furnish abstract images, in which one can at most make out trench lines and a landscape pockmarked with shell craters. The aerial photography and panoramic shots of the front convey a sense of great emptiness. Usually there is no enemy in sight—indeed, no soldiers at all. And where ruined hamlets or villages do not testify to the effects of martial violence, there is

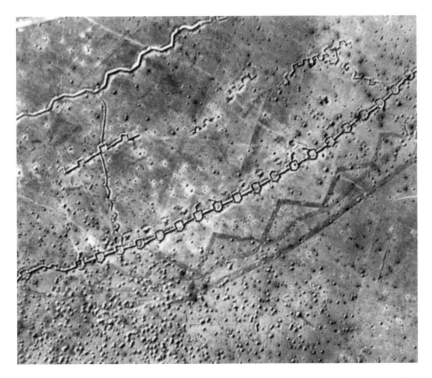

Abstraction and emptiness: the geometric landscape of war—aerial photo of German trenches at Oppy

not necessarily anything to suggest a battle zone, especially if the enemy's trench systems have been adapted to the landscape.

After the first few months, with the shift on the western front to positional warfare, the massive impact of long-range heavy artillery dominated the soldiers' experience at the front and made the killing process largely anonymous. The enemy that killed was seen not as another human being but as an impersonal "it." The danger of death, present in every section of the front where there was actual combat, was impossible to predict: shelling could start at any moment, and anyone could be killed or wounded by it. The power of chance, which decided whether you survived the war or not, became a constant leitmotif.[122] In September 1915, for example, Robert Musil received the impact of an Italian flechette that landed right next to him. (Flechettes were steel darts, up to 15 centimeters long, which fighter pilots dropped from their aircraft.) For Musil, the experience had the force of an initiation, in which unawareness of the projectile combined with awareness of the immediate proximity of death: "The piece of shrapnel or airman's dart up in Tenna: the sound has already been perceptible for a long time. The noise made by a whistling or rushing wind. Getting louder and louder. Time seems to pass very slowly. Suddenly something went into the ground right next to me. As if the ground were being swallowed up. No memory of any air-wave. But this must have been so since I instinctively wrenched my upper body to one side and, with feet firmly planted, made quite a deep bow. No trace of fright as I did so, not even any purely nervous response such as palpitations that otherwise manifest themselves with any sudden shock even when there is no sense of fear. Afterward a very pleasant feeling. Satisfaction at having had the experience. Almost pride, being taken up into a community, baptism."[123]

This sense of exposure to death was not limited to actual battle. Jean Dartemont described a changed perception of sky and sunset (read: nature and time), which before the war had been symbols of peace but had now become dangerous traps if they caused the soldier to drop his guard: "The rose-pink morning light, the silence of dusk, the warmth of midday, all these are traps. Happiness is a ruse, preparing us for an ambush. A man feels a sudden sense of physical well-being and raises his head above the parapet: a bullet kills him. A bombardment goes on for hours but there are only a few victims, while a single shell fired for want of anything better to do lands in the middle of a platoon and wipes it out. A soldier comes back from the long nightmare of Verdun and on an exercise a grenade detonates in his hand, tearing off his arm, ripping open his chest."[124]

Dawn and dusk acquired important meaning in the soldiers' eyes: preparations for major offensives took place in the light of a new day; the sky appeared in a special light from the trenches. But the old idea of the sky as a symbol for hope and peace, as a universal locus of human purification or even salvation, gave way to heightened fear on the soldiers' part. The heavens lost their traditional aesthetic and moral significance. Daybreak became the danger zone, and the German word *Morgengrauen* (*Grauen* has the dual sense of [day]break and horror) reflected this wartime shift in perception.[125]

The proximity of death and the randomness of danger resulted in a permanent stress situation and a huge psychological burden on soldiers. Battle had no beginning or end in the traditional sense, and therefore no markers from which some degree of security could be derived. The killing zone at the front was not only the space where attacks and enemy counterattacks were launched but also the area where long-range artillery could have an impact at any moment. You could feel safe only when you got outside it. On the other hand, the dominance of mechanized warfare meant that the enemy remained invisible within ever more intricate defensive systems. The oppressive reality of trench warfare disguised the fact that, after the devastating losses of the early weeks of the war, trenches did make soldiers considerably safer in the face of unprotected attacks across open territory, especially as they were constantly built up and reinforced in the course of 1915. Casualty rates therefore fell appreciably with the shift to positional warfare in late 1914.[126]

Frontline soldiers experienced a paradox of the war: short, highly concentrated situations of combat during attacks and counterattacks were followed by periods of stagnation when the men often had to sit still and wait, either in the trenches or in rest areas behind the front.[127] The constant work of perfecting the defensive systems and rear communication zones also played a role in keeping the masses of soldiers busy outside periods of combat. After his first few days at the front in the peak of Summer 1915, Chevallier's alter ego Dartemont could note, "I had been astonished to find myself in the middle of the war yet not be able to find it, unable to accept that in fact the war consisted precisely of this stasis. But I had to *see* it, so I clambered up on a fire-step and stuck my head above the parapet. Through the tangle of barbed wire an embankment very much like ours could be seen less than a hundred meters away, silent as if abandoned, yet full of eyes and gunsights focused on us."[128] Robert Michaels, a captain and cavalryman in the Austrian army, explained in a letter to his son that, contrary to all historical experience, soldiers on the new battlefields had to retreat and conceal themselves at the sight of the enemy. This was leading to a novel relationship to space. The point now was not to make oneself seen as a soldier or officer, to display one's presence by means of uniforms, decorations, and flags, but rather to use space always in such a way that one was invisible to the enemy. Land warfare, Michaels concluded, was being waged increasingly in trenches and dugouts, the war at sea was being transferred to submarines, and in the air pilots were trying to fly as high as possible so as to avoid ground fire.[129]

It was not only in retrospect that the trench became an iconic locus of the war—the place where people experienced most clearly the distinctive super-imposition of fear and boredom, mortal danger and stagnation, as well as the geographical and climatic conditions of various regions.[130] Together with the machine gun and the gas mask, the trench deeply marked the experience of war for millions of soldiers on the western front, but it was also a key element in other battle zones such as nonmountainous areas of the southern front (the Isonzo, for instance), the Balkans on the Macedonian front starting in Salonica, and northern sections of the eastern front that were relatively stable between 1915 and 1917. Where war of movement dominated—in south-ern sections of the eastern front between the Pripet marshes and Romania, which witnessed major Russian offensives in 1916 and 1917—the trenches remained rather improvised. Outside Continental Europe, in Africa and the Near East, they were an exception because war of movement with small units was the normal feature of that war. Only in Mesopotamia and Gaza were trench systems worth speaking of constructed in 1916 and 1917.[131]

Constant improvements on the western front in the course of 1915 created a wide area of phased, interlinked trench systems that provided cover for the supply of fresh troops, munitions, and food to the most advanced posi-tions. If trenches at the very front had to be abandoned in the face of enemy attack, these staggered defenses prevented a frontal breakthrough, and the ever more sophisticated organization of areas to the rear gave defenders the possibility to regroup in the trenches that remained secure and to bring up fresh troops and supplies. This whole system, more and more polished over time, made it hard for the enemy to advance and hold new territory on more than a temporary basis. Furthermore, German trench systems on the western front were in most cases more robust than those of the Allies. While German troops were able to defend the territory they had occupied in 1914, having usually secured the more elevated positions, the Allied commanders tended to accept trenches as at best a temporary expedient, so as not to weaken the offensive resolve of their men and encourage their latent cowardice. Senior officers gave up this attitude only slowly and after much hesitation.[132]

On the Somme, many German trenches right on the frontline were more than 4 meters deep, and dugouts as much as 12 meters, in order to give sol-diers effective shelter from artillery bombardment. Suitable ladders were

Trenches and barbed wire: the microcosm of everyday life—a French infantryman at Verdun, Winter 1916–1917

required to reach the firing line above. The ever more elaborate dugouts and tunnels certainly offered protection, but many soldiers suffered torments climbing down into the confined spaces. Henri Barbusse described one such experience in his novel *Le Feu,* which as mentioned was first published in 1916: "There are two entries, very low and very narrow, on the level of the ground. This one is flush with the mouth of a sloping gallery, narrow as the conduit of a sewer. In order to penetrate the Refuge, one must first turn round and work backwards with bent body into the shrunken pipe. . . . Once inside you have a first impression of being trapped—that there is not room enough either to descend or to climb out. As you go on burying yourself in the gulf, the nightmare of suffocation continues that you progressively endured as you advanced along the bowels of the trenches before foundering in here.

On all sides you bump and scrape yourself, you are clutched by the tightness of the passage, you are wedged and stuck. I have to change the position of my cartridge pouches by sliding them round the belt and to take my bread bags in my arm against my chest."[133]

Further refinements to the trench system included planking, piled sandbags, special loopholes, and mobile barbed-wire obstacles that could be opened to clear assault paths toward the enemy. Soldiers wore special breastplates to protect themselves against shrapnel. Thus, along with the modernization of weapons technology in twentieth-century warfare, armies resorted to very traditional measures to protect individual soldiers. Zigzag lines were meant to prevent enemy raiders from firing on whole trench systems, and they did limit the effect of shrapnel or fragmentation bombs. Dugouts, forward listening posts, "saps" (covered trenches at a 90-degree angle) from which patrols fanned out in the no-man's-land between enemy lines, and tunnels leading toward the enemy's frontline completed the immediate area of the front.

The reality of positional warfare: breastplates for frontline troops, 1916–1917

The increasingly complex zone of trenches for the purposes of protection, supply, and communication, which added up to a system more than 40,000 kilometers long on the western front, gave new arrivals the impression of an impenetrable labyrinth. Clear points of reference were often lacking, as in the crater-pocked strip of no-man's-land usually 100 to 200 meters wide.[134] In a diary entry in July 1916, during the Battle of the Somme, Ernst Jünger described confusion as "one of the greatest dangers," since a unit that wandered off course a little usually got lost; "the many holes mean it can easily bump into some English, not to mention the shells constantly crashing down. And if you fall into enemy hands, you can't count on pardon. Here everyone knows it's do or die and there is enormous bitterness. Why take prisoners, when you'll have to struggle through the barrage to get them to the rear?"[135] In these conditions, dead comrades even came to serve as markers: "And everywhere full of dead men, tossed and ripped apart a hundred times over. Whole firing lines lie before the positions, our gully is filled with corpses lying on top of one another in layers. We can't advance three spade's lengths without . . . coming across a body part. Dead men to left and right of the approaches. They have fallen, perhaps been wounded, comrades walked on in the agitation of death. Dead men on the approach paths neatly indicate whether you are still heading in the right direction."[136] Many soldiers lost their way, especially on night marches. One English soldier, Charles Carrington, reported, "When moving about in the trenches you turn a corner every few yards, which makes it seem like walking in a maze. It is impossible to keep your sense of direction and infinitely tiring to proceed at all. When the trenches have been fought over the confusion becomes all the greater. Instead of neat, parallel trench lines, you make the best use of existing trenches which might run in any direction other than the one you would prefer, until an old battlefield, like that of the Somme, became a labyrinth of trenches without any plan."[137]

A new kind of soldiers' microcosm took shape, an experiential space with its own rules and communication habits. In this space everyday life had little in common with the idea of uninterrupted struggle, of permanent switching between attack and counterattack. On the western front from the Channel to the Swiss frontier—geographically western only from the German viewpoint—there were zones of intensive combat and others where all might be quiet for weeks or months at a time. In the latter areas, as in the Vosges, soldiers developed a practice of informal rules and agreements across enemy lines; these went far beyond ad hoc local truces or the kind of meetings in no-man's-land that took place at Christmas 1914. Gabriel Chevallier described how this informal communication worked, after an exchange of fire between the French and German trenches on the Vosges front: "The trench, almost leveled, is being pegged out by a working party in a long line, their rifles lying on the ground beside them. Twenty meters away, other shovels are clanging and you can clearly see shadows bending over the ground. The Germans are working on their side, and this part of the front is just one big building site. Accompanied by a sergeant, I walk several meters out beyond our working party, driven by curiosity as much as bravado. A German shadow begins to cough loudly, to point out that we are breaking the rules, going beyond the limits of neutrality. We cough in our turn to reassure this vigilant watchman."[138]

This "live and let live" principle, operating below the leadership level, provided a minimum of security to soldiers on each side by making violence a rule-bound ritual event for which the men in the trenches could prepare themselves.[139] Older practices involving ritualized forms of violence showed through in the microcosm of the modern front. By this time, however, there was a situational logic of survival within an experiential space dominated by instruments of violence—a logic counterbalancing the randomness of mechanized killing and being killed. It had little to do with political motives or a conscious rejection of the war, still less with disguised support for the enemy. Rather, it was an appeal to the reason of those who sought a minimum of security to survive in a particular danger zone. Arranged truces to exchange food, tobacco, and newspapers; to recover the dead and wounded from no-man's-land; or to swap information about planned artillery barrages or the detonation of forward explosive charges were supposed to give the enemy a chance to get out of harm's way. The smaller the no-man's-land between the frontline trenches, the more intensely such agreements were struck. Hence a section of front where the German and French trenches were just under 10 meters apart counted among the safest on the whole western front.[140] Against this background, local geographical conditions played a key role in the soldiers' lives: high groundwater levels in coastal sections of the front in the north or Flanders made it more difficult to get through the day, and particularly to excavate dugout shelters, whereas a regular "mole war," with a distinctive subterranean microcosm, developed in the Argonne region.[141]

Unlike in December 1914 or again in 1917, large-scale troop fraternization was quite exceptional. However, special conditions affecting everyone on one section of the front might lead to temporary truces, as in mid-December 1915, when heavy rain in the area of Neuville-Saint-Vaast flooded the trenches so badly that men from both sides gathered in no-man's-land and in some cases began to sing the "Internationale." Although in theory such understandings made the participants liable to severe punishment, and although officers tried to eliminate them whenever possible (for example, by swapping units in affected areas of the front), the penalties for NCOs and men remained within limits when compared with those for other offenses. The system was subtly tolerated at the local level, often being a reflex action on the soldiers' part to intolerable living conditions.[142]

For any new arrival at the front, death and survival became key points of reference. The proximity of death made it difficult to classify soldiers in hindsight as either perpetrators or victims.[143] The reality of their lives could not be simply reduced to a killing instinct or a special national culture of violence, nor to the image of men ruthlessly sent to the slaughter by generals or the class system. On returning from his first offensive action in 1915, the *poilu* Jean Dartemont found the trench from which the original attack had been launched and that had meanwhile been shelled by German artillery. The young soldier was not prepared for the many faces of death that there reflected the colossal force of the weapons in use: "Corpses contorted into every possible position, corpses which had suffered every possible mutilation, every gaping wound, every agony. There were complete corpses, serene and perfectly composed like stone saints in a chapel; undamaged corpses without any evident injuries; foul, blood-soaked corpses like the prey of unclean beasts; calm, resigned, insignificant corpses; the terrifying corpses of men who had refused to die. . . . And then there were the pieces of corpses, the shreds of bodies and clothes, organs, severed members, red and purple human flesh, like rotten meat in a butcher's, limp, flabby, yellow fat, bones extruding marrow, unraveled entrails, like vile worms that we crushed with a shudder. . . . To escape such horror, I looked out at the plain. A new and greater horror: the plain was blue. The plain was covered with our comrades, cut down by machine guns, their faces in the mud, arses in the air, indecent, grotesque like puppets, but pitiable like men."[144]

Although such episodes and the high casualty rate in particular battles marked contemporary images of the First World War, and especially recollections of the western front, the killing and the danger of being killed were very unevenly distributed in time and space and across the generations. Periods of extreme peril under shellfire and infantry attack alternated with the greatest possible inactivity and monotony. Not constant deployment right at the frontline but a demoralizing mix of action, rest, and waiting in reserve was the stuff of daily life for most soldiers. An average British battalion spent 42 percent of the war at the front, 38 percent in reserve close to the front, and 20 percent in a rest position.[145] In 1915, French units on the western front were used in offensives on 100 out of 365 days.[146] Often it was the move from rest

Living with death: Italian soldiers in trenches

areas to the front or a return from home leave that triggered disquiet among soldiers or, later in the war, even insubordination. The mutinies of Spring 1917 in the French army did not begin in frontline trenches, but rather in reserve positions and rest areas, when men weary from earlier attacks were ordered back to the front.

The German army in August and September 1914 suffered the highest casualty rates (12.4 percent and 16.8 percent, respectively)—that is, the number of dead, wounded, missing, and captured as a percentage of the total strength of units deployed. Subsequently, its monthly losses on the western front averaged only 3.5 percent until Spring 1918, but then they increased once more. On the eastern front, in 1916–1917, the corresponding ratios were roughly two-thirds of those in the west. In terms of age, the toll more and more affected young soldiers, particularly conscripts with little experience of the front. Nearly half of the German and British dead were between ages 19 and 24; men older than 30 accounted for 30 percent of the fighting strength of units, but only one-tenth of the numbers killed. In 1917 and 1918, just under 25 percent of the war dead were soldiers aged between 18 and 20. Losses were particularly high among the American forces who, with no previous experience of the war, began to arrive on the western front in early 1918.[147]

After Summer and Fall 1914, when classical infantry weapons were still being used on the western front, the deployment of artillery changed the typical pattern of injuries. Between 1914 and 1917, 76 percent of the French wounded were casualties of shelling, while in the German army only 16 percent owed their wounds to infantry munitions. The proportion of casualties from hand grenades and poison gas was even lower (1–2 percent and 1.7 percent, respectively). Thus there was a glaring discrepancy between the actual physical effects of these weapons (especially poison gas) and what the media imagined. On the other hand, the ideal in every army had long been an infantry attack by men with the will to fight at close quarters in the enemy trenches, whereas in reality such classical methods scarcely figured in combat any more. Only 0.1 percent of all wounds were inflicted by sabers, knives, or bayonets. One final symptom of the extreme conditions was the high percentage of soldiers who died not from the effect of weapons but from pulmonary or gastrointestinal infections. This phenomenon grew worse because of food supply problems at the front, and it explains the devastating consequences of the Spanish flu epidemic in the army during and after Summer 1918. Despite the improved medical care in comparison with previous wars, one-tenth of German and one-sixth of Austro-Hungarian troops died of such illnesses.[148]

Everyday life in the trenches also depended on the climate, on cold and damp, on the presence of vermin (especially rats and lice), and on hunger and thirst if artillery fire had caused supply problems. Patrols and guard duty caused lack of sleep. Despite temporary agreements across the lines and the rotation of active periods and rest at the rear, the constant possibility of death, as well as random strikes in the killing zone and elsewhere, placed the soldiers under permanent stress. A focus on individual battles obscures the fact that, from 1915 on, as many soldiers died in circumstances such as night patrols, minor skirmishes, or excavation work (with its exposure to shelling) as in the actual battles. Fear that a bombardment would bury them alive in a dugout or tunnel was so widespread that it often became a synonym for "war neurosis."[149] War no longer left room for idealized hand-to-hand combat, a model of playing by the rules derived from the situation of the duel. Hence national rhetoric and explanations of the war corresponded less and less to the real world of soldiers' lives and experiences, where they had to manage as best they could and get to know the particular rules and dangers. To survive did not mean pursuing the ideal of patriotic sacrifice, but holding out and enduring.

Life at the front was more varied than the image of "field gray" uniformity suggested, primarily because modern warfare entailed huge functional differences not only among infantry, artillery, cavalry, and air force units but also between combat troops and supply and maintenance units. In the soldiers' eyes, the *embusqué* type, the "shirker," existed both back home and at the front—for example, among messengers or members of artillery and cavalry units, who were usually deployed behind the frontlines and had a better chance of surviving the war unscathed.[150] The new role of machinery and technology in the war bred a mixture of fascination and horror, but it also speeded up the training of specialists. In gas weaponry, artillery, and reconnaissance, expert knowledge was required to assess their precise effects. Not only field-gray soldiers in the trenches but also engineers of abstract killing made their mark on the war.[151]

In this mechanized warfare, killing became a form of work for many soldiers. With its emphasis on materials, resources, and troop strengths, the war reminded them of the division of labor, "just in time" production, and Taylorism in modern industry. Traditional conceptions of obedience and heroic conduct were increasingly overlaid with technical-functional forms of behavior or downright bureaucratic procedures. The soldier felt himself to be a war worker, a specialist in killing and violence.[152] The day-to-day discourse of civilian work, harking back to prewar times, often dominated the way in which troops described combat missions. Thus, one German soldier on the western front compared the effect of machine guns to that of industrial machinery: "You only notice that when you're behind a machine like that working at full capacity. The whole job takes place on the ground—mostly 30 seconds of fabulous high-speed work to prepare the machine gun for firing—and then the business of murder gets going. It's got to feel very special to lie behind a machine gun as it goes to work on advancing infantry—you see them coming and aim this terrible hailstorm at them."[153]

Soldiers saw themselves less as perpetrators than as victims of technologically demanding weapons, gunfire, and systematic violence, which were visible to them at most for brief moments in the shape of actual enemy troops. It was a largely depersonalized experience, but its psychological effects were all the greater for that. As a result, frontline troops tended not to regard the enemy in the light of the images that had dominated society at the beginning of the war and were still present back home. Rather, the soldiers emphasized the common experiences on either side of the front, where the dangers and living conditions were more or less the same; the enemy remained the enemy, but again and again the situation made him feel a comrade. The very distance from commanders at the rear, the difference between the relative equality of the soldier's lifeworld and the critical attitude of the military hierarchy, was a key support for this way of looking at things. Jean Dartemont put it as follows: "So it is that the shout sometimes heard from the German trenches, '*Kamerad Franzose!*' is quite probably sincere. Fritz is closer to the *poilu* than to his own field marshal. And the *poilu* is closer to Fritz, because of the suffering they share, than to the men in Compiègne. Our uniforms are different but we are all proletarians of duty and honor, miners who labor in competitive pits, but above all miners, with the same pay and risking the same explosions of firedamp."[154]

Life at the front spawned a special kind of communicative culture, including informal and official trench newspapers that were produced on the spot. In the French army alone there were no fewer than 400 such papers. News could be reported in them that inspired more confidence than the censored information available in the official press, but most important of all was the fact that they spoke the soldiers' vernacular.[155] Although their vocabulary highlighted differences between the military and home fronts, close links with the homeland and the often-repeated hope of one day returning to the old way of life became increasingly important themes as the war dragged on. The front was not a world apart, but a sphere connected in manifold ways, through countless letters and packages, with the home society. These links and cohesion were one of the main reasons why, despite the military crises, French soldiers held out as they did.[156] Correspondence with soldiers' wives shows how intense the exchanges could be about life back home and the everyday grind at the front. The numerous letters between Paul Pireaud and his wife Marie, for example, between the years 1914 and 1919, represented an attempt to participate in each other's experiences—Paul in life on the land in their native village, in the gathering of the crop, and Marie in the dangers of the front. The correspondence could not produce physical closeness, but it did bring emotional sharing and therefore an element of continuity and stability, so that they could cope with the extreme situation of the war and their long separation.[157] In contrast, the notebooks of many soldiers, as well as letters between sons and parents, siblings and spouses, demonstrate the limits of what could be said and undermine the illusion of a world unchanged by war. At any event, the changes on the home front were already unmistakable in the first year of the war. When the gunner Herbert Sulzbach left his parents' home in Frankfurt on May 12, 1915, and returned to the front, he noted, "Such a departure, again for the war, had been imagined differently, and in this too it is clear how jaded we are becoming. . . . Of course, farewells are probably worse for those who remain at home."[158]

Satire directed at officers to the rear, for example, and more generally a sarcastic undertone in the soldiers' language were ways of expressing and coping with the gulf between expectations and actual experiences at the front. Irony and humor created a distance from the extreme impressions. Terminology often covered up existential experiences, downplaying them and rendering them innocuous.[159] Behind a little word like *cafard* (melancholy) might stand profound anxiety states and bouts of depression brought on by nervous stress at the front.[160] The language of the French *poilus,* as of the German field-grays or the British Tommies, distanced itself from the patriotic hype, although precisely among French soldiers a defiant sense of defending their country played an important role at such times as the Battle of Verdun in 1916. Even then it was not a question of perpetuating national heroics. When the *poilus* referred to themselves as *bonhommes,* the idea of "poor guys" resonated in the word. One of their other favorite terms for themselves was the acronym P.C.D.F. (*Pauvres Couillons du Front*), that is, Poor Sods of the Front—and it was no accident that the German expression *Frontschwein* ("pig of the front") evoked similar living conditions.[161]

The extreme situation at the front stemmed not least from what the men and their NCOs and officers saw as a mismatch between high casualties and nonexistent successes—a perception more or less common to all fronts. Regarding the impasse of infantry attacks in the West, the French officer Saint-Jouan wrote at Easter 1915, "When the order is given to climb up to the edge of the trench, no one makes a move. The officers are put in a position where, having ordered an attack, they are powerless toward their unruly soldiers. Completely beside themselves, they then suddenly sally forth and run straight to their death. That's suicide."[162] But what held the soldiers together, what got them through the day between the two extremes of waiting and staring death in the face? It was not the overheated patriotism of August 1914, nor the comradeship that was so often overdrawn after the war, but rather the experience of a survival-oriented microcommunity created by chance. There, mutual trust and knowledge that they could count on their fellows were existentially necessary. Jean Dartemont described it as a veritable surrogate family: "We were such a disparate bunch in that squad, and quarreled so often, but we were nevertheless a little family."[163] It is true that, because of deaths and injuries and furloughs, the composition of these little groups was liable to fluctuate, but they were still a key point of reference. This also affected the men's personal motivation to fight, which depended less on the abstractions of national or fatherland than on the identity of their company or regiment, the immediate community of the front, and the references provided by their home region, family, and occupation. In the

British army, whose "Pals Battalions" extended social-occupational relations and contexts from the prewar years, but also in German and French regiments with their sometimes strong regional roots, loyalty to one's unit was an important element in the reinforcement of fighting morale.[164]

The historian Marc Bloch observed that the fear of death was usually less strong in actual battle than in the time spent preparing for it or on the way up from the rear to the killing grounds. A key reason for this was thoughts of personal honor, coupled with concern for one's own group at the front.[165] This further marked the soldier's sense of duty, which was dependent on the specific situation, on the danger zone, and on the distance between the front and the rear. Gabriel Chevallier's alter ego Jean Dartemont vividly described this: the "idea of duty varies according to one's place in the hierarchy, one's rank, and the dangers one faces. Among soldiers it comes down to a simple solidarity between men, in a shell-hole or a trench, a solidarity that doesn't consider the campaign as a whole or its aims, and isn't inspired by what we like to call ideals, but by the needs of the moment. . . . The further one gets from the front, the more the idea of duty is separated from risk. In the highest ranks it is entirely theoretical, a pure intellectual game. It merges with concern for one's responsibilities, reputation and advancement, unites personal success with national success, which are in opposition for those doing the fighting."[166] As a result, many ordinary soldiers felt great respect for their platoon or company leaders. These NCOs and lieutenants shared the same dangers and concrete experiences with the men under them, and in this way gained reliability and authority in their eyes. But ordinary soldiers "held them in deepest contempt" if they threw their weight around "without having proved themselves."[167]

Comradeship rested above all on a mechanism of mutual trust, an expectation that in principle each would stand by the others, because only then was it possible to handle the extreme danger of life at the front. Trust stood for reliability, which meant being able to count on the others' behavior as a counterweight to the random presence of death. It appealed to unwritten rules and served the common aim of survival.[168] And often it was associated with the subjective view that solidarity was possible only among men who knew one another and shared the experience of having become, as it were, prisoners of the front: "If a German should come to attack me, I know for sure that I will do all I can to kill him. So that he doesn't kill me, above all; and then because I am responsible for the safety of four men in our bunker, and if I don't shoot I could expose them to danger. I am bound to these farmers. . . . The solidarity of a chain gang."[169]

War at the front brought together men from every social stratum and every region of a country that had never before been so affected. As a soldier in the war, Marc Bloch noticed how many recruits from Brittany understood the French language only with great difficulty and therefore repeatedly found themselves in danger at the front.[170] Men from southern France, according to Jean Dartemont, encountered in the trenches of the north a country they had never seen before: "These people experience the north as an exile. They say: 'We've come to fight for others. It isn't our country that's being attacked.' To them, their country is the shores of the Mediterranean, and they have no worries about their frontiers. They are astonished that people can fight tooth and nail over cold regions, blanketed in snow and fog for six months of the year."[171]

The front community was thus rather different from the comradeship so idealized and mystified after the war; nor did it develop by way of patriotic fervor. Soldiers from rural Bavaria, for instance, displayed an anti-nationalist attitude—or anyway, little enthusiasm for the war—in their letters home. They did not see themselves as fighting for something clearly defined, but lived on the expectation that they would get some home leave after the battle. Particularly for farming people, it was important that they not lose contact with their villages and families, who had to keep looking after their land and animals. Although they increasingly turned against their superior officers, things did not reach the point of large-scale mutinies. One reason for this was the affinity between their living conditions before the war and their everyday lives at the front: a combination of monotonous rations, hard physical labor, and command and obedience. The hierarchy of officers, NCOs, and ordinary soldiers felt to some like a continuation of the relationship between overseers and farm laborers. Soldiers from a farming milieu generally coped better with army culture and conditions at the front than did volunteers from a middle-class background, who were used to more varied activities and better food.[172]

All in all, the war was quite a negative experience for most Bavarian soldiers; it forced them to put up with a lot of hardships to survive. All this had little to do with the inflated notions of army comradeship and a male community of the front that were dear to Nazi ideologues in particular.[173] Bavarian soldiers acted more from instinct, and their trench community resulted from a need to keep adapting to changed circumstances in order to ensure their survival. Herein lay the limitations of comradeship. As soon as the zone of immediate danger was behind them, comradeship played a very subordinate role.[174]

Many of these experiences were more or less the same in all armies, but in the year 1915 there were some characteristic differences. In the Russian army, the idea of a nation at war was rather alien and incomprehensible to most ordinary soldiers. Their everyday concern was to defend their own, which meant their local region, the Tsar, and the Orthodox religion. These were concrete things on which to pin their thoughts. What Russia amounted to exactly when they left their village lifeworld was usually unclear. So long as the enemy did not threaten their home district, many saw no reason to continue the fighting. In the early weeks of the war, a farm agent from Smolensk noted down the words of one Russian soldier: "What devil has brought this war on us? We are butting into other people's business." Another remarked, "We have talked it over among ourselves. If the Germans want payment, it would be better to pay ten rubles a head than to kill people." General Brusilov had no illusions about the gulf between patriotic propaganda and the thinking of most soldiers: "The drafts arriving from the interior of Russia had not the slightest notion of what the war had to do with them. Time after time I asked my men in the trenches why we were at war, . . . who these Serbians were, [and] no one could say. They were equally doubtful as to what a Slav was."[175]

In contrast to soldiers on the western front, however, Russian soldiers in 1915 were characteristically beginning to show signs of unrest and war weariness. The crass differences between a callous officer elite (which hardly seemed to notice the huge casualties) and ordinary soldiers were compounded by the development of serious supply problems.[176] In the spring of that year, one man wrote to his wife of the unbearable living conditions, which he attributed mainly to the officers' behavior: "The officers want to break our spirits by terrorizing us. They want to make us into lifeless puppets." Another spoke of officers who assembled 28,000 troops to witness the flogging of five soldiers, because they had left the barracks without permission to go and buy bread. The bitterness in the rank and file thus came not only from the mismatch between casualty rates and military progress but also from the discrepancy between petty offenses and punitive sanctions.[177]

6. SHIRKERS, PROFITEERS, AND TRAITORS
Economic Pressures, Social Conflicts, and Political Volatility on the Home Front

The effort to supply the front with artillery munitions had run into difficulties by late 1914, and things came to a head in spring of the following year. The structural challenge underlying this was felt by all the belligerent countries between Fall 1914 and Spring 1915.

The munitions crises became the first test of the switchover to a war economy, with all its political and social costs. There were a number of reasons for the supply problems: army headquarters had massively underestimated the quantities that would be needed to fight a short campaign. In the first weeks of the war France lost more than half of its heavy industry in the north of the country, while Russia found itself cut off from imports as the war progressed. Within a few weeks, the Allied blockade forced Germany into a complete reorganization of war materials management. In Britain too, the battles of Spring 1915 made it clear that economic "business as usual" was not going to win the war. But as the munitions crisis there grew into a political scandal, it pointed to a changed relationship between the armed forces, the press, and the world of politics.

When British forces mounted attacks in May 1915 on Aubers Ridge, in support of French offensives in Artois, their lack of success was not due only to the massive reinforcement of German defenses and trench systems earlier in the year. Many German machine-gun positions had survived bombardment partly because the British had at their disposal just 20 percent of the number of artillery shells they had used at Neuve Chapelle. British and Indian losses amounted to 11,500 men, whereas the Germans lost fewer than 1,000. When the BEF commander in chief John French, after the battle, ordered an additional 22,000 artillery shells to be transferred to Gallipoli, it illustrated the dual burden on Britain to supply both the western front and the southeastern Mediterranean and highlighted the conflict over the most appropriate strategy to be pursued. However, this was no longer just a quarrel between the army and politicians. Lord Northcliffe—the leading figure in the British press world, having published the *Daily Mail* and *Sunday Dispatch* since before 1900, founded the *Daily Mirror* in 1903, and taken over the *Observer* in 1906 and the *Times* in 1908—and Charles Repington, a former colonel and now military correspondent for the *Times,* were both present at French's headquarters when he made the decision.[178] And both men ensured that the munitions shortfall took on the dimensions of a public scandal. This conscious collaboration between military and media also marked subsequent developments. Repington's article (for which French supplied important information) appeared on May 14, 1915, under the headline, "Need for Shells: British attacks checked. Limited supply the cause. A Lesson from France," and savagely blamed the shortage for the death of British soldiers.[179] By no means did the press act in this as an institution serving the higher aims of national war propaganda, submissive to the military or to leading politicians. The point for French was to stir up criticism of shortcomings on the western front due to the Gallipoli enterprise, in order to put the western front back at the center of military operations, while for Northcliffe the aim was to turn the screws on the Asquith government.[180] This reflected Northcliffe's enormous self-confidence and his faith in the political power of the popular press in the war situation. The still current notion that newspapers degraded themselves into pure propaganda instruments, meekly following official accounts of the war, is therefore wide of the mark.

Reports that French had leaked information on the munitions shortage not only to the *Times* and David Lloyd George (a cabinet member) but also to the opposition leaders Balfour and Andrew Bonar Law led to a veritable political crisis. This deepened with the return of Lord Fisher as first sea lord and his damning criticisms of the Dardanelles campaign. Asquith felt compelled to expand the Liberal cabinet to form a coalition with the Conservatives; Lloyd George became head of a newly created ministry of munitions, which lost no time in pointing up the urgency of the problem. But contrary to Northcliffe's exaggerated view of his powers, it was not his press campaign that had led to these consequences. Rather, Asquith himself was seeking to counter the accusation that the political leadership of the country had been too indecisive and failed to rise to the challenges of the war.[181]

The special ministry of munitions headed by Lloyd George—an important innovation for Britain—continually expanded its powers and duties. It took responsibility not only for the production of shells and artillery pieces but also for the technological development of weapons systems, including tanks, and other key areas of the arms industry. In 1916 and 1917, the control of mineral resources and fuel imports was added to its portfolio.[182] But the establishment of the new ministry in 1915 also operated as a symbolic break. Although Lord Kitchener as war minister continued to enjoy wide popularity, campaigns in the press had damaged his reputation as a national war hero. At the same time, French too was drawn into the scandal. Supporters of Kitchener protested Northcliffe's campaign and publicly burned copies of the *Times* in front of the London Stock Exchange. But the main political figure to profit from it all was David Lloyd George: he presented himself over the coming months as a particularly energetic minister, who could solve the crisis by systematically drawing top industrialists into armaments organization and the state bureaucracy. This was a misleading picture, however, which Lloyd George himself skillfully cultivated in the public arena. The additional munitions stocks that he commissioned only began to come onstream in October 1915, whereas Kitchener's much-criticized war ministry had managed to increase munitions production nineteen-fold in the first six months of the war.[183]

With the Welsh-born Lloyd George, a new political type came to the fore in British wartime politics. Thanks partly to his rhetorical brilliance, he had risen to become leader of the radicals within the parliamentary Liberal Party, serving first as trade minister and from 1908 as chancellor of the exchequer; after his opposition to the Boer War he had represented the pacifist course of the Left Liberals. Entrusted as a Welshman with responsibility for the problem of the United Kingdom's four nationalities, he came out in favor of Irish home rule. With his demands for a German-style pension insurance scheme, a progressive income tax (first introduced in 1909), and higher inheritance taxes, he stood at the head of the social-reformist wing of the British Liberals, who in the Parliament Act of 1911 found a way of overcoming the resistance of the House of Lords. At the latest by the Morocco crisis of 1911, however, he distanced himself from the radical pacifism of the Left Liberals and, in his Mansion House speech, became one of the harshest critics of German foreign policy. Although he remained skeptical about British involvement during the crisis of July 1914, the violation of Belgian neutrality was the spur for him to change his mind and support a war on the Continent. Lloyd George remained in the government as the sole representative of Left Liberalism and soon adapted to the prospect of a long war. This, he was convinced, called for a new financial basis, a major arms drive, and in the medium term the introduction of general conscription. Above all, he realized that the institutionally underdeveloped British state—a legacy of the nineteenth century—had to undergo fundamental change if it was to mobilize and centralize the necessary resources.

What did this turn to a war state mean in Britain? Lloyd George's new ministry of munitions created an institutional basis for state intervention in the economy, which had previously been unknown in Britain.[184] In particular, the tendency to include systematic management of raw materials in the state-controlled war economy was reminiscent of Rathenau's measures in Germany in Fall 1914. In Britain too, industrial firms important to the war effort were methodically registered and subjected to state control. Unlike in Germany, however, where the pressure to act was especially great because of the early effectiveness of the Allied blockade, radical measures such as the confiscation of strategic raw materials remained the exception. Given how the war at sea developed, the British war economy could continue to draw on the global resources of the Empire.[185]

From 1915 on, the war also pushed Britain toward closer and closer cooperation between science and the economy. Since the war ended the import of scientific and technological know-how from German universities, British scientists and engineers developed basic industrial materials of their own. In 1916 the Belarus-born chemist Chaim Weizmann, who had studied in Germany and taught at Manchester University since 1904, became director of the Admiralty-supported munitions laboratory; there he developed the bacterial fermentation method for the production of acetone, essential to the production of cordite, a smokeless military propellant. Not by chance did Weizmann's efforts recall the research of Fritz Haber in Germany. Both men were Jews—but whereas Haber put his science at the service of the

German state, Weizmann became the leader of the British Zionists and went on to play a key role in the founding of a Jewish state in Palestine that the war itself had brought closer. The war put pressure on the sciences to develop new products and technologies, but it also offered a unique opportunity for scientists to serve their state and nation by distinguishing themselves in these fields.

These changes at the level of institutions and personnel marked a watershed for Britain in 1915. The tradition of free, unregulated markets with minimal government intervention gave way to a state-regulated and state-controlled war capitalism and the beginnings of a wartime corporatism. It anticipated many future experiments in a mixed economy.[186] But apart from this focus on the potential of expanded ministerial bureaucracies, another characteristic interest of Lloyd George's was the systematic involvement of the press. This had already become apparent in August 1914, when he began to construct a War Propaganda Bureau under Charles Masterman (called Wellington House after its location), which in 1917 was swallowed up by the Information Ministry.[187] By early September 1915, well-known writers, journalists, and artists, especially painters and graphic designers, were being recruited to produce publications and artworks in the spirit of the War Propaganda Bureau. Along with more than one thousand special flyers that were dropped behind enemy lines, the monthly *Nelson's History of the War,* which went through twenty-four editions beginning in February 1915, proved a great success. The *Report of the Committee on Alleged German Outrages,* published in early 1915, had a major international echo as well. Translated into more than twenty languages, produced and illustrated with the means available to the popular press, this Bryce Report, as it was known, made an essential contribution to the image of barbaric German troop behavior. As in the cultural war between intellectuals, claims and counterclaims were competitively ratcheted up. Just a few days after publication of the Bryce Report, a German government White Book pilloried the uncivilized conduct of the Allies and, above all, in line with the *franc-tireurs* panic, that of Belgian soldiers.

Of course, as Northcliffe's role in the "shell crisis" had shown, these institutional forms could not totally control the press landscape. Yet the creation of the War Propaganda Bureau demonstrated the importance given to public opinion as a special factor in the war; this was true from very early on in all the belligerent countries and became all the more pertinent with the rising death toll. In Britain's case, the introduction of conscription in January 1916 meant that public pressure for enlistment, centered on a particular image of the war and a moral obligation to do one's duty, had to be built up via the media. Other countries founded similar propaganda organizations for this purpose: the Kriegspresseamt in Germany, the k.u.k.-Kriegspressequartier in Vienna, the Maison de la Presse in France, and the Committee on Public Information in the United States immediately after it joined the war.

In the course of 1915, the stalemate plus high casualty figures on the western front, together with the failure of the Gallipoli campaign, fueled doubts in British society about the conduct of the war. It seemed to fit less and less with the country's experiences of war in previous centuries: it was not possible to rest content with subsidizing Continental allies to do the fighting, nor was this a war that could be decided by the Royal Navy alone. The lessons of 1915 were rather that the war could not be won in short order and that it had to be fought as a land war in Europe and many other theaters. Long casualty lists and reports of poison gas use, but also the munitions crisis and the high civilian losses from the sinking of the *Lusitania* in May 1915 and the German U-boat campaign against merchant shipping, brought the war increasingly to the fore in people's everyday consciousness. Moreover, these developments strained Britain's industrial capacity and emphasized how little its comparatively small and unprofessional state institutions had been prepared for a long war. At a number of levels, the conflict struck home more than any other had in the past. Refugees told of the barbaric German conduct of the war in Belgium. And the first Zeppelin raids, or the shelling of towns on the south coast by German battleships, shrank the perceived geographical distance from events on the Continent.

Against this background, there was a change in the way people viewed loyalty and betrayal. Suspicion was directed not only at the external enemy but also at "enemy aliens" inside Britain; events such as the sinking of the *Lusitania* increased the preparedness to take action against Germans, or even ethnic minorities in general. Spy mania spread, as it had done in Summer 1914, and in the wake of the "shell crisis" the Conservative mass media

Hunting the internal enemy: anti-German disturbances after the sinking of the *Lusitania*, London 1915

demanded not only a change of political course but also the mass internment of foreigners. In Summer 1915 the country saw ethnically motivated rioting of a kind it had never experienced before; German-owned businesses were pillaged in Hull, Liverpool, and London, but excesses also occurred in other towns and cities, directed at foreigners so much as suspected of supporting the German cause. Various motives were mixed up in these attacks: the Lusitania riots of Summer 1915 in Hull and London, for example, mainly targeted food stores belonging to people of German origin, especially butchers and bakers. These were not classical hunger riots (in which people losing out from the war became active); the looting was often carried out by organized groups and was not always triggered by current events. It was no accident that the violence mainly affected working-class districts and areas where families had been hit hardest by the war with Germany. In Hull, for instance, it was concentrated in the part of the city where many families depended on deep-sea fishing for a living; many fathers, brothers, and sons had either been interned in Germany at the beginning of the war or were threatened daily by German sea mines and submarines.[188]

In this working-class milieu, then, economic factors and war-related causes lay behind the wave of anti-German violence, but as the months and years went by there was a change in both the motives and social profile of people involved in such actions. The year 1915 saw the founding of the Anti-German Union, out of which the British Empire Union (BEU) developed in the following year. In Summer 1915, later strongholds of the BEU such as Brighton and Oxford did not experience any anti-German disturbances, but from 1916 the proportion of middle-class members in these organizations increased as they underwent an ideological turn. The BEU thus became a rallying point for anti-socialist and in some cases anti-Semitic forces, which from 1917 wanted to use violent means to ward off the Bolshevik danger supposedly represented by the Labour Party, but which also turned their fury against pacifist currents. It is estimated that by the end of 1918 the BEU had over 10,000 members, organized in more than fifty local branches. Large anti-German demonstrations took place in London's Hyde Park, along with poster campaigns and a petition with more than 1.2 million signatures calling for the mass internment of enemy aliens.[189]

In 1915, however, the increasing pressure on the societies at war did not manifest itself only in the exclusion of supposed internal enemies. The domestic war effort also became the focus of attention. Controls and regulation, as well as tighter discipline on everyone's part, were meant to secure the achievements of each society; any official measure, any encroachment on people's habits and traditions, could now be justified as a patriotic necessity. A good example of this was the campaign initiated by Lloyd George against alcohol abuse. As in Russia at the beginning of the war, it was feared that alcoholism would play into the hands of the enemy. Prominent supporters of the campaign, including the King himself, vowed not to touch a drop for the duration of the war. But not a few opponents of the Liberal Party saw this as an attempt to exploit the new wartime conditions to revive earlier abstinence campaigns.[190]

In this, as in other spheres, the war catalyzed social tensions and conflicts whose origins went back far beyond 1914; only now these were addressed with different means and a different vocabulary. The discourse of loyalty changed.

Even before 1914, clashes between unionized workers and employers had raised the question of how British workers would conduct themselves in a future war. Many entrepreneurs, but also leading politicians, feared that a wartime economy with high unemployment and steep price increases would severely test the workers' loyalty and that mass strikes would weaken the front.

After the early months of war, British society in Spring 1915 showed evidence of the first changes: the leap in joblessness following the outbreak of war soon fell away with the mass enlistment of volunteers in the New Armies and the rising demand for labor; the war even offered a livelihood to many who had lost hope of finding a job. At the same time, inflation started moving upward in 1915 and eroded real wages for many workers, even if total incomes remained stable or actually increased as a result of overtime and the employment of other family members.[191]

Although social tensions did not at first lead to major conflicts, there were two regional exceptions in 1915 that indicate particularly clearly the changes that were taking place. In the traditionally militant mining districts of South Wales, where conflicts had already pitted workers and owners against each other before 1914, strikes broke out in 1915 against the employers' refusal to increase wages in line with the extra profits they were making from war-related production. The workers also had expected to benefit from the fact that the Royal Navy's demand for high-grade anthracite coal had given a boost to Welsh mining. Lloyd George quickly realized that the strike could limit the operational capacity of the navy in a crucial period of the war, and the so-called Treasury Agreements that he pushed through would apply to other social conflicts during the war. In fact, these involved a compromise between the two sides of industry, with the government acting as the arbiter in labor relations. On the one hand, the Munitions of War Act prohibited strikes in industries essential to the war effort and made any change at the workplace dependent on the employer's agreement. Trade unions had to accept the suspension of existing wage agreements for the rest of the war, as well as the practice of "dilution," that is, the opening of jobs to unskilled workers and women. On the other hand, the government made a concession to the unions by introducing a war profits tax that limited net corporate gains from the war; the nation's sacrifice for the war effort should not lead to excessive individual profits or accentuate the disparities in society.[192] The effective of these measures should not be exaggerated. But fiscal policy clearly had greater weight in Britain than in Germany, where funding of the war through taxes played a much smaller role.[193]

Another locus of social conflict in 1915 was the industrial centers of Glasgow. The housing situation there, with often dire sanitation and insalubrious living quarters right next to the factories, had long been a source of conflict between workers' representatives and local entrepreneurs and landlords.[194] Trade union mobilization was therefore especially high in working-class areas along the so-called Red Clydeside. From 1909 to 1914 alone, membership in the Scottish Trades Union Congress soared from 129,000 to more than 230,000, while the number of strikes quadrupled during the same period in comparison with the period between 1900 and 1909. Women and unskilled workers often played a particularly important role in these actions.[195] In the run-up to August 1914, many workers in Glasgow mobilized against war, and the antiwar movement and resistance to the Munitions of War Act continued under the newly founded Clyde Workers' Committee. When talks failed to reach a compromise, the leaders of the committee were arrested under the Defence of the Realm Act and sentenced to terms of imprisonment.[196] Glasgow, with its key munitions industry, remained a center of socialist activity, and on Sunday afternoons in 1915 the teacher and diehard revolutionary John Maclean was able to continue holding what had been the largest Marxist Sunday schools anywhere in Europe.[197] At the same time, the first attempts at social corporatism were being made by workers' and employers' representatives. The Munitions of War Act not only limited the trade unions' scope for action; it also created more flexible conditions for them to have a greater say at the local level.[198]

In June 1915, however, another social conflict erupted in the working-class areas of Glasgow. When a number of landlords exploited the absence of men on war service to impose often dramatic rent increases, workers' wives began to set up local tenants' associations and to organize a rent boycott. Under the leadership of Mary Barbour, herself the wife of a shipyard worker, the women gained the support of the local Independent Labour Party. Their protests ranged from demonstrations against evictions to the occupation of houses and apartments, in many cases involving hundreds of people. Some women removed policemen's trousers in order to make them look ridiculous. On November 17, a demonstration of several thousand women in Glasgow, "Mrs Barbour's Army," as it was called, became well known outside the region and soon won the support of shipyard and munitions workers. This was a new phenomenon, which made the Glasgow rent strike a model to be taken up in other industrial cities. But the government quickly stepped in to prevent the development of countrywide resistance and a weakening of war-related production. A new Rent Control Act, passed in November 1915, significantly improved the legal rights of tenants vis-à-vis landlords in working-class districts.[199]

These forms of protest were linked to older working-class traditions, but the tensions and conflicts in 1915 revealed a new tendency. The rent strikes, in particular, expressed a new language of patriotism, a new vocabulary to use the situation created by the war for the strikers' own interests. "Profiteer" and "shirker" became negative terms referring to people like employers or landlords who benefited economically from the absence of men at the front—a form of behavior that, in the eyes of trade unionists and workers' wives, was not only a provocative violation of the social truce but carried an unpatriotic stigma and could be regarded as indirect support for the enemy. At one demonstration on October 8, 1915, the slogans on placards were a clear sign of how nationally defined enemy categories could be taken up and applied to the social-economic situation in Britain. Children, for example, carried banners with the words "While my father is a prisoner in Germany, the landlord is attacking our home," or "My father is fighting in France, we are fighting the Huns at home." Such language vilifying the "landlord Huns" used the fate of men on active service or in captivity to extract social improvements on the home front.[200] Nor was the home society only a linguistic battleground. Behind the widespread use of the term "Kaiserism" to attack manufacturers, mine owners, or landlords was taking shape a new consciousness among working-class families and, in particular, large numbers of women.[201] The linguistic opposition between war profiteer and shirker, on the one side, and soldier, war worker, and working mother or wife, on the other, reflected a new constellation. It foregrounded war service and work for the nation at war, providing the basis for a definition of loyalty in terms of service and compensation in return. This obligated the government, under wartime conditions, to intervene if the balance between the two was in danger.

In the case of Britain, the changed world of work in 1915 did not manifest itself only in reduced unemployment and a growing demand for labor in industries essential to the war effort. Women were increasingly taking on jobs that men had left to become soldiers. But it was a question not so much of housewives starting new work for the first time as of a shift within the realm of female employment; that is, it mainly concerned women who had previously worked in the textile industry or as domestics. Despite all the posters showing women in arms factories, however, the process did not take place only or primarily in industrial firms, but rather in the retail trade and the service sector. At first the unions were critical of this development, as they were more generally of the opening of jobs to unskilled men and women, fearing that it would weaken the position of their skilled membership base. The government in London, and especially Lloyd George, leaned on the unions to accept "dilution" and mass female employment, and with this official support, a number of prominent suffragettes such as Emmeline and Christabel Pankhurst (who had been harassed by the police for their campaigning before 1914) added to the pressure. Their demand for "women's right to serve" also used the war situation to popularize the idea that women were indispensable to the life of the nation, while opposing voices could be held up as an unpatriotic weakening of the home front.[202] In this respect the war indirectly opened up possibilities of political participation, increasing the scope for action and nurturing hopes for change that would last beyond the end of the war.

In the course of 1915, it became clear that the number of volunteers in Britain would not be sufficient to offset the casualties on the western front and elsewhere. Until the introduction of conscription in January for unmarried men and, in May 1916, for all adult males, there were intense debates on the need for such an unprecedented measure—one that all major Continental countries had adopted in the second half of the nineteenth century. The Liberals recoiled from state-imposed conscription, not least because they knew from history that it had been identified with authoritarian, or anyway un-English, political principles. But the war, with its high casualty rates, had put such considerations into perspective, if not rendered them completely obsolete. The Conservatives, for their part, supported compulsory military service, even though the associated potential for social and national conflict was evident enough. Resolute opposition came mainly from the Labour Party and the trade unions, which feared moves toward "industrial conscription." While the property-owning classes found it easier to avoid conscription and other burdens of war, the risks and sacrifices tended to be loaded onto the shoulders of the workers, as more and more people came to realize in 1915. The imposition of conscription thus fueled wartime social tensions; the contrast became ever sharper between fathers who had volunteered to perform their patriotic duty and "shirkers" or "profiteers" who stayed home and dodged the front or benefited financially from the war.

The conscription debate also polarized opinion in the Empire, as events in Australia and especially Canada showed in 1916. The apprehensions were greatest of all, however, in relation to Ireland and Britain itself, where the first consequences were already making themselves felt in 1915.[203] Since conscription was a priori unpopular as an imposition from London, it put in danger the precarious internal peace that had prevailed since August 1914. Despite the high casualties, the main feeling in all parts of Ireland in 1915, albeit for differing reasons, was a readiness to prove people's loyalty through war service. The pro-union Ulster Volunteer Force in the north became the core of the 36th Ulster Division, and the unionist leader Sir Edward Carson—in striking contrast to John Redmond, the leader of the Irish Parliamentary Party—joined the new coalition government in a move symbolizing the internal political truce. Whereas the unionists thereby sought to emphasize their opposition to home rule for Ireland, many Irish nationalists in the south also volunteered to serve in the army. Other organizations such as the Irish Volunteers quarreled bitterly and in some cases split over whether to support the war.[204] The 16th Irish Division, like the 36th Ulster Division, fought on the western front. Many Irish people argued that it was, among other things, a war for the rights and independence of small nations like Serbia and Belgium, which therefore also served the cause of an independent Ireland. In the case of Belgium and Ireland, there was also the underlying image of Catholic nations under the heel of Protestant occupation forces—British in Ireland, Prussian-German in Belgium. But the personal motives of volunteers in these units cannot be reduced to the distinction between Ireland and

Ulster, or between the Irish independence struggle and loyalty to London. Often other factors, such as the social-economic position of the young men in question, played a key role in their decision to enlist.[205] War service could sometimes lighten the economic burden of families with many children, while honor and reputation counted for more among the better off. Only during the first months of the war did it become clear that Ireland, with its strong agricultural base, would actually benefit considerably from the increased demand for manpower and farm produce. Indeed, it experienced a veritable boom essentially because of the war.

Finally, the idea that the clash between Irish nationalists and pro-British loyalists was simply transposed to the armed forces should be set against the common belief at the time that the shared experience of war would have a unifying effect. In the 10th Division, for example, supporters of the union and of Irish independence fought together at Gallipoli.[206] According to John Redmond, this might lay the basis for a future united Ireland: "I pray that whenever a battalion of the Irish Brigade goes into action there may be a battalion of the Ulster Division alongside of them. I need not point the moral to you. That is the way to end the unhappiness and the discords and the confusion of Ireland. Let Irishmen come together in the trenches and risk their lives together and spill their blood together and I say there is no power on earth that when they come home can induce them to turn as enemies one upon another."[207]

But when conscription began in 1915 in response to the volunteer shortfall, radical Irish nationalists took up the issue to promote violent resistance to the British war state. The critical military situation and the actions of the British military bureaucracy made conscription appear as the instrument of a colonial occupation regime. Talk of liberation through force appeared more and more alongside the loyalty discourse that many Irish employed in the hope of following through on home rule. This process was aided by the programmatic and organizational split in the ranks of Irish nationalists, as one section staked everything on a radical strategy that set it apart from the parliamentary course of the home rule supporters. James Connolly, the leader of the nationalist and socialist-oriented Irish Citizen Army, already advocated in 1915 an armed uprising. But more decisive was a splinter group within the Irish Volunteers, strongly marked by the culture of violence of the

Irish Republican Brotherhood founded in 1858. Under the leadership of the charismatic Gaelic teacher Patrick Pearse, who had founded the Volunteers in 1913 and joined the Brotherhood in 1914, this small militant faction vehemently opposed what it saw as the strategic compromise being pursued by Irish politicians in parliament. Pearse turned the Brotherhood into a secret organization. The funeral on August 1, 1915, of Jeremiah O'Donovan Rossa—who had belonged to the nineteenth-century Fenian movement for Irish independence and, following an amnesty, emigrated to the United States—was used by the nationalists to argue in public for an uprising against British rule. In a graveside speech reported in all the papers, Pearse expressed this programmatic break with the August 1914 line of loyalty to Westminster. The British government, he said, cherished the view that it had pacified Ireland: "They think that they have purchased half of us and intimidated the other half. They think that they have foreseen everything, think that they have provided against everything; but the fools, the fools, the fools!—they have left us our Fenian dead, and while Ireland holds these graves, Ireland unfree shall never be at peace."[208] Pearse set his sights on independence: London's war would be the opportunity for Ireland's freedom; a bloody beacon was necessary to reorient Irish nationalism. Weaving together Christian and Celtic themes, Pearse gambled on a binding blood sacrifice, which would place the fighters of the Brotherhood in a line of continuity with the martyrs of the Catholic faith and Irish freedom.[209] So came about the plan for an armed uprising at Easter 1916, less as a real chance to achieve Irish independence than as a signal for struggle. In Spring and Summer 1916, the great costly battles on the western front and the huge burdens on British society itself were overlaid with a civil war situation in Ireland.[210]

In France too, pressure was visibly mounting on the home society. On the national holiday, July 14, the French ministry official Michel Corday noted in Paris the contrast between the previous year's images of enthusiastic support for the war and the popular mood in 1915: "Silent crowds of people. Wounded men, some of them with limbs amputated, soldiers on leave in greatcoats faded by the sun. As many people collecting money as there are spectators, and they are asking for contributions to a variety of benevolent causes. The regiments march past with their bands; remember that all these men are on their way to the slaughter." Another of Corday's observations reflected the agonizing stalemate at the front: "the small flags marking the frontlines on the department's war maps had cobwebs on them."[211]

Whereas in Germany the Allied blockade created acute problems in the first weeks of war, there was not the same pressure on the other side of the Rhine for a complete reorganization of the war economy. The sharp rise in unemployment in France following the outbreak of war soon receded as a result of conscription, and in general the economy took longer than in Germany to adjust to the conditions of wartime production, another reason for this being that the industrialized northeast of the country, near the Belgian border, became part of the hinterland of the front. From early 1915 there was a pronounced manpower shortage that posed a threat to arms production; thousands of soldiers were withdrawn from the front and sent back to their factories. In agriculture, although the war had broken out in August, the employment of women, old people, and children had made it possible to gather the harvest successfully. The absence of men at the front together with a shortage of machinery and fertilizer did mean that output levels were down from the previous year, but France, unlike Germany, experienced no really major supply problems or hunger crises in Winter 1914–1915 or during the further course of the war. Eventually, despite the loss of important industrial centers, French industry successfully carried out the switch to a war economy. Between Summer 1915 and the end of the war, the production of shells increased tenfold and that of powder and explosives sixfold. At its peak in 1918, the French arms industry was turning out 1,000 new artillery pieces a month, and 261,000 shells and 6 million cartridges a day. Of the 1.7 million men and women working on arms production in 1917, no fewer than 1 million (of whom 400,000 were women) comprised new categories of workers. In addition there were mobilized workers and soldiers under military orders reassigned from the front, as well as 175,000 foreigners (mainly from the French colonies) and more than 30,000 prisoners of war.[212]

These figures indicate the extent to which the French economy was re-geared to meet war needs over a two-year period. To many contemporaries, the country came to seem the center of the Allied war effort and

OPPOSITE: Allied weaponsmiths: Citroën poster for standard shrapnel shells

FABRICATION DES OBUS SHRAPNELLS

ANDRÉ
CITROËN

POUR LA FRANCE LA RUSSIE L'ITALIE
ET LA ROUMANIE

the weaponsmith of the war, playing a role altogether comparable to that of the United States in the Second World War. Firms such as Renault and Citroën became major arms producers in a short space of time—a structural change with far-reaching implications, since it laid the basis for the twentieth-century French arms industry. The impressive output increases also had a political dimension: French politicians could now argue that the country was demonstrating how a democratic republic could pass the test of industrial warfare. Back in 1911 the socialist intellectual Marcel Sembat had doubted that this was possible: the Third Republic, he argued, would not be able to wage a protracted modern war with all that it involved; it would have to secure peace because a consistent war policy was imaginable only in a monarchy.[213]

The output successes, however, disguised internal tensions and conflicts resulting from the concentration on war production. In France, too, the munitions crisis at first led to institutional changes. Sembat (now minister for public works) placed the Socialist Albert Thomas, an acolyte of Jean Jaurès and leading supporter of the *union sacrée,* in charge of centrally coordinating the production of goods essential to the war effort. In May 1915, as undersecretary of state, Thomas took responsibility for the supply of artillery in particular, and in December 1916 he went on to become armaments minister and a member of the Supreme War Council. In line with the vision of reformist socialism, Sembat also used the switchover to war production to achieve advances in employer-worker relations. Working closely as a minister with the CGT labor federation, he pushed through a number of measures focused on collective wage agreements, workers' participation in management, and state arbitration in wage disputes, which not only recognized the unions as representatives of workers' interests but also continued the prewar course of reformist socialism to safeguard the wartime social peace.[214]

Unlike in Germany, the military did not operate in France as a key player in the war economy; this is clear from the fact that by 1915 arms production had been transferred from the war ministry to the civilian leadership and that in 1916 it was placed under a special ministry headed by Thomas. State and economy, too, remained more clearly separate in France: the economic centralization and coordination so characteristic of Germany and Britain, with their burgeoning state bureaucracies in control of raw material distribution, did not materialize in France for a long time. Its arms industry was organized on a regional basis, and the Comité des Forges, the central interest group of the French coal and steel industry that took on the task of coordination, retained a relative distance from the state. It is true that a Bureau of Economic Studies was founded in Paris in 1915 to tie together the regional interests. But only in 1917 did the ministerial pressures on industry intensify, when raw materials management was transferred to various state-supervised consortiums and joint stock companies.[215]

What did change in 1915, however, were attitudes to the social costs of the burgeoning war economy. When the demand for labor in the arms industry rose after the first few months of war, it led in France also to a heightening of social tensions. As in Britain, the French labor unions feared that the opening of jobs to unskilled workers and women would play into the employers' hands by lowering the wages of skilled (mostly unionized) workers and releasing them for service at the front. In the course of the year, attitudes hardened toward the *embusqués,* the "shirkers" suspected of avoiding the dangers of the front. But who could rightly count as unavailable for military service, and what were the criteria? Any transfer from the front to factory or vice versa could decide whether the person in question lived or died, and the publication of daily casualty lists brought this home to everyone at the time. This sharpened the problem of social integration and national loyalty, since war service for the republic could be justified only if there was an egalitarian distribution of burdens and sacrifices. Contemporary discourse pointed up this new context: it was enough to mention the *embusqués* (or "shirkers" in Britain or *Drückeberger* in Germany) to remind people of the egalitarian ideal and the gratitude due to war casualties.[216]

When thousands of soldiers were shipped back from the front in late 1914 and early 1915 to maintain arms production, it happened without methodical checking of selection criteria. As the casualty numbers rose, so too did the pressure on politicians to develop a clear and transparent system to distinguish between available and unavailable workers. Behind this lay the concept of an *impôt du sang* or blood tax, related to Jacobin-republican principles of equality, that all adult French males were expected to deliver. The very credibility of the nation at war depended on whether it was capable of justly distributing the burdens of sacrifice; the demand for loyalty presupposed a transparent fairness institutionally underwritten by the state. Accordingly, the Loi Dalbiez of August 1915 was supposed to ensure the "appropriate distribution and better employment of mobilized or mobilizable males" by checking every worker's availability and selecting men in accordance with strict criteria. The Loi Mourier of August 1917 stood in the same tradition of state verification and classification. Both laws showed the scale of the pressure exerted on politicians by labor unions, political parties, and soldiers. The criterion of "importance to the war effort" bound the military front and wartime society ever more closely together, with an enormous impact at the political level.[217]

In practice, however, neither of these laws solved the problem that trust in a fair distribution of sacrifices was on the wane. Of the 88,000 men who were sent to the front under the Loi Mourier, only 6,000 came from firms essential to the war effort, whereas 73,000 older soldiers were ordered back from the front to work in the homeland. The labor unions did stand up for factory workers to prevent their transfer to the front, but their close cooperation with the authorities was a condition for their recognition by the state. Government agencies had to make efforts to stabilize the *union sacrée* with the *impôt du sang*, while at the same time meeting the needs of the war economy. It was acknowledged that output increases could mostly be obtained only with skilled workers and that they were therefore more effectively deployed on the home front than in the trenches. But the realization that this deployment back home was going on intensified the impression of an unjust system.[218] The extent to which the term *embusqué* became synonymous in 1915 with the issue of unfair classification can be seen from a cartoon on the effects of the Loi Dalbiez that appeared in *L'Humanité* in December. In it, two pedestrians who notice a soldier with amputated legs sitting on an improvised wheelchair ask each other whether he too should not be considered a shirker. As civilian monitors of the law, they symbolize the growth of suspicion in French society that could be turned against anyone. The *embusqué* (like the "shirker" or *Drückeberger*) was not only a personal coward. All these terms acquired a new wartime meaning charged with moral and patriotic sentiments. As the negative counterpart of the *poilu*—the simple, honorable, brave combatant embodying equality of sacrifice and the traditions of the republican citizen-soldier—the *embusqué* symbolized a breach of loyalty and betrayal of the principles of the nation at war. This contrast could be used at any moment for political purposes; it also reflected the close link between front and homeland and the precarious structure of the *union sacrée*.

Unlike in Britain and France, the "civil truce" in Germany led to a situation where the military played a key role from the beginning in the development of the home society and the war economy. The willingness of the SPD and unions to submit to the domestic political compromise initially won them at least symbolic recognition: for example, the authorities no longer prevented sales of the SPD party paper, *Vorwärts*.[219] In 1915, however, SPD or union participation in government was still a long way off. But their vigorous support for the civil peace had much to do with a fear of being accused of unpatriotic behavior—a persistent reflex, also underlying their approval of war credits in Summer 1914, in response to their stigmatization as the "enemy within" in the post-1871 Reich. On the other hand, this tendency to offer repeated proof of their loyalty to the nation exacerbated conflicts inside the party, as events in the course of 1915 would show.[220]

The war economy in Germany, as elsewhere, owed much to the soaring demand for labor that caused the sharp rise in unemployment at the beginning of the war to subside in late 1914. The army and industry began to compete for what manpower was available. This situation was further complicated by strong decentralization within the framework of the Deputy General Commands and civilian administrations. At any event, the polycracy of players and partly competing authorities contradicted the image of a well-ordered rational-bureaucratic state prepared in advance for a long war. Many improvised decisions led in fact to a system that was scarcely equal to the huge and (in scale) unprecedented burdens on the economy. This soon became evident with regard to manpower. Whereas the military wanted to enlist as quickly as possible all soldiers fit for action, entrepreneurs tried to hang on to their skilled workers, fearing that otherwise they would not be able to fulfill the plethora of arms contracts. By late 1915 hard bargains were being struck among the war ministry, the civilian authorities, and private businesses, the latter newly represented under the umbrella of the Kriegsausschuss der deutschen Industrie. As a result, 600,000 recruits fit for military action (roughly 20 percent of the arms industry workforce) were released from service at the front. This figure rose to 1.2 million by Fall 1916 and to 1.7 million in 1917, but even then it was too small to meet the skyrocketing demand. As in other belligerent countries, the shortfall was made up primarily by women and youngsters and in the longer term by prisoners of war and forced laborers.[221] The close link between war economy and occupation regime was most evident in Russian Poland and Belgium, from where large numbers of men were deported for forced labor in Germany.[222]

The raw materials dependence of Germany and Austria-Hungary was acutely felt from the first weeks of the war. The problems of mobilization, production, and supply thus became evident earlier, and with graver effect, in the Central Powers than in France or Britain.[223] As much as 43 percent of German exports consisted of raw materials, until the British blockade of the North Sea and the Channel cut Germany off from the world market and caused a growing trade deficit. Freight that did reach German ports in spite of everything could hardly be paid for. At first it was still possible to import dual-purpose goods, suitable for both peacetime and wartime production, via

The other war economy: satirical cartoon depicting hard-pressed farmers in Denmark, 1915

neutral Denmark, Sweden, Norway, and Holland; even British goods such as pewter, wool, cotton, meat, and tea were exempt.[224] But the limited success in British eyes, as well as the deployment of German submarines, led to the introduction of a full-scale blockade in March 1915, with the result that all shipping and any links with the ports of the Central Powers, as well as any indirect trade via neutral ports, were prohibited. Germany was thus denied all imports from overseas, though not from other countries in Continental Europe. Swedish iron ore, Norwegian nickel, Dutch and Danish foodstuffs, as well as Romanian oil (after the country's military defeat in 1916), could still get through.[225] Some sectors in neutral countries actually benefited from the growth in German demand. Danish farmers, for example, obtained higher prices for their produce, so that the image of its depressed agriculture became the object of satire.

In the early months of the war, the German imports crisis spawned an ever more obscure complex of institutions centered on the raw materials department under Rathenau and the numerous military-industrial companies.[226] The relationship between economy and state thus became increasingly multilayered. Representatives of each branch were well placed to assert their interests and could employ tried-and-tested methods to achieve them. But since they could not simply instrumentalize military-industrial companies, they were unable to impose a really independent policy between state and economy. Rather, they operated as an instrument for the enforcement of state (that is, mainly military) guidelines. Or, best of all, the military bodies functioned as a control room of the war economy. Yet even their power and predefined authority could not change the fact that many decision-making processes remained segmented and by no means corresponded to the ideal of "strong government." Conflicts within the military, as well as with business representatives and civilian bodies, were the order of the day.[227]

The German war economy displayed an ever-greater tension between theoretical-programmatic plans and assumptions, on the one hand, and actual experiences and pressures to improvise, on the other. The military raw materials companies prioritized industries essential to the war effort, whose workforce increased by 44 percent, while consumption goods industries such as textiles and foodstuffs, but also craft industry and small businesses, suffered under the wartime conditions. In particular, small- to medium-sized businesses were at a disadvantage in the allocation of raw materials. It is true that the German war economy developed a distinctive mix of private and top-down bureaucratic elements. But the contemporary term "war social-ism," with its hopes for better integration of workers and employers, was misleading, since in the end the role of state planning remained quite lim-ited. In practice, the model of a state-socialist "social economy," envisaged by Rathenau in his book *Von kommenden Dingen* (1917), failed to material-ize. Instead, entrepreneurs were able to assert their interests through effi-cient lobbying, while the Reich treasury department under Karl Helfferich exercised considerable restraint in the use of its powers.[228] In particular, the Kriegsausschuss der deutschen Industrie gained greater influence than state bodies over the war economy, however much the government tried to centralize contracts by setting up new organizations, such as the Central Purchasing Society founded in September 1915 as a food import monopoly and the War Nutrition Bureau founded in 1916.[229] These bureaucratic mea-sures changed nothing fundamental: the ultimately unregulated relationship between limited supply and enormous demand often permitted sizable profit margins in industries vital to the war effort, difficult though it is to calculate the profits of war, especially if inflation, depreciation, and investment are taken into account.[230]

The distinction between peace industry and war industry became ever clearer over time. Many export-oriented firms quickly lost their markets because of the blockade, and not all could offset this through war-related business as successfully as the chemicals firm Bayer Leverkusen managed to do; it had previously exported 85 percent of its output, but took advantage of new basic materials (as produced in the Haber-Bosch nitrogen fixation process) and made up the shortfall. The boom in war-related branches of industry could not, however, prevent a 40 percent drop in total industrial output during the war. The main contributory factors to this were the mas-sive problems in the supply of fuel and raw materials, labor shortages, and productivity decreases due to the employment of unskilled (and, from 1916, increasingly undernourished) manpower.[231]

In Germany, as in other countries, the large expansion of state orders already pushed up prices considerably by 1915. Early in the year, politicians reacted to the strongly decentralized ordering system by setting up no fewer than forty different procurement bodies, and in a further effort at centralization the war ministry clamped down on middlemen to keep some control over prices. A system developed in which the military authorities ensured the supply and procurement of raw materials and manpower, while no intervention was made in the profits of the arms industry until Summer 1917. This was in sharp contrast to the policy of Lloyd George and his ministry in Britain, which gave a signal to the trade unions by taxing profits as early as 1915.[232]

In comparison with the industrial profits resulting from preferential military orders, social measures in Germany remained modest. Since many firms were able to offload part of their risks and development costs onto the war economy as a whole, the fair distribution of the burdens of war became a focus of policy disputes. Right from the start, the "free" (that is, socialist) trade unions declared that for the duration of the war they would forego strikes and other means of fighting to increase wages. But such concessions did not prevent the de facto suspension of many protective regulations covering female and youth labor, as well as the fast-expanding sector of home-based work.

On the other hand, new social emphases began to appear after the first few months of the war—not as a result of particularly labor-friendly policies on the employers' part or an adequate conception of state responsibilities, but often simply because of a realization that some compromises in social policy were necessary to avoid risks to the war economy and therefore to Germany's military survival. One measure in 1915 was the development of voluntary wage arbitration boards, against the determined opposition of the workers, who feared that these would weaken the unions. In the end, the arbitration boards proved to be an important institutional basis for the Auxiliary Service Act of December 1916, which was supposed to enlarge the pool of labor for the arms industry, but also to lead to recognition of the unions as representatives of industrial workers. In 1915, employers and unionists responded to the rising number of disputes over higher wages that took place in the movement between jobs. When the war ministry in January 1915 threatened to stop giving orders to firms that took on workers without the consent of their former employers, the Berlin Metalworkers Association raised a storm of protest. In response, a Military Committee for Berlin Metal Enterprises was set up to reach consensual decisions at weekly meetings.

The representation of employers and unions on this committee, and their recognition of each other as official representatives, marked an important step toward a parity-based institution.[233]

In the early months of the war, high unemployment resulted in considerable social problems. By late July 1915, the unions' support funds were paying out more than 200 million marks to their members. Unprotected jobless workers, on the other hand, had to rely on the slender support provided by local councils. And by no stretch of the imagination could it be said that women with husbands at the front, and often without work themselves, were adequately provided for. Their husbands' pay did not go far, and in many cases their wives had to turn to local welfare services and charities. Homelessness was also a growing risk because of rent increases. Thus, in early August 1914, the Bundesrat issued an order allowing a three-month postponement of payment for debtors, and local boards were set up to arbitrate disputes between landlords and tenants.[234]

The other key problem was the food supply. In 1915, however, there was still a conviction that Germany was not dependent on imports: "The first anxious question when war broke out was: will we have enough to eat? Thank God, yes; our harvest will last us a year. If that were not so, we would have been defeated a long time ago; all the courage of our heroes would not have been able to save us." The war therefore showed that Germany's might and future survival rested not "on the water" but "on our home soil."[235] However, contrary to a widespread belief that Germany was self-sufficient in food, even before 1914 it was the world's largest importer of agricultural produce (38 percent of its total imports). The shortage of farm labor, which deportees from occupied parts of eastern Europe could only partly fill as the war advanced, as well as interruptions in the supply of fertilizer, led to a decline in the area under cultivation. Agricultural output fell by one-third during the course of the war, cattle production by 40 percent, grain production by 36 percent, and potato production by 35 percent. The direct consequences by Fall 1914 were rising food prices and growing tensions between the SPD and union representatives (who saw a threat to the social peace) and farmers who saw the blockade as a chance to boost their profits.[236]

In view of these developments, the public mood in Germany began to change in Summer 1915—although the authorities tried to give the

Satiety imagined: Prussian home army troops resisting the British naval blockade, German postcard, Leipzig, 1914–1915

impression, by issuing thousands of propaganda postcards, that the food supply was secure. A Berlin police report in June 1915 stated, "Margarine has become scarcer and more expensive. . . . Other foodstuffs have remained high in price. No fall is expected. Someone whose pay has increased considerably because of the war can live as before under the present circumstances." All other households were cutting down more and more; people calmly endured these privations, so that no "hunger revolts" were to be feared. "But the higher cost of living does affect people's mood, especially as there is no end in sight to the war . . . and, as a result of skillful agitation, there is a stronger sense that many of the higher prices are almost entirely due to unscrupulous speculation."[237] By September the warnings were becoming clearer: the "fruit-lessness of most measures to lower prices" not only had a "disheartening" effect but politicized the conflict, by "converting many more" to the demand for an early peace, "especially as radicalism busily continues its 'underground work' to this end."[238]

In October 1914 the government had already brought a maximum price decree into force, and special institutions were created following the example of the military-industrial companies responsible for raw materials management. Thus, in November 1914 a War Grain Company took over central supervision of all grain imports, including their distribution. Rivalry soon developed among institutions with partly overlapping competences: most notably, alongside the military-industrial companies, procurement agencies run by the military, local councils, and large enterprises began to compete with one another to purchase and distribute food. The consequences of this structural inefficiency were already visible by the winter and spring of 1914–1915, in the shape of bread-grain and potato bottlenecks, and bread cards were introduced for Berlin in January and the whole country in June. New authorities sprang up thick and fast, but their mania for regulation and control reflected not so much coherent strategies to deal with crises as a need to improvise in the face of growing shortages. From the Imperial Grain Agency (June 1915), through the Imperial Potato Agency (October 1915) and an Imperial Price Controls Board to the authorization for courts to declare the last peacetime prices legally binding, what took shape was less a state-run command economy than a shortage economy. The development of corporatist-type authorities reached a climax in the founding of the War

Nutrition Bureau in May 1916, with August Müller on its board as the first Social Democrat to hold a government position.

Despite all the official efforts, it soon became clear that more and more foodstuffs—30 to 50 percent at the peak—were being traded on black markets. There was a creeping criminalization of daily life. In 1915 the Imperial Health Ministry carried out surveys that showed evidence of undernourishment, especially in the large cities. Although agricultural imports from occupied Romania staved off disaster in Winter 1915–1916, the constantly worsening food supply turned into the beginnings of a crisis of the wartime state and its capacity to provide the civilian population with a fair and adequate minimum. That same winter, the first demonstrations and hunger riots took place in a number of urban centers.[239] The estimate of 700,000 civilian casualties from the Allied blockade is debatable, but the food crisis certainly made people more susceptible to illnesses.[240] The frenetic activity of new authorities created an expectation that the state would solve the supply problem—only disappointment that this corresponded less and less to the reality finally eroded the authority of the state and the credibility of government agencies.[241]

The limitations of state controls and food security policy are illustrated by the so-called pig murders of Spring 1915. Before the outbreak of war, Germany had largely supplied its own meat, especially pork. But after the war halted imports of fodder (mainly Russian barley), the authorities organized an inventory in early 1915 and discovered two completely opposite action logics. Since most farmers feared requisitioning of their fodder grain and potatoes, they reported considerably lower stocks than they actually held, also hoping that this pseudo-shortage would push up prices. The authorities, on the other hand, under pressure from rising food prices, feared that large stocks of farm animals would lead to a shortage of bread grain, and so they ordered the slaughter of more than five million pigs and the holding of their preserved meat in reserve. The economic sequel showed just how little official measures could interfere with the logic of the market. At first prices fell because of the pork glut, but then they rose in the second half of the year as massive shortages appeared. Finally, the authorities set maximum prices, but these remained ineffectual because much of the additional meat output had long been diverted to the black market.[242]

The society of shortage led to novel phenomena such as Ida Boy-Eds's war cookbook *Des Vaterlandes Kochtopf,* which had an insert claiming that in war the "kitchen question" had become an "arms question"; it showed ways to "effectively counter the English starvation frenzy."[243] In 1915 Georg Simmel described the paradoxical correlation between rising food prices and the savings behavior of various social classes: "People used to lobster salad, young carrots, and partridge" would now eat only "fresh herrings, old carrots, and chopped lights," and were convinced that "the worse something tasted, the more it served the fatherland." But the exact opposite was true: "So long as cheap food could be got at the market without restriction, it might have been a virtue for the well-off to stick to simplicity. But now, when quantities are limited and can hardly be increased, the well-off must abstain from it as much as possible, for the benefit of those who cannot afford anything more expensive." If the rich cut down on spending, they will cause "stocks of things on which the poor rely" to run short.[244]

But the emergence of the war economy had another consequence. As in Britain and to some extent France, the wartime corporatism forced a basic rethink of the relationship between economy and state, employers and industrial workers, as well as the development of new models for the integration and cohesion of modern industrial societies up to and beyond the end of the war. Although in principle the problem affected all belligerent countries, a particularly lively debate developed in 1915 in Germany, where the effects of economic warfare on people's daily lives were especially severe. In these conditions, some writers put forward ideas for a new economic and social constitution arising out of the war—ideas that at first linked up with a debate before 1914 on the problems of the German nation-state. In 1901 Karl Helfferich had put his finger on these problems when he noted that Germany had "an agrarian politics in an industrial state" and addressed the integration deficits of the young nation-state.[245] The successful industrial society, in his view, was bound up with a retrograde distribution of political power among the groups in society. The result was two conflicting strategies: an "agrarian" nation-state relied externally on a great-power politics, in which the army, based on an autarkic agrarian sector, could remain largely independent of industrial workers and a bourgeois officer corps. As a thoroughgoing industrial state, however, the German Empire had to orient itself to the world market. According to this interpretation, the Schlieffen Plan and a short war would render superfluous the mobilization of industry and therefore an alliance with the industrial working class.[246] Against this "agrarian" viewpoint, however, stood the conviction of military leaders like Ludendorff that war would require mobilizing the economy and joining together with the industrial working class. War radicalized liberal imperialism, whose motto "social reform internally, power externally" had been outlined by Friedrich Naumann in 1900.[247]

Unlike in France and Britain, no substantive political or social concessions were made under the aegis of the social truce. Chancellor Bethmann Hollweg did favor a "farsighted social policy," but at the same time he demanded the "reform of Social Democracy in a national and monarchical direction."[248] In 1915, the outlines of a war society with newly allocated roles of winners and losers were becoming discernible. In a war that had to be waged not only militarily but also industrially, certain industries and their workforces gained in importance. While these profited economically, incomes fell in agriculture and the bourgeois middle classes, especially among senior employees and officials in areas not directly necessary to the war effort; conflicts became unavoidable as factors such as property and education declined in importance compared with functions in the war economy. Not by chance did these problems come together in the nutrition issue, with its underlying question of whether the wartime state was capable of sharing the burdens fairly. In Germany, too, the rampant enemy-image of "profiteers" and "winners from the war" bound the military and domestic fronts more closely together. In a book published in 1915 under the title *Wucher und Kriegsgewinn* (Profiteering and War Gains), we read, "Profiteering has become the common custom in Germany! That sounds harsh, but it is demonstrably true. The authorities basically accept it and only combat 'excesses' of the general price friction. When hundreds of thousands of our brothers are shedding their blood, and hundreds of thousands more are losing their jobs and livelihood, to defend our borders, it should not be tolerated that those who remain at home are amassing fortunes out of their graves and affliction."[249]

At the same time, there was a search for new models of social cohesion and integration, with one eye already on the postwar world. New programmatic terms were introduced for the future changes and opportunities. Thus, when

Walther Rathenau and his colleague Wichard von Moellendorff coined the terms "new economy" and "social economy," they emphasized that industrialized mass warfare would lead to a social-corporate balancing of interests and transcend the traditional definition of class loyalties. The fact that many spoke of "social economy" and "war socialism" as synonymous, whether or not they approved of it, proved the nexus between national integration and social participation. Conservative economists went so far as to derive the "community of a national labor state" from the wartime social economy.[250]

The term "national community" (*Volksgemeinschaft*) also gained currency in this context. First used in 1870 by both anti-Semites and Zionists, and then around the turn of the century by the youth movement and various nationalist and military groups, it had referred since 1914 to the cross-class and interdenominational mobilization of all the forces of society and industry to defend the nation-state established in 1871.[251] The idealized, classless nation promised the integration of all its members with equal rights. This explained why it was precisely Social Democrats, the Catholic Center, and German Jews who took up the term *Volksgemeinschaft*, in opposition to the exclusive conservative vision of the nation. Nation and socialism seemed to be drawing closer to each other. But this was feasible only if a strong war state, a neutral institution above parties and interest groups, distributed goods fairly and thereby strengthened people's experience of constituting a single nation at war. In 1915 Max Scheler put it as follows: "A first discovery made possible by the war, and bound up with the form of the 'war experience' in all its abundance, is the reality of the nation as a spiritual person." The nation, in peacetime "more a symbolic concept for its members," had now become "truly visible and tangible to the mind's eye."[252]

But not only social theorists and economic experts were formulating new concepts. In 1915 the Social Democrat Rudolf Hilferding, based on his prewar and post-1914 criticisms of the SPD's strategic focus on social gains rather than the issue of political participation, coined the term "organized capitalism." This referred to the new conception of the economy that had come about as a result of the war. The idea of a revolutionary collapse of capitalism, he argued, was no longer appropriate to a highly developed industrial society such as that of Germany. The proletariat had flexibly established itself within existing capitalism, where the living conditions of industrial workers had been constantly improved through the policies of the SPD and labor unions. The dominance of finance capital, growing ever stronger since the 1890s, involved the "conversion of anarchic capitalism into an organized capitalist economic order." The state-organized formation of monopolies and oligopolies, which had been accelerated by the war, was further reinforcing this tendency.

Hilferding concluded that, as the war economy was already demonstrating, the future development of society would consist in the evolutionary development of capitalism. But he criticized the profoundly undemocratic organization of this process, whereby the workers submitted to the economic monopolies and state institutions, while the SPD and unions supported this course.[253] Instead of socialism overcoming capitalist society, what was appearing was "the society of organized capitalism, better adapted than before to the immediate material needs of the masses."[254] In the face of this, socialists should use the prerequisites for the achievement of socialism that the war itself had created, and work with the state to establish a democratic economic order. As the war impelled a shift toward organized capitalism, the issue of political participation became decisive. This was the point at which Hilferding parted company with the SPD leadership, for whom social and political improvements were also conceivable within the framework of the monarchic state.

For most people in the home society, however, the war economy with its daily experience of shortages, black markets, and unequal burdens and profits stood in sharp contrast to such projections and discussions. This too was becoming clear in 1915, but the contrast would acquire a sharper edge over the next few years. As the war state resorted to the *Volksgemeinschaft* ideology to justify ever-greater efforts and sacrifices, the widening gulf between expectations and actual experiences created a huge potential for conflict. In 1915 the civil peace was still holding, but the popular mood was changing with the realization that the war was locked in a stalemate. This in turn made the population an ever more important object of state supervision. In October 1915, the responsibility for government censorship, which had been operating in the framework of the regional Deputy General Commands, was transferred to a new central War Press Bureau and considerably tightened. In practice, self-censorship by publishers and journalists proved even more effective than the often-improvised official censorship.[255]

Politically, the debate over military objectives intensified in the course of 1915. It became evident that no really clear war aims had been formulated in August 1914 and that in 1915 many players were trying to define their position in view of the deadlock on the western front and the successes in the east. The spelling out of war aims then triggered a polarization that affected the organization of divergent political interests. From 1915 the Right, with its Independent Committee for a German Peace, deployed a widespread network to gain a hearing for its positions. The five leading business associations waged a campaign under the influence of Heinrich Claß, the chairman of the All-German Association. Meanwhile, a petition with 1,347 signatures— including 352 professors, 148 judges and attorneys, 158 clerics, 182 industrialists, and 252 artists, writers, and publishers—was submitted to the Reich chancellor on July 8, 1915. It demanded, as part of any peace settlement, the French Channel coast and sizable reparations, the incorporation of the whole of Belgium, and the ceding of Russia's Baltic provinces and other settler territories; Britain would be required to recognize German's position on the seas and beyond, to guarantee the freedom of the seas, and to pay as high reparations as possible.[256] Although this blast provoked a countermemorandum with more moderate demands, in which the historians Hans Delbrück and Friedrich Meinecke played a role, the debate showed that the so-called annexationists envisaged a peace that would not only achieve economically motivated conquests in the west but also implement major German settlement projects and population transfers in eastern Europe.[257] Such aims no longer had anything in common with a defensive war.

Friedrich Naumann's vision of *Mitteleuropa* (the title of a book published in 1915), stretching from the North and Baltic Seas to the Alps, and from the Adriatic to the southern rim of the Danubian plain, also belonged to this context of spatially defined war aims. He understood central Europe as a "highly articulated fraternal land, a defensive league, an economic area," where, "in the stress of the world war, all historical particularism should be erased insofar as it tolerates the idea of unity."[258] The war had meant for it an "interruption in the world economy": "By the will of England, we were almost completely cut off from large-scale foreign trade." Germans, Austrians, and Hungarians had been living in an "economic prison," but after the war only central Europeans would experience the "closed commercial state"—an allusion to the ideal of an autonomous nation-state, as outlined in Johann Gottlieb Fichte's *Der geschlossene Handelsstaat* (1800)—which "by fate and national predisposition has been realized here in wartime."[259] This marked an abandonment of Germany's orientation as a global economic power and a return to a conception of itself as a continental economic and political power.

The debate showed the link between ever-higher casualties and ever more expansive war aims, since only the achievement of these could justify the cost in human lives. On March 15, 1915 the president of the Prussian House of Lords, Count von Wedel-Piesdorf, argued that, while Germany had lost its colonies, no enemy was present on its own territory and it occupied Belgium and parts of France and Poland: "Germany, however, cannot declare itself content with this. We must demand more after the huge sacrifices we have endured, in human lives as well as goods and chattel. We can put our sword back in its scabbard only when Germany has an assurance that our neighbors will not descend upon us as they have done this time."[260] On June 19, 1915, the left-wing SPD deputies Eduard Bernstein, Hugo Haase, and Karl Kautsky attacked these far-reaching objectives as an erosion of the political truce, incompatible with the defensive war supported by their party. The SPD, they thought, should ask itself whether its principles allowed it "to side with those whose aims blatantly contradicted the declaration of our parliamentary group on August 4, 1914, in unison with the International, condemning any war of conquest."[261] Subsequently, the group's support for war credits began to decline. Whereas in August 1914 a total of 78 fraction members had voted for war credits and only 14 against, the picture in 1915 was as follows: in March, 77 yes to 23 no; in August, 72 yes to 36 no; and in December, 66 yes to 44 no. Tensions within the group were now unmistakable.[262]

With no end in sight for the war, leftist socialists in Germany and elsewhere tended to display stronger opposition. In September they tried to revive socialist pacifism and to restore the international cooperation broken in Summer 1914. The result was the conference held at Zimmerwald in Switzerland in September 1915, on the initiative of the Swiss Social Democrat Robert Grimm.[263] There too, however, the divisions between the various strategies were manifest. It is true that the delegates—who included Vladimir Ilyich Lenin and Grigorii Zinoviev for the Russian Social Democratic

Labor Party, and Adolf Hoffmann and Georg Ledebour for the German SPD—issued a manifesto, *To the Workers of Europe*, that criticized the imperialist war and the willingness of various sections of the European Left to support their governments, and called for a peace without annexations on the basis of national self-determination.[264] But individual voices pointed in a different direction: Lenin, for one, called for the war between states to be transformed into a revolution and an international civil war, a people's war of all the oppressed against their oppressors. Tensions remained palpable, and at the follow-up meeting at Kienthal in late April 1916 the differences between moderate and radical delegates could no longer be bridged. Finally, at the Stockholm conference in September 1917, the socialist parties of the belligerent countries failed to adopt the idea of a mass strike to force an end to the war. The attempts to breathe new life into the International therefore remained unsuccessful. While the large socialist parties criticized the social and economic effects of the war in their home countries, the majority stuck to the civil peace in their foreign policy. What the exile conference in Sweden showed above all was a sharpening of evolutionary and revolutionary strategies vis-à-vis the war. In 1917, Lenin would then apply his own conception in Russia in a historically unique situation.[265]

7. MULTIETHNIC SOCIETIES AT WAR
From Undisputed Loyalty to the Escalation of Ethnic Violence

Many social and economic developments occurring in other wartime societies were also observable in the Habsburg monarchy. Yet its multiethnic character and special languages of loyalty on the home front differentiated it from Britain, France, and Germany.[266] The economy of Austria-Hungary was not initially prepared for a long war, although some sectors profited enormously from the conversion to arms production. The Škoda machine builders, for example, founded in Pilsen in 1859, had already been an important prewar arms producer and constructor of battleships, and with the war it became the largest arms corporation in Austria-Hungary. By 1918 it delivered almost 13,000 artillery pieces of all calibers to the armed forces. As a whole, however, the economy continually shrank during the war years. One reason for this, following a short period of high unemployment immediately after the outbreak of war, was the shortage of skilled labor in particular, as well as the interruption of import-export links. Economically, the Dual Monarchy increasingly resembled a fortress under siege, partly because its government and military leadership underestimated the decisive importance of key sectors for the war effort. When fighting with Russia initially halted access to petroleum facilities in Galicia, little attention was paid in either Austria-Hungary or Russia. Unlike the British forces, who, sensitized by the Royal Navy to the interconnectedness of energy resources, mobility, and military capacity, destroyed the Romanian oilfields before the Germans could capture them in 1917, the Russians left the Galician facilities largely intact before their withdrawal. The fact that the war was also a battle over energy resources was for a long time unclear to most military commanders and politicians. This was a fundamental difference between the First and Second World Wars.[267]

Vienna reacted to the British naval blockade by following the German wartime model of raw materials management: it centralized branches of the economy important for the war effort, and by the end of the war a total of ninety-one military agencies had been founded. In 1915—after the early shock of adjustment—the economy stabilized to some extent, most noticeably in the coal and iron sectors, and this assured a relatively high level of arms production. The resulting social costs were a massive increase in the working week from 80 to 110 hours and the employment of numerous women for a low hourly wage.[268] But the wartime boom remained limited in time and sectors, so that by 1916 the output figures for coal, iron, and steel were beginning to decline.

Other aspects of the war economy affected people's lives even more directly. Steep price rises followed official recourse to the printing of money. As in Germany, war loans were issued with a big media fanfare to avoid tax hikes, but although they were initially popular, they netted less and less money as the war went on and exacerbated the problems of inflation and food shortages. The eighth and last loan, available from May to June 1918, brought in a mere quarter of the target sum. The loan subscription figures reflected the dwindling trust in the future of the monarchy, especially among Czechs, who in 1918 finally introduced their own banknotes. By early 1915, the money supply in Austria-Hungary had reached twice the prewar level, and by 1918 it would increase tenfold. In contrast to other wartime societies, Austria-Hungary did not manage to set effective legal curbs on the resulting price rises.[269]

Induced by the blockade, the temporary loss of farmland in Galicia, and a lack of competent official coordination, the cost of living doubled between Summer 1915 and 1916. Emergent black markets began to criminalize people's daily lives. The failure of the authorities to maintain adequate supplies for civilians, particularly in large Cisleithanian cities such as Vienna and Prague, was becoming apparent by the beginning of 1915. Until early 1917 there was no food supply board covering the whole monarchy. Flour already had to be rationed by March 1915. The problem only grew worse with the large influx of refugees from areas on the eastern front, which led to clashes in Vienna and created a real parallel between the struggle of women for their daily bread and the war being fought by their menfolk at the front.[270] A decree issued by the Vienna city hall on February 2, 1915, stated that the commercial production of cakes ("so-called ring cakes, doughnuts, strudels, butter pastry and yeast dough, biscuits, and so on") was permissible on only two days a week. From 1915, popular reactions in Austria-Hungary were one reason why the social and economic shortages led to ethnic-national lines of conflict on the home front. This conversion process, discernible in the growing criticism in Austria of Hungary's unwillingness to deliver farm produce on a large scale, could at any moment acquire a political dimension.[271]

In the Austrian part of the Empire—the term "Austria" for the Cisleithanian half became common usage in late 1915—the AOK high command acquired ever-greater influence on domestic politics and endangered the civil peace in two respects. First, it undermined the influence of the labor unions, which stepped up their activity in view of the supply crises ahead, while at the same time continuing to emphasize their loyalty. The First of May in 1915, and again in 1916, was celebrated under the slogan "Endurance"; workers demonstratively refrained from work stoppages to underline their solidarity with soldiers at the front.[272] At the same time, well-known unionists were watched and immediately arrested if they made critical remarks (for example, on capitalism as the cause of the war). It thus became more and more difficult to defend the social truce in a convincing manner. Alongside these social tensions, multiethnic complexities disturbed the delicate pre-1914 balance between parts of the monarchy, as conflicts began to develop beneath the multiple avowals of loyalty. With the help of a new monitoring service in Vienna, the military was able to enforce its orders in the provinces despite the lack of parliamentary control or other political counterweights. At many levels, however, a dual structure led to rivalry and conflict between military institutions and the civilian authorities. In contrast to western Europe, it became more and more difficult to define the home front, since the war of movement in the east blurred the boundaries and did not allow them to stabilize for long. Repeated changes of occupation power, together with the military frontier and the lack of a fixed boundary, left their mark on the region. The situation in combat zones and in the vicinity of the military fronts differed considerably from that in provinces more remote from the fighting. Thus, the military resorted to tougher measures in areas close to the front in Bosnia-Herzegovina, Galicia, and Moravia or, beginning in Spring 1915, close to the border with Italy;[273] there the treatment of civilians was especially dependent on the military situation. The reverses suffered in Winter 1914–1915 against Russian forces offered a pretext for massive reprisals against the non-German and non-Hungarian population.

The basis for these actions was a set of emergency decrees that restricted civil rights in combat zones and gave sweeping powers to military tribunals. Hangings on gallows, at first staged in public to maximize the effect and recorded in numerous photos, were potent symbols of this policy toward civilians; the main victims were Ruthenians and Poles in Galicia (where lists of "Russophiles" were also drawn up), Bosnians and Serbs in the Balkans, and, from Spring 1915, also Italians. Fear of spies and enemy collaborators made arrests and hostage taking daily events under the de facto military rule. As early as August 1914, an Imperial military order prescribed, "So long as troops are in or close to these locations, hostages absolutely must be levied after notification is received—and in any case these should consist primarily of the most notable and influential individuals. Wherever the least sign of support for the enemy is observed, the action should be completely ruthless. No measure is harsh enough in such cases."[274] Although there was a danger that the foreign media might use these policies to demonstrate the inhumanity of the Central Powers, the treatment of alleged spies was no secret in the home societies. On May 23, 1915, for example, a photograph in the weekly

Wiener Hausfrau showed a man under arrest who had clearly been branded a Jewish spy and was awaiting execution: "In the eastern theater of war," the article read, "espionage plays a far greater role than in the west, where it occurs only in isolated instances. Russian Poland, Galicia, etc. is the real center of traitors to the fatherland, of those sad souls who are ready to serve the enemy, often for a mere pittance. . . . Of course no one can have any sympathy for such people; they meet a well-deserved end."[275]

Operations along the south of the eastern front often brought about changes between Austro-Hungarian and Russian occupation. The actions of the military authorities in areas close to the front, most notably in Galicia, triggered large-scale refugee movements; thousands of Ruthenians, including many Orthodox Jews, were forced to leave the land of their birth. This migration intensified the already tense supply situation in the western cities of the Reich, soon unleashing anti-Semitic responses in Vienna and Bohemia. Measures in parts of South Tyrol bordering Italy against individuals regarded as disloyal also followed the pattern of exclusion. In that area more than 100,000 people were evacuated from their homeland in May 1915, since it counted as a region close to the front where the authorities feared that the population would collaborate with the Italians. In South Slav regions, what amounted to a military dictatorship took shape under the Croat general Stjepan Sarkotić, the governor of Bosnia-Herzegovina and Dalmatia. The Bosnian parliament, the Sabor, and local councils were abolished; Serb schools and associations were closed and use of the Cyrillic alphabet prohibited. But the AOK could not impose this style of repression against opposition groups in other parts of the monarchy.[276]

The home front in the Habsburg monarchy was as diverse as the traditions, structures, and expectations in its constituent parts. This was clearest in areas not close to the front. In Bohemia, tensions between the AOK and Czech politicians began to increase in late 1914, but the prime minister, Stürgkh, managed to limit the political influence of the military and to avoid a rapid escalation of conflicts. Anti-Russian enemy-images, often cited in Summer 1914 to justify Austria-Hungary's entry into the war, had in fact little purchase among the Czech population, and the war added greater urgency to the question of Bohemia's long-term prospects within the monarchy. Nevertheless, one cannot speak of a national Czech resistance to the war—however many Czech national historians tried to present this after 1918 as the dominant trend on the home front. If we discount this twofold retrospect—the Austrian search for Czech "traitors" as the cause of the downfall of the monarchy and the quest of Czech historians for wartime secessionism and nation-building—it becomes clear that the situation was more complicated.

In parallel to the military successes of the Central Powers against Russia in 1915 and 1916, many Czechs remained loyal to the Austrian emperor and the dynasty as symbols of the monarchy, even if expressions of support by local administrations, schools, and churches may often have been stage-managed.[277] Nevertheless, tensions were mounting: 74 percent of the 4,600 people detained for political reasons in Bohemia were Czechs. In contrast to German politicians, who demonstratively affirmed their support for the Austrian war effort, Czech parties and leading politicians distanced themselves ever more plainly in late 1914 and 1915. A good example in this respect was Karel Kramář, the leader of the Young Czech group on the Imperial Council in Vienna, its vice president from 1907, and later the first prime minister of Czechoslovakia. Convinced that the war signified a clash between the Slav and Germanic worlds, he stepped up his resistance to the monarchy after August 1914. After he spoke of his vision of an independent state of the Czechs and Slovaks to the Russian foreign minister, he was arrested in mid-1915 and, despite his parliamentary immunity, tried and sentenced for high treason (while the same charges were dropped against Josef Scheiner, the president of the Sokol gymnastic association). Amnestied in 1917, Kramář was able to continue pursuing his goal of Czech statehood in a domestic political situation then quite different from that in 1915.[278]

Elsewhere, too, official measures against oppositionists or sections of the population suspected of collaboration with the enemy sharpened the criticism of Viennese politicians. Arrests of leading national politicians, such as the Slovene Franc Grafenauer in Carinthia or the Croat Tresić Pavičić in Dalmatia, fueled the mistrust. Many of the men in question were amnestied in 1917 and were able to resume their political activity, but the mood was different in this final period of the war and they found a greater echo in the public.[279]

The AOK aimed to increase its influence in Bohemia by replacing a civilian with a military governor. Openly directed against the prime minister, Stürgkh, who kept on good terms with Kramář, this policy reflected the tense relationship between the civilian government and the military leadership in Vienna. Conrad von Hötzendorf had Bohemia in mind in Spring 1915 when he had this to say after the Italians joined the war: "The restrictions and obligations caused by the war may tempt the unpatriotic population, spurred on by unscrupulous agitators, to engage in the most dangerous acts, especially as the state power confronting them has given signs of a disturbing weakness and has by no means sufficient troops at its disposal to make a rebellion seem hopeless from the start."[280] The arrest and trial of Kramář and other Czech politicians had an alarming effect on large sections of the Czech public, creating potential martyrs and fueling national political expectations.

At this time Tomáš G. Masaryk was developing a radical alternative from abroad. A member of the Imperial Council in Vienna from 1900 to 1914, he traveled to the Netherlands in Fall and Winter 1914, and then to Italy and finally Switzerland. Warned that he might be arrested if he returned home, he decided to remain abroad with his daughter and founded in Geneva an organization of Czech political exiles. On July 6, 1915, the anniversary of the death of the national martyr Jan Hus, he called for the dissolution of Austria-Hungary and the formation of an independent Czech state. At first he spoke for only a minority of Czechs, but in exile a tangible alternative began to appear for the first time. As an exiled former member of the Imperial Council, Masaryk further offered a bridge to the Slovaks in Upper Hungary by developing the idea of an independent binational state. He thus went far beyond the majority Czech policy geared to obtaining a greater say within the monarchy. In the course of 1915, the group around Masaryk organized "external action" in western capitals, which was funded mainly by Czechs and Slovaks living in the United States. At the same time, Masaryk's comrade-in-arms Edvard Beneš waged an intensive media campaign in France to convince the Allies to accept a binational Czechoslovak state as part of a new order for east central Europe. Special attention was given to imprisoned soldiers and to deserters from the Imperial army: they were urged to fight under their own commanders on the Allied side and to emphasize the demand for an independent state. The resulting Czechoslovak Legion eventually comprised 11,000 men in France, 23,500 in Italy, and more than 75,000 in Russia. But such a development was not yet foreseeable in 1915.[281]

For German Austrians, the negative stereotype of unreliable Czechs was becoming in 1915 a fixed part of a burgeoning culture of mistrust. It began to poison the domestic political climate of the Cisleithanian half of the Empire.[282] Whereas in 1914 such reproaches had referred only to Czechs who responded half-heartedly to the call-up, many German Austrians in 1915 accused Czech soldiers of deserting en masse to the Russians. The mistrust reached a peak in 1917, when an official questionnaire sought the views of ethnic German representatives in the Imperial Council on "the conduct of Czechs in the world war." The replies frequently referred to the 28th, 35th, and 75th Infantry Regiments, all with Czech majorities, that were alleged to have deserted during battles in April 1915 and April 1917. In reality, the 28th Regiment had been almost completely wiped out by a Russian attack in Spring 1915. The War Ministry, having been informed of the supposed desertions, had ordered the dissolution of the unit. And although the facts were clarified at a subsequent trial and the unit was reestablished, an impression remained of betrayal and desertion—especially as the rehabilitation was not made public.

The Battle of Zborów in July 1917 also saw no mass desertions. Rather, the Austro-Hungarian forces were ordered to withdraw, having been caught off guard by the Kerensky offensive so soon after the February revolution in Russia. In order to hide their own responsibility, the army commanders spread the accusation that the Czechoslovak Legion, consisting of former Czech prisoners of war, had fought on the Russian side and encouraged Czechs in the Habsburg ranks to defect. Unlike in 1915, the Czech units in 1917 were not exonerated; German Austrians in the Vienna parliament used the accusation of betrayal, in the changed domestic climate, to block any political concessions to the Czech population. In accepting these stereotypes after 1918—whether to explain the defeat and dissolution of the Habsburg monarchy as a result of Czech treachery or to justify the heroic struggle for a Czechoslovak state by reference to supposed resistance during the war— the respective national historians crafted a reality of their own making.[283] In fact, the rising desertion rates during the war do not explain the military reverses of Austria-Hungary, which were due to strategic mistakes, wrong assessments, and supply inadequacies.

In a way, the adventures of the *Good Soldier Schwejk* corresponded at a literary level to German-Austrian images of the Czechs. When Jaroslav Hašek published his picaresque novel in 1921, it owed its impact above all to the portrait of the war years from the vantage of a new Czechoslovak state, in which the search was on for figures with whom the people could identify. The wily soldier Schwejk, who manages to dodge service at the front and exposes the imaginary idyll of the Habsburg monarchy as a mixture of bureaucracy, prejudices, stupidity, and arrogance on the part of the German Austrian elite, appeared with hindsight to embody the reluctance of various nationalities to go to war for the Imperial regime. But that is exactly what they did in 1914 and 1915—and the novel's picture of the monarchy, drawn in the light of subsequent developments, did not mirror the situation during the war, but corresponded to an altogether different way of thinking.[284]

A distinctive mix of loyalty and skepticism also developed in other parts of the monarchy. Much as politicians and diplomats in other countries used delaying tactics after August 1914 to play off the Allies against the Central Powers and to take profit from their competing offers, so too did many representatives of ethnic groups in the Dual Monarchy temporize to strengthen their bargaining position. The question in 1915 was not whether to remain in the monarchy or struggle for an independent state, but how to use loyalty as a means of achieving maximum leeway and pursuing extensive autonomy within the Empire at some future date. The activities of Masaryk and Beneš abroad, as well as the creation of Czech units in Russia in 1915, did not yet represent majority opinion inside Bohemia.

In general, the debate about future structures and reform of the dual monarchic system continued to intensify. In 1915, Conrad von Hötzendorf himself was pushing for a negotiated peace with Serbia and Russia to pacify the South Slav regions, so that forces could be released for the war with Italy. He therefore called for a reform package that would address, among other things, the oppression of ethnic minorities in Hungary: "The petty harassment of neighbors and the gagging of non-Magyar nationalities must end, and attention must be given to the incorporation or attachment of the South Slavs to the monarchy—with increased rights for the Croats and the creation of a central parliament for the whole monarchy."[285] Wherever politicians could assert themselves in the competition with the military authorities—as in Carniola under Ivan Šušteršič (the Catholic leader of the Slovenes) or in Croatia in the Hungarian part of the Empire—the bargaining led to limited concessions. It was no accident that the Hungarian government permitted the reopening of the Croatian parliament in June 1915, after Italy had decided to enter the war on the Allied side. On the one hand, many Croats supported the war because Italy had been making demands on Croatian territory and had received assurances that London would back its claims. On the other hand, a majority of the parliament in Zagreb demanded that the Imperial government should give greater priority in the long term to an enlarged Croatia within the monarchy. In this context one could see what the war meant for a multiethnic society: loyalty became a political currency, in the hope that it would force through future changes beneath the threshold of secession. But the multiplicity of such bargaining strategies fueled a dynamic of expectations that the monarchy could less and less credibly address as the war continued from year to year.

Two episodes illustrate, in contradictory ways, how closely the military and home fronts were interrelated in the Russian Empire, too, and how in the first year of war a gap within Russian society opened up between expectations and experiences. In the early months, many women set off for the front, not only to work as nurses but also, dressed as men, to take an active part in the fighting. Indeed, beginning in February 1917 there was an actual women's battalion, which had recruited more than 2,000 volunteers by May. Large numbers of children and young people also left home for the front, either alone or in small groups—a phenomenon, unknown in other countries, which turned into a mass movement. Stories in the media and schoolbooks about child heroes probably played a large role in this: they presented the war as an adventure or extension of children's play, in which the struggle for the endangered fatherland appeared as a sacred national duty for one and all. In a survey conducted in Kiev, for example, 41 percent of boys and 33 percent of girls stressed that they were willing to take part in the war as soldiers or nurses. However, the military and the Interior Ministry eventually had to accept that this movement posed a major problem, since thousands of children and young people were traipsing around near the front without food and resorting to theft and muggings. Later, in the civil war that followed 1917, these "wild ones" would make cities and rural districts unsafe places to be; childhood enthusiasm, with its instilled patriotic fervor for the war, turned into a criminalization of everyday life.[286]

The other episode in Russia illustrating the nexus between front and home society occurred in 1915, during the military crisis that followed the breakthrough by German and Austro-Hungarian forces. That summer, the problems of the Russian army culminated in constant unrest among new recruits and an increasing number of desertions (already 500,000 by August, according to one estimate). Social motives intermingled with a hatred of officers and widespread exhaustion. The high number of prisoners, especially among poorly trained and equipped auxiliary troops, also points to a crisis of discipline, cohesion, and loyalty, since it must be assumed that more and more soldiers deliberately allowed themselves to be captured. At the time, this was a response to often-disastrous supply problems and a high casualty rate resulting from inflexible military tactics. Although the army leadership in 1915 ensured that reports of mass captures and desertions did not reach the public, the government and the right-wing press began a systematic campaign that indirectly accused Russian prisoners-of-war of betrayal and directly associated the military front with the home front. Some lists of deserters were published to curb defeatist tendencies, since their families lost all support and in some cases were even cast out of their communities. Appeals for donations to help prisoners were prohibited, so as to discourage a further weakening of the army through the loss of prisoners to the enemy.[287]

All this shows how much conditions on the Russian home front had changed by 1915. After the successful mobilization in August 1914, Russia shared many of the experiences of other wartime societies. The early months of the war had brought successes in Galicia against Austro-Hungarian forces and reverses in East Prussia against the German army, with the result that by the end of 1914 the war of movement had given way to positional warfare. In Russia, too, a munitions shortage exacerbated the difficulty of making the transition from a peacetime economy to a protracted war. In comparison with other belligerent countries, however, this adjustment process was markedly slower and more tortuous. It is true that arms production quadrupled between 1914 and 1916, but such achievements were far from sufficient to cover the enormous needs of the front. Material shortages were compounded by infrastructure problems: the means to move troops and goods, especially locomotives and railroad wagons, were in short supply and suffered from a lack of efficient central organization, as did the industries vital to the war effort.[288]

The supply crisis grew worse after the German offensives of Spring and Summer 1915 forced the Russians into a major retreat. Large areas in Galicia, Russian Poland, Ukraine, Belarus, and Lithuania, with their important industrial centers and farmlands, were lost for the mobilization of the home front. In addition, the enemy inflicted heavy casualties and eventually took more than a million prisoners of war. To offset these losses, recruitment had to be continually stepped up, taking in all men under 40 and those who had previously been the only breadwinners in their family. This led to regional and local resistance. When it was thought necessary in 1916 to impose conscription even in traditionally exempted regions, this provoked a large-scale armed uprising among the Muslim population against the tsarist war state.[289]

Paralleling the situation in areas close to the front in the Habsburg monarchy, the tsarist authorities expelled and deported a million people of German and Jewish origin to the Russian interior or Siberia. Beginning in 1915 the war of movement, with its frequent changes of occupier, caused huge flows of refugees, which grew to six million by early 1917 and further worsened the supply situation in the cities. In Summer 1915 there were violent excesses against supposedly unreliable and disloyal groups in Russian society who, in the case of Jews, Germans, or Catholic Poles, were accused of collaboration or espionage. At the beginning of the war, the regime confiscated property near the front belonging to *Reichsdeutsche,* Germans living in Russia under the jurisdiction of the Reich, and over the subsequent months similar measures were applied first to Volhynia Germans and then to all individuals and families of German origin, including the Baltic German nobility. German-owned companies and businesses were also taken over.[290] The more critical Russia's military position became, the more the fate of Germans living there worsened. In one dramatic case, in Moscow in May 1915 as a response to the Central Powers breakthrough at the front, acts of violence were committed on a large scale against people with a German name.[291] How far things went is clear from the fact that in November 1915 the army was forced to protect Russian officers with German names.[292] Often rumors contributed to this hysterical climate of suspicion. Anti-Jewish pogroms also occurred in this context, particularly in areas where the army had assumed control over the civilian population or where Jews living in Galicia and Poland were indiscriminately regarded as untrustworthy.[293]

The dominance of military over civilian institutions helped to swell the rising tide of suspicion in 1915. As in the German-ruled Ober Ost, but less systematically than in areas occupied by Austro-Hungarian troops in Galicia and the Balkans, the Russian authorities subjected the civilian population to ethnic-religious classification and exclusion.[294] On both sides, ever-greater numbers of people were deprived of their rights and driven out, whether in the wake of military reversals (the Russian case) or on the basis of a utopian fantasy of German conquest and rule (in the Ober Ost). Violence became an accepted instrument in dealings with the civilian population. The boundaries between ethnically alien groups in occupied or frontline areas and supposedly disloyal or untrustworthy foreigners within one's own population became more and more blurred.

In 1915, then, the discourses of loyalty changed in the multiethnic society of the Russian Empire, and this affected the solidarity initially shown by ethnic groups in outlying regions. For example, Russian Muslims had demonstratively stood shoulder to shoulder with the Empire in August 1914; their parliamentary group in the Duma had voted in favor of the war credits. Yet the distrust of Muslims displayed by state institutions had persisted. Local policemen were automatically suspicious of Muslims in the Volga and Ural regions. And as in earlier wars against the Ottoman Empire, especially the Balkan wars, it was feared that they might collaborate with Turkish Muslims on the other side of the border. In late 1914, the authorities gave the green light for a congress that went on to found a Central Committee of Social Organizations of the Muslims of Russia, but the widespread expectation of political concessions from the government in Petrograd came to nothing. When their hopes were dashed, Muslim representatives in the Duma joined the liberal-centrist Progressive Bloc that had sprung up in opposition to the tsarist government after the string of military defeats. In the brief session of the Duma held in Summer 1915, the deputies from non-Russian ethnic groups took precise stock of the changed situation. Together with Latvians,

Lithuanians, Estonians, Armenians, and Jews, they demanded "equal state and national rights for all peoples in Russia"; all laws that accorded a lesser legal status to various ethnic or religious groups should be revoked. Thus, before 1916–1917 it was already becoming clear that the government could no longer expect unconditional cooperation and extensive compliance on the part of non-Russians. The special position of ethnic minorities was more and more recognizably associated with political opposition to the Tsar's war government.[295]

Why, despite these many problems following the crisis of Summer 1915, did Russia achieve a relative stability that allowed it to mount a successful offensive under General Alexei Brusilov in Summer 1916 on the southwestern front? Tsar Nicholas and his government moved to adopt a series of measures in Summer 1915 that would be of benefit to the war industries in particular. For the first time, government officials and representatives of local and regional enterprises and corporate bodies formed a number of bureaus to boost arms production. The same tendency was visible in the creation of war industry committees, but it was precisely there that intense competition for state orders developed among companies in Petrograd and Moscow. The war promised huge profits, and unlike in Britain these were not trimmed by high taxes. The conversion to a war economy forced entrepreneurs to forge agreements and corporate ties with one another. But in view of their profits from the war, their wide-ranging criticism of the government struck many industrial workers as insincere. The outlines were already appearing of the political-social conflict between political leadership and elite groups (especially in the business world), and between those elites and urban workers and underclasses, which would shape the revolutionary constellation in 1917.[296]

Another factor contributing to stability was the creation of new institutions beyond the established state. Already in 1914, an All-Russian Union of Zemstvos (those noble-dominated self-management bodies in the countryside, one of the chief results of the great reforms of the 1860s) came into being, along with an All-Russian Union of Cities, which looked after the innumerable wounded and refugees and became involved in the supply of troops at the front. When the two organizations fused in 1915 to become the Zemgor, it soon enjoyed a far higher reputation than the state institutions, which had become the epitome of bloated, inefficient administration, corruption, and clientelism, made all the worse because many members of the upper and middle classes found a civic niche there to escape the draft.[297]

The fact is that in 1915 the Russian war economy achieved a remarkable improvement in performance. By 1916 the production of artillery shells had doubled. Aided by higher import volumes of Allied weaponry, this enabled Russia to overcome the crisis of Summer 1915 and laid the basis for the counteroffensive of 1916. The initial success of this military operation was not the result of new tactics, but the reflection of intensive economic mobilization. The efforts came at a high social cost, however, since the increased output for the war entailed major supply problems for the population. The large numbers of soldiers killed, wounded, or captured further intensified the manpower shortage back home. Thus, while the contingent of workers in the Russian engineering industry rose by 66 percent between 1914 and early 1917, the labor shortage in the countryside increased dramatically. Unskilled, politically unorganized women left there in droves for the large cities, where they found living conditions that the mass of refugees from areas near the front had made worse than ever—this was another parallel to the situation in the Habsburg monarchy. The continual influx into the industrial agglomerations was a threat to agricultural production, however, compounding the loss of territory since Spring 1915 and the destruction of transport infrastructure. Between 1914 and 1916, grain deliveries to Petrograd fell by no less than 44 percent, while the cities in general became social flashpoints because of the substandard housing, poor hygiene, and inadequate health care. Factory conditions also deteriorated as a result of such measures as the lifting of the ban on night work for women and children.[298]

The war accelerated an urbanization that had already been underway before 1914.[299] In the capital, there was a major process of industrial concentration, with 80 percent of all workers during the war years working in 130 enterprises. Wages did rise from 1916, but they could not keep up with the price increases. Impoverishment in urban working-class districts was a high price to pay for the increased arms output and created a potential for protest and conflict, as black markets, soaring rents, and food price inflation added to the precariousness of life in the wartime cities. After an early period of patriotic solidarity with the regime that extended beyond the upper and middle classes, strikes and demonstrations began to leave their mark on public life. Although radical socialist groups were by no means dominant among urban workers, the tendency for opposition to take political forms was unmistakable.[300]

The situation in 1915 did not only have far-reaching consequences for social and economic relations; it also changed the political landscape of Russia. The top man in the Zemgor was Prince Georgii Lvov, a representative of the Liberals, who became the first prime minister of the Provisional Government after the revolution of February 1917. In 1915 he joined a new political group. Like the creation of the Zemgor, the establishment in Summer 1915 of the Progressive Bloc of all moderate groups in the Duma under the leadership of the Democrat Pavel Milyukov reflected a widespread sense that governments had not been equal to the challenges of the war. Since 1914 there had been four prime ministers and five interior, three exterior, three defense, and four agriculture ministers—a lack of continuity that posed a long-term threat to public trust in the Tsar. The demands of the Progressive Bloc highlighted urgent problems that already pointed to a crisis of political confidence, integration, and loyalty within the Empire. They called not only for a "ministry of social trust" but also for attention to the special needs of workers and the non-Russian nationalities—a characteristic association of the potential for ethnic and social conflict. The Poles, they argued, should gain a solid autonomy status, while other ethnic groups and the Jews should enjoy greater rights. Labor unions should be officially recognized as representatives of the workers in order to defuse tensions in the cities and industrial centers.

At the height of the military crisis following the German-Austrian breakthroughs in Summer 1915, Tsar Nicholas took personal command of the armed forces; he was thus one of the few monarchs who tried to live up to the ideal of the royal commander in chief, the *roi connétable*, thereby exposing himself to the danger that, with no one else in supreme charge, any defeat would further undermine his legitimacy.[301] This would be an important factor over the following months, since it meant that, against the wishes of many advisors and army chiefs, Nicholas went to the front and left a political vacuum behind in the capital. The previous supreme commander, Grand Duke Nikolai Nikolaevich, assumed command on the Caucasus front, taking the consequences for his failed attempt to curb the influence that the (originally German) Tsarina Alexandra Fyodorovna and her confidant Grigorii Rasputin had over military decisions.

Rasputin came from a peasant family in western Siberia and had acquired a high profile as an itinerant preacher and miracle worker. His influence on the Tsarina, and indirectly on the Tsar, rested on Alexandra's confidence that he could cure Crown Prince Alexei of his severe hemophilia. Distrust of the Tsarina was growing among the public as well as in high political and military circles; rumors of sexual orgies at the Tsar's palace mingled with suspicions that, as the sister of the grand duke of Hesse-Darmstadt, she was actively collaborating with the enemy. This combination of a latent legitimacy crisis with scandal at the court (not affecting the Tsar personally but his inner circle) was reminiscent of the situation in France in the late 1780s, when a hostile press campaign had accused Queen Marie Antoinette, an Austrian princess, of various sexual transgressions. In Russia too, in 1915, the creeping erosion of the Russian monarchy also began with criticisms of a foreign consort. The accusations were baseless, but their impact on a public reeling from military defeats and supply crises was almost as great as if they had been true; a gallery of actual people could be reproached with betrayal of the soldiers and workers, wives and mothers, who had to endure the main burden of the war. The practice of transnational marital alliances, established in European dynasties before 1914, ran up against an aggressive wartime nationalism that no longer spared the family of the Tsar.[302]

Whereas, at the height of the crisis of Summer 1915, the Tsar had still been willing to make concessions, his attitude hardened again in the fall after the military and economic situation had become more stable. Not the least of the reasons for this was the Tsar's autocratic conception of his rule, in which he embodied the Russian nation and could not tolerate any permanent representative role in politics for the Duma, the Zemgor, or other forms of wartime corporatism. His strong penchant for political symbolism reached a peak in the combination of the black two-headed eagle, the personal flag of the Romanov dynasty, with the Russian tricolor.[303] But in 1915 this language of national-dynastic war patriotism was less and less capable of heading off a collision course with the country's political and military elites and ever-larger sections of society. In October, the appointment of the ultra-reactionary, anti-Semitic leader of the Duma Right, Alexei Khvostov, as interior minister squandered the political credit the Tsar had earned from the temporary military and economic stabilization, demonstrating his readiness to take on the Progressive Bloc without openly opposing it. This also dashed the hopes of non-Russian nationalities for political concessions, especially in western parts of the Empire hardest hit by the war. The Tsar's U-turn played such havoc because people directly attributed the new appointment of reactionary politicians to the influence of the Tsarina and Rasputin. From Fall 1915, plans for a coup d'état to break the Tsarina's power and eliminate Rasputin circulated within the political-parliamentary and military elite, and even within the Tsar's family circle. The sacral, mythical aura of the ruler, with his claim to a direct bond with the Russian people, had by now been severely damaged. The revolutionary legitimacy crisis of Spring 1917 was not yet on the horizon, but possible cracks in the system of tsarist rule were already becoming visible. Developments in 1915 gave the regime some breathing space, enabling it to make a final military push, but by this time much more than the continuation of the war depended on the outcome of the offensive.[304]

While ethnic tensions and suspicions about the loyalty of supposedly hostile aliens came to a head in the Habsburg monarchy and the Russian Empire, ethnic violence in the Ottoman Empire erupted into genocide against Armenian Christians.[305] Rafael de Nogales, a Latin American serving as a cavalry officer in the Ottoman army, learned of the scale of this violence in 1915. On June 18, Turkish officers openly reported to him that systematic killing of Armenians and other Christians would begin in the region of Siirt. When Nogales arrived there, he saw a hill on the main street covered with "thousands of half-naked and still bleeding bodies, lying in heaps, tangled, as if in a last embrace of death. Fathers, brothers, sons, and grandsons lay as they fell from the bullets or the murder. . . . Flocks of vultures sat on top of the heap, picking the eyes out of the dead and dying, whose rigid gaze still seemed to mirror terror and inexpressible pain, while carrion dogs sank their sharp teeth into entrails still pulsing with life." Nogales observed the police and the Muslim population in the act of plunder, and concluded that this was not a spontaneous pogrom but a systematic operation involving the local authorities and police.[306]

By 1920 the Armenian genocide would cost 800,000 to a million lives.[307] How can such an escalation be explained? The original idea of Ottomanism, which involved integrating the different religions of the Empire, had already been under increasing pressure before 1914—not least because of the expulsion of Muslims from lost territories in southeastern Europe. The presence of these refugees fueled tensions among the various ethnic-religious groups within Ottoman society. Although the Armenians and other Christian communities were systematically isolated and murdered only in the context of the world war, the suspicion directed against non-Muslims had roots in the previous period, and there had already been pogrom-like episodes in the late nineteenth century. After the Balkan wars, Russia and Germany, in particular, pushed for internal changes in the Ottoman regime in order to increase their influence. At the same time, there were discussions about the creation of two autonomous Armenian provinces under the supervision of the international powers. For the Young Turk elite, this would have further undermined the territorial integrity of the Ottoman Empire, adding

Genocide in the shadow of war: Armenian children dead from starvation, approximately 1915–1916

parts of the Anatolian heartland to the areas lost in southeastern Europe and North Africa.

The government suspended these plans as soon as the world war began, since the Young Turk elite associated them with the kind of external influence that highlighted the impotence of the Empire. It also began to develop plans of its own for a predominantly national-Turkish economy. Until then, trade and industry had been in the hands of foreign businesses, particularly Jewish or Christian merchants who benefited from special tax exemptions. In the first months of war, the government executed a policy turn against non-Muslim entrepreneurs and merchants, and between 1916 and 1918 more than eighty new businesses would be founded, often on the basis of property confiscated from Greeks or Armenians. With the rise of war nationalism in Turkey, non-Muslim population groups had been exposed to a systematic practice of exclusion well before the military crisis began to bite in Spring 1915.[308]

As the war advanced, the victimization of Armenians went from economic dispossession to outright murder. One of the main motives for this in the minds of the Young Turk elite was the chain of foreign policy humiliations and military defeats; an aggressive nationalism espoused the vision of a monoethnic state that would ensure the cohesion and viability of the Empire, replacing the traditional idea of different ethnicities and religions living side by side. The political and military elites represented an empire in transition, which had to make use of the modern concept of the nation. The Young Turks saw this ethnic homogeneity as the guarantee for future internal development and external political survival—a political current that had been growing stronger since the effective coup d'état by the radical right wing of the Young Turks following the Balkan wars in 1913.[309] The outcome in the Balkans seemed to confirm that the Ottoman Empire might have a future only if its Turkish element was reinforced and the influence of all supposedly disloyal groups was curtailed.

After the outbreak of war, the idea began to spread that the Armenians constituted a danger to the Ottoman armies, that they were collaborating with Russian troops and carrying out espionage on their behalf. The experience of earlier defeats, together with humiliations after the Balkan wars and the mass expulsion of Muslims from southeastern Europe, reinforced this perception. Greeks and Armenians, their shops and businesses often looted and destroyed in the coastal towns of Asia Minor, began to be deported soon after August 1914, and many Greeks took refuge across the Aegean. But eastern Anatolia, close to the Russian front in the Caucasus, became the real flashpoint after the Sarikamish disaster in January 1915, when a Turkish counteroffensive across the mountain passes was repulsed with heavy casualties. The readiness to use violence against Armenians intensified with the rivalry between Russian and Young Turk ideas of what should happen to the contested areas.[310] When Russian units advanced into Anatolia in Spring 1915, one of their objectives was to gain territory for Russian settlers. In this they received support from Armenian nationalists, who were also reported to be raising demands for a state of their own. The Young Turk leadership now feared secession and a general destabilization of the Empire.

In this situation, rumors of large-scale desertions from Armenian units in the Ottoman army seemed to confirm the accusations of betrayal. Although the war minister, Enver Pasha, demonstratively thanked the Armenian patriarch on February 21, 1915, for the "devotion and heroism of Armenian soldiers," the government was already preparing to strike. Armenian troops were disarmed, forced into labor battalions, and finally, between April 1915 and September 1916, systematically murdered.[311] Leading intellectuals were arrested as early as April—a first group of 235, followed by more than 2,300 over the next few weeks, only few of whom would survive the subsequent deportation. This wave of repression took place in the context of the Allied landing on the Gallipoli peninsula and the uprising of the Armenian population in the city of Van, which the Turkish military had deliberately provoked. In the fears of Young Turk officers, a threat behind the lines, the danger of a Russian breakthrough, and anti-Armenian violence formed a single picture. Local contexts and subjective perceptions favored a cumulative radicalization of violence—but the decisive factor in this concrete situation was an already existing Young Turk strategy.[312]

In Spring 1915, German embassy officials were in no doubt about what was happening, and they sent long and detailed reports to Berlin. On April 12, even before the Van uprising, the German consul in Aleppo wrote to the Reich chancellor: "After my return, Celal Bey—the *wali* of Aleppo— informed me that . . . a current which tends to regard Armenians in general as suspect or hostile appears to have gained the upper hand in the Turkish government."[313]

The sites of anti-Armenian massacres that occurred even before the systematic deportations were also hotspots in the war. In May 1915, a successful spring offensive carried the Russian Caucasus armies into the city of Van, which had been under Ottoman siege since the Armenian uprising. The Russians then succeeded in making further advances with the help of Armenian volunteer units, the so-called Ararat Legion. The Turks eventually managed to halt them, but in June 1915, under the impact of the Ottoman military crisis, there were massacres in the mainly Armenian towns of Bitlis and Mush. There too, however, the "stab in the back" narrative of Armenian betrayal and collaboration with the Russians cannot explain the scale of the violence—at any event, the Van uprising began only some time after the Turkish preparations for systematic killings had been concluded.[314] The ethnic dimension of the war continued on both sides: when the Russian forces again evacuated Van in August 1915, they took more than 200,000 people with them to the border, and the Russian chief of staff gave an order for the frontier areas to be destroyed and hostile population groups driven out.[315]

The German consular report of May 15, 1915, from Erzurum gave a nuanced view of the situation. To describe the events in Van, the consul referred not only to Russia's significance as protector of the Armenians but above all to the various economic and political reasons why the Muslim population acted against Armenians: "As Your Excellency recognizes, the Armenians of Turkey have always looked upon Russia as their natural protector, and Russia too has always claimed and exploited this right to protect them. The fact that Russian Armenians enjoy greater security and better economic conditions has considerable appeal for the broad mass. On the other hand, the consideration that a stronger Russian influence will inevitably bring a danger of denationalization has remained limited to the Armenians' spiritual leaders."[316] The conduct of the Ottoman authorities, including their systematic action against the Armenians, was reported to many other ambassadors and consuls—those of Britain and the United States, for example. Moreover, German representatives had very detailed information at their disposal. A telegram sent by Ambassador Wangenheim to the Auswärtiges Amt on May 31, 1915, stated,: "Enver Pasha intends to prevent further Armenian espionage and mass uprisings, by using the wartime emergency to close a large number of Armenian schools, to suppress Armenian newspapers, to ban Armenian postal correspondence, and to resettle in Mesopotamia all families from currently insurgent Armenian centers who are not completely without fault." Wangenheim expected this to arouse great attention abroad, but he argued that Germany should seek to "tone down, not completely block" such measures, since the "Armenian subversive activities fostered by Russia" threatened "Turkey's continued existence" and might weaken the military position of the Central Powers.[317] In a report to the Reich chancellor, dated June 17, 1915, Wangenheim described the systematic nature of the Turkish actions and left no doubt about their purpose: "Resettled people are forced to leave their dwellings either immediately or within a few days, so that they have to abandon their homes and most of their movables, without being able to take even the bare necessities for the journey. On arrival at the destination, they find themselves helpless and defenseless amid a hostile population. . . . There is no way the government will support people driven out in this way with money, food, and so on." "Military defeats were not the only reason for such measures"; it was apparent—and Interior Minister Talaat Pasha had openly admitted it—that the Ottoman Empire "wants to the use the world war to clear away its internal enemies— the indigenous Christians—without being troubled by diplomatic intervention from abroad." This was not "temporary neutralization," the Armenian patriarch told Wangenheim, but "expulsion" and "extermination."[318]

In June 1915, Turkish anti-Armenian policy reached a new level. Repressive measures were no longer kept secret, but became more or less institutionalized through a "provisional law on the measures to be taken by the army against individuals who contravene government measures in wartime." Talaat Pasha gave the ideological justification for this at a session of the Council of Ministers, when he defined the goal of establishing an ethnically homogeneous Turkish core of the state "free from alien elements."[319] The underlying idea was to ensure the supremacy of Muslim Turks over other population groups in the Empire and to impose this model by means of systematic violence, mass deportations, and mass killings. The traditional *millet* structure and Ottomanism, which had sought to integrate all ethnic and religious groups, retreated definitively into the background.[320]

On this basis, local and military authorities proceeded to expel the whole Armenian civilian population to the steppes of northern Syria. The violence shifted into death marches across the Anatolian highlands, which, it was assumed, scarcely anyone would survive, both because of the geographical-climatic conditions and because the columns included large numbers of children, women, and old people. Targeted attacks were also made by the Teşkilât-i Mahsusa, a special organization controlled by the Young Turks party and consisting of Muslim and Turkish refugees from the Caucasus and Balkans, as well as Kurds; it was a straightforward instrumentalization of the Muslim-Christian polarization resulting from the refugee flows after the Balkan wars. The practical implementation of this policy could not be explained simply by the proximity of the Russian front, since some of the deported Armenians came from far-flung areas such as Aleppo. Moreover, the expulsion of other Christian groups, such as the Assyrian Chaldeans in the southeast, testified to a wider turn against ethnic-religious minorities. Only the old Armenian communities in Smyrna and Constantinople, and large Catholic communities, were spared such measures; in Smyrna the German army inspector-general, Otto Liman von Sanders, opposed deportation for military reasons, and elsewhere the presence of international observers had to be taken into account.[321]

The planned mass killings were not "genocide by neglect," and they also went well beyond the forced resettlements and deportations experienced before 1914.[322] In many cases, the operations began with the looting of Armenian property by the Turkish and Kurdish population, egged on by the local authorities. The intention was not simply the ethnic cleansing of areas through the expulsion of local people; the Turkish authorities did not aim to resettle them in Russian Armenia, but rather to organize deportations and death marches that would leave few if any survivors. The German military was involved in the planning and, to some extent, the execution, of these measures. Ethnic factors played no role for them, as they did for Turkish nationalists. What counted were military considerations—above all, the strengthening of the eastern Anatolian front against the Russians and the consolidation of the German-Ottoman alliance.[323]

The ethnic violence did not end in 1916 once most of the Armenians had been killed. With the collapse of the tsarist regime in 1917, Russian forces withdrew from Ottoman areas and from the Armenian-populated provinces of Ardahan and Kars that had been part of the Russian Empire. When Turkish troops advanced into these areas, more massacres took place. The revolutions of February and October 1917 in Russia prompted the Young Turk leaders to plan for a pan-Turkic empire in the east that could compensate for the territorial losses in the west. The driving idea behind this was the ethnic-religious homogeneity of a future nation-state. The role of such plans for the Young Turk elite became evident when Enver Pasha, already thinking of the threatened Ottoman defeat in the war, sent his brother Nuri off to the east with an irregular "Army of Islam." In September 1918, Turkish troops even managed to occupy the oilfields of Baku.[324]

The anti-Armenian operations of the Turkish civilian and military authorities were by no means unknown to the public abroad; they were not a genocide in the shadow of war that did not interest anyone. Apart from the German government, American politicians, intellectuals, and activists had detailed information at their disposal. The crime was well documented at the time—and the refusal of politicians to intervene had nothing to do with deficient knowledge, but reflected the Allies' fear, after the disastrous Gallipoli experience, that they would have to embark on another military venture.[325] The main country where the Armenian genocide would resonate after 1918 was Germany. Armin Theophil Wegner, who in 1915 had participated as a German medical orderly in campaigns in the Ottoman Empire and enjoyed considerable freedom to travel, gave lectures at which he displayed the numerous photographs he had taken at the time. His aim was to mobilize political support for the Armenians and to argue that, "after the experiences of recent years," there was no longer much difference between their fate and that of the Germans and Austrians.[326] The background to this interest was, on the one hand, the discussion on German involvement in the Armenian genocide (which the theologian Johannes Lepsius had fueled in 1919 by publishing the documents of the Auswärtiges Amt),[327] and, on the other hand, the not-guilty verdict that a Berlin court returned in 1921 on the Armenian Soghomon Tehlirian (who had shot the former Ottoman interior minister Talaat Pasha, one of the main figures responsible for the crimes). At the trial, Lepsius had a chance to speak at some length as an expert witness, declaring that in his view there was no doubt about the systematic and calculated nature of the killings.[328] When Adolf Hitler, on August 22, 1939, ordered German field commanders to launch the invasion of Poland, explaining his plans "to send men, women, and children of Polish origin ruthlessly and pitilessly to their death," he added the rhetorical question: "Who still speaks today of the annihilation of the Armenians?"[329] At any event, it would be wrong to assume that this collective ignorance or lack of interest applied in the period after 1918.

8. JUSTIFYING WAR, UNDERSTANDING VIOLENCE
Intellectual Responses to the Wartime Experience

With the western front deadlocked, there was no end in sight as the casualty figures mounted and the economic and social costs of the war became clearer. But how were these efforts to be justified? The sometimes shrill cultural war among intellectuals continued into the second year: countless essays and articles were joined on the interpretation market by monographs that methodically constructed enemy-images and reassuring narratives. The criteria differentiating the two sides were made more and more explicit as the rising death toll increased the pressure to justify the conflict. In Britain, intellectuals stuck to the perception of cultural differences that had been dominant both there and in Germany since the outbreak of war, as expressed in *Why We Are at War: Great Britain's Case* and the German equivalent, the "Manifesto of the Ninety-Three."[330] The British self-image, in which parliamentary monarchy was identified with a historically rooted freedom of thought, was not the only striking element in this respect. It could, of course, be effectively counterposed to autocratic rule and Prussian-German militarism, but the domestic tensions over suffrage rights, social policy, and home rule for Ireland, as well as the external alliance with the tsarist autocracy, meant that it was by no means free of contradictions.

Earlier interest in German modernization successes, in areas such as social policy, education, and technological-industrial development, faded amid the programmatic hostility to power politics based on war and violence. One Oxford theologian stressed that the "age of German footnotes" was over, and Leonard Hobhouse attributed German excesses in the war to a continuum stretching back to Hegel's deification of the state: "In the bombing of London I had just witnessed the visible and tangible outcome of a false and wicked doctrine. . . . In the Hegelian theory of the god-state all that I had witnessed lay implicit."[331] Nevertheless, the British perception of Germany remained ambiguous: reports in the popular press about Germany's conduct in the war and accounts of Belgian refugees bolstered the image of barbaric militarism, but not everyone identified this with the German people as a whole or allowed it to eclipse an older appreciation of German literary, artistic, and musical culture. Militarism and barbaric war making seemed to characterize the autocratic elite of Prussia-Germany and to underlie its reactionary political culture; the war, it was thought, would overcome all that. Ernest Barker, a Fellow at New College, Oxford, placed his hopes in a development of parliamentary democracy, a reform of the Prussian three-class franchise system, and an end to feudal remnants and nationalism directed against national minorities: "Democracy in an industrial society will be different from a landed aristocracy. Militarism will not suit its book. Exclusive nationalism will not be its gospel. It will not lay heavy hands on Danes or Poles."[332]

In France, Jacques Bainville outlined in his *Two Histories Face to Face* (1915) a long conflict between Germany and France that culminated in the world war. Here too the author took a programmatic distance from "war after the German fashion, the savage war of armed nations," which must become the "saddest record of mankind."[333] German atrocities in Belgium made a powerful impact on French journalism. The historian Ernest Lavisse and the Germanist Charles Andler, in their work *German Theory and Practice of War* (1919, orig. French 1915), painted a picture of a country trapped in militarism that expressed itself in the barbaric conduct of war; this they contrasted with the French self-image of a humane republic fighting for the whole of humanity. Similarly, the sociologist Émile Durkheim, in his analysis of Heinrich von Treitschke's lectures on politics, diagnosed a peculiarly German orientation to ruthless power politics, to the supposed right of a rising nation-state to contravene all the principles of international law.[334]

The Franco-German clash over interpretations of the war mirrored the role of political and historical argument in the often-intricate relations between the two countries. To enlist the German "ideas of 1914" against the French "ideas of 1789" was to load the debate with historical self-images and enemy images. This was an important crystallization of the ways in which people positioned themselves in Germany at the time: the fraternal quarrel between Heinrich and Thomas Mann, for instance, expressed itself as a conflict between western European / transatlantic conceptions of democracy and an ostensibly apolitical retreat into German culture in the center of Europe. Had it not been for the conflict with France, this opposition would have been unimaginable. In 1915 the dispute became visible with the publication of two programmatic essays. In *Frederick and the Great Coalition,* Thomas Mann evoked the situation at the beginning of the Seven Years' War, when Prussia had found itself encircled by its Austrian, Russian, and French enemies, in order to justify German policy in August 1914 in the face of what seemed to him an analogous problem.[335]

In his view, the Prussian attack on neutral Saxony corresponded to the German occupation of Belgium in August 1914: Frederick's decision to violate "a neutrality that stood on paper, whereas its own betrayal did not so stand, was actuated by the sternest necessity." Mann justified this by the right of a rising state inseparable from its historical mission. In this too, Prussia's action served as a model for Germany in Summer 1914: "He was not in the right in so far as right is a convention, the voice of the majority, the judgment of humanity. His right was the right of the rising power, a problematical, still illegitimate, untested right, which had first to be fought for and won. . . . Only when success had shown him to be the agent of destiny, only then would he be in the right and proved to have been always in the right."[336] The war in 1756 had been an "offensive war"—since a "young, rising power is always psychologically on the attack" and Frederick obligingly picked a fight—but it had also been a "defensive war," since Prussia was indeed encircled and on the point of being annihilated. In Prussia's case, the "toughest, most desperate defense" necessarily found salvation "in the form of attack."[337] The eighteenth century was thus summoned to endow wartime Germany with the right of a historically rising power.

While Thomas Mann clung to such ideas for the time being, they had long been crumbling for his brother. Already before 1914, his novels *Der Untertan* (translated as *Man of Straw*) and *Professor Unrat oder das Ende eines Tyrannen (Small Town Tyrant)* had shown him to be a sharp critic of Wilhelmine society. In his vision of France and its revolutionary legacy, which was by no means free of idealization, he had castigated the willingness of the German bourgeoisie to knuckle under to an authoritarian state with many feudal remnants. Behind its ostensibly modern character, German society was a cocktail of aggressive nationalism and obsessions with material progress, and even the SPD and the labor unions had allowed themselves to be drawn in too deeply. In 1915 Heinrich Mann published a long essay in the monthly *Die Weißen Blätter* on the French naturalist writer Émile Zola, who in his eyes had become a hero for democrats and resolute republicans through his defense of the unjustly imprisoned Jewish army captain Alfred Dreyfus. As background, Mann examined Zola's engagement before 1870 against the regime of Napoleon III, the political and social situation of France in the 1850s and 1860s, and the transition to a democratic republic following the defeat in the Franco-Prussian war of 1870–1871. But in 1915 every German reader realized that Mann was evoking the regime of Napoleon III to comment on the German situation a year after the outbreak of the world war. The force of the text derived from this oscillation between historical France and contemporary Germany, but also from the indirect confrontation with the positions of his brother.

Heinrich Mann interpreted the defeat of the French Second Empire in 1870 as a new beginning for republican democracy: "But democracy is here a gift of defeat. The increment of general happiness, the increase in human worth, seriousness, and strength as they return, and an intellectuality prepared for action: gifts of the defeat." For Mann, victory and defeat were ciphers for the inner state of society: "Those who have the truth gain victory. Defeat is confirmation that you are living a lie. What is decisive in [Zola's novel] *La Débâcle?* That the army lacks faith. No one really believes any longer in the Empire for which they are supposed to vanquish. They believe at first in its power; they think it is all but invincible." Power, Heinrich Mann was convinced, must be based on right. Otherwise, the notion of the fatherland is devalued: "Now the oppressors really are what they have long brazenly claimed to be: the fatherland! Not only must you fight for those who are the fatherland; you must falsify things like them, commit injustice like them, besmirch yourself like them. You become contemptible like them. What still distinguishes you from them? You are beaten even before the defeat."[338]

While France loomed large in the dispute between the Mann brothers, Britain was the main focus for German intellectuals in 1915. This weakened the Russian enemy-image in the world of German journalism—the element that had been so decisive in Summer 1914 in lining up the SPD behind the civic peace. The ideological clash with Britain stretched well beyond the salutation "God punish England!" although this certainly reflected the spread of an anti-British sense of identity. The enemy-image went further than anti-French and anti-Russian conceptions of the time—after all, many German authors conceded that the French fought valiantly and honorably for a particular goal, and that Russian soldiers had no idea what the war was about. In contrast to new integrative concepts such as "social economy" or "war socialism," Britain's conduct of the war was thought to embody a dishonorable capitalism that paid little heed to its own casualties, corresponding to the idea of the mercenary army as opposed to the nation under arms. As early as October 1914, in a piece entitled *England und Wir* (England and Us), Wilhelm Dibelius remarked that British imperialists and businessmen had hoodwinked ordinary English people. The war was not being waged against that England; its target was "pettiness" and puritan hypocrisy.[339] In 1915, Werner Sombart and Max Scheler went a stage further and dissolved the distinction between elites and common people, replacing it with a Manichaean vision of incompatible national essences. In his book *Händler und Helden: Patriotische Besinnungen* (Merchants and Heroes: Patriotic Reflections), Sombart played skillfully on stereotypes of the small-minded English "shopkeeper" and heroic German individuals who saw struggle as a test of historical selection. He interpreted the war as a clash between two fundamental principles: English materialism and comfort against the German willingness to surpass oneself in a given situation. For the British, war was not an existential test but a sport. When the German cruiser *Emden* was sunk, the British press concentrated mainly on the ship's master; "The heroic Captain Müller was praised to the skies. When he came to London . . . he would be the most celebrated of men. Why? Because he had performed heroic deeds out of loyalty and a sense of duty to the Kaiser? Oh, no! Because he had outstanding sporting achievements to his name! . . . Perhaps nowhere has the complete commercialization of war appeared as clearly as in this unconscious conflation of war and sport. For sport was born from the innermost soul of the merchant, who can never ever see the point of war."[340] The war showed German soldiers to be embodiments of

Goethe's classicism and Nietzschean heroism, against the mercenary symbolizing the English sickness of total commercialism and moral degeneracy.[341] For Sombart, then, militarism was nothing other than "the heroic spirit raised to the martial spirit": "It is Potsdam and Weimar supremely united. It is 'Faust' and 'Zarathustra' and Beethoven scores in the trenches. For the Eroica and the Egmont overture are genuine militarism."[342] Similarly, Max Scheler distinguished between the utilitarianism and materialism of the British, geared to utility, pragmatism, and discretion, and the values of the German warrior nation, which boldly and capably exposed itself to dangers and distinguished itself by its chivalry, loyalty, and self-sacrifice, its sense of honor and glory.[343]

What did this flood of reassuring self-images and ideological demarcations show? If one leitmotif began to take shape in 1915, it was the challenge to the ideas of progress embodied by Germany. This meant that justifications of the war were also debates over claims to modernity, and it disclosed an asynchronicity of historical development processes in Imperial Germany. The Janus face of the German nation-state, as bearer of culture and efficient military machine and the juxtaposition of modernity and progress with barbarism and lawbreaking, was a key point of reference in numerous writings that either defended or condemned Germany: it could be seen in the self-definition of German authors who, against a backdrop of corporatism, social economy, and war socialism, turned their backs on British capitalism, or in the critique by French or British writers of the German ideal of a strong state, or in the perceived ambiguity of cultural and scientific achievements and the wartime loss of inhibitions about violence.

In 1915, the American sociologist Thorstein Veblen got to the heart of this coexistence of modern economic and technological development with backward political-constitutional structures in his book *Germany and the Industrial Revolution*. Germany, he argued, had learned from Britain's industrialization and by 1914 had almost overtaken its former model, but it lacked the positive experience of a political revolution to secure its freedoms. This explained how it was that agrarian elites such as the Junkers east of the Elbe and the Prussian military elite enjoyed a special extra-constitutional position in the power structure. As a representative of the American "Progressive Era," Veblen advocated early entry of the United States into the war, on the grounds that the Anglo-American world would only then be able to impose the model of democracy and self-determination against the archaic combination of militarism and authoritarianism.[344]

In 1915, the sociologist and philosopher Georg Simmel made a very different assessment of the role of the United States and the global dimension of the war. American aid to Britain was not so much an expression of friendship between the two countries as America's "first great practical thrust to accelerate the western change of course in world history." European countries were committing "hara-kiri" in the war, and even if Germany came out stronger in the end Europe as a whole would be weakened by the "irrecoverable loss of prestige that Europeans have suffered in Africa and throughout the East as a result of the war." Simmel downplayed the importance of Alsace-Lorraine or the Trentino, for the possession of which tens of thousands of soldiers had died. A year into the war, he diagnosed a fundamental shift in the tectonics of global power: "Together we could have preserved the peace in Europe . . . , to maintain Europe's and indeed England's world position vis-à-vis the rising powers of America and perhaps also East Asia. . . . And it is the destiny of this war to sharpen Europe's acute problems and internal suffering to the most egregious levels, at the very moment when this inner pathology—in the form of war within Europe—threatens us with a danger that has never existed before in world history."[345]

In 1915, when the new dimensions of violence could not be overlooked in the home societies, the Viennese psychoanalyst Sigmund Freud presented a first balance sheet in his *Reflections on War and Death*. His starting point was the blow struck to the prewar idea of "cultural cosmopolitanism": "The war in which we did not want to believe broke out and brought—disappointment. It is not only bloodier and more destructive than any foregoing war, as a result of the tremendous development of weapons of attack and defense, but it is at least as cruel, bitter, and merciless as any earlier war." It had nothing in common with the humanitarian ideals of the prewar age; indeed, it "places itself above all the restrictions pledged in times of peace, the so-called rights of nations, it does not acknowledge the prerogatives of the wounded and of physicians, the distinction between peaceful and fighting members of the population, or the claims of private property." The intensification of violence, both internally and externally, the engulfment of the whole of society, threatened in the long term "to leave a bitterness which will make impossible any reestablishment of these ties for a long time to come."[346]

Freud stressed, however, that this disappointment rested on an illusion. The achievements of culture, including precisely the bourgeois-liberal hope that international law might overcome the principle of war, was no more than a thin veneer, a surface beneath which quite different drives operated that could be neither tamed nor channeled. Freud thus forcefully contradicted the ideal of societies and states rendered more peaceful through the advance of law and culture. The "feeble morality of states in their external relations which have inwardly acted as guardians of moral standards, and the brutal behavior of individuals of the highest culture of whom one would not have believed any such thing possible," proved that the opposite was the case.[347] The war and the spread of violence on a mass scale underlined the fact that a relapse into an older mental state could happen at any time. This explained the complete loss of inhibitions that Freud saw around him. Unlike participants in the "cultural war" of the early weeks and months after August 1914, he expressed a deep skepticism that, not by chance, reminds one of Carl Schmitt's conception of the friend-enemy distinction as the foundation of the political, or of certain premises on which Thomas Hobbes based his theory of the state. At any event, the transformation of the prewar world of culture into the reality of war demonstrated that one could not simply place one's trust in the promises of reason and demystification.

The new character of war, the quantitative scale that made chance less of a factor, was understood by Freud as a heightening of existence: "It is obvious that the war must brush aside this conventional treatment of death. Death is no longer to be denied; we are compelled to believe in it. People really die and no longer one by one, but in large numbers, often ten thousand in one day. It is no longer an accident. Of course, it still seems accidental whether a particular bullet strikes this man or that, but the survivor may easily be struck down by a second bullet, and the accumulation of deaths ends the impression of accident. Life has indeed become interesting again; it has once more received its full significance."[348] Freud contrasted the cultured bourgeois individual of the pre-1914 period to the "primitive man" who again becomes visible in war and exposes the achievement of peaceableness as something superficial: "Our unconscious is just as inaccessible to the conception of our own death, just as much inclined to kill the stranger, and just as divided, or ambivalent, towards the persons we love as was primitive man. But how far we are removed from this primitive state in our conventionally civilized attitudes towards death! It is easy to see how war enters into this disunity. War strips off the later deposits of civilization and allows the primitive man in us to reappear. It forces us again to be heroes who cannot believe in their own death, it stamps all strangers as enemies whose death we ought to cause or wish; it counsels us to rise above the death of those whom we love."[349] One year after the outbreak of the war, Freud was arguing that we should recognize death as a constant possibility, and that to suppress the thought of it inevitably leads to neurosis. Only by exposing the illusory potency of cultural achievements can we really experience life and make it endurable.[350]

Freud's reflections expressed not only an insight of scientists and journalists but something that had long been part of everyday experience. Like many others of his generation, Franz Göll from Berlin (b. 1899) developed a marked skepticism about conventional ideals of humanity, in view of the thousands of war veterans and the wartime changes in ordinary life. To experience the war on a daily basis, to see the casualties of its violence, had a profound impact on people's consciousness. Instead of maintaining their faith in progress, they increasingly focused on man's destructive animal powers.[351]

9. SEVENTEEN MONTHS OF WAR
Radicalization and Extension beneath a Surface of Stasis and Movement

The second year of hostilities put into perspective most of the prewar military prognoses and strategic expectations; the dynamic of new experiences revealed a war on which traditional concepts had less and less purchase. Yet practically all commanders stuck to the premises of conventional offensive tactics, without finding answers either to the battlefield asymmetry of long-distance and defensive weapons, heavy artillery and machine guns; to the increasing complexity of positional systems; or to the problems associated with massed infantry attacks to break through the enemy lines. The first months of the war already refuted the idea that it would be over quickly, and all attempts in 1915 to force the issue—by means of new offensives, new technologies, and new belligerent countries—failed to secure a decisive advantage.

(1) In 1915 the war oscillated between stagnation on the western front and possible movement on the eastern. In the new war zones too, from Gallipoli to the Alps, defense proved to be superior in principle, even when the defenders were outnumbered. The reasons for this did not have to do only with the incapability and inflexibility of commanding officers. In some battles, the basic problem was inadequate coordination between artillery and infantry or imprecise reconnaissance of enemy positions. Where artillery and infantry worked properly together, it was not impossible to break through enemy lines. The shift to war of movement in the east was due above all to the superior artillery of the Central Powers, but this increased the focus on gun numbers and shell size, and hence on the war of technology and materiel. The great hope at the beginning of 1916 was that the development of ever more powerful artillery would create new openings for infantry attacks to break through enemy lines. The artillery war, however, reinforced all the aspects of industrial warfare, and the munitions crises of 1915, with their social and political costs, underlined the growing dependence of the military front on the industrial capacity and social cohesion of the home societies. This too was a precondition for the "total battles" of 1916.

(2) Most prognoses about the war readiness of the belligerent countries and societies proved to be mistaken, nowhere more so than in the multiethnic empires. The Ottoman Empire, driven almost entirely from the European continent by the Balkan wars and seen as a classical example of unstoppable decline, acquitted itself better in the world war than most had predicted. This was due not only to German military aid but also to the fact that Ottoman forces benefited from robust defense, as Gallipoli impressively demonstrated. Their tactical and operational efficiency became clear at Kut al-Amara in 1916 and even in the Gaza-Beersheba operations in 1917, and right up to the final months of the war they remained an enemy to be taken seriously. The frequent claim that the Ottoman army had only quantitative superiority is therefore misleading.[352] Approximately 500,000 men, mostly of Arab or Armenian origin, deserted in the course of the whole war—a high rate in comparison with Britain, France, or Germany, but not significantly greater than in other multiethnic armies. The casualty rates, often quoted

to cast doubt on the quality of the Ottoman armed forces, were also not significantly higher than those of other armies. Characteristic was the widening gap between the jihad rhetoric and the actual practice of war. Although the war minister, Enver Pasha, had unrealistic expectations of the army, his commanders did not cherish the illusion that they could reconquer the Ottoman territories lost before 1914.[353]

The Russian army, which the German general staff before 1914 had compared to an unstoppable "steamroller," soon faced major problems in the supply of weapons, war material, and, above all, munitions; it also suffered high casualty rates due mainly to rigid battlefield tactics. The prediction that mass desertions would cause the multiethnic Habsburg armies to collapse in short order proved incorrect; their setbacks came about not because of their multiethnic composition but because the AOK high command was incapable of bringing strategic objectives into line with the available resources. Its insistence on taking decisions independent of the German OHL also reflected an overestimation of itself that was all the more apparent because of the limited means at its disposal. In 1915, as in 1914, there was a lack of coordination between top German and Austro-Hungarian commanders. The successful operations against Montenegro and the driving of the Serbs toward northern Albania even strengthened Conrad von Hötzendorf's resolve to keep a free hand vis-à-vis the OHL.

(3) The war spread in 1915 because the key players hoped that this would achieve the decisive breakthrough that had been tactically unattainable on the western front. But the advances on the eastern front took the Central Powers into empty space left behind by the Russians, without forcing the Tsar to sue for a separate peace. The expansion of the war was visible spatially in new fronts such as Gallipoli and Salonica, technologically in the use of poison gas and submarine warfare, and politically in the quest of military leaders and governments for new alliance partners. In the cases of Italy and Bulgaria, the wait-and-see neutrality that had operated since Summer 1914 gave them the chance to bargain over territory for their nation-states, which irredentist nationalists sought to "complete" through war. While the Allies promised the Italians a lot in the London treaty, the Germans considered that the successful campaign against Serbia would encourage the Bulgarians to join the war on their side and sew up the Balkan front as far as the Salonica

enclave. Particularly in the Italian case, however, the actual course of the war dashed the high hopes of gains in territory and prestige. The mechanisms of positional warfare, with an asymmetry of expenditure, casualties, and results, were present also in the extreme conditions of the Alpine front, and French and British commanders reacted with disappointment to the Italians' failure to deliver the hoped-for successes. Notwithstanding the two new fronts, in the Alps and in southeastern Europe in the Salonica region, the weakening of the Austro-Hungarian army had no decisive effect on the war.

(4) At the end of 1915, the high commands of all the belligerent powers drew a sober balance sheet. The second year of war had seen a flurry of offensives on the western front and successes for the Central Powers on the eastern front, but nowhere had there been a decisive breakthrough. The high losses for minimal gains in the west did not lead to a fundamental review of strategic and tactical assumptions. Indeed, the Allied conference in Chantilly signed up to further offensives to liberate areas on both the eastern and western front under German or Austro-Hungarian occupation, as well as Trieste. In the belief that the German army would seek a decision in the east, there was support for a long-haul war of attrition that Germany would not be able to win.

On the German side, Falkenhayn continued to think in terms of possible victories. Yet throughout 1915 both he and Conrad von Hötzendorf showed signs that they feared exhaustion. Complex calculations began as to how the Central Powers could continue the war when there were no longer enough resources and "human material."[354] Falkenhayn gradually retreated from the idea of a great battle to roll over the enemy defenses. In a conversation with Walther Rathenau in late November, he pointed out that the French "had attempted a breakthrough with more guns than we possessed in total, but had failed to achieve it."[355] And in his so-called Christmas memorandum— in all likelihood a later analysis written in 1920 of the Battle of Verdun in 1916—Falkenhayn wrote that 1915 had shown the need for a larger German offensive on the western front. France, he argued, had been weakened both militarily and economically by the war on its own territory, Russia's offensive capacity had been decisively curtailed after the German successes of Summer 1915, Serbia's army was as good as finished, and Italy had been excluded as a key factor for the Allies. Britain was the only reason why these successes had not yet paid off: its "immense pressure on its allies" was shaping the war and forced Germany to treat it as its main enemy.

The conclusion, for Falkenhayn, was that Germany should intensify its submarine warfare and aim for a military decision against France on the western front; an "advance on Moscow" would become an "endless drain" on resources and soon stretch them to breaking point. Therefore, the aim should no longer be to break through the enemy front at all costs, but to weaken the French army as much as possible in the long term: "Behind the French sector of the western front, there are objectives in reach for the defense of which the French leadership is forced to commit the last man. If it does this, France's forces will bleed away; there is no escaping it, whether or not we achieve our actual objective. If it does not do this and the objective falls into our hands, the impact on morale in France will be immense. . . . The objectives we are talking about are Belfort and Verdun. The above points apply to both. But it is Verdun for choice."[356]

5

**WEARING DOWN
AND HOLDING OUT**
1916

"THE LANDSCAPE is unforgettable for anyone who has seen it. A short time
ago, this area still had meadows and forests and cornfields. None of that
to be seen any more. Literally no blade of grass, not one tiny little blade.
Every millimeter of earth is plowed up and replowed, the trees . . . uprooted,
mangled, and ground up. The houses shelled flat, the stone bricks atomized
to powder. The railroad tracks twisted into spirals, the hills worn down: in
short, everything turned into desert."[1] On July 28, 1916, during the Battle
of the Somme that had been raging since the beginning of the month, Ernst
Jünger wrote these impressions in his war diary. Only later did he return
to them in compiling his famous book *In Stahlgewittern* (Storm of Steel),
which made the death-defying young lieutenant and storm troop leader
one of the most influential war writers of the interwar period. The diary
itself, with its descriptions often written in a dugout, was by no means free
of such stylized presentations, which offered a way for Jünger to cope with
the constant presence of death. But the diary generally recorded his impressions in a more direct manner, with less filtering and protection, than the
book he published in 1920.[2]

Soldiers were aware at the time that the Verdun and Somme battles
in the spring and summer of 1916 were giving a new quality to the war.

Kresten Andresen, a Danish conscript in the Prussian army, recorded in early August 1916 that hardly any of the Danish comrades with whom he had enlisted in Summer 1914 were still alive. The new-style barrage fire and 38-centimeter shells made him think he was beholding "a monster from the sagas." Andresen soon fell in his turn—which meant that, like so many others in these battles, he disappeared without trace, not leaving a body to be identified. The remains of dead soldiers, often not immediately recoverable, were further mangled, shredded, and in the end literally broken up in the subsequent fighting. In one of his last letters home Andresen—who in Summer 1914, as a member of Germany's Danish minority, had shown no patriotic enthusiasm for the war—trenchantly summarized the change in his own experience of the conflict: "At the beginning of the war, in spite of all the terrible things, there was a sense of something poetic. That has now gone."[3] This was also true of the colors of war: no more did brightly colored uniforms enhance the soldiers' public presence physically and culturally. The gray greatcoats of British officers had become trench coats, and these would also influence fashions back home. When even the typical German spiked helmets were given a coating in that color, "field gray" became a byword for the ordinary soldier. Only the red regimental number marked his particular identity.

What lay behind this new experience of war? At the beginning of 1916, the central question for political and military leaders on the western front was how to reconvert the stasis and stagnation of positional warfare into a war of movement. The year 1915 had brought no decision on the western front, but new opportunities had opened up in the east for the Central Powers; while the Allied offensives in Artois and Champagne had failed at a high price in casualties, German and Austro-Hungarian forces had achieved a summer breakthrough on the eastern front. However, it had not been possible to force St. Petersburg into a separate peace, and in the end Russia had again succeeded in mobilizing its military and economic resources. On the western front, despite the huge losses in 1915, Allied commanders had stuck to the principle of offensive warfare and delayed the construction of defensive lines so as not to weaken the fighting spirit of their troops. The Germans, on the other hand, had intensively built up their positions, which more often than not were situated on higher ground. One of the lessons of the first

North Sea

NETHERLANDS

GERMAN REICH

Ostend
Nieuport
Flanders
Dunkirk
Bruges
Antwerp
Diksmuide
Ghent
Ypres
Passchendaele
Messines
Armentières
Neuve Chapelle
Lille
Tournai
Loos
Vimy
Douai
Arras
Maubeuge
Cambrai
Havrincourt
Le Cateau-
Cambrésis
Picardy
Amiens
St. Quentin
La Fère
Montdidier
Noyon
Laon
Juvigny
Compiègne
Soissons
Brussels
Louvain
Maastricht
Aachen
BELGIUM
Liège
Mons
Charleroi
Namur
Spa
Malmedy
Dinant
Ardennes
LUXEMBOURG
Mézières
Sedan
Semoy
Luxembourg
Aisne
Argonne
Longwy
Reims
Étain
Briey
Verdun
Metz
Lorraine
Château-
Thierry
Marne
Épernay
Châlons-sur-Marne
Montmirail
Champagne
St. Mihiel
Paris
Nancy
Toul
Lunéville
FRANCE

Allied attacks
German attacks
Farthest German advance, 1914
Approx. frontline from 1914–15
to winter 1916–17
Allied territorial gains in 1916–17

Troyes

Épinal

0 10 20 30 40 50 km

Map 7. Western Front, 1915–1917

seventeen months of the war was the dominance of mechanized warfare and the war of materiel, with its heavy artillery and vast quantities of munitions. This lineup connected events at the front with the war economies of the home countries.

The year 1916 gave the greatest impetus yet to mechanized warfare and the "battle of materiel"—and at the same time, with its high casualty figures, showed the limits of any attempt to decide the war by means of large-scale frontal attacks. The battles of Verdun and the Somme shaped people's vision of the western front and the collective imagination of the world war, and they have continued to do so down to the present day. Together, they accounted for an estimated total of 1.5 million dead, wounded, and missing. Each individual loss carried the reality of war into the societies of Britain, France, and Germany, but also of Canada, Australia, New Zealand, and India. By the end of the year, there was scarcely one large family that did not number at least one casualty among its husbands, brothers, sons, or grandsons.

Furthermore, the third year of war made it ever clearer how tightly the various theaters of war in Europe and beyond were intermeshed with one another. More than ever, the task was to redistribute resources, to redeploy troops when necessary to places where the danger was greatest. The link between Verdun and the Somme, the British aid to French troops, the Russian southeastern offensive to take some pressure off the Allies on the western front, the transfer of German troops from Verdun to the Somme, the German assistance to Austria-Hungary in Summer 1916 against the major Russian offensive under General Brusilov, the refusal of the German OHL in May and June to support the Austrian campaign against Italy in the Tyrol—all these marked the total context of the war. Strategic priorities had to be repeatedly redefined to take account of the situation on new or existing fronts and theaters. Romania's entry into the war against the Central Powers, together with the coup d'état in Greece and the emergence of another front in Macedonia, further extended the war in southeastern Europe.

Each new offensive came with expectations that it would decide the war. The sharpening of decision-making processes and awareness of their consequences increased the pressure on the players responsible for them, and in 1916 disappointed expectations tended more and more often to threaten a credibility and legitimacy crisis for military and political leaders. The search for guilty parties was matched by the sudden rise of savior figures, one of the hallmarks of this year of the war. After the failure of Verdun and the entry of Romania into the war on the Allied side, the former head of the German OHL, Falkenhayn, was replaced by Hindenburg and Ludendorff at the head of the Third OHL.[4] In France the popular hero of Verdun, Robert Nivelle, took over at the end of the year from Joseph Joffre, whose reputation had been based on his role in 1914 at the Battle of the Marne. In Britain, David Lloyd George relieved Asquith as prime minister. Old monarchs, too, got caught up in this succession of military and political upheavals: while the cult surrounding Hindenburg—whose paternal figure featured in numerous monuments and pictures in Germany—increasingly pushed the Kaiser into the background, the question of Austria-Hungary's future became more urgent after the death of Emperor Franz Joseph in November 1916. Although the assassination of Prime Minister Stürgkh in October was the action of a single individual (Friedrich Adler, son of the Social Democrat Party leader Viktor Adler), it was a powerful indication of how deep the crisis of confidence had become. The assassination reflected the rising tide of protest against official prowar policies, the antidemocratic regime, and the dire supply situation. Finally, in Russia, the gulf continued to widen between the tsarist autocracy and large sections of the elite and the general population. At the end of December 1916, the murder of the ostensible faith healer and confidant of the empress, Grigorii Rasputin, by members of the Russian elite close to the court, illuminated in a flash the erosion of tsarist rule. Each in their different ways, the loyalties and institutions based on dynastic rule were losing respect and credibility.

1. TOTAL BATTLES, STRATEGIC DEAD ENDS, TACTICAL INNOVATIONS
The Transition to Modern Warfare on the Western Front and the High Seas

The starting point for new developments on the western front was the Allied conference at Chantilly in early December 1915, when the supreme commanders of the French forces and the BEF, Joffre and French, agreed on a common course with General Yakov Zhilinsky from Russia and the commanders of the Italian and Serbian armies. The shared assumption was that in 1916

Germany would continue its war of attrition at a lower level and seek a decisive breakthrough on the eastern front after its successes there in the previous year. Although the Allies did not go so far as to establish a joint supreme command, they were able to develop a number of special arrangements. Meanwhile, the rivalry between the commanders of the Central Powers was so intense that it stood in the way of any meaningful cooperation between Falkenhayn and Conrad von Hötzendorf.[5] The Austro-Hungarian monarchy, with its new foreign minister, István Burián, declared victory over Italy to be its principal war aim, in the hope that this would put its international prestige on a more stable long-term footing, but Conrad von Hötzendorf was unable to convince the OHL that an offensive in the Tyrol should take priority over operations on the western front. In 1916, therefore, the Central Powers may be said to have been pursuing different strategies in the different theaters of war.[6] Only the setbacks in the Tyrol and the major crisis following the early successes of the Brusilov offensive compelled Vienna to make a turnaround in Summer 1916. The German and Austro-Hungarian decision-making structures became effectively coordinated for the first time, but the price was high, insofar as the Imperial army lost any real ability to mount independent operations of its own. To the Empire's economic dependence on Germany was now added military dependence on the OHL and the German armed forces.

These developments increased the pressure on Germany to act, but the basic problems started before then. As early as January 1916, Falkenhayn had warned the Kaiser that neither the Dual Monarchy nor the Ottoman Empire could continue fighting much beyond the fall. Falkenhayn's decision to launch a large-scale operation on the western front should also be seen in this light.[7] He did not believe that the war could be decided on the eastern front, because he feared that a deep retreat by Russian forces there would pose a problem of overextension for the Central Powers. In his so-called Christmas memorandum—which, according to his postwar memoirs, he presented to the Kaiser in December 1915—he argued for a great battle at Verdun to bring about the systematic weakening of France. In November 1914, with the war of movement becoming bogged down in the west, he had already spoken to the German chancellor, Bethmann Hollweg, of his skepticism about the general course of the war. In his view, if Russia, France, and Britain held together, it would be impossible for Germany to win the war in a manner that offered any hope of acceptable peace terms. He therefore proposed a separate peace with Russia or France that ruled out annexations. Falkenhayn stuck to this assessment over the coming months. Unlike many German commanders, he did not believe in a military breakthrough on the western front—and in support of this he could point to the massive French losses in the offensives of 1915, which, despite their great efforts, had not achieved a breakthrough. Falkenhayn's calculation in choosing the Verdun option was that the lightning capture of such a symbolic strategic point—the fortifications of Verdun—would compel the French to try to retake it and then the German defenders, by holding the line, would impose huge losses on the enemy and systematically wear him down.[8]

The so-called Christmas memorandum, with its symptomatic metaphor of "bleeding away," was thus not just a case of retrospective sense-making on Falkenhayn's part, conducted with hindsight about the casualties suffered at Verdun and the eventual outcome of the war. However cynical the logic of attrition may have been, various statements of his since late 1914 suggest that he was thrashing around for a concept that would meet the requirements of Germany's overall situation in the war, including the impossibility of major frontal breakthroughs.[9] On December 3, 1915, he had a discussion with the Kaiser: "General von Falkenhayn unfolds to [His Majesty] a serious picture of the war situation, with the conclusion that a blow must be struck in the *west* [sic] to bring about a decision, and that all available forces must be readied for this! He wants to attack at Belfort, because he has the best flank support there. When, he did not say."[10] While Falkenhayn's basic option was for a great battle on the western front, it cannot be said that he had a fully coherent vision. Nor did the actual planning of the battle proceed in the way he depicted in his later memoirs: it was not he but Crown Prince Wilhelm, as commander of the Fifth Army, and his chief of staff, Schmidt von Knobelsdorf, who set the objective of attack. Falkenhayn himself feared that an attack against the heavily fortified city-fortress might tie down too many troops.[11]

The result—as in the case of later disputes between British commanders on the Somme—was a disastrous compromise. The German attack took place at Verdun because its distinctive curving front was supposed to facilitate an assault on many sides and to compel the French to withdraw troops from other sections of the front. Moreover, the fact that the defenders could be supplied only along a small corridor between Bar-le-Duc and Verdun was supposed to make their position highly vulnerable. Yet the German forces only attacked east of the Meuse River, not also against the heights on its west bank. Their main objectives were Douaumont and Vaux, the great outer forts in the east of Verdun.[12]

One special feature of Verdun's geography was the ring of heights above the Meuse. There were historical reasons why this location was strategic: it was here that the Meuse intersected with the road link from Metz to Paris. Surrounded by the Woevre Plain, the Moselle River, and Metz in the east, and by the Argonne Forest with its opening to Champagne in the west, Verdun had always had symbolic importance in the Franco-German history of conflict. Under German rule between 925 and 1552, Verdun was then awarded to France in the Treaty of Westphalia in 1648 and built up into a fortress

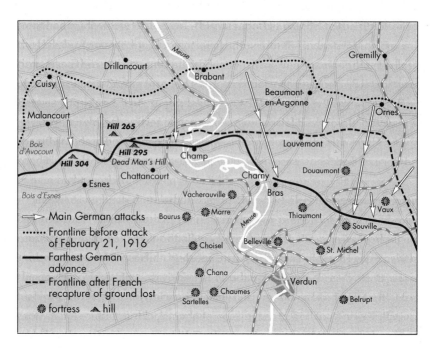

Map 8. The Battle of Verdun, 1916

by Errard de Bar-le-Duc and Vauban in the seventeenth century. In 1792 it was captured by Prussian troops and then retaken by the French army; it fell again to Prussian-German forces in 1870 and only reverted to France in September 1873. The transfer of Lorraine to the German Reich in 1871 meant that the border ran across the Woevre Plain. This exposed position induced the French military leadership over the subsequent decades, and most intensively before 1914, to make Verdun itself impregnable. Three rings with a total of twenty forts, including at Douaumont and Vaux to the east, and numerous prepared positions surrounded the town.[13] In September 1914 the German advance had ground to a halt before reaching Verdun. Since no further offensive ensued in the next few months, and since the German invasion of Belgium had shown how effective heavy artillery could be against outer forts, the French reduced their fort garrisons and placed heavy weapons of their own in sectors of the front farther to the west. All the same, the German attack plans underestimated the geographical peculiarities of Verdun. The alternation of hills, forest, and ridges offered decisive advantages to defending forces, because they could operate there very effectively from fortified dugouts, trenches, and machine-gun positions.[14]

On February 21 at 8:12 A.M., a German long-barrel gun set to work. The first shell, with a caliber of 38 centimeters, landed 22 kilometers away in the vicinity of the bishop's palace in Verdun, opening an attack of unprecedented strength designed to eliminate fortifications and defensive positions. In the first 18 days of the battle, three million shells of all calibers were fired from a total of 1,400 artillery pieces—the equivalent of thirty munitions trains a day. In the thinking of commanders in the battles to come, most notably on the Somme, this massing of artillery fire was supposed to guarantee success. The same tactic had been tried before in 1915, but never with the intensity seen in Spring and Summer 1916. But even such intensive bombardment could not overcome the limitations of the whole plan: artillery fire on this scale precluded any surprise effect, and in practice it was never possible to destroy all the defensive positions. Moreover, the numerous impacts and shell craters made it difficult for troops to advance across the terrain, especially if the infantry was deployed in classical lines.

In another respect too, the Battle of Verdun marked the transition to a new battlefield reality. A German soldier's equipment included flamethrowers and phosphorus gas (in use at Fort Vaux), and for many soldiers a steel helmet had replaced the traditional spiked leather helmet for the first time. As in other armies, this was a response to the large number of head wounds from shell splinters. While the light French steel plate "Adrian" helmet offered only limited protection, the wide-brimmed British MK1 proved a solid defense against shrapnel. The M16 steel helmet developed in Germany, with its cutout section for the eyes and its protruding neck protection, became an iconic image of the frontline soldier, assimilated after the war for political uses.[15] Effective it certainly was, but its 1.3 kilos of chrome nickel steel were on the heavy side. And only in late 1917 would it be issued to all German troops at the front.[16]

The battle situation and geographical peculiarities at Verdun meant that attacks in lines were out of the question. So-called storm troopers were therefore deployed against individual outer forts, in accordance with the model of the first storm battalion of 1915 under Captain Willy Rohr. Unlike the French and British armies, which addressed the problems of positional warfare mainly by the long-term development of armored vehicles, the German military relied on infantry detachments and innovative tactics. The storm units in question were small, highly trained, and well equipped, consisting of infantrymen and sappers with flexible and mobile weapons such as light machine guns and, by the end of the war, the first machine pistols, as well as hand grenades, flamethrowers, and light mortars. The regulation issue no longer consisted of the usual backpack, but rather "2 sandbags with hand grenades hanging round the neck over both shoulders," a "medium wirecutter," and a "folding trench shovel."[17] These units made themselves as small as possible in the intervening space, as they advanced to breach enemy positions at previously identified weak points or to create confusion behind enemy lines. They engaged in direct combat, but at first they functioned as training units to introduce other frontline troops to the new tactics. Thus, they carried out practice operations on models of enemy positions specially built at the rear, exemplifying the general tendency to methodical planning and execution of attacks.[18]

Although artillery fire and infantry attacks dominated the scene at Verdun, both the German and French armies made their first systematic use of aircraft, which would become increasingly important as the war went on. For

War booty and technological advances: display of captured German fighters, Paris

the German engineer Anton Fokker, 1915 was the year of a key technological innovation: the synchronization of propeller motion and machine-gun
fire, in such a way that German pilots could use their onboard guns in the
direction of flight. Although the Germans then had the upper hand in aerial
combat, the French air force protected supply lines during the Battle of Verdun and located German artillery positions. In fact, aerial observation was
essential to the course of the battle. A young pilot by the name of Hermann
Göring, wounded in Alsace as a lieutenant at the beginning of the war and
then transferred to flying duties, delivered a precise report on the French
forts, for which he was personally received and decorated by the German
crown prince.[19]

Verdun was not a decisive battle in the strategic sense. Since the German
forces could not achieve their original objectives, Falkenhayn's real aim was
not achieved either. In contrast to memories of the war and to public perceptions of it even today in France and Germany, the battle was not the bloodiest
of the conflict. But it did exemplify the mismatch between outlay, casualties,

and results—and hence the inability to find an adequate answer to the killing power of modern weapons on a limited battlefield. After German units took the thinly manned Fort Douaumont on February 25, their further advance was halted by fire from the Meuse heights to the west and other strongly entrenched positions.[20] The soldier Julius Marx wrote of the fighting at Douaumont in his diary entry for March 24, 1916: "March-off again at one in the morning. . . . One of my people is thrown from his horse, a man from the artillery column has an arm torn off, another is badly wounded in the head, and yet another screams in terrible pain. And we stay there without cover, unable to help."[21]

The high casualty rates on both sides indicate the intensity of the battle. In the first five days the French lost 24,000 men, of whom 15,000 were taken prisoner. In the first 10 days, the losses on the German side already totaled 26,000. While the writer Romain Rolland diagnosed "an increasingly revolutionary mood" in France and recorded rumors on the home front and among combat troops—"generals shot, Joffre and Gallieni in opposition . . . the government showering soldiers' wives with support"—the soldier Jean Norton Cru wrote in April 1916 of the reality of the battlefield. It had nothing in common with the images of hand-to-hand combat conjured up at home and in the press: "The bayonet attack, as described in the newspapers, is a myth that certain loudmouthed vacationers perpetuate in coffee houses. In reality the men saddled with cartridge pouches, bread bags, and water bottles cannot use their bayonet at all; a hefty blow with a stick would disarm them."[22] The high casualties had an impact on all soldiers. On July 7, 1916, the French infantryman René Arnaud recorded that he and his men had been issued with new collar patches, as sizable losses had led to the merging of two brigades; his old regiment, No. 337, no longer existed. Many in his own brigade tried to report sick before a new action in Verdun. A crowd of them surrounded the battalion doctor, "clinging to him like drowning men to a lifebuoy. . . . In short, there was a general state of disintegration."[23]

In the second phase of the battle, strong French resistance inflicted heavy losses on the German attackers on the Meuse heights. Sustained fire skimmed several meters of rock from "Hill 304" and "Dead Man's Hill." On June 23, the Germans made a last major push with 73,000 men via the Vaux and Fleury forts, from where they could see the Meuse at Verdun, the real

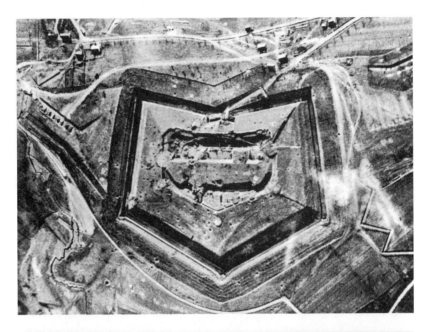

Verdun as a symbol of total military force: Fort Douaumont before and after the battle, 1916

object of attack, in the distance. Because of Allied preparations for the Somme battle, more and more German soldiers were transferred there in May and June, and offensive operations gradually petered out.[24] This gave the other side the opportunity to recapture the forts of Douaumont and Vaux in a final phase of the battle. By the end of August, the total losses in dead, wounded, missing, and captive stood at 315,000 French and 281,000 Germans. This corresponded to a ratio of 1.1 to 1—far below the 3:1 or even 5:1 that German commanders had hoped for.[25] Although the final balance sheet of casualties is hard to determine—the highest estimates are 377,000 French and 337,000 Germans—the fighting between February and December 1916 must have resulted in the death, wounding, or capture of more than a half-million soldiers.[26]

But what made Verdun the "total battle"?[27] Why did it seem like the watershed of the war? The first reason was the extreme density of violence in a relatively small space: some ten million shells, weighing 1.35 million tons, were fired on an area of 26 square kilometers.[28] This led to the only instance during the war of two overlapping experiences of violence: the mechanized warfare of long-range heavy artillery and fierce hand-to-hand combat for tiny gains of territory.[29] The landscape around Verdun would remain contaminated for decades by the deadly ordnance, and large parts of it remained no-go areas.

But this is not all there was to the "total battle," for the symbolic charge of events at Verdun was part of the battle itself and resonated well beyond it. The military and political consequences crossed a "difference threshold" in the war; the defense of Verdun became in France the decisive moment when the whole nation was put to the test, while Germans saw the tactically insignificant capture of Fort Douaumont in February as a beacon for the future. From that point on, the French military leadership related to Verdun as the key defensive position for the entire front. Whereas Joffre was accused of having underestimated the danger of a German attack, the commander of the Second Army, Philippe Pétain, managed to stabilize the situation, having taken command of Army Group Center in April 1916. Pétain's later career, and the charisma surrounding him as a national savior amid a military crisis, invited comparison with the role of Hindenburg in Germany. Already 60 years old in 1916, having been a colonel on the brink of retirement at the beginning of the war, Pétain had risen since Summer 1914 to become commander of the Second Army. By 1915 his opposition to *attaques à outrance*, suicidal actions at any cost often without adequate artillery preparation, had earned him great popularity among ordinary French soldiers.[30]

During the first weeks in Verdun, Pétain pursued a triple strategy that soon gave him the reputation of savior in the hour of crisis. The three planks were: positions should be defended under all circumstances; infantry attacks should take place only after massive artillery barrages; and, in anticipation of high casualties, a rotation system should ensure that as many units as possible shared the burden.[31] The last point, together with the automatic dissolution of units with losses higher than 50 percent, did indeed strengthen the esteem in which soldiers held Pétain, but it gave other commanders the impression that he was acting too defensively and was incapable of winning either the battle or the war. The *noria* (water wheel) or rotation system, also known as the paternoster system (an allusion to the revolving elevator of that name), meant that, by mid-July and the beginning of the Somme battle, eighty of ninety-five divisions (or, by December 1916, 78 percent of all French regiments) had taken part in the Battle of Verdun. Only twenty-three divisions were ever deployed twice.[32] On the one hand, this ensured a realistic chance of survival and headed off protests or mutinies; on the other hand, many relatively inexperienced soldiers were thrown into battle, and knowledge of local conditions was lost whenever there was a changeover. Most important, however, this mechanism made Verdun a reference point for the whole army, so that two-thirds of all soldiers could be identified as Verdun veterans. The whole of French society was involved in this process via the soldiers and their links to their home regions. The battle thus played a special role, even during the war, as a locus of collective experience and memory. An integrative symbolic language of national defense took shape around it, imbuing each individual with a spirit of self-sacrifice and unconditional perseverance. When the Fort Vaux commander Major Raynal, already wounded from an earlier battle, refused to make an appeal for help with his last carrier pigeon before he surrendered with more than 600 men dying of thirst, he and the pigeon became a symbol of this attitude. The bird made it to headquarters with the news, but died from battlefield gases and was decorated with a medal. Raynal himself was taken captive by the Germans, and after the war he returned to Mainz with French occupation forces and became its city commander in 1920.[33]

The problem of supplying Verdun was seen as a national duty and vividly illustrated the interaction of homeland and front. Verdun's geographical location in an arc of the front meant that 500,000 soldiers and 170,000 animals could be supplied only along a 60-kilometer strip of land between Bar-le-Duc and Verdun and a parallel narrow-gauge railroad. Between February 27 and March 6, at the height of the battle, a total of 190,000 men and 23,000 tons of munitions were sent in via this route. On average, 50,000 tons of supplies and 90,000 soldiers a week were transported there. In June, one vehicle was passing on the road every 14 seconds.[34] Roads and rail lines were divided into six sectors, which were maintained by thousands of engineers and laborers. The army leadership requisitioned thousands of motorized trucks from the whole of France, producing a transport shortage in other parts of the country that doubled the price of vegetables in Parisian markets. Maurice Barrès, whose widely read editorials in the *Echo de Paris* celebrated the ideal of the home front, described the road into Verdun as a *voie sacrée*, underlining the importance of the nation in the defensive war.[35]

A final element in the symbolic discourse was the persuasiveness and credibility of the military leaders. For the French *poilus* these characteristics were particularly true of Pétain, who in a distinctive mix of defensive theory and understanding for the soldiers' situation exemplified the will to hold out. He was thus able to prevent the distance between men and officers from developing into a crisis of communication and legitimacy—the kind of crisis that did indeed occur in Spring 1917. When the Germans mounted heavy attacks on Hill 304 on the left bank of the Meuse, Pétain expressed the spirit of stubborn defense and perseverance in his famous order of the day for April 10, 1916: "Each man must pitch in and ensure another success like yesterday's. . . . Be brave, we'll get the better of them [*Courage, on les aura*]!"[36] In the end, the French side managed to weave the battle and its casualties into a heroic, credible narrative of national defense of the republic and the values it embodied, and at the same time to recognize practical limits to the burden that could be placed on the soldiers. Verdun thereby became a test case for the defensive capacity of the French nation and its readiness to mobilize and focus all its forces, to oppose the attackers' will with the defenders' will to hold out. This was the context in which President Poincaré visited Verdun on September 13 and symbolically decorated it with the cross of the Légion d'Honneur.[37] In 1916, Pétain's appeal as national savior rested not on a cult of the offensive and an unconditional will to attack, but on defense of his homeland against the German aggressor. When large-scale mutinies broke out in Spring 1917 after the failure of further French offensives, he finally took supreme command of the army. Then too, it was his commitment to defensive action that prevented an escalation of the crisis. This posture, combining a national salvation myth with a will to stay the course, would eventually carry him to the head of the state following France's defeat in 1940.

Later in 1916, however, Pétain's attitude was criticized as overly pessimistic, and it was not he but Robert Nivelle who replaced Joffre in December as supreme commander. Nivelle came to appear as the real victor of Verdun in the eyes of military and political leaders. His watchword on June 23, when German troops took the village of Fleury—"Do not let them through, comrades!"— gave fitting expression to the symbolic image of Verdun as the site of national defense.[38] Nivelle's consistent use of the "creeping barrage" (*barrage roulant*) was based on improved collaboration between artillery and infantry, which had first come into effect in the second battle of Champagne in Fall 1915.[39] In contrast to so-called drumfire, designed to wipe out an enemy position over a period of days, the creeping barrage advanced at well-defined intervals by 50 to 100 meters at a time. The idea behind this was to force enemy infantry to remain in their trenches, while one's own units advanced under the protection of a wall of fire and eventually poured into the enemy positions. This tactic presupposed intensive shelling, but also—and most important— precise spatial and temporal coordination between artillery and infantry forces. In the final phase of the Battle of Verdun, it was mainly such coordination on the French side that resulted in success. Recapture of the forts of Douaumont and Vaux was hailed as a symbolic victory. But the French also benefited from the Russian June offensive on the eastern front and from the beginning of the Somme battle in July. These developments prevented the German military from deploying all the troops it had earmarked for Verdun.

Nivelle's meteoric rise to become head of the army by December 1916 mainly had to do with hopes that the success in Verdun, won at great sacrifice and on a limited battlefield, could be transferred to the whole of the western front. This reflected an increasing disorientation, or, indeed, despair in late 1916 about the reality of positional warfare, and it explained the high expectations for the offensive plan for Spring 1917 devised by the new supreme commander. The bloody failure of the Nivelle offensive at Chemin des Dames then led to the crisis of the French army and home front, and to the replacement of Nivelle with Pétain. Verdun marked the further course of the war by virtue of the two men's fates alone. Nivelle and Pétain stood for competing narratives about who should be seen as the real victor of the battle. Whereas Pétain enjoyed a good reputation among ordinary soldiers, because his defensive tactics aimed to avoid unnecessary casualties, Nivelle appeared to the political and military leaders around Clemenceau, Joffre, and Foch as an innovative commander who, with his élan and commitment to the offensive, could be trusted to bring about the conclusion to the war that they did not think Pétain was capable of achieving.[40]

The view of the battle was very different on the German side. Since there was nothing comparable to the French system of frontline troop rotation, the burden of service at the front was much higher for German soldiers. As a rule, German units were deployed for five to seven days in the two forwardmost lines, then withdrawn for four to five days to rest areas outside the killing zone. But extremely high losses whittled down the number of replacement troops, so that the same units had to spend more and more time in the combat zone and less and less behind the lines. The Württemberg Infantry Regiment no. 122, for example, was deployed for up to six weeks right at the front or on standby.[41] Unlike French soldiers, who, however great the losses, felt they were fighting to defend their homeland from attack and occupation, and who at Verdun feared a German breakthrough to the heartlands of France, many German soldiers became increasingly aware of a discrepancy between high casualty rates and minimal territorial gains. In the face of enemy defensive fire, therefore, Verdun increasingly became for them the bloody "man-grinder" on the Meuse.[42]

Other costs of this "total battle" also became visible. Not only were there more frequent disciplinary cases against soldiers; numerous symptoms of mental exhaustion were reported on both the German and French sides, on top of the many dead and physically injured. Crown Prince Wilhelm blamed Falkenhayn for the annihilation of his army at Verdun, and hence also for an unprecedented weakening of the German armed forces.[43] The worsening mood among German soldiers was typical of this new context, expressing itself not in open resistance or antiwar politics but in officers' worries about the survival strategies of their men. Thus, on October 27, 1916 Crown Prince Wilhelm, as supreme commander of his army group, addressed his officers about an alarming fact: "One of the most regrettable consequences of the corrosive effects of heavy fighting on the western front is our comparatively high losses in unwounded prisoners." Nevertheless, he insisted, "it must generally be considered shameful for a troop contingent to be taken prisoner with gun in hand. . . . Rather perish honorably than live without honor!"[44]

The military results of Verdun were at variance with the soldiers' experiences and with the explanations in the official press. For example, in early November 1916 the German *Kriegsecho* hailed the battle as proof of unprecedented martial heroism: "What our troops have given in crisp daredevilry, stubborn holding of new gains, cheerful endurance of unheard-of hardships and horrors, and unfailing joy in attack, is at the very summit of heroism." Since by then it had long been clear that the battle was not decisively weakening the Allies, it took some effort to describe the advantage gained at such a high price: "What they have gained in struggle is considerable: we have in our sights the Verdun basin, the town itself, the bridges over the Meuse, and the railroad lines, and we can direct our fire effectively at all these points. Verdun's value as a cornerstone of France's defenses may not yet have been nullified, but it has been greatly reduced, and its importance as a bridgehead and base for attack has been completely eliminated."[45]

In essence, Falkenhayn's strategy at Verdun had been a failure: the battle had not weakened but strengthened the defensive resolve of French politicians. Similarly, the British would later show at the Somme that, despite terrible casualties, there could be no question of their leaving the alliance and withdrawing from the European battlefield. But no less important, as at the Marne in Fall 1914, were the contrast between positive and negative myths surrounding the battle; the focus on the two enemies, France and Germany; and the symbolic political charge on both sides, which began with the battle itself and extended into the post-1918 cultures of remembrance. The dashing of high German hopes gave rise to explanatory constructs, as after the battle of the Marne and again in 1918–1919 with the "stab in the back" myth.[46] Not only military leaders but also the home front were made responsible for the bloodletting that marked the image of the "Verdun fighter" in countless memoirs. The vision of patriotic sacrifice and heroic death in battle, in a just war to defend the fatherland, lost more and more of its credibility.[47] In the scale of violence in a limited space, the all-out mobilization and symbolic concentration in one place, Verdun acquired the same kind of significance that attached to Stalingrad in the Second World War.[48]

The gap between expectations and results also had political consequences, and soon the public reputation of leading military and political players was on the line. The battle advanced and destroyed careers in short order: while it consolidated the image of Pétain as national savior and of Nivelle as energetic commander, the former commander, Joffre, came under intense pressure. What would have been unthinkable in Germany actually happened in France in Summer 1916, when parliament insisted on summoning and questioning the military top brass. On June 22, at a secret session of the National Assembly, the future defense minister André Maginot—who had himself been wounded in late November 1915—criticized Joffre for his decisions in the context of the battle. Although Joffre's popularity as victor of the Marne prevented his immediate dismissal, his influence continued to wane, and in December 1916 he was shifted to a ceremonial function under the pretext of promotion to marshal.

On the German side, too, the battle made deep inroads into the military leadership structure, considerably weakening Falkenhayn's position in particular. When Romania joined the war in August 1916 on the side of the Entente, he was finally removed and replaced with Hindenburg and Ludendorff, placed at the head of the Third OHL. Only the British chief Douglas Haig hung on, despite the huge losses at the Somme, although a political crisis led to the formation of a new government under Lloyd George at the end of the year. In the shadow of these changes, the paths of future politicians in the "age of extremes" intersected at the Battle of Verdun: Hermann Göring made his name as a pilot, while Captain Charles de Gaulle was taken prisoner during the fight for the village of Douaumont. Although he attempted to escape on several occasions, he remained in German captivity until 1918, getting to know the future Russian marshal Mikhail Tukhachevsky in a camp for officers.

In the end, a mere 15 kilometers of territory changed hands at the price of a half-million dead and wounded, but no more than before did the disproportion lead to a policy review on the western front. At Verdun, too, the Germans did not succeed in decisively weakening the enemy. The next offensive was supposed to force the issue by means of even more intense artillery bombardment and the deployment of even more human material. Paradoxically, therefore, the high death toll actually reinforced the doctrine of the offensive: the war continued because any yielding, any compromise, any renunciation of unconditional victory, would devalue all the past sacrifices and call into question the legitimacy of the nations at war. The war fed on itself, as it were. Each new sacrifice prolonged the conflict by hardening the resolve on all sides to win the victory that would give sense to the sacrifice. None of the military commanders could free themselves from this logic.

Beginning in July 1916, the experiences of Verdun were repeated with role changes and greater quantitative inputs at the Battle of the Somme. There were the same mechanisms of attack and defense, the same outlay / results miscalculation, and the same inability to come up with a strategic answer to the challenges of modern war other than the deployment of more and more soldiers and ever-greater firepower, resulting in ever-greater losses. While the British and French initially planned to break through the German front with a full-scale attack, and only subsequently changed this aim to a massive weakening of the enemy, the Somme became the "German Verdun" for soldiers on the other side, a defensive battle for survival. The period between July 1 and November 18, 1916, witnessed by far the costliest battle of the First World War, which was at the same time a prelude to the military violence later in the twentieth century. Douglas Haig's argument that the massive losses weakened the Germans' long-term capacity for major offensive operations was a retrospective attempt to give some meaning to the battle. Unlike Falkenhayn, the British supreme commander expected that it would be possible to turn the positional warfare back into a war of movement and to force a decision through fresh offensives. Such thinking left no room for the possibility that the paralysis would continue until one of the players collapsed under the burden of its demographic, economic, social, and political problems.

At a meeting between Joffre and Haig (who had replaced French in December 1915 after the disillusioning experiences on the western front), it was agreed in late May 1916 to mount a joint offensive in the area between

Beaumont-Hamel and the Somme marshes. Since the Battle of Verdun was still continuing, the French could field only sixteen divisions instead of the forty originally planned. This circumstances intertwining the two battles meant that the British had to be the mainstay of the attack, so that the battle also became a test for Kitchener's New Armies.[49] For the British high command, the aim was to demonstrate that the British political and military leadership was committed to the war on the Continent in support of its French allies more than to the war at sea, in the Near East, and in Africa. The conditions in Summer 1916 were quite different from those in the previous year: Haig, the new supreme commander, had at his disposal not only more than twelve divisions of regular troops but also an additional thirty divisions of the New Armies. After the number of volunteers had fallen in 1915, a Military Service Act in January 1916 had introduced conscription for the first time, making what seemed a virtually inexhaustible supply of soldiers available to commanders. The munitions crises of the previous year also seemed to have been overcome through vigorous measures to boost output in the British war economy.[50]

Yet in Summer and Fall 1916 on the Somme, the discrepancy between quantitative improvements and qualitative problems proved to be the key reason for the high casualty figures. More shells were being fired than ever before, but roughly one-quarter of them were duds. The British army had more soldiers than ever, but time pressure meant that their battle training and experience at the front were inadequate, while gaps in the officer and NCO corps had not been fully filled after the high casualties of the previous year. The Allied superiority in soldiers and munitions was evident. But the bald figure of 3,000 artillery pieces concealed the fact that this included only 400 heavy guns that could be effectively deployed against German positions. At first, with 201 French and 185 British aircraft against 129 German machines, the Allies enjoyed an air superiority that permitted excellent reconnaissance of enemy artillery. Yet the one-sided focus on breaking through the front overlooked the fact that in many ways local conditions suited the defensive tasks of the German troops, and that they had had enough time to entrench themselves in hillside positions largely reinforced with concrete, as well as in a number of abandoned villages.[51] The high expectations on the Allied side rested mainly on an improved supply situation at the outset, not on a change in strategy or battlefield tactics or on a more nuanced view of the effectiveness of the available weapons.

The quantitative advantages of the attacker had to be set against the fact that the British high command disagreed over what were realistic objectives on the western front and which expectations were unrealizable from the outset. While Haig pursued a maximal aim—a full-scale breakthrough that the cavalry could then use to turn positional warfare into a war of movement leading to a great battle behind the German frontlines—Henry Rawlinson, the commander of the British Fourth Army, openly doubted whether a breakthrough was feasible. Based on the experience of the past year, he favored a "bite and hold" tactic of many small attacks on discrete sections of the enemy front, which could then be held and used to drive back the enemy step by step.[52] To this end, the artillery was supposed to concentrate on the first line of the German front. The outcome of this dispute was a disastrous compromise: Haig gained acceptance for his view that the artillery should bombard not only the forwardmost German trenches but the whole zone of three staggered trench systems. This may have suited his breakthrough scenario, but it limited the effect of the artillery barrage beginning on June 24, 1916, that prepared the ground for the infantry offensive. A total of 1.5 million shells weighing 12,000 tons were fired—the equivalent of one ton per square meter of battlefield. In addition, British sappers carried mines along s seventeen tunnels right up to the German frontline. After these preparations, British commanders ruled out the possibility that the attack would encounter major resistance.

The reality was different. The British soldier Robert Cude had already spent 10 months at the front in France, but he had never experienced a major battle. In late May 1916 he returned from a 10-day furlough to his East Kent Regiment, also known as the "Buffs," which was a typical example of Kitchener's New Armies. Cude's task as a "runner" was, if possible, to carry news by bicycle between the battalion command post and individual units. His diary entries reflect the perspective of ordinary soldiers at the beginning of the battle, their hopes and disappointments. On his way back to the front, he already pondered the growing distance between the reality at the front and at home: "Am beginning to long for trenches again, for I get fed up with civilization."[53] On June 24, he recorded with fascination the British artillery barrage. While hoping that the enemy positions would be destroyed, he saw how many shells fell wide and killed his own fellow soldiers: "Today 3.30 A.M. the guns start the preliminary bombardment. As day succeeds day we notice more and more artillery getting into action. Jerry is getting it now. Plenty of rain first two or three days. We are getting a goodly number of casualties, for a good many of our shells are falling short."[54]

The seven-day bombardment was the longest softening-up operation of the war so far. On July 1, a bright summer's day, the shelling intensified into drumfire, before the British began the attack on the enemy trenches. It was characteristic of the mentality of many soldiers that the image of a sporting contest occurred to them at this moment: "7.22 A.M. Every gun for eight minutes gave of their best and the din was terrific. Punctual to time 7.28 A.M. two minutes before the line advanced Captain Neville . . . kicks off the football that is to take the boys over to Jerry. He is killed as his leg is uplifted after kicking the ball. . . . E. Surrey and Queens go over singing and shouting and the ball is punted from one to another."[55] But then Cude observed the German resistance: "Jerry's machine gun opens a terrific fire on our chaps and the first wave is speedily decimated. Others jump forward and fill the gaps. I am aghast at the accuracy of the fire. He has plenty of machine guns and is making a frightful carnage." Nevertheless, the march-off on this summer's day continued to impress Cude: "It is a wonderful sight and one that I shall not forget. War such as this, on such a beautiful day seems to me to be quite correct and proper! On a day such as this one, one feels a keen joy in living even though living is, to say the least of it, very precarious. Men are racing to certain death, and jesting and smiling and cursing, yet wonderfully quiet in a sense, for one feels that one must kill, and as often as one can."[56]

Yet Cude's next entry, at 10:00 A.M. on the same morning, paints a thoroughly different picture of the battlefield: "Boys are still fighting in the trenches and dugouts and I must say that considering the grueling Jerry has had and the opposition he is met with, he is fighting a battle for life itself. No quarter is asked or given in a good many places and today I was astounded to think that men could fight so bitterly. The reason is not far to seek, for tens of thousands of our men are lying low, never to rise again. They are England's flower. The men that England can ill afford to spare. As far as my eye takes me, I can see rows of dead." Over the next few days, Cude writes of the numerous burials. His own 55th Brigade had lost 3,000 dead, wounded, and missing. Since most of them were volunteers, enrolled in Pals Battalions by place of origin, even by street or place of work, these losses were especially severe back home, for they affected strong relationships, groups of school friends, workmates, or neighbors.[57]

The British offensive, launched on July 1 with such great expectations, ended in failure and a high death toll. But the widespread idea that British troops, weighed down with heavy backpacks, left the trenches unprotected in their tens of thousands and advanced in classical lines across 200–400 meters of no-man's-land into the range of German machine guns is not accurate. Only twelve to seventeen of the eighty British battalions went over the top; the others had been waiting all night directly before the German lines, came together in no-man's-land, and attacked in small groups, giving evidence of more flexible battlefield tactics. To this extent, it was not such a clear-cut anachronistic scenario in which the bravery of ordinary soldiers contrasted with the incompetence of arrogant officers, as the later image of "lions led by donkeys" would suggest.[58] What does seem really anachronistic is the sixteen German soldiers pierced by lances during a cavalry attack of the 7th Dragoon Guards—a final harking back to the premodern warfare that had all but vanished amid the battle of materiel.[59]

What, then, were the reasons for the catastrophe? A large part of the troops in question, and particularly of the New Armies, had little battle experience—unlike the German units, most of which had spent more than two years at the front. There was also an underlying communication deficit among the high command, the field commanders, and the officers in assault formations. The traditional centralized chains of command forced officers in the frontline to keep reporting back to their superiors, who, being some distance away, seldom appreciated the situation on the ground. The asymmetry between weapons systems and communications was plain to see: heavy artillery fire regularly interrupted telephone connections, and the burgee or flare link between officers in no-man's-land and artillery positions in the rear scarcely functioned in a pitched battle. Such communication was essential, however, if infantry advances were to dovetail with artillery fire.

The plans envisaged that the infantry would attack behind a wall of fire, ideally laid down 100 meters in front of the advancing troops. This was supposed to take out the enemy defenders, so that one's own men could leap directly into their trenches. In practice, however, the wall of fire proved to be inflexible. Detailed plans prescribed that the artillery would automatically push the wall forward every two minutes, without taking into account the true situation of the advancing infantry. Many units took longer to get through the plowed-up no-man's-land filled with shell craters, and so they fell ever farther behind the wall of fire. This growing distance meant that the impact of artillery on the enemy defenses gradually fizzled out. In the end, the preliminary bombardment also proved inadequate: it was spread over too wide an area encompassing three trench systems; it involved too many shrapnel shells and too few heavy guns; and many of the shells were duds. Consequently, far more of the heavily fortified German trenches and dugouts—some 10 to 12 meters deep in the chalky soil—remained intact than the Allied planners had anticipated. Finally, the British supply and transport system was incapable of supporting attacks for a long period of time. This made the British position extremely vulnerable to counterattack.[60]

In essence, the first day on the Somme confirmed the lesson of earlier battles: well dug-in defenders could withstand the most intense artillery barrage and, even if weakened by effective weapons such as mobile machine guns, could hold out against numerically far superior enemy forces.[61] At any event, the heavy German casualties did not lead to a collapse of the defenses. Reinforcements could be speedily brought up via a complex seven-tier system of rear positions measuring more than eight kilometers across. British hopes of a breakthrough gave way to the experience of huge casualties: on July 1, 1916 the BEF lost 57,470 men, including 19,240 dead, against German losses of roughly 8,000 men—a ratio of 7:1. The first of July thus became by far the bloodiest day in the history of the British army, its losses then being higher than in the whole of the Crimean, Boer, and Korean Wars combined.[62] The toll was particularly great in certain Empire units: the First Newfoundland Battalion at Beaumont-Hamel lost 91 percent of its strength—26 officers and 658 men—in the space of 40 minutes. The 36th Ulster Division also suffered enormous casualties during the capture of the so-called Schwaben Redoubt near Thiepval—a prize that had to be given up the same day because nearby units were unable to maintain contact. In the first two days of the offensive, the 36th Division lost more than 2,000 men. The death of so many northern Irish unionists acquired huge symbolic significance, vividly contrasting with the resistance to conscription in parts of southern Ireland and the Easter Rising by radical republicans in Dublin in April of the same year. The experience of war, with its radical language of sacrifice, thus deepened the opposition between the competing nationalisms of the loyalist pro-British unionists and the Irish Republicans, with long-term consequences for the different cultures after the war.[63] The mutual recrimination and instrumentalization disguised the fact that the great majority of Irish soldiers on the western front deplored the Easter Rising and continued to fight loyally in their various units.[64]

French attacks to the south were more successful than the British operations on the Somme. They showed that the thinking of Haig and Rawlinson was not completely unrealistic, even if it took little account of the robust German defenses and the inexperience of Kitchener's New Armies. The problem was not only faulty tactics but, most important, inflexible operational methods.[65] Successful local breaches in the defenses, as well as the large number of Germans taken prisoner, indicated that French sectors of the front were applying important lessons from Verdun. They directed artillery fire only at the first German complex of trenches, and small groups and columns were deployed to exploit the peculiarities of the terrain. The French forces were also helped by the fact that the German positions were less robust there than farther north. Although a major breakthrough on the Somme never happened, the battle continued for some time. The main aim of British commanders was to wear down the enemy and to inflict heavy casualties that precluded any counteroffensive. By mid-July the British forces had lost another 25,000 men. Even though German casualties were still less than half of the British, by July 10 the German Second Army had lost 40,200 dead, wounded, and captive. This was significantly more than during the first 10 days of the Battle of Verdun, and it forced the withdrawal of more and more units from there to the Somme.

From mid-July on, the two battles were thus intermeshed with each other—a development that reached a climax with Falkenhayn's decision on September 11, 1916, to pass over to a "strictly defensive posture" at Verdun.[66] In this situation, Haig calculated that fresh attacks could force the Germans to transfer more troops, and he prolonged the battle with many individual operations such as the one at Fromelles in Artois, where Australian troops were sent into action; their losses there were even higher than at Gallipoli.[67]

The Somme battle demonstrated the increasing importance of the Empire troops: nine of fifty-three divisions came from the Dominions: four each from Australia and Canada and one from New Zealand. Furthermore, there was one South African and one Newfoundland brigade within the British divisions.[68] The persistently high toll continued to have an impact far away in the home societies of the Empire, giving a decisive impetus to a new stage of nation-building; the war casualties made them seem more than mere auxiliaries in the service of London.

Beginning in September 1916, the Allies stepped up their efforts to address with new technologies the dilemma of positional deadlock.[69] On September 15, armored vehicles with the cover name "tanks" (after a British prototype reminiscent of a water tank) were deployed for the first time. Conceived as "land battleships," combining armor, firepower, and mobility, they were intended to facilitate breakthroughs of the enemy front and to eliminate artillery positions to the rear; infantry or cavalry alone could not fulfill these functions, because of the effectiveness of long-range and defensive weapons. The British had been intensively developing armored vehicles since 1915 and the French since the middle of 1916, whether fitted with guns to clear the way for infantry or with machine guns for close combat. Whereas the Entente powers, after the experiences of 1916, opted decisively for new weapons—Britain and France had produced 1,865 and 3,977 tanks, respectively, by the end of the war— the German military leadership turned to modified infantry tactics with the development of storm troops and storm battalions. The Somme experience reinforced German skepticism about the new armored weapons: because of technical problems, only nine of the forty-nine tanks shipped to France made it across no-man's-land. The OHL armaments program focused more on submarines than armor. Only in 1917 did there exist a German armored combat vehicle ready for production, the A7V, and in 1918 there were still only twenty of them capable of deployment.

Technical problems notwithstanding, British tanks helped to make some territorial gains on the Somme that previous weaponry had not been able to achieve, even though the vehicles were not concentrated in battle formations, as experts recommended, but used on an ad hoc basis for infantry support. The fighting at Cambrai in November 1917 began to show the potential of the new tanks to revolutionize the battlefield. They were the main factor in the Allied tactical successes of Summer 1918, particularly the offensives near Soissons and Amiens in July and August.[70]

The use of aircraft also reflected the quest for technological answers to the problem of positional warfare. On the one hand, they were intended to combine mobility, reconnaissance, and spatial mastery; the Albatros D2 did succeed in restoring German air superiority, following on from the decisive breakthrough of the Fokker machines in the synchronization of propellers and machine guns in Fall 1915. As with the first tanks, the main function of aircraft was to support ground troops and to identify enemy artillery positions and supply lines, but they did not play a major role in combat operations on the ground. At the Somme the German air force improved the quality of reconnaissance, enabling the artillery to operate more precisely and, beginning in the fall, to take much of the sting out of Allied offensives.

But the significance of the air force went far beyond these functions. Consciously encouraged and supported by the military leadership, it occupied an important place in the patriotic media campaign, where pilots fought an idealized war that had little in common with the bloody reality of the airborne hunt and chase. As the enemy became invisible to millions of soldiers and the killing more anonymous on both sides, as it became more and more difficult to tell individual soldiers apart, and as machines and materiel increasingly dominated the battlefield, the contrast with fighter pilots could be staged all the more effectively. The press focused on them as individual personalities, as brave warriors with a sense of fair play, as chivalrous heroes showing respect for the enemy. This vision harkened back to the era of free movement and the duel played by the rules—a reality that no longer existed either on the ground or in the air. Flying in an Albatros D2 over the Somme battlefield, Manfred von Richthofen notched up the first of the eighty kills he would achieve before his own death in April 1918; he was the archetypal media hero, decorated with the Pour le Mérite order, christened the "Red Baron" because of the color of his airplane, and held up as a model to young people in the book *Der rote Kampfflieger* (1917).[71] Richthofen personified the war—in his spirit of adventure, his constant heroism and daredevilry, his martial prowess and technical skill fighting nature and the enemy, and his challenge to the limits of the possible. This imagined war contained both forward-looking and backward-looking elements: a fascination with modern technology, but also the ideal of chivalry and a sports-like measurement of individual courage and expertise.[72]

But this celebration of individual heroes and the nexus of chivalry and self-sacrifice, so often present in picture postcards, could not alter the sobering balance sheet of the great battles on the western front.[73] After the Battle of the Somme, the mismatch between spatial gains and casualty figures could hardly be overlooked. In approximately 150 days of fighting, the Germans lost 10 kilometers of a front stretching 35 kilometers across, but their withdrawal to the heavily fortified Siegfried Line in early 1917 allowed them to stabilize the whole front. British and Empire forces lost 420,000 men, the French 204,000; altogether the Allies suffered 146,000 dead or missing. On the other side, German losses amounted to 465,000 men, including 164,000 dead and missing.[74]

With total losses of 1.1 million on the Somme and a half-million at Verdun, a reassessment became all the more urgent. Controversies over the role of the British commander in chief, Douglas Haig, therefore involve more than a biographical evaluation of a leading military player of the world war. Ultimately what was and is at stake is the verdict on the great battles of 1916 on the western front and the purpose of the casualties they entailed. Soon after the war was over, public opinion became more critical of the performance of British commanders, and Haig in particular was accused of sticking too long to conventional offensive tactics in the face of enormous losses. The image of "lions led by donkeys" contrasted the bravery of ordinary soldiers with the incompetence of senior officers.[75]

The career of Basil Liddell Hart was symptomatic of the changing contemporary judgments and the disillusionment of many frontline officers. Serving as a captain on the Somme, Liddell Hart wrote this in a letter during the battle: "Terrible though this carnage is, it has got to be gone through with. I endeavor to behave as an Englishman and a Christian. Somehow I would not have liked to have missed it. It is a wonderful experience."[76] After the war, however, Liddell Hart became one of the harshest critics of the top brass. Like many of his generation, he was disappointed with the generals'

OPPOSITE: Adventure, technology, and chivalry: the pilot as idealized war hero—German poster appealing for war loans

Und Ihr?

Zeichnet Kriegsanleihe

limited intelligence and analytic incompetence, and with the petty intrigue, disloyalty, and dishonesty of the memoirs of leading officers that neglected both the achievements of ordinary soldiers and the responsibility of commanders. Access later to new information about the battle on the Somme made Liddell Hart even more critical in his judgment. As a "captain instructing the generals," he published his own history of the war in 1934, in which he accused General Haig of having no feel for the reality of the battlefield. Weeks of preliminary bombardment had eliminated any surprise effect, while disputes among commanders had limited the effectiveness of the artillery. The Somme battle had been "an object-lesson in supreme negation"; Haig himself had stuck to his position with "bulldog tenacity," underestimating the enemy and happily going on with the battle. The infantry on both sides had been used up as "cannon fodder for the artillery."[77]

The main accusation, then, was that Haig believed for too long in the possibility of a breakthrough, whereas from mid-1916 most senior officers preferred Rawlinson's "step by step" tactics. After the experiences of 1915 and 1916, most commanders wanted to pursue limited objectives, with the deployment of new weapons such as the tank. According to the so-called all arms doctrine, moreover, specialists from infantry and sapper units, armed with machine guns, flamethrowers, light mortars, and mobile technology, were supposed to work together to clear obstacles under the protection of heavy artillery fire. Only close cooperation among all sections of the army, which did not exhaust the infantry too quickly, promised to bring lasting results.[78] Haig, for his part, clung to the possibility of a frontal breakthrough right up to the third Flanders battle in 1917. There was more than a little denial of reality in this.

The Somme, however, was not a defeat for the Allies; in fact, it took some of the pressure off the French in Verdun and, by inflicting heavy casualties, barred any German initiative for further attacks. Haig's responsibility for the high Allied losses on the Somme—comparable to that of German commanders for their losses in Verdun—lay in his pursuit of overambitious, unrealistic objectives and his neglect of the specific conditions on the ground. Other factors were the poor coordination among fighting units and branches of the armed forces, and inadequate time management in the face of geographical peculiarities and climatic conditions.[79]

Haig's supporters argued quite differently, emphasizing his achievement as an "educated soldier." In their view, he had certainly not been a cold, unfeeling technician of war, installed at the rear with no understanding of the consequences of his decisions for hundreds of thousands of soldiers. He had been attentive to their concerns during the war and after 1918 had supported adequate care for veterans and war invalids. The large turnout at his funeral, including numerous ex-soldiers, contradicted the idea that his men had been passive victims of incompetent commanders.[80] Some revisionist interpretations go even further, attributing a definite logic to Haig's tactical choices and insisting that in the long run they helped to decide the war. The basis for this argument is Haig's own formulations after the Battle of the Somme. He had to admit that the original objectives had not been achieved. On November 21, 1916, however, his main focus was not on territorial gains, but on irreversible weakening of the German forces. Nor did he reflect on the discrepancy between high casualties and meager advances: "We must expect a very severe struggle and our utmost efforts will be required, but the results of the Somme battle fully justify confidence in our ability to master the enemy's powers of resistance. It is true that the amount of ground gained is not great. That is nothing. The strength of the defenses overcome and the effect on the defenders are the real tests. Time after time in the last five months the Allies have driven the enemy, with heavy loss, from the strongest fortifications that his ingenuity could conceive and his unwearying labor could construct. Time and again his counter-attacks have been utterly defeated. If the memory of these experiences should fade during the winter, a few successes by us at the beginning of next year's campaign will bring it back. The full value of these results will become evident in the future."[81]

The revisionist thesis built on this assessment to argue that Haig was the mainstay of the battle of materiel and attrition necessary to weaken the Germans in the long term and that their losses had to be so high that nothing could compensate for them. Such was the logic of the battle and in the end its great success: Haig realized that the German army could be weakened only through a costly campaign to wear it down. This was a legitimate strategy because the war could not be decided on other fronts, in Italy, eastern Europe, and the Balkans or in the Near and Middle East. In this perspective, there were really two battles on the Somme, in which the aim was not to relieve the French at Verdun but to achieve purposive Allied cooperation: the first, beginning in July, was fought with a traditional conception of warfare; the second, beginning in September, was the expression of a modern operational approach.[82]

The verdict on the battles of 1916 depended and still depends on one's perspective and criteria. Measured by the high hopes of the army commanders—Falkenhayn's plan to wear down the enemy as the prelude to a separate peace with Russia or France, or Haig's vision of a frontal breakthrough relaunching a war of movement and putting a final decision in the cards—the German approach collapsed at Verdun and the Franco-British on the Somme. Only after these objectives had gone by the board did Haig, in particular, revert to a different approach. His justification then for the high casualties was not to achieve a decisive breakthrough on the western front, but to wear the enemy down through repeated attacks and to render it incapable of new offensives. Haig himself developed the logic of attrition only after high casualties had thwarted his original idea of a frontal breakthrough and posed the question of how to justify his military action.[83]

If the military relationship of forces and the task of compensating for exorbitant losses were taken as the key problematic, then it was possible to argue after the Somme battle that it had weakened the German offensive capability on the western front. However, in view of the proven effectiveness of defensive tactics, such arguments remained tenuous at the time of the battle and depended on a number of unknowns. They completely left out the course of the war on the eastern front and its conclusion in the winter of 1917 that enabled the Germans to transfer troops to the west.[84] The fact remains that in 1916 it was impossible to predict exactly how much the enemy could be worn down and when that might become a decisive factor in the war. On the British side, Haig had originally associated the battle with far-reaching objectives, which in the end could not be realized. Seen from a post-1918 vantage point, the logic of attrition may offer an explanation for the high casualties, but in 1916 it was by no means clear how things would work out. At any event, the Somme battle finally settled the dispute between "westerners" and "easterners" in Britain: the war against the Central Powers, it was now agreed, could only be decided on the western front, not in the southeastern Mediterranean, the Near East, or Mesopotamia.[85]

Another aspect was more important in the long run: the experiences of Verdun and the Somme triggered some hard thinking in every army about new technologies and battle tactics. The war changed its face. After more than two years, the idea of attack at any price seemed less convincing, because no army could sustain for long the high casualty rates that this implied. Against this background, a start was made on decentralizing command structures, communications, and troop deployment. More attention was given to actual battlefield conditions, weapon effects, and the possibilities for effective defense. War freed itself of nineteenth-century ideas and conceptions: such was the military "difference threshold" that the year 1916 represented for the world war.

This was also apparent in the war at sea, where the German focus shifted in 1916 from battleships to submarines. First, however, in May 1916 came the Battle of Jutland (Skagerrak)—the only really major engagement of the war between the British and German navies. It was essentially over in an hour, and though magnified on both sides for propaganda purposes, it demonstrated the limited significance of a great naval battle between expensive battleships. Indeed, its real importance was its precipitation of a search for alternatives. On the German side, the emphasis fell on submarine warfare.[86] The very fact that the battle of May 1916 took place at all was not the result of extensive planning; rather, the discovery by British radio intelligence of German naval operations against merchant shipping off Skagerrak led to the mobilization of the British battle fleet. This then developed into the greatest sea battle in history up to that time. The Grand Fleet suffered sizable losses: fourteen ships against the German eleven, or 115,025 tons against the German 61,180. The human casualties totaled 6,094 sailors and officers on the British side and 2,551 on the German.[87] The German navy chalked up a noteworthy success, but it changed nothing essential in the relationship of forces between the two fleets.[88] Wilhelm II's reaction was exuberant: "The English fleet has been beaten! The first huge hammerblow has been struck, the aura of English world supremacy has been torn down, the tradition of Trafalgar torn to shreds."[89] Beneath the triumphalist surface, however, the climate in the German navy was beginning to change. The perceived victory over the British foe did not translate into a stable loyalty, and beginning in Summer 1917 the first disturbances broke out in the High Seas Fleet. Not the least reason for these was the promotion policy:

fifteen of the twenty-eight commanders at the Battle of Jutland became rear admirals by the end of the war, but the deck officers who proved their mettle in it were given no comparable recognition. The common experience of the battle did not therefore strengthen cohesion, since the naval command treated the various ranks very differently. Even more important, officers on active duty set themselves apart in the daily routine of life on board, stoking tensions between them and their crews.[90]

The daily round in the navy was fundamentally different from life at the front. Officers had expected that the war at sea would last a long time and, above all, that the battle fleets of Germany and Britain, so present in the public imagination, would play a key role in deciding the war. But there were almost no major assignments until the brief, almost incidental, Battle of Skagerrak. This increased the pressure on officers to justify their actions, not least before crews who often rode at anchor for weeks or months at a time. A few months after Jutland, the German officer Ernst von Weizsäcker noted in his diary entry for September 27, 1916, "Reading about the heavy fighting by the army keeps making me think of how little use the navy is. It sits around idle—and that includes submarines and airships. Its usefulness in the war bears no relation to what is sacrificed for it, in terms of money, political hostility, and concessions in domestic politics."[91]

The lessons of the battle soon gave rise to new strategic conceptions with political implications. The first lesson, the huge importance of reconnaissance, led to efforts to improve radio intelligence and cooperation between surface ships and submarines, as well as coordination with zeppelins and aircraft. But the fundamental problem remained: the role of the flagship in providing tactical leadership for large formations in a narrow space loaded the head of the fleet with enormous responsibility, at a time when he could form only an imperfect judgment of the situation. There was a wide gulf between the effectiveness of weapons and the speed of large battleships, on the one hand, and the possibilities for reconnaissance of enemy ships, on the other. So long as no radar was available, navies could rely on nothing more than visual aids. The inadequate means of communication therefore made operations with large naval forces extremely risky.

On the German side, Admiral Scheer continued after Summer 1916 to regard the large battleship as the "cornerstone of naval power." But he was realistic about the chances of a war at sea against Britain: "With a favorable succession of operations the enemy may be made to suffer severely, although there can be no doubt that even the most successful result from a high sea battle will not compel England to make peace. The disadvantages of our geographical situation as compared with that of the Island Empire and the enemy's vast material superiority cannot be coped with to such a degree as to make us masters of the blockade inflicted on us. . . . A victorious end to the war at not too distant a date can only be looked for by the crushing of English economic life through U-boat action against English commerce. Prompted by the convictions of duty, I earnestly advise Your Majesty to abstain from deciding on too lenient a form of procedure."[92] The German naval command distanced itself from the concept of a "risky fleet," because it feared a major battle with heavy losses.[93] Instead, its focus shifted to submarine warfare.

In March 1916, the civilian government of the Reich was able to get its way again, when submarine action was limited to the context of German naval operations.[94] Otherwise, in accordance with international law, U-boats were to target only armed merchant vessels and to leave passenger ships undisturbed. Amid this controversy Admiral Tirpitz, a forceful proponent of unrestricted submarine warfare, resigned from his position at the Imperial Naval Office.[95] When further incidents and vehement criticism from the United States led to abandonment even of the more limited strategy, the naval command saw it as a sign of government weakness vis-à-vis the main enemy, Great Britain. This tightly circumscribed any political opposition on the government side to the eventual resumption of unrestricted submarine warfare in February 1917.[96]

In Spring 1916, it became clear that the naval command was using the public to put pressure on the chancellor, whom it saw as weak and pliable, and therefore as an obstacle to all-out war against Britain. In mid-March, a memorandum drawing on information from the navy and pushing for a victorious peace with annexations was sent to members of the Reichstag, with more than 90,000 signatures including those of the historian Dietrich Schäfer and various right-wing national-conservative politicians, professors, and journalists. Distributed in 750,000 copies, this document clearly showed how the nationalist Right was aggressively using the issue of submarine warfare and the general intensification of the war to turn the people's mood against the chancellor.[97]

2. SPACE AND MOVEMENT
The Price of Expansion into Southeastern Europe and the Near East

Anyone who visits the battlefields on the Meuse and the Somme today finds a remembrance landscape with numerous military cemeteries, monuments, and museums. The fallen are present on the former western front as they are back home, in the white crosses, the war memorial inscriptions, the lists of the dead. Things look very different in eastern Europe, where there appear to be no memorial sites for soldiers killed in 1916 on the front between Lake Narach and Galicia, and except for experts hardly anyone knows where the battles took place. The "total battles" of Verdun and the Somme have come to symbolize the futility of the battles of materiel, and their presence in the remembrance cultures of western Europe obscures the proportions of the world war as a whole. For however high the losses of the German, French, British, and Empire forces on the western front, the casualty rates there were considerably lower than in many armies of eastern and southeastern Europe. Thus, the share of dead, wounded, and missing in Serbia and Romania clearly exceeded those in Canada, Australia, and New Zealand. Serbia had a relatively large army, 700,000 strong, but 35 percent of its forces died or were wounded or missing—a casualty rate twice as high as the armies of the western Allies and significantly more than the 20 percent or so of the armies in the Ottoman Empire, Romania, and Bulgaria. By this criterion, Serbia was ahead of France, Germany, and Australia, and also of a further group consisting of New Zealand, Austria-Hungary, Great Britain, Belgium, Italy, and Canada.[98]

The reasons why casualty ratios and retrospective perceptions vary so much and the western front receives incomparably more attention than the eastern front have to do primarily with the differential processing of war memories after 1918, the differential weight of the war in national remembrance cultures, and the ways in which the effects of the war persisted in in the postwar societies themselves. This in turn reflects the new political order established after the war in eastern, east central, and southeastern Europe. In countries where the First World War appeared mainly as a prelude to the battles for national independence, the fallen soldiers who had fought under the command of the multiethnic empires were given little attention.

Their war service was not congruent with the borders and loyalties of the new nation-states that came into being in the aftermath of the world war.

Another factor appeared in the course of 1916. Whereas the societies of western Europe associated the high losses on the western front with the comparatively limited spaces of military action there, the huge casualties in eastern Europe somehow got lost in the long front stretching from the Baltic to the eastern Mediterranean and the Black Sea, large sections of which, unlike on the western front, witnessed offensives, breakthroughs, and territorial gains. In 1916 there were no actual sites in the east comparable to Verdun or the Somme that might have compressed the violence and casualties in people's memory. The naming of offensives by army or geographical region (Galicia, for example), rather than by an individual battle, disguised the scale of casualties, which was part of the perception of the western front during the war itself and shaped the national remembrance cultures when it was over. Wartime experiences retained a media presence in western Europe thanks to veterans associations, monuments, and days of remembrance, while the symbolically compressed image of the frontline combatant at Verdun or the Somme lent itself to political instrumentalization. By contrast, large parts of eastern and southeastern Europe formed a crisis zone even after 1918, the collapse of the multiethnic empires often being followed by civil wars and a difficult process of state-building. Yet to regard the world war until 1917 as a mere prelude to civil and national wars is to devalue the war service of many soldiers in the multiethnic armies of Austria-Hungary, Russia, and the Ottoman Empire.

This makes it all the more important to factor in military events other than the great western battles in the third year of the war. By the end of 1915, Austria-Hungary had suffered enormous losses in dead, wounded, missing, and captive soldiers. This reflected the military efforts on various fronts against Russia and Italy and in the Balkans, but the situation in 1916 also demonstrated how limited the territorial gains had been on all these fronts— especially in view of the fact that German troops had achieved the key breakthroughs against Russia in Summer 1915. Still, the AOK under Conrad von Hötzendorf continued to look to fresh offensives, partly to demonstrate the autonomy of the Austro-Hungarian army on important strategic issues. By March 1916 its strength was back to 2.3 million men, including 900,000 ready for action. Isolated successes on the southeastern front, particularly the conquest of Montenegro, reinforced the determination of the army command to attack in South Tyrol and break through the Italian front in the direction of Padua and Venice, relieving the threatened positions on the Isonzo and forcing Italy out of the war. The German OHL was little informed about these details, and it refused to withdraw German troops from Verdun to support action on a front that Falkenhayn did not see as crucial to the outcome of the war. It was therefore mainly Austro-Hungarian troops from Galicia who were transferred to the Tyrol. Tensions within the AOK, as well as the geographically favorable position of the Italian defenders, caused the offensive to break down in May and June 1916; the Austro-Hungarian commanders had learned nothing from previous experiences about the superiority of defensive operations. Artillery stocks proved inadequate and provisions were held up, and large parts of the Imperial forces became unfit for service because of various illnesses. The long-term gain of 19 kilometers of territory was bought at the high cost of 43,000 men, against the loss of 76,000 Italians. A major breakthrough had failed to materialize. War production companies in Austria-Hungary were able to boost output, and for a long time the drafting of millions of soldiers made up for the casualties, but the tactical mobility of large units did not improve. Even when artillery preparations and infantry attacks were effectively coordinated, as in 1915 at Tarnów and Gorlice or in 1916 during the Brusilov offensive, any breakthroughs did not lead to a decision in the war.[99]

The failure of the Austro-Hungarian offensive in the South Tyrol had a demoralizing effect on large numbers of officers and men and weakened the front against Russia.[100] The AOK's insistence on autonomy made it seem less and less credible, because offensive operations increasingly overstretched its forces. When the great Russian offensive under General Brusilov got underway in Galicia in early June 1916, it encountered a weakened enemy that was soon on the brink of catastrophe. According to Allied agreements, Russian offensives were supposed to take pressure off the French and Italian fronts at Verdun and in the South Tyrol. Mobilization of Russia's war economy meant that its forces were better equipped than in 1915, and another aim of the Brusilov offensive was to improve the public reputation of the Russian army, which had taken a hard knock after the major retreat forced on it the previous year.

Nevertheless, Russian troops suffered a major defeat at Lake Narach in northern Belarus. The field commanders did concentrate in principle on just one point of the German front, but otherwise they repeated the methods of earlier battles, overestimating the effects of the Russian artillery and underestimating the capacity of the defenders to withstand drumfire in well-fortified bunkers and dugouts. Despite adequate munitions and a 3:1 superiority in artillery, 350,000 Russian soldiers were unable to achieve a breakthrough against 75,000 men on the German side. While the artillery neither coordinated properly with the infantry nor concentrated its fire effectively, some commanders proceeded to apply the traditional tactics of attack. The army group under General Pleshkov sent classical infantry lines across a no-man's-land more than 1,000–2,000 meters wide that offered no cover, while NCOs took up position behind them and fired on stragglers or fleeing soldiers. Repeated attacks on the same sections of front resulted in losses as high as 100,000 men, against 20,000 on the German side. Coming as it did after the experiences of the previous year and the hopes fueled by Russian war propaganda, the battle shattered the prestige and self-confidence of the old officer elite, most of whom afterward argued against any further offensive.[101]

This situation gave General Brusilov, the commander of the southwestern Galicia front, an opportunity to propose an offensive plan of his own against the Austro-Hungarian forces—especially as French and Italian pressure on the Tsar had been increasing since the beginning of the Tyrol offensive.[102] Although the war economy was in better shape than in 1914 and 1915, the supply of munitions to the Russian army remained precarious. In fact, only one-third of the artillery and infantry munitions were produced in Russia; the rest had to be imported with considerable difficulty and then transported west on long routes to the front. Brusilov decided to attack, even though part of the Russian army had only Japanese guns and captured weapons, and the artillery was largely firing French and British gas shells. The early success of the offensive, which began on June 4, 1916, was due to the fact that the commanders did not repeat the egregious errors of earlier offensives. Instead, they transferred innovative French attack tactics to the eastern theater. It became clear under what conditions a frontal breakthrough and a return to war of movement were possible, even if the attackers did not have numerical superiority and their artillery was distinctly inferior. Brusilov relied on a multiple surprise effect, planning huge explosions at the enemy's most advanced positions and bringing his own assault troops as close as possible to the enemy tunnels and trenches, thereby narrowing the no-man's-land that needed to be crossed. A short, intense bombardment, directed mainly at machine-gun positions, and a number of feint attacks across the width of the front would then make it impossible for the enemy to send replacements to the critical points. Another reason for the success of the offensive was that the Austro-Hungarian commanders no longer believed the Russians capable of staging one and had withdrawn troops from Galicia for their own offensive in the Tyrol.

In fact, the Brusilov offensive led to Russia's greatest breakthrough of the war and marked the Allies' most significant territorial gain since August 1914. Russian troops advanced as much as 75 kilometers and captured Czernowitz, inflicting particularly heavy losses on the Austro-Hungarian army. The Seventh Army under General Pflanzer-Baltin lost 57 percent of its combat strength and was driven back to the foothills of the Carpathians; the First Viennese Regiment even lost 77 percent, so that it could no longer be considered a combat unit. More important still, the large numbers of prisoners and deserters implied that the army's motivation and cohesion were beginning to crumble. Although another Russian push seemed unlikely—the Austro-Hungarian headquarters at Teschen was 350 kilometers away—there were panicky reactions within the AOK.[103] On the home front, the hunt was on for scapegoats, and the question of the loyalty of the multiethnic troop formations returned to the fore. Josef Redlich, a professor of constitutional and administrative law and member of the Moravian parliament and the Imperial Council in Vienna, noted on June 14, 1916, "People in Teschen are very 'downhearted.' The axed Archduke Josef Ferdinand is shifting the blame onto the high command, saying that he vainly tried to warn them that his forces were not sufficiently numerous. Many Ruthenians and Poles are said to have crossed sides. The Russians have cleverly used the troop fraternization often reported last winter on the eastern front!"[104]

In these circumstances, Conrad von Hötzendorf was finally compelled to ask for German support. After the experience of Summer 1915, he was increasingly skeptical about the future of the Dual Monarchy. But now he had to accept not only German dominance but the fact that the war would last until the Germans were victorious or declared a ceasefire;[105] meanwhile, German commanders were put in place right down to the battalion level. Although Austro-Hungarian generals remained at the top to conceal what was going on, Germans took over the actual reins of command. Hans von Seeckt, for example, who, together with August von Mackensen, had been the brains behind the breakthroughs of Summer 1915, became chief of staff and therefore de facto commander of the Seventh Army, though still formally subordinate to Pflanzer-Baltin.

In July 1916, then, things were becoming critical for the Central Powers, as the fighting became more intense in the three zones of Verdun, the Somme, and Galicia. Their forces on the eastern front were numerically inferior, 421,000 men against the enemy's 711,000, but they were able to stabilize the situation there, while Brusilov, after the Russian breakthroughs, had to fear German counterattacks on his weakened northern flank. At this point he changed tactics and again wagered on high-cost attacks against sections of the enemy front where close coordination between infantry and artillery was lacking. However, the Russian offensive began to falter in August 1916 and, because of its fast-rising casualties (by then significantly higher than those of the Central Powers), came to a complete standstill in September. The high number of desertions on the Russian side illustrated the extent to which its troops were exhausted.

With their high casualties and above all their structural, military, and political consequences, the four months of battles on the eastern front had a much deeper impact on the course of the war than did Verdun and the Somme, even though those battles commanded much greater attention at the time and have continued to do so until the present day. The Russian offensive led to breakthroughs in the enemy front and territorial gains that would have been decisive on the western front, and in its opening phase it highlighted what could be achieved through rigorous tactical adaptations to the conditions of the war. The largest Allied gains of the war so far must, however, be set against losses from which neither Russia nor Austria-Hungary was able to recover. Although the estimates for all sides vary, the Russian forces probably lost something close to a million dead, wounded, missing, and captive, plus only 58,000 through desertion. Austria-Hungary lost 600,000

men, including roughly 400,000 prisoners (200,000 by mid-June); this practically halved the armed forces of the Dual Monarchy in this theater of the
war. German losses were as high as 350,000 men.[106] This gives a casualty
total well above two million for the fighting on the eastern front between
March and September (including the battle on Lake Narach), compared with
approximately 1.6 million for the more protracted Verdun and Somme battles
together. But in the collective memory of east European societies, those two
million have been eclipsed by the victims of subsequent violence, from the
October Revolution of 1917 and the ensuing civil war through the Stalinist
terror of the 1930s and the Second World War to the early years of the 1950s.

This comparison of casualty figures highlights the fact that this period of
fighting on the eastern, rather than the western, front showed the first signs
of the mechanism that would eventually shape the final phase of the world
war. The key factor in this denouement was not battlefield breakthroughs,
since all territorial gains remained provisional and were associated with
losses too high to be sustained for long, but rather the wearing down of the
enemy's forces. At the end of this process, the exhaustion was so great that
military structures and the legitimacy of political systems began to crumble.
This is precisely what made the events on the eastern front between March
and September 1916 a decisive watershed for the Habsburg monarchy as well
as the tsarist empire. In France, Britain, and Germany, too, the enormous
losses opened up breaks in the wartime consensus and doubts about the conduct of the war. But at first these remained at the level of isolated expressions
of views. Although the discontent was quite diffuse, not yet representing
a substantive challenge to cohesion in the army, it was becoming apparent
on both the Russian and Austro-Hungarian side that the ties holding entire
units together were beginning to loosen.

In late 1916, casualty tolls, military setbacks, and a demoralizing exhaustion were widening the gap in Russia between the mass of peasant-soldiers
and their officers, who mostly came from aristocratic families or the urban
upper classes. In many places, officers found themselves physically threatened and reacted with paralysis. In Austria-Hungary, the decline in the power
of Conrad von Hötzendorf and the AOK in general accelerated after Summer
1916, corresponding to the subordination of the political leadership of the
Dual Monarchy to the German OHL. North of Lemberg (Lvov), German

officers took command of Austro-Hungarian units, while to the south they only nominally operated under the leadership of Archduke Karl, with von Seeckt in de facto control. All future operations had to be agreed to by the German commanders. The German Kaiser now functioned as supreme commander of all the armed forces, while Franz Joseph had to be consulted only on matters affecting the territorial integrity of the Dual Monarchy. The relative weight of the two partners in the alliance was evident from the fact that around this time Germany had to shore up Austria-Hungary to the tune of 100 million reichsmarks a month.[107] From late Summer 1916, the two armies of the Central Powers became effectively coordinated for the first time, albeit under German dominance. In contrast to the period between 1914 and Summer 1916, there was now a central command of all troops serving in the Central Powers; this would be one of the reasons for the military successes on the eastern front and against Italy from then until 1918.[108]

In southeastern Europe, too, the war entered a new phase in Summer 1916. As in the cases of Italy and Bulgaria, the entry of Romania into the war in 1916 and of Greece in 1917 reflected far-reaching ambitions at the cost of neighboring states. Many politicians looked forward to the completion of nation-building processes and the expansion of their own nation-states, and this gave rise to an aggressive war nationalism geared to territorial gains. Such tendencies were fueled by competing offers from the Central Powers and the Entente. Romanian and Greek leaders feared that neutrality would make them seem weak in the game of power politics and put them at a disadvantage, if not exclude them altogether, when it came to redrawing the map of the region.

Romania, which had developed as an independent state after the Crimean War out of the two Danube principalities of Moldavia and Walachia, had not taken part in the two Balkan conflicts after the turn of the century, nor joined the Balkan League in 1912 against the Ottoman Empire. Nevertheless, it had made territorial gains at Bulgaria's expense in southern Dobruja during the Second Balkan War. Its foreign policy orientation may be compared to the developments in Italy. Its membership in the Triple Alliance, which it joined in 1883, had become significantly weaker, and on the outbreak of war in August 1914 it too, like Italy, had declared itself neutral. Although King Carol I (himself related to the Prussian Hohenzollerns) favored a rapprochement with the Central Powers, Prime Minister Ion Brătianu forced through his policy of wait-and-see neutrality.[109] As early as October 1914 he was pursuing a "bargaining" strategy similar to that of the Italian and Bulgarian governments. While Germany and Austria-Hungary offered only Russian Bessarabia and held out the prospect of economic interdependence with the Central Powers, the Allies' promises fired the vision of a Greater Romania.[110] The anti-Habsburg mood in the country, stronger since Vienna had supported Bulgaria in the Balkan wars, had been directed since 1914 mainly against the policies of the Hungarian prime minister Tisza. The Bremen merchant Ludwig Roselius could not alter this hostility with an extensive German propaganda campaign, costing more than forty million marks by 1916, to ensure that Romania at least remained neutral.[111]

The Allies' proposal was that Romania should gain from Austria-Hungary the territory of Transylvania plus Banat and parts of Bukovina, but other considerations also came into play in the situation in Summer 1916. The contemporaneous Allied intervention in Greece showed the dangers of continuing with a course of uncertain neutrality. The government feared losing Dobruja to Bulgaria, which had joined the war in 1915 on the side of the Central Powers, and the successful Russian offensive seemed to make this a favorable moment for Romania to make the leap. So it was that the Allies got their way in August 1916 with the Treaty of Bucharest. In the hope of carving out a Greater Romania at the expense of Bulgaria and Austria-Hungary, Romania joined the war on August 27, creating another front for the Dual Monarchy, more than 600 kilometers long, in addition to the Russian and Italian ones.

The crisis of Summer 1916, featuring the Verdun and Somme battles, the Brusilov offensive, and the failed Austro-Hungarian offensives against Italy in the Alps, was exacerbated by Romania's entry into the war. As head of the German OHL, Falkenhayn had not expected such a step at that point in time—and this became the immediate reason for his replacement.[112] The Austro-Hungarian military now experienced its third crisis, on top of its problems in the South Tyrol and the disastrous Russian breakthroughs in the Carpathians. For the second time in just three months, the Dual Monarchy was forced to turn urgently to Germany for help. After Falkenhayn had been removed and given a field command in the war against Romania, the appointment of the Third OHL under Hindenburg and Ludendorff and the establishment of a central command raised the clout of the Central Powers in southeastern Europe.

Romanian forces scored initial successes with the capture of Hermannstadt (Sibiu) and Kronstadt (Braşov). They were numerically superior, as the needs of other fronts compelled the Central Powers to keep redistributing their troops. Yet the Romanian attack ended in a major defeat. In contrast to the Serbian and Bulgarian armies, the Romanians could not draw on experience gained in the Balkan wars of 1912–1913. Poor transport infrastructure also created supply problems, and after the Brusilov offensive eased off, the Central Powers were able to redeploy for a counteroffensive on the Romanian front. Under Falkenhayn's command in Transylvania and Mackensen's in Dobruja, they pushed the Romanians back into their heartlands. The centralized command structure of the Central Powers was now proving highly successful for a strongly multiethnic army including units from all their allies; 46 percent of troops belonged to units from Austria-Hungary, 32 percent from Bulgaria and the Ottoman Empire, and only 22 percent from Germany. At the beginning of December 1916, German troops occupied Bucharest, in a campaign fought in the shadow of the Russian summer offensive and again involving high numbers of casualties. Of the 750,000 men in the Romanian army, 163,000 were killed or wounded and 147,000 taken prisoner. But the country did not capitulate. In 1917, with the rural population mobilized by promises of land reform, it even managed to halt the Central Powers' offensive for a short time, before Russia's exit from the war and its internal political situation forced Romania to agree to a ceasefire in November 1917.[113]

In Summer and Fall 1916, a turning point in the war was shaping up in east central and southeastern Europe. While the Austro-Hungarian military lost its capacity for independent operations because of high casualty rates, its de facto subordination to German commanders improved coordination between the Central Powers. Russia's military and political leadership faced a new challenge, now that the Brusilov offensive and Romania's entry into the war had lengthened the front in southeastern Europe by more than 300 kilometers. Large sections of the Russian elites had always regarded with great skepticism the idea of a common struggle alongside the Romanians, although the alliance contained a great strategic potential for a decisive blow against Austria-Hungary. On the Romanian side, often critical attitudes to

Russia went back a long way. When nearly a million Russian soldiers retreated into the Moldavian enclave, it was feared that this would put a huge burden on the population and lead to the imposition of an occupation regime.[114] For the Russian leadership, an invasion of Ukraine by the Central Powers was looming large, with its own exhausted troops distributed along a wider front than before. From early October 1916 mutinies broke out on a large scale, and the cohesion of the Russian army began to crumble as tensions between officers and men turned into open protests. This process not only heralded the end of the tsarist army but also had a direct impact on the already volatile internal political situation.[115]

A special situation developed in Greece in Summer 1916. Unlike in Romania, the dispute over possible entry into the war pitted two conceptions of nation-building and two ideological camps against each other. A civil war was looming in the shadow of the great war, a "war within the war" that would have long-term consequences for the political polarization and instability of the country later in the twentieth century. Massive Allied pressure, going as far as military intervention and the establishment of a de facto occupation regime, contributed decisively to this constellation. The world war blurred the boundaries between "internal" and "external" and, in a short span of time, fundamentally altered the room for maneuver available to politicians.[116] King Constantine (a brother-in-law of the German Kaiser and commander in chief of the Greek army) and the future dictator Ioannis Metaxas favored a policy of benevolent neutrality toward the Central Powers. The camp associated with those two men advocated a monarchic-oligarchic order and a romantically glorified nation; Greece, in line with the ideal of antiquity, was not to stretch beyond the frontiers of the nation-state that had emerged from the Balkan wars. On the other side, Prime Minister Eleftherios Venizelos pursued the vision of a Greater Greece, comparable to the ambitions of the Romanian government and the Italian interventionists in 1915. Fear of being passed over in a future carve-up fanned this variant of irredentist nationalism, whose vision of a Greater Greece, spread over two continents and five seas, involved the liberation of territories hitherto excluded from the nation-building process.[117] This position was mainly supported by the bourgeois-liberal elites, who favored an orientation to the Allies and especially Britain.

Since the outbreak of war in 1914, the Allies and the Central Powers had competed for Greece's support, but their rival promises had had quite contradictory effects. When the Treaty of London of 1915, concluded in the wake of the Ottoman entry into the war, held out the prospect of extensive territorial gains for Italy in Asia Minor, the champions of a Greater Greece feared that this would weaken their position and dash their hopes for a land grab at the expense of the Ottoman Empire. In September 1915, after the pro-monarch camp clashed with the prime minister and a majority of parliament over whether to join the war in alliance with Serbia against Bulgaria, Entente troops landed at Salonica (Thessaloniki). Originally opened after the Gallipoli debacle to stabilize Serbia and to weaken Austria-Hungary, the Salonica front had lost much of its significance for the Allies after the collapse of Serbia at the end of 1915. But now Greek leaders leaning toward the Central Powers found themselves confronted with what amounted to an occupation regime, which often directly intervened in Greece's internal conflicts and placed its sovereignty in question.[118]

The crisis escalated in August 1916 when the monarchist government wanted to hand Greek troops over to Germany and Bulgaria. Officers and supporters of Venizelos staged a putsch, and Venizelos himself, dismissed by the king, formed an alternative government against a backdrop of mounting British and French pressure. In November, Allied troops landed at the Athenian port of Piraeus to disarm the monarchists—an intervention that, together with the naval shelling of Athens, accelerated the drift to civil war. After large parts of the country had been occupied, King Constantine abdicated in June 1917, Venizelos took over again as prime minister, and a pro-Allied parliamentary majority decided at the end of the year to join the war against the Central Powers.[119] This assured Greece of a say at the peace negotiations, where it was awarded territory in Thrace and Asia Minor from the legacy of the Ottoman Empire.[120] But the vision of a Greater Greek nation-state ended in catastrophe in 1922, when the new Turkish state under Mustafa Kemal succeeded by force of arms in revising the terms of the Treaty of Sèvres. This outcome deepened the ideological division within Greece, perpetuating it late into the twentieth century.[121] The post-1918 reversal of perceived victory into military defeat poisoned the internal political climate for decades to come and became a major handicap for the Greek nation-state.

Contrary to the expectations of nearly all military observers after the Ottoman Empire joined the war on the side of the Central Powers, its armed forces held their own at Gallipoli and maintained the blockade of the Black Sea. But it was not only in the Dardanelles that their defensive operations blossomed into remarkable successes. In Mesopotamia, they initially halted and bottled up a British-Indian expeditionary corps, forcing a whole division to surrender in late April 1916 at Kut al-Amara south of Baghdad. More than 13,000 men were taken prisoner.[122]

Thus, the situation remained precarious for the Allies in the Near and Middle East and the southern Mediterranean, especially as the broken supply lines through the straits continued to create difficulties for Russia. Nevertheless, the British and French did not originally plan to divide up the Ottoman Empire after a military victory. As the foreign ministers Grey and Delcassé emphasized in January 1915, London and Paris were convinced that in the long run they had to support the Ottoman Empire as an international player. While the French feared for the investments they had made there before 1914, British political and military leaders viewed with horror the mere possibility that the humiliation of the Sultan and Caliph would fuel jihad among India's Muslims and undermine the foundations of the British Empire in Asia.

Only the crisis facing their Russian ally had changed this baseline situation since 1915. Petrograd's request for military support after its setbacks against German troops in 1915, together with fears that Russia might sign a separate peace and leave the war, contributed to a change of mind, especially in the British government.[123] Overcoming considerable resistance, Foreign Minister Grey established in a secret treaty of March-April 1915 that Russia would be awarded Constantinople and other territories in the Ottoman Empire, including the western shores of the straits, parts of eastern Thrace, northeastern Asia Minor, and northern Armenia and Kurdistan. In return, Tsar Nicholas left France and the other Allies free to draw the border with Germany and to pursue territorial demands in Syria, Cilicia, and Palestine, with the exception of the holy sites.[124] At a critical juncture, and without having fought with its own troops in the Dardanelles, Russia thus gained for the first time a real prospect of achieving its number one war aim: domination of the straits between the Black Sea and the Mediterranean. This was a long-term strategic concept that embodied the nationally charged ambitions of Russian Slavophiles.[125] To keep Russia in the war, the British government was also prepared to modify the 1907 Treaty of St. Petersburg, which had envisaged the division of Iran into three zones of influence; now the southern part of the neutral zone would be added to the British sphere and the northern part, including Tehran, would go to Russia.[126]

These agreements of Spring 1915 had a number of immediate consequences. In effect, the Allies accepted the division of the Ottoman Empire after a military victory, since the pledges to Russia prejudiced any future claims by other players, whether Britain and France themselves or Italy and Greece. These pledges aroused far-reaching expectations and increased the pressure to act. It could already be foreseen that the carve-up of the Ottoman Empire would mainly correspond to the strategic interests of Britain and France, not to the home areas or the wishes of more than twenty ethnic groups in the region. This game of power politics, overriding traditional attachments or interests, was highly reminiscent of the arrangements that came out of the Congress of Vienna in 1814–1815.

In 1915–1916, the special Anglo-French responsibility for the future political order in the Near East was already becoming clear, British policy in particular setting the course for the region down to the present day.[127] The basic problem, even at this early stage, was the contradictory nature of British strategy, another result of the mismatch between objectives and military resources that made compromises necessary on the ground. The region, with Egypt and the Suez Canal, was so important for the global infrastructure of the British Empire that London could not contemplate giving up influence and control there.[128] As in eastern and southeastern Europe, the search was on for partners in the contest with the Central Powers: British diplomats courted Arab tribal leaders and promised that they would be dealt into a future reallocation of territory if they provided military support against the Ottoman Empire.[129]

In the correspondence between the leader of the Hejaz and sharif of Mecca, Hussein ibn Ali, and the British high commissioner in Egypt, Sir Henry McMahon, the most important issues in 1915 and 1916 were the future of the Arab lands in the region and the terms for an Arab uprising against Ottoman rule; another point was the encouragement of Arab soldiers in the Ottoman armed forces to desert. There were hints of British support for an Arab kingdom and hence for Arab independence after the war, but the shape of future borders was already creating difficulties. The districts of Mersina and Alexandretta, as well as parts of Syria, were to be excluded on the grounds that they did not count as purely Arab areas. And British diplomacy stressed Britain's special responsibility to protect the holy sites in Palestine against external attack and to guarantee their inviolability. These formulations, in particular, gave cause for conflict; the British government and McMahon himself repeatedly emphasized, after the correspondence became known, that Palestine had been excluded from the promise of an independent Arabia. The basic thrust of British policy, including its support for Arab independence, continued when the defeat of the Ottoman Empire loomed on the horizon. After 1917, when the new Bolshevik government in Russia publicly dissociated itself from earlier agreements concerning the Ottoman Empire, the British government reaffirmed its support in principle for Arab independence in the "Hogarth message" of 1918.[130]

The Arabs, too, participated in this strategy of mutual promises, which on both sides aroused great expectations that were not fulfilled in political reality. Thus, Arab leaders informed the British secret service in Egypt that Arab soldiers would desert en masse from the Ottoman army and join the struggle for Arab independence, whereas in practice no such events took place. A real credibility problem arose, because the Arabs viewed British statements as a pledge of an independent state, whereas the Sykes-Picot agreement of May 1916 foresaw the division of the region into two zones controlled by the British and the French, respectively. On the whole, these developments were reminiscent of the intensive discussions on war aims and the many competing promises to possible alliance partners in Europe. There, as in the Middle East, high casualties and the need to justify them increased the likelihood of extensive territorial changes after the victory. On the other hand, the contradictory war aims and policy commitments reduced the scope for alternatives and peace feelers on the basis of compromise. In the Middle East, the contradictory positions of Britain and France sooner or later damaged the credibility of the Allies, who were pursuing their own strategic and territorial interests in the region.

A good example of these contradictory positions was the Sykes-Picot agreement itself, essentially an Anglo-French balancing of interests in the tradition of nineteenth-century colonial deals.[131] Mark Sykes from the Arab Bureau in Egypt and Charles François Georges Picot, the representative of France since January 1916, agreed in May on the parts of the Near and Middle East that would become the zones of influence of the two belligerents after victory; they did so in an exchange of notes that were later officially endorsed and also confirmed by Russia. Despite later major changes, especially Russia's exit from the war in 1917–1918, the agreement basically prefigured the postwar political structure of the region. It distributed the Ottoman booty as sized up in 1915: France would receive the Syrian coastal region, including today's Lebanon, as well as the province of Mosul with its important oilfields, while Britain would take Baghdad and Basra provinces in what is now Iraq, as well as the Mediterranean strongholds of Acre and Jaffa. An international administration was planned for Palestine, but its form remained vague and left room for various interpretations. In the British and French zones of influence thus defined, the two alliance partners undertook to promote Arab independence and its conversion into statehood. But these plans, too, were not spelled out at first: was there to be one independent Arab state, a monarchy, an independent federation of Arab states with an Arab at its head, or an Arab solution under British and French supervision?[132]

But there were even more fundamental problems. For the discussion of an independent Arab state passed over the ethnic and social reality of the region; there could be no talk of a homogeneous pan-Arabism, a clear-cut secessionist nationalism directed against the Ottoman Empire. Quite different tendencies were dominant in different regions—Arabism, Lebanism, Syrianism, and Iraqism—and only a small minority initially embraced the aim of an Arab state. Besides, these heterogeneous currents were themselves not mass movements but elite phenomena, while large parts of the population knew nothing of such ideas or had no interest in them.[133]

Both before and after the Arab revolt, the separatists on whom the British relied in the world war were organized in mostly secret societies under the sharif of Mecca. But the relations of the rebels with one another—between Hashemites and Arabs, Iraqis and Syrians, Egyptians and inhabitants of the Hejaz region—were highly intricate and volatile. Moreover, the success of the revolt did not give rise to a unified movement, but underlined the ethnic complexity of the many regions. At least four different currents may be identified. In addition to advocates of an Arab state, there were supporters of a Greater Syria, which would have comprised the territory of today's Syria, Lebanon, Palestine, and Israel. Others were in favor of an independent Lebanon and an independent Iraq. Although the Hashemite-led pan-Arab tendency became dominant during the war, mainly thanks to British support, it represented only one option and was by no means uncontroversial.[134]

A final complication was the fact that in 1916 the British government took more and more seriously the position of the group around Chaim Weizmann, an early enthusiast for the basic ideas of Zionism set out in Theodor Herzl's book *The Jewish State*. As leader of the Zionists in Britain, Weizmann succeeded in drawing together the political and practical dimensions of Zionism. Politically, he opposed any idea of establishing a Jewish state in Uganda, Argentina, or South Africa, opting instead for the historical territory of Palestine. But he was not thinking only of settlements by a Jewish religious community, such as those he had seen on a trip to Palestine in September 1907; he had set his mind on the foundation of a full-fledged state there. Varying degrees of emancipation in western Europe, he argued in 1916, had led to a situation where many individual Jews were increasingly integrated into society, and their sense of Jewish solidarity had receded even more during the war. In eastern Europe the spirit of solidarity was greater, because of outbreaks of violence and discriminatory laws, but experiences of occupation and frequent regime changes meant that there too the situation remained very complicated. Only a state of their own in Palestine could offer a lasting solution and strengthen the feeling of all Jews that they belonged to a Jewish nation.[135]

The motives of British politicians in supporting the creation of a Jewish state in Palestine, as the Balfour Declaration did in November 1917, were multifaceted and contradictory, ranging from an explicit Christian philosemitism to anti-Semitic stereotypes. Many argued that an effort should be made to enlist the international influence of Jews, especially in North America, for a world war against the Central Powers. But the rather vaguely formulated declaration of support in 1917, which was eventually made public under pressure from Weizmann, had a dynamic of its own that clashed with British war aims in the region and the foundations of their strategy.

3. HUNGER AND SHORTAGES, COMPULSION AND PROTEST
The Tectonics of Societies Struggling to Survive

As the supply of volunteers fell in Britain in 1915, despite a persistently high level of casualties, the debate over conscription became more intense.[136] The basic political lineup soon took shape. The introduction of conscription in January 1916 marked a decisive change for British Liberals in particular, modifying the nineteenth-century liberal heritage and traditional positions on state action. But conscription also had major repercussions in the British Empire, as developments in Australia and Canada demonstrated. For many people at the time, it came to symbolize a "war state" that was encroaching in the lives of millions. This kind of state had not existed before in Britain; indeed, for a long time it had entered into the Continental enemy-image, serving to demarcate Britain as a parliamentary system with enshrined liberties from absolute monarchies able to call upon standing mass armies. This underlay the "Whig interpretation of history," marked by successful struggles for freedom and the victory of parliamentary sovereignty against the armies and power claims of absolutist Catholic monarchs.[137] For many Liberals, then, the end of voluntary enlistment in 1916 spelled the end of Britain's long tradition of liberties; it seemed to obey the principles of the Prussian military state against which the war was being fought.

In 1915, the keywords "conscription" and "compulsion" had already informed the opposition of many Liberals to the expanding war state as well as extra-parliamentary forms of protest, at a time when Asquith's Liberal government was running the country. The crisis of political liberalism was looming in the context of war.[138] While "compulsion" stood for ever-greater regulation and intervention by Lloyd George's arms ministry in the free movement of labor and the activity of the trade unions, "conscription" was for many Liberals synonymous with a military state that increasingly restricted individual freedom. In June 1915 an article in the *Westminster Gazette,* a mouthpiece of the "New Liberals," argued that the war had created a special situation: "We place no limits on the claims of the State to the service of its individual citizens in a struggle in which its honor, and it may be its existence, is at stake."[139] But the closer that conscription came, the greater were the fears that the country might betray its historical freedoms by adopting "Prussianism" under the pressure of the war and its casualty toll. What played no role in this debate, however, was the participatory dimension of the defense of the mother country, in the tradition of the French Revolution. In October 1915, a letter to the editor of *The Nation* even went so far as to identify conscription with the betrayal of liberal principles and the end of the Liberal Party: "We go to war professedly to fight for freedom, and are rapidly introducing industrial and military slavery here. . . . There will be no Liberal Party as we have known it. It is abdicating its birthright; it will have lost its soul."[140]

It was by no means an intellectual or political minority alone that had such reservations in early 1916. By the end of the year there were more than a million objectors to conscription, only 1 percent of whom gave an opposition to war in principle as their reason. The initially staggered draft aroused more protests. But professional motives were predominant in these, especially among the self-employed, while married men saw the exemption of bachelors as unjust. Although the million or more objections to the draft did not reflect a pacifist groundswell or a general war weariness, they indicated an important shift in the public mood. The appeal to each man's sense of duty and obligation to his mother country, which had dominated official discourse at the beginning of the war, was increasingly overshadowed by a critical awareness of the grave personal, familial, and professional consequences of military service. The call-up imposed by the government considerably strengthened this tendency.[141]

The conscription debate was particularly conflictual in Ireland. Although its introduction was deferred there, the mere prospect provoked resistance to measures that many saw as bound up with a regime based on war and occupation.[142] At the beginning of the war, it had by no means been expected that the Irish conflict would escalate into the Easter Rising of 1916 and its subsequent repression. Some 200,000 Irish, 60 percent of them Catholics, volunteered for military service, and more than one-quarter of all Irish soldiers belonged to the British professional army and non-Irish units. This was largest military mobilization that Ireland had ever experienced. Altogether, however, the deferment of conscription meant that the call-up was smaller than in other parts of the United Kingdom.[143]

Although the political truce was already becoming brittle in 1915, the real escalation came with the action of a radical minority of southern Irish nationalists. The Easter Rising of April 24–29, 1916, was a perfect example of how world war and national liberation struggle were linked to each other. The radicalization destroyed the balance between unionists and nationalists constructed with such difficulty in August 1914, and their rival positions burst forth again beneath the surface truce. Only the bloody insurrection, however, created the possibility for a narrative that continued to operate far into the twentieth century and became a key reference for all players in the "Irish Troubles." Since August 1914 unionists in the North and nationalists in the South had taken part in the war and supported the mobilization, but had done so with opposing interests and expectations that had by no means disappeared. Two small, but highly militant, organizations stood behind the rising: the socialistic Irish Citizen Army around James Connolly, who had been pressing for action since 1915, and the group around Patrick Pearse, which, though a minority within the Republican Brotherhood, looked to the impact that a blood sacrifice would have on the Irish struggle. Each opposed any constitutional, evolutionary strategy, regarding it as a betrayal of the cause of Irish independence. In their view, the wartime situation of the government in London should be used to strike a resounding blow for freedom, putting the national movement back on the right track after a period of compromise.

For the insurgents, the Easter Rising was neither a guerrilla war nor an isolated terrorist action, but an open military conflict. It asserted their claim to represent a sovereign nation with its own armed forces. Not by chance did they choose the religious feast of Easter, with its themes of resurrection, but the proclamation of April 24 (mainly attributable to Pearse) emphasized the historical continuity of the struggle: "In the name of God and of the dead generations from which she receives her old tradition of nationhood, Ireland, through us, summons her children to her flag and strikes for her freedom. . . . In every generation the Irish people have asserted their right to national freedom and sovereignty; six times during the past three hundred years they have asserted it in arms. Standing on that fundamental right and again asserting it in arms in the face of the world, we hereby proclaim the Irish Republic as a Sovereign Independent State." The fighters could have had no illusion about their chances of immediate success—which made it all the more important to emphasize the theme of sacrifice for the nation that would set an example for the future: "In this supreme hour the Irish nation must, by its valor and discipline, and by the readiness of its children to sacrifice themselves for the common good, prove itself worthy of the august destiny to which it is called."[144]

Approximately two thousand members of the Irish Citizen Army and the Irish Volunteers took part in the fighting, using Dublin's main post office as their military headquarters. It took British army units, with quite a high proportion of Irishmen, four days to crush the rising; 450 insurgents lost their lives, and 15 political leaders, including Connolly and Pearse, were tried by military tribunals and executed. The action by no means rested on the support of a mass movement; one did develop, however, in the wake of the violence of British troops in Dublin under General John Maxwell. This identification with the Irish national martyrs led to the collapse of loyalty to Britain in the war. Instead of cooperation between Irish nationalism and British liberalism, a massive confrontation loomed between nationalism and unionism. The Easter Rising thus ended in a characteristic paradox: the military fiasco and the trials and executions of its leaders were converted into a massive mobilization of radical Irish nationalists. In this sense, the rising worked as a signal and as a powerful continuation of the anti-British narrative of sacrifice and martyrdom. Patrick Pearse expressed his understanding of this in his speech from the dock: "We seem to have lost. We have not lost. To refuse to fight would have been to lose; to fight is to win. . . . You cannot conquer Ireland. You cannot extinguish the Irish passion for freedom. If our deed has not been sufficient to win freedom, then our children will win by a better deed."[145] Sinn Féin, the Irish republican party and political force behind the independence movement under Éamon de Valera, turned against any policy of compromise and distanced itself from the old strategy of seeking home rule for Ireland. In 1918 it did not take up the seats it had won in Westminster, and the next year it founded an Irish parliament that did not recognize the government in London. For Sinn Féin supporters, the Easter Rising of 1916 became the decisive reference point in the nation's political history.[146] Now began a real guerrilla war against the British army.

The Irish uprising was associated with the world war at two levels, through Germany's involvement and through the effects on northern and southern Irish units on the western front. Roger Casement, from an Irish Protestant family in the Dublin area, had long been active in the British diplomatic service and had played a key role in uncovering atrocities against the civilian population in Belgian Congo, before his retirement in 1911. He then joined the paramilitary Irish Volunteers and became a forceful champion of Irish independence. After the outbreak of war, he worked intensively to enlist German government support for an Irish uprising, making contact with the embassy in New York and traveling via Norway to Germany in Fall 1914. Although his plan to raise a national Irish unit from prisoners of war held in Germany did not bear fruit, he managed to induce the German army to supply weapons and the German government to make a declaration of support. Casement was not involved in planning the Easter Rising, however. German weapons were shipped on a Norwegian freighter, but the British intercepted radio communications and seized the vessel on April 21, 1916. The German captain subsequently blew up the ship and its cargo. Casement himself, set ashore on Ireland's southwest coast by a German submarine, was arrested before the start of the rising and in June 1916 was indicted in London for high treason and sabotage. Arthur Conan Doyle and George Bernard Shaw, among others, appealed in vain for leniency. The British authorities tried to tarnish Casement's reputation by publishing diary sketches (whose genuineness would be hotly contested for years) that supposedly proved his homosexuality.[147]

As in the trial of the Dublin insurgents, the authorities in London could not prevent Casement from becoming a heroic martyr of Irish independence after his execution in early August 1916. His speech from the dock, which played an important part in this legend, emphasized that an occupation power could not enforce loyalty: "Loyalty is a sentiment, not a law. It rests on love, not on restraint. The government of Ireland by England rests on restraint, and not on law; and since it demands no love, it can evoke no loyalty." Casement further argued that Irish hopes for the implementation of home rule had not been fulfilled, despite their military service during the war. He directly associated the Irish sacrifices at the front with this denial of the right to national independence. What the British had promised other nations in order to win them as allies, they refused to the Irish people—a contradiction that called into question the credibility of the British government: "We are told that if Irishmen go by the thousand to die, not for

Ireland, but for Flanders, for Belgium, for a patch of sand in the deserts of Mesopotamia, or a rocky trench on the heights of Gallipoli, they are winning self-government for Ireland. But if they dare to lay down their lives on their native soil, if they dare to dream even that freedom can be won only at home by men resolved to fight for it there, then they are traitors to their country, and their dream and their deaths are phases of a dishonorable phantasy. . . . Ireland is being treated today among the nations of the world as if she were a convicted criminal."[148]

However, it was not German military assistance but the changed perception of Irish casualties at the front that revealed the momentous consequences of the nexus of war and civil war. The fight against conscription in Ireland, which would reach a climax in Spring 1918, deepened the chasm between supporters of loyalist and republican nationalism; both camps associated Ireland's internal situation with the question of loyalty in the war and instrumentalized it to justify their position. In view of the high death toll, many Irish soldiers at the fronts felt aggrieved by the uprising, and pro-British unionists took the opportunity to accuse Irish nationalists of betrayal.

In the middle of the war, conflict was already raging over the historical significance of events. In rival narratives, the Easter Rising myth opposed the unionist countermyth of the 36th Ulster Division's blood sacrifice at the Battle of the Somme, although the 16th Irish Division also suffered heavy losses there.[149] When football teams from the two units played each other before 3,000 spectators, one wag on the Ulster side wondered "if we shall get into trouble for fraternizing with the enemy."[150] The rivalry thus deepened across generations as the common experience of war failed to have an integrative effect. Moreover, the special combination of national and religious lines of conflict overlapped with social class identity: workers' solidarity did not assert itself across the divide, and an independent socialist labor movement capable of reconciling the two sides failed to develop.[151]

The external and internal crisis factors—massive British casualties on the western front with no decisive breakthrough, new dangers on the home front resulting from unrestricted U-boat warfare, the conflicts in Ireland, and ever-greater problems in financing the war with loans from the United States—threw the Asquith government onto the defensive in late 1916.[152] Asquith, whose own son fell on the Somme, found himself less and less capable of defending his position against the tide of criticism in the British popular press. When he finally resigned in December 1916, the publisher Lord Northcliffe attributed it to the power of his press, as indeed did his left-liberal critics. They feared that the war had enormously increased the power of the press barons, along with that of an increasingly centralized state, and saw this as a direct threat to Britain's liberal society.[153]

More generally, moderate political forces were coming under pressure in 1916 in both Britain and France. Liberal Party and Labour Party supporters turned their backs on the government in the British lower house, fearing that in the name of "compulsion" and "conscription" the war state would encroach more and more on private life. On the other side, many British Conservatives as well as the republican Right in France accused their government of not fighting the war with sufficient energy. "Defeatism" and "pacifism" became code words to be used on every occasion against political opponents. In December 1916 Lloyd George formed a new government, whose structure pointed in a different direction: important decisions would henceforth be made by a small, six-member war cabinet with almost dictatorial features. The long-established understanding of the cabinet as an executive committee of the lower house receded into the background, effectively suspending the traditional parliamentary focus of the political culture in favor of an active, regulatory war state.[154] As in Germany, France, and Italy, there was serious discussion of whether industries essential to the war effort should be nationalized. In a series of articles titled "The Elements of Reconstruction" in July and August 1916, the *Times* newspaper—above all suspicion of socialist propaganda—called for a "national plan" against the "chaotic world of individualistic businesses run for unchecked private profit"; the ideal was a new "system of amalgamated businesses in which the public interest [was] the controlling shareholder." In 1918, the government drew up a balance sheet: the world war had brought with it "a transformation of the social and administrative structure of the state, much of which is bound to be permanent."[155]

Lloyd George was a new-style politician, who seemed better equipped than Asquith and most Liberals to face the challenges of an interminable war.[156] Like Clemenceau who became premier in 1917 in France, he represented a charismatic war politician, who since 1915 had built up the arms ministry as his basis of popularity and came to embody the interventionist war state. Asquith's fall and the new Tory-dominated cabinet thus strengthened the importance in people's minds of a new kind of extra-parliamentary legitimacy. Although a large number of Liberals left the government with Asquith, the internal civic peace continued to hold for the time being in Westminster.[157] But the first fault lines were appearing: Lloyd George himself looked to a rebuilding of political camps in accordance with their position on the war. He deliberately tried to boost those Liberal and moderate Conservative MPs who, in contrast to sections of Labour and the Left Liberals, supported the new government's policy. Firing accusations of pacifism, defeatism, and failure to support the nation at war, he played a key role in splitting the Liberal Party and forcing it onto the political defensive. Far more than a political watershed, what loomed at the end of 1916 in wartime Britain was a dilemma for political liberalism.

Although Britain had undergone radical, tradition-breaking changes in the two years since Summer 1914, although it had converted its peacetime economy into a war economy, although the war state had successfully mobilized its own resources and those of the Empire, and although it had recruited a mass army, sustained high casualties on the European fronts and elsewhere, and weathered the Irish crisis of Summer 1916—it nevertheless stood on the brink of financial bankruptcy and a realization that it could continue the war only with American help. All this illustrated how deeply the war had changed the position of individual countries and the leeway available to them.[158]

Between 1914 and 1916, Britain had pursued four parallel objectives. First, from the very beginning, Britain had sought to maintain global maritime supremacy in the contest with Germany, in order to safeguard access to the resources of the Empire. Second, it had increasingly become the center for the funding of the war in the whole Entente. Third, London had sought to win strategic allies among formerly neutral states—although its policy toward Italy, Romania, and Greece, as well as in the Near and Middle East, had led there to a wave of mutually conflicting expectations, especially for territorial acquisitions from the future breakup of the Ottoman Empire. This sowed the seeds of disappointment, above all in the Near and Middle East. Fourth, Britain had been forced to give up its traditional geopolitical strategy—concentration on a navy with global reach and a small land army for colonial operations—and to develop a Continental-style mass army. This had far-reaching implications for domestic politics as well as for Britain's society and war economy, and it served to inflame the situation in Ireland.

Against this background, the Somme battle of 1916 operated as a watershed in the British wartime experience: Kitchener's original policy of defensively eroding the German war machine gave way to a strategy of offensive attrition. This reflected a realization that the Central Powers could not be overcome unless the British made a comprehensive military commitment to the western front. Only the Somme battle fully revealed the break with the tradition of seeking to impose British interests mainly through global maritime supremacy, financial investment, and protection of the population at home. In 1914 and 1915, Britain's leaders had still seen the war as a limited conflict; the relatively low casualty rates of the British army, in comparison with those of the French and especially the Romanian or Serbian, supported this link, which was also precisely understood in Whitehall. In Summer 1916, Lloyd George sensed that the country had to made sacrifices of a different order if it was to win the war. On May 30, 1916, he argued against Asquith (then still prime minister) that "this war would ultimately be decided by superiority in quality and quantity of material, and by the wearing down of the enemy in numbers."[159] The Battle of the Somme demonstrated that the British leadership was prepared to suffer the consequences.

But the funding of the Allies and the construction of a mass army, however great the mobilization in the societies of the Empire, seriously overstretched Britain's economic capacities. Its economic and monetary independence began to crumble in 1916. As early as 1914 U.S. loans and war material began to acquire increasing importance, but it was only in November 1916 that the full scale of the dependence became clear as the American credit line threatened to dry up. On November 28, 1916, an influential group of American bankers advised its investors not to award any more credits to the belligerent countries, and particularly not to Great Britain. When the Federal Reserve Board issued similar warnings, the Conservative leader and chancellor in Lloyd George's cabinet, Andrew Bonar Law, had to admit that Britain faced bankruptcy if it did not receive further American loans. Panic spread in Whitehall. Foreign Minister Grey confessed on November 21, "In previous wars we had given our Allies the full support of our fleet and of our money. In this war, for the first time we were given the fullest support, not only naval and financial, but also in merchant shipping and material, and we had for the first time created a large army. . . . Our resources were very considerable, but they were not inexhaustible."[160]

By the time that Asquith fell at the end of the year, Britain could in a sense afford neither defeat nor victory—a continuation of the war was possible only with direct American involvement. Thus, well before the United States entered the war in Spring 1917, Britain's economic and monetary dependence had acquired dimensions that were less and less consistent with its leaders' image of it as the foremost European power and global naval power or as the economic and financial center for the Allied war efforts.

The longer the war went on, the more the role of the British Empire changed. Once the number of volunteers plummeted and it became necessary to write off Kitchener's strategy of deciding the war in the west with Britain's own mass armies, the new war coalition formed in December 1916 under Lloyd George charted a new course. More than ever it had become necessary to multiply the efforts of the whole Empire.[161] Newly created institutions such as the Imperial War Conferences, the Imperial War Cabinet, and the Imperial Development Board were supposed to help in politically acknowledging the military achievements of the Empire and its changed role in the war—although the major political and military decisions were made in the small circle of the war cabinet and the BEF leadership.[162] But the societies of the Empire developed more heterogeneously than these new institutions and the expressions of solidarity made in 1914 and 1915 would lead one to suppose. While the British government expected the Empire to contribute more to the war, conflicts were shaping up in various parts of the Empire with their own war states.

Even where secessionist movements or violent coup attempts did not occur—as they did in South Africa at the beginning of the war and Ireland in 1916—resistance to state encroachment became more intense. South Africa and Ireland witnessed bloody conflicts, because the threshold of violence was lower there, while the protests in Australia and Canada were more like those in other countries. In Canada, not only Anglophone areas but the Québécois too had declared their solidarity with Britain at the beginning of the war. But there, as in Australia, conflicts related to conscription opened deep rifts in society. These escalated in 1917 and again brought to the surface older tensions over the status of Quebec.

The self-image of all these societies centered less and less on the provision of mere material assistance to the British war effort, foregrounding instead their own military achievements. The war was no longer seen as an experience of Canadian, Australian, New Zealand, or Indian soldiers under British command, but rather a distinctively Canadian, Australian, New Zealand, or Indian contribution with important nation-building implications. Unlike earlier wars, the global conflict was not exhausted in the idea of a common struggle by a homogeneous empire. European battlefields became symbolic sites where the nation's martyrs gave their lives and, as such, sites of national remembrance after the end of the war. Australians and New Zealanders would commemorate Gallipoli, Canadians Vimy Ridge, Newfoundlanders Beaumont-Hamel, Welshmen Mametz Wood, Australians Pozières, and the Irish of Ulster and southern Ireland the Somme. But while this was generally true of the white dominions, a dual hierarchy governed perceptions in accordance with the political order of the Empire and the racial-ethnic segregation of its societies. Thus, the South African Brigade troops deployed

Racial segregation at the front: laborers of the South African Native Labour Corps with white officers in France

in 1916 in the defense of Delville Wood were held in lesser regard than their Canadian or Australian counterparts. Black draftees were generally excluded from combat service, being used in France, if at all, only as auxiliaries in the South African Native Labour Corps and then only under special conditions.

Participation in the war fueled national and anticolonial ideas among soldiers from the British colonies. Promises were made in the recruitment of troops from Jamaica, and many Jamaicans later referred to them in recalling the lives lost on the battlefield. But hopes for a better status for the colonies within the Empire, or even recognition of their inhabitants as full citizens, ended in disappointment. By contrast, the white settler colonies of Australia, New Zealand, and Canada managed to combine Imperial loyalty with a distinctive role in the war.[163] But this too came at a price, for the practice of racial-ethnic exclusion was not limited to South Africa, where the war tended to reinforce the division between the races. Of the 620,000 Canadian soldiers, roughly 4,000 members of indigenous peoples served as snipers or scouts at the front or auxiliaries behind the lines, but also in some cases as fighter pilots; 17 were even promoted to officers. German troops admired the Canadians, of both European and indigenous origin, for their special qualities in battle. But the deployment of Canadian First Peoples took place against the background of their problematic situation in Canada itself: they enjoyed no democratic rights, were mostly marginalized in native reserves, and were seen as an expensive burden on the state. Still, they continued a tradition that went back to the eighteenth century, when their ancestors had loyally supported the British Crown, and even now they associated their role in the armed forces with hopes of political recognition and legal equality. Back home, indigenous peoples supported the war: they subscribed to war loans despite widespread poverty, sent many aid packages to Europe, and took part in patriotic festivities without heeding the prejudices against them within Canadian white society. There, as in other countries, the soldiers who made it back after 1918 became disillusioned when their war service received scant recognition and nothing changed in their precarious status at either an everyday or political level.[164]

The integration problems of Empire societies were also apparent in Australia, where Prime Minister Hughes failed in his policy of expanding the war effort. In 1916 and 1917, bills to introduce unrestricted conscription were rejected—which highlighted the limits of the war state in a political system involving regular participation. While the social pressure on men to volunteer for the army increased appreciably in 1916, the government promoted the ANZAC myth and stepped up propaganda against supposedly disloyal "enemy aliens." In the dominions too, therefore, external and internal enemy-images reinforced each other.[165] The prowar policies of the Australian government affected many areas of ordinary life, as in the strong action it took against prostitution and sexually transmitted diseases to protect the health and fighting capacity of soldiers, or in the strict limits on opening hours for bars and hotels. In view of the fact that most soldiers were posted not in Australia but in Europe and the Near East, these were completely exaggerated measures that nevertheless showed how war in faraway places could change everyday life and foster a regime of suspicion, controls, and regulations. Prime Minister Hughes, however, overestimated the capacity of the economy and the resolve of the population to keep increasing the war effort. No central direction of the economy was yet in place even by 1916, and military and political leaders increasingly showed themselves to be ill prepared and overstretched.

All the same, the dominions bore their share of the burdens of war and suffered an increasing proportion of the casualties on the western front, while policy decisions tended to become more decentralized within the Empire. The global war thus made itself felt at several levels for the dominions: in its economic and political effects on the home societies, in institutional changes within the Empire, and in the soldiers' experiences of war on the fronts in Europe and the Near and Middle East.[166]

One particularly instructive aspect of the gap between experiences of war and rising political expectations was the developments in India. The implications of the war in terms of casualties and economic effects were evident; it stimulated Indian industry by reducing or eliminating imports from Europe (in the textile industry, for example), but it also caused an economic crash and, in the form of higher inflation, affected large parts of the country and the impoverished rural population.[167] At first the hardships were widely accepted, because large sections of the middle strata expected a new order to emerge from a war in which Britain, the Empire, and India itself had actively participated. One contemporary observer spoke for many when he emphasized the opportunities: the war had put the clock forward fifty years and opened the way for advances unthinkable before 1914.[168]

On the other hand, German hopes of provoking a widespread anti-British revolt in India via the Ottoman Empire and an Islamic jihad came to nothing. There were isolated riots against British rule in Bengal and Punjab, which were put down under the Defence of India Act that had come into force in 1915, and by the end of the war a total of forty-six people had been tried and executed, and another sixty-four sentenced to long terms of imprisonment. This was a long way from a politically explosive anticolonial movement, but tensions did begin to grow from 1916 on.[169] Bal Gangadhar Tilak, a nationalist politician released in June 1914 after six years in prison, gained increasing influence in the Indian National Congress (INC) following the death of two prominent leaders of its moderate wing. He and the radical currents around him began in 1916 to build a home rule movement with branches all over India, which opposed the course pursued by moderate figures in the INC. Characteristic of the moderates was Annie Besant, originally from England, who had made India her adopted country and founded in 1915 an Indian Home Rule League, calling for India to become a "free nation within the British Empire, under the Imperial Crown." It did not call the Empire into question, nor did it signify a demand for the country's formal independence.[170]

The real test for the INC came with Mahatma Gandhi in Spring 1916. As a lawyer in South Africa from 1907 to 1914, he had made a name for himself among Indian settlers there by taking part in passive resistance to the discriminatory policies of the Transvaal government. His influence in the INC began to increase after his return to India in 1915.[171] When the Hindu University Central College demanded by Annie Besant opened in Benares in early 1916, Gandhi, in the presence of the viceroy and a number of regional maharajahs, used the opportunity to make a speech openly criticizing British rule in India. By then, reference to the war was no longer enough to hold back the rising tide of expectations within the Indian national movement. Taking the example of education, Gandhi developed the basic ideas behind independence: "The only education we receive is English education. . . . But suppose that we had been receiving during the past fifty years education through our vernaculars, what should we have today? We should have today a free India, we should have our educated men, not as if they were foreigners

Spy mania and the rule of suspicion: poster for Léon Daudet's spy novel *The World's Vermin*, issued by the nationalist Action française movement, 1916

in their own land but speaking to the heart of the nation." Given the rural poverty in the country, the display of jewelry by office holders at the occasion seemed to Gandhi to represent an oriental, historically imagined India, not the present social and political reality: "I compare with the richly bedecked noble men the millions of the poor. And I feel like saying to these noble men, 'There is no salvation for India unless you strip yourselves of this jewelry and hold it in trust for your countrymen in India.'" For Gandhi there was no doubt that Indians had to actively demand their freedom, not wait for the British government to make voluntary concessions: "If we are to receive self-government, we shall have to take it. We shall never be granted self-government. Look at the history of the British Empire and the British nation; freedom loving as it is, it will not be a party to give freedom to a people who will not take it themselves."[172]

Anyone walking through the French capital in Summer 1916 would not necessarily have realized at first sight that it was a city at war, from which the front could be reached in just a couple of hours. What initially struck the observer as a peacetime idyll, however, soon revealed itself to be a changeable surface. Tourists strolled in Paris in late July 1916, and vacationers were heading for the Atlantic coast, where scarcely one hotel room was still available. Yet the war was omnipresent beneath the well-ordered façade, creating its own universe on the home front too. The numerous soldiers on leave caused prostitution to soar in the cities, especially Paris, where it was fully tolerated by the authorities. At the same time, arrests for illegal prostitution rose 40 percent. Although condoms were issued to soldiers, the spread of sexually transmitted diseases (STDs) in the cities and ports of France became an ever-greater problem. In 1915 no fewer than 22 percent of Canadian soldiers were treated for an STD. Men grown desperate from battle and ready to try anything to avoid returning to the front engaged in the extreme practice of infecting themselves with STD pathogens. A regular trade sprang up in TB bacilli and gonorrhea pus, which soldiers rubbed onto their sexual organs.[173]

In 1916 tensions in the *union sacrée* became more evident. Spy mania and a climate of suspicion continued to hold sway. Questions as to exactly what national defense meant and how victory was possible could no longer be fobbed off with references to August 1914. A striking example of this was developments in the conservative Catholic milieu. Claire Ferchaud, born in

1896 into a Catholic farming family in the Vendée, reported having religious experiences at an early age. Encouraged by the local priest, she spent longer and longer periods living a solitary existence sunk in prayer. In the course of the war, her religious experience became even more intense, until she finally believed that she had been given a national mission, not unlike that of Joan of Arc in the Hundred Years' War with England. In 1916 she claimed that Christ had instructed her to save the fatherland, and shortly afterward, her family home of Loublande became a place of pilgrimage. Thousands of believers, including many women from well-off bourgeois families, saw in the young woman's appearance a sign that France could be saved. Given the critical situation on the western front, such ideas solidified into a full-blown hope for peace. Claire Ferchaud thus formed a projection surface for a decidedly Catholic interpretation of the war, and it was precisely here that differences within the *union sacrée* became more pronounced.[174]

In keeping with this Catholic savior myth, the outcome of the first battle of the Marne was interpreted as a religious miracle brought on by prayers at a service in the basilica of Sacré Cœur (itself built after the defeat of 1870–1871).[175] The cult of the Sacred Heart received fresh impetus in 1915, and Catholic attempts to change the national holiday to June 14 provoked massive resistance among republicans. Still, symbols associated with the Sacred Heart were very popular among soldiers at the front. Appeals to defend the fatherland could scarcely conceal the conflict between secular republicans and Catholics, and an army decree issued in August 1917 forbade the display of such images.

The later life of Claire Ferchaud reflected the tensions within the *union sacrée*. In December 1916 she was officially called to testify before an episcopal commission, and she gained the support of a bishop. In January 1917 she then turned to the country's president, sending him a short letter, and in March, after the intervention of a conservative senator, she traveled to Paris for an audience with Poincaré. She asked him to add the Sacred Heart symbol to the tricolor, and to take up the struggle against freemasons as a demonstration of France's loyalty to the faith. The Catholic renewal project failed: Poincaré gave no undertaking, because such a pro-Catholic and pro-clerical policy would have challenged the *union sacrée* and the secular basis of the Third Republic. The religious vision clashed with a political culture that had no time for it. In the end, Claire Ferchaud got nowhere with her demand for the nation at war to be placed under the Sacred Heart, in a symbolic act that would have atoned for its sins (anticlerical policies and *laïcité* as the cornerstones of the republic since the 1880s) and gained divine support for a French victory. What was so remarkable in this episode was that elements in the Catholic milieu made the republican political elite indirectly responsible for the military crises of the war and the failure to achieve victory. After letters along similar lines to leading generals failed to produce results, the archbishop of Paris criticized Ferchaud for claiming to have received direct instructions from God; he ended support for her project and she returned to Loublande. Without official recognition from the Vatican, she withdrew to a convent as "Sister Claire of the Crucified Jesus," where she remained the focus of much local attention for the rest of her life. She died in 1972.[176]

Conflicts within the *union sacrée* were also becoming conspicuous at a political level. The high casualties on the western front brought the debate on war aims to a head, increasing the pressure for compensation to be claimed in advance. In particular, the Comité des Forges under its general secretary Robert Pinot went well beyond the previous position of demanding the return of Alsace-Lorraine and the reestablishment of an independent Belgium. As to the army, Joffre demanded the left bank of the Rhine, the creation of satellite states, a Saar dependent on France, and further bridgeheads on the right bank of the Rhine. Action Française, the right-wing nationalist organization founded in 1898, went the furthest by calling for the outright annexation from Germany of territory on the left bank. The public debate on war aims now began to excite criticism among Socialists.[177] The discussion thus became a catalyst for domestic political conflicts.

Tensions developed in 1916 between parliament and the military leadership, as pressure continued to mount on the army to justify the high casualties on the western front. A reinvigorated parliament managed to assert political control, having already since late 1914 moderated the militarization of the country's economy and administration. Unlike in Germany, where such a relationship would have been unthinkable, the groups in the National Assembly, both at sessions of parliament and in the *comités secrets* (whose proceedings were not made public), critically examined the role of army commanders before and after the Battle of Verdun. The battle may thus be seen as a turning point in the development of parliamentary politics. Above all, the senate army commission chaired by Georges Clemenceau vociferously accused Joffre of having underestimated the likelihood of a German attack.[178] In this situation, neither Joffre, popular victor of the Marne in 1914, nor the war minister Millerand was able to maintain the primacy of military headquarters. It lost more of its power when Nivelle replaced Joffre in December 1916, while the appointment of the Socialist Albert Thomas as arms minister in late November 1916 seemed at first to reinforce the *union sacrée*.[179]

Nevertheless, by the end of the year it was no longer possible to disregard the critical mood in the country and the people's war weariness. The *union sacrée* still held, but beneath the surface of patriotic declarations pressure was growing to make the next offensive under Nivelle the last, decisive battle of the war. Only this, it seemed, would give meaning to the earlier casualties and prevent a dual crisis from breaking out at the front and at home. Yet when these high hopes were shattered in Spring 1917, it became a threefold crisis: large-scale mutinies in the army combined with strikes in major industrial centers, while the fourth new cabinet in a year reflected the political instability.

These developments, together with the army's relative loss of power and the blow to its credibility with the changeover from Joffre to Nivelle and finally, in 1917, to Pétain, cleared the way for a new type of politician in France. Clemenceau's programmatic motto as charismatic war premier—"*Je fais la guerre*"—underlined his claim to be concentrating all forces on military victory. This personalization of politics at the moment of crisis was reminiscent of Lloyd George in Britain. Clemenceau's visits to the front and his eventual appointment of Foch as supreme Allied commander—which in 1918 made it possible for the first time to coordinate all Allied forces effectively on the western front—pointed in the same direction.[180] The price for this personalization was a Bonapartist style of government, which would seal the end of the *union sacrée* in 1917.

In France, too, the authorities established tight controls in 1914 in the shape of censorship and countless prefects' reports on the popular mood. But in practice the censorship was repeatedly circumvented and had only limited effect. In 1916, for example, the founding of the paper *Le Canard enchaîné* offered a forum for satirical criticism,[181] and the publication of

Barbusse's *Le Feu*—which followed an age-old pattern of sin, damnation, and redemption, but above all made survival and physicality its central focus—demonstrated even more clearly the niches and loopholes available in French wartime society. In Barbusse's novel, banks, financial interests, and assorted profiteers lay behind the moral abyss of the war; it converted individuals into an undifferentiated mass of human flesh at the mercy of the great battles. Barbusse, like Walter Benjamin, saw the body as the physical shell of the self, so that the war's physical sacrifices also made a sacrifice of individuality. He placed his hopes in a vague socialist internationalism that would make war a thing of the past.[182] As an early volunteer marked by his experiences at the front, he adopted a more and more critical attitude to the war. In 1917 he became a founding member of a socialist-pacifist veterans organization, the Association Républicaine des Anciens Combattants (ARAC), and after the war he helped to create a peace movement that enlisted the likes of Romain Rolland and Heinrich Mann. Barbusse's war diary *Le Feu,* with its characteristic subtitle "The Story of a Squad" and its focus on a small combat unit, was remote from patriotic rhetoric, yet in 1916 it won the Prix Goncourt, the most important French literary prize. As perhaps the great pioneer of war literature, corresponding to Erich Maria Remarque's later *All Quiet on the Western Front* in Germany, *Le Feu* managed to evade censorship in 1916 by appearing as a serialized novel. Only a few passages drew complaints that they displayed openly pacifist tendencies.

In 1916, its second year of war, Italy experienced rapid growth of its war industry. In a sense it was catching up with the other belligerent countries. One striking aspect there was the increasing involvement of the military authorities in the industrial mobilization; close cooperation between the army and capital and labor developed at the local and regional level. Despite isolated work stoppages, there were no major strike waves in 1916—partly because of draconian military sanctions, but partly too because of government social provisions such as compulsory extra payment for overtime and night work. By late 1916, with labor shortages more and more of a problem since the summer, workers in industries essential to the war effort were earning 40 percent more than other male industrial workers. Politically, Italy developed into a highly repressive war society, in which basic civil rights were suspended and the military acquired ever-greater political influence. When Salandra criticized the supreme commander Cadorna after the Austro-Hungarian offensive of Summer 1916, he lost a vote of confidence in parliament and had to resign. For Italy, too, the conflict between military leadership and civilian government, and the army's insistence on preserving its influence, were determining factors—although for the time being, unlike in France, the military retained the upper hand.[183]

The military crisis facing the Central Powers led in Summer 1916 to fundamental changes in the German war economy, society, and politics. When fighting intensified on the various fronts—Verdun, the Somme, Galicia (with the Russian offensive), and Romania's entry into the war—another supply crisis threatened to erupt. The demand for munitions shot up from July, while the burdens of war had highly varied consequences for different sections of the population. On August 31, just two days after he had replaced Falkenhayn as head of the OHL, Hindenburg presented a radical program outlining the ends and means of the war economy. The so-called Hindenburg Program To Meet the Needs of the Army envisaged a rapid quadrupling of arms production, while also seeking military control and centralization of war industries, resources, and, especially, manpower. Compulsory labor was to play an even greater role than before, with the employment of Poles and Belgians on a large scale.

In August 1916, then, the Third OHL was under a threefold pressure to act: it seemed essential to concentrate all efforts on the war economy, along with the military commitment on the western front and the stabilization of Germany's ally in the southeast. As with previous military decisions, Hindenburg presented the program in person to the Kaiser and the Reich leadership, and once more he functioned as a symbolic figure consciously staged for the media—a strict, paternal war hero; a brave, unshakable embodiment of the will to hold out; a model for frontline soldiers and factory workers alike. He radiated the confidence and authority that the monarch increasingly lacked. The "Iron Hindenburg"—a giant figure displayed in many cities into which iron nails sold to the public could be driven—gave expression to this image of steadfastness and self-sacrifice.[184]

But Hindenburg was neither the central intellect in OHL strategic planning nor the brains behind the new-style war economy that began to take shape in 1916. Again it was Ludendorff who proved to be the architect of modern

warfare; he was convinced that only the most extensive centralization of politics and warfare could address its challenges. He saw his book *Kriegführung
und Politik,* first published in 1922, as a radical continuation of Clausewitz's
thinking. A belief in perpetual struggle was in his view decisive. When victory
and annihilation were the only alternatives, and compromises as in earlier
peace agreements were no longer options, political and military leadership
had to be united and concentrated; and only military men knew how to fulfill
the political exigencies of a nation at war. In retrospect, Ludendorff thought
that politics since August 1914 had ultimately revolved around total war; it
required the total mobilization of all resources, which only a great military
leader could implement. At least as an idea, this meant unshackling war
from all conditions and all political-constitutional restrictions—an incipient
tendency in other countries too. In France Charles Maurras, invoking the
absolute needs of the nation at war, called for a kind of military king, while
in Italy Mussolini saw a radical war state as the only chance to survive the war
and to achieve national aggrandizement.[185]

In working out the program, Ludendorff drew on proposals submitted by
the OHL department head responsible for weapons and munitions, Lieutenant Colonel Max Bauer, who was in close touch with influential businessmen
such as Carl Duisberg and Gustav Krupp. The Hindenburg program concentrated on personnel recruitment plus a swift and massive increase in arms
production, if possible by Spring 1917. The aim was that "eventually anyone
usable for the war should go to the front." Since Germany, even with these
measures in place, would be inferior to its enemies, industry in the age of
"mechanized warfare" had to make up for this demographic shortfall: "People
must more and more be replaced with machines." This explained the focus
on heavy artillery, machine guns, mortars, and aircraft.[186] Output had to
be doubled in the case of ammunition and mortars, or even tripled in that
of artillery and machine guns. This economic dimension of the war had
already come to the fore in the battle of materiel. But now it did not only
relate to effectiveness in killing the enemy and to the numbers of soldiers
sent to the front, taken away from it, or capable of being replaced; it also
established a close connection between war demography and mechanized
warfare that was directly relevant to the wider society at home. In essence,
machines were supposed to compensate for human losses. War Minister

Wild von Hohenborn spoke of this in September 1916 to representatives of industry: "The more we eat into our reserves of human material, the more must machines, guns, machine guns, shells, and so forth take the place of men—from which it follows that we must not only keep in step with our enemies but actually surpass them."[187]

The setting of new priorities for the war economy brought the OHL and the arms industry even closer together. This was most evident in the creation of a supreme war office in the Prussian war ministry, whose director, General Wilhelm Groener, had previously been head of the railroad department on the general staff and then transferred to the war provisions office; he thus became one of the key figures in the army's takeover of civilian administrative functions. This process contributed to the creeping transformation of the political-constitutional system, in which military experts seemed increasingly to personify the interventionist state.[188] The sociologist Max Weber observed this trend with growing skepticism. In a conversation with Joseph Redlich in early June 1916, he lamented the "shortage of outstanding men in the Reich: the much-celebrated German organization and administration had failed in many respects." Above all, Weber was suspicious of the relations between public finances and the business world: "he said the worst would be state-run monopolies; it was necessary to preserve the powerful factor of independent industrialists and their office staff as pillars of the German economy; German civil servants always needed an invigorating counterpart in the shape of private entrepreneurs, engineers, and office staff. This dualism of 'state' and 'free' in relation to the national life ran through the whole of German history."[189]

The Hindenburg program envisaged that funding issues would take second place to the expansion of arms production; unproductive enterprises and those not important to the war effort would close down. Closely related to this was the Auxiliary Service Act of December 2, 1916, which provided in principle for the compulsory labor mobilization of all men between 17 and 60 not liable for military service. Huge restrictions were placed on the freedom to choose one's job and place of work. Bauer's original ideas had included a general obligation to work as the equivalent of military service; a lowering of the minimum working age to 15 years; the applicability of the act to both men and women; the closure of universities, including war-related departments, for the duration of the war; and the gearing of food supplies to the needs of war production, with rationed allocations for workers in "productive war sectors."

In the end, however, the legislation involved a compromise that also served the purposes of labor unions. The Reich government under Bethmann Hollweg sought to accommodate the SPD and the unions, so as to maintain the civil peace under increasingly difficult conditions. Firms with more than fifty employees had to introduce workforce committees, and employers and workers had parity on arbitration boards. While disputes between the OHL and the Reich government, as well as between conservative entrepreneurs and unions, became more frequent, cooperation among state, military, and unions grew deeper in the context of the wartime mobilization.[190] Confidence in the reform-oriented war state, which recognized the unions as representatives of industrial workers, fueled major hopes for the future. The union official Wilhelm Jansson wrote on December 11, 1916, "Only complete fools can imagine that the German worker would be better off under the rule of Cossacks or English or French soldiers than in the Germany of universal suffrage and social reform. The unions' position in the war follows from this. A defeat for Germany would inevitably be a severe blow to the working class."[191]

Problems soon appeared, however, with the practical implementation of the Hindenburg program, which in the end was not based on a coherent plan, but was a reaction to the crisis of Summer 1916. Output increased, to be sure, but later than planned, and the first results were discernible only in Winter 1917–1918. At the same time, the radical switchover to war production worsened the coal bottleneck, overstretched the transportation system, and left the economy well short of its targets until Fall 1917.[192] Despite enormous demand and intensive efforts, German industrial output fell by no less than 30 percent by 1918. The Hindenburg program, too, proved unable to compensate for the growing shortage of raw materials and manpower, while the ever more poorly supplied working population reached the limits of what it could produce.

In a conversation he had with Ludendorff in mid-February 1917, Walther Rathenau analyzed the problems in implementing the Hindenburg program: "no one had borne in mind that a country which is absolutely occupied with making supplies for the war is not ready to be launched into a gigantic construction program." Large numbers of manufacturers had been "chivvied into building a great number of new factories," which were still "just begun or half-finished" because of the shortage of construction materials. "Transport conditions had been accepted as they were, with no thought for the increased quantity of goods in circulation and increased production." Rathenau drew Ludendorff's attention to a basic problem that was also evident in relation to the Auxiliary Service Act: "One of the causes of disorganization lies in overorganization, in the way committees and advisory bodies are constantly expanding, in the way attention is paid to deputies, interested parties, and parliaments, so that they have now reached the stage where directions and principles cannot be adhered to because of committee meetings, conferences, and the work of organization."[193]

In hardly any sphere other than food supply was there such a marked tendency to create new, unclearly demarcated, and therefore competing authorities and institutions. This multiplicity reflected the growing shortages of food, and more generally of everyday products and materials. In March 1916 there was formed an Imperial Clothing Authority and an Imperial Meat Authority, in April an Imperial Sugar Authority and an Imperial Coffee and Tea Board, and in May an attempt was finally made to draw these agencies together through the establishment of a War Food Office.[194] The administrative polycracy fueled ever-greater expectations that improved organization would overcome the shortages, albeit through a de facto military dictatorship of the Third OHL. However, the daily experience of administrative rivalry and inefficiency damaged the authority of the German war state.

Food supply problems eventually became a vector of politicization. The British naval blockade was not the only cause of the everyday experience of shortages. At first, imports from neutral countries, a fairly high self-sufficiency rate, and access to conquered farmlands compensated for the shortfall. But the situation worsened considerably in Summer 1916, when the Hindenburg program put the German war economy on a new footing, enforcing the primacy of arms production to the detriment of consumption goods and the agricultural sector. Together with the shortage of farm labor and fertilizer, this shift accelerated the slide in agricultural production. In Britain and France, by contrast, the government went out of its way to ensure that supplies to the population were maintained as long as possible and that areas under cultivation were systematically expanded. There too, shortages eventually affected the economy and led to food rationing, but whereas the situation in Germany was growing worse in the winter of 1916–1917, major repercussions were felt in Britain only in the last year of the war.[195]

As many as 700,000 people died in Germany as a direct or indirect result of inadequate provisions. The effects of the Allied naval and commercial blockade were tangible by late Fall 1914, and from Summer 1917 Germany had to rely almost entirely on its own limited resources.[196] Most of the civilian deaths cannot have been due to starvation: under normal circumstances, the national rationing system introduced in 1916 covered people's minimum needs, if they lost weight and adjusted their activity accordingly; German miners, for example, were clearly able to continue their hard work on the allocated rations, without major adverse effects. The widespread feelings of hunger did not therefore correspond to an absolute shortage of food, but rather to the use of substitute ingredients, such as sawdust or cornmeal in the production of bread. Still, the situation did deteriorate considerably in the so-called turnip winter of 1916–1917 and again in Summer 1918.[197] And the supply deficiencies certainly had grave consequences, for although people could survive on the daily rations their susceptibility to illness rose sharply. From Summer 1916 on, many of Berlin's poor suffered adverse health effects and directly attributed them to food supply problems.

Subjectively, hunger and shortage became distinctive features of the home front in Germany. Already in late 1914 signs of shortage were becoming apparent, and in 1915 police reports mentioned the creeping criminalization of daily life—the result of inflation and black markets—as a public order issue. The Heidelberg historian Karl Hampe also recorded these changes. On June 5, 1916, he noted in his diary, "It looks as if the fruit harvest will be very good. . . . So with a bit of luck we'll be over the shortages of the coming weeks. Here things are still reasonably OK despite many interruptions, and it is ridiculous and undignified that irregularities still occur before the butcher's shops on the high street. . . . We ourselves now eat a little roast at most every eight to ten days. . . . In Leipzig . . . there must already be real undernourishment, and riots are said to have occurred in the streets."[198]

Chancellor Bethmann Hollweg emphasized that the supply bottlenecks were due not to the blockade—Germany produced enough to feed itself—but to speculation and black markets, to the unscrupulousness of war profi-teers. In the search for guilty parties, the police and press acted as regular go-betweens, targeting egoistic dealers and speculators as the equivalent of shirkers at the front. In particular, the press strengthened local protests by accepting the motivation behind them. This, too, created unrealistic expectations that the war state was capable of solving the problem.[199] Food and hunger became dominant issues precisely at the midpoint in the war: September–October 1916. On October 1, after 26 months of war, Karl Hampe observed, "Summer time is over. Anyone capable of it can sleep an hour lon-ger. The earlier evening darkness is disagreeable.—Tomorrow, mushroom-hunting on the Königstuhl [hill, near Heidelberg]. Groceries and delicacies play a quite different role in life from the one they used to have. Instead of flowers you give a lady chocolate, because now it's something special. Today Baethgen is bringing us a dozen eggs from Galicia, and Anschütz will give us a sack of potatoes to thank us for looking after the children. The sense of taste becomes more valuable and sometimes demands to stand on the same level as the enjoyment of art. It makes one fear a lurch into material things in the period after peace comes."[200]

The gulf between the monarch's lifeworld and everyday existence in Ger-man society was virtually unbridgeable. As the "turnip winter" was beginning in early November 1916, Wilhelm II was busying himself at his headquarters with the problems of his beloved hunting ground in East Prussia. Lunch on November 4 went as follows: "His Majesty attached such importance to Forester Baron Speck von Sternburg's report on deer stocks in Rominten that he read it out at the lunch table. He met with silence, and yet eloquent disapproval, when the report spoke of the plan to buy up carrots as fodder to improve antler formation."[201]

On account of such burdens, the funding of the war became an ever-greater problem. In 1914 the Reichsbank had shared the view that it would be a short war, but the exorbitant costs of the conflict soon emptied the state coffers in the Spandau citadel in Berlin. To avoid endangering social cohesion by making daily life even more difficult for a population already weighed down by the human losses at the front, the government did not increase taxes to cover the deficit. (In fact, at an average of 14 percent, the tax rate in Germany was considerably lower than in France or Britain, for example.) Instead, the war was funded from loans and an increased money supply that pushed up inflation. The thinking behind war loans, which state institutions, banks, and savings banks promoted in large-scale operations as a patriotic duty for all Germans, was based on the idea that a victorious peace would bring a high level of reparations; only then would the loans and interest be paid in full. The war loans therefore strengthened collective behavior that ruled out expectations of a compromise peace or even a defeat. With an interest rate of 5 (or, from 1916, 4.6) percent, the bonds seemed an attractive proposition, especially as the shortage of goods to buy meant that quite a lot of money was floating around. The number of small subscribers, up to 2,000 marks, kept climbing until the fourth loan issue in March 1916, but many then shunned the fifth issue in Fall 1916 in the wake of the high casualties and meager results at Verdun and the Somme. Large investors increasingly took their place, lured by expectations of a sizable tax benefit.[202]

The climbing public debt and the monetary and credit inflation also led to a change in the relationship between central and local government.[203] The costs of providing for widows and orphans largely fell on urban and rural authorities, which had to resort in part to foreign loans. The change in all spheres of life was palpable in the cities: Freiburg, for example, because of its closeness to the Vosges and French air raids, had a strong atmosphere of a frontline city. The local war economy and the invasive regulation and bureaucratic control had an impact on the situation of wage earners. The winter of 1916–1917 was particularly harsh, as the food crisis reached into the most private areas of people's lives. New dietary and sartorial practices took hold, while disabled soldiers became part of the scene on city streets. Death—in the shape of funerals, obituaries, and stories circulating among neighbors—was naturally part of everyday life. Even wildlife was affected, as many hedgerows were stripped bare and various species of birds were driven out.

The collective narrative of national survival, which referred repeatedly to August 1914 as the defining moment, came under increasing pressure as a result of wartime experiences. In view of the uneven burdens of war and the obvious difficulties faced by its victims, the social consensus began to change despite the official propaganda campaigns. Conflicts developed within social groups and milieus as loyalties and self-images came to reflect new polarizations.[204] Münster provides a good example: the largely Catholic population of this city in Westphalia was vocally integrated into the national community at the beginning of the war, and patriotic priests took up the theme from church pulpits. But things changed later. While the Catholic elite continued to adhere to the conventional political and social order, workers were ever more forceful in their demand for reforms. Class affiliation became more important than the (Catholic) milieu.[205]

The year 1916 also brought a period of upheaval for parliamentary politicians and political parties. The Auxiliary Service Act of December 1916 had an important political dimension for the Reich chancellor, since its implicit recognition of labor unions as the representatives of industrial workers corresponded to his efforts to extend the social truce. The large parliamentary majority in favor of the law (235–19) brought together MPs from the Left Liberals, the Catholic Center, and the Social Democratic Party (SPD), while the 143 abstentions among those who until then had supported the chancellor—that is, from the conservative parties and the National Liberals—expressed a view that the concessions to workers and unions had gone too far. The "no" votes came from SPD members critical of the war.[206]

In 1916, despite the attempts to prolong the civil peace through concessions and worker-friendly discourse, the rifts in German society and politics were unmistakable. Large sections of the population saw the distribution of the burdens of war as unjust. Many pointed to the large output increases and noted the restructuring of capital in favor of the upper classes, whose members also owned tangible assets in the form of land, enterprises, and buildings that shielded them to some extent from price inflation.

Kaiser Wilhelm II operated less and less as the personification of the nation at war and more and more as a shadowy emperor who sent robotic orders to the front and signed memorial sheets by the thousand for soldiers killed in action.[207] In his stead, Hindenburg and the OHL in general took center stage. Other symbols had virtually no effect. Thus, an inscription (*Dem deutschen Volke*—To the German People) had been planned as far back as 1893 for the façade of the Reichstag, but had never materialized because of various objections and the Kaiser's own lack of support. Finally, after the press revived the idea in 1915, Arnold Wahnschaffe, the undersecretary at the chancellor's office, offered the government's (and hence Wilhelm's) approval, referring to the new "circumstances" in 1916. The proposal passed without further ado, and the inscription was put up shortly before Christmas 1916.[208]

By then, however, the idea of a politically integrated nation under the aegis of a symbolically upgraded parliament clashed with the emergence of sharp political conflict. This had become apparent at a Reichstag debate on emergency powers on March 24, 1916, when the spokesman for the critical wing of the SPD, Hugo Haase, emphasized that there would be no victors and vanquished at the end of the war, but "only defeated peoples bleeding from millions of wounds." In response, the finance secretary Helfferich attacked Haase personally and accused him of treason; he had dared in parliament "to utter words liable to give the enemy heart and encouragement and therefore to prolong the war."[209] This prefigured the legend of a "stab in the back" for troops at the front, but the debate also reflected a deepening of conflicts inside the SPD. The eighteen deputies under Haase's leadership who voted against the approval of fresh credits were subsequently expelled from the party; they went on to form a "Social Democrat Working Group" of their own in parliament, out of which the Independent Social Democratic Party of Germany (USPD) crystallized in 1917.

In another respect, too, it became clear that it was no longer possible to speak of an idealized nation at war in the spirit of August 1914. Early on, nationalist anti-Semites had begun to harp on the supposed benefits that Jews derived from the war; the Reichshammerbund (Reich Hammer League), for example, had put together "war reports" on the military and civilian activities of German Jews. Since Jews had been promoted to higher posts in the military and the state administration, such anti-Semites feared that this changed status would continue even after the end of the war, and they therefore sought to discredit Jews in general. This was helped along in October 1916 when the Catholic Center Party politician Matthias Erzberger, from the Reichstag budget committee, demanded that people employed in war companies should be listed by age, gender, income, and religion. Although the government rejected this proposal, a so-called census of Jews did take place in the armed forces: the Prussian war ministry justified this by referring to frequent complaints that Jews were disproportionately seeking to avoid military service. The shock haunted Jewish soldiers: "I feel as if I've received a terrible slap in the face," wrote Georg Meyer, two months before he was killed in action. The Frankfurt police chief noted that Jews there "remained alienated and were very reserved about my efforts to raise donations."[210]

Although no results were published during the war, the census of Jews in 1916 marked a parting of the ways. The accusations of shirking were nothing new, but for the first time the German state took over this argument from nationalist anti-Semites and based its surveys on them. For Jews, too, this meant a new kind of classification and exclusion, and many took a hard look at their Jewishness for the first time. Nor was the impact only psychological. In the statistics for one motorized unit, we read the following about Jewish soldiers: "The NCOs and men specified in the above order shall, if available, be promptly sent into the field—to places where they are completely exposed to enemy fire."[211] In contrast to Germany, the Austro-Hungarian army did not carry out an explicit census of Jews; the tradition of integrating various ethnic groups continued even under the military conditions of 1916.

4. POLICY CHANGE
From the Limits of the Imperial Order to the Crisis of Political Legitimacy

Two deaths marked the year 1916 in the Habsburg monarchy: the assassination of Prime Minister Stürgkh in October and the passing of the emperor in November. Already for people at the time, both events crystallized the volatility of the political order and the failing confidence in the cohesion of the monarchy. Earlier and more extensively than in Germany or the Entente countries, the social and economic consequences of the war generated political unrest in Austria-Hungary. Food shortages, runaway inflation, and housing problems shaped everyday life for hundreds of thousands of people, especially women, in large cities such as Vienna and Prague. Although Vienna and Prague, unlike Galicia and the Tyrol, were not close to the actual fighting, the burdens of war had worsened there since late 1915; half of the bakeries in Prague, for example, had closed in December because of a flour shortage. In 1916 the supply of potatoes plummeted, and turnips could not substitute entirely for them. The call-up of farmers and laborers, together with a drift from the country to the industrial centers, led to a shortage of agricultural labor, with the result that output fell considerably in 1915 and 1916. Since the Hungarian government refused to send more food to the western half of the Empire—it could barely manage to feed its own population—prices rose for agricultural produce from Hungary and fueled the mistrust on both sides. The response of the authorities in the western part of the Empire— from comprehensive rationing of food and consumer goods to the setting of maximum prices—did not alter the essential problems; indeed, it displayed the growing helplessness of the state.

The food shortages and the difficulty of providing for thousands of wounded soldiers were compounded by the refugee problem. As a consequence of the war of movement and the frequent changes of rule, large sections of the population from Galicia, especially Jews, were forced to flee to central areas of the country. Though citizens of the Empire, they encountered an ever more aggressive xenophobia in the overcrowded cities, where local people tended to exclude them and to scapegoat them for the supply shortages. In particular, the presence of east European *Ostjuden* in the metropolises fostered negative ethnic-religious stereotypes.[212] The nationalist propaganda of German youth movements in Bohemia operated quite openly with anti-Semitic imagery.

The shortages both threatened and shored up social cohesion. Protests grew in response to the shortages and the inability of the authorities to come up with appropriate solutions. In the Czech lands, the number of demonstrations in protest at the situation increased from 31 in 1915 to 70 in 1916, 252 in 1917, and 235 in 1918 (up to October).[213] Even if there was no sign that these were turning into a national polarization or mass demands for an independent state, people were changing their attitude to social cohesion on the home front.[214] The decisive factor in this was the constant worsening of the food supply situation, particularly in the large cities. The daily struggle for food in Vienna became a defining experience of the home front. Rising prices, the black marketization of more and more consumer goods, the housing crisis, and the influx of refugees made life a struggle for survival in which neighbors turned into competitors for the available supplies. Many women began to interpret the social woes and the latent criminalization of everyday life, but also their reactions to it and their ability to hold out, as an expression of war sacrifice equivalent to the combat role of their sons, brothers, and husbands at the front.[215] This attitude had many consequences: the individual experience of holding out in a crisis, transferred from the front, helped to stabilize women and society back home, while massive conflicts and tensions accumulated beneath the surface. The hunger revolts from May 1916 represented a further escalation, as the politicization of protest increasingly eroded the legitimacy of the authorities in Vienna.[216]

In the Habsburg monarchy, the determination to hold out showed visible cracks where the multiethnic character of society inflamed the issue of burden sharing and revived prewar conflicts that had been merely postponed in Summer 1914. The civil truce agreed to in 1914 changed in character, as the attitude of the Social Democrats clearly displayed.[217] In late March 1916, the national conference of the Social Democratic Workers' Party, under its chairman Viktor Adler, called for a comprehensive federalization of the monarchy: "A satisfactory lasting peace in southeastern Europe, which meets the needs of its peoples, can be achieved only by structuring Austria-Hungary as a democratic federal state, where all nations, enjoying the same rights and the same opportunities for development, combine their strength into a great political and social entity to which a free, independent Poland in the north and an independent league of free Balkan peoples in the south can adhere in their own and in the common interest."[218]

Although the party spoke of overcoming the traditional dualism, the Social Democrats stuck to the monarchy as a constitutional framework—it was not up for negotiation. Adler, in particular, still thought that the Central Powers would soon emerge victorious, and so demands for peace played no role, even if the Social Democrats already rejected the expansionist war aims of the conservative Right. A change came only with the military crisis of Summer 1916, which pushed the monarchy to the brink of catastrophe and strengthened its dependence on Germany. From then on, the demand for a peace without annexations or reparations was openly voiced. Early in November, the Party Conference issued this statement: "The government should be vigorously challenged to declare in public, after agreement with its allies, that the Central Powers are prepared at any time to open peace negotiations, on condition that all powers renounce direct or indirect annexations and war reparations."[219]

Tensions in Bohemia kept rising in 1916. At the beginning of June, Josef Redlich commented on the sentences handed down to various Czech politicians, including the popular Karel Kramář, who together with Josef Scheiner, the leader of the national armed movement of the Prague Sokol, had been arrested in May 1915 and accused of high treason. The trial and the reactions to their death sentences (which were later commuted to a term of imprisonment and ended with the amnestying of Kramář in 1917) appeared to Redlich symptomatic of the relations between Germans and Czechs: "With his [Kramář's] judgment," he noted in his diary on June 3, 1916, "the nearly forty years of Czech advancement within Austria" had come to an end, since the authorities had opted for confrontation rather than cooperation. The outcome would inevitably be "complete destruction of the idea of the empire" and disintegration of the monarchy. He could not understand the Germans who "politically, if not humanly, rejoice at the sentence on Kramář." He saw this as the "start of the most intense and dangerous battles within the Austro-Hungarian monarchy and the Austrian state."

In Redlich's eyes, the unequal constitutional treatment of Hungarians and Czechs reached its highpoint in 1916: both had demonstrated their francophilia during the war, but now only the Czech leaders had to suffer the consequences. Redlich considered the official policy toward Poland a further danger to the cohesion of the monarchy. If one considered that "Poles, even government ministers, had acted in a largely Russophile manner since 1905 and openly declared their existence as part of Austria to be no more than a temporary burden," then one would gain "the right vantage point for this whole sad development of Czech affairs and Czech public figures."[220] Redlich's assessment highlighted the fact that any outcome of the war might not simply be the maintenance of the unstable constitutional structure of the unequal monarchy. For this close observer of events and representative of liberalism, who never held an influential government position until he was appointed in 1918 as "liquidator of the old Austria," the idea of the Empire could be saved by forming a parliamentary government, federalizing the monarchy, and according autonomy rights to its individual peoples.[221] He was all too aware of the challenges that the Habsburg monarchy faced for its existence amid the reality of war; the monarchic-dynastic framework for the containment of ethnic diversity was no longer appropriate at a time when expectations were rising on all sides. With its origins in early modernity and the age of absolutism, the "centuries-old imperial empire and state made up of so many nations and tribes" was so difficult to preserve because "the liberal principles of individual political freedom and the nationalist principles of popular freedom were supposed to apply simultaneously for all the constituent lands and peoples."[222] The war generated not only an enormous dynamic of expectations but also multiple contradictions that continually called these principles into question, while everyday experiences increasingly undermined the legitimacy of the war state.

The loyalty of Czechs—as the course of the war until then had shown—was dependent on the military situation. It also was characterized by a cautious "bargaining" approach, a critical weighing of the costs and opportunities of a future within the monarchy. In the relationship between Czechs and Germans, this served again and again to confirm the mutual negative stereotypes: many Germans clung to their "national vested rights," because they thought they could detect an aggressive nationalism and a tendency to shirking on the part of the Czechs. The accusation of mass desertion by Czech units may not have been accurate, but it could be publicly instrumentalized as a political weapon. After the successful military operations against Russia in Summer 1915, the German nationalist parties developed ever more ambitious plans for a de facto Germanization of the Cisleithanian half of the Empire. Their Easter 1916 program asserted that the aim now was to enshrine the German position once and for all, effectively marginalizing other ethnic groups. Galicia, for example, would acquire a special status, thereby excluding Poles and Ruthenians from the future Imperial Council, while Bohemia would be governed along ethnic lines to neutralize the majority Czech population. German would become the official language of the state. The mistrust of Czechs grew apace when the new government in Vienna, under Clam-Martinic and Seidler, gave their support to this program.

In 1916, the main trend among Czechs was still one of situational loyalty to Vienna. So long as the war went reasonably well for the monarchy, as it did until Spring and Summer 1916, symbolic gestures of loyalty to emperor and dynasty were a matter of course in schools and churches and in numerous messages to the Kaiser. But the war with Russia was never popular, and fears grew that a victory for the Central Powers would further increase the Teutonic weight within the monarchy and promote Germanization and harsh AOK practices in Bohemia.[223]

As the situation on the Russian front became critical in Summer 1916, the relationship between public loyalty and symbolic distance changed. But the wearing of Slavic symbols or flouting of order in everyday life, often through symbolic resistance of the kind later expressed in the literary figure of the soldier Schwejk, cannot be straightforwardly equated with a mass tendency to seek constitutional independence. Such actions also reflected a growing war weariness and spirit of protest, especially against the AOK top brass, which focused on petty restrictions or on official measures that were felt as a provocation—for example, the dissolution of the Sokol association in late 1915 and the cancellation of the quincentenary celebrations of the burning of Jan Hus, the national Czech martyr, when all references to him, or to leaders of the Bohemian revolt executed after 1618, were removed from school textbooks, postcards, and even the Prague city hall. The authorities also took steps to suppress the Czech language.[224] Attitudes to the eight war loans issued up to the end of the war were revealing: Czechs made up only 20 percent of the subscribers, far below the percentage of Germans and Jews in Bohemia (Franz Kafka's family being one case in point).[225] Confidence in the traditional structure of the Habsburg monarchy was thus waning among Czechs because of the military situation in Summer 1916 and because of the growing dominance of Germans within the Central Powers and in the Cisleithanian half of the Empire.

In parallel to these developments, exile circles developed into a second political space linking the independence movements with the Allies. The far from conflict-free relations between the exiles and their home societies were an indicator of the reduced room for maneuver and the gradual turning away from the monarchy as a constitutional framework. This was not yet so apparent in 1916, but the activities of exile politicians and their commitment to national independence fed back into their home societies, representing a permanent political alternative to which people there had to relate.[226] This was most striking in the case of Czech exiles. At first, Masaryk's plans for a state of Czechs and Slovaks remained quite vague; he was anyway skeptical of too great a reliance on Russia, where the authorities viewed Czech expatriates with suspicion. Czech politicians came together in a secret society to promote the idea of an independent state among Western governments, and cooperation with exile groups in Allied countries and the United States was closely coordinated.[227] Alongside London, Paris developed as a center for these activities, with Masaryk's close colleague Edvard Beneš as its key

figure. But it was only in late 1915 that the two men established serious contacts with Slovak representatives, a breakthrough coming with the October
agreement of Czechs and Slovaks to work together in the United States to
solicit political support. The Comité d'action tchèque à l'étranger, an umbrella
organization founded on November 14, 1915, publicly announced the goal
of an independent state. The formation of a Czechoslovak National Council
followed in February 1916.[228]

Masaryk, as chairman of the National Council, became more and more
prominent after the arrest of leading politicians in Bohemia, but it was not
easy to exert effective influence from abroad. First, the Allies were by no
means convinced that the dissolution of the Habsburg monarchy and the
foundation of new independent states were inevitable, and for a long time
they remained wedded to the idea of a reformed monarchy with greater
autonomy for the various nationalities. Second, Masaryk's plans for a Czech
Legion as the visible core of a future sovereign state initially found no support. In Russia, the authorities permitted only the creation of small military
units, not a full-fledged legion with its own commanders, but at least such
units were a starting point. Third, the programs of Czech politicians in Prague
and exile organizations under Masaryk cannot be said to have been congruent. Even in the third year of the war, and for all their criticisms of Habsburg
dualism, the Czech parties still saw their future as lying within a reformed
federal monarchy. In January 1917 the Czech Union assured Karl, the new
monarch, that "the Czech nation, in the future as in the past," viewed "the
conditions for its development under the scepter of the Habsburgs." The
occasion for this declaration of loyalty may have been the royal inauguration,
but it was not merely rhetorical. Only in the course of 1917, with the growth
of political tensions back home, as well as changes in Austria-Hungary's
foreign policy situation and the attitude of the Allied powers, did politicians
living abroad acquire the scope to exert greater influence.[229]

The death of Franz Joseph on November 21, 1916, was a symbolic watershed for people at the time. Josef Redlich noted the emperor's integrative
force, based on a monarchic-dynastic continuity expressed in his rule stretching across generations: "On Thursday, November 21, at nine in the evening,
Emperor Franz Joseph died a peaceful death. With him ends the Francisceian
Austria that began in 1792, when Maria Theresa's son Leopold II passed

away. When Franz Joseph was born my grandfather was 25 years old; when he ascended the throne my father was 9; and when my father died at the age of 57 the emperor outlived him by almost another 21 years. He outlived the generation of Ferdinand I, the generation of the revolution, the men of 1866 and the generation of the occupation of Bosnia, the social-political generation of the 1880s, and the capitalist and imperialist generation that had Franz Ferdinand as its center. And he has died amid the generation that is battling its way through the world war."[230]

The emperor's death exacerbated the crisis of confidence, especially among the Czech population.[231] The defense of Czech interests against Germanization did not as such go beyond the limits of a national movement rooted in the nineteenth century and operating within the framework of the multiethnic monarchy. Still, Czech politicians took a major step forward in criticizing the dualist system and the dangers of a full-scale Germanization of Cisleithania: they held that the objective of a federal monarchy that recognized and upgraded the constitutional position of Czechs and Slovaks and South Slavs was not achievable without drawing on Hungarian territory. Although these demands did not call into question the existence of the monarchy, they were no longer reconcilable with the traditional dualist system and the territorial integrity of Hungary. These tensions resulted in polarization within the Habsburg monarchy, so that by the end of 1916 national contrasts had become an instrument in political disputes.[232]

Just a couple of days before the Kaiser's death, Czech members of the last prewar imperial council founded the Czech Union. A national committee took shape on the initiative of the political parties, creating for the first time a common institutional basis and fundamental agreement about how they should proceed.[233] Thus, the winter of 1916–1917 became a turning point in the internal politics of the Habsburg monarchy. On October 21, Prime Minister Karl Stürgkh was shot by Friedrich Adler, son of the Social Democratic Party leader Viktor Adler. His motive was not only opposition to the war: he was also protesting the lack of parliamentary government since Spring 1914, which in his view had increasingly led to an army-supported dictatorship. The assassin was sentenced to death, but this was commuted by the emperor and he was eventually released in an amnesty in 1918. The assassination, followed by the Kaiser's death in November, highlighted the political tensions in the third year of war and the fragility of the integrative personal symbols at the disposal of the monarchy. Together with the glaring shortages and exhaustion in the large cities, the social and economic costs of the war, and the evident dependence on Germany, this situation reinforced the polarization within the monarchy as a whole.

Franz Joseph's successor, the 29-year-old Karl, had served mainly as a military commander after the assassination of the original crown prince Franz Ferdinand; he was placed in this role to bolster the popularity of the monarchy. But neither in the spring offensive against Italy in 1916 nor in the operations against Romania had he been able to make a real mark on his own; the fact that he gave his name to the southeastern army front had done nothing to change the dominance of the German commanders. After the emperor's death, Karl's swift coronation as king of Hungary on December 30, 1916, accompanied by the Calvinist István Tisza in the St. Matthew church in Budapest, appeared symptomatic of the attempt to preserve the dualist system with all its contradictions and to demonstrate the unbroken continuity of the dynasty.[234] Politically, however, the new king—whose youth emphasized the contrast with the transgenerational figure of Franz Joseph as bulwark of the monarchy—immediately came under pressure. While he had to overcome tensions between the two parts of the monarchy and to organize a reform of the dualist system that addressed the fears of the Czechs and South Slavs, he also faced the external political and military challenge of acting with some degree of independence vis-à-vis Germany and the Third OHL.

Volatility was also apparent in Hungarian society.[235] Romania's entry into the war and the attack on Transylvania taxed the resources of István Tisza, the Hungarian prime minister, since he had repeatedly justified the internal political truce by arguing that it was necessary to guarantee the country's security. The military threat from Russia and Romania in the summer and fall of 1916 made such claims appear less credible. At the same time, criticism of the Tisza regime intensified the opposition outside parliament: the leader of the Independence Party, Count Mihály Károlyi—who in 1918 would became chairman of the Hungarian National Council, assume the premiership, and proclaim the republic—demanded that Austria-Hungary end its political-military dependence on Germany and pushed for peace talks with the Entente powers. The search was underway for alternatives to a continuation of the war alongside Germany.

Pressure mounted on Budapest to introduce reforms such as an opening of the suffrage to all ethnic groups and social strata. Yet nothing of substance was done before late 1918. The regime under Tisza and his successor Wekerle remained elitist, closed both to the workers' political representatives and to non-Magyar sections of the population;[236] even critics of Tisza such as Károlyi supported the course of ethnic-national exclusion. The policy of Magyar imperialism therefore continued within Hungary—one reason being a fear that in the long run the dominance of the Magyar elite would otherwise be questioned. The main victims were Slovaks and Transylvanian Romanians. No fewer than 3,000 alleged "traitors" were interned in a camp at Sopron in late 1916. At the same time, the expulsion of Social Democrat and labor union representatives from parliament widened the gulf between the parliamentary and extra-parliamentary public spaces.[237]

All in all, a fundamental reform of the monarchy seemed inevitable by the end of 1916, both because of political developments within the two parts of the Empire (especially the reorientation among Czechs, Slovaks, and Slovenes) and because the policies of the government and the AOK made it impossible to continue with the status quo. In November 1916 the Kingdom of Poland, though dependent on the governments in Berlin and Vienna that set it up, emerged in principle as a national Polish state, changing the balance between the parts of the Habsburg monarchy and showing the scope for changes in east central Europe.

Max Weber—who was deeply involved in the discussions on Poland—emphasized how much Germany's orientation to the east and to the west depended on its future political shape. He rejected a German annexation of Polish territories, as well as any idea of a German-Austrian protectorate. Courland (a region in Latvia) under German rule seemed to him a pure illusion. Above all, he argued for Germany to adopt a long-term orientation to the West, free of obligations to Austria-Hungary in line with Friedrich Naumann's vision of *Mitteleuropa*. A clear demarcation from Russia was essential—and this gave meaning to a Polish state. Independent Latvia and Lithuania would constitute the future borderlands with Russia.[238]

The case of Poland made it clear that the attempts of the Central Powers to gain new allies, by holding out the prospect of national advances, set up a dynamic in 1916–1917 that would be more and more difficult to control. After the offensives of Summer 1915 and the conquests in eastern Galicia, Lvov, and Russian Poland, German and Austro-Hungarian administrative areas had been created in Poland; the authorities did collaborate with the Poles, but they made no substantial concessions to the independence movement. In fact, even the limited collaboration of Poles within structures laid down by the Central Powers forced elements of the national movement to take the road of exile. Roman Dmowski, for instance, the leader of the National Democrats, fled via Russia and Sweden to Switzerland, where he founded a new Polish National Committee in August 1917 and, together with Poles living in the United States, sought to enlist western Allied support for an independent state. However, the scope for Polish operations abroad only really expanded from 1917 on.

Inside the country, Poles did approach the new authorities with a view to collaboration, but many members of the independence-oriented national movement were disappointed with the policies of the Germans and Austrians, especially after Polish administrative bodies set up after the withdrawal of Russian troops were dissolved in September 1915. Numerous National Democrats then refused any further cooperation. Piłsudski, too, felt let down and pinned his hopes on secret military units to fight for independence— relying on the Central Powers, it is true, but with the Poles' own forces. The main instrument was to be a Polish army, in line with his operations in August 1914 against the Russians in Kielce.[239]

The longer the war lasted, and the more remote a victory over Russia seemed, the more significance Poland acquired for the Central Powers. This forced them to make concessions. In mid-November 1915, two high schools reopened in Warsaw, and permission was given for a Polish militia. After the independence movement established a central national committee in December 1915 under Piłsudski's unofficial leadership, it issued the Declaration of the Hundred in February 1916 calling for an independent state with its own army as a token of political sovereignty. But neither this document nor the two governors' proclamation of the Kingdom of Poland as a constitutional monarchy on November 5, 1916, gave a precise definition of the territory of the future state. In the end, the policy of the Central Powers remained inconsistent, reflecting as it did the ever-changing operational situation in the war. The Germans and Austro-Hungarians wanted to gain Polish support, but they were not willing to grant a truly independent state; their aim in setting up the Kingdom of Poland was in effect to create a satellite state. The leaders of the Polish independence movement began to look instead, from late 1916, to a sharpening of the political instability inside Russia. In particular, they hoped that the dramatic changes that occurred there in 1917 would give them a better bargaining position with Berlin and Vienna. The more uncertain the situation became in Russia, the greater interest the Central Powers had in a stable Poland.[240]

More than any other group in the Habsburg monarchy, the Jews experienced the complexity of the relationship between loyalty to the war state and their own identity. Three factors were of special importance: the role of the monarchy as guarantor of their rights as citizens (although these were increasingly flouted as the war went on, especially for Jewish refugees from Galicia); integration into their respective national cultures, such as German and Czech culture in Prague; and the relationship to their existence as Jews.[241] These reference points were by no means mutually exclusive; indeed, they continually overlapped with one other. Franz Kafka's perception of the war, for example, did not begin and end with the oft-quoted laconic diary entry for August 2, 1914: "Germany has declared war on Russia. Swimming in the afternoon"—as if that was all the war meant for him.[242] On April 4, 1915, he wrote to his fiancée Felice: "I suffer most from the war because I am not there myself." He also often expressed empathy with Jewish refugees from Galicia and shell-shocked soldiers.[243] As we have seen, Kafka's family subscribed to war loans, exemplifying the confidence that many Jews had in the survival of the monarchy; they hoped that, as the only higher institution, it would be able to contain national tensions and stem exclusive senses of belonging. As the wartime experiences of shortage and suffering became more acute, however, the more Jews had to recognize that others were scapegoating them and subjecting them to ethnic-religious exclusion. Daily encounters with Jewish refugees from Galicia brought this home in all its force.

But the war also confronted many Jews with their own Jewishness in an increasingly hostile milieu. This was true for liberal, assimilated Jews who observed the quite different reality of life for Orthodox Jews from Galicia, but it was also apparent in the development of Zionism. In 1916 the soldier

Hugo Bergmann, signing an article "from the field," described how the war was challenging the traditional passivity of Jews and forcing them into a new self-assertiveness, which pointed beyond the usual religious ceremonies and rituals toward a popular movement of their own. Bergmann noted a "new chapter in our age-old passive history." Jews had to stop believing "that this holiday Jewishness, this Jewishness at home, still amounts to anything. The war has inevitably brought us to a sense of reality and a critical attitude toward everything empty and imaginary. That kind of Jewishness, no longer rooted in life, is only a word . . . ; for us everything depends on whether we have learned in war to distinguish appearance from being, and whether we shall have the strength to create a truly Jewish national movement."[244]

There can be no doubt that Jews were particularly affected by the dealings of wartime authorities with multiethnic, multireligious populations and by the incipient trend toward territorial changes in eastern Europe. In a future Lithuanian state, for example, Jews would form one of the largest population groups alongside Poles and Lithuanians; they were even the majority in cities such as Vilnius. This created major tensions. In Poland, a dual line of conflict—with the administration of the Central Powers and with ethnic Poles—developed for Jews.[245] The attitude of Jewish civilians to the occupation forces in Ober Ost also changed as they became increasingly critical of the practice of forced labor. Jewishness was more and more a status imposed from above—but its defining criteria oscillated between religion and nationality. Whereas in the Kingdom of Poland the authorities recognized Jews as a religious community, in Ober Ost they treated them as a nationality—so little did discussions of status permit conclusions regarding actual conditions of existence. Such distinctions were important, however, as the struggle of Jews for recognition as a nationality within the Habsburg monarchy amply demonstrated. Nationality status, it was hoped, would be the basis for extensive rights that offered better protection against anti-Semitic currents.

In Russia, too, a high-profile killing in late 1916 fueled tensions in wartime society. When members of the court and the Duma assassinated Rasputin, the miracle healer and confidant of the Tsarina, on December 31, 1916, their action brought the year to a dramatic end. The shock of the frontal breakthroughs in 1915 and subsequent military developments had led the Russians, with French and British help, to mobilize the war economy again in late 1915 and early 1916.[246] Although this improved supplies to the army in Spring and Summer 1916, contributing to the initial successes of the summer offensive, Russia's general economic situation and the supply of the cities, in particular, remained precarious. The burdens of war hopelessly overloaded the transport infrastructure—even if this was less a sign of backwardness than a result of the booming war economy. The Russian railroads were already running at capacity in peacetime—and the huge challenge of supplying domestic industry, the big cities, and the long frontlines from the Baltic to the Black Sea stretched them to breaking point. Furthermore, the country was cut off from its main import routes in the Baltic and the Black Sea. Allied weapons and munitions deliveries, on which Russia relied to continue the war, had to be laboriously transported across long stretches of land. This may have been adequate for a short offensive, but in 1916 the Russian war economy was not up to a longer war of materiel.

As in other war societies, the switchover from a peacetime to a war economy promoted a general trend to centralization. In Russia, too, it was hoped that various new boards and authorities would master the tasks of economic mobilization by means of targeted reorganization. The Central War Economy Committee founded in 1915 and the Committee for the Development of Russia's Productive Forces attached to the Academy of Sciences were examples of the unprecedented opportunities that the war offered to scientists and engineers. By highlighting the country's infrastructure problems, the war seemed to present a chance to press ahead with modernization in areas such as transport and electrification. Another indication that the war served as an engine of development was the fact that cooperation with the Allies established whole new branches of industry in Russia; arms-centered collaboration with the French and Italian firms Renault and Fiat, for example, kick-started the twentieth-century Russian automobile industry.[247]

Yet these processes came at a high social cost. The shift of resources to key war industries meant that large sections of consumer goods production lagged behind. The consequences of this were different for the rural and urban populations: the migration of many families from the country to work in the industrial centers initially intensified the food supply problem, and a number of peasants took advantage of the situation. Not threatened themselves because they had their own means of subsistence, they withheld much of their produce or sold it at a high profit on the burgeoning black markets that the authorities could never adequately control. The food supply situation thus became more and more difficult in the big cities.

Similar developments tended to occur in other belligerent countries, especially the Habsburg monarchy. But in Russia, when the last military offensives became bogged down in Summer and Fall 1916 without having achieved any real success, the discontent began to escalate into a legitimation crisis of the tsarist state. The supply problem and galloping inflation, together with the social implications of the rural exodus in terms of overcrowded housing and poor hygiene, rapidly eroded confidence in traditional authorities. The war had stoked demands for an efficient solution to problems, above all in the cities, but officials there were less and less capable of ensuring an adequate food supply. The proportion of bread and fodder cereals that farmers marketed across regions sank from 12.4 percent between 1909 and 1913 to a mere 7.4 percent in 1915.[248] As it became clearer that the authorities could not handle the challenges, the critical social and economic situation began to generate political protest. Strikes and demonstrations—which had been occurring since Summer 1915 in parallel to the mutinies in the army—began to increase markedly from Fall 1916.[249]

These protests also had an effect on the standing of figures at the head of the Empire. The Tsar himself, who had taken command of the armed forces in Summer 1915 as the Central Powers were breaking through the front, became the focus of political protest along with the top brass. The Brusilov offensive, despite its initial successes, was unable to stem this erosion of legitimacy by the fall of 1916. As other belligerent countries would soon realize, the high toll at the front raised expectations that the next offensive, waged at the cost of new casualties, would bring the war to an end. Often this prospect was the only way to motivate Russian soldiers to fight. But the failure to achieve this in Summer 1916 on the southeastern front, comparable to the failure of the French Nivelle offensive in Spring 1917 and German experiences in Spring and Summer 1918 on the western front, dashed these ever-rising expectations and led to a deep disillusionment that sought a way to ventilate itself politically. Insofar as the lack of military success devalued earlier casualties, people began to doubt the sense of the war. Until 1916 the mechanism continued to function, but from Summer and Fall 1916—first of all in Russia—high casualties, growing exhaustion on the home front, military deadlock, and a massive crisis of confidence came together in a potent mix. In Russia, this drove the negative spiral leading to the fall of the tsarist regime in early 1917.

In one key respect, Russia's internal situation in late Summer and Fall 1916 differed from the exhaustion in other wartime societies: the loss of political credibility and the erosion of monarchic legitimacy developed much faster because political institutions such as the Duma had neither the experience nor the self-confidence to counter this process. Moreover, political and military representatives of the Tsarist Empire became alienated not only from the urban masses whose livelihood was threatened but also from the elites themselves, whose great fear was of a social revolution from below. For a time this constellation turned the Duma and the supraregional authorities, organized in the All-Russian Union of Zemstvos and the All-Russian Union of Cities, into alternative political platforms.[250] The Progressive Bloc, formed in 1915 under Pavel Milyukov and now representing three-quarters of deputies, engaged in open criticism, but this did not conceal the fact that parliament was unequal to a showdown with the Tsar.[251] As members of a relatively new institution, most deputies lacked the kind of strong constitutional or even parliamentary self-assurance that would have made them capable of resolute opposition. When the military situation had stabilized in Summer 1915, the Tsar effectively suspended the policy of reforms, appointed a conservative-reactionary government, and in September (on the advice of the geriatric prime minister Ivan Goremykin) dissolved the Duma as he had done in previous situations of conflict. In November 1916, following a series of defeats, signs of military and social-economic exhaustion, and a new wave of protests, the Duma, having been recalled in February, once more became the center of political argument.[252] On November 1, Milyukov—as leader of the Constitutional Democrats in the Duma—criticized the failures and omissions of the Tsar's government. But unlike earlier performances, his speech openly posed the question of legitimacy, rhetorically asking after each paragraph whether "stupidity or treachery" lay behind the government's negligence.[253]

Outside parliament, too, the person of the Tsar came under attack more and more frequently. An oppositional stance knit together various sections of the elite—from the war industry committees through the Duma groups to army commanders. By holding the Tsar personally responsible for the situation, they distracted attention from their own shortcomings and incorrect assessments. And by presenting him as an obstacle to military success, they increasingly eroded the basis of his rule. In this situation, the Rasputin affair served to catalyze a latent crisis of legitimacy. Rasputin's allegedly sexual relationship with Tsarina Alexandra, a German by origin, and the supposed influence he had on her and Russian politics, right up to the personal decisions of the Tsar, created a surface in Summer 1916 onto which all negative attributes of personal disloyalty and national behavior could be projected. The public scandal surrounding these issues underlined the fact that the monarch's special aura and sacralized rule, still so apparent in August 1914, were losing their effect. Things had already reached the point that, when Rasputin was murdered on the last day of the year by Duma deputies and the Tsar's nephew Felix Yusupov, Nicholas took no action against the assassins. It seemed an admission of impotence and a harbinger of his own downfall.[254]

In December 1916, at the end of a year in which renewed economic mobilization and high casualties had allowed Russia to achieve its most significant breakthroughs of the war, the dominant mood was one of disappointment with the military results and divisions on the home front. These took the form of conflict among the elites, between the Tsar and government, and within the Progressive Bloc in the Duma, but also of tense relations among the traditional parliamentary elites, the industrial committee, the army leadership, and the urban underclasses. Bourgeois as well as noble elite members feared a descent into revolution on the streets. Furthermore, the turn against the Tsar disguised the divergence of interests and expectations between the elites and the urban masses.[255] Confidence in the existing institutions was crumbling, but it remained unclear what would take their place. As a vacuum of rule developed at the head of the state and the military situation remained volatile, mistrust continued to spread among the key political players.[256] Duma Liberals, as champions of constitutional change, misjudged the mood in the country and at the front. Committed to the war and to the unity of the Russian Empire, they relied on the ideal of a society of citizens equal before the law, in line with the French model of 1789. Once the autocracy had fallen, a Russian nation in arms would continue the struggle against the Central Powers, as the French had waged the revolutionary wars of the 1790s.

The tensions, however, were not only of a political and social nature. As in Britain and the British Empire, military recruitment practices in 1916 caused ethnic conflicts to escalate. Long-dormant tensions came to the surface when the Russian war state encroached on local structures. Moreover, new criteria of ethnicity and class came to the fore within the army, increasingly supplanting the categories of status and religion traditionally used in dealings with the population of the Empire, and traditionalists and conservatives lost ground within the military leadership. This trend had a number of consequences: while ethnic Germans living in Moscow had their property confiscated, and Jews were exposed to spontaneous, though officially supported, attacks, extensive promises were made in border regions, especially Galicia and Poland, in an attempt to gain support against the Central Powers. At the same time, the army created ethnic units in the hope that they would heighten cohesion and combat motivation, especially among the Caucasian Muslims, who were originally recruited as volunteers but were now included in the conscription system. The practice of categorizing the population by class and ethnicity would become even more pronounced in the civil war that developed after 1917.[257]

Never before had Russia seen so many people in movement. This basic experience gave millions of peasant soldiers their first real glimpse of the ethnic diversity of the Empire, but they experienced it more as a constant danger than as an enrichment or opportunity. Hence their mistrust and their suspicion that peripheral peoples—in the Baltic, in Poland, the Caucasus, and parts of Ukraine—were unreliable and disloyal. For soldiers stationed on the western fringes of the Empire, the foreignness of these territories increased the fear of espionage and treason.[258] It was an experience that would mark a whole generation of soldiers and later Bolsheviks. In the dual enemy-image that resulted, the external foe existed alongside spies and traitors behind the front who withheld support and loyalty from the army and against whom it was necessary to act with no holds barred.[259] This juxtaposition of internal and external enemies existed in other wartime societies, but nowhere else did it so quickly assume radical forms or have such radical consequences.

Events in the Caucasus in 1916 seemed to confirm the suspicions of disloyalty, unreliability, and treachery. There conflicts flared up not with the introduction of conscription, as they did in Britain, for example, but after the extension of the draft to a multiethnic context. The huge losses of officers and men, as well as the buildup for offensives against the Central Powers, compelled the Russian government to enlist soldiers and laborers in parts of the Empire that had previously been exempt, particularly those in Central Asia with a Muslim population. When a decree of June 25, 1916, drafted 390,000 native *inorodtsy* for labor service in the vicinity of the front, a resistance movement sprang up that should not be underestimated and that pointed back to earlier causes. In November, the local boss of the tsarist secret police, Vladimir F. Sheleznyakov, listed what he saw as the five main reasons for the revolt: (1) Cossack units had stolen cattle from Kazakhs living in the area; (2) the land question had become a source of conflict when more and more settlers moved into the region, especially since 1906, taking the best pasture-land from nomads and often driving them out; (3) this led to increasingly fraught relations between Kazakhs and Russian settlers; (4) appreciation had not been shown for the self-sacrifice that local Kazakhs displayed at the beginning of the war in the form of voluntary donations, many of which had been swallowed up by the corrupt bureaucratic apparatus; and (5) corruption in the Russian secret police meant that the term "gendarme" had become synonymous with "racketeer."[260]

This view highlighted the extent to which colonial practices within the Empire had led to crisis by the year 1916. From 1906 on, the state-promoted introduction of eastern Slav settlers had displaced nomadic peoples on a massive scale in Central Asia—a policy that, together with deliberate Russification, was supposed to strengthen the cohesion of the multiethnic empire after its defeat in the war with Japan. Another reason why many Muslims experienced the mobilization as a forced imposition was that they felt at the mercy of a corrupt administration serving the Russian power elite—a situation they tended to personalize in the secret policeman Sheleznyakov and the rebel leader Kanat Abukin, whom the colonial administration had badly disappointed.[261] Thus, in Summer 1916 a long-simmering conflict escalated between nomadic herdsmen and Russian settlers from European parts of the Empire, who had been supported by the Russian government since the late nineteenth century. Colonial practices had already hardened the attitudes of army officers, bureaucrats, settlers, nomads, and the local population. But only the world war caused the conflict to burst into the open, because pressure on the Russian war state to mobilize all available resources broke down traditional constraints. Ethnically and ideologically motivated violence did not therefore begin only in 1917 and continue until 1922, with the revolution, the civil war, and the founding of the Soviet Union. In Central Asia, it stemmed more from the gradual radicalization of all social players, on the sides of both colonizers and colonized, since the late nineteenth century.[262]

The local and regional rebellions developed into a major conflagration, the largest uprising to occur between the February Revolution of 1905 and the October Revolution of 1917. It swept up the whole of Central Asia, including Kyrgystan, Kazakhstan, and the Trans-Caspian region, fusing the resistance together with religious themes. Attacks on Russian officials and colonial symbols such as the railroad were also seen as part of an Islamic jihad against untrustworthy colonizers.[263] The suppression of the revolt was brutal partly because Russia saw it as a challenge both to its war state and to its colonial rule. General Kuropatkin, the governor of Turkestan, ordered the spatial separation of Russians and Kazakhs, and it has been estimated that hundreds of thousands died or were expelled (more than 200,000 were moved to the Chinese part of Turkestan). Following the decimation of the nomadic population and the destruction of their means of subsistence, more farmers were resettled there from the European part of the Russian Empire.[264]

The extent to which the multiethnic character of the Empire affected the Russian war effort became unmistakable in the course of 1916. Unlike in the Ottoman sphere of influence or in Asia, the Central Powers had some prospect of success in exploiting ethnic divisions and thereby working to accelerate the breakup of the Russian Empire. With regard to Poland, all the players attempted to weaken their enemy by offering concessions. The exploitation of ethnic diversity—which before 1914 had led to external intervention at most in the case of the Ottoman Empire—became a common instrument of strategy in 1916. Russians, Austrians, and Germans made rival and inherently contradictory promises in relation to east central and eastern Europe, trying to outdo one another in ways that challenged the legitimacy of their empires. Russia's promises lost credence early in the war, when the Central Powers captured large swathes of non-Russian territory, and the way was then open for Vienna and Berlin to proclaim a de facto Kingdom of Poland. What at first sight appeared to be national liberation under the aegis of a war of movement turned out to be a calculation on Germany's part, in particular, that symbolic concessions on the national question could gain it new dependent allies for the war.[265]

The German military relied on the same strategic combination of promises and military mobilization in its dealings with other national movements in eastern Europe. Thus, supporters of the Finnish national movement fielded twenty-seven units of their own in the Baltic, under the umbrella of the Prussian Fusilier Battalion, while the League of Foreign Peoples, founded with German support in Stockholm in May 1916, consciously used ethnic conflicts as a weapon against Russian domination. The spectrum of its delegates ranged from Poles, Baltic Germans, Jews, and Ukrainians through Lithuanians, Latvians, and Belarusians to Georgians and Muslims, taking in various ethnic and religious groups that would turn in 1917 to President Wilson and his advocacy of the right to national self-determination. The Congress of Nationalities held in Lausanne, together with the *Bulletin des Nationalités de Russie* that first appeared in September 1916, operated as important platforms from which to gain international public support for the concerns of non-Russian nationalities. This tendency to internationalization—a new feature not yet discernible as such in the period before 1914—put the imperial elites under growing pressure, even before Woodrow Wilson's declaration of Spring 1917 and the Bolshevik revolution in October made the idea of national self-determination a global reference point.

5. HUMAN MATERIAL AND THE BATTLE OF MATERIEL
Planning, Frontline Experiences, Ways of Coping

Why did 1916 represent such a watershed in the war? In late 1915, the idea of deciding the war through ever more violent frontal attacks in a concentrated space began to give way to a different conception. From then on, the aim was to wear down and exhaust the enemy by inflicting heavy losses in men and materiel: it was to be a protracted process, rather than one big battle. This shift, however, reflected the disorientation of army commanders in the face of colossal firepower and the strength of defensive weaponry.[266]

The idea of wearing the enemy down was a novelty in the history of military strategy. For Carl von Clausewitz, "exhaustion" had no strategic value of its own: battles would decide the issue by virtue of the resolve and strength on either side. He did, it is true, point out that "fatigue" and "exhaustion of the stronger side" had often led to peace, but he insisted that this should not be seen as the ultimate objective of defense; rather, the "aim of the defense must embody the idea of waiting—which is after all its leading feature."[267] The military historian Hans Delbrück, in his *Geschichte der Kriegskunst,* counterposed a "wearing down" strategy (*Ermattungsstrategie*) to the concept of overcoming and crushing the enemy.[268] If—as in the case of Frederick the Great in the Seven Years' War—the "available means of war" were insufficient to "completely overcome the enemy state," it was necessary "to force it toward pliability and peace not so much by defeating it as by exhausting it." Yet Delbrück was convinced that this only applied to "the old monarchic system," whose rulers did not seek a conclusive battle. Since the French Revolution, in contrast, all wars had been all-out conflicts, in which all sides had sought a decisive battle.[269]

The military view of the relationship between costs and benefits, casualties and territorial gains, changed considerably amid the post-1914 realities of war. At least linguistically, it was not a First World War innovation to regard men in battle as a material resource; Theodor Fontane, for example, described British soldiers in the Crimean War in 1854 as "raw human material," and Houston Stuart Chamberlain, in his bellicose, vitalist work *The Foundations of the Nineteenth Century,* argued that "the struggle which means destruction for fundamentally weak . . . human material" strengthens the strong.[270] But it was only after 1914 that the term really entered the administrative vocabulary: "human material" corresponded to thinking centered on quantitative resources, on an economy of casualties, death rates, and killing power. It combined the experiences of men and machines with a demand for objectivity and scientific planning, decisively overshadowing the heroic elements still present in the nineteenth century. In the idea that it was possible to plan the course and outcome of a war, "human material" took its place alongside "war materiel." On August 31, 1916, in a submission to the German war minister *On Personnel Replacement and War Materiel,* Hindenburg stressed, "There is no doubt that future offensives will set even stronger tests for our capacity to resist, since our enemies have not only (1) almost inexhaustible human material, but also (2) an industry almost equal to that of all other countries. On (1), our human supplies are limited in comparison with the enemy's human material. . . . Men, as well as horses, must be increasingly replaced with machines."[271] The dynamic of the war of materiel is apparent in a German service manual for mine warfare in 1916, which states on the subject of trench fortifications, "If sandbags are lacking, the trench should be stopped up with earth, or even enemy corpses."[272] Thus, dead bodies, albeit of enemy soldiers, were reduced to the function of ensuring one's own survival.

In 1920, Ernst Jünger's preface to his *Storm of Steel* addressed this change in the experience of war. The book took up the metaphor of human material: "The monster's shadow is still raging above us. The most colossal thing in wars is still too close for us to take it all in, let alone to visibly crystallize its spirit. One aspect, however, emerges clearly from the flood of experiences: the paramount importance of matter. The war peaked in the battle of materiel; machines, iron, and explosives were its factors. Even human beings were considered as material." This world of materiel turned war into work, front into workplace, soldiers into workers.[273]

The war brought a new cult of enumeration, of quantifiability: it was also a war of lists and questionnaires. Comparative casualties, the unit cost of killing, the efficiency of military force: all these concerns were not invented by later historians, but were an important part of planning at the time, a specialist field of study that operated with cause-effect assumptions and scenarios. A particular conception of reality developed within the general staffs and ministries—one that became more and more remote from the soldiers' experience but had a deep, long-term impact on the home societies, where people registered very precisely the effects of war (for example, aerial bombardment) on the civilian population. After the war, H. A. L. Fisher remarked to Virginia Woolf that no one could afford to have another war, because in ten years the Germans would be able to "blot out London by their airplanes. It cost us £1000 to kill a German at the Battle of the Somme; now it costs us £3,000."[274]

A good example of this demographic economy of war may be found in the writings of Erich von Falkenhayn. Looking back at Summer 1916, in an attempt to justify his plans for the Battle of Verdun, he formulated a distinctive logic of perseverance in a war that could not be won by the classical criteria of victory and defeat. In his eyes, the war had not been fought "for the sake of glory or land"; it had been a struggle for "the survival of our nation," which we could not achieve by "physically crushing all our enemies in the literal sense of the word." Rather, it had been necessary to calculate the cost of defeating the enemy. Enemies therefore had to be shown once and for all that they were "incapable of paying the price to defeat us." This entailed a new view of the economy of resources: "To ensure that the Central Powers 'held out' [had] obvious significance," and "coolly calculated husbanding of the available weapons of war" was becoming as "immeasurably important" as the "resolute foregoing of warfare whose challenges exceeded our capacity to hold out." Only dogged perseverance held out the promise of victory; the logic of the war of materiel did not allow for a compromise and the end of the war before the complete exhaustion and collapse of one side. "If the Central Powers did not hold out—if they did not prove their martial resolve and their capacity for war longer than the other side—everything for which they had been fighting up to then would have no value. Not only would the war be lost, but they would be threatened with annihilation. If they held out, they would win the war—and it could only be won, given the strategic position of Germany and its allies against the forces of almost all the rest of the world. It made no difference to the final outcome whether our actual battlefield experiences yielded greater or lesser results."[275]

But, over and above such retrospective thinking, what marked the soldiers' actual experiences in and after 1916? The grievous shortage of officers had made itself felt in the early months of the war, making it necessary to accelerate the training of new ones. Modern warfare, based on attrition and the battle of materiel, had helped to shape a new vision of the officer: he was no longer a traditional heroic figure, a visible sacrifice in the struggle on behalf of the nation. Patriotic elements tended to give way to the image of a tried-and-tested leader taking action on the spot. It is therefore misleading to think that the war bred a general hatred of officers among the men under their command. In reality, soldiers drew a sharp distinction between staff officers at the rear and those present in the zones of death, where they shared the dangers and the living conditions with everyone else. Identification with the unit, a sense of belonging to a regiment that embodied the link with the home region, was an important motivating factor—nowhere more so than in the German army.[276] There it was not the abstract ideas of nation, class, and honor but the defense of an actual homeland that increasingly came to the fore and affected soldiers' daily lives. But this also raised the problem of how to legitimize a war that aimed at extensive territorial annexations.[277]

Family and homeland played a huge role in stabilizing soldiers emotionally, as countless invocations of the mother figure demonstrate. This was apparent not only in letters home but also in everyday practice at the front itself, where officers and NCOs took on the role of carers in addition to their purely military function. In March 1917, the British officer Lionel Hall recognized this presence of quasi-familial structures and the way in which they maintained the men's fighting spirit: "We are a very cheerful crowd—officers and men. We play all sorts of children's games with the men. There is something wonderfully pathetic about the private soldier in France. He is just a child, sometimes querulous, but always trustful."[278]

Part of the soldier's experience at the front was a new image of himself and of others. Like comradeship, however, this was often projected back after the end of the war—a process clearly observable in the writing of Ernst Jünger. In June 1916, as a young frontline officer and brigade leader, he directly experienced the Battle of the Somme: the massive use of artillery, the communication problem, the changing landscape, and the battlefield disorientation. On July 24, 1916, he noted, "We got our steel helmets. The steel helmet gives soldiers a wild appearance."[279] But later, in *Storm of Steel*, he presents a new vision of the frontline soldier as a symbol of modern warfare: "A runner from a Württemberg regiment . . . was the first German soldier I saw in a steel helmet, and he straightaway struck me as the denizen of a new and far harsher world. . . . The impassive features under the rim of the steel helmet and the monotonous voice accompanied by the noise of the battle made a ghostly impression on us. A few days had put their stamp on the runner, who was to escort us into the realm of flame, setting him inexpressibly apart from us."[280] This stylized account, barely hinted at in the diary Jünger kept at the time, also served to characterize the soldiers. The result was an eclectic mix of historical and progressive features, the frontline soldier being set primarily in the tradition of the early modern guardsman. But Jünger combined this with the conventional ethos of chivalry in combat and the new concept of objectivity—the expression of a particular kind of professionalism bound up with the extreme conditions of life at the front. "There was in these men a quality that both emphasized the savagery of war and transfigured it at the same time: an objective relish for danger, the chevalieresque urge to prevail in battle. Over four years, the fire smelted an ever-purer, ever-bolder warrior-hood."[281] The war reminded Jünger of manual "work" and the men's uniforms of working "kit."[282] His main focus was on the storm troop leader, his own role in the war. Jünger saw him as the true hero of the war: "the aristocrat of the trench, with hard, determined visage, brave to the point of folly, leaping agilely forward and back, with keen, bloodthirsty eyes, men who answered the demands of the hour, and whose names go down in no report."[283]

While nation and patriotism played a subordinate role in the soldiers' understanding of their experience, their home region, city, or village—often conjured up by impressions of nature at the front—became all the more important.[284] Jünger's diary also contains virtually no affirmations of patriotism or national interpretations of the war; these first appear at various points in his published novel of the war.[285] After the Battle of Verdun, many French soldiers began to criticize, at least implicitly, the official justifications of the war. On July 26, 1916, for example, Jean Norton Cru noted that the old formula "For Wife and Children" no longer rang true, especially for the countless "bachelors, widowers, and youngsters." To fight for "other people's wives and children" presupposed the kind of "noble sentiments" that scarcely existed any more. Convinced that "the soldier of 1916" was not fighting "for Alsace, for the annihilation of Germany, or for the fatherland," he laid the stress instead on "attitudes, custom, and compulsion": the ordinary soldier fought "because he could not do otherwise. He will go on fighting because a quiet submission to the unchangeable appeared in the second year of the war, replacing the early enthusiasm and the discouragement of the first winter." The main feeling, then, was not one of heroic sacrifice for the nation, but a hope that the war would end sooner rather than later: "We hoped that the suffering and the mortal perils would soon be over, yet for all their volatility they became a permanent condition over time." The front shaped its own special time, measured in terms of watch duties and replacements, attacks, periods of waiting, and furloughs. All this turned the men's thoughts away from their eventual return home: "We swapped home for dugout, family for comrades. . . . We can hardly imagine that the situation may change, that we will ever go back home. We still live with the hope, but we no longer count on it."[286] The struggle for home leave became a veritable obsession. In October 1916, the ministerial official Michel Corday reported on the mood among the troops. Albert J., one man on leave from the front, spoke of "the soldiers' hatred for Poincaré," whom they held responsible for starting the war. "He points out that what makes the men take part in attacks is the fear of appearing cowardly to the others. He also says—with a laugh—that he is thinking of getting married since that will give him the right to four days' leave and a further three days when a child is born. Also, that he hopes he will get the certificate exempting him from military service once he has produced six little ones."[287] The criticism of politicians, though not of the Republic as such, made it clear how important were traditional notions of virility, courage, and soldiering. No one wanted to be thought of as a coward or traitor—a fact that remained important even under the extreme conditions of the frontline battlefield.

On the eastern front, too, soldiers' attitudes changed in the course of 1916. Despite their military successes, the Central Powers had by no means solved their supply problems, and many German and Austro-Hungarian soldiers criticized the unfair distribution of burdens between the rear and the front, staff officers and combat troops. The writer Hans Carossa, in his *Roumanian Diary,* recorded his experiences as a military doctor during the German offensive of Fall 1916 in Romania. He carefully noted how the men more and more often tested the limits of obedience. One day in October, they were beside themselves with joy when they came across a store with cheese wheels, but then it turned out that the food was putrid. A private by the name of Kristl "proposed sending the cheeses to the Kaiser's court at Spa. He spoke so loudly that the major could not help hearing, but as he had known for a long time that Kristl was looking for trouble so as to get home again by way of prison, he paid no attention to the man's insolence."[288] On October 24, Carossa reported how the seasoned Lieutenant Levernz, held in high regard by his men, reacted to the indiscipline in his unit: "A dispassionate survey of the situation could diagnose it as an acute outbreak of an evil which has been lurking among us for some time. The war is dragging on into the third year; the soldier, usually without any vocation for his task, scantily fed, insufficiently clothed and shod, granted leave of absence only rarely, and then discouraged by the discouragement at home, loses his nervous energy and his discipline. The officers know it, and, the younger ones especially, let many things pass out of embarrassment, ignoring offensive remarks, persuading themselves that these are not maliciously intended and that everything will be all right when the enemy is sighted. This lax and ambiguous behavior is bound to appear undignified and unworthy to a man like Leverenz with the real soldier's temperament, and now that he is applying the full weight of his authority to bring order within his own jurisdiction at least, one is bound to sympathize with him as with a doctor who risks a touch-and-go operation."[289]

In each country, the war tested the nervous strength and willpower on which its resolution essentially depended. From early on, great attention was therefore paid to soldiers' emotions, and this increased even more after the great battles of 1916 on the western front. A key concern was the feelings of fear and the ways in which soldiers coped with them—a subject that Walter Ludwig addressed in his Tübingen thesis of 1919 on *Die Psychologie der Furcht im Kriege*.[290] During the war, Ludwig had collected some 200 essays from a course for aspiring officers and special schools for the wounded, having asked men there to describe their own experiences "from the field regarding what the soldier thinks at the moment of greatest danger in order to overcome the fear of death."[291] Although the context of their statements and the general military milieu need to be taken into account, these documents allow certain conclusions to be drawn about affective patterns and reactions and coping strategies.

The soldiers in question reported primarily on their experiences under heavy artillery fire. One response to feelings of fear and "inner trepidation" was to "initiate lively conversations with comrades," and "the presence of a comrade of whom they had grown especially fond" did indeed bring relief to many. Concepts of chance and probability also played a major role: "I never felt a real fear of death," one man noted, "because I always thought to myself that not every bullet strikes."[292] Another record showed how diversely soldiers handled the stress of protracted heavy bombardment: "As if by chance, my eyes fall on a soldier aged around 25; he is writing to his family back home; he keeps looking at a photo beside him (probably of his wife); he seems to have quite forgotten the danger. . . . Over there sits an older man who is turning gray; he has a book on his lap, the New Testament, and is eagerly reading it. Another cracks jokes, which might make people laugh out loud if they were in a different situation. Another man is crying; he's in a pretty bad way. Over there two men are conversing with each other; they're already happy that they might get decorated once the whole mess is over."[293]

Differences in the impact of weaponry feature prominently in Ludwig's records. The ubiquitous machine gun was much feared at the beginning of the war, but soldiers soon grew accustomed to it. Many continued to dread enemy artillery and mines carried up to the frontline. At the front the experience of asymmetry was direct: the gap between static offensive tactics and effective defensive weapons heightened the sense of insecurity and impotence. Combat gas made a powerful impression at first, but the introduction of protective masks soon allayed that fear too. In contrast, quite a few reported panic reactions at the thought of flamethrowers, against which they felt particularly defenseless.[294]

What many soldiers found most worrying was not acute combat, but the long periods of waiting, of passive endurance. "This kind of situation (when troops must hold out under fire without acting) is one of the most difficult moments in war. If you are condemned to passivity, you can't help feeling the mental distress more keenly; and the pressure to do something is then often so strong that you would gladly move to another place, even if that would put you in even greater danger. The very urge to do something, and the prospect of that happening, set up an active tension that is not much bothered with the suffering."[295] The end of home leave, or the return of troops from a rest area to the frontline, was often a critical phase, with railroad stations as particularly sensitive zones. Not by chance did mutinies and protest actions repeatedly develop at such junctures.

How did soldiers cope with these strains and these feelings of fear? Many spoke of distractions such as music or smoking, and in his work Ludwig methodically compiled a list of the factors named in individual or group reports "that serve to counter fear."[296] One is struck by the prominence of religion, home, and immediate community in these results. In comparison, factors highlighted in official propaganda and accounts of the war—discipline, bravery, patriotism—play a minor role. In his conclusions, Ludwig emphasized "manifestations of the social instinct" that had an effect "through reflection":

Phenomena that counteract fear, according to the testimony of soldiers

Phenomenon	Mentions
Religious impulses	90
Memories of home	65
Social emotions (community, comradeship)	54
Fatalism	44
Weighing the degree of possible evil	36
Indifference	33
General hopefulness	30
Humor	30
Dutifulness and empathy	29
Feelings of activity and passivity	26
Combat emotions	21
Narcotics	20
Rejection of fear	18
Faith in personal invulnerability	17
Discipline	16
Memories of past life	16
Fearlessness	15
Patriotism	11
Curiosity	10

Source: Ludwig, *Beiträge zur Psychologie der Furcht im Kriege.*

"thoughts of the family, home region, and fatherland. The first two of these are usually mentioned together and, apart from religious thoughts, are the themes most often stressed. . . . Thoughts of the fatherland are less conspicuous. . . . Thoughts of the family and home region appear in various hues: sometimes as concern about their circumstances and state of health; sometimes as longing for familiar domesticity and beloved parents, or a wish to say a last farewell to them; sometimes as an awareness of facing danger to protect those under threat, making it easier to accept difficulties; sometimes as an ardent desire to return and be reunited with them."[297]

But the soldiers' experiences always had other dimensions too. The diversity of living conditions and impressions brought paradoxes of their own: the coexistence of terror and beauty, death zones and battlefield tourism, existential threat and radical judgment. On October 19, 1916, on a troop transport to Romania, Hans Carossa witnessed a scene in the Transylvanian commune of Parajd (today's Praid) that intertwined such contradictory impressions as horror and closeness to nature, exposure to death, and a sense of meaning: "The station was beset by countless bands of refugees, and from the street leading out of it we saw Austrian stretcher-bearers advance carrying three small muffled shapes. These were the children of a refugee family who had found a live hand-grenade while playing, and in wrestling over it had touched it off. The explosion had killed the mother outright as she was lighting a fire for cooking and severely wounded the three children. The grandmother, a Saxon from Transylvania, walked beside the silent procession weeping and saying that the emperors and kings of the whole world should be told about such happenings, so that their consciences might be touched and they might stop making those godless wars. Meanwhile, the sun had all at once cleared the mists, and lit up a high mountain which filled us all with amazement. . . . This glorious apparition enchanted everybody; even the old grandmother fell silent; and as for me, dare I admit that in a second the heart-rending sight of the three wounded children was blotted out?"[298]

In 1916, Harry Graf Kessler underwent an unusual role change. On the eastern front he had classified peoples and spaces with a colonial gaze. Then, after a transfer to the western front, he experienced the Battle of Verdun from the viewpoint of an officer at the rear, hearing only indirectly of battlefield operations. While hundreds of thousands of soldiers were fighting in a narrow space just a few kilometers away, Kessler used the time to make an excursion. His battlefield tourism took him to nearby Sedan, where on Easter Monday he toured by car the site of the battle in 1870–1871 and visited the house where Bismarck and Napoleon III met afterward. Writing of the house owner Madame Fournaise-Liban, the visit by Wilhelm II, and the simultaneous presence of two wars from different periods, he noted on April 24, "Today's war is making her rich; yesterday, 600 visitors. . . . The visiting Kaiser signed himself in in French: Guillaume II, etc. With the war going on! Then on to Schloss Bellevue, where the act of surrender was signed in

'70. Fresh French graves from 1914 lie in the field towards Sedan, close to the façade; a mortar shell smashed into the stone next to the entrance gate beneath the clock."[299]

What Ludwig Wittgenstein sought was not safety behind the lines but mortal danger. Without it, his *Tractatus Logico-philosophicus* would have remained a treatise on logic, as it had been when he first drafted it in 1915. The existential threat, in which he was faced with the immediate presence of death, radicalized his thinking; his posting in late March to a combat unit on the Russian front (an artillery unit of the Seventh Austrian Army Corps) triggered intensive reflection on the nature of death. At the front, he made sure he was assigned to dangerous observation posts that were exposed to enemy fire. On May 5, 1916, he noted, "Only then will the war really begin for me. And—maybe—also life. Perhaps the nearness of death will bring light into life. God enlighten me! I am a worm, but through God I become a man." Then Wittgenstein experienced the Brusilov offensive at close quarters, his unit suffering heavy casualties. His impressions of this and the constant encounter with death helped to change his approach to the *Tractatus*. On July 8, 1916, he wrote in his diary, "Fear in the face of death is the best sign of a false, i.e. a bad life." The search for a religious answer passed into the search for a distinctive ethic. The self as bearer of morally binding values came to the fore—through a direct processing of his wartime experiences. When his unit retreated through the Carpathians, he noted the difference between the philosophical Ego and the pure will to survive, which knew nothing of moral considerations: "Yesterday I was shot at. I was scared! I was afraid of death. I now have such a desire to live. And it is difficult to give up life when one enjoys it. This is precisely what 'sin' is, the unreasoning life, a false view of life. From time to time I become an animal. Then I can think of nothing but eating, drinking, and sleeping. Terrible! And then I suffer like an animal too, without the possibility of internal salvation. I am then at the mercy of my appetites and aversions. Then an authentic life is unthinkable." Only after these experiences at the front did the *Tractatus* acquire its fundamental positions on ethics and the meaning of life.[300]

Beyond the individual and social dimension, a global perspective was also part of the experience of the front. Just as, on the Salonica front, French colonial troops from Asia fought alongside troops from the British dominions, and many ethnic groups rubbed shoulders with one another; so too did as many as fifty nationalities fight on the Yser in Belgium. European soldiers, often for the first time, encountered people from societies outside Europe as they fought alongside large numbers of soldiers and auxiliaries from the colonies; this contact with a previously exoticized Other led to a variety of reactions. On the one hand, soldiers admired the "wild warriors" and their martial qualities of courage and fortitude, as well as what they saw as a seemingly natural cruelty that commanders did not refrain from utilizing in combat. The *tirailleurs sénégalais,* Maoris, or Indian troops aroused curiosity but also a subliminal fear, while the deployment of black troops in Allied units provoked German accusations of barbarian warfare.[301] On the other hand, British and French officers remained convinced that the "noble savage" was like an exceptionally strong child, who needed to be led by white Europeans. This sense of superiority expressed itself in racist comments regarding not only colonial troops but also ethnic minorities within European armies. The stereotyping of Bretons or Scots, Canadians or Australians, demonstrated the preservation or deepening of more or less subtle demarcations in life at the front. Common experiences there by no means erased ethnic boundaries or hierarchies.[302]

The global dimension of European fronts went far beyond the deployment of Allied soldiers from the colonies. The example of Chinese auxiliaries shows how the experience of war also had a long-term impact on overseas societies. Between August 1916 and the end of the war, the British and French recruited some 140,000 workers in China and transported them to Europe. Roughly 100,000 joined the BEF, the rest being placed under the command of the French authorities. Most of the Chinese were immediately set to work building fortifications and trenches on the western front, where thousands would lose their lives. Some were also employed in factories producing materiel for the war. Recruited mainly in northwestern China, they were first shipped to Canada after undergoing a medical examination. But since local workers feared that the Chinese might stay on and compete for their jobs, the reality is that they were effectively interned there. This heralded a practice at the end of the war, in response to demobilized soldiers' fear of competition from colonial troops still living in Europe. The Chinese mostly faced harsh conditions on the European fronts, as well as racial prejudices, especially on the part of American overseers after Spring 1917. But they also had a range of new experiences, since in many cases it was their first encounter with the West. Not only did they witness the patriotic defense of French soldiers; they also came to understand the scale of wartime industrial production, the meaning of workers' rights, and the role of women in society. Several thousand Chinese remained in France after the war, many marrying there and founding families of their own.

The Chinese laborers were part of the Allied resource mobilization outside Europe, but they also marked an important phase in China's early twentieth-century development marked by new national and international orientations. For in allowing the British and French to recruit local workers, the government in Beijing was pursuing an important objective: participation in the European war was supposed to help overcome China's purely passive role as an object of internationalization, as a mere sphere of influence of the great powers. Furthermore, the context of this policy was an ever more intensive confrontation with ideas and models from the West.[303] The export of its labor emphasized China's claim to have a say in shaping the postwar world. President Wilson's program for a new world order therefore fell on fertile soil among the intellectual and urban elites of China—which added to the disillusionment that set in after 1918 as the peace treaties took effect.[304]

At least as important were the experiences of the Chinese in Europe and the feedback into China. When he came across Chinese laborers on the western front in France, the Chinese intellectual Yan Yangchu—known in the West as James Yen—understood the enormous significance of education. He began to organize literacy courses and published a special newspaper for Chinese auxiliary workers. In the 1920s, on the basis of his time in Europe, he campaigned for mass education back home in China. His movement eventually comprised as many as five million school and university students, including Mao Zedong, who volunteered to serve as a schoolteacher. Yen assumed that land reforms could be successful only if the population had a minimum of education; this reform would also help to avert a violent revolution. But above all else his movement embraced the ideal of decentralized structures, fighting both against the power of a centralized state and against influences and intervention from abroad.[305]

6. BODIES AND NERVES
The New Contours of the War Victim

In 1916, Elias Canetti left Vienna with his mother and two younger brothers and went to live near Zurich, in neutral Switzerland. There, as he later recalled in his autobiography, he was walking with his mother one day on the Limmat embankment when he saw a group of badly wounded French officers, dressed in resplendent uniforms, come across a group of German invalids. Such an encounter was quite common in Zurich, where wounded officers from both sides often came to convalesce. Canetti recalled, "I still remember how I shuddered from head to foot: What would happen now, would they charge one another? We were so disconcerted that we did not step aside in time and suddenly found ourselves between the two groups who were trying to pass each other; we were enclosed, right in the middle." Canetti expected that the two groups, holding each other responsible for their plight, would continue the war in words or gestures. But that was not the case: "No face was twisted with hate or anger. . . . They gazed calmly and amiably at one another as though there were nothing odd about the situation; a few saluted. They moved a lot slower than other people, and it took a while, it seemed like an eternity until they had gotten by each other. One of the Frenchmen turned back, raised his crutch aloft, waved it about a little, and then cried to the Germans, who were already past: '*Salut!*' A German who had heard it did the same, he too had a crutch, which he waved, and he returned the greeting in French: '*Salut!*' One might think, upon hearing this, that the crutches were brandished threateningly, but that wasn't the case at all, they were simply showing each other, by way of farewell, what had remained for them jointly: crutches."[306]

Over and above all national differences and patriotic energies, crutches and prostheses symbolized a basic community of experience: soldiers had become war victims, paying for their combat role with an injured body or a damaged psyche. Care and support were key terms in the public perception of wartime societies. Millions of men felt stigmatized by physical or mental impairment when they returned and brought the war back into the midst of their homeland. The novelty of this was bound up with the qualitative and quantitative increase of weaponry, with the concentration of deep-penetration artillery in limited spaces. In France, for example, this resulted in 2.8 million wounded in the course of the war, half of whom were wounded twice and another 300,000 three or four times. All in all, postwar Europe would house seven million invalids, including 350,000 with severe disabilities.[307]

What these bald figures leave out, moreover, is that physical injuries needed ongoing treatment more often than in earlier wars, not least because they forced the revision of conventional medical approaches or the development of new therapies. Until 1914, the dominant view among French army doctors had been that no abdominal operations could be performed in a major war, as the injuries in question gave little practical chance of survival and could not justify the expense of surgery. Yet the large number of abdominal injuries soon forced a rethink.[308] Although death rates following such operations remained high, they fell from roughly 70 percent in the 1914–1916 period to 50 to 60 percent in the last two years of the war. Experience at the front with major injuries, together with the limited resources available to overstretched field surgeons and the impossibility for them to administer aftercare, made it necessary to introduce new methods: the so-called guillotine amputations, for example, which took much less time than traditional ones. The costly preservation of limbs as an alternative to amputation became possible only after the front had stabilized to some degree, allowing field hospitals to be set up and complicated bone fractures to be successfully healed.[309]

The conditions at the beginning of the war, presenting new problems and a low ratio of medical staff to patients, made it essential to improve the initial screening of wounded patients and the grading of injuries by severity and treatability. The French army doctor Victor Pauchet reported that, on the Marne between September 7, 1914, and February 7, 1915, his field hospital received a total of 9,670 wounded and performed 1,590 operations, including 170 cranial procedures and 203 amputations.[310] The relatively low death rate in this case (31 percent for amputations) was due to the fact that the wounded men had already been screened on the battlefield and at special collection points. The principle of triage—the sorting and classification of wounded soldiers—went back to earlier wars. Following experiences in the Caucasus and Crimea, the Russian surgeon Nikolai Ivanovich Pirogov (1810–1881) developed a method of "patient dispersion" prior to treatment, whereby wounded men were divided into five groups and sent to different centers;

War victims and public care: poster for the German War Care Services exhibition, 1916

this helped to avert the chaos of overcrowding, to guarantee some degree of order, and therefore to increase the chances of survival. The world war required constant adaptation of this system to the new battlefield conditions.

For many medical personnel, the war signified patriotic service to individual casualties as well as the collective body of the nation. Associated with this was a new self-image and conception of their role: doctors were waging their own war, so to speak, against illness, injury, and death.[311] Problems arose in practice, however, as thousands of doctors with no previous military experience had to be hastily recruited and integrated into complex army organizations. In Britain a crisis developed in 1917, since the military and political leadership of the country had neglected the coordination of civilian medical personnel.[312] The mobilization of doctors combined the provision of care with patriotic service, social distinction with scientific progress. Significantly, the war meant that often doctors rapidly became acquainted with the treatment methods used in other countries: Allied field medics, for example, took over the practice of blood transfusions for the first time from American and Canadian colleagues. The use of orthopedic prosthetics, with its special techniques, was taken up and further elaborated, as was the field of bone prosthetics; Ferdinand Sauerbruch developed the "Sauerbruch hand" after his experiences as an army doctor. The prosthetic industry experienced a veritable boom everywhere. Advances also took place in the treatment of massive head injuries, aphasia research into the loss of discursive abilities, and surgery on the face and jaw.

Invalids gave the war a face—nowhere more so than in the physiognomy of individual victims. In September 1920 Erich Kuttner, an SPD deputy and journalist, published a report in the party daily *Vorwärts* that described his experiences at Berlin hospitals treating severely wounded soldiers: "A man comes into the small office wearing a bandage across the middle of his face. He takes it off and I find myself staring at a round palm-sized hole, which stretches from his nostrils to the lower jaw. His right eye is shattered, the left one half shut. While I am speaking with him, I see the whole space inside his mouth open before me: larynx, gullet, windpipe, as in an anatomical specimen. But what kind of hairy lump is this, which, like a carillon, swings loose in the cavity on a few sinews and ligaments? I am told it is an unsuccessful nose that was supposed to replace the poor man's original one. By now he

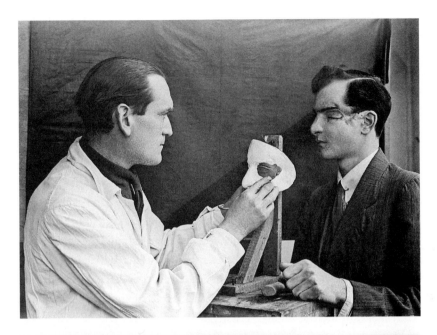

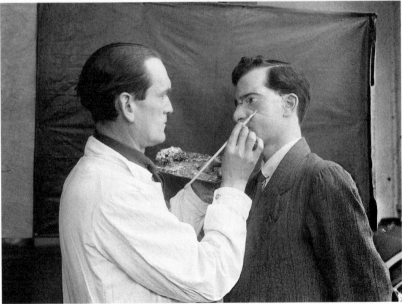

Facial reconstruction of a disfigured British soldier

has been through eighteen operations. But not even that is a record. Soon I get to meet people with 30 or 36 behind them."[313]

The significance of these injuries went far beyond the physical consequences for the victim. Precisely because a facial wound meant a loss of individuality and recognizability, it often attracted special attention during the war itself. Widespread rumors that disfigured soldiers were being treated at special centers, so that the shock of seeing them would not weaken the public resolve, testified to the horror that the idea of soldiers without a face inspired. In reality, no such secret centers existed. Indeed, soldiers with facial injuries were not passive invalids: in France they founded organizations like the Union des blessés de la face to represent their interests.[314] But they were also utilized for political purposes, since individual victims served as a radical illustration of the costs of war. At the signing of the Versailles treaty, five severely disfigured French soldiers, the *cinq gueules cassées*, paraded in front of the German delegation in the Hall of Mirrors, symbolizing the injured French nation and the enemy's moral guilt for the war. On the German side, in his pacifist book *Krieg dem Kriege* (War on War, published in 1924), Ernst Friedrich used photos of disfigured soldiers to indicate the scale of the violence and the futility of the war.[315]

Other injuries were not so conspicuous. In November 1914, Dr. Albert Wilson wrote in the *British Medical Journal* that he did not think psychologists would have to handle many cases during the war; most problems could be treated with alcohol and plenty of fresh air.[316] The reality was very different, however, for the war gave rise to new images of sickness that doctors could not comprehend with the traditional categories. After the first few months of positional warfare and heavy artillery bombardment, an increasing number of soldiers on all fronts showed symptoms that could not be attributed to visible injury: the war seemed to have struck their bodies like a bolt of lightning. Their whole body shook; they suffered from contortions, paralysis, and spasms.[317] Many became temporarily or permanently deaf or dumb. This new picture soon found a vocabulary: while German army doctors spoke of "war shakes," their British counterparts described the new phenomenon as "shell shock."[318] From the beginning, such soldiers had to face suspicions that they were faking symptoms to obtain home leave, exemption from war service, or later a disability pension. Officers and doctors then had to decide whether it was a genuine case of physical or psychological injuries sustained in the war.

Early on, neurologists and psychiatrists emphasized that Germans had particularly strong nerves, which gave them a decisive advantage over all enemies. But psychologists also foregrounded their own discipline. In 1916 Max Dessoir wrote that the war, as "a military, political, and economic process," was so fused with the psychological dimension that this "appeared partly as its cause, partly as its concomitant, and partly as its consequence." Hence "the oft-repeated words that we shall be victorious because we have the better nerves, that the moral element tips the scales, that it comes down to the mood in the population and the armed forces. There can be no doubt that only they who keep the psychological conditions in view can fully understand the great event of the war."[319] The war, then, was a stroke of luck for the psychological profession. Karl Bonhoeffer, one of the leading psychiatrists in Imperial Germany, saw it as "a gigantic experiment" making it possible to observe, on a large scale, phenomena that "in peacetime we can study only in isolated cases."[320]

The reality of war set novel tasks for neurologists and psychologists. For example, when it turned out that only 15 percent of amputees wore their prostheses, military psychologists were asked to find a solution to the problem. But primarily they concentrated on the neurological consequences of service at the front: if they determined that there was a causal relationship between trauma and neurosis, the soldiers in question were entitled to compensation. Thus, either war neuroses were seen as a constitutional disorder aggravated by military service, or their traumatic origin was questioned and the patients were accused of shirking and faking. Since psychiatrists had to differentiate genuine illness from "accidental, purposive, or pension-related neuroses"—to use the new wartime terminology—their own perceptions contributed to the fair distribution of the burdens of war.[321] Neurosis, it was commonly believed, "was activated through expert investigation"; not only *timor belli* but also a "wish for benefits" kept symptoms alive. Consideration of the strains on wartime society and the long-term implications for the economy partly shaped the perspective with which medical specialists operated. In 1916 a conference of neurologists and psychiatrists unanimously called for "the final settlement of compensation claims in the form of a lump sum payment"; this would be "in the interests of the injured parties as well as of the whole national labor force."[322]

Since patients had to participate actively in any therapy, they even seemed to be linked to the doctor in a struggle. Practitioners carried out experiments that, in appealing to the principle of trauma and countertrauma, often effectively involved forms of torture, though only with enlisted men rather than officers. Bedwetters were locked up in rooms without a toilet and let out to urinate only at specific hours. Patients with hysterical vomiting had to eat more than others under special supervision, and if they threw up they were forced to swallow the vomit again. Soldiers who had lost their voice were struck without warning on the larynx with a bullet probe to induce a curative cry of fear. Electric shocks were also used in the same context.[323]

One reason why the outbreak of neurological symptoms seemed so alarming was that it challenged the professional self-image of officers and soldiers as brave male warriors with nerves of steel. As in the prewar world of work, the war emphasized that physical fitness and nervous strength were twin conditions for success. This focus on individual willpower and strong nerves, as the keys to combat ability and perseverance, was closely bound up with the fixation on attack and the idea of a decisive battle. All that now seemed in danger: war neurotics represented an unmanly condition that clashed with the ideal of martial resolve; they had a breakdown of individual discipline and control over the body. Yet again the war became a crisis of nerves, mobilizing doctors in a fight against the "internal enemy" within the soldier. This also modified the academic metaphors used to describe doctors in the war: their struggle for the nerves of individual soldiers was at the same time a struggle for the collective body of the nation.

The perception of war neurotics and their symptoms changed in the course of the war. In Britain, special institutions were created to handle the "shell shocked"—for example, the Craiglockhart Special Hospital for Officers.[324] In Germany, the conference of the Society of German Neurologists in September 1916 marked a decisive shift to the view that the illness resulted not from anatomical injury but from psychological causes that doctors could treat. Euphoria began to develop about a possible victory over weak nerves and hysteria—two key terms even before the war in critical analyses of European societies and the fragility of all their achievements.[325]

Therapeutic methods ranged from verbal suggestions in the form of military orders through hypnosis to extremely painful, sometimes even deadly, treatment with electric shocks. Doctors repeatedly made use of surprise attacks.[326] Not infrequently the results were compared to religious miracles. People referred to "the power of the doctor's personality" and the special atmosphere surrounding the cure: "The reputation of the hospital may be so great that the patient becomes healthy as soon as he arrives there, and one is spontaneously reminded of the quotation: 'Rise, take up thy bed, and walk, thy faith has helped you.'"[327] Photographs and film helped to make successful treatments part of medical theory.[328] Although French army doctors applied similar therapies, they were not so inclined to euphoria. They initially assumed the illness to be only a mild, passing disorder that specialists could treat at the front so that the soldier in question could swiftly return to active duty. But it eventually became clear that quick results were not possible, and a pessimistic attitude began to spread.[329]

The image of "shell shocked" soldiers also had a racist dimension, especially in Britain. After the king personally asked the Empire to supply troops in 1915, many units with white soldiers felt themselves increasingly threatened by blacks from the African colonies. The possibility that war could trigger a crisis of white masculinity had already arisen in the Boer War, when there had been heated debates in Britain about the degeneration of the white race as a consequence of industrialization and urbanization.[330] Against this background, the high number of casualties on the western front in and after 1914 intensified the fear that the strongest and healthiest British males would die in combat, since it was precisely they who had volunteered for service, and that in the long term this would weaken the demographic foundations of the whole Empire. The authorities avoided using black soldiers—from Jamaica, for example—for fear that these "martial races" would prove physically bolder and mentally more resilient than the British and call into question the differentiation principle within the Empire, where racial hierarchies were strongly bound up with traditional gender roles. This theme came to the fore in the context of "shell shock." Although before the war Indians and Jamaicans had served under white officers in the Caribbean, India, and Africa, it was now decided to block the deployment of Jamaicans alongside white soldiers; instead, they were to serve in a British West Indies Regiment specially created for them. Racial segregation was carried over to the front.[331]

Many elements of mechanized warfare were incorporated into the treatment and rehabilitation of war invalids. Machines had killed or injured individual bodies; now they were supposed to help in their recovery.[332] Hospitals reproduced the tendency of mechanized warfare to erase differences, to standardize soldiers, and to interpret the war in a primarily economic and demographic perspective in which efficiency was paramount. Thus, the treatment and care of British soldiers in hospital followed quasi-military regulations. With the exception of officers, all soldiers had to wear the same blue, often ill-fitting, hospital uniforms, which identified them as victims of war rather than self-sacrificing heroes. The men saw them as symbols of their exclusion from wartime society and a visible barrier between themselves and other patients.[333]

In many literary works on the war, the ideal of the "whole man" who preserves his physical and psychological integrity played an important role. War novelists—from Henri Barbusse to William Faulkner—took masculinity as a key reference, while associating feminine qualities with uncontrolled emotion, as well as dependence and primitiveness.[334] At the same time, however, the moment of death was a major leitmotif; it was then that the wounded soldier asked for physical contact, a kiss or an embrace, that gave him special attention. This recalled the sense of closeness to the mother, even if many writers pointed to this contact's romantic or sexual connotations. But in the actual situation at the front, the main point was to confirm once again the soldier's bodily presence in a world of death. Touch and intimacy died with the individual's body, and neither photographs nor literary texts nor monuments could compensate for them. This dimension of experience, however much addressed and however important the physical contact that family members later had with war monuments, could never be represented.[335]

The same was true of the pain that a wounded soldier felt. The combination of intimacy and marginality featured prominently in the notebooks kept by British nurses. Their impressions at the front were marked by closeness to the patients, but it was impossible for them really to measure their physical suffering. In the end, there was no adequate language for it: "The pain of one creature cannot continue to have a meaning for another," wrote one nurse. "It is almost impossible to nurse a man well whose pain you cannot imagine. Deadlock."[336]

The huge number of invalids was itself a novel challenge for the wartime governments. Who was a war victim? Who should be entitled to public care and provision? Contemporary discourse is revealing on such matters.

The term "cripple," still the one mainly in use in the early years of the war, connoted a fear that ostensible invalids might obtain state benefits by trickery. The term "pension psychosis" was a direct expression of this exacerbation of distribution conflicts that did not spare the war wounded. Beginning in May 1915, the term "war invalid" replaced "cripple" in Prussia, emphasizing that state policy recognized the new quality of war victims. But it also had a limiting function, since the group of war victims could in principle be extended much further to include widows, orphans, and people in the occupied territories. In Germany as in other countries, traditional policy instruments and charitable work were quite insufficient to cope with the flood of war invalids. Although the prewar legislation was soon amended, provision remained on a precarious footing. From December 1914, a special welfare agency marked by bourgeois traditions of philanthropy provided care for the war disabled, and from September 1915 an Imperial committee managed incoming donations and government funds. But the law enacted in May 1920 guaranteed no more than minimal provision worthy of the name. The scant funds available for it meant that recipients had to rely on other income or family help.[337]

The authorities, but also the public, expected invalids to show self-discipline, to make themselves useful so that they could return as soon as possible to the world of work and reduce the costs for the community.[338] Categories relating to efficiency were thus consciously applied to the war wounded, the fear being that an army of men unable or unwilling to work might endanger future economic growth. It was hoped that scientific and technological advances would compensate for war injuries and mobilize patients for work, if necessary by coercion. Publicity featuring ever more sophisticated hand, arm, and leg prostheses accustomed society to the new kinds of injuries that could not be concealed in public. Indeed, the pictures used in such ads held out the promise that war invalids could be fully reintegrated into civil society; they must not be in a position to claim free board and lodging after the war. This corresponded to the ideal formulated in 1915 by the Berlin doctor Konrad Biesalski: "(1) not favors but work for war cripples; (2) return home to the same circumstances as before, and if possible to their old jobs; (3) dispersion among the active population as if nothing has happened; (4) the status of cripple does not exist if there is an iron will to overcome impediments to mobility; (5) all groups, beginning with the wounded themselves, should be educated as widely as possible about this."[339]

Enthusiasm about new breakthroughs in prosthetics and operation techniques, indeed a whole culture of body part replacement, testified to a utopian vision of complete compensation for war injuries. Not only did prostheses appear to serve as full substitutes; they perfectly fitted contemporary notions of a modern conveyor-belt industry based on an extensive division of labor. One article underlined this link between care for injured soldiers and the Taylorist system: "In this respect, the production of prostheses in their various forms and parts is nothing other than the realization of Taylor's demand for tools to be adapted to the worker's special abilities."[340]

Nor did this vision apply only to ordinary soldiers. On December 1, 1913, Paul Wittgenstein, brother of the philosopher Ludwig Wittgenstein and son of a celebrated Viennese industrialist, made his debut as a concert pianist in the great hall of the Wiener Musikverein in a performance with the Vienna Tonkünstler Orchestra. In August 1914, he was mobilized and sent to the eastern front, where he sustained such bad injuries that his right arm had to be amputated. After a period in Russian prisoner-of-war camps, he returned to Vienna in December 1915 and resumed his career as a left-handed pianist. As a patron of the arts, he popularized piano works for the left hand and came to symbolize the successful reintegration of war invalids; the idea of overcoming physical disability through an iron will helped to displace the concept of victimhood. Wittgenstein's musical repertoire linked up with nineteenth-century German traditions and helped to establish a canon—as if the hiatus of the First World War had not occurred and had had no aesthetic consequences.

Finally, war victims had a decisive function in interpretations of the war, both as players—post-1918 veterans, for example—and as objects of political instrumentalization. Over time, the war spawned real competition between positive and critical myths. At first the German military tried to give patriotic meaning to the massive loss of life—nowhere more clearly than in the myth of the youthful volunteers at the battle of Langemarck, whose deaths were supposed to exemplify the heroic self-sacrifice of the whole nation. In the case of the British dominions, the Canadian and Australasian soldiers killed in action significantly contributed to the process of nation formation and emancipation from a purely imperial mentality. In this, the idea of military victory increasingly gave way to celebrations of heroism in a no-win situation, where men had to endure and survive under extreme conditions. The lauding of a special kind of comradeship should be seen in this context. By contrast, the myth of the "lost generation" or the trope of "cannon fodder" responded critically to the mounting casualties; soldiers were presented not as active subjects dying for the nation and its values, but as passive victims of military irresponsibility and incompetent officers. The image of the soldier sent to the slaughter, forced to wage war for the speculators and profiteers of a thoroughly unjust economic order, eventually associated the casualty toll with hopes of a revolutionary mobilization.[341]

Images of death and injury could therefore be used for various purposes, entering into the political and social conflicts of the belligerent countries. The hostility to shirkers, *embusqués,* or *Drückeberger* owed much of its effect to the insinuation that they mocked the self-sacrifice of soldiers at the front. Appeals to their better nature became part of the discourse of the time, giving special moral force to the demand for equitable burden sharing; it reminded people that the cohesion of the wartime community was not a matter of course, but could be jeopardized if they lost sight of the invalids. References to internal treachery at moments of crisis—such as the mutinies and mass desertions in Russia (late 1916), France (Spring 1917), and Germany (from late Summer 1918)—were certainly no accident. The core of this political-ideological narrative was that traitors in the home society were denying the sacrifice of combat troops, stabbing them in the back, and undermining national defense. For all the ideological differences, the common element in the *gueules cassées* on display at Versailles, the images of disfiguration in later pacifist literature, and the postwar arguments of revisionist politicians was an insistence that all the deaths and injuries should not have been in vain. The resulting effect was enormous, combining as it did political agendas with the actual suffering of millions of soldiers and their families.

The German war neurosis debate was also susceptible to political instrumentalization; soldiers could apply "weak will" metaphors also to the psychological frailty of society back home. In the field—many doctors would argue in Summer 1919—war neurotics had been unfit for combat because of their disorder. In 1918–1919, however, "psychopathic leaders" had an impact on a population weakened by years of war and unleashed a "hysterical mass psychosis." The large numbers of "war weary" soldiers in hospital, and of mentally unstable women in German society, were unable to put up effective resistance to this phenomenon. Comparisons between capable soldiers at the front and "lesser beings" at home showed how the "stab in the back" legend could become associated with the debate on nervous conditions.[342]

All in all, the war changed the image of the war victim. This had much to do with a transformation of bodily images and practices, and it had major implications for the understanding of war heroes in every society. Whereas, at the beginning of the war, a wound was still seen as a mark of the soldier's role as a heroic model for the fatherland, this image could not hold up in the face of vast numbers of wounded and disabled. Bodies displaying physical and mental damage led to a shift in the traditional picture of the heroic male warrior: this image no longer only highlighted his self-sacrifice in combat but also included his successful treatment and reintegration into the world of work. Severely disabled war heroes found their way back into employment, overcoming physical injury and restoring their manly status through willpower and discipline. Invalids did not rely on a passive role or a claim to financial support. In this sense, the ideology of a strong will continued to operate: a belief that it was possible to overcome the strongest defenses and a technologically superior enemy also applied to soldiers wrestling with themselves. Thus, everyone involved in the process of cure and rehabilitation appeared as a combatant: doctors in the fight against feigning and weakness of will, prosthetics technologists achieving victories on the front of the human body, and, above all, wounded soldiers who converted their stigma into a new self-image and avoided becoming a burden on the national community. Saying nothing about the dimension of individual suffering, multiple traumas, and paths back to family, job, and society, all the more did these projections exhibit the collective fears of postwar societies.[343]

The war victim, then, was a highly ambivalent figure. He was part of the community, but at the same time stood outside it. He differed from others by virtue of the visible, or perhaps only imaginable, stigma of his wound, and he had to struggle to reintegrate into society through willpower, discipline, and self-mastery.[344]

7. DISCOURSES OF WAR
Communication, Control, and the Limits of Opinion Formation

On July 28, 1916, at the height of the Somme battle, Ernst Jünger recorded his impressions in his diary: "This terrible array of artillery in this great battle is creating novel forms of war, which in particular make it extremely difficult to make contact with others. Even the telephone cable is immediately blown to pieces. Communication with the artillery and combat troop officers can take place only by means of flares, across kilometers ruled only by explosives. Not even the regiment or division knows where we actually are and where the front now lies. The English . . . do not know where we are, nor do we know where the English are—although we are often no more than 20 meters from each other. Often someone groping his way across shell holes, like an ant across a sandy path, falls straight into a crater occupied by the enemy. Forward communication is bad, too."[345] Breaks in communication were part of the soldier's experience at the front, entailing lack of news and information and disoriented wandering on the battlefield. The very gulf between this reality and the commanders' plans underlined the exceptional importance of various dimensions of communication in the First World War.

Any war involves an especially dense web of exchanges and understandings by means of language, pictures, and enactments—and the world war intensified this experience insofar as media and communications were understood and deployed as weapons with a mass impact of their own. This gave rise to a plethora of competing interpretations. The media dimension included—alongside official claims to control oral exchanges, texts, and images—an autonomous logic and dynamic that repeatedly eluded steering mechanisms. Communication was thus a key dimension: the military conduct of the war, the coordination of millions of soldiers, the mobilization of homeland societies, the links between soldiers and families, the men's own interpretations of their experience, the attribution of meaning to the conflict, attempts to justify it or criticize it—all this would have been unthinkable without communication, language, and media.

Communication during the war presupposed a particular infrastructure, based on technological innovations as well as traditional methods. Just as, despite the growing importance of motor vehicles, millions of horses continued to transport soldiers and provisions from railroad stations to frontline positions, so the development of the telephone and radiotelegraphy did not alter the fact that more than 300,000 carrier pigeons had to be used to convey information.[346] Still, the period after 1914 did see the continuation of earlier developments. During the battle of Mukden in the 1905 Russo-Japanese war, Marshal Oyama was able for the first time to string telephone lines to the front covering a distance of up to 20 kilometers. After 1914, a huge technological buildup got underway. The intelligence corps in all armies soared from a total of 25,000 men and 800 officers to 185,000 and 4,400, respectively. The German army, in particular, installed new telephone lines and established special intelligence departments, dispensing wherever possible with traditional messengers. A single army corps received as many as 5,000 calls a day. In 1917, the German field telephone network extended over 920,000 kilometers. Yet this modernization had another side to it: the new communication technologies called into question the traditional military hierarchies and a command structure that essentially relied on direct interaction

The unevenness of war: a tank and carrier pigeon

War communications: a German field telephone

between physically present interlocutors. The telephone changed this setup. On the side of the Allies, this development occurred at a slower pace.

At any event, the intensity of battlefield violence continually interfered with communications, so that for a long time commanders at the rear had to rely on traditional runners, bikers, and pigeon carriers. At one critical juncture in the Marne battle, Moltke as head of the OHL even sent his staff officer Richard Hentsch to obtain a firsthand view of the situation—an episode that highlights how important, but also how time costly, such personal intelligence gathering could be. Communication in battle between infantry and artillery positions was a common but important challenge, especially as the success of attacks depended on it. Flashing optical signals also served a purpose, but often they were not sufficiently visible during an actual battle. While radio apparatuses were still in their early days, Morse communications between aerial observers and ground stations, as well as radiotelephony in the case of Allied air forces, played a major role.[347]

Communications also had a special global dimension, and the link between information technologies and opinion markets became apparent right at the beginning of the war. Since the late nineteenth century, radio communication via undersea cable had become ever more important for press agencies and the flow of news around the world. In Summer 1914, when London and Berlin realized after a few days just how crucial their rival justifications of the war were in attracting American public support, British naval units cut the cables between Continental Europe and the United States. This gave British politicians a decisive advantage over the coming years, since their own underwater links meant that they could disseminate their view of events across the Atlantic, while the news agencies of the Central Powers could operate outside Europe only by complicated alternative routes.[348] Control over the channels of intelligence and communication technologies directly affected the reach of wartime propaganda.

War as a struggle for control over opinions did not relate only to communication with other countries. At least as important was the struggle for the population at home, ranging from systematic observation of popular moods, press censorship, and active efforts to influence public opinion. All the wartime societies witnessed the emergence of new institutions such as military press offices and information bureaus. After social tensions and economic problems increased in Germany in 1915 as a result of the British blockade, a war press office was established in October to monitor the mood inside the country and to influence it in a positive direction. Press censorship and official supervision of the developing film industry were supposed to serve the same purpose. The work of news agencies and press correspondents began to change during the course of the war. But these trends were much more contradictory than the usual understanding of war propaganda would suggest, since great discrepancies existed between what was claimed and what was really the case, between ostensible effects and actual practice. The idea that the government and the military had created a docile, dependent apparatus, and that this enabled them actually to control and steer opinion, failed to appreciate the complex reality.

Both German and French war reporters saw themselves first of all as patriots, who wished to put their talents to work in the war. This facilitated an early form of "embedding," in which journalists allowed the military leadership to use them for its own ends, restricting the scope for critical, investigative reporting. Many journalists remained on the margin of events, largely reliant on the information the military chose to hand out. Nevertheless, journalists were tolerated in Germany from the beginning, whereas in France the military leadership initially tried to exclude non-official war reporters. As the cultural war got underway, however, the authorities came to recognize the importance of journalists and increasingly had recourse to their services. The most popular issues varied considerably between the two countries: while war reporters in France highlighted the destruction in occupied areas, the German news was dominated by images of a war that seemed like a continuation of home life at the front and in occupied enemy territory. The papers were full of well-fed, good-humored soldiers.[349]

A special relationship developed between war reporters and the military authorities—building on tendencies in the prewar period. The military leadership in Britain and Germany recognized the media as important sources of news, but at the same time they were anxious to maintain confidentiality. The old reactive attitude to their national media changed rapidly from 1914 on. Since it proved impossible to break the deadlock in the positional war, and since the stability on the home front was not without limits, the army leadership and governments concentrated on the boosting of war propaganda through a stronger media input.[350]

The state and military authorities thus regarded a close link between control and communication as a precondition of social stability; news and commentary appeared decisive factors in the mobilization of the population and the preservation of internal cohesion. The British press enjoyed greater leeway than the German, which had to put up with more interference by the authorities. In the period up to May 1918, 174 newspapers in Germany were banned outright or for several days, and the number of directives issued by the censorship was considerably higher. But the tighter controls in Germany, together with the greater preparedness to suppress news, also led to an earlier loss of public credibility. Neither in Germany nor in Britain, however, were relations between journalists and officialdom marked by permanent conflict: the image of critical, independent journalists heroically committed to the truth, on one side, and the strict practice of government censorship on the other, did not correspond to the reality. Rather, the two sides bargained with each other and settled for numerous special arrangements and understandings. Often this involved negotiations over access to information and the adjustment of news reports to take into account the interests of the political and military leadership. Journalists, army leaders, and politicians established their own networks—although, as the scandal of the munitions crisis in Britain showed, this did not prevent the development of conflicts.

Against this common background, the differences between the two countries, already apparent before the war, continued to widen. Since the British newspaper market was more centralized, with fewer titles, larger print runs, and wider distribution, the press magnates and newspaper owners played an important role in shaping public opinion in close interaction with the political elite. Informal contacts—for example between Lord Riddell, the owner of the *News of the World,* and Lloyd George—repeatedly had an effect. The fact that the press in Britain tended to act as a "fourth estate," in contrast to its distinctly less self-assertive counterpart in Germany, had implications for the confidence that Whitehall had in the press and its owners.[351] But the view that wartime propaganda was key to the victory over Germany—a view that many newspapermen expressed in Britain even during the war—was a long way from the truth. Rather, it reflected wishful thinking on the part of press barons such as Lord Northcliffe, who were keen to translate their media power into a clear-cut political role. In reality, the influence of Northcliffe's Enemy Propaganda Department at the Ministry of Information was quite limited. The popular series of anti-German articles that had appeared before the war—in the *Daily Mail,* for instance—or the campaigns against Kitchener and Asquith in the munitions crisis of 1915 suggested an interdependence that did not exist in reality. Press influence in government decisions was anyway slight, and Lloyd George coolly rejected Northcliffe's request to take part in the Paris peace conference. His capacity to stir up fears in the popular press did not translate into any clearly defined political influence.[352]

Much as the need for official war propaganda was recognized in all belligerent countries, obstacles to its development made themselves felt in practice. In the Ottoman Empire, high costs together with relatively low literacy rates limited the effect of government propaganda. Along with strict censorship, the protracted war kept up pressure on the media to draw a positive picture of the regime's war effort. A new illustrated magazine *Harp Mecmuasi* (War Journal) was established, and in July 1915 a group of artists was invited to the Gallipoli front to get an idea of the fighting there and to depict it for the official media. But the government's efforts in this war of words were not very successful: the relatively high fees paid to journalists and artists bore no relationship to the effect they produced. The increasingly impoverished population simply did not have the spare cash to buy expensive newspapers and magazines.[353]

From 1916, the limits and ambiguities of war propaganda were expressed most clearly in the way that the media in the Central Powers treated the issue of food supplies. Posters and brochures in Germany and Austria-Hungary featured rationing, bread and flour cards, and economy drives while offering the prospect of a victory that would improve the situation: "But once we triumph at the Kremlin / We'll have our bread rolls again." But from the winter of 1916–1917, the pointed denials of hunger, with staged photos of well-fed soldiers before well-laid tables, must have seemed like a provocation to German and Austrian civilians.[354]

Therein lay a dilemma of wartime communication: the restrictions and food rationing, the introduction of ever-tighter controls, were presented as efficient, prudent actions on the part of the authorities, while national enemy-images, in an attempt to distract attention from internal problems, painted Britain in particular as the cowardly instigator of a starvation blockade. However, this picture evoked in propaganda turned into its opposite. For countless articles, posters, and postcards gave the impression that Germany did not have to rely on food imports, that it was economically autarkic and could not be brought to its knees by the British blockade. The task of supplying the civilian population therefore appeared as no more than a challenge of government organization and coordination. Official propaganda thus set the criteria for judging the efficiency and credibility of the wartime state. It aroused expectations that were increasingly disappointed in reality and could easily turn against the government itself. In 1917, official campaigns suggested that unrestricted submarine warfare could finally break the stranglehold. But when the supply situation worsened again, the authority of state institutions began to crumble. In this process, women were by no means silent sufferers on the home front, but rather key players in society's struggle to see the war through to the end. Because of their increasingly precarious living conditions—their death rates shot up in the final months of 1918—women became particularly skeptical of official pronouncements.[355]

The state's claim to monitor its own population, to check on its moods and to influence interpretations of the war, was an important feature of the communications war. But over the years this monitoring provoked reactions diametrically opposed to what the authorities intended. One crisis symptom was the spread of rumors and the general desire to obtain reliable information and uncensored news. Since the population was aware of the censorship, there was increasing distrust of what the newspapers printed—and this limited in advance the effectiveness of official attempts to steer public opinion. Early in 1917, French mutineers asked German soldiers to let them see their trench newspapers, since they no longer trusted their own press.

Rumors therefore became more significant as soldiers at the front and people back home saw the gaps in official reporting and the deficiencies of the censored news. In Britain, the Defence of the Realm Act represented a watershed, breaking as it did with liberal traditions and the political culture of a country that accorded a secure place to the press. Some attempts had been made even before 1914 to create a political police along Continental lines, but with the passage of this law Britain's distinctive liberal path seemed to have come to an end. In response to the crises of 1917, and especially the revolution in Russia, the police, intelligence service, and army commanders aligned their various practices to prevent the development of a Bolshevik-style movement in Britain's industrial centers. In Germany, the credibility of the official press suffered more with each passing year, as the gap between everyday experience and official propaganda became ever more apparent. This fueled the general loss of credibility and the eventual legitimation crisis of the war state and its representatives.[356] On the one hand, the state strengthened its capacity to monitor, control, and steer opinion; its knowledge of popular moods became more and more extensive. But a number of factors—for example, the detailed reports from police chiefs—alarmed the country's rulers, while despite everything their scope to mold public opinion remained limited. Above all, public knowledge of the scale of opinion monitoring laid the state itself open to attack—and official propaganda set the criteria that enabled people to formulate more clearly the conflict between ideal and reality. Although the war did not produce a totalizing surveillance state, tendencies in that direction could not be overlooked. The growing public distrust of the state was matched by official skepticism about the loyalty and reliability of the population. This constellation marked Germany in particular during the last two years of the war. Lieutenant Colonel Nicolai, the head of Abteilung IIIb, acknowledged in August 1918 that "the two-front war in east and west" had been superseded by "a war on two fronts against the external and internal enemy."[357]

The ambiguities of official control and obstinacy, and the emergence of discursive niches, also made a mark on communication among soldiers. Their correspondence as well as trench newspapers helped to stabilize relations between front and homeland and allowed them to exchange experiences with other soldiers. The field correspondence of various nations showed many similarities. Thus, comradeship and friendship in the trenches, shared experiences, and increasingly difficult living conditions were points of reference for German and British soldiers alike. Although their letters resorted again and again to models and stereotypes from the press that sought to justify the war, national enemy-images played a rather minor role in the actual interpretation of their experiences. German soldiers, especially, tended to distinguish sharply between a defensive war (with which they could still identify) and an unjustifiable offensive war. While clear enemy-images tended to recede on the western front, talk of uncivilized Slavs was very common in letters home from men on the eastern front.[358] As for the German occupation authorities in eastern Europe, their semantics and vocabulary were shot through with a sense of insecurity and estrangement in what they saw as an uncivilized part of the world.[359]

The letters sent via the army postal service reflected the linguistic conventions of the prewar period. Responding to the upheaval in their lives, many soldiers took refuge in an idealized private world: images of the secure social space of their home area, family, and workplace, which they hoped to find unchanged on their return, helped to stabilize them in an extremely insecure situation. The reality of mechanized warfare and mass society and the contrast between prewar world and wartime experience appear much less often in the letters. As the war dragged on, soldiers also reacted more testily when their hoped-for return to the imagined order at home seemed to be in danger. This explains not only the widespread criticism of shirkers and war profiteers, and the fear that their homeland might not be sufficiently supportive of the army at the front, but also an anxiety that foreign auxiliaries or demobilized colonial soldiers might unsettle the traditional order at home. These again pointed to common experiences and a common language among various groups within the army. The boundaries between "the top" and "the bottom" certainly did not disappear, but nor did the semantics of home and privacy indicate a skewed, polarized wartime society divided by status and class.[360]

National differences were most evident in the soldiers' correspondence when they addressed social-cultural developments and political contexts. Socialist visions of the postwar order in Germany referred to a "free people," while Irish Catholics called for a free Ireland. On the British side, despite the conflict over Ireland, the political consensus and trust in the country's liberal-parliamentary system tended to remain stable. But in Germany the wartime consensus and the national image of 1914, with the Prussian-German monarchy standing behind them, began to lose more and more of their credibility from 1916 on. Against the backdrop of military crisis, hunger, and eventual defeat and revolution, the semantic cohesion of the nation at war gave way to more polarized political discourses. Other leitmotifs, too, pointed to substantial differences in the interpretation of the war. The war as a test of nerves was present in the field correspondence, but the interpretive model centered on "nervousness" meant different things according to the situation of the frontline combatant. In British texts, the dominant features were trust in the spirit of attack, an awareness of human vulnerability, and a focus on new weapons technologies such as the tank, whereas the letters written by German troops adhered more to defensive models. The metaphor of "iron-clad Roland" gave expression to a bearing of individual bravery and perseverance. In 1917–1918 this model became less and less convincing to ordinary soldiers, but many officers stuck with it to the very end of the war.[361]

Last but not least—and despite the censorship—correspondence from the front was a medium for critical examination of living conditions there or back home. In fact, the two often belonged together: soldiers' complaints about officers, especially those at the rear, who knew the front only as a point on their maps, came side by side with criticism of munitions workers whose strike action threatened the cohesion of the front and the homeland itself. In an anonymous letter, one wounded soldier wrote to the German crown prince: "If you drive us once more into the fire as lightmindedly as you have often done before, we'll stick a few bullets into your hindquarters so that you too know what they taste like."[362]

By no means was the soldiers' correspondence a neutral medium: it was already being used for various purposes during the war. Selected letters were published to give the legitimacy of an eyewitness account to positive images of the war, while many others that expressed criticism of the war were weeded out. Even SPD members considered that letters describing abuse of soldiers should be suppressed, so as not to undermine the will to "hold out" at the front. Anthologies such as Philipp Witkop's *Kriegsbriefe gefallener Studenten* (War Letters of Fallen Students) thus contributed to the emergence of a particular narrative: the image of unconditional bravery and self-sacrifice, and later of an army undefeated in the field, simply omitted the increasingly critical attitude of many soldiers.[363] Such publications set leitmotifs that would also feature prominently after the war in radio broadcasts, photospreads, and motion pictures. Again and again, the war would be presented as an adventure, a protracted and enhanced summer holiday camp. The reality of the front, the mismatch between casualties and military stagnation of which soldiers were keenly aware, was left out of the picture.

Another dimension of communication was the contacts among soldiers themselves, with army newspapers as a particularly important field. An example of official press activity in the Austro-Hungarian Empire was the *Soldaten-Zeitung,* which the military leadership hoped would instill a patriotic attitude in its readers. The paper's mission was to highlight the achievements of the wartime state and army, to combat irredentist currents, and to affirm the unity of the monarchy. None other than Robert Musil wrote a series of articles for it in 1916. In the anniversary issue for the emperor, dated August 18, 1916, one of his pieces quoted a text of the Imperial Secret Council, written by Lieutenant Colonel Franz Graf Harrach of the Landsturm army reserve, the model for Count Leinsdorf in Musil's *Man without Qualities.* The article hailed the monarch as the embodiment of the Empire's unity in war—but also revealed how shaky this focus on personal identification was, since just a few months later the emperor's death raised the question of what would replace him as a symbol spanning the generations: "Our emperor! What a wealth of love and reverence, of memory and hope, these two words excite. Four generations have already sworn him allegiance. . . . Now, in these two years of terrible strife, his name and our memories of him imbue the whole army of his soldiers. For him they proudly march to the field of battle, for him they fight and lay down their lives; their breaking eye gazes in spirit after him, the ardently loved, the one tested by suffering." What endured in this monarch, beyond his actual political influence, was a sort of emotional credibility, since "he, the loving father of his subjects, who has borne and suffered so much, is stricken deep in his heart by the inevitable cruelties of the war."[364]

The hundred or more German soldiers' newspapers were more widely read and more popular than those of the Allies. Trench papers such as *Der Drahtverbau* or *Der bayerische Landwehrmann* addressed local and regional issues relevant to particular units at the front, the initiative for them having come from the men themselves. Until 1916 the frontline press—which displayed a distinctive candor and humor in its depiction of life at the front—was left more or less untroubled. But then the army press bureau began to flex its muscles. In view of the military situation, the growing criticism of living conditions at the front, and the more frequent disciplinary problems, there was pressure to control press content more closely and to centralize communication channels. The military authorities actively sought to shape soldiers' views in favor of continuing the war—which presupposed leadership with regard to interpretation and opinion formation and explained the efforts in 1917 to introduce patriotic education for soldiers. In this way, the German army leadership tried to establish a monopoly on the communication of wartime experiences.

Members of the army press bureau, most of them from the educated middle classes and often with a background in education or journalism, set about translating war experiences into the language of the prewar period. Themes that did not serve the aim of military endurance were excluded. From 1916, there was a change in how soldiers were depicted. Discarding the earlier humorous treatment of raw recruits, the frontline press concentrated on the need to halt the enemy under all circumstances, to hold the front against attack, and to protect the homeland from the realities of war. Appeals were made to duty and willpower and strong nerves—terms whose male connotations stood out. The ideal frontline combatant was serious and self-disciplined, embodying invincibility by virtue of his inner attitude. This mythical construct was all the more important because it only operated

OPPOSITE: "It's me, can't you see?" Communications and endurance: from a German newspaper *Die Sappe* (The Sap), produced at the front in northern France

DIE·SAPPE

HERAUSGEGEBEN VON
KARL·M·LECHNER

BAY·RES·INF·RGT·
19·RGT·STB

NORDFRANKREICH

— Dös bin ih kennst mi net? —

in combination with the opposing image of a home society that failed to offer adequate support to its intrepid fighters. From 1916, the war appeared less and less as a defensive war, as it had in 1914 and even 1915. The early consensus, which had been so important in integrating workers, began to crumble in late Fall 1916—and this became apparent on both the military and the home fronts, as the Reichstag resolution calling for a negotiated peace would demonstrate in Summer 1917. Faced with calls for peace from the SPD, the army leadership concentrated on propaganda for a victorious end to the war, arguing that this alone would justify the enormous loss of life and lastingly ensure the security of the homeland. The propaganda now also contained sharply racist enemy-images, especially of colonial troops fighting on the Allied side. The gulf between front and homeland widened, as in many soldiers' bitter complaints about barroom strategists who thought they knew everything, but were ignorant of the real situation at the front. Soldiers also expressed fears that they would find their local society changed on their return, perhaps with a role reversal between men and women. From late 1917 on, the basic features of the "stab in the back" legend were becoming clear—the legend that the Right would later manipulate for its own ends. The polarization between the front and German society in general grew ever sharper, as military setbacks and the fading hopes for a decisive victory on the western front were blamed on lukewarm support back home.[365]

Over time, the war exposed the limits of the control and steering of communication. In fact, the crisis of political legitimacy often began as a crisis of language and communication or an actual breakdown of communication— and in many cases an encounter with prettified official pictures of the war, so different from everyday experiences, proved to be the trigger for open criticism. Wartime discourses and media also offered a forum for subversion and alternative interpretations. Knowledge of the conditions of censorship and control meant that the media of the wartime states lost much of their credibility and power to convince. This allowed rumors and suspicions to spread with their special dynamism.

Willful semantics that obeyed no official guidelines were part of the discourses of war. Language could be instrumentalized from below to assert social and political interests, as the references to shirkers, *embusqués*, or *Drückeberger* illustrate. In the early part of the war, the discrepancy between private perceptions and official interpretations could still be contained within a widespread use of sarcasm. But beyond a certain point, it developed into a veritable crisis of communication. This was most evident in Germany, where official discourse aroused great expectations that the state could solve all the problems of the home society. When everyday experience gave the lie to the picture handed down from above, the credibility of the state began to crumble.

8. THE CRISIS OF REPRESENTATION
Images and Stagings of the War

On July 12, 1916, shortly before 7:00 P.M., a man was hanged in the courtyard of the castle in Trento. According to the records of the Austrian military authorities, death occurred "8.5 minutes after the hanging began." Fabio Filzi was executed along with Cesare Battisti, an Austrian citizen from Trento and a member of the Tyrol regional parliament. Battisti had volunteered to serve in the Italian army at the beginning of the war, argued in press articles for the Italian-speaking Trentino to be included in the Italian nation-state, and finally fought as a troop leader. On July 11, 1916, he and Filzi were captured during an Austrian attack, interrogated in Trento, and sentenced to death for high treason, after the military court had discounted Battisti's immunity as a member of parliament. The Austro-Hungarian authorities consciously staged the conviction, sentencing, and execution of Battisti,[366] eager to make the maximum public impact with their treatment of this symbolic figure of South Tyrolean irredentist nationalism. It was, so to speak, an act of revenge for Italy's treason in joining the war in May 1915 on the side of the Entente. In this war of symbols and images, the photograph of Battisti's staged public execution played a decisive role.[367]

The authorities duly notified the population of Trento of the time when a cart was to carry Battisti through the streets to the castle. Still in Italian uniform, he was pointedly photographed in chains—as if to underline the traitor's subjugation. At the execution itself, Battisti had to wear civilian clothing to demonstrate that he was not recognized as an Italian officer entitled to prisoner-of-war status. The execution, too, had a clearly theatrical character. The hangman, Josef Lang, specially brought in from Vienna, performed on a previously constructed stage. Numerous soldiers gathered together in the courtyard, many taking photographs either on a personal basis or as official war photographers. The execution and Battisti's death were thus recorded many times over. One photo, taken immediately after he died, showed the grinning hangman together with onlookers and army personnel. It seemed to express in exemplary fashion the triumph of a patriotic self-image and the punishment of treason.

But the dynamic of these pictures soon escaped the control of Austro-Hungarian officialdom. Their circulation far beyond Trento and South Tyrol demonstrated how the photograph had become a powerful weapon in a war of communication. Photos of the execution soon reached Italy, where the authorities disseminated them as proof of the cruelty of the Austro-Hungarian conduct of the war. Indeed, things went so far that Vienna was forced to prohibit the printing of pictures of Battisti's or Filzi's capture and execution. On the Italian side, however, a process of recasting and reinterpreting the event was by then well underway. Battisti's martyrdom, reproduced in thousands of picture postcards, became a symbolic sacrifice for

Putting the enemy on display and avenging betrayal: Cesare Battisti after his capture by Austro-Hungarian forces (left) and after his execution in Trento (right), 1916

the Italian nation. Moreover, Italian illustrators showed a version of the execution in which Battisti appeared with an open white shirt, as the popular hero willing to die for the cause, an allusion to heroes of the Risorgimento that made him appear far more resolute than his executioner. The main opposition became that between an individual national hero, whose bravery in the face of death was proof of his moral superiority, and the cowardly Austro-Hungarian military.[368] Nor did the political instrumentalization end in 1918. Four years later, in *The Last Days of Mankind,* Karl Kraus used a retouched version of the photo of the execution scene as "a group portrait of Austro-Hungarian humanity . . . a monument to our executioners' black humor, transformed into the scalp of Austrian culture."[369]

Photography and motion pictures became crucial war media, but they conveyed polyvalent messages. The example of Battisti's execution showed how quickly control over images could unravel. The rivalry that developed in relation to photos and films therefore increased the pressure on the authorities to set interpretations in advance to steer the reception process. One element fueling this rivalry was the fact that, in addition to professional war photographers, many soldiers took amateur snapshots. Technological advances and the availability of cameras and film material led to the coexistence of official war pictures with privately photographed war scenes—a combination that would also mark the Second World War.[370]

Both official and private photographs on the western front focused mainly on discrete events such as a monarch's visit to the troops, on the fascination of new technology, or on everyday life at the front. But to the east and the south, the colonial gaze at the Other, at newly conquered territories and unfamiliar peoples, was an additional factor. In many photos of Austro-Hungarian officers, the racist deprecation of Serbs and Russians was apparent. But the camera also recorded the execution of numerous civilians behind the lines, whom the Imperial courts found guilty of espionage on Russia's behalf. Unlike in the Second World War, it was not prohibited to photograph such executions, but from the third year of the war they were increasingly withdrawn from public view because the Austro-Hungarian authorities feared criticism of their practices in occupied areas. After the reinstatement of the parliament in Vienna in 1917, many deputies took particular issue with the reprisals against civilians and the large number of executions behind the frontlines.[371] But neither the private snapshots nor the character of the war they documented could be taken back. The images continued to circulate and were susceptible to instrumentalization. The medium eluded official channeling and controls.[372]

Private snapshots portrayed moments of the war—but they did not claim to extract the specific nature of the war or to lend universal significance to a personal experience. But could photographers or artists convey an adequate picture of the war at all? The medium of photography showed that classical painting techniques could no longer depict the new battlefield; quite different forms of representation were required to do this.[373] People at the time were acutely aware of this crisis: "This war," we read in a literary and artistic magazine from 1916, "cannot be depicted in pictures. No artist can give us a total impression of the things that go on in night and fog, under the earth and above the clouds. . . . The death-defying men who march past and pounce on the enemy in battlefield canvases of the old school have disappeared; communication trenches have swallowed them up."[374] For those who looked at them, photographs contained information that was not actually visible in the image. The beholder, with everything he or she knew beforehand, became an interpreter of the image in a quite novel way.[375]

The sculptor Erich Stephani, writing in *Deutsche Kunst und Dekoration* on October 1, 1918, lamented the trend in the visual arts during the world war. No work, he argued, had yet captured the special emotional quality of the war and processed it in a convincing artistic manner; nor had the supposedly "grandiose experience" brought forth a new artistic language. It was therefore no accident that the public turned to "authentic photography" to form a picture of the war. The "deficient pictorial quality of the modern battlefield" and the "mechanization of military technique" discernible in positional warfare were causing the individual combatant to disappear. The "tendency for individual physical performance to become invisible" was one essential reason why "the observing eye of the artist took no part."[376]

Against this background, the escape into conventional themes in the mass media is hardly surprising. Of the 28.7 billion items of German forces mail sent between front and home during the war, approximately 25 percent were picture postcards. These included many "agitation cards" (*Hetzpostkarten*) with stereotypical depictions of Germany's enemies, but also patriotic

"I pray to the Lord each day / For my beloved so far away." Convention, kitsch, and homesickness: a German picture postcard

themes such as the "watch on the Rhine." In the early months, postcards from the various theaters of war showed soldiers leading a mostly nonviolent everyday existence, often with a touch of humor. But romantic themes were the favorites by far.[377] Like war posters, the picture postcards conveyed an image of the war that became increasingly remote from the soldiers' actual experience.

In this imagery, violence was largely filtered out, rendered innocuous, or represented in the pictorial language of the nineteenth century, as we can see most clearly in numerous studio photos of soldiers in uniform, standing with all their equipment and rifles with fixed bayonets. Popular postcards and prints showed men and women, loyalty, and life back home. Harking back to the social romanticism of prewar times, marriage and the family appeared indestructible institutions. The great majority of soldiers depicted were getting on in years, well-fed paterfamilias figures. The modern frontline assault trooper did not appear in such pictures, although some posters for war loans used him as a symbol for the will to hold the front. The war itself appeared static in the picture postcard world—a long wait in preparation for fresh attacks, with weapons almost never visible. Images of a peaceful everyday life made the war seem like a holiday outing. The dominance of materiel and machines in the war was evident in postcards of German technical achievements, with pictures of submarines, Zeppelins, or 42-centimeter mortars. There was dying on the cards, but no killing; there were countless rapiers and sabers, the stuff of dueling. Death itself featured at most in pictures of burials and well-kept cemeteries; the perspective was that of the victim rather than the perpetrator. On these postcards chivalrous warfare lived on, as did the romantic transfiguration of lives laid down for the fatherland. What was missing from these traditional images was any religious connotations; the war took place without Christian consolation.[378]

On the Allied side, too, picture postcards were hugely important as a mass medium. Countless examples depicted the French GI, the *poilu,* as a republican citizen-soldier, often with clear references to the ideal of the French revolutionary army.[379] As with the *Feldgrauen* (German field-gray troopers) and the British "Tommies," the connection to trusted wives and stable families was often played up. The postcard images—that together with posters, prints, and brochures were also sold at the popular *journées patriotiques* organized back home from 1915 on—showed wives and children in ever new variations, their patriotism evident in living for the return of the husband and father. They embodied the promise that the social and private world of the prewar era could be preserved.[380]

In contrast to Germany, images of colonial troops played a large role in French picture postcards, symbolizing France's imperial resources as well as emphasizing the bravery and martial qualities of these men that justified their recruitment.[381] As in Germany, mechanized warfare came down to nothing more than a mixture of technical perfection and individual heroism, to cannons, tanks, and aircraft plus fighter ace chivalry.[382] One difference, however, was that countless French postcards featured destruction in the homeland itself, German violence against the civilian population, whereas in Germany the only comparable examples came from the beginning of the war, with images of the devastation wrought by Russian troops in East Prussia. The French images seared the idea of *France meurtrie* (wounded France) into the country's memory, holding out the hope of a victory that would bring redress for collective and private suffering.[383]

Modernism had a hard time of it in this wartime mass culture; it would be wrong to infer from postwar modernist art and literature that similar trends had been present in the mass media during the war.[384] The widely circulating images of the war did not reflect a twentieth-century cultural springtime, but rather a late blossoming of nineteenth-century traditions with their promise of security and private harmony.[385] This is clear from the allusions to an idealized homeland. German posters inviting subscriptions to war loans wove local area, region, and nation together, presenting such loans as a patriotic duty that symbolized participation in the real war. Publicity for the sixth loan in March 1917, for example, played on the familiar theme of the defense of homeland, family, and relatives; the focus was not on the nation as an abstract category, but on the home region with which soldiers at the front and those who remained behind could identify. Sketches for posters showed swords or knights as protectors of German landscapes, villages, and industries, but also of the homeland and family, repeatedly symbolized by images of a mother and child. Home was consciously associated with historical references, but also with elements of modern life.[386]

Local or regional allusions also existed in British war posters, but like the cultural-national stylization of Shakespeare and the Tudor age, the dominant metaphor of "thatched cottages, leafy lanes, and rural folk," remained thoroughly English and anti-proletarian in its essence.[387] The pictorial language of Britain's wartime society was based on the historical and cultural space of traditional "Englishness." It ignored not only the conflicts in Ireland but also social-political change, the effective suspension of parliamentary rule, and the growing role of a centralized, interventionist state. Its most distinctive feature, however, was its anti-proletarian thrust. Army and navy propaganda was mistrustful of the industrial working class—as attentive trade union leaders soon realized. Such "disdain for the lower orders" was expressed, for example, in war posters that placed two images side by side: "one of a silent factory, and the other of a battery silent presumably from want of ammunition," the implication being that "the guns are silent because the workers who should be making shells are on strike."[388]

The conventional nature of the content said nothing, however, about the use to which the latest media technologies were put. Film, for example, established itself as a new means to convey a certain image of the war. But the German military leadership discovered this special potential later than its counterparts in Britain and France. In early July 1917, Ludendorff stressed that the war had proved "the phenomenal power of pictures and film as means of instruction and influence"; it was beyond doubt that "film would not lose its huge significance as a means of exerting political and military influence." Therefore, it was absolutely essential for a favorable conclusion to the war that "film should operate with maximum vigor wherever German influence [was] still possible." Ludendorff emphasized its role in German propaganda abroad and called for the centralization of the film industry in Germany, so as to convey a uniform view of the war to the population. The OHL accordingly promoted the founding of the famous UFA corporation (Universum Film Aktiengesellschaft) on December 18, 1917.[389]

The British authorities were quicker to spot the global potential of the medium. This was borne out with the success of *The Battle of the Somme*, which opened in British cinemas in August 1916—while the battle was still taking place. The two camera operators, Geoffrey Malins and John McDowell, were sent to the front between Albert and Bapaume to record the British attack, in expectation of a major breakthrough. Its novelty was that the film was more than the usual short war news report shown before the main feature. Commissioned by the British Committee for War Films, it was meant to boost the morale of wartime society by making the public realize that a breakthrough at the front would force an end to the grueling positional warfare. By mid-1917, the film was already showing in eighteen lands of the Empire and in Allied countries in Europe. It was seen by twenty million people in Britain alone—the biggest success so far in the country's cinema history. While Newfoundlanders celebrated Beaumont-Hamel and Ulster's citizens Thiepval as symbolic sites on the Somme, the film emphasized the military achievement of the Empire as a whole. The full ferocity of the battle was largely glossed over, but the filmmakers made every effort to create a realistic impression. Indeed, this was crucial to an authentic picture of the war, since only then could the message be conveyed that it affected not only the mother country, and that the support of the Empire had long been more than simply economic.[390]

Alongside confident men smiling and winking at the camera, the film showed exhausted troops and the shipping out of German prisoners and wounded British soldiers; there were few shots, though, of dead bodies in shell craters. The real climax came with the detonation of a British mine on July 1 at 7:20 A.M. at Beaumont-Hamel—an iconic image of the western front associated with the hope that massive explosions could break open enemy positions for a frontal assault. Yet the focus on this isolated action concealed the sobering reality of the battlefield: the fact that, while mines might destroy frontline German positions, the huge resulting craters slowed the advance of British infantry, giving German troops a chance to rebuild effective defenses and to call up fresh reserves.[391]

Above all, *The Battle of the Somme* highlighted the basic problem of how modern warfare could be presented at all. It was hardly possible to take in the battlefield, and a tall order even to film exploding shells. Therefore certain scenes—barrages and infantry attacks, especially—had to be reenacted in exercise areas; the reality of war could not have been conveyed without a fictitious, staged element. This resource used the style of authenticity to give the audience an impression of documentary immediacy, making it possible to get across the message of the film. The tension between the promise of authenticity and the representability of war anticipated a basic problem that would persist for the rest of the twentieth century.[392]

The war also entered the museums of Europe, where major collections began to be assembled as early as Summer 1914. In a German Red Cross guide of 1916 we read that its special exhibitions, mainly consisting of weapons and trophies captured from the enemy, were intended to present the "palpable successes of our troops to the population remaining behind in the homeland." In view of the high casualty toll, the "difficulties of the raging battles" were illustrated by "our enemy's instruments of war," while stress was laid on the links between the military front and the home society. The sight of the enemy's weapons was supposed to elicit "a sense of gratitude to our brave troops," who "defend our borders so manfully and keep the visible horrors of war at a distance."[393]

The Verband deutscher Vereine für Volkskunde, the German ethnological federation, immediately began to collect everything that might have any bearing on the war. The exceptional situation made ethnologists euphoric, because it gave them the opportunity to explore the people's soul, with the military forces mail service and soldiers' journals providing some of the most important items. In contrast to such poorly structured collections, often improvised under acute time pressure, Wilhelm Pessler, the future director of the Fatherland Museum in Hanover, pursued a different track. Between 1915 and 1917, in his book *Das historische Museum und der Weltkrieg*, he argued that, along with the general presentation of the war in major museums such as the Berlin Zeughaus, historical museums in garrison towns and provincial cities should add special sections on the war to their existing collections. This meant paying close attention to local contexts. Pessler envisaged the organization of exhibits as quickly as possible, to encourage the population to identify with the war.

Many curators saw that, by making the war a reality to the museum visitors' senses and emotions, their work was one of patriotic instruction, education, and mobilization. "There is no point in mechanically stringing together an endless array of captured artillery pieces and machine guns; it can at most produce an overwhelming momentary sense of stupefaction. The object on display must come alive; the visitor must be able to see for himself how this or that instrument of war functions; his imagination must be stimulated, so that it keeps working and trying to solve tasks."[394]

Thoughts of soldiers killed in action were supposed to be the central focus. This soon became problematic at local war exhibits, however, for the military feared that numerous photos of fallen soldiers and references to the high death toll at the front might have an adverse effect on the war effort at home. At first, the displays were therefore mainly of military equipment and captured weapons. To increase public knowledge, curators soon began to organize war stagings along with the displays, complete with panoramas, realistic backdrops, and walk-through replicas of trenches and military positions. On November 19, 1915, a Prague newspaper reported, "Since it reopened, the Prague trench has been at center of the liveliest public interest. On Sundays in particular, thousands of visitors make their way to the Kaiserinsel to see the large-scale military installation, which offers so much that is interesting and instructive."[395] Sections of battlefield were reproduced at the Zoological Gardens in Berlin, the fairground in Frankfurt, and (in early 1918) Trafalgar Square in the heart of London. In Hanover, a field position with trenches and underground bunkers attracted public attention. It included, "in military detail, many thousand meters of communications trenches and advance posts, a main position, a second position, and an artillery position. It also contains all kinds of obstacles and protective devices: on the one hand, barbed wire enclosures and entanglements, concealed wire barriers, trip wire, and wolf pits; on the other hand, bombproof shelters with every accessory, other dugouts for machine guns, underground passages, and listening posts."[396]

The war became a visitor experience, in which sophisticated replicas promised a vicarious authenticity. Pessler himself went so far as to suggest an acoustic element, on the grounds that droning weapons would make a deep impression on visitors: "Perhaps a phonograph in a special hall of the museum could reproduce an extract from this huge mass of sounds at a decisive battle."[397] Although such exhibits seemed to bring the war closer to the society at home, they completely screened out the individual experience of injury and death or the disappearance of family members. The process of aestheticization, in the artful visualization of the war, left out the actual experience of cruelty. Artificial trenches gave visitors a sense of security, even coziness, which might work in the Grünewald woods in Berlin, but not at the front.[398]

While curators developed innovative ideas to fulfill the promise of authenticity, representations of the enemy went no further than conventional stereotypes. Models of Russian soldiers showed drunken, ragged hordes, while Frenchmen used cannons as champagne coolers, and effeminate British soldiers wore Scottish kilts. The introduction of "auxiliary peoples" from the colonies unleashed a whole spectrum of racist prejudices on the German side. The Allies were accused of barbarism in their conduct of the war, which was said no longer to have anything in common with the wars of the past.[399]

An interest in visualizing the war as authentically as possible also lay behind the advent of a real battlefield tourism, which began even before the conflict ended. The area of the Marne battle, for example, which had had a special aura since Fall 1914, became a popular destination for organized trips; the battlefield was easy to reach from the French capital. A cult of material objects developed around the experiential space of the front: battlefield tourists gathered German spiked helmets, uniform buttons, cartridge cases, and shell splinters, while full-fledged collectors' markets for them sprang up back home.[400]

Reenactments played a major role in photographs, moving pictures, and exhibits. But could the war actually be put on stage? The theater reacted to the war, and the changed conditions of communication became apparent precisely in the theaters and circuses. Technology enabled elaborate stagings of the war, which also made use of film and sound recordings. The theater functioned as an imaginative space for women back home, for soldiers on leave from the front, and for war invalids. The military theater, created for soldiers and by soldiers, was a European phenomenon. But the international theatrical scene fragmented in Summer 1914 among so many national cultures. It was not only plays on the world war that found their way onto the stage; producers also turned to older works to address the question of the nation at war.[401]

In Germany, many theaters in Summer and Fall 1914 promoted the idea of a people's war against a world of enemies, as part of a wider process of community-building on the streets as well as the stage. But things began to change in Spring 1915, and the rhetoric of a nation at war receded in the theatrical world. The stage became more of a forum, where experiences on both the military and home fronts were addressed. Suddenly speculators, profiteers, and shirkers entered the scene, but fear of a feminization of society also made itself felt. Plays and stage settings often reflected the shortage of men and soldiers' fears of a questioning of gender roles in a society where the husband was no longer self-evidently the breadwinner and family head. Women therefore did not appear on stage as war workers or even pioneers of the political women's movements, but rather as traditional mother figures.

The rhetoric of a nation at war also faded in theaters at the front. Instead, they focused on combatants as victims, though without presenting a fundamental critique of the war. Stage productions did not simply mirror official interpretations of the war. Often, humor and ironical detachment were used to address the reversal of gender roles—with men in dresses and women in trousers, for example—so that the theater became an important space to vent male fears. But the example of the Bavarian NCO Ferdinand Weisheitinger—who, under the name Weiß Ferdl, had been a popular singer before the war—illustrated the limits of criticism. As his patriotic compositions were received less and less well by soldiers at the front, he increasingly probed their fears and feelings of impotence. But he never called the war itself into question.[402]

9. TWENTY-NINE MONTHS OF WAR
Expectations and Experiences Halfway through the War

By 1916, the war had become a global phenomenon on the daily news horizon. In his diary entries for June 6 and 9, the Heidelberg history professor Karl Hampe found it natural to record a whole range of events from around the world: the sinking of the British warship *Hampshire,* on which the war minister Lord Kitchener perished on his way to Russia; the fighting around Fort Vaux at Verdun; the offensive against Italian troops in South Tyrol; "Austria's Bessarabian front" in the face of the Russian offensive; the Allied blockade of Greek coasts and the deepening of the internal crisis in Greece; the death of Yuan Shikai, the general and president of the Chinese Republic, and the prospect of destabilization in East Asia, with Japan as the main beneficiary; and the U.S. presidential campaign, against a background of increasing criticism of Germany. On June 9, Hampe also mentioned a letter to an acquaintance who, as "commandant of Grootfontein" in Southwest Africa, had been interned by the British; any future correspondence would have to be sent via a "committee in Lausanne."[403] A few diary entries covered practically all the important theaters of war in Europe and elsewhere, as well as developments in East Asia and the United States. All the events in question were linked with one another and had multiple feedback effects. An attentive reader like Hampe could draw the global connections even from the limited and censored information available to him—indeed, by 1916 it went almost without saying that in this war everything was connected with everything else. The news world seemed to shrink geographical distance, creating a new awareness that what happened in the United States or East Asia might be relevant to the future course of the war.

(1) The year 1916 initiated a formal change in the war; it was a watershed between the early phase and the 1917–1918 period. On the one hand, the year saw the last blossoming of the cult of the offensive, at the battles of Verdun and the Somme. The artillery barrages and troop deployments reached a new crescendo, so that Verdun and the Somme came to symbolize the battle of materiel on the western front and a resource economy in which man was little more than a quantifiable input. The two battles were iconic figures of the slaughter, but they too brought no strategic decision. As the expected breakthroughs failed to materialize, new justifications were found for the high death toll; the objective was no longer to decide the war in a great battle, but to bleed, tire, and wear down the enemy. Instead of the great *percée,* a series of pinpricks (*grignotage*).

(2) But the outcome of the battles posed more sharply than ever the question of the relationship between investment and yield. This now directly

affected the legitimacy of political and military leaders. The year therefore became one of dismissals and new appointments: Falkenhayn and Joffre lost their posts, and Asquith was replaced by Lloyd George. A new type of war leader took office, owing his position to the crisis of 1916 and bowing without compromise to the new conditions in order to produce results. For all the differences, this characteristic was common to Hindenburg's and Ludendorff's Third OHL in Germany, Nivelle in France, and the charismatic Lloyd George in Britain. The other new feature was the increasingly short half-life periods, since the belligerent countries could not afford the indefinite continuation of a war with such high casualties and such a huge waste of resources. This gave rise to expectations that the war would come to an end with the next great effort. A paradoxical mechanism became discernible: the cost of the war ensured its continuation; only victory could justify the high casualties already sustained and give them a meaning. Any compromise, any concession, would have meant betrayal of the fallen soldiers. The higher the death toll, the more extensive became the war aims: a victorious peace, with annexations and financial levies, would prevent any future repetition of such a war. This limited the scope for the peace feelers that Woodrow Wilson put forth in late 1916.

(3) A one-sided focus on the western front, which still lingers today, distracted attention from the space where more soldiers died in 1916 and where the exhaustion of two multiethnic empires was already foreshadowed. At first the Russian offensive was more successful than any earlier Entente campaign in restarting a war of movement; deep penetration of the front took Austria-Hungary to the brink of catastrophe. The military and economic dependence of the Dual Monarchy on the German Reich was unmistakable. But when the Brusilov offensive ran out of steam, having incurred enormous casualties, Russia's extreme exhaustion was also foreseeable; mutinies and assaults on officers were early signs of a crisis of military authority. At the same time, the war expanded into southeastern Europe with Romania's decision to enter the fray and what amounted to an Allied intervention in Greece. In both cases, the catalyst was the vision of an enlarged nation-state that would conclude the process of nation-building. Competition among the main players to gain new allies fueled a wait-and-see bargaining strategy in the objects of their attention, limited though their military weight remained. Both the Central Powers and the Entente aroused far-reaching expectations

in these countries and encouraged the development of rival nationalisms. While Greece slid into civil war, the formal establishment of a Kingdom of Poland in November 1916 raised hopes there that would be dashed in the later course of the war. In all these cases, the result would be enormous problems, contradictions, and a loss of political credibility for the war states.

(4) Meanwhile, in the Near and Middle East, the Allies moved away from a policy that had involved preservation of the Ottoman Empire. The prospect of a future carve-up of the Empire unleashed intense rivalry, with competing promises and offers of compensation. Russian claims to the straits and Constantinople were matched by Italian and Greek hopes of acquisitions in the Aegean and Asia Minor. British policies were especially contradictory: on the one hand, London tried to win over the Arabs, so that they would organize revolts to weaken the structures of Ottoman rule from within. On the other hand, the quid pro quo of an independent Arab state clashed with the Sykes-Picot agreement, which defined separate British and French spheres of influence in the Near East, and the British government drew closer to the aims of the British Zionists around Chaim Weizmann that would eventually feed into the Balfour Declaration in 1917.

(5) The year 1916 posed major challenges for the internal structure of the multiethnic empires. Earlier fault lines and conflicts reasserted themselves under the new wartime conditions: the Easter Rising in Ireland and the gradual reorientation of the Indian national movement in the case of the British Empire, or the major revolt against conscription in tsarist Central Asia. In the Habsburg Empire, the Dual Monarchy proved ever less suited to the challenges of the war. Symptoms of this were the gradual politicization of the supply crisis on the home front, the ethnicization of social-economic conflicts over distributive justice amid the burdens of war, and the growing nationalization of politics in Cisleithania and Hungary. Only this explains why the death of the emperor was seen as so symbolic. It is true that he had increasingly withdrawn since 1914, leaving the field open to the rivalry of commanders and politicians (Conrad von Hötzendorf on one side, Tisza and Burián on the other). But with his passing in November 1916, the monarchy lost its most credible and tangible embodiment of the idea of a supranational empire. The lack of anyone to provide an equivalent emotional reference fueled criticism of the functions and achievements of the monarchy.

(6) German hopes of anticolonial movements in the British Empire came to nothing, but beyond such instrumental fantasies the war did change the global relationship of forces. The permanent mobilization of resources forced the European belligerent states to withdraw from a number of markets elsewhere, and this gave an impetus to local industry and commerce—in India, for example, but also in China and many parts of Latin America. The year 1916 was a key turning point for Britain itself. From the end of the year, in view of the heavy casualties on the western front as well as developments in the Near East, the whole of the Empire was being called upon to step up its contribution to the war. But this was more than just an effort in support of London: it brought about particular experiences for soldiers and societies in India, South Africa, Australia, New Zealand, and Canada, as well as in many African and Pacific colonies. In all these regions, participation in the war changed people's view of the traditional Imperial hierarchy and promoted a distinctive consciousness—whether as part of wartime nation-building or as an anticolonial impulse. These processes no longer revolved around the idea of a homogeneous empire.

(7) The year 1916 brought an inward and outward totalization of the war in attempts to gain new alliance partners, in new military offensives, and not least in a more intense mobilization of war economies and home societies. While the war continued without a decision, societies were marked internally by the struggle to hold out, in an everyday climate of shortages and constraints, surveillance and suspicion. The scale of the erosion became clearest in Russia toward the end of the year, and in outlines also in Austria-Hungary. Military exhaustion and economic overexertion passed into a crisis of political legitimacy.

(8) The shift in the war was also visible in another respect. The nation, so often invoked in Summer 1914 as the reference that gave the war collective meaning, increasingly lost this function in the face of the battles of materiel and the reality of attrition and fatigue at the front and at home. As the casualties mounted and more radical technological instruments were deployed, the war aims themselves became more radical and domestically controversial, and the earlier justifications lost much of their power to convince. Appeals to the nation sufficed less and less to motivate the efforts that people were called upon to make. Thus, in 1916 other justificatory formulas began to appear,

centered on the survival community at the front, on ethnic conflicts in the societies at home, or on a new tendency to exclude or segregate communities and to blur the boundaries between internal and external enemies. This connected the census of Jews in 1916 with the brutalization of occupation regimes, whether in Belgium (where new electrified fences on the Dutch border pointed to what was to come later in the century) or in the behavior of the Austro-Hungarian army toward civilians in Serbia. The most potent long-term alternatives to the nation and the nation-state would come in 1917 from Petrograd and Washington: two variants of a consistent internationalism offered a program for violent world revolution and a democratic moralization of politics under the banner of national self-determination, respectively. The fascination, and fear, that greeted the spread of the Bolshevik October Revolution, as well as the enthusiasm, indeed messianic expectation, of the responses to Woodrow Wilson, not only in Europe but especially in India, China, Korea, and South America, testified to one thing in particular: the justifications that drove the mobilization for war in Summer 1914, with their calls for sacrifice in the name of the nation, had begun to lose their legitimacy. In this sense, the transition from 1916 to 1917 marked a decisive turning point in the war. It also qualifies the idea of a long-term continuum, a single violent era comparable to the Thirty Years' War, stretching from 1914 to 1945. To understand why the war from which soldiers returned home in 1918 was so different from the one for which they left in the summer and fall of 1914, it is necessary to grasp the nature of this shift in 1916–1917.[404]

6
EXPANSION AND EROSION
1917

THE YEAR 1917 became one of global transitions, of a change in the shape of history.[1] Not only did the tactics and technology of warfare change once again, but the world war was combined with revolution and civil war in Russia. While the war on the eastern front seemed to be giving way to new forms of violent conflict, the violence of full-scale war spread on the western front. The arrival of new players, especially the United States, expanded the conflict militarily and ideologically, and a global wave of new expectations fused with the program put forward by President Woodrow Wilson.

But there was more, much more. Countless war posters in 1917 featured the new model tanks, the ultimate military machines that were supposed to break through the German lines, to relaunch the war of position and finally end the war. Another momentous development was the artistic flight from the war, from its endless casualties and its destruction of cultural symbols such as the library of Louvain or the cathedral at Reims that had witnessed the coronation of French kings. In this fourth year Pablo Picasso, who as a Spaniard was not directly involved in the war, created the huge stage curtain for the ballet *Parade* at the Ballets Russes production at the Théâtre du Châtelet in Paris. Its mixture of historical, folkloric, and abstract themes heralded a major change in the art world. The marked disparity among artistic approaches pointed to a crisis of representation, which became evident precisely in the genre of war art.[2] Traditional narratives had lost credibility in the face of mass slaughter at the front; the modern battlefield no longer allowed for images of heroic combat, but it also placed a question mark over empathy with individuals and a focus on their vulnerable bodies and minds. Something else came to the fore in art: the splitting of matter in cubism, its outright explosion in futurism, and a turn to objectless images. At the same time, however, a new cult of the object developed in the everyday culture of the age, and it was no accident that Picasso, in his wartime studio in Paris, began to put together still lifes out of trivial castaways.[3] The war itself brought forth a new aesthetic, not only in the countless souvenirs that soldiers fashioned in the trenches out of spent cartridge cases and shell fragments but also in the publicity for medical prostheses and facial reconstruction.[4] The aesthetics of compensatory substitutes supported the idea that an artificial hand seemed to function as well, if not better, than a natural hand.[5]

1. CRISES AND INNOVATIONS
The Asynchronicity of Space and Twentieth-Century Warfare

New military and political leaders had become active in 1916, Hindenburg and Ludendorff taking over at the Third OHL in the summer, and David Lloyd George as British prime minister in December. In France, the following year saw Pétain rise to head of the army and Clemenceau to head of the government. The crisis of military and political credibility gripped all countries to one degree or another: it was a result of the drain on their strength in 1916 and of the widening gap between expectations and experiences; between aims, casualties, and achievements. Therefore, hopes focused ever more on ending the war with the next offensive. But in early 1917 such heightened hopes could at any moment turn into disappointment, as the mutinies at the French front and the Russian revolutions in February and October 1917 showed.

On the German side, the successes in eastern Europe encouraged a greater willingness to take risks to achieve final victory—hence the decision on January 9, 1917, to launch unrestricted submarine warfare, followed a month later by Austria-Hungary in the Mediterranean. The high casualties suffered in the battles of 1916 forced the German armies into a defensive posture on the western front, but Berlin had to find an answer to the British blockade, to the global dimensions of the war, and, most important, to the mobilization of the resources of the British Empire. The naval officer Albert Hopman had high hopes for the declaration of unrestricted submarine warfare on February 1, not least because it promised to restore the reputation of the navy: "I have awaited today with great tension, and I felt quite a relief when the newspaper brought news this morning of the beginning of intensified submarine warfare. . . . Hopefully it will soon go swimmingly, and all will be up with Albion's proud dominance. Then the future of Germany, and especially its navy, will rest for all time on solid rock, and its rightful position amid the pack of liars would have fallen to it centuries ago, if we had not, with the exception of Frederick the Great and Bismarck, had such pathetic politicians."[6] The top brass in the navy, as at the OHL, were also confident that their U-boats would yield quick results. On April 1, Hopman wrote, "I feel an unshakable faith that submarine warfare will bring a decision within 3–4 months, in such a favorable sense that we will be able to dictate the peace. Hopefully other factors, such as the food question, national political currents, etc., or men of Bethmann Hollweg's ilk, will not make the settlement come too early."[7] Still, unrestricted submarine warfare was a risky business. The sinking of passenger ships in 1915, causing the deaths of numerous civilians from neutral countries, had increased the pressure on the United States to enter the war—which it finally did in April 1917, in a move that, in view of their growing economic and military exhaustion, was all the more in the interests of France and Britain. Berlin had greatly underestimated the consequences of its action in the Atlantic.

German plans in 1917, however, did take account of developments in the previous year. They avoided major offensives like Verdun, opting instead to dig in on the western front and to improve the forces' general position through a number of tactical retreats. On the other hand, the internal destabilization in Russia seemed to offer an opportunity to launch an offensive on the eastern front that would force that enemy power into a separate peace. Similar scenarios were envisaged in relation to Italy. As for Britain, the idea was to hit it hard with submarines before the possible declaration of war by the United States and the arrival of American troops in Continental Europe.[8] Meanwhile, greater tactical flexibility and rationalization would be introduced into operations on the western front; defense was again seen as the most effective form of warfare there, at least in a transitional period until Germany solved its problem of having to fight on several fronts and until it had sufficient forces to mount a decisive offensive campaign.[9]

This rethinking was visible in the so-called Siegfried Line, which stretched from Arras to St. Quentin and Vailly, running up to 50 kilometers behind what had until then been the German frontline. This meant giving up the exposed arc from Arras through Péronne, Noyon, and Soissons—an adjustment that not only released twenty divisions but cut across all Allied planning for Spring 1917, catching the enemy completely unaware and forcing it to develop new offensive operations. The Germans systematically built massive concrete defenses and machine-gun posts, unfurled acres of barbed wire, and, most important, arranged defensive positions in a new depth, relying more than they had before on the lessons they had learned from experience. The retreat between March 16 and 20 was the first time they had given back territory on the western front—an area measuring up to 110 kilometers from north to south and up to 45 kilometers from east to west. Operation Alberich, as it was called, involved the methodical deportation of 100,000 civilians to positions farther back from the front and the leveling of all roads, bridges, railroad lines, and buildings in that area. Military arguments fed into a "scorched-earth" policy, which in the Allied view was further proof after Belgium of the barbaric German conduct of the war. In 1919 at Versailles, French demands for reparations still referred to these measures taken in Spring 1917.[10]

The year 1917 brought the final transition to a different kind of war. The costly tactics of attrition used in 1916, which had brought no breakthroughs but had raised huge hopes that the war would soon be over, were discontinued. After the failure of the French spring offensive and the mass mutinies in the army, no one could ignore the exhaustion and the political and social dangers that it carried. This explained the emphasis on new tactics and technologies. On the German side, the planned withdrawal to the Siegfried Line meant abandoning the principle that captured territory should be held under all circumstances, and Ludendorff's defense in depth and new infantry tactics represented an adaptation to the western battlefield reality. The embodiment of this was the new storm trooper. Meanwhile, the Allies wagered on new combinations of weaponry, including the tank, which first

The soldier as frontline worker: members of the new German storm battalions, 1917

proved its potential at Cambrai in November 1917 in a display of armor, firepower, and mobility.[11]

After the experiences of the previous year and General Nivelle's counterattacks at Verdun, the French military leadership hoped that it would be able to continue the successes on the western front. The high casualties and exhaustion led French soldiers to set their sights on an end to the war, hoping that one last big effort would be enough to finish the job. In contrast to the British tactic of advancing step by step and holding new gains—represented at the Somme mainly by Rawlinson against Haig—Nivelle continued after Verdun to think that a major offensive could smash a way through; massive artillery bombardment of German positions would be followed by a rolling wave of fire, and finally tanks would clear the space for the infantry to attack. The breakthrough would be so deep that German artillery positions would be taken out as far as 10 kilometers behind the enemy lines. In addition, much was expected of simultaneous French and British attacks in Artois and the Aisne and Champagne regions. But the planned attack on the whole arc between Arras and Reims was thwarted by the German withdrawal to the Siegfried Line. Reworked plans for a pincer movement, involving a British offensive in Artois and a French offensive against the heights above the Chemin des Dames and east of Reims, led at first to conflicts among the Allied commanders. The popular Nivelle threatened to step down, and a political crisis ended only with the resignation of Prime Minister Briand and the formation of a new cabinet under Alexandre Ribot. The military and political leadership was acting under enormous pressure, given the exorbitant hopes that the next offensive would decide the war. In the end, Nivelle succeeded in winning the support of the British.[12]

But the British attack around Arras against the German-held Vimy Ridge, which began in early April 1917 and gave a major role to Canadian troops, ended in failure. One reason for this was German air superiority, with Richthofen a key player; the British lost seventy-five machines—one-third of their total force of fighter aircraft—before the battle had even begun.[13] The German media exalted Richthofen and other pilots as knightly heroes, in sharp contrast to the real conditions of the war in the air. The chances of survival were slim, as the light-weight machines had weak engines, offered little cover for the crew, and easily caught fire. Parachutes were disdained, clashing as they did with the warrior cult, and since the aircraft of the time did not yet have starter motors, a stall in mid-air left the pilot helpless. Air battles took place at a height of three to six kilometers. Pilots in the open cockpit therefore suffered from the extreme cold, which also created problems with the lubrication system.[14]

The aerial disasters of April 1917 made it difficult for the Allies to locate artillery positions from the sky and to direct fire with any precision. The familiar combination of intense bombardment—2.7 million shells were fired off—and high casualties was rewarded with meager territorial gains of at most six kilometers. It is true that the Vimy Ridge itself was captured on April 12, but the operation did not bring real relief for the French offensive. British and Canadian losses amounted to 160,000 men, those of the German army to 120,000–130,000.[15]

The next great French offensive, beginning on April 16, was directed at the Chemin des Dames, a crest line north of the Aisne with a pathway that had been fortified since the eighteenth century; it had a large number of caves, which the Germans had built up into defensive positions. Nivelle's original plan envisaged that two days would be enough for his troops to control not only two rivers, the Aisne and the Ailette, but also the crest line of the Chemin des Dames. But the great hopes vested in the offensive soon resulted in disappointment, as the attacks ran into the sand and no major breakthrough was achieved at any point. There too the German air superiority had an impact by limiting the ability of the French to conduct reconnaissance and to direct artillery fire against the deep defensive positions. What had worked in the narrow space at Verdun proved ineffective here: fire waves and infantry attacks were not properly coordinated, and on the very first day more than sixty tanks were lost. Wet weather and uneven terrain left armored vehicles highly vulnerable.

The offensive cost 120,000 dead, wounded, and missing, including 40,000 on the first day alone, while the 20,000 Germans taken prisoner were far below the target set by the French top brass. By May 9 no more than three kilometers had been taken, at the cost of 187,000 dead or captive against 103,000 on the German side. It proved impossible to seize the Chemin des Dames, and the persistent heavy bombardment soon led to ammunition shortages. At times there was a breakdown in medical care in the French army.[16]

Although the Nivelle offensive did not differ fundamentally from previous battles, the dashing of hopes turned this time into a major crisis of confidence that affected large parts of the army. On May 15, the war minister Painlevé replaced Nivelle with Pétain, and Foch was appointed supreme commander. Large-scale mutinies, fraternization with German soldiers, and the crossing of 20,000 men over to the Germans were alarming symptoms of the crisis. Pétain's response consisted not least in the abandonment of further offensive planning.[17] Militarily, the failure of the Nivelle offensive meant that France shifted to a purely defensive war until the summer of 1918.

With France deadlocked and with the United States still months away from deploying its first units on the western front, the pressure on the British army increased in Summer 1917. At the same time, the political situation in Russia meant that the eastern ally might exit the war after a fresh offensive by the Central Powers in eastern Europe. The British offensives of 1917 were therefore meant to show the enemy that the Allies now had the military will and ability to force a decision by means of large-scale operations. The result was the third battle of Flanders; after July 1916 and the Somme, October 1917 became the most costly month of the war for the British armed forces.

In June 1917, after meticulous preparation and the digging of numerous tunnels, the British carried out their first attack on the Messines Ridge south of Ypres; the largest mine explosion in the war up to that point wrecked the German positions and killed thousands of German soldiers. The surprise factor, the coordination of fire waves and infantry advance, as well as the use of gas and tanks, added up to a real success, and in the end the British managed to take the ridge. But their attempt to apply this tactic again at Passchendaele, in the third battle of Flanders, ended in failure. For the first time, the British commanders selected a battlefield on the western front without regard for their French allies. It was chosen partly because of the proximity of Channel ports that could ensure adequate supplies and partly because the Germans could not stage a tactical retreat from there as they had done at the Somme in Spring 1917. But the attacks at Messines had put the Germans on their guard and induced them to fortify their defensive positions. After a fortnight-long artillery bombardment, the British attacks began on July 31, but merely repeated the experiences of previous battles;

small territorial gains of no more than three kilometers were won at the price of huge casualties—as many as 32,000 in a single day. Heavy rain and the tactical destruction of canals meant that large parts of the battlefield had sunk into the mud, so that it was impossible to deploy heavy weapons or tanks. Nevertheless, Haig ordered the attacks to continue, with the help of troops from the Dominions.[18] On October 12 as many as 27,000 New Zealanders lost their lives, making it the bloodiest day in that country's history. The casualties also included 38,000 Australians (including a record 26,000 in October alone) and 30,000 Canadians.

This death toll made Passchendaele, together with the Somme, a byword for the British war on the western front, but it led to no major breakthrough and again expressed the disproportion between casualties and results. What everyone would remember was not the Canadian occupation of the totally ruined village of Passchendaele at the beginning of November, but the image of soldiers wading through deep mud. All told, the United Kingdom and Empire forces lost approximately 245,000 men, against 200,000 on the German side. Owing to the high groundwater level, the German troops had built numerous concrete positions for machine guns and artillery pieces, but as it turned out the British could not rely on aerial reconnaissance and were unable to give the artillery precise target locations. Only the new-style "all arms platoons"—that is, combat units consisting of infantrymen with rifle grenades and machine guns along with engineers, which had greater tactical flexibility than the German storm battalions—proved a success.[19] The third battle of Flanders, where the British casualties were exceeded only by those of the Somme battle, also failed to achieve any of its objectives; the key railroad junction at Roulers remained in German hands, the Belgian coast was not freed, and the German flank was not penetrated. Indeed, massively weakened by the battle, the BEF was at first unable to offer much resistance to the major German offensive in April 1918. All the more did the hopes of the western allies rest on the American forces.[20]

Although 1917 saw no breakthrough on the western front, the tactical and technological changes there were unmistakable. By the end of the year Haig was willing to adopt a more flexible defensive posture,[21] but the biggest innovations, on both the British and the German sides, appeared at the Battle of

Cambrai in late November and early December. The British deployed more than 450 tanks after a brief artillery bombardment, showing for the first time what armor could achieve under favorable geographical and climatic conditions. Moving over dry, flat terrain 15 kilometers wide, two-thirds of the tanks were able to reach the German lines, followed by six infantry divisions and cavalry, and supported by 400 aircraft. The initial penetration to a depth up to seven kilometers was greater than at the Flanders battle in July. In these first signs of a move beyond positional warfare, the well-trained British infantry units showed that, if there was time to prepare for battle, they were capable of applying the lessons of the previous year. But since the British had no reserves to call upon, they were unable to exploit their successes. Nor were the artillery or the supply chains up to the task; only the cavalry front riders got as far as Cambrai, and the town itself was never taken.[22] The Germans responded with a consistent use of the storm troop tactic: small units equipped with machine guns, hand grenades, flamethrowers, and mortars infiltrated enemy lines and caused mayhem before the infantry proper went into action. Counterattacks employing this tactic caused the British to lose their territorial gains and one-third of their tanks.

Dismayed by the loss of their tanks, the British failed to focus on what went well in the battle, particularly the coordination of artillery, tanks, infantry, and aircraft. German commanders, on the other hand, felt safe in the knowledge that their infantry had overcome the "tank horror."[23] This boosted confidence in their defensive capacities and the effectiveness of storm troop tactics, but also made them think that they had been right not to prioritize the development of armored units.[24] However, the Battle of Cambrai showed not only that tanks could effectively support infantry advances but also that, if used in large numbers and in the right terrain, they could operate as offensive weapons in their own right. In combination with other weapons, tanks were beginning to relaunch a war of movement—this was the critical import of Cambrai for the future wars of the twentieth century.

But 1917 was by no means a watershed only for the western front.[25] Nowhere else were military and political developments, front and homeland, war and crisis, as dramatically intertwined as they were in Russia. The situation at the front had an impact on Russian internal politics, and vice versa, giving rise to a quite special situation. Contrary to German and Austrian

Technological progress and vulnerable mobility: British tanks at the Battle of Cambrai, 1917

expectations, however, the February Revolution that overthrew tsarist rule did not bring the Russian war effort to an end. From May on, the Provisional Government and its war minister Alexander Kerensky gambled on continuing the war on the Allied side. Although Kerensky in principle favored a peace without annexations or reparations, he was adamant that it must involve an honorable settlement for Russia. With an eye on the example of revolutionary France after 1792, he believed that the revolution had set Russia on the way to a civil society in which each citizen would serve by birth as a defender of the fatherland; the boost to morale would transform the tsarist army of subjects into a citizens' army, and a combination of political participation and national defense would allow a victorious conclusion to the war. The military consequence of such thinking was the last big push by Russian forces that began in June 1917, which Kerensky personally supported with visits to the front and numerous speeches to soldiers.[26]

The main target of operations was Lvov on the southwestern front, although smaller attacks were also launched on the western and northern fronts and against Romania. On June 29, an unprecedented artillery barrage got underway on the eastern front. But in a repetition of the Brusilov offensive, Russian troops were unable to sustain their initial successes and isolated breakthroughs. Russian losses in just four days of July numbered some 80,000, against 16,000 on the German side, so that despite Kerensky's urging it proved impossible to continue the attacks. The Russians then called off the offensive on July 15 and began to prepare for a German counteroffensive. Signs of disintegration became evident in Russian units, especially in those containing non-Russian nationalities such as Poles, Ukrainians, and Finns.[27]

The German attacks in the Baltic in late 1917, featuring highly effective storm troop tactics in the battles around Riga, effectively brought to an end the war between Russia and the Central Powers that had begun in August 1914. The lack of synchronization between western and eastern fronts was by then a decisive factor, but the differences between northern and southern sectors of the eastern front were also enormous. In a city such as Warsaw, as well as in large parts of Galicia, people lived more or less as they had done in peacetime, whereas on the Macedonian front, the southwestern city of Salonica—a multiethnic port where, around the turn of the century, six or seven languages had been spoken, and where the 70,000 Jews had had Greeks, Armenians, Turks, Albanians, and Bulgarians as neighbors—was destroyed by a catastrophic fire in August 1917.[28]

Just a few days before the outbreak of the October Revolution, when it looked increasingly likely that Russia would leave the war, there was a dramatic turn of events on the Alpine front that brought Italy to the brink of military disaster. By late 1917 resources on all sides were so exiguous that any military reverse could decide the war;[29] all the more abrupt and surprising, in the extreme conditions of the high Alps, was the transition from a year of bitter positional warfare to a war of movement.

The eleven previous battles on the Isonzo had involved the same mechanisms that characterized the war of position on the western front: small territorial gains for completely disproportionate losses of men, with no decisive breakthrough. But in the summer and early fall of 1917, the Italian superiority

OPPOSITE: Map 9. Eastern Front, 1917–1918

Eastern front at Brest–Litovsk ceasefire, Dec. 15, 1917

Farthest Central Powers advance until Brest–Litovsk peace treaty, Mar. 3, 1918

Russian territory occupied by Central Powers

Advance of the Central Powers (Feb. 1918)

Kerensky offensive (July 1917)

Allied intervention after treaty

Central Powers intervention after treaty

Murmansk

Arkhangelsk

Finland

Helsinki

Petrograd (St. Petersburg)

Stockholm

Tallinn (Reval)

Pskov

Tver

RUSSIA

Baltic Sea

Riga

Moscow

Liepāja (Libau)

Vitebsk

Smolensk

Tula

Dvina

Kaunas

Königsberg

Vilnius

Minsk

Mogilev

Orel

Danzig

Grodno

Gomel

Kursk

Tannenberg

Brest-Litovsk

Byelgorod

Warsaw

Kharkov

Wrocław

Kiev

Ukraine

Dniepr

Rostov on Don

Kraków

Lvov

Taganrog

Galicia

Czernowitz

Dniester

Bug

Bessarabia

Moldavia

Crimea

Novorossiisk

Vienna

Odessa

Budapest

AUSTRIA-HUNGARY

Sevastopol

Drava

ROMANIA

Black Sea

to Baku

Sava

Bucharest

Constanţa

Belgrade

Wallachia

Danube

OTTOMAN EMPIRE

0 100 200 300 400 500 km

Constantinople

due to the fact that the enemy had to fight on several fronts was gradually beginning to tell. Thus, the Italian supreme commander Cadorna was able to field thirty-eight divisions at the tenth Isonzo battle, against fourteen on the Austro-Hungarian side under General Boroević, and as many as fifty-four against twenty in the subsequent battle. The 315,000 Italian casualties were larger than the 235,000 on the Austro-Hungarian side. In August and September 1917, the Italians even managed to capture the Bainsizza Plateau in western Slovenia and to shift the front to within 15 kilometers of Trieste, provoking a crisis in the Austro-Hungarian armed forces. Although gloom and discontent over the casualty toll was spreading among Italian soldiers, further increasing high desertion rates, Cadorna felt confident that the fall would bring a decisive victory over the weakened enemy.

In this situation, Emperor Karl asked the Germans for help, which they were able to give after the end of the Russian Kerensky offensive. At first Hindenburg and Ludendorff remained skeptical, however, fearing that Austria-Hungary would be unlikely to fight on in the event of victory over Italy and Russia's possible exit from the war; they were also under growing pressure at home, faced with persistent supply problems that fueled national political conflicts. On the other hand, defeat by Italy might lead the Dual Monarchy to sign a separate peace. The two scenarios together emphasized how little room for maneuver existed in late 1917. In the end, the OHL transferred the 14th Army under Otto von Below from the eastern front to the Alps—partly to exercise control over the Austro-Hungarian allies. But the decision to mount a relief attack in the upper reaches of the Isonzo, between Flitsch and Tolmein, was taken from an objective position of weakness: the thirty-five Austro-Hungarian divisions faced forty-one on the Italian side.[30] Only at the center of the attack, near Caporetto (Karfreit), did the Central Powers have a clear numerical superiority. Although the Italian high command had intelligence reports that an attack was being planned, Cadorna stuck to the view that attrition in the previous battles made it impossible for the enemy to take the offensive. It was a miscalculation that reflected thinking in the final period of the war—a confidence that the enemy was on the brink of collapse concealed the exhaustion in one's own ranks. Mutually reinforcing illusions about one's own resources and the enemy's weakness sustained the continuation of the war until one side actually collapsed. This point was growing closer, as sudden dramatic events in the deadlocked fronts (the Alps in Fall 1917 and the western front from Summer 1918) demonstrated.[31]

The scale of the turnaround on the Isonzo front took both sides by surprise, as local breakthroughs had far-reaching consequences for an enemy accustomed to positional warfare. The success of the initially limited offensive that the Central Powers launched on a small sector of the front on October 24, 1917, rested on several factors: their heavy barrages and massive use of gas—1,600 gas shells in the space of four and a half hours—combined with bad weather to knock out the Italian artillery at Tolmein at an early stage in the battle;[32] the tactic of infiltrating enemy lines with storm troops, in which young German officers like Erwin Rommel distinguished themselves, paid off handsomely; and rapid advances into the valleys cut off the Italian supply routes. Caporetto fell on the afternoon of October 24, and by the end of the day the penetration was up to 20 kilometers deep. More than 20,000 Italian soldiers were taken prisoner; and Godirna and Udine were captured on October 30. Further attacks spread confusion and panic, so that the orderly retreat ordered by Cadorna on October 25 was hardly a possibility. Fleeing soldiers and civilians jammed the roads, greatly exacerbating the situation, and Italian units in the combat areas began to disintegrate. Since all reserves were tied down on the front from Lake Garda to the Isonzo, the Italian high command was unable to assemble enough troops for a counteroffensive. Finally, with the situation continuing to worsen, it was forced to pull its forces back into the Dolomites. The front then stabilized behind the Piave River, a mere 35 kilometers from Venice, when the Central Powers too lacked the troops to press on with the attack.[33]

The Caporetto disaster escalated into a crisis for the war state and the whole of Italian society, bringing it to the brink of collapse. By November 10, the country had lost half of its fighting strength, with 30,000 dead and wounded, and 370,000 taken prisoner; 3,000 machine guns and nearly half of all artillery pieces had fallen into enemy hands.[34] To stabilize Italy militarily and to prevent an enemy breakthrough into the heart of the north, the British and French supreme commanders deployed five and six divisions, respectively, between Brescia and Venice, obtaining in return the replacement of Cadorna with Armando Diaz.[35]

This marked the beginning of intense debate in Italy over who was responsible for the outcome of the battle. The military commanders, especially Cadorna, argued that the blame did not lie with themselves or their troops, but with a combination of socialist propaganda and defeatism at home that had undermined the fighting capacity of the armed forces. An Italian stab in the back legend, diverting attention from various failings and omissions, thus took shape long before the counterpart in Germany in Fall 1918.[36] Mussolini, in particular, exploited the military shortcomings of the national state and the crisis of *irredenta* nationalism, turning Isonzo into a byword for the weakness of the liberal regime and its inability to ensure the nation's survival and complete its unification. The self-empowerment of the Fascists fed on this negative myth in a new cult of violence.[37]

Caporetto confronted Italy for the first time with the fact that it had overestimated its strength and misjudged the relationship between its war aims and the resources available to it. The mobilization of society in support of the battle produced a degree of cohesion that had not existed in 1915, when entry into the war had revealed political splits and deficits at the level of national integration.[38] In late 1917 the military and political leadership was forced to adjust its war aims to its real possibilities, in a process of retreating from the maximalist demands of the London treaty. Instead of planning to acquire new territories in southeastern Europe, it now sought an agreement with the Serbs and drew closer to the positions of the South Slav Committee, which for the first time gained a political voice within the circle of the Allies.[39]

These dramatic developments stemmed from what the Central Powers had planned to be no more than a relief operation, since they no longer believed that they had the resources for a frontal breakthrough. In late 1917 the war entered a decisive stage. The battles since 1915 had considerably weakened all sides, with the result that local breakthroughs could suddenly lead to a critical juncture for the war as a whole, but also that the attacking army no longer had the resources to mount many further offensives or to repel major counterattacks. This increased the danger as well as the likelihood of unexpected developments. A possible scenario for the end of war began to appear on the horizon—not victory or defeat in a last great battle, but rather the sudden collapse of one side in the manner of a building long hollowed out from the inside.

For the Austro-Hungarian army, which contributed the bulk of the attack-ing forces on the side of the Central Powers, the battle showed that even in late 1917 there could be no talk of a breakup of its multiethnic composition. Many Slav soldiers continued to fight loyally—one reason being that Italy's entry into the war in 1915, seen as treason to the Dual Monarchy, had given rise to a common enemy-image for all ethnic groups within the army. Unlike in the war against Russia, which Czech soldiers could never see as the main enemy, the Italian enemy-image fueled a general mobilization. The Habsburg army remained operational despite its severe crises, and in favorable circum-stances it was still capable of achieving successes in alliance with German forces. This differentiated it from the Russian army, which had been more or less paralyzed since the failure of the Kerensky offensive.[40]

Harry Graf Kessler gave an impression of the mood in the OHL supreme headquarters, which he visited in early October 1917. The main hope there was that the French army would disintegrate. Ludendorff, "stouter, but still as pink, fresh, and energetic as a year ago," thought that "the French army is truly getting tired. That as well is the only way he can explain to himself their lack of activity. Since the spring they had done as good as nothing." The American entry into the war had yet had little effect: "Up to now they have sent in total 30,000 men, so two divisions. That is as good as nothing on the western front." In the evening there were celebrations for Hindenburg's birthday; he pointed to a globe, obviously a present, and said he had "always wanted such a thing. Here at least you could find all the little republics that have declared war against us. . . . White bread—now a rarity in Germany—a quite good Mosel wine, soup, venison, two birthday cakes. All simple but well done and plentiful as in a good country home." Kessler observed "a thor-oughly pan-German mood . . . against Alsace-Lorraine" among staff officers. Hindenburg "reported tranquilly that he had received birthday wishes from Scheidemann, Albert, and David. 'I am going to buy a baker's cap next.' His popularity gives him pleasure but spiced with irony. He sits in the middle of his enormous fame without vanity, with a kind of grandfatherly good humor that he expresses in short sentences. His voice sounds like hoarse thunder, like that of some old thunder god Wotan, but with undertones of laughter." Kessler noted the contrast between the field marshal and the headquarters boss: while Hindenburg sometimes looks like a "huge packet of healthy nerves and force, a kind of boxer, a genius of weighty agility, a mixture of Wotan and Eulenspiegel, whose pranks are called Tannenberg, Bucharest, Riga," Ludendorff appears "more intellectual, a constantly mobile intellect. . . . [He is] a great talent certainly, probably with sudden intellectual inspirations and illuminations, a sharp critical understanding to eliminate the fantastic from among them, and the tenacity, the force, the practical talent to implement the others." In society, Hindenburg only briefly joined the conversation that Ludendorff sustained: "I imagine that this will also be the case in part when Ludendorff reports to him. The staff creates around both of them a platform and an atmosphere. That is the innermost cell of the world war, the tiny, powerfully tense feather spring driving and ordering the entire affair."[41]

In November 1917 a new situation was taking shape for the Central Powers. On the western front, tactical retreats and defensive fortifications had enabled the Germans to repel the French spring offensives. Large-scale mutinies suggested that France had lost its capacity for major offensives, and after the third battle of Flanders the same tendency was apparent on the British side; American troops had not yet been seriously deployed. To the east, however, the war was effectively over by November 1917. Russia's exit, giving the Central Powers an opportunity to transfer forces to the western front, seemed in the cards, while Caporetto had thrown the Italian military into crisis. In the east and the south, a renewed war of movement had opened up the possibility of an end to the war on those fronts. In Germany, the news reports had a truly liberating effect. In early December 1917, Harry Graf Kessler quoted military observers: "The basic strategic problem of the war is being torn up—the problem that has defined it as a contest between two power groups, one surrounded in its inner lines, the other encompassing the enemy on all sides and fighting in the outer lines. Should Russia completely leave the fray, we will no longer have to wage a war on two or three fronts, but rather a war in which the hitherto encircled powers fight with no one to their rear."[42]

In view of the clear signs of troop depletion and exhaustion, the successes of the Central Powers increased the pressure to end the war victoriously in the limited time during which the army and the home society could continue to hold out. At the same time, such hopes of victory—which outweighed all other considerations in Germany's political and military leadership until late Summer 1918—reduced the scope for a peace agreement with the Allies.

2. NEARING THE LIMITS
Soldiers between Deviance and Protest, Captivity and Politics

For France, 1917 became the *année impossible,* the "impossible year," when the gap widened between war aims and available resources, and when military crisis and social exhaustion gave rise to massive protests that threatened the *union sacrée* through army mutinies and strike movements at home.[43] This combination of elements, together with the lack of military successes, forced the country into a second mobilization, which had a military, political, and social dimension and pushed the *union sacrée* markedly to the right. A new kind of wartime regime replaced the domestic political truce of August 1914, bringing to power the charismatic premier Georges Clemenceau and excluding the Socialists from government. The most important consequence of this second mobilization was that hopes for peace rose once more—but to be credible, its results would have to reflect all the sacrifices, privations, and efforts that the war had brought. Thus, 1917 saw a major change threshold, a shift to projections and expectations that could not—or not entirely—become political reality in postwar France. Without the crisis of 1917, we cannot really grasp the basic feature of that period: that is, the fixation of France's political and military leadership on security and on compensation for the wartime death toll.

What was the breaking point for soldiers? Why did they go on fighting? What drove them to look for military breakthroughs, despite casualty rates as high as 20 percent in many units? Why did their motivation at some point turn into protest and resistance? The two explanatory poles on offer today—compulsion and repression, consent and persuasion—draw too readily on one-sided ideal types to account for the complex situation and motivation of combat troops. For a regime of coercion alone could not have held the mass armies together for so many years. And consent, after the great battles of 1916 on the western front, did not mainly involve fighting patriotically for the fatherland; national rhetoric had run into the sands of positional warfare and the battle of materiel. Republican patriotism may have motived the defense against German invasion in Summer and Fall 1914, but in 1916–1917 it had lost a great deal of its persuasive power. At any event, the official war propaganda increasingly seemed to soldiers like "brainwashing."[44]

If any combat motivation was common to all soldiers, it was the idea that the micro-community of immediate comrades could not be left in the lurch. What maintained order in the armed forces was neither the abstract quantities of nation and republic nor the traditional top-down command structure, but a horizontal discipline arising directly out of the comradely milieu on which each soldier's life largely depended. The will to survive, and not so much a readiness for heroic self-sacrifice, was the motive force driving the frontline community. Its key references were a sense of responsibility toward comrades and attention to immediate superiors, who, unlike the commanders behind the lines, were exposed to the same dangers that ordinary soldiers faced. This experiential context could be politicized only to a limited extent. For Francisque Vial, a soldier in the French territorial army, discipline came "from below," "from the respect and affection that the soldier felt for conscientious and good leaders." They had not gone to the front "in order to talk about class struggle"; this was an "egalitarian, democratic army," indeed a "fraternal army." Although such terms might at first sight appear to belong in the tradition of the French Revolution, what lay behind them was primarily the soldiers' own experiences. The platoon was fraternal and egalitarian because all were exposed to the same dangers, the same proximity of death.[45] This consensus within the soldiers' microcosm did not decrease in the course of the war. While national justifications for the conflict became more fragile, the ties joining soldiers to one another grew deeper as a result of their common experiences. Thus, the war itself generated the mechanisms for soldiers to continue fighting it. Louis Mairet expressed this in a paradox: "The warrior prevents the end of the war."[46]

In 1917 this consensus within the French army was challenged. After the slaughter at Verdun, hopes were all the higher that Nivelle's successful counteroffensives could be followed through in a last great effort to end the war. These hopes foundered at Chemin des Dames. The French army did not achieve its planned breakthrough (percée) of the enemy front, at most inflicting a few pinpricks (grignotage).[47] But it would be too simplistic to attribute the mutinies to the failed offensive per se; the casualty levels were high, but not significantly higher than in earlier battles. The decision to relieve Nivelle of his command on May 15, on the grounds that he was the main figure responsible for the failure, was therefore not enough to stem the mutinies; the issue was not the shortcomings of one player, but a fundamental crisis of trust and credibility. What happened in April and May 1917 may be understood as a "revolution of rising expectations." The dashing of these hopes and the resulting disillusionment turned into protest and resistance because there was no longer any perspective of a decisive breakthrough to end the war. This made soldiers wonder what the point was of all the efforts and sacrifices, both past and future. Their basic motivation—trust in their own survival and a rapid end to the war—began to dissolve.

Since the beginning of the war, there had been isolated incidents when one or more men refused to obey an order. On average, twenty to twenty-three death sentences were handed down each month, though these were usually commuted to terms of imprisonment. By Spring 1917, however, whole groups of soldiers declined to return to their positions at the front after a period of rest behind the lines. They were not conscientious objectors who laid down their weapons in the field or refused to climb out of the trenches to attack the enemy. The critical periods for desertions were those when soldiers felt most acutely the contrast between the killing zone and rear positions or home leave. Railroad stations, train journeys, and moments of transition between rest and combat developed into particular flashpoints, with alcohol often playing a role. Men gathered together and organized spontaneous demonstrations at which they raised a whole range of demands. Soldiers laid down conscious political markers when they sang the "Internationale," waved red flags, or threatened to march on Paris. Disciplinary proceedings dealt with more than isolated cases of disobedience; nearly half of the French army was affected. In sixty-eight divisions, there were approximately 250 incidents in which men collectively refused to obey orders. Five divisions in the Chemin des Dames attack zone between Soissons and Reims were a prime example. The peak of unrest was in May and June 1917, but local mutinies continued until January 1918. The total number of active mutineers was probably between 30,000 and 50,000, but this figure conceals the effect on other soldiers, who faced the question of the circumstances under which they would continue to fight.

Actively or passively, therefore, the mutinies involved hundreds of thousands of soldiers, almost all of them in infantry units. Most came from the lower middle classes and, typically for French infantrymen, were farmers. Sometimes there were violent protests and assaults on officers; for instance, against General Bulot, the commander of a brigade in the Second Division, whom the men accused of sending them to the slaughter in attacks that made no military sense.[48] The mutinies also had an impact on society at home. On July 19, 1917, the French infantryman René Arnaud saw in a theater in Noyon how some soldiers in the audience greeted with jeers the customary singing of the "Marseillaise" at the end of the evening. In Spring and Summer 1917, many officers even prevented the playing of the anthem, fearing that its references to struggle might encourage revolutionary sentiments.[49]

The mutineers' contradictory demands reflected the experience of soldiers during the previous years. This was no antiwar movement or revolutionary class struggle, but an attempt to recover human dignity amid the conditions at the front, with a special focus on the poor provisions and the inadequate system for relief and home leave. Many protests started in connection with furlough trains, since soldiers were particularly worried about the conditions that their families had to face. In 1916, letters and packets from family members had reassured them that supplies were still getting through back home, but the situation deteriorated in the long winter of 1916–1917. If *poilus* referred in their letters and requests to the formula "provided the civilians hold out," this involved not so much an ironic dismissal of "shirkers" at home as a real fear for their families' survival and the stability of the home front.[50] Protests against injustice therefore related to the home front as well—and not only to food supplies or factory conditions but also to the rumored use of black colonial troops against women protesting or on strike. A basic sense of insecurity took hold: many soldiers feared that their long absence and the new tasks of their women back home were challenging their traditional roles as breadwinners and family heads.[51]

The central demand for an end to the war grouped these themes together— but not in the sense of a pacifist movement. Mutineers did not wish to stop defending their country, but they did demand a realistic prospect of survival and a just peace that would keep France safe and justify their time of service at the front. Spring 1917 was a critical moment in the political awareness of

French soldiers, who thought of themselves in the tradition of the *soldats-citoyens* of the Great Revolution. The conflict between direct and representative democracy, which had surfaced in ever-new variants since 1789, broke out once more, as the soldiers' resistance appealed directly to the general will (*volonté générale*) of the nation. It was this, rather than parliament, that they saw as the true origin of sovereignty. The government and commanding officers seemed to have lost sight of the principle of the *volonté générale* and the consequences of the war for millions of French men and women. In their letters and petitions, the *poilus* reminded deputies in the National Assembly that the fate of France was in the hands of its soldiers.[52]

Why did the mutinies not lead to the collapse of France? Many senior officers reacted to them quite passively, convinced that younger colleagues would regain the trust of the rebellious soldiers and restore order in the ranks.[53] Pétain, appointed as Nivelle's successor to bring the mutiny to an end, tried at first to isolate the active elements from those who just went along; the army leadership would heap blame on a few instigators and avoid having to admit a general crisis of loyalty, and the great majority of mutineers would be given a chance to return to their units at the front. Pétain went out of his way to praise one commander who, having surrounded a group of rebels with reliable cavalry units (mostly consisting of colonial troops noted for their loyalty), offered them a deadline to resume active service. Relying on his reputation among the *poilus*, Pétain was eventually able to contain the mutineers by addressing some of their specific demands and making improvements in food supply and home leave regulations. Most important, however, he gave up the idea of further offensives—at least until American troops had reached the western front in larger numbers.[54]

In late 1916, after Pétain's espousal of a defensive strategy at Verdun, the army leadership had treated him with skepticism and chosen Nivelle instead. By Summer 1917, however, he alone seemed capable of bringing the situation under control. Once the soldiers had decided by a majority to return to combat duties at the front, the sanctions against a small number of their leaders kicked in. Roughly 10 percent of those who had refused to obey orders were put on trial: 3,427 were found guilty; 554 were sentenced to death, and in the end 49 were actually executed; more than 1,300 had to serve heavy terms of forced labor. The official statement on the matter referred to defeatist currents in the home society. And a new wave of spy mania and conspiracy theories gripped the country in Spring and Summer 1917 in the context of the army mutinies and strike movements.[55] But the military declarations made virtually no mention of the officers whose duty it had been to maintain discipline. The mutineers were externalized, as it were, appearing not as evidence of a breakdown in discipline and shaky national loyalty, but as the result of organizational problems and political agitation by a handful of troublemakers.[56]

The crisis shattered the trust of many soldiers in the political institutions and leaders of France, but not their basic attachment to the principles of the republic and the need to defend it from German attack—that was the bottom line as far as the movement was concerned. Reliable commanders and politicians were able to get things back under control. Some 20,000 men deserted to the Germans, and local fraternizations and exchanges of soldiers' newspapers with German troops (reflecting a loss of confidence in their own press) should also be seen as crisis symptoms, even though, in comparison with the armies of Russia and Italy, the numbers remained manageable.[57] But the situation of the French army was quite different from others on the western front: although the German and British armies also faced similar demands from the troops and suffered high casualties at Verdun and the Somme in 1916 and at the third battle of Flanders, neither had to deal with the same kind of refusal to obey orders.[58] The reactions of French soldiers had to do with the earlier hope that, given the mismatch between battlefield casualties and results, a last great effort would bring a speedy end to the war. Disappointment then turned into active resistance because the mutineers' demands were still essentially imbued with the principle of wartime service for the nation under attack. The link between this minimum consensus and France's culture of political protest, its tradition of direct appeals to the nation, explains why events escalated as they did—but it also indicates the limits of that escalation and how it could be overcome. After the spring and summer of 1917, France remained in a precarious situation, but it did not fall apart.

The mutinies in the French army were not an isolated phenomenon. But group protests and demands were a very different thing from individual decisions to desert. Conduct that deviated from the norms of military discipline was therefore quite diverse—and hardly a novelty in the history of warfare in general or this war in particular. In 1917, however, new symptoms became visible: protests multiplied, in some cases acquiring mass forms and a new political dimension, albeit with typical differences that became clearer as the war went on.

Disobedience always had a structural and an individual dimension. The British writer Siegfried Sassoon (b. 1886) enlisted in the world war as a volunteer and recorded his experiences as an officer with a penetrating eye. The loss of close friends made him more and more critical, in a series of poems that both exposed the senseless slaughter and glorified the heroism.[59] Sassoon's radical conclusion was a pacifism that crystallized in June 1917 in an open letter of protest; he saw it as "an act of wilful defiance of military authority." Sassoon maintained that the war was being deliberately prolonged by people who had the power to end it. "I am a soldier," he wrote, "convinced that I am acting on behalf of soldiers. . . . I have seen and endured the sufferings of the troops, and I can no longer be a party to prolonging those sufferings for ends which I believe to be evil and unjust." He thought his public protest might "help to destroy the callous complacence with which those at home regard the continuance of agonies which they do not share and which they have not sufficient imagination to realize."[60] Sassoon's open letter was read out in parliament by an MP who manifestly supported him, and it was published in several newspapers. But although it had a national echo, the really decisive point was that most of Sassoon's comrades, while sharing many of his criticisms, condemned his refusal on principle to carry on fighting.[61]

Desertion rates and the number of courts-martial give some idea of the scale of dissidence in the ranks. During the war a total of 18 German and 269 British soldiers were tried and executed—whereas 10,000 German soldiers and no British suffered the same fate in the Second World War.[62] These figures point to a key difference between military cultures and qualify any notion that the army elite in Germany was uniquely autocratic. Between 1914 and 1918, the British army was strongly marked by conventional ideas of discipline and obedience, as expressed in the use of capital punishment inherited from the nineteenth century; draconian measures were imposed both in British society and in the armed forces for a number of offenses. In the German army, by contrast, the basic principles of the constitutional state—a key achievement of liberals in the post-1871 nation-state—entailed careful examination of individual cases and a graduated sentencing policy in military courts. This contradicts the idea that the German army was an institution and a social milieu completely isolated from the gains in civilian life.[63] By contrast, the large number of executions in Italy—more than 1,000 soldiers in the course of the war—is remarkable.[64] The backdrop was not only the trying experience of positional warfare under extreme Alpine conditions, in which fruitless attacks increasingly undermined trust in officers, but also the traumatic break that the war represented for many young men from parts of Italy where the idea of a united nation meant little to nothing.

The dissidence in the ranks was characterized by more than desertion and mutiny, however. Protest and resistance always had a local dimension, reflecting the microcosm of the frontline community and its sense of justice. We can see this clearly in the mutiny of September 9–12, 1917, at Étaples near the French Atlantic coast, where a British training camp that also processed units from the Empire had a reputation for especially fierce discipline. When a New Zealand soldier was arrested by the hated military police and court-martialed for desertion, some of his immediate comrades who demanded his release refused to obey orders. Violent clashes, including the killing of one of the men, led to solidarity actions that soon spread to the whole camp. In the end, the military police were physically driven out, and on September 12, in a clear sign of nerves, the authorities sent in loyal regular units with a high proportion of officers to take action against the mutineers. Along with the regular units' use of clubs, the presence of a machine-gun unit acted as a threat and underscored the authorities' determination to take extreme measures. The crushing of the mutiny was followed by numerous courts-martial, but only one soldier, identified as a ringleader, was sentenced to death and executed.[65]

Captivity in enemy hands was another experience for millions of soldiers. The Italian army alone lost 600,000 men in this way, some 100,000 of whom died in Austrian and German prisoner-of-war (POW) camps. Unlike their French or British counterparts, the Italian prisoners were generally suspected back home of desertion and received hardly any support.[66] Paolo Monelli, a 25-year-old mountain trooper, found himself in Summer 1918 in the Austrian camp at Hart, where he passed his days in an atmosphere of monotony, hunger, and lack of privacy: "Today is like yesterday. Nothing changes. Today like yesterday like tomorrow. Reveille in the gloomy dormitories, evening inspection to make sure it is all dark and, bracketed between those two points, a meaningless existence in which people have stopped thinking of the future. . . . Hatred of the comrades whom the Austrians have forced you to become close friends with, the miasma of humanity, the dreadful stench of five hundred inmates, a hungry and egotistical herd, twenty-year-old bodies condemned to masturbation and inactivity."[67] There was a new dimension, both quantitative and qualitative, to this experience of captivity. Between 6.6 and 8 million men, roughly 10 percent of the total mobilized, became prisoners of war in the course of the First World War.[68]

Since the beginning of the century, a code of practice had existed for the treatment of prisoners of war; it was not as if they had no rights at all, as in antiquity. The Hague Convention of 1907 on the Laws and Customs of War on Land established that prisoners came under the jurisdiction of the enemy government, but that units in charge of them should not subject them to arbitrary action. They were to be treated humanely, their personal property safeguarded, and their religious practices respected. Article 20 of the convention stipulated that prisoners should be repatriated as soon as possible after peace returned.[69] However, these norms said little about the actual conditions that millions of soldiers would endure in the First World War. As their status as prisoners became ever more precarious, blurring the distinction between combatants and noncombatants, they were subjected to physical violence at the hands of their guards. In the German context, written and graphic propaganda often associated prisoners with negative enemy-images, although it is a matter of dispute whether brutalization was a general tendency and what it involved in detail. At any event, the practice of regarding POWs as combatants and questioning their protected status pointed to a basic feature of the war; that is, a sharper definition of criteria of national, ethnic, or racial affiliation. Application of these criteria had a direct impact on the status and living conditions of prisoners, but the practices remained inconsistent. For example, the German military authorities in Zossen-Wünsdorf established a "crescent camp" for Muslim prisoners of war. On the one hand, it was supposed to address their distinctive religious needs, and indeed the first mosque in Germany was built there. On the other hand, inmates were not only methodically registered as Muslims but presented as racial aliens—in a deprecatory tone that suggested their inferiority. African and Asian prisoners were photographed thousands of times for the "National Types" series of picture postcards; camps became the setting for field studies by ethnologists and medical researchers. Special events, such as Indian spring festivals, were straightforwardly staged for the cameras. Africans had to dance before camp commandants, and so-called Indian chiefs were put on display. All this betrayed a mixture of fascination and revulsion with regard to the Other, a combination of curiosity and distance that could turn violent at any moment. Prisoners appeared as exotic creatures, but at the same time as "savages," who could be manipulated to confirm the model of racial inferiority and the superiority of Western civilization. The leitmotif remained the spectacle of "our enemies' ethnic circus."[70]

A second feature of wartime captivity was the development of an international perspective, which in some cases—Britain in 1915 or France in 1917, for example—could have a moderating influence on public opinion. Traditional POW problems such as epidemics and undernourishment were increasingly felt to be unacceptable. A third element, however, was the treatment of prisoners as an economic resource and the violence to which they were often exposed in special labor detachments.[71] The close link between captivity and forced labor generated a dual system of labor battalions near the front and POW camps in the enemy homeland. In Germany, the treatment of prisoners worsened in the last period of the war, from 1916 on, and violence became an everyday phenomenon in the final months. Mere reference to Germany's military culture, with violence not only situational but an established norm, cannot explain this tendency to brutalization.[72] Economic factors were also important, as were the widespread food shortages in society at large.[73]

Thousands of civilians were also interned in camps. More stringent criteria of national affiliation and loyalty could suddenly turn someone into an enemy alien: this applied in all the belligerent countries and was a sign of the dual—external and internal—war that gave rise to a climate of suspicion and mistrust. On the other hand, the example of British internees in the Ruhleben Camp near Berlin shows how important the perception of such camps abroad was for the civilians detained there. After mutual accusations of atrocities in the early months of the war, closer international attention had a direct positive effect on conditions of internment. One country's practices would be repeatedly changed in the light of the way in which its own internees were being treated by the enemy. This was a key difference between the First and Second World Wars.[74]

The conditions of captivity covered a wide spectrum, depending on differences in nationality, rank, or place of internment. After the war, in keeping with the anti-German propaganda of the time, numerous French memoirs of life in prison camps highlighted the inhumane, uncivilized conditions. Most descriptions of the German captors closely corresponded to negative stereotypes, but there were also quite different voices. Georges Connes, for instance, spoke out against French enemy-images and offered a more nuanced view of the German guards; he experienced them not as barbarians but as courteous human beings.[75] Admittedly this was the perspective of a privileged officer, interned in Mainz close to the French border, who received weekly packages from his family that kept him better fed than those who guarded him. Officers were permitted to organize theater groups, choirs, and educational courses. Above all, the letters and packages that kept them in touch with France over long periods of time helped to shape their living conditions and emotional state.[76] Russian POWs had no such possibility at any time in the war. Nevertheless, their treatment was incomparably better than that of their comrades in the Second World War, whose deaths were deliberately calculated as a result of undernourishment and forced labor.

For their part, soldiers from the multiethnic empires experienced captivity as a sign of the growing weakness of their empire and monarch, which were evidently less and less capable of guaranteeing their security.[77] This fueled a new national consciousness among many soldiers—no longer as subjects of the Tsar, the Austrian emperor, or the Sultan, but as Finns or Poles, Latvians or Ukrainians, Czechs, Slovaks, or Croats. This tendency became all the stronger because prisoners of war were often segregated in accordance with national or ethnic categories—and because the authorities of the custodial power sought to exploit tensions within the empires and, later in the war, agreed to the request of exiled politicians to form special national combat forces out of imprisoned soldiers or deserters. The best-known case in point was the Czechoslovak Legion, which illustrated the military and political importance that such units had as symbols for newly emerging nation-states.[78]

When the war came to an end and POWs from the empires were released, tens of thousands of the Tsar's or Emperor's former soldiers returned to homelands where the old state or political order no longer existed. The new nation-states had major problems in reintegrating soldiers, and especially POWs; unless they went on to fight in a national legion, their service in the old empire did not fit the self-image of the times. This eminently political dimension of wartime captivity became clear early on in the Habsburg monarchy. At the beginning of 1918, the AOK instructed the Austro-Hungarian war press headquarters to publish edifying news and reports of successes to counter defeatist currents in society and centrifugal tendencies in the empire. The editor responsible for the paper *Heimat,* first published in early March 1918, was the writer Captain Dr. Robert von Musil. Since the October Revolution in Russia, the work of editors was mainly driven by fear that soldiers returning from Russian captivity might, so to speak, infect the home society ideologically with the virus of revolution. On May 30, 1918 one article complained, "Our prisoners of war are returning from Russia. After lengthy internment, they are coming back to their home country. They have experienced a great deal, undergone many difficulties. They have felt the heavy hand of tsarist rule and witnessed the great turnaround, the revolution that has raised the lowest to the highest. The force of this event has had a confusing effect on some, and now these infected individuals are returning home and fishing out the impressions they formed amid the chaos that prevails in Russia today, seeking to adapt them to our conditions. Although there are not many of them, . . . what they get up to is harmful and reprehensible. . . . All decent people returning home therefore have a duty to be constantly on their guard and to put in custody any man who wishes to bestow Russian conditions on us—even before he has caused any harm."[79]

The fight of French soldiers to improve conditions at the front and to uphold republican values, and the encounter of POWs from the Central Powers with the revolution in Russia, were not the only aspects of politicization. In Germany, the impetus came from a sense that exhaustion was not only a military tactic but also affected the symbols of the traditional order and from a new way of seeing and relating to political developments at home. This combination would acquire decisive significance in the final phase of the war. For many soldiers a kind of vacuum began to appear, since old institutions like the monarchy had long been losing credibility, while the revolutions in Russia offered a model for possible political and social change.[80]

The longer the war lasted and the more its character changed, the more the tangible means of appreciation of military honor shifted. At the beginning of the war, the German army expressed the "gratitude of the fatherland" in the form of highly regarded medals and decorations—particularly the Iron Cross, originally created in 1813 by the Prussian king Friedrich Wilhelm III in the war against Napoleonic France, reintroduced in 1870–1871 by Wilhelm I for the Franco-Prussian War, and authorized on August 5, 1914, by Wilhelm II for the duration of the world war. The medals culture served to ratify norms and models of conduct, and especially to maintain hierarchies and render them visible. In the case of the Iron Cross, the continuity of political history was also an important factor: it placed the world war in a line with the national conflicts of 1813 and 1870–1871, even though the reality fit such an interpretation less and less.

In essence, medals highlighted individual bravery in the face of the enemy, an exceptional readiness for self-sacrifice, heroism in action, and outstanding leadership. But their massive use in the course of the war tended to have an inflationary effect that eroded their credibility. Since top officers or the Kaiser himself became visible to most soldiers only at award ceremonies, military decorations indirectly widened the gap between the front and positions at the rear: the medal thus became another symbol of an order facing turmoil. Images of Wilhelm II bestowing medals, in a mechanical repetition of the same movements, seemed to confirm the impression that he was no more than a shadow emperor. The individual decoration lost its meaning through popularization. The war of attrition, with its posture of steadfast endurance, also contradicted the original intention of emphasizing individual heroism. Only later, in the Weimar Republic, did war veterans again enhance the status of the Iron Cross, reviving it as proof of individual self-sacrifice during the war.[81]

Even more important were the political developments in German society. In a speech at a decoration ceremony on May 31, 1917, at which he rounded on Social Democrats and other proponents of a parliamentary monarchy, the captain of the SMS *Helgoland* tried to make a link between external enemies and the ideological enemy at home. The splits in the home front, the hatred of war profiteers and alleged pacifists and defeatists, appeared more and more to signal a danger behind the lines. The stab in the back legend was not manufactured post hoc to explain the defeat in the war; it had already been operating long before. "Once the House of Hohenzollern has been overthrown they will compel us to accept a parliamentary form of government similar to that in England and in France. Which means that, just like them, we shall be ruled by merchants, lawyers, and journalists. In those countries, whenever they grow tired of a general or a military leader they simply dismiss him. . . . You must oppose all those who want to introduce parliamentary government into Germany, and you must never forget that the greatness of Germany stands and falls with her imperial dynasty, with her army, and with her young navy. Remember one thing: the social democrats in all the countries we are at war with desire to destroy us."[82] The navy's sensitivity to political developments was no accident: class distinctions between officers and men were highly conspicuous, so that the military hierarchy was seen as strongly class based. Sailors on warships and in port cities experienced on a daily basis the differences in accommodation, rations, and home leave regulations. In the eyes of many NCOs and ratings, the segregation of naval officers was especially provocative because the navy hardly saw any action, and the privileges of rank bore no relation to the dangers faced or deeds performed. This was quite different from the army, where young sergeants and lieutenants faced the same great dangers as the men they led, often earning the respect of ordinary soldiers.[83]

The sense of class boundaries was most widespread in the Russian army, where the year 1917 saw indignation turn into insubordination, open resistance, and mass desertions. Reports left no doubt that social tensions between aristocratic officers and ordinary soldiers, together with the Bolshevik agitation for peace, were eroding the cohesion of the army. One report described the atmosphere in early September on the northern front: "Deep distrust of officers and the supreme command is expressed everywhere. Combat readiness has plummeted, and in the present mood it is impossible to classify units into steadfast or less steadfast groups. Typically, artillery, cavalry, and technical units that used to be the most reliable have fallen away. Bolshevik propaganda has intensified; discipline is generally declining, and the masses are completely apathetic about the war. Officers are in an extremely difficult position."[84]

Furthermore, the actions of non-Russian soldiers reflected a breakdown of traditional loyalties. Men blamed the Provisional Government for the permanent supply problems in their homeland—but the really new element was the accusation that soldiers had to fight for a Russia that cared only about Russians and not about other ethnic groups. War experiences back home were, so to speak, ethnicized at the front. In a letter of September 1917 to the cabinet office of the Council of Ministers, 119 soldiers from Turkestan revealed how closely they linked the legality of the war—and hence their loyalty—to the fair treatment of all nationalities: "We, inhabitants of Turkestan, receive letters from our families in which every word is filled with horror and uncontrollable concern. Our families call us back to Turkestan, so that we, the breadwinners, can provide them with a livelihood and defend them from the government of the 'Socialists.' . . . We, the fathers of hungry families in Turkestan, have no possibility of sending anything even for our children—just because the Provisional Government had put power into the hands of cunning robbers and set up thieving officials who call themselves a 'food supply committee.' The Provisional Government itself does not care about the land of Turkestan. . . . But the Provisional Government calls on us, the sons of that territory, to defend the Russia that lets our children starve. Where is the logic in that? Where is the justice?"[85]

3. LENIN AND WILSON
Internationalism as Revolutionary Civil War and Democratic Intervention

Between April 6 and 9, 1917, in the space of 72 hours, the dimension of the war changed far beyond the military fronts of western, eastern, southern, and southeastern Europe and the high seas. At 3:20 P.M. on Easter Monday, April 9, three days after President Wilson had announced to Congress the American entry into the war against the German Empire, Vladimir Ilyich Lenin left his exile in Zurich on a special train heading in the general direction of Russia. At the time no one suspected what this trip would lead to, but within a few months the wartime context would make both Wilson and Lenin world-historic players.

When Lenin boarded that train, not many outside the Russian exile community in Switzerland knew his name or his ideas. In April 1917, he was 47 years old and had spent all of the previous 14 years abroad. While in school he had made contact with revolutionary currents, following the execution of his brother for an attempt on the life of Tsar Alexander III. Having become involved in student unrest in St. Petersburg, he put off his external bar exam, threw himself into the revolutionary movement as a lawyer, and forged close links with leaders of Russian Social Democracy. He conceived Marxism more and more as a theory of revolution that could be applied in Russia. In 1897, after his return from a trip to Europe, he was accused of political agitation and exiled to Siberia for three years, where he married his close collaborator Nadezhda Krupskaya in 1898.

In 1900 Lenin founded the exile paper *Iskra* in Munich, where he published *What Is to Be Done?* in 1902, a first attempt to systematize his political program. Unlike Karl Marx, he was not prepared to wait for a revolution to come at the natural point in the historical process, because that presupposed a developed industrial society and an advanced class consciousness among industrial workers. Instead, relying on efficient organization, he planned to take power by force when the opportunity presented itself; for this he needed a tightly organized cadre party of professional revolutionaries. Workers' councils, which sprang up in many big cities in Russia during the 1905 revolution, would be the second level of this new power structure.[86] The vanguard party would import revolutionary consciousness from outside into the Russian working class. At the second congress of the Russian Social Democratic Labor Party, these positions provoked lively clashes, which eventually led to a split within the organization in 1903 in Brussels. While the Mensheviks envisaged a new bourgeois-democratic order in Russia, Lenin's Bolsheviks insisted that workers and peasants should together pursue economic modernization within the framework of the revolution.[87]

In view of the revolutionary unrest and tsarist concessions in 1905 following Russia's defeat in the war with Japan, Lenin returned to Russia, but soon had to flee again. This second emigration continued until 1917, with stays in Geneva, Paris, Krakow, and Zurich. When war broke out in Summer 1914, Lenin was arrested in the Austrian part of Galicia on suspicion that he was a Russian spy, securing his release only after leading Austrian social democrats intervened on his behalf. After that he lived in Zurich—which at the time was not only the birthplace of the Dadaist movement around Hugo Ball at the Cabaret Voltaire but also a refuge for numerous radicals of the European Left who hoped for a revolution, but were sharply at odds with one another on many issues. Living in poverty with his wife, with some financial support from his mother, Lenin hoped that an opportunity would arise to take part in a revolution in Russia.

The German SPD's approval of war credits deepened Lenin's break with a political tradition that he had long considered exemplary. The European social democrats' decision to place loyalty to their nation-states above international workers' solidarity filled him with disgust; he saw them as having betrayed the cause of socialism in an imperialist war. His own vision was to convert the world war into an international civil war, which would eventually issue in proletarian revolutions.[88] Thus, in the struggle of all oppressed peoples against the imperialist big powers, or in the war of the victorious proletariat of one country against the surrounding capitalist world, it was the duty of socialists to take part in war. In such cases, war was nothing other than a continuation of revolutionary politics: "We are not pacifists and we cannot repudiate a revolutionary war," Lenin affirmed in Spring 1917.[89] Although he expected that the imperialist war would lead to revolution and civil war, he did not exclude another development if the proletariat was not victorious: "It would hurl Europe back several decades. That is improbable. But *not* impossible, for it is undialectical, unscientific, and theoretically wrong to regard the course of world history as smooth and always in a forward direction, without occasional gigantic leaps back."[90]

Lenin's vision of a violent international revolution was a minority position within the Left. At the two left-socialist conferences against the war, at Zimmerwald in 1915 and Kienwald in 1916, he was unable to win a majority for his opposition to socialist pacifism; the course of the war made him ever more given to doubt. In January 1917, in a talk he gave to Swiss socialists, he admitted with resignation, "We of the older generation may not live to see the decisive battles of this coming revolution. But I can, I believe, express the confident hope that the youth which is working so splendidly in the socialist movement of Switzerland, and of the whole world, will be fortunate enough not only to fight, but also to win, in the coming proletarian revolution."[91]

The dramatic change in Spring 1917 caught Lenin unprepared. Emigrés in Zurich had to rely on the papers for news about Russia, and these did not foresee the end of tsarist rule. One day in early March 1917, as Lenin was preparing for his daily visit to the library, a comrade he had befriended ran breathless into Siegelgasse 14 to report that the revolution against the Romanov dynasty, in power since 1614, had finally happened. The Tsar had abdicated, his brother Mikhail had given up his claim to the throne, and power was in the hands of the State Duma. Lenin saw in an instant that this situation created by the war represented a golden opportunity. Unlike in 1905, he lost no time and set off as quickly as possible for Russia, so that he could take a direct part in the action. The Allies would never allow a Bolshevik to transit through France, a journey through Ottoman territory seemed too fraught with danger, and it was too adventurous to think of flying over the fronts. The alternative was to get Russian socialists to sound out the German government as to whether they would permit him to cross Germany to Scandinavia, with the idea that he would then travel on to Petrograd.[92]

In fact, such plans suited the German strategy of promoting revolutionary groups to weaken Russia from within and to force it into a separate peace. Since late 1914 German diplomats in neutral countries—Switzerland, Denmark, and Sweden—had been using middlemen and informants to collect the names of Russian revolutionaries, and Lenin's name had been forwarded in March 1915 from Berne by Gisbert von Romberg. Lenin's program, which was conveyed shortly afterward to the German government, contained a peace proposal to the Central Powers that made no reference to the Allies. But at first Lenin was only one of a number of Russian exiles supported by Berlin. The Belarussian Alexander Helphand (aka Parvus)—who had himself been a socialist theorist, a fierce opponent of the tsarist regime, and an informant of the German ambassador in Denmark, Ulrich von Brockdorff-Rantzau—received a million reichsmarks in Spring 1915 to promote revolutionary activities in Russia. After the abdication of the Tsar in Spring 1917, Brockdorff-Rantzau and Parvus backed Lenin because they thought he could have the greatest impact in Russia. In the end, negotiations with the German ambassador in Berne took place through the good offices of a Swiss socialist. The government in Berlin agreed that Lenin could travel through Germany, and the OHL even offered to smuggle him across the eastern front into Russia itself, if he had problems in gaining admission to Sweden.

On April 9, 1917, Lenin set out from Zurich in a sealed train car for which he had requested extraterritorial status. A chalk line was drawn on the train separating German from Russian territory, since Lenin had insisted that there should be no further contact between the German officers and the Russian revolutionaries on board. Lenin, who worked on his April Theses during the journey, even created a set of signs to indicate when he wanted to use the toilet. At the railroad stations in Frankfurt and Berlin, the travelers saw for the first time the emaciated figures of soldiers and weary civilians about whom they had read in the Zurich press. From Rügen they took a boat to Copenhagen, moved on to Stockholm (where they fitted themselves out in new clothes), and then entered Russia without any problems—Lenin's first contact with his homeland in many years. His fear that troops loyal to the Provisional Government would arrest him at the frontier as a German spy and collaborator failed to materialize. The opportunity to take part in a revolution was therefore due to the war in two senses: the legitimation crisis of tsarist rule had deepened as a result of the war and the weariness on both the military and domestic fronts, and the willingness of the German government to further destabilize Russia, thereby improving the chances of a separate peace and a Russian exit from the war, made it possible for Lenin to return to the center of Russian politics in Spring 1917.[93]

The biography of the man responsible for the U.S. entry into the war in April 1917 looked very different. Two aspects set Woodrow Wilson apart from all other American presidents of the nineteenth and early twentieth centuries. First, he was not a professional politician of the classical type, having a background in neither law nor business but in the academic world, as a university professor and, most recently, president of Princeton University. Second, he came from the South, where he was born in 1856 in Virginia as the son of a Presbyterian preacher and brought up along strict Calvinist lines, and where he had experienced the Civil War firsthand. In 1885, following legal studies at Princeton, he wrote a dissertation, "Congressional Government," criticizing the undemocratic practices of American parliamentarism, which made him well known in other parts of the country. In his comparative study *The State* (1899), he occupied himself intensively with Germany and German political theory, which he was able to read in the original. In 1890 he was appointed as a professor in a politically oriented department of legal studies at Princeton, and in 1902, at the age of 42, he was elected president of the university. His term of office there, involving policy reforms that again brought him to nationwide attention, ended in 1910 in a grueling dispute, when Wilson's tendency to dogmatic-missionary inflexibility turned a majority of the professors against him.[94]

The conservative wing of the Democrats lost no time in recruiting him, and by the end of 1910 he was already governor of New Jersey. He took an ever-greater distance from the conservative Democrats, however, supporting instead the Progressive preference for an active state, socialist measures, and consistent action against the cartels and monopolies that had grown ever more powerful since the turn of the century. Wilson's policies in New Jersey, where he supported accident insurance for workers, made him a national figure and a candidate for the presidency, which he won in the election of November 1912. Twice, however, his campaign promises in relation to the war proved to lack substance. In 1912 people expected him to concentrate on domestic issues and to play no special role to foreign policy. And in 1916 he won a second presidential term with the slogan "he kept us out of the war"—a promise he failed to keep just a few months later.[95]

During his first term, along with regulation of the banking system, strong government supervision of the economy, and measures to ensure competition, President Wilson also concentrated on the flashpoint over the border in Mexico, where General Victoriano Huerta staged a putsch in 1913. Against the opposition of U.S. business and the European powers, he insisted on U.S. military intervention to impose democracy there—and indeed this conviction of the universal validity of democracy, and of the need to establish it by force if necessary (even if doing so contradicted the principle of national sovereignty central to the international order since the Congress of Vienna)—became a hallmark of Wilson's later approach to foreign policy. The intervention in Mexico lasted three years, and only in 1916 did the last American troops leave the country. This action also played a decisive role in 1917, when the German government offered Mexico an alliance with the prospect of regaining the territories it had lost to the United States in the nineteenth century. Germany was thus acting in a space of paramount importance to the United States. And when the British secret service intercepted the so-called Zimmermann Telegram, its publication made Germany appear the aggressor in a way that challenged the foundations of the Monroe

Doctrine.[96] Together with the intensification of submarine warfare in January 1917, this incident left Wilson with few alternatives other than entry into the war against Germany.[97]

After his close victory over the Republican C. E. Hughes in the 1916 presidential election, Wilson sent his trusted associate E. M. House to Europe to explore the possibilities for a compromise peace that ruled out victory for one side or the other. But the fruitlessness of these talks convinced Wilson that, if the United States actively intervened in the war, it could do nothing other than insist on a peace settlement geared to the principles of Progressivism. House's mission was also important in another respect: although economic interests tied the United States more closely to Britain and France, and although Wilson identified politically with the western Entente powers—but not with autocratic Russia—the soundings also revealed particular tensions and clashes of interest between the United States and Britain. The House / Grey memorandum of February 17, 1916, did give notice that America might enter the war if Germany continued to refuse serious peace talks. But the expectations of such a step differed enormously between Washington and London—and this already anticipated a basic conflict that would continue long after the end of the war. The British government sought to use the United States in its struggle with Germany, whereas the American leadership wanted to negotiate the earliest possible end to the war.

Most significantly, Wilson's special envoy House thought that the willingness in London to accept the American definition of a negotiated peace indicated basic agreement with the new peacetime order that Wilson had in mind—an order involving a fair compromise without annexations, recognition of the right of national self-determination, and an international system of collective security. If these principles were applied to the British situation, the memorandum would force Whitehall to address the problem of what a U.S. entry into the war and a Wilsonian peacetime order would mean for the future of the British Empire. In 1916, given the weakening of France and Russia, the British government had to rely on troops and resources from the Empire to shore up its central position in the land war on the western front. Yet the ideas put forward by House fundamentally contradicted Britain's global security interests—indeed, not only did they envisage no reallocation of the German colonies; they even suggested a strengthening of German positions in eastern Europe and the Near East, in compensation for the return of Alsace-Lorraine to France.[98]

This clash of interests was not resolved even after April 1917: Great Britain and the United States might wage a joint war against Germany, but that did not entail a partnership between the two countries. Militating against that were not only the imbalances stemming from Britain's economic and monetary dependence on American goods and loans but also British fears that a weakening of the Empire would not allow it to pull through the war at all. From this point of view, Wilson's emphasis on national rights and the right to self-determination contained an anticolonial thrust that could hardly be overlooked. At the same time, such rhetoric was at odds with actual American policies, which consciously pursued their own political and economic objectives. Thus, the war was manifestly affecting the traditional balance of power in a transatlantic perspective.[99]

In Spring 1916, Wilson was still convinced that his country had grown too close to the Allies. Not without reason did he mainly blame the governments in London and Paris for using the United States for their own ends, while he stuck to his own position and political objectives. Only German policies, especially the resumption of unrestricted submarine warfare, forced him to change tack. April 1917 thus marked a historical turning point. For the first time since it gained independence in the late eighteenth century, the United States became directly entangled in a European war.[100] In the nineteenth century, politicians had repeatedly affirmed the principle of non-involvement in Europe's interstate conflicts; this principle was fundamental to the country's stance as a young republic and peaceful trading nation. In 1917 people were aware of what Wilson's change of course represented. In *Our Times,* Mark Sullivan gave a popular account of the night of April 2: "To every person present, from members of the cabinet in the front row, to observers in the remote seats of the gallery, that evening was the most-to-be-remembered of their lives."[101]

The vision of a new world order that Woodrow Wilson set out in January 1917 was grounded on the right of nations to self-determination. In light of the ongoing war, small nations were to be on an equal level with the established powers: "No nation should seek to extend its polity over any other nation or people, but . . . every people should be left free to determine its own polity, its own way of development, unhindered, unthreatened, unafraid, the little along with the great and powerful." This demand was linked to Wilson's view that the war had its roots in "disregard of the rights of small nations and of nationalities which lacked the union and the force to make good their claim to determine their own allegiances and their own forms of political life."[102]

Wilson's conception of a "new diplomacy" challenged the classical European traditions of secrecy, which he saw as another cause of the war alongside the holding down of small nations. The new focus should be on the right of nations to self-determination, but also on the freedom of the seas, the publication of treaties between states, and a league of nations as the core of a new system of collective security. Thus Wilson had set his mind on liberalization and democratization of the world—but also on imposition of the interests of the United States as the economically strongest power.

Guided by this universalist program and this political mission to fight for democratic principles in Europe, Wilson's attitude to the war was also changing. Whereas in Summer 1914, as a liberal supporter of the Progressive movement, he had interpreted the war as a conflict of imperial interests reflecting the feudal-monarchic past of the European powers, he now drew a remarkable parallel with the American Civil War of the 1860s, which had given birth to a coherent, democratic nation, much as the world war was destined to lead to a united, democratic world community. The ideal of an organized society, based on "trust between state and citizen," was to be transferred to the world stage; this was the universalist promise of a dawning new age, in which the world war functioned as a "people's war," overcoming the archaic features of the reactionary classes of the past.[103] For all their ideological differences, Lenin and Wilson shared this focus on the international dimension, beyond the European states and their imperial protrusions: for the one, an international civil war would revolutionize all class societies; for the other a "people's war" would achieve the democratic principles of self-determination. In September 1918, Wilson developed his vision of a supranational order: the world war should end not in the resumption of traditional foreign policies but in a global internal policy; "national purposes have fallen more and more into the background and the common purpose of enlightened mankind has taken their place."[104]

The utopian visions of both Wilson and Lenin gained enormous appeal in a short time—partly because the war had so often shaken the premises of the liberal order on which European societies rested. In the new horizons taking shape, the war appeared to have redrawn many problems to such a great extent that the capacities of the traditional nation-states were no longer sufficient to resolve them. For Lenin, it was impossible to think of future wars as anything other than international civil wars. For Wilson, foreign policy needed to be understood as a global internal policy resting on an institutionalized system of collective security.[105]

4. REVOLUTIONS, COLLAPSING STATES, AND THE CONTINUITY OF VIOLENCE
Russia between International and Civil War

Russia acted as a beacon in world history from early 1917. But what explains the torrent of the two revolutions, in February and October 1917? Contrary to frequent claims, the war by no means deepened the country's backwardness, but actually triggered enormous economic mobilization and reorganization. At the same time, these processes of acceleration spawned social problems that increasingly eroded the credibility of the regime—both the tsarist government and the Provisional Government that succeeded it in Spring 1917.[106]

At the beginning of 1917, the Allies could count on quantitative military superiority over the Central Powers on nearly all the fronts of the war. This fueled their confidence that they could decide its outcome in the course of the year. But the situation on the eastern front differed considerably from that in the western and other theaters of the war. Until the mini-offensive in July and the German counterattacks, which led to the loss of eastern Galicia and Riga, there were no major military operations. Exhausted after the Brusilov offensive of Summer and Fall 1916 and the widening of the front with Romania's entry into the war, the Russian military leadership gave up further operations for the time being. Only the commencement of the Kerensky offensive changed the picture once more.

The upheavals of 1917 were not only the result of the military crisis, although it did seriously worsen things inside the country. The revolutionary situation stemmed more from the political and social erosion of Russian society. In the end, this erosion would lead to the disappearance of the war state and the continuation of violence in the civil war, in which ideological, social, and ethnic lines of conflict overlapped and mutually reinforced one another. The tsarist regime did not, however, collapse because Bolshevik agitation was so successful. In fact, the Bolsheviks played no significant role during the February Revolution, and until Lenin's arrival in Petrograd they were as confused and disoriented as many other political groups. Only in September did the Soviets, the workers' and soldiers' councils, have a Bolshevik majority. But even then it was not a will for revolutionary class struggle but the widespread food shortages that shaped the mood of people in the large cities, where hunger and disease stalked working-class districts and runaway inflation immediately wiped out wage increases and paralyzed economic life. The war economy and the military supply system, too, eventually ground to a halt.

In essence, this social-economic situation did not reflect the backwardness that many in Europe had identified with Russia before the war. Rather, it should be seen as an adjustment crisis expressing the deep and rapid changes that Russia had been experiencing since 1914. These changes included the mobilization of the economy, the soaring growth of the war industries, and an uncontrolled urbanization that came with high social costs. The production of war materials grew, and between 1914 and 1917 more banks than ever were founded. The weight of industrial workers in the population shot up: state factories employed a workforce of 400,000 in January 1917 (compared with 120,000 at the beginning of the war); 1.1 million people worked on the railroads (500,000 more than in 1914); and the numbers employed in mining doubled in the course of the war. In 1916–1917, the Russian railroads carried 113 million more passengers than in 1913–1914. All this movement mainly fed into the expanding cities, having a negative impact on the rural population and leading to labor shortages in agriculture.[107] In the few years after August 1914 the country experienced in fast motion the problems attendant on forced economic mobilization. Moreover, the change took place under extreme conditions, as imports from Germany as well as income from grain exports dried up. Russia had to develop more of its own industries, but this highlighted the basic problem of the economy: the fast-expanding industries and cities had to be supplied, but up until then Russian agriculture had not been geared mainly to the production of a surplus.

As in Germany and Austria-Hungary, the war in Russia relied financially not on special taxes but on war loans and ultimately the printing press; the money supply soared from 2,400 million rubles in 1914 to 19,000 million in the second half of 1917. Industry picked up speed with the erosion of the gold standard. By January 1917 prices had quadrupled, and by the time of the November Revolution they had increased tenfold. There was no regular or effective taxation of war profits—which heightened the sense of a social gulf between the war's winners and losers. War loans, with their characteristic blend of patriotic appeals and a 6 percent rate of interest, had a long maturity time, and high inflation gradually turned them into worthless assets.[108] Many people at the time saw the danger of an imminent collapse of the economic system and the political order, as neither the business world nor the authorities were capable of ensuring basic supplies to the population. The state therefore lost more and more credibility. Any wage increases were eaten up by runaway inflation, and as food shortages spread, money increasingly lost its primary function in everyday life. Inflation thus gave rise to a shadow subsistence economy, while supplies to the large cities decreased steadily from the end of 1916.

Agricultural production on the large estates declined because of conscription and the exodus to the industrial centers. Not only labor but also the fertilizer and machinery that used to be imported until 1914 were in short supply. Nevertheless, some farming sectors less dependent on machines and additional labor managed to stabilize, and in 1916, while grain output was declining, the livestock population actually increased because cows, for example, could graze on newly abandoned areas of land. The main problem underlying the supply difficulties was not harvest failure or other short-term production setbacks. There were certainly labor shortages, and farmland in western Russia was lost to the Central Powers, but on the other hand the high levels of grain exports came to an end. The real problem was the transportation and marketing of farm produce over large distances: the infrastructure was not capable of meeting the challenge. Furthermore, many farmers were unwilling to sell their products in other regions. They held grain back because of the high inflation and used it within their own subsistence economy—as animal fodder, for example. This microeconomic rationality was a response to the high prices for consumer goods such as shoes or clothing. Those who suffered the consequences were the inhabitants of large cities: in 1913–1914 they had bought 390 million pud (1 pud = 16.4 kilograms) of grain, but by 1916–1917, despite the huge growth of the cities, this figure had fallen to 295 million pud.[109] The result was hunger on a large scale and the impoverishment of millions.

In the transport sector, the adjustment crisis was due more to problems of quality than quantity. The number of locomotives grew from 17,036 (1914) to 18,757 (1918), and of wagons from 402,000 to 444,000, with further rolling stock imported from Britain and the United States. An additional 4,000 kilometers of track were laid by 1917. Yet, despite this investment, the railroad could not keep pace with the mass mobilization of the economy that was occurring in completely unplanned forms. The number of passengers increased from 235 million in 1914 to 348 million in 1916, and freight totals from 13,826 million pud before the war to 17,228 million in 1916.[110] It is true that the number of soldiers in the military railroad battalions rose from 40,000 to 250,000, and the number of civilian employees from 750,000 to 1.1 million, but the large proportion of unskilled workers rapidly lowered the level of technical maintenance; in 1917 one-quarter of all trains were out of service for technical reasons. Railroad workers were no longer—as political leaders had planned before the war—the vanguard of that engineering elite and labor aristocracy on whose loyalty the regime had been able to rely in 1905, when they had not taken part en masse in the strike wave of that year. Indeed, from Summer 1917 on, railroaders played an important role in the demoralization of the army and the politicization of the urban population, and the train itself provided a link between the revolutionary urban centers and the military front.[111]

The shortages on the national grain and food market, together with the failure of the transport infrastructure, symbolized the inefficiency and incompetence of the old regime and contributed to the politicization of popular protest. Russian soldiers at the front might believe in Kerensky's speeches calling on them to continue the war against the Central Powers. No more than French mutineers on the western front did they turn overnight into antipatriotic elements. But they felt much more strongly than their French comrades the everyday impotence of the state in relation to supplies. Still, the army did not simply disintegrate in Summer 1917, and in November there were still more than six million men at the front. There was a big difference between demoralization and surrender of the front. Claims that army structures were breaking up were a leitmotif in the explanations that officers later gave for the collapse of the old regime—after they themselves had experienced the waning of their authority. This was a kind of "stab in the back" legend in reverse, in which it was not the homeland that had stabbed the army in the back, but the disintegration of the army that had made the revolution possible.[112]

No doubt the supply breakdown hugely undermined the morale of troops. The issuing of paper money that no soldier could exchange for food, together with widespread alcoholism, further darkened the mood at the front. In the end, attacks on officers became an everyday occurrence. The strike movement in Summer 1917 was the result of a social revolution against the effects of the war economy and the failings of a war state that was no longer fulfilling its responsibilities. All this happened before the Bolshevik seizure of power, and it explains why there was scarcely any resistance to this revolution in Fall 1917. Only then did soldiers desert their units en masse and return to their native towns and villages, assuming that the war was effectively over. They wanted at all costs to be home when the Bolsheviks delivered on their promise of land redistribution. In the cities, inflation, food shortages, and widespread hunger had largely flattened the social differences between skilled and unskilled, long-established and newly recruited workers, but also, as a tendency at least, between men and women. This made it easier for a revolutionary spirit to develop among the masses. But people became susceptible to Lenin's promises only when they had suffered in their daily lives the fallout from the war-related economic crisis and the failings of the political and military authorities. The revolution was the outcome not so much of a distinctively Russian backwardness as of accelerated adjustment of the country's economy and society to wartime conditions.

In essence, then, Lenin profited from a breakdown that had been taking place over a long period. As mentioned, the first murders of officers at the front occurred before the Bolsheviks took power in October in a relatively bloodless coup. Compared with the number of Russian soldiers killed in the war or with the paroxysms of violence in the subsequent civil war, it was an almost peaceful revolution, which recalled Tocqueville's interpretation of the

French Revolution and the dismantling of feudal privileges in August 1789: it caused a building to collapse that had long been unoccupied. For this reason, the streetcars continued to run in Petrograd, as they did a year later, on November 9, in Berlin. The legitimacy of the monarchy had long since crumbled, and radical changes had already gone a long way when the October Revolution in Russia, or the revolutions of the following year in central Europe, became a historical reality. No particular violence was therefore necessary at the moment of the actual transfer of power, the formal change of system. Only subsequently, in clashes over the fate of the revolution, did it well and truly explode.

By late 1916 the credibility crisis of the tsarist regime was already looming. After the army and economy had once more been mobilized with the help of the Allies, the eventual failure of the Brusilov offensive in Fall 1916 had an effect that was all the more sobering because of the high hopes placed in it. The defeat of Romania, which had entered the war on the side of the Allies, meant a further widening of the front. But after the costly battles of 1916 another offensive was out of the question. Against this backdrop, a dual conflict took shape in Russian cities between the Tsar and the government, and between the State Duma (dominated by the bourgeoisie and aristocracy) and the urban underclasses. In early 1917, in the midst of a hard winter, the supply situation worsened in Petrograd and the other large cities. Grain shortages made hunger an everyday phenomenon, while lack of fuel led to transport interruptions. Work had to be suspended in many enterprises, and many workers were laid off because the machinery could no longer operate. The combination of these factors explains why protests began to intensify toward the end of February. The announcement that bread rationing would be introduced in March was the last straw for thousands of working men and women who at the time had no work and had received no pay. On February 23, women textile workers held a demonstration in Petrograd, which rapidly drew an influx from other factories. By the next day more than 200,000 were taking part in protest marches. This was no longer a traditional hunger revolt but a political movement, out of which came the demand for an end to tsarist rule. On February 25 a general strike was called, and there was looting of shops especially in Petrograd. The forces of order—the city police and the army—were paralyzed. Of course, the mobilization of war industries in the previous year, together with deliveries of Allied munitions and weapons via Arkhangelsk and Vladivostok, had improved the army's supply situation. But by early 1917 the Russian armed forces had suffered losses on the order of 2.7 million dead and wounded, not to speak of the four million prisoners of war. An explosive mixture existed in many barracks, as 2.3 million new recruits, many of whom had been coerced into military service, rubbed shoulders with disillusioned veterans and invalids or soldiers regarded as politically unreliable. Over the coming months the army garrisons would become focal points of revolutionary action.

In this tense situation, a characteristic dual structure took shape out of new political institutions and players, with rival claims to power that continued the political and social polarization of 1916. On February 27 the government stepped down. A "Provisional Committee for the Restoration of Public Order" was established within the Duma, while the parliament of the Petrograd Soviet developed as a workers' and soldiers' council with its own executive committee. Two-thirds of the Petrograd Soviet consisted of soldiers who had deserted from the army.[113] "Order No. 1" called for the creation of Soviets everywhere in the armed forces, whose approval would be needed for the implementation of orders from above. A start was made on the formation of an independent military organization, the Red Guards, while the traditional hierarchies began to break down in the army garrisons.[114]

Tsar Nicholas, who as supreme commander did not reside permanently in the capital, initially reacted as he had done in earlier political conflicts, demonstrating again that he could not properly assess the changed situation. For the army and parliament were now behaving in a quite new way. The Tsar's attempt to dissolve the Duma failed to take effect. While mutinies spread in the navy, with sailors soon in control of many warships and ports, the establishment of the Duma Provisional Committee marked a first decisive step against the regime and its political practices. On March 3, 1917, the chief of staff Mikhail Alexeev called on the Tsar to abdicate, not so much because of any military defeat but because he could no longer command political confidence.[115] Grand Prince Mikhail, appointed by his brother Nicholas because of the Tsarevich's parlous state of health, declined to ascend the throne in his place. This more or less peaceful transition from Romanov autocracy to a republic reflected the extent to which the war, with its high casualties and the

The price of freedom? The achievements of the revolution on the mountain of Russia's war dead, 1917

failings of the government on the home front, had already undermined the legitimacy of the monarchy. But the relatively small death toll from the revolution—500 dead, mostly in Petrograd—masked a deep divide that scarcely anyone had thought possible in Summer 1914, but that had suddenly become a warning sign for all the wartime societies and especially the monarchies of Continental Europe. The war had passed over into a revolution, and although its outcome remained uncertain, it would acquire a powerful dynamic of its own, both internally and externally, over the coming months.

Power initially fell into the hands of a newly formed Provisional Government under Prince Georgii Lvov, which was formed out of the Duma Provisional Committee after negotiations with the Petrograd Soviet. It was supposed to be "provisional" until democratic elections could be held for a constituent assembly, but the multiplicity of its tasks reflected the exceptional situation facing the country. The war was to be continued while major reforms turned Russia into a constitutional republic and a modern civil society, with equal rights guaranteed for all its citizens. At the same time, there was the challenge of organizing land reform and of redefining the relationship with the various nationalities in the old empire. Urban workers, soldiers at the front and in the garrisons, farmers, and ethnic minorities—all looked expectantly to the new regime, but the very heterogeneity of their expectations soon became a decisive burden for the Provisional Government. It remained a government at war, and its room for maneuver soon proved to be very limited. The basic feature that characterized the whole war made itself felt with a new virulence: the revolution in the midst of war aroused expectations that could not be fulfilled, and their disappointment damaged the credibility and authority of the new political players. This gave rise to the situation in Summer and Fall 1917, on which the Bolsheviks were eventually able to capitalize.[116]

In their own perception of themselves, the Russian revolutionaries of February 1917 were following on from the French Revolution of 1789, which they saw as the model for democratic change and a nation of citizens equal before the law. But their enthusiastic recourse to such French symbolism as the cockade or the "citizen" mode of address could not make up for the legitimacy deficit left by the Tsar's abdication: the Duma was not democratically elected, and it was anyway increasingly sidelined until its final dissolution on October 6. The elections to a constituent assembly were continually post-poned because of the war, just as the National Convention in the 1790s had repeatedly deferred the adoption of a constitution by reference to the war. In post-February Russia, politicians thus operated in a nonconstitutional space and kept delaying central political decisions. A political vacuum came into being, whose consequences were felt across the country. The need for land reform had become so urgent that the farming population itself began to take action, reviving the institution of the village commune and introducing reforms on their own authority. The supply crisis resulting from the war, but also the general uncertainty faced by farmers, had a catalyzing effect: the village communes themselves took possession of the land.[117]

How did these dramatic developments affect other belligerent countries in the spring of 1917? The Central Powers calculated that Russia's internal tensions and the fall of the Tsar would further destabilize the army and compel the Provisional Government to leave the war. Among the western Allies, it was mainly the left-wing and liberal parties that welcomed the change of regime; their alliance with an autocracy, which had been a problem for their political credibility since the beginning of the war, would no longer be an issue. As to President Wilson, the events in Russia enabled him to take the offensive in justifying the position of the United States: it was no accident that, in in his speech of April 2, 1917, to Congress on American entry into the war, he referred to the universal significance of the replacement of autocratic tsarist rule with a parliamentary-democratic form of government. Wilson used the example of Russia to expatiate on the link between democracy and peace: "A steadfast concert for peace can never be maintained except by a partnership of democratic nations. No autocratic government could be trusted to keep faith within it or observe its covenants. . . . Does not every American feel that assurance has been added to our hope for the future peace of the world by the wonderful and heartening things that have been happening within the last few weeks in Russia?" The revolution in Petrograd acted as a beacon for the democratic will to political self-determination. Wilson concentrated on the opposition between people and elites, which he would later turn against Germany: "Russia was known by those who knew it best to have been always in fact democratic at heart. . . . The autocracy that crowned the summit of her political structure, long as it had stood and terrible as was the reality of its power, was not in fact Russian in origin, character, or purpose; and now it has been shaken off and the great, generous Russian people have been added in all their naive majesty and might to the forces that are fighting for freedom in the world, for justice, and for peace."[118]

Only the revolutionary changes in Russia gave credence to Wilson's message that the struggle of Americans in the war against the Central Powers was serving to establish worldwide democracy and to liberate all peoples, including those of the enemy, from autocratic regimes and political repression: "We are now about to accept gage of battle with this natural foe to liberty and shall, if necessary, spend the whole force of the nation to check and nullify its pretensions and its power. We are glad, now that we see the facts with no veil of false pretense about them, to fight thus for the ultimate peace of the world and for the liberation of its peoples, the German peoples included: for the rights of nations great and small and the privilege of men everywhere to choose their way of life and of obedience." Wilson thus stood up against a war of territorial conquest or material gain. This spurning of the European tradition of war between states was part of what America's entry into the war promised for the future: "The world must be made safe for democracy. Its peace must be planted upon the tested foundations of political liberty. We have no selfish ends to serve. We desire no conquest, no dominion. We seek no indemnities for ourselves, no material compensation for the sacrifices we shall freely make. We are but one of the champions of the rights of mankind."[119]

But Wilson's effusive celebration of the Russian people's self-emancipation was only one side of the coin. For London and Paris feared what Berlin and Vienna hoped for: that Russia would exit from the war, either of its own volition or under the compulsion of internal destabilization. British and French leaders therefore stepped up their pressure on the new Provisional Government to continue the war. And when this seemed to be working, the German leadership in turn intensified its measures to destabilize the political situation within Russia. Such was the backdrop to Lenin's journey to Petrograd. At the same time, German commanders on the eastern front began to support systematic fraternization—for example, on the occasion of the Russian Orthodox Easter in April or on May the First—in the hope of weakening the Russian forces there.

In Spring 1917, the Provisional Government found itself in a precarious position. Its commitment to the war was alienating it from soldiers who had expected that the end of tsarist rule would soon put an end to the hostilities, while the rural population felt cheated when the government announced that the promised land reform would have to wait until the end of the war. The result was a special dynamic in the countryside, in which farmers and village communes took matters into their own hands—with implications for the front, where soldiers were eager to return home to avoid missing out on any redistribution.[120] A somewhat similar development occurred in the case of ethnic minorities, who became active when they saw their hopes of greater autonomy disappointed because the Provisional Government tied continuation of the war with recognition of the indivisibility of Russia. The first tendencies toward national autonomy became unmistakable.[121]

The real beneficiaries of these dashed hopes were the Bolsheviks. In the unstable political situation of Summer 1917, their outspoken promise to bring peace without annexations or reparations and to solve the land question fueled political radicalism in the urban centers and encouraged strivings for national independence in non-Russian parts of the Empire. As industrial workers and garrisoned soldiers turned against the war and blamed the new government for the lack of improvement in the disastrous supply situation, the nationalities on Russia's periphery made much of the Bolshevik commitment to the principle of national self-determination.

Alexander Kerensky, who gave his name to the military offensive of Summer 1917, soon emerged as the dominant figure in the Provisional Government. As leader of the Trudoviki group in the Duma and representative of the Socialist Revolutionaries (SRs), he embodied a program that combined democratic reforms with Russian patriotism. But despite his training in acting and rhetorical talents, Kerensky did not correspond to the type of the charismatic war leader as it had taken shape in the figures of Lloyd George and Clemenceau. As war minister in the government, he set out to integrate and moderate the Petrograd Soviet. He pursued this with a policy of cautious concessions, as in the official declaration of soldiers' rights and his approval of elections to army councils and military courts responsible for the punishment of soldiers. Kerensky saw the February Revolution as the equivalent of the liberation of the French people from monarchic absolutism.

Like the enthusiastic but naïve members of the National Convention in 1792, he believed it possible to transform a formally conceived nation of citizens with equal rights into a "nation in arms" and that doing so would enable the war to be decided.[122] The model in question, however, existed at best only in the mythology of the French revolutionary wars; the reality of wars since then looked very different. The French troops of 1792 had not primarily resisted the enemy out of particularly revolutionary or patriotic motives, but because experienced soldiers and new recruits had been successfully mixed together, and the privileges of aristocratic officers had been abolished. The meritocratic principle had precisely benefited young bourgeois officers such as Bonaparte. Thus, the French revolutionary armies had combined strict order and discipline with an attention to social mobility—that was an important element in their success.

In Spring 1917, the new government in Russia was intent on continuing the war whatever the circumstances, in order to ensure that the new democratic republic would be recognized as a player with equal rights fighting alongside the western European and transatlantic democracies. But the soldiers at the army's command expected a swift peace. After abolition of the traditional mechanisms of punishment, discipline in the army garrisons was on the decline. And a dual structure comparable to that at the political level was taking shape in the army: "Order No. 1" issued by the Petrograd Soviet showed that a new rival was being established alongside the old military hierarchy. In contrast to the traditional relations between officers and men, it issued a call for the election of soldiers' councils in all units of the army, which would answer to the Soviet rather than the army leadership. This was the context in which a fresh offensive against the Central Powers was launched in mid-June in Galicia under General Brusilov. Kerensky, who personally championed the offensive, had a realistic assessment of the Russian forces and gave many speeches at the front exhorting the troops to continue the war against the autocratic Central Powers. Their task, he argued, was to secure the revolutionary achievements of the spring. In the spirit of the war party in the French National Convention of 1792, he emphasized the link between self-sacrifice and newly won freedom. In this too, he fell victim to the historical myths surrounding the French revolutionary wars.

The unity of people and army? Provisional Government poster advertising war loans, 1917

Nevertheless, this last offensive against Germany and Austria-Hungary was further impressive evidence of Russia's economic and military mobilization. On the one hand, the Russian army had suffered massive losses: more than two million of the fifteen million Russians who took part in the war between August 1914 and October 1917 were killed or wounded, and another four million or so taken prisoner. On the other hand, despite high desertion rates, six million soldiers were still at the front in October 1917. At the beginning of the summer offensive, this figure was even higher: never before had more Russian soldiers been mustered against the Central Powers. Although industrial production had suffered interruptions since February, Allied deliveries of weapons and munitions ensured that the army was starting from a better position than in any campaigns of the previous three years. Quantitatively, the Russians were superior to the Central Powers in troop numbers and heavy artillery. At first, they achieved breakthroughs up to 30 kilometers deep in the Austrian part of Galicia, as in the Brusilov offensive of the previous year, but when the counterattacks began in early July the degree of exhaustion and war weariness on the Russian side became impossible to overlook. Desertions and mutinies ensued on an unprecedented scale—which played into the hands of the Bolsheviks, who had waged an intensive campaign at the front in May and June for an immediate peace.[123] More and more often, soldiers attacked officers who tried to force them to keep on fighting. Despite the relatively good equipment and a better supply situation than in previous years, the troops lost their cohesion as a fighting force. But was this really due to a lack of patriotism, as many officers assumed? The truth is that in Summer 1917 a general war weariness combined with the politically changed situation and uncertainty about what was happening back home. In the end, more and more men refused to take part in an offensive war that was not seeking to defend their homeland, but that was being fought in the non-Russian territories of Ukraine, Poland, Belarus, Armenia, Azerbaijan, Georgia, Moldavia, and the Baltic. In Galicia, too, they had to recognize that the aim was territorial aggrandizement. This seemed to question the viability of the Kerensky offensive.[124]

There was another factor. Events since February had rapidly negated the traditional symbolic language in the army and the idea of personal loyalty to the Tsar without replacing them with a convincing new symbolism. The radical shift from a centuries-old idea of the state embodied in the person of the monarch to one based on "liberty, equality, and fraternity" remained too abstract for the broad mass of peasant soldiers. The liberal nation of equal citizens did not have real roots; it lacked not only a social and political foundation but also a convincing figurehead. In the eyes of many, it was no more than a chimera entertained by a handful of politicians in Petrograd. This void at the level of identification worked in favor of the Bolsheviks, the only party that stuck consistently with the promise of "land and peace."[125]

Almost simultaneously with the German counterattacks, the situation deteriorated in Petrograd when the Bolshevik Red Guards, members of the Petrograd garrison, and Kronstadt sailors undertook a coup d'état in early July. It was meant to send out a signal against the war and the deployment of more troops at the front. But the uprising was crushed, many Bolsheviks were interned, and Lenin himself, branded a German agent, had to escape to Finland. In view of the military situation after the failed offensive, with the army in disarray and its command structures falling apart, but also because of the internal political situation, Kerensky (now the head of government) appointed Lavr Kornilov in mid-July as the new supreme commander. Soon seen as a charismatic military leader, Kornilov put himself forward as the man to restore discipline at the front and order in Russian society. His first step was to reintroduce the death penalty in military courts. He found support for this move both among tsarist officers, who had viewed with mounting anger Kerensky's concessions and the actions of the Petrograd Soviet against military traditions, and among the Octobrist and Kadet political groupings. These were supporters of the Conservative Liberal Union of October 17, founded in 1905, and the Constitutional Democratic Party, which had together formed in 1915 the Progressive Bloc opposition within the Duma, but had lost much influence as a result of Kerensky's policies.[126]

To avert the danger of further Bolshevik coup attempts, Kornilov stationed loyal units at places behind the front from which they could be quickly moved by train to Petrograd or Moscow. These measures increased the suspicion that the new commander in chief might play the role of a General Monck or a Bonaparte in the summer of 1917. In fact, Kornilov's relations with Kerensky deteriorated to such a degree that he decided to install a military dictatorship to stabilize the country and continue the war.[127] When he actually sent troops to Petrograd at the beginning of September, it appeared to be a rightist putsch against the conquests of the February Revolution, especially as he had previously claimed that the Provisional Government, having fallen under the influence of the Bolshevik-dominated Soviets, was playing into the hands of the German general staff, destroying social cohesion and putting the whole country in peril.[128]

The two sides of the future civil war were beginning to take shape. This division was all the more significant because Kerensky could no longer rely on the army and sought an alliance with the leaders and military forces of the Petrograd Soviet. The Bolshevik Red Guards, which he had disarmed after the July rising, were now mobilized again and turned into a key factor in the power equation. On September 9, Kerensky dismissed Kornilov, had him placed under arrest, and gave himself semi-dictatorial powers.[129] The real effect of this dramatic turn of events in late summer was that the liberal parties, which had seemed to be implicated in the putsch, as well as Kerensky and his Provisional Government, lost much of their political credibility, while the Bolsheviks were able to present themselves as defenders of the revolution against the counterrevolutionary threat from the Right. They considerably increased their share of the vote in the September and October elections to the Petrograd and Moscow Soviets, and in the changed climate Lenin was able to return from Finland.[130] But the situation in the army remained extremely shaky, as the hectic search continued for a stable leadership structure. Kerensky again appointed Alexeev as supreme commander to replace Kornilov, but after just a few days named the 41-year-old Nikolai Dukhonin as chief of the general staff. This rapid succession of personnel changes at the head of the army further undermined confidence in its command structures.[131]

The Bolshevik seizure of power in the October Revolution took advantage of this special constellation in which external pressure from the war and internal conflict between the Provisional Government and the military acted in combination, while the promise of land and peace appealed to soldiers and large sections of the rural population. In October 1917, these tendencies overlapped dramatically with each other.[132] German troops, benefiting from earlier experiences with storm troop tactics, started an offensive toward Riga and captured the city in early September. Meanwhile, German battleships advanced into the Baltic, protecting troop landings in mid-October on the islands of Ösel (Saaremaa) and Dagö (Hiiumaa) and destroying much of the

Russian Baltic fleet. Something that never happened on the western front or in the North Sea—a closely coordinated operation by the German army and navy—ended with great success in the Baltic. At that point (the middle of October), the end of the war in the east was in the cards, and it seemed possible for the German top brass to use the forces released after an armistice to mount an offensive in the west that would decide the war in favor of the Central Powers.

While Dukhonin noted with resignation that Russian sea power had been reduced to the status it had before Peter the Great's shipbuilding programs, the expectation in Petrograd was that German troops would actually march on the capital. When the Provisional Government under Kerensky evacuated Reval (Tallinn) and prepared its own transfer to Moscow, the leaders of the Petrograd Soviet saw this as treachery and formed a Military Revolutionary Committee on October 15 to defend the capital. It was vital for the success of the October Revolution that the Bolsheviks win the leadership of this committee, since they could then present themselves to the whole country as defenders of the revolution leading the struggle against the German enemy and the counterrevolution.[133] This twinning of the internal and external foe was reminiscent of 1792, when the Jacobins campaigned for a combined struggle against enemies of France abroad and enemies of the revolution at home.

The Bolshevik seizure of power in no way conformed to the ideas of Karl Marx. In his view, it would be at the end of the development of bourgeois society and the capitalist economic system that a spontaneous popular uprising would become historically necessary as a result of class conflicts in advanced industrial societies. Lenin, by contrast, set his sights from the beginning on the conquest of power by force—a coup d'état against the Provisional Government before the November elections to the Constituent Assembly. At first the events of October 25 and 26, 1917 (November 7 and 8 in the new calendar) occurred without significant bloodshed. Using the Second All-Russian Congress of Workers' and Soldiers' Deputies as their forum at the Smolny Institute, the Bolsheviks under Trotsky ensured their control of the Petrograd garrison under the auspices of the Military Revolutionary Committee and occupied strategic points in the city. After soldiers also took over the Winter Palace, the headquarters of the Provisional Government, posters announced the transfer of power to the committee of the revolution. Kerensky fled and took refuge in the U.S. Embassy.

In essence, this was a classical coup d'état, reminiscent of the situation after the 18th Brumaire in 1799. As in the coup staged by the revolutionary general Bonaparte, many people in Russia saw what happened in October 1917 as no more than another twist after all the power shifts and attempted putsches of the previous months. The so-called storming of the Winter Palace, the symbolic climax of revolutionary mass action in the eyes of later generations, was an invented tradition resting on Sergei Eisenstein's ostensible re-creation of events in his film *October*. The relative lack of violence reflected the extent to which the power and authority of the Provisional Government had already been eroded. A true revolution, in the sense of a structural political, social, and cultural turnaround, came only after the Bolsheviks had staked their claim to power and, over the next few months, set a host of deep changes in motion. Outside the cities, the Bolsheviks benefited from the support they received from large numbers of army deserters. Power there often fell into the hands of impromptu local militias mostly consisting of workers and soldiers, which could scarcely be controlled from the capital. In contrast to the relative order in Petrograd, many other parts of the country witnessed excesses and displays of violence under the influence of massive alcohol abuse; the end of the old regime, which had imposed strict prohibition at the beginning of the war, meant an end to that hated ban for many people in the countryside.[134]

On October 26, 1917, decrees issued by the All-Russian Congress of Soviets already signaled major changes and referred to the key promises made by the Bolsheviks in the previous months. They announced Russia's withdrawal from the war and called for efforts to achieve a peace without annexations or reparations. In a noteworthy parallel with Wilson's statements in April 1917, though within a completely different ideological perspective, Bolshevik foreign policy embraced the right of nations to self-determination. But at the same time, it appealed to war-weary workers of all countries, in the hope that the signal of the October Revolution would find an echo in other parts of Europe—in the Central Powers as well as the Entente countries. In a highly symbolic act, the Bolsheviks highlighted their withdrawal from the war coalition of 1914 by publishing the secret agreements on war aims that tsarist Russia had entered into with Britain and France. The western Allies then began to turn away from Russia, foreshadowing their intervention in the civil war that would last beyond 1920.

The dispossession of large landowners, the church, and the crown legalized the land redistribution that many farmers and village communities had already put into effect on their own initiative. The two decrees of October 26 also triggered a new wave of mass desertions, since an end to hostilities was now the official aim of the new rulers. A Council of People's Commissars, presided over by Lenin, was constituted as the new executive until the yet to be elected Constituent Assembly started its deliberations. The use of the new term "commissars" marked the break with the old political order symbolized by cabinets and ministers. From then on, rival players and institutions were systematically excluded: first, the existing Soviet executives, and in the end also the national assembly charged with drafting a constitution; the Constituent Assembly that issued from the theoretically democratic elections in November was forcibly dissolved by the Bolsheviks in early January 1918. The election results showed that there could be no talk of majority support for the Bolsheviks: the new rulers held their ground at best in the large cities, but countrywide they obtained only 22.5 percent of the vote. They could not have formed a parliamentary majority even with the Left SRs as their coalition partner, and the Socialist Revolutionaries supported by the peasantry won twice as many votes as the Bolsheviks.[135]

By late 1917 radical measures were being adopted in all conceivable areas of politics, economics, social life, culture, and the army, even if proclamations from Petrograd tell us nothing about what was happening on the ground elsewhere in this vast country. The will for a clean break with the past was plain enough—in everything from the principle of national self-determination; through workers' control over factories and enterprises, the elimination of traditional officialdom and the tsarist hierarchy of titles and service grades, the election of officers in all military units, and the nationalization of the banks; to the replacement of traditional courts by revolutionary tribunals. Abolition of the Julian calendar used by the Russian Orthodox Church brought a new system of marking the passage of time, a break between past and future and the beginning of a new historical epoch.

The Bolsheviks remained consistent on the question of the war. On November 21, 1917, after Lenin's call for a peace without annexations or

reparations found no positive response in any of the other belligerent countries, he instructed Dukhonin (whom Kerensky had appointed supreme
commander in one of his last official actions) to begin ceasefire talks with
Germany. Dukhonin, who earlier had allegedly continued the war and allowed
anti-Bolshevik generals to escape from detention, refused to obey the instruction. Accompanied by Red Guards, his planned successor Nikolai Krylenko
arrived in early December at army headquarters in Mogilev, where Dukhonin
was shot on the spot. A few days later, a ceasefire agreement was concluded
with the Central Powers.[136]

For Germany, Austria-Hungary, Bulgaria, and the Ottoman Empire, the
exit of Russia from the war coalition created the prospect of a decisive success. In November 1917, the basic strategic problem on the German side since
Summer 1914—a war on two fronts and the need to support Austria-Hungary
both militarily and economically—was suddenly solved. Both the Central
Powers and Russia had a great interest in the cessation of hostilities, and
the armistice between them was signed forthwith on December 5, 1917 (in
the new calendar). Fighting since 1915 had left Brest-Litovsk, the town in
Belarus between the two frontlines, almost completely destroyed, and yet
the German military preferred to hold the talks there rather than in neutral
Stockholm; the OHL wanted to emphasize that it, rather than the German
foreign office, would be in charge. It was clear to people at the time that they
were living in a quite special conjuncture. In early December, Harry Graf
Kessler wrote, "Today the Russian and German plenipotentiaries met for
armistice talks. The red fortress on the green island . . . is now the arena
for these negotiations that are world-historic in so many ways. The black-
crowned Russian eagle on the red fortress gates, Ludendorff, Tolstoy as the
inspiration of the anarchistic Russian commissars officially recognized by
two emperors, the broad, lazy, green-lined river completing this almost fairy-
tale gathering: what stuff for fantasy!"[137] In parallel with the peace talks
that opened in Brest-Litovsk on December 22, Ludendorff began to prepare
a large-scale offensive on the western front, which was meant to decide the
war before the presence of American troops and supplies made itself felt.

Despite Russia's precarious situation, Lenin figured that the war would
also accelerate the outbreak of revolution in other European countries, and
he therefore got Trotsky to play for time at the peace talks. The German

side eventually responded by ordering a further advance by their troops. An alternative possibility, which the Germans had sometimes supported with adventurous actions, now became a military reality; namely, the systematic breakup of the former empire through the promotion of national movements against Russia. In December 1917, the German government recognized the independence of Ukraine. And when Russian troops marched on Kiev to forestall this, Ukraine signed a separate peace with Germany and Austria-Hungary on February 9, 1918. With the prospect of the breakaway by a number of non-Russian nationalities and the creation of independent states with German support, the Bolsheviks found themselves with less and less room to maneuver.

The revolutionary changes in Russia were a warning sign for the legitimacy and survival of monarchic regimes throughout Europe. October 1917 witnessed the seizure of power by a radical ideological movement that called into question the liberal-constitutional political model and therefore the legacy of the bourgeois nineteenth century; it also marked a decisive turning point for the imperial model. What did the revolutions of February and October mean for the multiethnic structure of the former tsarist empire? How did the crisis of political legitimacy fit together with national political movements?[138] At first, the non-Russian periphery played a lesser role than in the 1905 revolution, partly because the centers of resistance in Poland and Latvian Courland that had been so important then were now occupied by the Central Powers. Where workers' councils sprang up—in Helsinki, Riga, or Odessa, for example, often spurred on by Russian workers and soldiers— tensions soon developed between these new organs of power and moderate national movements in the area. A second tendency, which accelerated from 1917 on, was the ethnicization of social and economic conflicts, as struggles over land redistribution came to be regarded in the light of national and ethnic affiliation. This trend applied especially to the peasant movement against landowners, which was expressed in the violent confiscation of land. Where the landowners were Poles and Russians, as they mostly were in Belarus and western Ukraine, the fight for land became interwoven with the struggle against an ethnically alien upper class. This was also the case with the clashes between Latvian farmers and German Baltic elites, for example, whereas nomads in eastern parts of the Empire had to deal mainly with Russian settlers. A third development was the formation of ethnic troop units, which played a considerable role in radicalization of the peasantry, as the example of the Latvian Rifle Brigade showed.[139] Their units originally consisted of volunteers, but from 1916 were largely made up of conscripts. Some 40,000 Latvians fought against the Germans between 1915 and 1917 as Russian army gunners. When their ranks were decimated in December 1916 and January 1917, however, and Russian officers did not follow through on costly but initially successful counterattacks against German positions, a protest movement began to grow. The gunners became increasingly sympathetic to the Bolsheviks and their promises of an end to the war. In May 1917, 35,000 Latvians finally sided with the Bolsheviks, forming a contingent that would play a key role in the revolution.[140]

This combination of the revolutionary political and social agenda with ethnic lines of conflict was a novelty on this scale. After the February Revolution, attempts were made to end discrimination against ethnic and religious minorities through a program protecting civil rights for all the inhabitants of Russia. Concessions to the Finns and Poles, however, who were promised autonomy or a revived kingdom, unleashed the conflicts they were intended to channel, because they were not extended to other regions and ethnic groups. This reinforced an impression of inequality. While the Provisional Government concentrated on the war and delayed political reforms, the national movements underwent a process of radicalization. In late September the government did subscribe in principle to the right of national self-determination within the Empire, but it felt like no more than a helpless gesture in the context of the country's defensive military situation and supply problems. The dynamism of the national movements could no longer be bottled up.[141]

The explosion of these national movements soon gave rise to a wide range of structures, demands, and strategies, in which social and ethnic-national lines of conflict overlapped with one another. Except in the case of Poland and Finland, the objective was to achieve greater autonomy, not secession and the founding of a separate state. Things went furthest in Ukraine, where peasants after the February Revolution could be mobilized both socioeconomically around the land question and nationally in the struggle against large Russian or Polish landowners—the two were intimately linked. In June 1917 the

Provisional Government recognized the Ukrainian Rada (central council) and representatives of the Ukrainian nation, but this led to an intensification of conflict on both sides. While the Cadets refused to accept the concessions and quit the government in Petrograd, the Ukrainian masses rejected the compromise because it offered no solution to the pressing social question. The Socialist Revolutionary Party, which associated the land question with the national question, benefited from this situation and grew to become the key political force.

Influenced by the impact of revolutionary events in areas not under German occupation, Latvians and Estonians too demanded greater autonomy—and the Bolsheviks gained considerable popularity among Latvian workers, peasants, and soldiers because of their policies combining land reform with peace and national self-determination. In Finland, the political situation in 1917 by no means generated a unitary national movement, but pointed instead toward civil war, since the movement in the majority Social Democrat parliament that sought the greatest degree of autonomy distanced itself from bourgeois forces more geared to cooperation with the Provisional Government. But while the military successes of the Central Powers in east central Europe and the Baltic, leading to the withdrawal of Russian troops and the erosion of Russian rule, created new leeway for Poles and Finns and bolstered their aspirations to independence, the situation in Transcaucasia was altogether different. There, in the proximity of the front with the Ottomans, a special committee dominated by Russians and Georgians looked to Russia to continue the war, while the Azerbaijani Musavat Party gained a considerable following with its demand for Russia to be given a federal structure.

The unleashing of ethnic-national conflicts amid war and revolution also had crucial importance for religious groups and minorities within the Russian Empire. While Jews welcomed the Provisional Government's acceptance in principle of equal rights, centrifugal tendencies in the various regions stood in the way of a Russia-wide Jewish congress. Muslims, in contrast, managed to organize their first countrywide congress in May 1917, which adopted a Musavat-style position in favor of the federalization of Russia.[142] A second congress in July 1917 then called for a Muslim "national assembly," in a characteristic coupling of social-revolutionary and ethnic-national positions. The same basic radicalization was visible among nomads in steppe regions;

there, traditional conflicts with new settlers flared up again when many Kazakhs and Kyrgyzs who had fled to China in 1916 after violent clashes over conscription returned to their ancestral territories. The year 1917 thus created new room for maneuver, and this led to new and complex lines of conflict. The end of tsarist rule dynamized the quest for new identities. In many places, a new consciousness linked up with older traditions, as in the case of Crimean Tatars or among the mountain peoples of the northern Caucasus who plotted an outright jihad against the Russians, referring back to the example of Imam Shamil in the nineteenth century.[143]

The February Revolution associated political and (to a growing extent) social-revolutionary demands with national and ethnic-religious issues, placing autonomy on the agenda even for Poles and Finns, though not their demands for formal independence. The social dimension was critical mainly because it affected the land question and the role of the peasantry as the mass base of the revolution. Many nationally minded parties moved more and more toward the agrarian-socialist positions of the Socialist-Revolutionaries (SRs), while the SRs supported demands for the federalization of Russia. The Bolsheviks, who remained in the minority with a few exceptions—some Baltic provinces, for example—supported the right to self-determination up to and including secession, because they hoped to use the mass base of the national parties for the revolution. For the Provisional Government, however, which postponed a comprehensive solution to ethnic-national conflicts until after the war, developments became increasingly out of its control, as military defeats further reduced its room for maneuver. The overlapping of war and political crisis with social-revolutionary and national movements explains the distinctive situation of turmoil in 1917.

The Bolshevik seizure of power in the October Revolution initially boosted hopes for a federal solution, especially after issuance of the Declaration of the Rights of the Peoples of Russia on November 2, 1917. In the Constituent Assembly elections of that month, the majority of non-Russians backed their respective national parties rather than Russian ones. In early January 1918 the Bolsheviks dissolved the assembly, setting their sights on centralized rule and placing the class struggle above the right to national self-determination. Many non-Russians interpreted this as the "victory of town over country, workers over peasants, and Russians over non-Russians." As Bolshevik rule became shakier and the advance of the Central Powers threatened to inflict military defeats, centrifugal tendencies asserted themselves again, though now with the aim of national independence. The link between military developments and formal declarations of independence speaks for itself: Finland, Estonia, Lithuania, Ukraine, Bessarabia, and Belarus had all declared independence by the time of the Brest-Litovsk peace treaty in early March 1918, to be followed in April by the Transcaucasian Federation. Meanwhile, other regions announced at least their autonomy.[144]

5. SHAKY PROMISES
The U.S. Decision to Enter the War and the Question of the American Nation

Anyone who visits Harvard University today encounters the legacy of the First World War in two striking pieces of architecture. In one the reference is transparent: the central building of the Harry Elkins Widener Memorial Library, the largest university library in the world, was opened in June 1915.[145] Its main staircase entrance features two murals with programmatic themes, which the president of the university commissioned in 1921 from John Singer Sargent. One of them symbolically depicts the salvation of Europe and freedom by the United States. The mural "The Coming of the Americans" shows U.S. soldiers—young white men—on their arrival in Europe. They are coming to the assistance of three female figures representing Britain, France, and Belgium. All three women look weary and exhausted, especially the pale woman in the background with a child on her arm, who symbolizes Belgium, which was raided in 1914. This interpretation of the war shaped people's perceptions in the United States, and the inscription emphasized its significance as an American crusade for the freedom of all peoples: "They crossed the sea crusaders keen to help / The nations battling in righteous cause."[146] Yet this retrospective view left out the controversies in the period leading up to America's entry into the war in Spring 1917—a perspective that opens up if one looks closely at the history of another building on the campus.

The Adolphus Busch Hall, the former Germanic Museum, feels almost like a foreign body amid the red brick of the old campus and the modern complex of scientific institutes—a mixture of church, cloister, and museum, it is built in a nearly perfect historicist style, with a reproduction of the famous Brunswick Lion in the garden and numerous German inscriptions on the façade. In fact, the history of the building reflects the high regard in which German culture and science were held in pre-1914 American academia—and the radical move away from it during the First World War. Around 1900, German universities were the model for progressive education and modern scientific standards. Numerous American graduates went to Germany to continue their studies—roughly 10,000 just by the year 1900—and on their return they helped to establish the high reputation of German scholarship in the United States. Charles Eliot, the president of Harvard from 1869, explicitly lauded the German model, and around 1890 it was even discussed whether to introduce the status of *Privatdozent* (a private teacher recognized by the university but compensated by student fees) there. Many professors in the humanities and sciences had had personal experience of Germany.

In 1914, Kuno Francke and Hugo Münsterberg were thought of as the two foremost representatives of German culture and science in the United States, and their biographies give us some idea of the radical break brought about by the war. Francke, a historian and literary theorist originally from Kiel, got to know Harvard through contacts with Charles Eliot; he taught in its German department from 1884 and became a professor there in 1896, with a special focus on German literature and history. In 1891 he married an American woman and acquired U.S. citizenship. Convinced of his mission, he began to campaign in 1897 for a Germanic Museum to be built on the campus, taking as its model various institutions such as the Germanic National Museum in Nuremberg and others founded in Germany since the middle of the nineteenth century. In 1891, with the opening of a Semitic Museum, Harvard had already tried to create a counterweight to the traditionally strong orientation to France.

Münsterberg, born in Danzig in 1863, studied physiological psychology with Wilhelm Wundt in Leipzig as well as medicine in Heidelberg, and his links with the American psychologist and philosopher William James took him to Harvard, where he taught social psychology from 1891 in the philosophy department. He went back to Freiburg in Germany in 1895, but because he was unable to continue his academic career there, he later returned to Harvard and became not only the founder of modern social psychology but also one of the most influential figures in the German American milieu. Unlike Francke, he never gave up his German citizenship, and he maintained close relations with the German embassy in Washington.[147] As an exchange professor, he taught in 1910–1911 in Berlin and founded the Berliner Amerika-Institut there.

The efforts to found a Germanic Museum at Harvard were supported by Charles Eliot, who repeatedly spoke of the high esteem in which German culture was held on the East Coast. In the 1880s the Boston Symphony Orchestra had a strong German imprint and German conductors. In 1901 the Germanic Museum Association was founded with Carl Schurz as its president. He was a figure who embodied the German and American legacy of the nineteenth century: he emigrated from Germany after the revolution of 1848, and during the American Civil War he fought as a general for the Northern states and served for a time as secretary of the interior. The list of the Museum Association's prominent members also included the U.S. ambassador in Berlin and the future president of Cornell University, Andrew D. White; Theodore Roosevelt, who became U.S. president in 1901; and the Berlin museum director Wilhelm Bode. The fundraising campaign at Harvard proved very successful, with Kaiser Wilhelm II and Chancellor Bernhard von Bülow among the participants. The Kaiser covered the costs of reproducing twenty-five monumental stone sculptures from the history of German art. When the German ambassador and Münsterberg were awarded honorary degrees at Harvard, Charles Eliot was effusive in his praise of Germany: he spoke of the "young and lusty German Empire, representative of an ancient people whose racial and institutional roots are intertwined with our own—of a people whose scholars and universities have for a century given example and inspiration to the learned world."[148] At the stone-laying ceremony for the museum on June 8, 1912, the Harvard Glee Club sang "Deutschland, Deutschland über alles."[149] The climate changed after August 1914, however, rapidly turning into one of cultural warfare between pro-German and anti-German intellectuals. Even before the United States entered the war, the perception of Germany in American society and the situation of Americans of German origin had undergone a dramatic shift.

A pro-British, pro-French mood swept academia in Summer 1914. A number of Allied support committees were founded, and thousands of young men, many of them students from East Coast colleges, volunteered to serve as ambulance drivers on the western front.[150] The former Harvard president and champion of the German academic tradition Charles Eliot now turned sharply against Germany: its "philosophy and religion have failed to work; her education has not developed in the people power to reason or good judgment; her efficiency even in war is not greater than that of her adversaries; and her ruling class is too stupid to see that their game of domination in Europe is already lost."[151]

Münsterberg, for his part, forcefully represented Germany's position, cultivating close links with politicians including Theodore Roosevelt. At Harvard he began a campaign against Eliot and his criticisms of Germany. But his book *The War and America* increasingly cut him off from the academic milieu of North America, earning him both the hostility of pro-Entente forces and idolization by supporters of Germany. Francke found himself facing a particularly acute loyalty dilemma because of his U.S. citizenship and his marriage to an American wife. The Germanic Museum, too, was caught in the crossfire between pro-German and anti-German propaganda. The German architect Bestelmeyer withdrew from the project, but the construction nevertheless continued. In May 1915 the sinking of the *Lusitania,* with its loss of life among American civilians, increased the anti-German pressure. The copy of the Brunswick Lion in the museum garden was covered with black paint, and some of the windows in the building were broken. The criticism directed at German Americans was often aggressive, referring to them as "hyphenated Americans" with questionable loyalties and demanding that they make an unambiguous commitment to the United States. While Münsterberg turned to President Wilson and used the votes of German Americans as an argument, Francke withdrew from the increasingly Germanophobic public arena. He did not agree with Münsterberg's radical pro-German stance and patriotic campaigning, and in Spring 1915 the two men finally broke with each other. Münsterberg grew increasingly isolated in the faculty, but he continued to make frequent pro-German speeches, until he collapsed and died on one such occasion in mid-December.

The Germanic Museum building was nearly finished when the United States entered the war in April 1917, and work on it was completed by the end of the year. At the same time, in the immediate vicinity, trainee American officers were being prepared by French officers for the war against Germany. For fear of riots, it was decided not to open the museum, which bore the two German names Busch and Reisinger on its inscription. The official explanation for the delay was the lack of coal to keep it heated, but the fact was that in just a few years the world war had made German science and culture a negative reference at Harvard. Only in April 1921, in a more relaxed climate of German-American relations, did it become possible to go ahead with the opening.[152]

Although the political leadership of the United States proclaimed strict neutrality after Summer 1914, the government position that the war was a purely European matter did not correspond to reality. In the multiethnic American society, it was simply impossible to escape emotional involvement, and many European immigrants expressed clear sympathies with their country of origin. Even more important, however, were the economic consequences of the war, since the British blockade of Germany limited American exports. Partly to compensate for this, President Wilson agreed as early as Fall 1914 that Britain and France could buy goods in the United States on credit. Political neutrality may have continued, but there could be no talk of economic neutrality—and the tension between the two would remain a feature of transatlantic relations.[153]

Nowhere was this plainer than in the relationship between the United States and Britain, which began to change in 1915 because of the increasingly tight financial position of the Allies, especially of the government in London, which was facing enormous pressure on the pound. The value of sterling fell in August 1915 from $4.86 to $4.65. American industrialists appealed to the president to grant larger credits to the Allies. The motives for this were more economic than political, since the loans were largely used to purchase imported American goods. Presidential advisers at the State Department pointed out that a British credit crisis would inevitably do major damage to American trade, with massive consequences for industrial production and employment levels in the United States; social unrest among American workers even seemed in the cards. Wilson responded promptly and let it be known that his government would not stand in the way of an increased credit line. The first bond sale to the tune of $5 million was soon followed by further loans, which mostly came from institutional lenders at a 6 percent rate of interest; in the end the total extended in the form of private loans came to $2 billion. This allowed the Allies to continue purchasing important war supplies in the United States, whereas it became increasingly difficult for the Central Powers to finance their war effort through loans. The United States virtually ceased to exist for them as a capital market. Credits helped Britain and France to continue the war, but at the same time they fueled an economic boom in the United States, making people there more aware not only of Britain's dependence on American goods but also of America's own vulnerability to the fortunes of war.[154]

The growing British interest in America's entry into the war should be understood in this light. The immediate cause was the German decision to resume unrestricted submarine warfare and the publication of the Zimmermann Telegram. When Arthur Zimmermann, the state secretary at the Auswärtiges Amt, sent a wire to Mexico on January 17, 1917, offering the government an alliance, he did so partly to back up the U-boat campaign against the United States. The German proposal envisaged that Mexico, in the event of a German victory, would recover the territories it had lost to the United States in the war of 1848: Texas, Arizona, and New Mexico. The British secret service intercepted and decoded the message, and by making it public Whitehall deliberately put the American government under pressure to join the war without delay. The German promises to Mexico affected a vital U.S. security zone and directly challenged its interests in Latin America as defined in the Monroe Doctrine. The reactions of American politicians and public figures were correspondingly robust. On April 6 the United States declared war on the German Reich.[155]

While Wilson associated the decision to go to war with his far-flung political objectives, the actual military dimension was at first modest: American soldiers, lacking any combat experience, had to be shipped to Europe and given suitable training before they saw any action. The supreme commander of U.S. troops in Europe, General John Pershing, insisted from the beginning that his units should remain autonomous, and he initially opposed any Allied training of his men. Flying in the face of the realities of positional warfare, he also argued for infantry attacks in open spaces, for which he believed U.S. troops to be especially suited because of the geographical conditions back home. Like the European commanders in Summer 1914, however, he underestimated the effectiveness of enemy defensive weapons. Pershing banked on the rifle as the key infantry weapon and set 600 meters as the minimum ground to be won in an attack, whereas French officers in 1917 figured on a maximum of 100 meters. This already suggested that there would be considerable conflict between British, French, and American commanders over tactics and weapon deployment. When the first large American contingents were deployed in late 1917 and early 1918, the lack of synchronization was plain to see: American officers applied tactics that their European counterparts had replaced since 1914 because of the high casualties they entailed.[156] The consequences were exorbitant losses on the American side.

While the military weight of the United States in Europe began to tell only in Spring 1918, changes in American society induced by the war had become discernible long before April 1917. The domestic political climate and conceptions of the American nation began to change after Summer 1914—as did attitudes to Germany after the deployment of German submarines in 1915. Ethnic groups in the United States—especially Germans and Austrians, but also the Irish—were increasingly viewed with mistrust. However, their electoral weight was also a factor that politicians took into account before 1917; people of German descent, for example, accounted for roughly 9 percent of the population. At any event, the pressure on supposedly disloyal members of society became ever greater from 1914–1915 on—and that included certain political and religious groups such as socialists, pacifists, or free church opponents of the war. More and more often, they came under suspicion of "un-American" conduct. Even where the war at first affected a country only indirectly, it intensified the problem of loyalties for ethnic groups in the United States associated with it. All this increasingly inflamed the debate over how the American nation should be defined. Not by chance did the government hold the national holiday celebrations on July 4, 1915, under the slogan "Many Peoples, but One Nation." At a moment when the United States was becoming more and more involved both economically and politically in the world war, President Wilson wanted to strengthen the cohesion of a multiethnic society.[157]

The so-called Preparedness Movement and the ideology of "100 Percent Americanism" developed against this background. Strongly influenced by the former president Theodore Roosevelt, the underlying fear was that the country would prove unprepared for war, both materially and in terms of people's collective consciousness as Americans. The movement was successful, especially on the East Coast, and was taken up by Wilson in his election campaign. The mood turned against all "hyphenated Americans" and their supposedly divided loyalties, not least those of German descent. It became a "test of attitude" whether one had a patriotic commitment to the American nation. Preparations for possible entry into the war thus went hand in hand with increased pressure to conform.[158]

But these developments also provoked a reaction. Discussion of the "melting pot" model of the American nation, which Theodore Roosevelt and Woodrow Wilson still espoused in 1916 in their presidential campaigns, became noticeably more strident.[159] Horace Kallen had already argued in 1915 that in practice the melting pot myth gave no immigrant the chance for individual affirmation, since it converted the Americanization model of the white Anglo-Saxon Protestant (WASP) elite into a fixed dogma. The aim of this model, in his view, was not to fuse different ethnic groups into a single American nation, but to suppress ethnic difference undemocratically in an "Anglo-Saxon Americanism."[160] The journalist and culture critic Randolph Bourne went further in "Transnational America," an essay he published in 1916. In light of the heated debate on Americanism in 1915–1916, he argued that the wartime horizon had refuted the premises of the melting pot ideal; the equation of Americanism with Anglo-Saxonism tied U.S. war preparations to the white, Anglo-Saxon model impregnated with British conceptions, and this only provoked resistance on the part of other ethnic groups. The United States was losing a unique opportunity to become a truly transnational society and to present a countermodel to that of the European continent of war. Bourne, then, was sketching the idea of an American cosmopolitanism.[161] Instead of assimilation, he saw dual citizenship as a necessary means to forswear in time of war any exclusive national identification with European societies. The key problem was to define affiliation unambiguously, in the sense of binding criteria for aliens and Americans: "We are all foreign-born or the descendants of foreign-born and if distinctions are to be made between us they should rightly be on some other ground than indigenousness."[162] This plea for social pluralism, against the greater stringency of criteria of affiliation and loyalty, may have been the isolated view of one intellectual who knew Europe from his own experience—but it counted all the more because it was formulated at the very moment when the practice of ethnic exclusion and the growing suspicion of supposedly disloyal or treacherous elements were hollowing out the liberal substance of all the societies involved in the war.

When the United States entered the war in April 1917, the dominant journalistic image of the country as an ethnic melting pot had trouble disguising the tensions and contradictions inherent in ideas of an American nation. Should this be seen as an ethnic-exclusive or a national-exclusive concept? The problem was posed clearly in a poster designed by Howard Chandler Christy in 1917, which encouraged Americans to purchase war loan subscriptions. Beneath the title "Americans All!" in large capital letters, it portrays a young white woman standing in front of an American flag. She is holding a laurel wreath over a roll of honor, whose very diversity testifies to the multiethnic origins of the American nation: "Du Bois, Smith, O'Brien, Cejka, Haucke, Pappandrikopolous, Abdrassi, Villotto, Levy, Turovich, Kowalski, Chriczanevicz, Knutson, and Gonzales."[163] As in the *Life Stories of Undistinguished Americans,* put together in 1906 by the journalist and civil rights activist Hamilton Holt, all the immigrant nationalities count as loyal Americans.[164] With the country going to war, it is implied, the loyalty of all immigrants lies with the American nation alone. Yet the towering female figure corresponds to the iconic white "American girl," an American version of the Eurasian Marianne, Britannia, and Germania. The national equality in diversity expressed in this poster refers to an imagined community dominated by its Anglo-Saxon origins. As the pamphlet *What Is It to Be an American?* put it in 1918, "Our backbone is Anglo-Saxon; the sinews of our vast body may come from a hundred hardy races, but our backbone comes from but one."[165]

The debate on Americanism had serious implications: the attitude of neighbors and authorities to supposed traitors and spies developed a dynamic of its own that was increasingly uncontrollable in many parts of the country.[166] But the precise meaning of loyalty and the point at which it became disloyalty remained unclear. The very lack of definition favored the dynamic of demands for proof of loyalty. What a loyal American should be was so indeterminate that the reproach of disloyalty could be instrumentalized in such a way as to shift the semantic boundaries.[167]

After the United States entered the war in April 1917, many German American newspapers found themselves compelled to fall in line with official justifications for the decision. Non-naturalized Germans were declared "enemy aliens" and placed under general suspicion of supporting German war efforts; a real surveillance hysteria began to develop. Immigrants of German origin, especially those who owned businesses, were directly attacked and their businesses ransacked. A state apparatus of control and institutions to disseminate an anti-German enemy-image took up position; the Committee on Public Information, for example, spread the image of vicious and cunning barbarians, driving it home with references to the Zimmermann Telegram and the resumption of unrestricted submarine warfare. A number of nongovernmental surveillance bodies such as the American Protective League (which had around 250,000 members) joined the fray, and seemingly untrustworthy neighbors were sometimes exposed to the vagaries of rough justice. Such vigilante practices, a legacy of the frontier, reflected the waves of immigrants since the 1890s and the revival of nativism with its potential for violence.

The collective hysteria did not stop short of targeting women of German descent, although only fifteen were actually interned. In Spring 1918 the measures were stepped up in view of the German military successes in Europe. On the other hand, the Sedition Act was partly an attempt to rein in vigilante tendencies; a total of 8,500 to 10,000 German "enemy aliens" were arrested under the official powers it introduced. In any case, by the end of the war, 8 percent of male Germans in the United States had been temporarily interned on suspicion of being "enemy aliens." Paradoxically, the witch hunts against Germans strengthened the assimilation of other ethnic groups—with the exception of African Americans. The anti-German operations served to ventilate nativism, and against this background the melting pot was celebrated as the result of a common war effort. Those branded as "enemy aliens" became an object onto which all manner of conspiracy theories were projected. The associated lines of demarcation helped to stabilize the national self-image.[168]

Americanization and spy mania, state-sanctioned violence, vigilante justice, aggressive social mobilizations—all these turned fellow citizens into suspects, neighbors into spies, friends into traitors. In 1918, one despairing

German American wrote of the pressure on family members and the numerous cases of nervous breakdown and suicide: "We are liable to be 'reported' by any moron and subjected to inquisitions by federal agents at every turn. These 'heart-to-heart talks,' as they are styled when there is not the least evidence for other action, officially counsel hate toward everything German, vilify our origins and our traditions, and, coming from the government itself, implant a rancor that does not heal. Can one wonder at the numerous suicides among German-Americans?"[169]

As in Britain, such developments increasingly blurred the boundaries between naturalized and non-naturalized Germans, between American citizens of German descent and immigrants without the rights of American citizens. Legislation was made considerably more stringent and basic political rights were greatly restricted, as the Espionage Act of June 1917 did in relation to the freedom of speech. Such measures also had a major impact on immigration policies, leading to greater exclusion and continuing the attempts evident since 1915 to enact more restrictive legislation. In February 1917 Congress overturned a presidential veto, and from May 1917 a new "literacy clause" made the immigration criteria even more restrictive. Fears grew that a tidal wave of immigration would flood the labor market after the war.[170] The idea of individual liberty was increasingly discredited after 1914 in both Britain and the United States. The American war state, too, developed more and more clearly into a repressive state, which at the end of the war would act with great vehemence against immigrants, dissidents, and unionized workers—always justifying its action by the argument that only national unity could confront the wartime challenges.[171]

In 1915–1916 there had been heated debate on how and whether the country needed to adjust to the war and on whether it was at all prepared to take part in it. Conscription eventually became a particularly controversial issue, as it did in Britain and Russia in 1916 and Canada in 1917. Although the practice of the Northern states in the Civil War under Abraham Lincoln tended to be overlooked, the introduction of compulsory military service meant a degree of state centralism and official intrusion in people's lives that was unprecedented for American society. After the passing of the Selective Service Act in May 1917, the call-up ensued in accordance with the inductees' abilities and economic circumstances. From early June 1917, all men aged between

21 and 30 were registered. President Wilson was aware of the implications of conscription, arguing that its main point was not to assemble an army, but to mold a nation for war. Resistance developed against these measures, especially from the ranks of American socialists and east European Jewish immigrants in New York. Nevertheless, unlike in Ireland, Canada, or Russia, there was little major or violent resistance, because the introduction of conscription was not accompanied by other political conflicts such as a struggle for national autonomy or independence.[172]

The divergence between claims and reality in relation to conscription was especially marked in the Southern states. In the mainly rural South, Washington's attempts to ensure the loyalty of the population soon ran into considerable practical problems: large numbers could neither read nor write and were often unable to understand their call-up papers. Besides, since the roll was very patchy in some areas, the authorities often lacked precise dates of birth. In practice it was race and class interests that determined how conscription was enforced. Since local committees were mostly put in charge of recruitment, prosperous white landowners—the very people who sat on the committees—played a central role in the process. They did what they could to ensure that poor white farmers, mainly involved in subsistence agriculture, were drafted into the army, leaving untouched the black laborers essential to larger farms. In plantation districts, this logic had the paradoxical result that African Americans were significantly less likely than poor white farmers to see action in Europe.[173]

In the South, several sources fed the antiwar mood: a tradition of agrarian radicalism, for which conscription by an overreaching state was a breach of the Constitution; pacifist currents with a strong evangelical influence; and draft avoidance by African American men to ensure their families' livelihood. The resistance, by no means limited to left-wingers and foreigners, thus forced the federal government to take new measures. It suspended a number of civil rights and recruited special agents to nail critics of the war or to track down people in the rural South who shirked the patriotic duty of subscribing to war loans.[174]

Members of indigenous tribes were also drafted into the army, where they, like African Americans, encountered everyday racism. Much as British and French officers appreciated soldiers from their colonies, American commanders valued the bravery of Indians and emphasized their warlike qualities. On the other hand, they openly doubted their intelligence and insisted that they should only perform simple tasks, seeing them as undisciplined and unreliable elements who needed strict leadership by white officers. Since experiments with segregated units had been unsuccessful in the late nineteenth century, the contingents that fought in the world war were racially mixed. In order to fulfill recruitment quotas and to protect white Americans, Indians were often classified as "whites." This did not assure them of equal rights, however, and they remained in an insecure position halfway between "citizen" and "alien"; often it was unclear whether they were liable to the draft at all. For all the romantic notions that Indians preserved their martial qualities intact, everyday practice in army units testified to their uncertain status.[175]

The ethnic diversity of American society crystallized in the composition of the army, which numbered recruits from forty-six different nationalities. A full 18 percent of soldiers recruited during the war had not been born in the United States, and a considerable number were second-generation immigrants.[176] Many came from countries that were now fighting one another in Europe, and this increased the pressure on ethnic minorities to demonstrate their loyalty to the United States. Practices inside the army also highlighted the religious diversity of American society: on the western front, for example, following the British example, Christian crosses were replaced with the Star of David on the graves of fallen Jewish soldiers.[177] At the same time, however, the multifaceted practice of racial separation and discrimination continued within the army.

African American recruits learned that military service brought no change in their political and social status. Wartime nationalism left room for a discrepancy between the imagined community and everyday racial exclusion. For African Americans, the war became an experimental terrain for social engineers and demographic or racial experts. Official IQ tests were designed to confirm the lower intelligence of black recruits. In 1916 the military psychologist Lewis Terman expected this research to show "significant racial differences in general intelligence, differences which cannot be wiped out by any scheme of mental culture." And Robert M. Yerkes, director of the World War I Testing Program, concluded that "the negro lacks initiative, displays little or no leadership, and cannot accept responsibility."[178]

Serious racial unrest broke out just four months after the United States entered the war. In late August 1917, African American soldiers of the 24th Infantry Regiment mutinied in Houston, when 150 men reacted to assaults by the local police on their comrades. The already tense situation in the city had escalated with the stationing of African American units. Ignoring their officers' orders, soldiers armed themselves and marched downtown, where violent clashes with white policemen and national guardsmen resulted in the deaths of sixteen white civilians (including four police officers) and four African American soldiers. A series of courts-martial, whose proceedings were the longest in U.S. history, handed down twenty-eight death sentences; nineteen soldiers were executed and forty-one condemned to life imprisonment.[179] In an instant, the episode revealed the emptiness of African Americans' hopes that, as in earlier wars such as the campaigns against Cuba and the Philippines, military service would allow them to assert their constitutional rights and improve their position in society, earning a

Whose American war? The fitting out of African American recruits

place in Wilson's vociferous crusade for democracy. The contrast between Wilson's promises abroad and the continuing racial discrimination at home was unmistakable.

The same discrepancy was evident in the partitioning of regional labor markets in the United States. As white landowners in the South attempted to hinder the migration of labor to the North, African American workers and intermediaries seeking to fill new vacancies in Northern factories found themselves forced to return home; whole railroad stations were blockaded. Southern landowners justified the exploitation of their laborers by referring to the war and the exigencies of national defense—a situation that, in the "red summer" of 1919, led to severe racial disturbances in the North. Outright gang warfare raged in Chicago in particular, resulting from competition between white workers and African American migrants from the South. Things grew worse with the demobilization of American soldiers returning from Europe. African American workers in the North also rejected black migrants from the South, fearing that they would undermine their own status.[180]

If units from plantation areas of the South are not considered, African American soldiers were generally overrepresented in comparison with whites from the Southern states. They often served in labor battalions and received markedly less intensive combat training—which translated into higher casualty rates on the western front.[181] Wilson, who in this respect was caught up in the racial prejudices of the bourgeoisie of the South, doubted the fighting morale of African American soldiers. Although he met with African American representatives after the Houston riots, nothing changed in the practice of discrimination within the U.S. Army.[182] All the same, the supreme commander of American forces on the western front, General Pershing, did what he could to promote a certain racial tolerance and explicitly acclaimed the deployment of African American soldiers.[183]

A final dimension of the American entry into the war was associated with the hopes of the liberal intellectual elite of Progressives. In April 1917 these too related to the great debate on the nature of the American nation and the meaning of its immigrant society over and above economic growth and material gain for individuals. The war in Europe also forced U.S. liberals to look hard at their own self-image and blueprint for the future,[184] particularly the role of the state and the scope for a liberal reform agenda. After 1910 the guiding light for politicians around Theodore Roosevelt was a program of national reconstruction—an institutional, political, and cultural renewal to strengthen the cohesion of American society—which in the eyes of many had been increasingly eroded since the 1860s by rapid social and economic change. Ideologically, this program was associated with the politics of the founding fathers Hamilton and Jefferson: national strength presupposed a democratic society. More specifically, the aim was to centralize political and economic decisions so that the state played a more active role. Here the U.S. entry into the war was a direct catalyst, since Wilson's organization of the war economy heralded the principle of an active, regulatory state. Celebrated by the influential group of Progressives around John Dewey as a kind of socialism or victory of political and economic planning, the American war economy prefigured the New Deal orientation of the 1930s under Franklin Delano Roosevelt. It was comparable, in its tendency to corporatist decision making, with developments in Germany and other European belligerent states, basing itself on specialized government agencies, associating the main industrial interest groups with the trade unions, and lending them official recognition. At the same time, these measures went hand in hand with an ideologically radical conception of Americanism, one that contained the promise of political and social participation, but in practice also developed strong tendencies toward aggressive nationalism and vigilantism.[185]

Progressive intellectuals around Herbert Croly, Walter Lippmann, and John Dewey emphasized in the spirit of Max Weber the importance of rational organization for modern industrial societies and the role of charismatic leadership figures. They saw the war as an opportunity to enhance the national integration of American society: the premises of "good administration," which Croly had outlined in 1915 in his book *Progressive Democracy*, would be put to the test in Spring 1917 and thereafter. President Wilson had geared the country up for entry into the war under the watchword of "military and industrial preparedness." The war—so left-liberal reformers hoped—would compel the United States to combine social integration with state economic rationality, and ideas embodying scientific thinking would eventually bring forth a new type of democracy. But these ambitious expectations ended in bitter disappointment. Even during the war, but particularly after 1918, leading Progressives had to recognize that the American variant of war socialism remained no more than a historical episode, and the internal and external hopes associated with Wilson were soon shattered.[186]

Unlike the German discussion of war aims, for example, the concept of the nation held by liberal intellectuals in the United States was not rooted in annexationist ambitions, but charted a new social and national democracy and a new vision of loyalty for the heterogeneous immigrant society. Progressives advocated an international system of collective security that would include the United States, but their main focus remained national politics. In February 1916, Lippmann already argued that the war had given Americans "a new instinct for order, purpose," thereby opening up the chance of an "integrated America." Croly too emphasized the idea of a "national purpose" that would redefine the common good beyond materialist culture and class interests. This vision of the nation was supposed to overcome both the stateless individualism of the pioneering age and the one-sided material-economic egotism of the second half of the nineteenth century. *The New Republic,* the mouthpiece of the Progressives, gave expression to these hopes of American liberals. In April 1917, following America's entry into the war, it wrote, "Never was a war fought so far from the battlefield for purposes so distinct from the battlefield."[187]

6. THE REVOLUTION OF RISING EXPECTATIONS
1917 as a Global Moment

The war had been global since 1914—on the world's oceans, in East Asia, in the African colonies. In 1917 the military situation in the Near and Middle East became more fraught, but what gave the year its global significance was the evident dynamic of expectations, in very different parts of the world, that the war might change in the long term the status of claims to power and political participation. The program of President Wilson was not so much the origin as a catalyst of this development, a symbolic embodiment of hopes for autonomy, independence, and self-determination stretching far back into the past. The contexts and traditions might vary widely, but these hopes were clearly multiplying worldwide in 1917. For politicians in Asia, South America, and the Arabian Peninsula, Wilson personified the horizon of expectations on which they visualized the end of the war and the future international order.[188]

The U.S. entry into the war triggered a global surge of political expectations and stimulated protest movements whose origins often went back quite a long time. Far beyond the warring states of Europe, many people looked to the American president as a figure of hope, counting on a new international order that would do more than just restore the status quo ante. This was true especially in China, Korea, and India. But it was not Wilson's ideas alone that drove hopes of an end to European colonial rule. Part of the global significance of that year was the fact that, in a short space of time, a network of informational channels and infrastructures spread news of Wilson's policies and the U.S. entry into the war all around the world, contributing decisively to a distinctive revolution of rising expectations.

The global dimension of communications made itself felt once more in the struggle for public opinion. The war thus also developed into a struggle over the reach of the major news agencies.[189] While Havas served the French colonial empire and southern Europe, the German Wolff Telegraphic Bureau took care of Habsburg, central Europe, Russia, and Scandinavia. The British Reuters agency covered the Imperial market, the United States, and East Asia. Only a few regions—Egypt, Greece, and the Ottoman lands—were supplied with news jointly by Havas and Reuters. At the beginning of the war, Reuters acted as an institution of the British Empire and methodically built up this position over the following years, opening offices in Bombay, Cairo, and Shanghai and supplying India, Egypt, and China with British news. For the United States the key agency was the Associated Press (founded in 1848), but Havas remained a formative influence in Latin America. Even before 1914 telegraphic technology had permitted the worldwide communication of news, and the media could take part in the war with no major time delay. In the United States, after the experience of the Zimmermann Telegram, there was an acute perception of how important a global and secure information network under national control could prove to be. The development of wireless networks took place in the same context, especially in relation to the Caribbean and Latin America.[190]

The German news agencies had been on the defensive since the beginning of the war. After the British navy cut the Atlantic cable between Continental Europe and North America, it became extremely difficult to convey the German view of the war on the American opinion market. In 1917 this applied even more to other parts of the world. The operations of Reuters, Havas, and Associated Press were truly global, and this gave the Allies a crucial advantage in the war of opinion. Most important was the contribution that Wilson's programmatic justifications of the war made to the development of a global news market. In the media war and the struggle for access to information, the differences in strategy between the main belligerent countries became ever clearer. In Germany, military leaders saw war propaganda as a part of tactics and allocated it to military intelligence. In France, the whole sphere came under the responsibility of foreign ministry officials. In Britain, efforts were made to attract authors and journalists for propaganda activity.

Only in the United States, however, did a highly professional organization develop after the decision to enter the war. It did not take long for the American leadership to understand the importance of world opinion and the struggle for interpretational jurisdiction in a global setting. Wilson's justification of the war and vision of a postwar order had to be presented as real alternatives to the traditional principles of the European state system, and not only communicated but efficiently marketed as American ideals. Wilson himself was convinced that a genuine and substantive transformation of international relations could succeed only if as much support for it as possible could be mobilized around the world: "Everything that affects the opinion of the world regarding us affects our influence for good." Only one week after the U.S. declaration of war, a Committee on Public Information was set up under the direction of the energetic George Creel, a convinced supporter of Wilson and the Progressives. Creel had extensive journalistic experience and continually sought to combine traditional methods with new techniques, including wireless communication, cinema, and radio, but also posters and photographs.[191] His aim was to promote a global understanding of how important a victory for the United States would be for the whole world. Accordingly, Creel's committee, linking up with the global Allied news agencies, preached the "absolute justice of America's cause, the absolute selflessness of America's aims" as the program of the president.[192]

Hardly anywhere did Wilson's message find such fertile soil as in India. In February 1917 the nationalist politician Ganghadar Tilak, released only in June 1914 after six years' imprisonment, resolutely campaigned to recruit as many soldiers as possible for the India Defence Force; he emphasized the necessity of defending not only India but also the rest of the Empire. One of his long-term concerns was to ensure that Indian soldiers had equal status with British subjects of European origin in India. With their calls for universal conscription, Indian nationalists sought to convey an idealized image of patriotic Indian citizens. The ever-greater need for soldiers and auxiliaries led to the recruitment even of members of lower castes and tribespeople, so that traditional social and cultural boundaries, especially between castes, tended to become less important during the war in certain places; for example, building sites. The outlines of a quite integrated model of military mobilization became discernible, although after the war ethnic criteria for army recruitment were tightened and participation in the war did not result in greater long-term social mobility.[193] Externally, the active participation of Indian soldiers in the war was used as a means of exerting political pressure on the British government, and the weight of national demands in the Indian public aroused fears in London that a mass movement might develop during the war. The government therefore aimed to strengthen moderate forces within the Indian National Congress through a policy of high-profile concessions. In August 1917 Edwin Montagu, the secretary of state for India, declared his support for "the increasing association of Indians in every branch of the administration and the gradual development of self-governing institutions." The promise of "responsible government" was meant to strengthen India's position as "an integral part of the British Empire."[194]

What captivated the Indian public at the time, however, was not this more accommodating British approach but the person and positions of the U.S. president, Woodrow Wilson. The popular press, in particular, paid relatively little attention to Montagu's declarations, especially as statements by the Allies—which since April 1917 included the United States—were not usually subject to press censorship. In fact, India became a prime target for the global propaganda offensive of the Committee of Public Information. As the year wore on, Wilson's insistence on the right to national self-determination overshadowed all other issues in the war reporting in India, where people increasingly suspected that other priorities for the British government, such as the threat to India from Afghanistan, the Ottoman Empire, Germany, or the Bolsheviks, were no more than pretexts for it to enshrine the status quo. Although Montagu's declaration went beyond all previous concessions on

India, it paled in comparison with Wilson's worldwide program. If the latter was applied to India, then the future of the country would lie in the hands of the Indian people, rather than the British government.[195]

Similar expectations marked the reception of Wilson's positions in China and Korea. But outside Europe, the hope of self-determination was not fulfilled in 1919, and the model of liberal democracy for which Wilson stood lost much of its persuasive power. The search then began in East Asia for alternative models. There too the year 1917 saw the start of a revolution of rising expectations. Far beyond Europe, people were looking for an end to the norms and institutions of the traditional order. This explains why the U.S. president came to be identified with messianic hopes. The results of the later peace talks and treaties would be measured against these high and wide-ranging expectations. The representatives of countries with a colonial or quasi-colonial status who went to Paris in 1919 to achieve objectives they associated with Wilson ended up bitterly disappointed.

The implicit formula "no contribution without representation" meant that conservative sections of the Indian colonial administration favored the least possible Indian participation in the war, whereas forces pushing for reforms sought the great possible involvement in order to secure a change in India's status. It was no accident that the country was represented by two Indian delegations at the Imperial Conference of 1917. When the pressure from London increased as the war continued, it became clear that a greater Indian contribution would not be possible without a clear pointer to "self-government" in the future. This idea that India would do more if Britain reached the heart of its people lay behind the Montagu declaration of August 1917 and its promise of "responsible government." But an explicit readiness to exercise repression was another way of handling Imperial diversity; the 1915 Defence of India Act sought to compensate for the dispatch of troops to Europe and the Near East by taking a harder line within India itself. This policy—which, without the promise of constitutional concessions, was also applied in Egypt—eventually led to massive unrest in both India and Egypt. Troop movements were also used to defuse military flashpoints: for example, when mutinies within the Indian 5th Light Infantry broke out in Singapore, leading to the deaths of several British officers, the regiment in question was immediately shipped to West Africa as a colonial police force. Such options were no longer available after the end of the war, and as the lack of fulfillment of wartime promises led to growing disenchantment, the illusion of a social truce within the Empire could no longer be sustained. A new period of conflict opened up. The words of the experienced Victorian proconsul Sir Harry Johnston, in a talk he gave in March 1919 to the African Society, also rang true for India and Egypt: the war marked the "beginning of revolt against the white man's supremacy."[196]

The link between wartime performance and self-determination was also apparent in other parts of the Empire. In Australia, voters rejected the introduction of conscription, but their decision can by no means be seen as a fundamental protest against the war; people there continued to support the country's participation alongside Great Britain.[197] As in Russia and Britain in 1916 and the United States in 1917, the introduction of conscription triggered huge conflicts in Canada by virtue of its multiethnic structure. In 1917, French Canadians engaged in large-scale resistance in Quebec, and seventeen Liberal Party deputies from the province voted against the measure. In Easter week 1917 and again in March 1918, there were bloody riots against implementation of the law, partly because the government had failed early on to include the francophone leader Wilfrid Laurier in the cabinet and to involve him in the decision-making. As the war dragged on, French Canadians found it much harder than those of British origin to identify with Britain's struggle alongside France. Francophone Canadians made up roughly 35 percent of the population, but a mere 5 percent of the troops in the Canadian Expeditionary Force. The clashes over the conscription issue reflected the generational, ethnic, and religious heterogeneity of Canadian society. Whereas relations between the largely Catholic Québécois and France had not been particularly strong for a number of generations, the census of 1911 had shown that every third male inhabitant between the ages of 18 and 45 was British-born. This explained the much greater identification that Canadians of British descent had with the old country. They considered that their casualties in the European war would benefit their claim to greater autonomy and nation-building, but in the end it was Canadians of British descent who fired on French Canadians in the conscription riots. As in the Irish case, religious and ethnic-national lines of conflict overlapped, and this would prolong the tension between the two communities well into the twentieth century. In addition there were the conflicts between old and new immigrants, and between town and country.[198] However, the scale of violence remained much lower there than in South Africa or Ireland, with no tradition of bloody conflict and no culture of violence. Because of the emergency regulations adopted in Canada, even conscription did not raise the rate of recruitment of soldiers above that of Australia (7 percent against 7.5 percent), which relied on voluntary service. Australians also suffered the highest casualty rates of all Imperial troops on the western front: 65 percent, in comparison with 59 percent for New Zealanders, 51 percent for British, and 49 percent for Canadians.[199]

The longer the war lasted, the less the diversity of the Empire could be compressed into a homogeneous "empire at war." This had at least three dimensions. Troops from the Dominions, India, and the colonies who were deployed on the various fronts attached importance to visible marks of their identity as members of the Australian Division, Canadian Corps, South African Brigade, Newfoundland, Rhodesian, or Gold Coast Regiment. But such titles did not mean that there was a straightforward causal relationship between the experience of war and nation-building. In many cases, a military communality developed for which the shared experience of "mateship" was often more formative than abstract invocations of a new dominion or even of the British Empire. A changed self-awareness, which soldiers took back to their home country, or which their home country used to process wartime experiences, was nevertheless unmistakable. It marked the Empire far beyond the end of the war.

Diversity among the societies of the Empire expressed itself first as a difference of interests, and then more and more often as a line of conflict defined by ethnicity or religion. It was not only that relations between Britain and various parts of the Empire became more conflictual; the societies themselves were becoming more complex. In the end, the Empire as a whole became more multifarious, especially as a result of Britain's new responsibilities in the Near East and Arabia following the breakup of the Ottoman Empire. Some suggested that the most surprising result of the war was British military supremacy in the whole Islamic world, from Constantinople to Singapore, but it could already be seen that this expansion contained the seeds of imperial overstretch. It highlighted the question of what kind of empire Britain could afford, in view of its demographic and economic weakening after 1918.[200]

But while relative weights shifted within the Empire, all the problems and ambiguities of the British conduct of the war were felt precisely in the Near East. This was the clearest example of the disparity between heterogeneous expectations of the postwar order and their outcomes of disappointment and fresh conflict, as well as of the presentation of the war as a global media event complete with heroic figures. The career of Thomas Edward Lawrence was possible only in the context of this media war and the space of the Arabian Peninsula. Promoted by the media as "Lawrence of Arabia," he already symbolized for his contemporaries a war so different, so much more exotic and colorful than the technological battlefields and anonymous slaughter on the European fronts. Only the stories of ace pilots and submarine commanders came close to his heroic narrative. The casting of Lawrence as a hero, prominent in the public eye, reflected the longing for an image of the war as personal adventure. In this border zone between reality and imagination, the individual turned into a larger-than-life figure, whose superhuman efforts and sacrifices proved his exceptional worth. Lawrence stood for an actual dimension of the war in the Near East, but he also epitomized the logic of the media war with its economy of public demand and media supply.

Born out of wedlock in 1888 in Wales, Lawrence had modest middle-class origins. He studied history at Oxford, developing an early interest in the Near East and the history of the Crusades, writing his final dissertation on the architecture of the crusader castles. His slight physique initially excluded him from military service. In 1910 he took part in archeological trips to the Hittite city of Carchemish on the Euphrates, also traveling to the Crusader castles in Syria, Lebanon, and Palestine. But the war interrupted his academic career. The former director of the Ashmolean Museum in Oxford, the archeologist David Hogarth, became head of the Arab Bureau in Cairo and of the British intelligence service branch that was of major importance for the wartime military and political development of the region.[201] Hogarth knew Lawrence from Oxford and, because of his linguistic skills and knowledge of the region, took him to Egypt. Lawrence's special expertise equipped him well to be used in the Near East, especially as the British army lacked sufficient local resources to back up its strategic objectives in the region.

In 1916, Lawrence, by now an army major, was instructed to support with British funds an uprising by the Emir of Mecca, Hussein ibn Ali. He managed to develop a personal relationship with the emir's son, Faisal, the later King

Faisal I of Iraq, whom he regarded as an integrative figure and even possible king of a united Arabia. But Lawrence's biography also brought out the contradictory nature of British objectives in the region: on the one hand, London tried to lure the Arab tribes into war against the Ottoman Empire with the promise of an independent state; on the other hand, the Sykes-Picot agreement of 1916 on the creation of British and French spheres of influence, and not least the promises made to Zionists of a Jewish homeland in Palestine, flew in the face of such a policy. Lawrence himself knew of these agreements, but he felt divided between loyalty to the British government and the struggle to gain the trust of his Arab contacts. His attitude to the Arabs shifted between criticism of British imperialism and skepticism toward the Arab tribes, which he did not consider ripe for independent statehood. He remained convinced that the Arabs still needed the leadership and guidance of a European power.[202] In November 1916, in describing the heterogeneous structure of Arab society, he wrote that the patriotism of the sharifs was worlds apart from the thinking of individual tribes: "Arab feeling in the Hejaz runs from complete patriotism amongst the Sherifs down to racial fanaticism in the ignorant. One thing of which the tribes are convinced is that they have made an Arab government, and consequently that each of them is it. The towns are sighing for the contented obstructionist inactivity of the Ottoman government, or for the ordered quiet of our own rule; the tribes know they are independent, and mean to enjoy their independence. This will not entail anarchy, since the family tie and the system of tribal responsibility will be tightened, but it will entail the practical disappearance or negation of central power in internal affairs."[203]

Lawrence's close personal contacts inspired a tendency for him to "go native": he partly took on the Bedouin lifestyle and distanced himself from Britain's traditional military culture. He could not give orders to his Arab partners, but played the role of moderator, acting as an interlocutor for local leaders, above all Faisal, and utilizing the considerable leeway this gave him. But it was Faisal more than Lawrence who actually probed the intricate system of relations and arrived at a common course of action among the often-discordant tribes.[204]

After the war, Lawrence worked for a short time as a Near East advisor to the British government, and at the Paris peace conference he and Faisal tried to give effect to the promise of Arab independence. But he could not prevail against the professional diplomats. He became more and more of an outsider at the Colonial Office and eventually left the diplomatic service. The eccentric side of his personality then came increasingly to the fore, and between 1922 and 1929, using a false name, he served again in the British army as an ordinary soldier. Finally, in May 1935, he lost his life in a motorcycle accident.[205]

In the southern Mediterranean and the Near East, following the disaster at Gallipoli, British strategy was essentially to forge an alliance with Arab tribes against the Ottoman Empire. Like the German generals and diplomats in Russia, the British were relying on a nexus of war and revolt.[206] The special geographical conditions of the Arabian Peninsula were an additional factor, since the British military saw this desert region, where the Ottoman army had great difficulty securing single-track supply lines, as ideal terrain for asymmetric guerrilla warfare. On the other hand, the harsh conditions posed a huge challenge, and the Arab tribes did not have any regular troops of their own. Organized as they were on a tribal basis, with often considerable tensions among themselves, the Bedouins stood no chance against an organized army complete with machine guns and artillery. But they did have special local knowledge and experience of the extreme climate, which became a decisive factor in the wide-open spaces of the desert. In this light, it was decided to concentrate on surprise attacks on Ottoman supply convoys, and indeed the real successes came in individual operations against the Hejaz railroad. The attacks tied up large numbers of Ottoman troops who could have been used against the British in other sections of the front. Lawrence himself played a part in this success—but the hyped-up postwar media image of him as a war hero in no way corresponded to his limited importance. During the war itself, he attracted little attention on either the Ottoman or the German side.[207]

A key event in the media legend was the attack on Aqaba from the land side on July 6, 1917, with a force of more than 2,000 men on camelback.[208] The city had strategic significance for the Ottoman army as its last remaining port on the Red Sea. Lawrence later idealized his own role in the operation in his bestseller *Seven Pillars of Wisdom*, first published in 1922. But contrary to his account, the attack was by no means of decisive military significance—nor, for that matter, should the effects of the Arab guerrilla war in general

The exotic hero of imperial war: Thomas Edward Lawrence

be overestimated. All the same, the capture of Aqaba did reflect the British strategy of employing varied means and tactics to keep up the pressure on the Ottoman army.

The really crucial element in the image of Lawrence that has come down to us is not his impact on the British campaign in the Near East, but rather the media mechanisms brought into play to reconstruct events and to attribute special personal qualities to him in response to the public expectations of the time. It was thus a rather fortuitous compilation that stood Lawrence in such good stead. The American journalist Lowell Thomas, who with his cameraman Harry Chase traveled first to Europe and then the Near East to report on the war, met Lawrence in late February 1918 in Jerusalem and later also in Aqaba. On both occasions a number of photos were taken of Lawrence in traditional Arab costume. Articles on the Arab revolt reached the American public along with these pictures, arousing great interest in Spring 1918. On March 2, 1918, Lowell Thomas gave an illustrated lecture in New York—the first of his so-called travelogs, which soon became regular shows with their own accompanying program. It was only this media celebration of the exotic war hero—in articles, pictures, and stage productions—that launched the real story of Lawrence's historical impact. It was not the unfathomable slaughter on the western fronts, but a highly individual adventurer, a cross-border hero straddling East and West, who occupied center stage and spoke to the imagination and fellow feeling of the public, mingling oriental stereotypes with mythical figures such as Achilles, Siegfried, or El Cid. This narrative continuum explains the fascination and suggestive quality of Lawrence of Arabia.[209] In a sense, the real person of Thomas Edward Lawrence was sacrificed to a media construct. This fueled an expectation on his part that his imagined position would translate into real political influence—an expectation that ended in disappointment at the Paris peace conference and in the British colonial service. After 1918 Lawrence fit less and less the reality of the time; his life became a succession of failed attempts to connect with his role.

Offensive operations by British troops were much more important that the Arab revolt and the attacks organized by Faisal and Lawrence. From June 1917, under the command of Field Marshal Edmund Allenby, the troops struck out from Egypt against Ottoman-held Sinai and Palestine. There, in contrast to the western front, no positional warfare ever developed; what counted was mobility. Large cavalry units once again entered the picture, sometimes sustaining considerable casualties. On December 9, 1917, Allenby marched into Jerusalem—a symbolic act recognizing the first tangible Allied victory occurring at the same time as the victory of the Central Powers over Russia. It also had a significance in political history, reminiscent of the Christian Crusades but also indicative of the weight of the British Empire. It boosted Lloyd George's confidence in the British military leadership.[210] Troops from New Zealand and India also took part in the attack on Amman, while Australian forces advanced across the Jordan River. Church bells rang out in Britain to mark the entry into Jerusalem—the first such occasion in the war.

The war in the Near East continued to be marked by its extreme geographical and climatic conditions, which made supply lines and logistical infrastructures decisive to the outcome. In this respect, it prefigured the experiences of German and British forces in the Second World War. The need to provide advancing troops with sufficient quantities of drinking water entailed the building of railroads and pipelines across the Sinai Peninsula. Still, in November 1917, supply problems forced the British to pull back despite the collapse of Turkish lines after the third battle of Gaza.[211] In these battles, the asymmetry of weaponry was a telling factor: a small number of aircraft operating against dense cavalry formations inflicted heavy losses in men and animals.[212]

A conflict in the British Imperial hierarchy intensified in the shadow of war. To maintain the logistical infrastructure, officers had to rely on tens of thousands of Egyptian forced laborers. Deployed behind the front, they were often subjected to draconian punishment that highlighted the racist prejudices in the British army. These tensions kept increasing from 1917 on and formed part of the background to the revolts against British colonial rule after the formal end of the war.[213] On November 9, 1917, as British forces advanced in Palestine and Arab leaders thought they could rely on British support for an independent state, the British government issued the Balfour Declaration. This had been preceded by difficult negotiations between the British foreign minister, James Balfour, and the British Zionist leader Chaim Weizmann. London declared its readiness to support the establishment of a national homeland for the Jewish people in Palestine. Although the rights of non-Jewish inhabitants were supposed to be protected, the formulations in the text remained vague on this point.[214]

The original version "a national home for the Jewish race" was altered to the more neutral "for the Jewish people."[215] The only Jewish minister in the British government, Edwin Montagu, criticized the document, fearing that it would provoke anti-Semitic reactions, especially as the war had largely discredited internationalist ideas and movements. The motives of the Zionists and the British were very different: while Weizmann pursued the Zionist objectives set out in the Basel program of 1897, the British government drew on a mixture of Christian philo-Semitic themes and anti-Semitic stereotypes. For the government in London openly built into its calculations the international weight of Jewry—in particular, the supposed power of Jews in the United States, which it hoped to mobilize against the Central Powers.[216] Once again, the British strategy to hasten the end of the war by mobilizing Allies around the world and instrumentalizing political influence had asserted itself. In practice, however, expectations were aroused that led to long-term conflict in the region—not least as a result of unclear formulations and contradictory signals.

In principle, the founding of a Jewish legion three months before issuance of the Balfour Declaration was part of this same context in the Near East. After the capture of Jerusalem in December 1917, the British military leadership began to transfer many troops to the embattled western front, where a major German offensive was expected the next spring. To continue the war against the retreating Ottoman forces, the British now fielded perhaps the most multiethnic army of the war, consisting of troops from Armenia, Burma, Algeria, Australia, New Zealand, India, South Africa, Italy, France, Singapore, Hong Kong, the West Indies, and Egypt—plus three Jewish battalions within the British Royal Fusiliers, the first purely Jewish combat units for 2,000 years. The British government had given non-naturalized Russian Jews a choice between joining the army and being repatriated to Russia. More soldiers were recruited from Palestine itself, but also from cities with a large Jewish community such as New York, Montreal, and Buenos Aires. The volunteers from the United States and Palestine included many future Israeli politicians, such as two heads of state, David Ben-Gurion and Yitzhak Ben-Zvi. Among the symbols of the Jewish battalion were the British and Zionist flags and the Star of David worn on uniforms. Soldiers received kosher food and made colloquial use of Yiddish. Although the units had limited military significance, their symbolic weight was enormous: they stood for the liberation of biblical lands from Ottoman rule. Like the Polish and Czech legions, they embodied the claim to political independence and defensive preparedness, although in practice the contradictory nature of British policy was evident too. After the victory over the Ottoman army, the importance of the Jewish legions was downplayed, and the press was even forbidden to report news about them to avoid provoking the Arabs. Considerable intra-Jewish tensions also came to light: North American Jews who wished to settle in Palestine after their wartime experiences there were rejected by the Zionists, who insisted on communication in Hebrew and a variant of agrarian communitarianism with which city-dwelling American Jews were unable to identify. At any event, in contrast to the patriotic national legions in east central Europe, the Jewish legions did not become a formative part of the Zionist self-image.[217]

7. SOCIAL POLARIZATION AND POLITICAL EROSION
The Limits of Consensus in the Home Societies

The official French image of the war—in newspapers and illustrated magazines, but also in letters from the front in which soldiers kept the censorship in mind—diverged more and more from the everyday reality. A mood of uncertainty and pessimism spread across the country in response to the heavy casualties of the battles of 1916 and the unpredictability of the efforts that would be required in the new year. On January 16, 1917, the French official Michel Corday noted that the press did not show the real France: "The almost total darkness that exists indoors because of the restrictions on lighting, or the gloomy, dim streets where the fruit merchants are illuminated by candles, or the dustbins that remain unemptied on the pavement until three in the afternoon because of a shortage of manpower, or the queues of anything up to three thousand people waiting outside the large grocery stores to get their sugar ration. Nor—to look at the other side the coin—will it show the huge numbers filling the restaurants, tea rooms, theaters, variety shows, and cinemas to bursting point."[218] The streets in Paris seemed all the more unreal to him because of the army mutinies. In June 1917 Corday observed "prostitutes with hats the size of parasols, knee-length skirts, bosoms bared, diaphanous stockings and made-up faces; young officers with unbuttoned collars and magnificent medal ribbons; Allied soldiers—muscular British, inoffensive Belgians, unfortunate Portuguese, Russians with impressive marching boots." But soldiers with fine medals on their chest also begged on the streets, and Corday was struck by the flourishing black markets and the everyday criminality. Chefs at top restaurants took on war veterans and invalids, as a way of displaying their patriotism.[219]

The French crisis of 1917 was not just a question of mutinies on the western front; in May and June there were also major waves of strikes. Although food supply was not as great a problem as in Germany, Austria-Hungary, or eastern and southeastern Europe, inflation was eating away at people's lives in 1917. Government funding of the war drove France to become ever more dependent on American loans, and a social-political credibility crisis began to call into question the *union sacrée* in its existing form.

The strikes breached the taboo on labor struggles for the duration of the war. But they did not simply reflect class conflicts; they were also marked by the change in gender roles and wartime perceptions of racial difference. In France, as in all the belligerent countries, women had a special importance. Unlike skilled workers who were sent back from the front to the factories, they were not liable to conscription and did not have to fear that the authorities would ship them off to the front as punishment for any revolt. The protests initially broke out in the textile industry, which was not directly important to the war effort; it employed large numbers of women as seamstresses or *midinettes*. Like the mutinous soldiers, the striking seamstresses set their sights not on political or social revolution, but on concrete improvements to their working and living conditions, consciously linking this issue to the idea of wartime service for the nation. Some 10,000 women in the industrial centers marched beneath the tricolor to emphasize their patriotic commitment. Their demands were for wage increases to compensate at least in part for the runaway inflation, and the introduction of a *semaine anglaise* that would leave Saturday afternoon free. Many women protested at the fact that they were paid less than men for the same work. Most strikingly, they also used the negative image of the *embusqué* or shirker to expose male foremen and supervisors and to lend weight to their demands. By pointing up their men's patriotic sacrifice at the front, they broadened the argument and developed a language of their own to articulate their interests. The demand for an end to the war also featured prominently in the strike wave, but like the mutinous soldiers, the female strikers did not abandon the consensus on national defense as such; their aim was not peace at any price, but a fair sharing of burdens on the road to a worthy peace. They backed up this demand, too, with references to the brave struggle of the *poilus* at the front, which obliged them to combat corruption and war profiteering and to track down *embusqués* in the workplace.

The massive use of colonial auxiliaries posed a particular problem in France. Strikers also directed their protests against them in Summer 1917, fearing that employers might use foreign workers to lower wages or to make French workers redundant, so that those workers would then have to reckon with the possibility of being sent to the front. In fact, labor migration did reach unprecedented proportions during the war: in addition to 600,000 soldiers, 220,000 workers came from the French colonies and China. This wartime phenomenon would extend far into the twentieth century and result in a change of perspective: the movement of French workers and products to the colonies was no longer the main focus, being replaced by the encounter of people from the colonies with French society.[220]

The resulting tensions were an important part of the background to the labor struggles of 1917 and thereafter. Violent protests were directed at workers from the colonies, and race became a key factor alongside class and gender. When the war ended in late 1918, the government was at pains to head off conflict by repatriating colonial workers as speedily as possible, especially as the demobilization of hundreds of thousands of French soldiers seemed imminent. Violent demonstrations took place in Paris and other major cities, in transport hubs and ports such as Marseilles, and there were repeated roundups of workers who were lying low to avoid being sent back to the colonies or China.

In May and June the strikes spread from the textile industry to metallurgical and munitions plants in the Paris region. Of 45,000 strikers, 75 percent were women—a figure that, considering that only 30 percent of the total workforce in the metal industry were women, underlines the extent of their mobilization. It also implies a special motivation on their part in the face of difficult living and working conditions, as well as an increased sense of themselves as workers and family breadwinners.[221] After some modest concessions and wage increases, the sanctions that followed were quite mild: sackings and arrests were the exception. Most of the women returned to their jobs, because none wanted to obstruct war-related production or to face accusations that they were endangering their own sons, brothers, or husband at the front. Further measures would be taken only after the end of the war. In Spring and Summer 1917, neither mutinies nor strikes crossed the threshold to revolution; protest and resistance did not call into question the basic consensus in favor of war against the German aggressor. What lay behind the struggle for fairer conditions was instead a political tradition of appealing to the nation and republican equality at moments of crisis— this did not undermine the political system, but upheld its core values and principles. By acting as a safety valve, the protests may therefore be said to have had a stabilizing effect.

This configuration reappeared in late 1917 and 1918 within the most radical sections of the strike movement. The authorities feared that these elements would aim at a political-social revolution in line with the model of the Bolshevik revolution in Russia. The Comité de défense syndicaliste, formed in late 1917 as a revolutionary organization, sought not only to organize a new strike movement but also to gain popular support for it by raising the demand for an immediate peace. In late May 1918, when the danger from the German offensive was at its greatest, the committee called on workers to strike in the main centers of the arms industry in the Loire basin and the Paris region. Many workers were prepared to end the war as swiftly as possible to give more weight to their demands, but the majority returned to work quite soon. Although the unity for national defense was becoming more fragile, and although the political character of the *union sacrée* had changed in 1917, the consensus did not break apart entirely. Even in the final months of the war, there was not a majority in favor of an uncompromising search for peace out of antipatriotic or revolutionary convictions—although France did repeatedly stand on the brink of collapse.[222]

Summer 1917 led to a political turnaround. In a speech in parliament lasting several hours, on July 22, 1917, Georges Clemenceau criticized the government for its lack of resolve to fight the war to the end; he accused Interior Minister Louis Malvy of not taking strong enough action to combat pacifism in the country. Indeed, Clemenceau explicitly charged the government with a lack of patriotism, presenting himself as the embodiment of the national will to achieve victory under all circumstances. Skillfully directing his fire at the secret committees of the Chamber of Deputies and the Senate, he emphasized how important it was that parliament should not become cut off from public opinion.[223] This was to stand by the core values of the republic. Despite the crisis and the arrest of isolated political opponents, the political order of the Third Republic survived, and parliamentary control of the army was not questioned. But at the end of 1917, the decision in principle to continue the war depended less on the new Clemenceau government formed on November 16 than on the soldiers returning to the front and the workers ensuring production in the factories.[224] What had changed was the representation of the political will to end the war victoriously. On November 20, in his first speech on taking office, Clemenceau gave expression to this will by subordinating everything to the link between the homeland and the soldiers fighting as the core of the nation: "One simple duty: to stand by the soldiers, to live, to suffer, to fight with them. To give up everything that does not belong to the *patrie.*" At the same time, he stressed that the strength of France's soul at the front and at home made everyone soldiers: the whole nation were *poilus,* so to speak. This was Clemenceau's response to the experiences of 1917: "Here the strength of the French spirit shows itself. What sets it to work and what leads it to wage war. Those silent factory soldiers deaf to bad proposals, those elderly farmers bent over their fields, those powerful women plowing the soil, those children who help out even though they are particularly weak: they too are our *poilus.* And later, when they think of this great work, they will be able say together with the men from the trenches: I was there." In the end, Clemenceau demanded absolute loyalty and absolute commitment to the war. The war against the Germans had its counterpart in the war against all defeatist enemies inside the country: "No more pacifist campaigns, no more German intrigues. Neither treason, nor semi-treason: the war. Nothing but the war."[225]

Clemenceau went on to become a premier of a new type, who, in the words of the British ambassador, operated as a super-minister combining multiple responsibilities and operating virtually as a one-man government.[226] His investiture was accompanied with a number of symbolic measures against alleged defeatism and treason. The press squeezed all it could out of the arrest, trial, and execution of Mata Hari as a German spy. The dancer, with the end of her career in sight, had tried to compensate for it by developing contacts with diplomats and military men. The scale of her alleged betrayal of secrets was modest, but the trial and sentence served as a demonstration of France's resolve to hunt down traitors and bring them to justice whatever their gender or reputation. The campaign against internal enemies reflected the credibility crisis that shook the country in 1917.[227]

The long-term consequences for French society of the mutinies and strike wave can hardly be overstated. They ratcheted up the climate of suspicion against supposed defeatists, pacifists, and aliens—not least people of German origin. The military leadership went out of its way to emphasize the political influences coming from society at home, so that its own image of itself would not be endangered. The authorities developed an outright obsession that would persist long after 1918: internal security; monitoring of suspects; and fear of spies, agents, and traitors overshadowed all other issues. Right into the 1930s, French intelligence would concern itself primarily with threats to national security from inside France, neglecting those associated with the rise of fascism and National Socialism. A fixation on frontier security also marked postwar defensive doctrines: while the search for internal enemies was ubiquitous, the French military dug in on the border with Germany, aiming to prevent any questioning of the army's loyalty such as that which developed in 1917 after failed offensives and high casualty rates. The Maginot Line—a hugely expensive system of fortifications set in concrete along the German frontier—ranked alongside intelligence activity inside the country as a byword for the strategic disorientation in postwar France.[228]

In wartime Britain, the enemy-images conveyed by official propaganda were often linked to actual experiences of people on the home front. Coastal shelling, together with the presence of thousands of Belgian refugees and intensive German air raids in 1917–1918, shaped the way in which the enemy was perceived. The reporting of German atrocities could also link up with popular models from the prewar period, such as the anti-German campaigns in the *Daily Mail*, owned by the press magnate Lord Northcliffe.[229]

The mechanisms of social inclusion and exclusion came to a head in relation to Jews of Russian origin, who in June and September 1917 were the targets of major rioting in Leeds and London, where many workers accused them of evading military service. On March 9, 1918, the *Morning Post* wrote of the background to the violence in London's East End: "British East Enders are soldiers and workers. The alien Jew East Enders are dealers and shirkers."[230]

After the German introduction of unrestricted submarine warfare, the fall in imports began to have an effect on British society. A strike wave occurred there too. The social and political fallout brought the question of burden sharing once more to the fore, but as in France there was no question of an antiwar movement or even a revolutionary movement with mass support. The readiness in principle to continue the war remained at a high level.[231] German submarines carried out some spectacular sinkings, and the British public reacted with alarm; the traditional strategic advantage of the island nation seemed to be in danger. After the Admiralty adjusted to the danger, however, the navy began to form convoys and sent out special ships to accompany and protect them.[232] This meant that the volume of imports was not as high as before, but more important, it considerably reduced the impact of the U-boat campaign. People in Britain did begin to feel the pinch, but the political and military leadership managed to head off a crisis of credibility that might have led to a politicized antiwar movement. The country was spared the full-scale bread rationing that had for some time been part of everyday life for millions of women and children in Germany and Austria-Hungary.

This objective situation needs to be distinguished from subjective perceptions, however. In the fall and winter of 1917–1918, the general mood in Britain took a sharp turn for the worse, as the accumulation of bad news crystallized into deeper doubts that a victorious end to the war was possible. From late 1916 the government had had to admit its financial dependence on the United States, and since spring the situation of the French army had considerably increased the burden on the British contingent on the western front. Haig's strategy of frontal attacks had led to high casualties with no decisive breakthrough; after the setback of the third battle of Flanders the political leadership under Lloyd George grew distrustful of Haig, and a continuation of his approach on the western front seemed to be ruled out.[233] Meanwhile, after the disaster at Caporetto, only a massive British and French intervention was able to prevent an Italian defeat in the Alpine war. In Russia, the Bolshevik revolution made it likely that the country would pull out of the war, solving the Germans' "two front" problem and freeing them for a major offensive in western Europe. But the dramatic events in Petrograd also had another dimension for the British: they increased their fear that war-weary industrial workers at home might link up with radical political movements, in line with the model of the Soviets. Internal threats were also overlapping with external ones, as German Gotha bombers carried out daily raids on London, killing more than 400 civilians and injuring another thousand.[234] From February 1918, sugar, margarine, and meat had to be rationed.

A growing sense that the British population could not be assured of adequate supplies in the long term led to a new wave of government measures, whose consequences, in the eyes of many, increased social inequality. Price guarantees, and in some cases extensive exemption from military service, were of benefit mainly to farmers; they gave a boost to British agriculture, which was as profitable as at any time before. Tenant farmers and their sons were exempt from income taxes and newly introduced taxes on war profits. This relative improvement, due largely to fears that the food supply would break down, fueled new conflicts within British society over "shirkers" and war "profiteers."

Another reason for the greater intensity of the debate on burden sharing was the worsening situation in the industrial centers. In many parts of Britain, it was no longer possible to plug labor shortages by employing more women, children, and prisoners of war. Not by chance, the strike wave of 1917 therefore began with protests by foremen in the metal and engineering industries against government/union agreements, particularly the Munitions of War Act, which had limited the freedom of workers to change jobs.[235] The strikers saw the labor shortages and the hiring of unskilled workers as a threat to their established positions and rights. The events in Russia also resonated with at least some of the strikers, who, for example, linked their demands on employers to distinctly political demands, such as the negotiated peace without annexations or reparations championed by the Bolsheviks. Although this politicization remained limited, it appeared to confirm the fears of the government, giving rise to an ideological enemy-image and a vehement anti-Bolshevism that would also express itself in British intervention in the Russian civil war.

While skilled workers fought against the loss of traditional rights, at least half of the strikes in 1917 were waged by unskilled workers. As in France, women and non-unionized workers played an important, though on the whole less clearly articulated, role in the strike movement. Their demands centered on local problems such as working conditions, workweeks sometimes as long as 60 hours, dangers to health, food shortages, and the rising price of food and housing. They often beefed up their demands with references to "shirkers" and "profiteers," but they were not a political movement with wider objectives and an ideological program. Nor can one speak of a unified workers' movement: the gap widened between shop stewards or skilled workers and unskilled workers.[236] The reaction of the authorities was symptomatic: a mixture of sanctions and concessions made it clear how seriously they took the strikes and how much they feared a possible extension and radicalization against the background of revolution in Russia. Individual ringleaders were isolated and arrested, while the propaganda of the National War Aims Committee was stepped up and given a social inflection. Government food subsidies were introduced, and arbitration boards were set up in workplaces to decide on bonus payments for families struggling to meet higher rents and food prices.[237]

The strikes did not reach the proportions seen in France, Germany, or Austria-Hungary, not to speak of Russia. Mostly brief and local, they did not seriously interfere with war-related production, and on the whole they were less militant than those of the period before the war. In Britain, as in France, the strike movement did not translate into a radicalized peace movement—indeed, discontent with working and living conditions was combined with a vociferous patriotism. To speak of serving the nation in the trenches or on the factory floor was to lend extra credibility to one's own position in contrast to that of "profiteers" and "shirkers." It was no accident that war loan subscriptions were particularly high in major strike centers such as Glasgow. The only exception was South Wales, where the origins of social conflict went back further and did not lose their force during the war.[238]

New kinds of class tensions also appeared in British society in 1917—particularly in the relationship between industrial workers (especially in war-related sectors) and white-collar employees. Rumors of colossal wages for munitions workers or the supposed selling of pianos to workers may have been exaggerated, but the tendencies at work were clear. By early 1918, the wages of unskilled workers had reached the level of office employees, and many members of the "middle classes" felt indignant that they were being made to pay the highest economic and personal price for the war. Unlike many farmers and workers, they had virtually no way of escaping military service, while their families had to bear additional burdens in the form of war taxes and higher rents in the cities. Nor could they fall back on growing their own food to escape the pressures of the black market, and unlike essential workers in industry they could not hope for bonuses or food subsidies.[239]

Targeting what they saw as privileged factory workers, whom they accused of ingratitude or lack of patriotism far from the dangers of the front, large sections of the old middle classes moved increasingly rightward and embraced an aggressive nationalism. In the final phase of the war, they called stridently for radical measures to be taken against aliens and alleged spies, blurring the boundaries between non-naturalized individuals and men and women who had long held British citizenship.

At the end of 1917, after the costly months of the three Flanders battles, Britain was nearing the end of its tether. Large sections of the public, but also of the political leadership, placed all their hopes on America's entry into the war and the relief it would bring to the western front. Long dependent on the United States to finance the war, the British were forced by the German offensives that began in Spring 1918 to mobilize their last reserves. Conscription was tightened up yet again, as companies faced increased pressure to send men off to fight, and the army began to recruit female volunteers to release men for service at the front. But it remained a controversial and politically delicate issue. In the Dominions, conscription either had to be abandoned or was implemented only at the cost of massive conflict in society. Australia rejected it twice in referendums, while in Canada the enforcement campaign led to wrenching tensions between anglophone and francophone parts of the country. In Ireland, too, where the go-ahead was given only after much hesitation, conscription became synonymous with the British war state and its coercive regime. This weakened the position of the Irish Parliamentary Party and its strategy of parliamentary and constitutional nation-building, which had gained some ground again since the Easter Rising in 1916; the main beneficiary was the more radical Sinn Féin, and in late 1917 and 1918 all the signs pointed to escalation and civil war.[240]

In Italy, the shock of Caporetto came toward the end of a year in which stress and exhaustion had increasingly coalesced into protests. Huge tensions and conflicts also emerged within Italian society, which had been divided since 1915 over entry and then continued involvement in the war. In Winter 1916–1917 food shortages had led to protests not only in the expanding arms industries but also in rural areas. These grew more serious in Summer 1917, when news of events in Russia reached Italy. While many farmers in the south attacked figures of authority and burned their call-up papers, workers destroyed state buildings in the towns and cities. In May there was serious unrest in Lombardy in particular, where men were subjected to draconian military law, and women made up more than 60 percent of the demonstrators. The most militant labor organizations were dissolved, and their officials, together with many workers, were sent to the front or to penal colonies.[241]

After the defeat at Caporetto, more and more parts of the north of Italy became war zones under de facto military control.[242] A new and strongly patriotic mobilization began to take shape, helping to ensure that the conflicts could be presented as a defensive war against a foreign aggressor. With the ending of offensive operations, the casualty figures declined, and army morale noticeably improved. On the home front, something like a political consensus, stretching even to the reform wing of the Socialists, developed for the first time around defense of the fatherland.[243]

In Germany, the 15-year-old schoolgirl Elfriede Kuhr wrote in her diary in September 1917 that the war had become a routine state of affairs that shaped everything in people's lives. The difference between war and peace seemed to grow fuzzy in the fourth year. The war "had become a kind of normal condition. We can hardly remember what peace was like. We scarcely think of the war any more."[244] This dominant presence of the war in home society grew stronger in Winter 1916–1917, when food supplies in Germany and Austria-Hungary deteriorated further as a result of the British blockade. Between February 5–18, and from February 26 to April 1, 1917, not even potatoes were available in the Neukölln district of Berlin—only cookies and rutabagas, which became a staple for months and gave their name to the "turnip winter," could be found. But the many ways of preparing rutabagas that the authorities recommended—as a pudding, in balls, in soups, stews, and salads, and as a puree or jelly—and the sarcastic description of them as "Prussian pineapples" did not make the people's diet more nourishing or appealing: just as onions or apples could not disguise the smell of the rancid fat in which they were fried, the official appeals to keep trying rutabagas became less and less persuasive.[245] Substitute foods were everywhere—and each new *Ersatz* developed by the chemical industry or the military authorities intensified the sense of shortage. In 1917, in the territory of the German Reich, there were no fewer than 837 types of substitute sausage, more than 1,000 stock cubes, 511 substitutes for coffee, and more than 6,000 for lemonade, fruit juice, beer, and wine.[246]

The gap grew ever wider between official press releases and nutrition advice, on the one hand, and people's daily experience in food stores, on the other. On February 18, 1917, at the height of the turnip winter, Interior State Secretary Helfferich oozed confidence as he emphasized at a session of the German Agricultural Council the decisive importance of the struggle against the British blockade: "German agriculture will fight the struggle against British farming in the right spirit, full of energy and resolute self-sacrifice, for, together with our industry, our army, and our navy, it will stake the latest and best on the great decision. If everyone does their duty in full . . . we shall make 1917 the year that changed the world."[247] In the same month, however, the war nutrition bureau declared in a handout: "Each baby is entitled to 500 grams of oatflakes a month, or roughly 17 grams a day, which is just enough. For infants in the second half-year of their lives, who should also have some pap, oats do not suffice. Perhaps some semolina or pearl barley will have been allocated on their food cards, or they will be given rusk mash or if necessary some mashed potato."[248]

The link between shortages and price inflation can be seen in an example from Munich. There meat consumption fell from 68 kilos a year per capita before the war to 21 kilos in 1917 and a mere 14 kilos in 1918. In November 1916, the weekly ration for adults was still 62.5 grams of fat. The Bavarian Price Monitoring Bureau then documented price increases. Where restrictions were in place, these were at first quite small: the price of a rye loaf in 1917 was 25 percent higher, and in 1918 50 per cent higher, than in 1914; quark cost 200 percent more in 1918, chicory coffee 71 percent more in 1917 and 140 percent more in 1918. But where there were no controls, process rocketed up: a pair of trousers cost 828 percent more in 1918 than in 1914, ladies' wear 1,233 percent more, and a cigarette 300 percent more. The growing

The criminalization of daily life: hunger revolts in Berlin, 1917

"hunger gap" between town and country brought thousands of people every weekend to the countryside around Munich, where they could trade objects of value for food. The authorities were more and more often unable to cope with the situation. How, for example, were 200,000 herrings to be distributed among 600,000 people living in 219,000 families?[249]

Another symptom of the worsening situation was the attempt to make shortages a patriotic equivalent of life at the front. Comparing the daily struggle of women for food to men's privations and achievements, the *Allgemeiner Wegweiser für jede Familie* wrote on April 7, 1917, "Three-quarters of an hour standing for flour doesn't do any harm. They stand in the trench much longer. . . . Saleswomen are now unbearably snooty with people stranded in the list of customers—our poor prisoners will also not find it easy to stand nearly two hours for cheese—it's a lot better than having the enemy stand in our country!"[250]

Against this background, the changes in the public mood constantly noted in police reports increased the pressure on the government and parliament. On March 28, 1917, in a letter to the *Frankfurter Zeitung*, Max Weber addressed the question of democratic participation: "The army that fought the battles should also have the main say in the postwar rebuilding of the fatherland"—although the editors left out his additional reference to "the army of labor, which makes it possible for the troops to fight out there."[251] For all the problems of everyday life, however, the situation in Russia supported more optimistic assessments, while the U.S. entry into the war made no great impression. On April 6, Karl Hampe noted in his diary that "militarily Russia [was] at the end of its tether" and that "soldiers there [were] blowing up munition dumps." The news from the Baltics was that the Allies in Paris and London regarded "Russia as a bankrupt estate": "If we in the east finally get some breathing space, the whole of the west, even with America, will have nothing on us." The next day, Hampe observed, "Remarkably, the entry of the United States (and Cuba!) into the war still cuts no ice. It may be wrong, but you feel that the war will be decided before America comes crashing in." In the very next sentence, Hampe moved on to his hopes in the domestic political effects of the current situation: "Something important is about to happen on the Prussian suffrage issue."[252]

On April 7, 1917, the Kaiser issued a proclamation promising reform of the Prussian three-class voting system. In part, this was a response to Allied propaganda and the Russian February Revolution: the political and military leaders of the Central Powers had to fear that—at least with the U.S. entry into the war—the monarchies in Germany and Austria-Hungary would come under ever greater pressure to justify their rule. Yet what the Kaiser actually said was extremely vague: Wilhelm held out the prospect of a direct and secret, but not an equal, ballot.[253] The Kaiser's Easter message had two important functions. On the one hand, it reflected the growing pressure on the monarchy and government to recognize the burdens of war on soldiers and workers, underlining the link between conscription and suffrage rights, between sacrifice on the battlefield and claims to political participation. Greater political equality, it could now be seen, was being considered not as a universally valid human and civil right, but as a reward for theoretically equal sacrifice in the war. On the other hand, the message highlighted the defensive position of the civilian government of the German Reich. The concessions in prospect were limited, but they aroused higher—and other—expectations and demands than the alternative models identified with Lenin in the East and Wilson in the West had done even before Spring 1917. German workers and their representatives in parliament and the trade unions reacted to the message with disappointment. This too made it clear that the political situation was becoming more polarized.

The scale of internal conflict and of the credibility crisis became even more apparent with the fall of the chancellor in July 1917. They reflected overlapping internal and external tensions, as the exhaustion of Germany's Austro-Hungarian ally had become as visible as the problems on the home front. Police reports highlighted the discontent among industrial workers, which the Kaiser's Easter message failed to contain and which caused the government and OHL to fear that the continuation of the war might put them in danger at a particularly critical moment. In view of these developments, SPD Reichstag deputies demanded on June 27 that the government should renounce all expansionist war aims and proceed with a consistent reform of the Prussian voting system based on equal suffrage. In early July, important figures in the SPD and the Catholic Center—most notably, Friedrich Ebert and Matthias Erzberger—criticized the decision to resume unrestricted submarine warfare, on the grounds that those responsible for it had criminally underestimated the danger of an American entry into the war.

On July 6, 1917, an Interparty Committee was formed from the ranks of the SPD, the Left Liberals and National Liberals, and the Catholic Center. (In Spring 1917, the division within the Left had hardened with the formal separation of the USPD [Independent Social Democratic Party of Germany], whose deputies had been excluded in 1916 and had initially organized themselves as a Social Democratic Working Group [SAG].) The establishment of the Interparty Committee, in the midst of war and a deepening credibility crisis of the monarchy, marked a political watershed. A transition from a constitutional to a parliamentary monarchy appeared on the horizon, reflecting debates in parliament and the gradual development of a parliamentary-democratic form of government with fixed majorities. Parliamentarization of the monarchy, which had not been achieved by 1914, was now advancing again because of the ever more pressing problems of the war. It thus did not begin with the reforms of October 1918, which made the chancellor formally dependent on the confidence of the Reichstag. Instead, the coalition involved in the Interparty Committee became the parliamentary force underpinning the constitutional changes. The crisis of 1917 that led to the removal of the chancellor, together with the tentative attempts to establish a parliamentary form of government, pointed ahead to the Weimar constitution, which would have been unthinkable without this preliminary effort. The problem, therefore, was not the impetus coming from within parliament, but the fact that the burdens of the war complicated the parliamentarization of the monarchy.[254]

Although Bethmann Hollweg had long fought against unrestricted submarine warfare, and although on July 9, at a session of the Privy Council, he had opposed the Kaiser and supported the introduction of equal suffrage in Prussia (which came into effect on July 11), he was still losing political support. This was mainly due to the attitude of the OHL, where Hindenburg and Ludendorff held it against him that he had backed a parliamentary motion in favor of peace. They called for Wilhelm II to dismiss him—since in the existing constitutional monarchy, parliament could not force the chancellor to resign through a vote of no confidence; only the Kaiser could decide his political fate. On July 13 Wilhelm then removed Bethmann Hollweg—who until Summer 1917 had managed to have a moderating effect on Imperial policies—and appointed the hitherto largely unknown Georg Michaelis to replace him. In any case, the scope for a peace agreement with the Allies was already narrow, as the war premiers Lloyd George and Clemenceau had shown in 1917 their determination to press for victory.

In July 1917, most Reichstag deputies saw peace efforts and constitutional reform as linked: they distanced themselves from government policy and signed up to the principle of a parliamentary monarchy. When the Reichstag adopted the motion in favor of peace on July 19, it simultaneously formed a committee to prepare a reform of the constitution—the fact that this finally ensued only in October 1918, with Germany's defeat already in the cards, should not make us forget its origins in the crisis of 1917. The forces behind the peace motion were those that formed the new parliamentary majority: the SPD, the Center Party, and the left-liberal Progressive People's Party—that is, the future Weimar coalition. It demanded an end to the war on the basis of a comprehensive agreement renouncing territorial gains, annexations, and economic reparations; the war would continue only if the Allies were not prepared to enter into talks. The peace resolution read, "Germany resorted to arms in order to protect its freedom and independence, to defend its territorial integrity. The Reichstag strives for a peace of understanding, for durable reconciliation among the peoples of the world. Territorial acquisitions achieved by force and violations of political, economic, or financial integrity are incompatible with such a peace. The Reichstag furthermore rejects all plans that envisage economic exclusion or continuing enmity among nations after the war. . . . As long, however, as enemy governments do not agree to such a peace, as long as they threaten Germany and its allies with territorial conquests and violations, the German people will stand together as one man, persevere unshakably, and fight on until its right and the right of its allies to life and free development is guaranteed. United, the German people is unconquerable."[255]

Max Weber criticized the Reichstag initiative. Although he vigorously supported democratization of the German political system, he felt in July 1917 that this core demand might leave itself open to the charge that reform would weaken Germany's fighting strength and give a boost to the enemy. Following the heated clashes in the Reichstag, he wrote in a letter dated July 12, "It wouldn't be clever to put too much stress on the link between peace and internal democratization, which does exist, of course. First, in the case of France, but also in that of England, it is highly questionable whether they will react to such extensive democratization with a greater preparedness for peace, rather than the presentation of impossible conditions. They hope that democratization will weaken Germany. Second, we must try to prevent reactionaries from later accusing us for decades that we helped other countries to impose on Germany a constitution that suited them. We cannot predict how strongly that will affect voters once peace has come. And if, despite democracy, peace does not come now . . . the disappointment will perhaps even work to the advantage of internal enemies."[256]

But the credibility of the peace resolution and moves toward parliamentary monarchy proved fragile for other reasons too. Despite the Reichstag majority, the heated argument surrounding both projects highlighted the extent of the political polarization in Germany and the erosion of the civil peace. Michaelis, the new chancellor, promptly distanced himself from the resolution, and the OHL did not feel bound by it. On September 2, the extreme Right responded by founding the German Fatherland Party as a rallying point for nationalist forces and organizations; the very date was politically and historically significant, being the anniversary of the victory over France, symbolizing the foundation of a German nation-state in 1871.

The founding declaration of the Fatherland Party attacked pro-peace politicians as defeatists: "Who does not yearn with all his heart for peace! The peace resolutions of the weak-nerved, however, only postpone peace. Our enemies, who are bent on the destruction of Germany, see in them only the symptoms of the collapse of German strength. And this at a time when, according to the testimony of our Hindenburg, our military situation is more favorable than ever before." It already evoked the alleged treachery of the "stab in the back" legend: "If we convince the enemy that he can have an honorable negotiated peace at any time, he has every reason to continue the war and nothing to lose. . . . We want no domestic strife! Amid domestic quarrels, we Germans too easily forget the war. The enemy forgets the war not for a moment!" At the same time, the declaration used the occasion to lash out at the western model of democracy: "German freedom towers above so-called democracy and all its vaunted blessings, which English hypocrisy and a Wilson want to coax onto the German people, in order to destroy a Germany whose armed might cannot be conquered. We do not wish to do England's business. . . . We will have no peace of starvation! In order to attain a speedy peace we must follow Hindenburg's command and keep our nerve. If we willingly bear shortage and deprivation, the German people will gain a Hindenburg peace, which will bring home the prize of victory for our immense sacrifices and exertions. Any other kind of peace represents a devastating blow to our future development."[257]

Chaired by Admiral Tirpitz and the agriculture boss Wolfgang Kapp, the Fatherland Party, with 1.25 million members, soon became the largest organization on the German Far Right before the rise of National Socialism. In its relatively broad recruitment, stretching from the conservative bourgeoisie to nationalist-minded workers, it came close to the type of a cross-class, cross-milieu people's party, prefiguring the foundation of the German Workers' Party and the National Socialist German Workers' Party in 1919–1920. With the support of the Pan-German League, German conservatives, and many National Liberals, it embraced expansionist war aims and turned most of its fire against the Social Democrats, seeing them as advocates of a peace

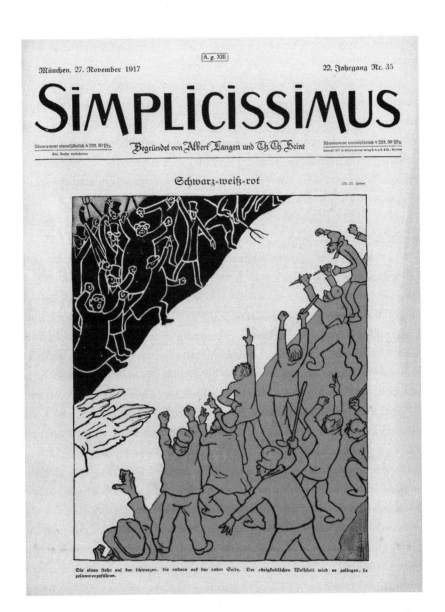

"Some stand on the black side, others on the red. The authorities in their wisdom manage to combine the two." Polarization on the home front, represented by the black, white, and red colors of the Imperial flag (*Simplicissimus*, November 27, 1917)

agreement that would betray all the Germans who had sacrificed their lives in the war.[258]

But the credibility of the resolution of Summer 1917 also suffered from the fact that the Reichstag majority who backed it did not extend their demand for a peace agreement to eastern Europe. When the Brest-Litovsk Treaty came up for ratification in the Reichstag in March 1918, the deputies in question had to recognize that this classical diktat of victors, with its aggressive demands for territory and other impositions, grossly contradicted the spirit and text of their resolution. Nevertheless, both the Left Liberals and the Center Party deputies voted for ratification.[259] Only the USPD voted against, while the SPD abstained.

The confidence in Ludendorff at the time, as the OHL's military and political architect of the war, is clear from the example of Walther Rathenau. After a conversation with Ludendorff on July 12, 1917, he noted in his diary the "incredibly complicated gear change in our power relations": "The chancellor can do nothing unless he has the approval of headquarters. At headquarters, Ludendorff is inhibited by Hindenburg, who swings this way and that as soon as the Kaiser taps him on the shoulder. The Kaiser himself feels he is acting constitutionally, and so the circle is closed. But this is not a question of dress regulations, but of world history." Yet Rathenau was sure that the "Hindenburg legend" was not everything, that the "real balance-sheet and the real impact of Ludendorff have sunk into the whole mass of educated people, if not into the common people." Ludendorff could now "rely on himself and did not need protection from superiors; this ensured his independent responsibilities."[260]

While political currents were polarizing both inside and outside parliament, the debate on war aims intensified once more and became the catalyst for internal political tensions. Not the least factor in this was the attitude of the OHL, which seemed quite optimistic in Summer 1917. On August 21, Hindenburg told the chancellor, "A look at all fronts shows that, at the beginning of the fourth year of war, we are in a more favorable position than ever before."[261] This assessment bolstered the demands of the nationalist organizations. The Pan-German League, for instance, focused on the western front in 1917: "Belgium must become German. . . . The so-called 'Belgian question' is actually not a Belgian question at all, but a German question, a

München, 30. Oktober 1917   A. g. XIII   Preis 40 Pfg.   22. Jahrgang Nr. 31

SIMPLICISSIMUS

Abonnement vierteljährlich 4 Mk. 50 Pfg.   Begründet von Albert Langen und Th. Th. Heine   Abonnement vierteljährlich 4 Mk. 50 Pfg.
Alle Rechte vorbehalten   Copyright 1917 by Simplicissimus-Verlag G.m.b.H. & Co., München

1517 — 1917

„Ich wünschte / daß alle Deutsche so gesinnt wären / daß sie sich kein Flecklein noch Dörflein plündern ließen / noch wegführen ließen / sondern wenn es zu solchem Ernste und Noth käme / daß sich wehrte / was sich wehren könnte / Jung und Alt / Mann und Weib / Knecht und Magd.''

Doctor Martin Luther

The mobilization of history: the quatrocentenary of the Reformation in 1917 question of Germany's destiny. . . . The country will be split into two parts, corresponding as closely as possible to the division of the population into Walloons and Flemings. . . . Both parts will be administered 'dictatorially' and preserve the position of the 'provinces' in the Roman Empire. . . . Those who have been Belgians until now will provisionally have no political rights within the Reich."[262]

The Pan-German chairman, Heinrich Claß, went a step further and identified the goal of German policy with the ideal of racial homogeneity and the need to segregate ethnic minorities in occupied areas. Non-German groups were for him no more than a mass of people at the disposal of the Germans. This pointed again to a nationalism with ethnic and racial connotations intensified by the war: "If we do not just become masters in a land acquired with the blood of the fallen and murdered, if we want to remain there, its inhabitants must obey us. Anyone who does not wish to do that will have the right to emigrate for a short period after the end of the war. Those who stay will have to be obedient. . . . The soil of the Reich must be kept clean; therefore we will not accept any coloreds in it, even if they come from our own colonies. . . . German universities are basically only for Germans and for foreigners of Germanic descent; other aliens will be permitted to attend them only if special political and economic circumstances justify it."[263] Such positions were also a response to divisions in the home front and the political erosion of its steadfast posture, which in the eyes of Claß and many others had been expressed in the Reichstag peace resolution. Similarly, the quatrocentenary celebrations of the Reformation in 1917—which affirmed the indissoluble unity between Luther and the German soul, and the firm resolve to fight for the national cause—pointed to the tensions within German wartime society. Beneath the surface, a theology of war with national overtones was beginning to change into a theology of crisis.[264]

Developments on the eastern front had a direct impact on the mood in Germany, as Harry Graf Kessler noted before Christmas 1917: "I found a mood strikingly different from before. People seem completely intoxicated with the idea that victory may be possible; that propaganda will hardly be necessary after the war, as we now have the prospect of victory and it will not matter whether people hate us or love us." There was even a hope "that Italy and France would not want to make peace just yet, so that we will first be able to gain our great victory over France before; then we would get a better peace." Everywhere people were talking about the huge increase in arms production, especially for heavy and long-range artillery. In contrast, there were concerns about overloaded infrastructure and the uncontrolled funding of the war, so that the challenges of the situation in this respect had greater importance for Kessler than the time window for a final decision to the war: "The state of the roads, the coal shortage, and the financial situation pose a threat to us. Our increased strength in men and heavy artillery on the western front is encouraging, as are the prospects of supplies from Russia."[265] But certain social constants were not lost on Kessler the chronicler: "Tiptoeing over the snow in front of me on Potsdamer Platz was a chic little lady dressed in the latest fashion: petite, trivial, timeless, despite her slightly ridiculous up-to-the-minute costume. How comical—like a wax figure in a museum of the future: 'Lady from the world war!' Short dress, high leather shoes, cloche hat and bird-of-paradise feathers on her head, nothing but boudoir vanity and convention amid all the killing. The war really makes as little impression on the woman as it does on nature; it destroys less than one thinks."[266]

The political situation in the Habsburg monarchy changed at the beginning of 1917, as the new emperor, only 29 years of age, showed in his first measures a will to change course. Within a few months, there were new political and military figures at the top of the regime: Sándor Wekerle replaced Tisza as Hungarian prime minister, and the emperor moved Burián to the finance ministry to make way for his trusted Count Czernin as foreign minister. Finally, Conrad von Hötzendorf—whose aggressive plans for expansion and annexation had set him at the opposite pole from Tisza—was removed in March 1917 as the head of the AOK, the army supreme command. Beginning with the conquests of Serbia and Montenegro and of Albania, he had argued for formal annexation in order to calm the Balkan trouble spots once and for all and to prevent any future infiltration by Russia or Italy. After Karl personally took over as commander in chief of the armed forces, Conrad von Hötzendorf assumed command of the Alpine front.[267]

At the same time that these decisions shifted the balance between Vienna and Budapest—the weight of Hungary under Tisza and Burián had been particularly strong since 1915—Karl gained greater freedom to implement the federalization plans that Tisza had so vigorously opposed. One idea was the conversion of dualism into a triple system, to include Serbia after its possible incorporation into the monarchy. Tisza had resisted this in particular, since it would inevitably have clipped Hungary's wings, but his insistence on Hungary's established status within the monarchy was based on a problematic political practice: it ignored the extra-parliamentary growth of social democracy and the trade unions, while also obscuring the multiethnic reality of Hungary itself. The relative stability of Hungarian internal politics was achieved on the premise that the representatives of both industrial workers and ethnic minorities should continue to be excluded from political participation in Budapest. In 1917, this was becoming a less and less convincing policy.[268]

The clear commitment of the new monarch to the traditional constitutional structure of the Habsburg monarchy, together with his coronation in Budapest as king of Hungary just two months after the death of Franz Joseph, highlighted the latent crisis of the dualist system. The contrast between this language of monarchic symbols and actual political practice became part of the everyday experience of millions. The Hungarian leadership insisted on preserving its country's economic autonomy. In the eyes of many in Cisleithania this considerably worsened their own supply situation, but from a Hungarian viewpoint Vienna's continued refusal to allow parliamentary involvement in policy decisions obstructed the proper functioning of the dualist system. Furthermore, policy toward Poland—where the founding of its own kingdom in November 1916 had involved a formal promise of constitutional independence—affected the balance within the monarchy as a whole and made a new order unavoidable after the end of the war. In Budapest, the fears of the political leadership were all the greater because Czech and South Slav politicians were more and more vehemently demanding a revision of the dualist system.

This internal situation was exacerbated by a paradoxical military development. In the course of 1917, Emperor Karl faced the problem of how to justify the war at a time when the burdens on society at home were giving rise to political protests, and when Austria-Hungary had already achieved its primary war aims against Serbia, Montenegro, Romania (with German help), and Russia, while also successfully repelling all Italian attacks on the Alpine front. Any further operation seemed to many soldiers to call into question the defensive self-image on which the monarchy had grounded the internal political consensus since Summer 1914.[269]

Open political conflict was becoming unmistakably clear as a result of supply problems in the large cities. In Vienna, in particular, the credibility of the municipal authorities—and therefore of the government itself—suffered from the fact that official declarations that it was ensuring food supplies blatantly contradicted what people witnessed in their everyday lives. Social-economic problems became increasingly ethnicized: for example, the mayor of Vienna accused the Hungarian government of being even more to blame than the British blockade for the hunger in his city. Galicia, the traditional bread basket for Cisleithania, was under Russian occupation until July 1917, and the leadership in Budapest was not prepared to supply the other half of the Empire with the fruit of Hungary's rich agricultural resources. The Hungarian government therefore resisted as long as it could the establishment of a joint food commission; only under the pressure of events was one eventually formed in February under General Ottokar Landwehr. But even then it could not have much effect, since it remained without executive powers and the authority to impose sanctions. Large sections of the Cisleithanian population reacted with undisguised hatred toward Hungarians and their government's insistence on economic autarky. The supply issue became increasingly politicized. The failings of the authorities not only undermined confidence in the traditional state structure but also served to illustrate the functional problems affecting the dualist system.[270]

Although internal conflicts grew noticeably more acute, it was still not possible to speak of an aggressive, irreversible tide of secessionist nationalism within the Habsburg monarchy. Czech developments were particularly instructive in this regard.[271] In 1917, the activities of politicians in Prague still differed markedly from those of the emigration. After President Wilson, in a first diplomatic initiative in December 1916, sought clarification about the aims of all the belligerent states, the Entente responded in January 1917 by referring for the first time to the "liberation of the Italians, Slavs, Romanians, and Czechoslovaks" from foreign rule—although without explicitly calling for the breakup of the Dual Monarchy. The formulation came down to one of greater autonomy for population groups within the monarchy. Count Czernin, for his part, organized a high-profile declaration of loyalty, which in late January even won the support of the Czech Union, emphasizing that the future of the Czech nation lay within the Habsburg monarchy.

This was a setback for the efforts of the foreign-based Czechoslovak National Council and for its claim to represent the interests of all Czechs and Slovaks living in their homelands. On the other hand, the developments of Spring 1917 in Russia, which led to the fall of the Tsar and hopes of a constitutional regime, also created new leeway for Czech exiles. Masaryk, in particular, felt encouraged to push for the formation of a Czech Legion in Russia, once the tsarist government, after much hesitation, had permitted the creation of the Družina in battalion strength out of Czech prisoners of war. When Czech units distinguished themselves at the Battle of Zborów in early July 1917, Masaryk's National Council was also formally recognized as the political authority behind the Czech Legion. This sent an important signal, and Czech units were also formed under their own commanders in France. In Italy, Czech and Slovak POWs began to form special labor battalions and, from Spring 1918, their own military units. Soldiers in prison camps experienced their national identity more strongly than before—their emotional ties to the monarchy were loosened, resulting in demands for an independent nation-state.[272]

The Russian February Revolution also affected developments in the societies of the Habsburg Empire, reinforcing fears in Vienna that the supply situation in large cities might contribute as in Petrograd to a revolutionary movement. Since social, economic, and political conflicts overlapped with ethnic tensions, the boundary between the struggle against external and internal enemies became increasingly unclear. When the Kaiser and the government in Vienna feared that they might lose control of events, they reacted with far-reaching concessions. The Imperial Council was recalled on May 30, 1917, on the basis of the 1911 election results, and the monarch and the government under Count Heinrich Clam-Martinic publicly relaxed censorship in a bid to stabilize the situation.[273]

Instead of fostering integration, however, these measures turned parliament and the press into new forums for public debates often tinged with nationalism and anti-Semitism. This was apparent in the insinuations of disloyalty that German nationalist politicians directed at Czech soldiers and in the general climate of suspicion surrounding certain national contingents within the multiethnic Austro-Hungarian army. The turn against Jews, Italians, and Czechs hardened into an everyday practice, violating not only the principle of equal rights but also traditions within the army. But from Summer 1917 on, debates in the Reichstag, inflamed by articles in the press, demonstrated how widely the fear of internal enemies had spread. The de facto equation of Jews with spies in Galicia was an especially crude example. As everyday relations between Jews and non-Jews gradually worsened, and as the supply and refugee problems were continually linked together, the supranational understanding of citizenship changed into one with distinctly ethnic connotations.[274] This led to a wave of aggressive anti-Semitism in the big cities that continued to the end of the war. The distribution crisis, which had originally had economic causes, began to fuel ethnic and religious antagonisms. Indeed, many members of the Vienna City Council openly blamed Jewish refugees for housing and food supply problems triggered by shortages and rising rents.

In Prague, in a move that recalled the treatment of east European Jewish workers in Germany, Jewish refugees were forbidden to use streetcars, because of suspicions that they had brought typhus fever into the city. In Hungary, demands were raised to deport Jewish refugees or to close the border in line with the German model. These developments, up to and beyond the end of the war, crystallized a major change in the status of Jewish refugees: no longer citizens of the Habsburg monarchy who had suffered ethnic expulsion, they came to be legally defined as homeless or stateless persons whose homeland had been literally lost through the breakup of the monarchy—and in the end as "enemy aliens," who were met with extreme mistrust and routine exclusion.[275]

The revival of parliamentarism in May 1917, together with the sudden easing of restrictions on communication, fueled high national expectations, the dynamic of which subsequently turned against the monarchy. In parliament and the mass press, it became clear in a flash how much the interests of the different parts of the monarchy had already diverged from one another. What had been conceived as integration along constitutional lines turned out to be the engine of disintegration.[276]

On May 17, 1917, 222 Czech writers and journalists published a manifesto calling on Czech deputies at the Imperial Council in Vienna to respect the rights and wishes of Czechs. At the official opening of the council, many deputies for the first time openly questioned the constitutionality of the Dual Monarchy and invoked the principle of national self-determination to argue that all parts of the Czech and Slovak nation should be combined in a single democratic state. This too was not yet an outright rejection of a common monarchical federation. But an end to dualism, now supported by a number of deputies, made the division of the monarchy a possible option—not only for exiled politicians but also for parliamentary groups in Vienna. Further concessions spurred on these developments in Summer 1917: Czech leaders around Kramař and Rašin were amnestied in July, at the very time when more sections of the population were nearing exhaustion and news was coming in of events in Russia. It was not so much the details of a radically different political model as the fact that the political situation was changeable in principle that appeared a sign of the times.[277]

After the easing of censorship regulations, a competitive market in political opinions opened up in the press as well as parliament. Until 1917 strict censorship and systematic monitoring of the press, based on the state of emergency throughout the monarchy, had illustrated how effective the war state could be—in sharp contrast to the central coordination of food supplies that was later introduced and was far less successful. In the course of 1917, however, the authorities in effect lost control of the media, and empire-friendly propaganda capable of influencing the public was lacking. Although Allied, especially Italian, propaganda against Austria-Hungary was closely monitored, the war press bureau was only an apparatus of control, rather than a proactive system of public relations. It therefore failed to communicate a positive self-image of the Imperial monarchy as a counterweight to the rise of national narratives, and by 1918, when campaigns to achieve this finally started in the army, it was already too late.[278]

Instead of the supranational patriotism for which the monarchy, the dynasty, and the army had stood as identity symbols before 1914, a wave of aggressive nationalisms washed over parliament and the press. This applied both to Magyars in Hungary and Germans in Cisleithania and also, by way of reaction, to the Czechs and South Slavs. In Hungary, the government continued the elitist Magyar course that ignored ethnic minorities, social democrats, and labor unions outside parliament. In Cisleithania, the government under Clam-Martinic embraced the radical demands of ethnic Germans and, in preparation for a possible new constitution, negotiated with German and Polish politicians over the imposition of a "German solution" by emergency decree, which would work to the disadvantage of the Czechs, Slovaks, and South Slavs. Pursuing the kind of bargaining strategy that had served other players so well during the war, Polish politicians sought to obtain more territory for an independent nation-state. But in early 1918, when the government in Vienna began to envisage a division of Galicia, they turned against the regime.[279]

In this context, the parliament in Vienna no longer acted as a supranational instrument of integration, but rather as a public forum where the nationalization of politics had to be negotiated. The dynamic that now developed was all but uncontrollable, as German and Czech deputies showed less and less willingness to compromise. The former sharpened their accusations that Czech politicians were under the influence of the Czech Legions abroad, fueling the mistrust of Czechs and other groups toward parliament and the Kaiser's political course. Along with federalization of the monarchy, their aim now was for Czechoslovaks and Slovenes to form states of their own.

The Czech manifesto of May 1917 had an enormous impact not only in Bohemia, where the party landscape began to change in the summer, but also, later that year, among the South Slavs. Starting in Slovenia, a movement spread out toward Bosnia and Dalmatia. Anton Korošec and other representatives on the Imperial Council in Vienna, together with members of the Catholic clergy, campaigned in demonstrations for a common state of Serbs, Croats, and Slovenes. Behind this idea of a trinational South Slav state—Yugoslavia—lay complex motives that were entangled with conflicting national interests: in 1917 the existing structure of the Habsburg monarchy no longer seemed to offer security against the aggressive nationalisms that had provoked the war and questioned the legitimacy of the Dual Monarchy from without and from within. Externally, Italy was making claims to territory in southeastern Europe, while internally the positions of ethnic Germans and Magyars encouraged the idea of a trinational state for the South Slavs. Yet even so the monarchy remained an overarching point of reference: commitment to a future Yugoslavia did not automatically mean giving that up. From late 1917, the South Slav movement could not simply be equated with political forces opposed to the continued existence of the monarchy. In March 1918, it still claimed to be seeking "freedom within a greater Habsburg Yugoslavia."[280]

The situation was complicated by the activities of Serb political leaders in exile, who, in the Corfu declaration of July 20, 1917, agreed on the postwar project of a South Slav nation-state in the form of a Serbian hereditary monarchy. After Russia, the traditional protector, dropped out of the picture, and Italian demands in the eastern Adriatic became increasingly overt, Serb leaders had to avoid becoming isolated. But there were still considerable tensions among exile politicians. While Prime Minister Pašić stuck to the plan of a Greater Serbia and demanded the straightforward annexation of neighboring territories, Prince Regent Alexander supported the idea of a federation under Serbian leadership—which had the support of the London-based Yugoslavia Committee under the Croat Ante Trumbić. Only after the collapse of Bulgaria in September 1918 did the exiled politicians return to a largely devastated country.[281]

A change in Allied attitudes to the future of the Habsburg monarchy eventually led to a stable political link between the national independence movements in exile and political forces in the various home countries. For a long time, Paris, London, and Washington had favored the continued existence of the monarchy, pursuing a separate peace with Vienna and recognizing the regime there as an important factor for stability in east central and southeastern Europe. A federalized Habsburg monarchy with greater autonomy for its individual parts seemed to conflict with this objective. Entente and U.S. policy still pursued the old strategy: the American declaration of war on Austria-Hungary came only in December 1917, and Wilson's Fourteen Points spoke only of autonomy for the peoples of the monarchy, not explicitly of its breakup. In January 1918 Lloyd George was still emphasizing that breakup was not a British war aim.

The outcome of the Sixtus affair in April 1918 was mainly responsible for the change in the Allied position. In March 1917 Emperor Karl had sent out peace feelers of his own that he had not cleared with the German government, using his brother-in-law Prince Sixtus of Bourbon-Parma, who had served as an officer in the Belgian army, to convey messages to President Poincaré of France in which he also expressed understanding for the return of

Alsace-Lorraine. In Karl's so-called Sixtus letter of March 24, 1917, he explicitly recognized France's military achievements in the war: "All the peoples of my empire are more than ever united in the common will to defend the integrity of the monarchy, even at the cost of the greatest sacrifices. . . . No one can dispute the military successes of my troops, especially in the Balkan theater. France too has given ample proof of its élan and its powers of resistance. We all unreservedly admire the traditional bravery of its army and the spirit of sacrifice of the whole French people." Above all, however, Karl stressed that there was no unbridgeable gulf between the Dual Monarchy and France: "It therefore gladdens me to see that, although we are enemies at the moment, no real conflicts of interest separate my empire from France, and that my lively sympathies for France, which are shared in all parts of the monarchy, gives grounds for the hope that we can avoid any future recurrence of a war for which I am not responsible."[282]

When the French government published the letters in Spring 1918, Karl had to distance himself from them officially before the German military leadership; his room for maneuver by then was so limited that the British and Americans no longer thought a separate peace with the Habsburg monarchy was a realistic possibility. Although the October Revolution and the Bolsheviks' announcement of a possible peace without annexations had complicated the situation in Fall 1917, the de facto diktat of the Brest-Litovsk treaty in early March 1918 had completely changed the picture in eastern Europe. It had greatly strengthened the Germans' hand and left the Austro-Hungarian government with little or no scope for a peace policy of its own. Only when the option of a separate peace crumbled did the exiled leaders of the national independence movements, and their request to form military units of their own in the struggle against the Central Powers, appear to the Allies in a different light.

Berlin's strengthened position also had implications for the Poles and led to open conflict with them later in the year. The contradiction between the Poles' national political expectations and the practice of the Central Powers in Poland had continued in early 1917: a Provisional State Council emerged in mid-January 1917 from the Central National Committee established toward the end of 1915, but it had to comply with the directives of the Central Powers, especially with regard to the military policy that was so important for the national movement. The German and Austro-Hungarian authorities did not allow Poland to have any independent armed forces; Polish units could be deployed only as auxiliaries within the German or Austro-Hungarian armies. The conflict escalated when Piłsudski asked Polish units to withhold an oath of allegiance to the German Kaiser and announced in early July 1917 that he was withdrawing from the State Council. He was placed under arrest and spent 1917–1918 in captivity in Germany. But this only enhanced his reputation as the political leader of the national movement—indeed, as a heroic martyr in the cause of an independent Poland.[283]

International developments in the course of 1917 created major new opportunities for the Polish national movement. The Provisional Government in Russia showed itself prepared to recognize an independent Polish state and actually permitted the formation of autonomous Polish military units. At the same time, the U.S. entry into the war, together with President Wilson's espousal of the right to national self-determination, offered new perspectives. His Fourteen Points declaration of January 1918 defined the restoration of an independent Polish state as an explicit Allied war aim. In response to the events in Russia and the new American position, the Central Powers were compelled to make fresh concessions, and on September 12, 1917, the Regency Council was formally recognized as the government of Poland. However, as soon as the military situation in eastern Europe turned in favor of the Central Powers, the Poles' national expectations were disappointed yet again. Berlin was determined to exploit the new room for maneuver it had won as a result of Russia's exit from the war in late 1917 and to establish a quite different order in east central Europe. Overriding the interests of the Polish independence movement, the German leadership therefore supported the independence of Ukraine by promising the incorporation of territories that had previously been part of Lithuania, while at the same time promoting national ambitions in the Baltic. The future of Galicia at first remained unresolved. The separate peace agreement between the Central Powers and Ukraine, signed on February 9, 1918, eventually included recognition of the autonomy of Ukrainians in east Galicia and the cession of formerly Polish territory around Chelm to Ukraine.[284]

Thus, after the military successes of late 1917, Poland was only one card in the hand of the Central Powers. As in other cases, new states would remain objects of policies mainly shaped in Berlin, not subjects acting in an independent capacity. No Polish representatives would be allowed to attend the talks at Brest-Litovsk, and independent Polish military units were disbanded.[285]

8. THE DUAL DEFENSIVE
Liberals in the War

In 1917, signs of a crisis of liberalism were multiplying in every belligerent country. What the war meant for the nineteenth-century liberal became clear. The traditional view that the political center was hollowed out only in the countries that lost the war in 1918, that left and right extremes were strengthened only in the war-induced passage from monarchy to republic in Germany or from empire to nation states in Austria-Hungary, is one-sided and therefore mistaken. The crisis of liberalism began earlier and was more extensive; it was also apparent in the future victor countries—Britain, France, and Italy—as well as in countries like Spain and Portugal that were not directly involved in the war.[286]

The conditions under which liberals operated in 1914 varied from country to country: the wide spectrum of political-constitutional possibilities reflected the stage of historical development each had reached, with constitutional and parliamentary monarchies at first dominating the scene alongside the parliamentary republics of France and the United States. The weakest foundations were those of the Russian Duma, which after 1906 was unable to develop into a stable forum for liberal politics. Prorogued by the Tsar in the event of conflict, the parliament and its liberal champions were lacking in political self-confidence. It is true that in 1915 they helped to form the Progressive Bloc opposition, but they eventually swallowed the tsarist clampdown in 1915–1916, losing the confidence that the Duma would have required in 1917 to assert itself against rival centers of power. In Austria-Hungary, the crisis of constitutional liberalism had been plain before 1914. With the parliament in Vienna adjourned since spring, Hungarian Magyars opted for repression against other ethnic groups—and so constitutional integration of the multiethnic monarchy did not succeed in either part of the Empire. In the German Reich, the tensions associated with nation-building had persisted since 1871 in the Reichstag. The chronological layers of liberalism in

Germany were, so to speak, converted into the complex suffrage laws, whose precise shape depended on the strength of the liberal parties. For whereas universal manhood suffrage in Reichstag elections tended to benefit the Social Democrats and the Catholic Center more than the liberal parties, electoral restrictions gave them the basis for considerable political success in many local areas. For many people at the time, the liberals' relationship to the Prussian three-class suffrage was the measure of their credibility in the future constitutional framework of the Lesser German nation-state that had emerged in the nineteenth century.

In all these cases, liberals mostly acted as an opposition force with no direct say in political decisions. In Italy, they came to power as part of the *destra storica,* the historical Right under Giolitti. But there the glaring contrast between a formal parliamentary monarchy and the reality of a deeply corrupt parliamentary system led to growing estrangement between parliament and the population of the country. Mounting criticism of the "liberal system," represented by Giolitti as prime minister before 1914, also raised doubts about the real animosity of national secular liberalism toward political Catholicism and socialism. In 1914–1915 liberalism was often identified with Giolitti's strategy of neutrality in the war, and therefore with the negative attributes of cowardice, defeatism, lack of patriotism, and betrayal of the *irredenta.*

In France, the strong role of parliament and the weakness of the executive, reflected in the succession of fifty governments between 1871 and 1914, were seen as a problematic legacy of the French Revolution and of constitutional liberalism. The question of whether a republic organized along these lines could survive in wartime therefore gave rise to heated debate. In Britain, not only did much more highly organized parties exist before 1914 but liberalism was actually in government again from 1906.[287]

Against this background, the world war marked the beginning of new crises and the continuation of certain prewar developments. As the war dragged on, it posed at least four new structural challenges to liberalism. The first of these came from tensions within national communities that both had to show themselves strong externally and to mobilize with determination internally. In practice, however, the quest for unrestricted loyalty meant that, as the principles of exclusion and inclusion asserted themselves in a climate of growing suspicion, the liberal paradigm of a plural society came under ever greater pressure to justify itself. Ideological mobilization under the aegis of an exclusive nationalism was a radical challenge to many liberal values in Europe. Thus, right at the beginning of the war, liberals experienced how quickly and easily emergency powers could entail the suspension of hard-won freedoms and civil rights.

Second, as army leaders in all wartime societies began to claim the right to shape political life, there was a change in the relationship between the civilian and military spheres. This was apparent in Britain in the clashes between Prime Minister Asquith and the BEF commander Sir John French, and later between Lloyd George and Haig, although eventually, in 1917–1918, civilian government emerged stronger from these conflicts. In France too, parliament stood up against the autonomous dynamic of the general staff, claiming not only a say in decisions but also political control over the military. By contrast, the Italian supreme commander Cadorna successfully refused for a long time to involve politicians in military decision making. In Austria-Hungary, the AOK enjoyed huge political influence because of the suspension of parliament until Spring 1917. And in Germany, the Third OHL under Hindenburg and Ludendorff demanded that political, economic, and social life should be subject to the primacy of the war effort, and it pursued policies of its own without regard to parliament or the government. There the military represented an extra-constitutional power center, which for a long time enjoyed high public confidence and increasingly overshadowed the Kaiser himself; the fall of Chancellor Bethmann Hollweg in Summer 1917 was therefore not an expression of strong opposition in the Reichstag, but reflected the power of the military leadership.[288]

The expansion of the war state was another challenge to liberals, who stood for political, economic, and social mobilization in the name of the war. It opened up new possibilities for the interventionist state; it was no accident that it also inspired wide-ranging hopes among Progressives in the United States. But the institutional expansion of the wartime states, their power in the economy, and their suspension of basic freedoms and civil rights for the sake of tighter supervision and control posed many liberals with a dilemma. The private sphere of the individual came more than ever before into the purview of state action.

Lastly, the war gave rise to new structures in the relationship among capital, labor, and the state. New forms of cooperation between entrepreneurs and state officials (exemplified by Rathenau in Germany or the railroad man

Eric Geddes in Great Britain), the many new hybrid models spanning the private and public sectors, new business groups such as the Zentralverein deutscher Industrieller or the Federation of British Industries, changes in the relationship between employers and unions—all these developments, in which the war state and its various agencies played a key role, redrew the options open to liberals. The bureaucratic mania for regulation, the highlighting of corporatist elements, and the debate on "organized capitalism" and the war's winners and losers called into question traditional liberal economic ideas, shifting the focus to social players who seemed more important than classical groups of the liberal bourgeoisie to the continuation of the war.[289]

Liberal crisis symptoms had already appeared before the outbreak of war. Then, within a few days or weeks, a certain style of politics and way of thinking, which for all the national differences had been a recognized legacy of liberalism, fell by the wayside. Practically everywhere basic rights were suspended on the pretext of the political-constitutional state of emergency. A dual structure of civilian and military authorities came into being, while parliaments—after the symbolic act of voting for war credits—took a back seat for the time being. Liberals actively participated in the various kinds of wartime social-political truce, but their main concern was to ensure the integration of forces on the Left. German liberals were prepared to postpone their agenda of political reform until the end of the war; many emphatically espoused the "ideas of 1914" against the "ideas of 1789" and intensively engaged in debates on the war. By 1915 the demands of Prussian National Liberals for an area of German settlement in eastern Europe were beginning to overlap with those of the Pan-German League.[290]

Liberals in many countries took part in the cultural war, and early on some strongly anti-liberal tendencies appeared in this context—for example, in the British philosopher Thomas Ernest Hulme or, on the German side, Max Scheler and Ferdinand Tönnies, each laying stress on the organic community against the principles of the plural society. These anti-liberal animosities were thoroughly transnational; they would grow considerably in the course of the war, again placing liberals on the defensive programmatically.[291]

Ideological polarization grew sharper in 1916 and especially in 1917—with noteworthy consequences for liberalism in Germany, but not only there. On top of defensive operations against Left and Right at home, Liberals had to face ideological competition from abroad, in the shape of the utopias of democratic egalitarianism and Bolshevik internationalism. The persuasiveness of liberal ideas had to be measured against the new political, social, and international models represented by Wilson and Lenin. In Petrograd, it was possible to see as in a laboratory how war and revolution were interlinked and how traditional institutions such as dynasty, monarchy, and empire could be swept aside in short order. The existence of a practical countermodel to which people could appeal gave added drama to the fact that by 1917 the political truce was crumbling in the western belligerent countries. Above all, the reform orientation of socialist and social-democratic parties in Europe seemed not only to meet the social and economic challenges (as well as formalizing the recognition of labor unions) but also to be actually superior to the liberal models of order. On the one hand, socialists were ministers in the wartime governments in Paris (Millerrand) and London (Arthur Henderson), though not in Berlin. On the other hand, tensions were rising in the Left over whether to support the continuation of the war. The USPD split in Germany highlighted what such conflicts could lead to. They reflected not so much ideological differences and the outcome of radical Left conferences in Zimmerwald and Kiental as the ever more pressing problems and social costs of the war since late 1916.

In 1917, the mobilization of the political Right against liberalism became more and more aggressive. In Germany, the maximalist war aims of the Pan-German League, supported by the Third OHL, exerted increasing pressure on the Bethmann Hollweg chancellery. The constitutional role of the German parliament played a role in the decision to resume unrestricted submarine warfare, and the military, brandishing Ludendorff's threat to resign, engineered the fall of the chancellor in a kind of negative coalition with parliamentary groups from the right to the center. It is true that a quite different lineup resulted from the peace resolution supported by previously cold-shouldered opposition parties. But on closer inspection it was clear how contradictory the role was that German liberals had played in this. The National Liberals were demanding greater powers for the Reichstag and the lifting of press censorship because they opposed what they saw as a weak chancellor and his course against maximalist war aims; Gustav Stresemann, in particular, criticized the "policy of accommodation and concessions."

The Left Liberals, on the contrary, sought to strengthen the government: Friedrich Naumann turned his fire against the "minister-deposers" and the "roaming in unconquered lands."[292] Although the National Liberals distanced themselves from the constitutional monarchy in the dispute over reform of the Prussian three-class electoral system, they showed no clear commitment to consistent parliamentarism. But the Left Liberals also shied away from conflict, with the result that Germany's "parliamentarization on the quiet" remained incomplete. Its association with hopes of a soft Wilsonian peace in 1918 became a burden in the long run.[293]

The year 1917 showed how problematic the role of parliament could be. Neither in Russia nor in Germany nor in Austria-Hungary did politics stabilize on a consensual basis of constitutional-parliamentary rule. Rather, the Duma, Reichstag, and Reichsrat became ideologically polarized arenas, as illustrated by the founding of the Fatherland Party in Germany in September 1917 as a rallying center for forces pursuing pan-German war aims. The split in the parliamentary Left between the SPD and USPD, and the nationalist conflicts between German and Czech deputies in the Reichsrat in Vienna, were further examples of the fact that parliaments did not provide an integrative basis in line with the constitution or a forum in which to seek consensus in small steps within the wartime societies.

But 1917 also brought a breaking of the liberal mold in France and Britain. The Briand cabinet, toppled even before the catastrophic Nivelle offensive and the mass mutinies, gave way to a new government under Ribot that was blamed all the more for the dual crisis. The polarization of the political spectrum was particularly evident in this paradigmatic situation of the liberal center. Criticism from the Left concentrated on responsibility for the military disaster and the mutinies, while the Right attacked the government for not pursuing the war consistently enough. Further changes of government finally led in November to the formation of Clemenceau's war cabinet, and the departure of the socialists from office more or less put an end to the *union sacrée* in its existing form. In practice, parliament sheltered behind the popularity of Clemenceau, who then used the war to establish himself as a charismatic politician embodying the will to victory.

In late 1916 Lloyd George showed a similar tendency in Britain, profiting from tensions within the Liberal Party over universal conscription and the growing state intervention in the economy. Many Liberal deputies and Labour representatives in the House of Commons distanced themselves from the Asquith government because they feared the encroachments of the centralist war state in more and more spheres of private life. The Conservatives, on the other hand, like the republican Right in France, accused the government of a lack of vigor in its conduct of the war; liberalism in office seemed to stand for "defeatism." After Lloyd George had formed a new cabinet, he sharpened the polarization by introducing measures that favored Liberal and Conservative MPs who supported his war policies. The nightmare scenario of a Labour / Left-Liberal coalition suspected of pacifism fit in very well with his plans. His campaigning and his equation of pacifism with defeatism certainly did much to deepen the split in the Liberals.

In 1917, the situation in nearly all the belligerent countries could be exploited in such a way as to throw liberalism onto the defensive. In another respect, too, it proved to be a fateful year for liberals; fears spread everywhere that the military war was being accompanied with a global economic war, in which the victor would in the long run assert itself by armed force. Consequently, the principles of free trade and lack of state intervention in the economy were being hollowed out in all the countries involved in the war. In Britain, the Conservatives dominated economic policy, arguing against the liberal free traders in favor of customs tariffs. In France, the government oriented itself more and more to the nationally defined interests of large industry, and in Germany the utopia of a highly autarkic, Germanicized economic area covering Continental Europe was being adumbrated.

All in all, the ideological hostility to liberalism grew considerably more strident from 1917 on. Writers invoking a decidedly nonpolitical bourgeois way of life appealed before and after 1918 to a nationally charged concept of "liberality" in order to demarcate themselves from the democratic-participatory connotations of liberalism. Many saw Thomas Mann as representative of this trend. In his *Reflections of a Nonpolitical Man*, written mainly in the last two years of the war, he emphasized a bourgeois, nonpolitical understanding of "liberality": if he was "liberal," it was only in the sense of "liberality and not liberalism. For my thinking is unpolitical—national but unpolitical—like that of Germans of bourgeois culture and like the Romantics, who knew no other political demand than the lofty national one for Kaiser and Reich."[294]

Max Weber, in his 1919 lecture on *Politics as a Vocation*, would historicize the traditional concepts of legitimate rule based on monarchs, dynasties, and empires, emphasizing the masses and democracy as new factors shaping politics in nation-states. But more generally, liberals in Germany saw how the war had shattered their traditional interpretive monopoly on the basic concepts of nation and citizenship.

For British liberals, on the other hand, society and the individual remained crucial references. But even such a prominent figure in the reform-oriented New Liberalism as John A. Hobson, who in 1916 had still embraced the ideal of organic British liberalism against state-centered Prussia, clearly believed in 1918 that there could be no return to the pre-1914 world of liberalism. A simple glance at the state showed this: "For no one can seriously argue that at the end of the war . . . the state can or will return to prewar conditions and the competitive *laissez-faire* which prevailed over the wide fields of industry and commerce."[295] Although he criticized the incursions of the British war state, he had to concede the following: "Any sudden lapse from the state socialism of wartime, with its enormous governmental control of engineering, agriculture, mining, transport, and other vital industries . . . into the prewar conditions, would spell disorder and disaster. The state must continue to retain a large proportion of this control and this spending power, if unemployment, industrial depression, a fall of wages, and something like social revolution are to be averted."[296]

After the U.S. entry into the war had raised the hopes of reform among Progressives around Walter Lippman, Walter Weyl, and Herbert Croly, inspiring their critique of the anti-state ideology of radical economic liberalism, a sobering up soon followed on a large scale. For although government regulation now operated through institutions such as the War Industries Board, the National War Labor Board, or the Food Administration, it went together with an exclusion of alleged traitors and "enemy aliens" that contradicted the liberal creed of diversity and tolerance. The end of the war meant not only the end of experiments with a proactive state but also a reversion to national isolation.

In the long term, then, the war put pressure on the liberal model of politics and on its plural vision of society. It was argued that, contrary to constitutional-parliamentary practice, modern states could survive a war only through bureaucratic-military expertise and the recruitment of specialists. The reconfiguration of premodern ideals of community, which was turned against liberalism after 1918, combined with new technologies to make the plural society appear atomistic. Social engineers, for whom the war had opened up new possibilities in areas such as pronatalism in France, now acquired increasing weight.

9. DEMOGRAPHY, CLASS, AND GENDER
The Contours of Postwar Societies

In 1917, the long-term structural features that would mark postwar societies were becoming more discernible. This applied first of all at the level of demography: conservative estimates put at roughly 12 percent—one in every eight—the percentage of mobilized soldiers who lost their lives between 1914 and 1918. Another 30 percent were wounded, and 10 percent were interned in POW camps. But such totals mask considerable differences between countries: in France, for example, 77 percent of all soldiers were wounded, killed, or taken captive, while the two million German soldiers who lost their lives represented the highest proportion of all the belligerent countries. Demographically, the heaviest toll was among men aged between 20 and 24: more than 70 percent of soldiers killed came from this age group. Of these, the proportion of farmers and farm laborers was higher than that of urban workers, who were often considered indispensable and spared service at the front. As the degree of industrialization decreased—moving, that is, from western to eastern, or northern to southern Europe—the share of the male rural population in the casualty total increased. Ultimately, members of upper social layers were at a particularly high risk of being killed. Mostly recruited as young officers at the start of the war and sent as platoon or company leaders to the front, they paid a higher than average price for the nation in the war.[297]

Global migration flows changed as a result of the war, following a period since the 1880s when millions of young families had left Europe, particularly for North and South America. Many of the classical host countries introduced more restrictive legislation—most notably the United States, where a nativist policy accompanied the turn against "enemy aliens." (Passports became a mass phenomenon after the war, when everyone traveling to another country had to show that he or she did not intend to settle there.) But while international migration slowed, huge numbers of people were on the move internally—above all to large cities and industrial conglomerations. Areas with new production facilities and workers' housing sprang up around many cities: the "red belt" around Paris, for example, would become a striking feature of the postwar period.[298]

Demographic trends showed major differences between countries. In Britain, the lot of workers tended to improve during the war, particularly of those in the most precarious situation, who now benefited from full employment, stable wages, and better health care, as well as from state assistance for mothers and children; child mortality declined in large parts of the country. However, many of these positive developments have to be set against the poor working and living conditions: wartime rent controls, for example, meant that many landlords no longer invested money in their rental accommodation. Many families drawn to the industrial centers, where the demand for labor was high, were not used to the often-extreme conditions there and were more susceptible to illness. In France, the differences from the prewar period were less significant, although there too workers generally benefited from some material improvements. In Germany and Austria-Hungary, in contrast, the situation rapidly deteriorated from 1916, when imbalances in the war economy and food supply problems became more and more apparent.[299] Whereas, in Britain and France, import-driven supply improvements headed off a process of impoverishment that might have had serious political consequences, the effects of the blockade and resulting shortages fueled new social conflicts in the Central Powers. The contrast was great between wage-dependent employees and owners of material resources and real estate, and between people living in the cities and country folk able to feed themselves. The criminalization of everyday life that began to take hold in 1916, particularly in the shape of black markets, increasingly eroded the legitimacy of an interventionist state responsible for the maintenance of supplies.[300]

The net wages of industrial workers tended to decline in most of the wartime societies, including Germany (1914: 100, 1918: 63) and France. Only in Britain did cooperation between the government and assertive labor unions, as well as a traditionally high readiness to take strike action, pay off in the form of relative wage stability (1914: 100, 1918: 96). Social homogenization was visible among employees in Germany, partly because of an increasingly critical attitude to vast profits and cartelization tendencies in the arms industry. Subjective class consciousness tended to rise, and industrial workers' organizations were the main beneficiaries, their membership figures showing a sharp increase after the end of the truce lineup in 1917.[301]

In each wartime society, status changes led to new lines of conflict.[302] This gave class a special character that eluded simple antagonistic models and involved new types of polarization. Thus, differences between workers in the arms sector and consumer goods industry, or between proletarian wage earners and the self-employed or civil servants, tended to overshadow traditional oppositions and class divisions between workers and employers or between workers on the factory floor and in white-collar jobs. Models of class antagonism could not encompass the different trends in city and country or government policies in favor of workers in vital war industries.

New social trends and the inequality between winners and losers became a dominant theme all over Europe; many people in France even thought they were a threat to national cohesion. In late September 1917, when Michel Corday visited the writer Anatole France on the Loire, he found a man who had become increasingly isolated. In 1914 France had signally held aloof from the intellectual warmongering, but then, at the age of 71, he had volunteered for the army and made a laughingstock of himself. In the fall of 1917 he was completely disillusioned about the state of French society and the flourishing of shameless profiteers with a major interest in the continuation of the war: "The overwhelming majority of people in Tours want the war to continue because of the high wages it has brought to the workers and the increased profits made by tradesmen. The bourgeoisie, whose only mental nourishment comes from the reactionary newspapers, has been completely won over by the idea of a war without end. In short, he declares, it is only the men at the front who are pacifists."[303]

In Britain, too, views about the moral economy of wartime sacrifice and the need for fairer burden sharing became more pronounced in 1917. Although these did not, as in France, crystallize into suggestive metaphors such as the blood tax (*impôt du sang*), tensions between winners and losers increased sharply. A gulf opened between Christian ideas of sacrifice, especially in the Anglican Church, and the reality of everyday life. Attempts to gloss over social differentiation and to idealize a cohesive national community of mourners stood in glaring contrast to the unequal distribution of sacrifices. The casualties of war included an especially high number of white-collar employees, while many farmers and arms sector workers were considered indispensable and not sent off to fight. The label "shirker" was more and more stridently directed against them. Industrial workers, in particular, also achieved considerable wage increases and social advances, the wartime improvement in their status being unmistakable. One political result of the burden on the middle classes was a hatred of the Left: anti-Bolshevism, anti-Semitism, and xenophobia became more and more common.[304] In a way, such animosities contributed to the development of more homogeneous classes, which became increasingly differentiated from one another with each passing year.[305]

In Germany, supply bottlenecks, rising prices, and wage trends led to new social positioning. The contrast between Christmas in 1915 and 1917 illustrated the change in everyday status and the massive belt tightening required for many a bourgeois married couple. The monthly magazine *Der Türmer* complained in 1917 that the middle classes were increasingly becoming the real victims of the war: "No war profits beckon for them, either as multi-million windfalls or as fourfold or fivefold wage increases. On the one hand, war profits make it possible to pay fantastic prices; on the other hand, they are rivaled by wages with which no civil servant's income can keep pace. Between the two lies the middle class. It carries the main burden of this starvation war. And it has not grumbled in complaint. It has not taken to the streets, although it has picked up no bonuses or Hindenburg handouts. The middle class has sacrificed the largest part of the millions that others have gained. Just ask the artisans whose materials were taken by the war, or the small storekeeper whose goods and prices are minutely allocated, or the houseowner who has to put up with large losses of rent."[306]

What was decisive in Germany was not so much the opposition between capital and labor as the variegated trends in war-related and other industries. The war economy had a better time of it than the peace economy. In the latter, indexed earnings fell from a base of 100 in 1913 to 85 in 1915 and 51 in 1917, whereas the decrease was considerably less in the war sector

(1915: 84, 1917: 82). The aggregated real wages of workers, taking productivity increases into account as well as real wage levels, changed mainly in the last two years of the war: they rose from a base of 100 in 1914, to 109 in 1915, and to 103 in 191, before falling to 87 in 1917 and 96 in 1918. The subjective perception of the contrast between wage earners and capital owners also changed, especially as patchy supplies and food shortages meant that any decrease in wages had an incomparably greater existential impact on workers than on recipients of income from capital, who generally had more money coming in as well as access to material assets.[307] As the perceived cracks in wartime society widened, the truce and new integrative concepts—from the "public economy" and "war socialism" to "national community"—came increasingly into question.

For representatives of bourgeois society such as industrialists and senior civil servants in Germany and France, the war was central to their self-image; both saw themselves as embodiments of the war state and the war economy. In addition to the sense of patriotic esteem, referring to national arguments enabled them to represent their interests better. Bourgeois perceptions and value concepts, and such distinctively bourgeois forms of participation as charity work and war loan subscriptions, seemed particularly in demand in the nation at war. But the war also brought major upheavals: French industrialists suffered from a loss of contracts and shortages of labor or raw materials, while many top officials in Germany had a feeling that their work was too little appreciated. Such relative loss of status increased expectations for the postwar period. In general, senior civil servants in Germany clung to ethnic models of interpretation: this was a reaction to their relative loss of status to the military and to new political players such as parliamentarians and trade union officials. The disparity between limited resources and far-flung expectations continued to grow: the widespread utopian visions of future colonial expansion spoke for themselves. Against this background, the war state in Germany tended to lose credibility and legitimacy, while the state elites in France, traditionally more insulated from the rest of the population, were able to maintain their status reasonably well.[308] Unitary republican patriotism proved remarkably stable among French prefects, and the occupation of France and the challenges of 1917 generally helped to motivate officials to make their own contribution to defense of the republic. It

Consumption and self-assurance: Christmas in Berlin, 1915

Coal shortage and a heat box: Christmas in Berlin, 1917

may be said, therefore, that the world war strengthened the continuity of older models of interpretation.[309]

But what did the war mean for men and women, for the relationship between the sexes and the perception of their social roles? One German woman wrote in 1915 about the outbreak of war: "A flood of feelings carried us away; we understood what was driving our men to leave. There was a strange frenzy in us to discard things, to make sacrifices for the general good. We felt impersonal and without needs of our own. That is how we led our families up to the threshold of war." While precisely recording the difference between men's and women's experience of the war, she noted above all how it initially reinforced traditional gender images: "We, however, stayed home. And while the men joined the iron snake, . . . we were destined to wait, to help, to hope, and to admire. The old womanless picture! But 'advanced' women had again become new and alien to us. We had felt equal with men, but the war brought back the old differences. What men had no longer felt inside themselves amid the customs and demands of modern culture—the hidden savagery of their blood—again came to light. And one thing in particular came to light: the heroic dimension. That is the big thing that women have experienced in these terrible, brutal times. Men have become men again, and women women. They go back to their old places as a matter of course. Once more there is inequality and mutual admiration, instead of the previous transparency among men and women with the same rights and the same aspirations."[310]

First of all, the war changed the demographic balance between men and women within the family. As early as Summer 1914, after their husbands, fathers, and brothers were called up, women played a key role in ensuring that the crops would be harvested. The war also determined the timescale of marriages and birth rates: these shot up at the beginning of the war, but then fell away just as sharply. Only in 1916, when there were longer periods of home leave before the major battles on the western front, did the number of marriages climb back up, to be followed by births nine months later. Most women had a remarkable capacity to adapt to demographic changes during and after the war. Although the number of unmarried women rose in the postwar period, it cannot be said that there was a generation of spinsters. Rather, many adjusted their choice of partners to the changed conditions: it often became possible to marry men from lower social strata. At least the end of traditional emigration flows of young men helped to compensate for the demographic effect of wartime casualties.

The end of the war brought a strong tendency to return to a male-defined social order. Veterans associations adhered to a conventional interpretation of gender roles, and more generally the war promoted a return of patriarchal models and older conceptions of men's role in society. In the long run, then, the war served less as an engine of female emancipation than as a boost to the subordinate image of wives and mothers. This explains the antipathy in many wartime societies to changes that affected women's autonomy and sexuality: whereas the Bolsheviks allowed abortion on demand, information about any kind of contraception was suppressed in France because of fears about population decline. There, a strong pronatalist policy developed under the impact of the heavy casualties among young men; demography became the object of long-range strategic calculation.[311]

In Summer 1914 the instrumentalization of gender images played an enormous role. War and battle were regarded as displays of masculine qualities—in line with the male composition of the army and widespread fears of a feminization of society. In the war's early months, many young men were afraid that it would come to an end too soon and prevent them from distinguishing themselves in action. The link between sexual attractiveness and participation in the war was clear during this period. Indeed, recruitment posters projected this image of soldiers as "real men," whether in their role as husbands defending their families or as bachelors who could prove their virility only in combat. British women were used in the campaign against men who did not immediately volunteer for military service, shown publicly taunting men with white feathers as a symbol of cowardice. Such shaming practices were based on a certain image of male bravery, which insinuated that certain individuals were not part of the national community. At the beginning of the war, the instrumental patriotism of middle-class women expressed itself in a variety of ways: while the French stressed the role of wives in giving emotional support to conscripts, the British mainly attempted to get women to pressure young men who were hesitating to sign up.

Gender images also played a key role in Allied propaganda about alleged German atrocities. Belgium was systematically depicted as a vulnerable woman, and the slogan, "Remember Belgium!," which featured on countless posters and postcards, showed the silhouette of a German soldier dragging a woman away. Her rape became the symbol of a violated, defenseless country, her defiled body representing the body of the nation. In German-occupied areas, real experiences lay behind such images: there was discussion in France about how women there should behave in the event that they became pregnant by German soldiers; it was eventually left up to them to decide whether to have the children adopted or to raise them themselves. At any event, violence against women—which has always been a part of war—also became a basis for the radicalization of self-images and enemy-images.[312] While brothels were organized for soldiers behind all the frontlines, it was taboo for any woman to have dealings with occupation troops.

As the months and years went by, the image of women in the war became increasingly ambiguous. The semantics of women as innocent victims of enemy violence remained intact, whether in allusions to the rape of nameless Belgian women or in the revulsion felt at the 1916 German execution of Edith Cavell, a British nurse shot in Brussels on suspicion of espionage. At the same time, however, women appeared as the cradle of danger, emotional instability, seduction, and corruptibility—qualities that contrasted with the willpower and resilience attributed to men at the front. In the critical gaze directed at the home society, it seemed important to test the validity of the values identified with the two sexes; this played a major role in the trial and execution of Mata Hari in 1917 as a German spy in France. Another danger identified with women was the communication of venereal diseases, against which soldiers were warned in countless leaflets.

Collective perceptions about how men and women should behave in the war, what was expected of them, and what was taboo did not remain static, but changed over time. This was true first of all at a structural level, especially in the mobilization of women for the economy. The number of women working in the British arms sector alone increased by 400,000 in the first year. In 1917 they accounted for 43.2 percent of all industrial workers in Russia and. at the beginning of 1918. for one-third of all munitions workers in France. But the total rate of female employment increased only slightly by 1918 in most of the belligerent countries. The image of a massive mobilization of women who had not previously gone to work is therefore deceptive; rather, female maids, farmhands, and textile workers often found themselves unemployed

The staging of role reversal: women in male occupations

and turned to the expanding war industries for work. In the United States, white women switched from housework to factory labor, while African American women gave up their traditional work on the land and took over vacated positions in domestic service. Contrary to what propaganda posters suggested, large numbers of women did not enter the labor markets of belligerent countries for the first time; what changed in the war was primarily the spectrum of female employment. The at least temporary improvement of women's wage levels during the war should be set against the considerable burdens it created in their daily lives, ranging from a 60-hour work week in Britain to the triple load of work, food provision, and child care. Women were not subjected to general labor service, although the German military leadership considered this as a possibility in 1916. At the same time, there were a number of social-political initiatives to improve working conditions for women in industry. In Germany, a special department operated under Marie-Elisabeth Lüders in the newly created War Office.[313]

Gertrud Bäumer, the German writer and campaigner for women's rights, who graduated in 1904 and went on to work as a schoolteacher and, from 1910, as chair of the Federation of German Women's Associations, looked in 1916 at the new role of women and carefully noted the demands and expectations associated with it. If one were "to give the broadest, most general name to what the war brought to maturity amid work and sacrifice, tears and despair, pride and jubilation, . . . nothing better could be found than the word: citizen. . . . After the availability of women ran up against the limits of inadequate vocational training in the first year of the war, the pressure of necessity meant that female participation developed to a quite unexpected degree in the second year. The retention of women even for difficult physical labor may become the Greek gift for the future." For women in the war found themselves in a difficult intermediate position: "Caught as it is between the self-interest of employers, who have only now fully discovered women's work, and male colleagues who fight against it, . . . between the theory of social hygienists and population experts who complain of the harm it does and the needs of the private sector that will drive even more women to work after the war, female employment in the Germany of the future has little prospect of harmonious solutions."[314] Despite these difficulties, however, she had the impression that an accelerated learning process was underway: "The war has simplified the global horizon for the whole people and given it an understanding of how to orient itself in immense spaces. Thrown backward and forward between the Balkans and Flanders, what facts has this male generation had to combine in order to grasp the meaning of its own action! How women have been able to forge political insights out of everything to do with the war economy—insights that no newspaper and no course in civics gave them so vividly!"[315]

In general, women tried as long as possible to avoid the extreme burdens of the war industry. New problems clouded the free spaces and new possibilities opened up by the war. One of these problems was stricter state supervision of women's private behavior: in particular, there was a growing fear of untrammeled female sexuality and infection with sexually transmitted diseases, as the Defence of the Realm Act and the Contagious Diseases Act showed in the case of Britain. Only women not suspected of immorality—which in practice meant marital infidelity—were supposed to receive state benefits. Here too the realities of a society at war nurtured the sway of suspicion and mistrust.[316]

The high proportion of women workers in the war industry led to considerable problems in 1918–1919, when the demobilization of millions of soldiers fueled overcapacity and an oversupply of labor. This increased the pressure to send women back into their traditional roles as housewives and mothers as fast as possible, so as to ensure jobs for men returning from the army. Nevertheless, women tended to remain more numerous than before the war in certain areas of the service sector and retail trade.[317] More generally, the wartime experiences of women—relations between the front and the home society, emotional closeness or estrangement between married couples, women's role as heads of families—continued to have their effects. Although it would be an exaggeration to equate the war with a general crisis of traditional masculinity, there were many signs of a fear of "unfaithful war wives" and a "battle of the sexes"—and the most frequent reaction to this was to fall back even more strongly on conservative notions of gender.[318]

But the war also upset traditional ideas of what counted as male or female; it challenged at least in part norms that were supposed to guarantee social cohesion. The tens of thousands of men who became nervous wrecks at the front, with no visible physical injuries at the end of the war, could not be reconciled with traditional notions of male willpower and bodily self-discipline; nor could conscientious objectors in this war be identified with the classical male qualities.[319] The image of the long-suffering patriotic wife or mother did not correspond to the minority of women who subscribed to a radical-feminist or left-socialist pacifism, as did Louise Saumoneau in France, Clara Zetkin and Rosa Luxemburg in Germany, or Sylvia Pankhurst in Great Britain. For the British suffragettes, the war was also a source of internal conflict and division: while her daughter Sylvia was vehemently opposed to the war, Emmeline Pankhurst argued forcefully for its continuation—partly because she expected the authorities to make concessions on the status of women in return for her cooperation.

Women were active in France and Britain during the crises of 1917 and were important players from late 1917 in the local strike movements that developed in Austria-Hungary and Germany. At the same time, many soldiers at the front grew more worried that new lines of conflict were being drawn back home; French mutineers demonstrated against the supposed deployment of colonial troops against striking women workers in Paris. In view of the high casualty rates at the front, the regulation that women should serve at the front only as nurses, not as soldiers, began to crumble in the course of

1917. While a Women's Army Auxiliary Corps was set up in Britain, regular combat battalions were formed with female troops in Russia after the February Revolution. Russian women had already played a key role in the proto-political hunger demonstrations, such as those organized on International Women's Day in March. In June, the Provisional Government began to put together a so-called Death Battalion out of female volunteers, the original initiative having come from, among others, the Siberian Maria Bochkarova, who had fought alongside her husband and remained in the army after his death. A number of newspapers published patriotic photos of her, together with a special message that the government made its own: if men refused to continue fighting, women should show what they were capable of in wartime. The deployment of women's battalions in the so-called freedom offensive of Summer 1917 was supposed to exert pressure on men in the face of a difficult military situation and high desertion rates.[320] In the end, some 300 women served in Summer 1917 in frontline areas, and a total of 5,500 to 6,500 were recruited for these units. Their last military operation was in October 1917, in the defense of the Winter Palace against the Bolsheviks.

These new role models—women as combat troops, men as conscientious objectors—remained the exception. Stricter adherence to conventional images was more typical of the war period, as we can see from the numerous picture postcards and novels dominated by homeland idylls and family life.[321] Conservative images featured in war literature by British female writers, who processed their experiences on the home front and presented them as part of the national war effort. They offered no criticism of the war, but reflected the expectations of the public and drew abundantly on themes from the prewar period.[322]

Even with regard to the suffrage, its later extension to women in many countries should not be placed in a direct causal relationship with the war. Female voting rights were already a heated issue before 1914, as the British suffragette movement demonstrated, and in Finland and Norway women had won the struggle by the time the war started. The Provisional Government in Russia provided for it as one of its first measures in 1917, and after 1918 nearly all European countries apart from France introduced female suffrage, mostly under socialist or social-democratic governments. In the United States, too, women's associations demonstrated before the White House; Alice Paul's

Role reversal: Russian women's battalions, 1917

National Woman's Party played a leading role in these, reminding President (or "Kaiser") Wilson that the democratic rights he was striving to achieve worldwide also had to be respected at home. The British Representation of the People Act of 1918 was based on an age qualification, giving women the right to vote after they reached 30; this excluded precisely those who had performed war service of one kind or another during the last few years of the war. In France, where the postwar focus was on wives and mothers, women won the right to vote only a quarter-century later, in 1944.[323]

Although governments in most of the belligerent states upheld a traditional view of women, excluding them from combat at the front, women developed other forms of symbolic participation, and many social norms underwent various changes in practice. At the end of the war, it became a matter of course that women in the British armed forces should wear khaki uniforms. Contact between unmarried men and women from all classes of society became more common than before the war, although certain misgivings remained decidedly in place. Behind the media focus on the patriotic duty of motherhood and the demand for more children lay concerns about female immorality and the birth of children out of wedlock. These fears put into perspective the political and cultural changes in many areas. For notwithstanding suffrage rights, changes in fashion, and employment opportunities, the chief impact of the war was conservative rather than innovative. The key element in women's lives during the war was something else: the common experience of work, of the struggle to survive, of caring for the wounded, and of mourning the dead. The war reinforced the image that most women had of themselves as mothers—mothers of future soldiers, but also mothers who, in breach of the law, insisted on burying their sons at home.[324]

Finally, the war was an enormous challenge for relationships and families. In this area too the nexus between front and home was by no means static; there were many different kinds of association and interaction, as the women violated in occupied France and the numerous letters between women and soldiers demonstrate. Emotional ties with brothers, fathers, and husbands at the front, including the fear of never seeing them again or the act of mourning after their death, formed one part of the picture. Women also had more concrete experience of the war, in the form of refugee influxes or air raids, for example. But the months of separation, together with a sense that their different lives at home and the front were drawing them apart and leaving them with less and less to say to each other, contributed to the estrangement of married couples. Flight into an imagined normality, or attempts to cling to a prewar image of homeland, family, and marriage, could help to stabilize things—but they came at a price. Women, in particular, clearly perceived this widening gap between illusion and reality. It fairly leaps to the eye in the correspondence between Anna and Lorenz Treplin (who had worked as a surgeon from 1901 at Eppendorf general hospital and from August 1914 in the army medical corps). Anna Treplin realized early on that there was no longer a relationship between them and that her husband was increasingly unable to relate to the everyday upbringing of their children. In September 1916, she commented drily on his constant references to the war: "Although it's very nice of you to keep believing so firmly (albeit vainly!) in the end to the war that we've heard about so much in the past two years, there is in my view absolutely no point in deluding ourselves on that score."[325] Even Lorenz Treplin's home leave increased the sense of alienation. After one three-week visit, the longest so far, he wrote in Spring 1917, "So, I've been sitting here again since yesterday evening and it's exactly as if nothing had happened, as if we'd dreamed in one night the whole three weeks that seemed so wonderfully long during the first few days. But you know, although the whole time was so splendid, there was something unsatisfying about being home only as a guest. And to some extent, this unsatisfied feeling superimposes itself on all the fine memories."[326]

In this correspondence, with all its bourgeois conventions, one is struck above all by the disciplined silence when the family had to accept dramatic losses. In Summer 1917 Anna and her children, who lived in Hamburg where the supply situation was deteriorating all the time, paid a visit to her husband's parents in the Ruhr countryside. She and her children fell ill there, and one of them died. Yet in his letters Lorenz Treplin does not let slip one word about this blow to the family, nor does he refer at all to the situation at home. It took a long time for the couple to find common ground again after the war and to overcome the strangeness that had developed between them as a result of the war and his personal sacrifices. Lorenz and Anna Treplin stopped writing to each other, but even after the war they never spoke with their children or in their own family about their wartime experiences. When the letters were found by chance in 1995, they were still tied together in the original bundle.[327]

10. ECONOMIC AND MONETARY TECTONICS
The Political Economy of a New World Order

The radical changeover from a peacetime to a wartime economy was a process that had no precedent. It became the engine driving a global economic and monetary interdependence that no one in Summer 1914 could have imagined. From the first months of the war, the exorbitant use of war materials and munitions, together with new logistical developments, gave a decisive boost to the war economies. A direct transport chain from production to consumption came into being on the western front as a result of the switch from war of movement to positional warfare; indeed, in many sections of the front, trains brought artillery shells right up to the firing positions. One sector of the British front 12 miles wide received 20,000 tons of supplies a day during the Battle of the Somme in 1916. The basic features of the new war economies soon became discernible: while the war ended trade relations between the Central Powers and the Entente, economic interdependence increased dramatically within the two sets of alliances. Between 1915 and 1918, half of all steel processed in France derived from imports from Britain and the United States. In 1916, some 40 percent of British munitions were shipped from America, and the same proportion of Russian munitions was imported from the Allied countries.[328] Despite this linkage, however, the main focus of war industries continued to be on national production.

In 1914 a total of 259 million people lived in Britain, France, and Russia, while the population of Germany and Austria-Hungary totaled no more than 118 million. The Entente therefore had 2.2 times more inhabitants, but its combined GNP was only 1.8 times higher than that of the Central Powers— which meant that it lagged behind in per capita terms. The main reason for this was the relatively low productivity in Russia. But the year 1917 changed the picture considerably, as Russia's exit from the war and America's entry strengthened the economic position of the Allies.[329]

In all the belligerent countries, industrial and agricultural output declined between 1914 and 1918—although in Britain GNP remained remarkably stable. Unlike in France and Russia, there was no actual fighting on British soil, and in contrast to the Central Powers, the country could draw on the enormous resources of the Empire. Whereas Germany and Austria-Hungary were directly affected by the British naval blockade, and whereas Russia's main trade routes were blocked in the Baltic and the Black Sea, Britain and France were able throughout the war to make up for national shortfalls by importing more products: this made it possible for France to survive even the severe economic crisis of 1917. After their isolation from the world market, the Central Powers stabilized at a lower level in 1916—though only at the cost of the major concentration on the arms industry, so that food supplies declined and increasingly threatened social cohesion.

Despite the growing dependence on American loans and a massive external trade imbalance, factors relating to prewar developments remained decisive for Britain's economic position. In 1913, 60 percent of world steamship capacity had been in British hands.[330] In combination with the Imperial transport infrastructure and the Royal Navy's protection of its merchant

Indexed GNP of Leading Belligerent States

Year	Britain	France	Germany	Austria-Hungary	Russia
1913	100	100	100	100	100
1914	97	84	92	90	95
1915	98	72	85	89	96
1916	94	81	81	80	80
1917	89	79	79	70	68
1918	87	66	76	62	
1919	92	72	68		
1920	101	77	77		

Source: Balderston, "Industrial Mobilization and War Economies," p. 220.

fleet, this ensured that the British economy had access to material and human resources. As we have seen, the economic relationship of forces between the Entente and the Central Powers was already 1.8:1 in 1914, and it rose further to 2.1:1 in 1915 and 1916, and to 3.7:1 in 1917, before falling back to 3.2:1 in 1918 after the collapse of further sections of French industry.[331]

The switch from peacetime to wartime economy did not only bring radical changes; it also involved major continuities between the prewar and war periods, especially with regard to the importance of the British Empire, transport capacity, and global shipping routes. But the continuities went even deeper. Several trends that had already existed in pre-1914 Germany, particularly in the arms sector, accelerated and intensified during the world war: for example, entrepreneurial demands for the national control and centralization of all economic resources; army pressure for total mobilization of the "nation under arms"; and a rise of technocratic statewide thinking, which made the organization of the economy dependent on weapons production and resource planning in a possible war of materiel.[332]

Economic mobilization for the war varied from country to country. Based on state spending as a share of GNP, it was particularly marked in Germany and France, and considerably less so in Britain and the United States. The aggregated total of state spending for the Entente countries was US$57.7 billion (in 1913 prices), of which $21.2 billion was for Britain (36.7 percent),

$9.3 billion for France (16.1 percent), and $17.1 billion for the United States (29.6 percent). The corresponding total for the Central Powers was $24.7 billion, of which $19.9 billion (or 80.6 percent) was for the German Reich. Thus, despite their greater mobilization of resources, the Central Powers at no point closed the economic gap with the Entente countries. On strictly economic criteria, if the costs of the war are correlated with casualty figures— conservatively estimated at 5.4 million in the Entente and approximately 4 million in the Central Powers—then the armies of the Central Powers killed more efficiently. The cost of killing one Central Powers soldier came to $14,300, against $4,500 for one Allied soldier.[333]

Altogether, only 30 percent of the costs of the war were funded from taxation, against 70 percent from loans. However, the share of state funding was distinctly higher in Britain and France than in the Central Powers. The problems of war finance were most apparent in Germany, because it was there that the debt burden, and hence money and credit inflation, increased most rapidly as a result. In 1914 the Reichsbank too had figured on a short war, and the state treasury held in the Spandau citadel was soon exhausted to pay for its exorbitant costs. In the 1914–1915 accounting year, only one-quarter of government expenditure was covered by current receipts, and from 1915–1916 this proportion dropped further to a mere 10 percent.[334]

To avoid making life even more difficult for a population already burdened by high casualties, and to reduce the dangers to social cohesion, the German government did not resort to additional taxation to pay for the war; the

State Spending as Share of GNP

Year	Germany	France	Britain	United States
1913	9.8	10.0	8.1	1.8
1914	23.9	22.3	12.7	1.9
1915	43.8	46.4	33.3	1.9
1916	50.3	47.2	37.1	1.5
1917	59.0	49.9	37.1	3.2
1918	50.1	53.5	35.1	16.6

Sources: Burhop, *Wirtschaftsgeschichte des Kaiserreichs,* p. 195; Broadberry and Harrison, "The Economics of World War I," p. 15.

share that came from this source (14 percent) was considerably lower than in France or Britain. Instead, it turned to loans and an increased money supply, the consequence of which was creeping inflation.[335] Part of the thinking behind the reliance on loans was that the war must end in victory, for only then would the loans be paid back in full by the enemy. This funding policy served to heighten public expectations that ruled out a compromise peace, let alone an acceptance of defeat.[336] From September 1916 the state debt exceeded the revenue from loans, and at the same time the money supply rose sharply—by 56 percent in 1917 and 76 percent in 1918. All told, the base money supply increased sixfold in Germany—from 7.2 billion marks in 1913 to 43.6 billion in 1918. Pressure mounted on cities and local communes, which were responsible for supplying the families of men at the front. The system of price controls and maxima prevented runaway inflation during the war years, but at best postponed the problem until the end of the conflict. Hyperinflation after 1918 wiped out the monetary assets of large parts of society, while allowing the state to reduce its debt level. The German public debt, which had already stood at 40 percent of GNP in 1913, would be down to a mere 8.4 percent by 1928.[337]

Inflation trends also varied internationally. In Britain, France, and Germany prices as a whole doubled between 1914 and 1918. In Russia they were four times higher in 1917 than they had been in 1914, while in Austria-Hungary they had quadrupled by the end of 1916. But governments in every country accepted inflation in the hope that it would prove to be only a temporary phenomenon and that after the war a return to the prewar gold standard would again regulate prices. It was precisely this confidence that drove the war at a monetary level.[338]

Since classical market economies could not have met the huge need for war goods in such a short time, the state became a key player in all war economies. Often it assumed the risks of industrial expansion, while allowing entrepreneurs to reap the profits in vital war industries. When the public saw what was happening, however, the wartime social consensus came under threat. Governments reacted to this mainly by introducing special taxes on war profits, although these played a much lesser role in Germany than in Britain or France. State regulation became more and more extensive in the course of the war, as local agencies took responsibility for food, rents, prices, raw material supplies, and relations between capital and labor. In Germany, bureaucratic-military intervention had supplanted market mechanisms by 1916–1917 at the latest—but the aim of central coordination and greater efficiency was not achieved. In many cases, the multiplication of authorities and competing jurisdictions meant that old-style requisitioning practices had to be resumed. This was most conspicuous in Britain, where new agencies intervened in railroad manufacturing, steel and munitions production, and rent and price controls; in 1917 the separation between summer time and winter time was introduced as a coal-saving measure. Above all, the British state became the world's most important player in key markets of the war economy, effectively taking over the textile market in its own country, as well as in Australia and large parts of the Empire. The Ministry of Munitions became the world's largest buyer and seller of war goods and increasingly drove out private sector competitors. Proactive intervention on such a scale was a novelty for a country where the Liberals had long relied on undisturbed market mechanisms and where institutionally—in terms of ministerial offi-cials and subordinate authorities—the prewar state had been much weaker than in Germany or France.

For the Allies, the pressure for economic and monetary cooperation gave these developments a global dimension, evident not least in the role of new players and institutions. In 1915, the J. P. Morgan banking house became the Allies' main agent for all purchases in the United States, and the establish-ment of the Inter-Allied Control Board meant that, after the U.S. entry into the war, a central structure reflected the degree of economic and financial interdependence.[339]

In the sphere of economic relations, it became clear in 1916–1917 how much the war was changing the relative weight of players around the world; the consequences would have a lasting impact on the twentieth century, precisely in parts of the world where the state had long remained neutral and did not become directly involved in the war. In Central and South America, the political and economic-monetary weight of the United States grew apace as European countries, particularly Britain, lost influence. The United States owed its political position to its rising importance for the export-dependent South American economies, after the war in Europe had massively interfered with traditional flows and shrunk trade ties with Britain and Germany. Not the least factors were the shortage of foreign currency and loss of purchasing power in the European war economies, which meant that they had to concentrate on imports of raw materials vital to the war effort. Naval battles at the beginning of the war, followed by the German U-boat campaign, made the shipping of goods on unprotected merchant vessels both dangerous and expensive. In the end, many commercial ships were taken over for use by the navy.

The British government aimed to wage the war with Germany on the commercial front too, thereby gaining increased long-term economic influence, but it did not achieve its ambitions. In 1916 it introduced the so-called Statutory Lists, which were supposed to penalize British companies that continued to do business in Latin America with German firms. But hopes of squeezing out German businessmen in the region and establishing an economic Greater Britain did not come to fruition.[340] It was not British but American companies that profited from the new constellation. Since Latin American states lacked large commercial fleets and the military strength to protect them, inter-American trade became considerably more important, especially after the opening of the Panama Canal on August 15, 1914, brought a major improvement to trade connections. Chile, for example, was able to switch its saltpeter exports, so important for fertilizer and munitions, from Europe to the United States. On the other hand, the collapse of grain and meat exports led to economic recession in Argentina and Uruguay; coffee exporters in Brazil, Colombia, Costa Rica, Nicaragua, and Guatemala suffered too, since coffee did not count as important to the war effort.

These economic developments were compounded by changes in the international finance market. New York virtually replaced the City of London as a provider of capital to Latin American states and businesses, so that after 1918 U.S. investment capital and U.S. firms became hugely important for the future development of the region. The building of new transport and communications infrastructure occurred in the same context, as did investment in agriculture, mining, and oil extraction.[341]

In 1917, the U.S. entry into the war directly affected the neutral countries in Europe. After the resumption of unrestricted submarine warfare, the deployment of German U-boats was a danger to neutrals too. The quantity of goods shipped to their ports fell by one-third, and many began to suffer supply problems of their own for the first time. The decline was particularly great in the case of American exports of grain, meat, fodder, oil, and metals to northern Europe. The total imports to neutral countries from the United States fell by three-quarters, with onward exports to Germany also affected.[342] Even in Switzerland, everyday hunger became a topic of discussion in Fall 1917.

Beyond the implications of the U.S. entry into the war, the year 1917 saw a shift in the centers of the global economy that would also have political consequences. A look at what it meant for Britain and the United States is particularly instructive. In the late nineteenth century, 40 percent of British capital resources were invested abroad, mainly in the Empire and Latin America, and by 1914 roughly half of total foreign investment around the world originated in Britain. Economically speaking, the United States had

The family members—Mr. and Mrs. Hunger, sons-in-law Anton Skinny and Fritz Fatless, Auntie Rations, and Niece Goshort— mourn the sad passing of their dear Mr. Breadloaf (postcard, Basel, 1917)

long since overcome its colonial status vis-à-vis the old country, which had been based on exports of raw materials and imports of food and led to a chronically negative trade balance. In the mid-1890s, moreover, the United States was well on the way to becoming one of the leading international lenders. President Wilson's policies were also designed to build up his country's influence in the world economy. The liberal vision of free trade as an instrument of peace and progress was part of this context, corresponding to the president's political universalism but also to the thoroughly down-to-earth interests of export-oriented American businesses.

The outbreak of war initially posed an economic and monetary challenge to the United States: the New York stock exchange had to close for four months, liquid capital was frozen, and the American export trade suffered severely from the lack of merchant shipping. But many entrepreneurs saw the growing Allied demand for American goods and capital as an opportunity to make some headway in regions where European players had been dominant. Business associations stepped up their pressure on Washington to use its strength to promote external trade.

Exports of goods and capital increased the significance of the dollar as a trading currency, as the Federal Reserve permitted transactions in dollars that had previously been effected in sterling. But in the long run the most important change was in the position of the United States as international lender. In 1914 the U.S. capital balance still showed debts to the tune of $3.2 billion, but then the war economy triggered a sudden turnaround that made the United States a net global creditor. Britain and France, in particular, absorbed huge quantities of American goods, while the level of American imports remained fairly constant. At first, the inward trade from the United States was financed with gold, and by 1917 the quantities crossing the Atlantic in the other direction had doubled. But the gold reserves of the European Allies were far from sufficient to pay for imports, and so the United States came to the fore as a supplier of credit. The flow of capital from the United States to the Allies supported the war boom of American industry long before it became likely that the country would enter the war. And by the time this happened, in April 1917, American loans to the British and French governments amounted to billions of dollars. The leading U.S. banks made New York their headquarters, and its stock exchange developed as a key center of the global capital market, at a time when the City of London was losing influence and drying up as a source of money.[343]

In Summer 1917, a major crisis illustrated the extent of changes in the world economy. Between April and June, the United States had provided the British government with loans in the region of $1 billion, but then the credit flow threatened to peter out and panic spread in Whitehall. The background to this crisis was a request by the J. P. Morgan bank, Britain's chief fiscal agent in the United States, that the American treasury should repay $400 million that Britain had received in loans before April that the U.S. government had underwritten. Market confidence in Britain's ability to repay this sum, despite the resources of the Empire that stood behind it, reached a low point in the summer. The way in which the British war cabinet responded to the U.S. ambassador, on July 16, 1917, revealed the degree to which it had become dependent on American loans: "If this financial breakdown should occur, it would be a deadly, perhaps a fatal, blow to the Allied cause. . . . The whole financial fabric of the Alliance will collapse. This conclusion will be a matter not of months but of days."[344] The U.S. treasury secretary William McAdoo wanted to use talks on the crisis to achieve far-reaching political and economic objectives: for example, that Britain should limit its investment in further development of its navy, thereby increasing the global maritime weight of the United States.

The U.S. entry into the war opened up huge advantages for its industry: German ships were impounded in American ports, the shares of German investors in American industries (especially chemicals and textiles) were seized, and many German technology patents were withdrawn. By 1917, then, the United States had more than compensated for the discontinuation of German imports. The war gave a powerful boost to the U.S. chemical and textile industries, in which the synergy of technological expertise and production growth was an important factor.[345]

Allied borrowing accelerated the boom in American exports, but it also made American industry dependent on Allied demand. When western European governments threatened in 1918 to stop importing U.S. pork, this was enough to trigger a crisis in American agriculture; the war-fueled expansion turned into overproduction, and prices plummeted. This context also limited Wilson's attempts in 1918–1919 to obtain political concessions from London or Paris by referring to the debt situation; the British and French governments knew how much the American economy depended on exports to Europe. The contradictions in Wilson's policy were carefully noted: he was pushing for political multilateralism, yet authorized economic bilateralism when it was a question of furthering U.S. economic interests. Wilson pleaded for the internationalization of politics, but hesitated to bring American economic resources into this new international order.[346]

These contradictions became all the more apparent as the war strengthened America's economic weight. Here lay the fundamental significance of the world war for the twentieth century: the American commercial fleet was 60 percent larger in 1919 than it had been before the war, and by 1922 it had grown 2.5 times since 1913. In 1919, for the first time since the Civil War of the 1860s, more U.S. goods were being transported on foreign routes than on the country's own rivers and coasts; 43 percent of America's foreign trade was being handled by its own ships. The export ratio doubled between 1914 and 1924, and U.S. products achieved a world market share of 15 percent. This development came mainly at the cost of British commerce in Asia and Latin America, where the Monroe Doctrine was, so to speak, extended to the economy. In 1929, 38 percent of imports in this region came from the United States, compared with 22 percent from Britain and 16 percent from Germany. One figure, above all, indicates the changes in the world economy resulting from the war and its political consequences: in 1914 the U.S. trade balance showed debts of $3.7 billion, whereas in 1919 the United States was in the black by the same amount. Without taking government loans into account, this figure would rise to $7 billion in 1924 and $8 billion in 1929.[347]

Another aspect of the U.S. entry into the war was that, following the spectacular wartime expansion of its industry, it did not invest the profits from it in the world economy after 1918. Instead, government and business began to seal off the U.S. economy more and more from the outside world. This was a major difference from the role played by Britain and its Empire in the nineteenth century. After 1918–1919, U.S. leaders staked a claim to world economic leadership that the wartime changes seemed to justify. But in practice their isolationism confuted that claim. Things would change decisively only a generation later, after the Second World War, and based on the knowledge of the disastrous effects that the discrepancy between economic-financial strength and political isolationism had produced.[348]

11. FORTY-ONE MONTHS OF WAR
The "Impossible Year" between Competitive Utopias and Illusions of Peace

On December 31, 1917, Harry Graf Kessler had his evening meal at the Hotel Kaiserhof restaurant in Berlin: "New Year's Eve meal for 25 marks: goose liver pâté, turtle soup, blue carp, spit-roasted young turkey and salad, sundae. Really good and a lot of it, even if 25 marks is more than double the peacetime price." The past year, he was in no doubt, had seen the "biggest turnaround in the state of the world," which neither he nor others at the time could have predicted. What with "the Russian revolution, the Russian peace, and America's interference in the war," it had been "one of the memorable years in world history."[349]

(1) What made 1917 the "impossible year"?[350] After the experiences of 1916, many had thought it impossible to continue the war with such high casualties, and it was no accident that the search for a possible peace became more intensive. However, the year had first transformed the military, social, and political exhaustion into a dynamic of rising expectations, and from there into a possible crisis. The example of France showed this: soldiers had expected that the extreme buildup of tension and the concentration on a last great offensive would finally end the war. But when the Nivelle offensive ended in failure, disappointment and disillusion turned into protest and resistance, which embryonically linked front and home society together. This was not only a trend in France in Spring and Summer 1917, but was even more pronounced in Russia after the Kerensky offensive and in Italy after the disaster of Caporetto. The cohesion of gigantic armies was in question, but the mutinies, desertions, and decomposition varied in scale, origin, and consequences. Whereas the Austro-Hungarian armed forces still held together against the Italian enemy, developments in Russian society in the spring eroded the cohesion of the army at the front. More and more soldiers wanted to be back home to solve the land question or engage in the struggle for national independence. In France it was neither radical pacifism nor socialist infiltration of the army that led to the mass mutiny in Spring 1917; the soldiers involved in it were fighting for concrete demands, including continuation of the war against the German aggressor and occupier of their country. A number of "stab in the back" legends sprang up amid these crises—in Russia as a reaction to the

failure of the Kerensky offensive, in France as part of a strategy to isolate mutinous soldiers and striking workers, and in Italy to deflect attention from the responsibility of commanders for military disaster.

(2) The year of exhaustion ushered in the second social mobilization since Summer 1914. It also represented a crucial test of the capacity of political systems to sustain the war under different conditions. The supply and efficiency crisis of the war states brought to a head the question of the relationship between casualties and promises of political participation—hence the new intensity of the debates in Germany on electoral reform. In 1917, Max Weber thoughtfully noted that the world war, with its experience of massive casualties among all sections of the population, made it increasingly impossible to go back on promises of universal and equal suffrage. But contrary to what the original advocates of universal suffrage had anticipated, the ideal was being realized in the struggle among nations and nation-states. Political equality did not develop as a universally valid human and civil right, but as compensation for "those equalities which the modern state offers all its citizens in a truly lasting and undoubted way: sheer physical security and the minimum for subsistence, but also the battlefield on which to die."[351]

(3) But the war states did not only face political protest against unfair burden sharing, the daily hardship of shortages, and, in the Central Powers, supply problems. With the two revolutions in Russia and the entry of the United States into the war, new political and social models appeared on the horizon. Whether as revolutionary civil war or as democratic interventionism, these new visions had a direct impact on politics in all the other belligerent countries. In Petrograd the nexus of war and revolution loomed, having in a short time eroded traditional ideas of monarchic or imperial legitimacy. Above all, however, Lenin and Wilson offered ways out of the war and, within very different perspectives, gave an answer to the problem of national self-determination.

The year 1917 did not bring "total war" as a reality, but it did demand total mobilization at the levels of army and society, economy, and politics.[352] The outcome was not "total" in the sense of completely blurring the boundary between military and home fronts, but the tendency or finality, the formulation of the aims of a process, may be described in that way. It was the year in which the totalization of war efforts appeared as a possibility, not least in the claims of the war regimes embodied by Clemenceau in France, Lloyd George in Britain, or Ludendorff in Germany. This totalization also affected the second post-1914 global expansion of the war. The wave of new declarations of war combined with new expectations that were ever more remote from European contexts, but would have long-term effects on them. The democratic definition of participatory rights and the principle of national self-determination were not only a promise to national minorities within the multiethnic Habsburg, Russian, and Ottoman Empires; they also stimulated anticolonial movements in Asia and Africa. Wilson rapidly came to symbolize the possibility of political change after the war was over. Here lay the global dimension of the criticisms of colonialism that developed in 1917—not through the Islamic holy war envisaged by the Central Powers in 1914, but through the agency of the American president. Wilson's program gave a new impetus to earlier developments in the colonial societies; the "Wilsonian moment" was thus less the origin of something new than an acceleration and concretization of positions that had been present for some time. At any event, models now existed for an exit from the war and a redefinition of political participation and autonomy, not only in Europe but also in colonial societies on other continents. The tensions among the new partners in Washington, London, and Paris were foreseeable, and they grew sharper in relation to military strategy and economic power relations.

(4) The significance of the U.S. entry into the war is not explained by highlighting the contrast between an old, exhausted Europe and a youthful America embodying new and progressive ideas. The leaderships in London and Paris could not simply compensate for Russia's impending exit from the war by drawing on American resources of men, capital, and goods. For the lineup after April 1917 was not just a continuation of the alliance of 1914, with a third partner to replace Russia; the United States brought with it an economic and international political agenda of its own, as well as a demand for military autonomy. Nor does the idea that North America dissolved the old Europe in April 1917 get us very far. The dependence of the European Allies on American capital and American war goods had begun much earlier, and this change at the level of political economy compelled the French, and *a fortiori* the British, leadership to adopt a transatlantic orientation long before the first U.S. troops landed in Europe. Within a few months the British and

French lost control of their own war finances, foreshadowing the transition to a new world economic order. To be able to continue the war, political leaders in London and Paris had to mutate into convinced Atlanticists.

But the contrast between Clemenceau, the authoritarian war premier of the old Europe, and Wilson, the idealist democrat, also needs to be put into perspective. For Clemenceau himself embodied thoroughly democratic values, albeit in a direct appeal to the people rather than through the traditional weight of parliament. And Wilson reflected the opposition between, on the one hand, far-flung democratic ideals and universalist claims, and, on the other hand, the practice of an ever more illiberal American society at war, in which vigilantism and racism were increasingly out of control.

(5) The political leaderships of the European war states confronted multiple challenges: the fair sharing of the burdens of war was under increasing pressure; the mobilization of national resources was nearing its limits (as Britain's dependence on the United States clearly showed); and the internal political truces of Summer 1914 were starting to crumble. A rethink was necessary, and the results of this were fundamental changes in the political landscape and increased political polarization. The Left, especially in Germany, was divided over the question of continuing the war. While the Right lambasted the war leaders as incompetent defeatists, liberals in every belligerent country found themselves on the defensive. Whether in Germany, Britain, France, or Italy, the new relationships between state authorities and economic players—the triangle of war state, labor, and capital—could be turned against traditional liberal principles under fire from accusations of defeatism and pacifism.

But the responses to this new lineup varied widely. In Britain and France, the charismatic war premiers Lloyd George and Clemenceau strengthened the role of the executive, without breaking their links with parliament. Although these links came under pressure in France—a widespread view was that if the war was won, it would be in spite, not because, of parliament—leading politicians in Paris and London did manage to act as something like mediators between the public and parliament, under the aegis of the patriotic war effort. Things were very different for the Central Powers. Here parliaments returned to the political stage in Spring and Summer 1917; the German Reichstag passed a peace resolution, and interparty alliances were formed in the newly recalled Imperial Council in Vienna. But the fall of Chancellor Bethmann Hollweg was a sign less of the strength of parliament than of the weight of the OHL in political decision making. The founding of the German Fatherland Party, as a counterthrust to the Reichstag peace resolution, highlighted the degree of the polarization. In Vienna, the recall of parliament and the easing of censorship showed how far the ethnicization of social and political conflicts had already advanced. Parliament and the press turned into forums for bitter disputes between rival nationalisms, such as those of German Austrians and Czechs in Cisleithania or Magyars in Hungary. In neither Berlin nor Vienna did parliament become an integrative force helping the wider society to see the war through to the end. What it displayed, rather, was the lines of conflict within society at large—plus, in the case of Vienna, the national polarization between parts of the Empire.

(6) Intensive peace feelers accompanied the exhaustion on the home fronts. Acting from a position of strength after the enactment of the law on auxiliary service and the victory over Romania in December 1916, Bethmann Hollweg sent a note to the United States that contained an offer of peace talks; it was partly meant to forestall an American initiative that, in the case of an armistice, would have required Germany to give back Belgium. At any event, there was no willingness on the German side at the time to restore Belgian sovereignty in line with Allied demands; Berlin saw the country's status as a card it could play in future peace talks. There was also the issue of Alsace-Lorraine, which the government could not contemplate returning to France. President Wilson's initiative in late 1916 also had no tangible result, especially as the German leadership was already threatening to resume unrestricted submarine warfare. Finally, Emperor Karl of Austria made no progress with his initiative, which led to a serious crisis of confidence with the OHL that ended in Karl's humiliating climbdown at German headquarters. After May 1918, there could no longer be any talk of Vienna's having room for maneuver in external politics.

The Reichstag peace resolution of Summer 1917 lost credibility because many deputies who had backed a peace agreement without annexations or reparations would vote with the large majority in March of the following year for the Brest-Litovsk diktat. Another significant event in August 1917 was Pope Benedict XV's peace proposal.[353] Although the U.S. entry into the war in April had initially made the situation more acute, the references on all sides to exhaustion and war weariness were by then so prominent that this approach by a neutral institution offered some prospect of success. The Pope had supported Emperor Karl's peace feelers in March, and rumors of British-French-Habsburg talks in Switzerland had strengthened the impression that there was some movement. For the Vatican, the February Revolution in Russia was a sign of economic, social, and political collapse, but fears among Catholics in Germany and the mutinies and strike waves in France were also important entry points. Furthermore, a number of international conferences, such as those of Catholic parliamentarians in Switzerland in February or of socialist delegates in Stockholm, seemed to confirm the great significance of the efforts to reach a peace agreement.

Benedict's peace proposal of August 1, 1917, went further than the earlier American and German initiatives. It did not consist of vague suggestions for an exchange of views or pronouncements on the rights and legitimate demands of nations, but outlined clear and precise steps with a view to ending the war and achieving a stable peace. The Pope called for simultaneous disarmament, a system of international arbitration to settle disputes, and recognition of the freedom of the seas. All sides should agree not to demand war indemnities, and occupied territories should be evacuated and restored. The Vatican hoped that it would be possible to mediate between the rival claims in a climate of mutual understanding. Finally, the Pope mentioned several specific territories: Belgium and northern France, but also the German colonies, would have to be handed back. Going beyond a simple return to the status quo ante, Benedict also stressed the need to examine competing claims in Armenia, the Balkan countries, and Poland.[354]

The Pope's efforts, including his proposals on many issues that the U.S. president would raise shortly in his Fourteen Points of January 1918, remained unsuccessful. In Germany, Bethmann Hollweg was not the kind of politician who could have credibly taken up and built on the proposals. More important, in view of the relatively favorable military situation, the OHL was quite unwilling to withdraw from occupied Belgium and France. Britain, for its part, was by then interested in much more than the fate of Belgium; it had far-reaching economic objectives and was concerned to ensure its maritime supremacy. In London as in Paris, the fear was that the Pope's efforts might interfere with the strategy of deciding the war with American military assistance. Besides, French political leaders, with their secular conception of the state, rejected any active role on the part of the Catholic church and the Vatican, which they saw as chiefly an instrument of the Central Powers and, in particular, the Dual Monarchy. Washington withheld support because the papal initiative called into question Wilson's role as mediator. Benedict XV mainly saw his proposal as a stand against the wartime radicalization of nationalism, the appeals of which to a supranational morality were increasingly unable to contain. In any case, the Vatican was not regarded in 1917 as a neutral party; its initiative was interpreted as an attempt to save the Habsburg monarchy and, more generally, to strengthen the political weight of Catholicism. There were many reasons for Benedict to defend the moral authority of the Catholic church: the anti-Catholic reflexes of French republicans, the events commemorating the Reformation in Germany, and the displeasure in Germany in December 1917 when church bells rang out in Rome—St. Peter's apart—and Te Deums were sung to celebrate Allenby's liberation of Jerusalem. His efforts, however, were unsuccessful.[355]

When the Wilsonian nexus of peace and worldwide democracy began to take shape toward the end of the year, Thomas Mann pointed to a basic problem: "World peace. . . . We humans should not get too many big ideas about morality. If we manage to achieve world peace, *a* world peace, we will not have reached it along the path of morality. Scheidemann said recently that democracy will make great strides on account of the general exhaustion. That does democracy no great honor—nor humanity for that matter. Morality out of exhaustion is not a very edifying morality."[356]

(7) The peace efforts failed in the end because the military situation was still unclear in 1917 and no state wanted to weaken its hand by agreeing to overhasty concessions. The year proved the significance of the thinning down of human and material resources. Thinking in time frames became more widespread: how long could such a war be kept up on the military and home fronts? The dangers looked greater than ever, for, as Caporetto had shown, even limited setbacks could dramatically accelerate and bring defeat closer. In 1917 the position of the Central Powers against Russia and Italy seemed to have improved, as had their defenses on the western front; Britain and France, after the failure of the spring offensives and the third battle of Flanders, now pinned their hopes on the United States.

In view of the developments in Russia, the German military saw no reason to doubt the possibility of peace with victory—so long as the home front remained stable and people were prepared to hold out and redouble their efforts. A new social mobilization also began in Britain and France in late 1917; the casualties of the previous four years made a compromise peace unthinkable for the leaderships in London and Paris. In a German perspective, there would be a window of opportunity between the end of the war with Russia (around the end of 1917) and the effective deployment of U.S. troops on the western front; Berlin underestimated the significance of the American entry into the war, hoping that the resumption of unrestricted submarine warfare would begin to tell first. On November 11, 1917, exactly a year before the armistice, Ludendorff made a highly favorable assessment of the situation on the eastern front and of the state of the Alpine front after Caporetto. But he could see that the Central Powers now had a very narrow time frame, which permitted of no alternatives: "The situation in Russia and Italy will probably allow us to strike a blow on the western front in the new year. The forces on the two sides will be roughly equal. Approximately 35 divisions and 1,000 heavy artillery pieces can be made available for an offensive. They will be enough for one offensive; a second major offensive—to create a diversion, for example—will not be feasible. Our whole situation requires us to strike as soon as we can, if possible by the end of February or early March, before the Americans can throw strong forces into the balance. We must hit hard at the British."[357]

This set out a major prerequisite for the coming year of the war. Awareness that victory was still possible led to high expectations that the war could soon be over, but their very height contained the possibility that the hopes would come crashing down and end in disillusionment and loss of legitimacy. The regimes and societies at war looked more and more like houses whose external walls alone were still standing and which the next blow might cause to collapse altogether. For many, the key question was therefore who could hold out for the last few meters and beat the enemy to the ground.

It was in 1917 that the paradoxical mechanism of the war's self-prolongation combined with actual scenarios for the end of the war. The more victims the war demanded, the less a compromise peace was in the cards, and the more military leaders focused on a victory that would justify all the casualties and efforts of the previous years. Peace with victory was therefore on the minds of people on all sides. This mechanism continued to operate until one side collapsed under the weight—but it remained open in Summer 1918 which side that would be. The end of the war, with all its far-reaching consequences, therefore came suddenly and caught the losers unprepared. The politically effective metaphor of a military victory, said to be within reach up to the end and snatched away only at the last minute, was based on the experiences and expectations of the latter part of 1917.[358]

7

ONRUSH AND COLLAPSE
1918

"GENUINE CRISES ARE RARE," wrote the Swiss historian Jacob Burckhardt in his lectures on world history, *Reflections on History*. He theorized a pathology of crisis as a phenomenon harboring many surprising elements, one being a decisive speeding up of history. A historical crisis manifests itself when the "world process" suddenly accelerates "in terrifying fashion": "Developments which otherwise take centuries seem to flit by like phantoms in months or weeks, and are fulfilled."[1] Did the last year of the world war constitute such a crisis?

It began with a contradictory juxtaposition. Signs of exhaustion seemed unmistakable on all sides, and a wave of strikes in January in Germany and Austro-Hungary showed that the justice of the war was being questioned more than before. The year 1917 had been one of mutinies and strikes, war weariness and collective exhaustion, social polarization and political reorientation—culminating in a radical utopianism bound up with violent revolution and the passage from world war to civil war in Russia. But this development did not continue in 1918 in the belligerent countries. Rather, a growing readiness to continue the war was discernible: the wish to see it end soon did not entail radical pacifism or strike action in the army. Instead, the final period of the war witnessed a renewed military, economic, and political mobilization. This began in Winter 1917–1918, in the awareness that a decision to the conflict was not far off. An important indicator was the decrease in the number of strikers: down in Germany from 667,000 in 1917 to 392,000 in 1918. In France the corresponding totals were 294,000 and 176,000. Only after the end of the war, in a context of revolution or demobilization, did the number of strikers shoot up again: to 2,321,000 in Germany and 1,151,000 in France.[2]

Meanwhile, on January 8, 1918, President Wilson set out before Congress his program for a new postwar international order. Most of what he had to say was already familiar, but the concise listing of the American position in Fourteen Points would become a key political reference in the last year of the war—although this was not yet foreseeable in January. Wilson declared certain principles of political freedom that had a claim to universal validity and were supposed to prepare the world for a democratic order. He wanted to transform the war between imperialist great powers into a crusade for democracy. Alongside the call for disarmament, the right to national self-determination (Point 10), which referred explicitly to the Habsburg monarchy and the Ottoman Empire, occupied a central place. The demand for unfettered national autonomy was not yet synonymous with the breakup of the multinational empires. But Point 13 explicitly mentioned the creation of a Polish state, and as to disputed colonial questions, Wilson stated that indigenous peoples should have a say in their future. He also turned against the European tradition of secret diplomacy, which he saw as part of the nineteenth-century states system. The demand that all international treaties should be made public (Point 1) was directed against a practice that he considered largely responsible for the outbreak of war in August 1914.

Another prominent aspect of the Fourteen Points was the liberal belief in free trade and the freedom of the seas, which required the opening of the Bosporus Strait to international shipping. These principles had a particular logic since the special interests of the United States—whose economic and financial power had grown enormously during the war—were part of the context of Wilson's program. He envisaged an end to the occupation regimes and the evacuation of occupied territories in France and Belgium in the west, Russia in the east, and Serbia, Montenegro, and Romania in the southeast of Europe. Alsace-Lorraine was to be returned to France and new Italian borders drawn in the Alps and the Adriatic; Serbia would be given access to the sea. Finally, Point 14 called for the founding of an international treaty organization binding all democratic nations to settle future conflicts in mutual respect for one another's territorial integrity.[3]

On January 24, 1918, the Central Powers rejected the Fourteen Points—a decision that reflected the favorable military situation in the east and the possibility of a breakthrough in the west. The German and American positions on the shape of a future peace would remain irreconcilable until the end of September. Then, on October 3, the official German request to the United States for an armistice explicitly referred for the first time to Wilson's list of demands, reflecting the dramatic changes of the previous nine months.[4]

At the beginning of the year, it was first and foremost the Allied commanders who were truly pessimistic. The war—in the view of many British and French officers—would continue far into 1919 or even 1920, for only then would the American military presence really begin to tell. The French army still seemed weak in the aftermath of the mutinies in 1917. The fear of many officers that a fresh outbreak remained possible prohibited any major offensive plans. The British armed forces were still absorbing the high number of casualties of the third battle of Flanders and the poor results of the tank deployment at Cambrai. Lloyd George openly doubted whether there would be political support for a costly new offensive on the western front. Italy was reeling militarily and politically in the wake of the Caporetto disaster, while Russia seemed to be sliding into the chaos of civil war and national independence struggles and could not be prevented from signing a separate peace with the Central Powers. Against this background, the Allies tensely waited for the Germans to launch another major offensive on the western front with troops transferred there from the east.

In 1918 everything seemed to be repeating itself, only faster and with higher stakes—but at the same time, everything was different. It became the year in which the war seemed to return to its temporal and spatial origins, to its first few months between August and October 1914 on the western front; this mirrored the realization of all involved that the war could only be decided there. In Spring 1918 a war of movement in the west suddenly became possible again—with penetrations of the front and territorial gains, but also with casualty figures on all sides that approximated the levels in the early weeks of the war. German hopes of a linkup between the western and eastern fronts were also revived, but within a reversed perspective. In 1914 a swift victory in the west would have enabled a decision in the east, solving the problem of a war on two fronts. In 1918, after the successes in the east, a victory on the western front and an end to the whole war seemed to be within reach. Once again, however, the hopes on the German side ended in disillusionment: while in Fall 1914 war of movement had turned into positional warfare of an unpredictable duration, the developments in Summer and Fall 1918 led to the defeat of the Central Powers. Spatially, too, the war in Summer 1918 returned to the places where it had been fought in 1914; German troops again stood before Paris, and as in September 1914 the Marne was the scene of a major turning point. But armies now had the experience of four years of war. Tactics and technologies had changed. Exhaustion was palpable on all sides, both at the front and in the home societies. Time windows were narrowing as more (in many places the last) resources were mobilized for the war. The leaders of the Central Powers were aware that little time remained to decide the conflict before their home fronts collapsed, while London and Paris not only had to cope with a major German offensive but also feared their increasing dependence on the United States. Any prolongation of the war would strengthen America's weight militarily, economically, and politically, reducing the influence of its western European partners in the postwar world.

This constellation gave rise to particular logics of action, associated with a readiness for higher stakes and risks. The deadly mechanism of the war, which had guaranteed its continuation over the previous four years, thus persisted until the end. The prospect of victory in the minds of political and military leaders stood in the way of a compromise peace, and only a complete victory could justify the enormous sacrifices of the past four years. This was the price to be paid for the expectations raised in all the belligerent states that any future peace would involve territorial gains, reparations, and security pledges that justified all the casualties, suffering, and social and economic burdens. As a consequence, the war ended only when one side grew so exhausted that it faced immediate collapse. Unlike in Summer and Fall 1914, the dominant feeling in 1918 was that there could not be many more attempts to bring the war to a victorious conclusion. The German side, buoyed up by the Brest-Litovsk treaty in the east, stuck to the classical model of peace with victory, but did not build the possibility of setbacks or even defeat into its calculations. It was therefore inevitable that any ending other than victory would arouse huge disappointment, with incalculable consequences for the cohesion of military structures and a secondary effect in the home societies.

The dramatic differences between January 1918 and mid-October of that year indicated that new developments had been coming thick and fast. The Central Powers' victory that had still seemed conceivable at the beginning of the year turned into an epoch-making defeat in the fall; the nine months in between saw a torrent of interrelated military decisions and an ever-tighter interlinking of the eastern and western fronts, the fronts in Italy, the southeastern Balkans (Macedonia), and the Near and Middle East.

At the same time, the face of the war changed once more, blurring the boundaries between military front and home society. This was particularly evident in aerial warfare, which was no longer just a question of reconnaissance and infantry support. The Germans began the systematic bombardment of Allied cities, and in 1918 twin-engine Gotha bombers and even four-engine Zeppelin-Staakens carried out raids on Paris and London. Already on June 13, 1917, as many as 162 civilians had lost their lives. The Allies, for their part, attacked German cities in the general vicinity of the western front: Stuttgart, Mainz, Metz, Mannheim, Karlsruhe, Freiburg, and Frankfurt. In many raids, the bombs were dropped from a great height, with the aim not so much of hitting strategic targets as demonstrating military power in the enemy homeland. In many cities, blackouts, sirens, searchlights, signal flares, air defense, and the taping of shop windows to contain shrapnel soon became part of everyday life.[5] There, the outlines of a different kind of phenomenon were appearing—the twentieth-century air war against the civilian population.

1. FROM FRONT TO SPACE OF VIOLENCE
Dictated Peace and Civil War in Eastern Europe

After the ceasefire between the Central Powers and Russia took effect in mid-December 1917, conflicts intensified among Bolshevik leaders about what to do next. Lenin had a realistic assessment of the situation at the beginning of 1918: he was inclined to accept harsh terms in the peace negotiations, in order to strengthen the position of the Bolsheviks at home and thereby secure the gains of the revolution. The impending civil war and national independence movements on the periphery made things difficult enough—and in his view they ruled out a continuation of hostilities with the Central Powers. But other Bolsheviks, convinced that the revolution would before long spread from Russia to other societies, did not agree. Nikolai Bukharin held that the war should be used consistently as a means of spreading the revolution. And Trotsky argued that, since it was just a matter of time before revolutions broke out in the Central Powers, Russia should settle for neither war nor peace, but stall as long as possible in the peace talks while doing everything to support revolutionary currents in Germany and Austria-Hungary.

This was designed to turn against the Central Powers the strategy that German leaders had employed in Spring 1917, when they facilitated Lenin's return to Russia in the hope of accelerating its internal collapse. Strike waves in the Central Powers in January 1918 seemed to lend credence to the Bolsheviks' hopes, and they stepped up their propaganda to encourage German and Austro-Hungarian soldiers to desert and fraternize with Russian troops. But this approach had limited success. Russia's release of two million (mostly Austro-Hungarian) prisoners of war was supposed to weaken the cohesion of the monarchy, and it is true that the returnees included many future leaders of the Left in Austria and southeastern Europe, including the Austrian Socialist Otto Bauer and the Hungarian and Yugoslav Communists Béla Kun and Josip Broz Tito.[6]

In any case, the Bolsheviks' most important measure to strengthen their long-term position in Russia pointed in a different direction; namely, the organization, from January 1918 on, of a loyal army of workers and peasants. Precisely because the military situation looked critical, Lenin increased the pace of this process. In February he consciously differentiated revolutionary warfare from traditional ideas of a people's militia or guerrilla warfare; defense of the October Revolution now demanded a turn to military professionalism. Lenin therefore rejected the calls of the Left Socialist Revolutionaries and anarchists for a people's war, insisting that strict centralization was a necessity in the reality of revolutionary war and that only a regular army, not a people's militia, could ensure access to all the economic resources crucial for the successful defense of the country: "There must be a lengthy, serious preparation for it [revolutionary war], beginning with economic progress, the restoration of the railways (for without them modern warfare is an empty phrase), and the establishment of the strictest revolutionary discipline and self-discipline everywhere."[7]

As the people's commissar for foreign affairs, Leon Trotsky led the Russian delegation at the Brest-Litovsk peace talks. Things took a sharp turn when he began playing for time with representatives of the Central Powers, most notably the German general Max Hoffmann. On February 9, 1918, Germany and Austria-Hungary signed a separate peace with Ukraine, turning the screws still tighter on the Bolsheviks. Still, on February 10, in line with his "neither war nor peace" strategy, Trotsky let it be known to his opposite numbers that his country would neither continue the war nor sign a peace treaty. The Central Powers reacted by expanding their territorial demands, so that now the strategically important Baltic and Black Sea coasts came up for grabs. When Trotsky then broke off the talks, German troops resumed their advance on February 18, immediately capturing Minsk and supporting the proclamation of an independent Belarus. In many places, facing no Russian resistance, they were even able to use the railroad: this explains the huge gains in such a short time and once again illustrates the character of the world war as a "rail war," in which the mobility of armies and transport infrastructures were of crucial importance. These developments led to more disputes within the Bolshevik leadership, but Trotsky and others who were relying on further revolutions in Europe then had to recognize that there was no alternative to a peace treaty. Lenin's argument won the day: the harsh conditions set by the Central Powers had to be accepted in order to stabilize the situation inside Russia.

Developments in 1918 on various fronts, most notably the Alps and southeastern Europe, illustrate the complexity of the period stretching from the ceasefire talks through the actual armistice to the start of formal peace talks and the signing and eventual ratification of a peace treaty. The end of the war did not come at one moment, with the cessation of hostilities and a peace agreement; it was a more intricate and protracted process. In eastern Europe in early 1918, the time before the signing of the final treaty agreement was used to advance and occupy new territory, thereby creating a *fait accompli* for the postwar order—a triumph of the territorial principle. When Ludendorff realized that the Bolsheviks were about to give way, he ordered his troops to advance even further. These operations clearly went beyond the original aim of forcing Russia into a separate peace and removing it as an ally of the western powers, which was intended to free resources for the war on the western front. The German sphere of influence was extended far beyond the frontiers of Ober Ost, with the creation of dependent satellite states at Russia's expense. The plan for the postwar order was that this military-imperial buffer zone would serve as the basis for German hegemony in Continental Europe.

Such conceptions were not uncontroversial. General Wilhelm Groener, commander of the German troops in Ukraine after the separate treaty of February 9, 1918, knew that this "bread peace" would give him access to the country's grain resources, improving supplies to the German and Austro-Hungarian home societies at a critical juncture of the war on the western front. According to Ludendorff's calculations, after a victory in the west, Ukraine and the Caucasus would also serve as the springboard from which to extend the war against the British Empire in India and Mesopotamia. But Groener had long considered such ambitions unrealistic, knowing that they conflicted with the real problems of occupation forces that had to operate with limited resources in a challenging war zone.[8]

After Central Powers troops entered Kiev on March 1 and Narva on March 2 without meeting any major resistance, the peace treaty was finally signed in Brest-Litovsk on March 3. This document, together with the peace treaty between the Central Powers and Romania signed in Bucharest in May 1918, marked the peak of German military power in eastern Europe. What happened in Courland, Lithuania, Poland, and Finland and what led in Ukraine to a de facto German protectorate proved the Bolshevik conception of a revolutionary-defensive war to be unrealistic. The talks at Brest-Litovsk had already demonstrated that the Bolsheviks had no military or foreign policy alternatives to a peace agreement. Once Lenin's hopes of further European revolutions failed to materialize, he pragmatically adjusted to the new situation. Only a peace agreement, even with harsh conditions attached, would allow the Bolsheviks to consolidate their power internally and to secure the revolution on that basis.

Stable conditions by no means resulted from the territorial changes that had come in short order between 1915 and Spring 1918. In areas where Russian rule had collapsed in the face of military offensives, the German occupation forces could at most stake a claim to an "eastern frontier empire"; new lines of conflict would overlap with one another there in 1918.[9] When German troops, after Brest-Litovsk, occupied a vast area comprising Belarus, Ukraine, the Baltic lands, and Poland, a vacuum developed in the former Ober Ost that not only fed German expansionist ambitions but also brought rival nationalisms onto the stage. An ephemeral grand duchy of Lithuania sought to link up with historical precedents to form a Lithuanian-Belarussian Empire, but it ran up against the claims of Poles and of the Lithuanian national movement, which was looking to create a nation-state of its own rather than a confederation.

Under the terms of the Brest-Litovsk treaty, Russia was obliged to recognize the independence of Finland, Estonia, Latvia, and Lithuania, as well as of Belarus and Ukraine.[10] The Ottoman leadership under Talaat Pasha also saw to it that Russia gave up all territories in the Caucasus that it had acquired since 1878. Thus, as a result of Brest-Litovsk, Russia lost roughly one-third of its urban population, 89 percent of its coal mines, 73 percent of its iron

Dividing the cake of Brest-Litovsk: the unequal alliance of the Central Powers—"In German arithmetic, two halves are never equal" (*Le Journal* [Paris], March 2, 1918)

industry, and 26 percent of its railroad network.[11] The size of lost territory, twice the size of the whole German Reich, covered nearly all the non-Russian parts of the former Romanov Empire. Furthermore, the treaty provided not only for reparations amounting to six billion marks but also for the granting of extra-territorial privileges to the Central Powers inside Russia, similar to those that had existed in the Ottoman Empire and China before 1914. The treaty said nothing about the release of the 2.6 million Russian soldiers (1.4 million in Germany and 1.2 million in Austria-Hungary) who had been taken prisoner during the war. A corridor of new states—Poland, Estonia, Latvia, Lithuania, Ukraine, and Georgia—came into being, initially under de facto German control, with the prospect of linking up with the oilfields of Azerbaijan.[12]

Brest-Litovsk was an all but ideal-typical dictated peace, which reflected the asymmetrical power relations and military constellation of the time— both between the Central Powers and Russia and between the German Reich and Austria-Hungary. After the bloody civil war and Allied interventions in Russia, only Armenia, Azerbaijan, Georgia, and Ukraine would be reconquered by 1921, while Poland, Finland, and the Baltic states would keep their independence throughout the interwar period. Russia therefore by no means recouped all the territorial losses it sustained in 1918, although the Brest-Litovsk treaty was declared invalid under the terms of the armistice of November 11 in the west and the subsequent Versailles treaty. The long-term consequences for Russia could hardly be overestimated. On the one hand, territorial revanchism became a central policy objective for all Soviet leaders after 1918—up to the Hitler-Stalin Pact of 1939, which provided for the recovery of areas lost in 1918. On the other hand, something like a core state of the Russian nation, roughly the size of today's Russian Federation, took shape after Brest-Litovsk and the foundation of the USSR as a union of individual republics.[13]

Lenin's argument that there was no alternative to Brest-Litovsk was based on the fact that the Bolsheviks lacked sufficient loyal forces and, faced with both external enemies and internal resistance, had no room to maneuver. The Bolshevik leaders assumed that the Central Powers would soon be defeated and that this would make the treaty obsolete. And they were also aware that it was more than just a peace treaty between two sovereign states:

the overlapping of civil war and world war had an existential significance for all involved. In August 1918, when much already pointed to a German defeat on the western front, German and Russian diplomats negotiated a supplement to the Brest-Litovsk treaty that was supposed to regulate relations between the two countries. The Russian delegate Adolf Abramovich Joffe referred in the talks to the fundamental differences between traditional diplomacy and the conditions under which the people's commissars were acting: "Herr von Kühlmann could make concessions, maneuver, tender his resignation, go home, and live off his estates; for Lenin or Trotsky or Joffe this was not possible; they had to realize their ideas or go under like Danton or Robespierre. It is not at all improbable that he, Joffe, will end up on the gallows. . . . 'There we are, that's the class struggle for you.'"[14]

For the German top brass, the successful conclusion to the war in the east demonstrated their capacity to force a peace with victory.[15] Brest-Litovsk turned out to be considerably harsher than the later Versailles treaty. For the moment, it strengthened the position of those who hoped to use it as the basis for a breakthrough on the western front and a wider victory in the war; it thus directly served to prolong the war. Despite Germany's high casualties, economic exhaustion, supply crisis, and increasing social tensions, the end of the war on the eastern front opened up new possibilities in the west. This was not only the view of the military leadership. A majority of the Center Party and left-liberal Reichstag deputies who in Summer 1917 had forcefully called for a compromise peace without annexations or indemnities voted to ratify the Brest-Litovsk peace treaty—only the USPD opposed it. Why, they now asked themselves, should the successful outcome in the east not also work in the west, especially as sizable military resources could be transferred there? The war had certainly not been finally decided in the east, but the end to the fighting there would facilitate a last offensive on the western front and help to bring the war to a victorious conclusion.

In the longer term, the perception of the Brest-Litovsk treaty in Germany shaped the image of eastern Europe as a potential space of German rule—a vision that would endure far beyond 1918 and the collapse of Ober Ost. However, the imagined future for the Baltic and other lands to the east was altered as circumstances changed, as ambitious plans for the colonial administration of the area eventually gave birth to new ideas that revolved around the categories of *Volk* and *Lebensraum*. The collapse of the German occupation regime after 1918 also fueled the image of the eastern lands as a largely unstructured, indeed chaotic, space with a culturally and racially underdeveloped population. Despite the annulment of the Brest-Litovsk treaty in 1919, the memory of the separate peace in the east remained firmly rooted in the German public; it was a widespread view that the successful outcome there had definitively shown what the German Empire could have achieved in the world war. In this perspective, the peace treaty also had an important ideological component: the German victory over Russia, as Golo Mann put it, brought about an "unacknowledged European achievement of the war," a hemming in of Russia and the Bolsheviks that would have to be built on in the future.[16] Many Germans concluded that if eastern Europe could not be cultivated and civilized as an area for colonization with the means deployed in the world war, more radical means would have to be used in the future. Most important, many *Baltikumer*—that is, members of the Freikorps forces deployed in the Baltic—developed fantasies after the war of a national resurrection of Germany in the east.[17]

For most Russians, the Bolshevik revolution and the end of the war with the Central Powers did not bring an improvement in everyday supplies and general living conditions—on the contrary. A journey from Odessa to Moscow in jam-packed trains took a whole week in early 1918. In Moscow itself most of the streets had no lighting. Many of the city's inhabitants deliberately wore shabby dress so as not to attract the attention of trigger-happy soldiers with red armbands. The guaranteed daily ration for one adult in January 1918 was 50 grams of bread and two potatoes.[18]

After Brest-Litovsk, these huge burdens were compounded by internal tensions that eventually erupted in the civil war. At first, only thirty-three of the sixty-six German divisions were transferred to the western front, so that considerable numbers of troops remained in the occupied areas and to some extent deliberately exacerbated conflicts between the Bolsheviks and their enemies. When the pressure on the Bolshevik leadership intensified—some accused them of treason because of their acceptance of the peace terms—Lenin left Petrograd on March 11 and moved into the Moscow Kremlin, while Trotsky, as the new commissar for war, concentrated on the task of organizing the Red Army of workers and peasants and making it a combat-effective force both internally and externally. Nearly all the old army commanders, including General Brusilov, went over to the "Whites"—a term that referred not to a homogeneous movement but to an often highly unstable collection of groups united only in their hostility to the Bolsheviks. In addition to officers from the tsarist army, the Whites comprised members of nearly all of Russia's former political currents—from monarchists to Mensheviks and Socialist Revolutionaries. This being so, the family of the Tsar developed into a dynastic rallying symbol of anti-Bolshevism, and so the Bolsheviks decided on a radical step. After Nicholas, his wife, the Tsarevich, and their other children fell into the hands of Bolshevik troops, they were shot in Ekaterinburg in July 1918.

The Red Terror and the Cheka—the organization to suppress counter-revolution created in late 1917 in the tradition of the political police—were seen as necessary means to secure the achievements of the revolution. The individual was no longer of importance: this was the symbolic dimension of the murder of the last tsar and his family. Felix Dzerzhinsky, the founder and first head of the Cheka, justified the execution in the press: "The Cheka is the defense of the revolution as the Red Army is: as in the civil war the Red Army cannot stop to ask whether it may harm particular individuals, but must take into account only one thing, the victory of the revolution over the bourgeoisie, so the Cheka must defend the revolution and conquer the enemy even if its sword falls occasionally on the heads of the innocent."[19]

In the countryside, it was clear that the October Revolution had not led to a redistribution of local power. Although in practice Bolshevik policies had turned more and more against their interests, farmers in central Russia generally remained loyal to the new system; they had done all in their power to support the revolution and certainly did not wish to see a White counter-revolution endanger their gains. However, in late 1917 and early 1918, their discontent played a major role in the new situation. After October, they managed to force through land redistribution and in effect became the dominant force at the local level. The conflicts between them and the Bolsheviks mainly had to do with the new regime's promotion of class struggle between rich and poor farmers, while the farmers themselves blamed the Bolsheviks for the disastrous food situation, the impact of the civil war, and the failure of early experiments with agricultural collectives. Still, at this stage there were no major revolts in the countryside. Only when the White forces, including many officers from the former landowning elite, had been beaten back did major conflicts develop with the Bolsheviks. On the whole, the relationship remained ambiguous: although farmers resisted enlistment into the Red Army, they defended the gains of October in their localities. In the long term, young farmers in particular saw the new Soviets as an opportunity for social advancement; the officials who staffed them rarely came from other parts of the country, but were the children of small farmers who had previously served in the tsarist army, the Red Army, or both.[20]

Various conflicts and power constellations overlapped in the civil war that lasted until 1921. It was far more than just a war between opposing regimes and ideologies, between Reds and Whites, Bolsheviks and supporters of the old tsarist autocracy. It was also a social conflict pitting armed peasants and local gangs against Reds and Whites alike, a struggle between workers and bosses, city and country. Then there were the ethnic lines of division: Cossacks against Chechens, Germans against Latvians, Jews against Ukrainians. This war of all against all fueled a dynamic of violence, in which the boundaries of political, ideological, national, and social animosities became increasingly blurred. A quite distinctive space developed, in which the end of the war between states coincided with the beginning of national independence struggles, fighting between Red and White armies, and intervention by foreign powers. German occupation units left behind in eastern Europe, Allied troops, and—a special case—the Czechoslovak Legion consisting of former prisoners of war all became players in the civil war.[21] Shortly after Russia's exit from the world war, British and French troops landed in Murmansk and Arkhangelsk in the north and Vladivostok in the far east of the country, their first objective being to take control of the ports and transshipment centers and to secure the war supplies delivered to their former ally. It was in these port cities that the global character of the war, with its mobilization of men from the most diverse regions of the world, was most directly visible. In Vladivostok, for example, Chinese, Mongols, Tatars, and Hindus rubbed shoulders with Russians, British, Americans, Romanians, French, Italians, Belgians, and Japanese.[22] After a series of local agreements with White forces, the Allied troops were then swiftly drawn into the civil war. On the Black Sea, they seized parts of the Russian fleet to use against the Turkish navy, which had been formed in 1914 out of German ships. Strategically important areas of the southeastern Mediterranean thus came under their control in 1918.

Since large sections of the White armies were active in non-Russian parts of the former tsarist empire, national independence struggles became entangled with the civil war. This was typical of the zone stretching from Finland to the Caucasus. The Central Powers repeatedly intervened in these conflicts well into the summer of 1918, seeking to expand their influence in an often-confusing situation. But their main aim in this final period of the war on the western front was to pump out as many economic resources as possible from the east, thereby stabilizing the situation on the home front. Accordingly, German troops were sent to Finland in April and Georgia in June. Local opponents of the Bolsheviks saw this as a welcome boost in their fight for national independence and against the Red Army, while the German military leadership was more interested in access to the Caucasian oilfields and in Summer 1918 occupied Baku on the Caspian Sea. The Habsburg navy endeavored to ship Ukrainian grain from along the Bug, Dniester, and Dnieper Rivers to the Black Sea and then up the Danube to the home country, but the collapse of the Bulgarian front in September 1918 blocked this route and put paid to hopes of an end to the supply bottlenecks. Still, these operations illustrated how, even after the formal end of the war in March 1918, eastern Europe continued to be marked by displays of violence, superimposed conflicts, and rival foreign interventions.[23]

The experience of Ukraine, many aspects of which would recur elsewhere in eastern Europe with the breakup of the multiethnic empires, also illustrates the complexity of the violence occurring after the formal end to the war on the eastern front. It shows why, at the moment when imperial state structures were collapsing, the path to national independence was sometimes not successful. As early as 1920 the whole of Ukraine was again part of other states. So it has to be asked why Ukraine did not achieve what the Czechs, Poles, Finns, Lithuanians, Estonians, and Latvians pursued and gained: a state of their own.

From Summer 1914, Ukraine had been a land where rival empires' claims to rule had collided, making the questions of affiliation and loyalty particularly difficult to answer. Ukrainians fought against one another, whether as Ruthenians in Habsburg uniform or Belarussians in Russian uniform. In Galicia, they were viewed with distrust by invading Russian troops and, in 1915, by the returning Austro-Hungarian army. When the Central Powers agreed in 1916 on the founding of an independent Polish state, the leaders in Berlin and Vienna looked on Ruthenians mainly as unreliable irredentists. Although the collapse of the tsarist regime in February 1917 ended the power of the Russian aristocracy and ushered in a relative liberalization, the Provisional Government stuck to the idea of an "indivisible Russia"; this was the starting point for the resistance of a Ukrainian independence movement. On June 10, 1917, the Rada (parliament) proclaimed the autonomy of Ukraine, triggering a conflict with the government in Petrograd. But in view of the political conflicts inside Russia and the continuation of the war with the Central Powers, the new Russian rulers were initially forced to recognize the Rada as the representative of the Ukrainian nation; they simply did not have the resources to open another front. This gave the Ukrainian independence movement at least some temporary room to maneuver.[24]

The final period of the war in the multiethnic empires, where independence struggles had been breaking out since 1917, typically was characterized by the ethnicization of political and social conflicts. Thus in Ukraine, spontaneous moves toward an agrarian revolution overlapped with the creation of peasant Soviets, and the social dimension of the land question with ethnic lines of conflict; so much was clear from the clashes between the Ukrainian national movement and non-Ukrainian political forces. The Russian urban population in Ukraine put its faith in Russian parties, while Jews aligned themselves with socialist and Zionist groups. In Ukraine, too, the October Revolution gave rise to expectations of far-reaching concessions to the various nationalities and of a radical land reform. Against this background, the Rada and the Bolsheviks cooperated with each other. But when it began to seem that the Bolsheviks were subordinating the right to self-determination to the revolutionary class struggle, the conflict between the two came to a head. Exploiting the military situation, the regime in Kiev proclaimed Ukrainian independence on January 12, 1918, but then Bolshevik troops occupied the city in February in the wake of the separate peace with the Central Powers. The German commanders offered to support the struggle against the Bolsheviks in return for Ukrainian food supplies, and the German entry into Kiev on March 1 seemed at first to crown this course with success.[25]

Very soon, however, the conflicts between the Rada and the Bolsheviks faded in comparison with those between Rada deputies and German occupation troops, whose main concern was to secure food supplies for their home country. When the fighting escalated, the German commanders dissolved the Rada and installed a so-called hetman in the shape of Pavlo Skoropadsky; it was an attempt to link up with old Ukrainian state forms. But the hetman's writ outside Kiev was very limited—yet another indication of the unclear situation and the multiplicity of power centers. Moreover, the Ukrainian National Union formed a directorate of its own, which, after the end of the war in the west, the German troop withdrawal, and the flight of the hetman in mid-December, took power in Kiev. Thus, the fourth government within a year was created at the head of the newly established Ukrainian People's Republic.

Against this background, Ukraine became a major theater of the civil war in 1919–1920: Bolshevik units fought against White troops, while Polish soldiers and Entente interventionist forces put in their oars, as did armed peasant formations and local bandits. This whole canvas—disintegrating state structures with a completely hollowed-out monopoly of violence, numerous regime changes, foreign military intervention, and a multiplicity of armed contenders—explains why the western Ukrainian territories came to be divided up among the new Polish and Czechoslovak nation-states and Romania. Altogether there were nine regime changes in Kiev up to Summer 1920. In Summer 1919 General Denikin, the White commander, made a grab for power and managed to chase the Bolsheviks out of Ukraine. But they came back at the end of the year, forcing the retreat of Polish troops under Piłsudksi, who had already been driven out by the Red Army in the summer. By 1921, with great effort and heavy casualties, the Bolsheviks finally succeeded in stabilizing the situation and crushing the resistance of peasant partisans.[26]

In Ukraine, the end of the war on the eastern front—which had pitted Germany, Austria-Hungary, and the tsarist empire against one another in August 1914—did not bring an end to violence; rather, it gave way to complex civil war constellations in which ideological, social, and ethnic lines of conflict overlapped and reinforced one another. The collapse of traditional state structures gave rise to a power vacuum, in which a number of players were able to operate largely uncontrolled. Alongside local warlords and bandits, other institutions and individuals—from the Rada and hetman to Allied interventionists and German or Austro-Hungarian commanders—also contended for power amid the chaos. This had an impact on German officers and soldiers in Ukraine, who were unable to operate effectively outside Kiev. After requisitioning brought them into conflict with the peasantry, whole villages were cut off from the outside world. The gulf between imagined and actual rule grew wider by the day, continually underlining the powerlessness of the occupation forces.

This chaotic situation also determined the character of the violence: the war that developed in Ukraine had no rules or clear boundaries. Whereas the interstate war up to December 1917 had in principle still recognized the identity of combatants and noncombatants, such distinctions became obsolete in many places. Everyone could be anyone's enemy. This confusion also marked the experience of many regular troops, who were often forced to operate autonomously because of the lack of central coordination. Desertion and breaches of discipline became increasingly common. Military force became uncoupled from higher political objectives, as it became a means for each individual to survive in an environment hostile to life. A swarm of bandits engaged in local and regional operations, stepping up their violence in response to retaliatory measures, so that excesses and outright atrocities, such as the mutilation of prisoners or the killing of the wounded, became the order of the day; systematic looting and expulsions repeatedly struck at the Jewish population in particular. The special dynamic of uncontrolled, random violence left its mark on a whole generation, with the result that violence did not disappear with the end of the civil war, but remained an individual and collective experience with which Stalin's later regime of terror was able to link up.[27]

The continuity of violence, but also its changing form, pointed to the widespread collapse of state structures after Spring 1917. In the resulting power vacuum, survival often depended on the possession of a weapon and a willingness to use it against all and sundry. In this context, with its multiplicity of players and lines of conflict, the Bolsheviks did not operate mainly as revolutionary ideologues or theoreticians, but rather as technicians of violence; it seemed a rational means of self-protection at the individual level, too, to use force offensively and proactively.[28] The result was a practice of unregulated violence, since no institutions or players were left who could have convincingly enforced rules; there was no longer confidence that anyone would feel bound by them.[29] In the Russian civil war, which together with its offshoots plagued the country until 1924, it seemed as if everyone had to be a perpetrator if they were not to become a victim. In the absence of reliable institutions, everyone had to take their survival into their own hands. And with no realistic chance to leave the space of war—for example, by fleeing abroad—the focus was increasingly on violence as the last remaining survival strategy. A long time would pass before the cycle of violence and counterviolence was broken. The scale of this phenomenon can hardly be overestimated: far more people perished in Russia during the civil war than in the whole of the world war up to the end of 1917.[30]

From the end of 1917, as the program of the October Revolution progressively came to be seen as a global threat, the animosity between Bolsheviks and their adversaries stretched far beyond the borders of Russia. The extension of these fears was exemplified in the case of the Russian soldiers on the Salonica front in northern Greece. As they heard of the upheavals back home in the course of 1917, some openly questioned the continuation of the war and began to form revolutionary committees, which created growing tensions with other Allied troops. When individual soldiers—who had formally served under French commanders—refused to carry out orders, all the Russians were disarmed, placed in the custody of loyal Moroccan troops, and deported to North Africa to perform forced labor. On the western front, too, the politicization of Russian soldiers under Allied command was plain to see, and in some cases uncertainty about events at home had a demoralizing effect. Conflicts developed especially after Russia formally left the war under the terms of the Brest-Litovsk treaty; some soldiers tried to link up with émigré circles in Paris, while others challenged the military hierarchy. Russian officers who placed their trust in the Tsar came under daily attack. In 1918, therefore, all European governments feared that the October Revolution would become international and penetrate the hearts and minds of their own soldiers and workers.[31]

2. ENDGAME
The War of 1914 Returns to the Western Front

The situation at the beginning of the year was dominated by the imminent end of the war in the east. For the first time since the Battle of Verdun in 1916, the German Reich found itself in a position to launch a major offensive. It would not just be a continuation of attrition tactics: it was supposed to usher in truly decisive battles on the western front, the aim being to carry out encircling operations like those against the Russian armies in Fall 1914 at the Battle of Tannenberg. Ludendorff, who was continually gaining influence, was aware of the risks that such an offensive would entail. On February 13, 1918, he told the Kaiser and the Reich chancellor: "The army in the west is waiting for the possibility to become active. It should not be thought that we shall have an offensive as in Galicia or Italy; it will be a violent contest that begins in one place, continues in another, and takes up a long time; it will be difficult but will end in victory." When Prince Max of Baden asked a week later what would happen if the offensive failed, Ludendorff's reply showed that the military leadership had no alternative plans: "Then Germany will simply go under." Commanders on both sides knew that everything depended on success in the west.[32]

Several factors at the beginning of 1918 contributed to Ludendorff's characteristic mix of optimistic assessments and high expectations. One of these was the relative weakness of the western European Allies. The French and Italian armies had been more or less paralyzed since 1917, because the failure of the Nivelle offensive, the mass mutinies and strike waves in France, and the Caporetto disaster on the Alpine front had largely broken their capacity to launch new attacks. This tended to be true for British troops as well after the third battle of Flanders in 1917. All the more important, therefore, was the potential American input into the war. Ludendorff was relying on U-boat operations, which in 1918 destroyed more tonnage than the Allies could replace. But they did not have much effect on U.S. troopships, which sailed in convoys and were successfully protected from attack.

Between May 1917 and November 1918, German submarines sank only two American troopships; a third sustained damage but managed to limp into the French port of Brest. Altogether, 2,079,880 American soldiers reached the European continent, and only 68 drowned. The limitation of German U-boats was that they were mainly a threat to unprotected merchant vessels, and despite the high number of kills they were unable at any point to interrupt the transatlantic flow of men and materials. In the course of 1918, the Allies increased their transport capacity by building new ships in the United States, so that by the late summer and fall the balance of forces had clearly shifted in favor of the Allies. The German military leadership had been guilty of an elementary miscalculation, since the level of the U-boat campaign was such that it allowed the Allies to compensate even for high losses on the western front. At the time of the armistice in November 1918, the American force of 1.4 million men at the front gave them almost exactly the same number of soldiers that the Germans had mustered at the beginning of their last major offensive. Not only were these U.S. troops considerably better fed and (from Fall 1918) better equipped; another 700,000 were in training camps in France, and an additional two million had been called up in the United States and were ready to be shipped to Europe. The factor hastening the end of the war was a fundamental change in the political and economic weight of the United States. By November 1918 there were more American soldiers on the European continent than there were troops from Britain and the Dominions.[33]

Yet the fact that only 175,000 American soldiers had landed in Europe by January 1918, and that they lacked experience of frontline combat and first had to be trained at special camps, seemed to German commanders in the spring to offer sufficient assurance that it would be a long time before the U.S. entry into the war could force a decision on the western front. For the OHL, therefore, it was not the American involvement but the weakness of Austria-Hungary and the Ottoman Empire, as well as war weariness on the home front, that represented the greatest danger. In the end, German commanders in 1918 were operating within a narrow time frame: with the eastern front out of the way, the war had to be ended before the presence of American troops and resources on the western front really began to have an impact. The period from Brest-Litovsk to the military turn in the second Marne battle thus was a special historical context. Put succinctly, the world war was decided militarily between early March and mid-July on the western front.

The situation of the Allies on the western front in early 1918 contributed to the optimism of the German OHL's assessments. Optimistic assessments particularly affected the British armed forces, who, having again suffered heavy losses and taken a massive blow in the battles of Fall 1917, were in a critical position. Passchendaele and Cambrai had become bywords in Britain for a loss of trust between the Imperial War Cabinet and the military leadership, symbolized by Lloyd George's lack of confidence in Haig. A continuation of offensive operations such as those at the third battle of Flanders seemed to be out of the question. In mid-December 1917 the chief of the Imperial General Staff, Sir William Robertson, had warned Lloyd George that British units and Empire troops needed to recover for some time in defensive positions before there could be any thought of fresh attacks. British hopes were therefore increasingly pinned on the American troops—even though this meant that the war might last even longer and increase the military and political weight of the United States in Europe. While the commander of the French reserve armies, General Fayolle, figured on an end to the war in Summer 1919 at the earliest, Haig was even more pessimistic: he did not think it was conceivable before 1920. Fearing the U.S. preponderance, Haig even argued in early 1918 that efforts should be made to conclude a compromise peace with Germany.[34]

At the beginning of the year, the pessimism at BEF headquarters was compounded by difficulties of communication among the army, brigade, and divisional staffs. This hindered a more intensive examination of the new German battle tactics, especially the staggered defense systems and the use of shock troops. After German forces initially made some deep breakthroughs in Spring 1918, forcing British troops to retreat hastily and give up large swathes of territory that they had won at great cost in the preceding months, the mood among officers and soldiers hit rock bottom. In the second half of 1918, Haig could claim at most symbolic leadership of the army. It is true that the tanks coming onstream in greater numbers were an important instrument for mobile attacks and gave the British new tactical options, but from Summer 1918 British commanders resorted with greater frequency to traditional tactics. Although many efforts were made to coordinate infantry, artillery, air, and armored weapons more effectively, British headquarters again concentrated on infantry-centered operations in which all other kinds of weaponry played a subsidiary role. The claim that massive and consistent use of tanks decided the war therefore needs to be treated with caution. For after the battle of Amiens, traditional tactics, mixed forms, and attrition of the enemy came once again to the fore; between August and November, British casualties against an increasingly demoralized German army would be just as high as in the months from March to May. Great though the losses had been at the third battle of Flanders in the previous fall, the following year turned out to be much bloodier than 1917 for the BEF.[35]

The American entry into the war posed new military problems. President Wilson had insisted from the outset on a separate army under American command and with its own combat section on the western front. The requirement that it should operate with its own strategy, its own commanders, and even its own supply links reflected American fears of becoming a mere adjunct of the British and French military. As the year wore on, however, this demand for independence—which also made itself felt in Wilson's search for a special U.S. status as associate rather than ally—came up against the reality of a war whose character had changed fundamentally over the previous four years. Only slowly did American officers learn to reconsider their traditional assessments and tactical doctrines—and the price of this learning process was high.[36]

The first operations proved that U.S. soldiers needed months of intensive preparation before they could be sent into battle. In January 1918, few combat-ready divisions were available on the European fronts, and most Allied commanders believed that the Americans could not be expected to provide palpable relief until 1919. In the critical situation of Spring 1918, moreover, American resistance to "amalgamation" or deployment under British command during the training period demonstrated the specific problems of a coalition war.[37] The U.S. supreme commander, General Pershing, was forced to compromise and to accept de facto amalgamation, both in training and in battle. Only then could American soldiers profit from the experience of comrades tried and tested in combat. The Americans went on to form their own army by late summer, and in September it managed to break through the Hindenburg Line between the Meuse and the Argonne Forest.[38]

The integration of American troops was not the only major challenge for the Allies. For a long time there had been no close or continuous cooperation between the French and British general staffs; the fact that they were fighting the same enemy did not mean there was a real coalition in practice between the military leaderships. Only the critical juncture of Spring 1918, brought on by German offensives, forced a change. For the first time, a joint supreme command of all Allied troops was created, under Marshal Foch, and what was designed to improve troop coordination soon developed into the central institution for the strategic conduct of the war. Its creation was motivated above all by logistical issues: when the Allies lost large chunks of territory to the Central Powers—on the eastern front in 1917 and on the western front in Spring 1918—only centralized command could ensure the supply of Allied troops and the home societies. This was Foch's special achievement, but also that of the Supreme War Council and the Allied Maritime Transport Council, two key institutions during the final year of the war. Foch operated as master of the possible, not indulging in grand strategic fantasies, but endeavoring to size up and exploit the situation at hand.[39] As a result, the Allies—unlike the Central Powers—generally managed to keep their troops and the home front adequately supplied and were more able to compensate for losses of soldiers and war goods in the late summer and fall.[40]

Why did the German army remain capable to the end of inflicting high casualties on the Allies? What lay behind its apparent efficiency as a killing machine? A look at a typical German unit, the 11th Bavarian Infantry Division (which was not an elite formation), puts some exaggerated assumptions into perspective.[41] What accounted for the Germans' relative military effectiveness was not a particular drive to kill, but a combination of other factors such as positive experiences in the war of movement on the eastern and southeastern fronts against Russia and Serbia. A strong sense of shared regional roots was especially visible in the Bavarian division, knitting together middle cadre as a cohesive element between commanders and ordinary soldiers; the relative leeway given to squad, platoon, and company leaders paid off. However, from 1916 on there were growing signs of troop demoralization in the face of high casualties and supply problems at the front, but German soldiers repeatedly demonstrated their capacity to adapt to circumstances and to use their resources accordingly. Given the casualty rates, the concentration on heavy artillery and the coordination of the different military branches were sheer necessities to compensate for the resource problems and diminishing possibilities of action. Military efficiency had to be increased because the casualty levels suffered up to 1916 could no longer be afforded.

In this light, what ensued was not so much a tactical revolution in warfare or a one-sided concentration by the OHL on intensive mechanized warfare, but rather an accumulation of discrete changes. The protracted deadlock on the western front distracted attention from these improvements and learning processes,[42] such as the deployment of special storm troops, the perfecting of staggered defense systems, the greater flexibility for NCOs and officers at the front, and so on. Nor should we overlook the new contradictions and ambiguities to which these led. Many divisional staff officers were uncertain in their response to the changes, often clinging to traditional conceptions of the offensive as the key to warfare. The will to continue the war by holding out in defensive positions remained fairly stable until the end, since by 1918 older soldiers were being continually mixed in with new recruits and were able to pass on lessons from their experience of the front.[43]

German plans for a major offensive in Spring 1918 were the most ambitious since the Battle of Verdun two years earlier. But unlike those of Spring 1916, the new offensives used a different set of tactics, deliberately avoiding frontal attacks in a broad line of advance. Attack formations were concentrated at a few key points between Flanders and Champagne, so as to break through the enemy front and advance far enough not only to knock out enemy artillery but also to resume a war of movement. The aim then was to encircle and defeat the enemy armies in great battles like the early ones on the eastern front, until the war was brought to a victorious conclusion. In Spring 1918 there was no sign of an interest in compromises or alternative plans; Hindenburg emphasized to the Kaiser that the western Allies had to be smashed if Germany's future political and economic position was to be secure.[44]

In preparation for the offensive, thirty-three divisions were transferred from the eastern front and the attack troops given methodical training. By early March 1918 the German side in the west had more than 192 divisions with a combat strength of 1.2 million men, against the Allies' 165 divisions. But many of the German divisions still had only half of their original fighting strength, and their supplies and technical equipment were inferior to those of the enemy. The bottlenecks so common in the Central Powers' territories had reached the German trenches on the western front. Thus, the average daily ration for German soldiers at the beginning of 1918 provided only 2,500 calories—considerably less than on the Allied side, where even in the relatively poorly supplied Italian army the target was 4,000 calories and the actual level still more than 3,000.[45]

On the one hand, Germany was again able to mobilize economic and military resources on a massive scale, so that Ludendorff could draw on 4,500 light and 2,500 heavy artillery pieces and significantly more aircraft (up from 1,200 in Spring 1917 to 2,600) than in previous operations. On the other hand, the motorization of German attack troops remained at a low level, because the experience of Cambrai in 1917 had allowed German commanders to think that they had overcome "tank fright." The few combat vehicles at their disposal scarcely counted in comparison with the 800 or so tanks on the British and French side.

German units had access to less than a quarter of the trucks available to the Allies (23,000 against 100,000), so that as in Summer 1914 they had to rely massively on horse-drawn vehicles—although in Spring 1918 there were fewer of them, and the horses were often undernourished. This was a considerable disadvantage in an attack whose explicit aim was to shift from positional warfare to a war of movement. On closer examination, even the Germans' numerical superiority was relatively small: 2.6:1 for attack troops, 2.5:1 in weaponry, and 3:1 in aircraft.[46] For an offensive associated with such high expectations, in which there were no alternatives other than a successful breakthrough, these initial ratios were too close for comfort.[47] Since the German military still occupied large swathes of eastern Europe in the hope of ensuring access to local resources, it had left a large number of troops there. Despite the Brest-Litovsk treaty, the two-front problem persisted in a different form; that is, as a resource dilemma split between the needs of the western front and those of occupying forces in a vast and complex area still prone to violence.

The German "Michael offensive" got underway on March 21, 1918, in the zone of the Somme battle of Summer 1916 between Arras and the Oise. It would be the largest offensive of any land war until the German campaign of 1940.[48] The operations were deliberately not preceded by days of artillery fire, as in previous offensives, but relied on a brief heavy bombardment as day was breaking. The German attack troops then advanced through thick

Map 10. German Offensives on the Western Front, 1918

fog toward the British lines, at first scoring only minor gains of territory. In the following days, however, they profited from dry weather and managed to recapture all the territory they had abandoned in Summer 1916 and Spring 1917 in the retreat to the Hindenburg Line. After the sixth day, the troops had advanced roughly 50 kilometers beyond the enemy lines. On the British side, these German successes triggered panic reactions: on March 24, Haig gave Pétain the impression that the British front could no longer hold and that he would have to abandon the defense of Amiens. Pétain, for his part, felt confirmed in his pessimism: the danger that the French would be cut off from the British was so great that only massive French support from southern sections of the front could prevent defeat. On the afternoon of March 25, Haig actually ordered his men to withdraw to the positions of 1916, and at that point even a retreat to the Channel ports was under consideration.[49] For the British military leadership and most of his commanders, at stake

Too late, too heavy, too few: German A7V tank with crew

were not only the outcome of the battle but also the future of the war on the western front—an unmistakable sign of the scale of the exhaustion. Since there seemed to be no scope for other options, the question of victory or defeat in the world war came to the fore.

The early German successes, which led to the capture of large numbers of British soldiers, appeared to vindicate the hopes of the OHL. If it was possible to move beyond positional warfare at this key point on the western front, there would be the prospect of forcing the enemy to fight in open ground, where the German military felt confident of its superiority. Optimism that the decisive turning point was just around the corner also gripped large parts of German society back home. On March 26, the chair of the Krupp board of directors, Alfred Hugenberg, wired his best wishes to Hindenburg on behalf of the mining association and the Essen board of commerce: "The peace with Russia . . . and the great victory of these days over the British are the two hammer blows resounding in all German hearts; all the protective shells and armor around them, which gradually condensed the trials and misconceptions of this long war, are starting to crack and crumble. Anyone who faint-heartedly doubted a German victory or never believed in one now sees it as a possibility within our grasp and must bow to the thought of victory."[50] Yet in a way, these words and the far-flung hopes mirrored the crisis of the "hold fast society." The crucial importance of the home front was also evident in Hindenburg's reply on March 31: "The events of the past few months tell us that the victory we need for the political and economic future of Germany cannot be torn from our grasp. We will gain it all the more decidedly, the more the homeland closes ranks behind the army's will to victory, and the more it is prepared to suffer the great and small hardships of a hopefully short period in order to wrest a brighter future for ourselves and those who come after us."[51]

In view of the critical situation, a meeting of leading Allied politicians and commanders was hastily organized in Doullens on March 26. In the talks that Poincaré and Clemenceau, Pétain and Foch held with the British top brass, and with Lord Alfred Milner as the representative of Lloyd George, it soon became clear that an energetic centralization of the command structures was the only way to counter the German attack. The most important result of the meeting was therefore the appointment of Foch as supreme commander of all the Allied armed forces. This was reminiscent of the crisis of the Central Powers during the Brusilov offensive of Summer 1916, which ended the OHL-AOK duality and forced the military leaderships to establish a single supreme command under de facto OHL dominance. In March 1918, Foch set the clear aim of holding the front under all circumstances, explicitly comparing the situation to the one faced in Fall 1914 on the Marne. He forbade the British commanders to retreat any farther. In return, the British troops—who had suffered huge casualties in the first six days of the German offensive—were reinforced with French reserves and four American divisions. The air supremacy lost to German pilots was largely regained in the zone of the Michael offensive, and French and British troops avoided being cut off from each other over an extensive area.[52] But this did not solve the crisis: German troops managed to seize Montdidier and Noyon, and by April 5, when the advance ended for the time being, they were only 110 kilometers from Paris. In 16 days they had lost 239,000 men, against 178,000 on the British and Empire side and 70,000 on the French. The 90,000 British troops captured by the Germans highlighted the scale of the crisis; never had the BEF lost such a high number in such a short time.[53]

Sensing that a final breakthrough was in the cards, the Germans now changed the focus of their attack. They no longer directed operations against the retreating British troops—Ludendorff thought they were beaten anyway—but concentrated on the French sections of the front, hoping to bring the war to a swift end by advancing on the Marne and Paris. Yet the daily arrivals of U.S. troops in the Channel ports did not enter into their calculations.[54] Moreover, supplies to the newly won territory became an almost insoluble problem for the Germans, given that the areas of the front on the Somme were virtual wasteland and nearly all the rail lines had been destroyed. This was the main reason why the German offensive front, initially 80 kilometers wide, had narrowed to 20 kilometers by March 27.[55]

Nevertheless, Ludendorff persisted with his plan and concentrated additional attacks on other sections of the front. Operation Georgette, lasting from April 9 to 29, moved along the River Lys toward the heights of Passchendaele, the eventual capture of which allowed German troops to press on toward the ruins of Ypres. In this battle, Portuguese units fighting on the Allied side lost more than 7,400 men. (In February Portugal had had to hand over German ships interned in its ports, whereupon the Reich declared war on it the following month. The government in Lisbon then recruited more than 200,000 men—the largest mobilization in the country's history.)[56]

The so-called Operation Blücher-Yorck, which lasted from May 27 to June 6, was mainly concentrated on the Chemin des Dames area, which the Allies managed to hold at great cost. German breakthroughs against the French frontlines north of the Aisne were more successful; they involved the largest deployment of German artillery of the whole war and, subsequently, the largest gains of territory. After 3,700 guns had loosed more than two million shells in the space of four and a half hours, German troops advanced across a zone 40 kilometers wide by 19 kilometers deep. In this area they really did force a resumption of the war of movement. Soissons soon fell, and on May 30 German cavalry units reached the Marne. At that point, the war returned to the decisive battle zone of September 1916. With the capture of Château-Thierry, German troops were less than 90 kilometers from Paris, and as in the late summer of 1914 German artillery bombarded the French capital.[57]

The use of long-range artillery had already begun in late March. Special guns weighing 140 tons, with 37-meter barrels and a range of more than 130 kilometers, were able to reach central areas of Paris thanks to new technology. A propellant charge could fire shells 40 kilometers straight up into the stratosphere; their flight path then passed through very thin layers of air, approximating the conditions of airless space.[58]

The German successes of this period were due to a number of factors: tactical innovations combined with combat experience, weapons proficiency, and the troops' hopes that a last great effort might finally end the war. Instead of the earlier battles of attrition, flexible surprise attacks and diversionary maneuvers were the order of the day. There were no daylong bombardments, but instead a maximum concentration of artillery fire in a short period of time, often during the night. This usually ceased after the firestorm had reached its farthest point. Loud hurrahs then issued from the German side, giving the impression that the attack was beginning and drawing the defenders out of their underground positions, whereupon the artillery began another massive barrage. Only then did the actual infantry attack get underway. Heavy artillery would play a key role right until the end of the war, but commanders were consistently able to achieve close coordination with the infantry. German storm battalions also employed infiltration tactics that often proved successful.[59]

But problems regularly developed as soon as the German attacks came to a standstill. Often commanders would try to force a decision by throwing in more troops—resulting in an exponential rise in casualties. On the other side, the British and French did not at first prepare German-style staggered defenses in depth; they improved on this score only in the course of the summer. However, the military situation clarified the division of responsibilities among the Allies and strengthened Foch's position as supreme commander. What had been conceived in March as merely a means to improve troop coordination developed into a strategy for conducting the war, for which significantly more contingents, including newly assigned American troops, became available. On the German side, the early breakthroughs brought considerable problems in their wake, particularly with regard to communication and coordination among great masses of men and materials, while the hopes placed on the concentration of German forces in the west began to evaporate. From May to June 1918, the military weight of the constantly growing American expeditionary force became impossible to ignore.

The aims of Operation Gneisenau, begun on June 9, were to consolidate the earlier advances, to link up the German armies at Compiègne, and to encircle the French troops. German and Allied losses in these and earlier attacks were finely balanced: 127,000 to 130,000 in Operation Blücher-Yorck and 30,000 to 35,000 in the Gneisenau offensive. But from June on, it became clear that, unlike the French and British—who could count on the constant influx of U.S. troops—the German side could no longer fill the holes left by its own casualties. On June 1, 1918, in a letter to the Reich chancellor, Crown Prince Rupprecht von Bayern complained of "the shortage of replacement troops and horses." Which side was victorious in the end depended on "who could manage longest with their supplies of men." According to Rupprecht, not even Ludendorff believed any longer that one decisive victory could crush the enemy; he was now pinning his hopes on the "sudden internal collapse of one of the western powers, in the manner of the collapse of the Russian empire. But east and west are fundamentally different, and none of the western states is as shaky as the Russian empire already was before the war." Germany, he concluded, should therefore be content with the status quo in the west: "The fact that one enemy in the east is completely finished is a victory for us; and even a peace in the west that brought us no gains would be a victorious peace."[60] By June 1918, however, the prospects of negotiating a peace with the Allies on the basis of the status quo ante—if the German leadership itself had wanted it—were slender indeed. By then London and Paris could count on the ever-rising numbers of U.S. troops in Europe, up from 78,000 in November 1917 to 220,000 in March 1918, including 139,000 ready for combat in Spring 1918. This increase was not yet decisive, but the Allies could be sure that in the medium term they would be able to compensate for their own casualties. Although a peace offer from the Central Powers had put some pressure on Wilson, Clemenceau and Lloyd George could exert pressure of their own by virtue of the interdependence of their war economies. As far as internal politics was concerned, the new social mobilization since late 1917 in France, Britain, and Italy had presupposed an unconditional will to victory, as embodied by the British and French premiers in particular. Any weakening of resolve would have called into question this (to a considerable extent political) war effort and therefore the cohesion of the home front. Most important, the forthrightness of the military and the feeling on both sides that victory was still possible spoke against peace initiatives. The fear that any hint of concessions would weaken their hand limited the scope for politicians to put out peace feelers.

Yet how desperate the situation was for the Allies can be seen from the mood in the French army. In early June 1918, many units were in the grip of panic, fearing the disintegration and collapse of the front; more and more soldiers in the streets claimed to have lost their regiments. Because of the high number of casualties in infantry regiments, an increasing number of cavalry units were being disbanded and reassigned as infantry—to the joy of many soldiers who treated with contempt the horsemen waiting behind the lines for the advance that never came. At the climax of the bloody fighting in the summer, army leaders resorted to desperate measures, even drawing on 17-year-olds not yet liable to conscription. Yet, many commanders did regain control of their units from mid-June on.[61] The Allied resistance gradually strengthened, not least because defense in depth had improved on the French side. The first major counterattacks began on June 11.

In these counterattacks the experiences of the previous years led to the introduction of new tactics. For the French infantryman René Arnaud, the newly arriving American soldiers were the most dramatic difference between 1914 and the immediate present. On June 3, 1918, he wrote, "An inexperienced officer newly arrived at the front with his head full of prescribed theories would probably have assumed he should continue advancing, which would have led to the majority of his men being killed for nothing. But by 1918 we had enough experience of the realities of the battlefield to stop ourselves in time. The Americans who had just left the front line close by, at Château-Thierry, did not have this experience for obvious reasons and we all know the enormous losses they suffered during the few months they were active."[62]

On all sides, then, the situation was extremely tense in mid-July as the Germans concentrated fifty-two divisions on the Marne. Despite the stubborn defense, they managed to cross the river, but on July 18, when a German victory seemed imminent, the Allies stabilized their frontline and began to organize counterattacks with an efficiently coordinated force of French and

Endgame: German soldiers enter British captivity at Reims

American infantry, 2,100 artillery pieces, 350 tanks, and 1,000 aircraft. By August 6 they had won back the recent German gains and were advancing on Soissons and Reims. The totals of dead, wounded, and captured were again roughly even, at 134,000 Allied and 139,000 German soldiers. But the high number of German prisoners (29,000) pointed to a new trend: whereas the first Marne battle in Fall 1914 had signaled the beginning of the end of the war of movement, the second battle in Summer 1918 initially marked the deepest advance by German troops on the western front—and then the beginning of the final phase of the war. From July 18 on, German troops were in continual retreat. It was certainly not yet the end of the war, but for the Germans it marked the transition from the last great offensive, with all its high hopes, to a defensive struggle, but one, in sharp contrast to Fall 1914, conducted with an awareness that they lacked the men or resources for further attacks. This was a point of no return—although the OHL initially regarded July 18 as an exception and did not believe there would be further Allied attacks. At first, subsequent events as well as the cohesion of German units and high losses on the Allied side masked the consequences of the military setback, but by the end of the month it was becoming clear to German commanders and soldiers that from then on it would be a defensive war, that the point of maximum advance lay in the past, and that they had lost the capacity for a decisive offensive, for a "Tannenberg" in the west.[63]

The Allied front stabilized, in part because of the constant influx of American troops. Their divisional strength corresponded to that of a German army corps, and in the period up to October U.S. commanders consciously relied on sheer numbers to compensate for lack of combat experience. Reinforcements also arrived from other combat areas: for example, British soldiers were brought in from other fronts, and the transfer of troops from the western front to the Near and Middle East or the Macedonian front came to a complete halt. Matters were complicated by the spread of Spanish flu in the summer and fall. It was a pandemic that struck armies and populations on all sides, but German troops proved especially susceptible because of their poor diet and the preceding months of combat. At its peak, nearly half of the 207 German divisions were affected. The Allies also suffered heavily from the epidemic during the counterattacks in the fall: a total of 360,000 American soldiers reported sick, including 100,000 of those stationed in

France; 25,000 American recruits, including 10,000 in Europe, died of the flu or from related lung infections.[64]

The slow German retreat from mid-July meant that the raised expectations of victory turned into fears of impending defeat. In the middle of July, the German artilleryman Herbert Sulzbach wrote, "We are very, very dejected, for if such a gigantic attack is not immediately successful it will be all over."[65] The German soldiers gazed at American prisoners with unconcealed envy. On August 6, 1918, Pál Kelemen recorded, "Their amazingly good physical condition, the excellent quality of their uniforms, the heavy leather in their boots, belts and such, the confident look in their eyes even as prisoners, made me realize what four years of fighting had done to our troops."[66] Many German commanders were no longer under any illusions. Major Alfred Niemann, since February 1918 the chief quartermaster in the Count Albrecht of Württemberg army group, wrote to Ludendorff on July 20 that time was now working against the Central Powers: "In the long run, the intellectual and moral superiority of the leadership cannot substitute for the dwindling popular energies and the growing shortage of potatoes. . . . The slogan 'Hold fast till the victorious end!' is only a slogan, a euphemistic expression for a voluntary 'honorable death.' . . . We must use our military strength as a means of exerting pressure, so long as we still have military superiority. If we are on our way down when we appear at the negotiating table, we will be playing without any trumps. Our means of exerting pressure will then decrease day by day."[67]

After July 18, in the ever-stronger Allied counterattacks, American troops provided for Foch the limitless reserve that had previously been expected from Russia. In this incipient endgame, the Allies relied on constant attacks against the Central Powers in every zone of battle: above all the western front, but also southeastern Europe in the form of British, French, and Serbian sallies on the Salonica front against Bulgarian and Hungarian forces. In addition, Italian attacks on the Alpine front aimed to hasten the disintegration of the Habsburg monarchy, while attacks were stepped up against Ottoman positions in the Near East and the Arabian Peninsula. This idea of wearing down the enemy on as many fronts as possible ultimately proved successful.[68] Allied breakouts from Amiens on the Somme began simultaneously with the battle on the Marne, a characteristic example of modern warfare in

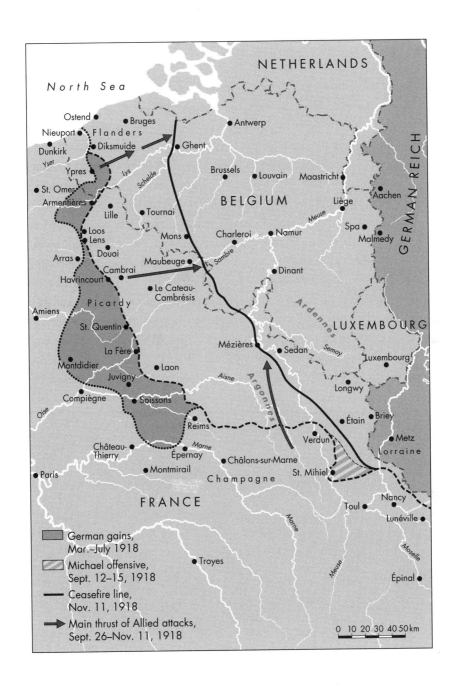

North Sea

NETHERLANDS

GERMAN REICH

Ostend • • Bruges • Antwerp
Nieuport •• Flanders
Dunkirk • • Diksmuide • Ghent
Yser
Ypres • Lys Schelde Brussels • • Louvain Maastricht •
St. Omer • Aachen •
Armentières • Liège •
Lille • Tournai BELGIUM
Loos • Mons • Charleroi • Namur Spa •
Lens • Meuse Malmedy •
Arras • Douai Maubeuge • Sambre
Cambrai • Dinant •
Havrincourt • Ardennes LUXEMBOURG
Le Cateau-
Cambrésis
Picardy
Amiens • St. Quentin • Mézières • Sedan Luxembourg •
La Fère • Semoy
Montdidier • Laon • Longwy •
Juvigny Aisne Argonne
Compiègne • Soissons • Étain • Briey •
Oise Reims • Verdun Metz •
Château- Marne St. Mihiel • Lorraine
Thierry • Épernay • Châlons-sur-Marne
Paris • Montmirail • Champagne Nancy •
FRANCE Toul •
Lunéville •
Marne
Moselle
German gains,
Mar.–July 1918 Troyes • Meuse Épinal •
Michael offensive,
Sept. 12–15, 1918
Ceasefire line,
Nov. 11, 1918
Main thrust of Allied attacks, 0 10 20 30 40 50 km
Sept. 26–Nov. 11, 1918

Map 11. Allied Counteroffensives on the Western Front, 1918

its tactics and use of technology. The aim of the Allied counteractions was to regain territory that German troops had overrun in the spring Michael offensive; the concentrated attack by fifteen infantry divisions, three cavalry divisions, 1,400 artillery pieces, 1,800 British and French aircraft, and 500 tanks that could be easily deployed on the relatively flat and dry terrain was certainly a success. Troops from the Dominions and the United States played a major role, with one American, four Canadian, and five Australian divisions deployed alongside five British ones. The combination of forces, backed up with rolling barrages and surprise attacks, was starting to bear fruit.

Ludendorff later described the Allied attacks from Amiens on August 8 as a "black day" for the German army. This assessment reflected the growing invulnerability of the tanks that drove deep into the German lines, creating an opening for infantry and cavalry units to advance. At the same time, air attacks targeted the rail and communications centers at Péronne and elsewhere, so that the Germans were unable to bring up reserves fast enough to critical points on the front. Nevertheless, the battle of Amiens showed that the German army could still inflict enormous casualties even when it was on the retreat. The new Fokker D7 airplane cost the British air force

Mobility and firepower: British tanks in the Amiens offensive, August 1918

ninety-seven machines on August 8 and robbed it of its superiority in the sky. Yet, German infantry units were no longer able to fill the gaps in their ranks left by the spring offensives and the Spanish flu. When the Allied fall offensives got underway, only forty-seven German divisions still counted as combat ready, and many other units were so depleted that they could no longer be actively deployed in battle.[69]

The result of the Battle of Amiens was a hole in the front 24 kilometers wide and a German retreat of 19 kilometers. The lost ground was not so important, but two related aspects were more alarming: the German commanders' attempts to organize counterattacks, in line with the traditional model, showed that their troops no longer had the required capacity; and the high number of captured German soldiers—who in some cases surrendered as whole units for the first time—indicated that the cohesion of the German army was beginning to crumble. Both the Allies and the Germans lost around 41,000 men, but the German losses included 33,000 taken prisoner, 16,000 of them in a single day. This was a qualitatively new development, for it showed that the generally stable defensive tactics and staggered defense systems could no longer stave off defeat.

The Battle of Amiens inaugurated the last major Allied offensive of the war, the so-called Hundred Days Offensive. Despite the critical situation at Amiens, there could be no talk of a German collapse: German troops continued to retreat to the Hindenburg Line, from where they had broken out to conduct the spring offensives, but not only did this line hold firm, its defenders inflicted heavy casualties on the Allies right up to the end of the fighting. On the other hand, another development casts doubt on the claim that the battle was a forerunner of modern twentieth-century warfare. For just as the virtually inexhaustible resources of American troops and war materiel began to make themselves felt and to influence the calculations of Allied commanders, the war returned once more to the cult of the offensive. Despite frequent claims to the contrary, modern warfare based on the coordination of different kinds of weaponry was not the model for the final phase of the war. Foch himself believed in the superiority of infantry attacks after suitable artillery preparation; the combination of those attacks with aircraft and tanks was for him of secondary importance at most. The presence of American soldiers, together with the knowledge that it would be possible to compensate even for very high casualties, led to a reconventionalization of warfare, a return to infantry attacks, machine guns, artillery fire, and poison gas, while the factors of mobility and efficient deployment of soldiers and weapons receded into the background. In the case of American troops—well fed and equipped, but without frontline experience—Pershing put his trust in open attack by massed infantry. The consequences were reminiscent of the early battles of Summer and Fall 1914.

In the endgame period, problems developed in Allied units despite the continual German retreat. From the beginning of August, the Australian army corps under General John Monash played an important role in the attacks and captured large numbers of prisoners. Yet a combination of high casualties and overly strict commanders resulted in a crisis of discipline. The desertion rate was four times higher than in the BEF—partly because Australian units meted out comparatively milder punishment and did not sentence deserters to death. In some cases, ordinary soldiers assaulted and even killed officers.[70]

So as not to give the Germans a chance to prepare for Allied attacks on the Hindenburg line by organizing a defense in depth, Foch established three offensive zones in late September: one north of the Somme in the direction of Cambrai and Sambre, where the aim was to advance into southern Belgium; one in the north, where units were supposed to push toward northern Belgium and the port city of Antwerp; and one in the south, where the American First Army was to attack the Argonne Forest west of Verdun with the objective of reaching Sedan. In all these operations, reliance on the offensive tactics of the early months of the war was evident in the trust that commanders placed in the newly available American resources. Admittedly the German defenders now had fewer and fewer with which to parry the attacks, but even a weaker defender, if sufficiently experienced, was capable of inflicting heavy casualties on the enemy; this would remain the case until the end of the fighting on the western front. Thus, the BEF lost roughly 314,000 men (including 49,000 Canadians) in the Hundred Days Offensive. It managed to drive the German troops back, but the German front did not collapse as the Austro-Hungarian front had in northern Italy. The Allies recaptured the Belgian coast, but Antwerp and Brussels remained in German hands. To the south, the Franco-American Meuse-Argonne offensive ended with quite small territorial gains, because German forces had fortified the Argonne Forest and were able to withstand for some time a combined attack involving 4,000 artillery pieces, 200 tanks, and 800 aircraft. It is true that in early November Allied troops finally reached the outer districts of Sedan, but the American casualties in particular were horrific: 117,000 men against 70,000 French and 120,000 Germans. The U.S. press covered up these losses with tales of heroism, referring, for example, to one soldier, Sergeant Alvin York of the 82nd Division, who single-handedly captured 132 Germans, and to the actions of the 93rd African American Division. This despite the fact that Allied, and especially American, officers had long resisted the use of African American troops.[71]

The same battle highlighted the deficiencies on the American side. Often untested units had to rely on the greater experience of British and French troops, especially with regard to artillery support, reconnaissance, and supplies. The attacks on German positions in the Meuse-Argonne offensive developed into the bloodiest battle in the history of the U.S. Army, in which 26,300 men lost their lives. (Compare this with the 12,900 Americans, less than half as many, killed in the battle of Okinawa during the Second World War.) The structural reasons for the American losses showed how little the United States, for all its economic potential, was prepared for an actual war. Its transport capacity was at first completely insufficient, so that by Summer 1918 few American divisions had even reached Europe, and those that did make it across the Atlantic suffered from poor motorization that affected the delivery of supplies. American soldiers were well fed, but for a long time the supply of modern weapons and ammunition to combat units failed to meet requirements. The new Browning machine gun became available to American troops only toward the end of the war. And the most intensive training behind the lines could not adequately prepare soldiers for the deadly efficiency of the machine guns, mortars, and gas directed at them from German defensive positions.[72]

Extremely high though the losses in dead and wounded were in certain actions, the late entry of the United States into the war meant that its total casualties were smaller than those of other countries. The average daily death toll for the 1,560 days of war between August 4, 1914, and November 11, 1918, was for Germany, 1,025; France, 888; Britain, 577; Serbia and Montenegro,

80 each; and Belgium, 65. The U.S. armed forces lost an average of 251 men a day from the beginning of April 1917. The peak losses of Verdun, the Somme, and the third battle of Flanders were already in the past when American soldiers began to come ashore in Europe. In the last 200 days of the war, from March to November 1918, the German armies lost 681 men a day, the French 908, the British 510, and the Americans 252 (on the roughly 14 percent of the western front that they held).[73]

The price was therefore very high for the dramatic developments on the western front and the military conclusion of the war—in this respect, too, they involved a return to the early period of Summer and Fall 1914. The costliest months of the whole war were August and September 1914 and those between March 21 and July 19, 1918.[74] In this final phase, the Germans lost a total of 641,000 men—mostly in divisions involved in offensive operations. This corresponded to roughly 50 percent of the total number of troops at the front in March 1918, and it was no longer possible to compensate for the losses. On the French side the losses totaled 433,000 and, among British and Empire soldiers, 418,000.

Another problem with the last major German offensive on the western front was its fragmentary character. A "Tannenberg" in the west seemed a possibility at best in early March and April, when the British front was crumbling before the German advance. Subsequently, any gains of territory were bought at such a high price that the chances of a decisive breakthrough faded fast; Ludendorff's almost symbolic focus on maintaining the threat to Paris made no difference in this regard.[75] Even in the most favorable case, the German armies would have lacked sufficient reserves to achieve further breakthroughs in the front, whereas the Allies deployed countless numbers of U.S. soldiers arriving every week, who at least quantitatively could fill the gaps left by the heavy French, British, and Empire casualties.

Disciplinary problems, especially relating to poor provisions, began to increase in the German army in the summer of 1918. Often, soldiers would stop marching when they came across food and alcohol in abandoned enemy positions. Attitudes to senior officers also deteriorated, and men might well refuse to salute them. But only in the late summer did signs appear that German units were losing their cohesion; only then did army high commands begin to report a massive increase in desertions and self-mutilation.[76] On

September 15, one soldier wrote this in a letter that was forwarded to the Prussian war ministry: "Now we have retreated on the whole front, not because we were forced to do so—for the German is a good soldier after all— . . . but because our combat troops do not want to stick it out any longer. What's the point of sacrificing themselves? Maybe for the fatherland and its holiest possessions? No, they all buried patriotism a long time ago. They no longer want to fight a war of conquest. . . . These views are shared by 95 percent of troops of every kind in the field."[77]

As German troops saw it, however, the end of the war was not the result of a concealed strike in the ranks since the summer, of mass mutinies, or of a complete breakdown of discipline.[78] There were no major mutinies up to the beginning of armistice talks in early October; they flared up only when soldiers no longer saw any point in continuing the war.[79] Nor did the mostly orderly march back to the home country suggest a self-image of chaotic collapse and defeat; claims to manly, heroic reliability in the field were maintained until the end, even if they did not correspond to the actual military situation. This was true *a fortiori* in eastern Europe, where German soldiers had succeeded in ending the war in March.

To be sure, the motive behind the comparative resilience of German soldiers was no longer war patriotism but personal perspectives and tangible individual expectations. Fear of an unknown enemy who could not be trusted became fused with an instinctive desire to defend homeland and family from the kind of destructive violence experienced at the front. So long as there was a realistic chance of winning the war in this sense and coming through it alive, this rationale remained intact; only in the late summer of 1918 did a breaking point loom for German soldiers. NCOs and young frontline officers, especially brigade, platoon, and company leaders, played a key role in this context.[80] They usually had the trust of the men under them, taking the initiative for self-demobilization and often leading the whole of their exhausted units into captivity or on the march back home. The fact that this passed only very late into a real erosion of military structures and discipline demonstrated the robustness of many German soldiers even after four years of war. Generally, excesses such as the looting of depots were seldom the expression of political radicalism, but rather reflected the sheer necessities of survival and access to food.[81]

Most French soldiers in Summer 1918 displayed a mixture of exhaustion and skepticism, especially with regard to the threat to Paris. But homesickness and a longing for peace did not exclude a determination to continue the war and achieve a peace that would justify the untold sacrifices of the previous four years. French soldiers' letters and mail censorship reports pointed to a rise in morale in Summer 1918 as counterattacks got underway against retreating German troops. But although there was less resistance in the ranks and German attacks were no longer to be feared, the mood remained volatile and always depended on the daily performance of the men's own units. Spanish flu was another factor darkening the situation.[82]

All in all, the final period of the war was marked neither by widespread strike action in the ranks of the contending armies nor by a consciously planned revolution in the home societies. Such reactions developed on the German side only after hopes of a victorious conclusion to the war in the west had been dashed. The sudden shift from remobilization to disillusion occurred especially in units that had suffered high casualties in the offensives and whose young company leaders realized that the war could no longer be won. Even then, however, many decimated units fought on because they wanted to protect their homeland as long as possible from the kind of destructive warfare they had come to know.[83]

The high losses between Spring and Summer 1918, which at times were the highest in the whole war, did not necessarily entail a collapse of the "hold fast society"—and this was a key link with the homeland. Many Germans expected victory until the final weeks of the war and were simply unable to imagine defeat. As Sebastian Haffner later wrote, "I no longer had any clear conception of peace, though I had some idea of the 'Final Victory.' The Final Victory—the grand total that would one day be the inevitable result of all the many partial victories mentioned in the military bulletins—was for me what the Last Day . . . is for a pious Christian. It was the stupendous climax of all those triumphant bulletins in which the numbers of prisoners, size of territory gained, and quantity of booty outdid each other. What would follow was beyond imagining. . . . Even in the months from July to October 1918 I confidently expected victory, although I was not so stupid as to fail to notice that the army bulletins were getting gloomier and gloomier, and that my expectation defied reason. Well, had not Russia been defeated?

Did 'we' not possess the Ukraine, which would provide all that was needed to win the war? Were our armies not still deep in France?"[84]

3. WARS OF DISSOLUTION
Anticipating the Postwar Period in Southern and Southeastern Europe

In parallel to developments on the western front, the situation worsened on other fronts in the summer and fall of 1918, especially in the southeastern Balkans and on the Austrian-Italian front. It became clear that players in the future victor-states were already beginning to create as many *faits accomplis* as possible in order to strengthen their bargaining position in the peace talks that would follow an armistice. Military and political leaders, as well as the general public, had huge expectations, and as soon as the prospect of victory suddenly arose, their focus of attention began to shift from the burdens of the war to what they could gain from the victory.

On the Macedonian front, too, there was a certain reversion to the origins of the war in 1914. Fall 1918 witnessed the liberation of Serbia, where the war had begun in late July 1914 with the shelling of Belgrade by Austro-Hungarian troops. In the Salonica enclave—so far a relatively minor front for the Allies, which in 1915 was supposed to have provided relief to the beleaguered Serbs and then received Allied troops from Gallipoli—a colorful assortment of soldiers from all over the world had gathered during the course of the war: French, British, and Empire troops, alongside French colonials from Indochina, Italians, Serbs, and Russians and, since 1917, a number of Greek contingents. But the strategic significance of the Macedonian front remained quite limited, and until Summer 1918 most of the casualties there were the result of illness rather than military action. Frequent disciplinary problems suggest that the endless waiting was becoming too much for many of the soldiers.

The French general Adolphe Guillaumat, having taken over command from his predecessor Sarrail, managed to integrate the multiethnic forces and to familiarize them with modern tactics. In June 1918, the command passed in turn to General Franchet d'Espèrey; British units were withdrawn for service in the Middle East, while Russian troops were disarmed for fear that they might provoke revolutionary disturbances or even support the enemy after Russia's exit from the war. Thus, in Summer 1918 the Allies had thirty-one divisions on the Macedonian front, with a total strength of 650,000 men. In mid-September, after a difficult process of coordination, they launched an attack on Bulgarian forces. French and Serbian units broke through the front at Dobro Pole, and British and Greek contingents at Lake Doiran. For the Greek army, which lost 3,900 men, it was the bloodiest battle of the war. The Bulgarian front effectively collapsed amid mass desertion and insubordination, and the retreating forces offered little or no resistance to the Allies. Emissaries from the Bulgarian king eventually requested an armistice, which was signed on September 29.[85]

Bulgaria's military collapse opened up a number of possibilities and fueled hopes of territorial changes among some Allied powers. While British and Greek troops conquered western Thrace and marched on Constantinople, the Italians concentrated on Albania and the Adriatic coast, from which Austro-Hungarian forces were now withdrawing. In the end, it was therefore mainly French and Serbian troops who advanced into a Serbia that had hitherto been occupied by Austria-Hungary. Their progress was swift, because fighting on the western front and in the Alps meant that few occupation troops had been left in the area.

These events opened the way for a new regime under a government of Serbian exiles headed by Pašić. By June 1917 they had isolated and passed sentence on the radical leaders of secret organizations that had supported the Black Hand and the Sarajevo assassin, Princip. Colonel Dimitrijević, one of those responsible for the escalation in Summer 1914, was executed in June—although the fact that this passed almost without notice emphasized the extent to which the war had moved on. With the Corfu declaration of Summer 1917, Serbian political leaders together with Croats and Slovenes had agreed on a kind of blueprint for the future that would involve the expansion of Serbia into the new transnational state of the South Slavs: Yugoslavia. After French and Serbian troops liberated Belgrade in early November 1918, Pašić returned to the capital and, a few days later, had the Serbian monarch proclaimed "King of the Serbs, Croats, and Slovenes."[86]

By the end of the war, therefore, politicians involved in peace talks could no longer ignore certain political and territorial *faits accomplis*—especially as the men around Pašić were quite deliberately appealing to the Wilsonian program of national self-determination. The Serbian leadership also laid great emphasis on a narrative of victimhood involving the violent expulsion of the army and much of the Serbian population in 1915. By depicting Serbia together with Belgium as the first victim of the war and comparing its agony to the biblical Golgotha, this narrative downplayed Serbian responsibility for the assassination of the royal couple in Summer 1914 and the escalation of a local conflict into a European war.

Just a few months lay between the Italian disaster of Fall 1917 at Caporetto, when only massive British and French help had averted collapse, and the effective rout of Austro-Hungarian forces on the Alpine front. Precisely because the exhaustion on both sides was so great, military developments there in Summer and Fall 1918 had a particularly dramatic character. Despite the depletion of their resources, the Austro-Hungarian military and political leadership decided on a final offensive, the background to which was Emperor Karl's secret peace overtures to France. When these had become public, Karl had had to assure the OHL and the government in Berlin that he had no part in them; the German military then demanded in Spring 1918 that Karl prove his loyalty and stabilize the alliance by launching another attack against Italy without German aid. The direction of this attack became a matter of dispute among Austro-Hungarian commanders: whereas Conrad von Hötzendorf sought a repetition of his (unsuccessful) offensive of 1916 in the Tyrol, General Boroević argued for an assault on enemy positions across the Piave River. Although huge problems in ensuring adequate supplies of food and munitions had considerably weakened his troops, the emperor gave the green light to both operations—with devastating consequences.

In the end, Conrad von Hötzendorf had too few infantry and Boroević insufficient artillery support. The so-called Second Battle of the Piave River, which was actually fought both on the Piave and in the Tyrol, began on June 15, 1918. Because of inadequate artillery cover, the Austrians eventually had to abandon their positions on the west bank of the Piave facing the city of Treviso, as well as on the bridgehead in the Venice lagoon at the mouth of the river that they had held since late 1917. Both sides were aware of the battle's significance, for any breakthrough of the front would decide which side ended the war as victor and which as loser. This time, the Italians managed at great cost to prevent an Austro-Hungarian breakthrough into their hinterland,

and by June 20 their defensive fire brought the attacks to a halt. However, these early successes, in which, again, thousands of Italians had been taken prisoner, could not be sustained. Indeed, Armando Diaz—who had replaced Cadorna as Italian supreme commander in 1917—went on to organize Italian counterattacks both on the Piave and in the Tyrol.[87] For Austria-Hungary, the battle signified the equivalent of what the second Marne battle meant in mid-July for the Germans on the western front; they could no longer compensate for their 150,000 or more dead and wounded and 25,000 prisoners, against the loss of 80,000 on the Allied side—even before the battle, the call-up had been extended to adult males born in 1900. The dismissal of Conrad von Hötzendorf in mid-July did nothing to alter the fact that the Dual Monarchy had lost for good the ability to conduct offensive operations.

After these successes, the Italians refrained from further attacks of their own; Diaz fended off British and French requests by referring to the exhausted state of his troops. But things changed in mid- and late October, when the collapse of the Central Powers seemed imminent. For the Italian leadership, the main tasks then were to occupy large tracts of territory claimed by Austria-Hungary before any armistice took effect and peace talks got underway and to take as many prisoners as possible in order to use them later as means of exerting political pressure. This jockeying for position in the future peace talks accounted for the drama of the final military actions on the Alpine front.

Another objective for the Italian military was to erase the memory of Caporetto. It was therefore no accident that the last attack on the Austro-Hungarian lines began on October 24, 1918, a year to the day since that disastrous battle. The fifty-one Italian divisions were supported by three British and two French divisions, as well as smaller American units. Czech forces, consisting, as in Russia, of former prisoners of war, also took part in the action against the army of the Dual Monarchy, demonstrating their political claim to nationhood. Although of limited military significance, the deployment of these units thus had much to do with the postwar period and the gaining of international support for an independent Czechoslovak state. Thus, from mid-October on, the operations on this front were about a reshaping of the postwar order.[88]

It was in this concluding phase of the war that Gabriele d'Annunzio carried out his famous propaganda flights. But even without the tens of thousands of leaflets, organized with the help of the British press magnate Lord Northcliffe and dropped by Italian aircraft over enemy lines and cities, the armies of the monarchy were no longer capable of countering attacks. On October 30, Italian troops captured Vittorio Veneto; it gave its name to the last battle on this front, which cut off the Austro-Hungarian armies in the south from those in the Tyrol. By this time, the military collapse of the Dual Monarchy was already looming, and it was accelerated by the Hungarian government's decision on November 1 to end the involvement of its troops.[89] Officers and men saw that withdrawal as a clear sign that the end was nigh for the monarchy as they had known it. Only one day after the fall of Vittorio Veneto, the military leadership of Austria-Hungary effectively gave up the Adriatic coast, and Habsburg naval units were handed over to the Yugoslav National Council at Pula and (the next day) at Cattaro. The military structures of the monarchy fell apart on the Alpine front, and within days tens of thousands of fleeing soldiers, deserters, and refugees were blocking the main transport routes. On November 2, the AOK offered to open talks with the Italian supreme command; an armistice was signed the next day and came into force on November 4.

The Italian military exploited major communication problems among the disintegrating enemy forces to launch further attacks. In expectation of the armistice, large sections of the Austro-Hungarian army gave up fighting 24 hours before their Italian counterparts, who took the opportunity to continue their advance. This had two consequences. On the one hand, the Italians made more territorial gains, even reaching Trieste, the symbol of *irredenta* nationalism, before the armistice took effect. On the other hand, these operations delivered large numbers of troops into Italian captivity: 135,000 Austro-Hungarian dead (against the Allies' 38,000) plus more than 360,000 prisoners of war were an extremely high price to pay in this final period—the latter figure accounting for a majority of the Austro-Hungarian soldiers who had not deserted by November 4.[90] Whereas Italian prisoners were soon able to return home, Italy hung on to its share of prisoners of war until 1919, using them as important leverage in the peace negotiations.

What this episode reflected was not Italian perfidy—as many claimed in postwar Austria—so much as a chaotic situation in which the largely paralyzed AOK was completely unprepared for the armistice talks and had only irregular contact with the military delegations.[91]

4. REMOBILIZATION AND COSTLY VICTORIES
The Price of Cohesion in the Allied Societies

After the strikes and mutinies of 1917 and the creeping exhaustion, no mass peace movement developed in France. There were calls for peace, but not at any price; a just settlement, consonant with the casualties and suffering, was seen as requiring victory over Germany. Even such a pitiless critic of the war as Henri Barbusse, in his articles "Why Are You Fighting?" and "To the End," wrote in 1917, "See this war through to the end, to the end of the misery, suffering, tragedy, and shame that war has spread on earth for millions of years; sacrifice yourselves to the end so that your children may not one day have to do what you have done." This idea that the war was a final, necessary effort to achieve a real and lasting peace would become a leitmotif. It also explains the messianic projects associated with President Wilson, who gave political expression to this basic feeling.[92]

And yet, the mood in the French capital hit a low point in late January 1918. A major reason for this were the systematic German air raids: on January 30 and 31, a force of twenty-eight bombers dropped 250 bombs on Paris and its suburbs, killing a total of sixty-five civilians. On March 11 another thirty-five people lost their lives. Although the air defenses functioned reasonably well, putting up more than 200 captive balloons into the approach corridors, the attacks demonstrated that Paris was again within reach of German weapons.[93] In view of Russia's impending exit from the war and the expected German offensive on the western front, the psychological impact of these raids should not be underestimated.

Although France did not experience supply bottlenecks comparable to those in Germany or Austria-Hungary, food rationing was introduced at the beginning of 1918, with a daily bread allowance of 300 grams for adults. Rumors spread of unrest in working-class districts and a new strike wave. All this underlined how tense and insecure the situation was. On January 31, Michel Corday—who had heard of the January strikes in Austria-Hungary—noted that British shipyard workers on the Clyde were also threatening to walk out again if there were no peace talks soon. The protests resulting from exhaustion gained an increasingly political character when concrete alternatives to the war emerged with the programs of Lenin and

Wilson: "This really does reveal a new challenge in the struggle between the people and their rulers—the people are demanding to know why their rulers are forcing them to fight. It has taken four years for this legitimate desire to come to the surface. It has already achieved its aim in Russia. Now it is raising its voice in England. It is beginning to break out in Austria. We do not know how strong it is in Germany and France. But the war has entered a new phase: a conflict between the shepherds and their flocks."[94]

Since the beginning of the March offensives, German troops had been shelling Paris as in 1914 with long-range artillery; more than 250 people were killed and over 600 wounded. During the Good Friday service on March 29, 1918, a shell hit the church of Saint-Gervais-Saint-Protais in the Fourth Arrondissement, killing nearly ninety civilians.[95] Although the military significance of this event was slight, the capital now felt directly threatened by German bombers and artillery; the situation of Fall 1914 and 1870–1871 seemed to be repeating itself. Even today, buildings in the Jardin du Luxembourg and on the Place de la République show the marks of shell bursts from the siege of Paris in 1871 and the hits received in Fall 1914 and Summer 1918. Once again, panic spread among the population and even more in the political elite. Members of the middle and upper classes drew large sums from their bank accounts and headed out of the capital. Stations and trains were crowded to overflowing, and the numbers residing in nearby cities like Orléans that were considered safe increased threefold in a short time. The Parisian local economy partly collapsed, because many stores closed and there were mass layoffs. Tighter rules meant that the censorship extended to cover not only letters and postcards but also the monitoring of telephone calls. While public confidence in official decrees and the press plummeted, spy mania and denunciations multiplied as in the early days of the war.[96]

The long-term obsession with security in French interwar politics had much to do with these experiences in the final period of the war and the sense of being at the mercy of an advancing enemy. The threat to the capital made it crystal clear that German troops were in the heart of the country and that in Spring 1918 there could no longer be any talk of an imminent defeat of the Central Powers.

Against this background, Clemenceau delivered a remarkable speech to the National Assembly on March 8, 1918. In the end, he argued, it was not material resources that would decide the war; the real problem was that Russia had exited from the war, but the United States was not yet present in sufficient strength on the European continent. The main issue again was the link between front and home society, the loyalty and cohesion of the whole nation. Clemenceau fully recognized the dangers of the situation and the narrow gap between victory and defeat; the winning side would be the one that could once again mobilize all its moral forces for a short period. While German military leaders called for strong nerves, he emphasized the moral cohesion of the nation and its faith in victory: "The longer the war lasts, the more you see develop the moral crisis that signifies the end of all wars. The . . . trial of armed strength, the brutalities, acts of violence, plunder, bloodbaths: that is the moral crisis in which one side or another ends up. The one that morally holds out the longest is the victor. And the great oriental people that suffered for centuries the trials of war succinctly formulated this idea: 'The victor is the one who believes he is not defeated for a quarter of an hour longer than his adversary.' That is my maxim of war. I have no other."[97]

Although the Allies began to stabilize the front in July and showed signs of a successful remobilization, deep pessimism continued to spread among the French civilian population. The shelling of Paris, the latent threat to the homeland far beyond the front, the German advances since March, the destruction of one city after another (Reims, Amiens, Soissons)—all these had sunk deep into the consciousness of many French men and women, exacerbating their fears that France might eventually meet the same fate as smaller countries. The Belgian and Serbian armies also fought on, even though their countries were occupied and seemed no longer to exist.[98]

The Italian remobilization, begun in the aftermath of the Caporetto disaster in Fall 1917, led to the first broad political consensus in that country since the beginning of the war. But it was accompanied by extreme repression and a frenetic search for alleged internal enemies and national traitors, whether directed at socialists or at Catholics supporting the Pope's peace initiatives. In this context, parliament also came under growing suspicion that it was a hotbed of pacifism and defeatism. The war efforts threw parliamentary liberalism more and more onto the defensive.[99]

As in Germany and Austria-Hungary, the economic burdens of the war led to strike waves in Italy in Spring 1918, most notably in the metallurgical and textile industries. Although these actions remained fairly limited—partly because the military authorities tried to keep the lid on them by calling up large numbers of workers—the labor unions were clearly gaining influence. The war minister, Alfredo Dallolio, recognized their importance and forced the employers to grant wage increases that improved living standards in the arms sector; union delegates were also allowed into the factories in an attempt to mitigate social conflicts. The dismissal of Dallolio in April 1918, after pressure from big industrialists, illustrated the scale of the tensions. When his successor turned to more pro-business policies, conflicts between workers and the state increased once again.[100] While the workers saw him as an agent of the military and industrialists, because of their wartime experiences and higher status they also expected the authorities to adopt social measures in their favor. This ambivalence would persist for some time. A further complication was the special situation of small farmers and rural laborers in Italy; they had suffered high casualties for the national state and expected comprehensive land reform after the war, especially in regions dominated by large landowners.[101]

In the midst of the battles on the western front, a major conflict erupted in Britain between military leaders and the government. The background to this was pressure on the war cabinet since the spring to reduce the scope of conscription and to focus more on food supplies and coal production.[102] The consequences of this policy led to a crisis in relations with the military. Major-General Frederick Maurice was soon relieved of his functions as director of military operations. He had been a close colleague of General Robertson, who a few weeks earlier had himself clashed with Lloyd George over mobilization and supply issues and ended up being fired. In a letter that he sent to several newspapers, Maurice accused the government of deliberately withholding troops from the western front and not keeping parliament informed of this. His criticisms sparked firm reactions from the Asquith-led opposition and widened the gulf between a section of the Liberal Party and the war cabinet. In the end, however, the Maurice affair strengthened Lloyd George, not only because he used the debate in the House of Commons to brand Maurice's letter as a betrayal of military secrets and to insist on political control over the armed forces but also because he succeeded in deepening the split among the Liberals. He skillfully turned the debate into a vote of confidence in his war policy: 295 MPs eventually voted for the government versus only 108 against, and while 98 Liberals sided with Asquith, 78 supported Lloyd George's course. The prime minister calculated that there would not be a majority in favor of a political turn in the final phase of the war, especially because Asquith did not enjoy a reputation as a strong war premier. In sharp contrast to developments in Germany at the time, the civilian political leadership thus asserted its primacy over the military.[103]

In view of the fighting on the western front, the government eventually had to step up army recruitment and to raise the maximum age of service from 41 to 50. Meanwhile, the Representation of the People Act, which passed parliament at the beginning of the year, extended the suffrage from eight to twenty million people (with only limited concessions to the suffragettes). Yet this did nothing to mitigate the social and political costs of the war.[104] Although the intensity of strikes subsided in the climate of remobilization, the growing burdens, especially on the middle classes, led to a wave of aggressive xenophobia and a widespread feeling that spies and traitors were at work. Such suspicions were directed not least at Jews—indeed, as early as February 1917 a non-Jewish journalist had spoken of an "Intern Them All" movement. On July 13, 1918, a large demonstration in Trafalgar Square demanded "the immediate internment of all aliens of enemy blood, whether naturalized or unnaturalized." The government did not respond to such calls, but the event itself highlighted the extent of the hysteria and a tendency to suspect ever larger numbers of collaboration with the enemy or, at least, of constituting a danger within. Disillusionment therefore remained widespread in the Anglo-Jewish population up to the end of the war. The hostility exhibited toward "enemy aliens" put their integration into British society into question—in addition, the government's pro-Zionist policy on the Palestine issue had asserted the primacy of foreign policy and security strategies over internal social aspects and reinforced many anti-Semitic prejudices.[105]

Even graver were the effects of the anti-Bolshevik mood in 1918. The press consciously situated the social unrest and the summer wave of local strikes in the context of supposed Bolshevik agitation—an amalgam that would continue beyond the end of the war into the demobilization period, which saw strikes in the arms industry and disturbances among exhausted soldiers returning from the war. Even the forces of law and order were affected, when discontented policemen marched in the streets of Liverpool and London. In

July 1919, unemployed ex-soldiers went so far as to destroy the town hall in Luton. Many newspapers saw all this as a Bolshevik threat to the internal stability of the kingdom, all the more frightening because it had swept up previously reliable sections of society.[106]

The special mix of tension and exhaustion, unfocused disquiet, xenophobia, and conspiracy hysteria gave rise to a surge of new or existing national-patriotic organizations, mostly directed against the enemy-image of Bolshevism. The National Security Union, the Liberty League, the British Commonwealth Union, the Comrades of the Great War, and the conservative Primrose League were just a few of the organizations in which a right-wing section of society made its public mark, inscribing on its banners the struggle to defend the nation against civil war. Rooted in the war and the confrontation with the Bolshevik revolution, it had considerable potential to develop into a far right movement that would put Britain's liberal heritage to the test.[107]

Militant anti-Bolshevism also had a more immediate political dimension in the context of the Allied military intervention in Russia and support for the Czechoslovak Legion involved in the civil war there. From late May, the Legion was the strongest military force in Siberia, and it was used as the basis for many operations by the Whites as well as the western Allies. The capture of important cities such as Samara, Kazan, and Ekaterinburg established control over supply routes into Bolshevik-held areas to the west.[108] In Summer 1918 a Central Russian Committee was founded in London to advise the British government. Anti-Bolshevik circles there forcefully opposed Lloyd George's initial appraisal of Trotsky as a possible interlocutor for the Allies, insisting that Bolshevik propaganda, and particularly its anti-imperialism, represented an enormous danger for Britain and the Empire in Asia and the Middle East. This was also the position of leading Conservatives around Churchill, Samuel Hoare, and Lord Curzon.[109] The Slavist Robert Seton-Watson and his journal *New Europe* campaigned intensively for Allied intervention in Russia—later supported by Russian émigrés in London such as Pavel Milyukov and Pyotr Struve.[110]

In the United States, too, major internal consequences of the war first became discernible in Winter 1917–1918. After shortages in the supply of coal and fuel, the government gradually centralized the war economy, but, unlike in Europe, with no overtones of war socialism or tangible concessions to the unions. One reason for this difference was that, aside from particular problems, the population remained better supplied and the economy as a whole received a great boost from war production.[111] It was already becoming clear that the United States was the only player that could benefit economically from the war. Although corporatist structures embracing labor, capital, and the state, so characteristic of the European war economies, were considerably weaker in the United States, there were incipient moves toward state intervention in favor of workers, such as the National War Labor Board, which in April 1918 announced a "new deal for American labor." Congress withheld concrete support for policies in this direction, but within the War Labor Policies Board headed by Felix Frankfurter one man would gather important experience for the New Deal policies later implemented in the Depression of the 1930s. That man was Franklin Delano Roosevelt.[112]

Hostility to "enemy aliens" in America, especially those of German origin, flared up again in the concluding period of the war. A swift succession of laws, from the Sedition Act through the Alien Act to the Espionage Act, were passed by late 1917, while vigilantism and the climate of suspicion went so far that even German breweries were seen as a danger, on the grounds that they supposedly used alcohol to turn workers against the war. The lynching of the German American Robert Prager in April 1918 forced the U.S. president to condemn the practice in general for the first time. In May 1918 the governor of Iowa, William L. Harding, proposed to ban the use of any foreign language in telephone calls, schools, or religious services.[113]

At the same time, the status of Italian and Jewish immigrants changed as a result of their participation in the war. In May 1918, Congress removed all conditions for the naturalization of soldiers who had fought in Europe, so that at the end of the war they received honorable discharges that entitled them to apply for full citizenship. More than 280,000 acquired this new status as a result of the war.[114]

Such hopes were not fulfilled for all who made their way back. But veterans from other ethnicities did not constitute a lost generation, a passive group of the disillusioned; they associated their wartime experience with the task of translating its sacrifices into claims to a new status in America. Often they turned to the "100 Percent Americanism" movement to justify this sense of entitlement, resolutely demanding their share in the victory. Thus, in New Haven as in New York, violent clashes occurred between these demobilized soldiers and other sections of the population. Jewish veterans in New York City demonstrated against the pogroms in eastern Europe. The new wave of nativism and aggressive Americanism that many soldiers encountered did not silence the new immigrants, and their role in American politics would become increasingly important in the course of the 1920s. On the one hand, Italians, Jews, and other ethnic groups seemed to lose the cultural war against Anglo-Saxon dominance; on the other hand, they recognized more than ever how important it was in the long run to assert their interests at the political level—and their participation in the war would remain a key argument in their favor.[115]

Still, there can be no doubt that such claims were put forward amid a highly tense situation in American society. A wave of strikes rolled over the country from May to December 1919. In addition, Spanish flu caused the death of more Americans than the fighting in Europe: more than 1,000 people succumbed in New Haven alone between September 1918 and the return of American soldiers, and the death toll in New York rose to 33,000. Millions of workers were hit hard by the conversion to peacetime production of a war economy that had been running at full blast. Within a few months of the end of the war, there were more than 100,000 new jobless in New York alone. Strike waves overlapped with demobilization from the army, resulting in collective fears that a new wave of immigration would endanger the country's economic and social equilibrium.

As in Britain, there was a huge right-wing mobilization on the American home front, given considerable momentum by the Bolshevik enemy-image. The American Legion was a particularly striking example: it eventually became the largest "vigilance society" of the postwar period. Originally founded by U.S. soldiers in France as a veterans organization, it gave its support to the "100 Percent Americanism" movement. After the end of the war, it worked closely with official counterespionage and other surveillance organizations and also played a major role in public life.

This was the background to the Red Scare of Summer 1919—a wave of hysteria based on fears of a communist revolution that was thought to lie behind a series of local bombings. In the so-called Palmer Raids, a large number of workers, left-wingers, and alleged defeatists were arrested. Many foreigners were interned again and in some cases deported.[116] In these actions, too, the American Legion played an important role. On May 1, 1919, for example, its members clashed violently in Cleveland and elsewhere with workers marching beneath red flags in a May Day demonstration. The Legion was also used against striking workers—for example, in November 1919 in Kansas City, in liaison with the governor of Kansas.

The final period of the war therefore had a Janus face in American society: one face offered hopes of modernization and a vast mobilization of social energies, but the other blurred the boundaries between an increasingly repressive war state and a civil society with xenophobic and aggressively nationalist features. It was no accident that the history of the racist Ku Klux Klan was closely bound up with the wartime development of American society. After 1914, and more intensely from 1917 on, the Klan was active in southern states and developed a distinctive culture of surveillance, control, and repression directed against loose women, enemy aliens, and anyone suspected of disloyalty. After the end of the war, its popularity increased, and in a short time it recruited more than 100,000 new members. The war had given it a spectacular boost.[117]

There were also sizable countermovements, however. The founding of the American Civil Liberties Union was another result of the world war and the peace movement, and in 1919–1920 it expressed protest against the surveillance state, encroachments on private life, and the suspension of various freedoms. The defense of civil liberties against the state was no longer a matter of course—after the wartime experiences it was necessary to fight for it.[118]

5. HOPES AND CRISES
Germany between Peace Utopias and the End of the Monarchy

On the side of the Central Powers, 1918 began with a crisis in their home societies. There was a wave of wildcat strikes, which reflected the supply crisis in the cities and industrial centers but, unlike earlier precedents, had distinctly political features. Once again, the new political models that had come to the fore with the Russian revolution and the U.S. entry into the war had a considerable impact. Most significantly, many workers were protesting against a prolongation of the war in pursuit of aggressive war aims, as the Brest-Litovsk peace talks had exemplified; the link between the strike wave, peace talks, and the discussion of Wilson's Fourteen Points was therefore not merely chronological. The military and foreign policy dimensions of the war could no longer be separated from developments within society and the rise of political protest movements. The programs associated with the names of Lenin and Wilson seemed to point to possible real alternatives—and that was enough to increase the pressure on the German political and military leadership.

In Germany, the main center of the strikes was initially in Berlin, but then they spread to Munich, Nuremberg, and Hamburg. On January 29, it was estimated that 150,000 workers had walked out in Berlin alone. At first, the strikes were mainly in the metallurgical industry and munitions factories, but in late January sailors on warships anchored in the North Sea got word of ongoing events. There, too, unrest mounted as news spread of the failure of the talks in Brest-Litovsk. Berlin workers as well as soldiers now feared that the war would continue, and so the workers' demands centered on peace without annexations or reparations.[119]

For the first time, new organizational forms were adopted from Russia. Workers' councils were elected—not as cells of a social-political revolution, however, but for the organization of protest action. The list of demands put forward by the Berlin workers included both immediate and longer-term objectives, but the general linkage of peace with extensive political reforms was one of the leitmotifs: "1. Rapid achievement of peace without annexations, without indemnities, and based on the right to national self-determination in accordance with the proposals of the Russian people's representatives; 2. Involvement of workers in the peace negotiations; 3. More substantial food supplies; 4. Suspension of the state of emergency, protection of the freedom of association and assembly; 5. An end to the militarization of enterprises; 6. Release of men under sentence and in detention; 7. Democratization of all state institutions, beginning with the introduction of universal, equal, direct, and secret suffrage for all men and women over the age of 20 in Prussia."[120]

The strikes were mainly organized by USPD shop stewards in metallurgical and munitions enterprises, as mentioned. Friedrich Ebert, then chairman of the majority SPD and later first president of the Weimar Republic, felt compelled to join the Berlin strike committee as a representative, in order to bring the strikes to an end as quickly as possible. In January and February, the protest movement was the key pretext for the Far Right and nationalist politicians (the German Fatherland Party, for example) to accuse the SPD and the rest of the Left of having betrayed the army. At the same time, however, the Far Left accused the SPD of class betrayal. Although there were some links between the front and the strike movement, a majority of soldiers were very critical of the major strikes in Berlin; they considered the workers to be privileged and feared that the strikes might prolong the war unnecessarily.[121] The German remobilization was marked by an awareness of the successful conclusion to the war in the east, which seemed to show what was still achievable despite all the privations. The continuing food crisis on the home front reinforced the image of an enemy prepared to use the most barbaric weapons against women and children. And soldiers on the western front were experiencing a war from which they had every reason to protect their homeland.[122]

Since the military leadership viewed the situation favorably and wanted to concentrate all its forces on a decisive offensive in the west, major political or social concessions were never likely. After the Brest-Litovsk diktat, a victorious peace in the west seemed within reach. However, the strike waves had an impact beyond the narrow time frame in which they occurred: not only did the protests have a political character closer to that of a peace movement than to hunger revolts, especially as Russian-style workers' councils were formed in Germany for the first time; they also permitted the forging of new links with the front. After the strikes were over, many workers whom the authorities had identified as ringleaders were drafted and sent off to fight at the front. But what had been conceived as a punishment developed into a gateway for political communication, since these very ringleaders served to pass on the mood in society to the front. This would play a major role in how soldiers reacted to the failure of the final major offensives.[123]

While military and political leaders focused on the peace talks in the east and preparations for the offensive in the west, the mood in German society remained volatile. More and more everyday goods were only available as ersatz materials: paper diapers saved on cellulose, and flour for bread was mixed with potatoes, beans, buckwheat, or horse chestnuts. Meat substitute was produced from pressed rice, which was then cooked in sheep tallow and served with wooden make-believe bones. The number of meat substitutes authorized for use in sausages rose to 837, and the number of coffee substitutes to 511. Outside the black market, the only available soles for shoes were made of wood. Iron replaced nickel in coins, while pans and roofing were produced from tin.[124]

The *Münstersche Zeitung* featured the "stomach question" on the occasion of Wilhelm II's birthday on January 27, 1918. One article that cleared the censors directly attacked the country's leadership: "The government was unable to counter the evil in time, allowing circumstances to take hold that enrage people and make them bitter." The burdens of war were less and less fairly distributed: "Broad layers of the people have to bear more of the burdens and sufferings of war than those circles whose wealth and talents, money and land assure them an adequate, sometimes more than adequate, existence even in days of direst need."[125] Thomas Mann provides a good example of how widespread was the image of unscrupulous speculators, even among those who did not go hungry. On September 20, 1918, at a performance of Wagner's *Parsifal* at the Prinzregenten Theater in Munich, he observed not only a "pleasant buffet in the intermissions" but also a "vulgar war profiteer's wife, large diamonds in her ears, picking her teeth with her stubby little finger after eating a twenty-mark portion of chicken."[126]

Doubts about the competence of the state authorities grew not only on the home front but also among many commanders. In a letter dated May 23, 1918, General Groener complained of the "jealousy between Berlin departments," in particular the Office of Economic Affairs and the War Food Office. The image of a polycracy of competing institutions and inefficient administration was gaining ground among a military focused on the coming offensives; the time seemed to have come for some kind of military dictatorship. Groener—who, as Ludendorff's replacement at the end of the war, would become the key military interlocutor for Germany's first republican government—wrote in May 1918, "There is only one rational form of government: the enlightened despotism of one man. Nothing rational ever comes out of the idle chatter in parliaments, commissions, delegations, committees, and so on."[127]

The gloom on the home front combined in the spring with a climate of tension among soldiers awaiting the decision on the western front. On March 30, 1918, in an article on "war psychology," Max Dessoir described the critical mood in the army and at home. Soldiers increasingly directed their hatred at "arrogant speeches and writings, bellicose professors, valiant newspaper editors, and indomitable clubroom idlers. The men out there expect from us greater resolve and steadfastness; they want order to prevail and the postwar period to be well prepared; they demand of the government that it take advantage of the military successes."[128]

In late August and early September, as the situation of the Central Powers was dramatically worsening on the various fronts, events started to occur thick and fast in Germany. This corresponded above all to the acceleration of a historic crisis, at once political, social, and military, in the sense that Jacob Burckhardt gave to the term. On top of the imminent military defeat came the fall of the regime, the revolution, and the founding of the republic. But the republic that existed at the end of the year—a year that had begun with success in the east and hopes of a victorious peace in the west—was more than just an "improvised democracy" in the context of military defeat; it was more than the outcome of a suddenly necessary attempt to soften the terms of a Wilsonian peace. It would be too simplistic to attribute the parliamentarization of the German monarchy and the transition to a republic solely to the circumstances in Fall 1918; they were not due only to a sudden reorientation in the military leadership as defeat approached. Strong forces in the Reichstag wanted the change and had been preparing for it at least since Summer 1917—although it is true that they had acted very cautiously because most Reichstag deputies had had their eyes fixed on the victory in the east and the possibility of a successful end to the war in the west.[129]

After the Austro-Hungarian peace initiative on September 14, the Allied ceasefire with Bulgaria, and the alarming situation on the western front, the OHL issued what amounted to a declaration of bankruptcy on September 28 and 29.[130] Ludendorff informed the Kaiser at OHL headquarters in Spa that the situation facing the German armies in the west made it urgently necessary to initiate armistice talks and to accompany this with a move to parliamentary government within Germany. In the hectic period that followed, the military leaders pushed for acceptance of Wilson's demands for political reforms, so that talks could get underway on the basis of the terms already outlined by the U.S. president. The decree establishing parliamentary rule was ready the next day, and under further pressure from the OHL, talks immediately began on the formation of a new government. On October 1 and 2, the situation took a dramatic turn when the prospective new chancellor, Prince Max of Baden, tried to win time to polish the application for armistice negotiations, while Ludendorff issued an ultimatum calling on the government to make an immediate offer to President Wilson: "The army cannot wait another 48 hours." On October 3, Hindenburg told Prince Max that the collapse of the Macedonian front and the weakening of German forces on the western front meant that it was no longer possible to fill the gaps left by casualties. As there was no "realistic prospect of forcing peace on the enemy," he proposed "to end the fighting, in order to spare the German people and its allies pointless sacrifices. Each further day [would] cost thousands of brave soldiers their lives."[131]

Max von Baden, appointed Reich chancellor the same day, formed a new government in close liaison with the Reichstag majority and with the support of the Center Party, the SPD, and the Left Liberals. This changed the constitutional monarchy into a parliamentary monarchy, in which the chancellor and his deputy were dependent on a majority in parliament, not on the emperor's confidence. The military leadership had by no means ordered a "parliamentary seizure of power." The Interparty Group of the SPD, the Center Party, and Left Liberals, founded in 1917, had already demanded a change to the constitution along these lines on September 28, and it was then prepared to translate into action the new self-confidence that the Reichstag had displayed in its peace resolution of Summer 1917. However, October 1918 did not belong to the German parliament—the Reichstag simply assembled on October 5 to receive the government declaration of the new chancellor and then went into recess until October 22. When the constitutional changes took effect on October 28, meeting the central objective at which many liberals and others had been aiming for decades, they had already been overtaken by political events. By the end of October, what was on the agenda was no longer a parliamentary-democratic and, above all, evolutionary development of the monarchy, but the abdication of the Kaiser and the possibility of a complete change of political system.

This perspective brought Ludendorff into conflict with the leaders of the Reichstag majority, who recognized that the constitutional reforms had made them responsible for bringing the war to an end. The situation was all the more paradoxical in that the Center Party and the SPD had been the main political forces blackballed after 1871 as enemies of the Reich; in October 2018 they were to be the liquidators of the war and political administrators of the imperial legacy. The SPD in particular—which, after its vote for war credits in August 1914, had been the largest opposition party in the country—had to assume political responsibility once more, in an immensely difficult internal and external situation. Tensions increased inside the SPD between internationalism and patriotic affirmation, between principled opposition and responsibility for the state.

It was only in early October, during negotiations over the formation of a new central government, that the OHL informed leaders of the parliamentary groups of the dire situation on the western front. Only then did it become altogether clear to many politicians that there was no longer any possibility of winning the war. But it was not the OHL leadership, Hindenburg or Ludendorff, who faced the parliamentarians. On October 2, the staff officer Erich von dem Bussche-Ippenburg was dispatched to Berlin, where he explained the situation to the parliamentary groups' leaders: lack of resources made it impossible to think of "forcing peace on the enemy." The Allies were able to absorb horrific casualties because of the arrival of American troops and materiel; meanwhile the large-scale use of tanks had broken the mental strength and will to resist among the German forces. Significantly, Bussche resorted to the "lack of nerve" model to explain the widespread "tank fright": when tanks "made a surprise appearance, the nerves of our men were not able to confront them."[132] This "lack of nerve" was also the explanation for "the high number of Germans taken prisoner." The "replacement situation" for the German forces was hopeless: "Only a callup of the 1900 cohort will raise battalion strength above 100, and then only as a one-off. Then our last reserves of men will be exhausted." The shock for the Reichstag deputies was enormous; it completely disoriented them. The euphoria that had prevailed just a few weeks earlier and the fanciful visions of peace through victory gave way to the reality of unavoidable defeat: "The deputies were devastated. Ebert turned deathly pale and could not utter a word; Stresemann looked as if something was happening to him."[133]

On the evening of October 3, Chancellor Max von Baden duly informed the U.S. president that the German government was seeking peace on the basis of Wilson's Fourteen Points. "In order to avoid further bloodshed," he wrote, "the German government is seeking the immediate conclusion of armistice agreements on land, at sea, and in the air." On October 21, this was followed up with an offer to evacuate the occupied territories and to cease submarine warfare.[134] For Thomas Mann, the triumph of the democratic virtue embodied by the western powers—which he rejected for Germany—now loomed ahead. On October 5, 1918, he wrote in his diary: "It is certainly a bit hard that it now depends on the wisdom of a Quaker whether Germany obtains a peace that does *not* inject into her bloodstream undying outrage against the turn of events." His conclusion was that "the worldwide triumph of democratic civilization in the political sphere" was an accomplished fact; the task now was "to preserve the German spirit," and consequently "one must recommend the separation of cultural and national life from politics, the complete detachment of the one from the other." This was also the thrust of his *Reflections of a Nonpolitical Man*, "against the fusion of the two realms, against the 'politicization' of Germany through the absolute domination, in the cultural sphere as well, of the victorious principle of democratic civilization."[135]

Some still opposed what they perceived as an overhasty entry into ceasefire talks. Walter Rathenau's article *"Ein dunkler Tag"* (A Dark Day), published in the *Vossische Zeitung* on October 7, sparked debate on the possibility of a people's guerrilla war, a *levée en masse* on the model of the French Revolution.[136] Arguing for such a popular levy and the creation of a "national defense department," Rathenau pointed out that scarcely more than half of German troops were currently stationed on the western front. Whereas the announcement of concessions suggested that the German front was breaking up, different armistice terms would be offered if it was thought that the front was stable and prepared for defensive operations. The new government had therefore been too rash: "We few issued reminders and warnings when no government thought of looking the truth in the face." People were "getting carried away prematurely, taking decisions prematurely. You don't begin talks by giving way—first you consolidate the fronts. . . . Has that been overlooked? Anyone who has lost his nerve must be replaced. . . . We want peace, not war—but not the peace of subjugation."[137] However, there was no support in either the military or political leadership for a people's war that called into question the cornerstone of the German war experience: the fact that at no point enemy troops had occupied German territory. The war was therefore ended politically, not through fighting on home ground: yet precisely this would be the starting point for the "stab in the back" legend.[138]

Thomas Mann, too, reacted against the idea of a *levée en masse*. This was a good example of how much confidence large sections of the German bourgeoisie still had in Hindenburg. Mann did not realize the riskiness of his maneuver and his flight from responsibility; he still believed that Germany deserved victory. Since people felt cheated out of this, and thus out of the prize for all their sacrifices, the rhetoric of democracy seemed to them like so much play-acting. The result was an even deeper skepticism about politics: the immediate present seemed to confirm that it was a dirty business. On October 12, Mann noted, "Mine is not the heroic stance. What I like about Hindenburg is that he refuses to play *va banque,* and that he has installed the 'popular government' so that it can make peace. Provided it is acknowledged . . . that Germany is the real victor in this war—insofar as 'war' is the proper word—there remains no other choice . . . but to view things from the comic side and declare the victory of the Allies a colossal humbug." It was necessary "to salute the new democratic world with good grace as a kind of world convenience that it will be quite possible to live with, assuming . . . that Germany obtains raw materials and is treated in general according to her merits." Germans would also have to "keep everything cultural, national, philosophical separate from politics and *free,* on a plane high above politics, something not in the least affected by democratic utilitarianism."[139]

The early days of October brought an admission of imminent military defeat, but the German population and political elites had not been prepared for the consequences. Until recently, official war propaganda had been insisting that the military situation was still open and that the German offensives on the western front had been successful. The naval officer Albert Hopman commented on the new government with a withering critique of Wilhelm II: "From *Sic volo sic jubeo* [This is what I want, this is what I order]"—Wilhelm's inscription on a photo he gave to a minister at the beginning of his time in government—"to that, what a tragicomedy!"[140]

It soon became perfectly clear that the persistent idea of peace through victory had not allowed a language in which to conceive of a compromise peace, let alone defeat. When it became necessary, after the failed offensives, to face the fact that the war was unwinnable, the consensus on holding out and continuing to fight also broke down. Theodor Wolff's observation on October 14, 1918, was concise and accurate: "Everything depended on the western front."[141] The sudden change in mood therefore reflected a breakdown in communication between the political leadership, the military elites, and the home population. When the offer of an armistice to Wilson became known on October 6, Hopman reacted with a helpless search for explanations. This led him to place all the blame on the Kaiser, exonerating the military of any responsibility: "World history is the last judgment. Germany will have to pay dearly for all the sins it has committed in the last three decades. It became politically ossified because of its blind trust, its slavish subordination to the will of a fool bursting with vanity and an exaggerated opinion of himself. No victory without struggle! Politically, we have not been struggling for the last three decades, only play-acting, playing like children lost in illusions and self-deception. Politically we have therefore remained children; we haven't become men, nor have we produced any. Now comes the bitter disappointment of a child who suddenly sees himself confronted with the harsh, cruel world. All our truly invincible military strength, our hard work, perseverance, and national energies have been wasted for nothing; the magnificent, well-nigh inexhaustible capital that Bismarck bequeathed has been lost."[142] With an eye on the popular mood, the authorities had recourse to the metaphor of failing nerves. The "strong nerves" of Germans, which in 1914 were seen as the guarantee of victory, seemed to have disappeared. A report by the Berlin police chief noted on October 29, "This sudden downturn in the mood . . . should be explained in terms of the psychology of the masses, who are used to swinging from one extreme to the other; the suggestive power of rumors; and the nervous overstimulation peculiar to large cities that has been dramatically increased by undernourishment and the general tension."[143]

The unexpectedly dramatic admission that the military situation was hopeless, together with the OHL's push for armistice talks within a few days, marked a fundamental turnaround. In view of the innumerable casualties of the preceding years, most people thought the main task was to end the war as quickly as possible, since a continuation of the slaughter made no sense if there was no prospect of victory. This was the basis for the peace movement that grew more radical in the course of the month and exerted increasing pressure on the new government under Max von Baden. For the first time, revolutionary groups also began to emerge—although there was no sign of a revolutionary mass movement. Fears spread that the concessions offered so far would not be enough to end the fighting in the near future. While the great majority of the peace movement was not driven by republican aspirations, there was now talk of the Kaiser's possible abdication if that would bring the end of the war closer.[144]

The radicalization was not the result of a long-present and growing tendency to revolution or even of an attempt to bring about a German October revolution along Bolshevik lines. The developments on October 1918 had more to do with the dynamic springing forth from Wilson's response to the German government's request for talks. In a letter dated October 17, Thomas Mann still firmly opposed "the democratic leveling of Germany" from without. Even the men in the St. Paul Church in 1848 (in Frankfurt during the revolution there) would in the end have recognized themselves in an Imperial Germany; so long as an emperor stood at the apex of the state, "the romantic, medieval Germany [was] not dead." But what Germany's enemies and the supporters of democracy had in mind was precisely the "deromanticization of Germany, its incorporation into rationalist civilization." Wilson now seemed to Mann "truly frightening," for the diplomat was gaining the upper hand over the philanthropist, and an increasing "joy and serenity in violence" was observable in him. On the other hand, there were no longer any alternatives: "To keep going militarily would be the only way of making him see things philanthropically, in terms of the League of Nations, and so on. But our soldiers say: 'If I gotta go over the top again, I'll defect.' Russification seems far advanced. And yet, the complete triumph of virtuous democracy, of the New York and London stock exchange, would be the biggest humbug in world history!"[145]

In his note of October 25, Wilson made it crystal clear that if the armistice talks took place only with military leaders and monarchical autocrats, Germany would have to surrender and would not be able to negotiate any concrete peace terms. The formulation of Wilson's reply may have reflected his goal to support a process of internal democratization in Germany. But at this time the German press itself was discussing more and more often the link between armistice, ending the war, and the Kaiser's abdication.[146]

Wilson's Fourteen Points, to which the German request for armistice talks referred, had been formulated back in January without close consultation with the other Allies. If they were to be used in October as the basis for armistice talks and peace negotiations, the political leaders in London, Paris, and Rome also had to be brought in. Wilson's negotiator Colonel House, however, who arrived in Europe on October 25, soon learned that the governments in question were not prepared to strengthen the credibility of Wilson's outlined principles by relating them to their own policies. Although the British, French, and Italian leaders agreed in principle to negotiate on the basis of the Fourteen Points, considerable disagreements among the Allies and the burdens for any new postwar order were already becoming apparent. In London, Paris, and Rome it was expected that Wilson's general call for disarmament would apply primarily to the Central Powers. They interpreted his central demand for greater autonomy in the multinational Habsburg and Ottoman Empires in such a way that the objective seemed to become completely independent nation-states and dissolution of the empires.[147]

The Fourteen Points, which Wilson had conceived as a universal, idealistic promise of justice without implying the shake-up of all political relations, now developed for the Central Powers into a political-territorial hiatus implying the drawing of completely new borders. This "border revolution," and above all the breakup of the European empires, was no longer like the land reparceling to which the inter-monarchic Congress of Vienna gave its blessing in 1815, even if it had an official character, in the sense that the governments in London, Paris, and Rome pushed it through. This revolution "from above" would have long-term consequences, whereas none of the attempted revolutions "from below" in the subordinate belligerent countries led to a repetition of the October Revolution.

Discussions with the Allies in late October 1918 suggested to American diplomats that the states on the losing side should from then on be excluded from real negotiations. It also became clear that the transition from war to peace was going to be a very unequal affair: the British rejected the principle of freedom of the seas, for example, because it would not have allowed them to maintain the blockade on German ports, and the French government demanded such large indemnities from Germany that a Wilsonian peace without reparations (on which the Central Powers had pinned their hopes) receded ever further into the background. When Wilson informed the German government on November 5 that the Allies were willing to negotiate on the basis of the Fourteen Points, the consequences of these quite diverse interpretations had not yet been fully thought through. Large parts of the German population expected lenient terms for an armistice and future peace, but such hopes would be dashed over the weeks and months ahead. This would pose an enormous burden for the new peacetime order.[148]

In parallel with the moves to a parliamentary system and the request to President Wilson, it had become clear since early October how little the German military leadership was ultimately prepared to allow political-parliamentary control, let alone to subordinate itself to a central government answerable to parliament. This was a crucial difference from the relationship between military and political leaders in Britain or France. Whereas Lloyd George and Clemenceau were able to assert the primacy of politics, the extensive political claims of the OHL led to a situation in which Ludendorff and Hindenburg refused to accept responsibility for the defeat. This made all the more important the question of to what extent the main representatives of the Empire, the monarchy, and the OHL leadership really were prepared to accept the consequences of the October reforms.

In practice very little, it soon appeared. German troops withdrawing from France and Belgium, drawing on the scorched-earth tactics tried in Spring 1917, systematically cut transport and communication links and destroyed industrial plants and mines, actions that could only have a negative effect on armistice negotiations. At the same time, the navy leadership—against the wishes of the new chancellor and Reichstag majority—planned a last operation of its own in the North Sea, so that it would not have to hand over its battle fleet to the British without a fight. And the monarch himself, placed under military protection at this key moment, left the increasingly unruly capital and betook himself to the supreme headquarters in Spa.[149] A political vacuum thus arose in Berlin, while the chancellor continued the change of course in internal politics and distanced himself from those who had led the OHL until then. On October 23, many political prisoners were released—including Karl Liebknecht, who would play a key role in events over the coming days and weeks. Three days later, Ludendorff's dismissal showed how deep the crisis of confidence between the military and political leaderships had become. The architect of the war, who had made his mark at Liège in 1914 and joined Hindenburg by Summer 1916 at the latest as the key player in the mobilization of German resources, fled the country and spent the rest of the war in a hotel room in Sweden. His replacement with General Groener demonstrated to many soldiers, and also to many sailors on battleships lying at anchor, what changes had suddenly become possible.[150]

The immense acceleration of change that gripped German society did not, however, lead to developments like those in Russia in 1917. The front did not simply collapse, nor did the army disintegrate: there was no paralysis or breakdown of its structures. In comparison with other armies, especially those of Russia and Italy, and in the end also of Austria-Hungary, the number of disciplinary proceedings remained fairly small. Hatred of officers was less pronounced than elsewhere, especially in the case of younger platoon or company leaders who shared the living conditions of their men at the front and were often held in higher regard than staff officers and commanders behind the lines.

Things were different in the navy, however, where tensions between officers and lower ranks had been rising throughout the war. Officers' privileges were seen as especially provocative because the battle fleet saw so little action at sea. Many younger officers, who were able to communicate better than their older peers with the crews, had been reassigned to the submarine fleet, while a distinctive traditional code of honor remained in place among the navy leadership. Local resistance to the final, senseless deployment of the navy escalated from October 27, with large-scale mutinies in the High Seas Fleet anchored at Wilhelmshaven. Behind these lay not only a widespread war weariness and fear of a pointless final action at sea but also the feeling that the navy leadership was consciously defying the will of the new government. How far the authority of naval officers had already been eroded became clear in their direct confrontations with sailors' representatives. Richard Stumpf reported on one such confrontation on November 4: "A war of words was fought between the ship's captain and a number of spokesmen for the demonstrators. The prize was the crew of the Baden, which was standing lined up on the upper deck. If the captain had been any kind of competent speaker, our spokesmen would have had to withdraw without winning over a single man. But both the officer, who was deathly pale, and the seamen's council made a rather poor job of it. The result was that about a third of the crew joined our ranks." The crews of other ships declared their solidarity, but the sailors' revolt was also part of the interface between hunger and politics. When Richard Stumpf asked his comrades to go ashore and join the demonstrations, the reply came back: "We're about to have lunch."[151]

The sailors' demands initially centered on improvements in their living conditions: better food rations and greater provision for home leave. But they also called for the creation of special committees to monitor military tribunals, a relaxation of disciplinary measures, and the release of comrades imprisoned in other ports. When the navy leadership had thousands thrown into jail in Wilhelmshaven and moved several ships of the line there, the men interpreted this as a sign that commanders were prepared to crush the de facto military strike by force, so as to prevent at all costs any repetition of the Russian events. Against this background, soldiers and sailors were also mobilized in other port cities and garrisons; protest actions took place especially in Kiel, going well beyond the original set of demands. Along with the release of imprisoned comrades, the aims now included the formation of soldiers' councils and the disarming of officers.

At this critical juncture, even the smallest concessions triggered a rush of increased expectations and political demands stretching beyond the particular context of the planned naval action and the detention of comrades. After the rebels had effectively taken power in Kiel on November 4, the movement began to spread throughout the Reich, revealing the depth of the legitimation crisis; the traditional state players and institutions, especially the military garrisons and urban police forces, seemed paralyzed. It is remarkable that, in this period from the beginning of the month to the climax on November 9, no particular violence was required. A regime change took place with little accompanying noise: the state did not have to be conquered, but seemed to throw in the towel.

In the movement spreading from Kiel, the key players were soldiers from local garrisons, industrial workers, union militants, and political representatives of the workers' parties. Although soldiers' and workers' councils were formed in many places, they were not based on a Bolshevik-style revolutionary mass movement or long-term revolutionary strategy; rather, they were improvised regimes, not centrally coordinated, that took power locally at a moment when the traditional state institutions had lost their authority. The German councils' movement of November 1918 was not the instrument of a red October Revolution; it became a dynamic instrument through which a large part of the population grappled with the possibility of a new political and social order.

The wave crossed into the northern port cities of Hamburg, Bremen, and Lübeck on November 5; reached Hanover on November 7; and then spread to Cologne and Düsseldorf on November 8 and onward to Frankfurt and Leipzig. Events had already come to a head in Munich on November 7, when Kurt Eisner proclaimed a republic and sealed the fate of the Bavarian Wittelsbach dynasty.

The poet Rainer Maria Rilke experienced the euphoria of liberation in that city. In a letter of November 7 to Clara Rilke, he wrote that in the past few days Munich had "given up some of its emptiness and quiet." Everywhere there were large gatherings in beer halls and in the open air. Rilke listened to speeches not only by Max Weber and the anarchist Erich Mühsam but also by many students and "men who had been four years at the front, all so simple and frank and of the people. . . . The fumes of beer and smoke and people did not affect one uncomfortably, one hardly noticed them, so important was it and so above all immediately clear that the things could be said whose turn has come at last, and that the simplest and most valuable of these things, insofar as they were to some extent made easily accessible, were grasped by the enormous multitude with a heavy massive approval. Suddenly a pale young worker stood up, spoke quite simply: 'Did you, or you, or you, any of you,' he said, 'make the armistice offer? and yet *we* ought to do that, not those gentlemen up there; if we take possession of a radio station and speak, we common people to the common people yonder, there will be peace at once.'"[152]

The climax on November 9 resulted from a number of overlapping events that had occurred that day in Berlin. Once again, as in early August 1914, a powerful dynamic was unleashed in the space of a few hours, neither completely random nor consciously steered. It was not a planned revolution, and the transition to a republic had not been expected to happen in that form, but the question of the Kaiser's abdication had been intensely discussed since the middle of October. On November 5, 1918, the *Frankfurter Zeitung* wrote of the "liquidation of the thirty-year rule of Kaiser Wilhelm II, or what was left of it, in the terrible catastrophe of this war that is also the Kaiser's catastrophe." He had come "to symbolize in the eyes of the world the policy that led Germany into the abyss. . . . Insofar as his system was supposed to uphold this always ego-driven policy before the times and before history. Dignity demands that he step down if that terrible policy collapses."[153]

The situation in Berlin unfolded at three levels. At the first of these, the wave of soldiers' and workers' protests reached the capital on November 9, when large demonstrations, including sizable sections of the Berlin army garrison, formed around midday. At the second level, Chancellor Max von Baden tried to prevail on the Kaiser (who was then hurrying to Spa) and the Crown Prince to renounce the throne; this corresponded to a hope fueled by Wilson's recent notes to Berlin that such a step would allow the war to be ended on acceptable terms. In seeking this abdication by the Hohenzollerns, however, the chancellor intended to preserve the monarchical state form on the basis of the October reforms. When Wilhelm hesitated to give him the go-ahead, Max von Baden eventually announced the Kaiser's abdication under the pressure of the situation in Berlin—without express authorization from army headquarters.

The third level of events concerned the SPD leaders in Berlin. Friedrich Ebert, in response to the ongoing mass movement, called for a new government that had the confidence of the people, stating that he was prepared to take over political responsibility himself. He replaced Max von Baden as chancellor and stressed that he intended to govern on the basis of the reformed Imperial constitution—which would have entailed not a republic but a parliamentary monarchy and the appointment of a regent. Representatives of the Majority Social Democrats (MSPD) accordingly supported early elections to a national constituent assembly; they were not thinking of a revolutionary transition to a republic—the national assembly was supposed to decide on this—nor of a social revolution, but rather of a provisional government with emergency powers. This government, based on the MSPD / Center Party / Left Liberal coalition dating back to 1917, only now with the addition of the USPD, was supposed to prevent a lurch into violence during the difficult period in which a new constitution was being elaborated. In upholding the October reforms and focusing on a national assembly with powers to draft a constitution, the leaders of the Majority Social Democrats distanced themselves from a revolutionary overthrow of the existing conditions. The proclamation of the republic by Philipp Scheidemann from a Reichstag balcony was not planned in advance, and Ebert's reaction to it was one of outrage. Scheidemann had acted on the spur of the moment, bending to pressure from the demonstrations and the declaration of intent by the Far Left around Liebknecht to declare a socialist republic of their own—which is what they did a few hours after Scheidemann took his action. This dual proclamation reflected the division of the Left resulting from the war—and it forced the MSPD to give up its original plan for a coalition government of socialist and bourgeois parties to ward off the looming "fraternal warfare" in the Left. The outcome was the formation of a Council of People's Representatives from leaders of the MSPD and the USPD.[154]

In her diary entry for November 9, 1918, the artist Käthe Kollwitz combined a sense of the enormity of the events with her individual experience of the war. While she welcomed the political revolution in the hope of a swift end to the war, personal grief over the loss of her son Peter remained her dominant feeling: "Today it's come true. This afternoon I walked through the Tiergarten to the Brandenburg Gate, where leaflets announcing the abdication were being handed out. A demonstration set out from the gate and I joined it. An elderly invalid came up and shouted: 'Ebert chancellor!—pass it on.' A rally in front of the Reichstag. Scheidemann proclaimed the republic from a window. . . . I saw soldiers rip off their cockades and laughingly toss them on the ground. So, now it's for real. We are experiencing it but don't really grasp it at all. I can't help thinking of Peter all the time—that he'd be here with us if he were alive. He too would tear off his cockade. But he's not alive, and when I last saw him and [he] looked more handsome than ever, he had the same hat with the cockade and his face was shining. I can't think of him any other way."[155]

In the evening edition of the *Berliner Tageblatt*, Theodor Wolff already tried to draw a first balance sheet: the acceleration of events was evident also in the rate at which events became historical. Unlike many other newspapermen, he did not simply emphasize the Kaiser's personal responsibility but also pointed to the monarch's passivity in the war and to associated shifts in the power structure. In his view, the Kaiser "operated with a fantastic misjudgment of the real circumstances." The real-life person had to be differentiated from the distorted picture drawn in the war propaganda: "He was neither the 'Attila' whose cruel, bloodthirsty image the Entente press tirelessly put out. We shall speak of the origins of this human catastrophe when peace has been concluded. Wilhelm II did not play the role of a figure leading his people and forging ahead, but only the role of someone pushed and pressured. His advisers, whether in positions of responsibility or not, maintained in their ignorance that a dazzling diplomatic success was certain if the operations were followed through to the end. Others whispered that if there was to be a war, it was better that it came at once. The Kaiser gradually gave way. . . . Wilhelm II was not the only initiator, but he did represent an absurd, short-sighted policy that misjudged all forces and ideas coming from abroad, and he symbolized an age and a spirit which, in its hubris and craving for power, brought on the catastrophe."[156]

The next day, at a 3,000-strong conference of Berlin soldiers and workers, it became clear that the situation in Germany did not permit a repetition of the Bolshevik revolution and that the majority of workers' and soldiers' councils approved of elections for a national constituent assembly. Dual power, divided between the Council of People's Representatives and the Petrograd-inspired Executive Council newly established out of the Berlin conference, failed to work. The critical period up to the adoption of a new constitution would be dominated not by revolutionary changes but by a threefold compromise between the key political and social players. This involved the collaboration of MSPD representatives on the Council of People's Representatives with ministerial bureaucracies and Reich departments whose leaders were close to the bourgeois parties; but it also involved coordination between the Council-based provisional government and the military leadership. The agreement reached on November 10 between Ebert and General Groener (Ludendorff's successor) expressed a common determination to safeguard public order and "the rule of law" in the critical period following the end of the war. Groener assured Ebert of the army's loyalty, while Ebert guaranteed that officers would retain the power to command and discipline troops in the upcoming demobilization. On November 15, a "central labor community agreement" signed by employers' associations and labor unions recognized the unions as the workers' representatives, provided for an eight-hour day and workers' committees in large enterprises, and established that entrepreneurs could preserve the existing economic order. This kept socialization off the agenda, while giving large industry a considerable degree of influence—all before the adoption of a new constitution and a reorientation of the political parties.[157]

These basic compromises marked the first period of the revolution as a largely nonviolent formal transfer of power, first in Berlin and then in the federal states where the MSPD and USPD formed the government in various constellations. Thomas Mann supported the new arrangements, bade farewell to the monarchy as a historical relic, and emphasized that the largely nonviolent revolution was the best proof of its consistency. On November 10, with a future German Austrian free state in mind, he wrote in his diary, "The imperial idea, the imperial name, was, as Bismarck put it, a great recruiting force for German unification fifty years ago. It is my conviction that today we need no longer fear for the unity of the Reich even without the Kaiser. Today the Imperial House is a romantic vestige, and Wilhelm II actually played his role in an appropriately nervous, highly overwrought, and provoking manner. In practice it is really dispensable. I repeat to myself and others that lack of resistance to a revolution proves its legitimacy and inevitability. I am content with the relative calm and orderliness with which, for the present at least, everything is taking place. The German revolution is after all German, though nonetheless a revolution. No French wildness, no Russian Communist drunkenness."[158]

The reactions to the events of November 9 were diverse. Karl Hampe—who, as a bourgeois intellectual, had identified with the German nation-state founded in 1871—described it the next day as "the most wretched day of my life! What has become of the Kaiser and the Reich? From the outside we face mutilation, indecision, and a sort of debt servitude; internally we face brutal class rule under the deceptive appearance of freedom, and civil war, starvation and chaos."[159] On November 12, the naval commander Albert Hopman found himself in Sevastopol, far from any German port, contemplating there too the breakdown of military discipline and the gradual loss of his power to command. His own units were committing acts of sabotage against Russian ships and taking everything they could turn into money. This prompted Hopman to make a general statement: "I am deeply depressed at this collapse of moral bearings on the part of our men. Just off home, and taking as much as possible with them. Brigands, Huns! The English are quite right. The German lacks any inner discipline. He is a machine pulled on a wire, with no soul and no self-control. . . . Holy Goethe, holy Bismarck, you lived in vain."[160]

In many respects, the suicide of Albert Ballin on November 9, 1918, symbolized the end of the empire. More than any other figure, this Jewish shipowner and personal friend of the Kaiser had long embodied the claims of the Reich to be a world power. His ship *Imperator,* epitomizing naval pride and efficiency, had been the German response to the wreck of the *Titanic,* and his commitment to the Berlin-Baghdad railroad had furthered the imperial visions to which large sections of the industrial elite adhered. His suicide, on the very day of Wilhelm's abdication, followed the shattering of his life's work, which seemed to be reflected in the demise of the German state founded in 1871. During the war, Ballin had found the Kaiser increasingly timid and passive, but his decision to kill himself did not come in response to the abdication; in fact, he had already wished the Kaiser a peaceful old age in exile and had even counseled him to step down earlier. Nor was Ballin a victim of the revolution; only later was there talk that Hamburg revolutionaries had put him on their blacklist and threatened him. What was decisive in the end was his disappointment with Wilson—and the fact that the war had destroyed his Hapag shipping company, once the largest in the world. There was no longer any future for him.[161]

A few weeks after the revolution, even those who had been euphoric about the changes in early November were showing signs of deep skepticism. Rilke, for example, wrote on December 19 that the great change concealed the "old lack of principle" beneath "the red flag"; a seductive "political dilettantism" threatened "to draw people outside the realm of their knowledge and customary practice" and inspire them "to seek themselves in the universal and introduce experimentation where only the wisest and most thoughtful approach can be effective." He went on to note how the longed-for peace had turned into a new polarization in the space of a few weeks. People had no time to catch their breath, because everyone was too busy "picking up the thousand fragments into which [the peace] fell from all our hands and broke." "We have never seen peace as a whole," although precisely that was needed: "to picture its magnitude, its sheer magnitude, after the turbid monstrosity of the war."[162]

6. BREAKUP WARS AND INDEPENDENCE STRUGGLES
The Dissolution of Continental Empires

In Austria-Hungary, as in Germany, the year began with a strike wave. Large demonstrations took place in the main cities and industrial centers—on January 13 in Budapest, January 14–25 in Vienna, and finally in Prague and Brno. The movement usually originated in the arms industry, and workers associated their protest against the announcement of food ration cuts with demands for an end to the war. News of the revolts spread in a few days to all the main cities of the Dual Monarchy. For the first time there were signs in Austria-Hungary that the wave of protests would spill into military garrisons, and in February disturbances and mutinies developed in the navy in the Adriatic port of Cattaro (today's Kotor).[163]

Meanwhile, socialist leaders from various parts of Austria-Hungary were struggling over the future of the monarchy. The overlapping of social, political, and national crises, so characteristic of the Dual Monarchy, was central to their positions, which were particularly at odds with one another in the case of the Austrian social democrats. While Karl Renner, the jurist and future premier (from 1918 to 1920) of the first Austrian republic, sought a solution to the nationalities question within an overarching monarchical state, Otto Bauer, the leading representative of Austro-Marxism, was already distancing himself from the monarchy. This was the context in which German Austrian, Czech, and Polish socialists adopted the nationalities program at their conference in Vienna, where the main document referred to the link between class development and nation-building that had emerged during the war: "History has subordinated the Czech nation to German and the Ukrainian nation to Polish and Russian foreign rule. It has robbed Poland of its independence and dismembered it. It has delivered a majority of the South Slav people in Austria, Hungary, and Bosnia over to foreign slave masters, while the rest of the South Slav people, living in small, powerless states that became the plaything of great power imperialism, was robbed of all possibilities of development." The starting point for those attending the conference was the "development of capitalism and democracy," since this had enabled the "Slav nations" to grow stronger: "They will no longer endure foreign rule and dismemberment. They demand their full right to self-determination. They will wrest it as soon as the full victory of democracy vanquishes the powers that enslave nations." German Austrian Social Democracy, "as a democratic and international party," supported the principle of national self-determination. But it also called on fraternal parties to fight "any attempt by their nations' bourgeoisies" to "enslave other nations in the name of the freedom of their own nation." This was an attempt to halt the spread of irredentist nationalism in all parts of the monarchy: "Czech Social Democracy must struggle unconditionally against the demand of the Czech bourgeoisie that the German territories of Bohemia and Moravia or the German and Polish areas of Silesia should be incorporated into the Czech state." In keeping with the ideal of international solidarity, the right to national self-determination was to be based only on "the full victory of democracy" and "the international class struggle."[164] The victory of democracy, it was firmly believed, would bring statehood to the Slav and Romance peoples. But by the same token, "German-Austria [would be separated] from the Austrian mixture of peoples as a distinctive polity. Once this is constituted, it may independently organize its relations with the German Reich in accordance with its own needs and wishes."[165] The most remarkable aspects of this position were that it tried to prevent national self-determination from fueling limitless competition among different nationalisms and that it rejected aggressive nationalism directed against ethnic minorities as a distinguishing characteristic of the bourgeoisie. At the beginning of 1918, the Left had still been convinced that an independent German Austrian state, one of whose long-term options would be union with the German Reich, was an obvious consequence if Wilson's forcefully asserted right to self-determination was to be taken seriously. The key question was what that state meant for the monarchy as a framework under international law. In 1918, Karl Renner for one still spoke in favor of a Habsburg "state of nationalities," which could "offer an example for the future national organization of humanity."[166]

By spring of that year, however, the reduced political leeway available to Austria-Hungary was becoming evident. On the one hand, the national independence movements in exile were stepping up their pressure and could increasingly rely on support from the Allied states. On April 8, 1918, the Congress of the Oppressed Nationalities opened in Rome—an important forum at which exiled politicians were able to solicit international support for their causes. Czech, Slovak, and South Slav delegates appealed to the Wilsonian right of nations to self-determination. Even more important were the political implications of Brest-Litovsk and the outcome of the Sixtus affair. Russia's exit from the war, together with the revelation of the Sixtus letters, had led to a clear change in the Allies' attitude to the Dual Monarchy. In mid-April, the letters from the French premier Clemenceau were published with the deliberate aim of torpedoing Austrian overtures and preventing a separate peace. The Allies were no longer interested in the survival of the Habsburg monarchy and more and more openly supported the exiled advocates of secessionism. The publication of the Sixtus letters triggered a storm of public outrage in Germany, where they were seen as an act of betrayal on the part of its Austro-Hungarian ally. Typical of the mood in Germany was Harry Graf Kessler's comment on April 15: "This verbal ranting, from safe areas well behind the bloody zone of battle, is quite nauseating in the middle of the war."[167] On May 12, as we have seen, Emperor Karl had to disown these peace feelers and became even more dependent on the German military leadership.

In May 1918, the Allies began to retreat from the idea of maintaining the Habsburg monarchy as a state federation and switched to support for the national legions and independence movements. The Czechoslovak Legion—formed in Russia out of Czech and Slovak prisoners of war from the Austro-Hungarian army—played a quite special role in this shift, having acquired great strategic significance with the development of the situation in Russia. When Allied troops tried in mid-May to evacuate it from the turmoil there, the 40,000-strong Legion became entangled in conflicts between the warring sides in the civil war, until in the end it sided with the Whites and took control of the strategically vital Trans-Siberian Railroad.[168] At the time, the Allies were still hoping to build a new front in the east, not least in order to salvage the copious war materials they had exported to Russia. This made the Legion an important factor in British and French policy toward Russia, and it explains why the exiled politicians around Masaryk were able to take advantage of the situation.

But the lines of conflict in the Russian civil war were also reflected in the Legion itself. The Bolsheviks made some attempts to recruit legionaries to the Red Army; "red" Czechs and Slovaks were offered the prospect of a swift return home, and 5,000 men actually did sign up. In late June, legionaries found themselves fighting on both sides in the battle at Penza; different ideological and national commitments resulted in fratricidal warfare. This had considerable long-term consequences, since it gave rise to two groups of legionaries and two rival narratives. The postwar Czechoslovak state punished as deserters those who had joined the Bolsheviks after they left Habsburg army units, whereas it hailed the act of leaving those units as an act of national liberation.[169]

In late June 1918, the U.S. government firmed up its support for the secessionist movements. Secretary of State Robert Lansing expressed his sympathy for Czechoslovak and Yugoslav efforts to found independent states, and on June 30 and August 3, respectively, the French and British governments finally recognized the Czechoslovak National Council as the official representative of the interests of the Czechoslovak people. At the same time, Masaryk succeeded in bringing together the Czech and Slovak organizations in the United States. On June 30, in Pittsburgh, they signed an agreement to establish a common state with federal structures and a separate Slovak parliament. London on August 9, and Washington in early September, then officially recognized the National Council as a "de facto belligerent government." These political moves—which perfectly illustrated the close link between nation-building and participation in the war—hastened the collapse of the Habsburg monarchy.

The Allied support for exile committees and national legions had a considerable impact on the political situation in the monarchy: conflicts among national groups intensified within the Imperial Council in Vienna, which had been recalled in May 1917; unresolved supply problems were given an ever more aggressive charge of ethnic animosity; and the parliament and the press, now largely free of censorship, became the forum for increasingly bitter disputes. It was therefore no accident that anti-Semitism in particular, which had already spread with the refugee influx into the big cities, reached a peak in June 1918 in Vienna. The so-called German National Council (Deutscher Volksrat) eventually made what amounted to a call for pogroms in the heart of the capital—and the fact that it was able to use the city hall draped in German colors as a public stage only heightened the effect.[170] At the Viennese municipal council, a representative by the name of Klotzberg spoke on October 9 of thousands of "Galician parasites" who had "cheated and robbed the people of Vienna in the crudest manner, without being charged with their deceitful handiwork—or if they were, the punishment was much too slight, where the wheel and the gallows would have been justified. (Shouts: Quite right!)"[171] For hardly any other group did the erosion and collapse of the Habsburg Monarchy end as dramatically as it did for the Jews. The monarchy had given them relative security as Imperial citizens and subjects, but the war increasingly eroded this status—and then, within a few months of its end, they were confronted with a completely new situation. With the constitutional secessions that saw the departure of Galicia, Bukovina, Bohemia, and Moravia, the Jewish community in the western part of the empire was divided among successor states into which it was more incorporated than integrated.[172]

On June 14, after completely inadequate preparations, the Austro-Hungarian army launched its offensive on the River Piave, which the German OHL saw as a test of loyalty. Its main purpose seems to have been to offset the demoralization in Vienna following the Sixtus affair, but the poorly fed and equipped soldiers suffered a grave defeat that fed back into the home society and fueled political tensions there. The next month, troop strengths on the southwestern front plummeted, as casualties reduced the 406,000 men in early July to 239,000 by October 1. The number of desertions shot up dramatically.[173] During the same period, Spanish flu began to spread in the army, claiming numerous victims among the weakened soldiers, and the authorities reported 700 new malaria cases a day in the area at the mouth of the Piave. In Infantry Regiment No. 73, the average weight of the men fell to 55 kilos, while the number of suicides showed a marked upward trend.[174]

The outcome of the battle severely damaged the reputation of the AOK and the monarchy. In parliament, deputies blamed both institutions for the lack of preparation and the pointless sacrifice of thousands of soldiers, and this led to a crisis of confidence between parliament and the Austro-Hungarian political and military leadership. In one closed session, the deputy Ignacy Daszyński quite openly threatened a revolution: "Parliament should pass the motion for these rogues and criminals to be brought to justice. Otherwise, the revolution will make order if no law punishes such crimes!"[175]

When Bulgaria's military collapse loomed at the end of September, the process of national secessions gathered speed, driven by exiled politicians such as members of the Czechoslovak National Council in Paris. On October 3, while pleading for the creation of a federation, the Austrian Social Democrats again explicitly recognized the right of the Slav and Romanian nations to self-determination, and at the same time the preliminary forms of national institutions continued to be organized. Between October 5 and 11, the Serbs, Croats, and Slovenes formed a national council in Zagreb, and a Polish national council was established in Krakow after the regency council had called for moves toward an independent Polish state.

With the military situation worsening by the day on the Italian and southern Balkan fronts, Austria-Hungary faced a crisis more or less comparable to Germany's. While the OHL pushed for acceptance of parliamentary rule, which was one of Wilson's main preconditions for armistice talks, the Habsburg foreign minister Burián also sought to demonstrate to the U.S. president that, in accepting his Fourteen Points, Vienna was serious about negotiations with the Allies. There too the pace quickened, and the result was Emperor Karl's proclamation of October 16, 1918, his "Manifesto to My Loyal Austrian Peoples." The military, in particular, had been pushing for a clear signal to be given, lest the Allies decide, at a conference due to begin in Paris on October 15, to fix the boundaries of a future Yugoslav state. As its room to maneuver narrowed, the political leadership wanted to be able to present a reform program for the federalization of the monarchy. But because it proved impossible to prevent the establishment of a trinational state of the South Slavs, the main aims of Karl's manifesto were to bolster the monarchy by achieving a solution at least to the Bohemian question.[176]

The federalization idea met with considerable resistance among German Austrians and in the Hungarian government. In fact, the text was self contradictory, because it in no way questioned Hungary's special constitutional status and therefore did not inspire confidence about the consistency of the planned reform. It read, "Austria must, in accordance with the will of its people, become a federal state, in which every nationality shall form its own national territory in its own settlement zone. This does not in any way presuppose the unification of the Polish territories of Austria with the independent Polish states. The city of Trieste together with its territories shall, in accordance with the wishes of its people, be accorded a special status. This reorganization, which will in no way affect the integrity of the countries of the Holy Crown of Hungary, will guarantee the independence of each individual national state; it will, however, also effectively protect common interests and bring them to bear wherever community is a necessity of life of the individual states. Of particular importance will be the union of all forces for a just and rightful solution of the great tasks resulting from the repercussions of the war."[177]

This final attempt to save the monarchy as an overarching state form no longer found support in the general population or among delegates from the various nationalities. According to a Vienna police report dated October 18, the manifesto had had no resonance "among the broad masses," because "the lower classes are interested only in the food situation and are rather indifferent to political events." German Austrian circles, in contrast, favored "attachment to the German Reich" given the reactions of "the non-German peoples, whose interpretation of the right to self-determination goes as far as a complete turning away from Austria."[178] The emperor's manifesto of the peoples, then, actually accelerated the formation of independent states and governments. The conduct of both Karl and the government in Vienna was at variance with the federalization plans, since in the previous year they had sided more and more clearly with Germans struggling to keep their own areas outside a possible Czechoslovak state; in Trautenau, for example, a separate German jurisdiction was established. A high-profile visit by the emperor to the German borderlands of Bohemia had had a symbolic impact; Prague already seemed to be the center of the Czech population. On the other hand, this political course of the leadership in Vienna damaged the credibility of the federalization plans and the projected devolution of power to the Czech majority. Instead of aiming to implement the emperor's reform program, the Czechs and Slovaks had set their sights on a unitary Czechoslovak state promising lasting protection against the demands of German Austrians and the pan-Germanic course of many Viennese politicians.[179]

After Wilson demanded full independence for Czechoslovaks and South Slavs on October 18, the jurist and politician Josef Redlich predicted, "Over the next few days, Wilson's note will probably result in the constitution of all Austrian national states. The strange thing is that up to now the army, police, and administration have operated flawlessly in the Slav lands as well: the state has thus now reverted to its true nature as the function of a historical apparatus of power!"[180] Wilson's declaration did indeed set off a chain reaction of secessions. On October 21, German Austrian representatives on the Imperial Council in Vienna declared themselves to be the provisional national assembly of a future German Austrian state, until such time as a permanent assembly could be formally elected. The objective was clearly an *Anschluss* to the German Reich in accordance with international law. The Social Democrat leader Victor Adler explained, "The German people in Austria should form its own democratic state, its German national state, which shall be completely free to decide how its relations with neighboring peoples and with the German Reich are to be regulated." Adler stressed that this state could unite with its neighbors in "a free federation of nations," if that was what "the nations in question wanted." But if they rejected that, "the German Austrian state— which would not by itself be a structure capable of economic development— would be forced to integrate into the German Reich as a separate federal state." "We demand," he concluded, "that the German Austrian state should have complete freedom to choose between these two associations."[181] On October 30, a separate German Austrian government was formed under the Social Democrat chancellor Karl Renner. And on November 12, one day after Emperor Karl left the country, came the proclamation of the Republic of German Austria and its union with the German Reich. As the peace treaties of 1919 would show, however, this consistent application of the Wilsonian principle of national self-determination was not destined to last.

Hungary, too, followed the logic of Wilson's note, declaring independence on October 24, less than a week after it was issued. The next day, Count Mihály Károlyi, the leader of the country's main opposition party, founded a Hungarian national council. Emperor Karl's recognition of him as prime minister on October 31 was a final attempt to preserve the constitutional link between the two parts of the empire of Austria and Hungary. But the situation was already escalating in Hungary. On that same day, soldiers supporting Károlyi's course shot Count Tisza, the figure symbolizing the traditional Habsburg monarchy and loyalty to Vienna. On November 1, even before the armistice on the Italian front was declared, Károlyi ordered all Hungarian troops to return home from the war.

This measure had dramatic consequences: it contributed to the military disintegration of the Austro-Hungarian army on the Italian front and provoked accusations that the Hungarians had betrayed the monarchy and that, because of the collapse of the front and the chaotic troop withdrawal, they were responsible for the Italian capture of hundreds of thousands of Austrian soldiers in the days before the armistice came into effect. The ethnicization of the war burdens now turned into the ethnicization of blame for the defeat. The end of censorship in Hungary contributed to this development, because in early November more and more outspoken newspapers began to trickle through to the western and Italian fronts, carrying the message that Hungarian troops fighting there should be withdrawn as soon as possible. One editorial set the tone: "Put an end to the bleeding in foreign lands for foreign purposes!"[182]

Other parts of the monarchy also declared independence in late October. On October 28, the Czechoslovak National Council in Prague proclaimed a national state, and the Allied governments officially recognized Masaryk as its provisional head of state; the next day, the Kingdom of the Serbs, Croats, and Slovenes was proclaimed in Zagreb. On November 3, almost in the shadow of these events, Italian troops occupied Trento and Trieste, and the armistice between Austria-Hungary and the Entente came into effect.

Although at this time increasing numbers of troops were returning from Russian captivity, and although workers' and soldiers' councils were being established in Austria-Hungary under the impact of events in Germany, it cannot be said that there was a revolutionary mass movement against the monarchy. Rather, the splitting away of one part of the empire after another made it clear that the writing was on the wall for the Dual Monarchy. There was something unreal about the monarch's final appearances: unlike Wilhelm II in Germany, Karl was not held personally responsible for the war and the way in which it had ended, but in the middle of Vienna, he seemed to be an emperor losing his empire. Not he personally, but the institution of the monarchy had lost its legitimacy in the wake of the dramatic developments and the erosion of confidence—because it seemed ever less capable of guaranteeing security and the basics of life to its citizens.

On October 28, when Josef Redlich visited the Hofburg palace to be sworn in as the last Habsburg finance minister, he noted, "The young gentleman speaks easily enough, but one does not sense that great matters really affect him differently from daily life. . . . And one thinks all the time: this is a way of conducting political business that doesn't seem right anymore."[183] One of the emperor's last public appearances, on October 30, unfolded with the traditional symbolism of the Dual Monarchy—almost as if the language of the monarchy was immune to all political, social, and national upheavals: "Around midday, the emperor arrived in Vienna from Schönbrunn [palace]. He drove in an open automobile along Mariahilferstrasse, completely undisturbed. He alighted in the inner castle courtyard, where the crowd gave him an ovation. The Hungarian guard battalion . . . marched in, as they do every day, with drums beating and in good order, and took up the castle guard with all the traditional military formalities. The flag was unfurled, and the band played [the imperial anthem] *Gott erhalte*."[184]

The last act unfolded in the institution that, together with the monarchy and the Catholic Church, had for centuries been the most important force bonding the multiethnic empire together. The metamorphosis of the monarchy into a system of new nation-states took place in the army; it was there that power effectively passed into the hands of national governments, before the Imperial units actually dissolved into national ones. As tensions grew in the course of the war, the so-called *Assistenztruppen*, stationed not at the front but in the interior, had assumed an ever more important role in maintaining the monarchical order. To be sure, the military authorities had tried for a long time to insulate them from national influences, so that in Bohemia *Assistenz* battalions were drawn from Magyar, Romanian, and German troops; in Moravia and Silesia, soldiers were from Styria and Lower Austria; and in South Slav areas from Magyar, German, and some Croat forces. But by Summer 1918, or at the latest by October, it was no longer clear whether these troops would obey their officers' order to fire if this was thought necessary to save the monarchy as a whole.[185] Moreover, not only had nationally minded officers begun to form conspiratorial groups within the army; some commanders were making contact locally with national committees and councils, seeing them as the political players of the future. On October 28, the war ministry itself finally empowered senior officers "to make contact with national councils in their area for the purpose of maintaining calm and order and providing for their troops in case of need."[186]

On October 30, Redlich noted the "complete inability of the government in Vienna to take action." In Bohemia and Moravia, "the whole state, with the military at its head, [had] abdicated." In Redlich's view, it was not a revolution from below that was sealing the end: "The generals are dissolving the state with the same stupidity and cowardice that they have shown in waging war."[187] On October 31, he noted how the monarchy was dissolving at an everyday level: "Street youths sometimes force officers to don the national cockade in place of the [uniform] rosette. The porter at army headquarters is selling the rosettes!"[188] In the end, the emperor discharged his army and agreed that it should be split up into national formations. On November 1, he gave the following order: "All military personnel—those at the rear forthwith, those in the field after their return home—must report to their superior officers which of the national armies in the making they are minded to join. . . . If the swearing of an oath is required on joining a national army, I hereby consent to the swearing of that oath."[189]

The asynchronous end was symbolic of the Habsburg monarchy. On November 4, already overtaken by events, the monarch gathered with AOK officers, government members, and top officials who had long given up on the empire for a high mass in St. Stephen's Cathedral in Vienna. As political and national upheavals unfolded outside, they celebrated the emperor's name day in the old forms of an imperial liturgy. The *Gott erhalte* anthem resounded once more, but its words, "Blood and treasure for our Kaiser, Blood and treasure for our fatherland," must have sounded almost ghostly as the monarchic knot unraveled after 51 months of war.[190]

On November 8, three days before the monarch announced his abdication, Redlich pondered the historical defeat and overthrow as he entered Schönbrunn palace: "At the moment when we received news of the proclamation of the Bavarian Republic, the revolution in Hamburg, and the takeover of the Kiel fleet by the sailors' council, when the old Imperial army shattered into a million atoms, when the emperor no longer had a trace of the old power of the royal house in either Vienna or Prague, Budapest or Agram [Zagreb], it seemed to me, in the soft light of a bright November day, that the deepest tragedy of earthly fame and human power was symbolized in the blithesome splendor of this proud seat of the House of Habsburg. In the adjutants' hall, the charming Countess Bellegarde strode across the floor looking every bit like a rococo marquise, elegant officers stood on duty, and everything had an aura of decay and decrepitude, and at the same time of the most refined, if now effete, culture! Will everything that will soon sink roots here be able to understand and continue this culture?" As the last Habsburg finance minister, Redlich was aware of the vastly complex problems associated with the breakup of the monarchy: the distribution of shared property, joint mortgages and war loans, banknotes and railroads. In retrospect, it seemed that Wilson's note of October 18, demanding recognition of the Yugoslav and Czechoslovak states, had made "the dissolution of the historical Habsburg and Austrian idea" inescapable. The "foundation of the German Austrian state" was no more than an inevitable consequence.[191]

Karl actually stepped down in two stages, symbolizing one last time the constitutional structure of the Dual Monarchy. But to the end he deliberately remained in his palace, unmolested, and, unlike Wilhelm in Germany, under no actual compulsion to act. On November 11 Karl renounced the imperial exercise of power, and two days later also abdicated as king of Hungary. In the eyes of the Vienna police chief Franz Brandl, this followed directly from the fact that the emperor no longer had any real power. On November 11, however, he mainly noted how in this situation—comparable to the one in Germany—the right-wing and conservative parties seemed paralyzed, whereas the Left for the time being held center stage: "You see and hear of no activity from the Christian Social or National German party leaders—as if the earth had swallowed them up! Red is triumphant! The emperor has given up the exercise of government business. He resisted for a long time. But to whom could he turn for support? The war has destroyed the priceless capital of devotion to the dynasty. Emperor Karl no longer enjoys anything but sympathy."[192] On this same day when the German Austrian republic was proclaimed, the Austrian socialist leader Victor Adler died of a heart attack. He did not witness the final scene in the passage from monarchy to republic.

The fact that the dynastic collapse in Austria-Hungary was more complex than in Germany stemmed from the intertwining of ethnic diversity and independence movements with attempts to initiate a social revolution on the model of the Russian October. A special encounter took place in Vienna in November 1918. Since Spring 1917, Egon Erwin Kisch had worked at the war press bureau in Vienna, and it was there that Robert Musil, his military superior, got to know him. At the end of the war, Kisch became one of the central figures in the revolution in Vienna. In November 1917 the left-wing action committee decided to establish a council of workers and soldiers in line with the Russian model and gave to Lieutenant Kisch (who in conspiratorial fashion often changed his name, uniform, and regimental particulars), among others, the task of accomplishing this. Musil knew what was going on, tolerated it, and provided Kisch with some protection. In his diary—in a tone similar to Thomas Mann's in Munich—he recorded his impressions of the events in Vienna. Like his fellow author in the Bavarian capital, he found himself bearing witness to a sluggish revolution that proceeded with neither sound nor fury; many others at the time also realized that the legitimacy of the old regime had long since been hollowed out and were struck by how inactive the new political forces appeared to be in many places. At any event, the threshold for regime change was extremely low. On November 2, Musil noted that the street protests were "up till now no worse than the constant national-political demonstrations." Only the formal withdrawal of the old authorities seemed to force the Left to take power, almost against its will: "If the Dynasty and the authorities had not positively surrendered power of their own accord, there might almost have been no revolution at all. The representatives of the sovereignty of the people moved only hesitatingly into the abandoned positions."

Musil attentively observed an enthusiasm for violence in Kisch, the new Red Guards commander. With the ending of the war against external enemies, the propensity to violence seemed to be turning inward under new ideological banners—although Musil, with the clarity of detachment, could tell the difference between reality and rhetorical-theatrical staging: "Kisch is making efforts to inject Bolshevism into the situation. 'This evening I'll have 4,000 rifles at my disposal. There's a lot of blood still to be shed,' he says with an expression of serious regret. (Four weeks ago he declared that the death of every extra man at the front was a crime!)" Kisch struck Musil as "hysterical," "concerned at any price to set himself at the center of an upheaval in the affairs of state. Spirit of the spirit of Expressionism. (But perhaps such delight in theatricals is a precondition for a role in history.)"[193] Yet in Vienna, too, the utopian vision of a Russian-style revolution did not last long. By November 18 Kisch would give up his post as commander of the Red Guards—although for the rest of his life he remained grateful to Musil for his support.

In the Ottoman Empire, the military had profited from the Russian Revolution, regaining lost territories in the Caucasus. For the political leadership, the situation even opened up the prospect of a pan-Turkic empire to the east—and so, a few months before the military collapse, troops were sent south into the Caucasus and plans were made to constitute an "army of Islam" out of irregular formations. As late as September, just a few weeks before the request for an armistice, Turkish forces occupied the oilfields of Baku. On the southern front in the Near East, however, British forces supported by Arab tribes pushed the Ottomans out of Arabia and Palestine, and then Syria and Mesopotamia; Baghdad, Jerusalem, Damascus, and Aleppo fell one after the other. In October 1918, after the head of government had quit and fled along with several ministers, a new government appointed by Sultan Mehmed VI applied for an armistice and, at first in close coordination with the British, turned to a policy of far-reaching concessions; it had little room to maneuver, given the seriousness of the military situation for both Turkey and its European partners. In this way, the sultan hoped to save the monarchy and dynasty and as many parts of the Empire as possible. Under Allied pressure, the Armenians were promised an independent republic. At the same time, there was a de facto return to older forms of external intervention: Britain would have the right for 15 years to appoint consuls to rule side by side with Ottoman governors in the provinces. A rivalry already began to appear with the Italian and Greek allies, particularly because the latter had plans for military operations in Asia Minor and on the west coast of Anatolia.[194]

Resistance to this policy of the sultan developed toward the end of the year, many younger officers seeing it as a betrayal of nationalist principles. In particular, the 38-year-old Mustafa Kemal, who had been heavily influenced by the Young Turks, sought to stabilize the Empire internally and to maintain it externally with a concept of the Turkish nation; he rose to become the head of the nationalist resistance to the sultan and his policy of appeasement. In practice, Kemal was able to rely on a network of nationalist associations and paramilitary organizations that the Young Turks had organized in the last year of the war to recruit supporters in the Anatolian provinces in close cooperation with local authorities.[195] With state structures in disarray at the end of the war, these "societies for the defense of national rights" became in effect the main actors in numerous towns and villages. Working together with local politicians, Muslim religious leaders, and landowners, they formed a front of resistance to the political leadership in Constantinople, which it accused of having unconditionally surrendered the country to the enemy.[196]

What happened after the end of the war had much to do with the competing aims of the various Allied powers. By early 1918, in response to the revolution and civil war in Russia, Lloyd George no longer supported the original Russian objective of keeping control of Constantinople and the Bosporus Strait and also dissociated Britain from French and Italian interests in Asia Minor. From then on, British policy involved the promise of national self-determination for the non-Turkish lands of the Ottoman Empire—which meant, above all, Arabia, Armenia, Mesopotamia, Syria, and Palestine. But it remained open how national self-determination would apply in practice, and this lack of precision greatly contributed to the future instability and insecurity in the region.[197]

Since 1917, British and Empire successes against Ottoman forces in the Near East had distracted attention from the continuing political problems in the region, which mainly stemmed from its multiplicity of ethnic groups and religions. There Arabian tribespeople lived side by side with Ismailites, Maronites, Shiites, Yazidis, European and Hebrew-speaking Jews, Turks and Europeans, and—to the north—Turkmen, Kurds, Armenians, Druze, Circassians, and Syrian Christians: a complex mix to which European concepts of nations and nation-states could not be transferred. During the war, many of these groups had held together solely by virtue of a common aim of ending Ottoman rule—an aspiration that had only intensified in the wake of the atrocities committed on all sides. Beyond this there was no unifying national concept. The Bedouins with their traditional values of tribal honor, independence, and equality were worlds apart from the small urban middle class and its ideas of an Arab nation. Just as Bedouins before 1914 could not be integrated into a European-style military structure, so they could not be forced, after the victory over the Ottomans, into a national state, the concrete significance of which remained altogether unclear.[198]

These problems soon overshadowed the military victory of the Allies and their regional associates. The capture of Damascus on October 3, 1918, seemed to complete the triumph of the Arab revolt,[199] but the war did not lead to an independent Arab state. Instead, the region saw the creation of artificial nation-states that immediately proved to be unstable; the new order in the Near East came down to the assignment of various ethnic and religious groups to new kingdoms under the tutelage of the League of Nations, whose political room to maneuver was limited by British and French interests that had already announced themselves in 1916 in the Sykes-Picot agreement. The postwar order that came into being, with its numerous readjustments of territory and population, was therefore reminiscent of the period following the Congress of Vienna in 1815. Palestine became a British mandated territory, Transjordan acquired the status (in 1923) of an independent emirate, and France assumed responsibility for Syria under a League mandate. Faisal, who as victor had entered Damascus in October 1918, lost the city, but became King Faisal I of the newly founded kingdom of Iraq. Lebanon was divided up. Faisal's father, as emir, continued to rule the holy cities of Mecca and Medina; his successor, Ibn Saud, would enlarge his realm and eventually found the kingdom of Saudi Arabia in 1932.

As if under a magnifying glass, Britain's problems in the region came into sharpest focus in the Arabian Peninsula and Mesopotamia. There the world war had been marked by an asymmetry between large open spaces and heterogeneous peoples on the one hand and strategic claims and limited resources on the other. This persisted far beyond the end of the war against the Ottoman Empire. British military leaders had little knowledge of the region and its multiethnic population, but operated with the idea that they had to make a success of their intervention there. Therefore army generals and colonial politicians repeatedly called on the help of local experts with appropriate linguistic skills. This explains the rapid rise of Lawrence and many other orientalists of the time, as well as of the traveler and politician Mark Sykes (who lent his name to the Franco-British agreement of 1916) and the archaeologist David Hogarth. Their on-the-spot assessments played a major role in shaping British policy in the Near East.[200] The mismatch between extensive ambitions and limited means of rule would continue to mark the region after 1918.

Why did the Continental European empires not survive the world war? The long-held answer, which referred to them as "prisons" from which small nations had to be wrested free, was a suggestive narrative that served to justify the new nation-states historically and helped them to achieve stability after 1918. But it could not explain the complex historical processes that led to the demise of the Russian, Habsburg, and Ottoman Empires.[201]

In the case of Russia, the consequences of the revolutions of 1917 overlapped with the ambitions of the victors of Brest-Litovsk. The victors' imperial-annexationist objectives eventually hastened their end and, along with the collapse of state structures, created the space for national secessionist movements to develop. But in essence, separation in accordance with the right to national self-determination was mainly designed to serve a new political order in east central Europe that Germany could dominate from the outside. After 1918, the Allies took over this space as a *cordon sanitaire*— and the various revisionist claims of the interwar period would center on it. The fact that the collective security guarantees of the 1925 Franco-Belgian-German treaty of Locarno applied only to the borders in the west, not to those in the east of Europe, would have a definite signaling effect. The zones that emerged after the collapse of empires in 1918 thus fueled visions of domination, penetration, and colonization, as well as constituting a space of violence marked by civil wars and ethnic conflicts.[202]

Things looked different for the Habsburg monarchy. For a long time the Entente had no plans to encourage its breakup, and its main problems were the internal ones of a society at war. Before the war, semi-authoritarian forms of government in both halves of the empire had disguised the full scale of internal conflicts, as had the de facto military rule of the AOK during the war. But the recall of parliament in Spring 1917 in Vienna made it the forum for an increasingly widespread ethnicization of social and economic conflicts. In the end, the transformation began before the military reverses of September 1918. The character of the disintegration confirmed this in a way, but the dissolution of the empire in Fall 1918 was a legal process. Contrary to widespread fears before 1914, the Habsburg monarchy did not disintegrate as a result of imperialist plans to carve it up or because of the rise of pan-Slavism. The breakup, when it came, did not revive the old territorial units out of which the monarchy had once been constituted historically; only the German Austrians insisted on the reunification of all Germans, in line with a pan-Germanic ideology that would acquire a hitherto unexpected dynamic and radicalism in the interwar period. In the end, it was remarkable how strong the national models of interpretation remained after the war—particularly among representatives of mass democratic parties of the Left, for whom there could be no talk of international solidarity. Otto Bauer, for example, argued that German Austria should join the German Reich and that Germans had a national superiority over their Slav neighbors. In July 1918, he stated in a speech, "We know the plans of imperialist politicians in foreign powers to take us into a largely Slav Danubian federation led from Prague, which would keep a watchful eye on Germany to ensure that it does not become strong again. . . . If we remain alone, this state will be nothing other than a very loose federation of these small countries, and we will lead a mini-state existence, a life of smallness and pettiness, in which nothing great can blossom, least of all the greatest thing we know: socialism."[203]

It would become clear in the years ahead what the breakup of the Habsburg monarchy and the rise of new nation-states with strong ethnic minorities really entailed. The war had led above all to a changed perception of the monarchy's borderlands as a political problem justifying radical solutions. Where linguistic and political boundaries intersected, as they did in the Tyrol, the war became a primal conflict over patriotism, loyalty, and betrayal; competition between nations was translated into a conflict between states. Only this could give rise to the idea that the internal enemy was a kind of fifth column of irredentist nationalism that called one's own state into question. With the end of the war and the breakup of the monarchy, this phenomenon multiplied and sank deeper roots. In the new post-Habsburg framework, some linguistic boundaries suddenly became political boundaries, as in southern Styria or Bohemia. Concepts developed and partly implemented in wartime, involving the resettlement of whole suspect populations away from border areas, were continued in the interwar period—only then as a solution to the problem of national minorities in the new nation-states.[204]

In the case of the Ottoman Empire, territorial redistribution was written into the Allied secret treaties from 1915–1916 on. But there too the whole contradictory character of Allied policy was apparent: British leaders raised Arab hopes of a state of their own, while the Balfour Declaration signaled to the Zionists support for a Jewish state, and arrangements with France defined special spheres of interest in the Near and Middle East. The division of the Ottoman Empire was accomplished militarily in the concluding period of the war. However, in the course of 1918, British, French, and Italian operations in Asia Minor and Arabia concentrated less on attacks against the retreating enemy than on the establishment of respective spheres of influence.

7. ARMISTICE OR SURRENDER
Ending the War in a Climate of Exhaustion

When did the world war end? And where did which war end? By late 1918 there had long been different spaces of violence: spaces of interstate warfare, but also of civil war and ethnic or national independence struggles, which reflected the chronological simultaneity of historically nonsimultaneous experiences. In early August 1914, the beginning of the war had represented a common reference point for millions of people across huge geographical distances—for the Prague writer Franz Kafka as much as for the driver Kande Kamara from the West African town of Kindia in French Guinea. The end of the war was less synchronized. November 11, 1918, ended the war between states in the west, but the armistice did not mean the end of violence in many other places: not in eastern, east central, and southeastern Europe; not in the disintegrating Russian, Habsburg, and Ottoman Empires, where interstate war led to state collapse and where world war passed into civil wars and ethnic conflicts, forming new fronts in which anyone—soldier or civilian—might be the enemy. Anyone who looks only at the much talked-of 11th hour on the 11th day of the 11th month will see only the end of the war between states in western Europe—although even at that moment major players from Summer 1914 such as the Russian and Habsburg Empires no longer existed.

Thus in parallel to the dramatic events in Germany and Austria-Hungary marking the end of the monarchies and the arrival of revolutionary changes, the war was coming to an end in western Europe. Wilson's latest reply, which reached Berlin on November 6, had confirmed the Allies' agreement to armistice talks. The German delegation that traveled to France that same day was led by the Center Party politician Matthias Erzberger, who in Summer 1917 had been one of the driving forces behind the Reichstag peace resolution. That which had characterized developments in October was continuing into November: the man leading the armistice negotiations was not an army general but a civilian Reichstag deputy, representing an institution that had had scarcely any influence on policy making during the war. (At no point did the OHL admit its responsibility for the defeat. The fact that it was representatives of the Reichstag parties who journeyed to France and eventually signed the armistice paved the way for Hindenburg, appearing before a parliamentary committee in 1919, to muddy the waters by denouncing a "stab in the back," a mythical left-wing betrayal on the home front. His claims to this effect would poison the long-term political climate in Germany, with fatal consequences, as the image of "November criminals" came to associate the republic with defeat and dictated peace terms in the eyes of many contemporaries.)[205]

On the morning of November 8, the German armistice delegation arrived in Compiègne, near Foch's headquarters. The terms on offer had nothing in common with the relatively lenient Wilsonian peace they had been expecting. They seemed to Erzberger an unacceptable diktat—even if Germany now found itself in the role it had forced on Russia eight months earlier at Brest-Litovsk. The Allies demanded the return of Alsace-Lorraine to France, the evacuation of all occupied territories in Belgium and France, the withdrawal of German troops from the left bank of the Rhine, and the establishment of Allied bridgeheads in Cologne, Mainz, and Koblenz. German-occupied territories in eastern Europe were also to be handed back, and the peace treaties of Brest-Litovsk and Bucharest declared null and void. Huge quantities of war materials and means of transport—trucks, railroad wagons, locomotives— were to be handed over, together with the entire fleet of battleships and submarines. All 535,000 French, 360,000 British, and 133,000 Italian prisoners of war were to be immediately released, while German prisoners—429,000 in France and 329,000 in Britain—were to remain in Allied hands until the conclusion of a peace treaty.[206] The naval blockade, too, would remain in place until then. The 72-hour ultimatum for the Germans to agree to these terms left no space for negotiations, especially in view of the political situation in Berlin on November 9. German headquarters in Spa pushed for better terms, but gave Erzberger a free hand to make a deal if that did not prove possible. Discussions among Groener, the Kaiser, and thirty-eight leading generals— Hindenburg was also present, but hardly said a word—indicated that there was no majority either for Rathenau's idea of a people's war or for a recall of the army to Germany to save the Hohenzollern monarchy. Eventually news arrived from Berlin that Max von Baden, without authorization, had announced the abdication of the Kaiser, that power had been handed over to Friedrich Ebert, and that a republic had been proclaimed twice over. In the afternoon, Wilhelm II traveled into exile in the Netherlands.

Only on the evening of November 10 did Ebert authorize the German delegation to sign the armistice. The war that had begun by train in August 1914, when millions of soldiers were transported to the fronts, would come to an end in a train carriage in the Compiègne Forest. Shortly after midnight on November 11, 1918, the German delegation returned to the carriage and continued negotiating for another three hours. All Foch was willing to offer was a few concessions on the repatriation of German troops; everything else remained unchanged. Around 5 A.M., Foch and the British First Sea Lord Admiral Rosslyn Wemyss signed the document for the Allies, and the German delegation followed suit. At 11 A.M., the guns fell silent on all fronts: on land, at sea, and in the air. But the symbolic history of Compiègne did not end in those early hours of November 11: a ghostly repetition of the scene, with roles reversed, would take place after the German victory in May 1940, when Adolf Hitler had the original carriage brought along for the representatives of France to sign the act of surrender, before he ordered the destruction of any reminder of the 1918 armistice.

The penultimate report from German army headquarters mentioned the last defensive engagements in a tone of military objectivity: "In fighting off American attacks east of the Meuse, the Brandenburg reserve infantry regiment No. 207, under its commander Lieutenant Hennings, and troops of the 192nd Saxon infantry division under Lieutenant v. Zeschau, commander of infantry regiment no. 183, distinguished themselves by successful counterattacks." The final report, on November 11, ended laconically: "Following signing of the armistice agreement, hostilities were ended on all fronts at midday today."[207]

The first British soldier killed in the war was the 16-year-old John Parr from Finchley, who had worked as a golf caddy and in Summer 1914 had hidden his true age in order to volunteer as soon as possible for the Middlesex Regiment. As a bicycle scout, he came across German cavalry north of Mons in Belgium and was shot in an exchange of fire. The last British soldier killed in the war was George Ellison, a mineworker from Leeds, who at the age of 40, on patrol near Mons, fell at 9:30 A.M. on November 11, 1918, just 90 minutes before the armistice came into effect. As a member of the 5th Royal Irish Lancers, he had fought all through the war on the western front. As chance would have it, it was discovered in 2008 that John Parr and George Ellison—who symbolize the beginning and end of the British deployment on the western front—lie buried in the Saint Symphorien military cemetery east of Mons, together with the last Allied soldier to die in action, the Canadian George Lawrence Price, who, two minutes before the ceasefire at 11 A.M., was shot by a German sniper in the village of Ville-sur-Haine, near the Canal du Centre in Belgium. The two British soldiers, from the beginning and end of the war, fell only a few kilometers from each other. Fifty-two months of war separated their deaths, but they had defended more or less the same piece of territory.[208]

News of the imminent armistice circulated among soldiers on the western front in the days leading up to November 11. On the day itself, trumpet signals announced the end of fighting at many places along the front, but in some sections hostilities continued, and soldiers died, up to the very last minutes before 11 A.M. Most then waited in their trenches to see whether the gunfire really would cease. There was some fraternization after the clock hands passed eleven, but that was not the general reaction. Corporal John Oborne, from the 4th Battalion, Devonshire Regiment, recalled, "At the armistice I was in a trench, and the Germans got out of theirs, bowed to us and walked off, and that was it. There was nothing to celebrate with—except biscuits."[209]

There was some jubilation on the victors' side, with isolated shouts and applause, but for many soldiers the main feeling was a calm and emptiness that expressed the exhaustion and grief after 52 months of war. At Maubeuge, Captain Oliver Lyttleton of the Grenadier Guards noted, "About ten A.M. one high-velocity shell roared into the town about five hundred yards from our house and frightened the life out of us. Then silence: silence, that is, except for the clucking of chickens, the creaking of cart wheels, mooing of cows, and other sounds of a country town on market day. We rode round the troops: everywhere the reaction was the same, flat dullness and depression. Winning in a war is a most exhilarating sensation, and we had not had many days in which to savour it. . . . We all felt flat and dispirited."[210]

The Belgian fighter pilot Willy Coppens, who was badly wounded shortly before the armistice and had to have a leg amputated, observed with growing repugnance how the surfeit of orders and medals was devaluing individual achievement. Looking back, he experienced the end of the war as a watershed, a moment of insecurity that drew a sharp line under a whole historical and biographical period. It was not a sense of victory or national liberation, but fear of what lay ahead, that shaped his perception of November 11: "I ought to have felt great joy but it was as if a cold hand took me by the throat. I was beset by anxiety about the future. I realized that a period of my life was over."[211] The Italian soldier Paolo Monelli also recorded a contradictory mix of joy and sadness and open-endedness: "This is going to be our evil inheritance, or our good inheritance, in any case our irretrievable inheritance—and we are going be fettered by our memories for ever."[212]

In Germany, as at the beginning of the war, large clusters of people formed in front of newspaper buildings and information boards. But there was no surge of unity, and many reactions reflected the political polarization in the country. In a number of incidents, people attacked officers who happened to be present and tore off their insignia or accused soldiers of having betrayed the fatherland.[213]

The political and military leadership of France basically presented November 11 as a German capitulation rather than an armistice, although in military terms that was far from the truth. What talk of surrender concealed was the fact that the French had never achieved a victorious military breakthrough; the Allies certainly had superiority, but the German front remained stable.[214] In the immediate aftermath of November 11, doubts persisted as to whether the armistice would hold and peace become a reality. The most common reaction was "Who would have believed it four months ago?" This indicated once again the limited distance between victory and defeat in subjective perceptions held since the exhaustion of Spring 1917.[215]

Large differences persisted between French society at home and soldiers at the front, whose awareness of the high casualties in the final battles made them more restrained in their reactions.[216] Newspapers displayed a characteristic mix of weary joy and sadness. *Le Petit Provençal*, for instance, summed up its impressions of November 11 as follows: "Everyone is vibrating. Enthusiasm is the order of the day. Yet some are sad as they mourn a loved one who disappeared in the 51-month storm. . . . If you see a mourning veil or black ribbon, people of Marseilles, you will fall silent!"[217] This too pointed to the leitmotif of the months and years ahead. Had the high price in casualties been worthwhile? Could the peace settlement justify it?

In many parts of southern Europe, local contexts set their stamp on the final period of the war and its aftermath. This was especially true in Italy, where the sequence of critical events was epitomized in the breath-taking biography of the Capuchin monk Pio, the later Padre Pio. Apparently he first learned of his stigmata in September 1918, when the danger of civil war was rising and when in some regions Spanish flu was causing very high mortality rates: 114.7 per 1,000 in Latium (1913: 1.1, 1917: 0.6), 104.8 in Calabria (1913: 2.4, 1917: 2.0), and 67.1 in Emilia (1913: 0.9, 1917: 0.7).[218] The coincidence of these developments with the end of the war suddenly made it seem like the end of times. The proximity of death was no longer a collective experience only at the front. Therefore the appearance of a redeemer figure was interpreted in religious terms as an answer to questions about God's presence in the war's catastrophic end-times. Pio rapidly became known beyond his home region—a development only possible thanks to modern means of communication. Indeed, his status as a popular saint was due to the same media and technologies that the war had developed as instruments of propaganda. His closeness to Mussolini and the milieu of the *fascisti* also helped things along.[219]

In many respects, the armistice terms of November 11 anticipated the peace treaty of the following year. The Allies had already achieved their main war aims against Germany: France regained control of Alsace-Lorraine and established the Rhine as its strategic boundary, and Britain was pursuing a long-term curtailment of German economic power. But the prejudicial character of the armistice was most apparent in the provision it made for internment of the German High Seas Fleet at Scapa Flow in Scotland. The Admiralty saw this as a symbolic victory that would vindicate the role of the Royal Navy, and it continued to push for the German fleet to be handed over. Admiral David Beatty made plans for this to be staged as an act of humiliation. Once he had taken custody of the seventy-four German ships, he forced the German commanders to place the Union Jack over the German flag as they made the crossing,[220] and in Scapa Flow itself they were required to disarm the ships and leave them with only skeleton crews on board. The German decision to scuttle the fleet there in June 1919 was an attempt to recover some military honor; during the war itself, neither the German nor the British navy had fulfilled the expectations held for it, and the thoroughly unheroic character of the "fleets in being" had underlined the contradiction with the image that naval officers on both sides had of themselves. The honorable scuttling seemed more acceptable than an incomplete, and ultimately unproven, defeat at the end of a war in which the ships had fought no battle.[221]

Despite these high-profile dimensions, the November armistice did not mean unconditional surrender: Germany as a whole was neither occupied nor divided, and the territorial core of the nation-state of 1871 remained intact. If the Allies had wanted to claim more, they would have had to continue the war, occupy Germany, and assume responsibility as an occupying power. But the exhaustion on the side of the victors was so great that the governments in London and Paris could not enforce such a scenario. A total victory after a war that had become total in 1917, entailing the complete disarmament and occupation of Germany, was simply not a realistic option.[222]

With the armistice, the orderly demobilization of millions of soldiers and the repatriation of prisoners of war became a major challenge. The terms agreed to on November 11, 1918, provided for Germany to evacuate occupied territories in short order and to demobilize its armies; some complete units had already set off back to Germany in the preceding weeks, led by younger officers. By early December, the high command of the army of the west reported that, of its total strength of 3.2 million soldiers, one million were heading home on their own initiative. To avoid greater disorder, the official German demobilization order was issued only on December 31. The degree of politicization among German soldiers certainly varied, but despite the hopes for a speedy end to the war there had been little concrete opportunity since 1916 for political agitation on the western front. On their return, many soldiers could not be given new assignments—against alleged insurgents, for example. They were placed under local commanders, then often proceeded to demobilize themselves as soon as they neared their home towns and villages.[223] Despite the enormousness of the organizational task, the total number of German soldiers shrank by half in less than two months, and by January 18, 1919, all the men in the army of the west were back on German soil. The 800,000 or so prisoners of war, however, would be released only in the second half of 1919 or in 1920.[224]

The soldiers were returning to a changed country. When Lieutenant Ernst Jünger's 73rd Fusilier Regiment entered Hanover on December 16, 1918, a band led it on its march to Waterlooplatz, but there were no accompanying cheers. People stood silent, and only a few here and there offered the soldiers flowers. The next day, the rather middle-class *Hannoverscher Kurier* reported, "Lawyer Lindemann added to the greetings of the workers' and soldiers' council by thanking the warriors and wounded and saying some words in honor of the dead who will never see their homeland again. Referring to the changed political conditions, he asked those returning home to help defend the newly won freedom. But freedom, he said, presupposes order, and everyone is primarily called upon to play a role in creating it; Bolshevism of any kind must be combated." The more left-wing *Volkswille* described the same scene with a strikingly different tone: "Lawyer Lindemann greeted the troops on behalf of the workers' and soldiers' council. Although the outcome of the war was different from what had been hoped, they were not to blame for this. Nor had their deeds been in vain. Something great had come to pass: the people had gained its freedom, and this freedom had to be secured. He therefore also asked the returning troops to stand solidly behind the present government and to fight against Bolshevism."[225]

On the Allied side, soldiers waited a long time to receive their discharges and to return to their families. Many French and British units were given new assignments—deployed as occupation troops in Germany, for example, or sent to the Near and Middle East. The letters of French soldiers contain ever-new variations on the theme of "When?" The fear that they might die of an illness or in an accident, having survived everything in 50 months of war, was especially prominent. The thought that the long years of absence and separate experience might have estranged them from their home town or village, their wife and children, also weighed heavily on their minds. And, as the correspondence between the husband and wife Pireaud illustrates, the fear of disillusionment at the moment of homecoming was another leitmotif of the time.[226]

The handling of soldiers from colonial societies was a source of distinctive conflicts during the demobilization period. The West India Regiment, which had performed wartime labor service on British sections of the western front, was subsequently assigned to military duties outside Europe. But none of this changed the racist segregation practiced by British officers, and the old hierarchy of the Empire persisted at the front. The men's frequent anger at the different levels of medical care, unfair pay differentials, and unequal disciplinary sanctions eventually led to two large-scale mutinies at the end of the war. While many colonial units were being demobilized after November 1918, an almost paranoid fear of black soldiers developed in both Britain and France, their supposed sexual attractiveness to white women being an especially common theme. Racially motivated attacks multiplied in various port cities. And after the soldiers returned home, their unfair treatment during the war became a potent symbol in the 1920s and 1930s for the nascent anticolonial independence movements. Marcus Garvey, the founder of the Universal Negro Improvement Association, had forcefully appealed in 1915 and 1916 for all parts of the Empire to support the British war effort. After 1918, however, he campaigned for recognition of the "citizens of Africa."[227]

Another dimension in Africa itself was the direct consequences of the war for the indigenous peoples. In East Africa, the recruitment of some 250,000 men as soldiers or auxiliary workers had huge implications: roughly 20,000 served in units of the King's African Rifles, but more than 200,000 men—equivalent to 75 percent of the adult male population of Malawi—were used as porters. The women, children, and old people who stayed behind had to face enormous problems: in particular, the shortage of agricultural labor led to harvest shortfalls and widespread starvation. Then came the ravages of Spanish flu: the death rate was around 12 percent among soldiers and 2.5 to 5 percent among porters, and when the epidemic struck the undernourished civilian population in 1919, five times more people died than during the whole of the war.[228] The demographic impact on the societies in question can hardly be overstated.

After the war, returning colonial troops looked on their country's social and economic problems with different eyes. Denied material or symbolic recognition for their war service by the British or French authorities, they came back to rising inflation and the levying of higher taxes by the colonial administration. The end of the war thus represented a transitional experience: many of the ex-soldiers in question lost their fear of colonial officials, no longer seeing them as omnipotent and realizing that they were more vulnerable than before.[229]

8. FIFTY-TWO MONTHS OF WAR, ONE MONTH OF PEACE
Indeterminacy of Victory and Defeat, Desynchronization of War and Peace

(1) In late 1917 and early 1918 the outcome of the world war was still open. The year 1918 would demonstrate, right up to its final months, how close victory and defeat were to each other. It would thus be wrong, on the basis of hindsight, to think that there was a simple continuum from the failure of the Schlieffen Plan in 1914 through the American entry into the war in Spring 1917 to the eventual defeat of the Central Powers in October and November 1918. At the beginning of 1918, the European Allies faced a difficult situation and were incapable of major offensives: France because of the mutinies of the previous year, Britain because of the heavy casualties it had sustained in the third battle of Flanders. After the Russian exit from the war, all hopes were pinned on the growing military presence of the United States. But the Brest-Litovsk treaty had rekindled old fears among the British leadership that India's position as the global strategic foundation of the Empire might be endangered.

For the Central Powers—primarily Germany—the successful end to the war in the east opened up the perspective of a final effort on the western front. But Brest-Litovsk also strengthened thinking in either-or categories and led to an underestimation of the long-term consequences, especially economic, of the U.S. entry into the war. The year seemed to begin much too favorably for Germany to consider a compromise peace. Woodrow Wilson's Fourteen Points, issued in January, therefore received serious consideration only when German hopes of a victorious peace—a repetition of Brest-Litovsk in the west—foundered in Fall 1918. The success in eastern Europe in March also reinforced the tendency of German political and military leaders to overestimate the strength of their position and to exclude alternative options—all the more so because the situation in German and Austro-Hungarian society was worsening and had already led in January to a wave of protests with clear political undertones. It seemed that the home fronts would not be able to withstand another hungry winter. This increased the pressure to end the war in 1918, before the American military presence in Europe brought palpable relief to the British and French.

(2) While these factors limited the window of opportunity for the Central Powers, the Allies had four interconnected resources at their disposal: the American entry into the war seemed to offer unlimited access to men and materials, and this, together with Britain's global maritime supremacy and transport capacities, yielded a time advantage over the Central Powers. British and French headquarters realized that if the war ended later, in 1919 or even 1920, it would strengthen the U.S. political position in Europe, but the additional resources that America provided could give them a decisive advantage: the Allies might profit militarily from a longer war, whereas the Central Powers could only address the problem of time working against them by intensifying the war and launching a major counterattack in the hope that one of their enemies would collapse. The time resource strengthened the Allies' position by enabling them to consider alternatives, whereas it reduced the options available to the Central Powers. While in 1915 the key issues had still been time and space, in the final months the relationship between time and access to global resources was decisive for the outcome of the war. This also explains the seemingly desperate attempts by German and Austro-Hungarian troops to secure grain from Ukraine or oil from the Caspian in order to alleviate the situation on the home front.

(3) Despite the more favorable long-term prospects for the Allies, there was still much skepticism in the British and French military in 1918: on the one hand, they did not rate the American Expeditionary Forces (AEF) war effort too highly, while also fearing that any increase in American input would reduce their own countries' political influence. On the other hand, they knew the degree of their own exhaustion and the still unbroken enemy potential, which made itself felt in the series of offensives on the western front between March and July but also on the River Piave and in Crimea. The outcome of these attacks, so different from the previous four years, would change the war fundamentally: it was no longer the same old story of small territorial gains followed by corresponding losses at the first opportunity. Instead, the German breakthroughs on the western front left the prospects for the end of the war truly open-ended. On the German side, the combination of

storm troop tactics with increased firepower and more accurate shelling proved successful, but poor motorization and supply problems were major weaknesses in view of their aim to shift from positional warfare to a war of movement and forcing decisive battles on the enemy. The significance of the threat to the French capital, including long-range shelling, was little more than symbolic.

In essence, these German attacks had been conceived without any real alternatives to fall back upon—and therefore no plans for a possible consolidation of German defensive positions. This was an expression of the narrowing time window, which forced the Central Powers to seek a decision in the west while the German armies there still had a sufficient offensive capacity. The OHL therefore gambled on a last major push to break through and achieve a decisive victory. There was no strategy to gain time by organizing a resilient defense that might convert French and British exhaustion into political room in which the Germans could maneuver. Again, the German architects of the war, for all the modernization of weaponry and all the economic mobilization over the past four years, remained trapped in narrow ways of thinking, able to contemplate a political solution to the war only when there was no longer any chance of military victory.[230]

For the German armed forces, the discrepancy between tactical advantages and open strategic flanks became ever clearer after the spring offensives got underway. Even tactical innovations could not change the fact that many German attacks concentrated on sectors of the front that ultimately brought no strategic advantage and that the Allies, in retreating, increased their time resources and gained the possibility to regroup and profit from the continuing arrival of American forces. From Summer 1918, these new troops would prove to be the most important development. The transition from grueling positional warfare to a possible war of movement also made it easier to remobilize the Allied forces; it was no accident that the fighting spirit of French soldiers gradually stabilized in June and July. While this constellation worked in favor of the Allied counteroffensives, by the summer the German troops were already exhausted by the offensives of the spring. By the end of April 1918 the Germans had lost 500,000 men, including 50,000 dead and missing, and the continuation of their offensives up to July 15, with a symbolic return to the battlefield of Fall 1914, simply emphasized that they saw no alternative and could only hope that one of the enemy forces might suddenly collapse. It is unlikely, though, that even a French collapse at the height of the battles in June and July 1918 would have meant a German victory that ended the war; the global implications of the European war for Britain and the United States were already too extensive.

By the time that the Allied counteroffensives began in August 1918, the offensive capacity of the German forces had already been broken. Still, their effective defense inflicted huge casualties, so that most Allied commanders did not think victory could be achieved before 1919. The collapse of the German army in Summer and Fall 1918 was due to tactical innovations and technological improvements on the Allied side, the centralization of the supreme command under Foch, and a preparedness to accept high casualties to make up for the Americans' limited battle experience: all these developments were in turn partly a response to the early success of the German spring offensives. When the prospect of victory vanished and the German armies began their gradual retreat, the soldiers' will to fight started to crumble. A disorderly rout was avoided, however, and local combat units retained their discipline for a very long time. The final period of the war was not characterized by individual desertions, but by a collective self-demobilization of small units under the leadership of young officers who largely enjoyed the trust of their men.

(4) In the final months, the face of the war changed again, displaying not simply some of the features of twentieth-century warfare but also a whole range of contradictory experiences. The intensification of aerial warfare, though far from the dimensions of the Second World War, not only affected sectors of the front but also included the bombing of enemy cities. Another strikingly modern feature was the way in which both sides applied the lessons of the previous two years in the coordination of all military branches; the combination of heavy artillery, armor, and infantry; and the tactical attention to reconnaissance, air superiority, and the use of gas. A tendency to greater flexibility was generally visible—for example, in the use of specialized units or storm battalions. The principles of a staggered defense in depth also repeatedly proved successful in the months up to the end of the war. These changes involved the whole sphere of logistics, transportation, supply, and communications, and the degree of motorization proved a key factor toward the end.[231] The American presence became more and more telling

with regard to supplies, logistics, railroads, and the stability of transport routes to the front.

Yet, for all the modern elements, some very traditional aspects continued to mark the war. Horses still carried most supplies from railroad stations to combat zones, especially on the side of the Central Powers, and the disastrous undernourishment of the animals reduced their carrying capacity and thus the amount of supplies that were delivered. At the time when German forces were punching holes in the front and moving from positional warfare to a war of movement, troop mobility became a decisive factor. And with the growing importance of motorization, reliable access to oil became a factor of strategic importance. The British leadership, in particular, had recognized early on this basic fact of modern warfare, and the main purpose of its attack on Mesopotamia in 1916 had been to secure oil supplies. In 1918, this connection was evident in the German advances on the Caspian Sea.

On the other hand, the war reentered conventional territory when Allied commanders were able to rely on American resources to compensate for heavy casualty rates. In the final counteroffensives from August on, the dominant feature was not the tanks, aircraft, and special units that would mark the war of the future, but in many cases a cult of the infantry attack. Not just tanks decided the war on the western front; the question of who could better offset their losses was also crucial.

With regard to the movement of men and materials, the Allies' global naval supremacy was not threatened at any time in the war, least of all the final months. The ever-closer coordination of transatlantic shipping was part of this picture. The threefold trend of the nineteenth century—industrial dynamism; the revolutionizing of transport and communications by means of railroads, steamships, and the telegraph; and the nexus of trade, migration, and the movement of commodities—displayed its full strategic significance for the first time in the world war. German submarines could not for long reduce the British lead in transportation capacity, which had already been enormous before the war. Besides, the U-boats were technically vulnerable, and the convoy system, together with aerial protection, proved a successful means of shipping troops across the Atlantic. Although the sinking of commercial vessels in 1918 was again a problem for the British home front, at no point did German submarines threaten to halt the flow of American soldiers and war goods. If necessary, the Allies could afford to soak up the losses, which could always be made good through increased ship production in the United States. The successful remobilization had a military, but also a key domestic political and social dimension for Britain and France. For although shortages and rationing increased in 1918, they were in no way comparable to the situation in Germany and Austria-Hungary, where food shortages in particular led to the criminalization of everyday life, politicization of protests, and progressive delegitimization of the war state.

(5) The war may still have been undecided militarily in Spring and Summer 1918, but conditions were rapidly changing on the home fronts. While the Allies managed to protect their war economies, the supply crisis in the Central Powers was turning into a credibility crisis for their political institutions, which was exacerbated in Austria-Hungary by the ethnicization of political and social conflicts. The use of Wilson's Fourteen Points as a framework for national independence movements, the activity of exiled politicians, the changed Allied attitude to the Habsburg monarchy after the Sixtus affair, and the new focus on foreign legions as a strategic factor (especially the Czechoslovak Legion in the Russian civil war) greatly shrank the political room to maneuver available to the Austro-Hungarian leadership. For some time, however, continuation of the monarchy with greater autonomy for its various nationalities remained a viable alternative; the fact that this did not happen in the end was due not only to internal factors, but above all to the Allies' strategic reorientation in Spring 1918 to the breakup of the Habsburg Empire.

In the western European war states, Lloyd George and Clemenceau achieved a remarkable new mobilization of their societies; the crisis of 1917, especially acute in France, did not last into 1918. There was a clear transfer of decision-making processes from parliament to closely knit war cabinets, and both men came to embody an inflexible political will to victory. As charismatic war premiers, they were able to draw on their popularity with the public, but in the end they did not turn away from the basic principles of parliamentary rule. Although tensions continued to mount, and although there were growing criticisms of parliament—it was sometimes argued, especially in France, that the war could be won not because of parliament but in spite of it—Clemenceau and Lloyd George were successful in mediating between parliament and the public. In clashes with military leaders, both asserted the primacy of politics—a point strikingly evident in the Maurice affair in Britain.

Things developed differently in the Central Powers, where Hindenburg and Ludendorff were the dominant military politicians. The credibility of the wartime regime depended on them, not on civilian institutions or individual protagonists in parliament and government. The monarchs stood in their shadow, and until October 1918 most parliamentarians shied away from conflict with them. Whereas French and British politicians acquired real expertise in military matters, most members of the German parliament and government were virtually blind to the activities of the OHL. Only when defeat began to loom in the late summer of 1918 did Germany's military leadership turn its attention to Wilson's Fourteen Points. The October reforms to parliamentarize the monarchy in Germany, like Emperor Karl's October manifesto to federalize the Dual Monarchy, were adopted in the hope that advance concessions might secure more lenient peace terms. In Germany, the future of the Reich was not up for negotiation, but in Vienna the issue was whether the monarchy could survive by establishing a federal constitutional structure with far-reaching autonomy for its various parts. The late concessions in Berlin and Vienna reflected the problems in both societies that had been unresolved at the outbreak of war in 1914 and that both empires had initially postponed in the hope that the war would be short and victorious. Now these problems returned to haunt them. Against a background of time pressure, military erosion, and potential social unrest, these changes in October demonstrated just how volatile the situation had become.

(6) The end of the war in the west did not involve unconditional surrender and the occupation of enemy territory, as some American politicians had initially demanded. In the end, the Allied leaderships accepted the orderly withdrawal of the German army, unwittingly providing fuel for the "stab in the back" legend and the idea that a German victory had still been within reach. But the absence of a decisive battle or visible capitulation, following the difficult and costly repulsion of still effective enemy forces, also reflected interests in the Allied camp. Whereas Pétain in France, for example, felt cheated out of a military victory—which he hoped would have dispelled his reputation as a purely defensive expert—other arguments prevailed in the

end. The mobilization of resources in 1917 and the remobilization in 1918 had pointed toward total war, but the treatment of the enemy in the final stages showed that that was still a long way off. There was no capitulation because the Allies feared the costs of continuing the war and occupying Germany. There was also a growing apprehension that Allied troops might become infected with Bolshevism and transmit it back into British and French society; Wilson also assumed that an occupation of Germany would symbolically humiliate the enemy and provoke a lurch into revolutionary violence. France, in particular, could no longer sustain such high levels of casualties, and the governments in both London and Paris were worried that if the war went on, they would lose influence to the United States and be forced at the eventual peace talks to make concessions affecting not only their position in Europe but also their global interests and colonial empires.[232] The enormous weight of the United States was making itself felt at several levels. Economically, it had been evident since 1914; monetarily, it had expressed itself in the granting of war loans to the European Allies since 1915; militarily, it had become a key factor since Summer 1918; and politically, it had been growing in the global arena since 1917, not so much in the form of a "Wilsonian moment," but more as a catalyst for older anticolonial movements in various societies outside Europe.

(7) Were there alternatives to the German strategic decisions of 1917–1918? There were two key moments that had enormous military and political consequences. One was the German decision, under the impact of the Skagerrak battle, to resume unrestricted submarine warfare in early January 1917; this pushed the United States into the war, even though Wilson kept delaying and was able to persuade Congress only when the British secret service intercepted and published the Zimmermann Telegram. The deployment of U-boats did not, however, bring the results that the military leadership had expected; it neither challenged the Allies' maritime supremacy nor effectively interrupted the transatlantic troopships. If submarines had been used earlier against commercial shipping in accordance with the rules of cruiser warfare, they would have offered a viable alternative. But the German military leadership did not choose that course, partly because it was convinced of the inherent superiority of the U-boat as a weapon of war, but, more important, because time pressure to end the war as quickly as possible was already mounting in Spring 1917.

The second crucial decision, after the signing of the Brest-Litovsk treaty in March 1918, was to throw everything into the western front—a consequence, in a way, of the first decision in January 1917. What lay behind it was again the idea of a victorious peace without compromises, a belief in Germany's military superiority, and a growing sense of time pressure as the home fronts seemed to be crumbling. In this situation, the advantages of a stabilizing defense in depth—which the Central Powers had themselves demonstrated—did not guide operational thinking. Yet the successes in 1917 at Caporetto, La Malmaison, the third battle of Flanders, and Cambrai had shown what possibilities a defensive strategy contained: the acute crisis facing the Italian army after Caporetto, and the high costs in men and materials that the French and British had paid on the western front, had highlighted the mismatch between input and yield after four years of war, and the fact that the Allies could not politically afford a repetition of the previous year's experiences would at least have increased the Germans' political room to maneuver. In late 1917, the Allied offensives failed to achieve any real breakthroughs on the western front and ran up against perfected German defensive strategies. At the same time, neither France nor Britain wanted to accept a victory that relied entirely on U.S. assistance, because Wilson's Fourteen Points were also a threat to their own position, especially in the overseas colonies.

Both German decisions—to resume unrestricted submarine warfare and to concentrate on offensives on the western front—had to do with the fact that, because of supply problems and their political implications, the Central Powers could not lose any time; they had to take advantage of a narrowing window of opportunity to decide the war before the deployment of American soldiers and resources had a palpable effect. Thus, as at key moments in the crisis of July 1914, a subjective perception of time limits was an important factor. The debates on war aims and all the unsuccessful peace feelers before Fall 1918—from the overtures of the Central Powers in 1916 through the initiatives of the Pope and Karl I to the parliamentary peace resolutions—demonstrated that in the end each side still had its reasons to push for victory and did not wish to spoil its chances through a premature willingness to compromise.

The failure of peace initiatives since 1916, and Wilson's turn in early 1917 away from his earlier moderate position, had already limited the scope for peace. By 1918 the U.S. economic and monetary commitment to the war was already too great, and the definition of global spheres of interest beyond the European heartlands was too far advanced. France and Britain had largely staked out their positions quite early on; their response to Wilson's peace initiative in January 1917 had contained the core demands on which they could not go back without losing credibility: the restoration of Belgium, Serbia, and Montenegro; the return of Alsace-Lorraine; and the breakup of the multiethnic Habsburg and Ottoman Empires through the "liberation of the Italians, Slavs, Romanians, Czechs, and Slovaks," as well as the peoples "subject to the Turks' bloody tyrannies."[233] Moreover, the German leadership—above all, the OHL—had become too caught up in either-or thinking. Even if it had brought other options to bear, such as a defensive strategy to gain time, Allied war aims were so fixed by early 1917 at the latest that the scope for negotiations was very slight.[234] But after the fall of Bethmann Hollweg, neither the monarch nor the government nor the Reichstag represented an effective counterweight to the largely uncontrolled power of the OHL.

(8) The armistice of November 11 repeated the asymmetry of Brest-Litovsk with a change in roles. Like the Russian Bolshevik leaders in March 1918, the German military no longer had any alternatives at its disposal; the country's political leadership had already ruled out the idea of waging a people's war on home ground, with all the unpredictable consequences it would have entailed. But only when all realistic prospects of successfully continuing the war had disappeared did the OHL push for a political declaration of bankruptcy on the basis of Wilson's Fourteen Points—and then it evaded its own responsibilities by appointing a parliamentary government as, so to speak, its political administrator. In a way, the regime change on November 9 had been prepared for on October 26: Ludendorff's withdrawal—after he had first rejected Rathenau's idea of a people's war, then described the Allies' terms as a violation of the nation's honor, and finally called on German soldiers to continue the struggle—marked the end in practice of the Third OHL installed in 1916, which had been moving toward a military dictatorship. This course of action allowed Hindenburg and Ludendorff not to recognize the armistice for what it was—the result of a military defeat for which they were essentially to blame—and to depict it instead as the result of external coercion that the politicians had failed to resist.[235]

(9) Two processes overlapped at the end of the war: the military defeat functioned as a catalyst for revolutions in the Central Powers, but the causes of these lay in the loss of political legitimacy, especially since 1916. The military defeat was hardly due to a revolutionary movement or social transformations. Self-demobilization and refusal to obey orders became a mass phenomenon in the army only when the prospect of victory had vanished, but then they did accelerate the political delegitimation of the militarized monarchies; the erosion of the war societies, in a context of constant shortages and criminalization of everyday life that turned into a credibility crisis of the war states, hollowed out the monarchies of the Central Powers. Their edifices then collapsed in November without any major resistance.

Despite the impact of an anti-Bolshevik enemy-image, the choice in this situation was not between a Bolshevik-style revolution and democracy. The emergent soldiers' and workers' councils mostly had a social democratic majority and saw themselves as transitional institutions, whose main task was to secure calm and order amid the demobilization of mass armies and the establishment of a democratic republic. The aims of the council movement were the democratization of state and society, army and public administration, and the socialization of the key industries. Only one section had a more radical vision of itself as a social-revolutionary vanguard along the lines of the Bolsheviks. A little later, in the confrontation over the council republics in Bremen and Munich, or in the crushing of the Spartacus rising and the riots of Spring 1919 in central Germany, disappointment over the SPD's course and the lack of political and social reforms ended in a wave of violence. This pattern was also seen in Admiral Horthy's liquidation of the Soviet regime in Hungary under the Communist Béla Kun and in the later establishment of an authoritarian regime under Marshal Piłsudski in Poland.

(10) Whereas the war began in Summer 1914 in a relatively synchronized manner, its ending was an example of pronounced asynchronicity. For western Europe, November 11 marked a decisive break, but this was not true for eastern Europe or the Ottoman Empire. When the world war ended in those latter areas, new spaces of violence opened up in a context of civil war, independence struggles, and conflicts over the outcome of the war.

8

OUTCOMES

Wars in Peace and Rival Models of Order, 1919–1923

THE WORLD WAR came to an end, but many wars continued or recommenced. At the end of 1918, it made quite a difference whether one was in Warsaw, Helsinki, or Lvov; in Trieste or Dublin; in Vienna, Prague, or Berlin. In the European conflict that had begun in August 1914, the interstate war between the Allies and the Central Powers, the guns fell silent at the latest on November 11, 1918. But the end of the war by no means signified an end to the story of violence—on the contrary. In many cases—Russia is a clear example—these asymmetrical post-wars, civil wars, and outbreaks of ethnic violence were hardly less bloody than the fighting in the world war. The complexity of the "postwar period," as it is known, eluded any simple distinction between war and peace or between continuity and radical change. What developed, rather, was a panorama of opposing and often overlapping situations.

In eastern Europe, the prelude to new conflicts often lay hidden in the diversity of postwar constellations;[1] the date November 11, 1918, therefore did not have the same significance that it had in western Europe. In Russia, despite its formal end, the interstate war was giving way to civil war by the end of 1917—a conflict that would last into the early 1920s and in which far more Russians would be killed than in the fighting of the world war. There the extreme shortage of life's necessities fostered the emergence of irregular violence. Yet insofar as reference was often made to Bolshevik violence in Russia, the civil war there was also a key element in the justification of paramilitary violence in many other parts of Europe. Wartime practices, involving a climate of suspicion, spy mania, and mistrust of supposedly hostile foreigners, were transposed to Bolshevik stereotypes, to revolutionary civil war, and to the international class struggle.[2] All this served to legitimate violence, and it was a transnational phenomenon. It reinforced a common enemy-image of Jewish-Slavic Bolshevism. Very soon after the end of the war, paramilitary anti-Bolshevik networks began to form in Germany, Austria, Hungary, Finland, Russia, and Italy.[3] In France, anti-Bolshevik propaganda helped to stabilize the political order of the Third Republic in the period of transition from war to peace.[4]

Along with civil war, independence struggles continued to make progress in eastern Europe—particularly in Finland, Poland, and the Baltic. After his release from German captivity, Piłsudski assumed dictatorial powers in Poland, reorganizing the government and forcing the withdrawal of German troops. In the shadow of the peace negotiations, he gambled on confrontation with a Russia weakened by civil war and Allied intervention, in order to expand eastward the territory of the newly emerging Polish nation-state. This military conflict, which was presented as a struggle for national independence, soon supplanted the post-1914 wartime experience in the historical memory of many Poles.[5] This displaced attention also applied to the Polish-Ukrainian conflict. In January 1919, a government formed the previous month in Kiev forced a short-lived unification with the West Ukrainian People's Republic founded in Lvov in November 1918. In bloody fighting with Ukrainian troops, the Poles occupied the city on November 21 and 22, and an anti-Jewish pogrom that lasted until November 24 led to deaths, woundings, and looting that also affected segments of the Polish and Ukrainian population. The background to this was an increasingly sweeping wartime perception among Ukrainians and Poles that the Jews of Lvov—a city where the occupier changed several times—were profiteers and collaborators, who always put themselves first and therefore counted as traitors. Later, in the 1920s and 1930s, war memorials and commemorations consolidated national self-images and enemy-images that had a strongly anti-Semitic tendency.[6]

In all these examples, the paramilitary violence of the Freikorps volunteers and assorted militias had enormous significance. This development, which began with the revolutions of 1917 in Russia, lasted until 1923–1924—that is, until the fighting subsided in the Ruhr, the civil war concluded in Ireland, and the Treaty of Lausanne brought conflict to an end in the former Ottoman Empire. The idea of November 11, 1918, as a watershed therefore needs to be put into perspective. Paramilitary violence continued after that in particular "shatterzones" of the former empires, where rival ideologies formed a tightly knit web of ethnic conflicts, nation-building processes, revolutions, and collapse of imperial state structures.[7]

On the other hand, the brutalization of conflicts in Finland after 1917 showed that there was no simple continuum between world war and civil war. In the civil war that broke out there in the wake of the October Revolution in Russia, bourgeois forces sought to disarm Russian troops still in the country, to bolster Finland's national autonomy, and to prevent a social revolution, while socialist forces pushed for cooperation with the new rulers in Petrograd. The creation of an armed Protection Corps under Karl Gustav Mannerheim (a former tsarist lieutenant-general openly sympathetic to the White counterrevolution in Russia) led to the organization of Red Guards and the establishment of a revolutionary government in Helsinki in January 1918. Mannerheim's White forces eventually prevailed, with the support of Finnish riflemen who returned from Germany in January 1918 but also of regular German troops. A total of 100,000 men on the Red side and 70,000 on the White took part in the civil war. But of the 29,000 who lost their lives, only 6,800 died in regular combat: the majority fell to the terror and reprisal measures on either side—an estimated 8,400 just in the mass killings perpetrated by the Whites. After the end of the fighting, an additional 80,000 people were rounded up as "Reds," and some 12,000 of these subsequently died in internment camps.[8] The Finnish civil war, one of the key watersheds in the country's history, developed such a dynamic of its own that the question of whether someone had fought in the world war or not became a secondary issue.[9]

In the Baltic states, paramilitaries left a strong mark on their nation-building processes; the connection between the two, against the background of the world war, was particularly close.[10] For German soldiers in the east, the end of the war in the west was all the harder to fathom because they had scored an overwhelming victory over Russia earlier in the year. In Russia, German forces did not withdraw immediately in November 1918 and often became entangled in fighting between Reds and Whites. In the guise of a Freikorps, many units actively supported movements struggling for national independence in non-Russian areas of the former tsarist empire. No doubt their thinking was that, although the war in the west was lost, they should at least maintain their positions in the Baltic, the main focus of German expansionist plans. As many as 40,000 German soldiers therefore continued to be deployed there, and in the ever-changing fronts between White and Red troops (in which units backed by the Allies also played a role) they gained experience of a brutal small war in which less and less distinction was made between combatants and civilians. Indeed, in this space of violence, it was much more difficult to identify the enemy than it had been on the western front. One member of a German Freikorps later described the situation: "In those days of high summer, the enemy lay in front of us, behind us, and between us."[11] Although the German units were forced to withdraw in the course of 1919, the experiences of the so-called *Baltikumer* lived on in the world of journalism. On the one hand, the experiences in the Baltic called into question traditional ethnic hierarchies, in which Poles, Czechs, and Latvians opposed the former Russian and German ruling stratum. On the other hand, anti-Bolshevik enemy-images linked up with traditional negative stereotypes of the eastern European population.

In Germany, the state after 1919 recaptured the public space over which it had effectively lost control in November 1918. There were close parallels to wartime experiences. Often, violent clashes were the result of unexpected resistance, as in soldiers' demonstrations calling for the release of imprisoned comrades. The use of firearms out of sheer panic, or amid rumors about officers' conspiracies or the shooting of hostages (as in late April in Munich), might suddenly acquire huge significance. The justification of violence as an emergency measure of self-defense and the mechanisms of overreaction under extreme stress were reminiscent of German attacks on the civilian population in Belgium at the beginning of the war.[12]

In the British Empire, the period after 1918 witnessed a range of revolts and civil war scenarios. In March and April 1919, several thousand Egyptians lost their lives in a wave of violent protests denouncing British rule and calling for national independence. On April 13, 1919, British colonial troops opened fire on marchers in the Indian city of Amritsar, and mass demonstrations throughout the country, initiated by the Indian National Congress, responded to the tightening of British control. Disappointment over the treatment of Indian soldiers returning home, together with the arrest of representatives in Amritsar of the Indian independence movement, played a role in these developments. The British use of machine guns cost the lives of more than 300 civilians, again demonstrating the pattern of asymmetrical violence in a colonial context. Finally, in Ireland the end of the war sharpened the tendencies to civil war. On January 21, 1919, the republican parliament proclaimed Irish independence—and this sparked off a civil war between armed IRA units and the British police and army. The British deployment of paramilitary Black and Tans against Irish nationalists was highly reminiscent of German Freikorps operations in the Baltic.[13] But in Ireland too there was no simple continuum between the violence of the world war and the postwar period, or between world war and civil war. And as in Poland, the active role of women as combatants in these conflicts would later be completely suppressed.[14]

It was not only in the British Empire that outbreaks of violence occurred outside Europe. In the repression of colonial revolts and resistance movements—in Libya against Italy, in North Africa against France, or in Morocco against Spain—the wartime experiences of violence often had a continuing effect. Technological know-how and new tactics were transposed to colonial contexts and further refined there. This was most striking in the case of weapons that emphasized the asymmetry between colonizers and colonized; that is, machine guns and poison gas.

In the Near East, amid the erosion of the Ottoman Empire, there were uprisings in Syria against the French army. The Ottoman Empire itself soon became the object of competing interests: Italy laid claim to areas in the Aegean and Asia Minor, while the Greeks landed troops of their own to advance the idea of a Greater Greek nation-state. A full end to the war in this region came only with the Lausanne treaty of 1923, which recognized the revisions by force of the Treaty of Sèvres. There too, November 1918 had ushered in a new period of violence, which Kemalist Turkish nationalists saw as a war of independence. But at the same time it was a period of civil war, with elements of asymmetrical violence. In 1919, although the Ottoman Empire still formally existed, it could not deploy any land forces of its own against Allied troops, and so the defense of Anatolia was mainly left to guerrilla forces, irregular units, and local gangs—to which Mustafa Kemal had to give a largely free hand. Against this background, a new wave of ethnic violence gripped the country, as multiethnic regions were subjected to a "demixing" process. The mass expulsion, persecution, and killing of Armenians continued until 1923, as did the forced migration of Greeks from Turkey and Turks from Greece. But the centuries-old mélange could not be disentangled so easily according to supposedly clear ethnic, linguistic, and religious criteria. On the island of Crete and in Macedonia there were Muslims who spoke only Greek, while many Anatolian Christians were fluent only in Turkish. In some parts of northern Greece, farmers had been forcibly converted to Islam in the nineteenth century, but had continued to celebrate Christian festivals, and in Salonica (Thessaloniki) the Dönmeh sect of converts to Islam practiced Jewish rituals.[15]

In this space, the continuity between war and postwar was especially striking. High desertion rates and loss of control in the Ottoman army led to a situation at the end of the war in which many soldiers were absconding with their weapons, including hand grenades and machine guns. The violence thus shifted from the fronts to the Turkish interior, giving rise to novel formations and combinations. In Thrace, for instance, Bulgarian, Macedonian, and Turkish units fought together against Entente troops—and similar multiethnic forces went into action against the Greek occupiers of Smyrna. A shared Muslim faith and reports of atrocities by Greek troops against Muslim civilians had a unifying effect on these groups, particularly in areas where Greeks represented barely more than 14 percent of the population. In the end, more than 1.2 million Muslims would flee from Thrace and western Anatolia.[16]

The mismatch between political ambitions and actual means of rule persisted after 1918 in the Near and Middle East, shaping British practices in their newly established mandates. In late nineteenth-century colonial conflicts, the machine gun had symbolized the asymmetry of force, and a similar capacity to control a much larger enemy by means of superior technology marked the post-1918 situation in the Near and Middle East. In the former Ottoman Empire, aerial observation and warfare became the primary instruments with which the British imposed their rule on mandated territories. When large Arab and Kurdish revolts broke out in Summer 1920,

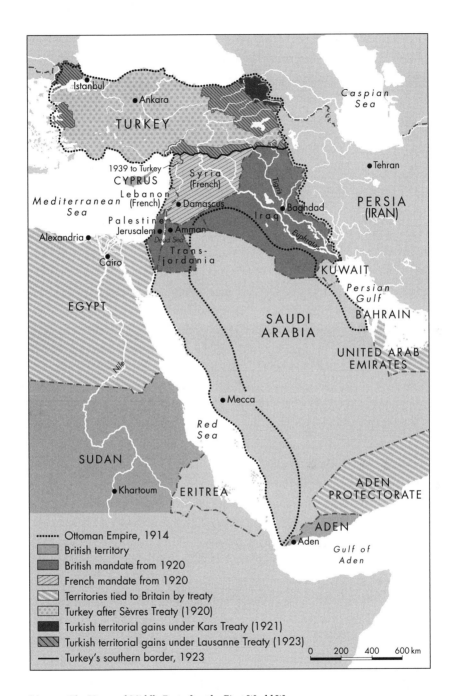

Istanbul

● Ankara

TURKEY

Caspian Sea

1939 to Turkey

CYPRUS

Syria (French)

Tigris

● Tehran

Mediterranean Sea

Lebanon (French)

● Damascus

PERSIA (IRAN)

● Baghdad

Iraq

Palestine

Jerusalem ● ● Amman

Euphrates

Alexandria ●

Dead Sea

Trans-jordania

● Cairo

KUWAIT

Persian Gulf

EGYPT

SAUDI ARABIA

BAHRAIN

UNITED ARAB EMIRATES

Nile

● Mecca

Red Sea

SUDAN

● Khartoum   ERITREA

ADEN PROTECTORATE

ADEN

● Aden   *Gulf of Aden*

Legend:

- ▪▪▪▪▪ Ottoman Empire, 1914
- British territory
- British mandate from 1920
- French mandate from 1920
- Territories tied to Britain by treaty
- Turkey after Sèvres Treaty (1920)
- Turkish territorial gains under Kars Treaty (1921)
- Turkish territorial gains under Lausanne Treaty (1923)
- ——— Turkey's southern border, 1923

0   200   400   600 km

Map 12. The Near and Middle East after the First World War

there was much public discussion in Britain as to whether it had been wise to assume responsibility after the war for the Mesopotamian provinces of Basra, Baghdad, and Mosul. The insurgents destroyed a large part of the infrastructure; British officers and some of their families fell victim to the violence. In August 1920, the number of armed rebels was estimated to be around 131,000.[17]

Only systematic use of the British air force succeeded in crushing the revolts. This then became the model for repressive police rule in Iraq. Bombing from the air did not differentiate between civilians and insurgents, and in this sense it anticipated RAF strategies in the Second World War. Before 1918 and in the aftermath of the war, British and Indian forces had repeatedly faced brutal violence in Mesopotamia and the Arabian Peninsula; British images of Arab fighters had centered on their use of snipers, their killing of wounded soldiers and prisoners, and reported looting of graves. Rumors of extreme brutality and inhumanity were rife. And particularly during the war years, it had been a common view in the British army that the inferiority of Arab civilization was expressed in its failure to differentiate between combatants and civilians. Many of these characteristics were then transposed to the way in which the British themselves fought the war—which helps to explain their willingness to use air power to enforce their claim to rule, offsetting their numerical inferiority with superior technology and tactics.[18]

With regard to the Continental empires and their successor states, a strong case can be made that there was a relative continuity in the experience of violence between 1908 and 1923. However, new developments after the end of 1918 explain the diversity of experiences from country to country and the tensions to which they gave rise. What felt like a period of defeat and humiliation for people in Germany, Austria, and Hungary; of disappointed expectations for Italy and Japan; and of severe defeat for Greece was for Irish, Poles, and Balts the beginning or completion of a national liberation struggle, which made the war years seem like the mere prelude to a process of nation-building by force.

Overall, therefore, the final months of 1918 witnessed a contradictory juxtaposition of end and beginning, an unexpected defeat plus a transition from formal war to other types of violence. The greater the distance in space and time from the western front of November 1918, the more blurred became the boundaries separating world war, breakup war, and civil war, or nation-building wars and ethnic violence—and the more difficult it was to differentiate between regular and irregular violence or between national, ideological, and social enemy-images. It is therefore no accident that the most suggestive explanations for the defeat all referred to internal betrayal and a "stab in the back"; they translated wartime enemy-images into metaphors that could be instrumentalized for domestic political purposes and allowed national and ideological elements to be welded together. The actual peace settlements were only sometimes associated with these experiences of violence—in the case of the Ottoman Empire, for example, where the Sèvres treaty was opposed with armed force. The treaty originally provided for a radical diminution of Turkish territory to a core around Constantinople and central Anatolia, the distribution of its former territories between Greece and European mandate-holders, and the creation of an independent Armenian state.

On June 28, 1919, at the Palace of Versailles, a scene took place in the Hall of Mirrors that illustrated the emotional charge of the treaty proceedings and the burdening of the postwar order with moral implications of guilt and responsibility. Before the German delegation was led into the hall,

The face of war guilt as a continuation of the war by other means: *Les cinq gueules cassées,* Versailles, June 28, 1919

five severely wounded French soldiers were placed near the table where the German politicians would be required to sign the documents without any discussion. The French prime minister Clemenceau added to the drama by silently shaking the hands of the *cinq gueules cassées* before the act of signature. Hundreds of thousands of picture postcards would later elevate the five soldiers to a symbol of the French war casualties—indeed, their disfigured features gave a face to the war itself, underlining the perception of German war guilt.[19]

Before the official talks began, the British prime minister Lloyd George had commissioned the painter William Orpen to record the Paris peace conference as its "official artist." Orpen, who had access to all conference rooms, produced portraits of all the main politicians and, most important, committed the signing of the treaty to canvas. Of that historic moment, he remarked that it "had not as much dignity as a sale at Christie's."[20] In general, the symbolic overloading of the peace talks and the Versailles treaty with allusions to the German Empire was impossible to overlook. Thomas Mann, for example, noted the rumor that Clemenceau planned to erect a statue of the Greek goddess Pallas Athena, the personification of wisdom, art, and science, in the hotel lobby where the German delegation would be handed the document. He saw this as a provocative attempt, after the experience of the war, to exclude Germany from the community of Western civilization. Yet to him, it was the German people that were "opposing Bolshevism with the last of its strength and a landsknecht's rectitude." "It is remarkable," he went on, "that the aged Frenchman whose twilight years are brightened by this peace has *slit* eyes. Perhaps he has some right of blood to kill off Western civilization and to bring in Asia and its chaos."[21]

In contrast to this symbolic continuation of the war, President Wilson mainly emphasized the link between the peace treaties and the founding of the League of Nations. After the conclusion of the peace talks, all future dangers of another war would be contained: "At the front of this great treaty is put the covenant of the league of nations. It will also be at the front of the Austrian treaty and the Hungarian treaty and the Bulgarian treaty and the treaty with Turkey. Every one of them will contain the covenant of the league of nations, because you cannot work any of them without the covenant of the league of nations. Unless you get the united, concerted purpose and power of the great Governments of the world behind this settlement, it will fall down like a house of cards. There is only one power to put behind the liberation of mankind, and that is the power of mankind. It is the power of the united moral forces of the world, and in the covenant of the league of nations the moral forces of the world are mobilized."[22]

Unprecedented in scale, with its large numbers of delegates and journalists,[23] the Paris peace conference was a laboratory of the twentieth century, an experimental space for the creation of a new world order geared to public opinion and the principles of collective security.[24] It opened with a deliberate emphasis on political history: that date, January 18, 1919, was the thirty-eighth anniversary of the proclamation of the German Empire in 1871 and the founding of the German nation-state. A total of thirty-two Allied and associate powers were present, but it soon became clear that effective decision-making processes were possible only within a smaller circle. The substantive issues were therefore decided within the Council of Four, which comprised the heads of state or government of the four main Allied powers (excluding Japan)—Wilson, Lloyd George, Clemenceau, and Orlando—although it was not long before the clash of interests among them became unmistakable. Wilson concentrated on the League of Nations and its mandated territories, seeing them as new instruments of collective security and a lasting peace. The charter of the League of Nations became part of the Versailles treaty and all other agreements signed on the outskirts of Paris. Alongside the constitutional organs of the League—its general assembly, council, and permanent secretariat—the International Labor Office and the Court of International Justice acquired great importance in the long term as subsidiary bodies. At first, only the Allies, the associate states, and thirteen neutral countries belonged to the League. In 1920 Wilson would fail to secure congressional approval for the ratification of the League and the entry into it of the United States.[25]

In the French perspective that Clemenceau represented, security vis-à-vis Germany was the main consideration; the revival of a strong Germany therefore had to be avoided under all circumstances. This explains not only his demand for a border on the Rhine but also later alliances with the new states of central Europe. The Little Entente with Poland and Czechoslovakia was meant to contain Germany also in the east. The French further demanded reparations for wartime casualties and damage, partly with the aim of limiting Germany's long-term economic strength. Lloyd George, for his part, pursued Britain's chief objective of keeping the German global position at a minimum, in terms both of commercial competition and of naval and colonial outreach. At the same time, however, in the so-called Fontainebleau memorandum, a sharp turn against the Russian Bolsheviks was reflected in his rejection of Germany's permanent weakening or even dismemberment; rather, it should remain a viable Continental power not only against the Bolshevik menace but also as a player capable of ensuring a long-term balance of power in Continental Europe.[26]

All the vanquished powers were excluded from the peace talks in Paris. In the end, representatives traveled there from many colonial societies in Africa and Asia, with high hopes that they could influence the U.S. president and assert the global validity of the right to national self-determination. Numerous submissions—from the First Pan-African Congress, the Young Algeria movement, Ho Chi Minh's movement for Vietnam, and so on—aimed to achieve a better political status vis-à-vis the colonial rulers, but consistently ended in disappointment.[27]

With a total of 440 articles in 15 sections, appendices, and supplementary treaties, the Versailles treaty between the Allies and the German Empire was at the time the longest and most complex peace agreement in history. On May 7, 1919, the fourth anniversary of the sinking of the *Lusitania,* the German delegation under Foreign Minister Count Ulrich von Brockdorff-Rantzau was handed the Allied peace terms. Direct negotiations were not provided for, so that the German politicians were only able to submit counter-proposals in writing. On June 16, the Allies rejected nearly every point made by the opposite side and emphasized even more than before that Germany alone was to blame for the war. Only a five-day ultimatum and a threat to occupy the territory of the Reich then eventually forced acceptance of the terms. Following the resignation of Philipp Scheidemann as prime minister—he had first been a member of the Council of People's Representatives and then been invited to form a government by the newly elected Reich president Friedrich Ebert—the Weimar National Assembly, elected in January 1919, bowed to the inevitable and voted by 237–138 with 5 abstentions to accept the Allied conditions. On June 28, Foreign Minister Hermann Müller and

Peace as forced migration: resettlement of German inhabitants of Alsace after the Versailles treaty of 1919

Transport Minister Johannes Bell signed the documents under protest in the Hall of Mirrors at the palace of Versailles.[28]

Part One of the treaty contained the Covenant of the League of Nations. Any future amendments were possible only under §19 of the covenant, but this possibility was excluded so long as Germany was not a member of the League of Nations. Territorial adjustments and boundaries were set out in Parts Two and Three. The peace treaties of Brest-Litovsk and Bucharest were declared null and void, and Danzig was treated as a League mandate. Alsace-Lorraine reverted to France. The Klaipeda region (Memelland) came under Allied administration. The newly created Polish state took control of the provinces of Poznan and West Prussia, as well as Pomerelia. East Prussia, minus Memelland, was now divided by a corridor from the Reich proper. The Hultschiner Ländchen became the Hlučin region of the new Czechoslovak Republic, and the Eupen-Malmedy cantons joined the Kingdom of Belgium. Masuria, Upper Silesia, and northern Schleswig were treated as special cases: referenda in 1920 and 1921 led to the incorporation of most of northern Schleswig into Denmark and of Upper Silesia into Poland. Article 80 of the treaty explicitly prohibited the incorporation of the German Austrian Republic into the German Reich. In addition, Britain and France occupied and administered the Territory of the Saar Basin as a League of Nations protectorate, which France made use of economically; a referendum was to decide on its final status in 1935. The articles in Part Four of the treaty ordered the evacuation of all German colonies, which became League mandates assigned to Britain and France. The forfeited German territory, apart from the colonies, amounted to 70,580 square kilometers, with a population of 7.3 million. This meant a long-term loss of part of Germany's zinc and iron ore production, one-quarter of its coal production, and one-sixth of its grain harvest.

Part Five specified certain military restrictions: the possession of heavy weapons, especially heavy artillery, tanks, warships over 10,000 tons, and submarines, was forbidden, as was the acquisition of military aircraft. Conscription and the general staff were abolished, the army was limited to a maximum of 100,000 men, and no reservists were to be trained. The navy could not exceed 15,000 men, six ships of the line, six small cruisers, twelve destroyers, and twelve torpedo boats. While weakening Germany militarily, these provisions were supposed to leave it capable of defending its eastern borders and, if necessary, suppressing internal revolution.

Parts Five to Fifteen, with their provision for sanctions, were particularly onerous. Wilhelm II and others were to be handed over as war criminals—although Germany never fulfilled this obligation. Article 231 explicitly defined Germany as the only guilty part in the world war and made this the legal basis for initially unspecified reparations; German demands for a revision of the treaty therefore concentrated on a rebuttal of this article. In practice, the signing of the peace treaty unleashed a flood of documentation and other publications concerning German war guilt, which still influence the most recent historical debates on responsibility for the outbreak of war.[29]

The reparations were initially defined as covering all war-related damage in the Allied countries. German advance payments were to total 20 billion gold marks in cash plus deliveries of goods. In January 1921, the Allies made their first total demand for payment, to the tune of 269 billion gold marks. After Germany refused to accept this and the Allies occupied Düsseldorf and Duisburg, the 1921 London ultimatum set the demand at 132 billion

gold marks in thirty-seven annual installments, together with simultaneous levies of 26 percent on German exports. The Dawes Plan of 1924 and
the Young Plan of 1929 issued further regulations, the Hoover moratorium
of 1931 deferred payment for one year, and the Lausanne Conference in 1932
agreed a final one-off payment of three billion gold marks, which was never
actually made.[30]

With the Allies already tied together monetarily by the war, a global nexus
took shape linking British and French war debts to the United States with
German reparations and U.S. loans to Germany. As a result, although the
United States withdrew politically and diplomatically from Europe, its economic and financial presence was an evident fact of life. France insisted on
high reparations so that it could cover its debts to the United States, while
the United States, after the period of inflation and in accordance with the
Dawes Plan, issued loans to Germany so that it could develop its economy
and improve its medium-term ability to keep up payments. The recall of
many of these short-term loans in 1928–1929, in a context of world economic
crisis, had a massive impact on the German economy.[31]

The extensive deliveries of goods under the terms of the treaty included
locomotives and railroad cars, 90 percent of the merchant fleet, all available
long-distance cables, 11 percent of the German cattle stock, and 40 million
tons of coal yearly for a period of 10 years to France, Belgium, Luxembourg,
and Italy. Germany property overseas was confiscated. A nonreciprocal most
favored nation clause would apply until 1925, supplemented by special rights
for the Allies in air transport and in German ports. German rivers and,
most important, the North Sea / Baltic canal were internationalized. German
troops had to withdraw from all formerly Russian areas in eastern Europe.
The entire left bank of the Rhine was occupied by Allied troops, as well as
bridgeheads on the right bank in the vicinity of Cologne, Mainz, and Koblenz;
this area, divided into three zones, would remain under Allied control for 5,
10, and 15 years, respectively. The demilitarized zone on the left bank was
supplemented by a 50-kilometer wide strip on the right bank, where the Germans were not allowed to build fortifications or station any military forces.

The harsh German terms imposed at Brest-Litovsk refute the widely prevailing idea in Germany that the Versailles treaty was a singular "dictated
peace." But Versailles did mark a break with the traditions of modern treaties

between 1648 and 1815: the concept of a decriminalized *iustus hostis* (just enemy) gave way to a moralization of politics and a blaming of only one side for the outbreak of war. Still, in contrast to May 1945, the Versailles treaty did not signify the unconditional surrender of Germany; its terms seemed to some too severe and to others too lenient. Germany found itself morally stigmatized, but did not completely lose its political or economic claim to be a European great power. Unlike in May 1945, the country continued to have the resources for a revisionist foreign policy—a position that reflected the by no means tension-free compromise among the victorious powers. The treaty expressed Anglo-American pressure on the new Continental equilibrium, thereby thwarting French plans, after the experiences of 1870 and 1914, for a long-term dismantling of Germany's great power status. One such plan might have involved the creation of a Rhine federation of small independent states dependent on France.

How was the complex legacy of the multiethnic empires addressed after the end of the war? And what were the medium- to long-term consequences?[32] The liquidation of the Habsburg monarchy and the Ottoman Empire entered international law as a result of the Paris peace agreements, which came into force between June 1920 and July 1921: that is, the treaties with German Austria on September 10, 1919, at Saint-Germain-en-Laye; with Bulgaria on September 27, 1919, at Neuilly; with Hungary on June 4, 1920, at Trianon; and with the Ottoman Empire on August 10, 1920, at Sèvres. Only Soviet Russia was missing, for, contrary to what Woodrow Wilson and Lloyd George had hoped, it was not represented at the Paris peace conference. The result was a divided peace; it would not apply to the whole of Europe, completely omitted large areas in Asia, and therefore lost much of its credibility and legitimacy. The internal destabilization of the Soviet state, which resumed the legacy of the Tsarist Empire, highlighted the limits of Wilson's policy of grounding the stability of international relations solely on the right of nations to self-determination. In contrast to the Habsburg monarchy, the multiethnic Tsarist Empire survived after 1917 in the shape of the Soviet Union.[33] There were several reasons for this. Whereas Germans and Hungarians had never constituted more than half of the population of the Habsburg Empire, Russians never formed less than 50 percent of the Soviet population—or two-thirds together with Belarussians and Ukrainians.[34] The Austro-Marxist debate on a

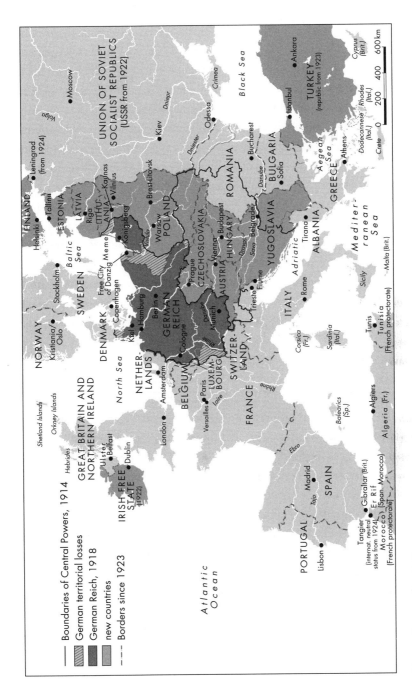

Map 13. Europe after 1918

Boundaries of Central Powers, 1914
German territorial losses
German Reich, 1918
new countries
Borders since 1923

GREAT BRITAIN AND NORTHERN IRELAND
IRISH FREE STATE (1922)
NORWAY
SWEDEN
FINLAND
DENMARK
NETHER-LANDS
BELGIUM
LUXEM-BOURG
GERMAN REICH
FRANCE
SWITZER-LAND
PORTUGAL
SPAIN
UNION OF SOVIET SOCIALIST REPUBLICS (USSR from 1922)
ESTONIA
LATVIA
LITHU-ANIA
POLAND
CZECHOSLOVAKIA
AUSTRIA
HUNGARY
ROMANIA
YUGOSLAVIA
BULGARIA
ALBANIA
GREECE
ITALY
TURKEY (republic from 1923)

Atlantic Ocean
North Sea
Baltic Sea
Mediterranean Sea
Adriatic
Aegean Sea
Black Sea

Shetland Islands
Orkney Islands
Hebrides
Ulster
Belfast
Dublin
London
Amsterdam
Paris
Versailles
Loire
Rhône
Ebro
Tajo
Lisbon
Madrid
Balearics (Sp.)
Algiers
Algeria (Fr.)
Tangier (internat. neutral status from 1924)
Gibraltar (Brit.)
Er Rif
Morocco (Span. Morocco)
Morocco (French protectorate)
Corsica (Fr.)
Sardinia (Ital.)
Rome
Tunis
Tunisia (French protectorate)
Sicily
Malta (Brit.)
Tirana
Crete
Athens
Rhodes (Ital.)
Dodecannese (Ital.)
Cyprus (Brit.)
Istanbul
Ankara
Sofia
Bucharest
Belgrade
Budapest
Vienna
Prague
Warsaw
Drava
Sava
Danube
Fiume
Trieste
Munich
Cologne
Berlin
Hamburg
Kiel
Copenhagen
Kristiania/Oslo
Stockholm
Helsinki
Tallinn
Leningrad (from 1924)
Moscow
Volga
Kiev
Dnieper
Dniester
Odessa
Crimea
Riga
Kaunas
Vilnius
Brest-Litovsk
Königsberg
Free City of Danzig
Meme
Kalau

0   200   400   600 km

federal solution to the problem of multiethnicity was meanwhile transposed to Russia, so that in the 1920s the Soviet Union faced the same problem that had taxed the Habsburg monarchy at the end of the war: the problem of political leadership of self-conscious nationalities. The Soviet answer was to combine a federal system with a tightly centralized Communist Party.

In the liquidation of the Habsburg monarchy, the principle of national self-determination was effectively set aside. Article 80 of the Versailles treaty established the independence of Austria, overriding German and Austrian decisions in favor of the constitutional unification of the two states. In the provisional constitution of the Republic of German-Austria, adopted on November 12, 1918, the new state was consciously defined as part of the German republic, and the Austrian constituent assembly confirmed this status in March 1919. The German National Assembly, for its part, approved this move on February 21, 1919, and Article 61, paragraph 2 of the Weimar constitution included German-Austria as a member of the Reich Council. With the ratification of the Versailles treaty, the German government had to declare this decision null and void in September 1919. The overwhelming majorities in some parts of Austria (such as the Tyrol and Salzburg) in favor of attachment to the German republic made no difference at all.[35]

The question of the frontiers of a German nation-state, having been raised but not answered in 1815 and 1848, was, so to speak, then deflected through the wars of 1866 and 1870–1871 and the resulting foundation of a smaller German / Prussian state. The treaties of Versailles and Saint-Germain now postponed the conflict again, and their credibility soon crumbled as postwar German and Austrian society came to see them as a "dictated peace." What the Allies refused in 1919 in the form of a democratically constituted German-Austrian republic, they would eventually accept in 1938 under quite different circumstances as a result of Adolf Hitler's act of military force. Indirectly, they thereby recognized the strategy of forcible revision of the Paris treaties, retrospectively highlighting the contradictions that had been built into them from the start. In 1938, Hitler could not only boast of having torn up the treaties of 1919–1920, but project himself as the man who had completed German history, restored the unity of the Reich, and erased the outcomes of 1848 and 1918.

Thus, the post-1918 liquidation of the Habsburg monarchy in the German and Hungarian successor states led to massive and persistent bitterness and fierce polarization at the level of internal politics.[36] In Austria, the treaty was seen as not only a diktat but an "annihilating peace." Unlike Germany, which, despite considerable losses of territory, retained great power status with its heartlands intact, Austria was regarded by many as a rump state that had lost much of its German-speaking population (South Tyrol with its 220,000 Germans plus 11,000 Ladins, Bohemia and Moravia with their more than three million people of German descent, as well as Silesia and, after the cession of further areas, parts of Lower Austria). While Austria counted in international law as a successor state to the Habsburg Empire, and therefore as a guilty party in the assignment of blame for the war, Czechoslovakia, Yugoslavia, and Romania enjoyed the status of victors. Under the right to self-determination, which Austria too had recognized with reference to Wilson's peace plans, the new Austrian republic would have had an approximate total of ten million inhabitants of German descent. In fact, the treaty of Saint-Germain and the ensuing referenda—in South Carinthia, for example—resulted in a population of little more than 6.5 million.[37]

The results of the Treaty of Trianon were seen as exceptionally harsh for Hungary.[38] As in the case of Germany and Austria, there were no real talks among the delegations. In January 1920 the Allies simply informed Budapest of the terms of the peace settlement, provoking outrage in the Hungarian public; they meant that Hungary would lose nearly 70 percent of the territory it had held at the beginning of the war, which had then contained more than 50 percent of the total Hungarian population. Like Austria, the Hungarian part of the defunct Dual Monarchy emerged with a greatly weakened state, encompassing no more than 93,000 square kilometers and 7.6 million inhabitants.[39] The greatest losses were to Slovakia (now part of the new Czechoslovak state), to Austria (which obtained Burgenland), to Yugoslavia (which acquired Croatia and Slovenia), and to Romania (which took over both Banat and Transylvania).[40]

The Hungarian-Romanian conflict shaped the context for this experience, which developed, so to speak, in the shadow of the postwar situation and ended with the downfall of Béla Kun's Bolshevik republic. Through its use of force, Romania imposed the territorial demands it had formulated in 1916, while the revolution in Budapest clearly reflected Hungarian national elements in the form of a social revolution. The shock in Hungary was thus based on various intertwined experiences: on the national humiliation of "de-Magyarization" associated with the Trianon peace terms; on external intervention; and on the internal paralysis resulting from ideological polarization, which eventually issued in Admiral Horthy's authoritarian regime.

Similarly drastic were the terms that the Neuilly peace treaty stipulated for Bulgaria. The refusal of the delegation leader and provisional prime minister, Todor Teodorov, to sign the acceptance statement changed nothing. Bulgaria lost further territory in addition to the sizable conquests it had made during the war, so that the 114,000 square kilometers that had constituted the state of Bulgaria in 1915 were whittled down to 103,000 square kilometers.[41]

There were striking parallels among the successor states most affected by the treaty terms. As in Germany, these terms led in Austria, Hungary, and Bulgaria to a twofold instability: the peace settlements and the status reduction associated with them virtually extended the war into the postwar period; while the forced acceptance of the terms imposed a heavy burden on the new republican governments as administrators of the imperial legacies, as their foreign policy sought to achieve the greatest possible revision of the agreements. The internal and external lines of conflict combined and overlapped with each other. Thus, the degree to which a revision of the treaties was pursued became a yardstick for the evaluation of political positions and was an important element in the ideological polarization of the postwar period. Bourgeois-liberal conceptions of the international order were further eroded by far left and far right accusations that they involved respect for the treaty terms.

The problems of ethnic-territorial restructuring and possible emancipation from the framework laid down in 1920 came into clear focus in the case of the Ottoman Empire. The situation there was, however, very different from that in the former Habsburg monarchy, primarily because the violent conflicts in which it was embroiled went farther back than 1914, to the beginning of the war with Greece in 1897 and the two Balkan wars of 1912–1913. Further complications were the Greek invasion of Smyrna (Izmir) in western Anatolia in May 1919 and the major internal unrest in various parts of the country.

On the one hand, this internal destabilization expressed the breakup of the Ottoman Empire, which had been considerably accelerated by the territorial losses in southeastern Europe. On the other hand—and this would become a key factor after 1918—the continuing internal and external crises had a both catalyzing and radicalizing effect on Turkish nationalism. The Moudros armistice agreement in October 1918 ushered in the de facto end of the Ottoman Empire.[42] For the leading protagonists in the Turkish national movement, its terms merely confirmed that the postwar order mapped out in Paris had to be revised at all costs. The formation of a Turkish nation-state therefore developed into an act of resistance against the Allied peace terms, exemplified by the major territorial reduction of Turkey in the Sèvres treaty.[43]

When Allied troops occupied Constantinople and advanced plans in March 1920 for the territorial division of Anatolia and the dissolution of the Turkish parliament, the inspector-general of Ottoman troops Mustafa Kemal (later known as Atatürk, "Father of the Turks") seized the initiative and convoked a new national assembly in Ankara, which would develop the foundations for a Turkish nation-state. At the same time, the leaders of the Turkish national movement recognized that this course against the Allied peace terms made external political support a necessity. In opposition to the Sèvres treaty of August 1920, they therefore sought to intensify collaboration with the Soviet state, which had been left out of the Paris treaties. Although the Sultan's government had signed the Sèvres treaty, the Turkish nationalists around Mustafa Kemal refused to recognize it. Their new collaboration with the Soviet leadership found expression in March 1921 in the Treaty of Friendship and Brotherhood between the two countries, which, on the Soviet side, was supplemented in 1922 by the Rapallo treaty with Germany. It may be said that the Paris treaty system was being successfully undermined from the periphery.[44]

Well before the foundation of the Turkish republic in October 1923, a breaking away from the Sèvres treaty framework therefore became apparent, revealing both the Allies' limited reach and the conflict of interests among them. In October 1920, just a few months after the treaty was signed, France signed a separate agreement with Turkey that threatened British positions in the southeastern Mediterranean and pushed Lloyd George into a dangerous maneuver that eventually accelerated his own political downfall. The British prime minister encouraged Greece to undertake a new military advance, which the Turkish national army repelled with such success that it was able to reconquer the city of Smyrna that it had lost in 1919. Only with difficulty did the units of the British Dardanelles army avert a catastrophe.[45]

These Turkish military successes permitted a renegotiation that eventually led in July 1923 to the Treaty of Lausanne, which recognized Turkey as a full and equal participant and represented a fundamental improvement on Sèvres.[46] This was a special case of early treaty revisionism and preparedness to use force in foreign policy, to which the Allies, just two years after the Paris treaties, seemed to have no response. It was a development that underlined the volatility and fragility of the postwar order, all the more because the formation of the Turkish nation-state was inextricably tied to new dimensions of violence in relation to ethnic minorities.[47] Under the Turkish republic (which officially came into being in October 1923) and its first president, Mustafa Kemal, a policy of full-speed modernization seemed to assimilate the western European model of a citizenship-based nation and a consistent separation of state and religion. But this went together with a violent policy toward ethnic minorities that openly contradicted the protections stipulated in the Paris negotiations and the principles of the newly established League of Nations.

The Turkish republic was thereby pursuing a policy whose roots went back a long time. After the Congress of Berlin in 1878, the Ottoman Empire had refused to ratify Article 61 of the agreements reached there, which had provided for protection of its Armenian minority; indeed in 1895–1896 and again in 1915 there had been waves of massacres of Armenians. The Sèvres treaty envisaged a free Armenia, and its liquidation at Lausanne in July 1923 meant that the Turkish republic recovered that territory. In 1925 it would also suppress an insurgent Kurdish movement with brute force, and in 1927 proceed to massive compulsory resettlement.[48]

Thus, Turkey successfully freed itself from the Paris treaty system through the foundation of a nation-state and the adoption of a violent course of action. This process highlighted the scale of the ethnic violence and repression, ranging from expulsion and forced resettlement—in the early 1920s, 2.35 million Greeks were driven from Turkey and 400,000 Muslim Turks from Greece, leading to an extensive depopulation of northern Greece—to massacres and a genocidal systematization of violence. The mass killings were one reply to the question of how ethnic homogeneity should be handled in a newly established nation-state geared to Western models. However, the break from the Paris treaty system also had the effect that Turkey made no major revisionist efforts after 1927 and remained neutral in the Second World War.

The strategy that Allied politicians and diplomats initially pursued with the Paris treaties came down to the foundation of new nation-states on the territory of the former multiethnic empires and the constitution of a stable international order by means of frontier changes and territorial reorganization. This strategy was applied most comprehensively in the Near and Middle East and southeastern Europe, because the multiethnic structures were especially strong there and the collapse of the empires had left behind a power vacuum and a lack of political direction. A number of new polities sprang up alongside refounded or expanded states. Finland, Estonia, Lithuania, Czechoslovakia, and Yugoslavia (the latter comprising Slovenia, Croatia, Serbia, Bosnia-Herzegovina, and Montenegro under Serbian leadership) were recognized in international law as independent players.[49] Poland was reconstituted as an independent state and expanded to include Polish Lithuania, Volhynia, East Galicia, West Galicia, parts of Upper Silesia, Poznan, and West Prussia. Romania obtained Transylvania, Bessarabia, and smaller areas to the south of Galicia. And in August 1921 Italy recognized Albania as an independent state. The cessions of territory that accompanied the dissolution of the multinational Habsburg monarchy and Ottoman Empire changed the map of Europe more profoundly than all previous European peace settlements of modern times.

In the end, however, the reconfiguation did not solve the multiple problems relating to national minorities but exacerbated them in various ways. For the Paris treaties in general and the Versailles treaty in particular could not fulfill the wide-ranging expectations in this respect and eventually turned disappointed hopes into bitter disappointment. Politics seemed to be a continuation of the war by other means. Large flows of refugees and migrants added to these structural problems: some 600,000 people fled to Germany after the Russian October Revolution alone. Many decisions to the disadvantage of the losers—Germany, Austria, and Hungary, as well as the Ottoman Empire at first—made the treaty framework appear unacceptable in the eyes of many contemporaries. This resulted in two sets of problems: the complexities of the ethnic picture could not be resolved by the formula of the right of nations to self-determination as it had been foregrounded especially by the U.S. president Woodrow Wilson; and the trust placed in former national minorities, which were expected to achieve an internally democratic and externally stable process of nation-building, proved to be illusory in most central and southeastern European countries in the inter-war period. The Turkish nation-state seemed to afford a positive example in contrast to unstable states like Yugoslavia. It suggested that the use of force—from compulsory resettlement to calculated deaths and killings on a mass scale—could be an effective instrument against ethnic complexity and tensions if states wielded sufficient power and were able to cover themselves internationally. In the case of Turkey, moreover, there was a long history of ethnic-religious violence, especially against Armenians.

The Paris treaties were not capable of solving the problems of national minorities.[50] It was not only in the Soviet Union that the problems persisted; many of the other newly founded states were by no means homogeneous, but contained a number of different nationalities.[51] The problem of the *Auslandsdeutschen* settled outside Germany, which was repeatedly raised by all German politicians after 1919, was therefore not an exception but the rule in many regions. The small Italian province of Venezia Giulia, for instance, was home to more than 500,000 Slovenes. The nationality mix was especially evident in Czechslovakia: in 1938 it had a population of just under 15 million, 43 percent of whom were Czech, 22 percent Slovak, 23 percent German, 5 percent Hungarian, 3 percent Ukrainian, and 4 percent Jewish. The problem that with others had unleashed the war in 1914 had thus by no means disappeared, but at most been postponed. The leitmotif of suppressed nationality, familiar from the *irredenta*, did not vanish from political discourse but tended to grow even stronger. In 1925, in a letter to the German crown prince, Gustav Stresemann recalled the "ten to twelve million fellow-countrymen . . . who now live under a foreign yoke in foreign countries."[52]

The elimination of two of the three Continental empires—the Habsburg monarchy and the Ottoman Empire—did not lead to a solution of the nationalities problem, but actually multiplied it by transposing it to the level of new multinational states. There, radical and exclusive conceptions of the nation excluded the possibility of federal structures, a commonwealth of peoples, or even effective protection for minorities. Emigration was no longer the option it had been in the nineteenth century, because the United States had considerably tightened its controls after 1918. The result was the new mass phenomenon of the stateless person. Until the introduction of the "Nansen Passport" in 1922—a document for stateless refugees and migrants named after the League of Nations high commissioner for refugees, Fridtjof Nansen—many lived without any legal protection, driven from their old places of residence and neither welcomed nor recognized in their new homes.

Although in 1919 the victorious Allied powers discussed general protection for minorities, covering such issues as equal opportunities, freedom of religious practice, cultural autonomy, and the corresponding fostering of national languages, they eventually rejected the idea because of the unpredictable consequences it would have for the traditional nineteenth-century notion of state sovereignty. Only particular treaties or bilateral agreements provided some protection for minorities; the issue was not taken up in the charter of the League of Nations. This provided scope for new kinds of ethnic violence. The influential British diplomat and politician James Headlam-Morley noted in his memoirs of the 1919 Paris peace talks, "At first there was a proposal, as far as I can recollect, that there should be inserted in the League of Nations some general clause giving [it] the right to protect minorities in all countries which were members of the League. This I always most strongly opposed . . . for it would have involved the right to interfere in the internal constitution of every country in the world. As I pointed out, it would give the right to protect the Chinese in Liverpool, the Roman Catholics in France, the French in Canada, quite apart from the more serious problems, such as the Irish. This point of view was, I think, not seriously opposed by any except the unofficial bodies who wished the League of Nations to be a sort of super-state with a general right of guarding democracy and freedom throughout the world. . . . My own view was that any right given to the League of Nations must be quite definite and specific, and based on special treaties entered into because of definite exceptional cases, and that such a right could only be recognized in the case of a new or immature state of eastern Europe or western Asia. Even if the denial of such a right elsewhere might lead to injustice and oppression, that was better than to allow anything which would mean the negation of the sovereignty of every state in the world."[53]

After his experiences at the European peace conference, a visibly disillusioned President Wilson declared in a speech to the U.S. Senate, "When

I gave utterance to those words [on the right to self-determination], I said them without a knowledge that nationalities existed, which are coming to us day after day. . . . You do not know and cannot appreciate the anxieties that I have experienced as the result of many millions having their hopes raised by what I have said."[54] Wilson's disenchantment mirrored the experience of ethnic situations in large parts of eastern and southeastern Europe, the complexity of which had been underestimated in the Paris peace treaties because it eluded the formula of national self-determination. That the practical application of the right to self-determination was neither consistent nor free of contradiction added to the problems. For the new states that arose in Continental Europe were not stable entities but complex multinational states whose internal and external order essentially depended on their treatment of minorities. A glance at the complicated loyalties in interwar Czechoslovakia suffices to demonstrate this.[55] In reality, what developed was a permanent potential for violence that could be mobilized from the outside at any time, involving aggressive scenarios of intervention.[56]

The outcome of the Paris peace talks was an intricate compromise among disappointed victors, definitely not between victors and vanquished. It ultimately satisfied neither the winners nor the losers of the war. Historians have rightly pointed out that, in comparison with other peace settlements, the manifold upheavals and challenges after the First World War meant that even to attempt a comprehensive solution would always be a major achievement. In a historical perspective, the Paris treaties closed the great era of European treaty diplomacy. Unlike Metternich, Talleyrand, and Hardenberg in 1815, or Bismarck, Disraeli, and Gorchakov in 1878, the political players after 1918 were no longer an isolated elite within the diplomatic arcana; Wilson, Clemenceau, and Lloyd George, but also the German, Austrian, Hungarian, Turkish, and Italian delegations, had to communicate their decisions and the results of the peace talks to their respective publics back home. The elections after 1918 therefore became virtual plebiscites,[57] in which the war was prolonged in the expectations that people had of the peace. This was true especially where there was a collective sense of having been cheated out of the fruits of victory or at least of a just peace settlement. There the result was a latent inward or outward bellicosity, which crystallized into scenarios of violence ranging from civil war, through terror against alleged traitors and campaigns of intervention or encirclement, to ideologically or racially motivated wars of expansion or annihilation. At first, however, the liberation of downtrodden nationalities and hence a revision of the Paris treaty system were key leitmotifs. The latency of violence, the thinking in paradigms of war, was a legacy of the precarious way in which people coped with the post-1918 aftermath of the world war. But the distance between idealistic statecraft and promises of collective security on the one hand and the reality of unfettered ethnic violence on the other pointed to another dilemma. In the age of political-ideological mass markets, appeals to the nation or the principle of national self-determination aroused collective expectations that increasingly limited the political room to maneuver. While nationalist ideologies dynamically raised the scope of what seemed feasible, practical complexities reduced the actual leeway available to political players. Totalized, ideologically motivated violence, both internal and external, appeared to be one answer to the difficulties. Indeed, the peace treaties and their aftereffects were a striking example both of this underlying dilemma and of the unleashing of violence in response to it.

Compared with the postwar settlements in 1763 (after the Seven Years' War), 1815, 1871, or 1945, the international order that took shape after 1919 remained effective for the shortest time. In the first place, it dissolved the previous pentarchy: Germany and Russia were initially excluded from the postwar order. The Habsburg monarchy had broken up. France and Britain counted at best as precarious winners, drained both economically and demographically. Only France stood unconditionally behind the treaty system, while the early departure of the United States removed it as a strong political partner. Congressional opponents headed by Senator Henry Cabot Lodge had appealed to isolationist traditions that dated back to the eighteenth century, polemically raising the question of whether American soldiers should be deployed in the interests of other powers. Lodge argued instead for a new "balance of power" and insisted that Congress should have a say in decisions about the deployment of troops abroad. A showdown then loomed when Wilson refused to consider any change to the treaty system. He returned to the United States and in the space of one week traveled more than 10,000 miles up and down the country, delivering more than forty speeches to mobilize support for the treaty. But instead of paving the way for compromise, his tendency to dogmatism reduced the scope for bargaining with his opponents. When he suffered a stroke, his circle of advisors kept his illness secret from the public.

But afterward he had only a very limited capacity to intervene in political discussions; the Senate refused to ratify the treaty, and in 1921 the United States concluded a peace treaty of its own with Germany, Austria, and Hungary.[58]

In contrast to 1815, the peace settlement harmed or excluded a number of countries—if they continued to exist at all. Notwithstanding critical perceptions at the time, the position of Germany was in fact relatively strengthened by the results of the Versailles treaty. Russia and the Habsburg monarchy, in contrast, suffered long-term exclusion or ceased to exist altogether as independent international players. Nor was Germany weakened by anything like the construction in 1815 of the German Confederation as an entity in international law. The political and economic unity of the country was not in question in 1919, and despite its military defeat the German Reich remained a key player in Continental Europe.

Another weakness of the Paris settlement was the assumption that all states would accept it. Turkey and China questioned its validity forthwith; Germany and Hungary agreed to ratify the treaties only under massive pressure and immediately began to think of how it could be revised in the future. When the Treaty of Versailles eventually came into force on January 10, 1920, American support for it was already in doubt, and the withdrawal of the United States from the process had considerably undermined its legitimacy. With the United States more or less out of the picture, the Italian leadership mainly pursued its own national objectives and took little interest in other matters, while France and Britain increasingly came at odds with each other over such issues as the German U-boats, application of the treaty terms in Silesia and Turkey, and the question of reparations for Russia. The delegations had given remarkably little thought to the actual implementation of the peace treaty, especially considering that many segments of the population in Germany, Hungary, Poland, and Turkey vehemently rejected its results. It soon became clear that it would be as difficult to secure the peace as it had been to win victory in the war.[59]

The provisional character of the treaty system thus became one of its hallmarks. Marshal Foch recognized that it was not a peace, but at best an armistice for the next 20 years. Although another war was not preordained, many problems remained, and—as the minorities problem in the new states of east central and southeastern Europe showed—the causes of the outbreak of war in 1914 had by no means been eliminated. There could be no talk of a stable system of collective security that could apply sanctions against any aggressor. Nor had the experience of total war by any means delegitimized war as a policy instrument. In the end, Lloyd George and Clemenceau also had to concede that the treaties were not the end of the story, but marked no more than the beginning of efforts to secure the peace. What future politicians would make of them was anyone's guess.[60] When Lloyd George compared the Paris conference of 1919 with the one in Vienna in 1814–1815, he concluded, "You then had to settle the affairs of Europe. It took eleven months. But the problems at the Congress of Vienna, great as they were, sink into insignificance compared with those which we have had to attempt to settle at the Paris Conference. It is not one continent that is engaged— every continent is affected."[61]

After the wartime experiences of death and destruction on an unprecedented scale, of revolution, civil war, devastated economies, and above all shattered certainties, the wish to return to some political normality was certainly great—but this very normality had largely contributed to the outbreak of war in 1914. High though the hopes had been that it would be the war to end all wars, they soon had little to do with the reality—the general exhaustion after 1918 was too extensive.

Economic criticisms of the treaties did not take long to appear. The Italian diplomat Count Carlo Sforza wrote in 1920, "The treaties of 1919 have multiplied the barriers between nations. In 1914 we had 24 customs areas and 13 monetary systems. Today we have 35 customs areas and 27 monetary systems. That means 6000 kilometers of new customs boundaries—at a time when industrial concentration and labor rationalization are increasingly the essential prerequisite of progress."[62] The most important critique came from John Maynard Keynes, whose book *The Economic Consequences of the Peace* took issue with the French reparations strategy in particular. In essence, he argued that the European states could not recover without deeper economic integration, but that Allied reparation demands, high debt levels, and high inflation (especially in Germany) stood in the way of this. Keynes thus reinforced the British government's growing skepticism about the treaty and its practicability. Two years later, in *A Revision of the Treaty*, he turned his attention to the United States and criticized the fact that there was no

Map 14.
A Political Map
of the World
after 1918

economic master plan for the postwar period—as there would be after 1945 with the Marshall Plan. He clearly saw that the problem of inter-Allied debt reached far beyond a problem of foreign trade balances. To be sure, the Dawes and Young plans would show that the United States was making an effort to solve the reparations problem at an economic and monetary level. But the basic problem remained: the liberal doctrine on which the

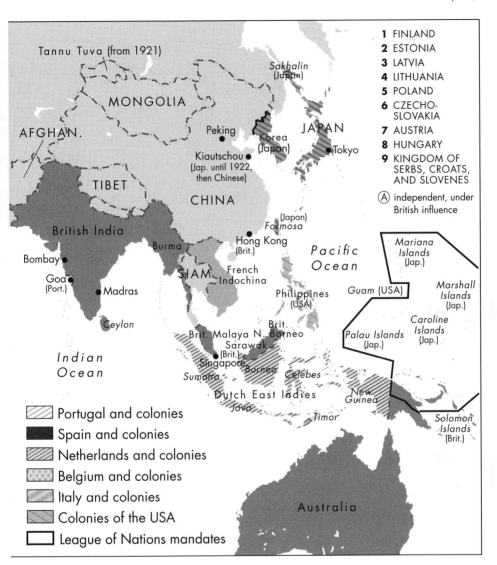

1 FINLAND
2 ESTONIA
3 LATVIA
4 LITHUANIA
5 POLAND
6 CZECHO-
   SLOVAKIA
7 AUSTRIA
8 HUNGARY
9 KINGDOM OF
   SERBS, CROATS,
   AND SLOVENES

Ⓐ independent, under
   British influence

Portugal and colonies
Spain and colonies
Netherlands and colonies
Belgium and colonies
Italy and colonies
Colonies of the USA
League of Nations mandates

Paris treaty system rested was not suited to the postwar economies. This was less a result of the peace treaties, as Keynes assumed, than of the war itself and the complex transition from a wartime to a peacetime economy. The European economies lost many of their prewar markets to new industries that had arisen in the war, but also to the economic powers that had profited most from the war: the United States and Japan.[63]

France emerged as a precarious victor from the war and the new peace-time order. The Third Republic had proved itself in the war, but the fact that leading politicians had expected a social and political revolution in the event of defeat pointed to a considerable degree of self-doubt. The human casualties and massive destruction inside the country continued to have their effect, leaving behind a widespread sense of demographic and military vulnerability. The population losses resulting from the war made nearly all subsequent governments focus more sharply on pronatalist policies, until demography came to appear the most important strategic resource for the future. Internationally, the country was in a difficult position. In contrast to Machiavelli's dictum that a vanquished enemy must be either wiped out or rehabilitated, the Versailles peace treaty produced neither the one nor the other outcome. At any event, Germany remained strong enough to hope for revisions to the treaty and humiliated enough to make this a "reason of state." The end of the Habsburg monarchy and the paralysis of Russia entailed a strengthening of Germany that could hardly be overlooked for long. Against this background, there was growing doubt in France as to whether the victory justified its countless war dead and its ruined economy. The recovery of the lost provinces certainly did not by itself compensate for the political insecurity. Yet in the end, French politicians clung to conventional nation-state interests defined in terms of territory: they demanded the return of Alsace-Lorraine and insisted on having their own sphere of interest in Syria. Not by chance did a serious crisis develop between Wilson and the French leadership with regard to the Saar question and sovereignty over the region.[64]

France's obsession with security vis-à-vis Germany expressed itself on a number of levels: in the encouragement of separatist tendencies in the Rhineland and southwestern Germany, in the symbolic humiliation of Germany through the deployment of black colonial soldiers in occupied zones, in the dogged insistence on reparation payments, and in the bilateral agreement with unstable successor states of the Habsburg monarchy, particularly Poland and Czechoslovakia. But in view of the cooling of political relations with Britain—which distanced itself more and more from the treaty after 1920—it was ultimately the Maginot Line that promised reliable protection against the neighbor in the east: it symbolized an emphasis on defense and fixed warfare, and a fixation on the status quo even in the figurative sense, resulting in the rejection of modern weapons technologies such as the tank.[65]

Thus, a subjective perception of internal and external threats to national security, a sense of latent weakness despite the victory in 1918, became a distinguishing feature of the interwar period. Jules Cambon—the chairman of the French ambassadors' conference, who before 1914 had served as ambassador in Berlin and in 1919 chaired the commissions on Poland and Czechoslovakia at the peace conferences—confided in 1921 to a younger colleague: "Young man, remember this: in the immediate future the difficulty will be to slide France reasonably smoothly into the ranks of the second-rate powers to which she belongs."[66]

In 1919, Britain was one of the undisputed victors of the war, but there too fractures were in evidence. The collapse of the Liberal Party was gathering speed, in parallel to the Labour Party's rise to become a potential governing party, and both developments went back to wartime changes in the political spectrum. Most significantly, the foundation of the Irish Free State in 1922 signified a relatively greater loss of territory than Germany had suffered in 1919. After the war, London had to face the growing self-assertiveness of the Dominions, and the presence of the Australian and South African prime ministers at the peace conference was more than just symbolic. The war had changed the relationship between empire and mother country: in the Dominions it had fueled a nation-building process that could no longer be reconciled with their traditional image as junior partners. New crisis symptoms had also begun to appear in Britain's growing economic and monetary dependence on the United States and in the danger of imperial overreach. Violent unrest in post-1918 Egypt and India, together with an increasingly evident discrepancy between pretensions to rule and limited resources, undermined the credibility of British policy in the Near East and the Indian subcontinent.[67]

The end of the Continental European empires and Germany's overseas colonies by no means entailed that imperial rule was petering out. Indeed, the British and French colonial empires reached their maximum extent after the war. In Africa, France gained territory in the Congo in 1922–1923 as well as 450,000 square kilometers of Togo and Cameroon, with their more than three million inhabitants. It also took over 150,000 square kilometers in the Middle East, with a further three million people. But France had fewer strategic and economic objectives than Britain in the region, and supporters of overseas expansion were far less incensed by Clemenceau's willingness to withdraw from the Mosul oilfields than by the relinquishment of the holy sites in Palestine, where the issue was more about French prestige and civilization, and the vision of a *France plus grande* in the north, south, and east of the Mediterranean. At any event, like Britain, France had to recognize its hopeless military inferiority in the Middle East. Its military concentration on the Rhine frontier, always in doubt, meant that its global room for maneuver remained limited.[68]

The hopes invested in Woodrow Wilson had been especially high in Italy since 1917; a veritable Wilson myth came into being, which colored perceptions of the United States in general. But this tendency came to an end in Spring 1919, when the dispute over Fiume led to deep disappointment over the terms of the peace settlement. In September 1919, Gabriele d'Annunzio captured the city with his band of irregulars; then it became a free state in 1920 under the terms of the Rapallo treaty between Italy and Yugoslavia and was finally incorporated into Italy under the Treaty of Rome in 1924. As a consequence, the Italian public became alienated from the peace treaty. The passage from idealization to disillusionment with America also weakened the governing liberals and discredited the legacy of the Risorgimento, promoting the negative countermyth of a *vittoria mutilata,* a truncated victory, which the Fascists were able to exploit for their own purposes.[69] Social tensions and deep political disenchantment combined with an all the more aggressive irredentist nationalism and cult of violence to strengthen the position of Mussolini and the Fascists, who argued that France and Britain had not adequately recognized Italy's wartime sacrifices and achievements. This accusation spread during the peace conference among all Italian political groupings, eventually even among democratic interventionists who defended Wilson's position. At the same time, the course of the peace conference alienated large sections of the American public from events and developments in Europe.[70]

Hungary illustrated more starkly than almost any other country the polarizing effects of the Paris peace conference. The downfall of the Habsburg monarchy had given rise, after a brief interlude of bourgeois government, to 133 days of a Soviet regime under the Transylvanian Béla Kun, who had

been released in 1918 from captivity in Russia and returned home as a supporter of the Bolsheviks. Many commissars in this short-lived dictatorship
were Jewish, like Kun himself. Their key focus was the creation of council
rule in line with the Soviet model in Russia, and they also planned a state
takeover of Jewish property. But their wrestling with the social consequences
of the war, together with the impending loss of large chunks of territory
under the terms of the peace treaty, ended in the establishment of violent
revolutionary tribunals. The successor regime of Admiral Horthy, the last
commander of the Austro-Hungarian navy, who marched into Budapest in
November 1919, continually referred to this experience of Soviet rule to
stigmatize liberalism and Bolshevism on ethnic-religious grounds, by characterizing both ideologies as Jewish. Béla Kun's Red terror was thus succeeded by a White terror that far right paramilitary groups and Horthy's
new national army directed against farmers, communists, and Jews—long
before the violently anti-Semitic Arrow Cross appeared on the scene. The
struggle against the Trianon treaty of June 1920, in which Hungary lost
nearly two-thirds of its former territory and more than half of its former
population (which had been subject to increasingly aggressive Magyarization
before 1918), then became the overriding objective of Horthy's policies. The
restoration of a Greater Hungarian state became associated with the aim of
isolating the Jewish urban middle classes, who were blamed for the defeat
and the political weakening of Hungary. Hungary thus became the first state
after the war to introduce a *numerus clausus* restricting the number of Jewish
university students.[71]

But the shock waves from the Paris peace conference reached far beyond
Europe. Spring 1919 marked a distinctive global moment—a negative counterpart, as it were, to the hopes and expectations that President Wilson had
identified in Spring 1917. As we have seen, national uprisings seemingly independent of one another began to take place in various parts of the world. In
early March, Korea witnessed a major revolt against the Japanese colonial
rule in place since 1910, while a wave of riots and demonstrations against
British rule gripped Egypt; then protests by the Indian national movement were
repressed by the British and reached a climax on April 13 at Amritsar. In China,
May 1919 marked the highpoint of the New Culture Movement, which promoted national renewal and an orientation to Western modernity, while also

advocating resistance to Japan's imperial order in East Asia.[72] The reason why these movements and uprisings coincided with one another in time had to do with disappointment that Wilson's program of national self-determination was not being applied in their own countries. After the press and propaganda there had turned Wilson into a political savior, the ensuing letdown was bitter indeed. The result was a global moment of anticolonial nationalism, which took the idea of national self-determination as its common point of reference. But the war and Wilson served more as catalysts of a longer process with political traditions that varied from country to country.[73]

In 1919, the Japanese political leadership demanded acceptance of the principle of racial equality in return for its recognition of the League of Nations. This clear signal of its interest in cooperation with the West, avoiding further international isolation, underlined the pro-Western, outward-looking orientation of the country's prime minister, Takashi Hara. The war had greatly increased the focus within Japan on its great power status and its overcoming of a sense of inferiority as a nonwhite power. But there were also economic aspects to its demands, such as the lifting of American and British curbs on immigration from Japan.[74]

Although they were among the victorious powers, not least economically, both Japan and the United States were shaken by internal disturbances. The war had enshrined the position of the United States as the world's largest creditor nation, but demobilization and the changeover to peacetime production triggered an economic crisis that in the South and in the industrial centers of the Midwest led to a wave of racial conflicts and social unrest. Anti-German hysteria was superseded by a new enemy-image—the Bolshevik menace—and the danger that eastern European migrants might bring it with them across the Atlantic led to a succession of measures tightening the immigration laws. Furthermore, many veterans and war invalids were disappointed by what they saw as a failure to recognize their war service—as late as 1932, in the middle of the Depression, 30,000 veterans organized a two-month march on Washington to draw attention to their plight. President Herbert Hoover's use of the army against the demonstrators caused his popularity to plummet and played a considerable role in the election of Franklin Delano Roosevelt later that year.[75]

The main problem of the new order after 1918 was the claim of leading players to be preventing a future war by a system of norms and statutes that remained inherently contradictory. Whereas President Wilson strove for a complete reorganization of Europe and the world under the aegis of democratic, universalist values, Britain stuck to its imperial rule and France to its territorial and economic war aims against Germany. At the same time, public opinion all around the world—far beyond the states that had entered the war in 1914—played a role in the peace negotiations that had never existed before in history. This increased the pressure on the delegations to achieve results in a fairly narrow time frame. What limited the flexibility of future politicians and diplomats was a direct legacy of the war; namely, the idea that the numerous provisions of the treaty should create a fundamentally unassailable postwar order. This led to the setting of high barriers for peaceful, gradual modifications in the future. Nevertheless, for all the shortcomings of the treaties signed between 1919 and 1923, a second world war was not inevitable so long as a new generation of politicians managed to find a compromise reconciling security interests, multilateralism, and flexibility—and to understand international treaties not as eternal truths or an outlet for political moralism, but as part of a time-sensitive quest for peace that had to be continued in the years ahead.

9

MEMORIES

Fragmented Experiences and Polarized Expectations

ON FEBRUARY 1, 1918, a French soldier was apprehended at the Gare des Brotteaux in Lyon; he came from a German prisoner-of-war camp, but had no military pass or other document to indicate his identity. He had evidently lost his memory. Although what he said was largely incomprehensible, it was possible to work out his name: Anthelme Mangin. After an odyssey from one hospital or psychiatric clinic to another, he ended up at a home in Rodez, in the southern French department of Aveyron. Its medical director, Dr. Fenayrou, took an interest in the unknown soldier and started a national campaign to trace his family. After Mangin's photo was published in the leading French newspapers, more than 300 families came forward claiming to recognize in him a lost husband, brother, son, or grandson—an example of the power of fictitious kinship at a time when hundreds of thousands were in mourning.[1]

Twenty of these families eventually competed with one another in court over the identity of Anthelme Mangin, so that the decision fell first to the authorities and finally to the courts. The hearings lasted a whole year. In the end, it proved possible to establish the man's identity when he paid a visit to Saint-Maur-sur-Indre in 1934 and was able to find his way alone from the station to his parents' home. Yet the legal tug-of-war continued for another four years. After Lucy Lemay filed an objection on the grounds that she was sure Mangin was her missing husband, a lengthy review of the case got underway. Only in 1938, when Pierre Monjoin finally received legal conformation that the unknown soldier was in fact his son Octave, did the latter return home to his father and brother. Two months later, both his father and brother lost their lives in an accident, whereupon Octave disappeared once and for all into a care home. After the Vichy government massively cut back on funding psychiatric facilities, the situation at such homes worsened considerably in 1941–1942, and on September 10, 1942, France's best-known unknown soldier died as a result of serious undernourishment. Interred at first in a mass grave, he was exhumed in 1948 and reburied in a ceremony attended by many veterans of the two world wars. In 2003, the granddaughters of one of the petitioners from the 1930s demanded a further exhumation and the carrying out of a DNA test.[2]

The case of Monjoin, who spent 20 years in care homes after 1918, then finally returned home, and spent his last 4 years in institutions following the death of his last two family members, was certainly very striking. But the endless legal battles over his person reflected a cruel burden left behind by the war. In France alone, at least 250,000 soldiers were recorded as missing after 1918: many of those killed in action, especially in the first weeks of the war, were not listed amid the retreats and horrific casualties, and the introduction of new heavy artillery meant that many corpses were impossible to identify. The associated trauma for many families—no evidence of death, no corpse, no final certainty, no definite place to grieve—was transposed to the whole society, as we can see from the huge resonance that Monjoin's fate had as a symbol for all the unknown soldiers. For years, stories about men who suddenly reappeared from the dead continued to fuel hopes of finding lost husbands, sons, or brothers. And the press's inflation of the numbers of missing from a quarter-million to 400,000 pointed to a deeper problem. The sometimes obsessional idea that a soldier might suddenly show up again also revealed uncertainty about how to cope with the sacrifice of the war, a fear of forgetting the dead too soon and devaluing their sacrifice, of returning too hastily to the everyday routine of the postwar period. The desperate courtroom battles over Monjoin, more than 20 years after he was taken into custody in Lyon, and the enormous public interest in the case testified to a deep and persistent sense of insecurity.

This episode illustrates how little individual experience was confined to the official commemoration of the war, how little personal memories—or struggles over them—necessarily linked up with collective remembrance. The gulf between the official cults of remembrance—which developed soon after the end of the war in countless war memorials, anniversaries, and textbook accounts—and the uniqueness of each individual's experience became an important feature of the interwar period. Official commemoration and individual memory might intersect with each other, but the one never merged into the other.

Even the basic conditions after November 1918 varied widely. Germany had not experienced the war on its own soil, but it had suffered two million dead and a military defeat. Nevertheless, German soldiers were welcomed home as heroes, "unvanquished in the field." The appropriation of the defeat therefore became a difficult process, which left its mark on the cultures of reminiscence. In Britain and the Empire, people mourned more than a million dead, but there too the war had not been fought on home ground. But although most returning soldiers were met by cheering crowds, that was not always the case. Memories of the war differed and began to compete with one another. Irish soldiers who had volunteered for the BEF came back to face an already established cult around the martyrs of the Easter Rising of 1916; their own wartime service was considered less valuable than that of the heroes of the independence struggle, especially in view of the civil war that began in 1918 and lasted until the creation of the Irish Free State in 1922. They did not seem to fit into the new state's culture of remembrance.

In contrast to Germany and Britain, France was directly and massively affected by the war, particularly in the north, which proportionately suffered the highest losses of all the major belligerent countries. But the memory of the war largely excluded the numerous civilian casualties in the occupied territories. Officialdom, but also the veterans associations, presented the ordinary soldier at the front, the *poilu*, as the figure embodying the war. In Belgium, by contrast, the focus was on the more than 20,000 civilian victims and the roughly 40,000 military casualties; the experiences of invasion and occupation mirrored each other. But in the first few months after the war, this dual memory turned with particular force against alleged collaborators, especially women accused of having had relations with German soldiers. In Italy, something like a unifying patriotic cult of the nation-state took shape for the first time in commemorations of the 600,000 war dead. At first, the national mourning overshadowed the enormous political tensions and conflicts, until Fascism took over the cult of the dead heroes and used it for its own purposes.[3]

The picture in eastern Europe was much more complicated. On the one hand, wars and violence continued to have an impact after November 1918; on the other hand, the end of the multinational Russian Empire and the Habsburg monarchy meant that completely new states sprang up with their own remembrance cultures. In many places, the minorities issue translated into particularly tense and difficult remembrance cultures. With Austria-Hungary no longer present as a state context, memories of the war divided along national lines, so that the new political frameworks and the quest for national narratives often had powerful effects. People in Austria and Hungary had to accept defeat and huge losses of territory, while in Czechoslovakia they felt part of a victorious nation. Before long, the official remembrance culture was concentrating on members of the Czechoslovak Legion in Russia: an idealized image of the legionary as a worker and head of a family, who had left the Austro-Hungarian army and formed the core of a national army symbolizing a new state, stood in sharp contrast to those who had sided with the Bolsheviks in Russia in 1918 and become guilty of a second desertion. Such men were branded as traitors and excluded from the nation-building process.[4] Also excluded were all Czechs and Slovaks who had continued fighting in the Habsburg armed forces until November 1918, for a state that no longer existed and whose historical legitimacy had been called into question by the justified claims of the Czechoslovak nation. The commemoration of Italian soldiers who had died fighting in the Austro-Hungarian army ran into similar difficulties; only in 2011 would a plaque in their memory be put up in Trento.[5]

The problem of multiethnic populations and of their distinctive wartime experiences that could not be straightforwardly incorporated into the new states was also evident in Yugoslavia. There the main focus was on the Serbs' exorbitant losses in the war, the occupation of their country, and their image of themselves as a martyr-nation, whereas the wartime experiences of Croats and Slovenes in the Austro-Hungarian army tended to be marginalized. In Poland, too, memories of the world war reflected the historical complexity:

Polish soldiers had fought on the German, Austro-Hungarian, and Russian sides, and the new Polish nation-state contained Ukrainian and Belarussian minorities with their own quite distinctive memories. In Poland, the remembrance culture and the theme of sacrifice and resurrection did not refer only, or even primarily, to the world war, but rather to the war of 1919 / 1920 against Soviet Russia and the border conflicts with Ukraine and Lithuania, which were seen as part of the struggle for national independence. It is true that, in Polish eyes, the world war had been the precondition for the birth of their own state, but it had also become a bitter fraternal struggle among Poles fighting on the different sides. Only a few distinct Polish regiments had fought on the Allied side or in the Austro-Hungarian army.[6]

Against this background, only soldiers who had fought in Polish regiments or in the post-1918 border wars counted unreservedly as national heroes in the Second Republic. The majority of Polish veterans, disparagingly referred to as *zaborczy*, had no place in this positive remembrance. However, membership in one of the international veterans associations, which were founded after 1918 and rapidly spread abroad, could integrate former soldiers into the national memory. These associations, beginning with the Fédération Interalliée des Anciens Combatants in the former Allied countries and expanding after 1925 with the Conférence Internationale des Associations de Mutilés et Anciens Combatants (which included former enemies and was decisively initiated by French and German veterans alike), arose in the context of similar challenges in all postwar societies, where one of their main functions was to rule on the claims of invalids and surviving dependents. The international struggle for social provision thus took its place alongside commemoration of the war and a political commitment to peace, finally enabling the *zaborcy* to enhance their position within postwar Polish society.[7] But their sometimes pacifist stand set them at odds with the growing militarization that came to a head with Piłsudski's putsch, and his foregrounding of the national border wars and the struggle of the Polish legions once more undermined the symbolic capital of the *zaborcy* war veterans. Still, their international networks survived at first, and in the 1930s these would serve as the basis for a policy geared to appeasement.[8]

On the Allied side, official commemorations after the end of the war featured both enthusiastic celebrations of victory and elements of mourning.

Belgium provided a characteristic example of this combination. When King Albert returned to Brussels on November 22, there were some wild scenes celebrating victory on the occasion of a parade by Belgian and Allied troops. But in his final speech there, the king emphasized the sacrifices of the living and the dead and went out of his way to include the civilian victims of the war.

The special features of the world war—the number of casualties, the burying of most of the dead near the front rather than at home, the listing of many casualties as missing because there were no identifiable corpses—marked the remembrance culture that began to take shape in 1919. This was already visible in many European capitals in July 1919 at the victory parades following the end of the peace conferences, when the erection of cenotaphs—empty tombs symbolizing the nameless victims—also represented an attempt to find a formal language for collective remembrance. In Paris, a cenotaph was placed before the Arc de Triomphe in the run-up to the national holiday on July 14, and one thousand veterans of the war marched at the front of the traditional military parade. In London, what was originally intended as a temporary cenotaph—erected on July 19 in the middle of Whitehall—soon became a key place of reference for the public commemoration of the war.

The hallmark of these commemorations was the democratization of sacrifice.[9] It was no longer a question of individual heroes or even particular monarchs or generals—the figures who had stood out in earlier memorials. The social hierarchy of heroism was dispelled, and the true war hero became the unknown, nameless, missing soldier. He would increasingly dominate official ceremonies, at least in most capitals of the former belligerent countries. Memorials to the Unknown Soldier were an expression of the scale of the casualties, but also of the depersonalization of death and the countless missing. Models of this kind were the Memorials to the Unknown Soldier at the Arc de Triomphe in Paris and Westminster Abbey in London, which were put in place as early as 1920. Similar memorials followed in Rome and Washington, DC, in 1921; Brussels, Prague, and Belgrade in 1922; and Bucharest and Vienna in 1923. They were not to be found, however, in Berlin or Moscow. While political differences over the war prevented a consensus in Germany on how to commemorate it, the October Revolution and its destruction of the Tsarist Empire precluded a distinct remembrance culture in Russia, where the oppressive reality of the civil war was another factor standing in its way.[10]

Remembering the war: The Unknown Soldier and the London cenotaph

The cult of the dead reached far beyond the capital cities—and in particular to the former battlefields on the western front. In many places—at the former Fort Douaumont near Verdun, for example—ossuaries were built alongside cemeteries to house the unidentifiable remains of countless soldiers. But often the military cemeteries reproduced the hierarchy of winner and losers; the areas made available for German cemeteries in France and Belgium or for Austro-Hungarian ones in Italy were usually much smaller than those for nationals or for the dead of Allied armies. The return of corpses to their home country posed a major problem. Whereas the British authorities had their dead buried in the vicinity of the front, the French and American authorities allowed the repatriation of corpses that could still be identified. No fewer than 20 percent of the French dead were eventually laid to rest in their hometowns and villages.[11]

The need to have dead soldiers buried at home to ensure a space for individual mourning is evident from many requests lodged with the authorities by wives, mothers, and sisters. Marie Geiger from Leutkirch, in the Allgäu region of southern Germany, wrote a letter to the Kaiser himself on May 12, 1918. Her husband had been killed on the western front on March 22, having served in the 124th Infantry Regiment since August 1914: "Thus, Your Majesty, I would like to beg most humbly if Your Majesty could be of help in transferring my husband's corpse back home . . . since it is a great sacrifice for a happy family to lose the breadwinner on the field of honor." On June 5, the 13th Acting General Command in Stuttgart, to which the Imperial Chamberlain's Office had forwarded the letter, asked the widow to submit another formal request. The outcome of the proceedings cannot be reconstructed from the surviving records.[12]

Numerous local memorials appeared in addition to national sites of mourning and remembrance, carrying the war into everyday life in societies far from any front. In Canada, Australia, and New Zealand, these served not only to remember the country's war dead but also to mark a key period of self-confident nation-building that was no longer limited to the image of a loyal empire. In postwar Anglo-American culture, allusions to the culture of antiquity played a large role in the war memorials. Greek civilization, with its familiar stylistic idioms and ecumenical character, seemed to offer a counterweight to the barbaric reality of the war. The healing of broken bodies and a faith in human resilience were common themes.[13] Again and again, classical devices were used to highlight the healthy, intact human body and the healing power of art.[14] Monumentalism, simplicity, and emotional restraint confined the pain and grief to certain zones of memory while foregrounding the warrior's individual heroism. His heroic sacrifice for all, alluding to themes of classical antiquity, appeared beautiful. War heroes were democratized—as national archetypes, as "Tommies," "Doughboys," or "Anzacs"—and in this way remembrance too tended to become more democratic. Emotional spaces arose in which mourners and the state related to each other. The language of heroism in memorials and commemorative events elevated the triumph of the individual over the anonymity of war and the stoical endurance of injuries. There too, veterans could see themselves not as wounded or survivors, but as heroes with an exceptional spirit of self-sacrifice.[15]

But the reality of the postwar period looked very different for many veterans. Their experiences back home, where they had to fight even for meager

A country fit for heroes? A British veteran and King George V at the Epsom Derby

benefits, did not correspond to the "land fit for heroes" promised by Lloyd George. Fobbed off with rhetorical platitudes, made to appear beggars and to fear the loss of all social protection, they raised their voices in criticism that would echo throughout the interwar period. The gap between expectations and experiences even applied to memories of the war, and many former soldiers referred to this in tones of skeptical irony and bitter disillusionment.[16] The postwar treatment of mentally ill soldiers often provoked clashes in which patients and relatives had to argue with psychiatrists and officials over benefits and the recognition of disabilities. Many sufferers from shell shock, for example, who during the war had been treated in special clinics, were given up as hopeless cases and ended up in state institutions that offered nothing in the way of psychotherapy. At any event, any communication between patients' lawyers and health experts petered out after the war. After a few years, most orderlies and doctors in state institutions no longer saw themselves as dealing with war victims, but treated them as mentally ill patients who happened to have a past in the army.[17]

The plethora of war memorials and mourning rituals and symbols disguised the fact that, in the postwar societies, relatives often found no consolation and were unable to accept the disappearance of their husbands, brothers, or sons. Many developed morbid obsessions; thousands ended up in psychiatric institutions.[18]

Through war memorials, the dead remained present in the society of the living, but also took their place in the political contexts of the time. Largely stereotypical in what they depicted and stated, the memorials in villages and small towns celebrated the heroism of ordinary soldiers. In 1921 an article in the *Weserzeitung* described the ideal type: "The memorial rises up in a sandy spot surrounded by barbed wire. The main body consists of large and small blocks. Cement joints lie on the surface like a network of varicose veins. On the baseplate, at the top of three steps, a shapeless monster with a large stone block for a head. A painted inscription in black letters cut into the stone. The names of the fallen on a recessed granite plate, polished black with gold lettering in the worst village grave style."[19] This alphabetical list became the symbol before which commemorations and local processions took place every year. Schools played a prominent role in these, as children were supposed to carry the regular honoring of the dead into the next generation. Pacifist connotations were nowhere to be found in this remembrance culture; the main focus was on the dead soldiers. Only in Belgium did civilians who died during deportation or were executed by the Germans as alleged *franc-tireurs* become part of the commemorations from the very beginning.

The memory of the war was most polarized in 1920s Germany and east central Europe. The monument erected in 1928 on Vítkov Hill in Prague highlighted the Legionaries as freedom fighters of the new nation-state, combining a museum with a mausoleum to those who died in the struggle for independence. The situation was quite different in Hungary. A Memorial to the Unknown Soldier stood on Heroes' Square in Budapest, but just outside the capital there was another memorial reminding people of the territories lost under the Treaty of Trianon; it soon became a rallying point for all radical irredentists.[20]

In Austria and especially Germany, the polarization of memory deepened existing political antagonisms. The Tannenberg memorial of 1927, in the form of a medieval crusaders' castle, was the largest project of its kind in the interwar period, mainly supported by right-leaning veterans associations and sometimes openly revanchist pro-monarchist groups. Funded by a countrywide donation drive, much of the initiative for it came from East Prussian soldiers' associations, which saw it as part of the struggle against the Versailles "diktat" and the resulting separation of East Prussia from the rest of the Reich. Although the Prussian government did not support the building of the monument, it sporadically contributed funds—as did President Hindenburg, on whose eightieth birthday it was eventually inaugurated. In the end, even the cabinet attended the opening ceremony—despite its annoyance over the exclusion of a Jewish rabbi. Clearly, nationalists tried to use the monument to promote revanchist claims in the east and to combat those allegedly responsible for November 1918.[21]

An attempt to raise a national memorial in central Berlin to the victims of the war ended in failure. The Neue Wache in the capital, originally built by Karl Friedrich Schinkel in 1816–1818 to accommodate the artillery administration and the Royal Life Guard, was until 1918 a site for the changing of the guard and military parades. In 1918 it lost this high-profile military function, but it seemed predestined for remembrance of the war because it was the place from which the mobilization and demobilization orders had been issued. Although thought had been given to the idea on previous occasions, it was only in 1930 that the Prussian government decided to create a site of remembrance there, and because of its national significance the Reich government lent its support. The list of architects who took part in the competition to design the memorial included Peter Behrens, Ludwig Mies van der Rohe, Hans Poelzig, and Heinrich von Tessenow. The winner was Tessenow's minimalist interior: a cube-shaped block of black granite was set up in the middle of the space, together with two candelabras. A gilded oak wreath lay on the altar-like monolith, and a simple inscription "1914 / 18" was embedded in the floor. In an allusion to the Pantheon in Rome, a circular aperture in the ceiling let some daylight into the otherwise crepuscular room.[22] But this very simplicity of form, so different from the monumentalism of the Tannenberg memorial, provoked endless controversy among various political camps, veterans associations, social organizations, and public authorities; so too did the location of the memorial and its inscription. Although Tessenow's Neue Wache, with its language of cool objectivity and recourse to traditional building materials, marked a turning point in the architectonic self-presentation of the Weimar Republic, it did not become an integrative national site of remembrance.[23] By the end of the Weimar Republic, there were probably more local war memorials in Germany than in any other country, most of the supporters and initiators having come from a conservative, nationalist, and in part even pro-monarchist milieu. But this national and local phenomenon deepened the political divide and the polarization of the remembrance culture.[24]

In scarcely any other period in modern times did war, death, and injury mark a postwar period so profoundly.[25] In addition to all the dead and mentally or physically wounded, the mistreated civilians, and violated women, there were millions of grieving widows and orphans and millions of people driven from their homelands. Millions of children and young people had grown up in the war and been socialized into hardship and shortage, knowing what it was like to live in a combat or occupation zone facing an enemy who was continually characterized as barbaric. But what did this lead to? What did it mean that millions of soldiers, each with his individual wartime experiences, now had to be reintegrated into society? Were the postwar societies in general, and young people in particular, necessarily more brutal than before?[26] In the complex reality, wartime experiences did not translate in linear fashion into a general brutalization of the younger generation. The later flood of picture books and movies, war literature and journalism, was important for the generation that had experienced the war as minors rather than active soldiers. But such media did not represent a direct continuation of wartime experiences.

Many factors and contexts determined continuity or discontinuity in the postwar period. For many German students, their personal experience of death and killing did not result in thoroughgoing disillusionment; military ideals and models were by no means discredited. For example, a student battalion formed in Tübingen immediately after 1918 highlighted the continuity of martial or military attitudes in Germany; in contrast, the ideal of soldierly duty lost much of its persuasiveness after 1918 among students in Cambridge. In Britain there was more of a tendency to internationalism, visible in a focus on peace themes and the multinational character of the British Empire, which many saw as a precursor of a League of Nations that would guarantee world peace.

Even more important than actual experiences of war were students' ideas about whether military action made any sense. In Germany, the perception of defeat was so deep and formative that it tended to level out the difference between those who had fought and those who had grown up in the war; picture books, movies, and commemorative events conveyed the same interpretations to both generations, qualifying any idea of a generation gap. German students, however, unlike their counterparts in Britain, were decisively affected by the chain of defeats stretching from November 1918 through the revolution and its threat to middle-class interests, to the Versailles peace treaty and social-economic downgrading as a result of inflation and depression. This succession of experiences prevented their turning away from the military ideals of the war generation, and it made this generation susceptible to political-ideological radicalization.[27]

In France as in Britain, there was no simple continuum of violence leading to a brutalized society after 1918. For teachers who had themselves taken part in the war, the dominant narrative at first was one of patriotic triumph and certainty that the casualties had not been in vain. But these interpretations, which were reflected in official accounts of the war, did not correspond to the individual memories of many teachers and students who returned to schools after 1918. Teachers therefore increasingly distanced themselves from textbook prettifications, which they could not reconcile with their own experiences and which did not meet their need for a space of mourning. Their own narratives resorted neither to triumphalism nor to victory euphoria, but highlighted the enormous costs and sacrifices of the war. In the 1920s, this linked up with the pacifist tendencies in French veterans' associations, often developing into outright criticism of the militaristic educational material and its glorification of the war. Many female teachers played a part in this: they had precious few other opportunities to air their critical view of the war in public, since French suffrage law still did not entitle them to vote.

This development had thoroughly practical implications. Many teachers encouraged exchanges between French and German schools, pen-pal friendships, and the learning of Esperanto. One particular initiative sought to give the anniversary of November 11 a peaceful inflection, instead of the emphasis on military victory. Although this did not succeed, the schoolbook image of the world war did change toward the end of the 1920s, no longer emphasizing heroism and patriotism but focusing on the terrible reality and the appalling scale of the casualties. All younger generations, it was said, had a duty to ensure at all costs that there would be no repetition of the war.[28]

The soldiers returned home, but the shadows of the war accompanied many of them. The Leonhard brothers, Ludwig and August, from the village of Bosen in the Saar, were born in 1893 and 1898 and were drafted into infantry regiments in 1914 and late 1916, respectively. After a brief home leave in April 1917, Ludwig Leonhard was killed on August 26 in the third battle of Flanders. In February 1919, August returned to his native village, where he got to know his brother's wife when she tried to obtain for her son the part of the paternal legacy due to him. In March 1922, August Leonhard married his brother's widow—something that happened in thousands of other families.

In 1925 Kurt Tucholsky wrote that the world war soldier returned as "a thing resembling a fairly good imitation of a human being," and the French writer and former soldier Léon Werth characterized the autobiographically inspired hero of his war novel as a man who, "once released from the war, soon understood that it had not restored him to life intact."[29] Part of the veteran's experience was his struggle for medical recognition: many neurological disorders and psychological problems only appeared after 1918, but as time went by doctors were less and less inclined to relate them to the war, and veterans often had to face the accusation that they were only looking for higher benefit payments. Many French doctors refused to recognize war traumas as the cause of mental disorders, pointing instead to allegedly hereditary defects, acquired weaknesses, or physical manifestations of psychological disturbances.[30]

Whereas male soldiers nevertheless obtained recognition of their physical injuries, this was by no means always the case with women who had volunteered as nurses and experienced the war close up in hospitals at the front. Their war service was scarcely mentioned, let alone recognized, and when they returned home they soon learned that society was eager to revert as quickly as possible to the prewar gender setup. In Britain, after the reform of February 1918, women over the age of 30 were entitled to vote, but most nurses in the Voluntary Aid Detachment had not reached that threshold. It cannot be said that there was much public interest in their fate or acknowledgment of their contribution to the war effort.[31]

The tourist battlefield: publicity poster, Brussels, early 1920s

The battlefield tourism that developed soon after 1918 was another way of remembering the war. The first signs had appeared during the war itself, and Baedeker-style guidebooks were published as early as 1917. Verdun became one major center where imagined horrors and publicity stunts, remembrance and consumption, were never far apart.[32] In 1928 Harry Graf Kessler, the chronicler of the war since August 1914, traveled once again to the Verdun battlefield and was struck by the differences in cemetery design that had far more to do with postwar resources than with shared wartime experiences: "The American dead lay here like billionaires in comparison with the impoverished European casualties in the other cemeteries." He found the anonymity there particularly oppressive: "The two German cemeteries at Consenvoye and Brieulles make a thoroughly bleak and mournful impression. Thousands of black wooden crosses with white, mostly illegible names painted on them, in a scree of heaped little stones without flowers—unloving and desolate. A cemetery worker told me that each downpour washes the names away, so that they have to keep being painted back, or else disappear."[33]

It was difficult for the soldiers' generation to talk about the war; their individual experiences of the battlefield often eluded verbal communication. As time went by, very different remembrance cultures took shape. For people in France, Britain, and Belgium, *la Grande Guerre,* the Great War, or *de Grote Oorlog* is still today a key reference point in their historical understanding of themselves. When the last *poilus* and Tommies died a few years ago, great attention was paid in Canada, Australia, and New Zealand to this moment of transition. It was quite different in Germany, however. Whatever conclusions were drawn there after 1918, and whatever memories remained of the First World War, another, more recent past—the past of the Second World War and the Holocaust—remains uppermost in people's minds. It continues to overshadow the memory of the 1914–1918 period in today's Germany.

10

BURDENS

The First World War and
the Century of Global Conflicts

IN 1923, five years after the end of the world war, Winston Churchill drew a first balance sheet. As First Lord of the Admiralty, the British navy minister, he had been mainly responsible for the Dardanelles campaign and had had to resign his post in 1915; he then fought as a major on the western front, until Lloyd George recalled him and appointed him munitions minister in 1917. In this capacity, he did much to promote the development of tanks as battlefield weapons. Looking back, he was clear about the differences between the world war and all previous wars: "The Great War through which we have passed differed from all ancient wars in the immense power of the combatants and their fearful agencies of destruction, and from all modern wars in the utter ruthlessness with which it was fought. All the horrors of all the ages were brought together, and not only armies but whole populations were thrust into the midst of them." The constant introduction of new weapons broke many taboos: "No truce or parley mitigated the strife of the armies. The wounded died between the lines: the dead moldered into the soil. Merchant ships and neutral ships and hospital ships were sunk on the seas and all on board left to their fate, or killed as they swam. Every effort was made to starve whole nations into submission without regard to age or sex. Cities and monuments were smashed by artillery. Bombs from the air were cast down indiscriminately. Poison gas in many forms stifled or seared the soldiers. Liquid fire was projected upon their bodies. Men fell from the air in flames, or were smothered, often slowly, in the dark recesses of the sea. The fighting strength of armies was limited only by the manhood of their countries. Europe and large parts of Asia and Africa became one vast battlefield on which after years of struggle not armies but nations broke and ran. When all was over, Torture and Cannibalism were the only two expedients that the civilized, scientific, Christian States had been able to deny themselves: and these were of doubtful utility."[1]

Churchill's panorama of horror referred to the legacies of the world war. But what had the war been? What did it bequeath to the twentieth century?

(1) People at the time were immediately aware that the impact of the war was not just a question of the scale of its casualties; the upshot of it all could not be measured by the millions of dead soldiers and civilians. There was something more fundamentally new in the character of the violence. Although unlike in the Second World War, the victims were still mostly soldiers, there was a new dimension of violence against the civilian population, especially in Belgium and northern France, in Serbia, Armenia, and many parts of eastern Europe. The bleeding of areas affected by the war, the ruined cities, factories, streets, and railroads, gave some idea of what future wars might hold in store. Many of the dead were from hitherto dependent peoples of the empires, in regions as different as Poland, India, Africa, and East Asia. And the lingering effects of the war included the army of wounded and the need for long-term public provision for war invalids. It was they who gave a face to the war in peace.

The war had revealed what was possible in the name of the nation and nation-state, and what was possible had become evident in the widespread breaking of taboos and loss of inhibitions. A specific kind of "European socialization," which had developed since the late seventeenth century against a background of religious civil wars, was entering into crisis.[2] That order had been based on the idea of a set of rules to regulate wars, to prevent conflicts from escalating between sovereign states, to channel violence and make it calculable. After the experiences of the French Revolution and the Napoleonic Wars, this order had again been operative in the period between 1815 and 1914—and for a long time the international order had proved flexible in adjusting to new nation-states and imperial outreach. But that epoch came to an end with the First World War. Between August 1914 and November 1918, European countries lost the ability to achieve external and internal peace on their own or to trust that it would continue in the long term. This marked a watershed in the global perception of Europe and the credibility of the international model represented by its states.

The victor of the world war was not a nation, a state, or an empire, and its outcome was not a world without war. The true victor was war itself—the principle of war and the possibility of total violence. In the long run, this weighed all the more heavily because it contradicted a leitmotif that had developed during the war and had for many been a decisive reason to continue it with all possible means. The hope that a last ferocious war had to be waged against the principle of war itself, the confidence that the world war was "the war that will end war," would end in bitter disappointment.[3] For as the world war came to an end, and despite all the rhetoric about a new international order, the principle of war—of violent change through the mobilization of all available resources—actually received a boost that would last long after 1918, not only in the areas of the collapsed Russian, Habsburg, and Ottoman Empires but also outside Europe.

The period immediately after November 11, 1918, already showed that military violence was still a method of choice: to establish or complete new nation-states, as in Ireland and Poland; to help an ideology to victory in a bloody civil war, as in Russia; or to revise the terms of a peace treaty, as in Turkey.[4] What had begun in Summer 1914 as essentially an interstate war branched out in 1917 into new forms of violence, often overlapping with one another, that lasted far beyond the formal end of the war in the west: wars of independence, nation-building wars, ethnic conflicts, and civil wars. These experiences called into question the rigid chronology of the 1914–1918 war. For eastern and southeastern Europe, it was more the period stretching from the Bosnian annexation crisis of 1908 through the Balkan wars of 1912–1913 to the Peace of Lausanne in 1923 that constituted a relative unity.

(2) Whether used against enemy troops or against civilians in occupied zones, the violence of the world war varied in time and space according to particular constellations. For all the excitement over planning and the

new technological or infrastructural developments, violence remained an instrument of domination, whose logic and dynamic repeatedly took it beyond the original political or strategic intentions. Violence was unpredictable, often surprising, and therefore so difficult to contain and channel. But it was not random, since there was a habit of its acceptance, an assumption that the massive use of violence was justified in emergency situations. This explains the link between situational stress and excesses of violence. In the world war, then, violence tended to become total: not only against enemy troops but also against factories and infrastructures, cultural symbols and buildings.[5]

Part of the experience was the anonymity resulting from the use of materials and machines. This produced a distinctive economy of violence, a weighing of the costs of killing and the effectiveness of human beings as means of warfare, which in principle could be calculated in the same way as other battlefield factors. Demographic abstraction, rather than individual casualties, took center stage. But with the mechanization of warfare came strategic disorientation, an invisible enemy, a permanent uncertainty and danger of death, countless bodies blown apart, mourning without corpses. The attraction of physical violence increased as the distance between weapons and the killing zone grew. All this diverted attention from the individual victims. But all the bureaucratization of killing, which made it seem the business of designers, engineers, and other specialists, changed nothing in the highly individual fear felt by survivors or in the grief for the dead.[6]

It was not the instruments of violence as such but their ideologization that contained elements of total war. After the excesses of the wars of religion, the early modern age had witnessed attempts to decriminalize the enemy, to recognize him as a *iustus hostis,* but during the world war they gave way to a moralization of politics and a focus on war guilt. As the war went on, the tendency to absolutize and instrumentalize the antagonism between friend and enemy, loyalty and betrayal, gave rise to more radical expectations and utopian visions of victorious peace and territorial control. Attempts were often made to legitimize ethnic violence—the Armenian genocide, for example, or the mass expulsions of Greeks and Turks—by reference to the right to self-defense. Since the distinction between external and internal foes was less and less clear and anyone could suddenly see himself surrounded by enemies, violence appeared to be an indispensable last resort to ensure survival in hostile surroundings. And the theme of self-defense lived on: in the defeated societies, for example, reference to the continuation of the war in the guise of the peace treaties was often used to justify defensive action even against the state itself, because of its acceptance of the treaty terms. This was a decisive argument for both the radical Right and the radical Left, for Freikorps, vigilante groups, and paramilitary associations.[7]

(3) During the war, a dynamic relationship developed between military fronts and home societies. Although the distinction between the two held up, especially on the western front, the boundary between combatants and noncombatants generally became more porous in occupied territories and the "shatterzones" of the empires after 1917–1918. Totalizing tendencies were apparent in the mobilization of resources and the ever-wider grip of the war state. But that did not amount to total war, as developments in 1918 would show. Although the war effort was stepped up and the violence became more intense, there was no unconditional surrender at the end of the war. The contradictory character of the peace settlement lay not least in the glaring contrast between its symbolic harshness and the fact that Germany, though humiliated, was able to retain its great power status. With regard to eastern and east central Europe and the demise of the Habsburg monarchy, it even came out of the war stronger than it had been in August 1914.

The relationship of the war state to the economy and society certainly changed: it became the crucial instance of mobilization and control. The war state's powers expanded through the occupation of foreign territory and the supply of war provisions, but also by virtue of its mediating role between capital and labor. These new tasks brought new protagonists and styles of politics to the fore. While the traditional monarchies receded more and more into the background, military leaders with lofty political ambitions, such as Hindenburg and Ludendorff in Germany, or charismatic politicians, such as Lloyd George in Britain or Clemenceau in France, appeared to personify modern warfare with its particular challenges and political will to victory. At the same time, however, the state fueled expectations of rational organization and efficient problem solving that often could not be fulfilled in practice or less and less as the war dragged on. Politicization in 1916 as a result of the worsening food supply in Germany and Hungary, when the criminalization of everyday life turned into a crisis of legitimacy, was a particularly striking example.

Totalizing tendencies in wartime societies created temporary opportunities and changes in social status, but the war did not necessarily serve as a vehicle of emancipation. Although the post-1918 return to traditional role models reduced most of the newfound opportunities for women, the war involved a certain repositioning of social groups, most evident in the case of industrial workers and the recognition of trade unions, but also in the relative loss of status of the middle classes. One particularly important result of the war was the projection of social enemy-images onto the political landscape of the postwar period: profiteers and speculators became synonymous with traitors, and behind this lay a fundamental critique of the traditional models of liberalism and capitalism.

In all wartime societies, the criteria of national affiliation and political loyalty became more exacting. Struggle against the external enemy was compounded by widespread suspicion of supposedly hostile aliens—businessmen in Moscow, for example, or artisans in London or Boston whose ancestors came from Germany or Austria-Hungary. The Irish in Britain, Jews in Germany, or left-wingers in a number of countries were also looked upon as disloyal elements who tended to weaken or undermine the national war effort. The result was a practice of inclusion and exclusion, and a sharpening of external and internal enemy-images. Putative threats provoked overreactions, nowhere more so than in Anglo-Saxon countries that had previously been spared the direct effects of war. Social conflicts and economic problems, including the demand for fair burden sharing, showed a striking tendency to become ethnicized: that is, to be viewed in terms of ethnic or racial lines of divide. The war brought a new intensity to social communication, spawning special slangs and vocabularies related to service, duty, and sacrifice or centered on the exigencies of endurance and perseverance. But many of these linguistic expressions of loyalty fell apart as the gap between expectations and experiences widened. For many people, the ever-tighter criteria for national affiliation eventually meant a basic uprooting, a sense of no longer being at home. In this sense, the war may be said to have produced a "utopia," a no-place.

(4) Why did the war not end earlier, despite the evident cost-benefit discrepancy and the many peace feelers put out in and after 1916? It ended only when the exhaustion on one side deactivated the mechanism that had ensured its continuation until then. Part of this mechanism was the openness of the military situation, which until the final weeks made victory seem a possibility for either side and any concession a potentially serious self-weakening. Furthermore, the colossal death toll, the army of invalids, and the host of impecunious widows and orphans made peace without victory seem a bleak and compromising prospect, which would devalue the sacrifices and rob any postwar social-political order of legitimacy. Paradoxical though it may seem, the ever-higher number of casualties barred any way back on all sides. But since the outcome was so unpredictable until late 1918, the eventual defeat came as such a surprise, such an inexplicable turnaround, that many attributed it to treachery behind the lines. This was a critical difference between 1918 and 1945. In May 1945, the unconditional surrender left no room for such constructs; the very principle of the German nation-state was set aside. In 1918, the impression lingered of an unexplained defeat or even of a victory that Germany had been cheated out of at the last minute. This poisoned the postwar political climate. References to a just-missed victory and guilty parties meant withholding acceptance of the defeat and obligating the nation-state to seek a revision of the treaty because only that could give it legitimacy after November 1918 and June 1919.[8] But this prolonged the war in the peace—internally within German society and externally in the context of the international order.

(5) Expectations and experiences diverged more than in any war before or since. Walter Benjamin wrote in 1933, "No, this much is clear: experience has fallen in value, amid a generation which from 1914 to 1918 had to experience some of the most monstrous events in the history of the world. . . . For never has experience been contradicted so thoroughly: strategic experience has been contravened by positional warfare; economic experience, by the inflation; physical experience, by hunger; moral experiences by the ruling powers. A generation that had gone to school in horse-drawn streetcars now stood in the open air, amid a landscape in which nothing was the same

except the clouds and, at its center, in a force field of destructive torrents and explosions, the tiny, fragile human body."[9]

Some generals in Summer 1914 may have doubted the possibility of a short war, but they could not have foreseen the scale of the war in 1916 or the nature of its outcome in 1918. But after 1918 there was a yardstick by which people could measure what was possible in modern warfare. In this way, the war acted as a great accelerator, a laboratory, a "space of potentiality." It seemed to facilitate political and social, but also scientific and technological, developments that many at the time had been unable to imagine. The acceleration also meant a revaluation and inversion of traditional values, both monetary and cultural. Part of the experience of war was thus a fascination with its technical and technological aspects—always in the hope that advances in fields such as gas weaponry or submarine warfare would lead to a breakthrough and final victory.

The reality of the war of materiel, however, soon escaped the justificatory paradigm of the nation at war. New thinking switched to coolly objective categories: the efficient use of resources, casualty ratios, per capita costs of killing, and so on. Demography, not the democratic nation, became the most important strategic resource—and its heroes were not political leaders or parliamentarians but self-appointed architects of the war, administrators of killing, and social engineers. Propaganda aside, the much-staged patriotism of Summer 1914 was soon overlaid with a cult of objectivity and with a sense of micro-societies struggling to survive at the front and at home; habits of endurance came to overshadow situational patriotism. This also changed the character of nationalism, which after the war became associated with a culture of violent empowerment, combining the mobilization of political, economic, and social resources with a tense coexistence of regressive cultural concepts and a progressive enthusiasm for technology.

(6) The war unleashed a succession of ever-rising expectations. This was apparent in the early strident debates on war aims and in self-images and enemy-images that became ever more radical as the casualties mounted. Players on all sides promised to mobilize new forces and to win new allies, whether among national movements in the multinational empires or among relatively new nation-states, which in the case of Italy, Greece, Bulgaria, or Romania sought to expand their territory and thereby complete the process

of nation-building. Hopes that participation in the war might change their place in the imperial configuration were part of this same context—which in the Habsburg monarchy came down to federalization with a greater degree of autonomy, and in the British Empire to home rule, dominion status, or outright independence. In the end, the appearance of President Wilson on the scene decisively strengthened and globalized this dynamic of diverse and often contradictory expectations—among Poles and Italians, Arabs and Indians, as well as in many Asian societies. The war again seemed an opportunity for worldwide restructuring in the name of universal principles, a chance to overcome imperial domination. The concept of national self-determination fueled manifold expectations of a comprehensive recasting of the European and global order. The entry of the United States into the war, at a point when the military, social, economic, and monetary exhaustion of the European belligerent countries had become all too obvious, decisively contributed to the elevation of Wilson into a kind of messianic savior-figure. Clearly, though, his policies led to a final surge of contradictory and ultimately incompatible expectations.

Such was the basic problem of the Paris peace treaties and the related attempts to create a new international order. For the hopes pinned on Wilson since 1917, and his media impact in South America, Asia, Egypt, India, and elsewhere, ended in bitter disappointment. The war constantly gave rise to excessive expectations, but since the postwar order blocked them (in China, Egypt, or India) or only partially fulfilled them (in Italy, for example), an unpredictable chain of disillusionment stretched far beyond the immediate victors and losers. This too sharpened debate after 1918 over the future viability of political and social models—liberalism and parliamentarism as much as capitalism and colonialism.

(7) The world war was a period of intensive conversion processes, involving transformations, reversals, and reinterpretations. This applied first of all to the idea of converting space into time, of obtaining a temporal advantage through the control of space, as in the British naval blockade or the Russian retreats of 1915. Germany, in contrast, faced the spatial problem of having to fight on two fronts, and it tried to solve this through the Schlieffen Plan in 1914 and again through its operations in the narrow time frame after March 1918. The military hope was that an ever-greater application of force

in a restricted space would result in a breakthrough and a return to a war of movement.

But the war led to many other transformations: the quantity of casualties, for example, produced a new quality in the status of war victims. The sacrifice of victimhood could be converted into political and social capital, into claims to political recognition and social participation, equal rights and social care. The war therefore strengthened a variety of negotiation processes; the diplomatic bargaining of neutral countries at the international level was mirrored by political attempts at the national level to translate loyalty into autonomy or independence, as the cases of Czechs and Poles, Irish and Indians, but also African and Asian colonial soldiers, eloquently highlighted.

Other important conversion processes involved the passage from war to revolution or from interstate war to civil war, as well as the translation of war regimes into new languages of loyalty, service, duty, and sacrifice. A major effect of the latter was the conversion of socially unequal burdens and economic distribution crises into ethnic-religious, national, or racial lines of conflict. This process was clearly visible from 1915–1916 on in the multiethnic empires, but also in other societies—where profiteers and speculators were equated with Jews, for example, or where food supply crises in the Habsburg monarchy were attributed to national egotism on the part of the Hungarians.

(8) The war called traditional concepts of political order into question—without putting a new model in their place. One of the complexities of the postwar period was thus a tense and often conflictual rivalry among new utopian visions. Liberalism, the substrate of the long nineteenth century, found itself on the ideological and political defensive, for it was precisely liberals who most acutely felt the wartime consequences of inclusion and exclusion in the name of national affiliations and loyalties; of the reign of suspicion, controls, monitoring, and coercion. One of the more sobering impressions was that the space for social pluralism and the private sphere of the individual were shrinking all the time. The war brought it home more and more how quickly and easily war states and emergency regulations could suspend basic rights fought for and won over decades. Another lesson for liberals was the way in which the war had delegitimized dynasties and monarchies, nation-states and empires, providing the ground for a

dynamic of violent revolutionary change in the name of new models of political order.

Particular antagonisms developed against liberalism—not in the form of specific critiques, but as systematic ideological oppositions. Nor was it only Germany that witnessed the development of war socialism and integrative conceptions of community, or only Britain that demonstrated the effects of compulsion and conscription by an ever-expanding state. Of special importance was the alternative between German-style war states, with their strong extra-constitutional and politically uncontrolled powers for the military, and the British or French model of parliamentary rule.

The rivalry between Wilsonian and Leninist utopias gave rise to confusion and insecurity, but the historical situation itself was open-ended; it created new free spaces and fired people's imagination in various ways. An example of this is the "either Rome or Moscow" discussion in Germany, which developed as part of the search for new geostrategic and cultural orientations. The Frankfurt writer and journalist Alfons Paquet saw no future for the Christian West that he identified with Rome; it no longer had a spiritual message to convey, having unleashed the world war with its technological civilization. The world-historical opposite was the Russian Revolution: "On the bedrock of Rome, the peoples of Europe have worked national life up into the greatest discord. . . . A new morality is taking shape under the spiritual influences of the awakening East."[10] It was no accident that a truly positive utopianism came into existence only with the First World War: the sociologist Karl Mannheim, for example, described it as future oriented, in contrast to ideology, which was addicted to the past.[11]

(9) A changed vision of politics came out of the First World War, as the example of Germany clearly illustrates. In "Politics as a Vocation," a lecture first given in 1918, Max Weber historicized the traditional conceptions of legitimate rule based on monarchs, dynasties, and empires and then emphasized—not least against liberals—the masses and democracy as the new factors conditioning politics in nation-states. He demanded a new analytic quality and rational purpose in politics: "Whoever wants to engage in politics at all, and especially in politics as a vocation, has to realize these ethical paradoxes. He must know that he is responsible for what may become of himself under the impact of these paradoxes. . . . He lets himself in for

the diabolical forces lurking in all violence. . . . He who seeks the salvation of his soul, of his own and of others, should not seek it along the avenue of politics, for the quite different tasks of politics can only be solved by violence."[12] In contrast to this attempt to replace normative conceptions with an ethics of responsibility in political action, others vehemently rejected the concept of politics altogether with its allegedly Western connotations. In this sense, following the hiatus of the First World War, Max Weber and Thomas Mann represent mutually antagonistic interpretations of a sped-up reality, whose transformations could no longer be expressed using traditional semantics. This was apparent precisely in their contrasting attempts to define an adequate conceptual approach to politics. Mann saw in politics a contempt for the intellect: "Politics makes people rough, vulgar, and stupid. Envy, impudence, covetousness, is all it teaches. . . . I do not want the parliamentary and party economic system that causes the pollution of all national life with politics. . . . I do not want politics. I want objectivity, order, and decency."[13]

But the debate on the essence of the political after the experiences of the world war also included other positions. According to Carl Schmitt in 1927, the "real political distinction" was between "friend and enemy." Only this made possible the conceptual definition without which there could be no criteria in the forms, processes, and contents of politics. All political concepts drew on this antagonistic opposition, whose "ultimate consequence" manifested itself "in war or revolution." But if the political reverted to the friend-enemy paradigm, with war as the "most extreme realization of enmity," then it could be argued that the permanent possibility of war was the precondition of the political itself: "The political does not reside in the battle itself, which possesses its own technical, psychological, and military laws, but in the mode of behavior which is determined by this possibility, by clearly evaluating the concrete situation and thereby being able to distinguish correctly the real friend and the real enemy." Thus, a world in which the "possibility of war" was "utterly eliminated" would be "a world without the distinction of friend and enemy and hence a world without politics."[14]

Part of the legacy of the war was the tension between nationalism and internationalism. All European protagonists in the conflict embraced the principle of the nation and the nation-state to win new allies, and in each case territorial ambitions drove the decision to join the war.[15] It also aroused contradictory expectations, which people could not shake off after the end of the war. Thus, not only hopes of political participation but also full-fledged nationalist horizons took shape, especially in the societies of the multinational empires. This explains Tomáš Masaryk's work in exile in London and the United States, the German support for Ukrainian and Finnish nationalists, the competition between Germans and Russians for Polish support in return for a promise of extensive national autonomy, the support of London and Paris for Palestinian and Arab independence movements against the Ottoman Empire, but also the British fears of Ottoman plans to stir Indians into revolt against British rule.

After the war, an ethnic-national model caught on in the new states, even though in most of the affected territories it was not possible to draw clear ethnic boundaries. Complex minority problems were a consequence. From the 1920s, German-speaking minorities in east central Europe became a key factor in German foreign policy and its efforts to revise the Versailles treaty. The new states in the region appealed to Wilson's principle of national self-determination, but they also contained large ethnic groups that did not see themselves as part of the nation in question, or were not seen by the state as part of it. This ethnicization of the idea of statehood entailed inadequate safeguards for minorities, since the new nation-states regarded the guarantees in the Paris treaties as unacceptable interference in their newly won sovereignty.

Wilson's hoped-for peace settlement under the aegis of democracy and national self-determination proved to be fragile: the nation-state did not become the active core of collective security; the International of peace remained a chimera. The League of Nations failed as the forum of a new security culture, because at no point could it offer a significant counterweight to the aggression and revanchist ambitions of nation-states. Indeed, by excluding the defeated countries at the outset, it actually encouraged forms of revisionist politics that deviated from its statutes. But the other international utopia also remained in play. The Communist International did not become the institution stabilizing international class solidarity, but rather the instrument of ideological polarization within European societies and the world as a whole.

Nevertheless, the war gave a definite impetus to the internationalization of such problems as the integration and repatriation of refugees and prisoners of war. In eastern Europe, more than a million prisoners of war were confronted with the fact that their home state had simply ceased to exist and that successor states were neither able nor willing to concern themselves with their release and repatriation. These issues stretched across national boundaries, and the activities of the League of Nations and other organizations such as the Red Cross unfolded in this context.

More important than this legacy and the international cooperation to overcome it was the utopian dimension of internationalism, its promise of an end to war between states. The abstract line from individual through family and nation to a single humanity was already a major theme for many people during the war. In 1916 Ernst Joël referred "to the paradoxical fact today . . . that the community of the truly patriotic is an international, supranational" community.[16] Henri Barbusse, the author of the savagely critical war novel *Le Feu*, emphasized in 1918: "Humanity instead of nation. The revolutionaries of 1789 said: 'All Frenchmen are equal.' We should say: 'All men.' Equality demands common laws for everyone who lives on earth."[17] This hope that the war and its gigantic sacrifices should not have been in vain, that they should lead to the creation of a new global order, has still not lost its normative claim today. But no one will claim that humanity, however much closer it has become, is a real subject of action. The disappointment of global hopes—"a war that will end war"—became a basic experience for people living in the twentieth century. Recent attempts to define a "global domestic politics" in contrast to the plural, state-centered foreign politics is an indication that the problems have shifted but not been solved. Reinhart Koselleck remarked in this regard, "Where wars used to be waged, civil wars are now unleashed."[18] There is still no end to the violence—on the contrary.

(11) The war marked the end of the classical European pentarchy as new global players appeared on the scene in the shape of the United States and Japan. This occurred not as a simple dissolution, a kind of *translatio imperii* in the shadow of war, but as a complex and contradictory overlapping process. The end of the Continental European empires and the maximization of the British and French colonial empires, as well as the transition from

zones of imperial rule to "imperial overstretching," were part of the legacy of the world war. Above all, the war left behind long-term zones of violence in eastern, east central, and southeastern Europe, where the accelerated collapse of state structures resulted in cycles of violence, expulsion, and civil war. There, mistrust of the staying power of political systems and the stability of personal lifeworlds, together with fears that violence might break out at any time, became the signature mark of the twentieth century. Long-term zones of conflict arose out of the collapsing land empires: they are still there today in the societies of former Yugoslavia, the Middle East, and Kurdish areas. The rise of political Islam after the end of the Ottoman Empire and the demise of the caliphate are other legacies of the war.

(12) Anyone who wishes to understand the First World War will do well not to treat it as a chronological block with a simple "before and after"; consideration of the range of diversity and difference thresholds is enough to cast doubt on the idea of a simple continuum. This war, seen from within the time of those who experienced it, is a particularly striking piece of evidence for the openness of the "future past" tense of history. At best, therefore, even in retrospect a degree of uncertainty remains about the outcome of things that had hitherto seemed familiar.[19]

In this perspective, it is too simplistic to see the First World War as the end of the nineteenth century and the beginning of the twentieth—for it always had elements of both continuity and discontinuity. The generation of frontline combatants might have become idealized targets for political-ideological mobilization, but for all their burdens, that did not mean an ongoing brutalization of all societies in the interwar period. There was no straightforward continuum from the trenches to the regimes of ideological violence in the 1920s and 1930s. The war did not simply continue in calls for a revision of the peace settlement; numerous veterans, as in France after 1918, rejected war in principle on the basis of their own experiences. What did change was how the potential for violence was seen against the background of a new kind of perplexity, an age of fractures that made it necessary to come up with new categories. No new stable order, whether social, political, or international, was discernible after 1918. But the new models of the Bolsheviks or the Italian Fascists turned unmistakably against the liberal legacy of the nineteenth century, not least in their propensity to violence and terror. This had to do with the diverse experiences of the world war, the passages from interstate war to revolution and civil war, as well as with the disappointed expectations common in many societies. At any event, in 1930 the model of the liberal-constitutional state and parliamentary government seemed to have no future.

After 1945, the history of unfettered violence amid the catastrophes and disintegration of the first half of the century gave way, at least in Europe, to a peaceful age marked by Cold War stability and the advent of democratic mass society, first in the west and after 1989–1991 also in the east. It seemed as if the second half of the century was being used to heal the wounds inflicted since August 1914. When the last surviving soldiers of the Great War died a few years ago, when the transition from communicative recollections to cultural memories was nearing completion, the public attention given to this temporal marker reflected a deeper layer of experience. The fact that this was much more intense in Britain and France than in Germany had historical reasons: it pointed to a continuing tendency in Germany for the Second World War and the Holocaust to be superimposed on the memory of the First World War; there the First World War is not the past but the pre-past. For a moment, the death of the last *poilu* and Tommy made visible those strata of time in which the earlier shines through in the later: that is, in our necessary knowledge of the essentially cruel and destructive history of violence, of what human beings can do to one another in modern warfare. That was and is not simply a deposited history; it is precisely not a pre-past, but an understanding of how we have arrived in the present.

At the end of *The Magic Mountain,* Thomas Mann takes leave of his hero Hans Castorp on the battlefield and asks whether "out of this worldwide festival of death, this ugly rutting fever that inflames the rainy evening sky all around, . . . love will someday rise up."[20] When Mann's children had to cancel their performance of *Pandora's Box* in 1914 because war had just broken out, a real box of horrors was let loose on Europe and the world: "At that very moment, a swarm of evils rushed out and spread in a flash over the earth. . . . And now misery in all its forms filled land, air, and sea; all manner of fevers laid siege to the earth, and death, which used to creep up slowly on mortals, quickened its step."[21] Many false paths, countless victims, and painful starts would be required before the extremes of violence unleashed in August 1914 could be trapped and bound again, and transformed with difficulty into a peaceful international order. Wherever this order is endangered, internally or externally, we are still today heirs of that war.

APPENDIX

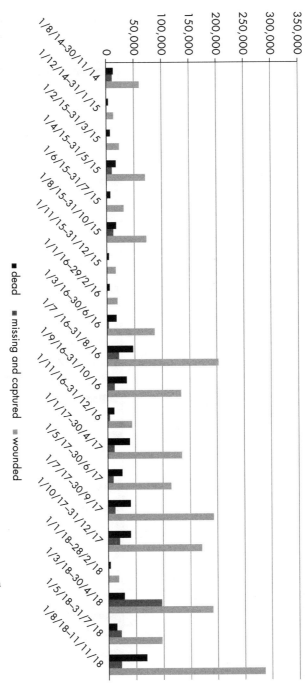

British and Empire losses on the western front, 1914–1918. Dates are in day / month / year format.

From McRandle and Quirk, *The Blood Test Revisited*, p. 677.

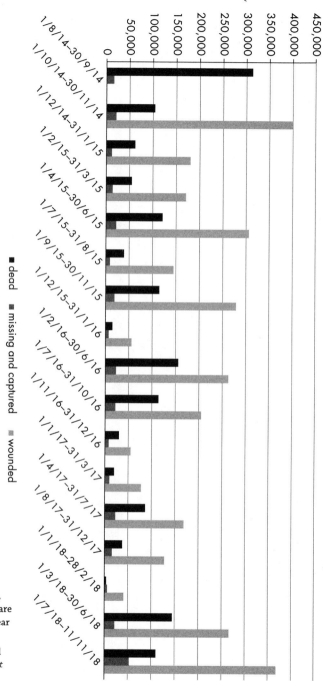

French losses on the western front, 1914–1918. Dates are in day / month / year format.

From McRandle and Quirk, *The Blood Test Revisited*, p. 678.

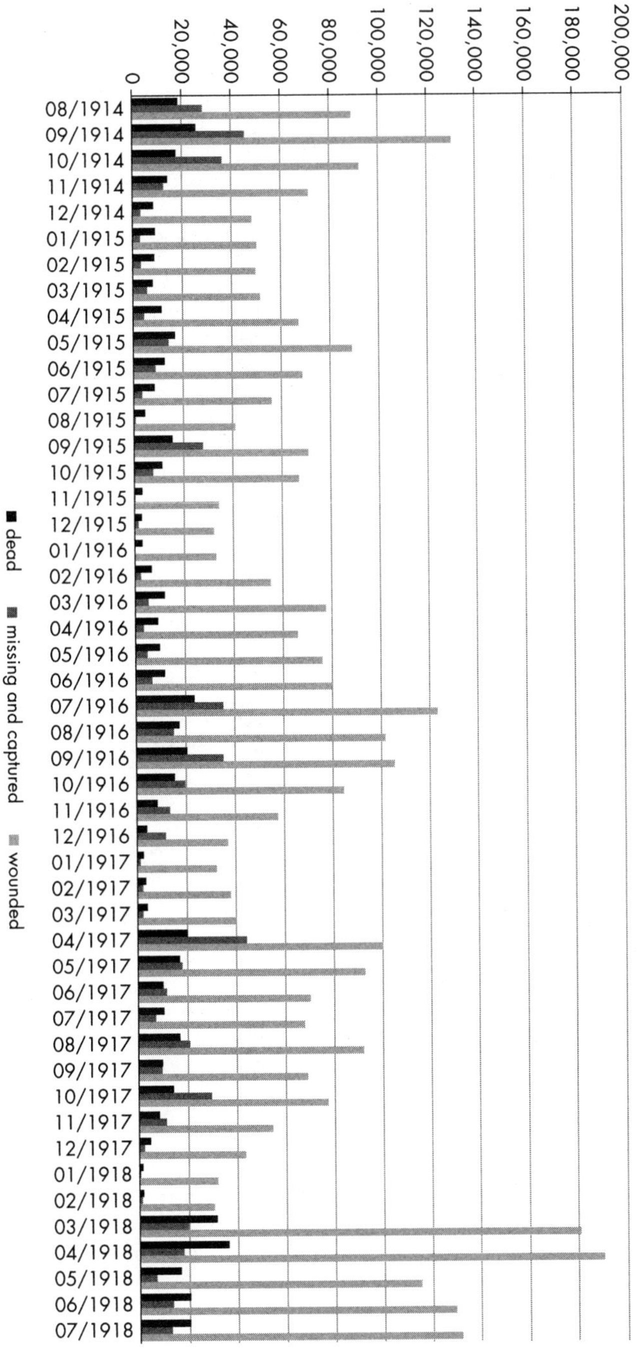
0
20,000
40,000
60,000
80,000
100,000
120,000
140,000
160,000
180,000
200,000
08/1914
09/1914
10/1914
11/1914
12/1914
01/1915
02/1915
03/1915
04/1915
05/1915
06/1915
07/1915
08/1915
09/1915
10/1915
11/1915
12/1915
01/1916
02/1916
03/1916
04/1916
05/1916
06/1916
07/1916
08/1916
09/1916
10/1916
11/1916
12/1916
01/1917
02/1917
03/1917
04/1917
05/1917
06/1917
07/1917
08/1917
09/1917
10/1917
11/1917
12/1917
01/1918
02/1918
03/1918
04/1918
05/1918
06/1918
07/1918
dead
missing and captured
wounded

German losses on the western front, 1914–1918.

From McRandle and Quirk, *The Blood Test Revisited,* pp. 684–685.

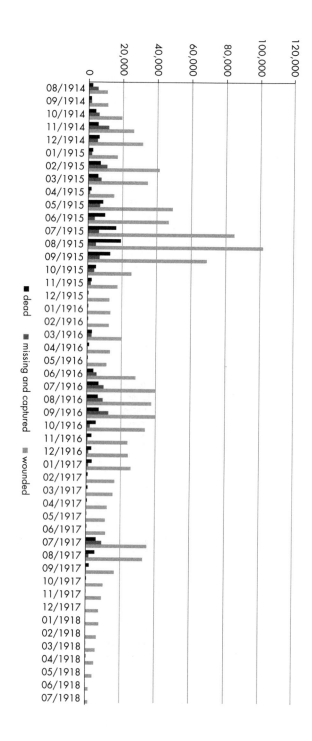

German losses on the eastern front, 1914–1918.

From McRandle and Quirk, *The Blood Test Revisited*, pp. 682–683.

NOTES

1. LEGACIES

1. Schwab, *Sagen des klassischen Altertums*, pp. 10–12.

2. Mendelssohn, *Der Zauberer*, vol. 2, pp. 1585–1587. Emphasis in the original.

3. Mann, *Tagebücher 1918–1921*, p. 65.

4. Ferro, *The Great War: 1914–1918;* Gilbert, *The First World War;* Beckett, *The Great War 1914–1918;* Strachan, *The First World War,* vol. 1; Ferguson, *The Pity of War;* Stevenson, *1914–1918;* Sondhaus, *World War One.*

5. Jünger, "Vorwort," in: idem, *Der Kampf um das Reich,* p. 529; Schramm, *Das Deutschlandbild,* pp. 333–335; Sondhaus, *World War One,* pp. 1–3.

6. Kennan, *The Decline of Bismarck's European Order,* p. 3; Mayer, *The Persistence of the Old Regime,* pp. 315–320; Mazower, *Dark Continent;* Schwarz, "Fragen an das 20. Jahrhundert," pp. 8–10; Prost and Winter, *The Great War in History,* p. 6; Wehler, "Der zweite Dreißigjährige Krieg," pp. 138–143; Kershaw, *Europe's Second Thirty Years War,* pp. 10–17; Traverso, *Fire and Blood;* Stern, "Der zweite Dreißigjährige Krieg," pp. 9–29.

7. Mann, *The Magic Mountain,* pp. xi–xii.

8. Weinrich, *Der Weltkrieg als Erzieher,* pp. 35–63.

9. Dittmann, "Parteidisziplin und Preußengeist," quoted in: Depkat, *Lebenswenden und Zeitenwenden,* p. 272.

10. Overmans, "Kriegsverluste," p. 665; Winter, "Demography," p. 249.

11. Matthew, *Gladstone,* p. vii.

12. Márai, *Bekenntnisse eines Bürgers,* pp. 11–12.

13. Taylor, *English History 1914–1945,* p. 1; Müller, *Contesting Democracy,* pp. 10–11.

14. Reinhard, *Geschichte der Staatsgewalt,* pp. 464, 467–469; Raphael, *Recht und Ordnung,* pp. 19–20; Maier, *Leviathan 2.0.,* pp. 204–205, 233, 278.

15. Tilly, *Reflections on the History of European State-Making,* p. 42; idem, *States and Nationalism,* pp. 187–204.

16. Gildea, *Barricades and Borders,* pp. 95–98; Diner, *Cataclysms,* p. 18.

17. Müller, *Contesting Democracy,* p. 13.

18. Troeltsch, "Das Neunzehnte Jahrhundert," p. 633; Langewiesche, "Das Jahrhundert Europas," pp. 32–33.

19. Hirschhausen and Leonhard, *Europäische Nationalismen*, pp. 11–45; idem, *Empires und Nationalstaaten*, pp. 107–110; idem, "Beyond Rise, Decline and Fall," in: idem (eds.), *Comparing Empires*, pp. 31–33.

20. Osterhammel, *Transformation of the World*, pp. 403–419, 629–633; Raphael, *Imperiale Gewalt*, pp. 19–37.

21. Osterhammel, *Transformation of the World*, pp. 458–461.

22. Angster, *Erdbeeren und Piraten*, pp. 283–294.

23. Maier, "Consigning the Twentieth Century to History," pp. 807–831; idem, "Transformation of Territoriality," pp. 32–55.

24. Langewiesche, "Eskalierte die Kriegsgewalt im Laufe der Geschichte?," pp. 12–36.

25. Ibid., pp. 29–48.

26. Mahan, *The Influence of Sea Power*, pp. 1–24.

27. Mahan, *Naval Strategy*; Hobson, *Imperialism at Sea*, chap. 4.

28. Leonhard, *Bellizismus und Nation*, pp. 725–739.

29. Krüger, *Kriegsbewältigung und Geschichtsbewusstsein*, p. 62; Hull, *Absolute Destruction*, pp. 7–10, 187–191.

30. Zollmann, *Koloniale Herrschaft und ihre Grenzen*, pp. 107–163.

31. Faust, *The Republic of Suffering*, pp. xi and 3.

32. Koselleck, "Hinter der tödlichen Linie"; Hölscher, *Die Entdeckung der Zukunft*, pp. 198–216.

33. Middendorf, *Massenkultur*, pp. 86–126.

34. Spengler, *Der Untergang des Abendlandes*, pp. 1081, 140; *Decline of the West*, II, pp. 416–418, and I, p. 105. Also, Geppert, "Oswald Spengler," pp. 112, 115–117.

35. Musil, *The Man without Qualities*, vol. 1, p. 53.

36. Freeden, *Liberal Languages*, pp. 107–128; Harris, "Epilogue," pp. 931–933.

37. Geyer, "Urkatastrophe," pp. 24–25.

38. Arendt, *Elemente und Ursprünge totaler Herrschaft*, p. 430; Geyer, "Urkatastrophe," p. 25.

2. ANTECEDENTS

1. Jessen, *Die Moltkes*, pp. 209–211.

2. Showalter, *Railroads and Rifles*, pp. 77–99; Walter, "Roonsche Reform oder militärische Revolution," pp. 192–193.

3. Förster, "Helmuth von Moltke und das Problem des industrialisierten Volkskriegs," pp. 103–115; idem, "Facing 'People's War,'" pp. 159–180.

4. "Über den angeblichen Kriegsrat in den Kriegen König Wilhelms I. (1881)," in: Stumpf (ed.), *Kriegstheorie und Kriegsgeschichte*, p. 600.

5. Moltke's letter of December 11, 1880 to Johann Kaspar Bluntschli, in: Stumpf (ed.), *Kriegstheorie und Kriegsgeschichte*, p. 488.

6. *Denkwürdigkeiten des General-Feldmarschalls Alfred Grafen von Waldersee*, vol. 1, p. 100; Busch, *Bismarck*, vol. 1, p. 273; Howard, *The Franco-Prussian War*, p. 380.

7. Moltke, "Rede im Reichstag vom 14. Mai 1890," in: Stumpf (ed.), *Kriegstheorie und Kriegsgeschichte*, pp. 504–505.

8. Schlieffen, "Million-Man Armies," pp. 206–207.

9. Moltke, "Rede im Reichstag vom 14. Mai 1890," in: Stumpf (ed.), *Kriegstheorie und Kriegsgeschichte*, pp. 505–506.

10. Leonhard, *Bellizismus und Nation*, pp. 45–110.

11. Schmitt, "The Turn to the Discriminating Concept of War," in *Writings on War*, pp. 30–74; and idem, *The Nomos of the Earth*, pp. 23, 112–114.

12. Kunisch, "Das 'Puppenwerk' der stehenden Heere," pp. 49–84; Burkhardt, "Die Friedlosigkeit der Frühen Neuzeit," pp. 509–574; Schilling, "Krieg und Frieden in der werdenden Neuzeit," pp. 13–22.

13. Robespierre's second speech against war, January 2, 1792, quoted (and translated) from: Markov (ed.), *Revolution im Zeugenstand*, vol. 2, pp. 210, 216, 218–219.

14. Clausewitz, *On War*, pp. 590–592; Leonhard, *Bellizismus und Nation*, pp. 268–282.

15. Schroeder, "The Transformation of European Politics," pp. 36–37.

16. Sellin, "Heute ist die Revolution monarchisch," pp. 335–361.

17. Georg Wilhelm Freiherr von Valentini, *Die Lehre vom Krieg*, pp. 203–205, 206.

18. Dehio, *Gleichgewicht oder Hegemonie*, pp. 194–195; Bridge and Bullen, *The Great Powers and the European State System*, p. 174.

19. Fisch, *Europa zwischen Wachstum und Gleichheit*, pp. 347–349.

20. Baumgart, *Europäisches Konzert und nationale Bewegung*, pp. 503–506.

21. Schieder, "Typologie und Erscheinungsformen," pp. 58–81.

22. Mulligan, *The Origins of the First World War*, pp. 180–186; Fisch, *Europa zwischen Wachstum und Gleichheit*, p. 348.

23. Hirschhausen and Leonhard, "Does the Empire Strike Back?," pp. 194–221; Leonhard, "Nations in Arms," pp. 287–308.

24. Wright, *A Study of War*, pp. 670–671; Alber, Eichenberg, Kohl, Kraus, Pfenning, and Seebohm, *State, Economy and Society*, vol. 1, pp. 361–449; Anderson, *The Ascendancy of Europe*, p. 317; Schremmer, *Steuern und Staatsfinanzen während der Industrialisierung Europas*, pp. 46–49, 100–101, 188; Fisch, *Europa zwischen Wachstum und Gleichheit*, pp. 348–349.

25. Rohrkrämer, *Der Militarismus der "kleinen Leute*," pp. 37–55, 266; Vogel, *Nationen im Gleichschritt*, pp. 279–291.

26. Rindfleisch, *Zwischen Kriegserwartung und Verrechtlichung*, pp. 73–86.

27. Churchill, *The River War*, p. 300; Ellis, *The Social History of the Machine Gun*, pp. 84–86.

28. Goldfrank, *The Origins of the Crimean War*, p. 289; Baumgart, *The Crimean War 1853–1856*, pp. 215–216; Fisch, *Europa zwischen Wachstum und Gleichheit*, p. 351.

29. Daniel, "Der Krimkrieg 1853–1856," pp. 61–63.

30. Schöllgen, *Imperialismus und Gleichgewicht*, pp. 418–419.

31. Bobroff, *Roads to Glory*, pp. 149–156.

32. Yapp, *The Making of the Modern Near East*, pp. 59–96; Höbelt, "Der Berliner Kongress als Prototyp internationaler Konfliktregelung," pp. 47–54.

33. Fisch, *Europa zwischen Wachstum und Gleichheit*, p. 354.

34. Ranke, *Serbien und die Türkei im neunzehnten Jahrhundert*, pp. vii–viii.

35. Kolb, "Stabilisierung ohne Konsolidierung?," pp. 189–195.

36. Afflerbach, *Der Dreibund*, pp. 88–92.

37. Hennock, *British Social Reform and German Precedents*, pp. 180–182; Morgan, "Lloyd George and Germany," pp. 755–766.

38. Mulligan, *The Origins of the First World War*, pp. 90–91.

39. Koselleck, "Hinter der tödlichen Linie."

40. Quoted [and translated] from Mombauer, *Die Julikrise*, p. 22.

41. Hewitson, "Germany and France," pp. 571–606.

42. Groß, *Mythos und Wirklichkeit*, pp. 102–104, 140–143.

43. Zuber, *Inventing the Schlieffen Plan*, pp. 135–219; Foley, "The Real Schlieffen Plan," pp. 91–115.

44. "Über die militärpolitische Lage und die sich aus ihr ergebenden Forderungen für die weitere Ausgestaltung der deutschen Wehrkraft, Denkschrift vom 21. Dezember 1912," quoted in: Ulrich, Vogel, and Ziemann (eds.), *Untertan in Uniform*, pp. 199–200.

45. Ritter, *The Schlieffen Plan*, pp. 81–102.

46. Kroener, *Militär, Staat und Gesellschaft im 20. Jahrhundert*, pp. 6–7.

47. Mombauer, *Die Julikrise*, pp. 17–18; Doughty, "French Strategy," pp. 427–454.

48. Clark, *The Sleepwalkers*, pp. 266–272.

49. Menning, *Bayonets before Bullets*, pp. 221–237; idem, "The Offensive Revisited," pp. 215–231; idem, *Russian Military Intelligence*.

50. Okey, *Taming Balkan Nationalism*, p. 257.

51. Clark, *The Sleepwalkers*, p. 104.

52. Miller, *The Shadow of the Past*, pp. 144–147.

53. Barraclough, *From Agadir to Armageddon*, pp. 5–15, 177–181.

54. Wesseling, *Soldier and Warrior*, pp. 77–101.

55. Krumeich, *Aufrüstung und Innenpolitik*, pp. 272–281; Porch, *The March to the Marne*, pp. 191–212.

56. Williamson, *The Politics of Grand Strategy*, pp. 167–204.

57. *Times*, July 22, 1911.

58. Epkenhans, *Die wilhelminische Flottenrüstung*, pp. 409–417; Hobson, *Imperialism at Sea*; Geppert and Rose, "Machtpolitik und Flottenbau," pp. 401–437.

59. Seligmann, *The Royal Navy and the German Threat*, pp. 109–131.

60. Rüger, *The Great Naval Game*, pp. 249–250.

61. Mojzes, *Balkan Genocides*, pp. 17–23.

62. Erickson, *Defeat in Detail*, pp. 338–345; Özcan, "Der deutsche Einfluss auf die türkische Armee," pp. 246–248.

63. Trotsky, *War Correspondence*, pp. 329–334, 345–379; Opfer, *Im Schatten des Krieges*, pp. 35–37.

64. Carnegie Endowment for International Peace, *Report of the International Commission*, p. 16.

65. Segesser, *Recht statt Rache*, p. 150.

66. Boeckh, *Von den Balkankriegen zum Ersten Weltkrieg*, p. 379; Hall, *Balkan Wars*, pp. 130–143; Höpken, "Archaische Gewalt," pp. 245–260; idem, "Performing Violence," pp. 213–249.

67. *Kölnische Zeitung*, October 1, 1912, quoted in: Keisinger, *Die Balkankriege*, p. 182.

68. Mojzes, *Balkan Genocides*, pp. 25–44.

69. Lieven, *Russia and the Origins*, pp. 28–50.

70. Clark, *The Sleepwalkers*, pp. 242–313, esp. 293–301.

71. Ibid., p. 301.

72. Ibid., p. 294.

73. Izvolsky to Sazonov, Paris, March 28, 1912: see Clark, *The Sleepwalkers*, p. 296.

74. Izvolsky to Sazonov, Paris, September 12, 1912: see Clark, *The Sleepwalkers*, p. 297.

75. Trumpener, "Germany and the End of the Ottoman Empire," pp. 111–40.

76. Kießling, *Gegen den "großen Krieg,"* pp. 154–192, 317–324.

77. Rose, *Zwischen Empire und Kontinent*, pp. 588–590.

78. Leidinger and Moritz, *Oberst Redl*, p. 236.

79. Röhl, "An der Schwelle zum Weltkrieg," p. 100. English translation from Adam Blauhut, trans., "The 'War Council' (December 1912)," German History in Documents and Images, http://germanhistorydocs.ghi-dc.org/sub_document.cfm?document_id=799.

80. Fischer, *War of Illusions*, pp. 162–167; Geiss, *Der lange Weg*, pp. 268–270; Mommsen, *Großmachtstellung und Weltpolitik*, p. 253; Röhl, "Vorsätzlicher Krieg?," pp. 193–215; Hildebrand, *Das vergangene Reich*, pp. 288–290.

81. Schöllgen, *Imperialismus und Gleichgewicht*, p. 428.

82. Engels, "Einleitung," pp. 350–351; Wehler, *Der Aufbruch in die Moderne*, pp. xxviii–xxix.

83. Herren, *Hintertüren zur Macht*, pp. 18–51; idem, *Internationale Organisationen seit 1865*, pp. 26–42.

84. Cooper, *Patriotic Pacifism*, pp. 60–87; Cortright, *Peace*, pp. 38–52.

85. Degen, "Basel im Zentrum der Friedensbewegung," pp. 30–41; idem, "Die europaweite Ausstrahlung," pp. 142–149.

86. Malkowsky (ed.), *Die Pariser Weltausstellung*, p. v.

87. Herren, *Internationale Sozialpolitik*, p. 239.

88. Goltz, *Das Volk in Waffen*, pp. 424–429, quoted in: Ulrich, Vogel, and Ziemann (eds.), *Untertan in Uniform*, pp. 202–203.

89. Kondylis, *Theorie des Krieges*, pp. 119–121; Schlieffen, "War Today," pp. 195, 198–199, 204; translation modified.

90. Dülffer, *Regeln gegen den Krieg*, pp. 331–348.

91. Spencer, *The Man versus the State* (1884), pp. 170–172.

92. Bloch, *Der Krieg*, vol. 1, pp. xv and xvii–xviii; Sheehan, *Where Have All the Soldiers Gone?*, pp. 28–30.

93. Bernhardi, *Germany and the Next War*, p. viii.

94. Sheehan, *Where Have All the Soldiers Gone?*, p. 38.

95. Ibid., pp. 32–34; Angell, *The Great Illusion*, pp. 40–43; Ceadel, *Living the Great Illusion*, pp. 87–152.

96. Thucydides, *The Peloponnesian War*, Book 1.

97. Kruse, "Imperialismus und Kriegspolitik," pp. 12–25.

98. Kehr, *Schlachtflottenbau und Parteipolitik*, pp. 445–448; Berghahn, *Der Tirpitz-Plan*, pp. 129–157; Wehler, *Deutsche Gesellschaftsgeschichte*, vol. 3, pp. 1152–1168.

99. Mulligan, *The Origins of the First World War*, pp. 175–176; Kruse, "Imperialismus und Kriegspolitik," pp. 17–20.

100. Vogel, *Nationen im Gleichschritt*, p. 279.

101. Fisch, *Europa zwischen Wachstum und Gleichheit*, pp. 358–359.

102. Bahners, "System der Hellhörigkeiten"; Kießling, *Gegen den "großen Krieg,"* p. 324.

103. Fisch, *Europa zwischen Wachstum und Gleichheit*, pp. 351–359.

104. Morton, *Thunder at Twilight*; Illies, *The Year before the Storm*; Emmerson, *1913: In Search of the World*.

105. Musil, *The Man without Qualities*, p. 390.

3. DRIFT AND ESCALATION

1. Franz Graf Harrach, quoted from: Kohler, *Der Prozess gegen die Attentäter*, pp. 158–59; Koerner (ed.), *Der Erste Weltkrieg*, vol. 1, pp. 16–18.

2. Mombauer, *Die Julikrise*, pp. 32–33.

3. Jerabék, *Potiorek*, pp. 82–96.

4. Dedijer, *The Road to Sarajevo*, pp. 445–447.

5. Čupić-Amrein, *Die Opposition gegen die österreichisch-ungarische Herrschaft*, pp. 399–406; Calic, *Geschichte Jugoslawiens*, pp. 70–71.

6. Berghahn, *Sarajewo*, pp. 7–9; Bihl, *Der Erste Weltkrieg*, pp. 43–44; Clewing and Schmitt (eds.), *Geschichte Südosteuropas*, pp. 544–545; Mombauer, *Die Julikrise*, p. 30.

7. Höpken, "Princip," pp. 781–782.

8. Kann, "Franz Ferdinand der Ungarnfeind," pp. 100–126; idem, *Der Thronfolger Erzherzog Franz Ferdinand*, pp. 127–156; Holler, *Franz Ferdinand von Österreich-Este*, pp. 117–149; Weissensteiner, *Franz Ferdinand*, pp. 174–199; Kronenbitter, "Franz Ferdinand," p. 501.

9. Quoted in: Mombauer, *Die Julikrise*, p. 29.

10. Sondhaus, *Franz Conrad von Hötzendorf*, p. 105.

11. Kraus, "Franz Ferdinand und die Talente," pp. 1–4.

12. Mombauer, *Die Julikrise*, pp. 34–35.

13. Zweig, *The World of Yesterday*, pp. 216–217.

14. Waal, *The Hare with Amber Eyes*, p. 178.

15. Clewing and Schmitt (eds.), *Geschichte Südosteuropas*, p. 546.

16. Zweig, *The World of Yesterday*, p. 218.

17. Kronenbitter, *The Militarization of Austrian Foreign Policy*, pp. 80–90.

18. Hantsch, *Leopold Graf Berchtold*, vol. 1, p. 549; Calic, *Geschichte Jugoslawiens*, pp. 68–69.

19. Quoted in: Mombauer, *Die Julikrise*, pp. 40, 38, 121.

20. Clewing and Schmitt (eds.), *Geschichte Südosteuropas*, p. 546.

21. Schieder, "Typologie und Erscheinungsformen," pp. 58–81.

22. Mulligan, *The Origins of the First World War*, pp. 180–186; Fisch, *Europa zwischen Wachstum. und Gleichheit*, p. 348.

23. Bairoch, "International Industrialization from 1780 to 1980," p. 292; Herrmann, *The Arming of Europe*, pp. 233–37; Stevenson, *Armaments and the Coming of War*, pp. 2–8; Mulligan, *The Origins of the First World War*, p. 181.

24. Hirschhausen and Leonhard, "Does the Empire Strike Back?," pp. 194–221; Leonhard, "Nations in Arms," pp. 287–308.

25. Hobson, "The Military-Extraction Gap," pp. 464–465; Mulligan, *The Origins of the First World War*, p. 184.

26. Hobson, "The Military-Extraction Gap," p. 479; Mulligan, *The Origins of the First World War*, p. 184.

27. Wright, *A Study of War*, pp. 670–671; Alber, Eichenberg, Kohl, Kraus, Pfenning, and Seebohm, *State, Economy and Society*, vol. 1, pp. 361–449; Anderson, *The Ascendancy of Europe*, p. 317; Schremmer, *Steuern und Staatsfinanzen während der Industrialisierung Europas*, pp. 46–49, 100–101, 188; Fisch, *Europa zwischen Wachstum und Gleichheit*, pp. 348–349.

28. Fischer, *War of Illusions*, p. 402; Förster, *Der doppelte Militarismus*, pp. 208–295; Mombauer, *Helmut von Moltke*, pp. 182–226.

29. Sösemann (ed.), *Theodor Wolff*, pp. 28–29.

30. Bihl (ed.), *Deutsche Quellen zur Geschichte des Ersten Weltkriegs*, p. 6; Young, "The Misunderstanding of August 1, 1914," pp. 644–665; Hünseler, "Die irische Bürgerkriegsgefahr," pp. 35–44; Ullrich, "Das deutsche Kalkül in der Julikrise," pp. 79–97.

31. Hildebrand, *Bethmann Hollweg*, p. 30; Mommsen, "Die deutsche Kriegszielpolitik," pp. 60–100.

32. Schulte, *Die Verfälschung der Riezler-Tagebücher*, pp. 71–85.

33. Afflerbach, *Der Dreibund*, pp. 813–848.

34. Fischer, *Germany's Aims in the First World War*, p. 57.

35. Quoted from: Vietsch, *Bethmann Hollweg*, pp. 186–188.

36. Clark, *The Sleepwalkers*, pp. 404–412.

37. Mombauer, *Die Julikrise*, p. 54.

38. Afflerbach (ed.), *Kaiser Wilhelm II. als Oberster Kriegsherr*, p. 130.

39. Quoted from ibid., pp. 51–52.

40. Schmidt, *Frankreichs Außenpolitik*, pp. 355–378.

41. Krumeich, *Aufrüstung und Innenpolitik*, pp. 219–271.

42. Quoted from Mombauer, *Die Julikrise*, p. 76.

43. "Das Ultimatum Österreich-Ungarns an Serbien (23. Juli 1914)," in: Philippoff (ed.), *Die Doppelmonarchie Österreich-Ungarn*, p. 153.

44. Mombauer, *Die Julikrise*, p. 41.

45. Ibid., pp. 63, 65.

46. Ibid., p. 74.

47. Quoted in: Calic, *Geschichte Jugoslawiens*, p. 71.

48. Clark, *The Sleepwalkers*, pp. 463–466.

49. Afflerbach (ed.), *Kaiser Wilhelm II. als Oberster Kriegsherr*, p. 130.

50. Bihl (ed.), *Deutsche Quellen zur Geschichte des Ersten Weltkriegs*, p. 10.

51. Buchner (ed.), *Kriegsdokumente*, vol. 1, p. 31.

52. Wilhelm II to Franz Joseph, July 30, 1914, in: Geiss (ed.), *Julikrise und Kriegsausbruch 1914*, vol. 2, no. 789, p. 378; Bittner and Uebersberger (eds.), *Österreich-Ungarns Außenpolitik*, vol. 8, no. 11026, p. 910; Geiss, "The Outbreak of the First World War," p. 81.

53. Quoted in: Mombauer, *Die Julikrise*, p. 81.

54. Ibid., pp. 83–84.

55. Ibid., p. 110.

56. Quoted in: Röhl, *Wilhelm II*, p. 1130.

57. McMeekin, *July 1914*, pp. 47–61, 125–35, 207–222; idem, *The Russian Origins*.

58. Mombauer, *Die Julikrise*, pp. 97–99, 102.

59. Bruch and Hofmeister (eds.), *Deutsche Geschichte in Quellen und Darstellung*, vol. 8, pp. 352–353.

60. Vietsch, *Bethmann Hollweg*, p. 190.

61. Nicholas II to Wilhelm II., July 31, 1914, in: Geiss (ed.), *Julikrise und Kriegsausbruch 1914*, vol. 2, no. 887, pp. 461–462; Afflerbach (ed.), *Kaiser Wilhelm II. als Oberster Kriegsherr*, pp. 131–132.

62. Mendelssohn, *Zeitungsstadt Berlin*, p. 253; Ludwig, *Juli 14*, pp. 97–98; Koszyk, *Deutsche Pressepolitik im Ersten Weltkrieg*, p. 99.

63. Mombauer, *Die Julikrise*, p. 107.

64. Ibid., p. 91.

65. Interview with Bethmann Hollweg, in: Geiss (ed.), *Julikrise und Kriegsausbruch 1914*, vol. 2, no. 1019, p. 574; Vietsch, *Bethmann Hollweg*, p. 192.

66. Afflerbach (ed.), *Kaiser Wilhelm II. als Oberster Kriegsherr*, pp. 132–133.

67. Jagow to Below, July 29, 1914, in: Geiss (ed.), *Juli 1914*, no. 91, p. 225; Moltke to Jagow, August 2, 1914, in: ibid., no. 179, pp. 359–364, esp. pp. 359, 361–362.

68. Mombauer, *Die Julikrise*, p. 110.

69. Bethmann Hollweg to Lichnowsky, August 3, 1914, in: Geiss (ed.), *Julikrise und Kriegsausbruch 1914*, vol. 2, no. 1018, p. 664.

70. Clark, *The Sleepwalkers*, pp. 542–544.

71. Mombauer, *Die Julikrise*, pp. 111–113. (See Sir Edward Grey's Speech on the Eve of War: 3 August 1914, "The Long, Long Trail," http://www.1914-1918.net/greys_speech.html.)

72. Reichskanzler von Bethmann Hollweg, "Erklärung im Reichstag am 4. August 1914," in: Fenske (ed.), *Unter Wilhelm II*, pp. 367–368. (English translation: *The German White Book*, World War I Document Archive, http://www.gwpda.org/papers/germwhit.html.)

73. Vietsch, *Bethmann Hollweg*, pp. 193–194. [See "Origin of the Term 'A Scrap of Paper,'" wwi.lib.byu.edu/index.php/Origin_of_the_Term_%22A_Scrap_of_Paper%22.)

74. Pöhlmann, *Kriegserklärungen*, pp. 637–638.

75. Braunthal, *History of the International*, vol. 1, pp. 320–356.

76. Beaupré, *Les Grandes Guerres*, pp. 9–29.

77. Gildea, *Children of the Revolution*, pp. 434–435.

78. *Vorwärts*, July 25, 1914.

79. Gildea, *Children of the Revolution*, pp. 434–435.

80. Vogt, "Hermann Müller," pp. 194–195; Hoffend, "Mut zur Verantwortung," pp. 26–27; Braun, *Die Reichskanzler der Weimarer Republik*, pp. 134–167.

81. Braunthal, *History of the International*, vol. 2, pp. 20–22; Becker and Krumeich, *Der Große Krieg*, p. 44.

82. Juillard, *La CGT devant la guerre*, pp. 47–62; Howorth, "French Workers and German Workers," pp. 71–97.

83. Quoted in: Fiechter, *Le Socialisme français*, p. 209; Gildea, *Children of the Revolution*, pp. 435–436.

84. "Erklärung von Hugo Haase für die Fraktion der SPD," August 4, 1914, in: Fenske (ed.), *Unter Wilhelm II.*, p. 371.

85. Kruse, *Krieg und nationale Integration*, pp. 223–225.

86. Sheehan, *Where Have All the Soldiers Gone?*, p. 63.

87. Afflerbach, *Der Dreibund*, pp. 834–848.

88. Schmidt, *Frankreichs Außenpolitik*, pp. 355–378.

89. Clark, *The Sleepwalkers*, p. 562.

90. Ibid., pp. 555–562.

91. Mombauer, *Die Julikrise*, p. 10.

92. Ullrich, "Zündschnur und Pulverfass," p. 53.

93. Förster, "Im Reich des Absurden," pp. 248–250; idem, "Vorgeschichte und Ursachen," p. 41.

94. Fisch, *Europa zwischen Wachstum und Gleichheit*, p. 358.

95. Fussell, *The Great War and Modern Memory*, p. 7; Förster, "Vorgeschichte und Ursachen," p. 41; Chickering, "Ein Krieg, der nicht vergehen will," p. 283.

96. Luhmann, *Trust and Power*, pp. 1–8; Seligman, *The Problem of Trust*, pp. 169–175; Frevert, *Vertrauen*, pp. 7–66.

97. Giddens, *Consequences of Modernity*, pp. 38–40; Hartmann, "Einleitung," p. 15.

98. Musil, *The Man without Qualities*, p. 12.

99. Written communication from Jagow to the German ambassador in Vienna, July 15, 1914, in: Bruch and Hofmeister (eds.), *Deutsche Geschichte in Quellen und Darstellung*, vol. 8, p. 347.

100. Hampe, *Kriegstagebuch*, pp. 99–101.

101. *Krieg-mobil*, quoted in: Ulrich, Vogel, and Ziemann (eds.), *Untertan in Uniform*, pp. 215–216.

102. Müller, *Die Nation als Waffe*, pp. 56–81.

103. Weber, *Hitler's First War*, p. 17.

104. Kessler, *Journey to the Abyss*, p. 739.

105. Friedrich Karl von Pourtales, *Am Scheideweg zwischen Krieg und Frieden. Meine letzten Verhandlungen in Petersburg Ende Juli 1914*, quoted in: Schulin, "Der Erste Weltkrieg," p. 61.

106. Stöcker, "Augusterlebnis 1914," pp. 37–52.

107. Zuckmayer, *Als wär's ein Stück von mir,* quoted in: Schulin, "Der Erste Weltkrieg," pp. 58–60.

108. Kafka, *Diaries, 1910–1923,* p. 301.

109. Ibid. See Cornwall, "The Wartime Bohemia," p. 38.

110. Quoted in Cornwall, "The Wartime Bohemia," p. 39.

111. *Mein Kampf* (http://greatwar.nl/books/meinkampf/meinkampf.pdf), p. 196, quoted in Schulin, "Der Erste Weltkrieg," pp. 61–62. See also Haas, *Die literarische Welt,* p. 41; Russell, *Autobiography,* pp. 226–227.

112. Evans (ed.), *Kneipengespräche im Kaiserreich,* nos. 344 (July 4, 1914), 346 (July 24, 1914), 347 (July 29, 1914), and 348 (July 29, 1914), pp. 413–416.

113. Blom, *Der taumelnde Kontinent,* pp. 453–459.

114. Rolland, "Conscience de l'Europe," quoted in: Schulin, *Der Erste Weltkrieg,* pp. 63–64.

115. Gide, *Journals,* July 30, 1914, p. 47; July 31, p. 48; August 1, p. 49; August 2, p. 42; August 3, p. 53.

116. Becker, "That's the Death Knell," pp. 20–22.

117. Becker, *1914 : Comment les Français,* pp. 329–357; Beaupré, "Construction and Deconstruction," pp. 41–57.

118. Clarke, *Voices Prophesying War,* pp. 93–130.

119. Strandmann, "The Mood in Britain," pp. 72–73.

120. Pennell, *A Kingdom United,* pp. 227–229.

121. Canetti, *The Tongue Set Free,* pp. 90–91.

122. Waal, *The Hare with Amber Eyes,* p. 213.

123. Sieg, *Jüdische Intellektuelle,* p. 61; idem, *Geist und Gewalt,* p. 108.

124. Rozenblit, *Reconstructing National Identity,* 39–58; Waal, *The Hare with Amber Eyes,* p. 213–214.

125. Strauss, "Reichstreue und Volkstreue," p. 387; Kilcher, "Zionistischer Kriegsdiskurs," p. 51; Sieg, *Jüdische Intellektuelle im Ersten Weltkrieg,* pp. 53–69.

126. Brussilow, *Meine Erinnerungen,* p. 84; Gilliard, *Thirteen Years,* p. 111; Figes, *A People's Tragedy,* p. 251.

127. Dowler, *Russia in 1913,* pp. 190–232.

128. Lohr, "The Russian Press," pp. 91–92.

129. Golder, *Documents on Russian History,* p. 21; Figes, *A People's Tragedy,* p. 250.

130. Figes, *A People's Tragedy,* pp. 251–252.

131. Lohr, *The Russian Press,* pp. 97–99.

132. Ibid., pp. 102–103.

133. Figes, *A People's Tragedy,* p. 252.

134. "Reservists Flock to the Consulates," in: *New York Times,* August 5, 1914.

135. Harbutt, "War, Peace, and Commerce," p. 321.

136. Sanders and Taylor, *British Propaganda,* pp. 170–172; Wüstenbecker, "Die Vereinigten Staaten," p. 218.

137. Daniel, *A Brief Time,* pp. 48–56, 450–452.

138. Altenhöner, *Kommunikation und Kontrolle*, p. 220; Raithel, Das *"Wunder" der inneren Einheit*, p. 376.

139. Altenhöner, *Kommunikation und Kontrolle*, pp. 217–218.

140. Kessler, *Journey to the Abyss*, p. 642; Riederer, "Einleitung," p. 25.

141. Müller, *Die Nation als Waffe*, p. 67; Riederer, "Einleitung," p. 25.

142. Bavendamm, *Spionage und Verrat*, pp. 186–215.

143. Weber, *Economy and Society*, p. 980.

144. Mollo and Turner, *Army Uniforms of the First World War*; Kraus, *Die feldgraue Uniformierung*, vol. 1, pp. 23–54; Bull, *Brassey's History of Uniforms*, pp. 65–84.

145. Snyder, *The Ideology of the Offensive*, pp. 199–216.

146. Citino, *The German Way of War*, pp. 89, 149.

147. Williamson, "Joffre Reshapes French Strategy," p. 147; Linnenkohl, *Vom Einzelschuß zur Feuerwalze*, p. 165; Sheehan, *Where Have All the Soldiers Gone?*, p. 71.

148. Clayton, *Paths of Glory*, pp. 26–30; Zuber, *The Battle of the Frontiers*, pp. 280–281.

149. Sheehan, *Where Have All the Soldiers Gone?*, p. 72.

150. Becker and Krumeich, *Der Große Krieg*, pp. 213–214.

151. Diner, *Das Jahrhundert verstehen*, pp. 44–45.

152. Schwarte (ed.), *Die Technik im Weltkriege*, pp. 19–59, 272–304; Linnenkohl, *Vom Einzelschuß zur Feuerwalze*, p. 187; Thoss, "Infanteriewaffen," p. 579.

153. Gascouin, *L'évolution de l'artillerie*, quoted in: Linnenkohl, *Vom Einzelschuß zur Feuerwalze*, p. 174.

154. Ibid. See also Storz, "Schrapnell," p. 820.

155. Gascouin, *L'évolution de l'artillerie*, quoted in: Linnenkohl, *Vom Einzelschuß zur Feuerwalze*, p. 175.

156. Ibid., pp. 165, 174–175; Thoss, "Infanteriewaffen," pp. 575–576.

157. Immanuel, *Die französische Infanterie*, p. 49; Montaigne, *Vaincre*, p. 120; Linnenkohl, *Vom Einzelschuß zur Feuerwalze*, p. 42.

158. Kaufmann, *Kommunikationstechnik und Kriegführung*, pp. 158–169.

159. Kessler, *Journey to the Abyss*, p. 646.

160. Ousby, *The Road to Verdun*, p. 9; Sheehan, *Where Have All the Soldiers Gone?*, pp. 73–74.

161. Tuchman, *The Guns of August*, p. 439; Craig, "The Revolution in War and Diplomacy," p. 196.

162. Englund, *The Beauty and the Sorrow*, pp. 60–61, 69.

163. Herrmann, *Randbemerkungen (1914–1917)*, quoted in: Johann (ed.), *Innenansicht eines Krieges*, p. 95.

164. *Prager Tagblatt*, morning edition, September 27, 1914, p. 2; Anz, "Motive des Militärischen," pp. 182–183.

165. Musil, *Diaries, 1899–1941*, pp. 173–174.

166. Bet-El, *Conscripts*, pp. 27–63.

167. Wilkinson, *Pals on the Somme*, pp. 49–64.

168. Arthur, *The Faces of World War I*, p. 37.

169. Bibbings, *Telling Tales about Men*, pp. 27–49, 233–235; Ellsworth-Jones, *We Will Not Fight*; Kennedy, A *History of the No-Conscription Fellowship*, pp. 1–27.

170. Sanborn, "The Mobilization of 1914," pp. 273–277.

171. Beşikçi, *The Ottoman Mobilization of Manpower*, pp. 312–314.

172. Palmer and Wallis (ed.), *Intimate Voices*, pp. 213, 215.

173. Lunn, *Memoirs of the Maelstrom*, pp. 65–73, 140–147.

174. Matthews, "Reluctant Allies," pp. 95–114; Killingray, "Military and Labour Policies," pp. 137–151.

175. Quinn, "The Impact of the First World War," pp. 171–185.

176. Greenstein, "The Nandi Experience," pp. 81–94; Lunn, "Kande Kamara Speaks," pp. 28–53; McLaughlin, "The Legacy of Conquest," pp. 115–136.

177. Fogarty, *Race and War*, pp. 270–293.

178. *Statistics of the Military Effort*, p. 756.

179. Ibid., pp. 756, 777.

180. Holland, "The British Empire and the Great War," p. 117.

181. Strachan, *The First World War in Africa*, p. 3; Stockwell, "The War and the British Empire," p. 37; Carrington, "The Empire at War," p. 642.

182. Morrow, *The Great War*; Omissi, *Indian Voices*; Smith, *Jamaican Volunteers*; Das (ed.), *Race, Empire and First World War Writing*.

183. Barrett, "Subalterns at War," pp. 156–176; idem, "Death and the Afterlife," pp. 301–320.

184. Vat, *The Ship that Changed the World*, pp. 183–202; Krüsmann, Langensiepen, and Nottelmann, *Halbmond und Kaiseradler*, pp. 9–28.

185. Nachtigal, *Die Murmanbahn*, pp. 126–127.

186. Tuchman, *The Guns of August*, pp. 161–190; Neugebauer, "Die Urkatastrophe des 20. Jahrhunderts," p. 62.

187. Bobroff, *Roads to Glory*, pp. 150–151.

188. Heubes (ed.), *Ehrenbuch der Deutschen Eisenbahner*, quoted in: Gall, *Eisenbahn in Deutschland*, pp. 63 and 69; Pohl, "Von den Staatsbahnen zur Reichsbahn," p. 71.

189. Heubes (ed.), *Ehrenbuch der Deutschen Eisenbahner*, p. 8, quoted in: Gall, *Eisenbahn in Deutschland*, p. 69; figures from Gall, *Eisenbahn in Deutschland*; Nipperdey, *Deutsche Geschichte*, vol. 2, p. 759; Spilker and Ulrich (eds.), *Der Tod als Maschinist*, p. 274.

190. Tuchman, *The Guns of August*, p. 200; Sattler, *Die deutsche Kavallerie*, pp. 41–43, 86–87.

191. Tuchman, *The Guns of August*, pp. 200–201.

192. Zuber, *Inventing the Schlieffen Plan*, pp. 220–280; Mombauer, "Der Moltkeplan," pp. 79–100.

193. Cornelißen, "Schlieffen-Plan," pp. 819–820.

194. Benvindo and Majerus, "Belgien zwischen 1914 und 1918," pp. 130–132; Benvindo, *Des hommes en guerre*, pp. 40–55.

195. Benvindo, *Des hommes en guerre*, pp. 63–72.

196. Schaepdrijver, *La Belgique*, pp. 137–211.

197. Benvindo and Majerus, "Belgien zwischen 1914 und 1918," pp. 133–135.

198. Ypersele, *Le roi Albert*, 92–101; idem, "Belgien," pp. 44–49.

199. Herr, *Die Artillerie in Vergangenheit*; Linnenkohl, *Vom Einzelschuß zur Feuerwalze*, pp. 80–82, 89–94; Storz, "Artillerie," pp. 344–349.

200. Herwig, *The Marne*, pp. 105–131.

201. Nebelin, *Ludendorff*, pp. 113–122.

202. Zuckerman, *The Rape of Belgium*, pp. 38–61.

203. Horne and Kramer, *German Atrocities, 1914*, pp. 120, 215; Herwig, *The Marne*, pp. 108–113.

204. Quoted in: Horne and Kramer, *German Atrocities, 1914*, p. 104.

205. Bihl, *Der Erste Weltkrieg*, p. 106.

206. Kessler, *Journey to the Abyss*, pp. 96–97.

207. Schöller, *Der Fall Löwen*; Schivelbusch, *Die Bibliothek von Löwen*; Lipkes, *Rehearsals*, pp. 257–294; Kramer, *Dynamic of Destruction*, pp. 6–30.

208. Gibson, *A Journal from Our Legation in Belgium*, p. 159, quoted in: Schivelbusch, *Die Bibliothek von Löwen*, p. 16.

209. *Times*, August 29, 1914; *Rotterdamsche Courant*, quoted in: *Berliner Tageblatt*, September 2, 1914, quoted in: Schivelbusch, *Die Bibliothek von Löwen*, pp. 26–27.

210. French, *British Strategy and War Aims*, pp. 13–16; Bourne, "Streitkräfte (Großbritannien)," pp. 886–887.

211. Koerner (ed.), *Der Erste Weltkrieg*, vol. 1, pp. 43–44.

212. Münchhausen, *Paris*, pp. 340–341.

213. Fischer, *World Power or Decline*, pp. 32–46; Koerner (ed.), *Der Erste Weltkrieg*, vol. 1, pp. 44, 47; Ferro, *The Great War: 1914–1918*, p. 240; Mommsen, *Bürgerstolz und Weltmachtstreben*, pp. 618–620.

214. Helfferich, *Der Weltkrieg*, vol. 2, p. 18; Mombauer, "The Battle of the Marne," p. 751.

215. Linnenkohl, *Vom Einzelschuß zur Feuerwalze*, p. 170.

216. Becker, "Marne," pp. 697–699.

217. Showalter, *Tannenberg*, pp. 293–295; Schwarzmüller, *Zwischen Kaiser und "Führer,"* pp. 93–95; Mombauer, "The Battle of the Marne," p. 752.

218. Herwig, *The Marne*, "Epilog." See also p. 222.

219. *Kriegs-Rundschau*, September 10, 1914.

220. Herwig, *The Marne*, pp. 266–306.

221. Afflerbach (ed.), *Kaiser Wilhelm II. als Oberster Kriegsherr*, p. 165.

222. Afflerbach, *Falkenhayn*, pp. 179–189.

223. Mombauer, "The Battle of the Marne," p. 760.

224. Sösemann (ed.), *Theodor Wolff*, pp. 52–53.

225. Becker and Krumeich, *Der Große Krieg*, p. 216.

226. Neugebauer, "Die Urkatastrophe des 20. Jahrhunderts," p. 36.

227. Koerner (ed.), *Der Erste Weltkrieg*, vol. 1, pp. 8–9.

228. Herwig, *The First World War*, pp. 103–105; Strachan, *First World War*, vol. 1, pp. 261–262; Mombauer, "The Battle of the Marne," p. 768.

229. Afflerbach, *Falkenhayn*, pp. 203–210; Deist, "Die Kriegführung der Mittelmächte," p. 253.

230. Mombauer, "The Battle of the Marne," p. 769.

231. Krumeich, "Langemarck," pp. 292–309; Becker and Krumeich, *Der Große Krieg*, pp. 216–218.

232. Unruh, *Langemarck*, pp. 9, 61–68.

233. Mann, *The Magic Mountain*, p. 705; Ketelsen, "Die Jugend von Langemarck," pp. 68–96; Schumann, "Deutschland, Deutschland über alles," pp. 29–44; Lehnert, "Langemarck," pp. 271–290; Neumann, "Kommentar," pp. 409–410.

234. Groß, "Im Schatten des Westens," pp. 49–62.

235. Sondhaus, *Franz Conrad von Hötzendorf*, pp. 158–164.

236. Linnenkohl, *Vom Einzelschuß zur Feuerwalze*, pp. 170–171; Bihl, *Der Erste Weltkrieg*, pp. 83–86.

237. Lyon, "A Peasant Mob," pp. 481–502.

238. Rothenberg, "The Austro-Hungarian Campaign against Serbia," pp. 127–146; Bihl, *Der Erste Weltkrieg*, p. 95.

239. Menzel, *Kriegsflüchtlinge in Cisleithanien*, p. 62; Holzer, *Die andere Front*, pp. 254–255.

240. Bihl, *Der Erste Weltkrieg*, p. 95; Calic, *Geschichte Jugoslawiens*, pp. 71–73; Cornwall, "Austria-Hungary and 'Yugoslavia,'" pp. 377–380; Clewing and Schmitt (eds.), *Geschichte Südosteuropas*, p. 547.

241. Kessler, *Tagebuch*, vol. 5, October 18, 1914, p. 432; Riederer, "Einleitung," p. 44.

242. Stone, *The Eastern Front*, pp. 37–69.

243. Pyta, *Hindenburg*, pp. 41–55; Nebelin, *Ludendorff*, pp. 123–146.

244. Rathenau, *Walther Rathenau, Industrialist, Banker, Intellectual, and Politician*, p. 200.

245. Nebelin, *Ludendorff*, pp. 43–64.

246. Braun, "Die Unterwerfung des deutschen Ordenslandes," quoted in: Riederer, "Einleitung," p. 33; Schenk, "Tannenberg/Grunwald," pp. 438–454.

247. Engelstein, "A Belgium of Our Own," pp. 441–473.

248. Liulevicius, *War Land on the Eastern Front*, pp. 23–25; Becker and Krumeich, *Der Große Krieg*, pp. 18–19.

249. Pyta, *Hindenburg*, pp. 91–113; Hoegen, *Der Held von Tannenberg*, pp. 177–192.

250. Gildea and Golz, "Flawed Saviours," pp. 441–442.

251. Hampe, *Kriegstagebuch*, September 15, 1914, p. 125.

252. Schröder, "An die deutschen Krieger," quoted in: Riederer, "Einleitung," p. 42; Koenen, "Der Russland-Komplex," pp. 51–75; Thum, "Ex oriente lux," pp. 7–15.

253. Kessler, *Tagebuch*, vol. 5, September 22 and 24, 1914, pp. 116–117; Riederer, "Einleitung," pp. 38–40.

254. Dettmann, *Ostfront*, quoted in: Liulevicius, "Der Osten als apokalyptischer Raum," p. 57.

255. Hampe, *Kriegstagebuch*, September 15, 1914, p. 124; September 30, 1914, p. 132; October 1, 1914.

256. Koenen, "Der Russland-Komplex," pp. 76–77.

257. "Saw Papeete Razed by German Shells," in: *New York Times,* October 8, 1914, quoted in: Sondhaus, *World War One,* p. 104.

258. Dickinson, *War and National Reinvention,* pp. 34–58.

259. Burdick, *The Japanese Siege of Tsingtao,* pp. 156–199.

260. Beasley, *Japanese Imperialism,* pp. 108–115.

261. Osterhammel, "Staat und Nation," p. 82.

262. Bennett, *Coronel and the Falklands,* pp. 13–42.

263. Hough, *The Great War at Sea,* pp. 87–98.

264. Peattie, *Nan'yō,* pp. 34–61; Hiery, *The Neglected War,* pp. 11–44.

265. Stachelbeck, *Deutschlands Heer und Marine,* pp. 69–84.

266. Ibid., pp. 88–97.

267. Samson, *World War I in Africa,* pp. 44–45.

268. Bührer, *Die Kaiserliche Schutztruppe,* pp. 401–478, esp. pp. 431–444.

269. Pesek, *Das Ende eines Kolonialreiches,* p. 156.

270. Hoyt, *Guerilla: Colonel von Lettow-Vorbeck,* pp. 29–36, 65–73.

271. Michels, *Der Held von Deutsch-Ostafrika,* pp. 234–242.

272. Anderson, *The Forgotten Front,* pp. 295–298.

273. Strachan, *The First World War in Africa,* pp. 1–12.

274. Paice, *Tip and Run,* pp. 392–393.

275. Sondhaus, *World War One,* pp. 119–20.

276. Engel, *1914. Ein Tagebuch,* quoted in: Johann (ed.), *Innenansicht eines Krieges,* p. 57.

277. "Erste und Zweite Balkonrede Wilhelms II.," in: Bihl (ed.), *Deutsche Quellen zur Geschichte des Ersten Weltkriegs,* pp. 45 and 49.

278. Gay, *The Cultivation of Hatred,* pp. 519–520.

279. Kruse, "Gesellschaftspolitische Systementwicklung," pp. 56–57.

280. Schulze, *State, Nations and Nationalism,* p. 270.

281. Matuschka, *Organisationsgeschichte des Heeres,* pp. 157–282.

282. Jarausch, *The Enigmatic Chancellor,* pp. 349–380; Kruse, *Krieg und nationale Integration,* pp. 31–41; Verhey, "Burgfrieden," pp. 400–402.

283. Schramm, "Militarisierung und Demokratisierung," pp. 476–497.

284. Deist, *Militär und Innenpolitik,* vol. 1, pp. xxxi–li; Kruse, "Gesellschaftspolitische Systementwicklung," pp. 56–57.

285. Deist, "Voraussetzungen innenpolitischen Handelns," pp. 126–138; Pöhlmann, "Stellvertretendes Generalkommando," pp. 525–526.

286. Führ, *Das k.u.k. Armeeoberkommando,* pp. 29–63.

287. Cornwall, "Austria-Hungary and 'Yugoslavia,'" pp. 375–377.

288. Kappeler, *The Russian Empire,* pp. 328–369.

289. "President Poincare's War Address, 4 August 1914," firstworldwar.com, http://www.firstworldwar.com/source/poincare_aug1914.htm; Caron, *La France des Patriotes;* Becker and Krumeich, *Der Große Krieg,* p. 79.

290. "Discours de Léon Jouhaux aux obsèques de Jaurès—4 août 1914," http://www.his toiresocialedeslandes.fr/p3_impact_win02.asp; Caron, *La France des Patriotes;* Becker and Krumeich, *Der Große Krieg,* pp. 80–81.

291. Sembat, *Faites la paix.*

292. Kruse, "Gesellschaftspolitische Systementwicklung," pp. 60–61.

293. Ibid., pp. 60–62; Saatmann, *Parlament, Rüstung und Armee,* pp. 326–328; Horne, "A Parliamentary State at War," pp. 211–236; Caron, *La France des Patriotes.*

294. Ewing and Gearty, *The Struggle for Civil Liberties,* pp. 90–93.

295. Panayi, "Introduction," p. 6; Reinecke, *Grenzen der Freizügigkeit,* p. 199; Panter, *Loyalitätskonflikte und Neuorientierungen,* p. 56.

296. Cassar, *Kitchener's War,* pp. 1–18.

297. French, "The Rise and Fall of 'Business as Usual,'" pp. 7–31; Kruse, "Gesellschaftspolitische Systementwicklung," p. 65.

298. Swartz, *The Union of Democratic Control,* pp. 28–45, 85–104; Robbins, *The Abolition of War,* pp. 48–92; Reimann, "Union of Democratic Control," pp. 937–938.

299. Hochschild, *To End All Wars,* pp. 14–15, 44–72.

300. Ullmann, "Kriegswirtschaft," pp. 200, 226.

301. French, *British Economic and Strategic Planning,* pp. 51–73, 98–123.

302. Burk (ed.), *War and the State,* p. 35.

303. Zilch, "Rohstoff bewirtschaftung," pp. 797–800.

304. *Der Große Krieg,* quoted in: Johann (ed.), *Innenansicht eines Krieges,* pp. 64–66.

305. Schweder, *Im kaiserlichen Hauptquartier,* quoted in: Johann (ed.), *Innenansicht eines Krieges,* p. 66.

306. Ullmann, "Kriegswirtschaft," p. 221.

307. Szöllösi-Janze, *Fritz Haber,* pp. 273–274.

308. Rathenau, "Deutschlands Rohstoffversorgung," pp. 26–27.

309. Quoted from: Gall, *Walther Rathenau,* p. 177.

310. Quoted from ibid., pp. 175–176, 178; Sabrow, "Walther Rathenau," pp. 786–787.

311. Gall, *Walther Rathenau,* pp. 184, 186–187.

312. Goebel, *Deutsche Rohstoffwirtschaft,* pp. 9–18; Feldman, *Army, Industry, and Labor,* pp. 45–52.

313. Rathenau, *Deutschlands Rohstoffversorgung,* p. 29.

314. Gall, *Walther Rathenau,* p. 184; Roth, *Staat und Wirtschaft,* pp. 116–146.

315. Zilch, "Rohstoffbewirtschaftung," pp. 799–800.

316. Gatrell, *Russia's First World War,* pp. 17–37, 108–131.

317. Pennell, *A Kingdom United,* p. 101.

318. Kresse, *Verdeutschung entbehrlicher Fremdwörter;* Rother (ed.), *Der Weltkrieg,* pp. 103–104.

319. I would like to thank Mareike König of the German Historical Institute in Paris for this reference.

320. Rostovcev, "The Capital University," p. 185.

321. Strandmann, "Nationalisierungsdruck und königliche Namensänderung," pp. 69–91.

322. Weber, "Religious Rejections," p. 335.

323. Englund, *Schönheit und Schrecken*, p. 36.

324. Quoted in: ibid., p. 33.

325. Kappeler, *The Russian Empire*, pp. 328–369.

326. Dziewanowski, *Joseph Piłsudski*, pp. 46–63.

327. Jędrzejewicz, *Józef Piłsudski*; Hecker, "Polen," pp. 777–779.

328. Davies, *Heart of Europe*, pp. 95–100, 113–128.

329. Kreiser, *Atatürk*, p. 76.

330. Aksakal, *The Ottoman Road to War*, pp. 37–39, 93–118; Trumpener, *Germany and the Ottoman Empire*, pp. 271–284, 367–370.

331. Deringil, *Turkish Foreign Policy*, pp. 58–64.

332. "Proclamation of Sultan Mehmed V, November 1914," firstworldwar.com, http://www .firstworldwar.com/source/mehmed_fetva.htm.

333. Quoted from: Hagen, *Die Türkei im Ersten Weltkrieg*, pp. 56–57; Kreiser, *Atatürk*, pp. 97, 78.

334. Zürcher, "Osmanisches Reich," p. 761.

335. Manela, *The Wilsonian Moment*, pp. 67–68.

336. Brown, *Modern India*, pp. 187–188.

337. Manela, *The Wilsonian Moment*, pp. 81–82.

338. Brown, "War and the Colonial Relationship," pp. 19–48; Cornelißen, "Indien," p. 571.

339. Carrington, "The Empire at War 1914–18," p. 606; Holland, "The British Empire and the Great War," p. 115.

340. Jeffery, *Ireland and the Great War*, pp. 10–11.

341. Fitzpatrick, *The Two Irelands*, pp. 51–55; Horne, "Irland," pp. 586–587.

342. Samson, *Britain, South Africa and the East Africa Campaign*, pp. 93–117.

343. Schramm, "Minderheiten gegen den Krieg," pp. 165–167.

344. Davenport, *South Africa*, pp. 245–249; Holland, "The British Empire and the Great War," p. 119; Nasson, "Südafrika," pp. 913–914.

345. Hesse, "O Freunde, nicht diese Töne"; Schwilk, *Hermann Hesse*, pp. 169–195.

346. Hofmannsthal, "Österreichs Antwort," p. 1; Schnitzler, *Tagebuch*, vol. 5, August 5, 1914, pp. 128–129; Waal, *The Hare with Amber Eyes*, p. 181.

347. Hampe, *Kriegstagebuch*, August 2, 1914, pp. 97–99; Flasch, *Die geistige Mobilmachung*, pp. 36–47.

348. Hübinger, "Ernst Troeltsch," pp. 926–927; Leonhard, "Über Nacht," pp. 205–230.

349. Troeltsch, "Nach der Erklärung der Mobilmachung," pp. 10–12, 15–16, 17–18.

350. Wilamowitz-Moellendorff, "Krieges Anfang, 27. August 1914," pp. 21–22, 23–24.

351. Klepsch, *Romain Rolland im Ersten Weltkrieg*, pp. 53–64.

352. "Brief Rollands an Hauptmann und seine Antwort," in: Schivelbusch, *Die Bibliothek von Löwen*, pp. 27–28. (Romain Rolland, "A Letter to Gerhart Hauptmann," World War One Centennial Gallery, http://jfredmacdonald.com/worldwarone1914-1918/german-14letter -gerhart-hauptmann.html.)

353. Ungern-Sternberg and Ungern-Sternberg, "Der Aufruf 'An die Kulturwelt,'" pp. 144–145; "To the Civilized World," pp. 284–285.

354. Bruch, "Aufruf der 93," pp. 356–357.

355. "Erklärung der Hochschullehrer des Deutschen Reiches," quoted in: Bruch and Hofmeister (eds.), *Deutsche Geschichte in Quellen und Darstellung*, vol. 8, p. 367.

356. Plenge, *1789 und 1914*, pp. 111–113; Leonhard, "Vom Nationalkrieg zum Kriegsnationalismus," pp. 204–240.

357. Bruendel, *Volksgemeinschaft oder Volksstaat*, pp. 16–18, 20–28, 110–116; Verhey, "Ideen von 1914," pp. 568–570. ("Ideas of 1914," Brill's Digital Library of World War I, http://referenceworks.brillonline.com/entries/brills-digital-library-of-world-war-i/ideas-of-1914-beww1_en_0300?s.num=1.)

358. Kurzke, *Thomas Mann*, pp. 217ff.

359. Ibid., p. 221.

360. Mann, "Gedanken im Kriege," pp. 27 and 31.

361. Kurzke, *Thomas Mann*, pp. 219–220.

362. Mann, "Gedanken im Kriege," p. 37.

363. Ibid., pp. 37–38; Sieferle, "Der deutsch-englische Gegensatz," pp. 139–60; Mendelssohn, *Der Zauberer*, vol. 2, pp. 1616–1617.

364. Grampp, "Besatzungsmacht Wagner," pp. 233–254.

365. Gildea, *Children of the Revolution*, pp. 437–443.

366. Hanna, *The Mobilization of Intellect*, pp. 106–141.

367. Rolland, *Au-dessus de la melée*, quoted from: Contamine, "Mourir pour la patrie," p. 1694.

368. Brüggemeier, *Geschichte Großbritanniens*, p. 108.

369. Wallace, *War and the Image of Germany*, p. 77.

370. Strandmann, "Germany and the Coming of War," pp. 87–89.

371. *Why We Are at War*, pp. 108–117; Hoeres, *Krieg der Philosophen*.

372. Quoted in: Figes, *A People's Tragedy*, p. 252.

373. Gleason, "American Identity and Americanization," pp. 31–58.

374. Oncken, *Deutschlands Weltkrieg und die Deutschamerikaner*, pp. 6–8.

375. Roosevelt, *Works*, vol. 10, p. 361 and vol. 18, p. 392; Bischoff and Mania, "Melting Pot-Mythen," pp. 526–528.

376. *Kölnische Volkszeitung*, December 22, 1914, quoted in: Johann (ed.), *Innenansicht eines Krieges*, pp. 88–89.

377. Publicity in: *Die Woche*, no. 47, November 21, 1914, and no. 51, December 19, 1914, quoted in: Johann (ed.), *Innenansicht eines Krieges*, unnumbered, between pp. 112 and 113.

378. Sösemann (ed.), *Theodor Wolff*, p. 71.

379. Hampe, *Kriegstagebuch*, December 25, 1914, p. 179 and December 27, 1914, p. 180.

380. Kessler, *Journey to the Abyss*, December 24, 1914, pp. 663–664.

381. Witkopp (ed.), *Kriegsbriefe gefallener Studenten*, quoted in: Johann (ed.), *Innenansicht eines Krieges*, pp. 96–97.

382. Barton, *Battlefields of the First World War*, p. 200.

383. Brown, *The Imperial War Museum Book*, pp. 44–49.

384. Jürgs, *Der kleine Frieden im Großen Krieg*, pp. 99–184; Rother (ed.), *Der Weltkrieg*, pp. 104–105; Wakefield, *Christmas in the Trenches*, pp. 1–35; Jahr, "Weihnachten 1914," pp. 957–959.

385. Englund, *The Beauty and the Sorrow*, p. 72.

386. Fussell, *The Great War and Modern Memory*, p. 7; Sheehan, *Where Have All the Soldiers Gone*, p. 69.

387. Stevenson, *The First World War*, pp. 297ff.

388. Bihl, *Der Erste Weltkrieg*, p. 95.

389. Beaupré, *Les Grandes Guerres*, p. 57.

4. STASIS AND MOVEMENT

1. French, *British Strategy and War Aims*, p. 15.

2. Quoted in: Holmes, *The Western Front*, p. 50.

3. Strachan, "Die Kriegführung der Entente," pp. 272–274.

4. Prior, *Churchill's "World Crisis,"* pp. 51–84.

5. Rudenno, *Gallipoli*, pp. 26–63.

6. Hart, *Gallipoli*, pp. 67–75.

7. Kreiser, *Atatürk*, pp. 437–449.

8. Prior, *Gallipoli: The End of the Myth*, pp. 110–144.

9. Ibid., pp. 190–209; Hart, *Gallipoli*, pp. 330–368.

10. Robertson, *Anzac and Empire*, pp. 178–181; Prior and Wilson, "Gallipoli," pp. 517–518.

11. Beaumont, "Nation oder Commonwealth," pp. 43–68.

12. Dawes and Robson, *Citizen to Soldier*, pp. 168–201.

13. Grace, "Our Little Army," quoted in: Pugsley, *Stories of Anzac*, p. 45.

14. Adcock, *Australasia Triumphant*.

15. Pugsley, *Gallipoli*, pp. 345–355.

16. Pugsley, *Stories of Anzac*, pp. 44–45, 58.

17. Farnie, *East and West of Suez*, pp. 530–549; Huber, "Connecting Colonial Seas," pp. 141–161; Huber, *Channeling Mobilities*.

18. Gust, *The Armenian Genocide*, pp. 156–165; Zürcher, *Osmanisches Reich*, p. 760.

19. Simkins, *Kitchener's Army*, pp. 79–103.

20. Holmes, *The Western Front*, p. 56.

21. Ibid., p. 55.

22. Williams, *Modernity*, pp. 83–104.

23. Prior and Wilson, *Command on the Western Front*, pp. 17–43.

24. Holmes, *The Western Front*, p. 56.

25. Ibid., pp. 56–59.

26. Baynes, *Morale*, pp. 51–91.

27. Kenyon, *Horsemen in No Man's Land*, p. 232.

28. Badsey, "Cavalry," pp. 138–174.

29. Holmes, *The Western Front*, pp. 59–60.

30. Englund, *Beauty and Sorrow*, pp. 162–163.

31. Quoted in: ibid., pp. 163–164.

32. Ibid., p. 164; Bourne, "Westfront," p. 964.

33. Tunstall, *Blood on the Snow*, pp. 210–212.

34. Sondhaus, *World War One*, pp. 128–144, 160–161.

35. Benvindo and Majerus, "Belgien zwischen 1914 und 1918," pp. 135–136.

36. Nivet, *La France occupée*, pp. 55–84, 85–114.

37. Benvindo and Majerus, "Belgien zwischen 1914 und 1918," pp. 177–179.

38. Majerus, *Die deutsche Verwaltung Belgiens*, p. 132.

39. Wandt, *Erotik und Spionage*, p. 207.

40. Majerus, "La prostitution à Bruxelles," pp. 5–42.

41. Thiel, "*Menschenbassin Belgien*," pp. 103–122, 201–238.

42. Benvindo and Majerus, "Belgien zwischen 1914 und 1918," pp. 135–141.

43. Neutatz and Radauer, "Besetzt, interniert, deportiert," pp. 9–26.

44. Liulevicius, *War Land on the Eastern Front*, pp. 247–277.

45. Strazhas, *Deutsche Ostpolitik im Ersten Weltkrieg*, pp. 276–277.

46. Westerhoff, *Zwangsarbeit im Ersten Weltkrieg*, pp. 181–246, 332, 339.

47. Angelow, "Der Erste Weltkrieg," pp. 178–194; Ortner, "Die Feldzüge gegen Serbien," pp. 123–142.

48. Neilson, *Strategy and Supply*, p. 141.

49. Cornwall, "Austria-Hungary and 'Yugoslavia,'" pp. 377–380.

50. Mitrović, *Serbia's Great War*, pp. 144–161.

51. Calic, *Sozialgeschichte Serbiens*, pp. 216–217.

52. Zhivojinovich, "Serbia and Montenegro," pp. 239–259; Hirschfeld, "Serbien," pp. 833–836.

53. Holzer, *Das Lächeln der Henker*, pp. 12–13.

54. Gumz, *The Resurrection and Collapse of Empire*, p. 1.

55. Ibid., p. 18.

56. Mitrović, *Serbia's Great War*, pp. 222–226, 240–243.

57. Opfer-Klinger, "Ein unaufgearbeitetes Kapitel," pp. 285–287.

58. Mayerhofer, *Zwischen Freund und Feind*, pp. 373–378.

59. Ansky, *The Enemy at His Pleasure*, p. 23.

60. Panter, *Jüdische Erfahrungen*, p. 60. Figures quoted in: *Staatliche Flüchtlingsfürsorge im Kriege 1914 / 15*; Panter, *Jüdische Erfahrungen*, p. 120; Adunka, "Der ostjüdische Einfluss auf Wien," p. 78; Habartová, "Jewish Refugees from Galicia and Bukovina," pp. 139–166.

61. Golczewski, *Polnisch-jüdische Beziehungen*, pp. 121–137; Prusin, *Nationalizing a Borderland*, pp. 66–74; Mick, *Kriegserfahrungen in einer multiethnischen Stadt*, pp. 79–181; Panter, *Loyalitätskonflikte und Neuorientierungen*, p. 94.

62. Wróbel, "The Jews of Galicia," p. 134; Panter, *Jüdische Erfahrungen*, pp. 115–116.

63. Scheer, *Zwischen Front und Heimat*, pp. 23–25.

64. Panter, *Jüdische Erfahrungen*, p. 48.

65. Cohn, "Zukunftsfragen," p. 565, quoted in: Panter, *Jüdische Erfahrungen*, p. 104.

66. Mordacq, *Le drame de l'Yser*, quoted in: Koerner (ed.), *Der Erste Weltkrieg*, vol. 1, p. 94.

67. *Berliner Tageblatt*, April 26, 1915, quoted in: Leitner, *Der Fall Clara Immerwahr*, p. 212.

68. Ibid., pp. 213–215.

69. Hanslian, *Der chemische Krieg*, vol. 1, pp. 9–37.

70. Lepick, *La grande guerre chimique*, p. 315.

71. Müller, "Total War," p. 103; Hull, *Absolute Destruction*, p. 214.

72. Szöllösi-Janze, *Fritz Haber*, p. 319.

73. Afflerbach, *Falkenhayn*, p. 261; Hull, *Absolute Destruction*, p. 214.

74. Müller, "Gaskrieg," p. 520.

75. Ibid., pp. 519–521; Martinetz, *Der Gaskrieg*, pp. 78–79.

76. Quoted in: Szöllösi-Janze, *Fritz Haber*, p. 325.

77. Halpern, *A Naval History*, pp. 44–47.

78. Herwig, "*Luxury Fleet*," pp. 226–248; Salewski, "Seekrieg," pp. 828–830.

79. Rohwer, "U-Boot-Krieg," p. 931.

80. Quoted in: Fenske (ed.), *Unter Wilhelm II.*, p. 385; Neugebauer, "Die Urkatastrophe des 20. Jahrhunderts," p. 65.

81. Rohwer, "U-Boot-Krieg," p. 931.

82. Ramsay, *Lusitania*, pp. 99–112.

83. Rohwer, "U-Boot-Krieg," p. 932.

84. Hopman, diary entry for October 27, 1915, in: Epkenhans (ed.), *Das ereignisreiche Leben eines Wilhelminers*, p. 720.

85. Sokol, *Österreich-Ungarns Seekrieg*, pp. 305–318; Rohwer, "U-Boot-Krieg," p. 932.

86. Stegemann, *Die deutsche Marinepolitik*, pp. 22–35; Salewski, "Seekrieg," pp. 829–830; Terraine, *Business in Great Waters*, pp. 11–16; Neugebauer, "Die Urkatastrophe des 20. Jahrhunderts," pp. 64–66.

87. Stumpf, *Warum die Flotte zerbrach*, entries for April 13, 1915, Whit Monday 1915, August 23 and November 7, 1915, quoted in: Johann (ed.), *Innensicht eines Krieges*, pp. 117, 125, 144; Englund, *The Beauty and the Sorrow*, p. 177.

88. Salvatore, "D'Annunzio," pp. 18–19.

89. D'Annunzio, "Rede von der Tribüne des Kapitols," p. 8.

90. Ibid., pp. 10–11.

91. Ernst, "Museale Kristallisation," pp. 309–320; Ballinger, "Blutopfer und Feuertaufe," pp. 175–202.

92. Janz, "Zur Historiographie," pp. 203–204.

93. Bosworth, *Italy*, pp. 377–417.

94. Woller, *Geschichte Italiens*, p. 68; Isnenghi, "Italien," pp. 99–101.

95. Bosworth, *Italy*, pp. 121–141.

96. Janz, "Zur Historiographie," p. 204.

97. Woller, *Geschichte Italiens*, p. 68; Isnenghi, "Italien," pp. 99–100.

98. Biguzzi, *Cesare Battisti*, pp. 511–576, 606–643.

99. Gatterer, *Erbfeindschaft Italien-Österreich*, p. 170; Sondhaus, *In the Service of the Emperor*, pp. 120–121.

100. Salvemini, *Opere*, vol. 4, pp. 164–165; Cattaruzza, "Das geeinte Italien," pp. 282–283.

101. Fellner, "Der Dreibund," pp. 19–82; Afflerbach, *Der Dreibund,* pp. 849–873.

102. Thompson, *The White War,* pp. 52–86.

103. Rauchensteiner, *Österreich-Ungarn und der Erste Weltkrieg,* pp. 100–105.

104. Langes, *Die Front in Fels und Eis,* pp. 133–144, 146–177; Schaumann, *Schauplätze des Gebirgskrieges;* Lichem, *Krieg in den Alpen,* vol. 1, pp. 84–95 and vol. 2, pp. 139–143; Storz, "Alpenkrieg," pp. 331–334.

105. Schindler, *Isonzo,* pp. 85–104, 175–193.

106. Haager, Hoffmann, Hutter, Lang, and Spielmann, *Die Tiroler Kaiserjäger,* p. 77; Mondini, *Alpini: Parole e immagini,* pp. 63–77.

107. Isnenghi, "Isonzo, pp. 589–590.

108. Woller, *Geschichte Italiens,* p. 70.

109. Schulze, *Staat und Nation in der europäischen Geschichte,* p. 281.

110. Woller, *Geschichte Italiens,* p. 72.

111. Sondhaus, *World War One,* pp. 368–370.

112. Friedrich, *Bulgarien und die Mächte,* pp. 186–189, 234–235.

113. Hall, *Bulgaria's Road to the First World War,* pp. 285–223; Crampton, *Bulgaria,* pp. 206–210; Höpken, "Bulgarien," pp. 399–400.

114. Smith, *The Embattled Self,* pp. 166–167.

115. Pairault, *Images de poilus,* p. 24.

116. Balzac, *Le Médecin de Campagne;* Doyle and Walker, *Trench Talk,* p. 60.

117. Déchelette, *L'argot des poilus,* p. 166.

118. Chevallier, *Fear,* pp. 37–38.

119. Lewin, "Kriegslandschaft," p. 441, quoted in: Bröckling, *Disziplin,* p. 202.

120. Jünger, *Storm of Steel,* p. 67; *In Stahlgewittern* (1978), p. 73.

121. Barton, *Battlefields of the First World War,* pp. 117, 294, 358.

122. Ritter, *Notizhefte,* p. 369.

123. Musil, *Diaries,* September 22, 1915, p. 184; Corino, *Robert Musil,* p. 238.

124. Chevallier, *Fear,* p. 239.

125. Fussell, *The Great War,* pp. 56–58; Ritter, *Notizhefte,* p. 413.

126. Ziemann, "Soldaten," pp. 156–157; illustrations 1–3 in the appendix to this book.

127. Ellis, *Eye-Deep in Hell,* pp. 26–42.

128. Chevallier, *Fear,* p. 43.

129. Leed, *No Man's Land,* p. 19.

130. Jones and Robertson, "Good Luck. . . . Dig In," pp. 91–114.

131. Sondhaus, *World War One,* pp. 198–202.

132. Bull, *Trench. A History of Trench Warfare,* pp. 59–94.

133. Barbusse, *Under Fire,* p. 165.

134. Wilson, *Landscapes of the Western Front,* pp. 134–136.

135. Jünger, *Kriegstagebuch,* August 28, 1916, p. 177.

136. Ibid.

137. Carrington, quoted in: Leed, *No Man's Land,* p. 78.

138. Chevallier, *Fear,* p. 171.

139. Sondhaus, *World War One*, p. 200; Ashworth, *Trench Warfare*, p. 101.

140. Ziemann, "Soldaten," pp. 160–161.

141. Werth, "Argonnen," p. 341.

142. Barton, *Battlefields of the First World War*, pp. 200–203.

143. Ziemann, "Soldaten," pp. 155–156.

144. Chevallier, *Fear*, p. 62.

145. Ziemann, "Soldaten," p. 159.

146. Miquel, *Les poilus*, pp. 189–240.

147. Ziemann, "Soldaten," p. 156; illustrations 1–4 in the appendix to this book.

148. Ibid., pp. 156–157.

149. Ulrich, "Schützengraben," p. 821.

150. Meyer, *Les Soldats de la Grande Guerre*, p. 37.

151. Leed, *No Man's Land*, p. 31.

152. Bröckling, *Disziplin*, pp. 203–204.

153. Ulrich and Ziemann (eds.), *Frontalltag im Ersten Weltkrieg*, p. 85, quoted in: Latzel, *Die Soldaten des industrialisierten Krieges*, p. 130.

154. Chevallier, *Fear*, p. 240.

155. Sondhaus, *World War One*, pp. 200–201.

156. Audoin-Rouzeau, *Men at War*, pp. 140–143.

157. Hanna, *Your Death*, pp. 23–24.

158. Englund, *Schönheit und Schrecken*, p. 142.

159. Watson, "Self-Deception and Survival," pp. 254–255.

160. Chevallier, *Fear*, p. 158.

161. Ibid., p. 160.

162. Meteling, *Ehre, Einheit, Ordnung*, p. 239.

163. Chevallier, *Fear*, p. 80.

164. Baynes, *Morale*, pp. 236–254.

165. Quoted in: Fink, "Introduction," p. 39.

166. Chevallier, *Fear*, pp. 160–161.

167. Ibid., p. 185.

168. Frevert, "Vertrauen," pp. 54–55; Kühne, "Vertrauen und Kameradschaft," pp. 245–278.

169. Chevallier, *Fear*, p. 188.

170. Fink, "Introduction," p. 40.

171. Chevallier, *Fear*, p. 243.

172. Ziemann, *Front und Heimat*, pp. 464–465.

173. Theweleit, *Männerphantasien*, vol. 2, pp. 239–287.

174. Ziemann, *Front und Heimat*, pp. 230–236.

175. Quoted in: Figes, *A People's Tragedy*, p. 258.

176. Beyrau und Shcherbinin, "Alles für die Front," pp. 155–156.

177. Quoted in: Figes, *A People's Tragedy*, p. 266.

178. Schramm, "British Journalism," pp. 56–59.

179. Holmes, *The Western Front*, p. 63.

180. Thompson, *Politicians, the Press and Propaganda,* pp. 42–65.

181. I am grateful to Ute Daniel for these suggestions.

182. Adams, *Arms and the Wizard,* pp. 180–181.

183. Holmes, *The Western Front,* p. 65.

184. Turner, *Lloyd George's Secretariat,* pp. 27–45; Grigg, *Lloyd George,* pp. 256–307.

185. Zilch, "Rohstoffbewirtschaftung," p. 800.

186. Winter, "Großbritannien," p. 55.

187. Hoeres, *Krieg der Philosophen,* pp. 102–103.

188. Gregory, *The Last Great War,* pp. 235–238.

189. Ibid., pp. 234–240.

190. Duncan, *Pubs and Patriots,* pp. 67–92.

191. Gregory, *The Last Great War,* pp. 112–151; Winter, "Großbritannien," pp. 51–57.

192. Clegg, *A History of British Trade Unions,* vol. 2, pp. 118–141; Gregory, "Britain and Ireland," p. 407.

193. Brüggemeier, *Geschichte Großbritanniens,* p. 117.

194. Butt, "Housing," pp. 29–55.

195. Gordon, *Women and the Labour Movement,* p. 239.

196. Glasgow Labour History Workshop, *The Labour Unrest in West Scotland,* pp. 18–40.

197. Duncan, "Independent Working-Class Education," p. 106.

198. Wendt, "War Socialism," pp. 117–149; Rubin, *War, Law and Labour,* pp. 39–42.

199. Melling, *Rent Strikes,* pp. 59–73.

200. Ibid., pp. 84–85, photograph of the demonstration.

201. Gregory, "Britain and Ireland," p. 407.

202. Ibid., pp. 407–408; Thom, "Women and Work," pp. 297–326.

203. Townshend, *Political Violence in Ireland,* p. 278.

204. Denman, *Ireland's Unknown Soldiers,* p. 33; Finnan, *John Redmond and Irish Unity,* p. 90.

205. Jeffery, *Ireland and the Great War,* pp. 8, 20; Fitzpatrick, "The Logic of Collective Sacrifice," pp. 1017–1030.

206. Orr, "200 000 Volunteer Soldiers," pp. 63–77; Gregory, "Britain and Ireland," p. 409.

207. Redmond, *A Visit to the Front,* p. 38.

208. Pearse, "O'Donovan Rossa," p. 137.

209. Edwards, *Patrick Pearse;* Moran, *Patrick Pearse,* pp. 133–173; Augusteijn, *Patrick Pearse,* pp. 323–344.

210. Fitzpatrick, *The Two Irelands,* pp. 51–58; Jeffery, *Ireland and the Great War,* pp. 37–68; Gregory, "Britain and Ireland," pp. 408–409.

211. Englund, *The Beauty and the Sorrow,* pp. 142–143.

212. Horne, *Labour at War,* pp. 73–75; Smith, "France," p. 420.

213. Sembat, *Faites un roi.*

214. Mollenhauer, "Albert Thomas," p. 921.

215. Antier, "1915," pp. 53–62; Ullmann, "Kriegswirtschaft," p. 223.

216. Boulanger, "Les embusqués," pp. 87–100.

217. Ridel, *Les embusqués,* pp. 153–172.

218. Horne, "L'impôt du Sang," pp. 201–223; Smith, "France," p. 421.

219. Johann (ed.), *Innenansicht eines Krieges*, p. 32.

220. Wehler, *Deutsche Gesellschaftsgeschichte*, vol. 4, pp. 45–47.

221. Ibid., pp. 47–49; Cornelißen, "Sozialpolitik," pp. 857–859.

222. Herbert, "Zwangsarbeit als Lernprozeß," pp. 285–304; Feldman, *Armee, Industrie und Arbeiterschaft*, p. 75; Mommsen, *Die Urkatastrophe Deutschlands*, pp. 80–81.

223. Herwig, *The First World War*, pp. 230–244, 254–270.

224. Hardach, *The First World War*, pp. 15–19; Burhop, *Wirtschaftsgeschichte des Kaiserreichs*, p. 196.

225. Hardach, *The First World War*, pp. 20–27; Burhop, *Wirtschaftsgeschichte des Kaiserreichs*, p. 197.

226. Rohlack, *Kriegsgesellschaften*.

227. Roth, *Staat und Wirtschaft im Ersten Weltkrieg*, pp. 420–421.

228. Mommsen, *Die Urkatastrophe Deutschlands*, pp. 82–83; Michalka, "Kriegsrohstoffbewirtschaftung," pp. 485–505; Krüger, "Kriegssozialismus," pp. 506–529.

229. Burhop, *Wirtschaftsgeschichte des Kaiserreichs*, p. 201.

230. Burchardt, "Zwischen Kriegsgewinnen und Kriegskosten," pp. 71–123; Baten and Schulz, "Making Profits in Wartime," pp. 34–56.

231. Wehler, *Deutsche Gesellschaftsgeschichte*, vol. 4, p. 50.

232. Ibid., pp. 52–53.

233. Ibid., pp. 55–56; Cornelißen, "Sozialpolitik," pp. 858–859.

234. Whalen, *Bitter Wounds*, pp. 95–106.

235. Jentsch, *Der Weltkrieg*, p. 189.

236. Wehler, *Deutsche Gesellschaftsgeschichte*, vol. 4, pp. 57–64.

237. "Bericht des Berliner Polizeipräsidenten," June 25, 1915, quoted in: Bihl (ed.), *Deutsche Quellen zur Geschichte des Ersten Weltkriegs*, p. 131.

238. "Bericht des Berliner Polizeipräsidenten," September 18, 1915, quoted in: Bihl (ed.), *Deutsche Quellen zur Geschichte des Ersten Weltkriegs*, p. 146.

239. Wehler, *Deutsche Gesellschaftsgeschichte*, vol. 4, pp. 58–61.

240. Offer, *The First World War*, pp. 51–53; idem, "The Blockade of Germany," pp. 169–188; Davis, *Home Fires Burning*, p. 117.

241. Roerkohl, *Hungerblockade und Heimatfront*, pp. 65–112; Huegel, *Kriegsernährungswirtschaft*, pp. 176–184.

242. Baudis, "Vom Schweinemord zum Kohlrübenwinter," pp. 129–152.

243. Insert in: *Die Woche*, 1915, quoted in: Johann (ed.), *Innenansicht eines Krieges*, p. 148.

244. Simmel, "Geld und Nahrung," p. 120.

245. Helfferich, *Beiträge zur neuesten Handelspolitik*, p. 259; Mai, "Der Erste Weltkrieg," p. 160.

246. Ibid., pp. 159–161; Offer, *The First World War*, pp. 45–47, 335–337.

247. Naumann, *Demokratie und Kaisertum*, p. 348.

248. Quoted in: Mai, *Das Ende des Kaiserreichs*, pp. 173–175; Mühlhausen, *Die Sozialdemokratie am Scheideweg*, pp. 649–671.

249. Haacke and Schneider, *Das Buch vom Kriege*, p. 161.

250. Krüger, *Nationalökonomen im wilhelminischen Deutschland*, p. 127; Mai, *Der Erste Weltkrieg*, p. 165.

251. Mai, "Verteidigungskrieg und Volksgemeinschaft," pp. 583–602.

252. Scheler, *Der Genius des Krieges*, pp. 119–120; Geschnitzer, Koselleck, Schönemann, and Werner, *Volk, Nation, Nationalismus, Masse*, pp. 391–392.

253. Winkler, "Einleitende Bemerkungen zu Hilferdings Theorie," pp. 9–18; Hilferding, "Arbeitsgemeinschaft der Klassen," pp. 63–76.

254. Hilferding, "Arbeitsgemeinschaft der Klassen," pp. 66–67.

255. Deist, "Zensur und Propaganda," pp. 156–159.

256. *Ursachen und Folgen*, vol. 1, quoted in: Johann (ed.), *Innenansicht eines Krieges*, pp. 131–132.

257. Mommsen, "Deutschland," p. 18.

258. Naumann, *Mitteleuropa*, p. 3.

259. Ibid., p. 135.

260. Quoted in: Johann (ed.), *Innenansicht eines Krieges*, pp. 112, 128.

261. Haase (ed.), *Hugo Haase*, quoted in: Johann (ed.), *Innenansicht eines Krieges*, p. 129.

262. Miller, *Burgfrieden und Klassenkampf*, pp. 113–33; Mühlhausen, "Sozialdemokratie," p. 856.

263. Miller, *Burgfrieden und Klassenkampf*, pp. 114–117.

264. Lademacher (ed.), *Die Zimmerwalder Bewegung*, vol. 1, pp. 160–169.

265. Mühlhausen, *Zimmerwalder Bewegung*, pp. 977–978.

266. Schulze Wessel, "Loyalität als geschichtlicher Grundbegriff," pp. 1–22.

267. Friedensburg, *Das Erdöl im Weltkrieg*, pp. 19–22; Frank, *Oil Empire*, p. 251.

268. Rauchensteiner, *Österreich-Ungarn und der Erste Weltkrieg*, p. 66.

269. Rauchensteiner, *Der Erste Weltkrieg*, pp. 577–604.

270. Healy, *Vienna and the Fall of the Habsburg Empire*, pp. 31–86.

271. Cornwall, "Austria-Hungary and 'Yugoslavia,'" pp. 375–377.

272. Rauchensteiner, *Der Tod des Doppeladlers*, p. 266.

273. Cornwall, "Austria-Hungary and 'Yugoslavia,'" pp. 372–375.

274. Quoted in: Holzer, *Die andere Front*, p. 254.

275. Ibid., p. 259.

276. Cornwall, "Austria-Hungary and 'Yugoslavia,'" p. 375.

277. Ibid., pp. 373–374.

278. Winkler, *Karel Kramář*, pp. 12–15, 276.

279. Cornwall, "Austria-Hungary and 'Yugoslavia,'" pp. 374–375.

280. Quoted in: Rauchensteiner, *Der Tod des Doppeladlers*, p. 265.

281. Hadler, "Die Herausbildung der tschechisch-slowakischen Zusammenarbeit," pp. 81–92; idem, "Tschechoslowakei," p. 929.

282. Mommsen, "Der Erste Weltkrieg," pp. 8–9.

283. Lein, *Pflichterfüllung oder Hochverrat*, pp. 199–202, 342–344, 417–421; Zückert, *Zwischen Nationsidee und staatlicher Realität*, pp. 80–95.

284. Cornwall, "Austria-Hungary and 'Yugoslavia,'" p. 374.

285. Quoted in: Rauchensteiner, *Der Tod des Doppeladlers*, p. 270.

286. Beyrau and Shcherbinin, "Alles für die Front," pp. 161–162.

287. Ibid., pp. 156–157.

288. Dahlmann, "Russland," p. 92.

289. Lohr, "Russia," pp. 482–483.

290. Lohr, "Nationalizing the Russian Empire," pp. 98–99, 102–103; Dahlmann, "Russland," p. 90.

291. Dönninghaus, *Die Deutschen in der Moskauer Gesellschaft*, pp. 370–467; Lohr, "The Moscow Riots," pp. 607–626.

292. Beyrau and Shcherbinin, "Alles für die Front," p. 154.

293. Gatrell, *A Whole Empire Walking*, pp. 16–32; Schuster, *Zwischen allen Fronten*, pp. 195–233.

294. Beyrau and Shcherbinin, "Alles für die Front," pp. 154–55.

295. Noack, *Muslimischer Nationalismus*, pp. 448–450.

296. Dahlmann, "Russland," pp. 92–93.

297. Ibid., p. 157.

298. Ibid., p. 93.

299. Hildermeier, *Geschichte Russlands*, pp. 1293–1311.

300. Hildermeier, *Die Russische Revolution*, pp. 117–121; Dahlmann, "Russland," p. 93.

301. Epkenhans, "Das Ende eines Zeitalters," p. 68.

302. Neutatz, *Träume und Alpträume*, p. 143.

303. Wortman, *Scenarios of Power*, vol. 2, p. 511.

304. Hildermeier, *Geschichte Russlands*, p. 1082; Neutatz, *Träume und Alpträume*, p. 143.

305. Barth, *Genozid*.

306. Quoted in: Englund, *The Beauty and the Sorrow*, p. 139.

307. Ther, *The Dark Side of Nation-States*, pp. 65–66.

308. Akçam, *Armenien und der Völkermord*, pp. 54–60; Zürcher, "Demographic Engineering," pp. 530–544.

309. Bloxham, "Determinants of the Armenian Genocide," pp. 23–50.

310. Somakian, *Empires in Conflict*, pp. 70–130.

311. Zürcher, "Ottoman Labour Battalions," pp. 187–196.

312. Bloxham, *The Great Game of Genocide*, pp. 70–96; Bloxham, "The First World War," pp. 274–275.

313. The consul in Aleppo to the Reich chancellor, April 12, 1915, quoted in: Gust (ed.), *Der Völkermord an den Armeniern*, pp. 129–130. Cf. notes 317 and 318.

314. Gust (ed.), *Der Völkermord an den Armeniern*, pp. 172–184.

315. Baberowski and Doering-Manteuffel, *Ordnung durch Terror*, p. 24; Kreiser, *Atatürk*, pp. 98–99.

316. The consul in Erzurum to the ambassador in Constantinople, quoted in: Gust (ed.), *Der Völkermord an den Armeniern*, p. 142.

317. The German ambassador in Constantinople to the Auswärtiges Amt, ibid., p. 154.

318. The German ambassador in Constantinople to the Reich chancellor, ibid., pp. 170–171.

319. Quoted in: Kreiser, *Atatürk,* p. 99.

320. Schwartz, "Imperiale Verflechtung," pp. 273–291.

321. Ibid., p. 99; Gust, "Armenier," pp. 342–343.

322. Zürcher, "Griechisch-orthodoxe und muslimische Flüchtlinge," pp. 623–627.

323. Blair, "Excuses for Inhumanity," pp. 14–30; Dinkel, "German Officers and the Armenian Genocide," pp. 77–133; Dadrian, *German Responsibility in the Armenian Genocide;* Dadrian, "The Armenian Question," pp. 59–85; Goltz (ed.), *Deutschland, Armenien und die Türkei;* Hosfeld, *Operation Nemesis;* Atılgan, *Österreichs Dilemma 1915.*

324. Gust, "Armenier," p. 343; Zürcher, "Osmanisches Reich," p. 761.

325. Winter, "Introduction," pp. 1–8; Adalian, "American Diplomatic Correspondence," pp. 146–184.

326. Wegner, *Die Austreibung des armenischen Volkes,* p. 89.

327. Lepsius, *Deutschland und Armenien.*

328. Gust (ed.), *Der Völkermord an den Armeniern,* pp. 56–60.

329. Quoted in: Albrecht, "Wer redet heute noch von der Vernichtung der Armenier?," p. 128.

330. Kellermann, *Der Krieg der Geister,* p. 28; Pulzer, "Vorbild, Rivale und Unmensch," p. 240.

331. Hobhouse, *The Metaphysical Theory of the State,* p. 6; Wallace, *War and the Image of Germany,* pp. 36–37; Pulzer, "Vorbild, Rivale und Unmensch," p. 241.

332. Barker, *The Submerged Nationalities,* p. 61.

333. Bainville, *Two Histories,* p. 288.

334. Winkler, *The Age of Catastrophe,* pp. 12–13.

335. Mann, "Frederick and the Great Coalition," p. 187.

336. Ibid., pp. 193, 200.

337. Ibid., pp. 187–189.

338. Mann, "Zola," pp. 179–180.

339. *Deutsche Vorträge Hamburger Professoren,* vol. 2, pp. 3, 8–9.

340. Sombart, *Händler und Helden,* pp. 47–48.

341. Ibid., pp. 34, 64, 108, 138.

342. Ibid., pp. 84–85.

343. Mommsen, "Das Englandbild der Deutschen," p. 229.

344. Winkler, *The Age of Catastrophe,* pp. 13–14.

345. Simmel, "Europa und Amerika," pp. 140–142.

346. Freud, *Reflections on War and Death* I, p. 8.

347. Ibid., p. 10.

348. Freud, *Reflections on War and Death* II, p. 19.

349. Ibid., p. 29.

350. Lohmann, "Schriften zum Thema Krieg und Tod," pp. 187–192; Fry, *Freud's War,* pp. 33–58.

351. Fritzsche, *The Turbulent World,* pp. 116–117.

352. Erickson, *Ottoman Army Effectiveness,* p. 167.

353. Erickson, *Ordered to Die,* pp. 214–216.

354. Afflerbach, *Falkenhayn,* pp. 351–352.

355. Rathenau, *Tagebuch 1907–1922*, p. 200; Janßen, *Der Kanzler und der General*, pp. 181–183.

356. Falkenhayn, *Die Oberste Heeresleitung*, pp. 176–177, 181–184.

5. WEARING DOWN AND HOLDING OUT

1. Jünger, *Kriegstagebuch*, pp. 176–177.

2. Kiesel, *Ernst Jünger im Ersten Weltkrieg*, pp. 621–647.

3. Englund, *The Beauty and the Sorrow*, pp. 288–289.

4. Pyta, *Hindenburg*, pp. 205–226; Nebelin, *Ludendorff*, pp. 211–216.

5. Afflerbach, *Falkenhayn*, pp. 341–350.

6. Pantenius, *Der Angriffsgedanke gegen Italien*, vol. 2, pp. 772–782.

7. Sondhaus, *World War One*, pp. 206–207.

8. Afflerbach, "Planning Total War," pp. 118–122.

9. Falkenhayn, *Die Oberste Heeresleitung*, pp. 177–184; Foley, *German Strategy and the Path to Verdun*, pp. 181–208.

10. Afflerbach (ed.), *Kaiser Wilhelm II. als Oberster Kriegsherr*, pp. 360–362.

11. Afflerbach, *Falkenhayn*, pp. 360–375.

12. Krumeich, "Verdun," pp. 942–943.

13. Holmes, *The Western Front*, pp. 83–84.

14. Krumeich, "Verdun," p. 942.

15. Gygi, "Shaping Matter," pp. 27–44.

16. Baer, *Vom Stahlhelm zum Gefechtshelm*, vol. 1, pp. 12–42.

17. *Anweisung für die Ausbildung beim Sturmbataillon*, p. 5, quoted in: Raths, *Vom Massensturm zur Stoßtrupptaktik*, p. 166.

18. Ibid., p. 167; Samuels, *Doctrine and Dogma*, pp. 7–56; idem, *Command or Control*, pp. 7–33; Gudmundsson, *Stormtroop Tactics*, pp. 55–72.

19. Martens, *Hermann Göring*, pp. 15–16.

20. Ousby, *The Road to Verdun*, pp. 76–109.

21. *Kriegstagebuch eines Juden*, quoted in: Werth, *Das Tagebuch Europas*, pp. 61–62.

22. Quoted in: ibid., pp. 68–69.

23. Englund, *The Beauty and the Sorrow*, p. 275.

24. Krumeich, "Verdun," p. 944.

25. Sondhaus, *World War One*, p. 209.

26. Horne, *The Price of Glory*, pp. 327–328.

27. Krumeich, "Verdun: un lieu," p. 127; Ferragne, "Allocution inaugurale," p. 9; Audoin-Rouzeau and Becker, *14–18, retrouver la guerre*, p. 40; Audoin-Rouzeau and Krumeich, "Les batailles," pp. 304–305.

28. Sondhaus, *World War One*, p. 210.

29. Krumeich, "Der Mensch als 'Material,'" p. 300.

30. Werth, *Verdun*, pp. 155–156.

31. Pétain, *La bataille de Verdun*, pp. 51–92.

32. Sondhaus, *World War One*, p. 208; Prost, *Verdun*, pp. 259–260.

33. Canini, *Combattre à Verdun*, pp. 70–73; Raynal, *Le Drame du Fort de Vaux*.

34. Holmes, *The Western Front*, pp. 101–102.

35. Englund, *The Beauty and the Sorrow*, p. 274; Petermann, *Rituale machen Räume*, p. 125.

36. Ministère de la Guerre, *Les armées françaises*, vol. 4 / 1, Annexes, vol. 3, p. 325.

37. Poincaré, *Au service de la France*, vol. 8, p. 347.

38. Ministere de la Guerre, *Les armées françaises*, vol. 4 / 2, Annexes, vol. 2, p. 403.

39. Canini, *Combattre à Verdun*, pp. 59–60.

40. Ferro, *Pétain*, p. 678.

41. Münch, *Verdun*, pp. 191–200.

42. Zweig, *Education before Verdun;* Ettighofer, *Verdun*, p. 105; Krumeich, "Le soldat allemand devant Verdun," pp. 77–88.

43. Herwig, "War in the West," p. 60.

44. Wandt, *Erotik und Spionage*, quoted in: Johann (ed.), *Innenansicht eines Krieges*, p. 214.

45. *Kriegsecho* 117, November 3, 1916, quoted in: Werth, *Das Tagebuch Europas 1916*, pp. 79–80.

46. Krumeich, "Verdun," p. 944.

47. Werth, *Verdun*, pp. 449–464.

48. Münch, *Verdun*, pp. 453–460, 482–486.

49. Prete, "Joffre and the Origins of the Somme," pp. 417–448.

50. Duffy, *Through German Eyes*, pp. 113–127.

51. Bull, *Trench. A History of Trench Warfare*, pp. 179–200.

52. Prior and Wilson, *Command on the Western Front*, pp. 77–80 and 141–144.

53. Robert Cude, May 27, 1916, in: Palmer and Wallis (eds.), *Intimate Voices from the First World War*, p. 193.

54. Robert Cude, June 24, 1916, in: ibid., p. 194.

55. Ibid., p. 194.

56. Ibid., p. 195.

57. Ibid., p. 195.

58. Blücher, *An English Wife in Berlin*, p. 211; Clark, *The Donkeys;* Prior and Wilson, *The Somme*, pp. 114–116; Hirschfeld, "Die Somme-Schlacht von 1916," p. 83.

59. Kenyon, *Horsemen in No Man's Land*, p. 32; Prior and Wilson, *The Somme*, p. 134.

60. Brown, *British Logistics on the Western Front*, pp. 109–134.

61. Foley and McCartney (eds.), *The Somme*, pp. 86–114.

62. Middlebrook, *The First Day on the Somme*, p. 246; Herwig, "War in the West," p. 61.

63. Loughlin, "Mobilising the Sacred Dead," pp. 133–154.

64. Horne, "Irland," p. 588; Fitzpatrick, *The Two Irelands*, pp. 52–54; Jeffery, *Ireland and the Great War*, pp. 37–68.

65. Philpott, *Bloody Victory*, p. 626.

66. Simkins, "Somme," p. 854.

67. Gilbert, *Somme*, pp. 121–124.

68. Sondhaus, *World War One*, p. 214.

69. Duffy, *Through German Eyes*, pp. 297–304.

70. Larson, *The British Army*, pp. 71–107; Harris, *Men, Ideas and Tanks*, pp. 47–78; Wright, *Tank*, pp. 54–110; Groß, "Tank," pp. 917–919.

71. Kilduff, *Richthofen*, pp. 107–24; Castan, *Der Rote Baron*, pp. 101–156, 177–205.

72. Kehrt, "Heldenbilder und Kriegserfahrung," pp. 223–238.

73. Frantzen, *Bloody Good*, pp. 75–96, 149–194.

74. Sondhaus, *World War One*, pp. 210–216; Herwig, "War in the West," pp. 60–62; Hirschfeld, "Die Somme-Schlacht von 1916," p. 87.

75. Blücher, *An English Wife in Berlin*, p. 211; Clark, *The Donkeys*.

76. Letter of July 15, 1916, quoted in: Liddell Hart, *Liddell Hart's Western Front*, p. 104.

77. Liddell Hart, *A History of the World War*, pp. 305–307, 309–311, 313–315, 319, 326; Bond, "Editorial Notice," p. 112.

78. Robbins, *British Generalship*, pp. 290–291.

79. Harris, *Douglas Haig and the First World War*, pp. 531–546.

80. Terraine, *Douglas Haig*, pp. 483–485.

81. Quoted in: ibid., p. 234.

82. Philpott, *Three Armies on the Somme*, p. 541.

83. Terraine, *Douglas Haig*, pp. 232–235.

84. Simkins, "Somme," p. 855.

85. Hart, *The Somme*, p. 531.

86. Halpern, *A Naval History of World War I*, pp. 310–329; Marder, *From the Dreadnought to Scapa Flow*, vol. 3, pp. 233–259.

87. Yates, *Flawed Victory*, pp. 215–225; Rahn, "Die Seeschlacht vor dem Skagerrak," p. 188.

88. Salewski, "Seekrieg," pp. 828–830.

89. Address by Wilhelm II, in: *Die deutsche Seekriegsleitung*, vol. 2, document 189, p. 98; Rahn, "Die Seeschlacht vor dem Skagerrak," p. 189.

90. Ibid., pp. 189–190.

91. Weizsäcker, *Die Weizsäcker Papiere*, p. 215, quoted in: Wolz, *Das lange Warten*, p. 467.

92. Scheer, *Germany's High Seas Fleet*, p. 169; "Immediatbericht des Kommandos der Hochseestreitkräfte," pp. 213–214.

93. Gordon, *The Rules of the Game*, p. 564.

94. Stegemann, *Die deutsche Marinepolitik 1916–1918*, pp. 36–43.

95. Kelly, *Tirpitz and the Imperial Germany Navy*, pp. 408–409.

96. Neugebauer, "Die Urkatastrophe des 20. Jahrhunderts," pp. 64–66; Salewski, "Seekrieg," pp. 829–830; Terraine, *Business in Great Waters*, pp. 17–39.

97. Hagenlücke, *Deutsche Vaterlandspartei*, p. 75; Epkenhans, "Vom Seekadetten zum Vizeadmiral," p. 78.

98. Winter, *The Experience of World War I*, p. 207; Geyer, "Gewalt und Gewalterfahrung im 20. Jahrhundert," pp. 243–44.

99. Artl, *Die österreichisch-ungarische Südtiroloffensive*, p. 178.

100. Sondhaus, *World War One*, pp. 216–218.

101. Stone, *The Eastern Front*, p. 231.

102. Dowling, *The Brusilov Offensive*, pp. 35–61.

103. Ibid., pp. 62–87.

104. Redlich, *Das politische Tagebuch*, vol. 2, June 14, 1916, p. 121.

105. Sondhaus, *Franz Conrad von Hötzendorf*, pp. 200–201.

106. Sondhaus, *World War One*, p. 223; Keegan, *The First World War*, pp. 304–305; Stevenson, *1914–1918: The First World War*, p. 197; Stone, "Brussilow-Offensive," p. 396.

107. Sondhaus, *World War One*, p. 230.

108. Ibid., pp. 233–235.

109. Torrey, "Romania's Decision to Intervene," pp. 95–120.

110. Hitchins, *Ionel Brătianu*, pp. 65–83.

111. Torrey, "Romania and the Belligerents 1914–1916," pp. 17–21.

112. Afflerbach, *Falkenhayn*, pp. 437–450; Janßen, *Der Kanzler und der General*, pp. 238–252.

113. Hitchins, *Rumania*, pp. 262–279; Torrey, "The Romanian Campaign of 1916," pp. 173–194; Torrey, "Romania Leaves the War," pp. 291–300.

114. Torrey, "Indifference and Mistrust," pp. 299–300.

115. Sondhaus, *World War One*, p. 231; Höpken, "Rumänien," pp. 806–807.

116. Despotopoulos, *Greece's Contribution*.

117. Dalby, *Eleftherios Venizelos*, pp. 55–75.

118. Leon, *Greece and the Great Powers*, pp. 438–489.

119. Leontaritis, *Greece and the First World War*, pp. 45–79.

120. Ibid., pp. 367–395.

121. Loulos, "Griechenland," pp. 534–537.

122. Townshend, *Desert Hell*, pp. 249–255.

123. Klieman, "Britain's War Aims in the Middle East," pp. 237–251.

124. Taylor, "The War Aims of the Allies in the First World War," p. 483; Stevenson, *French War Aims against Germany*, p. 27.

125. Linke, *Das zaristische Russland und der Erste Weltkrieg*, pp. 238–240.

126. Gehrke, *Persien in der deutschen Orientpolitik*, p. 90.

127. Tauber, *The Formation of Modern Syria and Iraq*, pp. 1–10; Catherwood, *Churchill's Folly*, pp. 41–62.

128. Monroe, *Britain's Moment in the Middle East*, pp. 23–49.

129. Fisher, *Curzon and British Imperialism in the Middle East*, pp. 66–110; Friedman, *British Pan-Arab Policy*, pp. 43–92.

130. Hurewitz, *Diplomacy in the Near and Middle East*, vol. 2, p. 15; Helmreich, *From Paris to Sèvres*, p. 6.

131. Barr, *A Line in the Sand*, pp. 7–36.

132. Fromkin, *A Peace to End All Peace*, pp. 342–345; Zürcher, "Sykes-Picot-Abkommen," p. 916.

133. Tauber, *The Emergence of the Arab Movements*, pp. 309–310.

134. Tauber, *The Arab Movements in World War I*, pp. 101–164.

135. Weizmann, "Introduction," pp. 6–8; Panter, *Jüdische Erfahrungen*, p. 145.

136. Adams and Poirier, *The Conscription Controversy in Great Britain*, pp. 119–170; Simkins, *Kitchener's Army*, pp. 138–161.

137. Leonhard, *Bellizismus und Nation*, pp. 83–85, 282–285, 464–472.

138. Jenkins, *Asquith*, pp. 387–404.

139. "Methods of Controversy," in: *Westminster Gazette*, June 2, 1915, quoted in: Freeden, *Liberalism Divided*, p. 20.

140. J. R. Tomlinson, "Liberalism and the War: Letter to the Editor," in: *Nation*, October 23, 1915, quoted in: Freeden, *Liberalism Divided*, p. 22.

141. Gregory, "Britain and Ireland," p. 410.

142. Adams and Poirier, *The Conscription Controversy in Great Britain*, pp. 217–230.

143. Fitzpatrick, *The Two Irelands*, p. 54.

144. "Proclamation of the Irish Republic. The Provisional Government of the Irish Republic to the People of Ireland, Dublin, 24 April 1916," quoted in: MacArthur (ed.), *The Penguin Book of Twentieth Century Speeches*, pp. 50–51.

145. Quoted in: ibid., pp. 51–51.

146. Laffan, *The Resurrection of Ireland*, pp. 77–168.

147. Fitzpatrick, *The Two Irelands*, pp. 58–63.

148. Roger Casement, "Speech from the Dock, Summer 1916," in: MacArthur (ed.), *The Penguin Book of Twentieth Century Speeches*, pp. 53, 57–58.

149. Dungan, *Irish Voices from the Great War*, pp. 130–150; Orr, "200,000 Volunteer Soldiers," pp. 63–77.

150. Quoted in: Bowman, *The Irish Regiments in the Great War*, p. 154.

151. Gregory, *Britain and Ireland*, pp. 409–410.

152. Ibid., p. 410; Broadberry and Howlett, "The United Kingdom during World War I," pp. 215–217.

153. Thompson, *Politicians, the Press and Propaganda*, pp. 103–122.

154. Schulze, *Staat und Nation in der europäischen Geschichte*, p. 281.

155. Ibid., p. 285; Marwick, *Britain in the Century of the Total War*, pp. 76–78.

156. Grigg, *Lloyd George*, pp. 475–503; Sharp, *David Lloyd George*, pp. 28–45.

157. Wilson, *The Myriad Faces of War*, pp. 408–423; Gregory, "Britain and Ireland," p. 410.

158. French, *British Strategy and War Aims*, pp. 244–249.

159. Quoted in: ibid., p. 247.

160. Quoted in: ibid., p. 248.

161. French, *The Strategy of the Lloyd George Coalition*, pp. 40–66.

162. Holland, "The British Empire and the Great War," p. 125.

163. Stanley, "He Was Black," pp. 213–230; Jeffery, "Writing out of Opinions," pp. 249–264; Smith, "Heaven Grant You Strength," pp. 265–282.

164. Winegard, *For King and Kanata*, pp. 12–22, 146, 170.

165. Segesser, *Empire und Totaler Krieg*, pp. 495–516.

166. Ibid., pp. 524–530.

167. Saini, "The Economic Aspects," pp. 141–176.

168. Speech by Madan Mohan Malaviya at the Imperial Legislative Council, March 23, 1917, quoted in: Manela, *The Wilsonian Moment*, p. 82.

169. Barrier, "Ruling India," pp. 75–108.

170. Quoted in: Manela, *The Wilsonian Moment*, p. 83; Brown, *Modern India*, pp. 188–198; Mukherjee, "The Home Rule Movement and Its Fallout," pp. 159–169.

171. Wolpert, "Congress Leadership in Transition," pp. 127–140; idem, *Gandhi's Passion*, pp. 82–98.

172. Mahatma Gandhi, Speech in Benares, February 4, 1916, in: MacArthur (ed.), *The Penguin Book of Twentieth Century Speeches*, pp. 48–49.

173. Englund, *The Beauty and the Sorrow*, p. 282.

174. Naour, *Claire Ferchaud*, pp. 29–55.

175. Jonas, *France and the Cult of the Sacred Heart*, pp. 198–243.

176. Jonas, *The Tragic Tale of Claire Ferchaud and the Great War*, pp. 62–95; Naour, *Claire Ferchaud*, pp. 87–122; Hanna, "The Tidal Wave of War," pp. 96–98.

177. Winkler, *The Age of Catastrophe*, p. 9.

178. Duroselle, *Clemenceau*, pp. 592–601.

179. Keiger, *Raymond Poincaré*, pp. 225–227.

180. Becker, "Frankreich," p. 35.

181. Ibid., p. 36.

182. Smith, *The Embattled Self*, pp. 69–72.

183. Procacci, "Popular Protest," pp. 31–58; Tomassini, "Industrial Mobilization," pp. 59–87; Morrow, *The Great War*, pp. 162–163.

184. Pyta, *Hindenburg*, pp. 115–153.

185. Schulze, *Staat und Nation in der europäischen Geschichte*, pp. 285–287.

186. Nebelin, *Ludendorff*, pp. 245–246, quoted in: Schulze, *Staat und Nation*, p. 246.

187. Geyer, "Hindenburg-Programm," p. 557.

188. Nebelin, *Ludendorff*, p. 258.

189. Redlich, *Das politische Tagebuch*, pp. 120–121.

190. Feldman, *Arms, Industry, and Labor*, pp. 197–234; Mai, *Arbeiterschaft in Deutschland*; idem, "Hilfsdienstgesetz," pp. 553–554.

191. Björnson, *Vom deutschen Wesen*, quoted in: Johann (ed.), *Innenansicht eines Krieges*, p. 223.

192. Geyer, "Hindenburg-Programm," pp. 557–58.

193. Rathenau, *Walter Rathenau: Industrialist, Banker, Intellectual, and Politician*, p. 216.

194. *Der große Krieg*, quoted in: Johann (ed.), *Innenansicht eines Krieges*, pp. 179–180, 182–183, 199.

195. Kruse, *Der Erste Weltkrieg*, pp. 99–103.

196. Davis, *Home Fires Burning*, pp. 22, 184.

197. Offer, *The First World War*, pp. 46, 51–53.

198. Hampe, *Kriegstagebuch*, June 4, 1916, p. 400.

199. Davis, *Home Fires Burning*, p. 117.

200. Hampe, *Kriegstagebuch*, October 1, 1916, p. 444.

201. Pless, November 4, 1916, in: *Regierte der Kaiser*, quoted in: Johann (Hg.), *Innenansicht eines Krieges*, p. 215.

202. Mommsen, *Die Urkatastrophe Deutschlands*, pp. 84–87.

203. Ullmann, *Der deutsche Steuerstaat*, pp. 88–96.

204. Chickering, *Freiburg im Ersten Weltkrieg*, pp. 493–520.

205. Nübel, *Die Mobilisierung der Kriegsgesellschaft*, p. 157.

206. Sondhaus, *World War One*, p. 340.

207. Röhl, *Wilhelm II*, pp. 1200–1208; Clark, *Kaiser Wilhelm II*, pp. 307–357.

208. Cullen, *The Reichstag*, pp. 44–45.

209. Haase (ed.), *Hugo Haase*, quoted in: Johann (ed.), *Innenansicht eines Krieges*, p. 181.

210. Pulzer, "The First World War," pp. 360–384.

211. Quoted in: Panter, *Jüdische Erfahrungen*, p. 184; Angress, "Das deutsche Militär und die Juden im Ersten Weltkrieg," pp. 77–146; Sieg, *Jüdische Intellektuelle im Ersten Weltkrieg*, pp. 90–95.

212. Rechter, *The Jews of Vienna and the First World War*, pp. 78–81.

213. Heumos, "Kartoffeln her oder es gibt eine Revolution," p. 256.

214. Cornwall, "The Wartime Bohemia of Franz Kafka," p. 44.

215. Ibid., p. 40; Healy, *Vienna and the Fall of the Habsburg Empire*, pp. 185–193.

216. Cornwall, "Austria-Hungary and 'Yugoslavia,'" pp. 376–377.

217. Mommsen, "Viktor Adler und die Politik der österreichischen Sozialdemokratie," pp. 378–408.

218. Neck, *Arbeiterschaft und Staat im Ersten Weltkrieg*, vol. 1, p. 160.

219. Ibid., p. 157.

220. Redlich, *Tagebuch*, vol. 2, June 3, 1916, pp. 118–119.

221. *Neue Freie Presse*, October 26, 1918.

222. Redlich, *Das österreichische Staats- und Rechtsproblem*, vol. 1, p. 89.

223. Cornwall, *The Wartime Bohemia of Franz Kafka*, pp. 40–41.

224. Havránek, "Politische Repression und Versorgungsengpässe," pp. 59–62.

225. Binder, *Kafkas Welt*, pp. 472–473.

226. Hadler, "Die Herausbildung der tschechisch-slowakischen Zusammenarbeit," pp. 83–92.

227. Hoensch, *Geschichte Böhmens*, p. 410.

228. Orzoff, *Battle for the Castle*, pp. 23–56.

229. Agnew, *The Czechs and the Lands of the Bohemian Crown*, pp. 166–167.

230. Redlich, *Tagebuch*, vol. 2, November 22, 1916, pp. 155–156.

231. Agnew, "The Flyspecks on Palivec's Portrait," pp. 86–112.

232. Cornwall, "Austria-Hungary and 'Yugoslavia,'" p. 381.

233. Rees, *The Czechs during World War I*, pp. 22–46.

234. Vermes, *István Tisza*, p. 370.

235. Ibid., pp. 348–366.

236. Galántai, *Hungary in the First World War*, pp. 256–263.

237. Cornwall, "Austria-Hungary and 'Yugoslavia,'" pp. 380–381.

238. Krumeich and Lepsius, "Einleitung," p. 5.

239. Borodziej, *Geschichte Polens*, pp. 75–77, 83–85.

240. Hecker, "Polen," pp. 778–779.

241. Rozenblit, *Reconstructing National Identity*, pp. 106–127; Cornwall, *The Wartime Bohemia of Franz Kafka*, p. 43.

242. Kafka, *Diaries, 1910–1923*, p. 301.

243. Cornwall, "The Wartime Bohemia of Franz Kafka," pp. 39–40.

244. Bergmann, "Der jüdische Nationalismus nach dem Krieg," p. 7; Kilcher, "Zionistischer Kriegsdiskurs im Ersten Weltkrieg," p. 66.

245. Zechlin, *Die deutsche Politik und die Juden*, pp. 198–123; Panter, *Jüdische Erfahrungen*, pp. 268–271.

246. Neilson, *Strategy and Supply*, pp. 141–166.

247. Gatrell, "Modernisation Strategies and Outcomes in Pre-Revolutionary Russia," p. 36; Neutatz, *Träume und Alpträume*, p. 141.

248. Gatrell, *Russia's First World War*, p. 171.

249. Lohr, "War and Revolution," pp. 659–661; Beyrau and Shcherbinin, "Alles für die Front," pp. 155–158; Neutatz, *Träume und Alpträume*, pp. 140–142.

250. Gleason and Porter, "The Zemstvo and Public Initiative," pp. 419–437.

251. Hamm, "Liberal Politics in Wartime Russia," pp. 453–468; Neutatz, *Träume und Alpträume*, pp. 142–153.

252. Dahlmann, "Russland," p. 91.

253. Hildermeier, *Die Russische Revolution*, p. 131.

254. Neutatz, *Träume und Alpträume*, p. 143.

255. Ibid., pp. 143–144; Haimson, *The Problem of Social Stability in Urban Russia*, Part One, pp. 619–642 and Part Two, pp. 1–22.

256. Hildermeier, *Die Russische Revolution*, pp. 131–132.

257. Sanborn, *Drafting the Russian Nation*, pp. 204–205.

258. Narskij, "Kriegswirklichkeit und Kriegserfahrung russischer Soldaten," pp. 249–262.

259. Baberowski, "Einführende Bemerkungen," pp. 150–151; Beyrau, *Der Erste Weltkrieg als Bewährungsprobe*, pp. 96–123.

260. Happel, *Nomadische Lebenswelten und zarische Politik*, pp. 55.

261. Ibid., pp. 303–306.

262. Ibid., pp. 307–324.

263. Kappeler, *The Russian Empire*, pp. 351–352.

264. Baberowski, "Diktaturen der Eindeutigkeit," pp. 48–49; idem, "Ordnung durch Terror," pp. 149–150.

265. Borodziej, *Geschichte Polens*, pp. 84–85.

266. Geyer, "German Strategy in the Age of Machine Warfare," pp. 527–597; Herwig, "War in the West," p. 63.

267. Clausewitz, *On War*, p. 613.

268. Delbrück, *Geschichte der Kriegskunst*, vol. 1, p. 613 and vol. 4, pp. 514–521; "Nachtrag. Über den Gegensatz der Ermattungs- und Niederwerfungsstrategie."

269. Delbrück, "Über die Verschiedenheit der Strategie Friedrichs und Napoleons," p. 241.

270. Chamberlain, *Foundations of the Nineteenth Century*, p. 276.

271. Hindenburg, "Über Personalersatz und Kriegsmaterial," p. 63.

272. *Vorschriften für den Stellungskrieg aller Waffen*, vol. 2, p. 69, quoted in: Raths, "Die Überlegenheit der Verteidigung," p. 396.

273. Jünger, *In Stahlgewittern* (1978), "Preface," p. iii.

274. Lee, *Virginia Woolf*, p. 345; I am grateful to Nicole Jordan for this reference.

275. Falkenhayn, *Die Oberste Heeresleitung*, pp. 245–246.

276. Meteling, *Ehre, Einheit, Ordnung*, pp. 274–292.

277. Watson, *Enduring the Great War*, pp. 44–84, 140–183.

278. Quoted in: Roper, *The Secret Battle*, p. 188.

279. Jünger, *Kriegstagebuch*, p. 167.

280. Jünger, *The Storm of Steel*, pp. 91–92. This passage, translated from Jünger's last revised edition of 1978, differs markedly from the original version published in 1920, incorporating in part the revisions first made in 1934: see Jünger, *In Stahlgewittern*, vol.1 (2013), pp. 206–209.

281. Jünger, *The Storm of Steel*, p. 140.

282. Ibid., p. 185.

283. Ibid., p. 216.

284. Langewiesche, "Gefühlsraum Nation," pp. 203–211.

285. Kiesel, "Ernst Jünger im Ersten Weltkrieg," pp. 624, 628–631.

286. Quoted in: Werth, *Das Tagebuch Europas 1916*, pp. 68–70.

287. Englund, *The Beauty and the Sorrow*, p. 307.

288. Carossa, *Roumanian Diary*, pp. 11–12.

289. Ibid., pp. 42–43.

290. Ludwig, *Beiträge zur Psychologie der Furcht im Kriege*.

291. Ibid., p. 6.

292. Quoted in: ibid., pp. 6–7.

293. Ibid., p. 7.

294. Ibid., pp. 22–23.

295. Everth, *Von der Seele des Soldaten im Felde*, p. 41; Ludwig, *Beiträge zur Psychologie der Furcht im Kriege*, p. 24.

296. Ludwig, *Beiträge zur Psychologie der Furcht im Kriege*, p. 48.

297. Ibid., p. 39.

298. Carossa, *Roumanian Diary*, pp. 25–26.

299. Kessler, *Tagebuch*, vol. 5, April 24, 1916, p. 532.

300. Monk, *Wittgenstein*, pp. 137–168; quotations from pp. 138, 141, 146.

301. Chielens, "Les troupes coloniales françaises sur le front en Flandre," pp. 51–88; Dendooven, "Les dominions et colonies britanniques," pp. 89–116; Dendooven, "Troupes de l'Inde britannique," pp. 117–130.

302. Koller, "Colonialisme militaire en France et dans l'Empire Britannique," pp. 11–22; Dendooven, "Les armées européennes," pp. 23–50; Dendooven, "Living Apart Together," pp. 143–157.

303. Dabringhaus, *Geschichte Chinas*, pp. 23, 48–49.

304. Xu, *Strangers on the Western Front*, p. 226; Xu, *China and the Great War*, pp. 258–265; Dabringhaus, *Geschichte Chinas*, p. 49.

305. Hayford, *To the People*, pp. 22–31.

306. Canetti, *The Tongue Set Free*, p. 165.

307. Delaporte, "Military Medicine," p. 296.

308. Delaporte, *Les Médecins dans la Grande Guerre*, pp. 15–86.

309. Delaporte, "Military Medicine," pp. 298, 300–302; idem, *Les Médecins dans la Grande Guerre*, pp. 89–157.

310. Delaporte, "Military Medicine," pp. 300–301.

311. Michl, *Im Dienste des "Volkskörpers,"* pp. 111–112, 273–281.

312. Whitehead, *Doctors in the Great War*, pp. 252–253.

313. Kuttner, *Vergessen*, quoted in: Ulrich, ". . . als wenn nichts geschehen wäre," p. 141.

314. Delaporte, *Les Gueules Cassées*, pp. 173–214.

315. Eckart, "Invalidität," pp. 584–586.

316. Winter, "The Strain of Trench Warfare," p. 84.

317. Michl, "Gehe hin, dein Glaube hat dir geholfen," pp. 219–227.

318. Leese, *Shell Shock*, pp. 13–47; Shephard, *A War of Nerves*, pp. 21–32.

319. Dessoir, *Kriegspsychologische Betrachtungen*, pp. 4–5; I am grateful to Andrea von Hohenthal for drawing my attention to this quote.

320. Bonhoeffer, *Erfahrungen aus dem Kriege*, p. 77, quoted in: Bröckling, *Disziplin*, p. 210.

321. Ibid., p. 211.

322. Quoted in: ibid., p. 227.

323. Ibid., pp. 213–220.

324. Ashplant, *Fractured Loyalties*, pp. 168–184.

325. Ullrich, *Die nervöse Großmacht*; Radkau, *Das Zeitalter der Nervosität*.

326. Lerner, "Hysterical Cures," pp. 79–101; idem, *Hysterical Men*, pp. 124–162.

327. Buttersack, "Die Suggestion und ihre Verwendung als Heilfaktor," p. 514, quoted in: Michl, "Gehe hin, dein Glaube hat dir geholfen," p. 221.

328. Ibid., pp. 223–225.

329. Michl, *Im Dienste des "Volkskörpers,"* pp. 218–231.

330. Leonhard, *Bellizismus und Nation*, pp. 791–797.

331. Smith, *Jamaican Volunteers*, p. 169.

332. Anderson, *War, Disability and Rehabilitation in Britain*, pp. 42–71.

333. Reznick, *Healing the Nation*, pp. 42–64, 99–115.

334. Philips, *Manipulating Masculinity*, pp. 41–84.

335. Das, *Touch and Intimacy in First World War Literature*, pp. 27, 109–136.

336. Ibid., p. 189.

337. Eckart, "Invalidität," pp. 584–586; Geyer, "Ein Vorbote des Wohlfahrtsstaates," pp. 230–277.

338. Cohen, *The War Come Home*, pp. 149–187.

339. Biesalski, "Wer ist der Führer in der gesamten Fürsorge," quoted in: Nieden, "Verdrängen durch Überspielen," p. 268.

340. Meyer, "Kriegsbeschädigtenfürsorge und Taylorsystem," p. 147, quoted in: Ulrich, ". . . als wenn nichts geschehen wäre," p. 150.

341. Ziemann, "Soldaten," pp. 165–166; Kruse, *Der Erste Weltkrieg*, pp. 58–60.

342. Kraepelin, "Psychiatrische Randbemerkungen zur Zeitgeschichte," pp. 171–183, quoted in: Geyer, *Verkehrte Welt*, pp. 99–100.

343. Kienitz, *Beschädigte Helden*, pp. 170–237, 344–353.

344. Goffman, *Stigma*, pp. 123–125.

345. Jünger, *Kriegstagebuch*, 28. Juli 1916, p. 176.

346. Pöppinghege und Proctor, "Außerordentlicher Bedarf für das Feldheer," pp. 103–117.

347. Kaufmann, *Kommunikationstechnik und Kriegführung*, pp. 159–169; idem, "Kommunikationstechnik," pp. 621–624.

348. Manela, *The Wilsonian Moment*, pp. 45–47; Wüstenbecker, "Die Vereinigten Staaten von Amerika," p. 218; Müller-Pohl, "Working the Nation State," pp. 101–123.

349. Lindner-Wirsching, "Patrioten im Pool," pp. 130–131.

350. Götter, "Wundermittel Medien?," pp. 16–23.

351. Marquis, "Words as Weapons," pp. 474–486; Altenhöner, *Kommunikation und Kontrolle*, pp. 83–88.

352. Thompson, *Politicians, the Press and Propaganda*, pp. 214–216.

353. Köroğlu, *Ottoman Propaganda and Turkish Identity*, pp. 72–110, 185–197.

354. Reimann, *Der Erste Weltkrieg*, pp. 72–73, 126.

355. Welch, *Germany, Propaganda and Total War*, p. 159.

356. Daniel, "Informelle Kommunikation und Propaganda," pp. 76–93; Altenhöner, *Kommunikation und Kontrolle*, p. 219.

357. Ibid., pp. 145–148, quotation on p. 148.

358. Reimann, *Der große Krieg der Sprachen*, pp. 186, 210–112.

359. Latzel, *Deutsche Soldaten—nationalsozialistischer Krieg*, pp. 156–182.

360. Kruse, *Der Erste Weltkrieg*, pp. 64–65.

361. Reimann, *Der große Krieg der Sprachen*, pp. 279–280.

362. Quoted in: Ulrich, *Die Augenzeugen*, p. 62.

363. Hettling and Jeismann, "Der Weltkrieg als Epos," pp. 205–234.

364. Quoted in: Corino, *Robert Musil*, p. 245.

365. Lipp, *Meinungslenkung im Krieg*, pp. 307–320.

366. Biguzzi, *Cesare Battisti*, pp. 539–756.

367. Holzer, *Die andere Front*, pp. 249–253.

368. Biguzzi, *Cesare Battisti*, pp. 589–606.

369. Kraus, *The Last Days*, p. 383.

370. Hüppauf, "Kriegsfotografie an der Schwelle zum neuen Sehen," pp. 205–233; idem, "Kriegsfotografie," pp. 875–909; Krumeich, "Kriegsfotografie zwischen Erleben und Propaganda," pp. 117–132.

371. Holzer, *Die andere Front*, pp. 255–256.

372. Hüppauf, "Fotografie im Ersten Weltkrieg," pp. 108–123.

373. Köppen, "Luftbilder," pp. 180–187.

374. Gaulke, "Kunst und Kino im Kriege," p. 619, quoted in: Riederer, "Einleitung," p. 71.

375. Hüppauf, "Ikonographie," p. 570.

376. *Deutsche Kunst und Dekoration* 22 (1918), quoted in: Johann (ed.), *Innenansicht eines Krieges*, pp. 331–332.

377. Didier (ed.), *In Papiergewittern*, pp. 156, 167–168.

378. Brocks, *Die bunte Welt des Krieges*, pp. 29, 50–51, 237–252.

379. Pairault, *Images de poilus*, p. 24.

380. Ibid., pp. 80–81, 84–85, 88–91.

381. Ibid., pp. 40–45.

382. Ibid., 56–61, 112–119.

383. Ibid., pp. 62–67.

384. Eksteins, *Rites of Spring*, pp. 300–331.

385. Winter, *Sites of Memory*, pp. 223–229.

386. Confino, *The Nation as a Local Metaphor*, pp. 9, 165, 168; illustrations in ibid., pp. 194–201.

387. Waugh, "Shakespeare's Warriors," pp. 113–124; Stopes, "Shakespeare and War," pp. 1057–1070; Rhys (ed.), *The Old Country*; Raleigh, *England at War*; Howkins, "The Discovery of Rural England," pp. 79–85; Coetzee, "English Nationalism and the First World War," p. 366.

388. Letter from Robert Williams, in: *Daily News and Leader*, June 15, 1915, quoted in: Coetzee, "English Nationalism and the First World War," pp. 364–365.

389. Zglinicki, *Der Weg des Films*, quoted in: Johann (ed.), *Innenansicht eines Krieges*, pp. 265–266.

390. Gregory, "Britain and Ireland," p. 410; Sorlin, "Film and the War," pp. 353–367.

391. Fraser, Robertshaw, and Roberts, *Ghosts on the Somme*, pp. 86–106; Kilb, "Blut in den Gräben"; Hammond, "The Battle of the Somme," pp. 19–38.

392. Smither, "A Wonderful Idea of the Fighting," pp. 149–168.

393. *Deutsche Kriegsausstellungen 1916*, pp. 5, 67.

394. Müller-Jarbusch, "Kriegs-Museen," quoted in: Zwach, *Deutsche und englische Militärmuseen*, p. 80; Pessler, *Das historische Museum und der Weltkrieg*, Part 1: pp. 68–75, 143–155, Part 2: pp. 91–104, 199–203, Part 3: pp. 52–82; Zwach, "Ein Volkskundler im Ersten Weltkrieg," pp. 14–31.

395. *Prager Tageblatt*, morning edition, November 19, 1915, p. 5; Anz, "Motive des Militärischen in Kafkas Erzähltexten," p. 177.

396. Pessler, *Das historische Museum* (1916), p. 94, quoted in: Zwach, *Deutsche und englische Militärmuseen*, p. 81.

397. Pessler, *Das historische Museum* (1916), p. 100, quoted in: ibid, p. 83.

398. Ibid., pp. 88–91.

399. Ibid., p. 85.

400. Englund, *The Beauty and the Sorrow*, p. 81.

401. Krivanec, *Kriegsbühnen*.

402. Baumeister, *Kriegstheater*, pp. 183, 156.

403. Hampe, *Kriegstagebuch*, June 7, 1916, pp. 401–402.

404. Jeismann, "Angstschweiß auf der Stirn Europas."

6. EXPANSION AND EROSION

1. Hölzle, "Formverwandlung der Geschichte," pp. 329–344.

2. Garnier and Le Bon (eds.), *1917*, pp. 228–231.

3. Ibid., pp. 236–337.

4. Saunders, *Trench Art*, pp. 35–51.

5. Spies, "Das Ende der Darstellbarkeit"; Garnier and Le Bon (eds.), *1917*, pp. 35–67.

6. Hopman, diary entry for February 1, 1917, in: Epkenhans (ed.), *Das ereignisreiche Leben*, pp. 954–855.

7. Hopman, diary entry for April 1, 1917, in: ibid., p. 971.

8. Stegemann, *Die deutsche Marinepolitik*, pp. 71–76.

9. Samuels, *Command or Control*, pp. 158–197.

10. Geyer, "Rückzug und Zerstörung," pp. 163–202; Sondhaus, *World War One*, p. 244.

11. Griffith, "The Extent of Tactical Reform," pp. 1–22.

12. Clayton, *Paths of Glory*, pp. 120–135.

13. Hart, *Bloody April*, pp. 115–120.

14. Englund, *The Beauty and the Sorrow*, p. 355.

15. Sondhaus, *World War One*, p. 253.

16. Ibid., p. 255.

17. Carré, *Les Grandes Heures du Général Pétain*, pp. 99–118; Amouroux, *Pétain avant Vichy*, pp. 77–123; Szaluta, "Marshal Pétain and the French Army Mutiny," pp. 181–210; Szaluta, "Marshal Pétain and French Nationalism," pp. 113–118; Fisher, *Philippe Pétain*, pp. 80–82; Azéma, "Pétain et les mutineries de 1917," pp. 80–85.

18. Wolff, *In Flanders Fields*, pp. 195–209.

19. Griffith, *Battle Tactics of the Western Front*, p. 79.

20. Bourne, "Flandern," pp. 492–494; Sondhaus, *World War One*, pp. 256–259.

21. Samuels, *Doctrine and Dogma*, pp. 111–168.

22. Connelly, *Steady the Buffs*, pp. 156–157.

23. Sheldon, *The German Army at Cambrai*, pp. 227–272.

24. Smithers, *Cambrai*, pp. 150–80.

25. Beckett (ed.), *1917: Beyond the Western Front*.

26. Abraham, *Alexander Kerensky*, pp. 214–221.

27. Stone, "Brussilow-Offensive," pp. 394–396.

28. Mazower, *Dark Continent*, pp. 60–62; Englund, *The Beauty and the Sorrow*, pp. 402, 434.

29. Schindler, *Isonzo*, pp. 243–265.

30. Schmid, "Die Überlegenheit des Angriffs," pp. 380–395.

31. Sondhaus, *World War One*, p. 260.

32. Radax, "Giftgas und das 'Wunder von Karfreit,'" pp. 49–51.

33. Monticone, *La battaglia di Caporetto*, pp. 146–81; Felberbauer, "Die 12. Isonzoschlacht," pp. 13–33.

34. Lichem, *Krieg in den Alpen*, vol. 3, pp. 293–308; Scheffl, "Die Kriegsgefangenen," p. 101; Sondhaus, *World War One*, p. 262.

35. Massignani, "Caporetto (Karfreit)," pp. 405–406.

36. Schindler, *Isonzo*, pp. 258; Sondhaus, *World War One*, p. 262.

37. Woller, *Geschichte Italiens*, pp. 74–75.

38. Janz, "Zwischen Konsens und Dissens," pp. 205–206.

39. Woller, *Geschichte Italiens*, pp. 75–76.

40. Sondhaus, *World War One*, pp. 259–264.

41. Kessler, *Journey to the Abyss*, October 3, 1917, pp. 781, 783–784.

42. Idem, *Tagebuch*, vol. 6, December 8, 1917, p. 211.

43. Becker, *1917 en Europe*.

44. Smith, "France," p. 424.

45. Vial, *Territoriaux de France*, p. 34, quoted in: Smith, "France," p. 424.

46. Mairet, *Carnet d'un combattant*, pp. 249–250, quoted in: Smith, "France," p. 424.

47. Smith, *Between Mutiny and Obedience*, pp. 99–124.

48. Becker, "Frankreich," pp. 710–711.

49. Englund, *The Beauty and the Sorrow*, p. 375.

50. Hanna, *Spaces of War*, p. 55.

51. Smith, *Between Mutiny and Obedience*, pp. 175–214.

52. Bock and Bonzon, "Il faut que vous sachiez ce qui se passe chez nous," pp. 167–180.

53. Smith, "The French High Command," pp. 79–92.

54. Pedroncini, *Les mutineries de 1917*, pp. 232–278, 302–306.

55. Bavendamm, *Spionage und Verrat*, pp. 246–267.

56. Smith, "France," pp. 426–427; Becker, "Frankreich," pp. 710–711; Pedroncini, *Les mutineries de 1917*, pp. 194–231.

57. Sondhaus, *World War One*, p. 256.

58. Becker, "Frankreich," p. 42.

59. Lane, *An Adequate Response*, pp. 87–120.

60. Sassoon, *Diaries 1915–1918*, pp. 173–174; Wilson, *Siegfried Sassoon*, pp. 373–376; Ashplant, *Fractured Loyalties*, p. 92.

61. Ashplant, *Fractured Loyalties*, pp. 92–93.

62. Jahr, *Gewöhnliche Soldaten*, p. 18.

63. Ibid., pp. 79–107, 333–338.

64. Englund, *The Beauty and the Sorrow*, p. 377.

65. Ibid., p. 381.

66. Janz, "Zwischen Konsens und Dissens," p. 202; Procacci, *Soldati e prigionieri italiani*.

67. Quoted in: Englund, *The Beauty and the Sorrow*, p. 466.

68. Hinz, "Kriegsgefangene," p. 641.

69. Idem, *Das Kriegsgefangenenrecht*, pp. 7–10; Rosas, *The Legal Status of Prisoners of War*, pp. 69–80.

70. Lange, "Recherches académiques sur les prisonniers de guerre," pp. 154–157; Mahrenholz, "Les enregistrements sonores ethnographiques," pp. 161–166.

71. Jones, *Violence against Prisoners of War*, pp. 371–374.

72. Ibid., pp. 374–376.

73. Hinz, *Gefangen im Großen Krieg*, p. 362.

74. Stibbe, *British Civilian Internees in Germany*, pp. 184–189.

75. Connes, *A POW's Memoir of the First World War*, pp. 37–76.

76. Becker, *Les Oubliés de la Grande Guerre*, p. 100.

77. Nachtigal, *Rußland und seine österreichisch-ungarischen Kriegsgefangenen*; idem, *Kriegsgefangenschaft an der Ostfront 1914 bis 1918*.

78. Leidinger and Moritz, *Gefangenschaft, Revolution, Heimkehr*, pp. 377–409.

79. *Heimat* 13, May 30, 1918, p. 2, quoted in: Corino, *Robert Musil*, pp. 256–257.

80. Kruse, *Der Erste Weltkrieg*, pp. 74–75.

81. Winkle, *Der Dank des Vaterlandes*, p. 243.

82. Englund, *The Beauty and the Sorrow*, pp. 359–360.

83. Ibid., pp. 361–62.

84. "Berichte über die Stimmung der Armee, 2. bis 10. September 1917," in: Lorenz (ed.), *Die Russische Revolution 1917*, pp. 295–296.

85. "Aus Briefen turkestanischer Soldaten ans Kabinett des Ministerrats, September 1917," in: ibid., pp. 293–294.

86. Service, *Lenin*, pp. 129–146.

87. Ibid., pp. 147–165.

88. Lenin, *Imperialism, the Highest Stage of Capitalism*.

89. Idem, "Report on the Current Situation," p. 237.

90. Idem, "The Junius Pamphlet," p. 310.

91. Idem, "Lecture on the 1905 Revolution," p. 253.

92. Service, *Lenin*, pp. 255–257.

93. Ibid., 257–264.

94. Schwabe, "Woodrow Wilson," pp. 278–280.

95. Ibid., pp. 282–283; Traxel, *Crusader Nation*, pp. 139–170.

96. Boghardt, *The Zimmermann Telegram*, pp. 90–128.

97. Schwabe, "Woodrow Wilson," pp. 283–284.

98. Woodward, *Trial by Friendship*, pp. 12–14.

99. Ibid., pp. 219–20.

100. Tucker, *Woodrow Wilson*, pp. 187–192.

101. Sullivan, *Our Times: America at the Birth of the Twentieth Century*, p. 512.

102. Wilson, "A Peace Worth Preserving," p. 27; idem, "Only One Peace Possible," p. 106.

103. Steigerwald, *Wilsonian Idealism in America*, pp. 33–38.

104. "An Address at the Metropolitan Opera House," September 27, 1918, quoted in: ibid, p. 37.

105. Fisch, *The Right of Self-Determination of Peoples*, pp. 129–137.

106. Stone, *The Eastern Front*, pp. 282–301.

107. Ibid., pp. 284–285.

108. Ibid., pp. 287–290.

109. Ibid., pp. 294–295.

110. Ibid., pp. 298–300.

111. Schenk, "*Mastering Imperial Space*," pp. 60–77.

112. Stone, *The Eastern Front*, p. 300.

113. Hasegawa, *The February Revolution*, pp. 313–427.

114. Sondhaus, *World War One*, p. 247.

115. Sellin, *Gewalt und Legitimität*, pp. 120–124.

116. Figes, *A People's Tragedy*, pp. 406–473.

117. Neutatz, *Träume und Alpträume*, pp. 147–151.

118. Wilson, "An Address to a Joint Session," April 2, 1917, p. 524.

119. Ibid., p. 525.

120. Wade, *The Russian Revolution*, pp. 127–143.

121. Kappeler, *The Russian Empire*, pp. 354–355.

122. Abraham, *Alexander Kerensky*, pp. 192–225.

123. Wildman, *The End of the Russian Imperial Army*, pp. 332–372, 379.

124. Beyrau and Shcherbinin, "Alles für die Front," pp. 156–161.

125. Lohr, "Russia," pp. 488–489.

126. Rosenberg, *Liberals in the Russian Revolution*; Katzer, *Die Weiße Bewegung in Russland*, pp. 72–75.

127. Figes, *A People's Tragedy*, pp. 451–455.

128. Curtiss, *The Russian Revolution of 1917*, pp. 143–144; Sondhaus, *World War One*, p. 264.

129. Katkov, *The Kornilov Affair*, pp. 83–104; Pipes, *The Russian Revolution, 1899–1919*, pp. 448–464.

130. McAuley, *Bread and Justice*, pp. 47–111.

131. Katkov, *The Kornilov Affair*, pp. 105–120; Figes, *A People's Tragedy*, pp. 453–455; Sondhaus, *World War One*, pp. 264–265; Neutatz, *Träume und Alpträume*, p. 149.

132. Wade, *The Russian Revolution*, pp. 232–254.

133. Lohr, "Russia," pp. 489–490.

134. Haumann, "Das Jahr 1917 in den Metropolen und in den Dörfern," pp. 59–72; Neutatz, *Träume und Alpträume*, pp. 154–158.

135. Ibid., p. 156.

136. Sondhaus, *World War One*, p. 267.

137. Kessler, *Journey to the Abyss*, December 2, 1917, pp. 794–795. Translation modified.

138. Kappeler, *The Russian Empire*, pp. 353–66; Wade, *The Russian Revolution*, pp. 144–169.

139. Schlürmann, "Vom Zarenadler zum Sowjetstern," pp. 19–24.

140. Figes, *A People's Tragedy*, p. 590.

141. Kappeler, *The Russian Empire*, pp. 356–361.

142. Noack, *Muslimischer Nationalismus im Russischen Reich*, pp. 499–510.

143. Kappeler, *The Russian Empire*, p. 361.

144. Ibid., pp. 365–366.

145. Bentinck-Smith, *Building a Great Library*, pp. 69–103.

146. Battles, *Widener: Biography of a Library*, pp. 63–66.

147. Goldman, *A History of the Germanic Museum*, pp. 1–9.

148. Quoted in: ibid., p. 8.

149. Ibid., pp. 13–14, 17, 31.

150. Klekowski and Klekowski, *Eyewitnesses to the Great War*.

151. Quoted in: Goldman, *A History of the Germanic Museum*, p. 37.

152. Ibid., pp. 37–45.

153. Keene, "The United States," p. 510.

154. Traxel, *Crusader Nation*, pp. 147–148.

155. Nassua, *"Gemeinsame Kriegführung, gemeinsamer Friedensschluss,"* pp. 50–79.

156. Smythe, *Pershing*, pp. 72–73.

157. Wüstenbecker, "Die Vereinigten Staaten von Amerika," pp. 219–220.

158. Higham, *Strangers in the Land*, pp. 195–212.

159. Gordon, *Assimilation in American Life*, pp. 115–131; Bischoff and Mania, "Melting Pot-Mythen als Szenarien amerikanischer Identität," pp. 513–536; Panter, *Loyalitätskonflikte und Neuorientierungen*, pp. 145–146.

160. Kallen, "Democracy versus the Melting-Pot," pp. 67–92.

161. Higham, "The Redefinition of America," p. 315.

162. Bourne, "Trans-National America," pp. 86–97, quoted in: idem, *The Radical Will*, p. 249; Matthews, "The Revolt against Americanism," pp. 4–31.

163. Quoted in: Sollors, "Konstruktionsversuche nationaler und ethnischer Identität," pp. 546–547.

164. Oliver, "Deconstruction or Affirmative Action," pp. 799–800.

165. Quoted in: Banta, *Imaging American Women*, p. 125.

166. Wüstenbecker, *Deutsch-Amerikaner im Ersten Weltkrieg*, pp. 177–214.

167. Panter, *Jüdische Erfahrungen*, p. 329.

168. Nagler, *Nationale Minoritäten im Krieg*, pp. 684–705.

169. Weldt, "A Plea for Tolerance," p. 356.

170. Nagler, *Nationale Minoritäten im Krieg*, p. 22; Daniels, *Guarding the Golden Door*, pp. 39–50; Panter, *Jüdische Erfahrungen*, pp. 329, 340.

171. Stears, *Progressives, Pluralists, and the Problem of the State*, pp. 140–141.

172. Panter, *Jüdische Erfahrungen*, pp. 235–236; Chambers, "Conscription for Colossus," pp. 297–311; Sterba, *Good Americans*, pp. 54–61; Fleming, *The Illusion of Victory*, pp. 86–87.

173. Keith, *Rich Man's War*, pp. 33–56.

174. Ibid., pp. 135–161, 200.

175. Britten, *American Indians in World War I*, pp. 51–72, 99–115.

176. Ford, *Americans All*, p. 3.

177. Panter, *Jüdische Erfahrungen*, p. 259.

178. Quoted in: Gould, *The Mismeasure of Man*, pp. 174, 179–180, 191–193; Schaffer, *America in the Great War*, pp. 3–5, 75–77; Shapiro, "Racism and Empire," pp. 155–173.

179. Haynes, *A Night of Violence*, pp. 254–296; Smith, "The Houston Riot of 1917," pp. 85–95.

180. McWhirter, *Red Summer*, pp. 114–126; Krist, *City of Scoundrels*, pp. 80–83, 104–105.

181. Mjagkij, *Loyalty in Time of Trial*, pp. 73–120.

182. Ibid., 123–125, 134–142.

183. Ibid., p. 142.

184. Leonhard, "Vom Nationalkrieg zum Kriegsnationalismus," pp. 204–240.

185. Vorländer, *Hegemonialer Liberalismus*, pp. 195–205.

186. Ibid., pp. 203–204; Croly, *Progressive Democracy*, p. 73; Forcey, The *Crossroads of Liberalism*, pp. 273–315; Rochester, *American Liberal Disillusionment*, pp. 88–104.

187. *The New Republic*, February 19, 1916, pp. 62–67, and April 21, 1917, p. 338.

188. Jansen and Osterhammel, *Dekolonisation*, pp. 29–32.

189. Manela, *The Wilsonian Moment*, pp. 46–47.

190. Winkler, *Nexus*, pp. 268–269.

191. DeBauche, *Reel Patriotism*, pp. 104–136.

192. Manela, *The Wilsonian Moment*, pp. 46–48.

193. Singha, "Front Lines and Status Lines," pp. 55–106.

194. Manela, *The Wilsonian Moment*, pp. 82–83; Brown, *Modern India*, pp. 197–199.

195. Manela, *The Wilsonian Moment*, pp. 83–84.

196. Quoted in: ibid., p. 121.

197. Holland, *The British Empire and the Great War*, pp. 127–128.

198. Ibid., p. 126; Brown and Cook, *Canada*, p. 303.

199. Bridge, "The Reason Why," pp. 11–12; Holland, *The British Empire and the Great War*, p. 128.

200. Carrington, "The Empire at War," p. 640; Holland, *The British Empire and the Great War*, p. 135.

201. Mohs, *Military Intelligence and the Arab Revolt*, pp. 7–11, 32–38.

202. Wilson, *T. E. Lawrence*, pp. 17–26.

203. Lawrence, *Nationalism among the Tribesmen*, p. 81.

204. Thorau, *Lawrence von Arabien*, pp. 108–158.

205. Wilson, *Lawrence of Arabia*, pp. 681–707.

206. McKale, *War by Revolution*, pp. 170–199.

207. Thorau, *Lawrence von Arabien*, pp. 79–92; Schüller, "Die Entstehungsgeschichte der Arabischen Revolte," pp. 155–162; Rink, "Lawrence und der Partisanenkrieg," pp. 163–172.

208. Janssen, "Kamele im Krieg," pp. 97–101.

209. Hoffmann, "Die Genese des Mythos Lawrence von Arabien," pp. 39–50.

210. Hughes, "Command, Strategy and the Battle for Palestine," pp. 113–130.

211. Grainger, *The Battle for Palestine*, pp. 109–47.

212. Englund, *The Beauty and the Sorrow*, p. 343.

213. Woodward, *Hell in the Holy Land*, pp. 35–38, 40–41.

214. Stein, *The Balfour Declaration*; Friedman, *Palestine*, vol. 1.

215. Quoted in: Panter, *Jüdische Erfahrungen*, p. 316.

216. Ibid., pp. 314–315; Gouttman, *The Balfour Declaration*, pp. 12–27.

217. Keren and Keren, *We are Coming, Unafraid*, p. 169.

218. Quoted in: Englund, *The Beauty and the Sorrow*, pp. 326–327.

219. Quoted in: ibid., pp. 366–367.

220. Stovall, "Colour-Blind France," pp. 33–55; idem, "The Color Line behind the Lines," pp. 737–769; Smith, "France," p. 428.

221. Downs, *Manufacturing Inequality*, pp. 119–146; Smith, "France," p. 427.

222. Becker, "Frankreich," p. 41.

223. Duroselle, *Clemenceau*, pp. 610–637.

224. Smith, "France," p. 428; Becker, "Frankreich," pp. 38–39.

225. Clemenceau, "Discours d'investiture," November 20, 1917, quoted in: Becker, *Clemenceau*, pp. 134–135; Dallas, *At the Heart of a Tiger*, pp. 501–502.

226. Becker, *Clemenceau, Chef de Guerre*, p. 97.

227. Smith, "France," p. 428.

228. I am grateful to Nicole Jordan, University of Chicago, for this reference.

229. Gregory, *The Last Great War*, p. 40.

230. Quoted in: Panter, *Jüdische Erfahrungen*, p. 223; Shukman, *War or Revolution*, pp. 32–48.

231. Gregory, "Britain and Ireland," pp. 411–412.

232. Terraine, *Business in Great Waters*, pp. 57–84.

233. Woodward, *Lloyd George and the Generals*, pp. 160–189.

234. White, *The Gotha Summer*, pp. 218–219; Canwell and Sutherland, *Battle of Britain 1917*, pp. 39–89.

235. Hinton, *The First Shop Stewards' Movement*, pp. 196–212; Gregory, "Britain and Ireland," p. 411.

236. Clegg, *A History of British Trade Unions*, vol. 2, pp. 168–174.

237. Whiteside, "Concession, Coercion or Cooperation?" pp. 107–122; Gregory, "Britain and Ireland," pp. 411–412.

238. Gregory, "Britain and Ireland," pp. 411–412.

239. Ibid., p. 412.

240. Gregory, "You Might as Well Recruit Germans," pp. 113–121.

241. Morrow, *The Great War*, p. 218.

242. Gibelli, "Italy," p. 471.

243. Janz, "Zwischen Konsens und Dissens," pp. 205–206; Procacci, "Aspetti della mentalita," pp. 261–290.

244. Elfriede Kuhr, September 10, 1917, quoted in: Englund, *The Beauty and the Sorrow*, p. 394.

245. Ibid., p. 330; Kotowski, Pöls, and Ritter (eds.), *Das Wilhelminische Deutschland*, quoted in: Johann (ed.), *Innenansicht eines Krieges*, pp. 242–243.

246. Ibid., p. 277.

247. *Der große Krieg. Eine Chronik von Tag zu Tag,* quoted in: ibid., p. 246.

248. Kriegs-Ernährungsamt (ed.), *Die Kriegsernährungswirtschaft 1917*, Berlin 1917, quoted in: ibid., pp. 247–248.

249. Geyer, *Verkehrte Welt*, pp. 42, 44.

250. *Allgemeiner Wegweiser*, quoted in: Johann (ed.), *Innenansicht eines Krieges*, p. 253.

251. Weber, "Ein Wahlrechtsnotgesetz des Reichs," p. 221; Krumeich and Lepsius, "Einleitung," p. 7.

252. Hampe, *Kriegstagebuch*, April 6 and 7, 1917, pp. 527–528.

253. Bergsträßer, *Die preußische Wahlrechtsfrage im Kriege*, pp. 1–12; Mommsen, *Die Urkatastrophe Deutschlands*, pp. 74–78.

254. Bermbach, *Vorformen parlamentarischer Kabinettsbildung in Deutschland*, p. 62.

255. *Der große Krieg. Eine Chronik von Tag zu Tag,* quoted in: Johann (ed.), *Innenansicht eines Krieges*, pp. 270–271; http://germanhistorydocs.ghi-dc.org/pdf/eng/1007_Reichstag's%20Peace%20Resolution_194.pdf.

256. Weber, *Briefe 1915–1917*, pp. 695–696; Mommsen, *Max Weber and German Politics*, pp. 244–266.

257. Pross (ed.), *Die Zerstörung der deutschen Politik,* quoted in: Johann (ed.), *Innenansicht eines Krieges,* pp. 284–286; http://germanhistorydocs.ghi-dc.org/sub_document.cfm?document_id=971.

258. Hagenlücke, *Deutsche Vaterlandspartei,* pp. 334–371.

259. Steglich, *Die Friedenspolitik der Mittelmächte 1917/18;* Epstein, *Matthias Erzberger und das Dilemma der deutschen Demokratie;* Ribhegge, *Frieden für Europa.*

260. Rathenau, *Tagebuch 1907–1922,* pp. 223–224.

261. Dehn (ed.), *Hindenburg als Erzieher in seinen Aussprüchen,* quoted in: Johann (ed.), *Innenansicht eines Krieges,* p. 280.

262. Pross (ed.), *Die Zerstörung der deutschen Politik,* quoted in: ibid., pp. 236–237

263. Ibid., pp. 297–298.

264. Greschat, "Reformationsjubiläum 1917," pp. 419–429; Albrecht, "Zwischen Kriegstheologie und Krisentheologie," pp. 482–499.

265. Kessler, *Journey to the Abyss,* December 22 and 23, 1917, p. 799.

266. Ibid., December 25, 1917, p. 800.

267. Sondhaus, *Franz Conrad von Hötzendorf,* pp. 200–204.

268. Vermes, *István Tisza,* pp. 367–401.

269. Cornwall, "Austria-Hungary and 'Yugoslavia,'" pp. 380–381.

270. Ibid., p. 377; Schulze, "Austria-Hungary's Economy in World War I," p. 90.

271. Agnew, *The Czechs and the Lands of the Bohemian Crown,* pp. 167–169.

272. Leidinger and Moritz, *Gefangenschaft, Revolution, Heimkehr,* pp. 377–409.

273. Höglinger, *Ministerpräsident Heinrich Graf Clam-Martinic,* pp. 172–186.

274. Panter, *Jüdische Erfahrungen,* p. 291.

275. Ibid., pp. 293–294; Healy, *Vienna and the Fall of the Habsburg Empire,* p. 9.

276. Cornwall, "Austria-Hungary and 'Yugoslavia,'" pp. 380–381.

277. Idem, "News, Rumour and the Control of Information," pp. 50–64.

278. Idem, *The Undermining of Austria-Hungary,* pp. 24–29, 268–287, 405–415; idem, "Austria-Hungary and 'Yugoslavia,'" pp. 380–381.

279. Höglinger, *Ministerpräsident Heinrich Graf Clam-Martinic,* pp. 132–157; Cornwall, "Austria-Hungary and 'Yugoslavia,'" pp. 381, 384.

280. Ibid., p. 382; idem, "The Experience of Yugoslav Agitation in Austria-Hungary," pp. 656–676.

281. Hirschfeld, "Serbien," p. 836.

282. "Kaiser Karl I., Der Sixtus-Brief, 24. März 1917," in: Kleindel (ed.), *Österreich. Daten zur Geschichte und Kultur,* p. 307.

283. Borodziej, *Geschichte Polens,* p. 87.

284. Schuster, *Zwischen allen Fronten,* pp. 30–31; Panter, *Jüdische Erfahrungen,* p. 288.

285. Borodziej, *Geschichte Polens,* pp. 86–89.

286. Turner, *The Challenge to Liberalism,* pp. 163–178.

287. Ibid., pp. 163–167.

288. Nebelin, *Ludendorff,* pp. 229–337.

289. Turner, *The Challenge to Liberalism,* pp. 175–178.

290. Langewiesche, *Liberalism in Germany,* p. 246.

291. Hoeres, *Krieg der Philosophen*, pp. 196, 439–440.

292. Langewiesche, *Liberalism in Germany*, p. 247.

293. Ibid., pp. 248–249.

294. Mann, *Betrachtungen eines Unpolitischen*, pp. 22–23.

295. "Capital, Labor, and the Government," quoted in: Freeden, *Liberalism Divided*, p. 28.

296. Hobson, *Democracy after the War*, pp. 164–165; Freeden, *Liberalism Divided*, p. 42.

297. Winter, "Demography," pp. 250–252.

298. Idem, "Paris, London, Berlin," pp. 3–24; Bonzon, "The Labour Market," pp. 164–195.

299. Winter, "Demography," pp. 255–256.

300. Torp, *Wachstum, Sicherheit, Moral*, pp. 40–58.

301. Kruse, *Der Erste Weltkrieg*, p. 101; Kocka, *Klassengesellschaft im Krieg*, p. 33; Winter, *The Great War and the British People*, p. 233.

302. Kruse, *Der Erste Weltkrieg*, pp. 99–110.

303. Quoted in: Englund, *The Beauty and the Sorrow*, p. 395.

304. Gregory, *The Last Great War*, pp. 113, 257.

305. Kruse, *Der Erste Weltkrieg*, pp. 102–104.

306. Haacke and Schneider, *Das Buch vom Kriege*, quoted in: Johann (ed.), *Innenansicht eines Krieges*, p. 240.

307. Kocka, *Facing Total War*, pp. 11–66; Ritschl, "The Pity of Peace," pp. 54–55; Burhop, *Wirtschaftsgeschichte des Kaiserreichs*, pp. 208–210.

308. Föllmer, *Die Verteidigung der bürgerlichen Nation*, p. 192; Kruse, "Gesellschaftspolitische Systementwicklung," p. 90; Mommsen, "Der Erste Weltkrieg und die Krise Europas," p. 31.

309. Föllmer, *Die Verteidigung der bürgerlichen Nation*, pp. 190–193.

310. *Deutschlands Frauen und Deutschlands Krieg*, pp. 33–34, quoted in: Schulin, *Der Erste Weltkrieg*, p. 64.

311. Winter, "Demography," pp. 257–260.

312. Grayzel, "Women and Men," pp. 264–266.

313. Kruse, *Der Erste Weltkrieg*, p. 108.

314. Bäumer, *Weit hinter den Schützengräben*, pp. 216, 219.

315. Ibid., p. 229.

316. Grayzel, "Women and Men," pp. 266–268.

317. Winter, "Demography," p. 256.

318. Daniel, *Arbeiterfrauen in der Kriegsgesellschaft*, pp. 139–147, 256–275; Canning, "Sexual Crisis and the Writing of Citizenship," pp. 169–172.

319. Grayzel, "Women and Men," pp. 268–270.

320. Englund, *The Beauty and the Sorrow*, pp. 384–385.

321. Grayzel, "Women and Men," pp. 270–272.

322. Potter, *Boys in Khaki, Girls in Print*, pp. 88–149.

323. Grayzel, "Women and Men," pp. 272–274.

324. Idem, *Women's Identities at War*, pp. 243–246.

325. Letter from Anna to Lorenz Treplin, September 3, 1916, in: Gudehus-Schomerus, Recker, and Riverein (eds.), *"Einmal muss doch das wirkliche Leben wieder kommen,"* p. 37.

326. Letter of April 28, 1917, in: ibid., p. 625.

327. Gudehus-Schomerus, Recker, and Riverein, "Einleitung," pp. 39–40.

328. Balderston, "Industrial Mobilization and War Economies," p. 218.

329. Burhop, *Wirtschaftsgeschichte des Kaiserreichs*, p. 192; Broadberry and Harrison, *The Economics of World War I*, p. 11.

330. Ibid., p. 227.

331. Burhop, *Wirtschaftsgeschichte des Kaiserreichs*, pp. 193–194; Broadberry and Harrison, *The Economics of World War I*, pp. 10–12.

332. Geyer, *Deutsche Rüstungspolitik*, pp. 83–85.

333. Burhop, *Wirtschaftsgeschichte des Kaiserreichs*, p. 195; Ferguson, "How (Not) to Pay for the War," p. 427.

334. Burhop, *Wirtschaftsgeschichte des Kaiserreichs*, pp. 210–211.

335. Balderston, "War Finance and Inflation," pp. 222–244; Gross, "Confidence and Gold," pp. 223–252.

336. Mommsen, *Die Urkatastrophe Deutschlands*, pp. 84–87.

337. Ferguson, "How (Not) to Pay for the War," pp. 409–434; Burhop, *Wirtschaftsgeschichte des Kaiserreichs*, pp. 212–213.

338. Balderston, "Industrial Mobilization and War Economies," pp. 223–224.

339. Ibid., pp. 224–226.

340. Dehne, *On the Far Western Front*, pp. 128–155, 159–190.

341. Rosenberg, *World War I and the Growth of United States Predominance*, pp. 31–76; Albert, *South America and the First World War*, pp. 41–42, 58; Fischer, *Die Souveränität der Schwachen*, pp. 47–53.

342. Burhop, *Wirtschaftsgeschichte des Kaiserreichs*, p. 197; Hardach, *Der Erste Weltkrieg*, pp. 37–38.

343. Kennedy, *Over Here*, pp. 296–306.

344. Quoted in: ibid., p. 319.

345. Ibid., pp. 311–315.

346. Ibid., pp. 332–335.

347. Ibid., pp. 337–338.

348. Ibid., pp. 346–347.

349. Kessler, *Tagebuch*, vol. 6, December 31, 1917, p. 234.

350. Becker, *1917 en Europe*.

351. Weber, "Suffrage and Democracy," pp. 82, 105.

352. Steglich, *Bündnissicherung oder Verständigungsfrieden*.

353. Stevenson, *The First World War*, pp. 162–169.

354. Pollard, *The Unknown Pope*, pp. 123–127.

355. Ibid., pp. 132–136.

356. Mann, "Weltfrieden?," p. 212; Llanque, *Demokratisches Denken*, pp. 103–135.

357. Quoted in: Nebelin, *Ludendorff*, p. 404.

358. Sheehan, *Where Have All the Soldiers Gone?*, p. 84.

7. ONRUSH AND COLLAPSE

1. Burckhardt, *Force and Freedom*, pp. 265–267.
2. Charle, *La crise des sociétés impériales*, p. 285; Beaupré, *Das Trauma des großen Krieges*, p. 23.
3. Waechter, "Vierzehn Punkte," pp. 949–951.
4. Schwabe, *Woodrow Wilson*, pp. 11–58.
5. Englund, *The Beauty and the Sorrow*, pp. 440–441.
6. Sondhaus, *World War One*, p. 421.
7. Lenin, "A Painful but Necessary Lesson," p. 64.
8. Baumgart, "Einleitung," pp. 29–30.
9. Snyder, *Bloodlands*, pp. 4–6.
10. Plakans, *A Concise History of the Baltic States*, pp. 298–307.
11. Neutatz, *Träume und Alpträume*, pp. 158–160.
12. Sondhaus, *World War One*, p. 423.
13. Kappeler, *The Russian Empire*, pp. 365–366.
14. Kessler, *Tagebuch*, vol. 6, August 18, 1918, p. 513.
15. Rabinowitch, *The Bolsheviks in Power*, pp. 181–209.
16. Mann, *Deutsche Geschichte des 19. und 20. Jahrhunderts*, p. 665; Liulevicius, "Die deutsche Besatzung," p. 103.
17. Liulevicius, "Die deutsche Besatzung," pp. 103–104.
18. Englund, *The Beauty and the Sorrow*, p. 428.
19. Figes, *A People's Tragedy*, pp. 641–642.
20. Figes, *Peasant Russia, Civil War*, pp. 354–356.
21. Neutatz, *Träume und Alpträume*, pp. 160–164.
22. Englund, *The Beauty and the Sorrow*, pp. 450–452.
23. Sondhaus, *World War One*, p. 424.
24. Kappeler, *Kleine Geschichte der Ukraine*, pp. 165–176.
25. Kappeler, *The Russian Empire*, p. 357.
26. Kappeler, *Kleine Geschichte der Ukraine*, pp. 170–176.
27. Schnell, "Ukraine 1918," pp. 166–168.
28. Baberowski, *Scorched Earth*, pp. 35–61.
29. Baberowski, "Verwüstetes Land," pp. 171–174.
30. Baberowski, *Kriege in staatsfernen Räumen*, pp. 291–310.
31. Englund, *The Beauty and the Sorrow*, pp. 448–450.
32. Nebelin, *Ludendorff*, p. 408.
33. Sondhaus, *World War One*, pp. 438–439.
34. Ibid., pp. 407, 410.
35. Travers, *How the War Was Won*, pp. 175–176.
36. Grotelueschen, *The AEF Way of War*, pp. 10–58.
37. Yockelson, *Borrowed Soldiers*, pp. 15–20.
38. Trask, *The AEF and Coalition Warmaking*, pp. 168–172.
39. Doughty, *Pyrrhic Victory*, pp. 461–507.

40. Greenhalgh, *Victory through Coalition*, pp. 163–185, 263–264.

41. Stachelbeck, *Militärische Effektivität im Ersten Weltkrieg*, pp. 351–356.

42. Geyer, "German Strategy in the Age of Machine Warfare," pp. 527–597; Afflerbach and Sheffield, "Waging Total War," pp. 61–90.

43. Stachelbeck, *Militärische Effektivität im Ersten Weltkrieg*, p. 345.

44. Stevenson, *With Our Backs to the Wall*, pp. 33–34.

45. Sondhaus, *World War One*, pp. 406–407.

46. Stevenson, *With Our Backs to the Wall*, p. 42.

47. Nebelin, *Ludendorff*, pp. 409–410; Kielmansegg, *Deutschland*, p. 635.

48. Stevenson, *With Our Backs to the Wall*, p. 42.

49. Nebelin, *Ludendorff*, p. 416; Harris, *Douglas Haig and the First World War*, pp. 454–456.

50. Quoted in: Nebelin, *Ludendorff*, pp. 414–415.

51. Quoted in: ibid., p. 415.

52. Duménil, "1918, L'Année de la 'Grande Bataille,'" pp. 229–256.

53. Sondhaus, *World War One*, pp. 410–411.

54. Nebelin, *Ludendorff*, p. 416; Deist, "Strategy and Unlimited Warfare in Germany," pp. 278–279.

55. Nebelin, *Ludendorff*, pp. 417–418.

56. Albes, "Portugal," p. 780.

57. Stevenson, *With Our Backs to the Wall*, pp. 78–88.

58. Taube, *Deutsche Eisenbahn-Geschütze*, pp. 18–28.

59. Englund, *The Beauty and the Sorrow*, pp. 452–453.

60. Schwertfeger, *Das Weltkriegsende*, quoted in: Johann (ed.), *Innenansicht eines Krieges*, pp. 315–316.

61. Englund, *The Beauty and the Sorrow*, pp. 483, 460.

62. Ibid., p. 461.

63. Stevenson, *With Our Backs to the Wall*, pp. 116–117.

64. Winter, "Demography," p. 250; Sondhaus, *World War One*, p. 432.

65. Quoted [and translated] from: Englund, *Schönheit und Schrecken*, p. 572.

66. Quoted from: Englund, *The Beauty and the Sorrow*, p. 474.

67. Schwertfeger, *Das Weltkriegsende*, quoted in: Johann (ed.), *Innenansicht eines Krieges*, p. 319.

68. Smith, "France," pp. 428–429.

69. Stevenson, *With Our Backs to the Wall*, pp. 117–125; Sondhaus, *World War One*, p. 432.

70. Sondhaus, *World War One*, pp. 426, 428.

71. Ibid., p. 432.

72. Ferrell, *America's Deadliest Battle*, pp. 148–156.

73. Mead, *The Doughboys*, pp. 347–353.

74. See charts 1–3 in the appendix to this book.

75. Sondhaus, *World War One*, pp. 413–415.

76. Jahr, *Gewöhnliche Soldaten*, pp. 149–151.

77. Quoted in: Ulrich and Ziemann (eds.), *Frontalltag im Ersten Weltkrieg*, p. 142.

78. Deist, "Verdeckter Militärstreik im Kriegsjahr 1918," pp. 146–167.

79. Jahr, *Gewöhnliche Soldaten*, pp. 161–167.

80. Deist, "Verdeckter Militärstreik im Kriegsjahr 1918," p. 160; Stachelbeck, *Militärische Effektivität*, pp. 344–345; Stephenson, *The Final Battle*, p. 65; Watson, *Enduring the Great War*, pp. 184–231.

81. Watson, *Enduring the Great War*, pp. 204–205; Ziemann, "Enttäuschte Erwartung und kollektive Erschöpfung," pp. 165–182.

82. Cabanes, *La victoire endeuillée*, pp. 12–24; Beaupré, *Das Trauma des großen Krieges*, p. 27.

83. Beaupré, *Das Trauma des großen Krieges*, p. 27.

84. Haffner, *Defying Hitler*, p. 19.

85. Sondhaus, *World War One*, pp. 415–416.

86. Ibid., pp. 415–418; Calic, *Geschichte Jugoslawiens*, pp. 79–82.

87. Pust, *Die steinerne Front*.

88. Thompson, *The White War*, pp. 328–382.

89. Neck (ed.), *Österreich im Jahre 1918*, pp. 104–113.

90. Sondhaus, *World War One*, pp. 418–420.

91. Rauchensteiner, *Der Tod des Doppeladlers*, pp. 617, 621.

92. Quoted in: Beaupré, *Das Trauma des großen Krieges*, p. 23.

93. Münchhausen, *Paris. Geschichte einer Stadt*, p. 344.

94. Quoted in: Englund, *The Beauty and the Sorrow*, pp. 428–429.

95. Miller, *Paris Gun*, pp. 66–67.

96. Englund, *The Beauty and the Sorrow*, pp. 453–454.

97. Quoted in [and translated from]: Winock, *Clemenceau*, p. 431.

98. Englund, *The Beauty and the Sorrow*, pp. 464–465.

99. Gibelli, "Italy," p. 472.

100. Morrow, *The Great War*, pp. 266–267.

101. Ibid., p. 267.

102. Ibid., p. 270.

103. Gooch, "The Maurice Debate 1918," pp. 211–268; Martin, "Asquith, the Maurice Debate and the Historians," pp. 435–444; Grigg, *Lloyd George*, pp. 489–512.

104. Morrow, *The Great War*, pp. 270–271.

105. *American Jewish Chronicle* 14, February 9, 1917, pp. 423–424, quoted in: Panter, *Jüdische Erfahrungen*, p. 325.

106. Northedge and Wells, *Britain and Soviet Communism*, p. 47; Graves and Hodge, *The Long Week-End*, p. 135; Lawrence, "Forging a Peaceable Kingdom," pp. 566–568.

107. Ruotsila, *British and American Anticommunism*, pp. 98–100; Neilson, *Britain, Russia, and the Collapse of the Versailles Order*, p. 45; Brüggemeier, *Geschichte Großbritanniens*, p. 126. I am grateful to Manuel Geist for the reference to this context.

108. Figes, *A People's Tragedy*, pp. 576–578.

109. Neilson, *Britain, Russia, and the Collapse of the Versailles Order*, p. 47.

110. Alston, *Russia's Greatest Enemy*, pp. 132–143. I am grateful to Manuel Geist for the references in this context.

111. Morrow, *The Great War*, p. 273; Keene, *The United States and the First World War*, p. 3.

112. Morrow, *The Great War*, p. 273.

113. Nagler, *Nationale Minoritäten im Krieg*, p. 22; Morrow, *The Great War*, p. 274; Panter, *Jüdische Erfahrungen*, pp. 330, 331.

114. Sterba, *Good Americans*, p. 200.

115. Ibid., pp. 202–203.

116. Heale, *American Anticommunism*, pp. 60–62; Higham, *Strangers in the Land*, pp. 222–233.

117. Capozzola, *Uncle Sam Wants You*, pp. 210–212.

118. Walker, *In Defense of American Liberties*, pp. 23–26, 42–47; Cottrell, *Roger Nash Baldwin and the American Civil Liberties Union*, pp. 119–134.

119. Englund, *The Beauty and the Sorrow*, p. 430.

120. *Der große Krieg. Eine Chronik von Tag zu Tag*, quoted in: Johann (ed.), *Innenansicht eines Krieges*, p. 304.

121. Beaupré, *Das Trauma des großen Krieges*, p. 23.

122. Ibid., p. 25.

123. Kröning, *Die Januar-Streiks in Berlin und Wien*, pp. 71–99.

124. Englund, *The Beauty and the Sorrow*, p. 470.

125. *Münstersche Zeitung*, January 27, 1918, quoted in: Nübel, *Die Mobilisierung der Kriegsgesellschaft*, p. 156.

126. Mann, *Diaries*, p. 8.

127. Quoted in Baumgart (ed.), *Von Brest-Litowsk zur deutschen Novemberrevolution*, p. 279.

128. *Moderne illustrierte Wochenschrift* 34 (1918), quoted in: Johann (ed.), *Innenansicht eines Krieges*, p. 309.

129. Kluge, *Die deutsche Revolution*, pp. 51–53.

130. Kolb, *The Weimar Republic*, p. 4.

131. Schwertfeger, *Das Weltkriegsende*, quoted in: Johann (ed.), *Innenansicht eines Krieges*, p. 333.

132. Sondhaus, *World War One*, p. 428.

133. Baden, *Erinnerungen und Dokumente*, quoted in: Johann (ed.), *Innenansicht eines Krieges*, pp. 332–333.

134. Sondhaus, *World War One*, p. 433.

135. Mann, *Diaries*, p. 12.

136. Baden, *Erinnerungen und Dokumente*, quoted in: Johann (ed.), *Innenansicht eines Krieges*, p. 335; Geyer, "Insurrectionary Warfare," pp. 459–527.

137. Quoted in: Thiel, *Die Generation ohne Männer*, p. 260.

138. Geyer, "Insurrectionary Warfare," pp. 474–475.

139. Mann, *Diaries*, p. 13.

140. Quoted in: Baumgart (ed.), *Von Brest-Litowsk zur deutschen Novemberrevolution*, p. 613.

141. Wolff, *Tagebücher 1914–1919*, vol. 2, October 14, 1918, p. 632, quoted in: Altenhöner, *Kommunikation und Kontrolle*, p. 306.

142. Quoted in: Baumgart (ed.), *Von Brest-Litowsk zur deutschen Novemberrevolution*, p. 615.

143. "Immediatbericht des Berliner Polizeipräsidenten an Wilhelm II., 29. Oktober 1918," quoted in: Altenhöner, *Kommunikation und Kontrolle*, p. 304.

144. Kluge, *Die deutsche Revolution*, pp. 51–69.

145. Mann, *Briefe II 1914–1923*, pp. 260–261.

146. Kolb, *The Weimar Republic*, pp. 6–7.

147. Cooper, *Woodrow Wilson*, pp. 441–445.

148. Sondhaus, *World War One*, pp. 434–436.

149. Kolb, *The Weimar Republic*, pp. 7–8.

150. Nebelin, *Ludendorff*, pp. 489–508.

151. Quoted in Englund, *The Beauty and the Sorrow*, pp. 492–493.

152. Rilke, *Wartime Letters*, pp. 100–101; Holthusen, *Rilke*, pp. 132–133.

153. *Der große Krieg. Eine Chronik von Tag zu Tag*, quoted in: Johann (ed.), *Innenansicht eines Krieges*, pp. 338–340.

154. Kolb, *The Weimar Republic*, pp. 7–9.

155. Kollwitz, *Die Tagebücher*, November 9, 1918, pp. 378–379.

156. Mendelssohn, *Zeitungsstadt Berlin*, quoted in: Johann (ed.), *Innenansicht eines Krieges*, pp. 344–345.

157. Kolb, *The Weimar Republic*, pp. 13–14.

158. Mann, *Diaries*, p. 20.

159. Hampe, *Kriegstagebuch*, November 10, 1918, p. 775.

160. Quoted in: Baumgart (ed.), *Von Brest-Litowsk zur deutschen Novemberrevolution*, p. 643.

161. Straub, *Albert Ballin*, pp. 257–261.

162. Quoted [and translated] in: Holthusen, *Rilke*, pp. 133–134; cf. Rilke, *Wartime Letters*, pp. 106–107.

163. Sondhaus, "Austro-Hungarian Naval Mutinies of World War I," pp. 195–212.

164. Quoted in: Neck (ed.), *Österreich im Jahre 1918*, pp. 42–43.

165. Quoted in: ibid., p. 44.

166. Mazower, *Dark Continent*, p. 45.

167. Kessler, *Tagebuch*, vol. 6, April 15, 1918, p. 358.

168. Fic, *The Bolsheviks and the Czechoslovak Legion*; Bradley, *The Czechoslovak Legion in Russia*.

169. Thunig-Nittner, *Die tschechoslowakische Legion in Russland*, pp. 61–90; Stegmann, *Kriegsdeutungen, Staatsgründungen, Sozialpolitik*, pp. 69–70.

170. Panter, *Jüdische Erfahrungen*, pp. 302–303.

171. Hoffmann-Holter, "Abreisendmachung," p. 138.

172. Panter, *Jüdische Erfahrungen*, pp. 304–305.

173. Haselsteiner, Plaschka, and Suppan, *Innere Front*, vol. 2, pp. 62–65.

174. Rauchensteiner, *Der Tod des Doppeladlers*, p. 592.

175. Neck (ed.), *Österreich im Jahre 1918*, p. 55.

176. Rumpler, *Das Völkermanifest Kaiser Karls*, pp. 29–64.

177. The proclamation transcript is available online: "To my faithful Austrian people! Proclamation by Emperor Karl on 16 October 1918," British Library, www.bl.uk/collection-items /to-faithful-austrian-people-emperor-karl.

178. Quoted in: Neck, *Arbeiterschaft und Staat im Ersten Weltkrieg*, pp. 707–708.

179. Cornwall, *The Wartime Bohemia of Franz Kafka*, pp. 45–46.

180. Redlich, *Tagebuch,* vol. 2, October 21, 1918, p. 305.

181. Neck (ed.), *Österreich im Jahre 1918*, p. 79.

182. Englund, *The Beauty and the Sorrow*, p. 490.

183. Redlich, *Tagebuch,* vol. 2, October 28, 1918, p. 310.

184. Windischgrätz, *Vom roten zum schwarzen Prinzen*, p. 386; Haselsteiner, Plaschka, and Suppan, *Innere Front*, vol. 2, p. 322.

185. Ibid., vol. 2, pp. 120–121.

186. Quoted in: ibid., p. 122.

187. Redlich, *Tagebuch,* vol. 2, October 30, 1918, p. 310.

188. Ibid., October 31, 1918, p. 311.

189. Quoted in: Haselsteiner, Plaschka, and Suppan, *Innere Front*, vol. 2, p. 332.

190. Rauchensteiner, *Der Tod des Doppeladlers*, p. 624.

191. Redlich, *Tagebuch,* vol. 2, November 8, 1918, pp. 315–316.

192. Brandl, *Kaiser, Politiker und Menschen*, pp. 265–266.

193. Musil, *Diaries,* pp. 201–202; Corino, *Robert Musil*, pp. 262–263.

194. Zürcher, "Osmanisches Reich," p. 761.

195. Kreiser, *Atatürk*, pp. 127–132.

196. Plaggenborg, *Ordnung und Gewalt*, pp. 222–223.

197. Adelson, *London and the Invention of the Middle East*, p. 154.

198. Nippa, *Zu den Beduinen Nord-Arabiens*, pp. 77–86.

199. Hughes, *Allenby and British Strategy in the Middle East*, pp. 89–110.

200. Satia, *Spies in Arabia*, pp. 239–262; Atia, "Mesopotamian Myths," pp. 247–252.

201. Fellner, "Der Zerfall der Donaumonarchie in weltgeschichtlicher Perspektive," pp. 246–248.

202. Bartov and Weitz (eds.), *Shatterzone of Empires*.

203. Bauer, "Acht Monate auswärtige Politik," speech delivered on July 29, 1919, quoted in: Fellner, "Der Zerfall der Donaumonarchie in weltgeschichtlicher Perspektive," p. 249.

204. Judson, *Guardians of the Nation*, p. 232.

205. Heinemann, *Die verdrängte Niederlage*, pp. 177–191.

206. Sondhaus, *World War One*, p. 436.

207. *Der große Krieg. Eine Chronik von Tag zu Tag*, quoted in: Johann (ed.), *Innenansicht eines Krieges*, p. 346.

208. Lichfield, "Two Soldiers Linked in Death by a Bizarre Coincidence"; Bostridge, "Charlotte and Jack."

209. Quoted in: Arthur, *Faces of World War I*, p. 270.

210. Quoted in: Best, *The Greatest Day in History*, p. 193.

211. Englund, *The Beauty and the Sorrow,* p. 504.

212. Ibid., p. 506.

213. Ibid., p. 498.

214. Smith, "France," pp. 428–430.

215. Englund, *The Beauty and the Sorrow,* p. 501.

216. Cabanes, *La victoire endeuillée,* pp. 23–70.

217. Beaupré, *Das Trauma des großen Krieges,* p. 21.

218. Tognotti, *La "spagnola" in Italia,* p. 155.

219. Krass, "Stigmata und Yellow Press," pp. 365–366; Luzzatto, *Padre Pio,* pp. 53–55, 60–72, 144–145.

220. Van der Vat, *The Grand Scuttle;* Krause, *Scapa Flow.*

221. Wolz, *Das lange Warten,* pp. 469–471.

222. Lowry, *Armistice 1918,* pp. 163–165.

223. Stephenson, *The Final Battle,* p. 44.

224. Bessel, "Demobilmachung," p. 428.

225. Kiesel, "Ernst Jünger im Ersten Weltkrieg," pp. 640–641.

226. Hanna, *Your Death Would Be Mine,* pp. 281–288.

227. Smith, *Jamaican Volunteers,* pp. 122–172; Grant, *Negro with a Hat,* pp. 95–115.

228. Page, *The Chiwaya War,* pp. 91–124.

229. Ibid., pp. 201–234.

230. Stevenson, *With Our Backs to the Wall,* p. 78.

231. Ibid., pp. 173, 243.

232. Ibid., pp. 540–543.

233. *Schulthess' Europäischer Geschichtskalender, 1917,* Part II, pp. 377–379, quoted in: Fenske, *Der Anfang vom Ende des alten Europa,* p. 43.

234. Ibid., pp. 39–48.

235. Krumeich, "Les armistices," pp. 981–987; Beaupré, *Das Trauma des großen Krieges,* p. 28.

8. OUTCOMES

1. Mick, "Vielerlei Kriege," pp. 311–326.

2. Rosenberg, "Paramilitary Violence in Russia's Civil Wars," pp. 21–39.

3. Gerwarth, "Fighting the Red Beast," pp. 52–71.

4. Horne, "Defending Victory," pp. 216–233.

5. Davies, *Heart of Europe,* pp. 100–105, 113–128; Hecker, "Polen," pp. 778–779.

6. Mick, "Wer verteidigte Lemberg?," pp. 189–216; idem, *Kriegserfahrungen in einer multiethnischen Stadt,* p. 318.

7. Bloxham, *The Final Solution;* Gerwarth and Horne, "Paramilitarism in Europe after the War," p. 7; Bartov and Weitz (eds.), *Shatterzone of Empires.*

8. Wegner, "Finnland," pp. 486–487.

9. Haapala and Tikka, "Revolution, Civil War, and Terror in Finland," pp. 72–84.

10. Balkelis, "Turning Citizens into Soldiers," pp. 126–144.

11. Bischoff, *Die letzte Front*, p. 150; Liulevicius, "Der Osten als apokalyptischer Raum," pp. 61–62.

12. I am grateful to Mark Jones, University College, Dublin, for this reference.

13. Gregory, "Peculiarities of the English," p. 58; Brüggemeier, *Geschichte Großbritanniens*, pp. 131–132.

14. Eichenberg, "Soldiers to Civilians to Soldiers," pp. 184–199.

15. Mazower, *Salonica: City of Ghosts*, pp. 305–370.

16. Plaggenborg, *Ordnung und Gewalt*, pp. 222–323.

17. Omissi, *Air Power and Colonial Rule*, p. 23.

18. Cox, "A Splendid Training Ground," pp. 157–184; Dodge, *Inventing Iraq*, pp. 131–156.

19. Audoin-Rouzeau, "Die Delegation der 'gueules cassées,'" pp. 280–287; Steller, *Diplomatie von Angesicht zu Angesicht*, pp. 462–464; Delaporte, *Gueules cassées de la Grande Guerre*.

20. Orpen, *An Onlooker in France*, p. 116; Plessen (ed.), *Idee Europa*, pp. 243–244.

21. Mann, "Friede," p. 249.

22. Wilson, "Address at the City Hall. Pueblo," September 25, 1919; Plessen (ed.), *Idee Europa*, p. 242.

23. Temperley (ed.), *A History of the Peace Conference of Paris*.

24. Boemeke, Feldman, and Glaser (eds.), *The Treaty of Versailles*; Krumeich (ed.), *Versailles 1919*; Steiner, "The Treaty of Versailles Revisited," pp. 13–33; Becker, *Le traité de Versailles*; Hay (ed.), *The Treaty of Versailles*; Kolb, *Der Frieden von Versailles*; Andelman, *A Shattered Peace*; Baycroft and Fischer (eds.), *After the Versailles Treaty*; Sharp (ed.), *The Versailles Settlement*.

25. Macmillan, *Paris 1919*, pp. 53–106.

26. Fink, "The Peace Settlement," pp. 543–547.

27. Manela, *The Wilsonian Moment*, pp. 141–175.

28. Kolb, *The Weimar Republic*, pp. 23–35.

29. Krumeich, *Juli 1914*, pp. 183–203.

30. Krüger, *Deutschland und die Reparationen 1918/19*.

31. Fischer, *Weltwirtschaftliche Rahmenbedingungen*; Heyde, *Das Ende der Reparationen*.

32. Leonhard, "Das Erbe der Vielfalt," pp. 361–385.

33. Rezun (ed.), *Nationalism and the Breakup of an Empire*; Chulos, *The Fall of an Empire, the Birth of a Nation*; Martin and Suny, *A State of Nations*; Birgerson, *After the Breakup of a Multi-Ethnic Empire*; Baron, *Homelands*.

34. Mummelthey, *Die Nationalitätenzusammensetzung des Russischen Reiches und der Sowjetunion*.

35. Kerekes, *Von St. Germain bis Genf*; Ackerl and Neck (eds.), *Saint-Germain 1919*; Fellner, *Vom Dreibund zum Völkerbund*.

36. Etschmann, "Die erste Republik Österreich," pp. 123–150; Barany and Gal, "Political Culture in the Lands of the former Habsburg Empire," pp. 195–248.

37. Jedlicka, "Saint Germain 1919," pp. 149–181; Ermacora, *Der unbewältigte Friede*.

38. Macartney, *Hungary and Her Successors*; Daruvar, *Le destin dramatique de la Hongrie*; Király (ed.), *Trianon and East Central Europe*; Borhi, "Towards Trianon"; Hajdu, "La Hongrie

dans les années de crise," pp. 37–51; Romsics, *The Dismantling of Historic Hungary;* Pastor, "Major Trends in Hungarian Foreign Policy," pp. 3–11.

39. Kovács, "Border Changes and Their Effect," pp. 79–86.

40. Botoran, "Romania in the System of the Paris Peace Treaties," pp. 136–145; Cassoly, "Les frontières de la Grande Roumanie," pp. 69–77; Berindei, "Mehrheit und Minderheiten im Nationalstaat Rumänien," pp. 315–326; Hausleitner, *Die Rumänisierung der Bukowina.*

41. Nestor, "Greece, Macedonia and the Convention of Neuilly," pp. 169–184; Damjanov, "Le traité de Neuilly et ses répercussions," pp. 56–69.

42. Ahmedov, "Les antagonismes interalliés," pp. 27–48.

43. Montgomery, "The Making of the Treaty of Sèvres," pp. 775–787; Helmreich, *From Paris to Sèvres;* Zürrer, "Der Friedensvertrag von Sèvres," pp. 88–114; Andonovski, "The Sèvres Treaty for Macedonia and the Macedonians," pp. 274–278; Macfie, "The Revision of the Treaty of Sèvres," pp. 57–88.

44. Neilson, *Britain, Soviet Russia and the Collapse of the Versailles Order.*

45. Kent, "British Policy, International Diplomacy and the Turkish Revolution," pp. 33–51; Karvounarakis, "Britain, Greece, and the Turkish Settlement," pp. 169–186.

46. Demirci, *Strategies and Struggles.*

47. Hirschon, *Crossing the Aegean.*

48. Beederian, "L'échec d'une percée internationale," pp. 351–371; Hovannisian, *The Republic of Armenia.*

49. Evans, *Great Britain and the Creation of Yugoslavia.*

50. Sheehan, "The Problem of Sovereignty in European History," pp. 1–15.

51. Langewiesche, *Reich, Nation, Föderation,* p. 97.

52. Möller, *Europa zwischen den Weltkriegen,* p. 35; Lendvai, "Sprengstoff im gemeinsamen Haus," p. 17; Schulze, *Staat und Nation in der europäischen Geschichte,* pp. 294–295.

53. Quoted in: Mazower, *Dark Continent,* pp. 56–57; Cohrs, *The Unfinished Peace after World War I.*

54. Quoted in: Manela, *The Wilsonian Moment,* p. 215.

55. Schulze Wessel (ed.), *Loyalitäten in der Tschechoslowakischen Republik.*

56. Sharp, *The Versailles Settlement,* pp. 205–206.

57. Leonhard, *Bellizismus und Nation,* pp. 835–836.

58. Keene, *The United States,* pp. 519–520.

59. Marks, *The Illusion of Peace,* pp. 27–28.

60. Clemenceau, *Grandeur and Misery of Victory,* pp. 355–367; Lloyd George, *The Truth about the Peace Treaties,* vol. 1, p. 6; Sharp, *The Versailles Settlement,* p. 200.

61. Sharp, *The Versailles Settlement,* p. 205.

62. Quoted in [and translated from]: Plessen (ed.), *Idee Europa,* p. 243.

63. Sharp, *The Versailles Settlement,* pp. 205–206.

64. Stevenson, *French War Aims against Germany,* pp. 198–202.

65. Smith, "France," pp. 429–430.

66. Quoted in: Jordan, *The Popular Front and Central Europe,* p. 5; Chastenet, *Quatre fois vingt ans,* p. 121.

67. Gregory, "Britain and Ireland," pp. 413–415.

68. Andrew and Kanya-Forstner, *The Climax of French Colonial Expansion*, pp. 237–240.

69. Gibelli, "Italy," pp. 472–475.

70. Rossini, *Woodrow Wilson and the American Myth*, pp. 186–187.

71. Lendvai, *The Hungarians*, pp. 373–388.

72. Dabringhaus, *Geschichte Chinas im 20. Jahrhundert*, pp. 23, 49, 57.

73. Manela, *The Wilsonian Moment*, pp. 141–175; Conrad, *What Is Global History?*, pp. 153–155.

74. Shimazu, *Japan, Race and Equality*, pp. 164–166.

75. Keene, "The United States," pp. 520–521.

9. MEMORIES

1. Naour, *The Living Unknown Soldier*, p. 198; Goebel, "Beyond Discourse," p. 383; Hanna, "The Tidal Wave of War," pp. 94–96.

2. Winter, "Forms of Kinship and Remembrance," pp. 40–60.

3. Janz, *Das symbolische Kapital der Trauer*.

4. Stegmann, *Kriegsdeutungen, Staatsgründungen, Sozialpolitik*, p. 275.

5. I am grateful to Paolo Pombeni in Bologna for this reference to the placque in Trento.

6. Ypersele, "Mourning and Memory," pp. 577–578.

7. Eichenberg, *Kämpfen für Frieden und Fürsorge*, pp. 72–100.

8. Ibid., pp. 223–229.

9. Prost, *War Memorials of the Great War*, pp. 11–43.

10. Ypersele, "Mourning and Memory," p. 579, Mosse, *Fallen Soldiers*, pp. 80–93.

11. Ypersele, "Mourning and Memory," p. 580.

12. Ulrich and Ziemann, *German Soldiers in the Great War*, pp. 184–185.

13. Inglis, "The Homecoming," pp. 596–597; Goebel, "Beyond Discourse," p. 380.

14. Winter, *Sites of Memory, Sites of Mourning*, pp. 78–116.

15. Carden-Coyne, *Reconstructing the Body*, pp. 311–315.

16. Fussell, *The Great War and Modern Memory*, pp. 31–38; Smith, "Paul Fussell's *The Great War and Modern Memory*," pp. 241–260.

17. Barham, *Forgotten Lunatics of the Great War*, pp. 167–221; Goebel, "Beyond Discourse," pp. 381–382.

18. Scates, *Return to Gallipoli*, pp. 216–219; Goebel, "Beyond Discourse," pp. 383–384.

19. Quoted in: Ulrich and Ziemann (eds.), *Krieg im Frieden*, p. 124.

20. Ypersele, "Mourning and Memory," p. 581; Cornwall, "Mémoires de la Grande Guerre," pp. 89–101.

21. Schenk, "Tannenberg/Grunwald," pp. 438–454.

22. Demps, *Die Neue Wache*.

23. Lange (ed.), *Geschichte der bildenden Kunst in Deutschland*, vol. 8, pp. 425–426, 454–455.

24. Ulrich and Ziemann (eds.), *Krieg im Frieden*, pp. 107–142, 164–170.

25. Geyer, "Das Stigma der Gewalt," pp. 678; Beaupré, *Das Trauma des großen Krieges*, p. 10.

26. Mosse, *Fallen Soldiers*; Schumann and Wirsching (eds.), *Violence and Society after the First World War*.

27. Levsen, *Elite, Männlichkeit und Krieg*, pp. 355–365.

28. Siegel, *The Moral Disarmament of France*, pp. 221–223.

29. Quoted [and translated] in: Beaupré, *Das Trauma des großen Krieges*, p. 9.

30. Thomas, *Treating the Trauma of the Great War*, pp. 171–174.

31. Ouditt, *Fighting Forces, Writing Women*, p. 44.

32. Harp, *Marketing Michelin*, pp. 89–125; Salzmann, "La bataille de Verdun," pp. 327–349; Heymel, *Touristen an der Front*, pp. 345–362; Riederer, "Einleitung. Ein Krieg wird besichtigt," pp. 67–69.

33. Kessler, *Tagebuch*, vol. 9, September 18, 1928, pp. 206–207.

10. BURDENS

1. Churchill, *The World Crisis*, vol. 1, pp. 10–11; Schulze, *State, Nations, Nationalism*, pp. 265–266.

2. Geyer, "Urkatastrophe," pp. 24–25.

3. Wells, *The War That Will End War*.

4. Hirschon, *Crossing the Aegean*.

5. Kramer, *Dynamic of Destruction*; Hohrath and Neitzel (eds.), *Kriegsgreuel*.

6. Lüdtke, "Thesen zur Wiederholbarkeit," pp. 284–285.

7. Geyer, *Verkehrte Welt*, pp. 379–396.

8. Kraus, *Versailles und die Folgen*, pp. 15–33.

9. Benjamin, "Experience and Poverty," pp. 731–732.

10. Paquet, "Rhein und Donau," pp. 25–26; Koenen, *Der deutsche Russland-Komplex*, p. 28.

11. Koselleck, "Zur Begriffsgeschichte der Zeitutopie," pp. 266–267.

12. Weber, "Politics as a Vocation," pp. 125–126.

13. Mann, *Reflections of a Nonpolitical Man*, pp. 187–189.

14. Schmitt, *The Concept of the Political*, pp. 30, 33, 37, 35; Nippel, "Krieg als Erscheinungsform der Feindschaft," pp. 61–70; Böckenförde, "Der Begriff des Politischen als Schlüssel," pp. 283–299; Vollrath, "Wie ist Carl Schmitt an seinen Begriff des Politischen gekommen?," pp. 151–168; Meier, *Carl Schmitt and Leo Strauss*.

15. Esch, "Zur historischen Verortung von 'ethnischer Säuberung' und Völkermord," pp. 27–28.

16. Joël, "Kameradschaft," p. 162.

17. Barbusse, *La lueur dans l'abîme*, p. 92.

18. Koselleck, "Patriotismus," pp. 238–239.

19. Ritter, *Notizhefte*, p. 266.

20. Mann, *The Magic Mountain*, p. 706.

21. Schwab, *Sagen des klassischen Altertums*, pp. 10–12.

BIBLIOGRAPHY

Abraham, Richard, *Alexander Kerensky: The First Love of the Revolution,* New York 1987.

Ackerl, Isabella, and Neck, Rudolf (eds.), *Saint-Germain 1919. Protokoll des Symposiums am 29. und 30. Mai 1979 in Wien,* Vienna 1989.

Adalian, Rouben P., "American Diplomatic Correspondence in the Age of Mass Murder: The Armenian Genocide in the US Archives," in: Winter (ed.), *America and the Armenian Genocide of 1915,* pp. 146–184.

Adams, Ralph J. Q., *Arms and the Wizard: Lloyd George and the Ministry of Munitions 1915–1916,* London 1978.

Adams, Ralph J. Q., and Poirier, Philip P., *The Conscription Controversy in Great Britain, 1900–18,* Basingstoke 1987.

Adcock, Arthur St. J., *Australasia Triumphant,* London 1916.

Adelson, Roger, *London and the Invention of the Middle East: Money, Power, and War, 1902–1922,* New Haven 1995.

Adunka, Evelyn, "Der ostjüdische Einfluss auf Wien," in: Peter Bettelheim and Michael Ley (eds.), *Ist jetzt hier die "wahre Heimat?" Ostjüdische Einwanderung nach Wien,* Vienna 1993, pp. 77–88.

Afflerbach, Holger, *Der Dreibund: Europäische Großmacht- und Allianzpolitik vor dem Ersten Weltkrieg,* Vienna 2002.

———, *Falkenhayn: Politisches Denken und Handeln im Kaiserreich,* Munich 1994.

——— (ed.), *Kaiser Wilhelm II. als Oberster Kriegsherr im Ersten Weltkrieg. Quellen aus der militärischen Umgebung des Kaisers 1914–1918,* Munich 2005.

———, "Planning Total War? Falkenhayn and the Battle of Verdun, 1916," in: Chickering and Förster (eds.), *Great War, Total War,* pp. 113–131.

Afflerbach, Holger, and Sheffield, Gary, "Waging Total War: Learning Curve or Bleeding Curve?" in: Jay Winter (ed.), *The Legacy of the Great War: Ninety Years On,* Columbia 2009, pp. 61–90.

Agnew, Hugh L., *The Czechs and the Lands of the Bohemian Crown,* Stanford 2004.

———, "The Flyspecks on Palivec's Portrait: Franz Joseph, the Symbols of Monarchy, and Czech Popular Loyalty," in: Laurence Cole and Daniel L. Unowsky (eds.), *The Limits of*

Loyalty: Imperial Symbolism, Popular Allegiances, and State Patriotism in the Late Habsburg Monarchy, New York 2007, pp. 86–112.

Ahmedov, Ahmed S., "Les antagonismes interalliés sur les problèmes turcs après l'armistice de Moudros jusqu'au traité de Sèvres," in: *Études Balkaniques* 19 (1983), pp. 27–48.

Akçam, Taner, *Armenien und der Völkermord: Die Istanbuler Prozesse und die türkische Nationalbewegung*, Hamburg 1996.

Aksakal, Mustafa, *The Ottoman Road to War in 1914: The Ottoman Empire and the First World War*, New York 2008.

Alber, Jens, Eichenberg, Richard, Flora, Peter, Kohl, Jürgen, Kraus, Franz, Pfenning, Winfried, and Seebohm, Kurt, *State, Economy and Society in Western Europe 1815–1975*, vol. 1, Frankfurt / M. 1983.

Albert, Bill, *South America and the First World War: The Impact of the War on Brazil, Argentina, Peru, and Chile*, New York 1988.

Albes, Jens, "Portugal," in: Hirschfeld, Krumeich, and Renz (eds.), *Enzyklopädie Erster Weltkrieg*, p. 780.

Albrecht, Christian, "Zwischen Kriegstheologie und Krisentheologie. Zur Lutherrezeption im Reformationsjubiläum 1917," in: Hans Medick and Peer Schmidt (eds.), *Luther zwischen den Kulturen: Zeitgenossenschaft—Weltwirkung*, Göttingen 2004, pp. 482–499.

Albrecht, Richard, "Wer redet heute noch von der Vernichtung der Armenier? Adolf Hitlers Geheimrede am 22. August 1939: Das historische L-3-Dokument," in: *Zeitschrift für Genozidforschung* 9 / 1 (2008), pp. 93–131.

Allgemeiner Wegweiser für jede Familie 1917, Berlin 1917.

Alston, Charlotte, *Russia's Greatest Enemy? Harold Williams and the Russian Revolution*, London 2007.

Altenhöner, Florian, *Kommunikation und Kontrolle: Gerüchte und städtische Öffentlichkeiten in Berlin und London 1914 / 18*, Munich 2008.

Amouroux, Henri, *Pétain avant Vichy: La guerre et l'amour*, Paris 1967.

"An Address at the Metropolitan Opera House, 27 September 1918," quoted in: Steigerwald, *Wilsonian Idealism in America*, p. 37.

Andelman, David A., *A Shattered Peace: Versailles 1919 and the Price We Pay Today*, Hoboken 2008.

Anderson, Julie, *War, Disability and Rehabilitation in Britain: Soul of a Nation*, Manchester 2011.

Anderson, Matthew S., *The Ascendancy of Europe 1815–1914*, 2nd edn., London 1985.

Anderson, Ross, *The Forgotten Front: The East African Campaign 1914–1918*, Stroud 2004.

Andonovski, Hristo, "The Sèvres Treaty for Macedonia and the Macedonians," in: *Macedonian Review* 11 (1981), pp. 274–278.

Andrew, Christopher M., and Kanya-Forstner, Alexander S., *The Climax of French Imperial Expansion 1914–1924*, Stanford 1981.

Angell, Norman, *The Great Illusion: A Study of the Relation of Military Power to National Advantage* (1910), 3rd edn., London 1911.

Angelow, Jürgen, "Der Erste Weltkrieg auf dem Balkan. Neue Fragestellungen und Erklärungen," in: Bauerkämper and Julien (eds.), *Durchhalten*, pp. 178–194.

Angress, Werner T., "Das deutsche Militär und die Juden im Ersten Weltkrieg," in: *Militärgeschichtliche Mitteilungen* 19 (1976), pp. 77–146.

Angster, Julia, *Erdbeeren und Piraten: Die Royal Navy und die Ordnung der Welt*, Göttingen 2012.

Ansky, Shloyme, *The Enemy at His Pleasure: A Journey through the Jewish Pale of Settlement during World War I* (1925), ed. by Joachim Neugroschel, New York 2002.

Antier, Chantal, "1915: La France en chantier," in: *Guerres mondiales et conflits contemporains* 219 (2005), pp. 53–62.

Anweisung für die Ausbildung beim Sturmbataillon, Berlin 1916.

Anz, Thomas, "Motive des Militärischen in Kafkas Erzähltexten seit August 1914," in: Engel and Robertson (eds.), *Kafka, Prag und der Erste Weltkrieg*, pp. 173–183.

Arendt, Hannah, *Elemente und Ursprünge totaler Herrschaft*, Frankfurt 1955.

———, *The Origins of Totalitarianism*, New York 1951.

Arthur, Max, *The Faces of World War I*, London 2012.

Artl, Gerhard, *Die österreichisch-ungarische Südtiroloffensive 1916*, Vienna 1983.

Ashplant, Timothy G., *Fractured Loyalties: Masculinity, Class and Politics in Britain, 1900–1930*, London 2007.

Ashworth, Tony, *Trench Warfare, 1914–1918: The Live and Let Live System*, London 1980.

Atia, Nadia, "Mesopotamian Myths," in: *History Workshop Journal* 71 (2011), pp. 247–252.

Atılgan, İnanç, *Österreichs Dilemma 1915: Türken oder Armenier?* Klagenfurt 2008.

Audoin-Rouzeau, Stéphane, "Die Delegation der 'gueules cassées' in Versailles am 28. Juni 1919," in: Krumeich (ed.), *Versailles 1919*, pp. 280–287.

———, *Men at War, 1914–1918: National Sentiment and Trench Journalism in France during the First World War*, Oxford 1992.

Audoin-Rouzeau, Stéphane, and Becker, Annette, *14–18: Retrouver la guerre*, Paris 2000.

Audoin-Rouzeau, Stéphane, and Becker, Jean-Jacques (eds.), *Encyclopédie de la Grande Guerre 1914–1918: Histoire et culture*, Paris 2004.

Audoin-Rouzeau, Stéphane, and Krumeich, Gerd, "Les batailles de la Grande Guerre," in: Audoin-Rouzeau and Becker (eds.), *Encyclopédie de la Grande Guerre 1914–1918*, pp. 299–311.

Augusteijn, Joost, *Patrick Pearse: The Making of a Revolutionary*, Basingstoke 2010.

Azéma, Jean-Pierre, "Pétain et les mutineries de 1917," in: *L'Histoire. Spécial: 14.18. Mourir pour la Patrie*, 107 (1988), pp. 80–85.

Baberowski, Jörg, "Diktaturen der Eindeutigkeit. Ambivalenz und Gewalt im Zarenreich und in der frühen Sowjetunion," in: idem (ed.), *Moderne Zeiten?* pp. 37–59.

———, "Einführende Bemerkungen," in: Groß (ed.), *Die vergessene Front*, pp. 147–152.

———, "Kriege in staatsfernen Räumen. Russland und die Sowjetunion 1905–1950," in: Beyrau, Hochgeschwender, and Langewiesche (eds.), *Formen des Krieges*, pp. 291–310.

——— (ed.), *Moderne Zeiten? Krieg, Revolution und Gewalt im 20. Jahrhundert*, Göttingen 2006.

———, "Ordnung durch Terror. Stalinismus im sowjetischen Vielvölkerreich," in: Isabel Heinemann and Patrick Wagner (eds.), *Wissenschaft—Planung—Vertreibung: Neuordnungskonzepte und Umsiedlungspolitik im 20. Jahrhundert*, Stuttgart 2006, pp. 145–172.

———, *Scorched Earth: Stalin's Reign of Terror*, New Haven 2017.

————, "Verwüstetes Land: Macht und Gewalt in der frühen Sowjetunion," in: idem and Metzler (eds.), *Gewalträume*, pp. 169–188.

Baberowski, Jörg, and Doering-Manteuffel, Anselm, *Ordnung durch Terror: Gewaltexzesse und Vernichtung im nationalsozialistischen und im stalinistischen Imperium*, Bonn 2006.

Baberowski, Jörg, and Metzler, Gabriele (eds.), *Gewalträume: Soziale Ordnungen im Ausnahmezustand*, Frankfurt / M. 2012.

Baden, Max, Prinz von, *Erinnerungen und Dokumente*, Stuttgart 1927.

Badsey, Stephen, "Cavalry and the Development of Breakthrough Doctrine," in: Griffith (ed.), *British Fighting Methods in the Great War*, pp. 138–174.

Baer, Ludwig, *Vom Stahlhelm zum Gefechtshelm. Eine Entwicklungsgeschichte von 1915 bis 1993*, 2 vols., Neu-Anspach 1994.

Bahners, Patrick, "System der Hellhörigkeiten: Die europäischen Mächte vor dem Ersten Weltkrieg," in: *Frankfurter Allgemeine Zeitung*, November 24, 1993.

Bainville, Jacques, *Two Histories Face to Face: France versus Germany*, Paris 1919 (French orig. 1915).

Bairoch, Paul, "International Industrialization from 1780 to 1980," in: *Journal of European Economic History* 11 (1982), pp. 269–333.

Balderston, Theo, "Industrial Mobilization and War Economies," in: Horne (ed.), *A Companion to World War I*, pp. 217–233.

Balderston, Thomas, "War Finance and Inflation in Britain and Germany, 1914–1918," in: *Economic History Review* 42 (1988), pp. 222–244.

Balkelis, Tomas, "Turning Citizens into Soldiers: Baltic Paramilitary Movements after the Great War," in: Gerwarth and Horne (eds.), *War in Peace*, pp. 126–144.

Ballinger, Pamela, "Blutopfer, and Feuertaufe," in: Gumbrecht, Kittler, and Siegert (eds.): *Der Dichter als Kommandant*, pp. 175–202.

Balzac, Honoré de, *Le Médecin de Campagne*, Paris 1834.

Banta, Martha, *Imaging American Women: Ideas and Ideals in Cultural History*, New York 1988.

Barany, George, and Gal, Susan, "Political Culture in the Lands of the Former Habsburg Empire. Authoritarian and Parliamentary Traditions," in: *Austrian History Yearbook* 29 (1998), pp. 195–248.

Barbusse, Henri, *La lueur dans l'abîme*, Paris 1920.

————, *Under Fire: The Story of a Squad*, New York 1935, reprinted 2015 (French orig. *Le Feu*, Paris 1916).

Barham, Peter, *Forgotten Lunatics of the Great War*, New Haven 2004.

Barker, Ernest, *The Submerged Nationalities of the German Empire*, Oxford 1915.

Baron, Nick, *Homelands: War, Population and Statehood in Eastern Europe and Russia 1918–1924*, London 2004.

Barr, James, *A Line in the Sand: Britain, France and the Struggle for the Mastery of the Middle East*, London 2011.

Barraclough, Geoffrey, *From Agadir to Armageddon: Anatomy of a Crisis*, London 1982.

Barrett, Michele, "Death and the Afterlife: Britain's Colonies and Dominions," in: Das (ed.), *Race, Empire and First World War Writing*, pp. 301–320.

————, "Subalterns at War: First World War Colonial Forces, and the Politics of the Imperial War Grave Commission," in: Rosalind C. Morris (ed.), *Can the Subaltern Speak? Reflections on the History of an Idea*, New York 2010, pp. 156–176.

Barrier, N. Gerald, "Ruling India: Coercion and Propaganda in British India during the First World War," in: Ellinwood and Pradhan (eds.), *India and World War I*, pp. 75–108.

Barth, Boris, *Genozid: Völkermord im 20. Jahrhundert: Geschichte, Theorien, Kontroversen*, Munich 2006.

Barton, Peter, *Battlefields of the First World War: The Unseen Panoramas of the Western Front*, London 2008.

Bartov, Omer, and Weitz, Eric D. (eds.), *Shatterzone of Empires: Coexistence and Violence in the German, Habsburg, Russian, and Ottoman Borderlands*, Bloomington, Ind. 2013.

Baten, Jörg, and Schulz, Rainer, "Making Profits in Wartime: Corporate Profits, Inequality, and GDP in Germany during the First World War," in: *Economic History Review* 58 (2005), pp. 34–56.

Battles, Matthew, *Widener: Biography of a Library*, Cambridge, Mass. 2004.

Baudis, Dieter, "'Vom Schweinemord zum Kohlrübenwinter.' Streiflichter zur Entwicklung der Lebensverhältnisse in Berlin im Ersten Weltkrieg (August 1914 bis Frühjahr 1917)," in: *Jahrbuch für Wirtschaftsgeschichte* (1986), pp. 129–152.

Bauerkämper, Arnd, and Julien, Élise (eds.), *Durchhalten! Krieg und Gesellschaft im Vergleich 1914–1918*, Göttingen 2010.

Baumeister, Martin, *Kriegstheater: Großstadt, Front und Massenkultur 1914–1918*, Essen 2005.

Bäumer, Gertrud, *Weit hinter den Schützengräben: Aufsätze aus dem Weltkrieg*, Jena 1916.

Baumgart, Winfried, *The Crimean War 1853–1856*, London 1999.

————, "Einleitung," in: idem (ed.), *Von Brest-Litowsk zur deutschen Novemberrevolution*, pp. 13–48.

————, *Europäisches Konzert und nationale Bewegung. Internationale Beziehungen 1830–1878. Handbuch der Geschichte der Internationalen Beziehungen in 9 Bdn.*, vol. 6, Paderborn 1999.

———— (ed.), *Von Brest-Litowsk zur deutschen Novemberrevolution. Aus den Tagebüchern, Briefen und Aufzeichnungen von Alfons Paquet, Wilhelm Groener und Albert Hopman, März bis November 1918*, Göttingen 1971.

Bavendamm, Gundula, *Spionage und Verrat: Konspirative Kriegserzählungen und französische Innenpolitik, 1914–1917*, Essen 2003.

Baycroft, Timothy, and Fischer, Conan (eds.), *After the Versailles Treaty: Enforcement, Compliance, Contested Identities*, London 2008.

Baynes, John, *Morale: A Study of Men and Courage: The Second Scottish Rifles at the Battle of Neuve Chapelle 1915*, London 1987.

Beasley, William G., *Japanese Imperialism 1894–1945*, Oxford 1987.

Beaumont, Joan, "Nation oder Commonwealth? Der gefallene Soldat und die nationale Identität," in: Jörg Echternkamp and Manfred Hettling (eds.), *Gefallenengedenken im globalen Vergleich. Nationale Tradition, politische Legitimation und Individualisierung der Erinnerung*, Munich 2013, pp. 43–68.

Beaupré, Nicolas, "Construction and Deconstruction of the Idea of French War Enthusiasm in 1914," in: Kettenacker and Riotte (eds.), *The Legacies of Two World Wars*, pp. 41–57.

———, *Das Trauma des großen Krieges 1918–1932/33*, Darmstadt 2009.

———, *Les Grandes Guerres 1914–1945*, Paris 2012.

Becker, Annette, *Les Oubliés de la Grande Guerre, humanitaire et culture de guerre 1914–1918: Populations occupées, déportés civils, prisonniers de guerre*, Paris 1998.

Becker, Jean-Jacques, *1914. Comment les Français sont entrés dans la guerre. Contribution à l'étude de l'opinion publique printemps-été 1914*, Paris 1977.

———, *1917 en Europe: L'année impossible*, Brussels 1997.

———, *Clemenceau, Chef de Guerre*, Paris 2012.

———, *Clemenceau: L'Intraitable*, Paris 1998.

———, "Frankreich," in: Hirschfeld, Krumeich, and Renz (eds.), *Enzyklopädie Erster Weltkrieg*, pp. 31–43.

———, *Le traité de Versailles*, Paris 2002.

———, "Marne," in: Hirschfeld, Krumeich, and Renz (eds.), *Enzyklopädie Erster Weltkrieg*, pp. 697–699.

———, "That's the Death Knell of Our Boys . . . ," in: Patrick Fridenson (ed.), *The French Home Front 1914–1918*, Oxford 1992, pp. 17–36.

Becker, Jean-Jacques, and Krumeich, Gerd, *Der Große Krieg: Deutschland und Frankreich im Ersten Weltkrieg*, Essen 2010.

Beckett, Ian F. W., *The Great War 1914–1918*, Harlow 2001.

——— (ed.), *1917: Beyond the Western Front*, Leiden 2009.

Beckmann, Rasmus, and Jäger, Thomas (eds.), *Handbuch Kriegstheorien*, Wiesbaden 2011.

Beederian, Arthur, "L'échec d'une percée internationale. Le mouvement national arménien (1914–1923)," in: *Relations Internationales* 31 (1982), pp. 351–371.

Benjamin, Walter, "Experience and Poverty (December 1933)," in: idem, *Selected Writings*, vol. 2, *1927–1934*, ed. by Michael Jennings, Howard Eiland, and Gary Smith, Cambridge, Mass. 1999, pp. 730–736.

Bennett, Geoffrey, *Coronel and the Falklands*, London 1962.

Bentinck-Smith, William, *Building a Great Library: The Coolidge Years at Harvard*, Cambridge, Mass. 1976.

Benvindo, Bruno, *Des hommes en guerre: Les soldats belges entre ténacité et désillusion, 1914–1918*, Brussels 2005.

Benvindo, Bruno, and Majerus, Benoît, "Belgien zwischen 1914 und 1918: Ein Labor für den totalen Krieg," in: Bauerkämper and Julien (eds.), *Durchhalten*, pp. 127–148.

Berghahn, Volker R., *Der Tirpitz-Plan: Genesis und Verfall einer innenpolitischen Krisenstrategie unter Wilhelm II.*, Düsseldorf 1971.

———, *Sarajewo, 28. Juni 1914: Der Untergang des alten Europa*, Munich 1997.

Bergmann, Hugo, "Der jüdische Nationalismus nach dem Krieg," in: *Der Jude* 1 (1916), pp. 7–13.

Bergsträßer, Ludwig, *Die preußische Wahlrechtsfrage im Kriege und die Entstehung der Osterbotschaft 1917*, Tübingen 1929.

Bericht des Berliner Polizeipräsidenten, 25. Juni 1915, quoted in: Bihl (ed.), *Deutsche Quellen zur Geschichte des Ersten Weltkriegs,* p. 131.

"Bericht des Berliner Polizeipräsidenten, 18. September 1915," quoted in: Bihl (ed.), *Deutsche Quellen zur Geschichte des Ersten Weltkriegs,* p. 146.

"Bericht Bethmann Hollwegs über die Unterredung mit Wilhelm II. am 5. Juli 1914," in: Geiss (ed.), *Julikrise und Kriegsausbruch 1914,* vol. 1, no. 22, p. 85.

Berindei, Dan, "Mehrheit und Minderheiten im Nationalstaat Rumänien 1918–1945," in: Heiner Timmermann (ed.), *Nationalismus und Nationalbewegung in Europa 1914–1945,* Berlin 1999, pp. 315–326.

Bermbach, Udo, *Vorformen parlamentarischer Kabinettsbildung in Deutschland: Der Inter-fraktionelle Ausschuss 1917/18 und die Parlamentarisierung der Reichsregierung,* Cologne 1967.

Bernhardi, Friedrich von, *Germany and the Next War* (1912), London 1914.

Beşikçi, Mehmet, *The Ottoman Mobilization of Manpower in the First World War: Between Voluntarism and Resistance,* Leiden 2012.

Bessel, Richard, "Demobilmachung," in: Hirschfeld, Krumeich, and Renz (eds.), *Enzyklopädie Erster Weltkrieg,* pp. 427–430.

Best, Nicholas, *The Greatest Day in History: How, on the Eleventh Hour of the Eleventh Day of the Eleventh Month, the First World War Finally Came to an End,* New York 2008.

Bet-El, Ilana R., *Conscripts: Lost Legions of the Great War,* Stroud 1999.

Beyrau, Dietrich, "Der Erste Weltkrieg als Bewährungsprobe. Bolschewistische Lernpro-zesse aus dem 'imperialistischen' Krieg," in: *Journal of Modern European History* 1 (2003), pp. 96–123.

Beyrau, Dietrich, Hochgeschwender, Michael, and Langewiesche, Dieter (eds.), *Formen des Krieges: Von der Antike bis zur Gegenwart,* Paderborn 2007.

Beyrau, Dietrich, and Shcherbinin, Pavel P., "Alles für die Front: Russland im Krieg 1914–1922," in: Bauerkämper and Julien (eds.), *Durchhalten,* pp. 151–177.

Bibbings, Lois S., *Telling Tales about Men: Conceptions of Conscientious Objectors to Military Service during the First World War,* Manchester 2009.

Biesalski, Konrad, "Wer ist der Führer in der gesamten Fürsorge für unsre heimkehrenden Krieger?" in: *Tägliche Rundschau,* January 18, 1915.

Biguzzi, Stefano, *Cesare Battisti,* Turin 2008.

Bihl, Wolfdieter, *Der Erste Weltkrieg 1914–1918: Chronik—Daten—Fakten,* Vienna 2010.

—— (ed.), *Deutsche Quellen zur Geschichte des Ersten Weltkriegs,* Darmstadt 1991.

Binder, Hartmut, *Kafkas Welt: Eine Lebenschronik in Bildern,* Reinbek 2008.

Birgerson, Susanne Michele, *After the Breakup of a Multi-Ethnic Empire: Russia, Successor States, and Eurasian Security,* Westport, Conn. 2002.

Bischoff, Josef, *Die letzte Front: Geschichte der Eisernen Division im Baltikum 1919,* Berlin 1935.

Bischoff, Volker, and Mania, Marino, "Melting Pot-Mythen als Szenarien amerikanischer Identität zur Zeit der New Immigration," in: Giesen (ed.), *Nationale und kulturelle Iden-tität,* pp. 513–536.

Bittner, Ludwig, and Uebersberger, Hans (eds.), *Österreich-Ungarns Außenpolitik von der bosnischen Krise 1908 bis zum Kriegsausbruch 1914: Diplomatische Aktenstücke des österreichisch-ungarischen Ministeriums des Äußeren*, vol. 8: *1. Mai bis 1. August 1914*, Vienna 1930.

Björnson, Björn, *Vom deutschen Wesen: Impressionen eines Stammverwandten 1914–1917*, Berlin 1917.

Blair, Susan K., "Excuses for Inhumanity: The Official German Response to the 1915 Armenian Genocide," in: *Armenian Review* 37 / 4 (1984), pp. 14–30.

Bloch, Ivan, *Is War Now Impossible? Being an Abridgment of the War of the Future in Its Technical, Economic, and Political Relations*, Whitefish, Mont. 2008.

Bloch, Joachim von, *Der Krieg. Übersetzung des russischen Werkes des Autors: Der zukünftige Krieg in seiner technischen, volkswirtschaftlichen und politischen Bedeutung*, 6 vols., Berlin 1899.

Blom, Philipp, *Der taumelnde Kontinent: Europa 1900–1914*, Munich 2008.

———, *The Vertigo Years: Europe, 1900–1914*, New York 2010.

Bloxham, Donald, "Determinants of the Armenian Genocide," in: Richard G. Hovannisian (ed.), *Looking Backward, Moving Forward: Confronting the Armenian Genocide*, New Brunswick 2003, pp. 23–50.

———, *The Final Solution: A Genocide*, Oxford 2009.

———, "The First World War and the Development of the Armenian Genocide," in: Ronald G. Suny, Fatma M. Göçek, and Norman M. Naimark (eds.), *A Question of Genocide. Armenians and Turks at the End of the Ottoman Empire*, Oxford 2011, pp. 260–275.

———, *The Great Game of Genocide: Imperialism, Nationalism, and the Destruction of the Ottoman Armenians*, Oxford 2005.

Blücher, Evelyn, *An English Wife in Berlin*, London 1921.

Bobroff, Ronald Park, *Roads to Glory: Late Imperial Russia and the Turkish Straits*, London 2006.

Bock, Fabienne, and Bonzon, Thierry, "Il faut que vous sachiez ce qui se passe chez nous . . . 246 lettres de militaires français au Parlement en 1917," in: André Loez and Nicolas Mariot (eds.), *Obéir / désobéir. Les mutineries de 1917 en perspective*, Paris 2008, pp. 167–180.

Böckenförde, Ernst-Wolfgang, "Der Begriff des Politischen als Schlüssel zum staatsrechtlichen Werk Carl Schmitts," in: Quaritsch (ed.), *Complexio Oppositorum*, pp. 283–299.

Boeckh, Katrin, *Von den Balkankriegen zum Ersten Weltkrieg: Kleinstaatenpolitik und ethnische Selbstbestimmung am Balkan*, Munich 1996.

Boemeke, Manfred F., Feldman, Gerald D., and Glaser, Elisabeth (eds.), *The Treaty of Versailles: A Reassessment after 75 Years*, Cambridge 1998.

Boghardt, Thomas, *The Zimmermann Telegram: Intelligence, Diplomacy, and America's Entry into World War I*, Annapolis 2012.

Bond, Brian, "Editorial Notice," in: Liddell Hart, *Liddell Hart's Western Front*, pp. 106–112.

Bonhoeffer, Karl, "Erfahrungen aus dem Kriege über Ätiologie psychopathologischer Zustände mit besonderer Berücksichtigung der Erschöpfung und Emotion," in: *Allgemeine Zeitschrift für Psychiatrie* 73 (1917), pp. 76–95.

Bonzon, Thierry, "The Labour Market and Industrial Mobilization, 1915–1917," in: Robert and Winter (eds.), *Capital Cities*, pp. 164–195.

Borhi, László, "Towards Trianon," in: *Hungarian Quarterly* 41 (2000), pp. 129–134.

Borodziej, Włodzimierz, *Geschichte Polens im 20. Jahrhundert*, Munich 2010.

Bostridge, Mark, "Charlotte and Jack: The Pacifist Campaigner and Her Brother, the Commander-in-Chief: How Families and Friendships Were Split by the First World War," in: *Times Literary Supplement*, July 1, 2011, p. 4.

Bosworth, Richard J. B., *Italy, the Least of the Great Powers: Italian Foreign Policy before the First World War*, Cambridge 1979.

——, *Italy and the Approach of the First World War*, London 1983.

Botoran, Constantin, "Romania in the System of the Paris Peace Treaties (1919–1920)," in: *Romania, Pages of History* 12 (1987), pp. 136–145.

Boulanger, Philippe, "Les embusqués de la première guerre mondiale," in: *Guerres mondiales et conflits contemporains* 192 (1998), pp. 87–100.

Bourne, John M., "Flandern," in: Hirschfeld, Krumeich, and Renz (eds.), *Enzyklopädie Erster Weltkrieg*, pp. 489–494.

——, "Streitkräfte (Großbritannien)," in: Hirschfeld, Krumeich, and Renz (eds.), *Enzyklopädie Erster Weltkrieg*, pp. 884–891.

——, "Westfront," in: Hirschfeld, Krumeich, and Renz (eds.), *Enzyklopädie Erster Weltkrieg*, pp. 960–967.

Bourne, Randolph S., *The Radical Will: Selected Writings, 1911–1918*, ed. by Olaf Hansen, New York 1977.

——, "Trans-National America," in: *Atlantic Monthly* 118 (July 1916), pp. 86–97.

Bowman, Timothy, *The Irish Regiments in the Great War: Discipline and Morale*, Manchester 1999.

Bradley, John F. N., *The Czechoslovak Legion in Russia, 1914–1920*, Boulder, Colo. 1991.

Brandl, Franz, *Kaiser, Politiker und Menschen: Erinnerungen eines Wiener Polizeipräsidenten*, Vienna 1936.

Braun, Bernd, *Die Reichskanzler der Weimarer Republik: Zwölf Lebensläufe in Bildern*, Düsseldorf 2011.

Braun, Fritz, *Die Unterwerfung des deutschen Ordenslandes durch die Polen im 15. Jahrhundert. Zum 500. Geburtstag der Schlacht Tannenberg 15. Juli 1410*, Berlin 1910.

Braunthal, Julius, *Geschichte der Internationale*, 3 vols., 2nd edn., Hannover 1974; *History of the International*, vol. 1, *1864–1914*, London 1966; vol. 2, *1914–1943*, London 1967.

Bridge, Carl, "The Reason Why: Australia and the Great War," in: *Quadrant* 38 (1994), pp. 11–12.

Bridge, Francis R., and Bullen, Roger, *The Great Powers and the European State System 1815–1914*, 2nd edn., London 2005.

Britten, Thomas, *American Indians in World War I: At Home and at War*, Albuquerque 1997.

Broadberry, Stephen N., and Harrison, Mark (eds.), *The Economics of World War I*, Cambridge 2005.

——, "The Economics of World War I: An Overview," in: idem (ed.), *The Economics of World War I*, pp. 3–40.

Broadberry, Stephen N., and Howlett, Peter, "The United Kingdom during World War I: Business as Usual?," in: idem (eds.), *The Economics of World War I*, pp. 206–234.

Bröckling, Ulrich, *Disziplin: Soziologie und Geschichte militärischer Gehorsamsproduktion*, Munich 1997.

Brocks, Christine, *Die bunte Welt des Krieges: Bildpostkarten aus dem Ersten Weltkrieg 1914–1918*, Essen 2008.

Brown, Ian M., *British Logistics on the Western Front 1914–1919*, Westport, Conn. 1998.

———, *The Imperial War Museum Book of the Western Front*, London 1993.

Brown, Judith M., *Modern India: The Origins of an Asian Democracy*, Oxford 1985.

———, "War and the Colonial Relationship: Britain, India and the War of 1914–18," in: Ellinwood and Pradhan (eds.), *India and World War I*, pp. 19–48.

Brown, Robert C., and Cook, Ramsay, *Canada, 1896–1921: A Nation Transformed*, Toronto 1974.

Bruch, Rüdiger vom, "Aufruf der 93," in: Hirschfeld, Krumeich, and Renz (eds.), *Enzyklopädie Erster Weltkrieg*, pp. 356–357.

Bruch, Rüdiger vom, and Hofmeister, Björn (eds.), *Deutsche Geschichte in Quellen und Darstellung*, vol. 8: *Kaiserreich und Erster Weltkrieg 1871–1918*, Stuttgart 2000.

Bruendel, Steffen, *Volksgemeinschaft oder Volksstaat: Die "Ideen von 1914" und die Neuordnung Deutschlands im Ersten Weltkrieg*, Berlin 2003.

Brüggemeier, Franz-Josef, *Geschichte Großbritanniens im 20. Jahrhundert*, Munich 2010.

Brussilow, Alexej Alexejewitsch, *Meine Erinnerungen*, Berlin 1988.

Buchner, Eberhard (ed.), *Kriegsdokumente: Der Weltkrieg 1914 in der Darstellung der zeitgenössischen Presse*, vol. 1: *Die Vorgeschichte: Der Krieg bis zur Vogesenschlacht*, Munich 1914.

Bührer, Tanja, *Die Kaiserliche Schutztruppe für Deutsch-Ostafrika: Koloniale Sicherheitspolitik und transkulturelle Kriegführung, 1885 bis 1918*, Munich 2011.

Bull, Stephen, *Brassey's History of Uniforms: World War One German Army*, London 2000.

———, *Trench: A History of Trench Warfare on the Western Front*, Oxford 2010.

Burchardt, Lothar, "Zwischen Kriegsgewinnen und Kriegskosten: Krupp im Ersten Weltkrieg," in: *Zeitschrift für Unternehmensgeschichte* 32 (1987), pp. 71–123.

Burckhardt, Jacob, *Force and Freedom: Reflections on History*, New York 1943.

Burdick, Charles Burton, *The Japanese Siege of Tsingtao: World War I in Asia*, Hamden, Conn. 1976.

Burhop, Carsten, *Wirtschaftsgeschichte des Kaiserreichs 1871–1918*, Göttingen 2011.

Burk, Kathleen (ed.), *War and the State: The Transformation of British Government, 1914–1919*, London 1982.

Burkhardt, Johannes, "Die Friedlosigkeit der Frühen Neuzeit: Grundlegung einer Theorie der Bellizität Europas," in: *Zeitschrift für Historische Forschung* 24 (1997), pp. 509–574.

Busch, Moritz, *Bismarck: Some Secret Pages of His History, Being a Diary Kept by Dr. Moritz Busch during Twenty-five Years' Official and Private Intercourse with the Great Chancellor*, reprinted from the edition of 1898, vol. 1, New York 1970.

Butt, John, "Housing," in: Robert A. Cage (ed.), *The Working Class in Glasgow, 1750–1914*, London 1987, pp. 29–55.

Buttersack, Felix, "Die Suggestion und ihre Verwendung als Heilfaktor: Kriegsärztlicher Vortrag mit Demonstrationen, gehalten am 29. September 1917 in Stuttgart," in: *Medizinisches Correspondenz-Blatt des Württembergischen Ärztlichen Landesvereins* 48 (1917).

Cabanes, Bruno, *La victoire endeuillée: La sortie de guerre des soldats français (1918–1920)*, Paris 2004.

Calic, Marie-Janine, *Geschichte Jugoslawiens im 20. Jahrhundert*, Munich 2010.

———, *Sozialgeschichte Serbiens, 1815–1941: Der aufhaltsame Fortschritt während der Industrialisierung*, Munich 1994.Canetti, Elias, *The Tongue Set Free* (German orig. 1977), New York 1983.

Canini, Gérard, *Combattre à Verdun: Vie et souffrance quotidiennes du soldat 1916–1917*, Nancy 1988.

Canning, Kathleen, "Sexual Crisis and the Writing of Citizenship: Reflections on States of Exception in Germany 1914–1920," in: Alf Lüdtke and Michael Wildt (eds.), *Staats-Gewalt: Ausnahmezustand und Sicherheitsregimes. Historische Perspektiven*, Göttingen 2008, pp. 167–213.

Canwell, Diane, and Sutherland, Jonathan, *Battle of Britain 1917: The First Heavy Bomber Raids on England*, Barnsley 2006.

"Capital, Labor, and the Government," *Nation*, March 16, 1918.

Capozzola, Christopher, *Uncle Sam Wants You: World War I and the Making of the Modern American Citizen*, Oxford 2008.

Carden-Coyne, Ann, *Reconstructing the Body: Classicism, Modernism, and the First World War*, Oxford 2009.

Carnegie Endowment for International Peace, Division of Intercourse and Education, *The Other Balkan Wars: A 1913 Carnegie Endowment Inquiry in Retrospect with a New Introduction and Reflections on the Present Conflict by George F. Kennan*, Washington, DC 1993.

———, Publication No. 4: *Report of the International Commission to Inquire into the Causes and Conduct of the Balkan Wars*, Washington, DC 1914.

Caron, François, *La France des patriotes*, Paris 1985.

Carossa, Hans, *A Roumanian Diary* (German orig. 1924), New York 1930.

Carré, Henri, *Les Grandes Heures du Général Pétain: 1917 et la crise du moral*, Paris 1954.

Carrington, Charles, "The Empire at War 1914–18," in: idem, Ernest A. Benians, and James Butler (eds.), *The Cambridge History of the British Empire*, vol. 3, *The Empire-Commonwealth 1870–1919*, Cambridge 1967, pp. 604–644.

Casement, Roger, "Speech from the Dock," in: MacArthur (ed.), *The Penguin Book of Twentieth Century Speeches*, pp. 52–59.

Cassar, George H., *Kitchener's War: British Strategy from 1914–1916*, Washington 2004.

Cassoly, Anne-Marie, "Les frontières de la Grande Roumanie. Approche géopolitique," in: *Revue Roumaine d'Histoire* 35 (1996), pp. 69–77.

Castan, Joachim, *Der Rote Baron: Die ganze Geschichte des Manfred von Richthofen*, Stuttgart 2007.

Catherwood, Christopher, *Churchill's Folly: How Winston Churchill Created Modern Iraq*, New York 2004.

Cattaruzza, Marina, "Das geeinte Italien und das Dilemma des Irredentismus, in: Sacha Zala (ed.), *Die Moderne und ihre Krisen: Studien von Marina Cattaruzza zur europäischen Geschichte des 19. und 20. Jahrhunderts*, Göttingen 2012, pp. 261–283.

Ceadel, Martin, *Living the Great Illusion: Sir Norman Angell, 1872–1967*, Oxford 2009.

Cecil, Hugh, and Liddell, Peter (eds.), *Facing Armageddon: The First World War Experienced*, London 1996.

Chamberlain, Houston S., *The Foundations of the Nineteenth Century* (German orig. 1899), Munich 1911.

Chambers II, John W., "Conscription for Colossus. The Progressive Era and the Origin of the Modern Military Draft in the United States in World War I," in: Peter Karsten (ed.), *The Military in America: From the Colonial Era to the Present*, New York 1986, pp. 297–311.

Charle, Christophe, *La crise des sociétés impériales: Allemagne, France, Grande-Bretagne. Essai d'histoire sociale comparée*, Paris 2001.

Chastenet, J., *Quatre fois vingt ans*, Paris 1974, p. 121, quoted in: Jordan, *The Popular Front and Central Europe*, p. 5.

Chevallier, Gabriel, *Fear* (French: *La Peur*, 1930), London 2010.

Chiari, Bernhard, and Groß, Gerhard Paul (eds.), *Am Rande Europas? Der Balkan—Raum und Bevölkerung als Wirkungsfelder militärischer Gewalt*, Munich 2009.

Chickering, Roger, "Ein Krieg, der nicht vergehen will. Zur Frage des methodischen Fortschritts in der Historiographie des Ersten Weltkriegs," in: Sven Oliver Müller and Cornelius Torp (eds.), *Das Deutsche Kaiserreich in der Kontroverse*, Göttingen 2009, pp. 281–289.

———, *Freiburg im Ersten Weltkrieg: Totaler Krieg und städtischer Alltag 1914–1918*, Paderborn 2009.

Chickering, Roger, and Förster, Stig (eds.), *Great War, Total War: Combat and Mobilization on the Western Front, 1914–1918*, Cambridge 2000.

Chielens, Piet, "Les troupes coloniales françaises sur le front en Flandre," in: idem and Dendooven (eds.), *Cinq Continents au front*, pp. 51–88.

Chielens, Piet, and Dendooven, Dominiek, *Cinq Continents au front: La Première Guerre mondiale*, Brussels 2008.

Chulos, Chris J., *The Fall of an Empire, the Birth of a Nation: National Identities in Russia*, Aldershot 2000.

Churchill, Winston, *The River War: An Historical Account of the Reconquest of the Soudan* (orig. 1899), New York 2013.

———, *The World Crisis*, vol. 1, London 1923.

Citino, Robert M., *The German Way of War: From the Thirty Years War to the Third Reich*, Lawrence 2005.

Clark, Alan, *The Donkeys*, London 1961.

Clark, Christopher, *Kaiser Wilhelm II: A Life in Power*, London 2000.

———, *The Sleepwalkers: How Europe Went to War in 1914*, London 2012.

Clarke, Ignatius F., *Voices Prophesying War—Future Wars 1763–3749*, 2nd edn., Oxford 1992.

Clausewitz, Carl von, *On War*, ed. and trans. by Michael Howard and Peter Paret, Princeton 1976.

———, "Vom Kriege. Hinterlassenes Werk des Generals Carl von Clausewitz, Berlin 1832/34," in: Stumpf (ed.), *Kriegstheorie und Kriegsgeschichte*, pp. 9–423.

Clayton, Anthony, *Paths of Glory: The French Army 1914–18*, London 2003.

Clegg, Hugh A., *A History of British Trade Unions since 1889*, vol. 2: *1911–1933*, Oxford 1985.

Clemenceau, Georges, "Discours d'investiture," November 20, 1917, quoted in: Becker, *Clemenceau*, pp. 133–137.

———, *Grandeur and Misery of Victory*, London 1930.

Clewing, Konrad, and Schmitt, Oliver J. (eds.), *Geschichte Südosteuropas: Vom frühen Mittelalter bis zur Gegenwart*, Regensburg 2011.

Cochet, François (ed.), *1916–2006—Verdun sous le regard du monde*, Paris 2006.

Coetzee, Frans, "English Nationalism and the First World War," in: *History of European Ideas* 15 (1992), pp. 362–368.

Cohen, Deborah, *The War Come Home: Disabled Veterans in Britain and Germany, 1914–1939*, Berkeley 2000.

Cohn, Willy, "Zukunftsfragen des deutschen Judentums," in: *Allgemeine Zeitung des Judentums* 48, November 26, 1915, pp. 565–566.

Cohrs, Patrick O., *The Unfinished Peace after World War I: America, Britain and the Stabilisation of Europe, 1919–1932*, Cambridge 2006.

Confino, Alon, *The Nation as a Local Metaphor: Württemberg, Imperial Germany and National Memory, 1871–1918*, Chapel Hill 1997.

Connelly, Mark, *Steady the Buffs! A Regiment, a Region, and the Great War*, Oxford 2006.

Connes, Georges, *A POW's Memoir of the First World War: The Other Ordeal*, Oxford 2004.

Conrad, Sebastian, *What Is Global History?* Princeton 2016.

Contamine, Philippe, "Mourir pour la patrie. Xe–XXe siècle," in: Pierre Nora (ed.), *Les lieux de mémoire*, vol. 2, Paris 1997, pp. 1673–1698.

Cooper, John Milton, *Woodrow Wilson: A Biography*, New York 2011.

Cooper, Sandi E., *Patriotic Pacifism: Waging War on War in Europe, 1815–1914*, New York 1991.

Corino, Karl, "Robert Musil—Genauigkeit und Seele," in: idem, *Robert Musil*, pp. 10–17.

———, *Robert Musil: Leben und Werk in Bildern und Texten*, Reinbek 1989.

Cornelißen, Christoph, "Indien," in: Hirschfeld, Krumeich, and Renz (eds.), *Enzyklopädie Erster Weltkrieg*, pp. 571–573.

———, "Schlieffen-Plan," in: Hirschfeld, Krumeich, and Renz (eds.), *Enzyklopädie Erster Weltkrieg*, pp. 819–820.

———, "Sozialpolitik (Deutsches Reich)," in: Hirschfeld, Krumeich, and Renz (eds.), *Enzyklopädie Erster Weltkrieg*, pp. 857–859.

Cornwall, Mark, "Austria-Hungary and 'Yugoslavia,'" in: Horne (ed.), *A Companion to World War I*, pp. 371–385.

———, "The Experience of Yugoslav Agitation in Austria-Hungary," in: Cecil and Liddell (eds.), *Facing Armageddon*, pp. 656–676.

———, "Mémoires de la Grande Guerre dans les pays tchèques, 1918–1928," in: John Horne (ed.), *Démobilisations culturelles après la Grande Guerre: 14–18*, in: *Aujourd'hui—Today—Heute* 5 (2002), pp. 89–101.

———, "News, Rumour and the Control of Information in Austria-Hungary, 1914–1918," in: *History* 77 / 249 (1992), pp. 50–64.

———, *The Undermining of Austria-Hungary: The Battle for Hearts and Minds*, Basingstoke 2000.

————, "The Wartime Bohemia of Franz Kafka: The Social and National Crisis," in: Engel and Robertson (eds.), *Kafka, Prag und der Erste Weltkrieg*, pp. 37–48.

Cortright, David, *Peace: A History of Movements and Ideas*, Cambridge 2008.

Cottrell, Robert C., *Roger Nash Baldwin and the American Civil Liberties Union*, New York 2000.

Cox, Jafna L., "A Splendid Training Ground: The Importance of the Royal Air Force and Its Role in Iraq, 1919–32," in: *Journal of Imperial and Commonwealth History* 13 (1985), pp. 157–184.

Craig, Gordon Alexander, "The Revolution in War and Diplomacy, 1914–39," in: idem, *War, Politics, and Diplomacy*, New York 1966, pp. 194–205.

Crampton, Richard J., *Bulgaria*, Oxford 2007.

Croly, Herbert, *Progressive Democracy*, New York 1915.

Cullen, Michael S., *The Reichstag: German Parliament between Monarchy and Federalism*, rev. edn., Berlin 2004.

Čupić-Amrein, Martha M., *Die Opposition gegen die österreichisch-ungarische Herrschaft in Bosnien-Hercegowina (1878–1914)*, Berne 1987.

Curtiss, John Shelton, *The Russian Revolution of 1917*, Princeton 1957.

D'Annunzio, Gabriele, *Rede von der Tribüne des Kapitols am 17. Mai 1915*, Hamburg 1992.

Dabringhaus, Sabine, *Geschichte Chinas im 20. Jahrhundert*, Munich 2009.

Dadrian, Vahakn N., *German Responsibility in the Armenian Genocide: A Review of the Historical Evidence of German Complicity*, Watertown 1997.

————, "The Armenian Question and the Wartime Fate of the Armenians as Documented by the Officials of the Ottoman Empire's World War I Allies: Germany and Austria-Hungary," in: *International Journal of Middle East Studies* 34 (2002), pp. 59–85.

Dahlmann, Dittmar, "Russland," in: Hirschfeld, Krumeich, and Renz (eds.), *Enzyklopädie Erster Weltkrieg*, pp. 87–96.

Dalby, Andrew, *Eleftherios Venizelos: Greece*, London 2010.

Dallas, Gregor, *At the Heart of a Tiger: Clemenceau and His World 1841–1929*, London 1993.

Damjanov, Simeon, "Le traité de Neuilly et ses répercussions sur les relations interbalkaniques (1919–1923)," in: *Études Balkaniques* 16 (1980), pp. 56–69.

Daniel, Silvia, *A Brief Time to Discuss America: Der Ausbruch des Ersten Weltkriegs im Urteil amerikanischer Politiker und Intellektueller*, Göttingen 2008.

Daniel, Ute, *Arbeiterfrauen in der Kriegsgesellschaft: Beruf, Familie und Politik im Ersten Weltkrieg*, Göttingen 1989.

———— (ed.), *Augenzeugen: Kriegsberichterstattung vom 18. zum 21. Jahrhundert*, Göttingen 2006.

————, "Der Krimkrieg 1853–1856 und die Entstehungskontexte medialer Kriegsberichterstattung," in: idem (ed.), *Augenzeugen*, pp. 40–67.

————, "Informelle Kommunikation und Propaganda in der deutschen Kriegsgesellschaft," in: Siegfried Quandt (ed.), *Der Erste Weltkrieg als Kommunikationsereignis*, Giessen 1993, pp. 76–93.

Daniels, Roger, *Guarding the Golden Door: American Immigration Policy and Immigrants since 1882*, New York 2004.

Daruvar, Yves de, *Le destin dramatique de la Hongrie: Trianon ou la Hongrie écartelée*, Paris 1989.

Das, Santanu (ed.), *Race, Empire and First World War Writing*, Cambridge 2011.

———, *Touch and Intimacy in First World War Literature*, Cambridge 2005.

Davenport, Thomas R. H., *South Africa: A Modern History*, 4th edn., London 1991.

Davies, Norman, *Heart of Europe: The Past in Poland's Present*, rev. edn., Oxford 2001.

Davis, Belinda Joy, *Home Fires Burning: Food, Politics, and Everyday Life in World War I Berlin*, Chapel Hill 2000.

Dawes, John N. I., and Robson, Leslie L., *Citizen to Soldier: Australia before the Great War: Recollections of Members of the First A. I. F.*, Melbourne 1977.

DeBauche, Leslie M., *Reel Patriotism: The Movies and World War I*, Madison 1997.

Déchelette, François, *L'argot des poilus: Dictionnaire humoristique et philologique du langage des soldats de la Grande Guerre de 1914* (orig. 1918), Paris 2004.

Dedijer, Vladimir, *The Road to Sarajevo*, London 1967.

Degen, Bernard, "Basel im Zentrum der Friedensbewegung," in: Degen, Haumann, Mäder, Mayoraz, Polexe, and Schenk (eds.), *Gegen den Krieg*, pp. 30–41.

———, "Die europaweite Ausstrahlung des Kongresses," in: Degen, Haumann, Mäder, Mayoraz, Polexe, and Schenk (eds.), *Gegen den Krieg*, pp. 142–149.

Degen, Bernard, Haumann, Heiko, Mäder, Ueli, Mayoraz, Sandrine, Polexe, Laura, and Schenk, Frithjof Benjamin (eds.), *Gegen den Krieg: Der Basler Friedenskongress 1912 und seine Aktualität*, Basel 2012.

Dehio, Ludwig, *Gleichgewicht oder Hegemonie: Betrachtungen über ein Grundproblem der neueren Staatengeschichte*, Krefeld 1948.

Dehn, Paul (ed.), *Hindenburg als Erzieher in seinen Aussprüchen*, Leipzig 1918.

Dehne, Phillip, *On the Far Western Front: Britain's First World War in South America*, New York 2009.

Deist, Wilhelm, "Die Kriegführung der Mittelmächte," in: Hirschfeld, Krumeich, and Renz (eds.), *Enzyklopädie Erster Weltkrieg*, pp. 249–271.

———, *Militär, Staat und Gesellschaft: Studien zur preußisch-deutschen Militärgeschichte*, Munich 1991.

———, *Militär und Innenpolitik im Weltkrieg 1914–1918*, 2 vols., Düsseldorf 1974.

———, "Strategy and Unlimited Warfare in Germany: Moltke, Falkenhayn and Ludendorff," in: Chickering and Förster (eds.), *Great War, Total War*, pp. 265–279.

———, "Verdeckter Militärstreik im Kriegsjahr 1918?," in: Wolfram Wette (ed.), *Der Krieg des kleinen Mannes. Eine Militärgeschichte von unten*, Munich 1992, pp. 146–167.

———, "Voraussetzungen innenpolitischen Handelns des Militärs im Ersten Weltkrieg," in: idem, *Militär, Staat und Gesellschaft*, pp. 126–138.

———, "Zensur und Propaganda in Deutschland während des Ersten Weltkrieges," in: idem, *Militär, Staat und Gesellschaft*, pp. 153–163.

Delaporte, Sophie, *Gueules cassées de la Grande Guerre*, Paris 2004.

———, *Les gueules cassées: Les blessés de la face de la Grande Guerre*, Paris 1996.

———, *Les Médecins dans la Grande Guerre*, Paris 2003.

————, "Military Medicine," in: Horne (ed.), *A Companion to World War I*, pp. 295–306.

Delbrück, Hans, *Geschichte der Kriegskunst*, vol. 1: *Das Altertum*, Berlin 1900.

————, *Geschichte der Kriegskunst*, vol. 4: *Die Neuzeit*, Berlin 1920.

————, "Über die Verschiedenheit der Strategie Friedrichs und Napoleons," in: idem, *Historische und Politische Aufsätze* (orig. 1887), 2nd edn., Berlin 1907, pp. 223–301.

Demirci, Sevtap, *Strategies and Struggle: British Rhetoric and Turkish Response: The Lausanne Conference 1922–1923*, Istanbul 2005.

Demps, Laurenz, *Die Neue Wache: Entstehung und Geschichte eines Bauwerks*, Berlin 1988.

Dendooven, Dominiek, "Les armées européennes loin du monolithe ethnico-culturel," in: idem and Chielens (eds.), *Cinq Continents au front*, pp. 23–50.

————, "Les dominions et colonies britanniques sur le front en Flandre," in: idem and Chielens (eds.), *Cinq Continents au front*, pp. 89–116.

————, "Living Apart Together: Belgian Civilians and Non-White Troops and Workers in Wartime Flanders," in: Das (ed.), *Race, Empire and First World War Writing*, pp. 143–157.

————, "Troupes de l'Inde britannique dans le Westhoek, 1914–1919," in: idem and Chielens (eds.), *Cinq Continents au front*, pp. 117–130.

Denman, Terence, *Ireland's Unknown Soldiers: The 16th (Irish) Division in the Great War*, Dublin 1992.

Depkat, Volker, *Lebenswenden und Zeitenwenden: Deutsche Politiker und die Erfahrungen des 20. Jahrhunderts*, Munich 2007.

Der Große Krieg: Eine Chronik von Tag zu Tag: Urkunden, Depeschen und Berichte aus der Frankfurter Zeitung, Frankfurt 1914–1918.

Deringil, Selim, *Turkish Foreign Policy during the Second World War: An "Active" Neutrality*, Cambridge 1989.

Despotopoulos, Alexandros I., *Greece's Contribution to the Outcome of Two World Wars*, Athens 1993.

Dessoir, Max, *Kriegspsychologische Betrachtungen*, Leipzig 1916.

Dettmann, Ludwig, *Ostfront: Ein Denkmal des deutschen Kampfes in Bildern und Tagebuchblättern*, Berlin 1938.

Deutsche Kriegsausstellungen 1916. Im Einverständnis und mit Unterstützung des Königlich Preußischen Kriegsministeriums veranstaltet vom Zentralkomitee der Deutschen Vereine vom Roten Kreuz, Berlin 1916.

Deutsche Vorträge Hamburger Professoren, vol. 2, Hamburg 1914.

Dickinson, Frederick R., *War and National Reinvention: Japan in the Great War, 1914–1919*, Cambridge, Mass. 1999.

Didier, Christophe (ed.), "1914–1918," quoted in: *In Papiergewittern 1914–1918. Die Kriegssammlungen der Bibliotheken*, Paris 2008.

Diner, Dan, *Cataclysms, A History of the Twentieth Century from Europe's Edge*, Madison, WI 2008.

Dinkel, Christoph, "German Officers and the Armenian Genocide," in: *Armenian Review* 44 / 1 (1991), pp. 77–133.

Dittmann, Wilhelm, "Parteidisziplin und Preußengeist: War unsere Parteiorganisation 'preußisch'?," in: *Neuer Vorwärts* 238, supplement, December 31, 1937.

Dodge, Toby, *Inventing Iraq: The Failure of Nation Building and a History Denied*, London 2003.

Dönninghaus, Victor, *Die Deutschen in der Moskauer Gesellschaft: Symbiose und Konflikte (1494–1941)*, Munich 2002.

Doughty, Robert A., "French Strategy in 1914: Joffre's Own," in: *Journal of Military History* 67 (2003), pp. 427–454.

——, *Pyrrhic Victory: French Strategy and Operations in the Great War*, Cambridge, Mass. 2005.

Dowler, Wayne, *Russia in 1913*, DeKalb, Ill. 2012.

Dowling, Timothy C., *The Brusilov Offensive*, Bloomington, Ind. 2008.

Downs, Laura, *Manufacturing Inequality: Gender Divsion in the French and British Metalworking Industries, 1914–1939*, Ithaca 1995.

Doyle, Peter, and Walker, Julian, *Trench Talk: Words of the First World War*, Stroud 2012.

Duffy, Christopher, *Through German Eyes: The British and the Somme, 1916*, London 2006.

Dülffer, Jost, *Regeln gegen den Krieg? Die Haager Friedenskonferenzen von 1899 und 1907 in der internationalen Politik*, Berlin 1981.

Duménil, Anne, "1918, l'année de la 'Grande Bataille': Les facteurs militaires de la défaite allemande," in: idem, Nicolas Beaupré, and Christian Ingrao (eds.), *1914–1945: L'ère de la guerre*, vol. 1, Paris 2004, pp. 229–256.

Duncan, Robert, "Independent Working-Class Education and the Formation of the Labour College Movement in Glasgow and the West of Scotland, 1915–1922," in: idem and Arthur McIvor (eds.), *Militant Workers: Labour and Class Conflict on the Clyde 1900–1950*, Edinburgh 1992, pp. 106–128.

——, *Pubs and Patriots: The Drink Crisis in Britain during World War I*, Liverpool 2013.

Dungan, Myles, *Irish Voices from the Great War*, Dublin 1995.

Duroselle, Jean-Baptiste, *Clemenceau*, Paris 1988.

Dziewanowski, Marian K., *Joseph Piłsudski: A European Federalist, 1918–1922*, Stanford 1969.

Eckart, Wolfgang U., "Invalidität," in: Hirschfeld, Krumeich, and Renz (eds.), *Enzyklopädie Erster Weltkrieg*, pp. 584–586.

Edwards, Ruth Dudley, *Patrick Pearse: The Triumph of Failure*, New York 1977.

Ehlert, Hans, Epkenhans, Michael, and Groß, Gerhard P. (eds.), *Der Schlieffenplan: Analysen und Dokumente*, Paderborn 2006.

Eichenberg, Julia, *Kämpfen für Frieden und Fürsorge: Polnische Veteranen des Ersten Weltkriegs und ihre internationalen Kontakte, 1918–1939*, Munich 2011.

——, "Soldiers to Civilians to Soldiers: Poland and Ireland after the First World War," in: Gerwarth and Horne (eds.), *War in Peace*, pp. 184–199.

Eksteins, Modris, *Rites of Spring: The Great War and the Birth of the Modern Age* (orig. 1989), Boston 2000.

Ellinwood, DeWitt C., and Pradhan, C. D. (eds.), *India and World War I*, New Delhi 1978.

Ellis, John, *Eye-Deep in Hell*, London 1976.

——, *The Social History of the Machine Gun*, London 1975.

Ellsworth-Jones, Will, *We Will Not Fight: The Untold Story of the First World War's Conscientious Objectors*, London 2007.

Emmerson, Charles, *1913: In Search of the World before the War*, New York 2013.

Engel, Eduard, *1914. Ein Tagebuch. Mit Urkunden, Bildnissen, Karten*, vol. 1: *Vom Ausbruch des Krieges bis zur Einnahme von Antwerpen*, vol. 2: *Von der Einnahme Antwerpens bis zum Ende des Jahres 1914*, Brunswick 1915.

Engel, Manfred, and Robertson, Ritchie (eds.), *Kafka, Prag und der Erste Weltkrieg*, Würzburg 2012.

Engels, Friedrich, "Einleitung" [to Sigismund Borkheim: *Zur Erinnerung an die deutschen Mordspatrioten, 1806/1807*, Hottingen 1888], in: idem and Karl Marx, *Werke*, 39 vols., supp. vol. Parts 1–2, 13th edn., Berlin 1981.

Engelstein, Laura, "A Belgium of Our Own: The Sack of Kalisz, August 1914," in: *Kritika: Explorations in Russian and Eurasian History* 10 (2009), pp. 441–473.

Englund, Peter, *The Beauty and the Sorrow: An Intimate History of the First World War*, New York 2012.

——, *Schönheit und Schrecken: Eine Geschichte des Ersten Weltkriegs, erzählt in neunzehn Schicksalen*, Berlin 2011.

Epkenhans, Michael, "Das Ende eines Zeitalters: Europäische Monarchen und ihre Armeen im Ersten Weltkrieg," in: Winfried Heinemann and Markus Pöhlmann (eds.), *Monarchen und ihr Militär*, Potsdam 2010, pp. 59–74.

—— (ed.), *Das ereignisreiche Leben eines "Wilhelminers": Tagebücher, Briefe, Aufzeichnungen 1901 bis 1920 von Albert Hopmann*, Munich 2004.

——, *Die wilhelminische Flottenrüstung 1908–1914: Weltmachtstreben, industrieller Fortschritt, soziale Integration*, Munich 1991.

——, "Vom Seekadetten zum Vizeadmiral: Stationen einer Karriere im wilhelminischen Deutschland," in: idem (ed.), *Das ereignisreiche Leben*, pp. 21–83.

Epkenhans, Michael, Hillmann, Jörg, and Nägler, Frank (eds.), *Skagerrakschlacht: Vorgeschichte—Ereignis—Verarbeitung*, Munich 2009.

Epstein, Klaus, *Matthias Erzberger und das Dilemma der deutschen Demokratie*, Frankfurt 1976.

Erickson, Edward J., *Defeat in Detail: The Ottoman Army in the Balkans, 1912–1913*, Westport, Conn. 2003.

——, *Ordered to Die: A History of the Ottoman Army in the First World War*, Westport, Conn. 2001.

——, *Ottoman Army Effectiveness in World War I: A Comparative Study*, London 2007.

Ermacora, Felix, *Der unbewältigte Friede. St. Germain und die Folgen, 1919–1989*, Munich 1989.

Ernst, Wolfgang, "Museale Kristallisation: Il Vittoriale degli Italiani," in: Gumbrecht, Kittler, and Siegert (eds.), *Der Dichter als Kommandant*, pp. 309–320.

Esch, Michael E., "Zur historischen Verortung von 'ethnischer Säuberung' und Völkermord," in: Mathias Beer, Dietrich Beyrau, and Cornelia Rauh (eds.), *Deutschsein als Grenzerfahrung. Minderheitenpolitik in Europa zwischen 1914 und 1950*, Essen 2009, pp. 15–34.

Etschmann, Wolfgang, "Die erste Republik Österreich im Spannungsfeld zwischen Demobilisierung, Abrüstung und paramilitärischer Aufrüstung 1918–1923," in: *Jahrbuch für Zeitgeschichte* (1984–1985), pp. 123–150.

Ettighofer, Paul, *Verdun: Das große Gericht*, Gütersloh 1936.

Evans, James, *Great Britain and the Creation of Yugoslavia: Negotiating Balkan Nationality and Identity*, London 2008.

Evans, Richard J. (ed.), *Kneipengespräche im Kaiserreich: Die Stimmungsberichte der Hamburger politischen Polizei 1892–1914*, Reinbek 1989.

Everth, Erich, *Von der Seele des Soldaten im Felde*, Jena 1915.

Ewing, Keith D., and Gearty, Conor A., *The Struggle for Civil Liberties: Political Freedom and the Rule of Law in Britain 1914–1945*, Oxford 2000.

Falkenhayn, Erich von, *Die Oberste Heeresleitung 1914–1916 in ihren wichtigsten Entschließungen*, Berlin 1920.

Fansa, Mamoun, and Hoffmann, Detlef (eds.), *Lawrence von Arabien: Genese eines Mythos. Begleitband zur Sonderausstellung "Lawrence von Arabien,"* Mainz 2010.

Farnie, Douglas A., *East and West of Suez: The Suez Canal in History 1854–1956*, Oxford 1969.

Faust, Drew Gilpin, *The Republic of Suffering: Death and the American Civil War*, New York 2008.

Felberbauer, Franz, "Die 12. Isonzoschlacht: Der Operationsplan und seine Durchführung," in: Rauchensteiner (Hg.), Waffentreue, S. 13–33.

Feldman, Gerald D., *Armee, Industrie und Arbeiterschaft in Deutschland 1914–1918*, Berlin 1985.

——, *Army, Industry and Labor in Germany 1914–1918*, Princeton 1966.

Fellner, Fritz, "Der Dreibund: Europäische Diplomatie vor dem Ersten Weltkrieg," in: idem, *Vom Dreibund zum Völkerbund*, pp. 19–82.

——, "Der Zerfall der Donaumonarchie in weltgeschichtlicher Perspektive," in: idem, *Vom Dreibund zum Völkerbund*, pp. 240–249.

——, "Die Mission Hoyos," in: idem, Heidrun Maschl, and Brigitte Mazohl-Wallnig (eds.), *Vom Dreibund zum Völkerbund*, pp. 112–141.

——, *Vom Dreibund zum Völkerbund: Studien zur Geschichte der internationalen Beziehungen 1882–1919*, ed. by Heidrun Maschl and Brigitte Mazohl-Wallnig, Vienna 1994.

Fenske, Hans, *Der Anfang vom Ende des alten Europa: Die alliierte Verweigerung von Friedensgesprächen 1914–1919*, Munich 2013.

—— (ed.), *Unter Wilhelm II. 1890–1918*, Darmstadt 1982.

Ferguson, Niall, "How (Not) to Pay for the War: Traditional Finance and 'Total' War," in: Chickering and Förster (eds.), *Great War, Total War*, pp. 409–434.

——, *The Pity of War*, London 1998.

Ferragne, André, "Allocution inaugurale," in: Claude Carlier and Guy Pedroncini (eds.), *La bataille de Verdun*, Paris 1997, pp. 7–10.

Ferrell, Robert H., *America's Deadliest Battle: Meuse-Argonne 1918*, Lawrence 2007.

Ferro, Marc, *The Great War: 1914–1918*, London 1973.

——, *Pétain*, Paris 2009.

Fic, Victor M., *The Bolsheviks and the Czechoslovak Legion: The Origin of Their Armed Conflict (March–May 1918)*, New Dehli 1978.

Fiechter, Jean-Jacques, *Le Socialisme français de l'Affaire Dreyfus a la Grande Guerre*, Geneva 1965.

Figes, Orlando, *Peasant Russia, Civil War: The Volga Countryside in Revolution (1917–1921)*, Oxford 1989.

———, *A People's Tragedy*, London 1996.

Fink, Carole, "Introduction," in: Marc Bloch, *Memoirs of War, 1914–15*, Ithaca 1980, pp. 15–73.

Fink, Caroline, "The Peace Settlement, 1919–1939," in: Horne (ed.), *A Companion to World War I*, pp. 543–557.

Finnan, Joseph P., *John Redmond and Irish Unity, 1912–1918*, Syracuse 2004.

Fisch, Jörg, *Europa zwischen Wachstum und Gleichheit 1850–1914*, Stuttgart 2002.

———, *The Right of Self-Determination of Peoples: The Domestication of an Illusion*, Cambridge 2015.

Fischer, Fritz, *Germany's Aims in the First World War*, New York 2007.

———, *War of Illusions: German Policies, 1911–14*, London 1975.

———, *World Power or Decline: The Controversy over Germany's War Aims in the First World War*, New York 1974.

Fischer, Thomas, *Die Souveränität der Schwachen. Lateinamerika und der Völkerbund, 1920–1936*, Stuttgart 2012.

Fischer, Wolfram, *Weltwirtschaftliche Rahmenbedingungen für die ökonomische und politische Entwicklung Europas, 1919–1939*, Wiesbaden 1980.

Fisher, Didier, "Philippe Pétain: Le Mythe et l'Histoire (1856–1940)," in: *Bulletin du Centre d'histoire de la France contemporaine* 5 (1984), pp. 80–82.

Fisher, John, *Curzon and British Imperialism in the Middle East 1916–19*, London 1999.

Fitzpatrick, David, "The Logic of Collective Sacrifice: Ireland and the British Army, 1914–1918," in: *Historical Journal* 38 (1995), pp. 1017–1030.

———, *The Two Irelands 1912–1939*, Oxford 1998.

Flasch, Kurt, *Die geistige Mobilmachung: Die deutschen Intellektuellen und der Erste Weltkrieg. Ein Versuch*, Berlin 2000.

Fleming, Thomas J., *The Illusion of Victory: America in World War I*, New York 2004.

Fogarty, Richard S., *Race and War in France: Colonial Subjects in the French Army, 1914–1918*, Baltimore 2008.

Foley, Robert T., *German Strategy and the Path to Verdun: Erich von Falkenhayn and the Development of Attrition, 1870–1916*, Cambridge 2006.

———, "The Real Schlieffen Plan," in: *War In History* 13 / 1 (January 2006), pp. 91–115.

Foley, Robert T., and McCartney, Helen (eds.), *The Somme: An Eyewitness History*, London 2006.

Föllmer, Moritz, *Die Verteidigung der bürgerlichen Nation. Industrielle und hohe Beamte in Deutschland und Frankreich 1900–1930*, Göttingen 2002.

Forcey, Charles, *The Crossroads of Liberalism: Croly, Weyl, Lippmann, and the Progressive Era 1900–1925*, New York 1961.

Ford, Nancy G., *Americans All! Foreign-Born Soldiers in World War I*, College Station 2001.

Förster, Stig, *Der doppelte Militarismus: Die deutsche Heeresrüstungspropaganda zwischen Status-quo-Sicherung und Aggression 1890–1913*, Stuttgart 1985.

———, "Facing 'People's War': Moltke the Elder and Germany's Military Options after 1871," in: Peter H. Wilson (ed.), *Warfare in Europe, 1815–1914*, Aldershot 2006, pp. 159–180.

———, "Helmuth von Moltke und das Problem des industrialisierten Volkskriegs im 19. Jahrhundert," in: Roland G. Foerster (ed.), *Generalfeldmarschall von Moltke: Bedeutung und Wirkung*, Munich 1991, pp. 103–115.

———, "Im Reich des Absurden: Die Ursachen des Ersten Weltkrieges," in: Bernd Wegener (ed.), *Wie Kriege entstehen. Zum historischen Hintergrund von Staatenkonflikten*, Paderborn 2000, pp. 217–252.

———, "Vorgeschichte und Ursachen des Ersten Weltkrieges," in: Rother (ed.), *Der Weltkrieg*, pp. 34–41.

François, Etienne, and Schulze, Hagen (eds.), *Deutsche Erinnerungsorte*, vol. 1, Munich 2001.

Frank, Alison, *Oil Empire: Visions of Prosperity in Austrian Galicia*, Cambridge, Mass. 2005.

Frantzen, Allen J., *Bloody Good: Chivalry, Sacrifice, and the Great War*, Chicago 1989.

Franz, Eckhart G., "Familienbande: Die Häuser Romanow und Hessen-Darmstadt," in: Ralf Beil (ed.), *Russland 1900: Kunst und Kultur im Reich des letzten Zaren*, Cologne 2008, pp. 113–121.

Fraser, Alastair H., Robertshaw, Andrew, and Roberts, Steve, *Ghosts on the Somme: Filming the Battle, June–July 1916*, Barnsley 2009.

Freeden, Michael, *Liberalism Divided: A Study in British Political Thought 1914–1939*, Oxford 1986.

———, *Liberal Languages: Ideological Imaginations and Twentieth Century Progressive Thought*, Princeton 2005.

French, David, *British Economic and Strategic Planning 1905–1915*, London 1982.

———, *British Strategy and War Aims, 1914–1916*, London 1986.

———, "The Rise and Fall of 'Business as Usual,'" in: Burk (ed.), *War and the State*, pp. 7–31.

———, *The Strategy of the Lloyd George Coalition 1916–1918*, Oxford 1992.

Freud, Sigmund, *Reflections on War and Death* (German orig. 1915), Charleston 2015.

———, *Studienausgabe*, vol. 9: *Fragen der Gesellschaft, Ursprünge der Religion*, Frankfurt 1974.

Frevert, Ute, "Vertrauen—eine historische Spurensuche," in: idem (ed.), *Vertrauen*, pp. 7–66.

——— (ed.), *Vertrauen: Historische Annäherungen*, Göttingen 2003.

Friedensburg, Ferdinand, *Das Erdöl im Weltkrieg*, Stuttgart 1939.

Friedman, Isaiah, *British Pan-Arab Policy 1915–1922: A Critical Appraisal*, New Brunswick 2010.

———, *Palestine: A Twice-Promised Land*, vol. 1: *The British, the Arabs, and Zionism, 1915–1920*, New Brunswick 2000.

Friedrich, Wolfgang-Uwe, *Bulgarien und die Mächte 1913–1915: Ein Beitrag zur Weltkriegs-und Imperialismusgeschichte*, Wiesbaden 1985.

Fritzsche, Peter, *The Turbulent World of Franz Göll: An Ordinary Berliner Writes the Twentieth Century*, Cambridge, Mass. 2011.

Fromkin, David, *A Peace to End All Peace: Creating the Modern Middle East 1914–1922*, London 1989.

Fry, Helen, *Freud's War*, Stroud 2009.

Führ, Christoph, *Das k.u.k. Armeeoberkommando und die Innenpolitik in Österreich 1914–1917*, Graz 1968.

Fussell, Paul, *The Great War and Modern Memory* (1975), with a New Introduction by Jay Winter, Oxford 2013.

Galántai, József, *Hungary in the First World War,* Budapest 1989.

Gall, Lothar, "Eisenbahn in Deutschland: Von den Anfängen bis zum Ersten Weltkrieg," in: idem and Pohl (eds.), *Die Eisenbahn in Deutschland,* pp. 13–70.

——, *Walther Rathenau: Portrait einer Epoche,* Munich 2009.

Gall, Lothar, and Pohl, Manfred (eds.), *Die Eisenbahn in Deutschland: Von den Anfängen bis zur Gegenwart,* Munich 1999.

Gandhi, Mahatma, "Speech in Benares on 4 February 1916," in: MacArthur (ed.), *The Penguin Book of Twentieth Century Speeches,* pp. 47–49.

Garnier, Claire, and Le Bon, Laurent (eds.), *1917: Exposition présentée au Centre Pompidou-Metz du 26 mai au 24 septembre 2012, galerie 1 et grande nef,* Metz 2012.

Gascouin, Firmin E., *L'évolution de l'artillerie pendant la guerre,* Paris 1920.

Gatrell, Peter, "Modernisation Strategies and Outcomes in Pre-Revolutionary Russia," in: Markku Kangaspuro and Jeremy Smith (eds.), *Modernisation in Russia since 1900,* Helsinki 2006, pp. 21–37.

——, *Russia's First World War: A Social and Economic History,* Harlow 2005.

——, *A Whole Empire Walking: Refugees in Russia during World War I,* Bloomington, Ind. 1999.

Gatterer, Claus, *Erbfeindschaft Italien-Österreich,* Vienna 1972.

Gaulke, Johannes, "Kunst und Kino im Kriege," in: *Die Gegenwart. Zeitschrift für Literatur, Wirtschaftsleben und Kunst* 44/45 (1916), pp. 618–620.

Gay, Peter, *The Cultivation of Hatred,* New York 1993.

Gehrke, Ulrich, *Persien in der deutschen Orientpolitik während des Ersten Weltkrieges,* 2 vols., Stuttgart 1960.

Geiss, Imanuel, *Der lange Weg in die Katastrophe: Die Vorgeschichte des Ersten Weltkrieges 1815–1914,* 2nd edn., Munich 1991.

—— (ed.), *Julikrise und Kriegsausbruch 1914: Eine Dokumentensammlung,* 2 vols., Hannover 1963–1964.

—— (ed.), *July 1914: The Outbreak of the First World War, Selected Documents,* London 1967.

——, "The Outbreak of the First World War and German War Aims," in: *Journal of Contemporary History* 1 (1966), pp. 75–91.

Geppert, Alexander C. T., "Oswald Spengler: Der Untergang des Abendlandes," in: Uffa Jensen, Habbo Knoch, Daniel Morat, and Miriam Rürup (eds.), *Gewalt und Gesellschaft: Klassiker modernen Denkens neu gelesen,* Göttingen 2011, pp. 112–121.

Geppert, Alexander C. T., and Kössler, Till (eds.), *Wunder: Poetik und Politik des Staunens im 20. Jahrhundert,* Frankfurt 2011.

Geppert, Dominik, and Rose, Andreas, "Machtpolitik und Flottenbau vor 1914. Zur Neuinterpretation britischer Außenpolitik im Zeitalter des Hochimperialismus," in: *Historische Zeitschrift* 293 (2011), pp. 401–437.

Gerwarth, Robert, "Fighting the Red Beast: Counter-Revolutionary Violence in the Defeated States of Central Europe," in: idem and Horne (eds.), *War in Peace,* pp. 52–71.

Gerwarth, Robert, and Horne, John, "Paramilitarism in Europe after the War: An Introduction," in: idem (eds.), *War in Peace,* pp. 1–18.

—— (eds.), *War in Peace: Paramilitary Violence after the Great War,* Oxford 2012.

Geyer, Martin, "Das Stigma der Gewalt und das Problem der nationalen Identität in Deutsch-land," in: Christian Jansen, Lutz Niethammer, and Bernd Weisbrod (eds.), *Von der Aufgabe der Freiheit: Politische Verantwortung und bürgerliche Gesellschaft im 19. und 20. Jahrhundert, Festschrift für Hans Mommsen*, Berlin 1995, pp. 673–698.

——, "Ein Vorbote des Wohlfahrtsstaates: Die Kriegsopferversorgung in Frankreich, Deutschland und Großbritannien nach dem Ersten Weltkrieg," in: *Geschichte und Gesell-schaft* 9 (1983), pp. 230–277.

——, "Hindenburg-Programm," in: Hirschfeld, Krumeich, and Renz (eds.), *Enzyklopädie Erster Weltkrieg*, pp. 557–558.

——, *Verkehrte Welt: Revolution, Inflation und Moderne, München 1914–1924*, Göttingen 1998.

Geyer, Michael, *Deutsche Rüstungspolitik 1860–1980*, Frankfurt 1984.

——, "German Strategy in the Age of Machine Warfare, 1914–1945," in: Peter Paret (ed.), *Makers of Modern Strategy From Machiavelli to the Nuclear Age*, Princeton 1986, pp. 527–597.

——, "Gewalt und Gewalterfahrung im 20. Jahrhundert. Der Erste Weltkrieg," in: Spilker and Ulrich (eds.), *Der Tod als Maschinist*, pp. 241–257.

——, "Insurrectionary Warfare: The German Debate about a levée en masse in Octo-ber 1918," in: *Journal of Modern History* 73 (2001), pp. 459–527.

——, "Rückzug und Zerstörung 1917," in: Hirschfeld, Krumeich, and Renz (eds.), *Die Deutschen an der Somme*, pp. 163–202.

——, "Urkatastrophe, Europäischer Bürgerkrieg, Menschenschlachthaus—Wie Historiker dem Epochenbruch des Ersten Weltkrieges Sinn geben," in: Rother (ed.), *Der Weltkrieg*, pp. 24–33.

Gibelli, Antonio, "Italy," in: Horne (ed.), *A Companion to World War I*, pp. 464–478.

Gibson, Hugh, *A Journal from our Legation in Belgium*, New York 1917.

Giddens, Anthony, *The Consequences of Modernity*, Stanford 1990.

Gide, André, *Journals*, vol. 2: *1914–1927*, New York 1948.

Giesen, Bernhard (ed.), *Nationale und kulturelle Identität: Studien zur Entwicklung des kolle-ktiven Bewusstseins in der Neuzeit*, 3rd edn., Frankfurt / M. 1996.

Gilbert, Martin, *The First World War: A Complete History*, New York 1994.

——, *Somme: The Heroism and Horror of War*, London 2006.

Gildea, Robert, *Barricades and Borders: Europe 1800–1914*, London 1987.

——, *Children of the Revolution: The French, 1799–1914*, Cambridge, Mass. 2008.

Gildea, Robert, and Goltz, Anna von der, "Flawed Saviours: The Myths of Hindenburg and Pétain," in: *European History Quarterly* 39 (2009), pp. 439–464.

Gilliard, Pierre, *Thirteen Years at the Russian Court*, London 1921.

Glasgow Labour History Workshop, "The Labour Unrest in West Scotland 1900–14," in: William Kenefick and Arthur McIvor (eds.), *Roots of Red Clydeside 1910–1914? Labour and Industrial Relations in West Scotland*, Edinburgh 1996, pp. 18–40.

Gleason, Philip, "American Identity and Americanization," in: Oscar Handlin, Ann Orlov, and Stephen Thernstrom (eds.), *Harvard Encyclopedia of American Ethnic Groups*, Cam-bridge, Mass. 1980, pp. 31–58.

Gleason, William, and Porter, Thomas, "The Zemstvo and Public Initiative in Late Imperial Russia," in: *Russian History* 21 (1994), pp. 419–437.

Goebel, Otto, *Deutsche Rohstoffwirtschaft im Weltkrieg einschließlich des Hindenburg-Programms*, Stuttgart 1930.

Goebel, Stefan, "Review Article. Beyond Discourse? Bodies and Memoirs of Two World Wars," in: *Journal of Contemporary History* 42 (2007), pp. 377–385.

Goffman, Erving, *Stigma: Notes on the Management of Spoiled Identity*, New York 1963.

Golczewski, Frank, *Polnisch-jüdische Beziehungen, 1881–1922: Eine Studie zur Geschichte des Antisemitismus in Osteuropa*, Wiesbaden 1981.

Golder, Frank A., *Documents on Russian History, 1914–1917*, New York 1927.

Goldfrank, David M., *The Origins of the Crimean War*, London 1994.

Goldman, Guido, *A History of the Germanic Museum at Harvard University*, Cambridge, Mass. [1989].

Goltz, Colmar von der, *Das Volk in Waffen: Ein Buch über Heerwesen und Kriegführung unserer Zeit* (orig. 1883), Berlin 1899.

Goltz, Hermann (ed.), *Deutschland, Armenien und die Türkei 1895–1925: Dokumente und Zeitschriften aus dem Dr.-Johannes-Lepsius-Archiv an der Martin-Luther-Universität Halle-Wittenberg*, 3 vols., Munich 1998–1999.

Gooch, John, "The Maurice Debate 1918," in: *Journal of Contemporary History* 3 /4 (1968), pp. 211–228.

Gordon, Andrew, *The Rules of the Game: Jutland and British Naval Command*, London 1996.

Gordon, Eleanor, *Women and the Labour Movement in Scotland, 1850–1914*, Oxford 1991.

Gordon, Milton, *Assimilation in American Life: The Role of Race, Religion, and National Origins*, New York 1964.

Götter, Christian, "Wundermittel Medien?—Medienbeziehungen der britischen und deutschen Militärführung in der ersten Hälfte des 20. Jahrhunderts," in: *Militärgeschichtliche Zeitschrift* 70 (2011), pp. 15–26.

Gould, Stephen Jay, *The Mismeasure of Man*, New York 1981.

Gouttman, Rodney, "The Balfour Declaration. Philosemitism?" in: *Journal of Judaism and Civilization* 3 (2001), S. 12–27.

Grace, A. A., "Our Little Army," in: *New Zealand Herald*, August 1, 1914.

Grainger, John D., *The Battle for Palestine 1917*, Woodbridge 2006.

Grampp, Hermann, "Besatzungsmacht Wagner: Der französische Kriegsbann von 1914," in: Müller and Zalfen (eds.), *Besatzungsmacht Musik*, pp. 233–254.

Granier, Gerhard (ed.), *Die deutsche Seekriegsleitung*, 4 vols., Koblenz 1999–2004.

Grant, Colin, *Negro with a Hat: The Rise and Fall of Marcus Garvey*, Oxford 2008.

Graves, Robert, and Hodge, Alan, *The Long Week-End: A Social History of Great Britain 1918–1939*, London 1985.

Grayzel, Susan R., *Women's Identities at War: Gender, Motherhood, and Politics in Britain and France during the First World War*, Chapel Hill 1999.

———, "Women and Men," in: Horne (ed.), *A Companion to World War I*, pp. 263–278.

Greenhalgh, Elizabeth, *Victory through Coalition: Britain and France during the First World War,* Cambridge 2005.

Greenstein, Lewis J., "The Nandi Experience in the First World War," in: Page (ed.), *Africa and the First World War,* pp. 81–94.

Gregory, Adrian, "Britain and Ireland," in: Horne (ed.), *A Companion to World War I,* pp. 403–417.

———, *The Last Great War: British Society and the First World War,* Cambridge 2008.

———, "Peculiarities of the English? War, Violence and Politics: 1900–1939," in: *Journal of Modern European History* 1 (2003), pp. 44–59.

———, "You Might as Well Recruit Germans: British Public Opinion and the Decision to Conscript the Irish in 1918," in: idem and Pašeta (eds.), *Ireland and the Great War,* pp. 113–121.

Gregory, Adrian, and Pašeta, Senia (eds.), *Ireland and the Great War: "A War to Unite Us All?"* Manchester 2002.

Greschat, Martin, "Reformationsjubiläum 1917: Exempel einer fragwürdigen Symbiose von Politik und Theologie," in: *Wissenschaft und Praxis in Kirche und Gesellschaft* 61 (1972), pp. 419–429.

Griffith, Paddy, *Battle Tactics of the Western Front: The British Army's Art of Attack, 1916–18,* London 2000.

———, *British Fighting Methods in the Great War,* London 1996.

———, "The Extent of Tactical Reform in the British Army," in: idem (ed.), *British Fighting Methods in the Great War,* pp. 1–22.

Grigg, John, *Lloyd George: From Peace to War, 1912–1916,* Berkeley 1985.

Groß, Gerhard P. (ed.), *Die vergessene Front: Der Osten 1914/15. Ereignis, Wirkung, Nachwirkung,* Paderborn 2006.

———, "Im Schatten des Westens: Die deutsche Kriegführung an der Ostfront bis Ende 1915," in: idem (ed.), *Die vergessene Front,* pp. 49–62.

———, *Mythos und Wirklichkeit: Die Geschichte des operativen Denkens im deutschen Heer von Moltke d. Ä. bis Heusinger,* Paderborn 2012.

———, "Tank," in: Hirschfeld, Krumeich, and Renz (eds.), *Enzyklopädie Erster Weltkrieg,* pp. 917–919.

Gross, Stephen, "Confidence and Gold: German War Finance 1914–1918," in: *Central European History* 42 (2009), pp. 223–252.

Grotelueschen, Mark E., *The AEF Way of War: The American Army and Combat in World War I,* Cambridge 2007.

Gschnitzer, Fritz, Koselleck, Reinhart, Schönemann, Bernd, and Werner, Karl F., "Volk, Nation, Nationalismus, Masse," in: Otto Brunner, Werner Conze, and Reinhart Koselleck (eds.), *Geschichtliche Grundbegriffe,* vol. 7, Stuttgart 1992, pp. 141–432.

Gudehus-Schomerus, Heilwig, Recker, Marie-Luise, and Riverein, Marcus, "Einleitung," in: idem (eds.), *"Einmal muss doch das wirkliche Leben wieder kommen,"* pp. 9–43.

——— (eds.), *"Einmal muss doch das wirkliche Leben wieder kommen!" Die Kriegsbriefe von Anna und Lorenz Treplin 1914–1918,* Paderborn 2010.

Gudmundsson, Bruce I., *Stormtroop Tactics: Innovation in the German Army, 1914–1918*, New York 1995.

Gumbrecht, Hans U., Kittler, Friedrich, and Siegert, Bernhard (eds.), *Der Dichter als Kommandant: D'Annunzio erobert Fiume*, Munich 1996.

Gumz, Jonathan E., *The Resurrection and Collapse of Empire in Habsburg Serbia, 1914–1918*, Cambridge 2009.

Gust, Wolfgang (ed.), *The Armenian Genocide: Evidence from the German Foreign Office Archives, 1915–1916*, New York 2013.

———, "Armenier," in: Hirschfeld, Krumeich, and Renz (eds.), *Enzyklopädie Erster Weltkrieg*, pp. 341–344.

———, *Der Völkermord an den Armeniern: Die Tragödie des ältesten Christenvolkes der Welt*, Munich 1993.

Gygi, Fabio, "Shaping Matter, Memories and Mentalities. The German Steel Helmet from Artefact to Afterlife," in: Paul Cornish and Nicholas J. Saunders (eds.), *Contested Objects: Material Memories of the Great War*, London 2009, pp. 27–44.

Haacke, Ulrich, and Schneider, Benno, *Das Buch vom Kriege, 1914–1918: Urkunden, Berichte, Briefe, Erinnerungen*, Ebenhausen 1933.

Haager, Christian, Hoffmann, Paul, Hutter, Franz, Lang, Eberhard, and Spielmann, Anton H., *Die Tiroler Kaiserjäger. Die Geschichte der Tiroler Eliteregimenter: Gründung, Einsätze, Ausrüstung*, Cremona 1996.

Haapala, Pertti, and Tikka, Marko, "Revolution, Civil War, and Terror in Finland in 1918," in: Gerwarth and Horne (eds.), *War in Peace*, pp. 72–84.

Haas, Willy, *Die literarische Welt: Erinnerungen*, Munich 1960.

Haase, Ernst (ed.), *Hugo Haase: Sein Leben und sein Wirken*, Berlin 1929.

Habartová, Klára, "Jewish Refugees from Galicia and Bukovina in East Bohemia during World War I in Light of the Documents of State Administration," in: *Judaica Bohemiae* 43 (2007–2008), pp. 139–166.

Hadler, Frank, "Die Herausbildung der tschechisch-slowakischen Zusammenarbeit im Exil während des Ersten Weltkriegs," in: Mommsen (ed.), *Der Erste Weltkrieg und die Beziehungen zwischen Tschechen, Slowaken und Deutschen*, pp. 81–92.

———, "Tschechoslowakei," in: Hirschfeld, Krumeich, and Renz (eds.), *Enzyklopädie Erster Weltkrieg*, pp. 929–930.

Haffner, Sebastian, *Defying Hitler: A Memoir*, London 2002.

Hagen, Gottfried, *Die Türkei im Ersten Weltkrieg: Flugblätter und Flugschriften in arabischer, persischer und osmanisch-türkischer Sprache aus einer Sammlung der Universitätsbibliothek Heidelberg, eingeleitet, übersetzt und kommentiert*, Frankfurt 1990.

Hagenlücke, Heinz, *Deutsche Vaterlandspartei: Die nationale Rechte am Ende des Kaiserreiches*, Düsseldorf 1997.

Haimson, Leopold, "The Problem of Social Stability in Urban Russia, 1905–1917, Part I," in: *Slavic Review* 23 (1964), pp. 619–642 and "Part II," ibid. 24 (1965), pp. 1–22.

Hajdu, Tibor, "La Hongrie dans les années de crise. Apres la Premiere Guerre mondiale, 1918–1920," in: *Guerres mondiales et conflits contemporains* 200 (2001), pp. 37–51.

Hall, Richard C., *Balkan Wars 1912–1913: Prelude to the First World War*, London 2000.

————, *Bulgaria's Road to the First World War,* New York 1996.

Halpern, Paul G., *A Naval History of World War I,* Annapolis 1994.

Hamm, Michael F., "Liberal Politics in Wartime Russia: An Analysis of the Progressive Bloc," in: *Slavic Review* 33 (1974), pp. 453–468.

Hammond, Michael, "*The Battle of the Somme* (1916): An Industrial Process Film that 'Wounds the Heart,'" in: idem and Michael Williams (eds.), *British Silent Cinema and the Great War,* Basingstoke 2011, pp. 19–38.

Hampe, Karl, *Kriegstagebuch 1914–1919,* ed. by Folker Reichert and Eike Wolgast, 2nd edn., Munich 2007.

Hanna, Martha, *The Mobilization of Intellect: French Scholars and Writers during the Great War,* Cambridge, Mass. 1996.

————, "Spaces of War: Rural France, Fears of Famine, and the Great War," in: Daniel Brewer and Patricia M. E. Lorcin (eds.), *France and Its Spaces of War: Experience, Memory, Image,* Basingstoke 2009, pp. 45–58.

————, "The Tidal Wave of War," in: *European History Quarterly* 38 (2008), pp. 93–100.

————, *Your Death Would Be Mine: Paul and Marie Pireaud in the Great War,* Cambridge, Mass. 2006.

Hanslian, Rudolf, "Der Gasangriff," in: idem (ed.), *Der chemische Krieg,* vol. 1: *Militärischer Teil,* 3rd edn., Berlin 1937.

Hantsch, Hugo, *Leopold Graf Berchtold: Grandseigneur und Staatsmann,* vol. 1, Graz 1963.

Happel, Jörn, *Nomadische Lebenswelten und zarische Politik: Der Aufstand in Zentralasien 1916,* Stuttgart 2010.

Harbutt, Fraser J., "War, Peace, and Commerce. The American Reaction to the Outbreak of World War I in Europe 1914," in: Holger Afflerbach and David Stevenson (eds.), *An Improbable War: The Outbreak of World War I and European Political Culture before 1914,* New York 2007, pp. 320–334.

Hardach, Gerd, *The First World War, 1914–1918,* New York 1987.

Harp, Stephen L., *Marketing Michelin: Advertising and Cultural Identity in Twentieth Century France,* Baltimore 2001.

Harris, J. Paul, *Douglas Haig and the First World War,* Cambridge 2008.

————, *Men, Ideas and Tanks: British Military Thought and Armoured Forces, 1903–1939,* Manchester 1995.

Harris, José, "Epilogue: French Revolution to 'Fin de Siècle': Political Thought in Retrospect and Prospect, 1800–1914," in: Gregory Claeys and Gareth Stedman Jones (eds.), *The Cambridge History of Nineteenth-Century Political Thought,* Cambridge 2011, pp. 893–933.

Hart, Peter, *Bloody April: Slaughter in the Skies over Arras, 1917,* London 2005.

————, *Gallipoli,* London 2011.

————, *The Somme,* London 2005.

Hartmann, Martin, "Einleitung," in: idem. (ed.), *Vertrauen: Die Grundlage des sozialen Zusammenhalts,* Frankfurt 2001, pp. 7–34.

Hasegawa, Tsuyoshi, *The February Revolution: Petrograd, 1917,* Seattle 1981.

Haselsteiner, Horst, Plaschka, Richard G., and Suppan, Arnold, *Innere Front. Militärassistenz, Widerstand und Umsturz in der Donaumonarchie 1918,* vol. 2: *Umsturz,* Vienna 1974.

Haumann, Heiko, "Das Jahr 1917 in den Metropolen und in den Dörfern," in: idem (ed.), *Die Russische Revolution 1917*, Cologne 2007, pp. 59–72.

Hausleitner, Mariana, *Die Rumänisierung der Bukowina: Die Durchsetzung des nationalstaatlichen Anspruchs Großrumäniens 1918–1944*, Munich 2001.

Havránek, Jan, "Politische Repression und Versorgungsengpässe in den böhmischen Ländern 1914–1918," in: Mommsen (ed.), *Der Erste Weltkrieg und die Beziehungen zwischen Tschechen, Slowaken und Deutschen*, pp. 47–66.

Hay, Jeff (ed.), *The Treaty of Versailles*, San Diego 2002.

Hayford, Charles W., *To the People: James Yen and Village China*, New York 1990.

Haynes, Robert V., *A Night of Violence: The Houston Riot of 1917*, Baton Rouge 1976.

Heale, Michael J., *American Anticommunism: Combating the Enemy Within, 1830–1970*, Baltimore 1990.

Healy, Maureen, *Vienna and the Fall of the Habsburg Empire: Total War and Everyday Life in World War I*, Cambridge 2004.

Hecker, Hans, "Polen," in: Hirschfeld, Krumeich, and Renz (eds.), *Enzyklopädie Erster Weltkrieg*, pp. 777–779.

Heinemann, Ulrich, *Die verdrängte Niederlage: Politische Öffentlichkeit und Kriegsschuldfrage in der Weimarer Republik*, Göttingen 1983.

Helfferich, Karl, *Beiträge zur neuesten Handelspolitik*, Berlin 1901.

———, *Der Weltkrieg*, vol. 2: *Vom Kriegsausbruch bis zum uneingeschränkten U-Bootkrieg*, Berlin 1919.

Helmreich, Paul C., *From Paris to Sèvres: The Partition of the Ottoman Empire at the Peace Conference of 1919–1920*, Columbus 1974.

Hennock, Ernest P., *British Social Reform and German Precedents: The Case of Social Insurance 1880–1914*, Oxford 1987.

Herbert, Ulrich, "Zwangsarbeit als Lernprozeß," in: *Archiv für Sozialgeschichte* 24 (1984), pp. 285–304.

Herr, Frédéric G., *Die Artillerie in Vergangenheit, Gegenwart und Zukunft*, Charlottenburg 1925.

Herren, Madeleine, *Hintertüren zur Macht: Internationalismus und modernisierungsorientierte Außenpolitik in Belgien, der Schweiz und den USA*, Munich 2000.

———, *Internationale Organisationen seit 1865: Eine Globalgeschichte der internationalen Ordnung*, Darmstadt 2009.

———, *Internationale Sozialpolitik vor dem Ersten Weltkrieg: Die Anfänge europäischer Kooperation aus der Sicht Frankreichs*, Berlin 1993.

Herrmann, David G., *The Arming of Europe and the Making of the First World War*, Princeton 1996.

Herrmann, Georg, *Randbemerkungen (1914–1917)*, Berlin 1919, quoted in: Johann (ed.), *Innenansicht eines Krieges*, p. 95.

Herwig, Holger H., *The First World War: Germany and Austria-Hungary 1914–1918*, London 1997.

———, *"Luxury Fleet": The Imperial German Navy, 1888–1918*, London 1987.

———, *The Marne 1914: The Opening of World War I and the Battle that Changed the World,* New York 2009.

———, "War in the West, 1914–16," in: Horne (ed.), *A Companion to World War I,* pp. 49–65.

Hesse, Hermann, "O Freunde, nicht diese Töne!," in: *Neue Zürcher Zeitung,* November 3, 1914.

Hettling, Manfred, and Jeismann, Michael, "Der Weltkrieg als Epos," in: Hirschfeld, Krumeich, and Renz (eds.), *"Keiner fühlt sich hier mehr als Mensch,"* pp. 205–234.

Heubes, Max (ed.), *Ehrenbuch der Deutschen Eisenbahner,* Berlin 1930.

Heumos, Peter, "Kartoffeln her oder es gibt eine Revolution: Hungerkrawalle, Streiks und Massenproteste in den böhmischen Ländern 1914–1918," in: Mommsen (ed.), *Der Erste Weltkrieg und die Beziehungen zwischen Tschechen, Slowaken und Deutschen,* pp. 255–286.

Hewitson, Mark, "Germany and France before the First World War: A Reassessment of Wilhelmine Foreign Policy," in: *English Historical Review* 115 (2000), pp. 570–606.

Heyde, Philipp, *Das Ende der Reparationen: Deutschland, Frankreich und der Youngplan 1929–1932,* Paderborn 1998.

Heymel, Charlotte, *Touristen an der Front: Das Kriegserlebnis 1914–1918 als Reiseerfahrung in zeitgenössischen Reiseberichten,* Berlin 2007.

Hiery, Hermann Joseph, *The Neglected War: The German South Pacific and the Influence of World War I,* Honolulu 1995.

Higham, John, "The Redefinition of America in the Twentieth Century," in: Hartmut Lehmann and Hermann Wellenreuther (eds.), *German and American Nationalism: A Comparative Perspective,* Oxford 1999, pp. 301–325.

———, *Strangers in the Land: Patterns of American Nativism 1860–1925,* New Brunswick 1955.

Hildebrand, Klaus, *Bethmann Hollweg—der Kanzler ohne Eigenschaften? Urteile der Geschichtsschreibung,* Düsseldorf 1970.

———, *Das vergangene Reich: Deutsche Außenpolitik von Bismarck bis Hitler 1871–1945,* Stuttgart 1995.

Hildermeier, Manfred, *Die Russische Revolution 1905–1921,* Frankfurt 1989.

———, *Geschichte Russlands: Vom Mittelalter bis zur Oktoberrevolution,* Munich 2013.

Hilferding, Rudolf, "Arbeitsgemeinschaft der Klassen?" (1915), in: Cora Stephan (ed.), *Zwischen den Stühlen oder über die Unvereinbarkeit von Theorie und Praxis: Schriften Rudolf Hilferdings 1904 bis 1940,* Berlin 1982, pp. 63–76.

Hindenburg, Paul von, "Über Personalersatz und Kriegsmaterial. An den Herrn Kriegsminister, 31. August 1916," in: *Urkunden der Obersten Heeresleitung 1916–1918,* ed. by Erich Ludendorff, Berlin 1920, pp. 63–65.

Hinton, James, *The First Shop Stewards' Movement,* London 1973.

Hinz, Joachim, *Das Kriegsgefangenenrecht: Unter besonderer Berücksichtigung seiner Entwicklung durch das Genfer Abkommen vom 12. August 1949,* Berlin 1955.

Hinz, Uta, *Gefangen im Großen Krieg: Kriegsgefangenschaft in Deutschland 1914–1921,* Essen 2006.

———, "Kriegsgefangene," in: Hirschfeld, Krumeich, and Renz (eds.), *Enzyklopädie Erster Weltkrieg,* pp. 641–646.

Hirschfeld, Gerhard, "Die Somme-Schlacht von 1916," in: idem, Krumeich, and Renz (eds.), *Die Deutschen an der Somme*, pp. 79–90.

——, "Serbien," in: idem, Krumeich,and Renz (eds.), *Enzyklopädie Erster Weltkrieg*, pp. 833–836.

Hirschfeld, Gerhard, Krumeich, Gerd, and Renz, Irina (eds.), *Die Deutschen an der Somme 1914–1918. Krieg, Besatzung, Verbrannte Erde*, Essen 2006.

—— (eds.), *Enzyklopädie Erster Weltkrieg*, 2nd edn., Paderborn 2004.

—— (eds.), *"Keiner fühlt sich hier mehr als Mensch . . ." Erlebnis und Wirkung des Ersten Weltkriegs*, Essen 1993.

Hirschhausen, Ulrike von, and Leonhard, Jörn, "Beyond Rise, Decline and Fall—Comparing Multi-Ethnic Empires in the Long Nineteenth Century," in: Leonhard and idem (eds.), *Comparing Empires*, pp. 9–34.

——, "Does the Empire Strike Back? The Model of the Nation in Arms as a Challenge for Multi-Ethnic Empires in the Nineteenth and Early Twentieth Century," in: *Journal of Modern European History* 5 (2007), pp. 194–221.

——, "Europäische Nationalismen im West-Ost-Vergleich: Von der Typologie zur Differenzbestimmung," in: idem (eds.), *Nationalismen in Europa*, pp. 11–45.

——, *Nationalismen in Europa: West- und Osteuropa im Vergleich*, Göttingen 2001.

Hirschon, Renée, *Crossing the Aegean: The Consequences of the 1923 Greek-Turkish Population Exchange. An Appraisal of the 1923 Compulsory Population Exchange between Greece and Turkey*, New York 2004.

Hitchins, Keith, *Ionel Brătianu. Romania*, London 2011.

——, *Rumania: 1866–1947*, Oxford 1994.

Hitler, Adolf, *Mein Kampf*, vol. 1: *Eine Abrechnung*, Munich 1933, pp. 172, 176–177, quoted in: Schulin, *Der Erste Weltkrieg und das Ende des alten Europa*, pp. 61–62.

Höbelt, Lothar, "Der Berliner Kongress als Prototyp internationaler Konfliktregelung," in: Chiari and Groß (eds.), *Am Rande Europas*, pp. 47–54.

Hobhouse, Leonard T., *The Metaphysical Theory of the State*, London 1915.

Hobson, John A., *Democracy after the War*, London 1917.

Hobson, John M., "The Military-Extraction Gap and the Wary Titan: The Fiscal Sociology of British Defence Policy, 1870–1913," in: *Journal of European Economic History* 22 (1993), pp. 461–506.

Hobson, Rolf, *Imperialism at Sea: Naval Strategic Thought, the Ideology of Sea Power, and the Tirpitz Plan, 1875–1914*, Boston 2002.

Hochschild, Adam, *To End All Wars: A Story of Loyalty and Rebellion, 1914–1918*, Boston 2011.

Hoegen, Jesko von, *Der Held von Tannenberg: Genese und Funktion des Hindenburg-Mythos (1914–1934)*, Cologne 2007.

Hoensch, Jörg K., *Geschichte Böhmens: Von der slavischen Landnahme bis zur Gegenwart*, 3rd edn., Munich 1997.

Hoeres, Peter, *Krieg der Philosophen: Die deutsche und die britische Philosophie im Ersten Weltkrieg*, Paderborn 2004.

Hoffend, Andrea, *"Mut zur Verantwortung"—Hermann Müller: Parteivorsitzender und Reichskanzler aus Mannheim*, Mannheim 2001.

Hoffmann, Detlef, "Die Genese des Mythos Lawrence von Arabien," in: idem and Fansa (eds.), *Lawrence von Arabien*, pp. 39–50.

Hoffmann-Holter, Beatrix, *"Abreisendmachung": Jüdische Kriegsflüchtlinge in Wien 1914 bis 1923*, Vienna 1995.

Hofmann, Tessa (ed.), *Der Völkermord an den Armeniern vor Gericht: Der Prozess Talaat Pascha. Stenographischer Bericht über die Verhandlungen gegen den des Mordes an Talaat Pascha angeklagten armenischen Studenten Salomon Teilirian* (orig. 1921), 3rd edn., Göttingen 1985.

Hofmannsthal, Hugo von, "Österreichs Antwort," in: *Neue Freie Presse*, September 24, 1914, morning edition.

Höglinger, Felix, *Ministerpräsident Heinrich Graf Clam-Martinic*, Graz 1964.

Hohrath, Daniel, and Neitzel, Sönke (eds.), *Kriegsgreuel: Die Entgrenzung der Gewalt in kriegerischen Konflikten vom Mittelalter bis ins 20. Jahrhundert*, Paderborn 2008.

Holland, R., "The British Empire and the Great War, 1914–1918," in: Judith M. Brown and William Roger Louis (eds.), *The Oxford History of the British Empire*, vol. 5, *The Twentieth Century*, Oxford 1997, pp. 114–137.

Holler, Gerd, *Franz Ferdinand von Österreich-Este*, Vienna 1982.

Holmes, Richard, *The Western Front*, London 1999.

Hölscher, Lucian, *Die Entdeckung der Zukunft*, Frankfurt 1999.

Holthusen, Hans Egon, *Rilke*, Hamburg 1987.

Holzer, Anton, *Das Lächeln der Henker: Der unbekannte Krieg gegen die Zivilbevölkerung 1914–1918*, Darmstadt 2008.

———, *Die andere Front: Fotografie und Propaganda im Ersten Weltkrieg*, Darmstadt 2007.

Hölzle, Erwin, "Formverwandlung der Geschichte: Das Jahr 1917," in: *Saeculum. Jahrbuch für Universalgeschichte* 6 (1955), pp. 329–344.

Höpken, Wolfgang, "Archaische Gewalt oder Vorboten des 'totalen Krieges'? Die Balkankriege 1912 / 13 in der europäischen Kriegsgeschichte des 20. Jahrhunderts," in: Ulf Brunnbauer (ed.), *Schnittstellen: Gesellschaft, Nation, Konflikt und Erinnerung in Südosteuropa*. Munich 2007, pp. 245–260.

———, "Bulgarien," in: Hirschfeld, Krumeich, and Renz (eds.), *Enzyklopädie Erster Weltkrieg*, pp. 399–400.

———, "Performing Violence. Soldiers, Paramilitaries and Civilians in the Twentieth Century Balkan Wars," in: Alf Lüdtke and Bernd Weisbrod (eds.), *No Man's Land of Violence: Extreme Wars in the 20th Century*, Göttingen 2006, pp. 213–249.

———, "Princip, Gavrilo," in: Hirschfeld, Krumeich, and Renz (eds.), *Enzyklopädie Erster Weltkrieg*, pp. 781–782.

———, "Rumänien," in: Hirschfeld, Krumeich, and Renz (eds.), *Enzyklopädie Erster Weltkrieg*, pp. 804–807.

Horne, Alistair, *The Price of Glory: Verdun 1916* (orig. 1962), London 1993.

Horne, John (ed.), *A Companion to World War I*, Malden, Mass. 2010.

———, "Defending Victory: Paramilitary Politics in France, 1918–1926," in: Horne and Gerwarth (eds.), *War in Peace,* pp. 216–233.

———, "L'Impôt du Sang: Republican Rhetoric and Industrial Warfare in France, 1914–1918," in: *Social History* 14 (1989), pp. 201–223.

———, "Irland," in: Hirschfeld, Krumeich, and Renz (eds.), *Enzyklopädie Erster Weltkrieg,* pp. 586–589.

———, *Labour at War: France and Britain, 1914–1918,* Oxford 1992.

———, "A Parliamentary State at War: France 1914–1918," in: Art Cosgrove and J. I. McGuire (eds.), *Parliament and Community,* Belfast 1983, pp. 11–236.

Horne, John, and Gerwarth, Robert (eds.), *War in Peace, Paramilitary Violence in Europe after the Great War,* Oxford 2012.

Horne, John, and Kramer, Alan, *German Atrocities, 1914: A History of Denial,* Hamburg 2001.

Hosfeld, Rolf, *Operation Nemesis: Die Türkei, Deutschland und der Völkermord an den Armeniern,* Cologne 2005.

Hough, Richard, *The Great War at Sea 1914–1918,* Oxford 1983.

Hovannisian, Richard G., *The Republic of Armenia,* vol. 3: *From London to Sevres, February–August 1920,* Berkeley 1996.

Howard, Michael, *The Franco-Prussian War: The German Invasion of France 1870–1871,* 2nd edn., New York 2001.

Howkins, Alun, "The Discovery of Rural England," in: Robert Colls and Philip Dodd (eds.), *Englishness: Politics and Culture, 1880–1920,* London 1986, pp. 79–85.

Howorth, Jolyon, "French Workers and German Workers: The Impossibility of Internationalism, 1900–1914," in: *European History Quarterly* 15 (1985), pp. 71–97.

Hoyt, Edwin P., *Guerilla: Colonel von Lettow-Vorbeck and Germany's East African Empire,* New York 1981.

Huber, Valeska, *Channelling Mobilities: Migration and Globalisation in the Suez Canal Region and Beyond,* Cambridge 2013.

———, "Connecting Colonial Seas: The 'International Colonisation' of Port Said and the Suez Canal during and after the First World War," in: *European Review of History—Revue européenne d'histoire* 19 (2012), pp. 141–161.

Hübinger, Gangolf, "Ernst Troeltsch," in: Hirschfeld, Krumeich, and Renz (eds.), *Enzyklopädie Erster Weltkrieg,* pp. 926–927.

Huegel, Arnulf, *Kriegsernährungswirtschaft Deutschlands während des Ersten und Zweiten Weltkriegs im Vergleich,* Konstanz 2003.

Hughes, Matthew, *Allenby and British Strategy in the Middle East 1917–1919,* London 1999.

———, "Command, Strategy and the Battle for Palestine, 1917," in: Beckett (ed.), *1917: Beyond the Western Front,* pp. 113–130.

Hull, Isabel Virginia, *Absolute Destruction: Military Culture and the Practices of War in Imperial Germany,* Ithaca 2005.

Hünseler, Wolfgang, "Die irische Bürgerkriegsgefahr im Kalkül der deutschen Großbritannienpolitik in der Julikrise," in: *Militärgeschichtliche Mitteilungen* 32 (1982), pp. 35–44.

Hüppauf, Bernd, "Fotografie im Ersten Weltkrieg," in: Spilker and Ulrich (ed.), *Der Tod als Maschinist,* pp. 108–123.

———, "Ikonographie," in: Hirschfeld, Krumeich, and Renz (eds.), *Enzyklopädie Erster Weltkrieg*, pp. 569–570.

———, "Kriegsfotografie," in: Michalka (ed.), *Der Erste Weltkrieg*, pp. 875–909.

———, "Kriegsfotografie an der Schwelle zum neuen Sehen," in: Bedrich Loewenstein (ed.), *Geschichte und Psychologie*, Pfaffenweiler 1992, pp. 205–233.

Hurewitz, Jacob C., *Diplomacy in the Near and Middle East: A Documentary Record*, vol. 2: *1914–1956*, Princeton 1956.

Illies, Florian, *1913. The Year before the Storm*, New York 2013.

Immanuel, Friedrich, *Die französische Infanterie*, Berlin 1905.

"Immediatbericht des Kommandos der Hochseestreitkräfte über die Seeschlacht vor dem Skagerrak vom 4. Juli 1916 (Dokument 2)," in: Epkenhans, Hillmann, and Nägler (eds.), *Skagerrakschlacht*, pp. 205–214.

Inglis, Kenneth Stanley, "The Homecoming: The War Memorial Movement in Cambridge, England," in: *Journal of Contemporary History* 27 (1992), pp. 583–605.

Isnenghi, Mario, "Isonzo," in: Hirschfeld, Krumeich, and Renz (eds.), *Enzyklopädie Erster Weltkrieg*, pp. 589–590.

———, "Italien," in: Hirschfeld, Krumeich, and Renz (eds.), *Enzyklopädie Erster Weltkrieg*, pp. 97–104.

Jahr, Christoph, *Gewöhnliche Soldaten: Desertion und Deserteure im deutschen und britischen Heer 1914–1918*, Göttingen 1998.

———, "Weihnachten 1914," in: Hirschfeld, Krumeich, and Renz (eds.), *Enzyklopädie Erster Weltkrieg*, pp. 957–959.

Jansen, Jan C., and Osterhammel, Jürgen, *Dekolonisation: Das Ende der Imperien*, Munich 2013.

Janssen, Elmar, "Kamele im Krieg—eine Kavallerie für unkonventionelle Kampfeinsätze," in: Pöppinghege (ed.), *Tiere im Krieg*, pp. 85–102.

Janßen, Karl-Heinz, *Der Kanzler und der General: Die Führungskrise um Bethmann Hollweg und Falkenhayn (1914–1916)*, Göttingen 1967.

Janz, Oliver, *Das symbolische Kapital der Trauer: Nation, Religion und Familie im italienischen Gefallenenkult des Ersten Weltkriegs*, Tübingen 2009.

———, "Zwischen Konsens und Dissens. Zur Historiographie des Ersten Weltkriegs in Italien," in: Bauerkämper and Julien (eds.), *Durchhalten*, pp. 195–213.

Jarausch, Konrad H., *The Enigmatic Chancellor: Bethmann Hollweg and the Hubris of Imperial Germany*, New Haven 1973.

Jedlicka, Ludwig, "Saint Germain 1919," in: *Anzeiger der Österreichischen Akademie der Wissenschaften: Philosophisch-Historische Klasse* 113 (1976), pp. 149–181.

Jędrzejewicz, Wacław, *Józef Piłsudski: A Life for Poland*, New York 1982.

Jeffery, Keith, *Ireland and the Great War*, Cambridge 2000.

———, "'Writing out of Opinions:' Irish Experience and the Theatre of the First World War," in: Das (ed.), *Race, Empire and First World War Writing*, pp. 249–264.

Jeismann, Michael, "Angstschweiß auf der Stirn Europas," in: *Frankfurter Allgemeine Zeitung*, July 31, 2004.

Jenkins, Roy, *Asquith*, London 1986.

Jentsch, Carl, *Der Weltkrieg und die Zukunft des deutschen Volkes*, Berlin 1915.

Jerabék, Rudolf, *Potiorek: General im Schatten von Sarajewo*, Graz 1991.

Jessen, Olaf, *Die Moltkes: Biographie einer Familie*, Munich 2010.

Joël, Ernst, "Kameradschaft," in: *Das Ziel: Aufrufe zu tätigem Geist*, ed. by Kurt Hiller, Munich 1916, pp. 156–166.

Johann, Ernst (ed.), *Innenansicht eines Krieges: Bilder—Briefe—Dokumente*, Frankfurt 1968.

Jonas, Raymond, *France and the Cult of the Sacred Heart: An Epic Tale for Modern Times*, Berkeley 2000.

———, *The Tragic Tale of Claire Ferchaud and the Great War*, Berkeley 2005.

Jones, Heather, *Violence against Prisoners of War in the First World War: Britain, France and Germany, 1914–1920*, Cambridge 2011.

Jones, Shaun M., and Robertson, Kirsty, "'Good Luck . . . Dig In!' The Experience of Trench Warfare during World War I," in: Timothy C. Dowling (ed.), *Personal Perspectives: World War I*, Santa Barbara 2006, pp. 91–114.

Jordan, Nicole, *The Popular Front and Central Europe: The Dilemmas of French Impotence, 1918–1940*, Cambridge 1992.

Judson, Pieter M., *Guardians of the Nation: Activists on the Language Frontiers of Imperial Austria*, Cambridge, Mass. 2006.

Juillard, Jacques, "La CGT devant la guerre, 1900–1914," in: *Mouvement Social* 49 (1964), pp. 47–62.

Jünger, Karl (ed.), *Deutschlands Frauen und Deutschlands Krieg. Ein Rat-, Tat- und Trostbuch: Gesammelte Blätter aus Frauenhand*, Stuttgart 1916.

———, *Kriegstagebuch 1914–1918*, ed. by von Helmuth Kiesel, Stuttgart 2010.

———, *In Stahlgewittern* (orig. 1920), in: idem, *Sämtliche Werke*, Erste Abteilung, *Tagebücher*, vol. 1, Stuttgart 1978.

———, *In Stahlgewittern. Historisch-Kritische Ausgabe*, 2 vols., ed. by von Helmuth Kiesel, Stuttgart 2013.

———, *Storm of Steel*, New York 2016.

———, "Vorwort," in: idem (ed.), *Der Kampf um das Reich*, Essen (1929), in: idem, *Politische Publizistik 1919 bis 1933*, ed. by Sven Olaf Berggötz, Stuttgart 2001, pp. 527–536.

Jürgs, Michael, *Der kleine Frieden im Großen Krieg. Westfront 1914: Als Deutsche, Franzosen und Briten gemeinsam Weihnachten feierten*, Munich 2003.

Kafka, Franz, *Diaries, 1910–1923*, p. 301.

———, *Tagebücher, Textband*, ed. by Hans-Gerd Koch, Michael Müller, and Malcolm Pasley, in: Franz Kafka, *Schriften, Tagebücher, Briefe: Kritische Ausgabe*, Frankfurt 1990.

Kallen, Horace, "Democracy versus the Melting-Pot: A Study of American Nationality (1915)," in: Werner Sollors (ed.), *Theories of Ethnicity: A Classical Reader*, New York 1996, pp. 67–92.

Kann, Robert A., "Der Thronfolger Erzherzog Franz Ferdinand und seine Einstellung zur böhmischen Frage," in: idem, *Erzherzog Franz Ferdinand Studien*, pp. 127–156.

———, *Erzherzog Franz Ferdinand Studien*, Munich 1976.

———, "Franz Ferdinand der Ungarnfeind?" in: idem, *Erzherzog Franz Ferdinand Studien*, pp. 100–126.

Kappeler, Andreas, *Kleine Geschichte der Ukraine*, Munich 1994.

———, *The Russian Empire: A Multi-Ethnic History*, New York 2013.

Karvounarakis, Theodossios, "Britain, Greece, and the Turkish Settlement. An Overview of Events, Policies, and Relations, 1920–1922," in: *Modern Greek Studies Yearbook* 14 (1998), pp. 169–186.

Katkov, George, *The Kornilov Affair: Kerensky and the Break-Up of the Russian Army*, London 1980.

Katzer, Nikolaus, *Die Weiße Bewegung in Russland. Herrschaftsbildung, praktische Politik und politische Programmatik im Bürgerkrieg*, Cologne 1999.

Kaufmann, Stefan, "Kommunikationstechnik," in: Hirschfeld, Krumeich, and Renz (eds.), *Enzyklopädie Erster Weltkrieg*, pp. 621–624.

———, *Kommunikationstechnik und Kriegführung, 1815–1945: Stufen telemedialer Rüstung*, Munich 1996.

Keegan, John, *The First World War*, New York 1999.

Keene, Jennifer D., "The United States," in: Horne (ed.), *A Companion to World War I*, pp. 508–523.

———, *The United States and the First World War*, London 2000.

Kehr, Eckart, *Schlachtflottenbau und Parteipolitik, 1894–1901: Versuch eines Querschnitts durch die innenpolitischen, sozialen und ideologischen Voraussetzungen des deutschen Imperialismus*, Berlin 1930.

Kehrt, Christian, "Heldenbilder und Kriegserfahrung. Zum Habitus deutscher Militärpiloten im Zeitalter der Weltkriege," in: Jörg Echternkamp, Wolfgang Schmidt, and Thomas Vogel (eds.), *Perspektiven der Militärgeschichte: Raum, Gewalt und Repräsentation in historischer Forschung und Bildung*, Munich 2010, pp. 223–238.

Keiger, John F. V., *Raymond Poincaré*, Cambridge 1997.

Keisinger, Florian, *Die Balkankriege und die öffentliche Meinung in England, Deutschland und Irland 1876–1913*, Paderborn 2008.

Keith, Jeanette, *Rich Man's War, Poor Man's Fight: Race, Class, and Power in the Rural South during the First World War*, Chapel Hill 2004.

Kellermann, Hermann, *Der Krieg der Geister: Eine Auslese deutscher und ausländischer Stimmen zum Weltkriege 1914*, Weimar 1915.

Kelly, Patrick J., *Tirpitz and the Imperial Germany Navy*, Bloomington, Ind. 2011.

Kennan, George F., *Bismarcks europäisches System in der Auflösung: Die französisch-russische Annäherung 1875–1890*, Frankfurt 1981.

Kennedy, David M., *Over Here: The First World War and American Society*, New York 1980.

Kennedy, Thomas C., *A History of the No-Conscription Fellowship 1914–1919*, Fayetteville 1981.

Kent, Marian, "British Policy, International Diplomacy and the Turkish Revolution," in: *International Journal of Turkish Studies* (1985–1986), pp. 33–51.

Kenyon, David, *Horsemen in No Man's Land: British Cavalry and Trench Warfare, 1914–1918*, Barnsley 2011.

Kerekes, Lajos, *Von St. Germain bis Genf. Österreich und seine Nachbarn 1918–1922*, Budapest 1979.

Keren, Michael, and Keren, Shlomit, *We Are Coming, Unafraid: The Jewish Legions and the Promised Land in the First World War,* Lanham 2010.

Kershaw, Ian, "Europe's Second Thirty Years War: The Twentieth-Century World and Beyond," in: *History Today* (2005), pp. 10–17.

Kessler, Harry Graf, *Berlin in Lights: The Diaries of Count Harry Kessler, 1918–1937,* New York 2000.

———, *Journey to the Abyss: The Diaries of Count Harry Kessler, 1880–1918,* New York 2011.

———, *Das Tagebuch,* vol. 5: *1914–1916,* ed. by Ulrich Ott and Günter Riederer, Stuttgart 2008.

———, *Das Tagebuch,* vol. 6: *1916–1918,* ed. by Günter Riederer with Christoph Hilse, Stuttgart 2006.

———, *Das Tagebuch,* vol. 9: *1926–197,* ed. by Sabine Gruber and Ulrich Ott, Stuttgart 2010.

Ketelsen, Uwe, "Die Jugend von Langemarck. Ein poetisch-politisches Motiv der Zwischenkriegszeit," in: Rolf-Peter Janz, Thomas Koebner, and Frank Trommler (eds.), *"Mit uns zieht die neue Zeit." Der Mythos Jugend,* Frankfurt 1985, pp. 68–96.

Kettenacker, Lothar, and Riotte, Torsten (eds.), *The Legacies of Two World Wars: European Societies in the Twentieth Century,* Oxford 2011.

Kielmansegg, Peter Graf, *Deutschland und der Erste Weltkrieg,* Stuttgart 1980.

Kienitz, Sabine, *Beschädigte Helden: Kriegsinvalidität und Körperbilder 1914–1923,* Paderborn 2008.

Kiesel, Helmuth, "Ernst Jünger im Ersten Weltkrieg: Übersicht und Dokumentation," in: Jünger, *Kriegstagebuch,* pp. 596–647.

Kießling, Friedrich, *Gegen den "großen Krieg?" Entspannung in den internationalen Beziehungen 1911–1914,* Munich 2002.

Kilb, Andreas, "Blut in den Gräben, Rauchsäulen am Horizont," in: *Frankfurter Allgemeine Zeitung,* August 31, 2011.

Kilcher, Andreas B., "Zionistischer Kriegsdiskurs im Ersten Weltkrieg," in: Engel and Robertson (eds.), *Kafka, Prag und der Erste Weltkrieg,* pp. 49–72.

Kilduff, Peter, *Richthofen: Beyond the Legend of the Red Baron,* London 1993.

Killingray, David, "Military and Labour Policies in the Gold Coast during the First World War," in: Page (ed.), *Africa and the First World War,* pp. 137–151.

Király, Béla Kálmán (ed.), *Trianon and East Central Europe: Antecedents and Repercussions,* Boulder, Colo. 1995.

Kleindel, Walter (ed.), *Österreich: Daten zur Geschichte und Kultur,* Vienna 1978.

Klekowski, Edward J., and Klekowski, Libby, *Eyewitnesses to the Great War: American Writers, Reporters, Volunteers and Soldiers in France, 1914–1918,* Jefferson, N.C. 2012.

Klepsch, Michael, *Romain Rolland im Ersten Weltkrieg: Ein Intellektueller auf verlorenem Posten,* Stuttgart 2000.

Klieman, Aaron S., "Britain's War Aims in the Middle East in 1915," in: *Journal of Contemporary History* 3 (1968), pp. 237–251.

Kluge, Ulrich, *Die deutsche Revolution 1918 / 1919,* Frankfurt 1985.

Kocka, Jürgen, *Facing Total War: German Society, 1914–1918,* ACLS Humanities E-Book, 2008.

Koenen, Gerd, "Der deutsche Russland-Komplex: Zur Ambivalenz deutscher Ostorientierungen in der Weltkriegsphase," in: Thum (ed.), *Traumland Osten*, pp. 16–46.

———, *Der Russland-Komplex: Die Deutschen und der Osten 1900–1945*, Munich 2005.

Koerner, Peter (ed.), *Der Erste Weltkrieg 1914–1918*, vol. 1: *Vormarsch und Stellungskrieg*, Munich 1968.

Kohler, Josef, *Der Prozess gegen die Attentäter von Sarajewo, nach dem amtlichen Stenogramm der Gerichtsverhandlung aktenmässig dargestellt*, Berlin 1918.

Kolb, Eberhard, *Der Frieden von Versailles*, Munich 2005.

———, "Stabilisierung ohne Konsolidierung? Zur Konfiguration des europäischen Mächtesystems 1871–1914," in: Peter Krüger (ed.), *Das europäische Mächtesystem im Wandel. Strukturelle Bedingungen und bewegende Kräfte seit der Frühen Neuzeit*, Munich 1996, pp. 189–195.

———, *The Weimar Republic*, 2nd edn., London 2005.

Kolb, Eberhard, and Schumann, Dirk, *Die Weimarer Republik*, 8th ed., Munich 2013.

Koller, Christian, "Colonialisme militare en France et dans l'Empire Britannique," in: Chielens and Dendooven (eds.), *Cinq Continents au front*, pp. 11–22.

Kollwitz, Käthe, *Die Tagebücher*, ed. by Jutta Bohnke-Kollwitz, Berlin 1989.

Kölnische Volkszeitung, December 22, 1914.

Kondylis, Panajotis, *Theorie des Krieges: Clausewitz—Marx—Engels—Lenin*, Stuttgart 1988.

Köppen, Manuel, "Luftbilder. Die Medialisierung des Blicks," in: Gerhard Paul (ed.), *Das Jahrhundert der Bilder 1900 bis 1949*, Göttingen 2009, pp. 180–187.

Köroğlu, Erol, *Ottoman Propaganda and Turkish Identity: Literature in Turkey during World War I*, London 2007.

Koselleck, Reinhart, *Begriffsgeschichten*, Frankfurt 2006.

———, "Hinter der tödlichen Linie. Das Zeitalter des Totalen," in: *Frankfurter Allgemeine Zeitung*, November 27, 1999.

———, "Patriotismus: Gründe und Grenzen eines neuzeitlichen Begriffs," in: idem, *Begriffsgeschichten*, pp. 218–239.

———, "Zur Begriffsgeschichte der Zeitutopie," in: idem, *Begriffsgeschichten*, pp. 252–273.

Koselleck, Reinhart, Spree, Ulrike, and Steinmetz, Willibald, "Drei bürgerliche Welten: Zur vergleichenden Semantik der bürgerlichen Gesellschaft in Deutschland, England und Frankreich," in: Hans-Jürgen Puhle (eds.), *Bürger in der Gesellschaft der Neuzeit*, Göttingen 1991, pp. 14–58.

Koszyk, Kurt, *Deutsche Pressepolitik im Ersten Weltkrieg*, Düsseldorf 1968.

Kotowski, Georg, Pöls, Werner, and Ritter, Gerhard A. (eds.), *Das Wilhelminische Deutschland: Stimmen der Zeitgenossen*, Frankfurt 1965.

Kovács, Zoltán, "Border Changes and Their Effect on the Structure of Hungarian Society," in: *Political Geography Quarterly* 8 (1989), pp. 79–86.

Kraepelin, Emil, "Psychiatrische Randbemerkungen zur Zeitgeschichte," in: *Süddeutsche Monatshefte* 16 (1919), pp. 171–183.

Kramer, Alan, *Dynamic of Destruction: Culture and Mass Killing in the First World War*, Oxford 2007.

———, "Greueltaten: Zum Problem der deutschen Kriegsverbrechen in Belgien und Frankreich 1914," in: Hirschfeld, Krumeich, and Renz (eds.), *"Keiner fühlt sich hier mehr als Mensch . . . ,"* pp. 85–114.

Krass, Urte, "Stigmata und Yellow Press. Die Wunder des Padre Pio," in: Geppert and Kössler (eds.), *Wunder,* pp. 363–394.

Kraus, Hans-Christof, *Versailles und die Folgen: Außenpolitik zwischen Revisionismus und Verständigung 1919–1933,* Berlin 2013.

Kraus, Jürgen, *Die feldgraue Uniformierung des deutschen Heeres 1907–1918,* vol. 1, Osnabrück 1999.

Kraus, Karl, "Franz Ferdinand und die Talente," in: *Die Fackel* 400–403 (July 10, 1914), pp. 1–4.

———, *The Last Days of Mankind* (German orig. 1922), New Haven 2015.

Krause, Andreas, *Scapa Flow: Die Selbstversenkung der Wilhelminischen Flotte,* Munich 2001.

Kreiser, Klaus, *Atatürk: Eine Biographie,* Munich 2008.

Kresse, Oskar, *Verdeutschung entbehrlicher Fremdwörter,* Berlin 1915.

Krieg-mobil! 19. von . . . [sic!], 5th edn., Berlin 1913.

Kriegs-Ernährungsamt (ed.), *Die Kriegsernährungswirtschaft 1917,* Berlin 1917.

Kriegstagebuch eines Juden, Frankfurt 1964.

Krist, Gary, *City of Scoundrels: The Twelve Days of Disaster that Gave Birth to Modern Chicago,* New York 2012.

Krivanec, Eva, *Kriegsbühnen: Theater im Ersten Weltkrieg. Berlin, Lissabon, Paris und Wien,* Bielefeld 2012.

Kroener, Bernhard, *Militär, Staat und Gesellschaft im 20. Jahrhundert (1890–1990),* Munich 2011.

Kronenbitter, Günther, "Franz Ferdinand," in: Hirschfeld, Krumeich, and Renz (eds.), *Enzyklopädie Erster Weltkrieg,* p. 501.

———, "The Militarization of Austrian Foreign Policy on the Eve of World War I," in: Günter Bischof, Michael Gehler, and Anton Pelinka (eds.), *Austrian Foreign Policy in Historical Context,* New Brunswick 2006, pp. 80–90.

Kronenbitter, Günther, Pöhlmann, Markus, and Walter, Dierk (eds.), *Besatzung: Funktion und Gestalt militärischer Fremdherrschaft von der Antike bis zum 20. Jahrhundert,* Paderborn 2006.

Kröning, Peter, *Die Januar-Streiks in Berlin und Wien,* n.p. 1987.

Krüger, Dieter, "Kriegssozialismus: Die Auseinandersetzung der Nationalökonomen mit der Kriegswirtschaft 1914–1918," in: Michalka (ed.), *Der Erste Weltkrieg,* pp. 506–529.

———, *Nationalökonomen im wilhelminischen Deutschland,* Göttingen 1983.

Krüger, Gesine, *Kriegsbewältigung und Geschichtsbewußtsein: Realität, Deutung und Verarbeitung des deutschen Kolonialkriegs in Namibia 1904 bis 1907,* Göttingen 1999.

Krüger, Peter, *Deutschland und die Reparationen 1918 / 19: Die Genesis des Reparationsproblems in Deutschland,* Stuttgart 1973.

Krumeich, Gerd, *Aufrüstung und Innenpolitik in Frankreich vor dem Ersten Weltkrieg: Die Einführung der dreijährigen Dienstpflicht,* Wiesbaden 1980.

———, "Das Kaiserreich unterschätzte 1914 Englands Macht," in: *Die Welt,* September 12, 2013.

———, "Der Mensch als 'Material'": Verdun, 21. Februar bis 9. September 1916," in: Stig Förster, Markus Pöhlmann, and Dierk Walter (eds.), *Schlachten der Weltgeschichte. Von Salamis bis Sinai,* Munich 2001, pp. 295–305.

————, *Juli 1914. Eine Bilanz*, Paderborn 2013.

————, "Kriegsfotografie zwischen Erleben und Propaganda," in: Ute Daniel and Wolfram Siemann (eds.), *Propaganda*, Frankfurt 1994, pp. 117–132.

————, "Langemarck," in: François and Schulze (eds.), *Deutsche Erinnerungsorte*, vol. 1, pp. 292–309.

————, "Les armistices," in: Audoin-Rouzeau and Becker (eds.), *Encyclopédie de la Grande Guerre*, pp. 981–992.

————, "Le soldat allemand devant Verdun. Variations du souvenir," in: Cochet (ed.), *1916–2006—Verdun sous le regard du monde*, pp. 77–88.

————, "Verdun," in: Hirschfeld, idem, and Renz (eds.), *Enzyklopädie Erster Weltkrieg*, pp. 942–945.

————, "Verdun: Un lieu pour une mémoire commune?," in: Jacques Morizet and Horst Möller (eds.), *Allemagne-France. Lieux et mémoire d'une histoire commune*, Paris 1995, pp. 121–139.

———— (ed.), *Versailles 1919 : Ziele—Wirkung—Wahrnehmung*, Essen 2001.

Krumeich, Gerd, and Lepsius, Mario R., "Einleitung," in: *Max Weber Gesamtausgabe*, Abteilung II: *Briefe*, vol. 9: *Briefe 1915–1917*, ed. by idem, *Tübingen* 2008, pp. 1–18.

Kruse, Wolfgang, *Der Erste Weltkrieg*, Darmstadt 2009.

———— (ed.), *Eine Welt von Feinden: Der Große Krieg 1914–1918*, Frankfurt 1997.

————, "Gesellschaftspolitische Systementwicklung," in: idem (ed.), *Eine Welt von Feinden*, pp. 55–91.

————, "Imperialismus und Kriegspolitik," in: idem (ed.), *Eine Welt von Feinden*, pp. 11–54.

————, *Krieg und nationale Integration: Eine Neuinterpretation des sozialdemokratischen Burgfriedensschlusses 1914/15*, Essen 1993.

Krüsmann, Jochen, Langensiepen, Bernd, and Nottelmann, Dirk, *Halbmond und Kaiseradler: Goeben und Breslau am Bosporus, 1914–1918*, Hamburg 1999.

Kühne, Thomas, "Vertrauen und Kameradschaft. Soziales Kapital im 'Endkampf' der Wehrmacht," in: Frevert (ed.), *Vertrauen*, pp. 245–278.

Kunisch, Johannes, "Das 'Puppenwerk' der stehenden Heere: Ein Beitrag zur Neueinschätzung von Soldatenstand und Krieg in der Spätaufklärung," in: *Zeitschrift für Historische Forschung* 17 (1990), pp. 49–84.

Kurzke, Hermann, *Thomas Mann: Life as a Work of Art. A Biography* (orig. 1999), Princeton 2002.

Kuttner, Erich, "Vergessen! Die Kriegszermalmten in Berliner Lazaretten," in: *Vorwärts*, September 8, 1920, quoted in: Ulrich, ". . . als wenn nichts geschehen wäre," pp. 140–156.

Lademacher, Horst (ed.), *Die Zimmerwalder Bewegung: Protokolle und Korrespondenz*, 2 vols., The Hague 1967.

Laffan, Michael, *The Resurrection of Ireland: The Sinn Féin Party, 1916–1923*, Cambridge 1999.

Lane, Arthur E., *An Adequate Response: The War Poetry of William Owen and Siegfried Sassoon*, Detroit 1972.

Lange, Barbara (ed.), *Geschichte der bildenden Kunst in Deutschland*, vol. 8: *Vom Expressionismus bis heute*, Munich 2006.

Lange, Britta, "Recherches académiques sur les prisonniers de guerre (non-blancs) en Allemagne, 1915–1918," in: Chielens and Dendooven (eds.), *Cinq Continents au front*, pp. 153–160.

Langes, Gunther, *Die Front in Fels und Eis: Der Weltkrieg 1914–1918 im Hochgebirge*, 4th edn., Bozen 1972.

Langewiesche, Dieter, "Das Jahrhundert Europas: Eine Annäherung in globalgeschichtlicher Perspektive," in: *Historische Zeitschrift* 296 (2013), pp. 29–48.

———, "Eskalierte die Kriegsgewalt im Laufe der Geschichte?," in: Baberowski (ed.), *Moderne Zeiten*, pp. 12–36.

———, "Gefühlsraum Nation. Eine Emotionsgeschichte der Nation, die Grenzen zwischen öffentlichem und privatem Gefühlsraum nicht einebnet," in: *Zeitschrift für Erziehungswissenschaft* 15 (2012), pp. 195–215.

———, *Liberalism in Germany*, Princeton 2000.

———, *Reich, Nation, Föderation: Deutschland und Europa*, Munich 2008.

Larson, Robert H., *The British Army and the Theory of Armored Warfare, 1918–1940*, Newark 1984.

Latzel, Klaus, *Deutsche Soldaten—nationalsozialistischer Krieg? Kriegserlebnis—Kriegserfahrung 1939–1945*, Paderborn 1998.

———, "Die Soldaten des industrialisierten Krieges—'Fabrikarbeiter der Zerstörung?' Eine Zeugenbefragung zu Gewalt, Arbeit und Gewöhnung," in: Spilker and Ulrich (eds.), *Der Tod als Maschinist*, pp. 125–141.

Lawrence, Jon, "Forging a Peaceable Kingdom: War, Violence, and Fear of Brutalization in Post-First World War Britain," in: *Journal of Modern History* 75 (2003), pp. 557–589.

Lawrence, Thomas E., "Nationalism among the Tribesmen, 26. November 1916," in: Malcolm Brown (ed.), *T. E. Lawrence in War and Peace: An Anthology of the Military Writings of Lawrence of Arabia*, London 2005, pp. 80–82.

Lee, Hermione, *Virginia Woolf*, London 1996.

Leed, Eric, *No Man's Land: Combat and Identity in World War I*, Cambridge 1979.

Leese, Peter, *Shell Shock: Traumatic Neurosis and the British Soldiers of the First World War*, Basingstoke 2002.

Lehnert, Herbert, "Langemarck—historisch und symbolisch," in: *Orbis Litterarum* 42 (1987), pp. 271–290.

Leidinger, Hannes, and Moritz, Verena, *Gefangenschaft, Revolution, Heimkehr: Die Bedeutung der Kriegsgefangenenproblematik für die Geschichte des Kommunismus in Mittel- und Osteuropa 1917–1920*, Vienna 2003.

———, *Oberst Redl. Der Spionagefall. Der Skandal. Die Fakten*, St. Pölten 2012.

Lein, Richard, *Pflichterfüllung oder Hochverrat? Die tschechischen Soldaten Österreich-Ungarns im Ersten Weltkrieg*, Vienna 2011.

Leitner, Gerrit von, *Der Fall Clara Immerwahr: Leben für eine humane Wissenschaft*, Munich 1993.

Lendvai, Paul, "Sprengstoff im gemeinsamen Haus. Nationalitätenkonflikte in Osteuropa," in: *Europäische Rundschau* 2 (1991), p. 17.

———, *The Hungarians: A Thousand Years of Victory in Defeat*, London 2003.

Lenin, Vladimir I., "Imperialism, the Highest Stage of Capitalism," in: *Collected Works* 22, Moscow 1964, pp. 185–304.

————, "The Junius Pamphlet," in: *Collected Works* 22, Moscow 1964, pp. 305–319.

————, "Lecture on the 1905 Revolution," in: *Collected Works* 23, Moscow 1964, pp. 236–253.

————, "A Painful but Necessary Lesson" (February 25, 1918), in: *Collected Works* 27, Moscow 1972, pp. 62–66.

————, "Report on the Current Situation" (May 7, 1917), in: *Collected Works* 24, Moscow 1964, pp. 228–243.

Lentin, A., "Decline and Fall of the Versailles Settlement," in: *Diplomacy & Statecraft* 4 (1993), pp. 358–375.

Leon, George B., *Greece and the Great Powers, 1914–1917*, Thessaloniki 1974.

Leonhard, Jörn, *Bellizismus und Nation. Kriegsdeutung und Nationsbestimmung in Europa und den Vereinigten Staaten 1750–1914*, Munich 2008.

————, "Das Erbe der Vielfalt: Die europäischen Empires und die Friedensverträge nach 1918," in: *Zeitschrift für Staats- und Europawissenschaften* 3 (2012), pp. 361–385.

————, "Nations in Arms und Imperial Defence—Continental Models, the British Empire and Its Military before 1914," in: *Journal of Modern European History* 5 (2007), pp. 287–308.

————, "'Über Nacht sind wir zur radikalsten Demokratie Europas geworden'—Ernst Troeltsch und die geschichtspolitische Überwindung der Ideen von 1914," in: Friedrich Wilhelm Graf (ed.), *"Geschichte durch Geschichte überwinden": Ernst Troeltsch in Berlin*, Gütersloh 2006, pp. 205–230.

————, "Vom Nationalkrieg zum Kriegsnationalismus—Projektion und Grenze nationaler Integrationsvorstellungen in Deutschland, Großbritannien und den Vereinigten Staaten im Ersten Weltkrieg," in: Hirschhausen and idem (eds.), *Nationalismen in Europa*, pp. 204–240.

Leonhard, Jörn, and Hirschhausen, Ulrike von (eds.), *Comparing Empires: Encounters and Transfers in the Nineteenth and Early Twentieth Century*, 2nd edn., Göttingen 2012.

————, *Empires und Nationalstaaten im 19. Jahrhundert*, 2nd edn., Göttingen 2010.

Leontaritis, George B., *Greece and the First World War: From Neutrality to Intervention, 1917–1918*, New York 1990.

Lepick, Olivier, *La grande guerre chimique: 1914–1918*, Paris 1998.

Lepsius, Johannes, *Deutschland und Armenien 1914–1918: Sammlung diplomatischer Aktenstücke,* (orig. Potsdam 1919), reprinted Bremen 1986.

Lerner, Paul, "Hysterical Cures: Hypnosis, Gender and Performance in World War I and Weimar Germany," in: *History Workshop Journal* 45 (1998), pp. 79–101.

————, *Hysterical Men: War, Psychiatry and Politics of Trauma in Germany 1890–1930*, Ithaca 2003.

Levsen, Sonja, *Elite, Männlichkeit und Krieg: Tübinger und Cambridger Studenten 1900–1929*, Göttingen 2006.

Lewin, Kurt, "Kriegslandschaft," in: *Zeitschrift für angewandte Psychologie* 12 (1917), p. 441, quoted in: Bröckling, *Disziplin*, p. 202.

Lichem, Heinz von, *Krieg in den Alpen: 1915–1918*, 3 vols., Augsburg 1993.

Lichfield, John, "Two Soldiers Linked in Death by a Bizarre Coincidence," in: *The Independent*, November 8, 2008.

Liddell Hart, Basil H., *A History of the World War 1914–1918*, London 1934.

———, *Liddell Hart's Western Front: Impressions of the Battle of the Somme with War Letters, Diary and Occasional Notes Written on Active Service in France and Flanders 1915 and 1916*, ed. by Brian Bond, London 2010.

Lieven, Dominic, *Russia and the Origins of the First World War*, London 1983.

Lindner-Wirsching, Almut, "Patrioten im Pool: Deutsche und französische Kriegsberichterstatter im Ersten Weltkrieg," in: Daniel (ed.), *Augenzeugen*, pp. 113–140.

Linke, Horst-Günther, *Das zaristische Russland und der Erste Weltkrieg: Diplomatie und Kriegsziele 1914–1917*, Munich 1982.

Linnenkohl, Hans, *Vom Einzelschuss zur Feuerwalze. Der Wettlauf zwischen Technik und Taktik im Ersten Weltkrieg*, Bonn 1996.

Lipkes, Jeff, *Rehearsals. The German Army in Belgium, August 1914*, Louvain 2007.

Lipp, Anne, *Meinungslenkung im Krieg: Kriegserfahrungen deutscher Soldaten und ihre Deutung 1914–1918*, Göttingen 2003.

Liulevicius, Vejas G., "Der Osten als apokalyptischer Raum. Deutsche Fronterfahrungen im und nach dem Ersten Weltkrieg," in: Thum (ed.), *Traumland Osten*, pp. 47–65.

———, "Die deutsche Besatzung im 'Land Ober Ost' im Ersten Weltkrieg," in: Kronenbitter, Pöhlmann, and Walter (eds.), *Besatzung*, pp. 93–104.

———, *War Land on the Eastern Front: Culture, National Identity, and German Occupation in World War I*, Cambridge 2000.

Llanque, Marcus, *Demokratisches Denken im Krieg: Die deutsche Debatte im Ersten Weltkrieg*, Berlin 2000.

Lloyd George, David, *The Truth about the Peace Treaties*, vol. 1, London 1938.

Lohmann, Hans-Martin, "Schriften zum Thema Krieg und Tod," in: idem and Joachim Pfeiffer (eds.), *Freud-Handbuch. Leben—Werk—Wirkung*, Stuttgart 2006, pp. 187–192.

Lohr, Eric, "The Moscow Riots of May 1915," in: *Kritika: Explorations in Russian and Eurasian History* 4 (2003), pp. 607–626.

———, *Nationalizing the Russian Empire: The Campaign against Enemy Aliens during World War I*, Cambridge, Mass. 2003.

———, "Russia," in: Horne (ed.), *A Companion to World War I*, pp. 479–493.

———, "The Russian Press and the 'Internal Peace' at the Beginning of World War I," in: Troy R. E. Paddock (ed.), *A Call to Arms. Propaganda, Public Opinion and Newspapers in the Great War*, Westport, Conn. 2004, pp. 91–113.

———, "War and Revolution, 1914–1917," in: Dominic Lieven (ed.), *The Cambridge History of Russia*, vol 2: *Imperial Russia, 1689–1917*, Cambridge 2006, pp. 655–669.

Lorenz, Richard (ed.), *Die Russische Revolution 1917: Der Aufstand der Arbeiter, Bauern und Soldaten. Eine Dokumentation*, Munich 1981.

Loughlin, James, "Mobilising the Sacred Dead: Ulster Unionism, the Great War and the Politics of Remembrance," in: Gregory and Pašeta (eds.), *Ireland and the Great War*, pp. 133–154.

Loulos, Konstantin, "Griechenland," in: Hirschfeld, Krumeich, and Renz (eds.), *Enzyklopädie Erster Weltkrieg*, pp. 534–537.

Lowry, Bullitt, *Armistice 1918*, Kent, Ohio 1996.

Lüdtke, Alf, "Thesen zur Wiederholbarkeit: Normalität und Massenhaftigkeit von Tötungsgewalt im 20. Jahrhundert," in: Helga Breuninger and Rolf Peter Sieferle (eds.), *Kulturen der Gewalt: Ritualisierung und Symbolisierung von Gewalt in der Geschichte*, Frankfurt 1998, pp. 280–289.

Ludwig, Emil, *Juli 14: Vorabend zweier Weltkriege* (1929), Hamburg 1961.

Ludwig, Walter, *Beiträge zur Psychologie der Furcht im Kriege. Inaugural-Dissertation zur Erlangung der Doktorwürde einer hohen Philosophischen Fakultät der Universität Tübingen*, Leipzig 1919.

Luhmann, Niklas, *Trust and Power*, Chichester 1979.

Lunn, Joe H., "Kande Kamara Speaks: An Oral History of the West African Experience in France 1914–18," in: Page (ed.), *Africa and the First World War*, pp. 28–53.

———, *Memoirs of the Maelstrom: A Senegalese Oral History of the First World War*, Portsmouth 1999.

Luzzatto, Sergio, *Padre Pio: Miracles and Politics in a Secular Age*, New York 2007.

Lyon, James M. B., "'A Peasant Mob': The Serbian Army on the Eve of the Great War," in: *Journal of Military History* 61 (1997), pp. 481–502.

MacArthur, Brian (ed.), *The Penguin Book of Twentieth Century Speeches*, 2nd edn., London 1999.

Macartney, Carlile A., *Hungary and Her Successors: The Treaty of Trianon and Its Consequences 1919–1937*, Oxford 1937, London 1968.

Macfie, A. L., "The Revision of the Treaty of Sèvres: The First Phase (August 1920–September 1922)," in: *Balkan Studies* 24 (1983), pp. 57–88.

Macmillan, Margaret, *Paris 1919: Six Months that Changed the World*, New York 2003.

Mahan, Alfred T., *The Influence of Sea Power upon History, 1660–1783* (orig. 1890), Gretna 2003.

———, *Naval Strategy Compared and Contrasted with the Principles of Military Operations on Land*, Boston 1911.

Mahrenholz, Jürgen-K., "Les enregistrements sonores ethnographiques dans les camps de prisonniers allemandès durant la premiere guerre mondiale," in: Chielens and Dendooven (eds.), *Cinq Continents au front*, pp. 161–166.

Mai, Gunther, *Arbeiterschaft in Deutschland 1914–1918: Studien zu Arbeitskampf und Arbeitsmarkt im Ersten Weltkrieg*, Düsseldorf 1985.

———, *Das Ende des Kaiserreichs: Politik und Kriegführung im Ersten Weltkrieg*, 2nd edn., Munich 1993.

———, "Der Erste Weltkrieg," in: Hans-Ulrich Wehler (ed.), *Scheidewege der deutschen Geschichte: Von der Reformation bis zur Wende 1517–1989*, Munich 1995, pp. 159–171.

———, "Hilfsdienstgesetz," in: Hirschfeld, Krumeich, and Renz (ed.), *Enzyklopädie Erster Weltkrieg*, pp. 553–554.

———, "Verteidigungskrieg und Volksgemeinschaft. Staatliche Selbstbehauptung, nationale Solidarität und soziale Befreiung in Deutschland in der Zeit des Ersten Weltkrieges 1900–1925," in: Michalka (ed.), *Der Erste Weltkrieg*, pp. 583–602.

Maier, Charles S., "Consigning the Twentieth Century to History: Alternative Narratives for the Modern Era," in: *American Historical Review* 105 (2000), pp. 807–831.

————, "Leviathan 2.0: Die Erfindung moderner Staatlichkeit," in: Akira Iriye and Jürgen Osterhammel (eds.), *Geschichte der Welt*, vol. 5: *1870–1945:Weltmärkte und Weltkriege*, ed. by Emily S. Rosenberg, Munich 2012, pp. 33–286.

————, "Transformation of Territoriality 1600–2000," in: Gunilla Budde, Sebastian Conrad, and Oliver Janz (eds.), *Transnationale Geschichte: Themen, Tendenzen und Theorien*, Göttingen 2006, pp. 32–55.

Mairet, L., *Carnet d'un combattant (11 février 1915–16 avril 1917)*, Paris 1919.

Majerus, Benoît, "Die deutsche Verwaltung Belgiens in den zwei Weltkriegen," in: Kronenbitter, Pöhlmann, and Walter (eds.), *Besatzung*, pp. 131–146.

————, "La prostitution à Bruxelles pendant la Grande Guerre: Contrôle et pratique," in: *Crime, Histoire et Sociétés* 7 (2003), pp. 5–42.

Malkowsky, Georg (ed.), *Die Pariser Weltausstellung in Wort und Bild*, Berlin 1900.

Manela, Erez, *The Wilsonian Moment: Self-Determination and the International Origins of Anticolonial Nationalism*, Oxford 2009.

Mann, Golo, *Deutsche Geschichte des 19. und 20. Jahrhunderts*. expanded edn., Frankfurt 1958.

Mann, Heinrich, "Zola," in: idem, *Essays und Publizistik*, vol. 2: *Oktober 1904 bis Oktober 1918*, ed. by Manfred Hahn with Anne Flierl and Wolfgang Klein, Bielefeld 2012, pp. 147–208.

Mann, Thomas, *Betrachtungen eines Unpolitischen*, in: idem, *Große Kommentierte Frankfurter Ausgabe*, vol. 12 / 1, ed. by Hermann Kurzke, Frankfurt 2009.

————, *Diaries, 1918–1939*, London 1983.

————, "Frederick and the Great Coalition," in: idem, *Three Essays*, New York 1929 (German orig. 1915), pp. 143–215.

————, "[Friede?]," in: idem, *Große kommentierte Frankfurter Ausgabe*, vol. 15 / 1, p. 249.

————, "Gedanken im Kriege," in: idem, *Große kommentierte Frankfurter Ausgabe*, vol. 15 / 1, pp. 137–141.

————, *Große kommentierte Frankfurter Ausgabe*, vol. 15 / 1: *Essays II 1914–1926*, ed. by Hermann Kurzke, Frankfurt / M. 2002.

————, *Große kommentierte Frankfurter Ausgabe*, vol. 22: *Briefe II 1914–1923*, ed. by Thomas Sprecher, Frankfurt / M. 2004.

————, *The Magic Mountain* (orig. 1924), trans. by John E. Woods, New York 1995.

————, *Reflections of a Nonpolitical Man* (orig. 1918), trans. by Walter D. Morris, New York 1983.

————, *Tagebücher 1918–1921*, ed. by Peter de Mendelssohn, Frankfurt 1979.

————, "Weltfrieden?" (December 27, 1917), in: idem, *Große kommentierte Frankfurter Ausgabe*, vol. 15 / 1, pp. 212–215.

Márai, Sándor, *Bekenntnisse eines Bürgers* (orig. Hungarian: 1934), Munich 2000.

Marder, Arthur J., *From the Dreadnought to Scapa Flow: The Royal Navy in the Fisher Era*, vol. 3: *Jutland and After (May 1916–December 1916)*, 2nd edn., London 1978.

Markov, Walter (ed.), *Revolution im Zeugenstand: Frankreich 1789–1799*, vol. 2: *Gesprochenes und Geschriebenes*, Frankfurt / M. 1987.

Marks, Sally, *The Illusion of Peace: International Relations in Europe, 1918–1933*, Basingstoke 2003.

Marquardt, Sabine, *Polis contra Polemos: Politik als Kampfbegriff der Weimarer Republik,* Cologne 1997.

Marquis, Alice G., "Words as Weapons: Propaganda in Britain and Germany during the First World War," in: *Journal of Contemporary History* 13 (1978), pp. 467–498.

Martens, Stefan, *Hermann Göring: "Erster Paladin des Führers" und "Zweiter Mann im Reich,"* Paderborn 1985.

Martin, Gred, "Asquith, the Maurice Debate and the Historians," in: *Australian Journal of Politics and History* 31/3 (1985), pp. 435–444.

Martin, Terry, and Suny, Ronald, *A State of Nations: Empire and Nation-Making in the Age of Lenin and Stalin,* Oxford 2001.

Martinetz, Dieter, *Der Gaskrieg 1914–1918: Entwicklung, Herstellung und Einsatz chemischer Kampfstoffe,* Bonn 1996.

Marwick, Arthur, *Britain in the Century of Total War,* London 1968.

Massignani, Alessandro, "Caporetto (Karfeit)," in: Hirschfeld, Krumeich, and Renz (eds.), *Enzyklopädie Erster Weltkrieg,* pp. 405–406.

Matthew, Henry C. G., *Gladstone, 1809–1898,* Oxford 1997.

Matthews, Fred H., "The Revolt against Americanism: Cultural Pluralism and Cultural Relativism as an Ideology of Liberation," in: *Canadian Review of American Studies* 1 (1970), pp. 4–31.

Matthews, James K., "Reluctant Allies: Nigerian Responses to Military Recruitment," in: Page (ed.), *Africa and the First World War,* pp. 95–114.

Matuschka, E. von, "Organisationsgeschichte des Heeres 1890 bis 1918," in: Militärgeschichtliches Forschungsamt (ed.), *Handbuch zur deutschen Militärgeschichte 1648–1939,* vol. 3, Munich 1979, pp. 157–282.

Mayer, Arno J., *Adelsmacht und Bürgertum: Die Krise der europäischen Gesellschaft 1848–1914,* Munich 1984.

Mayerhofer, Lisa, *Zwischen Freund und Feind—Deutsche Besatzung in Rumänien 1916–1918,* Munich 2010.

Mazower, Mark, *Dark Continent: Europe's Twentieth Century,* New York 1998.

———, *Salonica: City of Ghosts—Christians, Muslims and Jews, 1430–1950,* New York 2005.

McAuley, Mary, *Bread and Justice: State and Society in Petrograd 1917–1922,* Oxford 1991.

McKale, Donald M., *War by Revolution: Germany and Great Britain in the Middle East in the Era of World War I,* Kent, Ohio 1998.

McLaughlin, Peter, "The Legacy of Conquest: African Military Manpower in Southern Rhodesia during the First World War," in: Page (ed.), *Africa and the First World War,* pp. 115–136.

McMeekin, Sean, *July 1914: Countdown to War,* New York 2013.

———, *The Russian Origins of the First World War,* Cambridge, Mass. 2011.

McRandle, James, and Quirk, James, "The Blood Test Revisited: A New Look at German Casualty Counts in World War I," in: *Journal of Military History* 70/3 (2006), pp. 667–701.

McWhirter, Cameron, *Red Summer: The Summer of 1919 and the Awakening of Black America,* New York 2011.

Mead, Gary, *The Doughboys: America and the First World War,* London 2000.

Meier, Heinrich, *Carl Schmitt and Leo Strauss: The Hidden Dialogue,* Chicago 1995.

Meisner, Heinrich Otto (ed.), *Denkwürdigkeiten des General-Feldmarschalls Alfred Grafen von Waldersee, auf Veranlassung des Generalleutnants Georg Grafen von Waldersee,* vol. 1, Stuttgart 1922.

Melling, Joseph, *Rent Strikes: Peoples' Struggle for Housing in West Scotland 1890–1916,* Edinburgh 1983.

Mendelssohn, Peter de, *Der Zauberer. Das Leben des Schriftstellers Thomas Mann,* vol. 2: *1905 bis 1918,* Frankfurt / M. 1996.

———, "The Offensive Revisited. Russian Preparations for Future War, 1906–1914," in: idem and David Schimmelpenninck van der Oye (eds.), *Reforming the Tsar's Army: Military Innovation in Imperial Russia from Peter the Great to the Revolution,* Cambridge 2004, pp. 215–231.

———, *Zeitungsstadt Berlin: Menschen und Mächte in der Geschichte der deutschen Presse,* Berlin 1959.

Menning, Bruce W., *Bayonets before Bullets: The Imperial Russian Army, 1861–1914,* Bloomington, Ind. 1992.

———, *Russian Military Intelligence, July 1914: What St. Petersburg Perceived and Why It Mattered,* unpublished ms., Cambridge.

Menzel, Walter, *Kriegsflüchtlinge in Cisleithanien im Ersten Weltkrieg,* diss., Vienna 1997.

Meteling, Wencke, *Ehre, Einheit, Ordnung: Preußische und französische Städte und ihre Regimenter im Krieg, 1870 / 71 und 1914–19,* Baden-Baden 2010.

"Methods of Controversy," in: *Westminster Gazette,* June 2, 1915.

Meyer, E., "Kriegsbeschädigtenfürsorge und Taylorsystem," in: *Zeitschrift für Krüppelfürsorge* 10 (1917–1918), pp. 145–150.

Meyer, Jacques, *Les Soldats de la Grande Guerre,* Paris 1966.

Michalka, Wolfgang (ed.), *Der Erste Weltkrieg. Wirkung, Wahrnehmung, Analyse,* Munich 1994.

———, "Kriegsrohstoffbewirtschaftung, Walther Rathenau und die 'kommende Wirtschaft,'" in: idem. (ed.), *Der Erste Weltkrieg,* pp. 485–505.

Michels, Eckard, *"Der Held von Deutsch-Ostafrika": Paul von Lettow-Vorbeck. Ein preußischer Kolonialoffizier,* Paderborn 2008.

Michl, Susanne, *Im Dienste des "Volkskörpers": Deutsche und französische Ärzte im Ersten Weltkrieg,* Göttingen 2007.

———, "Gehe hin, dein Glaube hat dir geholfen: Kriegswunder und Heilsversprechen in der Medizin des 20. Jahrhunderts," in: Geppert and Kössler (eds.), *Wunder,* pp. 211–236.

Mick, Christoph, *Kriegserfahrungen in einer multiethnischen Stadt: Lemberg, 1914–1947,* Wiesbaden 2010.

———, "Vielerlei Kriege: Osteuropa 1918–1921," in: Beyrau, Hochgeschwender, and Langewiesche (eds.), *Formen des Krieges,* pp. 311–326.

———, "Wer verteidigte Lemberg? Totengedenken, Kriegsdeutungen und nationale Identität in einer multiethnischen Stadt," in: Dietrich Beyrau (ed.), *Der Krieg in religiösen und nationalen Deutungen der Neuzeit,* Tübingen 2000, pp. 189–216.

Middendorf, Stefanie, *Massenkultur: Zur Wahrnehmung gesellschaftlicher Modernität in Frankreich 1880–1980,* Göttingen 2009.

Middlebrook, Martin, *The First Day on the Somme, 1 July 1916,* London 1971.

Miller, Gregory D., *The Shadow of the Past: Reputation and Military Alliances before the First World War*, Ithaca 2012.

Miller, Henry W., *Paris Gun: The Bombardment of Paris by the German Long-Range Guns and the Great German Offensives of 1918*, New York 1930.

Miller, Susanne, *Burgfrieden und Klassenkampf: Die deutsche Sozialdemokratie im Ersten Weltkrieg*, Düsseldorf 1974.

Ministère de la Guerre, État-Major de l'Armée, Service Historique (ed.), *Les armées françaises dans la Grande Guerre*, vol. 4 / 1: *Verdun et la Somme; Annexes*, vol. 3, Paris 1931.

Miquel, Pierre, *Les poilus: La France sacrifiée*, Paris 2000.

Mitrović, Andrej, *Serbia's Great War, 1914–1918*, London 2007.

Mjagkij, Nina, *Loyalty in Time of Trial: The African American Experience during World War I*, Lanham 2011.

Mohs, Polly A., *Military Intelligence and the Arab Revolt: The First Modern Intelligence War*, London 2008.

Mojzes, Paul, *Balkan Genocides: Holocaust and Ethnic Cleansing in the Twentieth Century*, Lanham 2011.

Mollenhauer, Daniel, "Thomas Albert," in: Hirschfeld, Krumeich, and Renz (eds.), *Enzyklopädie Erster Weltkrieg*, p. 921.

Möller, Horst, *Europa zwischen den Weltkriegen*, Munich 1998.

Mollo, Andrew, and Turner, Pierre, *Army Uniforms of World War One*, Littlehampton 1984.

Mombauer, Annika, "The Battle of the Marne: Myths and Reality of Germany's 'Fateful Battle,'" in: *The Historian* 68 (2006), pp. 747–769.

———, "Der Moltkeplan: Modifikation des Schlieffenplans bei gleichen Zielen," in: Ehlert, Epkenhans, and Groß (eds.), *Der Schlieffenplan*, pp. 79–100.

———, *Die Julikrise: Europas Weg in den Ersten Weltkrieg*, Munich 2013.

———, *Helmuth von Moltke and the Origins of the First World War*, Cambridge 2001.

Mommsen, Hans (ed.), *Der Erste Weltkrieg und die Beziehungen zwischen Tschechen, Slowaken und Deutschen*, Essen 2001.

———, "Einführung," in: idem (ed.), *Der Erste Weltkrieg und die Beziehungen zwischen Tschechen, Slowaken und Deutschen*, pp. 7–13.

———, "Viktor Adler und die Politik der österreichischen Sozialdemokratie im Ersten Weltkrieg," in: Isabella Ackerl (ed.), *Politik und Gesellschaft im alten und neuen Österreich: Festschrift für Rudolf Neck zum 60. Geburtstag*, Vienna 1981, pp. 378–408.

Mommsen, Wolfgang J., *Bürgerstolz und Weltmachtstreben: Deutschland unter Wilhelm II. 1890 bis 1918*, Berlin 1995.

———, "Das Englandbild der Deutschen und die britische Sicht seit dem Ende des 18. Jahrhunderts," in: Süssmuth (ed.), *Deutschlandbilder in Dänemark und England, in Frankreich und den Niederlanden*, pp. 215–234.

———, "Der Erste Weltkrieg und die Krise Europas," in: Hirschfeld, Krumeich, and Renz (eds.), *"Keiner fühlt sich hier mehr als Mensch . . . ,"* pp. 30–52.

———, "Die deutsche Kriegszielpolitik 1914–18: Bemerkungen zum Stand der Diskussion," in: Walter Laqueur and George L. Mosse (eds.), *Kriegsausbruch 1914*, 2nd edn., Munich 1970, pp. 60–100.

———, *Die Urkatastrophe Deutschlands: Der Erste Weltkrieg 1914–1918* (Gebhardt Handbuch der deutschen Geschichte), vol. 17, 10th edn., Stuttgart 2002.

———, *Großmachtstellung und Weltpolitik 1870–1914: Die Außenpolitik des deutschen Reiches*, Frankfurt 1993.

———, *Max Weber and German Politics, (1890–1920)*, Chicago 1984.

Mondini, Marco, *Alpini: Parole e immagini di un mito guerriero*, Rome 2008.

Monk, Ray, *Wittgenstein: The Duty of Genius*, New York 1990.

Monroe, Elizabeth, *Britain's Moment in the Middle East 1914–1971*, Baltimore 1981.

Montaigne, Jean-Baptiste, *Vaincre*, Paris 1913.

Montgomery, A. E., "The Making of the Treaty of Sevres of 10 August 1920," in: *Historical Journal* 15 (1972), pp. 775–787.

Monticone, Alberto, *La battaglia di Caporetto*, Udine 1999.

Moran, Seán F., *Patrick Pearse and the Politics of Redemption: The Mind of the Easter Rising 1916*, Washington 1994.

Mordacq, Henri, *Le drame de l'Yser : Surprise des Gaz (Avril 1915)*, Paris 1933.

Morgan, Kenneth O., "Lloyd George and Germany," in: *Historical Journal* 39 (1996), pp. 755–766.

Morrow, John H. Jr., *The Great War: An Imperial History*, London 2004.

Morton, Frederic, *Thunder at Twilight: Vienna 1913 / 1914 (1989)*, Cambridge, Mass. 2001.

Mosse, George L., *Fallen Soldiers: Reshaping the Memory of the World Wars*, Oxford 1990.

Mühlhausen, Walter, "Die Sozialdemokratie am Scheideweg—Burgfrieden, Parteikrise und Spaltung im Ersten Weltkrieg," in: Michalka (ed.), *Der Erste Weltkrieg*, pp. 649–671.

———, "Sozialdemokratie," in: Hirschfeld, Krumeich, and Renz (eds.), *Enzyklopädie Erster Weltkrieg*, pp. 856–857.

———, "Zimmerwalder Bewegung," in: Hirschfeld, Krumeich, and Renz (eds.), *Enzyklopädie Erster Weltkrieg*, pp. 977–978.

Mukherjee, Mridula, "The Home Rule Movement and Its Fallout," in: idem, Chandra, Bipan, Mahajan, Sucheta, Mukherjee, Aditiya, and Panikkar, K. N., *India's Struggle for Independence*, New Delhi 1988, pp. 159–169.

Müller, Jan-Werner, *Contesting Democracy: Political Ideals in Twentieth Century Europe*, New Haven 2011.

Müller, Rolf-Dieter, "Gaskrieg," in: Hirschfeld, Krumeich, and Renz (eds.), *Enzyklopädie Erster Weltkrieg*, pp. 519–522.

———, "Total War as the Result of New Weapons?" in: Chickering and Förster (eds.), *Great War, Total War*, pp. 95–111.

Müller, Sven Oliver, *Die Nation als Waffe und Vorstellung: Nationalismus in Deutschland und Großbritannien im Ersten Weltkrieg*, Göttingen 2002.

Müller, Sven Oliver, and Zalfen, Sarah (eds.), *Besatzungsmacht Musik: Zur Musik- und Emotionsgeschichte im Zeitalter der Weltkriege (1914–1949)*, Bielefeld 2012.

Müller-Jarbusch, Maximilian, "Kriegs-Museen: Ein Vorschlag," in: *Ostsee Zeitung*, April 30, 1916.

Müller-Pohl, Simone, "Working the Nation State: Submarine Cable Actors, Cable Transnationalism and the Governance of the Global Media System, 1858–1914," in: Isabella Löhr and Roland Wenzlhuemer (eds.), *The Nation State and Beyond: Governing Globalization Processes in the Nineteenth and Early Twentieth Centuries,* Heidelberg 2013, pp. 101–123.

Mulligan, William, *The Origins of the First World War,* Cambridge 2010.

Mummelthey, Reinhard, *Die Nationalitätenzusammensetzung des Russischen Reiches und der Sowjetunion von 1897 bis 1989,* Munich 1996.

Münch, Matti, *Verdun—Mythos und Alltag einer Schlacht,* Munich 2006.

Münchhausen, Thankmar von, *Paris: Geschichte einer Stadt: Von 1800 bis heute,* Munich 2007.

Münkler, Herfried, *Machiavelli: Die Begründung des politischen Denkens der Neuzeit aus der Krise der Republik Florenz,* new edn., Frankfurt 2004.

Musil, Robert, *Diaries, 1899–1941,* New York 1998.

———, *The Man without Qualities,* trans. by Sophie Wilkins and Burton Pike, New York 1995.

Nachtigal, Reinhard, *Die Murmanbahn: Die Verkehrsanbindung eines kriegswichtigen Hafens und das Arbeitspotential der Kriegsgefangenen (1915 bis 1918),* Grunbach 2001.

———, *Kriegsgefangenschaft an der Ostfront 1914 bis 1918: Literaturbericht zu einem neuen Forschungsfeld,* Frankfurt 2005.

———, *Russland und seine österreichisch-ungarischen Kriegsgefangenen (1914–1918),* Remshalden 2003.

Nagler, Jörg, *Nationale Minoritäten im Krieg: "Feindliche Ausländer" und die amerikanische Heimatfront während des Ersten Weltkriegs,* Hamburg 2000.

Naour, Jean-Yves Le, *Claire Ferchaud—La Jeanne d'Arc de la Grande Guerre,* Paris 2006.

———, *The Living Unknown Soldier: A True Story of Grief and the Great War,* London 2005.

Narskij, Igor, "Kriegswirklichkeit und Kriegserfahrung russischer Soldaten an der russischen Westfront," in: Groß (ed.), *Die vergessene Front,* pp. 249–262.

Nasson, Bill, "Südafrika," in: Hirschfeld, Krumeich, and Renz (eds.), *Enzyklopädie Erster Weltkrieg,* pp. 913–914.

Nassua, Martin, *"Gemeinsame Kriegführung, gemeinsamer Friedensschluss": Das Zimmermann-Telegramm vom 13. Januar 1917 und der Eintritt der USA in den 1. Weltkrieg,* Frankfurt / M. 1992.

Naumann, Friedrich, "Demokratie und Kaisertum" (1900), in: idem, *Werke: Politische Schriften,* ed. by Theodor Schieder, vol. 2: *Schriften zur Verfassungspolitik,* Opladen 1964, pp. 1–351.

———, *Mitteleuropa,* Berlin 1915.

Nebelin, Manfred, *Ludendorff: Diktator im Ersten Weltkrieg,* Munich 2010.

Neck, Rudolf, *Arbeiterschaft und Staat im Ersten Weltkrieg 1914–1918, A. Quellen,* vol. 1: *Der Staat, 1. Teil: Vom Kriegsbeginn bis zum Prozeß Friedrich Adlers, August 1914–Mai 1917,* Vienna 1964.

———, *Arbeiterschaft und Staat im Ersten Weltkrieg. 1914–1918, A. Quellen,* vol. 1: *Der Staat, 2. Teil: Vom Juni 1917 bis zum Ende der Donaumonarchie im November 1918,* Vienna 1968.

——— (ed.), *Österreich im Jahre 1918: Berichte und Dokumente,* Vienna 1968.

Neilson, Keith, *Britain, Soviet Russia and the Collapse of the Versailles Order, 1919–1939,* Cambridge 2006.

———, *Strategy and Supply: The Anglo-Russian Alliance, 1914–17,* London 1984.

Nestor, Stelios, "Greece, Macedonia and the Convention of Neuilly (1919)," in: *Balkan Studies* 3 (1962), pp. 169–184.

Neugebauer, Karl-Volker, "Die Urkatastrophe des 20. Jahrhunderts. Der Erste Weltkrieg 1914 bis 1918," in: idem (ed.), *Grundkurs deutsche Militärgeschichte*, vol. 2: *Das Zeitalter der Weltkriege 1914 bis 1945. Völker in Waffen*, 2nd edn., Munich 2009, pp. 1–85.

Neumann, Michael, "Kommentar," in: *Thomas Mann, Große kommentierte Frankfurter Ausgabe*, vol. 5/2, Frankfurt 2002, pp. 127–410.

Neutatz, Dietmar, *Träume und Alpträume: Eine Geschichte Russlands im 20. Jahrhundert*, Munich 2013.

Neutatz, Dietmar, and Radauer, Lena, "Besetzt, interniert, deportiert: Der Erste Weltkrieg und die Zivilbevölkerung im östlichen Europa," in: Alfred Eisfeld, Guido Hausmann, and Dietmar Neutatz (eds.), *Besetzt, interniert, deportiert: Der Erste Weltkrieg und die deutsche, jüdische, polnische und ukrainische Zivilbevölkerung im östlichen Europa*, Essen 2013, pp. 9–26.

Nieden, Gesa zur, "Verdrängen durch Überspielen: Musik, Krieg und Kriegsbewältigung am Beispiel des einarmigen Pianisten und Mäzens Paul Wittgenstein," in: Müller and Zalfen (eds.), *Besatzungsmacht Musik*, pp. 255–278.

Nippa, Annegret, "Zu den Beduinen Nord-Arabiens," in: Fansa and Hoffmann (eds.), *Lawrence von Arabien*, pp. 77–86.

Nippel, Wilfried, "Krieg als Erscheinungsform der Feindschaft," in: Schmitt, *Der Begriff des Politischen*, pp. 61–70.

Nipperdey, Thomas, *Deutsche Geschichte 1866–1918*, vol. 2: *Machtstaat vor der Demokratie*, Munich 1992.

Nivet, Philippe, *La France occupée 1914–1918*, Paris 2011.

Noack, Christian, *Muslimischer Nationalismus im Russischen Reich: Nationsbildung und Nationalbewegung bei Tataren und Baschkiren 1861–1917*, Stuttgart 2000.

Northedge, Frederick S., and Wells, Audrey, *Britain and Soviet Communism: The Impact of a Revolution*, London 1982.

Nübel, Christoph, *Die Mobilisierung der Kriegsgesellschaft: Propaganda und Alltag im Ersten Weltkrieg in Münster*, Münster 2008.

Offer, Avner, "The Blockade of Germany and the Strategy of Starvation, 1914–1918: An Agency Perspective," in: Chickering and Förster (eds.), *Great War, Total War*, pp. 169–188.

———, *The First World War: An Agrarian Interpretation*, Oxford 1989.

Okey, Robin, *Taming Balkan Nationalism*, Oxford 2007.

Oliver, Lawrence J., "Deconstruction or Affirmative Action: The Literary-Political Debate over the 'Ethnic Question,'" in: *American Literary History* 3 (1991), pp. 792–808.

Omissi, David, *Air Power and Colonial Rule: The Royal Air Force 1919–1939*, Manchester 1990.

———, *Indian Voices of the Great War*, Basingstoke 1999.

Oncken, Hermann, *Deutschlands Weltkrieg und die Deutschamerikaner: Ein Gruß des Vaterlandes über den Ozean*, Stuttgart 1914.

Opfer-Klinger, Björn, "Ein unaufgearbeitetes Kapitel südosteuropäischer Nationalgeschichte: Bulgarische Kriegsgreuel 1912–1918," in: Hohrath and Neitzel (eds.), *Kriegsgreuel*, pp. 279–292.

———, *Im Schatten des Krieges: Besatzung oder Anschluss—Befreiung oder Unterdrückung? Eine komparative Untersuchung über die bulgarische Herrschaft in Vardar-Makedonien 1915–1918 und 1941–1944*, Münster 2005.

Orpen, William, *An Onlooker in France, 1917–1919*, London 1921.

Orr, Philip, "200 000 Volunteer Soldiers," in: John Horne (ed.), *Our War: Ireland and the Great War*, Dublin 2008, pp. 63–77.

Ortner, M. Christian, "Die Feldzüge gegen Serbien in den Jahren 1914 und 1915," in: Jürgen Angelow (ed.), *Der Erste Weltkrieg auf dem Balkan: Perspektiven der Forschung*, Berlin 2011, pp. 123–142.

Orzoff, Andrea, *Battle for the Castle: The Myth of Czechoslovakia in Europe, 1914–1948*, Oxford 2009.

Osterhammel, Jürgen, "Staat und Nation nach dem Ersten Weltkrieg," in: Rother (ed.), *Der Weltkrieg*, pp. 82–89.

———, *The Transformation of the World: A Global History of the Nineteenth Century*, orig. 2009, Princeton 2014.

Ouditt, Sharon, *Fighting Forces, Writing Women: Identity and Ideology in the First World War*, London 1994.

Ousby, Ian, *The Road to Verdun: France, Nationalism and the First World War*, Garden City 2002.

Overmans, Rüdiger, "Kriegsverluste," in: Hirschfeld, Krumeich, and Renz (eds.), *Enzyklopädie Erster Weltkrieg*, pp. 663–666.

Özcan, Gencer, "Der deutsche Einfluss auf die türkische Armee," in: Chiaria und Groß (eds.), *Am Rande Europas*, pp. 241–258.

Page, Melvin E. (ed.), *Africa and the First World War*, New York 1987.

———, *The Chiwaya War: Malawians and the First World War*, Boulder, Colo. 2000.

Paice, Edward, *Tip and Run: The Untold Tragedy of the Great War in Africa*, London 2007.

Pairault, François, *Images de Poilus. La Grande Guerre en cartes postales*, Paris 2002.

Palmer, Svetlana, and Wallis, Sarah (eds.), *Intimate Voices from the First World War*, New York 2003.

Panayi, Panikos, "Introduction," in: idem (ed.), *Minorities in Wartime: National and Racial Groupings in Europe, North America and Australia during the Two World Wars*, Oxford 1993, pp. 3–24.

Pantenius, Hans Jürgen, *Der Angriffsgedanke gegen Italien bei Conrad von Hötzendorf. Ein Beitrag zur Koalitionskriegsführung im Ersten Weltkrieg*, 2 vols., Cologne 1984.

Panter, Sarah, *Jüdische Erfahrungen und Loyalitätskonflikte im Ersten Weltkrieg*, Göttingen 2014.

Paquet, Alfons, "Rhein und Donau," in: idem, *Rom oder Moskau: Sieben Aufsätze*, Munich 1923, pp. 26–55.

Pastor, Peter, "Major Trends in Hungarian Foreign Policy from the Collapse of the Monarchy to the Peace Treaty of Trianon," in: *Hungarian Studies* 17 (2003), pp. 3–11.

Pearse, Pádraic H., "O'Donovan Rossa: Graveside Panegyric," in: *Collected Works of Pádraic H. Pearse: Political Writings and Speeches*, Dublin [1916], pp. 133–137.

Peattie, Mark R., *Nan'yō: The Rise and Fall of the Japanese in Micronesia, 1885–1945*, Honolulu 1988.

Pedroncini, Guy, *Les mutineries de 1917*, Paris 1967.

Pennell, Catriona, *A Kingdom United: Popular Responses to the Outbreak of the First World War in Britain and Ireland*, Oxford 2012.

Percin, Alexandre, "Le massacre de notre infanterie 1914–1918, Paris 1921," quoted in: Linnenkohl, *Vom Einzelschuss zur Feuerwalze*, p. 175.

Pesek, Michael, *Das Ende eines Kolonialreiches: Ostafrika im Ersten Weltkrieg*, Frankfurt 2010.

Pessler, Wilhelm, "Das historische Museum und der Weltkrieg," in: *Museumskunde* 11 (1915), pp. 68–75, 143–155; *Museumskunde* 12 (1916), pp. 91–104, 199–203; *Museumskunde* 13 (1917), pp. 52–82.

Pétain, Philippe, *La bataille de Verdun*, Paris 1930.

Petermann, Sandra: *Rituale machen Räume—Zum kollektiven Gedenken der Schlacht von Verdun und der Landung in der Normandie*, Mainz 2006.

Philippoff, Eva (ed.), *Die Doppelmonarchie Österreich-Ungarn: Ein politisches Lesebuch (1867–1918)*, Paris 2001.

Philips, Kathy J., *Manipulating Masculinity: War and Gender in Modern British and American Literature*, Basingstoke 2006.

Philpott, William, *Bloody Victory: The Sacrifice of the Somme and the Making of the Twentieth Century*, Boston 2009.

———, *Three Armies on the Somme: The First Battle of the Twentieth Century*, New York 2010.

Pipes, Richard, *The Russian Revolution, 1899–1919* (orig. 1990), London 1997.

Plaggenborg, Stefan, *Ordnung und Gewalt: Kemalismus—Faschismus—Sozialismus*, Munich 2012.

Plakans, Andrejs, *A Concise History of the Baltic States*, Cambridge 2011.

Plenge, Johann, *1789 und 1914: Die symbolischen Jahre in der Geschichte des politischen Geistes*, Berlin 1916.

Plessen, Marie-Louise von (ed.), *Idee Europa: Entwürfe zum "Ewigen Frieden": Ordnungen und Utopien für die Gestaltung Europas von der pax romana zur Europäischen Union. Eine Ausstellung als historische Topographie. Katalogbuch zur gleichnamigen Ausstellung des Deutschen Historischen Museums*, Berlin 2003.

Pohl, Manfred, "Von den Staatsbahnen zur Reichsbahn 1918–1924," in: Gall and idem (eds.), *Die Eisenbahn in Deutschland*, pp. 71–108.

Pöhlmann, Markus, "Kriegserklärungen," in: Hirschfeld, Krumeich, and Renz (eds.), *Enzyklopädie Erster Weltkrieg*, pp. 637–638.

———, "Stellvertretendes Generalkommando," in: Hirschfeld, Krumeich, and Renz (eds.), *Enzyklopädie Erster Weltkrieg*, pp. 525–526.

Poincaré, Raymond, *Au service de la France, neuf années de souvenirs*, vol. 8, Paris 1930.

Pollard, John Francis, *The Unknown Pope: Benedict XV (1914–1922) and the Pursuit of Peace*, London 1999.

Pöppinghege, Rainer (ed.), *Tiere im Krieg: Von der Antike bis zur Gegenwart*, Paderborn 2009.

Pöppinghege, Rainer, and Proctor, Tammy, "Außerordentlicher Bedarf für das Feldheer—Brieftauben im Ersten Weltkrieg," in: Pöppinghege (ed.), *Tiere im Krieg*, pp. 103–117.

Porch, Douglas, *The March to the Marne: The French Army 1871–1914*, Cambridge 1981.

Potter, Jane, *Boys in Khaki, Girls in Print: Women's Literary Responses to the Great War 1914–1918*, Oxford 2008.

Pourtalès, Friedrich Karl von, *Am Scheideweg zwischen Krieg und Frieden: Meine letzten Verhandlungen in Petersburg Ende Juli 1914*, Berlin 1919.

Prete, Roy A., "Joffre and the Origins of the Somme: A Study on Allied Military Planning," in: *Journal of Military History* 73 (2009), pp. 417–448.

Prior, Robin, *Churchill's "World Crisis" as History*, London 1983.

———, *Gallipoli: The End of the Myth*, New Haven 2009.

Prior, Robin, and Wilson, Trevor, *Command on the Western Front: The Military Career of Sir Henry Rawlinson*, Oxford 1992.

———, "Gallipoli," in: Hirschfeld, Krumeich, and Renz (eds.), *Enzyklopädie Erster Weltkrieg*, pp. 517–518.

———, *The Somme*, New Haven 2005.

Procacci, Giovanna, "Aspetti della mentalità collettiva durante la Guerra. L'Italia dopo Caporetto," in: Diego Leoni and Camillo Zadra (eds.), *La grande guerra: Memoria, Esperienza, Immagini*, Bologna 1986, pp. 261–290.

———, "Popular Protest and Labour Conflict in Italy, 1915–18," in: *Social History* 14 (1989), pp. 31–58.

———, *Soldati e prigionieri italiani nella grande guerra*, Rome 1993.

"Proclamation of the Irish Republic. The Provisional Government of the Irish Republic to the People of Ireland, Dublin, 24 April 1916," in: MacArthur (ed.), *The Penguin Book of Twentieth Century Speeches*, pp. 50–52.

Pross, Harry (ed.), *Die Zerstörung der deutschen Politik: Dokumente 1871–1933*, Frankfurt 1959.

Prost, Antoine, "Verdun," in: Pierre Nora (ed.), *Erinnerungsorte Frankreichs*, Munich 2005, pp. 253–278.

———, "War Memorials of the Great War: Monuments to the Fallen," in: idem, *Republican Identities in War and Peace: Representations of France in the Nineteenth and Twentieth Centuries*, Oxford 2002, pp. 11–43.

Prost, Antoine, and Winter, Jay, *Penser la Grande Guerre: Un essai d'historiographie*, Paris 2004.

Prusin, Alexander Victor, *Nationalizing a Borderland : War, Ethnicity, and Anti-Jewish Violence in East Galicia, 1914–1920*, Tuscaloosa 2005.

Pugsley, Christopher, *Gallipoli: The New Zealand Story*, Auckland 1984.

———, "Stories of Anzac," in: Jenny Macleod (ed.), *Gallipoli: Making History*, London 2004, pp. 44–58.

Pulzer, Peter, "The First World War," in Michael A. Meyer (ed.), *German-Jewish History in Modern Times*, vol. 3: *Integration in Dispute 1871–1918*, New York 1997, pp. 360–384.

———, "Vorbild, Rivale und Unmensch. Das sich wandelnde Deutschlandbild in England 1815–1945," in: Süssmuth (ed.), *Deutschlandbilder in Dänemark und England, in Frankreich und den Niederlanden*, pp. 235–250.

Pust, Ingomar, *Die steinerne Front : Vom Isonzo zur Piave. Auf den Spuren des Gebirgskrieges in den Julischen Alpen*, 3rd edn., Graz 2009.

Pyta, Wolfram, *Hindenburg: Herrschaft zwischen Hohenzollern und Hitler,* Munich 2007.

Quaritsch, Heinz (ed.), *Complexio Oppositorum: Über Carl Schmitt,* Berlin 1988.

Quinn, Frederick, "The Impact of the First World War and Its Aftermath on the Beti of Cameroun," in: Page (ed.), *Africa and the First World War,* pp. 171–185.

Rabinowitch, Alexander, *The Bolsheviks in Power: The First Year of Soviet Rule in Petrograd,* Bloomington, Ind. 2007.

Radax, Felix, "Giftgas und das 'Wunder von Karfreit,'" in: Rauchensteiner (ed.), *Waffentreue,* pp. 49–63.

Radkau, Joachim, *Das Zeitalter der Nervosität: Deutschland zwischen Bismarck und Hitler,* Munich 1998.

Rahn, Werner, "Die Seeschlacht vor dem Skagerrak: Verlauf und Analyse aus deutscher Perspektive," in: Epkenhans, Hillmann, and Nägler (eds.), *Skagerrakschlacht,* pp. 139–196.

Raithel, Thomas, *Das "Wunder" der inneren Einheit: Studien zur deutschen und französischen Öffentlichkeit bei Beginn des Ersten Weltkrieges,* Bonn 1996.

Raleigh, Walter, *England at War,* Oxford 1918.

Ramsay, David, *Lusitania: Saga and Myth,* London 2001.

Ranke, Leopold von, *Serbien und die Türkei im neunzehnten Jahrhundert,* Leipzig 1879.

Raphael, Lutz, *Imperiale Gewalt und mobilisierte Nation, Europa 1914–1945,* Munich 2011.

———, *Recht und Ordnung: Herrschaft durch Verwaltung im 19. Jahrhundert,* Frankfurt 2000.

Rathenau, Walther, "Deutschlands Rohstoffversorgung: Vortrag, gehalten in der 'Deutschen Gesellschaft 1914' am 20. Dezember 1915," in: idem, *Gesammelte Schriften,* vol. 5: *Wirtschaft, Staat und Gesellschaft,* Berlin 1925, pp. 24–58.

———, *Tagebuch 1907–1922,* ed. by Hartmut P. von Strandmann, Düsseldorf 1967.

———, *Walther Rathenau: Industrialist, Banker, Intellectual, and Politician; Notes and Diaries 1907–1922,* ed. by Hartmut P. von Strandmann, rev. edn., Oxford 1987.

Raths, Ralf, "Die Überlegenheit der Verteidigung: Die Entwicklung der deutschen Defensivkonzepte im Grabenkrieg," in: Beckmann and Jäger (eds.), *Handbuch Kriegstheorien,* pp. 396–404.

———, *Vom Massensturm zur Stoßtrupptaktik: Die deutsche Landkriegstaktik im Spiegel von Dienstvorschriften und Publizistik 1906 bis 1918,* Freiburg 2009.

Rauchensteiner, Manfried, *Der Erste Weltkrieg und das Ende der Habsburgermonarchie 1914–1918,* Vienna 2013.

———, *Der Tod des Doppeladlers: Österreich-Ungarn und der Erste Weltkrieg,* Graz 1993.

———, "Österreich-Ungarn," in: Hirschfeld, Krumeich, and Renz (eds.), *Enzyklopädie Erster Weltkrieg,* pp. 64–86.

———, *Österreich-Ungarn und der Erste Weltkrieg: Bildband,* Graz 1998.

——— (ed.), *Waffentreue: Die 12. Isonzoschlacht 1917, Begleitband zur Ausstellung des Österreichischen Staatsarchivs,* Vienna 2007.

Raynal, Sylvain Eugène, *Le Drame du Fort de Vaux,* Paris 1933.

Rechter, David, *The Jews of Vienna and the First World War,* London 2001.

Reclams Universum, *Moderne illustrierte Wochenschrift 34 (1918).*

Redlich, Josef, *Das österreichische Staats- und Reichsproblem,* vol. 1, Leipzig 1920.

————, *Das politische Tagebuch Josef Redlichs,* vol. 2: *1915–1919,* ed. by Fritz Fellner, Graz 1954.

Redmond, John, *A Visit to the Front,* n.p. 1915.

Rees, H. Louis, *The Czechs during World War I: The Path to Independence,* New York 1992.

Regierte der Kaiser? Kriegstagebücher, Aufzeichnungen und Briefe des Chefs des Marine-Kabinetts Admiral Georg Alexander von Müller, 1914–1918, Göttingen 1959.

Reimann, Aribert, *Der große Krieg der Sprachen: Untersuchungen zur historischen Semantik in Deutschland und England zur Zeit des Ersten Weltkriegs,* Essen 2000.

————, "Union of Democratic Control," in: Hirschfeld, Krumeich, and Renz (eds.), *Enzyklopädie Erster Weltkrieg,* pp. 937–938.

Reimann, Brigitte, *Der Erste Weltkrieg: Wahrheit und Lüge in Bildern und Texten,* 3rd ed., Munich 2005.

Reinecke, Christiane, *Grenzen der Freizügigkeit: Migrationskontrolle in Großbritannien und Deutschland, 1880–1930,* Munich 2010.

Reinhard, Wolfgang, *Geschichte der Staatsgewalt: Eine vergleichende Verfassungsgeschichte Europas von den Anfängen bis zur Gegenwart,* Munich 1999.

Reznick, Jeffrey S., *Healing the Nation: Soldiers and the Culture of Caregiving in Britain during the Great War,* Manchester 2004.

Rezun, Miron (ed.), *Nationalism and the Breakup of an Empire: Russia and Its Periphery,* Westport, Conn. 1992.

Rhys, Ernest (ed.), *The Old Country,* London 1917.

Ribhegge, Wilhelm, *Frieden für Europa: Die Politik der deutschen Reichstagsmehrheit 1917 / 18,* Berlin 1988.

Ridel, Charles, *Les embusqués,* Paris 2007.

Riederer, Günter, "Einleitung : Ein Krieg wird besichtigt—Die Wahrnehmung des Ersten Weltkriegs im Tagebuch von Harry Graf Kessler (1914–1916)," in: Kessler, *Tagebuch,* vol. 5, pp. 9–71.

Rilke, Rainer Maria, *Wartime Letters of Rainer Maria Rilke, 1914–1921,* New York 1964.

Rindfleisch, Alexander, *Zwischen Kriegserwartung und Verrechtlichung: Die internationalen Debatten über das Seekriegsrecht 1904–1914,* Norderstedt 2012.

Rink, Martin, "Lawrence und der Partisanenkrieg. Eine Konzeption 'neuer' Kriege?" in: Fansa and Hoffmann (eds.), *Lawrence von Arabien,* pp. 163–172.

Ritschl, Albrecht, "The Pity of Peace: Germany's Economy at War, 1914–1918 and Beyond," in: Broadberry and Harrison, *The Economics of World War I,* pp. 41–76.

Ritter, Gerhard, *The Schlieffen Plan: Critique of a Myth,* London 1958.

Ritter, Henning, *Notizhefte,* 4th edn., Berlin 2010.

Robbins, Keith, *The Abolition of War: The "Peace Movement" in Britain, 1914–1919,* Cardiff 1976.

Robbins, Simon, *British Generalship during the Great War: The Military Career of Sir Henry Horne (1861–1929),* Farnham 2010.

Robert, Jean-Louis, and Winter, Jay (eds.), *Capital Cities at War: Paris, London, Berlin 1914–1919,* Cambridge 1997.

Robertson, John, *Anzac and Empire: The Tragedy and Glory of Gallipoli,* London 1990.

Robespierre, Maximilien, second speech against the war, January 2, 1792, in: *Oeuvres de Maximilien Robespierre*, vol. 7, pp. 74–92, Paris 1912–1967.

Rochester, Stuart, *American Liberal Disillusionment in the Wake of World War I*, University Park, Penn. 1977.

Roerkohl, Anne, *Hungerblockade und Heimatfront: Die kommunale Lebensmittelversorgung in Westfalen während des Ersten Weltkriegs*, Stuttgart 1991.

Rohkrämer, Thomas, *Der Militarismus der "kleinen Leute": Die Kriegervereine im Deutschen Kaiserreich 1871–1914*, Munich 1990.

Röhl, John C. G., "An der Schwelle zum Weltkrieg: Eine Dokumentation über den 'Kriegsrat' vom 8. Dezember 1912," in: *Militärgeschichtliche Mitteilungen* 1 (1977), pp. 77–134.

———, "Vorsätzlicher Krieg? Die Ziele der deutschen Politik im Juli 1914," in: Michalka (ed.), *Der Erste Weltkrieg*, pp. 193–215.

———, *Wilhelm II.: Der Weg in den Abgrund 1900–1941*, 2nd edn., Munich 2009.

Rohlack, Momme, *Kriegsgesellschaften (1914–1918): Arten, Rechtsformen und Funktionen in der Kriegswirtschaft des Ersten Weltkriegs*, Frankfurt 2001.

Rohwer, Jürgen, "U-Boot-Krieg," in: Hirschfeld, Krumeich, and Renz (eds.), *Enzyklopädie Erster Weltkrieg*, pp. 931–934.

Rolland, Romain, *Au-dessus de la melée : Lettre ouverte du 15 Septembre 1914*, Paris 1914.

———, *Journal des années de guerre, 1914–1919*, Paris 1952.

Romsics, Ignác, *The Dismantling of Historic Hungary: The Peace Treaty of Trianon 1920*, Boulder 2002.

Roper, Michael, *The Secret Battle: Emotional Survival in the Great War*, Manchester 2009.

Rosas, Allan, *The Legal Status of Prisoners of War: A Study in International Humanitarian Law Applicable in Armed Conflicts*, Helsinki 1976.

Rose, Andreas, *Between Empire and Continent: British Foreign Policy before the First World War*, London 2017.

———, *Zwischen Empire und Kontinent: Britische Außenpolitik vor dem Ersten Weltkrieg*, Munich 2011.

Rosenberg, Emily S., *World War I and the Growth of United States Predominance in Latin America*, New York 1987.

Rosenberg, William G., *Liberals in the Russian Revolution: The Constitutional Democratic Party, 1917–1921*, Princeton 1974.

———, "Paramilitary Violence in Russia's Civil Wars, 1918–1920," in: Gerwarth and Horne (eds.), *War in Peace*, pp. 21–39.

Rossini, Daniela, *Woodrow Wilson and the American Myth in Italy: Culture, Diplomacy, and War Propaganda*, Cambridge, Mass. 2008.

Rostovcev, Evgenij A., "The Capital University in a Time of War: Saint Petersburg / Petrograd 1914–1917," in: Trude Maurer (ed.), *Kollegen—Kommilitonen—Kämpfer. Europäische Universitäten im Ersten Weltkrieg*, Stuttgart 2006, pp. 177–188.

Roth, Regina, *Staat und Wirtschaft im Ersten Weltkrieg. Kriegsgesellschaften als kriegswirtschaftliche Steuerungsinstrumente*, Berlin 1997.

Rothenberg, Gunther Erich, "The Austro-Hungarian Campaign against Serbia in 1914," in: *Journal of Military History* 53 (1989), pp. 127–146.

Rother, Rainer (ed.), *Der Weltkrieg 1914–1918: Ereignis und Erinnerung,* Berlin 2004.

Rozenblit, Marsha, *Reconstructing National Identity: The Jews of Habsburg Austria during World War I,* Oxford 2001.

Rubin, Gerry, *War, Law and Labour: The Munitions Acts, State Regulation and the Unions, 1915–1921,* Oxford 1987.

Rudenno, Victor, *Gallipoli: Attack From the Sea,* New Haven 2008.

Rüger, Jan, *The Great Naval Game: Britain and Germany in the Age of Empire,* Cambridge 2007.

Rumpler, Helmut, *Das Völkermanifest Kaiser Karls vom 16. Oktober 1918: Letzter Versuch zur Rettung des Habsburgerreiches,* Munich 1966.

Ruotsila, Markku, *British and American Anticommunism before the Cold War,* London 2001.

Russell, Bertrand, *Autobiography,* London 1975.

Saatmann, Inge, *Parlament, Rüstung und Armee in Frankreich 1914 / 18,* Düsseldorf 1978.

Sabrow, Martin, "Walther Rathenau," in: Hirschfeld, Krumeich, and Renz (eds.), *Enzyklopädie Erster Weltkrieg,* pp. 786–787.

Saini, Krishan G., "The Economic Aspects of India's Participation in the First World War," in: Ellinwood and Pradhan (eds.), *India and World War I,* pp. 141–176.

Salewski, Michael, "Seekrieg," in: Hirschfeld, Krumeich, and Renz (eds.), *Enzyklopädie Erster Weltkrieg,* pp. 828–832.

Salvatore, Gaston, "D'Annunzio," in: D'Annunzio, *Rede von der Tribüne des Kapitols,* pp. 17–41.

Salvemini, Gaetano, *Opere,* vol. 4, Milan 1970.

Salzmann, Jean-Pierre, "La bataille de Verdun, un but touristique: Les guides Michelins des champs de bataille de la guerre de 1914–1918," in: Cochet (ed.), *1916–2006—Verdun sous le regard du monde,* pp. 327–349.

Samson, Anne, *Britain, South Africa and the East Africa Campaign, 1914–1918: The Union Comes of Age,* London 2006.

———, *World War I in Africa: The Forgotten Conflict among the European Powers,* London 2013.

Samuels, Martin, *Command or Control? Command, Training and Tactics in the German and British Armies, 1888–1918,* London 1995.

———, *Doctrine and Dogma: German and British Infantry Tactics in the First World War,* London 1992.

Sanborn, Joshua A., *Drafting the Russian Nation: Military Conscription, Total War, and Mass Politics, 1905–1925,* DeKalb, Ill. 2003.

———, "The Mobilization of 1914 and the Question of the Russian Nation: A Reexamination," in: *Slavic Review* 59 (2000), pp. 267–289.

Sanders, Michael, and Taylor, Philip M., *British Propaganda during the First World War, 1914–1918,* London 1982.

Sassoon, Siegfried, *Diaries 1915–1918,* ed. by R. Hart-Davis, London 1983.

Satia, Priya, *Spies in Arabia: The Great War and the Cultural Foundations of Britain's Covert Empire in the Middle East,* Oxford 2008.

Sattler, Alfred, *Die deutsche Kavallerie im Ersten Weltkrieg,* 2nd edn., Norderstedt 2004.

Saunders, Nicholas J., *Trench Art: Materialities and Memories of War,* Oxford 2003.

Scates, Bruce, *Return to Gallipoli: Walking the Battlefields of the Great War,* Cambridge 2006.

Schaepdrijver, Sophie de, *La Belgique et la Première Guerre Mondiale,* Brussels 2004.

Schaffer, Ronald, *America in the Great War: The Rise of the War Welfare State*, New York 1991.

Schaumann, Walther, *Schauplätze des Gebirgskrieges, 1915–1917*, 3 vols., Cortina d'Ampezzo 1972–1985.

Scheer, Reinhard, *Germany's High Seas Fleet in the World War*, London 1920.

Scheer, Tamara, *Zwischen Front und Heimat: Österreich-Ungarns Militärverwaltungen im Ersten Weltkrieg*, Frankfurt 2009.

Scheffl, Barbara, "Die Kriegsgefangenen," in: Rauchensteiner (ed.), *Waffentreue*, pp. 91–102.

Scheler, Max, *Der Genius des Krieges und der deutsche Krieg*, Leipzig 1915.

Schenk, Frithjof Benjamin, "Mastering Imperial Space?—The Ambivalent Impact of Railway-Building in Tsarist Russia," in: Leonhard and Hirschhausen (eds.), *Comparing Empires*, pp. 60–77.

———, "Tannenberg / Grunwald," in: François and Schulze (eds.), *Deutsche Erinnerungsorte*, vol. 1, pp. 438–454.

Schieder, Theodor, "Typologie und Erscheinungsformen des Nationalstaats in Europa," in: *Historische Zeitschrift* 202 (1966), pp. 58–81.

Schilling, Heinz, "Krieg und Frieden in der werdenden Neuzeit—Europa zwischen Staaten-bellizität, Glaubenskrieg und Friedensbereitschaft," in: idem and Klaus Bussmann (eds.), *1648: Krieg und Frieden in Europa. Politik, Religion, Recht und Gesellschaft*, Munich 1998, pp. 13–22.

Schindler, John R., *Isonzo: The Forgotten Sacrifice of the Great War*, Westport, Conn. 2000.

Schivelbusch, Wolfgang, *Die Bibliothek von Löwen: Eine Episode aus der Zeit der Weltkriege*, Munich 1988.

Schlieffen, Alfred von, "Million-Man Armies," in: *Alfred von Schlieffen's Military Writings*, ed. by Robert Foley, New York 2003, pp. 206–207.

———, "War Today," in: *Alfred von Schlieffen's Military Writings*, ed. by Robert Foley, New York 2003, pp. 194–205.

Schlürmann, Jan, "Vom Zarenadler zum Sowjetstern: Die Lettischen Schützenbataillone und Regimenter in der Kaiserlich Russischen Armee (1915–1917)," in: *Chakoten. Dansk Militaerhistorisk Selskab* 61 (2006), pp. 19–24.

Schmid, Johann, "Die Überlegenheit des Angriffs: Der Angriff aus Schwäche. Ein Phänomen im Widerspruch zur Clausewitz'schen Theorie von der 'größeren Stärke der Verteidigung,' untersucht am Beispiel der zwölften Isonzoschlacht 1917," in: Beckmann and Jäger (eds.), *Handbuch Kriegstheorien*, pp. 380–395.

Schmidt, Stefan, *Frankreichs Außenpolitik in der Julikrise 1914: Ein Beitrag zur Geschichte des Ausbruchs des Ersten Weltkrieges*, Munich 2009.

Schmitt, Carl, *The Concept of the Political* (1927), expanded edn., Chicago 2007.

———, *Der Begriff des Politischen: Ein kooperativer Kommentar*, ed. by Reinhard Mehring, Berlin 2003.

———, *The Nomos of the Earth in the International Law of Jus Publicum Europaeum* (1950), New York 2003.

———, "The Turn to the Discriminating Concept of War" (1938), in: idem, *Writings on War*, pp. 30–74, Cambridge, 2011.

Schnell, Felix, "Ukraine 1918: Besatzer und Besetzte im Gewaltraum," in: Baberowski and Metzler (eds.), *Gewalträume*, pp. 135–168.

Schnitzler, Arthur, *Tagebuch*, vol. 5: *1913–1916*, Vienna 1983.

Schöller, Peter, *Der Fall Löwen und das Weißbuch: Eine kritische Untersuchung der deutschen Dokumentation über die Vorgänge in Löwen vom 25. bis 28. August 1914*, Cologne 1958.

Schöllgen, Gregor, *Imperialismus und Gleichgewicht: Deutschland, England und die orientalische Frage 1871–1914*, Munich 1984.

Schramm, Gottfried, "Militarisierung und Demokratisierung: Typen der Massenintegration im Ersten Weltkrieg," in: *Francia* 3 (1975), pp. 476–497.

———, "Minderheiten gegen den Krieg, Motive und Kampfformen 1914–18 am Beispiel Großbritanniens und seines Empires," in: *Geschichte und Gesellschaft* 6 (1980), pp. 164–188.

Schramm, Martin, "British Journalism in the Great War," in: Frank Bösch and Dominik Geppert (eds.), *Journalists as Political Actors: Transfer and Interaction between Britain and Germany since the Late 19th Century*, Augsburg 2008, pp. 56–73.

———, *Das Deutschlandbild der britischen Presse 1912–1919*, Berlin 2007.

Schremmer, Eckart, *Steuern und Staatsfinanzen während der Industrialisierung Europas: England, Frankreich, Preußen und das Deutsche Reich 1800–1914*, Berlin 1994.

Schroeder, Paul, "The Transformation of European Politics," in: Wolfram Pyta (ed.), *Das europäische Mächtekonzert. Friedens- und Sicherheitspolitik vom Wiener Kongress 1815 bis zum Krimkrieg 1853*, Cologne 2009, pp. 25–40.

Schröder, Rudolf A., "An die deutschen Krieger," in: "Der Krieg—ein Flugblatt mit Beiträgen von Elsa Asenijeff u. a.," quoted in: Riederer, "Einleitung: Ein Krieg wird besichtigt," p. 42.

Schulin, Ernst, "Der Erste Weltkrieg und das Ende des alten Europa," in: *Funkkolleg Jahrhundertwende, Studienbrief 6*, Weinheim 1989.

Schüller, Tonia, "Die Entstehungsgeschichte der Arabischen Revolte," in: Fansa and Hoffmann (eds.), *Lawrence von Arabien*, pp. 155–162.

Schulte, Bernd F., *Die Verfälschung der Riezler-Tagebücher: Ein Beitrag zur Wissenschaftsgeschichte der 50iger und 60iger Jahre*, Frankfurt 1985.

Schulze, Hagen, *States, Nations, Nationalism: From the Middle Ages to the Present*, Malden, Mass. 1996.

Schulze, Max-Stephan, "Austria-Hungary's Economy in World War I," in: Broadberry and Harrison (eds.), *The Economics of World War I*, pp. 77–111.

Schulze Wessel, Martin, "Loyalität als geschichtlicher Grundbegriff und Forschungskonzept: Zur Einleitung," in: idem (ed.), *Loyalitäten in der Tschechoslowakischen Republik*, pp. 1–22.

——— (ed.), *Loyalitäten in der Tschechoslowakischen Republik 1918–1938: Politische, nationale und kulturelle Zugehörigkeiten*, Munich 2004.

Schumann, Dirk, and Wirsching, Andreas (eds.), *Violence and Society after the First World War*, Munich 2003.

Schumann, Willy, "'Deutschland, Deutschland über alles' und 'Der Lindenbaum.' Betrachtungen zur Schlußszene von Thomas Manns *Der Zauberberg*," in: *German Studies Review* 9 (1986), pp. 29–44.

Schuster, Frank M., *Zwischen allen Fronten: Osteuropäische Juden während des Ersten Weltkrieges, 1914–1919*, Cologne 2004.

Schwab, Gustav, *Sagen des klassischen Altertums*, ed. by Ernst Beutler, 3 vols., (orig. Leipzig 1909), Stuttgart 1956.

Schwabe, Klaus, "Woodrow Wilson 1913–1921: Kreuzzug für die Demokratie," in: Jürgen Heideking and Christof Mauch (eds.), *Die amerikanischen Präsidenten. 42 historische Portraits von George Washington bis George W. Bush,* 3rd edn., Munich 2002, pp. 278–290.

———, *Woodrow Wilson, Revolutionary Germany, and Peacemaking, 1918–1919: Missionary Diplomacy and the Realities of Power,* Chapel Hill 1985.

Schwarte, Max (ed.), *Die Technik im Weltkriege*, Berlin 1920.

Schwartz, Michael, "Imperiale Verflechtung und ethnische Säuberung," in: Peter Hoeres, Armin Owzar, and Christina Schröer (eds.), *Herrschaftsverlust und Machtverfall*, Munich 2013, pp. 273–291.

Schwarz, Hans-Peter, "Fragen an das 20. Jahrhundert," in: *Vierteljahrshefte für Zeitgeschichte* 48 (2000), pp. 1–36.

Schwarzmüller, Theo, *Zwischen Kaiser und "Führer": Generalfeldmarschall August von Mackensen. Eine politische Biographie*, Paderborn 1995.

Schweder, Paul, *Im kaiserlichen Hauptquartier: Deutsche Kriegsbriefe*, 2 vols., Leipzig 1915.

Schwertfeger, Bernhard, *Das Weltkriegsende. Gedanken über die deutsche Kriegführung 1918*, Potsdam 1937.

Schwilk, Heimo, *Hermann Hesse. Das Leben des Glasperlenspielers*, Munich 2012.

See, Klaus von, *Die Ideen von 1789 und die Ideen von 1914: Völkisches Denken in Deutschland zwischen Französischer Revolution und Erstem Weltkrieg*, Frankfurt 1975.

Segesser, Daniel Marc, *Empire und Totaler Krieg: Australien 1905–1918*, Paderborn 2002.

———, *Recht statt Rache oder Rache durch Recht? Die Ahndung von Kriegsverbrechen in der internationalen wissenschaftlichen Debatte 1872–1945*, Paderborn 2010.

Seligman, Adam B., *The Problem of Trust*, Princeton 2000.

Seligmann, Matthew S., *The Royal Navy and the German Threat, 1901–1914: Admiralty Plans to Protect British Trade in a War against Germany*, Oxford 2012.

Sellin, Volker, *Gewalt und Legitimität: Die europäische Monarchie im Zeitalter der Revolutionen*, Munich 2011.

———, "Heute ist die Revolution monarchisch: Legitimität und Legitimierungspolitik im Zeitalter des Wiener Kongresses," in: *Quellen und Forschungen aus italienischen Archiven und Bibliotheken* 76 (1996), pp. 335–361.

Sembat, Marcel, *Faites un Roi sinon Faites la Paix*, 4th edn., Paris 1911.

Service, Robert, *Lenin: A Biography*, London 2000.

Shapiro, Herbert, "Racism and Empire: A Perspective on a New Era of American History," in: Norbert Finzsch and Dietmar Schirmer (eds.), *Identity and Intolerance: Nationalism, Racism, and Xenophobia in Germany and the United States*, Cambridge 1998, pp. 155–173.

Sharp, Alan, *David Lloyd George: Great Britain*, London 2008.

——— (ed.), *The Versailles Settlement: Peacemaking after the First World War, 1919–1923,* 2nd edn., New York 2008.

Sheehan, James J., "The Problem of Sovereignty in European History, American Historical Society Presidential Address 2005," in: *American Historical Review* 111 (2006), pp. 1–15.

———, *Where Have All the Soldiers Gone? The Transformation of Modern Europe*, New York 2008.

Sheldon, Jack, *The German Army at Cambrai*, Barnsley 2009.

Shephard, Ben, *A War of Nerves: Soldiers and Psychiatrists in the Twentieth Century*, Cambridge, Mass. 2001.

Shimazu, Naoko, *Japan, Race and Equality: The Racial Equality Proposal of 1919*, London 1998.

Showalter, Dennis E., *Railroads and Rifles: Soldiers, Technology, and the Unification of Germany*, Hamden 1997.

———, *Tannenberg: Clash of Empires*, Hamden 1991.

Shukman, Harold, *War or Revolution: Russian Jews and Conscription in Britain, 1917*, London 2006.

Sieferle, Rolf Peter, "Der deutsch-englische Gegensatz und die 'Ideen von 1914,'" in: Gottfried Niedhart (ed.), *Das kontinentale Europa und die britischen Inseln: Wahrnehmungsmuster und Wechselwirkungen seit der Antike*, Mannheim 1993, pp. 139–160.

Sieg, Ulrich, *Geist und Gewalt: Deutsche Philosophen zwischen Kaiserreich und Nationalsozialismus*, Munich 2013.

———, *Jüdische Intellektuelle im Ersten Weltkrieg: Kriegserfahrungen, weltanschauliche Debatten und kulturelle Neuentwürfe*, Berlin 2002.

Siegel, Mona L., *The Moral Disarmament of France: Education, Pacifism, and Patriotism, 1914–1940*, Cambridge 2004.

Simkins, Peter, *Kitchener's Army: The Raising of the New Armies, 1914–16*, Manchester 1988.

———, "Somme," in: Hirschfeld, Krumeich, and Renz (eds.), *Enzyklopädie Erster Weltkrieg*, pp. 851–855.

Simmel, Georg, "Europa und Amerika. Eine weltgeschichtliche Betrachtung (4. Juli 1915)," in: idem, *Gesamtausgabe*, vol. 13 / II, pp. 138–142.

———, "Europe and America in World History," in *European Journal of Social Theory* 8/1, pp. 63–72.

———, "Geld und Nahrung (28. März 1915)," in: idem, *Gesamtausgabe*, vol. 13 / II, pp. 117–122.

———, *Gesamtausgabe*, ed. by Otthein Rammstedt, vol. 13 / II: *Aufsätze und Abhandlungen 1909–1918*, ed. by Klaus Latzel, Frankfurt 2000.

Singha, Radhika, "Front Lines and Status Lines: Seoys and 'Menial' in the Great War 1916–1920," in: Ravi Ahuja, Katrin Bromber, Dyala Hamzah, Katharina Lange, and Heike Liebau (eds.), *The World in World Wars: Experiences, Perceptions and Perspectives from Africa and Asia*, Leiden 2010, pp. 55–106.

Smith, C. Calvin, "The Houston Riot of 1917, Revisited," in: *Houston Review* 13 (1991), pp. 85–95.

Smith, Leonard V., *Between Mutiny and Obedience: The Case of the French Fifth Infantry Division during World War I*, Princeton 1994.

———, *The Embattled Self: French Soldiers' Testimonies of the Great War*, Ithaca 2007.

———, "France," in: Horne (ed.), *A Companion to World War I*, pp. 418–431.

———, "The French High Command and the Mutinies of Spring 1917," in: Cecil and Liddle (eds.), *Facing Armageddon*, pp. 79–92.

———, "Paul Fussell's *The Great War and Modern Memory*: Twenty-Five Years Later," in: *History and Theory* 40 (2001), pp. 241–260.

Smith, Richard, "'Heaven grant you strength to fight the battle for your race': Nationalism, Pan-Africanism and the First World War in Jamaican Memory," in: Das (ed.), *Race, Empire and First World War Writing*, pp. 265–282.

———, *Jamaican Volunteers in the First World War: Race, Masculinity and the Development of National Consciousness*, Manchester 2004.

Smither, Roger, "'A Wonderful Idea of the Fighting': The Question of Fakes in 'The Battle of the Somme,'" in: *Historical Journal of Film, Radio and Television* 13 (1993), pp. 149–168.

Smithers, Alan Jack, *Cambrai: The First Great Tank Battle*, London 1992.

Smythe, Donald, *Pershing: General of the Armies*, Bloomington / Ind. 1986.

Snyder, Jack, *The Ideology of the Offensive: Military Decision Making and the Disasters of 1914*, Ithaca 1984.

Snyder, Timothy, *Bloodlands: Europa between Hitler and Stalin*, New York 2010.

Sokol, Hans Hugo, *Österreich-Ungarns Seekrieg 1914–1918*, Vienna 1933.

Sollors, Werner, "Konstruktionsversuche nationaler und ethnischer Identität in der amerikanischen Literatur," in: Giesen (ed.), *Nationale und kulturelle Identität*, pp. 537–570.

Somakian, Manoug J., *Empires in Conflict: Armenia and the Great Powers, 1895–1920*, London 1995.

Sombart, Werner, *Händler und Helden: Patriotische Besinnungen*, Munich 1915.

Sondhaus, Lawrence, "Austro-Hungarian Naval Mutinies of World War I," in: Jane Hathaway (ed.), *Rebellion, Repression, Reinvention: Mutiny in Comparative Perspective*, Westport, Conn. 2001, pp. 195–212.

———, *Franz Conrad von Hötzendorf: Architect of the Apocalypse*, Boston 2000.

———, *In the Service of the Emperor: Italians in the Austrian Armed Forces 1814–1918*, New York 1990.

———, *World War One: The Global Revolution*, Cambridge 2011.

Sorlin, Pierre, "Film and the War," in: Horne (ed.), *A Companion to World War I*, pp. 353–367.

Sösemann, Bernd (ed.), *Theodor Wolff, der Chronist. Krieg, Revolution und Frieden im Tagebuch, 1914–1919*, Düsseldorf 1997.

Spencer, Herbert, "The Man versus the State" (1884), in: idem, *Political Writings*, ed. by John Offer, Cambridge 1994, pp. 61–175.

Spengler, Oswald, *Decline of the West*, New York 1927.

———, *Der Untergang des Abendlandes: Umrisse einer Morphologie der Weltgeschichte* (1918), Munich 1923.

Spies, Werner, "Das Ende der Darstellbarkeit," in: *Frankfurter Allgemeine Sonntagszeitung*, August 19, 1912.

Spilker, Rolf, and Ulrich, Bernd (eds.), *Der Tod als Maschinist: Der industrialisierte Krieg 1914–1918*, Bramsche 1998.

Stachelbeck, Christian, *Deutschlands Heer und Marine im Ersten Weltkrieg*, Munich 2013.

———, *Militärische Effektivität im Ersten Weltkrieg: Die 11. Bayerische Infanteriedivision 1915 bis 1918*, Paderborn 2010.

Stanley, Peter, "'He was black, he was a White man, and a dinkum Aussie': Race and Empire in Revisiting the Anzac Legend," in: Das (ed.), *Race, Empire and First World War Writing*, pp. 213–230.

Statistics of the Military Effort of the British Empire during the Great War, 1914–1918, London 1922.

Stauda, Johannes, *Der Wandervogel in Böhmen 1911–1920*, 2 vols., Reutlingen 1978.

Stears, Marc, *Progressives, Pluralists, and the Problem of the State: Ideologies of Reform in the United States and Britain, 1909–1926*, Oxford 2002.

Stegemann, Bernd, *Die deutsche Marinepolitik 1916–1918*, Berlin 1970.

Steglich, Wolfgang, *Bündnissicherung oder Verständigungsfrieden: Untersuchungen zu dem Friedensangebot der Mittelmächte vom 12. Dezember 1916*, Göttingen 1958.

——, *Die Friedenspolitik der Mittelmächte 1917/18*, Wiesbaden 1964.

Stegmann, Natali, *Kriegsdeutungen, Staatsgründungen, Sozialpolitik: Der Helden- und Opferdiskurs in der Tschechoslowakei, 1918–1948*, Munich 2010.

Steigerwald, David, *Wilsonian Idealism in America*, Ithaca 1994.

Stein, Leonard, *The Balfour Declaration*, London 1961.

Steiner, Zara, "The Treaty of Versailles Revisited," in: Michael Dockrill (ed.), *The Paris Peace Conference, 1919. Peace without Victory?* Basingstoke 2001, pp. 13–33.

Steller, Verena, *Diplomatie von Angesicht zu Angesicht: Diplomatische Handlungsformen in den deutsch-französischen Beziehungen 1870–1919*, Paderborn 2013.

Stephenson, Scott, *The Final Battle: Soldiers of the Western Front and the German Revolution of 1918*, Cambridge 2009.

Sterba, Christopher M., *Good Americans: Italian and Jewish Immigrants during the First World War*, Oxford 2003.

Stern, Fritz, "Der zweite Dreißigjährige Krieg," in: idem, *Der Westen im 20. Jahrhundert: Selbstzerstörung, Wiederaufbau, Gefährdungen der Gegenwart*, Göttingen 2008, pp. 9–29.

Stevenson, David, *Armaments and the Coming of War: Europe 1904–1914*, Oxford 1996.

——, *The First World War and International Politics*, Oxford 1988.

——, *French War Aims against Germany 1914–1919*, Oxford 1982.

——, *1914–1918: The First World War*, New York 2004.

——, *With Our Backs to the Wall: Victory and Defeat in 1918*, London 2011.

Stibbe, Matthew, *British Civilian Internees in Germany: The Ruhleben Camp, 1914–1918*, Manchester 2008.

Stöcker, Michael, "Augusterlebnis 1914," in: *Darmstadt: Legende und Wirklichkeit*, Darmstadt 1994.

Stockwell, J., "The War and the British Empire," in: John Turner (ed.), *Britain and the First World War*, London 1988, pp. 36–53.

Stone, Norman, "Brussilow-Offensive," in: Hirschfeld, Krumeich, and Renz (eds.), *Enzyklopädie Erster Weltkrieg*, pp. 394–396.

——, *The Eastern Front 1914–1917* (orig. 1975), London 1998.

Stopes, Charlotte, "Shakespeare and War," in: *Fortnightly Review* (June 1915), pp. 1057–1070.

Storz, Dieter, "Alpenkrieg," in: Hirschfeld, Krumeich, and Renz (eds.), *Enzyklopädie Erster Weltkrieg*, pp. 331–334.

——, "Artillerie," in: Hirschfeld, Krumeich, and Renz (eds.), *Enzyklopädie Erster Weltkrieg*, pp. 344–349.

——, "Schrapnell," in: Hirschfeld, Krumeich, and Renz (eds.), *Enzyklopädie Erster Welt-krieg*, p. 820.

Stovall, Tyler, "The Color Line behind the Lines: Racial Violence in France during the Great War," in: *American Historical Review* 103 (1998), pp. 737–769.

——, "Colour-Blind France? Colonial Workers during the First World War," in: *Race and Class* 35 (1993), pp. 33–55.

Strachan, Hew, "Die Kriegführung der Entente," in: Hirschfeld, Krumeich, and Renz (eds.), *Enzyklopädie Erster Weltkrieg*, pp. 272–280.

——, *The First World War*, vol. 1: *To Arms*, Oxford 2001.

——, *The First World War in Africa*, Oxford 2004.

Strandmann, Hartmut P. von, "Germany and the Coming of War," in: idem and Robert J. W. Evans (eds.), *The Coming of the First World War*, Oxford 1988, S. 87–124.

——, "The Mood in Britain in 1914," in: Kettenacker and Riotte (eds.), *The Legacies of Two World Wars*, pp. 58–76.

——, "Nationalisierungsdruck und königliche Namensänderung in England: Das Ende der Großfamilie europäischer Dynastien," in: Gerhard Albert Ritter and Peter Wende (eds.), *Rivalität und Partnerschaft: Studien zu den deutsch-britischen Beziehungen im 19. und 20. Jahrhundert*, Paderborn 1999, pp. 69–91.

Straub, Eberhard, *Albert Ballin: Der Reeder des Kaisers*, Berlin 2002.

Strauss, Ludwig, "Reichstreue und Volkstreue," in: *Jüdische Rundschau* 41 / 42 (1914), p. 387.

Strazhas, Abba, *Deutsche Ostpolitik im Ersten Weltkrieg: Der Fall Ober Ost, 1915–1917*, Wies-baden 1993.

Stumpf, Reinhard (ed.), *Kriegstheorie und Kriegsgeschichte: Carl von Clausewitz und Helmuth von Moltke*, Frankfurt 1993.

Stumpf, Richard, *Warum die Flotte zerbrach: Kriegstagebuch eines christlichen Arbeiters*, Berlin 1927.

Sullivan, Mark, *Our Times: America at the Birth of the Twentieth Century*, ed. by Dan Rather, New York 1996.

Süssmuth, Hans (ed.), *Deutschlandbilder in Dänemark und England, in Frankreich und den Niederlanden: Dokumentation der Tagung "Deutschlandbilder in Dänemark und England, in Frankreich und den Niederlanden" 15.–18. Dezember 1993*, Baden-Baden 1996.

Swartz, Marvin, *The Union of Democratic Control in British Politics during the First World War*, Oxford 1971.

Szaluta, Jacques, "Marshal Pétain and the French Army Mutiny of 1917," in: *Third Republic* 6 (1978), pp. 181–210.

——, "Marshal Pétain and French Nationalism: The Interwar Years and Vichy," in: *European Nationalism: History of European Ideas* 15 (1992), pp. 113–118.

Szöllösi-Janze, Margit, *Fritz Haber 1868–1934: Eine Biographie*, Munich 1998.

Taube, Gerhard, *Deutsche Eisenbahn-Geschütze: Rohr-Artillerie auf Schienen*, Stuttgart 2001.

Tauber, Eliezer, *The Arab Movements in World War I*, London 1993.

——, *The Emergence of the Arab Movements*, London 1993.

——, *The Formation of Modern Syria and Iraq*, London 1995.

Taylor, A. J. Percivale, *English History 1914–1945*, Oxford 1992.

———, "The War Aims of the Allies in the First World War," in: idem and Richard Pares (eds.), *Essays Presented to Sir Lewis Namier*, London 1956, pp. 475–505.

Temperley, W. V. (ed.), *A History of the Peace Conference of Paris*, 6 vols. (orig. 1920–1924), 2nd edn., London 1964.

Terraine, John, *Business in Great Waters: The U-Boat Wars, 1916–1945*, London 1989.

———, *Douglas Haig: The Educated Soldier*, London 1963.

Ther, Philipp, *The Dark Side of Nation-States: Ethnic Cleansing in Modern Europe*, New York 2014.

Theweleit, Klaus, *Männerphantasien*, 2 vols., Frankfurt 1977–1978.

Thiel, Jens, *"Menschenbassin Belgien": Anwerbung, Deportation und Zwangsarbeit im Ersten Weltkrieg*, Essen 2007.

Thiel, Rudolf, *Die Generation ohne Männer*, Berlin 1932.

Thom, Deborah, "Women and Work in Wartime Britain," in: Richard Wall and Jay Winter (eds.), *The Upheaval of War: Family, Work and Welfare in Europe, 1914–1918*, Cambridge 1988, pp. 297–326.

Thomas, Gregory M., *Treating the Trauma of the Great War: Soldiers, Civilians and Psychiatry in France, 1914–1940*, Baton Rouge 2009.

Thompson, J. Lee, *Politicians, the Press and Propaganda: Lord Northcliffe and the Great War, 1914–1919*, Kent, Ohio 1999.

Thompson, Mark, *The White War: Life and Death on the Italian Front 1915–1919*, New York 2008.

Thorau, Peter, *Lawrence von Arabien: Ein Mann und seine Zeit*, Munich 2010.

Thoss, Bruno, "Infanteriewaffen," in: Hirschfeld, Krumeich, and Renz (eds.), *Enzyklopädie Erster Weltkrieg*, pp. 575–579.

Thucydides, *The Peloponnesian War*, trans. and ed. by Steven Lattimore, New York 1998.

Thum, Gregor, "Ex oriente lux—ex oriente furor : Einführung," in: idem (ed.), *Traumland Osten*, pp. 7–15.

——— (ed.), *Traumland Osten: Deutsche Bilder vom östlichen Europa im 20. Jahrhundert*, Göttingen 2006.

Thunig-Nittner, Gerburg, *Die tschechoslowakische Legion in Russland: Ihre Geschichte und Bedeutung bei der Entstehung der 1. Tschechoslowakischen Republik*, Wiesbaden 1970.

Tilly, Charles, "Reflections on the History of European State-Making," in: idem (ed.), *The Formation of National States in Western Europe*, Princeton 1975, pp. 3–83.

———, "States and Nationalism in Europe 1492–1992," in: John L. Comaroff and Paul C. Stern (eds.), *Perspectives on Nationalism and War*, Amsterdam 1995, pp. 187–204.

"To the Civilized World," in: *North American Review*, vol. 210, no. 765 (August 1919), pp. 284–287.

Tognotti, Eugenia, *La "spagnola" in Italia: Storia dell'influenza che fece temere la fine del mondo (1918–19)*, Milan 2002.

Tomassini, Luigi, "Industrial Mobilization and the Labour Market in Italy during the First World War," in: *Social History* 16 (1991), pp. 59–87.

Tomlinson, J. R., "Liberalism and the War: Letter to the Editor," in: *Nation*, October 23, 1915.

Torp, Claudius, *Wachstum, Sicherheit, Moral: Politische Legitimation des Konsums im 20. Jahrhundert,* Göttingen 2012.

Torrey, Glenn, "Indifference and Mistrust: Russian-Romanian Collaboration in the Campaign of 1916," in: *Journal of Military History* 57 (1993), pp. 279–300.

——, "Romania and the Belligerents 1914–1916," in: idem, *Romania and World War I,* pp. 9–29.

——, *Romania and World War I: A Collection of Studies,* Iasi 1998.

——, "Romania Leaves the War: The Decision to Sign an Armistice, December 1917," in: idem, *Romania and World War I,* pp. 291–300.

——, "The Romanian Campaign of 1916: Its Impact on the Belligerents," in: idem, *Romania and World War I,* pp. 173–194.

——, "Romania's Decision to Intervene: Bratianu and the Entente, June–July 1916," in: idem, *Romania and World War I,* pp. 95–120.

Townshend, Charles, *Desert Hell: The British Invasion of Mesopotamia,* Cambridge, Mass. 2011.

——, *Political Violence in Ireland: Government and Resistance since 1848,* Oxford 1983.

Trask, David F., *The AEF and Coalition Warmaking: 1917–1918,* Lawrence 1993.

Travers, Tim, *How the War Was Won: Command and Technology in the British Army on the Western Front, 1917–1918,* London 1992.

Traverso, Enzo, *Fire and Blood* (French: 2007), London 2016.

Traxel, David, *Crusader Nation: The United States in Peace and War and the Great War, 1898–1920,* New York 2006.

Troeltsch, Ernst, "Das Neunzehnte Jahrhundert" (1913), in: idem, *Gesammelte Werke,* vol. 4: *Aufsätze zur Geistesgeschichte und Religionssoziologie,* ed. by Hans Baron, Tübingen 1925, pp. 614–649.

——, "Nach der Erklärung der Mobilmachung, 2. August 1914," in: Wende (ed.), *Politische Reden,* vol. 3, pp. 9–19.

Trotsky, Leon, *War Correspondence of Leon Trotsky: Balkan Wars, 1912–13,* New York 1990.

Trumpener, Ulrich, "Germany and the End of the Ottoman Empire," in: Marian Kent (ed.), *The Great Powers and the End of the Ottoman Empire,* London 1984, pp. 111–140.

——, *Germany and the Ottoman Empire 1914–1918,* Princeton 1968.

Tuchman, Barbara W., *The Guns of August,* New York 1962.

Tucker, Robert W., *Woodrow Wilson and the Great War: Reconsidering America's Neutrality 1914–1917,* Charlottesville 2007.

Tunstall, Graydon Allen, *Blood on the Snow: The Carpathian Winter War of 1915,* Lawrence 2010.

Turner, J. A., "The Challenge to Liberalism: The Politics of the Home Fronts," in: Hew Strachan (ed.), *The Oxford Illustrated History of the First World War,* Oxford 1998, pp. 163–178.

Turner, John, *Lloyd George's Secretariat,* Cambridge 1980.

"Über die militärpolitische Lage und die sich aus ihr ergebenden Forderungen für die weitere Ausgestaltung der deutschen Wehrkraft, Denkschrift vom 21. Dezember 1912," in: *Kriegsrüstung und Kriegswirtschaft: Anlagen zum ersten Band,* Berlin 1930, pp. 178–180.

"Über den angeblichen Kriegsrat in den Kriegen König Wilhelms I." (1881), in: Stumpf (ed.), *Kriegstheorie und Kriegsgeschichte,* pp. 591–601.

Ullmann, Hans-Peter, *Der deutsche Steuerstaat: Geschichte der öffentlichen Finanzen vom 18. Jahrhundert bis heute,* Munich 2005.

———, "Kriegswirtschaft," in: Hirschfeld, Krumeich, and Renz (eds.), *Enzyklopädie Erster Weltkrieg,* pp. 220–232.

Ullrich, Volker, "Das deutsche Kalkül in der Julikrise 1914 und die Frage der englischen Neutralität," in: *Geschichte in Wissenschaft und Unterricht* 34 (1983), pp. 79–97.

———, *Die nervöse Großmacht: Aufstieg und Untergang des deutschen Kaiserreichs 1871–1918,* Frankfurt 1997.

———, "Zündschnur und Pulverfass," in: *Die Zeit,* September 12, 2013, p. 53.

Ulrich, Bernd, ". . . 'als wenn nichts geschehen wäre': Anmerkungen zur Behandlung der Kriegsopfer während des Ersten Weltkriegs," in: Hirschfeld, Krumeich, and Renz (eds.), *"Keiner fühlt sich hier mehr als Mensch . . . ,"* pp. 140–156.

———, *Die Augenzeugen: Deutsche Feldpostbriefe in Kriegs- und Nachkriegszeit 1914–1933,* Essen 1997.

———, "Schützengraben," in: Hirschfeld, Krumeich, and Renz (eds.), *Enzyklopädie Erster Weltkrieg,* p. 821.

Ulrich, Bernd, and Ziemann, Benjamin (eds.), *German Soldiers in the Great War: Letters and Eyewitness Accounts,* Barnsley 2010.

——— (eds.), *Krieg im Frieden: Die umkämpfte Erinnerung an den Ersten Weltkrieg. Quellen und Dokumente,* Frankfurt 1997.

Ulrich, Bernd, Vogel, Jakob, and Ziemann, Benjamin (eds.), *Untertan in Uniform: Militär und Militarismus im Kaiserreich 1871–1914. Quellen und Dokumente,* Frankfurt 2001.

Ungern-Sternberg, Jürgen von, and Ungern-Sternberg, Wolfgang von, *Der Aufruf "An die Kulturwelt": Das Manifest der 93 und die Anfänge der Kriegspropaganda im Ersten Weltkrieg,* Stuttgart 1996.

Unruh, Karl, *Langemarck: Legende und Wirklichkeit,* Koblenz 1986.

Ursachen und Folgen: Eine Dokumentensammlung, vol. 1: *Die Wende des Ersten Weltkrieges und der Beginn der innenpolitischen Wandlung 1916 / 1917,* Berlin 1958.

Valentini, Georg Wilhelm Freiherr von, *Die Lehre vom Krieg, Dritter Theil. Der Türkenkrieg,* Berlin 1822.

Vat, Dan van der, *Grand Scuttle: The Sinking of the German Fleet at Scapa Flow in 1919,* Edinburgh 2012.

———, *The Ship that Changed the World: The Escape of the* Goeben *to the Dardanelles in 1914,* London 1985.

Verhey, Jeffrey, "Burgfrieden," in: Hirschfeld, Krumeich, and Renz (eds.), *Enzyklopädie Erster Weltkrieg,* pp. 400–402.

———, "Ideen von 1914," in: Hirschfeld, Krumeich, and Renz (rds.), *Enzyklopädie Erster Weltkrieg,* pp. 568–570.

———, *The Spirit of 1914: Militarism, Myth, and Mobilization in Germany.* Cambridge 2000.

Vermes, Gabor, *István Tisza: The Liberal Vision and Conservative Statecraft of a Magyar Nationalist,* New York 1985.

Vial, F., *Territoriaux de France,* Paris 1919.

Vietsch, Eberhard von, *Bethmann Hollweg: Staatsmann zwischen Macht und Ethos*, Boppard 1969.

Vogel, Jakob, *Nationen im Gleichschritt: Der Kult der "Nation in Waffen" in Deutschland und Frankreich, 1871–1914*, Göttingen 1997.

Vogt, Martin, "Hermann Müller," in: Wilhelm von Sternburg (ed.), *Die deutschen Kanzler: Von Bismarck bis Kohl*, Berlin 1998, pp. 191–206.

Vollrath, Ernst, "Wie ist Carl Schmitt an seinen Begriff des Politischen gekommen?" in: *Zeitschrift für Politik* 36 (1989), pp. 151–168.

Vorländer, Hans, *Hegemonialer Liberalismus: Politisches Denken und politische Kultur in den USA 1776–1920*, Frankfurt 1997.

Vorschriften für den Stellungskrieg aller Waffen, vol. 2: *Minenkrieg*, Berlin 1916.

Waal, Edmund de, *The Hare with Amber Eyes*, London 2010.

Wade, Rex A., *The Russian Revolution 1917*, Cambridge 2000.

Waechter, Matthias, "Vierzehn Punkte," in: Hirschfeld, Krumeich, and Renz (eds.), *Enzyklopädie Erster Weltkrieg*, pp. 949–951.

Wakefield, Alan, *Christmas in the Trenches*, Stroud 2006.

Walker, Samuel, *In Defense of American Libertie: A History of the ACLU*, New York 1990.

Wallace, Stuart, *War and the Image of Germany: British Academics 1914–1918*, Edinburgh 1988.

Walter, Dierk, "Roonsche Reform oder militärische Revolution? Wandlungsprozesse im preußischen Heerwesen vor den Einigungskriegen," in: Karl-Heinz Lutz, Martin Rink, and Marcus von Salisch (eds.), *Reform, Reorganisation, Transformation: Zum Wandel in deutschen Streitkräften von den preußischen Heeresreformen bis zur Transformation der Bundeswehr*, Munich 2010, pp. 181–198.

Walther, Peter (ed.), *Endzeit Europa: Ein kollektives Tagebuch deutschsprachiger Schriftsteller, Künstler und Gelehrter im Ersten Weltkrieg*, Göttingen 2008.

Wandt, Heinrich, *Erotik und Spionage in der Etappe Gent*, Vienna 1928.

Watson, Alexander, *Enduring the Great War: Combat, Morale and Collapse in the German and British Armies, 1914–1918*, 2nd edn., Cambridge 2009.

——, "Self-Deception and Survival: Mental Coping Strategies on the Western Front, 1914–18," in: *Journal of Contemporary History* 41 (2006), pp. 247–268.

Waugh, Arthur, "Shakespeare's Warriors," in: *Fortnightly Review* (January 1915), pp. 113–124.

Weber, Max, *Economy and Society. An Outline of Interpretive Sociology*, 2 vols., Berkeley 1978.

——, "Ein Wahlrechtsnotgesetz des Reichs. Das Recht der heimkehrenden Krieger," in: idem, *Gesamtausgabe, Abteilung I*, vol. 15, *Zur Politik im Weltkrieg*, ed. by Wolfgang Justin Mommsen with Gangolf Hübinger, pp. 215–221.

——, *Gesamtausgabe, Abteilung II*, vol. 9, *Briefe 1915–1917*, ed. by Gerd Krumeich and Mario Rainer Lepsius, Tübingen 2008.

——, "Politics as a Vocation" (orig. 1918), in: *From Max Weber: Essays in Sociology*, ed. by H. H. Gerth and C. Wright Mills, New York 1946, pp. 77–128.

——, "Religious Rejections of the World and Their Directions," in: *From Max* Weber, ed. by H. H. Gerth and C. Wright Mills, New York 1946, pp. 323–359.

——, "Suffrage and Democracy in Germany" (1917), in: idem, *Political Writings*, ed. by Peter Lassman and Ronald Speirs, Cambridge 1994, pp. 80–129.

Weber, Thomas, *Hitler's First War*, Oxford 2011.

Wegner, Armin T., *Die Austreibung des armenischen Volkes in die Wüste: Ein Lichtbildvortrag*, ed. by Andreas Meier, Göttingen 2011.

Wegner, Bernd, "Finnland," in: Hirschfeld, Krumeich, and Renz (eds.), *Enzyklopädie Erster Weltkrieg*, pp. 483–487.

Wehler, Hans-Ulrich, "Der Aufbruch in die Moderne 1860 bis 1890: Armee, Marine und Politik in Europa, den USA und Japan," in: Michael Epkenhans and Gerhard Paul Groß (eds.), *Das Militär und der Aufbruch in die Moderne 1860 bis 1890. Armeen, Marinen und der Wandel von Politik, Gesellschaft und Wirtschaft in Europa, den USA sowie Japan*, Munich 2003, pp. xxi–xxix.

———, "Der zweite Dreißigjährige Krieg: Der Erste Weltkrieg als Auftakt und Vorbild für den Zweiten Weltkrieg," in: *Spiegel Special: Die Ur-Katastrophe des 20. Jahrhunderts*, 1 (2004) pp. 138–143.

———, *Deutsche Gesellschaftsgeschichte*, vol. 3: *Von der "Deutschen Doppelrevolution" bis zum Beginn des Ersten Weltkrieges 1849–1914*, Munich 1995.

———, *Deutsche Gesellschaftsgeschichte*, vol. 4: *Vom Beginn des Ersten Weltkriegs bis zur Gründung der beiden deutschen Staaten 1914–1949*, 2nd edn., Munich 2003.

Weinrich, Arndt, *Der Weltkrieg als Erzieher: Jugend zwischen Weimarer Republik und Nationalsozialismus*, Essen 2013.

Weissensteiner, Friedrich, *Franz Ferdinand, der verhinderte Herrscher*, Vienna 2007.

Weizmann, Chaim, "Introduction," in: Harry Sacher (ed.), *Zionism and the Jewish Future*, London 1916, pp. 6–8.

Weizsäcker, Ernst von, *Die Weizsäcker-Papiere 1900–1932*, Berlin 1982, p. 215, quoted in: Wolz, *Das lange Warten*, p. 467.

Welch, David, *Germany, Propaganda and Total War 1914–1918*, London 2000.

Weldt, Gerald L., "A Plea for Tolerance," in: *New Republic* 14, April 20, 1918.

Wells, Herbert G., *The War that Will End War*, London 1914.

Wende, Peter (ed.), *Politische Reden*, vol. 3: *1914–1945*, Frankfurt 1994.

Wendt, Bernd-Jürgen, "War Socialism—Erscheinungsformen und Bedeutung des Organisierten Kapitalismus in England im Ersten Weltkrieg," in: Winkler (ed.), *Organisierter Kapitalismus*, pp. 117–149.

Werth, German, "Argonnen," in: Hirschfeld, Krumeich, and Renz (eds.), *Enzyklopädie Erster Weltkrieg*, p. 341.

———, *Das Tagebuch Europas 1916: Schlachtfeld Verdun—Europas Trauma*, Berlin 1994.

———, *Verdun: Die Schlacht und der Mythos*, 2nd edn., Bergisch Gladbach 1982.

Wesseling, Henk L., *Soldier and Warrior: French Attitudes toward the Army and War on the Eve of the First World War*, Westport, Conn. 2000.

Westerhoff, Christian, *Zwangsarbeit im Ersten Weltkrieg. Deutsche Arbeitskräftepolitik im besetzten Polen und Litauen 1914–1918*, Paderborn 2012.

Whalen, Robert W., *Bitter Wounds: German Victims of the Great War, 1914–1939*, Ithaca 1984.

White, C. M., *The Gotha Summer: The German Daytime Air Raids on England, May to August 1917*, London 1986.

Whitehead, Ian, *Doctors in the Great War,* Barnsley 1999.

Whiteside, Noel, "Concession, Coercion or Cooperation? State Policy and Industrial Unrest in Britain, 1916–1920," in: Leopold Haimson and Giulio Sapelli (eds.), *Strikes, Social Conflict and First World War: An International Perspective,* Milan 1992, pp. 107–122.

Why We Are at War: Great Britain's Case. By Members of the Faculty of Modern History, 3rd edn., Oxford 1914.

Wilamowitz-Moellendorff, Ulrich von, "Krieges Anfang, 27. August 1914," in: Wende (ed.), *Politische Reden,* vol. 3, pp. 20–29.

Wildman, Allan K., *The End of the Russian Imperial Army: The Old Army and the Soldiers' Revolt (March–April 1917),* New Jersey 1980.

Wilkinson, Roni, *Pals on the Somme 1916: Kitchener's New Army Battalions Raised by Local Authorities during the Great War,* Barnsley 2006.

Williams, John F., *Modernity, the Media and the Military: The Creation of National Mythologies on the Western Front 1914–1918,* Abingdon 2009.

Williamson, Samuel R. Jr., "Joffre Reshapes French Strategy, 1911–1913," in: Paul Kennedy (ed.), *The War Plans of the Great Powers, 1880–1914,* rev. edn., London 1985, pp. 133–154.

——, *The Politics of Grand Strategy: Britain and France Prepare for War, 1904–1914,* Cambridge, Mass. 1969.

Wilson, Jean M., *Siegfried Sassoon: The Making of a War Poet: A Biography (1886–1918),* London 1998.

Wilson, Jeremy, *Lawrence of Arabia: The Authorised Biography of T. E. Lawrence,* London 1989.

——, "T. E. Lawrence: Vom Traum zur Legende," in: Fansa and Hoffmann (eds.), *Lawrence von Arabien,* pp. 17–26.

Wilson, Ross J., *Landscapes of the Western Front: Materiality during the Great War,* New York 2012.

Wilson, Trevor, *The Myriad Faces of War: Britain and the Great War 1914–1918,* Cambridge 1986.

Wilson, Woodrow, "Address at the City Hall Auditorium in Pueblo, Colorado," September 25, 1919. *The American Presidency Project,* www.presidency.ucsb.edu/ws/?pid=117400.

——, "An Address to a Joint Session of Congress, April 2, 1917," in: *The Papers of Woodrow Wilson,* ed. by Arthur S. Link, vol. 41: *January 24—April 6, 1917,* Princeton 1983, pp. 519–527.

——, *Americanism: Woodrow Wilson's Speeches on the War, Why He Made Them and What They Have Done—the President's Principal Utterances in the First Year of War,* ed. by O. M. Gale, Chicago 1918.

——, "Only One Peace Possible, Address to Congress Answering a Peace Offensive, February 11, 1918," in: *Americanism: Woodrow Wilson's Speeches on the War,* pp. 103–109.

——, "A Peace Worth Preserving, Address to Congress on Essential Terms of Peace, January 22, 1917," in: *Americanism: Woodrow Wilson's Speeches on the War,* pp. 22–28.

Windischgrätz, Ludwig, *Vom roten zum schwarzen Prinzen: Mein Kampf gegen das k.u.k. System,* Berlin 1920.

Winegard, Timothy C., *For King and Kanata: Canadian Indians and the First World War,* Winnipeg 2011.

Winkle, Ralph, *Der Dank des Vaterlandes: Eine Symbolgeschichte des Eisernen Kreuzes 1914 bis 1936*, Essen 2007.

Winkler, Heinrich A., "Einleitende Bemerkungen zu Hilferdings Theorie des Organisierten Kapitalismus," in: idem (ed.), *Organisierter Kapitalismus*, pp. 9–18.

——— (ed.), *Organisierter Kapitalismus: Voraussetzungen und Anfänge*, Göttingen 1974.

———, *The Age of Catastrophe: A History of the West, 1914–1945*, New Haven 2015.

Winkler, Jonathan R., *Nexus: Strategic Communications and American Security in World War I*, Cambridge, Mass. 2008.

Winkler, Martina, *Karel Kramář (1860–1937): Selbstbild, Fremdwahrnehmungen und Modernisierungsverständnis eines tschechischen Politikers*, Munich 2002.

Winock, Michel, *Clemenceau*, Paris 2007.

Winter, Denis, "The Strain of Trench Warfare," in: James Hannah (ed.), *The Great War Reader*, College Station 2000, pp. 84–94.

Winter, Jay (ed.), *America and the Armenian Genocide of 1915*, Cambridge 2003.

———, "Demography," in: Horne (ed.), *A Companion to World War I*, pp. 246–262.

———, *The Experience of World War I*, New York 1989.

———, "Forms of Kinship and Remembrance in the Aftermath of the Great War," in: idem and Emmanuel Sivan (eds.), *War and Remembrance in the Twentieth Century*, Cambridge 1999, pp. 40–60.

———, *The Great War and the British People*, London 1985.

———, "Großbritannien," in: Hirschfeld, Krumeich, and Renz (eds.), *Enzyklopädie Erster Weltkrieg*, pp. 50–63.

———, "Introduction: Witness to Genocide," in: idem (ed.), *America and the Armenian Genocide of 1915*, pp. 1–8.

———, "Paris, London, Berlin 1914–1919: Capital Cities at War," in: Robert and idem (eds.), *Capital Cities*, pp. 3–24.

———, *Sites of Memory, Site of Mourning: The Great War in European Cultural History* (orig. 1995), Cambridge 1998.

Witkop, Philipp (ed.), *Kriegsbriefe gefallener Studenten*, Munich 1928.

Wolff, Leon, *In Flanders Fields: The 1917 Campaign*, London 1958.

Wolff, Theodor, *Tagebücher 1914–1919: Der Erste Weltkrieg und die Entstehung der Weimarer Republik in Tagebüchern, Leitartikeln und Briefen des Chefredakteurs am "Berliner Tageblatt" und Mitbegründers der Deutschen Demokratischen Partei*, ed. by Bernd Sösemann, 2 vols., Berlin 1984.

Woller, Hans, *Geschichte Italiens im 20. Jahrhundert*, Munich 2010.

Wolpert, Stanley, "Congress Leadership in Transition: Jinnah to Gandhi, 1914–20," in: Ellinwood and Pradhan (eds.), *India and World War I*, pp. 127–140.

———, *Gandhi's Passion: The Life and Legacy of Mahatma Gandhi*, Oxford 2001.

Wolz, Nicolas, *Das lange Warten: Kriegserfahrungen deutscher und britischer Seeoffiziere 1914 bis 1918*, Paderborn 2008.

Woodward, David R., *Lloyd George and the Generals*, London 1983.

———, *Hell in the Holy Land: World War I in the Middle East*, Lexington 2006.

———, *Trial by Friendship: Anglo-American Relations 1917–1918*, Lexington 1993.

The Works of Theodore Roosevelt, National Edition in 20 Volumes, New York 1926.

Wortman, Richard S., *Scenarios of Power: Myth and Ceremony in Russian Monarchy*, vol. 2: *From Alexander II to the Abdication of Nicolas II*, Princeton 2000.

Wright, Patrick, *Tank: The Progress of a Monstrous War Machine*, London 2000.

Wright, Quincy, *A Study of War*, 2nd edn., Chicago 1965.

Wróbel, Piotr, "The Jews of Galicia under Austrian-Polish Rule, 1869–1918," in: *Austrian History Yearbook* 25 (1994), pp. 97–138.

Wüstenbecker, Katja, *Deutsch-Amerikaner im Ersten Weltkrieg: US-Politik und nationale Identitäten im Mittleren Westen*, Stuttgart 2007.

———, "Die Vereinigten Staaten von Amerika: Widerwillige Teilnahme am Ersten Weltkrieg," in: Bauerkämper and Julien (eds.), *Durchhalten*, pp. 217–237.

Xu, Guoqi, *China and the Great War: China's Pursuit of a New National Identity and Internationalization*, Cambridge 2005.

———, *Strangers on the Western Front: Chinese Workers in the Great War*, Cambridge 2011.

Yapp, Malcolm E., *The Making of the Modern Near East 1792–1923*, London 1987.

Yates, Keith, *Flawed Victory: Jutland 1916*, Annapolis 2000.

Yockelson, Mitchell A., *Borrowed Soldiers: Americans under British Command, 1918*, Norman, Okla. 2008.

Young, Harry F., "The Misunderstanding of August 1, 1914," in: *Journal of Modern History* 48 (1976), pp. 644–665.

Ypersele, Laurence van, "Belgien," in: Hirschfeld, Krumeich, and Renz (eds.), *Enzyklopädie Erster Weltkrieg*, pp. 44–49.

———, *Le roi Albert: Histoire d'un mythe*, Ottignies 1995.

———, "Mourning and Memory, 1919–45," in: Horne (ed.), *A Companion to World War I*, pp. 576–590.

Zechlin, Egmont, *Die deutsche Politik und die Juden im Ersten Weltkrieg*, Göttingen 1969.

Zglinicki, Friedrich von, *Der Weg des Films*, quoted in: Johann (ed.), *Innenansicht eines Krieges*, pp. 265–266.

Zhivojinovich, D., "Serbia and Montenegro," in: Nándor F. Dreisziger and Béla K. Kiraly (eds.), *East Central European Society in World War I*, Boulder 1985, pp. 239–259.

Ziemann, Benjamin, "Enttäuschte Erwartung und kollektive Erschöpfung: Die deutschen Soldaten an der Westfront 1918 auf dem Weg zur Revolution," in: Jörg Duppler and Gerhard Paul Groß (eds.), *Kriegsende 1918: Ereignis, Wirkung, Nachwirkung*, Munich 1999, pp. 165–182.

———, *Front und Heimat: Ländliche Kriegserfahrungen im südlichen Bayern 1914–1923*, Essen 1997.

———, "Les soldats et l'effondrement de l'armée allemande en 1918," in: Pietro Causarano, Olivier Feiertag, Valeria Galimi, François Guedj, Romain Huret, Isabelle Lespinet-Moret, Jérôme Martin, Michel Pinault, Xavier Vigna, and Mercedes Yusta (eds.), *Le siècle des guerres: Penser les guerres du premier XXe siècle*, Paris 2004, pp. 141–149.

———, "Soldaten," in: Hirschfeld, Krumeich, and Renz (eds.), *Enzyklopädie Erster Weltkrieg*, pp. 155–168.

Zilch, Reinhold, "Rohstoffbewirtschaftung," in: Hirschfeld, Krumeich, and Renz (eds.), *Enzyklopädie Erster Weltkrieg*, pp. 797–800.

Zollmann, Jakob, *Koloniale Herrschaft und ihre Grenzen: Die Kolonialpolizei in Deutsch-Südwestafrika 1894–1915*, Göttingen 2010.

Zuber, Terence, *The Battle of the Frontiers. Ardennes 1914*, Stroud 2007.

———, *Inventing the Schlieffen Plan: German War Planning 1871–1914*, New York 2002.

Zuckerman, Larry, *The Rape of Belgium: The Untold Story of World War I*, New York 2004.

Zückert, Martin, *Zwischen Nationsidee und staatlicher Realität: Die tschechoslowakische Armee und ihre Nationalitätenpolitik 1918–1938*, Munich 2006.

Zuckmayer, Carl, *Als wär's ein Stück von mir: Horen der Freundschaft*, Vienna 1966.

Zürcher, Erik-Jan, "Demographic Engineering, State-Building and the Army—The Ottoman Empire and the First World War," in: Leonhard and Hirschhausen (eds.), *Comparing Empires*, pp. 530–544.

———, "Griechisch-orthodoxe und muslimische Flüchtlinge und Deportierte in Griechenland und der Türkei seit 1912," in: Klaus J. Bade, Pieter C. Emmer, Leo Lucassen, and Jochen Oltmer (eds.), *Enzyklopädie Migration in Europa. Vom 17. Jahrhundert bis zur Gegenwart*, Paderborn 2007, pp. 623–627.

———, "Osmanisches Reich," in: Hirschfeld, Krumeich, and Renz (eds.), *Enzyklopädie Erster Weltkrieg*, pp. 758–762.

———, "The Ottoman Conscription System in Theory and Practice, 1844–1918," in: *International Review of Social History* 43 (1998), pp. 437–449.

———, "Ottoman Labour Battalions in World War I," in: Hans-Lukas Kieser and Dominik J. Schaller (eds.), *Der Völkermord an den Armeniern und die Shoah: The Armenian Genocide and the Shoah*, Zurich 2002, pp. 187–196.

———, "Sykes-Picot-Abkommen," in: Hirschfeld, Krumeich, and Renz (eds.), *Enzyklopädie Erster Weltkrieg*, p. 916.

Zürrer, Werner, "Der Friedensvertrag von Sevres: Ein kritischer Beitrag zur Problematik der Neuordnung des nahöstlichen Raumes nach dem Ersten Weltkrieg," in: *Saeculum. Jahrbuch für Universalgeschichte* 25 (1974), pp. 88–114.

Zwach, Eva, *Deutsche und englische Militärmuseen im 20. Jahrhundert: Eine kulturgeschichtliche Analyse des gesellschaftlichen Umgangs mit Krieg*, Münster 1999.

———, "Ein Volkskundler im Ersten Weltkrieg: Wilhelm Pessler und die Kriegsmuseen," in: *Zeitschrift für Volkskunde* 95 (1999), pp. 14–31.

Zweig, Arnold, *Education before Verdun* (German orig. 1935), New York 1936.

Zweig, Stefan, *The World of Yesterday*, New York 1943.

ACKNOWLEDGMENTS

To all Fellows of the School of History of the Freiburg Institute for Advanced Studies (FRIAS) from 2007 to 2012—for their focus and informality, attention and discussion, inspiration and interested curiosity;

to colleagues at Freiburg and far beyond: Volker Berghahn, Roger Chickering, Christopher Clark, Ute Daniel, Ulrich Herbert, John Horne, Nicole Jordan, Edward J. Klekowski, Gerd Krumeich, Dieter Langewiesche, Charles S. Maier, Dietmar Neutatz, Paolo Pombeni, Joachim von Puttkamer, Gottfried Schramm, James J. Sheehan, Jakob Tanner, and Thomas Weber—for exchanges and contradiction;

to Sabine Mischner, my first, and last, unerring reader—for her patience, attention, and thoughtfulness in matters large, small, and minute;

to my coworkers Theo Jung and Friedemann Pestel—for all their corrections and salutary composure toward the author;

to my past and current assistants: Andrés Antolín Hofrichter, Claudia Gatzka, Svenja Goltermann, Julia Heinemann, Andrea von Hohenthal, Athanasia Koiou, Roman Köster Sonja Levsen, Armin Owzar, Sarah Panter, Fabian Rausch, Christina Schröer, and Jörg Später—for their suggestions and translations, calm concentration, professionalism, and, above all, a good working atmosphere;

to the whole team at Freiburg: Jonas Baumann, Dominique Brossier, Bastian Max Brucklacher, Konradin Eigler, Marcus Gaidetzka, Manuel Geist, Martin Gerth, Patrik Gihr, Konrad Hauber, Gesine Hübner, Christoph Koller, Anna Mashi, Pia Masurczak, Kelly Minelli, Friederike Nehmer, Sebastian Petznick, Jan Stoll, Christoph Streb, and Tobias Winter—for their tremendous commitment, absolute reliability, and great patience;

to the Minda de Gunzburg Center for European Studies of Harvard University and its directors David Blackbourn and Grzegorz Ekiert—for a year of reading and writing and a balance of generosity, intellectual stimulation, and peace;

to the librarians at the Harry Elkins Widener Memorial Library of Harvard University—for the fulfillment of every wish and access to the place that for now comes pretty close to paradise;

to the Baden-Wuerttemberg Ministry of Sciences, Research, and Arts—for the means permitting my retreat into reading and writing;

to Wolfgang Beck, Detlef Felken, Sebastian Ullrich, and Carola Samlowsky at the C. H. Beck publishing house—for the right mix of trustfulness, intelligent attention, and gentle pressure;

to my family: always and first of all;

to the whole team at Harvard University Press, in particular Ian Malcolm, and my translator Patrick Camiller, who allowed me to rediscover my own book;

and in memory of my grandfather August Leonhard (1898–1976) and his brother Ludwig (1893–1917).

Freiburg, Advent 2017

ILLUSTRATION CREDITS

Archiv für Kunst und Geschichte (AKG): pp. 270, 519 (Universal History Archive /
Universal Images Group), 532 (*right*), 553

Bibliothek für Zeitgeschichte Stuttgart: p. 505

Bibliothek für Zeitgeschichte / Württembergische Landesbibliothek: p. 535

Bibliothèque de Documentation Internationale Contemporaine (BDIC): p. 117

bpk: p. 297

Bridgeman Art Library: p. 845

Centre for the Study of Civil War, International Peace Research Institute: p. 11

Constable & Robinson: p. 293

Corbis: p. 628

culture-images: pp. 125, 603

Deutsches Historisches Museum: pp. 337, 708

Getty Images: pp. 145, 298, 317 (Topical Press Agency), 641 (Popperfoto), 889
(Central Press / Freier Fotograf)

Imperial War Museum: pp. 130 (Q 53517), 137 (Q 30067), 267 (Q 48951), 507 (*top*)
(Q 30456), 507 (*bottom*) (Q 30457), 559 (Q 6432), 657 (Q 110883), 699 (Q 106252),
754 (Q 11086), 881 (Q 14965), 889 (Art. IWM PST 3951—Artist unknown)

Kharbine Tapabor: pp. 327, 453, 663, 695

Nicolaische Verlagsbuchhandlung GmbH, Berlin: pp. 690, 691 (Birgit Jochens,
Deutsche Weihnacht)

Österreichische Nationalbibliothek: p. 286, 532 (*left*)

ullstein bild: pp. 23, 119 (TopFoto), 198 (TopFoto), 207 (Heritage Image Partnership /
Artist: Joseph Swain), 243 (Süddeutsche Zeitung Photo / Scherl), 302 (Leone), 364

(Archiv Gerstenberg), 395 (Roger-Viollet / Maurice Branger), 397 (*top* and *bottom*), 415, 518, 748 (Süddeutsche Zeitung Photo / Scherl), 758 (Photo 12 Collection), 849 (Roger-Viollet)

Universität Odense: p. 332 (Axel Thiess)

ILLUSTRATIONS TAKEN FROM BOOKS

Antonelli, Quinto, and Leoni, Diego (eds.), *Il popolo scomparso: Il Trentino, i Trentini nella prima guerra mondiale (1914–1920)*, Rovereto 2003: p. 258

Didier, Christophe (ed.), *In Papiergewittern 1914–1918. Die Kriegssammlungen der Bibliotheken*, Paris 2008, p. 127: p. 529

Garnier, Claire, and Le Bon, Laurent (eds.), *1917: Exposition présentée au Centre Pompidou-Metz du 26 mai au 24 septembre 2012*, Metz 2012: pp. 597, 665

Strachan, Hew, *The Oxford Illustrated History of the First World War*, Oxford 1998: p. 449, p. 729

INDEX

Page numbers followed by *f* indicate photographs and illustrations; those followed by *t* indicate tables.

struggles near end of war, 770–772; early twentieth century conflicts and military scenario development, 39–44, 51–53; economy and population in, 191, 197; *élan* and, 160; factors contributing to victory or defeat, 826–835; financial and class differences in, 686–687; financial credit from U.S., 619–620; food supplies, 463–464; gas attacks and, 265; gender and roles during war, 697; German bombing of, 725, 770–771, 828; German scorched-earth withdrawal tactics and, 790; growing crisis after Franz Ferdinand's assassination, 78–80, 82–85, 89, 91–93; hero worship of Ronarc'h, 161–162; illusions about end of war, 712–713; intellectuals and justifications for war, 220–221, 372–373; journalists and, 521, 524; mechanized warfare, early in war, 129–131, 130*f*, 132–133, 135; memories of war and, 877, 887–888, 890; militarization, war economy, and *union sacrée*, 186–189; military situation in 1918, 740; missing persons after war, 876; mobilization and military spending before 1914, 31–32, 31*f*, 32*f*; motives for war and risk policies of, 102, 104, 106–107; mutiny of troops, 567–573; national movements, before 1914, 34, 35; nineteenth century alliances of, 28; *offensive à outrance* concept, 165; Paris peace conference and Versailles Treaty, 847–848, 850, 864, 868–870; Plan XVII of, 44, 46, 104, 105, 130, 154, 231; political and societal changes from war, 454–458; pessimism of army in 1918, 723; postcards of war events, 536; in postwar period, 841, 857, 863, 873; propaganda and, 633; public reactions at start of war, 116–119, 117*f*, 124, 127; public reactions to armistice, 821; reality of war in 1916, 388; Russian Revolution

and, 600, 608–609; socialists' support for war, 96–99; social polarization and political conflicts in, 645–650, 712, 715; suffrage in, 698, 699; support for war in, 94, 96–98; Syria and, 814; tear gas use, 264–265; U.S. commanders and, 621; violence against population, 892; war debts to U.S., 851; war plans for 1917, 554–556; wartime economy and, 325–331, 327*f*, 702–705, 709–710, 714–715

France, Anatole, 687

France meurtrie (wounded France) idea, 536

Francke, Kuno, 616, 617, 618

Franco-Prussian War (1870–1871), 22–25, 94–95

Franc-tireurs, 23, 36, 79, 151, 166, 260, 315, 884

Frank-Caro process of cyanide synthesis, 196

Franke, Victor, 178

Frankfurter, Felix, 776

Frankfurter Zeitung, 657–658

Franz Ferdinand, archduke, 476, 477; assassination of and initial reactions to, 71–77; failure of de-escalation efforts after death of, 77–87; as heir presumptive, 46, 74–75

Franz Joseph, emperor of Austria and king of Hungary, 74, 75, 78, 87, 110, 185, 200, 429; death of, 389, 469, 475–477, 545

Frederick and the Great Coalition (T. Mann), 373

Frederick II, the Great, 112, 130, 212, 373, 490, 551

Free trade, Fourteen Points and, 722

Freiherr von der Goltz, Colmar, 58

Freikorps, 838–839, 840, 841, 895

French, John, 154, 190, 238, 239, 311, 313, 389, 679

French Congo, 46, 47, 869